The four "bottom line" practices that managers and companies must deliver to their customers

Quality

Customers' expectation of a product or service must be met and exceeded. Managers must ensure attractiveness, lack of defects, reliablity, and dependability in everything the organization produces.

Cost

Goods and services must be valuable and at prices the customer is willing to pay. To accomplish this goal, managers must keep costs under control to allow the company to set fair prices that cover costs and achieve profit.

Innovation

Managers should constantly strive to quickly create new competitive goods and services that customers value. This practice is the key to staying ahead of competitors.

Speed

Organizations must respond to market needs quickly by introducing new products first; quickly delivering customer orders; and responding quickly to customer requests.

Management

Building Competitive Advantage

Management

Building Competitive Advantage

Fourth Edition

Thomas S. Bateman
The University of North Carolina

Scott A. Snell
Pennsylvania State University

Boston Burr Ridge, IL Dubuque, IA Madison, WI New York San Francisco St. Louis
Bangkok Bogotá Caracas Lisbon London Madrid
Mexico City Milan New Delhi Seoul Singapore Sydney Taipei Toronto

Irwin/McGraw-Hill

A Division of The **McGraw-Hill** *Companies*

MANAGEMENT: BUILDING COMPETITIVE ADVANTAGE

This book is printed on acid-free paper.

international 2 3 4 5 6 7 8 9 0 VNH/VNH 9 3 2 1 0 9
domestic 3 4 5 6 7 8 9 0 VNH/VNH 9 3 2 1 0 9

ISBN 0-256-26142-3
ISBN 0-07-304025-8 (Business Week set)

Vice president and editorial director: *Michael W. Junior*
Publisher: *Craig S. Beytien*
Senior sponsoring editor: *John E. Biernat*
Developmental editor: *Christine Scheid*
Marketing manager: *Ellen Cleary*
Senior project manager: *Mary Conzachi*
Senior production supervisor: *Madelyn S. Underwood*
Designer: *Kiera Cunningham*
Cover image: *©John Stili*
Photo research coordinator: *Sharon Miller*
Photo researcher: *Sarah Evertson*
Supplement coordinator: *Kimberly D. Stack*
Compositor: *PC&F*
Typeface: *10/12 Times Roman*
Printer: *Von Hoffmann Press, Inc.*

Library of Congress Cataloging-in-Publication Data

Bateman, Thomas S.
Management: building competitive advantage/Thomas S. Bateman, Scott A. Snell.—4th ed.
p. cm.
Includes index.
ISBN 0-256-26142-3 (alk. paper),—ISBN 0-07-304025-8 (Business Week Set : alk. paper)
1. Management. I. Snell, Scott, 1958– . II. Title.
HD31.B369485 1999
658.4—dc21 98-8256
CIP

INTERNATIONAL EDITION

When ordering the title, use ISBN 0-07-115444-2

http://www.mhhe.com

For my parents, Tom and Jeanine Bateman
and Mary Jo, Lauren, T.J., and Jamie
and
My parents, John and Clara Snell,
and Marybeth, Sara, Jack and Emily

About the Authors

Thomas S. Bateman

Thomas S. Bateman is a chaired professor of management at the Kenan-Flager Business School of the University of North Carolina, where he teaches courses in organizational behavior to undergraduates, M.B.A. students, Ph.D. students, and practicing managers. He also is spending two years in Europe as a visiting professor at the International Institute for Management Development (IMD), one of the world's leaders in the design and delivery of executive education. Dr. Bateman completed his doctoral program in business administration in 1980 at Indiana University. Prior to receiving his doctorate, Dr. Bateman received his B.A. from Miami University.

In addition to UNC–Chapel Hill and IMD, Dr. Bateman has taught at Texas A&M, Tulane, and Indiana Universities. Dr. Bateman also taught an undergraduate course in Europe where students visited with the managers of companies such as Porsche, Löwenbräu, Caterpillar, and the Scotland office of Hewlett-Packard.

Dr. Bateman is an active management researcher, writer, and consultant. He has served on the editorial boards of major academic journals, and has presented numerous papers at professional meetings on topics including managerial decision making, job stress, negotiation, employee commitment and motivation, group decision making, and job satisfaction. These articles appeared in professional journals such as the *Academy of Management Journal, Academy of Management Review, Journal of Applied Psychology, Organizational Behavior and Human Decision Process, Journal of Management, Business Horizons, Journal of Organizational Behavior, Decision Sciences,* and *Financial Times Mastering Management Journal.*

Dr. Bateman's current consulting and research centers around entrepreneurship in the United States, Central Europe, and Southeast Asia. He is currently working closely with companies including Nokia, Singapore Airlines, EMC, and Lego.

Scott A. Snell

Scott A. Snell is associate professor of business administration at Pennsylvania State University. He holds a B.A. in psychology from Miami University, as well as an M.B.A. and Ph.D. in business administration from Michigan State University. During his career, Dr. Snell has taught courses in human resources management, principles of management, and strategic management to undergraduates, graduates, and executives. He is actively involved in executive education and serves as faculty director for Penn State's Strategic Leadership Program, as well as faculty leader for programs in human resources management. In addition to his teaching duties, Dr. Snell also serves as director of research for Penn State's Institute for the Study of Organizational Effectiveness.

Professor Snell has worked with companies such as AT&T, GE, IBM, Merck, and Shell to address the alignment of human resource systems with strategic initiatives such as globalization, technological change, and total quality management. As these companies compete more through the talents of their people, developing and deploying human capital as the foundation of core competencies has taken on increased importance. Along these lines, Dr. Snell has been conducting studies sponsored by the Society for Human Resource Management and Human Resource Planning Society of how leading-edge companies manage their people for competitive advantage.

Dr. Snell's research has been published in the *Academy of Management Journal, Academy of Management Review, Human Resource Management, Human Resource Management Review, Industrial Relations, Journal of Business Research, Journal of Management, Journal of Managerial Issues, Organizational Dynamics, Organization Studies,* and *Strategic Management Journal.* In addition to this book, Dr. Snell is coauthor of *Managing Human Resources,* and is on the editorial boards of *Academy of Management Journal, Journal of Managerial Issues, Digest of Management Research,* and *Human Resource Management Review.*

Preface

The story, appearing May 6, 1998, was a business blockbuster: *The Wall Street Journal Europe* reported secret meetings surrounding a possible merger between America's Chrysler Corporation and Germany's Daimler-Benz AG.*

The next day, the *WSJE* printed the news that Chrysler's board and Daimler's managing board had just approved the merger. A single new company would be created, incorporated in Germany. The merger was described as "stunning in size and scope" and a "once-unthinkable combination." It was to be the biggest industrial merger in history, one that would change forever the face of the industry.

Playing off the big news, the *Journal* printed separate articles about 1) Juergen Schrempp, the Daimler chairman who was orchestrating the deal, including descriptions of his career and management style; 2) the successes (and failures) of global mergers; 3) U.S. reaction to the heavy flow of German investment into the United States, including the 1998 purchase of Random House by Bertelsmann; 4) the effect of the proposed merger on Japanese competitors; 5) reactions of regulatory agencies around the world; 6) potential synergies between Chrysler and Daimler-Benz; 7) the business plan driving the deal; 8) the political intrigue surrounding the negotiations; and 9) the crucial role of labor and employee relations in determining the success of the new company.

Most analysts raved about the deal. Each company would benefit, they said. As examples, Chrysler would improve quality (for instance, in off-road vehicles), and Daimler-Benz could now enter Asia in the low- to medium-priced market segments. And the global reach would be extraordinary.

But how to make the merger work? Work fast, was the advice. A revered business leader said, "The single most important thing in a merger is to move fast." Another stated, "Go fast even if it hurts."

In reporting the Daimler-Chrysler merger, the *Journal* made an important observation: That what is *not* remarkable about the merger is that one player is based in Stuttgart and the other in Detroit. Big deal. Transnational combinations occur all the time. "Forget globalization the buzzword; say hello to globalization the reality," the reporter wrote. Or as the No. 2 executive at Bertelsmann put it, "There are no German and American companies. There are only successful and unsuccessful companies." Of course, there are American companies, and companies in every country of the world that operate primarily domestically. But the bigger points the executive was making about globalization and hard business results are vital ones.

Consistent with these current business realities, this is the first management text to focus hard on success—that is, on results. You will read later about how we do this.

Furthermore, this is the first management text to be written from two continents. One author wrote from the United States, the other while on a two-year appointment in Europe. Reflecting current realities, in writing this book our goal was—and we believe, the result is—a text that maintains the American domestic foundation while incorporating a rich and balanced global perspective.

---

* S. Lipin, "In the Fast Lane: Daimler and Chrysler conduct secret talks on $35 billion deal," *The Wall Street Journal Europe,* May 6, 1998, pp. 1, 10; and D. Lavin, "Big Wheels: Daimler and Chrysler raise hard question about global deals," *The Wall Street Journal Europe,* May 7, 1998, pp. 1, 6.

In many ways, the Daimler-Chrysler story is a metaphor for today's management opportunities and challenges. Think of the topics reflected in the story—globalization, corporate strategy, the "human element" of business, leadership, decision making, mergers, culture, quality, costs, speed, managing change, creating futures, and so many others—and learn more about them in the following pages.

Our goals

Our mission with this book is threefold: to inform, instruct, and inspire. We hope to *inform* by providing descriptions of the important concepts and practices of modern management. We hope to *instruct* by describing how you can take action on the ideas discussed. In other words, you will learn practical applications that will make you more effective in ways that benefit both you and your organization.

We hope to *inspire* not only by writing in a positive, interesting, optimistic way, but also by providing a real sense of the unlimited opportunities ahead of you. Whether your goal is starting your own company, leading a team to greatness, building a strong organization, delighting your customers, or generally forging a positive future, we want to inspire you to take positive actions.

We hope to inspire you to be both a thinker and a doer. We want you to think about the issues, think about how to become a better manager, think about the impact of your actions, think before you act. But being a good thinker is not enough; you also must be a doer. Management is a world of action. It is a world that requires timely and appropriate action. It is a world not for the passive, but for those who commit to positive accomplishments.

We also hope to inspire you to keep learning. Keep applying the ideas you learn in this course, read about management in sources outside of this course, and certainly keep learning about management after you leave school and continue your career. Make no mistake about it, learning about management is a personal voyage that will last years, an entire career, your entire lifetime.

Competitive advantage

Today's world is competitive. Never before has the world of work been so challenging. Never before has it been so imperative to your career that you learn the skills of management. Never before have people had so many vast opportunities with so many potential rewards.

You will compete with other people for jobs, resources, and promotions. Your organization will compete with other firms for contracts, clients, and customers. To survive the competition, and to thrive, you must perform in ways that give you an edge over your competitors, that make the other party want to hire you, buy from you, and do repeat business with you. You will want them to choose you, not your competitor.

To survive and thrive, today's managers have to think and act strategically. Today's customers are well educated, aware of their options, and demanding of excellence. For this reason, managers today must think constantly about how to build a capable workforce and manage in a way that delivers the goods and services that provide the best possible value to the customer.

By this standard, managers and organizations must perform. The four types of performance, on which the organization beats, equals, or loses to the competition, are *cost, quality, speed,* and *innovation.* These four performance dimensions, when done well, deliver value to the customer and competitive advantage to you and your organization. We will elaborate on all of these topics throughout the book. You can read the inside front cover for a brief overview.

Good managers find ways to make their organizations successful. The ways to do this are to build competitive advantage in the forms of cost competitiveness, quality, speed, and innovation. Because of the importance of the four sources of competitive advantage—which really are goals that every manager should constantly try to achieve and improve upon—we refer to them frequently throughout the book. The idea is to keep you focused on a type of "bottom line," to make sure you think continually about "delivering the goods" that make both the manager (you) and the organization a competitive success.

Results orientation

An important theme of this book, then, is how to manage in ways that deliver *results*—results that customers want. When you deliver high-quality, innovative products, quickly, and at a competitive price, you are achieving the results that can give you the competitive edge. And keep in mind, these are the same results that your competitors strive for as they try to gain an edge over you.

This approach makes this book unique among management texts. Rather than offering only concepts and processes, which nonetheless are integral parts of this text, we have a clear results orientation that is essential to success. The concepts and processes are means to an end, or the ways by which you can achieve the results you need.

Topical currency

It goes without saying that this textbook, in its fourth edition, remains on the cutting edge of topical coverage, as updated via both current business examples and recent management research. Chapters are thoroughly updated and students are exposed to a wide variety of important current topics, including:

Life cycle analysis
Ecocentric management
Entrepreneurship in the inner city
Human capital
Psychological contracts
Virtual office
Coaching
Boundarylessness
Open-book management
Technology audit
New overseas markets
Product and process innovation
Core competencies
Learning organizations
European unification
Privatization
NAFTA
Technology leadership
Rightsizing
Transnational teams
Customer service
Crisis management
Empowerment
Codetermination
Strategic HRM
Post-heroic leadership
Cross-functional teams
Network organizations
Sexual harassment
Mass customization
Benchmarking
Corporate political activities
Strategic alliances
Competitor analysis
The MBA Enterprise Corps., working to bring the free market to Eastern Europe and Southeast Asia

This list, of course, is just a sampler of the comprehensive coverage offered by this text. We have done our very best to draw from a wide variety of subject matter, sources, and personal experiences.

Forging the future

By highlighting the sources of competitive advantage and using a clear results orientation, we continue our efforts to create a new generation of management texts. Our previous edition was more integrative than other texts and was the first to devote major coverage to the vital management topics of managing in our natural environment and managing workforce diversity. And, we have broken the traditional mold by encouraging students to "forge the future," including more coverage of career management in the first and last chapters.

Still, in this edition we retain the traditional functional organization. Even though the world has changed, it is not chaos. A functional approach still is useful in that it provides students and instructors with a framework within which to tackle dynamic issues. Moreover, we of course give full coverage to all the topics all management texts emphasize: globalization, total quality, change, ethics, teams, and so on.

As this textbook forges the future for management texts, we want to influence students to forge *their* futures. Throughout the text, a proactive rather than passive approach to management is encouraged. For example, Chapter 7, New Ventures, doesn't merely describe small business management; it inspires readers to create new ideas and new businesses. And Chapter 18, World Class Futures, speaks to the importance of creating a great future, not just being ready for the future and adapting to it. We highlight the "Genius of the 'and' " and being both a leader and a learner.

With your help, we want to influence business in the future. Through our mission of informing, instructing, and inspiring, we hope you will apply these ideas to create your own organizations and/or make the organizations in which you work more successful and outstanding.

A team effort

This book is the product of a fantastic Irwin/McGraw-Hill team. Moreover, we wrote this book believing that we would form a team with the course instructor and with students. The entire team is responsible for the learning process.

Our goal, and that of the instructor, is to create a positive learning environment in which you can excel. But in the end, the raw material of this course is just words. It is up to you to use them as a basis for further thinking, deep learning, and constructive action.

What you do with the things you learn from this course, and with the opportunities the future holds, *counts*. As a manager, you can make a dramatic difference for yourself, and for other people. What managers do matters, *tremendously*.

Outstanding pedagogy

Management: Building Competitive Advantage is pedagogically stimulating and is intended to maximize student learning. With this in mind, we used a wide array of pedagogical features—some tried and true, others new and novel:

- Learning Objectives, which open each chapter, identify what students will learn by reading and studying the chapter.
- Opening quotes provide a thought-provoking preview of chapter material. The quotes are from people like Peter Drucker (on management), Jack Welch (on strategy), Henry David Thoreau (on ethics), Julius Caesar (on leadership), and Charles Kettering (on change and the future).
- Setting the Stage describes an actual organizational situation and provides a rich introductory example of the chapter topic. Setting the Stage is placed before the text material as a practical application.

- Boxed inserts describing current examples and controversial issues are found throughout the text.
- "From the Pages of Business Week" highlights recent *Business Week* articles in each chapter.
- Icons representing the four running themes of the book—cost, quality, speed, and innovation—are placed at appropriate points in the text to indicate an extended example, best practice, or issue for discussion. The icons continually reinforce and enhance the learning of these important themes.

End-of-chapter elements

- Key Terms are page-referenced to the text and are part of the vocabulary-building emphasis. These terms are defined in the glossary at the end of the book.
- A Summary of Learning Objectives provides clear, concise responses to the learning objectives, giving students a quick reference for reviewing the important concepts in the chapter.
- Discussion Questions, which follow the Summary of Learning Objectives, are thought-provoking questions that test the student's mastery of concepts covered in the chapter and ask for opinions on controversial issues.
- Concluding Cases provide focus for class discussion.
- A Video Case or Video Exercise appears at the end of each chapter. These cases/ exercises reinforce the concepts presented in the videos for each chapter.
- Two Experiential Exercises are included in each chapter. Most of them are group-based, and many involve outside research.

End-of-part elements

- An Integrating Case appears at the end of each of the five parts of the book.
- Two short Case Incidents also focus on managerial problems that include issues from multiple chapters and are a stimulating arena for discussion.
- Part I has a new in-basket exercise, which we believe is an excellent exercise for early in the course.

Comprehensive supplements

For the student

- A study guide online with content written by Sue Stewart-Belle of Texas A&M University—Corpus Christi, will provide students with not only a study aid, but the ability to match their wits against students across the country who are using our text.

For the instructor

- Instructor's Manual, prepared by Carol Smolinski, University of North Carolina, contains chapter outlines, suggested discussion questions and answers for Setting the Stage, two lecturettes for each chapter, suggested answers to end-of-chapter Discussion Questions, suggested answers to the Concluding Case discussion questions, objectives and teaching tips for the experiential exercises, discussion questions and suggested answers for Case Incidents and Integrating Cases, and a Video Guide.
- Test Bank, prepared by Amit Shah, Frostburg State University, contains approximately 100 questions for each chapter and consists of true/false, multiple-choice, fill-in, matching, and essay questions.

- PowerPoint Presentation software, also written by Sue Stewart-Belle, contains tables and figures from the text plus additional graphic material. A self-contained viewer is packaged with each disk so that those who do not have the PowerPoint software can easily view the presentation.
- Color acetates from the PowerPoint slides are also available.
- Videos are available for each chapter. A videoguide that ties the videos closely to the chapter can be found in the Instructor's Manual.
- Computerized Testing enables you to pick and choose questions and develop tests and quizzes quickly and easily on the computer. Available for Windows or Mac users.

Acknowledgments

This book could not have been written and published without the valuable contributions of many individuals.

Our reviewers over the last three editions contributed time, expertise, and terrific ideas that significantly enhanced the quality of the text. The reviewers of the fourth edition are:

Debra A. Arvanites
Villanova University

Barbara Boyington
Brookdale Community College

Diane Caggiano
Fitchburg State College

Ron Dibattista
Bryant College

Dale Dickson
Mesa State College

William Jedlicka
William Rainy Harper College

Augustine Lado
Cleveland State University

Bert Nyman
Rockford College

Marc Siegall
California State University—Chico

Robert J. Ash
Rancho Santiago College

Charles A. Beasley
State University of New York—Buffalo

Hrach Bedrosian
New York University

Charles Blalack
Kilgore College

Mary A. Bouchard
Bristol Community College

Eugene L. Britt
Grossmont College

Lyvonne Burleson
Rollins College—Brevard

Elizabeth A. Cooper
University of Rhode Island

Anne C. Cowden
California State University—Sacramento

Michael W. Drafke
College of DuPage

J. F. Fairbank
Pennsylvania State University

Alan J. Fredian
Loyola University—Chicago

Steve Garlick
Devry Institute—Kansas City

John Hall
University of Florida

Donald E. Harris
Oakton Community College

Frederic J. Hebert
East Carolina University

Durward Hofler
Northeastern Illinois University

Thomas O. James
Benedictine College

Elias Kalman
Baruch College

Gus L. Kotoulas
Morton College

Catherine C. McElroy
Bucks County Community College

David L. McLain
Virginia State University

Joseph B. Mosca
Monmouth College

James J. Ravelle
Moravian College

Joseph C. Santora
Essex County College

Many individuals contributed directly to our development as textbook authors. Dennis Organ provided one of the authors with an initial opportunity and guidance in textbook writing. John Weimeister has been a friend and adviser from the very beginning. The entire Irwin/McGraw-Hill team demonstrated continued and generous support for this book. John Biernat was a great champion for the project, and is a talented editor and good friend. Kurt Strand is, too! What a team!

We thank Mary Conzachi and the production team for their diligence, perseverance, and professionalism. They kept us on schedule—the best they could—and produced a great looking book. Maryellen Krammer and Christine Scheid—what a super tandem of DEs. Maryellen had the tricky job of getting us out of port, through the harbor, and into the open sea. Christine then took the helm and helped us navigate from deep water back to shore. Together, these two colleagues and friends made us laugh, kept us to task, gave us great advice, and made us remember what a joy it can be to work with an excellent team. We can't forget Kimberly Stack, who somehow, someway was able to organize and deliver all of our supplements. Together, we can all take great pride in our product.

Finally, we thank our families. Our parents, Jeanine and Thomas Bateman and Clara and John Snell, provided us with the foundation on which we have built our careers. They continue to be a source of great support. Our wives, Mary Jo and Marybeth, demonstrated great encouragement, insight, and understanding throughout the entire process. Our children, Lauren (who also helped with clerical work!), T. J., and Jamie Bateman, and Sara, Jack, and Emily Snell, are an inspiration for everything we do.

Thomas S. Bateman
Lausanne, Switzerland

Scott A. Snell
State College, PA

Contents in Brief

Contents

Management

Building Competitive Advantage

Part One

Foundations of Management

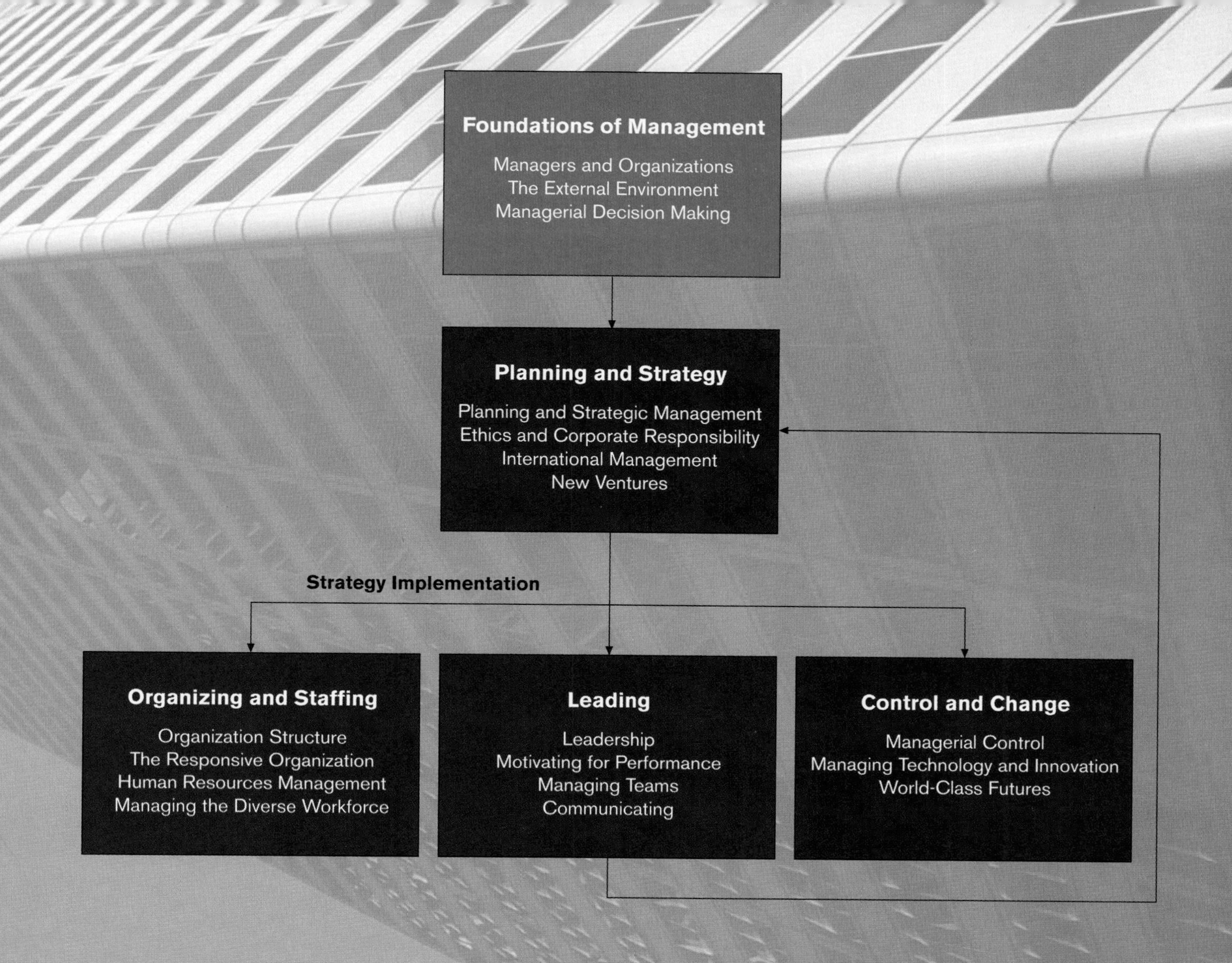

The three chapters in Part I describe the foundations of management. Chapter 1 introduces key functions, skills, and competitive goals of effective managers. Chapter 2 describes the external environment in which managers and their organizations operate. Chapter 3 discusses the most pervasive managerial activity—decision making. Sound decision-making skills are essential for effective managerial performance.

Chapter One
Managers and Organizations

Management means, in the last analysis, the substitution of thought for brawn and muscle, of knowledge for folklore and tradition, and of cooperation for force.

—*Peter Drucker*

Chapter Outline

Management and Its Functions
- The Functions of Management
- Performing All Four Management Functions

Management Levels
- Top-level Managers
- Middle-level Managers
- Frontline Managers

Why Study Management?
- Managers Are Universal
- Management by Common Sense
- Management by Experience

Organizations

Managing for Competitive Advantage
- Cost Competitiveness
- Quality
- Speed
- Innovation
- Delivering All Four

Management Skills
- Technical Skills
- Conceptual and Decision Skills
- Interpersonal and Communication Skills

Change and the Future of Management
- Globalization
- Total Quality
- The Learning Organization
- An Eye on the Future

Your Career in Management

Learning Objectives

After studying Chapter 1, you will know:

1. The functions of management.
2. The nature of management at different organizational levels.
3. How you can benefit from studying management.
4. The nature of organization.
5. The keys to gaining advantage over your organization's competitors.
6. The skills you need to be an effective manager.
7. The current forces shaping management practice today and for the future.
8. What to strive for as you manage your career.

Setting the Stage

Young Managers, Big Challenges

• Nicola Foulston is 29 years old, chief executive officer of Brands Hatch Leisure, and 1997 recipient of a Businesswoman of the Year award in the United Kingdom. The company's core businesses are four auto race tracks, which under her leadership have become highly profitable. She is now launching a chain of outdoor adventure parks built around the racing theme. Her success is accredited to her unique management style, bold creativity, strong character, and the fact that she usually makes the right decisions.

• Jamie Bonini was named manager of Chrysler Corp.'s big-van plant in Windsor, Ontario, at the age of 33. Sales were flat, and Bonini was faced with the task of launching a new van. He had to win the support of his 84 managers, 1,800 workers, and local union officials. Other managers had wanted the job, and they saw Bonini as young and inexperienced. Many expected, and some even wanted, him to fail. He made some mistakes, but within one year he was able to overhaul the outdated manufacturing system, change the factory's culture, and improve productivity and morale.

• George Jackson was recently named president and CEO of Motown Records. Motown had been plagued by years of disappointing results and poor management. Jackson is trying to restore Motown's great legacy by making the company profitable and an industry leader once again. He is under pressure; not only is the company struggling, after years of brilliance under Berry Gordy, but several prominent black-owned businesses have failed in recent years. As Clarence Avant, Motown's chairman emeritus, put it, "White people can afford to lose Pan Am, Montgomery Ward, or Woolworth's. There are a million other white-run institutions. Blacks cannot afford to lose even one." Jackson will need both knowledge of business fundamentals and managerial creativity.

Jill Barad, CEO of Mattel, has her own approach to managing that spells success for the company. *[Daniel Simon/Gamma Liaison]*

• Jill Barad is one of the most prominent female chief executives in America. She is highly competitive and has outperformed her rivals in her company and industry. After many successes in product design and marketing, including giving the Barbie doll a makeover and reestablishing it as the world's best-selling doll, she was named CEO at Mattel. She is doing things differently from her predecessor, including selling assets and focusing more on the longer term than on quarterly targets. Having always succeeded despite long odds and personal skeptics, she says she will continue to exceed expectations.

Sources: M. Yost, "Young CEO Revs up U.K. Corporate Engine," The Wall Street Journal, *June 12, 1997, p. 4; L. Bannon, "She Reinvented Barbie: Now, Can Jill Barad Do the Same for Mattel?"* The Wall Street Journal, *March 6, 1997, pp. 1, 7; and G. Stern, "Old Chrysler Plant Has Young Manager Rattling the Culture,"* The Wall Street Journal, *April 22, 1997, pp. 1, 6.*

Intel chairman Andy Grove is a model of effectiveness *and* efficiency. Working out of a 175-square-foot cubicle, Grove produces an average annual return to Intel investors of 28.8 percent. *[Christopher Irion]*

"Setting the Stage" portrays a fascinating and diverse group of managers in a variety of industries: music, automobiles, toys, racing, and theme parks. They don't have a lot in common. As you can see, however, they are all highly successful managers in their chosen careers. Throughout this textbook you will read about many other managers who have attained significant achievements in their organizations and industries. The purpose of this book is to provide you with ideas and tools that will help you become a successful manager, too.

Many people assume that being a good manager will come to them naturally. Some believe it is nothing more than common sense. Some have in their minds a stereotype of the traditional supervisor in a bureaucratic organization. But management is not what it used to be. Managers traditionally have worked within tradition and convention, by the rules, by the numbers, by the book, in the here and now. Power derived from being the boss, controlling resources, having access to information that others did not, and being able to command and control other people.

But things have changed. Managers today still must be able to analyze and control resources. They now must also be able to rethink, redo, and reenergize. They must live for the future, not just the here-and-now. And in stark contrast to the past, previous experience can now hurt more than it helps, if the experience is in a past business environment that no longer exists, or if it blinds a person to current and future realities and opportunities. Managers must lead their organizations into a highly uncertain future.[1]

Management and its functions

management The process of working with people and resources to accomplish organizational goals.

Management is the process of working with people and resources to accomplish organizational goals. Good managers do those things both effectively and efficiently. To be *effective* is to achieve organizational goals. To be *efficient* is to achieve goals with minimum waste of resources, that is, to make the best possible use of money, time, materials, and people. Some managers fail on both criteria, or focus on one at the expense of another. The best managers maintain a clear focus on both effectiveness *and* efficiency.

The functions of management

functions of management The four basic management processes consisting of planning, organizing, leading, and controlling.

What can managers do to be effective and efficient? The management process, properly executed, involves a wide variety of activities, including planning, organizing, leading, and controlling. These basic activities, described below and discussed throughout the book, are the traditional **functions of management.**

planning The management function of systematically making decisions about the goals and activities that an individual, a group, a work unit, or the overall organization will pursue in the future.

Planning

Planning is specifying the goals to be achieved and deciding in advance the appropriate actions taken to achieve those goals. Planning activities include analyzing current situations, anticipating the future, determining objectives, deciding in what types of activities the company will engage, choosing corporate and business strategies, and determining the resources needed to achieve the organization's goals.

A few years ago a businessman announced his plans to create a new national television network out of a small collection of stations. People laughed at first, but CBS, ABC, and NBC are not laughing at the Fox network now.[2] BMW developed a clear long-term plan to change from a high-cost German company into a true global car company, and then acted decisively by building a plant in South Carolina and purchasing Rover from British Aerospace.[3] Small firms, too, such as those owned by CPAs and plumbers, can benefit greatly from comprehensive planning.[4] Plans set the stage for action and for major achievements.

Plans are developed for entire organizations, for specific work units, and for individuals. These plans may cover long periods of time (five years or more) or a short time horizon (days or weeks). They may be very general (e.g., to improve profits through new product development) or very specific (e.g., to reduce product defects by 10 percent over the next month). In each case, however, managers are responsible for gathering and analyzing the information on which plans are based, setting the goals to be achieved, and deciding what needs to be done. Part II of this book focuses on planning, and covers topics such as strategy, ethics, new ventures, and the global environment.

organizing The management function of assembling and coordinating human, financial, physical, information and other resources needed to achieve goals.

Organizing

Organizing is assembling and coordinating the human, financial, physical, informational, and other resources needed to achieve goals. Activities include attracting people to the organization, specifying job responsibilities, grouping jobs into work units, marshalling and allocating resources, and creating conditions so that people and things work together to achieve maximum success. The chapters in Part III discuss organizing.

For example, when Dorothy Terrel of Digital Equipment Corporation was asked to manage the computer company's high-density interconnect and multichip module operation, her organizing and staffing skills proved essential. Her challenge was to transform a high-tech, nonmanufacturing operation into a high-volume producer of endurance technology for high-end office products. Terrell was chosen for the job because she had a thorough knowledge of the company, had an extensive network of business and community contacts in the Boston area, and could, in her words, "put technical minds together." In three years Terrell built the staff and plant management team from 200 to 1,200, was producing quality products at a competitive cost, and controlled a budget of more than $300 million at the new facility.[5]

leading The management function that involves the manager's efforts to stimulate high performance by employees.

Leading

Leading is stimulating people to be high performers. It is directing, motivating, and communicating with employees, individually and in groups. Leading involves close day-to-day contact with people, helping to guide and inspire them toward achieving team and organizational goals. Leading takes place in teams, departments, and divisions, and at the tops of entire organizations.

Livio DeSimone is chief executive officer of 3M, one of the great corporations of the world. The main tenets of his leadership philosophy include creating a cooperative work environment, maintaining constant communications, giving people some freedom to pursue their ideas, being honest at all times (with bad news as well as good), assigning people tasks that allow them to learn and grow, and publicly praising and rewarding people who do their jobs well.[6] Of course, Mr. DeSimone's leadership style is far more complex than this brief description; Part IV will elaborate on the best approaches to leading, motivating, communicating, and forging teamwork.

controlling The management function of monitoring progress and making needed changes.

Controlling Comprehensive plans, solid organization, and outstanding leaders do not guarantee success. The fourth function, **controlling,** monitors progress and implements necessary changes.

When managers implement their plans, they often find that things are not working out as planned. The controlling function makes sure that goals are met. It asks and answers the question, "Are our actual outcomes consistent with our goals?" It makes adjustments as needed.

Specific controlling activities are to set performance standards that indicate progress toward long-term goals; to monitor performance of people and units by collecting performance data; to provide people with feedback or information about their progress; to identify performance problems by comparing performance data against standards; and to take actions to correct problems. Budgeting, information systems, cost cutting, and disciplinary action are just a few of the tools of control.

Successful organizations, large and small, pay close attention to how well they are doing. They take fast action when problems arise and are able to change as needed. Part V covers control-related topics, including organizational control processes, operations management, innovation, and change.

Performing all four management functions

As a manager, your typical day will not be neatly divided into the four functions. You will engage in all of these activities, but usually not independently or sequentially. You will be doing many things more or less simultaneously. You will spend over 60 percent of your time meeting with many different people, and spend perhaps one and a half days per week on the telephone, discussing and deciding a vast variety of issues.[7] On average, your encounters with others will last about two minutes, and your quiet time without interruption will last less than 10. Your days will be busy and fractionated, spent dealing with interruptions, meetings, and firefighting. There will be plenty to do that you wish you could be doing but can't seem to get to. These activities will involve all four management functions.

Some managers are particularly interested in, devoted to, or skilled in a couple of the four functions but not in the others. The manager who does not devote adequate attention and resources to *all four* functions will fail. You can be a skilled planner and controller, but if you organize your people improperly or fail to inspire them to perform at high levels, you will not be an effective manager. Likewise, it does no good to be the kind of manager who loves to organize and lead, but who doesn't really understand where to go or how to determine whether you are on the right track. Good managers don't neglect any of the four management functions. Knowing what they are, you can periodically ask yourself if you are devoting adequate attention to *all* of them.

In the following example, recent MBAs describe their work experiences in central Europe. Virtually everything in their messages pertains to the functions performed by managers the world over.

The MBA enterprise corps: Spreading management skills

Selected graduates of the top U.S. business schools took their first jobs not making big paychecks with a Fortune 500 corporation but earning about $150 per month in Hungary, Poland, and the Czech Republic. They are members of the MBA Enterprise Corps, an organization based in Chapel Hill, North Carolina, and modeled after the Peace Corps. The MBAEC's mission is to help former communist countries successfully manage the transition to a free-market society of private rather than government-run enterprises.

These MBA Enterprise Corps members are meeting in Slovakia with political and business leaders to learn about the current economic and political situation.
[Courtesy MBA Enterprise Corps]

The corps members engage in all four management functions: planning, organizing, leading, and controlling. Following are some excerpts (a few paraphrased) from letters corps members wrote back to the United States while overseas:

On the management challenges:

- I'm engineering a new organizational structure to optimize the utilization of our scarce resources. The division has little managerial experience as we know it, but our director is determined that, with my advice, we can create a fully functioning, modern, competitive company.
- My role is to help in creating a general business strategy. The biggest problem is the enormous bureaucracy of the firm.
- The most fundamental of business skills—such as how to conduct business meetings—are not well developed. Overcoming resistance to change will be difficult.
- At times the place feels like it has the potential to be the next McKinsey of Poland, and at others it seems that it could explode and disintegrate at any moment.

On planning and decision making:

- I'm here to help implement needed changes. The problem is that there is absolutely no means of predicting the future. I've been attempting to persuade people to prepare a strategy under each possible scenario, but the people's general reaction to uncertainty is: It's safer to continue what we're doing now and wait to see what happens.
- I have spent a lot of my time developing three-month marketing plans. I had wanted to develop six-month plans, but there are too many changes occurring in the market and economy for us to effectively plan that far in advance.
- Decisions are based more on basic common sense, gut feelings, and trust than on what the numbers say.
- The village elders are hoping we could come up with a use for a deserted Soviet tank base in western Hungary. It's located in a swamp, is run down, and probably has a great deal of damage. If you have any ideas, let me know.

On the rewards:

- There is a world of opportunity here. It's a very rewarding experience. When I make a suggestion, their eyes light up as if I have just made a revelation. It's really fun.
- I am constantly required to apply the things I've learned in a new and different manner. In many ways, I believe I've learned as much from my Polish counterparts as I have taught to them.
- The most critical traits for corps members are curiosity, a wide range of interests, and large doses of courage and humility. This has been the most interesting, intellectually challenging adventure I have ever undertaken. ●

figure 1.1
Management levels

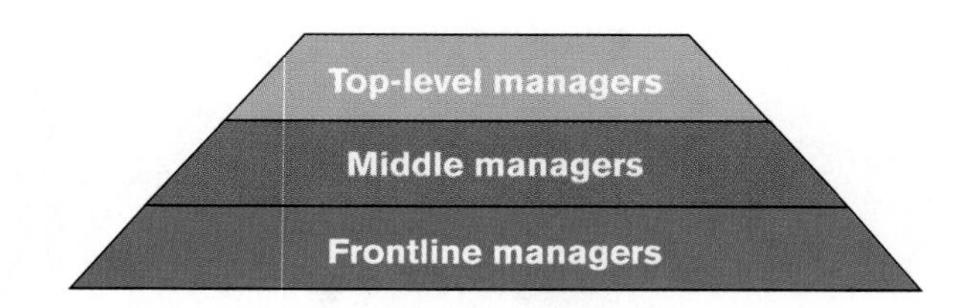

Management levels

Different managers emphasize different activities or exhibit different management styles. Recall the successful managers described in "Setting the Stage." These individuals do not manage using identical techniques.

There are many reasons for these differences, including the managers' training, personalities, and backgrounds. However, you will find that the organizational level at which the manager operates often influences the mixture of important functions and skills. Organizations (particularly large organizations) have many levels. In this section, you will learn about the types of managers found at three different levels in virtually all large organizations: top-level, middle, and frontline. Figure 1.1 shows the levels these managers occupy within the large organization.

Top-level managers

top-level managers Senior executives responsible for the overall management and effectiveness of the organization.

Top-level managers are the senior executives of an organization and are responsible for its overall management. Typically top-level managers, often referred to as *strategic managers,* focus on long-term issues and emphasize the survival, growth, and overall effectiveness of the organization.

Top managers are concerned not only with the organization as a whole, but also with the interaction between the organization and its external environment. This interaction often requires managers to work extensively with outside individuals and organizations.

The chief executive officer (CEO) is one type of top-level manager found in large corporations. This individual is the primary strategic manager of the firm. Others include the chief operating officer (COO), company presidents, vice presidents, and members of the top executive committee.

To some people, the CEO seems all-powerful. But it is an exceedingly demanding position that, like all other positions, can be managed well or poorly.

CEO disease: how *not* to lead

The CEO job easily can go to one's head. *Fortune* magazine described the "CEO Disease"–the belief of some CEOs that they are omnipotent, with the result being poor leadership. Most CEOs don't have the disease. Those who do have it exhibit the following symptoms. They

- Believe they can do no wrong and refuse to admit any mistakes.
- Surround themselves with people who say yes to their every whim.
- See themselves as the individual genius on whom success depends.
- Use degradation and humiliation to control people.
- Blame others for the CEO's own mistakes.
- Don't interact with "underlings."

- Want to make every decision, even if others know more of the relevant facts.
- Are overly preoccupied with being ahead of other CEOs in salary and perks.
- Relish media attention, not so much for the company but for personal fame and gain.

CEO Disease does not enhance the CEO's power. Instead, it leads to his or her demise. It hurts the company, in part by harming employee motivation and creating a we-versus-them atmosphere. By learning the material in this text, you will know the keys to avoiding the disease: a humble awareness of the complexities of management, an understanding of how to make decisions, a knowledge of what kinds of people to hire, an understanding of how to generate employee involvement instead of cynicism, and other things that make for good leadership and effective management.

Source: J. Byrne, W. Symonds, and J. Siler, "CEO Disease," *Fortune,* April 1, 1991, pp. 52–60; D. J. Cornwall, "The Demise of the Imperial CEO," *Fortune,* February 8, 1993, p. 38; and M. Cox and J. L. Roberts, "How the Despotic Boss of Simon & Schuster Found Himself Jobless," *The Wall Street Journal,* July 6, 1994, pp. A1, A8.

Traditionally, the role of top-level managers has been to set overall direction by formulating strategy and controlling resources. But now, top managers are more commonly called upon to be not only strategic architects but also true organizational leaders. As leaders they must create and articulate a broader corporate purpose with which people can identify, and one to which people will enthusiastically commit. Effective top leaders treat people as valued members of the organization. Thus Percy Barnevik, one of the most revered business leaders in Europe, strives to create an environment in which people are motivated to work for an organization in which they are proud to belong.

Middle-level managers

middle-level managers
Managers located in the middle layers of the organizational hierarchy, reporting to top-level executives.

As the name implies, **middle-level managers** are located in the organization's hierarchy between top-level management and the frontline managers described below. Sometimes called *tactical managers,* they are responsible for translating the general goals and plans developed by strategic managers into more specific objectives and activities.

Traditionally, the role of the middle manager is to be an administrative controller who bridges the gap between higher and lower levels. Middle-level managers take corporate objectives and break them down into business unit targets; put together separate business unit plans from the units below them for higher-level corporate review; and serve as linchpins of internal communication, interpreting and broadcasting top management's priorities downward, and channeling and translating information from the front lines, upward.

The evolving role of middle managers now requires them to be not only administrative controllers but also developmental coaches to the people who report to them. They should support the activities of their people, and coach people to become more entrepreneurial and innovative. Paul Guehler of 3M describes his job as "to help develop the people to develop the business."[8] Waldemar Schmidt of ISS, who recently became CEO, constantly contacted his frontline managers to say "Well done!" and "How can I help?"

Middle managers should ensure that those reporting to them keep long-term strategic objectives and short-term, more immediate operating priorities in balance. For example, Paul Guehler forced one of his frontline managers to make major cuts in his units in order to meet financial objectives, but at the same time fought against attempts to close the unit down and worked to line up support and resources for the manager's proposed development initiatives.

Frontline managers

frontline managers Lower-level managers who supervise the operational activities of the organization.

Frontline managers, or *operational managers,* are lower-level managers who supervise the operations of the organization. These managers often have titles such as supervisor or sales manager. They are directly involved with nonmanagement employees, implementing the specific plans developed with middle managers. This role is critical in the organization, because operational managers are the link between management and nonmanagement personnel. Your first management position probably will fit into this category.

Traditionally, frontline managers have been directed and controlled from above, to make sure that they successfully implement operations in support of company strategy. But in leading companies, the role has expanded. Whereas the operational execution aspect of the role remains vital, in leading companies frontline managers are increasingly called upon to be innovative and entrepreneurial, managing for growth and new business development.

As examples, Andy Wong took over a struggling division at 3M, fought some battles, focused attention on new goals, reenergized a discouraged team of people, introduced new products, and found new markets for old products. His unit became a showcase within 3M—quite an honor in a company known for its innovative and successful business units. When Don Jans managed Westinghouse's relays business unit, he was urged to milk the declining but modestly profitable operations. But when ABB bought Westinghouse's power transmission and distribution business, which included the relays business unit, Jans and his team were able to turn the mature business into one that looked like a new growth company. Export sales skyrocketed, new products were introduced, operating profits doubled, and the foundation was laid for long-term expansion into a major new growth area.

These and other outstanding front-line managers are not only *allowed* to initiate new activities, but are *expected* to by their top- and middle-level managers. And they are given freedom, incentives, and support to find ways to do so.

Table 1.1 elaborates on the traditional and changing aspects of different management levels. You will learn about each of these aspects of management throughout this course.

Working leaders with broad responsibilities

You may have noted that several times we have qualified our descriptions of managerial levels by referring to large organizations. These descriptions represent the traditional model for large organizations. But the trend today is toward less hierarchy and more teamwork. Small companies have become more common and important as large corporations lay off people, those people and other entrepreneurs start their own firms, and these smaller firms prove themselves capable of beating the giants with specialized products and strategies and the ability to adapt quickly to change.

In these small firms—and in those large companies that have adapted to the times—managers have strategic, tactical, *and* operational responsibilities. They are *complete* businesspeople; they have knowledge of all business functions, are accountable for results, and focus on serving customers both inside and outside their firms. All this requires the ability to think strategically, translate strategies into specific objectives, coordinate resources, and do real work with lower-level people.

In short, today's best managers can do it all; they are "working leaders".[9] They focus on relationships with other people and on achieving results. They are hands-on, working managers. They don't just make decisions, give orders, wait for others to produce, and then evaluate results. They get dirty, do hard work themselves, solve problems, and produce value.

table 1.1
Transformation of management roles and tasks

	Frontline managers	Middle-level managers	Top-level managers
Changing roles	• From operational implementers to aggressive entrepreneurs	• From administrative controllers to supportive coaches	• From resource allocaters to institutional leaders
Primary value	• Driving business performance by focusing on productivity, innovation and growth within frontline units	• Providing the support and coordination to bring large company advantage to the independent frontline units	• Creating and embedding a sense of direction, commitment and challenge to people throughout the organization
Key activities	• Creating and pursuing new growth opportunities for the business	• Developing individuals and supporting their activities	• Challenging embedded assumptions while establishing a stretching opportunity horizon and performance standards
	• Attracting and developing resources and competencies	• Linking dispersed knowledge, skills, and best practices across units	• Institutionalizing a set of norms and values to support cooperation and trust
	• Managing continuous performance improvement within the unit	• Managing the tension between short-term performance and long-term ambition	• Creating an overarching corporate purpose and ambition

Source: C. Bartlett and S. Goshal, "The myth of the generic manager: New personal competencies for new management roles." *California Management Review* Vol. 40, No. 1, fall 1997, pp. 92–116.

Why study management?

Sometime during this term, a member of your class (who did not study this chapter) will make a statement similar to one of the following:

"Why should I study management? I'm going to be an accountant."

"Why should I study management? It's all common sense."

"Why should I study management? Experience is the best teacher."

On the surface, these statements seem to have merit. Let's consider each argument.

Managers are universal

Managers work in all types of organizations, at all levels, and in all functional areas. Large and small businesses, hospitals, schools, governments, and churches benefit from efficient and effective management. The leaders of these organizations may be called executives, administrators, principals, or pastors, but they are all managers and are responsible for the success or failure of the organization. This success or failure is reflected in a manager's career. For example, when a CEO saves a failing corporation, the board rewards this success with bonuses and stock options. When a professional football team starts losing, the owner fires the coach, not the team.

The success of any organization, including the military, depends on effective management.
[Randy Taylor/Sygma]

Even the military is not exempt from the need for good management. In his book *The Straw Giant,* Arthur Hadley describes a long list of U.S. military disasters and fiascoes from World War II through the operations in Iran, Lebanon, and Grenada.[10] He cites a variety of reasons for these problems, most of which were management related: inadequate and mismanaged human resources, overcontrol from Washington, lack of coordination among the different branches of the military, and poorly allocated resources. Conversely, many of these basic management activities have been executed much more effectively in recent years. No matter where you intend to work, effective managers are a necessity.

Managers are also found in each functional area of an organization. Accountants are promoted to accounting department heads and project team leaders, sales representatives become sales managers, writers become editors, and nurses become nursing administrators. Management skills are important to anyone who intends to pursue a career. Beginning to prepare now for a career in management will yield benefits sooner than you may think.

Management by common sense

Many of the basic ideas you will learn in this course do not sound revolutionary or earth shattering: Managers should plan for the future; organizations should adapt to their environments; and managers should identify things their employees value and offer them as rewards for high performance. Most of this sounds like common sense.

Although some of the management concepts discussed in this text may seem obvious, developing them on your own or putting them into practice in the proper way, at the right time, and under appropriate conditions is difficult. If management was all common sense, there would not be so many failing companies, and so many people who complain about their incompetent bosses. Our natural ability to make the right decision or take the proper action—our common sense—can be improved greatly through systematic study.

Management by experience

One successful entrepreneur often makes statements like "Management can be learned only from the school of hard knocks." This person never took a business course; instead, he learned everything on his own. Although he was fired from two jobs and failed in three previous business attempts, he is now the owner of a thriving firm with sales of $100 million. This person believes a textbook and a college course cannot replace the experience he gained from his years in business.

Although this book alone cannot replace the knowledge and skills you will develop through experience, a management course can offer valuable preparation and supplement your experience. Many of the concepts covered in this text will help you make sense out of your experiences more quickly. These concepts will provide you with a head start in your management career. Furthermore, this text is an organized summary of the experiences of many managers. The management research reported here is another form of experience. Through this course, you can learn from the experiences of others and perhaps avoid being fired twice or failing the first three times you start a business.

Organizations

Managers operate in organizations. Exactly what is an organization? An organization is not a random group of people who come together by chance. It is consciously and formally established to accomplish certain goals that its members would be unable to reach by themselves. For example, a business organization has objectives to (1) make a profit for its owners, (2) furnish its customers with goods and services, (3) provide an income for its employees, and (4) increase the level of satisfaction for everyone involved.

A hospital delivers health care services. A professional sports team is organized to win games and make money. A charitable organization attempts to raise funds to alleviate some social problem. The managers of these organizations are responsible for achieving those objectives.

systems theory A theory stating that an organization is a set of interdependent elements, which in turn are interdependent with the external environment.

organization A managed system designed and operated to achieve a specific set of objectives.

system A set of interdependent parts that processes inputs into outputs.

Systems theory, which takes a comprehensive view of organizational processes, provides a way to more completely understand organizations. An **organization** is a managed system designed and operated to achieve a specific set of objectives. As Figure 1.2 shows, a **system** processes inputs (such as raw materials) into outputs (products). Business inputs typically are called *resources.* Most businesses use a variety of human, financial, physical, and informational resources. Managers function to transform these resources into goods and services, the products of the business.

Important concepts from systems theory include open versus closed systems, efficiency and effectiveness, subsystems, equifinality, and synergy.

Open versus closed systems

A *closed system* does not interact with the outside environment. Although few systems actually take this form, some of the classical

figure 1.2
Open-system perspective on an organization

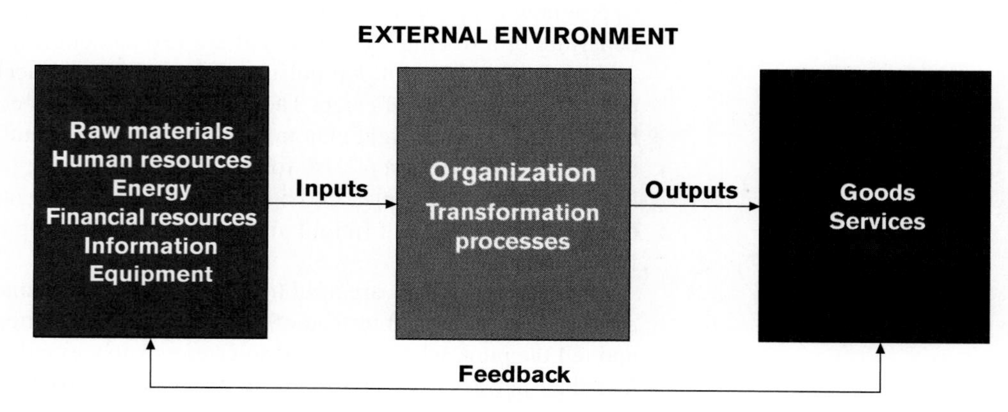

approaches to management treated organizations as closed systems. The assumption was that if managers improve internal processes, the organization will succeed. Clearly, however, all organizations are *open systems,* dependent on inputs from the outside world, such as raw materials, human resources, and capital, and outputs to the outside world that meet the market's needs for goods and services.

Figure 1.2 illustrates the open-system perspective. The organizational system requires inputs, which the organization transforms into outputs, which are received by the external environment. The environment reacts to these outputs through a feedback loop, which then becomes a new input for the ongoing cycle of the system.

Efficiency and effectiveness The closed-system focus of the classical theorists emphasized the internal efficiency of the organization; that is, these perspectives addressed only improvements to the transformation process. In systems theory terms, **efficiency** is the ratio of outputs to inputs. Systems theory highlights another important dimension for managers: effectiveness. **Effectiveness** is the degree to which the organization's outputs correspond to the needs and wants of the external environment. The external environment includes groups such as customers, suppliers, competitors, and regulatory agencies.

efficiency The ratio of outputs to inputs.

effectiveness The degree to which the outputs of the organization correspond to the outputs desired by organizations and individuals in the external environment.

Subsystems Systems theory also emphasizes that an organization is one level in a series of **subsystems.** For instance, American Airlines is a subsystem of the airline industry and the flight crews are subsystems of American Airlines. Again, systems theory points out that each subsystem is a component of the whole and is interdependent with other systems.

subsystems Interdependent components of a system.

Equifinality The concept of **equifinality** states that there are many avenues to the same outcome. Instead of maintaining that there exists "one best way," systems theory suggests that many different combinations of subsystems, ideas, and methods can lead to the same goal. The validity of this principle is clear in many businesses today. For instance, Domino's Pizza has been very successful with a low-cost, high-volume strategy, while Pizza Hut has been equally successful with a more full-service strategy.

equifinality Principle that states there are many avenues to the same outcome, and not just one best way.

Synergy Systems theory also highlights the concept of **synergy,** which states that the whole can be greater than the sum of its parts. For example, 3M has applied its core technology of adhesives to many products, from industrial sealers to Post-it™ notes. 3M has not had to start from scratch with each product; its adhesives expertise provides synergies across products.

synergy The sharing of benefits across system parts, resulting in a whole that is greater than the sum of its parts.

See how many of the elements of systems theory you can identify in the arrival and departure of a Boeing 737. On board are 130 passengers, 4,000 pounds of luggage, and 2,000 pounds of freight. All must be removed and replaced by an equivalent number of people and poundage of cargo. The following procedures occur: (1) As passengers disembark, the pilot loads flight plan information into the aircraft computer; (2) workers clean the cabin; (3) caterers replenish food, drinks, and snacks; (4) a fuel truck loads 5,300 gallons of fuel into the wings; (5) baggage crews unload luggage and freight; (6) new people board, and luggage and freight are loaded; and (7) ramp agents "push" the plane away from the gate.

A number of tactics are used to speed up the turnaround times. Six or seven baggage employees can be used instead of three or four. Flight attendants can inventory leftovers and tell the pilot, who calls ahead so caterers know exactly what is needed. Cleaners do a less-than-perfect job, tidying up on an as-needed basis. Passengers face stricter rules regarding arrival times and carry-on luggage. (Southwest Airlines saves even more boarding time by not assigning seats.) And the crew really has to hustle.

When such tactics are used to improve turnaround, some crew members complain about the time pressure, and passengers lose some amenities. But business travelers now are a little more likely to be able to complete their business in one day. And airlines that significantly reduce turnaround times can get more flights daily out of their planes, and can sell thousands more tickets per day.[11]

Figure 1.3 begins to convey that real systems are more complex than the basic model of Figure 1.2. It shows some of the many important elements of the organization's external environment and indicates that those elements both provide inputs to and receive outputs from the organization. As you progress through this course, you will learn more about these complex interdependencies.

Great Organizations

Because this course is about managers and organizations, you may be interested in the results of a survey that *Fortune* magazine conducts each year. The survey asks executives, board members, and financial analysts to rate the 10 largest companies in their industries on the following eight key attributes of reputation:

1. Quality of management.
2. Quality of products.
3. Innovativeness.
4. Long-term investment value.
5. Financial soundness.
6. Ability to attract, develop, and keep talented people.
7. Community and environmental responsibility.
8. Use of corporate assets.

figure 1.3
Expanded systems view

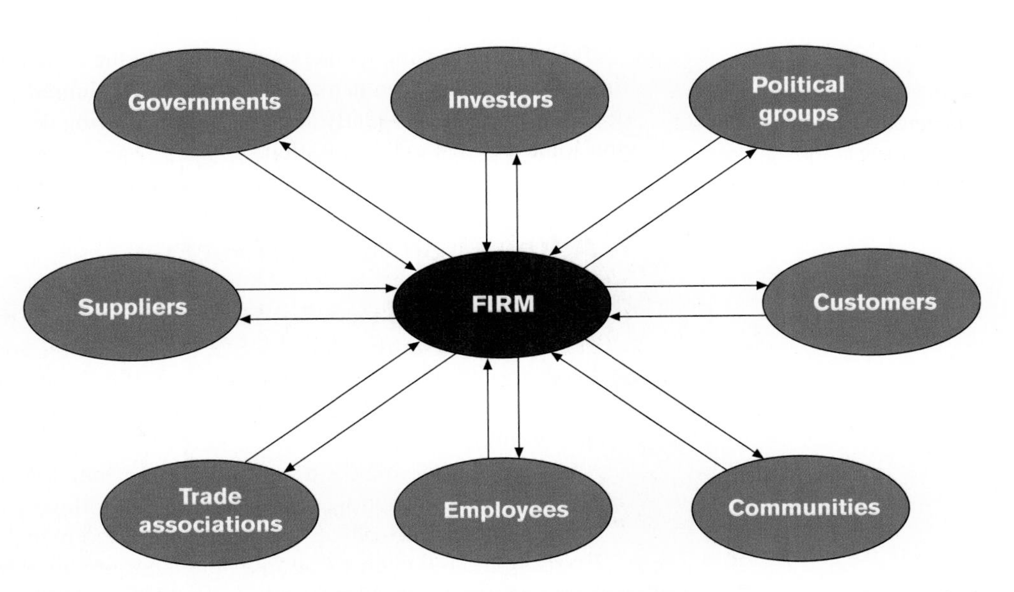

Source: T. Donaldson and L. Preston, "The Stakeholder Theory of the Corporation: Concepts, Evidence, and Implications," *Academy of Management Review* 20 (1997) pp. 65–91.

table 1.2
The world's most admired companies

For 1998, *Fortune* magazine determined their list of America's most admired companies in a new way. They simply asked 12,600 ballot recipients which companies, regardless of industry, they admired most.

And the winners are:

1. General Electric
2. Microsoft
3. Coca-Cola
4. Intel
5. Hewlett-Packard
6. Southwest Airlines
7. Berkshire Hathaway
8. Disney
9. Johnson & Johnson
10. Merck

Source: Anne Fisher, "The World's Most Admired Companies," *Fortune*, October 27, 1997, p. 40.

Table 1.2 shows the winners worldwide. In the United States, Rubbermaid has several times in the 1990s been named the single most-admired corporation.[12] Why do you think certain firms are consistently admired? The following description of Rubbermaid may give you some answers to this question.

Admiration for Rubbermaid

Fortune magazine calls Rubbermaid a "master of the mundane and a champion innovator." Under CEO Stanley Gault and now Wolfgang Schmitt, Rubbermaid has for years been one of the most successful and admired companies in the United States. How do they do it? What is its great strengths?

One of Rubbermaid's great strengths is that it does not depend on any single product or on any single person. What the company does rely on is 5,000 products for home, office, and recreation. And to improve continuously, Rubbermaid relies on its people. Its managers care about the company and its products, and they know that teamwork is a wellspring of new ideas. Teams of five to seven people from different functional areas (marketing, manufacturing, finance, and so on) focus their productive efforts on particular product lines. Rubbermaid executives believe that organizing by teams is the key to their success.

The products themselves are not very fancy–they include mail boxes, mops, dust mitts, spatulas, drink coasters, and ice cube trays. In addition to improving these constantly, Rubbermaid introduces new products at a rate of one per day–and 9 out of 10 succeed. With this in mind, CEO Schmitt sets special goals for his company, among them: (1) entering a new product category every 12 to 18 months; (2) getting 33 percent of sales from products introduced in the past five years; and (3) getting 25 percent of revenues from non–U.S. markets by the year 2000.

The details that people at other companies don't take seriously are studied carefully by dedicated Rubbermaid employees. As *Fortune* put it, "Engineers pour over blueprints of beverage coolers and sandwich keepers with the same intensity General Dynamics might bring to an F-111." Rubbermaid's laundry baskets are ergonomically engineered to fit comfortably against the waist; its mailboxes have flags that pop up automatically to show they have mail.

The innovative people of Rubbermaid get their ideas from everywhere. A recent trip to the British Museum and its Egyptian antiquities led a team to 11 new product ideas. The ancient Egyptians had a lot of well-designed kitchen utensils. Why not learn from them?

Rubbermaid has faced some problems. The price of resin, the basic raw material in production, has doubled in a short period, and a low-cost competitor is doing well. But Rubbermaid's speed and innovation are carrying it through the rough waters. The company spends money on design, production, and whatever else can have immediate impact on speed and innovation. Wolfgang Schmitt states, "Ingenuity of design to create the best combination of quality, price, timeliness, service, and innovation is our best defense against copycats and our best way to delight customers." (Kanter et al., p. 151) "Today's consumers are unwilling to sacrifice quality and other things for a good price. They expect–and Rubbermaid aims to deliver–it all." (p. 153)

Rubbermaid's policy, constantly discussed and vigorously pursued, is to delight consumers and customers. The entire organization is focused on delighting.

Sources: R.M. Kanter, J. Kao, and F. Wiersema, *Innovation: Breakthrough Thinking at 3M, DuPont, GE, Pfizer, and Rubbermaid.* (New York: HarperBusiness, 1997); A. Farnham, "America's Most Admired Company," *Fortune,* February 7, 1994, pp. 50–54.

Innovation, attention to detail, challenging goals, continuous improvement, good leadership, motivated people, awareness of what customers value, constant desire to learn. . . these and other things you will learn about in this course typify the great companies, and the great managers.

Managing for competitive advantage

Management is about helping your firm survive and win in competition with other companies. If your firm is well managed, it is far more likely to be a success and a leader in the highly competitive business world.

To survive and win, you have to gain advantage over your competitors. You need to be better than your competitors at doing valuable things for your customers. You gain competitive advantage by adopting management approaches that satisfy customers through cost competitiveness, high-quality products, speed, and innovation.[13]

The cost overruns of Denver International Airport overshadowed its value to airline customers.
[AP Photo/Joe Mahoney/Wide World Photos]

Cost competitiveness

cost competitiveness
Keeping costs low in order to achieve profits and price so that they are attractive to consumers.

Cost competitiveness means that your costs are kept low enough so that you can realize profits and price your products (goods or services) at levels that are attractive to consumers. Needless to say, if you can offer a desirable product at a low price, it is more likely to sell. Southwest Airlines is a good example of a company that has a big cost advantage over its rivals, in that it can reduce prices and survive fare wars.[14]

You can offer low prices by managing your costs and keeping them down. This means being efficient: accomplishing your goals by using your resources wisely and minimizing waste. If your cost structure is competitive (as low as or lower than your competitors'), your success is not guaranteed. But you cannot be successful without a competitive cost structure.[15]

Costs include money spent on inputs, transformation processes, and delivery of outputs to the market. Raw materials, equipment, capital, manufacturing, marketing, delivery, and labor are just some of the costs that need to be managed carefully.

The Denver International Airport became an international embarrassment when it came in more than $1 billion over budget and carriers were asked to pay per-passenger operating costs that were three times those charged at the existing Stapleton Airport.[16] Major league baseball owners did a poor job of keeping their labor costs down, although they were able to keep raising ticket prices for years. But when they claimed they were in financial trouble and tried to halt rising salaries, the players struck. Many businesses and people were hurt financially by the owners' and players' inability to agree on a fair way to control costs.[17]

People are a central topic of this course. One obvious, simplistic way to reduce costs is to cut back the labor force, or to provide low wages and benefits. But a better way to achieve favorable costs is to pay people fairly and make sure they add more value to your products than your competitors' employees add to theirs.[18]

Quality

A CPA in Michigan says, "People are more aware than ever that you are judged by the quality of your product above all."[19] Larry Harmon, a highly successful plumber in California, wants to start franchising: "I think the nation is ready for a national franchised plumbing company—as long as it is high quality."[20] Brio America, a division of the Swedish maker of high-quality toys, distributes through small specialty toy stores rather than the huge toy merchants. Why? The specialty stores "sell toys based on what is in the package rather than what is on the package."[21] In other words, they focus on quality products that provide the value customers want.

quality The excellence of a product, including such things as attractiveness, lack of defects, reliability, and long-term dependability.

Quality is the excellence of your product, including its attractiveness, lack of defects, reliability, and long-term dependability. The importance of quality, and standards for acceptable quality, have increased dramatically in recent years. Firms cannot get by offering poor-quality products as they could a few years ago. Customers now demand high quality and value, and will accept nothing less.

Providing world-class quality requires a *thorough* understanding of what quality really is.[22] Quality can be measured in terms of performance, additional features, reliability (failure or breakdowns), conformance to standards, durability, serviceability, and aesthetics. Only by moving beyond broad, generic concepts like "quality," to identifying the more specific elements of quality, can you identify problems, target needs, set performance standards more precisely, and deliver world-class value. For example, as the following examples illustrate, there are many aspects to providing customers with world-class service.

Achieving world-class service quality

What can organizations do to achieve one of the most important dimensions of world-class excellence–great service quality?

- *Provide basic service:* Fundamentals are more important than fanciness. Performance is key, not empty promises. Automobile repair customers expect competence, respect, and explanations. Hotel customers want a clean and safe room, and want to be treated like guests. Insurance customers want their agents to keep them informed, be on their side, play fair, protect them, and deliver prompt results. These are not the extravagant, inflated, unreasonable expectations that some executives attribute to today's customers.
- *Be reliable.* Perform the promised service dependably and accurately. Hard Rock Cafe's philosophy is: Be careful and don't make a mistake in the first place–but if a mistake does occur, correct it before it reaches the customer.
- *Listen to customers:* Learn from customers the strengths and weaknesses of your company's service. Develop a complete service quality information system. It took them 15 years to learn it, but the downtown Chicago Marriott Hotel discovered that 66 percent of all guest calls to housekeeping were requests for irons and ironing boards. So they put irons and ironing boards in all guest rooms.
- *Listen to employees:* Learning what's on the employees' minds is as important to good customer service as doing customer research. Employees often know what reduces service quality, because they see the service delivery system in action on a daily basis. They may even see early signs of a service breakdown before customers are exposed to it.
- *Solve problems:* When a problem arises, some firms make things worse. The best service providers *encourage* customers to complain, respond quickly and personally, and have a system in place for solving problems.
- *Surprise customers:* Service providers must be reliable. Beyond that, they can surprise and even delight customers with special courtesy, competence, commitment, and action. Don't meet customer expectations: exceed them, maybe even dramatically. They will never forget it, and they will tell their friends.
- *Be fair:* This is the essence underlying all customer expectations. Ask yourself: Is it fair to the customer? Does it look fair in his or her eyes? Customers won't return if they don't trust your company to deal with them fairly. A service guarantee sends the fairness message clearly. For example, Hampton Inn offers the night's stay for free to dissatisfied customers; almost nine out of ten guests who invoke the guarantee say they will return.

Source: L. Berry, A. Parasuraman, and V. Zeithaml, "Improving Service Quality in America: Lessons Learned," *The Executive,* May 1994, pp. 32–45. ●

Speed

speed Fast and timely execution, response, and delivery of results.

Speed often separates the winners from the losers in the world of competition. How fast can you develop and get a new product to market? How quickly can you respond to customer requests? You are far better off if you are faster than the competition—or if you can respond quickly to your competitors' actions.

One of the biggest problems in the fashion industry—called by some the dirtiest secret in the industry—is the speed with which expensive designer originals are turned into low-priced knockoffs or "interpretations."[23] Photographs taken at fashion shows are faxed overnight across the world, factories turn out samples a few hours later, and the samples can be shipped anywhere by the next day. Retail stores sell them in their private-label collections at the same time they offer the original designs in their pricier departments. Competitors' sheer speed is driving fashion designers crazy—and eroding their profits.

Innovation

Two Stanford business professors recently completed a study of 18 great companies. Impressed with all the companies, the authors still were able to choose one above them all that they believed would be the most successful over time. That company was 3M, and the reason is its extraordinary ability to innovate.[24]

innovation Introduction of new products.

Innovation is the introduction of new goods and services. Your firm must adapt to changes in consumer demands and to new sources of competition. Products don't sell forever; in fact, they don't sell for nearly as long as they used to, because so many competitors are introducing so many new products all the time. Your firm must innovate, or it will die. Like the other sources of competitive advantage, innovation comes from people; it must be a goal; and it must be managed. You will learn how 3M and other great companies innovate in later chapters.

Delivering all four

Don't assume you can settle for delivering just one of the four competitive advantages: low cost alone, or quality alone, for example. The best managers and companies deliver them all. And small firms that can provide multiple advantages over larger, more powerful companies can seize the competitive edge. For example, in custom software development, big-name corporations take a long time and charge big daily fees that can add up seemingly forever. Sapient Corp. was founded in 1991 on the premise that customers who want new software systems would love to be given a guaranteed delivery date and a fixed price. With this combination of speed and low price, relative to its famous competitors, Sapient is off to a flying start.[25]

Michael Dell started Dell Computer in his dorm room and used a low-cost, direct-sales approach to making his company the driving force in the PC business. Dell's manufacturing costs are the lowest in the industry. Dell says, "We will be the lowest-cost provider, period." Dell's competitors are scrambling to match it, but right now it is impossible for them to match Dell's low prices.[26]

But low cost is not the only thing at which Dell excels. Dell builds and ships PCs within 36 hours of receiving an order. All of its suppliers know they must deliver parts to Dell within one hour. At the same time, Dell computers have consistently held some of the highest quality ratings in the industry. Nonetheless, Michael Dell recently became obsessed with improving quality even further.[27] The sensitive hard drive needed to be handled less during assembly, he decided. Revamping the production lines, he has reduced the number of touches from more than 30 per drive to fewer than 15. Rejected hard drives fell by 40 percent, and the overall PC failure rate by 20 percent.

From his dorm room, Michael Dell took on giants IBM, Apple, and Compaq. The amazing success of Dell computer is due to its low cost, speed, quality, and innovation. *[Reuters/Toshiyuki Aizawa/Archive Photos]*

Low cost, speedy delivery, quality improvements . . . all these changes also suggest an innovative company. As another example, Dell buyers can configure their own model on Dell's website and see how their customized PC is priced by features on the screen. Intel's Andy Grove says, "Dell has always been able to figure out the next wrinkle to stay ahead. It's in their genes."[28]

Remember three key points about these sources of competitive advantage: First, they represent the crucial results that your firm, and you, must achieve. Second, each is directly affected by your decisions and actions and by the decisions and actions of others with whom you work. Third, it is *how you manage* that determines how well you and your people achieve competitive advantage and deliver the valued results. Because of the importance of focusing on the sources of competitive advantage, and because managers can easily and often lose sight of them, we will highlight them with icons in the margins throughout the book.

Management skills

Performing management functions and achieving competitive advantage are the cornerstones of a manager's job. However, recognizing and understanding this does not ensure success. Managers need a variety of skills to *do* these things *well.* Skills are specific abilities that result from knowledge, information, practice, and aptitude. Although managers require many individual skills, which you will learn about throughout the text, consider three general categories: technical skills, interpersonal and communication skills, and conceptual and decision skills.[29] When the key management functions are performed by managers who have these critical management skills, the result is a high-performance work environment.

Technical skills

technical skill The ability to perform a specialized task involving a particular method or process.

A **technical skill** is the ability to perform a specialized task that involves a certain method or process. Most people develop a set of technical skills to complete the activities that are part of their daily work lives. When you leave school, you will have a set of technical skills that will provide you with the opportunity to get an entry-level position. Accounting majors will develop many of the basic skills needed to conduct an audit. Information systems majors will have important computer skills. Marketing majors may know pricing, market research, and sales techniques.

The technical skills you learn in school will also help you as a manager. For example, your basic accounting and finance courses will develop the technical skills you need to understand and manage the financial resources of an organization. Managers may rely less on their basic technical skills as they rise through an organization, but these skills give them the background for their new responsibilities, as well as an appreciation of the activities of others in the firm.

Conceptual and decision skills

conceptual and decision skills Skills pertaining to a manager's ability to recognize complex and dynamic issues, examine the numerous and conflicting factors such issues involve, and resolve the problems for the benefit of the organization and its members.

Conceptual and decision skills involve the manager's ability to recognize complex and dynamic issues, to examine the numerous and conflicting factors that influence these issues or problems, and to resolve the problems for the benefit of the organization and everyone concerned. As you acquire greater responsibility, you must exercise your conceptual and decision skills with increasing frequency. You will confront issues that involve all aspects of the organization and must consider a larger and more interrelated set of decision factors. Such decisions have profound effects on the success of the organization.

Managers use these skills when they consider the overall objectives and strategy of the firm, the interactions among different parts of the organization, and the role of the business in its external environment. A major portion of this text is devoted to enhancing your conceptual and decision skills, but remember that experience plays an important part in their development.

Interpersonal and communication skills

interpersonal and communication skills People skills; the ability to lead, motivate, and communicate effectively with others.

Interpersonal and communication skills influence the manager's ability to work well with people. These skills are often called the *people skills.* Managers spend the great majority of their time interacting with people.[30] Because managers must deal with others, they must develop their abilities to lead, motivate, and communicate effectively with those around them. The ability to get along with many diverse types of people and exchange information with them is vital for a successful management career.

A recent *Fortune* article decried the lack of communication and other "people" skills among recent MBAs launching their management careers.[31] It is vital to realize the importance of these skills in getting a job, keeping it, and performing well in it. As one expert commented, "In many, many companies, the reason a manager fails is not because he doesn't have the technical skills. It's because he doesn't have the people skills."[32]

While there are still plenty of traditional managers around, concentrating on being the boss, giving orders, and carefully monitoring employees, many believe that the manager of today and of the future must focus more on interpersonal skills such as being a team player, sharing information with others, and teaching and helping people learn. Table 1.3 asks you to consider whether you are (or will be) a traditional manager, or the contemporary manager needed now and in the future.

Change and the future of management

Table 1.3 barely begins to describe how managers must change. Time keeps passing, and things keep changing. This may sound obvious, but it isn't to those managers and firms that fail to adapt. If you don't anticipate change and adapt to it, you and your firm will not survive in a competitive business world.

Effective managers must be comfortable with change and willing to act in the face of uncertainty. Bob Galvin, Motorola's CEO until his son took over in 1997, announced at a meeting that the company was too bureaucratic and must begin large-scale change. But he didn't say how. He purposely left it vague and uncertain so that his managers could be creative and experiment. Some managers wallowed in the ambiguity, stuck in the fact that they didn't know what Galvin was looking for. Others—energized instead of frustrated and inhibited by the uncertainty of the situation—used the challenge as an opportunity to try new things.[33]

What would have been your reaction to Galvin's challenge? Good management will require you to make difficult decisions and take action even if it is not clear exactly what needs

table 1.3
Which kind are you?

Traditional Manager	Contemporary Manager
Thinks of self as a manager or boss.	Thinks of self as a sponsor, or internal consultant.
Follows the chain of command	Deals with anyone necessary to get the job done.
Makes more decisions alone.	Invites others to join in decision making.
Hoards information.	Shares information.
Tries to master one major discipline, such as marketing or finance.	Tries to master a broad array of managerial disciplines.
Looks "up" for direction and answers.	Questions, collaborates, and negotiates with others to find solutions
Accepts and does repetitive work.	Learns new ways to contribute.
Sees others primarily as bosses and competitors.	Creates relationships based on common purpose, mutual respect, and exchange of information.
Demands long hours.	Demands results.

Sources: B. Dumaine, "The New Non-Manager Managers," *Fortune,* February 22, 1993, p. 81; and C. Hakim, *We Are All Self-Employed,* (San Francisco: Berrett-Koehler, 1995).

to be done. *Fortune* magazine described the managers of the world's most admired companies as being "willing to take risks so bold they may cause shareholders, stock analysts, and employees to seriously question their sanity." Even Royal Dutch/Shell, the world's most profitable company, is reinventing itself amid tremendous uncertainty. Says Shell's exploration and production director Robert Sprague, "We are moving forward briskly into the fog."[34]

Here is a brief introduction to just a few of the major changes currently having profound effects on the practice of management. We will revisit these topics throughout the book.

Globablization

William Johnson has the responsibility for taking Heinz global. Entry into Europe, China, Argentina, and Africa look promising.
[Theo Westenberger/Liaison International]

For U.S. and non–U.S. managers alike, isolationism is a thing of the past.[35] This must be so for organizations to survive worldwide competition in a global marketplace. U.S. companies are no longer the unrivaled stars of the business world. The great companies of the world now include Sony, Honda, Bayer, and BMW.

Multinational enterprise have sales offices and production facilities in countries all over the world. Corporations such as Bertelsmann, Reuters, Citicorp, ASEA Brown Boveri, and Nestlé are "stateless": They operate worldwide without reference to national borders.[36] At Heinz, building foreign businesses will be one of William Johnson's biggest challenges.[37] International sales account for 43 percent of Heinz's revenues, but much of that comes from the mature European markets. Heinz must now sell baby food in China, pet treats in Argentina, and ketchup in Africa.

Even small firms that do not operate on a global scale must make important strategic decisions based on international considerations. Many small companies export their goods. Many domestic firms assemble their products in other countries. And *every* organization is under pressure to improve its products in the face of intense competition from high-quality foreign producers. Firms today must ask themselves, "How can we be the best in the world?"

A Spanish manufacturing firm, BH SA, is bent on becoming a global powerhouse in bicycle manufacturing.[38] American Peter Grisley, one of the founders of the sport of mountain biking and a legendary bicycle designer, is part of BH's management team. The goal is to put European riders on Grisley-designed, BH-built bikes, and then use the American's reputation to go after the U.S. mountain bike market. Grisley says, "The Basques have the best manufacturing equipment in the world and they're the best craftsman I've ever come across." Moreover, costs are low, and "I couldn't have made these bikes [at this cost] anywhere else in the world."

Total quality

Everyone connected with the business world in the past decade has heard a great deal about quality, and total quality management, or TQM. You read about the importance of high-quality products earlier, as one of the four pillars of competitive advantage. **Total quality management** refers broadly to an integrative management approach to customer satisfaction through a wide variety of tools and techniques meant to achieve high-quality goods and services.[39]

total quality management An integrative approach to management that supports the attainment of customer satisfaction through a wide variety of tools and techniques that result in high-quality goods and services.

The TQM philosophy of *continuous improvement* asks people throughout the company to constantly upgrade and do better everything the company does. This can entail improving anything from the company's products to its methods of production to its ways of managing its people. Many of the ideas you read about in this book can be implemented in the spirit of continuous improvement.

Germany's superb Mittelstand (mid-sized companies) have a passion for continuous improvement, and they abhor the status quo.[40] They work to stay ahead of the competition, but they don't do this by focusing on the competition. This is because they themselves are the market pacesetters. They set the pace because they focus constantly on outdoing themselves.

The learning organization

As the old rules for doing business become obsolete, firms must be flexible and adaptable to rapidly changing times. Firms, like people, must continually learn new things and avoid obsolescence. Rather than merely reacting to change, they must *anticipate* change and stay ahead of it.

In the **learning organization,** employees are given the opportunity to know what's going on, think constructively about the important issues, look for opportunities to learn new things, and seek creative solutions to problems.[41] Learning organizations are committed to openness to new ideas, to generating new knowledge, and to spreading information and knowledge. Learning organizations seek high levels of collaboration among people from different business disciplines. Learning organizations are more successful at continuous improvement.

learning organization An organization skilled at creating, acquiring, and transferring knowledge, and at modifying its behavior to reflect new knowledge and insights.

Companies like McKinsey, 3M, Sony, Johnson & Johnson, Corning, Mitsubishi, and General Electric are learning organizations. The best management practices you will learn about in this book are found at companies that are doing better than the competition because they are willing to learn and try new things.

From the Pages of BusinessWeek

Top Managers of the Year

Business Week annually identifies 25 "Top Managers," a diverse group who share one common characteristic: They break from the pack and outperform competitors. Recent examples are:

Ellen Marram of Tropicana Beverage, who bought Dole Food's juice business so that Tropicana is now in 23 nations, is planting groves in China, and is pushing new products like calcium-added juice all over the world. She has achieved double-digit quarterly profit increases for three years running.

William George of Medtronic, the world leader in heart pacemakers. He has increased R&D spending, tightened up on costs, won approval to apply its pacemaker technology to other diseases such as Parkinson's, and the company now realizes 70% of sales from new products.

Jeanne Jackson of Banana Republic, who has successfully distinguished the retailer from its rival Gap, opened new flagship stores and increased revenues dramatically.

Scott McNealy, chief executive of Sun Microsystems, whose high-risk strategy has positioned the Java programming language as the most serious challenger to Microsoft's software dominance. Sun Microsystems has achieved booming sales of its UNIX computers in the corporate computing market, in the face of Microsoft's growing presence.

James Sinegal of Costco, the discount warehouse, keeps the lid on costs and pushes high-profit services to the point that it is closing in on Wal-Mart's legendary 13% margins.

Donald Fites of Caterpillar faced heavy losses a few years ago and undertook a huge restructuring. The company is vulnerable due to the Asian economy, as 51% of its revenues come from overseas, but he vows to reach $30 billion by 2010.

Michael Ruettgers "has gone from nothing to leader of the $10 billion corporate data storage business" in 5 years. CEO of EMC, he has beaten IBM and other formidable rivals thanks to a two-year technology lead. He charges premium prices, profits are at over half a billion dollars, and EMC shares have gone through four stock splits.

Michael Dell redefines the PC industry again and again. Sales are growing 50% annually, the company is driving hard into overseas markets, and Internet sales are at over $3 million per week and growing.

Robert Louis-Dreyfus wears sneakers and jeans to work as CEO of Adidas. He moved production out of high-cost Germany, boosted marketing, bought equipment-maker Salomon, and is now second only to Nike. And he is taking on Nike on Nike's home turf, the U.S.

Discussion questions

1. What common themes do you see in these selections? What differences?
2. Whom else would you consider a strong candidate for "top manager" honors? Why?

Source: "The 25 top managers of the year," *Business Week,* January 12, 1998, pp. 22–34. ●

An eye on the future

As the business environment continues to change, there will be winners and losers. Not to oversimplify at this point, as you will be reading about these topics in greater detail, but it seems clear that progressive organizations are engaged in the following historic shifts:[42, 43]

- *From* bureaucracy as the key to efficiency *to* flexibility and involved people as the keys to success.
- *From* business-as-usual *to* continual change and innovation.
- *From* believing that people are cogs in a machine, to be used and controlled, *to* believing that people throughout the organization can and must contribute in a myriad of ways to provide competitive advantage and success.

- *From* relying solely on individual accountability and performance *to* relying also on collaboration and teams.
- *From* focusing internally on the boss *to* focusing externally on the customer.
- *From* using communication and technology to control people *to* using communication and technology to inform and empower people.
- *From* top management and technical experts making most of the important contributions *to* all employees adding significant value.
- *From* concern for looking busy *to* focus on real results.

That last one is crucial. Effective managers never lose sight of their responsibility for getting results. They cannot blame others, or neglect their own responsibility. A recent article in *Harvard Business Review* titled "Whatever Happened to the Take-Charge Manager?" was highly critical of American managers in recent years; they had abdicated their responsibilities, turning to consultants for ready-made answers and faddish solutions to their problems, and counting on the consultants to make decisions for them.[44] In contrast, the best managers know that the responsibility for good decisions is theirs, never let fads and fashions interfere with their focus on hard results, apply their own practical judgment, pick and choose carefully the best management ideas, adapt those ideas to the unique characteristics of their own companies, and constantly seek creative and workable new solutions.

Your career in management

In the United States, the power axis of management has changed over the years. After World War II, engineering and manufacturing expertise was highly valued and provided a common path to career success in business. In the 1960s, marketing emerged as the powerful function. In the 1970s, it was finance. Now, one function does not (and should not) dominate; the current business environment demands people and processes that synthesize various specialized functions into general management.

Career paths within organizations have reflected this change. Traditionally, people's careers advanced through promotions up the hierarchy within a single business function or discipline. Now, career progress is more likely to include lateral moves across disciplines. Figure 1.4 depicts traditional, vertical career paths within single functions and the current move toward career paths that include sideways moves providing more general experience and demanding more general skills. Whatever your current interests and expertise, you should assume that you will need to become more of a generalist and to view the business and manage from a broader, strategic, general perspective.

What can you do to help ensure a successful management career for yourself in these challenging times? As the discussion above suggests, it will help if you can become both a specialist and a generalist.[45] Seek to become a *specialist:* you must be an expert in something. This will give you specific skills that help you provide concrete, identifiable value to your firm and to customers. And over time, you should learn to be a *generalist,* knowing enough about a variety of business or technical disciplines so that you can understand and work with different perspectives.

It is also important to be both self-reliant and connected with other people.[46] To be *self-reliant* means to take full responsibility for yourself, your actions, and your career. You cannot count on your boss or your company to take care of you. A useful metaphor is to think of yourself as a business, with you as president and sole employee. Table 1.4 gives some specific advice about what this means in practice.

Being *connected* means having many good working relationships, and being a team player with strong interpersonal skills. For example, those who want to become partners in

figure 1.4 Organizational careers: From vertical to horizontal paths

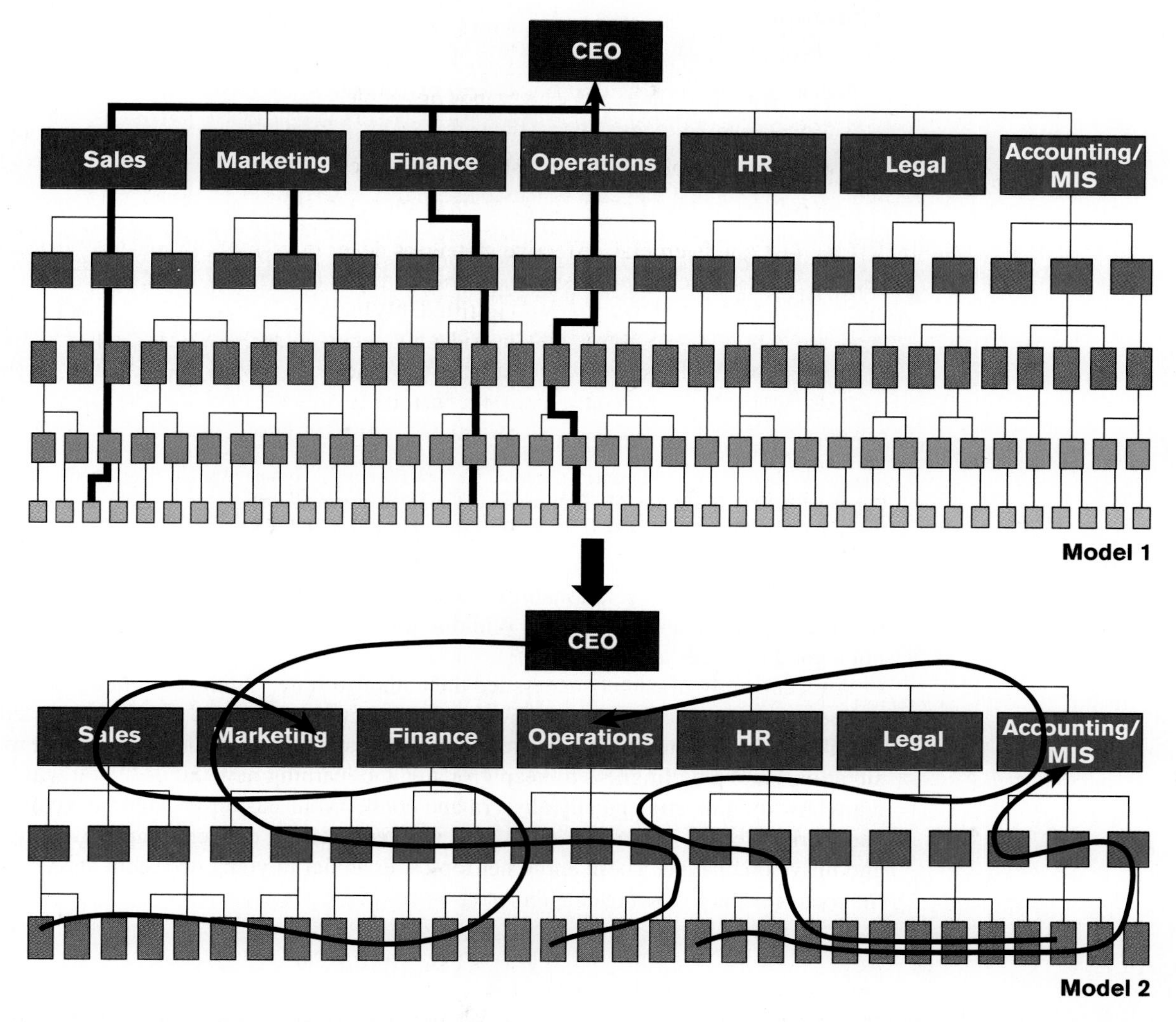

Source: Reprinted by permission of the publishers, from M. Peiperl and Y. Baruch, "Back to Square Zero: The Post Corporate Career," *Organizational Dynamics,* Spring 1997, pp.7–22. © 1997 American Management Association, New York. http://www.amanet.org. All rights reserved.

professional service organizations like accounting, advertising, and consulting firms, strive constantly to build a network of contacts. Their goal is to work not only with lots of clients but also with a half-dozen or more senior partners, including several from outside their home offices and some from outside their country.

Few would argue against the usefulness of having such a strong network of allies. Just ask Jay Alix, a successful advisor to and acquirer of troubled companies who has helped restructure Wang Laboratories, Unisys, and National Car Rental System. Believing that in his competitive business getting hired is not a function of competence alone, but also of whom you know, Mr. Alix prides himself on his networking prowess. He stays in constant touch with hundreds of people, and calls his network of contacts "the daisy chain."[47]

Look at this another way: All business is a function of human relationships.[48] Building competitive advantage depends not only on you but on other people. Management is personal. Commercial dealings are personal. Purchase decisions, repurchase decisions, and

table 1.4
Keys to career management

Vicky Farrow of Sun Microsystems gives the following advice to help people assume responsibility for their own careers:

1. Think of yourself as a business.
2. Define your product: what is your area of expertise?
3. Know your target market: to whom are you going to sell this?
4. Be clear on why your customer buys from you. What is your "value proposition"–what are you offering that causes him to use you?
5. As in any business, strive for quality and customer satisfaction, even if your customer is just someone else in your organization–like your boss.
6. Know your profession or field and what's going on there.
7. Invest in your own growth and development, the way a company invests in research and development. What new products will you be able to provide?
8. Be willing to consider changing your career.

Source: W. Kiechel III, "A Manager's Career in the New Economy," *Fortune,* April 4, 1994, pp. 68–72.

contracts all hinge on relationships. Even the biggest business deals—takeovers—are intensely personal and emotional. Without good work relationships, you are an outsider, not a good manager and leader.

A recent study of career success led the author to state, "In the current economic environment, people who fear competition, want security, and demand stability are often sinking like rocks in water."[49] Success requires high standards, self-confidence in competitive situations, and a willingness to keep growing and learning new things.[50] You will need to learn how to think strategically, discern and convey your business vision, make decisions, and work in teams. You will need to cope with uncertainty, deliver competitive advantage, and thrive on change. These and other topics, essential to your successful career, provide the focus for the following chapters.

Key terms

Conceptual and decision skills, p. 24
Controlling, p. 8
Cost competitiveness, p. 20
Effectiveness, p. 16
Efficiency, p. 16
Equifinality, p. 16
Frontline managers, p. 12
Functions of management, p. 6
Innovation, p. 22
Interpersonal and communication skills, p. 24
Leading, p. 7
Learning organization, p. 26
Management, p. 6
Middle-level managers, p. 11
Organization, p. 15
Organizing, p. 7
Planning, p. 7
Quality, p. 21
Speed, p. 22
Subsystems, p. 16
Synergy, p. 16
System, p. 15
Systems theory, p. 15
Technical skill, p. 23
Top-level managers, p. 10
Total quality management, p. 26

Summary of learning objectives

Now that you have studied Chapter 1, you should know:

The functions of management.

Managers work with people and resources to achieve organizational goals. The primary functions of management are planning, organizing, leading, and controlling. Planning is analyzing a situation, determining the goals that will be pursued, and deciding in advance the actions needed to pursue these goals. Organizing is assembling the resources needed to complete the job and grouping and coordinating employees and tasks for maximum success. Leading is motivating people and stimulating high performance. Controlling is monitoring the progress of the organization or the work unit toward goals and then taking corrective action if necessary.

The nature of management at different organizational levels.

Top-level, strategic managers are the senior executives and are responsible for the organization's overall management. Middle-level, tactical managers translate the general goals and plans developed by strategic managers into more specific objectives and activities. Frontline, operational managers are lower-level managers who supervise the operations of the organization.

How you can benefit from studying management.

This text will examine each management function and give you a solid foundation of knowledge and action ideas for your career. The ideas presented should supplement your common sense and experience, and help you avoid mistakes and create positive results.

The nature of organization.

An organization is a managed system designed and operated to achieve a specific set of objectives. This system processes human, financial, physical, and informational resources into outputs. These outputs are the goods and services demanded by the external environment. Meeting these demands allows an organization to achieve its goals.

The keys to gaining advantage over your organization's competitors.

Because management is a competitive arena, you need to deliver value to customers in ways that are superior to your competitors'. The four pillars of competitive advantage are low cost, quality products, speed, and innovation.

The skills you need to be an effective manager.

To execute management functions successfully, managers need technical skills, conceptual and decision skills, and interpersonal and communication skills. A technical skill is the ability to perform a specialized task involving a certain method or process. Conceptual and decision skills help the manager recognize complex and dynamic issues, analyze the factors that influence those issues or problems, and make appropriate decisions. Interpersonal and communication skills enable the manager to interact and work well with people.

The current forces shaping management practice now and in the future.

Management thought and practice continue to evolve. Among the major forces and ideas now revolutionizing work—and for which you need to be prepared—are globalization, total quality, the learning organization, and many other ongoing changes. You will be learning more about them throughout this book and course.

What to strive for as you manage your career.

Great managers maintain their focus on getting results, and can make decisions and take action in the face of change and uncertainty. Keeping in mind several goals will help you succeed in your career: be expert in something valuable; know about all the business functions; take full responsibility for yourself and your career; and strive for good working relationships with other people.

Discussion questions

1. Identify and describe a great manager. What makes him or her stand out from the crowd?

2. Have you ever seen or worked for an ineffective manager? Describe the causes and the consequences of the ineffectiveness.

3. Name a great organization. What makes it great?

4. Name an ineffective organization. Why did you label it as such?

5. Which companies are in *Fortune*'s most recent "Most Admired" list? Why did they make the list?

6. Give examples you have seen of firms that are outstanding and weak on each of the four pillars of competitive advantage.

7. Describe your use of the four management functions in the management of your daily life. Discuss the importance of technical, decision, and interpersonal skills at school and in jobs you have held.

8. Analyze your school as an open system. Identify and explain the major elements of systems theory.

9. Review Table 1.3. Which type of manager are you or will you be? Give examples of both types you have seen or for which you have worked. For which do you prefer to work, and why?

10. What are your strengths and weaknesses as you contemplate your career? How do they correlate to the skills and activities identified in the chapter? How would you go about improving your managerial skills?

11. Devise a plan for developing yourself and making yourself attractive to potential employers.

Concluding Case

Jamie Bonini at Chrysler

You read briefly about Jamie Bonini at the beginning of the chapter, in Setting the Stage. An engineer by training, Bonini was named plant manager of Chrysler's big-van plant in Windsor. He was 33 years old. Within a year, *The Wall Street Journal* hailed him as one of the new breed of managers who are reshaping the U.S. auto industry's manufacturing plants. The article also suggested he would be equally successful in other industries.

At the same time, *Forbes* magazine selected Chrysler as its Company of the Year. They selected Chrysler based on its results, its ways of operating, and its superb management. "We think Chrysler has superior management—not just at the very top but deep down in the organization." (p. 83)

Chrysler, like many other American companies, is teaching its foremen new ways of managing: giving more power to workers, rather than exercising top-down, management-by-intimidation. Previously at some of Chrysler's manufacturing plants, managers were described as acting like drill sergeants, quality problems were abundant, and the people were demoralized. Dennis Pawley, who is in charge of Chrsyler manufacturing worldwide, decided to change things dramatically, and among other things appointed the young and inexperienced Bonini to the Windsor job.

The plant was one of the least automated in the industry, with hundreds of manual jobs. Sales were stagnant, and the plant was scheduled to launch a new van. Adding to the challenges was the resentment of other managers who were passed over for the promotion, and the skepticism of many who thought Bonini was not up to the job. Looking back, he said, "I was scared. There were moments when I thought, 'I'm in over my head.'"

But he went to work, and within a year, productivity, sales, and morale were all up. You can learn elsewhere how he did it. But what would you do if you were in his shoes?

After his success at the Windsor plant, Bonini was offered a position in Latin America, to run an engine plant that Chrysler is building with BMW of Germany. He was torn; he wanted to stay at Windsor to see the new van launched, and people were upset that he was leaving them. But he felt he couldn't turn down the offer. He took the job, and he may now have an impact on car building in other parts of the world.

Chysler was selected Company of the Year by *Forbes* magazine in part because of the quality of its management team. *[Jonathan Becker/Contact Press Images]*

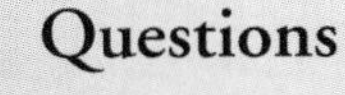

Questions

1. If you were taking the job in Windsor, what would be your reaction? What strengths and shortcomings would you bring to the position?

2. What would be a *bad* way to start out as the new manager? What mistakes should you try to avoid?

3. What would be your short- and long-term goals? What actions would you take?

4. How would you prepare for the international assignment?

Sources: J. Flint, "Company of the Year," *Forbes,* January 13, 1997, pp. 83–87; and G. Stern, "Old Chrysler Plant Has Young Manager Rattling the Culture," *The Wall Street Journal,* April 22, 1997, pp. 1,6. ●

Video Case

Managers and organizations: A skill development journal

The principles of effective management are nearly universal; that is, they apply to almost any type of organization. Whether it is a large or small business, nonprofit organization, or a hospital, they all benefit from efficient and effective management. The leaders of these organizations go by various titles, but they are all responsible for carrying out the goals of the organization. In trying to reach these goals, managers are most effective when they understand the four key functions of management: planning, organizing and staffing, leading, and controlling.

Purpose:

Each of the four critical areas of management requires special knowledge and a set of skills that can be developed in part through training, but also must be integrated with your life experiences. This textbook will provide you with a lot of information about effective management, and your personal management experiences will provide equally important training. This exercise is designed to help you integrate your formal training with your life experiences in the four important areas of management.

Materials:

A notebook dedicated to your development as a manager, and the respective sections you'll divide it into, will serve as your journal for significant information and life experiences in each of the four important areas of management. In the notebook, you'll provide yourself with an ongoing account that will help you develop your management effectiveness throughout this semester and beyond.

Procedure:

1. Divide your notebook into four approximately equal sections. If you have them, use divider tabs to mark the beginning of each section. The divider tabs should be labeled as follows: "Planning," "Organizing and Staffing," "Leading," and "Control and Change."

2. Divide the first few pages in each section into two equal columns by drawing a line down the middle of the page. As you fill your notebook over the coming weeks of the semester, do the same for new pages as you get to them.

3. On the top of the left-hand column write "Formal Training" and on the top of the right-hand column write "Experience."

4. As you move through the chapters of the book, watch additional videotapes, and listen to your instructor and classmates, record significant ideas, techniques, and tools in the "Formal Training" side of your journal in the appropriate section. Make sure you date each entry, and leave plenty of room beneath each to add additional material.

5. As your managerial experience grows through your work, participation in student groups, or other outside activities, record your experiences in the right-hand column of your journal. Try to place records of your life experiences next to corresponding records of your formal training.

6. Use your journal to note discrepancies between your formal training and your life experiences. You should discuss discrepancies in class, and get feedback and ideas from your instructor and classmates. What tools and techniques have been effective for you? Which ones ineffective?

7. If you're going to continue business education and aspire to higher levels of management, you may want to continue or even expand your journal-keeping activities. Almost any management skill can be developed more quickly if you take an active approach to integrating your formal training and life experiences.

Experiential Exercises

1.1 Effective managers

Objectives

1. To better understand what behaviors contribute to effective management.

2. To conceive a ranking of critical behaviors that you personally believe reflects their importance to your success as a manager.

Instructions

1. Below is a partial list of behaviors in which managers may engage. Rank these items in terms of their importance for effective performance as a manager. Put a 1 next to the item that you think is most important, 2 for the next most important, down to 10 for the least important.

2. Bring your rankings to class. Be prepared to justify your results and rationale. If you can add any behaviors to this list that might lead to success or greater management effectiveness, write them in.

Effective managers worksheet

______ **Communicates and interprets policy so that it is understood by the members of the organization.**

______ **Makes prompt and clear decisions.**

______ **Assigns subordinates to the jobs for which they are best suited.**

______ **Encourages associates to submit ideas and plans.**

______ **Stimulates subordinates by means of competition among employees.**

______ **Seeks means of improving management capabilities and competence.**

______ **Fully supports and carries out company policies.**

______ **Participates in community activities as opportunities arise.**

______ **Is neat in appearance.**

______ **Is honest in all matters pertaining to company property or funds.**

1.2 Career Planning

Objectives

1. To explore your career thinking.

2. To visualize your ideal job in terms as concrete as possible.

3. To summarize the state of your career planning, and to become conscious of the main questions you have about it at this point.

Instructions

Read the instructions for each activity, reflect on them, and then write your response. Be as brief or extensive as you like.

Career Planning Worksheet

1. Describe your ideal occupation in terms of responsibilities, skills, and how you would know if you were successful.

2. Identify 10 statements you can make today about your current career planning. Identify 10 questions you need answered for career planning.

10 statements

1.

2.

3.

4.

5.

6.

7.

10 questions

1.

2.

3.

4.

5.

6.

7.

10 statements

8. ______________________________

9. ______________________________

10. ______________________________

10 questions

8. ______________________________

9. ______________________________

10. ______________________________

Appendix
The Evolution of Management

For thousands of years, managers have wrestled with the same issues and problems confronting executives today. Around 1100 B.C., the Chinese practiced the four management functions—planning, organizing and staffing, leading, and controlling—discussed in Chapter 1. Between 350 and 400 B.C., the Greeks recognized management as a separate art and advocated a scientific approach to work. The Romans decentralized the management of their vast empire before the birth of Christ. During medieval times, the Venetians standardized production through the use of an assembly line, building warehouses and using an inventory system to monitor the contents.[1]

But throughout history most managers operated strictly on a trial-and-error basis. The challenges of the industrial revolution changed that. Management emerged as a formal discipline at the turn of the century. The first university programs to offer management and business education, the Wharton School at the University of Pennsylvania and the Amos Tuck School at Dartmouth, were founded in the late 19th century. By 1914, 25 business schools existed.[2]

Thus, the management profession as we know it today is relatively new. This appendix explores the roots of modern management theory. Understanding the origins of management thought will help you grasp the underlying contexts of the ideas and concepts presented in the chapters ahead.

Although this appendix is titled "The Evolution of Management," it might be more appropriately called "The Revolutions of Management," because it documents the wide swings in management approaches over the last 100 years. Out of the great variety of ideas about how to improve management, parts of each approach have survived and been incorporated into modern perspectives on management. Thus, the legacy of past efforts, triumphs, and failures has become our guide to future management practice.

Early management concepts and influences

Communication and transportation constraints hindered the growth of earlier businesses. Therefore, improvements in management techniques did not substantially improve performance. However, the industrial revolution changed that. As companies grew and became more complex, minor improvements in management tactics produced impressive increases in production quantity and quality.[3]

The emergence of **economies of scale**—reductions in the average cost of a unit of production as the total volume produced increases—drove managers to strive for further growth. The opportunities for mass production created by the industrial revolution spawned intense and systematic thought about management problems and issues—particularly efficiency, production processes, and cost savings.[4]

Figure 1.A.1 provides a timeline depicting the evolution of management thought through the decades. This historical perspective is divided into two major sections: classical approaches and contemporary approaches. Many of these approaches developed simultaneously, and they often had a significant impact on one another. Some approaches were a direct reaction to the perceived deficiencies of previous approaches. Others developed as the needs and issues confronting managers changed over the years.

figure 1.A.1 The evolution of management thought

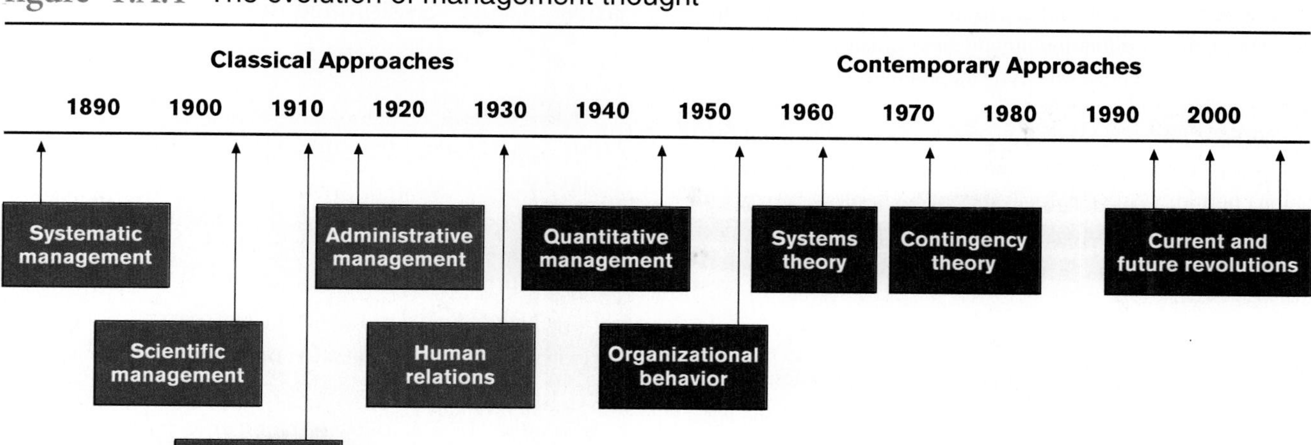

Production costs dropped as mass manufacturing lowered unit costs. Thus economies of scale was born, a concept that is alive and well in the modern manufacturing era.
[Martin Rogers/Tony Stone Images]

All the approaches attempted to explain the real issues facing managers and provide them with tools to solve future problems.

Figure 1.A.1 will reinforce your understanding of the key relationships among the approaches and place each perspective in its historical context.

Classical approaches

The classical period extended from the mid-19th century through the early 1950s. The major approaches that emerged during this period were systematic management, scientific management, administrative management, human relations, and bureaucracy.

Systematic management During the 19th century, growth in U.S. business centered on manufacturing.[5] Early writers such as Adam Smith believed the management of these firms was chaotic, and their ideas helped to systematize it. Most organizational tasks were subdivided and performed by specialized labor. However, poor coordination among subordinates and different levels of management caused frequent problems and breakdowns of the manufacturing process.

The **systematic management** approach attempted to build specific procedures and processes into operations to ensure coordination of effort. Systematic management emphasized economical operations, adequate staffing, maintenance of inventories to meet consumer demand, and organizational control. These goals were achieved through

- Careful definition of duties and responsibilities.
- Standardized techniques for performing these duties.
- Specific means of gathering, handling, transmitting, and analyzing information.
- Cost accounting, wage, and production control systems to facilitate internal coordination and communications.

Systematic management emphasized internal operations because managers were concerned primarily with meeting the explosive growth in demand brought about by the Industrial Revolution. In addition, managers were free to focus on internal issues of efficiency, in part because the government did not constrain business practices significantly. Finally, labor was poorly organized. As a result, many managers were oriented more toward things than toward people.

Table 1.A.1 lists some of the key concepts, contributions, and limitations of systematic management. Although systematic management did not address all the issues 19th-century managers faced, it tried to raise managers' awareness about the most pressing concerns of their job.

Scientific management Systematic management failed to lead to widespread production efficiency. This shortcoming became apparent to a young engineer named Frederick Taylor who was hired by Midvale Steel Company in 1878. Taylor discovered that production and pay were poor, inefficiency and waste were prevalent, and most companies had tremendous unused potential. He concluded that management decisions were unsystematic and no research to determine the best means of production existed.

In response, Taylor introduced a second approach to management, known as **scientific management.**[6] This approach advocated the application of scientific methods to analyze work and to determine how to complete production tasks efficiently. For example, U.S. Steel's contract with the United Steel Workers of America specified that sand shovelers should move 12.5 shovelfuls per minute; shovelfuls should average 15 pounds of river sand composed of 5.5 percent moisture.[7]

Taylor identified four principles of scientific management:

1. Management should develop a precise, scientific approach for each element of a one's work to replace general guidelines.
2. Management should scientifically select, train, teach, and develop each worker so that the right person has the right job.

table 1.A.1 Systematic management

Key concepts
Systematized manufacturing organizations.
Coordination of procedures and processes built into internal operations.
Emphasis on economical operations, inventory management, and cost control.
Contributions
Beginning of formal management in the United States.
Promotion of efficient, uninterrupted production.
Limitations
Ignored relationship between an organization and its environment.
Ignored differences in managers' and workers' views.

Frederick Taylor (left) and Dr. Lillian Gilberth (right) were early experts in management efficiency.
[Stock Montage, Inc.]

3. Management should cooperate with workers to ensure that the job matches plans and principles.
4. Management should ensure an equal division of work and responsibility between managers and workers.

To implement this approach, Taylor used techniques such as time-and-motion studies. With this technique, a task was divided into its basic movements, and different motions were timed to determine the most efficient way to complete the task.

After the "one best way" to perform the job was identified, Taylor stressed the importance of hiring and training the proper worker to do that job. Taylor advocated the standardization of tools, the use of instruction cards to help workers, and breaks to eliminate fatigue.

Another key element of Taylor's approach was the use of the differential piecerate system. Taylor assumed workers were motivated by receiving money. Therefore, he implemented a pay system in which workers were paid additional wages when they exceeded a standard level of output for each job. Taylor concluded that both workers and management would benefit from such an approach.

Scientific management principles were widely embraced. Other proponents, including Henry Gantt and Frank and Lillian Gilbreth, introduced many refinements and techniques for applying scientific management on the factory floor. One of the most famous examples of the application of scientific management is the factory Henry Ford built to produce the Model-T.

At the turn of the century, automobiles were a luxury that only the wealthy could afford. They were assembled by craftspeople who put an entire car together at one spot on the factory floor. These workers were not specialized, and Henry Ford believed they wasted time and energy bringing the needed parts to the car. Ford took a revolutionary approach to automobile manufacturing by using scientific management principles.

After much study, machines and workers in Ford's new factory were placed in sequence so that an automobile could be assembled without interruption along a moving production line. Mechanical energy and a conveyor belt were used to take the work to the workers.

The manufacture of parts likewise was revolutionized. For example, formerly it had taken one worker 20 minutes to assemble a flywheel magneto. By splitting the job into 29 different operations, putting the product on a mechanical conveyor, and changing the height of the conveyor, Ford cut production time to 5 minutes.

By 1914 chassis assembly time had been trimmed from almost 13 hours to 1½ hours. The new methods of production required complete standardization, new machines, and an adaptable labor force. Costs dropped significantly, the Model-T became the first car accessible to the majority of Americans, and Ford dominated the industry for many years.[8]

The legacy of Taylor's scientific management approach is broad and pervasive. Most important, productivity and efficiency in manufacturing improved dramatically. The concepts of scientific methods and research were introduced to manufacturing. The piecerate system gained wide acceptance because it more closely aligned effort and reward. Taylor also emphasized the need for cooperation between management and workers. And, the concept of a management specialist gained prominence.

Despite these gains, not everyone was convinced that scientific management was the best solution to all business problems. First, critics claimed that Taylor ignored many job-related social and psychological factors by emphasizing only money as a worker incentive. Second, production tasks were reduced to a set of routine, machinelike procedures that led to boredom, apathy, and quality control problems. Third, unions strongly opposed scientific management techniques because they believed management might abuse their power to set the standards and the piecerates, thus exploiting workers and diminishing their importance.

table 1.A.2 Scientific management

Key concepts
Analyzed work using scientific methods to determine the "one best way" to complete production tasks.
Emphasized study of tasks, selection and training of workers, and cooperation between workers and management.
Contributions
Improved factory productivity and efficiency.
Introduced scientific analysis to the workplace.
Piecerate system equated worker rewards and performance.
Instilled cooperation between management and workers.
Limitations
Simplistic motivational assumptions.
Workers viewed as parts of a machine.
Potential for exploitation of labor.
Excluded senior management tasks.
Ignored relationship between the organization and its environment.

Finally, although scientific management resulted in intense scrutiny of the internal efficiency of organizations, it did not help managers deal with broader external issues such as competitors and government regulations, especially at the senior management level. Table 1.A.2 summarizes some of the key concepts, contributions, and limitations of scientific management.

Administrative management The **administrative management** approach emphasized the perspective of senior managers within the organization, and argued that management was a profession and could be taught.

An explicit and broad framework for administrative management emerged in 1916, when Henri Fayol, a French mining engineer and executive, published a book summarizing his management experiences. Fayol identified five functions and 14 principles of management. The five functions, which are very similar to the four functions discussed in Chapter 1, include planning, organizing, commanding, coordinating, and controlling. Table 1.A.3 lists and defines the 14 principles. Although some critics claim Fayol treated the principles as universal truths for management, he actually wanted them applied flexibly.[9]

A host of other executives contributed to the administrative management literature. These writers discussed a broad spectrum of management topics, including the social responsibilities of management, the philosophy of management, clarification of business terms and concepts, and organizational principles. Chester Barnard's and Mary Parker Follet's contributions have become classic works in this area.[10]

Barnard, former president of New Jersey Bell Telephone Company, published his landmark book *The Functions of the Executive* in 1938. He outlined the role of the senior executive: formulating the purpose of the organization, hiring key individuals, and maintaining organizational communications.[11] Mary Parker Follet's 1942 book *Dynamic Organization* extended Barnard's work by emphasizing the continually changing situations that managers face.[12] Two of her key contributions—the notion that managers desire flexibility and the differences between motivating groups and individuals—laid the groundwork for the modern contingency approach discussed later in the chapter.

All the writings in the administrative management area emphasize management as a profession along with fields such as law and medicine. In addition, these authors offered many recommendations based on their personal experiences, which often included managing large corporations. Although these perspectives and recommendations were considered sound, critics noted

table 1.A.3 Fayol's 14 principles of management

1. *Division of work*–divide work into specialized tasks and assign responsibilities to specific individuals.
2. *Authority*–delegate authority along with responsibility.
3. *Discipline*—make expectations clear and punish violations.
4. *Unity of command*–each employee should be assigned to only one supervisor.
5. *Unity of direction*–employees' efforts should be focused on achieving organizational objectives.
6. *Subordination of individual interest to the general interest*–the general interest must predominate.
7. *Remuneration*–systematically reward efforts that support the organization's direction.
8. *Centralization*–determine the relative importance of superior and subordinate roles.
9. *Scalar chain*–keep communications within the chain of command.
10. *Order*–order jobs and material so they support the organization's direction.
11. *Equity*–fair discipline and order enhance employee commitment.
12. *Stability and tenure of personnel*–promote employee loyalty and longevity.
13. *Initiative*–encourage employees to act on their own in support of the organization's direction.
14. *Esprit de corps*–promote a unity of interests between employees and management.

table 1.A.4 Administrative management

Key concepts
Fayol's five functions and 14 principles of management.
Executives formulate the organization's purpose, secure employees, and maintain communications.
Managers must respond to changing developments.
Contributions
Viewed management as a profession that can be trained and developed.
Emphasized the broad policy aspects of top-level managers.
Offered universal managerial prescriptions.
Limitation
Universal prescriptions need qualifications for environmental, technological, and personnel factors.

that they may not work in all settings. Different types of personnel, industry conditions, and technologies may affect the appropriateness of these principles.

Table 1.A.4 summarizes the administrative management approach.

Human relations A fourth approach to management, **human relations,** developed during the early 1930s. This approach aimed at understanding how psychological and social processes interact with the work situation to influence performance. Human relations was the first major approach to emphasize informal work relationships and worker satisfaction.

This approach owes much to other major schools of thought. For example, many of the ideas of the Gilbreths (scientific management) and Barnard and Follet (administrative management) influenced the development of human relations from 1930 to 1955. In fact, human relations emerged from a research project that began as a scientific management study.

Western Electric Company, a manufacturer of communications equipment, hired a team of Harvard researchers led by Elton Mayo and Fritz Roethlisberger. They were to investigate the influence of physical working conditions on workers' productivity and efficiency in one of the company's factories outside Chicago. This research project, known as the *Hawthorne Studies,* provided some of the most interesting and controversial results in the history of management.[13]

The Hawthorne Studies were a series of experiments conducted from 1924 to 1932. During the first stage of the project (the Illumination Experiments), various working conditions, particularly the lighting in the factory, were altered to determine the effects of these changes on productivity. The researchers found no systematic relationship between the factory lighting and production levels. In some cases, productivity continued to increase even when the illumination was reduced to the level of moonlight. The researchers concluded that the workers performed and reacted differently because the researchers were observing them. This reaction is known as the **Hawthorne Effect.**

This conclusion led the researchers to believe productivity may be affected more by psychological and social factors than by physical or objective influences. With this thought in mind, they initiated the other four stages of the project. During these stages, the researchers performed various work group experiments and had extensive interviews with employees. Mayo and his team eventually concluded that productivity and employee behavior were influenced by the informal work group.

Human relations proponents argued that managers should stress primarily employee welfare, motivation, and communication. They believed social needs had precedence over economic needs. Therefore, management must gain the cooperation of the group and promote job satisfaction and group norms consistent with the goals of the organization.

Another noted contributor to the field of human relations was Abraham Maslow.[14] In 1943, Maslow suggested that humans have five levels of needs. The most basic needs are the physical needs for food, water, and shelter; the most advanced need is for self-actualization, or personal fulfillment. Maslow argued that people try to satisfy their lower-level needs and then progress upward to the higher-level needs. Managers can facilitate this process and achieve organizational goals by removing obstacles and encouraging behaviors that satisfy people's needs and organizational goals simultaneously.

Although the human relations approach generated research into leadership, job attitudes, and group dynamics, it drew heavy criticism.[15] Critics believed that one result of human relations—a belief that a happy worker was a productive worker—was too simplistic. While scientific management overemphasized the economic and formal aspects of the workplace, human relations ignored the more rational side of the worker and the important characteristics of the formal organization. However, human relations was a significant step in the development of management thought, because it prompted managers and researchers to consider the psychological and social factors that influence performance.

Table 1.A.5 summarizes the human relations approach.

Bureaucracy Max Weber, a German sociologist, lawyer, and social historian, showed how management itself could be more efficient and consistent in his book *The Theory of Social and Economic Organizations.*[16] The ideal model for management, according to Weber, is the **bureaucracy** approach.

Weber believed bureaucratic structures can eliminate the variability that results when managers in the same organization have different skills, experiences, and goals. Weber advocated that the jobs themselves be standardized so that personnel changes would not disrupt the organization. He emphasized a structured, formal network of relationships among specialized positions in an organization. Rules and regulations standardize behavior, and authority resides in positions rather than in individuals. As a result, the organization

table 1.A.5 Human relations

Key concepts

Productivity and employee behavior are influenced by the informal work group.

Cohesion, status, and group norms determine output.

Managers should stress employee welfare, motivation, and communication.

Social needs have precedence over economic needs.

Contributions

Psychological and social processes influence performance.

Maslow's hierarchy of needs.

Limitations

Ignored workers' rational side and the formal organization's contribution to productivity.

Research findings later overturned the simplistic prescription that happy workers are always more productive.

need not rely on a particular individual, but will realize efficiency and success by following the rules in a routine and unbiased manner.

According to Weber, bureaucracies are especially important because they allow large organizations to perform the many routine activities necessary for their survival. Also, bureaucratic positions foster specialized skills, eliminating many subjective judgments by managers. In addition, if the rules and controls are established properly, bureaucracies should be unbiased in their treatment of people, both customers and employees.

Many organizations today are bureaucratic. Bureaucracy can be efficient and productive. However, bureaucracy is not the appropriate model for every organization. Organizations or departments that need rapid decision making and flexibility may suffer under a bureaucratic approach. Some people may not perform their best with excessive bureaucratic rules and procedures.

Other shortcomings stem from a faulty execution of bureaucratic principles rather than from the approach itself. Too much authority may be vested in too few people; the procedures may become the ends rather than the means; or managers may ignore appropriate rules and regulations. Finally, one advantage of a bureaucracy—its permanence—can also be a problem. Once a bureaucracy is established, dismantling it is very difficult.

Table 1.A.6 summarizes the key concepts, contributions, and limitations of bureaucracy.

Contemporary approaches

The contemporary approaches to management include quantitative management, organizational behavior, systems theory, and the contingency perspective. The contemporary approaches have developed at various times since World War II, and they continue to represent the cornerstones of modern management thought.

Quantitative management Although Taylor introduced the use of science as a management tool early in the 20th century, most organizations did not adopt the use of quantitative techniques for management problems until the 1940s and 1950s.[17] During World War II, military planners began to apply mathematical techniques to defense and logistic problems. After the war, private corporations began assembling teams of quantitative experts to tackle many of the complex issues confronting large organizations. This approach, referred to as **quantitative management,** emphasizes the application of quantitative analysis to management decisions and problems.

Quantitative management helps a manager make a decision by developing formal mathematical models of the problem. Computers have facilitated the development of specific quantitative methods. These include such techniques as statistical decision theory, linear programming, queuing theory, simulation, forecasting, inventory modeling, network modeling, and break-even analysis. Organizations apply these techniques in many areas, including production, quality control, marketing, human resources, finance, distribution, planning, and research and development.

Despite the promise quantitative management holds, managers do not rely on these methods as the primary approach to decision making. Typically they use these techniques as a supplement or tool in the decision process. Many managers will use results that are consistent with their experience, intuition, and judgment, but they will

table 1.A.6 Bureaucracy

Key concepts

Structured, formal network of relationships among specialized positions in an organization.

Rules and regulations standardize behavior.

Jobs staffed by trained specialists who follow rules.

Hierarchy defines the relationship among jobs.

Contributions

Promotes efficient performance of routine organizational activities.

Eliminates subjective judgment by employees and management.

Emphasizes position rather than the person.

Limitations

Limited organizational flexibility and slow decision making.

Ignores the importance of people and interpersonal relationships.

Accumulation of power can lead to authoritarian management.

Rules may become ends in themselves.

Difficult to dismantle once established.

table 1.A.7 Quantitative management

Key concept
Application of quantitative analysis to management decisions.
Contributions
Developed specific mathematical methods of problem analysis.
Helped managers select the best alternative among a set.
Limitations
Models neglect nonquantifiable factors.
Managers not trained in these techniques and may not trust or understand the techniques' outcomes.
Not suited for nonroutine or unpredictable management decisions.

reject results that contradict their beliefs. Also, managers may use the process to compare alternatives and eliminate weaker options.

Several explanations account for the limited use of quantitative management. Many managers have not been trained in using these techniques. Also, many aspects of a management decision cannot be expressed through mathematical symbols and formulas. Finally, many of the decisions managers face are nonroutine and unpredictable.

Table 1.A.7 summarizes the quantitative management approach.

Organizational behavior During the 1950s, a transition took place in the human relations approach. Scholars began to recognize that worker productivity and organizational success are based on more than the satisfaction of economic or social needs. The revised perspective, known as **organizational behavior,** studies and identifies management activities that promote employee effectiveness through an understanding of the complex nature of individual, group, and organizational processes. Organizational behavior draws from a variety of disciplines, including psychology and sociology, to explain the behavior of people on the job.

During the 1960s, organizational behaviorists heavily influenced the field of management. Douglas McGregor's Theory X and Theory Y marked the transition from human relations.[18] According to McGregor, Theory X managers assume workers are lazy and irresponsible and require constant supervision and external motivation to achieve organizational goals. Theory Y managers assume employees *want* to work and can direct and control themselves. McGregor advocated a Theory Y perspective, suggesting that managers who encourage participation and allow opportunities for individual challenge and initiative would achieve superior performance.

Other major organizational behaviorists include Chris Argyris, who recommended greater autonomy and better jobs for workers,[19] and Rensis Likert, who stressed the value of participative management.[20] Through the years, organizational behavior has consistently emphasized development of the organization's human resources to achieve individual and organizational goals. Like other approaches it has been criticized for its limited perspective, although more recent contributions have a broader and more situational viewpoint. In the past few years, many of the primary issues addressed by organizational behavior have experienced a rebirth with a greater interest in leadership, worker participation and incentives, and productivity.

Table 1.A.8 summarizes the key concepts, contributions, and limitations of organizational behavior.

Systems theory The classical approaches as a whole were criticized because they (1) ignored the relationship between the organization and its external environment and (2) usually stressed one aspect of the organization or its employees at the expense of other considerations. In response to these criticisms, management scholars during the 1950s stepped back from the details of the organization to attempt to understand it as a whole system. These efforts were based on a general scientific approach called **systems theory.**[21] As you recall from Chapter 1, systems theory provides a way to interpret organizations. Systems theory takes a holistic view of the entire organizational system and stresses processes. Important concepts from systems theory include open versus closed systems, efficiency and effectiveness, subsystems, equifinality, and synergy, which you read about in Chapter 1.

Table 1.A.9 summarizes systems theory.

Contingency perspective Building on systems theory ideas, the **contingency perspective** refutes universal principles of management by stating that a variety of factors, both internal and external to the firm, may affect the organization's performance.[22] Thus, there is no "one best way" to manage and organize, because circumstances vary. For example, a universal strategy of offering low-cost products would not succeed in a market that is not cost conscious.

table 1.A.8 Organizational behavior

Key concepts
Promotes employee effectiveness through understanding of individual, group, and organizational processes.
Stresses relationships among employees, managers, and the work they perform for the organization.
Assumes employees want to work and can control themselves (Theory Y).
Contributions
Increased participation, greater autonomy, individual challenge and initiative, and enriched jobs may increase performance.
Recognized the importance of developing human resources.
Limitation
Some approaches ignored situational factors, such as the environment and the organization's technology.

table 1.A.9 Systems theory

Key concepts
Organization is viewed as an open system.
Management must interact with the environment to gather inputs and return the outputs of its production.
Organizational objectives must encompass both efficiency and effectiveness.
Organizations contain a series of subsystems.
There are many avenues to the same outcome.
Synergies exist where the whole is greater than the sum of the parts.
Contribution
Recognized the importance of the organization's relationship with the external environment.
Limitation
Does not provide specific guidance on the functions and duties of managers.

Situational characteristics are called **contingencies.** Understanding contingencies helps a manager know which sets of circumstances dictate which management actions. You will learn the recommendations for the major contingencies throughout this text. The contingencies include

1. The rate of change and degree of complexity in the organization's external environment.
2. The internal strengths and weaknesses of the organization.
3. The values, goals, skills, and attitudes of managers and workers in the organization.
4. The types of tasks, resources, and technologies the organization uses.

With an eye to these contingencies, a manager may categorize the situation and then choose the proper competitive strategy, organization structure, or management process for the circumstances.

Researchers continue to identify key contingency variables and their effects on management issues. As you read the topics covered in each chapter, you will notice similarities and differences among management situations and the appropriate responses. This perspective should represent a cornerstone of your own approach to management. Many of the things you will learn about throughout this course apply a contingency perspective.

Table 1.A.10 summarizes the contingency perspective.

table 1.A.10 Contingency perspective

Key concepts
Situational contingencies influence the strategies, structures, and processes that result in high performance.
There is more than one way to reach a goal.
Managers may adapt their organizations to the situation.
Contributions
Identified major contingencies.
Argued against universal principles of management.
Limitations
Not all critical contingencies have been identified.
Theory may not be applicable to all managerial issues.

Key terms

administrative management A classical management approach that attempted to identify major principles and functions that managers could use to achieve superior organizational performance, p. 40.

bureaucracy A classical management approach emphasizing a structured, formal network of relationships among specialized positions in the organization, p. 41.

contingencies Factors that determine the appropriateness of managerial actions, p.44

contingency perspective An approach to the study of management proposing that the managerial strategies, structures, and processes that result in high performance depend on the characteristics, or important contingencies, of the situation in which they are applied, p. 43.

economies of scale Reductions in the average cost of a unit of production as the total volume produced increases, p. 37.

Hawthorne Effect People's reactions to being observed or studied resulting in superficial rather than meaningful changes in behavior, p. 41.

human relations A classical management approach that attempted to understand and explain how human psychological and social processes interact with the formal aspects of the work situation to influence performance, p. 41.

organizational behavior A contemporary management approach that studies and identifies management activities that promote employee effectiveness by examining the complex and dynamic nature of individual, group, and organizational processes, p. 43.

quantitative management A contemporary management approach that emphasizes the application of quantitative analysis to managerial decisions and problems, p. 42.

scientific management A classical management approach that applied scientific methods to analyze and determine the "one best way" to complete production tasks, p. 38.

systematic management A classical management approach that attempted to build into operations the specific procedures and processes that would ensure coordination of effort to achieve established goals and plans, p. 38.

systems theory A theory stating that an organization is a set of interdependent elements, which in turn are interdependent with the external environment, p. 43.

Discussion questions

1. How does today's business world compare with the one of 40 years ago? What is different about today, and what is not so different?

2. What is scientific management? How might today's organizations use it?

3. Table 1.A.3 lists Fayol's 14 principles of management, first published in 1916. Are they as useful today as they were then? Why or why not? *When* are they most, and least, useful?

4. What are the advantages and disadvantages of a bureaucratic organization?

5. In what situations are quantitative management concepts and tools applicable?

6. Describe an open system. Using an example, explain the major elements of systems theory.

7. Why did the contingency perspective become such an important approach to management? Generate a list of contingencies that might affect the decisions you should make as a manager.

8. For each of the management approaches discussed in the chapter, give examples you have seen. How effective or ineffective were they?

Video Case

The evolution of management

The management profession, as we know it today, is relatively new, even though the issues and problems that confront managers have existed for thousands of years. Management emerged as a formal discipline at the turn of the century, when rapid industrialization called for better-skilled management of natural resources, capital, and labor. The various management approaches that have been developed can be divided into two major groups: classical and contemporary approaches.

The classical approaches, which extended from the mid-19th century through the early 1950s, emerged as managers tried to cope with the growth of American industry. These approaches were systematic management, scientific management, administrative management, human relations, and bureaucracy.

Systematic management represented the beginning of formal management thought in the United States. It emphasized the way in which manufacturing firms operated because most management problems were focused on manufacturing.

Scientific management was introduced around the turn of the century by Frederick Taylor, an engineer who applied scientific methods to analyze work and determine the best way to complete production tasks. Taylor stressed the importance of hiring and training the proper workers to do those tasks. One of the most famous examples of the application of scientific management is how the factory Henry Ford built to produce the Model-T. Ford used scientific management principles to yield higher productivity and efficiency. For example, by 1914, chassis assembly time had been trimmed from almost 13 hours to 1.5 hours.

Administrative management emerged at about the same time and emphasized the perspective of senior managers within the organization. It viewed management as a profession that could be taught.

The human relations approach to management evolved from the Hawthorne Studies conducted from 1924 to 1932 at the Western Electric Company outside Chicago. Various working conditions, particularly lighting, were altered to determine the effects of these changes on productivity. But researchers, led by Harvard professor Elton Mayo, were ultimately unable to determine any relationship between factory lighting and productivity levels. This led the researchers to believe the productivity was affected more by psychological and social factors. This approach highlighted the importance of the human element in the organization. However, critics believed the human relations philosophy of "the happy worker as a productive worker" was too simplistic.

The bureaucracy approach to management was developed by Max Weber, a German sociologist and social historian. He attempted to establish an overall management system by focusing on a structured, formal network of relationships among specialized positions in an organization. Bureaucracy allowed efficient performance of many routine activities.

The contemporary approaches to management, which have been developed since World War II, attempted to overcome the limitations of the classical approaches. The contemporary approaches include quantitative management, organizational behavior, systems theory, and the contingency perspective.

Quantitative management was aided by the development of modern computers. It emphasizes the application of a formal, mathematical model to management decisions and problems.

The organizational behavior approach to management promotes employee effectiveness through an understanding of the complex nature of individual, group, and organizational processes.

The systems theory of management, which originated in the 1950s, was a major effort to overcome the limitations of the earlier approaches by attempting to view the organization as a whole system. Systems theory introduced the concept of equifinality—that there is no "one best way" to reach a goal. And it stresses the notion of synergy—that the whole is greater than the sum of its parts.

The contingency perspective has most recently dominated the study of management. It asserts that situational characteristics, or contingencies, determine the management strategies that will be most effective. This approach argues that no universal principle should *always* be applied. Rather, managers, like those at Trek Bicycle, analyze situations and then, based on their analysis of key contingencies, make decisions regarding the most appropriate ways to manage. Trek, based in rural Wisconsin, has a very open-minded approach to managing, and meeting customer needs.

But the evolution of management doesn't end there. Management thought and practice continue to evolve. Current events and trends are shaping the future of business and management. Among the major forces now revolutionizing management are globalization, learning organization, and total quality management.

Globalization refers to the rise of multinational enterprises in the ever-expanding global marketplace. Even small firms that don't operate on a global scale must make important strategic decisions based on international considerations.

The learning organization is committed to openness, new ideas, generating new knowledge, and spreading information and knowledge to others. Continuing dialogue and open-mindedness with an eye toward achieving the organization's goals are the foremost concern. Tellabs, a Chicago-area manufacturer of telecommunications products and services, is a learning organization that has emphasized innovation, teams, and mentoring. It seems to be working. Tellabs' stock has increased by more than 1,600 percent over the last five years, outperforming every other publicly traded stock in the nation.

Total quality management refers to an approach to management that produces customer satisfaction by providing high quality goods and services. Its goal is to solve and then eliminate all quality-related problems. First National Bank of Chicago has an aggressive quality program that includes weekly performance review meetings. In the meetings, managers analyze dozens of charts that are designed to monitor the quality of their performance.

First National's Rich Gilgan said, "You can't manage what you don't understand. And you don't understand what you don't measure."

From the classical approaches, through the contemporary approaches, and into the forces now revolutionizing management, the history of past efforts, triumphs, and failures has become the guide to future management practice. Since the mid-19th century, change has been the constant in the evolution of management. The marketplace keeps changing, the technology keeps changing, and the workforce keeps changing. Today's manager must learn how to deal with the forces of change affecting management. Only by understanding the implications of change and the challenges it presents will you be prepared to meet them head-on.

Critical Thinking Questions

1. In general, how do contemporary approaches to management differ from classical approaches?

2. What are some modern organizational problems that are a result of classical approaches to managing?

3. The Hawthorne Studies are frequently cited as a turning point in management thought. What is the significance of this research?

Experiental Exercises

1.A.1 Approaches to management

Objectives

1. To help you conceive a wide variety of management approaches.

2. To clarify the appropriateness of different management approaches in different situations.

Instructions

Your instructor will divide your class randomly into groups of four to six people each. Acting as a team, with everyone offering ideas and one person serving as official recorder, each group will be responsible for writing a one-page memo to your present class. Subject matter of your group's memo will be "My advice for managing people today is . . . " The fun part of this exercise (and its creative element) involves writing the memo from the viewpoint of the person assigned to your group by your instructor.

Among the memo viewpoints your instructor may assign are:

- An ancient Egyptian slave master (building the great pyramids).
- Henri Fayol
- Frederick Taylor
- Mary Parker Follett
- Douglas McGregor
- A contingency management theorist
- A Japanese auto company executive.
- The chief executive officer of IBM in the year 2030.
- Commander of the Starship Enterprise II in the year 3001.
- Others, as assigned by your instructor.

Use your imagination, make sure everyone participates, and try to be true to any historical facts you've encountered. Attempt to be as specific and realistic as possible. Remember, the idea is to provide advice about managing people from another point in time (or from a particular point of view at the present time).

Make sure you manage your 20-minute time limit carefully. A recommended approach is to spend 2 to 3 minutes putting the exercise into proper perspective. Next, take about 10 to 12 minutes brainstorming ideas for your memo, with your recorder jotting down key ideas and phrases. Have your recorder use the remaining time to write your group's one-page memo, with constructive comments and help from the others. Pick a spokesperson to read your group's memo to the class.

Source: R. Krietner and A. Kinicki, *Organization Behavior,* 3d ed. (Burr Ridge, IL.: Richard D. Irwin, 1994), pp. 30–31.

1.A.2 The university grading system analysis

Objectives

1. To learn to identify the components of a complex system.
2. To better understand organizations as systems.
3. To visualize how a change in policy affects the functioning of an organization system.

Instructions

1. Assume that your university has decided to institute a pass–fail system of grading instead of the letter-grade system it presently has. Apply the systems perspective learned from this chapter to understanding this decision.
2. Answer the questions on the Grading System Analysis Worksheet individually, or in small groups, as directed by your instructor.

Discussion Questions

Share your own or your group's responses with the entire class. Then answer the following questions.

1. Did you diagram the system in the same way?
2. Did you identify the same system components?
3. Which subsystems will be affected by the change?
4. How do you explain differences in your responses?

Grading system analysis worksheet

Description

1. What subsystems compose the system (the university)? Diagram the system.

____

____

____

____

____

____

2. Identify in this system: inputs, outputs, transformations, feedback, system boundaries.

____

____

____

____

____

____

Diagnosis

3. Which of the subsystems will be affected by the change; that is, what changes are likely to occur throughout the system as a result of the policy change?

Source: J. Gordon, *A Diagnostic Approach to Organizational Behavior* (Englewood Cliffs, NJ: Prentice Hall, 1983), p. 38. Reprinted with permission of Prentice Hall, Inc., Englewood Cliffs, NJ.

Chapter Two
The External Environment

The essence of a business is outside itself.

–Peter Drucker

Chapter Outline

Learning Objectives

After studying Chapter 2, you will know:

1. How environmental forces influence organizations, as well as how organizations can influence their environments.
2. How to make a distinction between the macroenvironment and the competitive environment.
3. Why organizations should attend to economic and social developments in the environment.
4. How to analyze the competitive environment.
5. How organizations respond to environmental uncertainty.

Setting the Stage

Things Are Up in the Air At Boeing

There is perhaps no other industry that has undergone more environmental change than aerospace, and recent events at Boeing illustrate that fact. While contractors such as Boeing, McDonnell Douglas, and Lockheed Martin have traditionally enjoyed enviable funding from a big U.S. defense budget, they have had to turn their focus toward the private sector as government funding has dried up. Boeing is perhaps in a better position to make this adjustment than other U.S. aerospace firms because it has not relied so exclusively on defense contracts. The company has long been the world's biggest maker of civil aircraft, but a second division player in defense. Nevertheless belt tightening in Washington could severely limit this Seattle-based manufacturer's potential for growth.

Competition in the private sector of aerospace is much more intense than that of the defense industry. Rivalry among U.S. competitors—and from competitors abroad—puts constant pressure on costs and price relationships. For example, international firms such as Fokker and Airbus present strong competition because of their political and market strengths within Europe. Airbus, in particular, receives billions of dollars in subsidies from the governments of Europe to cover its operating losses. Meanwhile, technological advances have steadily increased the cost of airplane development. Boeing's latest development, the 777, cost an astounding $5.5 billion to build. Estimates are that the next generation of airplanes will cost even more.

But while some companies simply react to change in the environment, Boeing seems to be enacting change that alters the environmental landscape that other competitors see. For example, in designing the 777, Boeing kept costs down (a bit) and reduced development time by partnering with a host of suppliers and designers who subcontracted components of the overall project. Boeing's core skill has been its ability to bring all these pieces together to manufacture the entire aircraft. In addition, the company has signed innovative, exclusive contracts to supply customers such as American Airlines and Delta Airlines with transport planes for the next 20 years. These aggressive new contracts are part of the company's 20-year plan, called Vision 2016, to become an integrated and flexible aerospace company.

Executives at Boeing and McDonnell Douglas finalize their agreement of the biggest merger in aerospace history.
[Mannie Garcia/Gamma-Liaison}

Perhaps the biggest news, however, is Boeing's recent merger with McDonnell Douglas. Instead of competing head to head, the two decided that a cooperative strategy would prove more effective. To iron out the details of the merger, CEOs Philip Condit (from Boeing) and Harry Stonecipher (from McDonnell Douglas) met for four days in a Seattle hotel room to iron out the $14 billion stock swap that will create a company with $48 billion in combined revenues, have 65 percent of the world aircraft market, and be a strong number 2 player (behind Lockheed Martin) in defense. While the Boeing/MD merger is awaiting approval from the U.S. government, it has been getting a good deal of resistance from some U.S. competitors and especially foreign governments.

Sources: Lee Smith, "Air Power," Fortune, *July 7, 1997 pp. 134–136; "Industry Awaits Impact of Boeing Merger,"* Industrial Distribution, *February 1997 pp. 15–16; "And Then There Were Two,"* Financial World, *April 15, 1997 p. 70; J. A. Donohue, "When Big Is Bad,"* Air Transport World, *June 1997 p. 7; Andy Reinhardt, "Three Huge Hours in Seattle,"* Business Week, *December 30, 1996 p. 38–39;*

Boeing, like other organizations, is trying to compete in an environment characterized by intense competition, economic fluctuations, technological advances, government regulations, and other forces that directly influence its success. In this chapter, we will discuss how pressures outside the firm create an external context in which managers and their organizations operate.

As you learned in the first chapter, organizations are open systems that are affected by, and in turn affect, their external environments. By **external environment,** we mean all relevant forces outside the firm's boundaries. By *relevant,* we mean factors to which managers must pay attention to help their organizations compete effectively and survive.

external environment All relevant forces outside a firm's boundaries, such as competitors, customers, the government, and the economy.

Many of these factors are uncontrollable. Companies large and small are buffeted or battered about by recession, government interference, competitors' actions, and so forth. But their lack of control does not mean that managers can ignore such forces, use them as excuses for poor performance, and try to just get by. Managers must stay abreast of external developments and react accordingly. Moreover, as we will discuss later in the chapter, it sometimes is possible to influence components of the external environment. We will examine ways in which organizations can do just that.

Figure 2.1 shows the external environment of a firm. The firm exists in its **competitive environment,** which is composed of the firm and competitors, suppliers, customers, new entrants, and substitutes. At the more general level is the **macroenvironment,** which includes legal, political, economic, technological, demographic, and social and natural factors that generally affect all organizations.

competitive environment The immediate environment surrounding a firm; includes suppliers, customers, competitors, and the like.

macroenvironment The most general environment; includes governments, economic conditions, and other fundamental factors that generally affect all organizations.

A look ahead

In this chapter, we discuss the basic characteristics of an organization's environment and the importance of that environment for strategic management. Later chapters will elaborate on many of the basic environmental forces introduced here. For example, technology will be discussed again in Chapter 17. The global environment gets a thorough treatment in Chapter 6, which is devoted entirely to international management. Other chapters focus on ethics, social responsibility, and the natural environment. Chapter 18 reiterates the theme that recurs throughout this text: Organizations must continually change because environments continually change.

The macroenvironment

All organizations operate in a macroenvironment, which is defined by the most general elements in the external environment that can potentially influence strategic decisions. Although a top executive team may have unique internal strengths and ideas about its goals, it still must consider external factors before taking action.

figure 2.1 The external environment

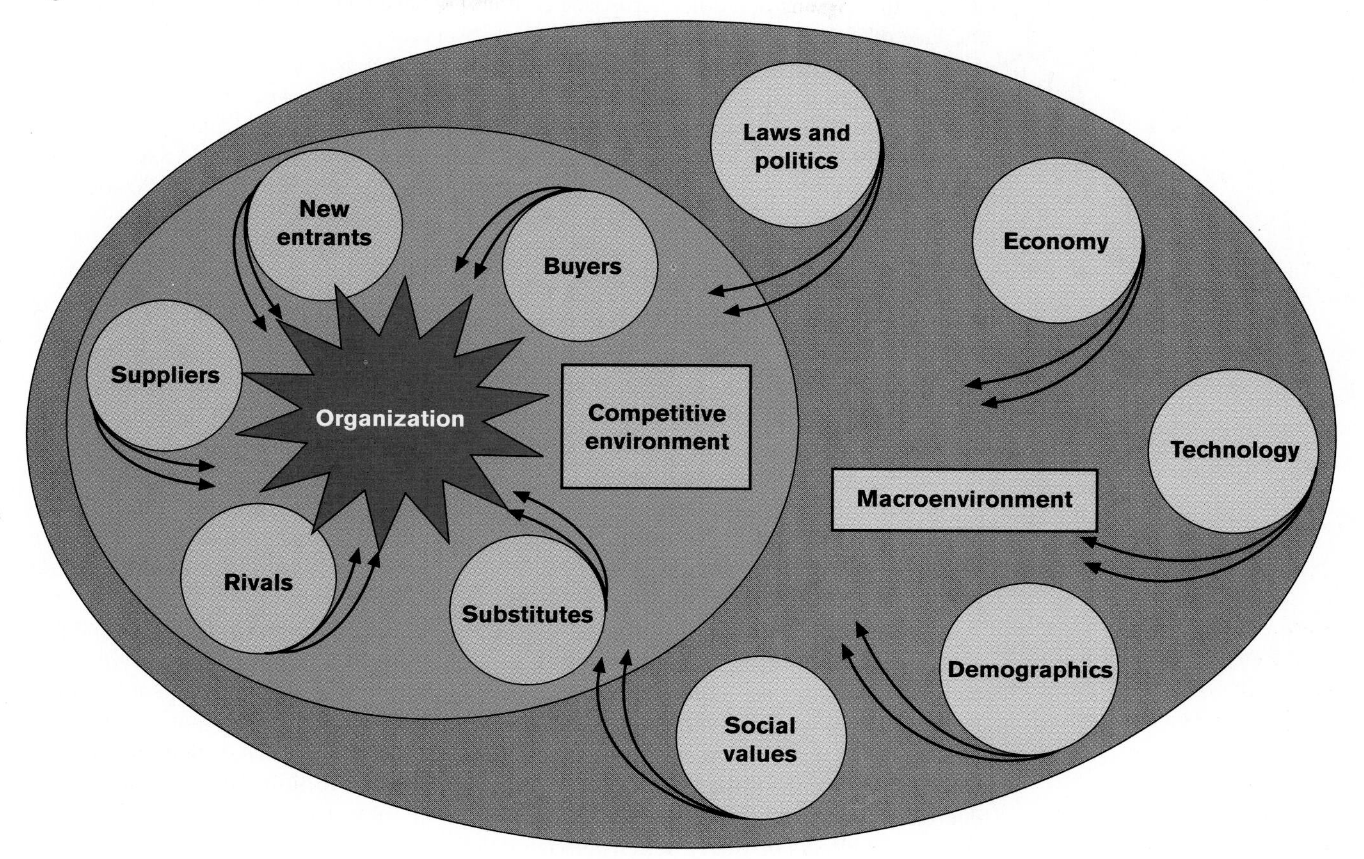

Laws and regulations

U.S. government policies both impose strategic constraints and provide opportunities. The government can affect business opportunities through tax laws, economic policies, and international trade rulings. One example of restraint on business action is the U.S. government's standards regarding bribery. In some countries, bribes and kickbacks are common and expected ways of doing business. But for U.S. firms, these are illegal practices. Indeed, some U.S. businesses have been fined for using bribery when competing internationally.

Regulators are specific government organizations in a firm's more immediate task environment. Regulatory agencies such as the Occupational Safety and Health Administration (OSHA), the Interstate Commerce Commission (ICC), the Federal Aviation Administration (FAA), the Equal Employment Opportunity Commission (EEOC), the National Labor Relations Board (NLRB), the Office of Federal Contract Compliance Programs (OFCCP), and the Environmental Protection Agency (EPA) have the power to investigate company practices and take legal action to ensure compliance with the laws.

For example, the Securities and Exchange Commission (SEC) regulates U.S. financial markets; since the insider-trading scandals, the SEC has dramatically changed investment houses' policies and practices. And the Food and Drug Administration (FDA) can prevent a company from selling an unsafe or ineffective product to the public. In the late 1980s, the FDA allowed the first biotechnology products to be marketed, creating the first profits in what will be a hugely profitable industry.

The government can offer strategic opportunities. For example, in "Setting the Stage," we saw that Boeing and other aerospace contractors have had to readjust their strategies in the face of defense cutbacks. However, some observers believe that the future of defense spending looks more promising. Boeing/McDonnell Douglas stands to win a large portion of the reported $150 billion that the Pentagon plans to spend over the next 15 years to develop new fighter aircraft. In addition, Boeing recently was awarded a prime contract to build the international space station and is in the process of becoming NASA's top supplier.[1] So while government laws and regulations place limits on what an organization can do, the government may also be a source of funding and revenues.

The economy

Although most Americans are used to thinking in terms of the U.S. economy, the economic environment is created by complex interconnections among economies of different countries. Wall Street investment analysts begin their workday thinking not just about what the Dow Jones did yesterday but also about how the London and Tokyo exchanges did overnight. Growth and recessions occur worldwide as well as domestically.

The economic environment dramatically affects companies' ability to function effectively and influences their strategic choices. Interest and inflation rates affect the availability and cost of capital, the ability to expand, prices, costs, and consumer demand for products. Unemployment rates affect labor availability and the wages the firm must pay, as well as product demand.

The overriding concern for the U.S. economy these days tends to be the size of the federal deficit. While both Republicans and Democrats are working together to reduce the deficit, Congress is not required to balance the budget each year, so the federal government continues to spend more than it takes in. The overspending is covered by loans, in the form of bonds, that the government issues to be paid back in the future. The situation is getting better. In 1990, the government racked up a debt of $220 billion, but that number had decreased to $107 billion by 1996 (its lowest point since 1981). Figure 2.2 shows the cumulative effects of yearly deficits on the national debt.[2]

figure 2.2
The growing debt

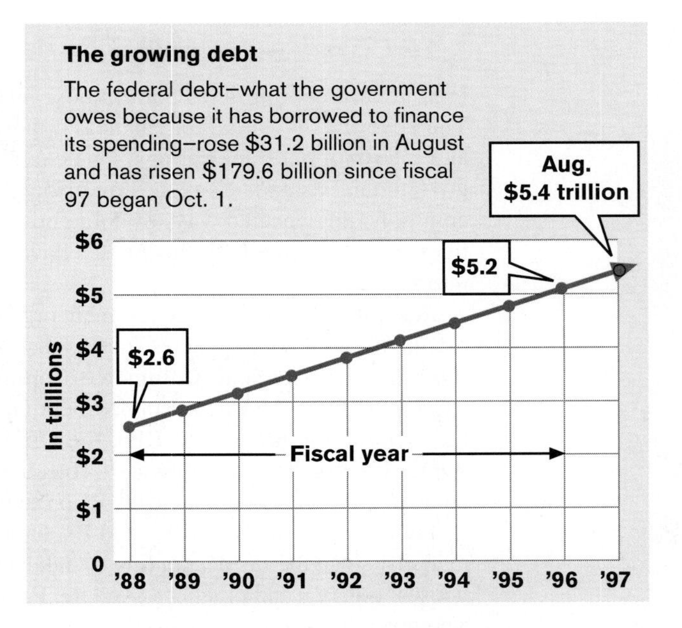

Source: Adapted and reprinted by permission of Harvard Business Review. From "How Competitive Forces Shape Strategy" by Michael E. Porter, *Harvard Business Review*, March/April 1997. Copyright © 1997 by the President and Fellows of Harvard College; all rights reserved.

Economic conditions change over time and are difficult to predict. Bull and bear markets come and go. Periods of dramatic growth may be followed by a recession. Every trend undoubtedly will end—but when? Even when times seem good, budget deficits or other considerations create concern about the future.

Technology

Today, a company cannot succeed without incorporating into its strategy the astonishing technologies that exist and continue to evolve. Technological advances create new products, advanced production techniques, and better ways of managing and communicating. In addition, as technology evolves, new industries, markets, and competitive niches develop. For example, the advent of computers created a huge industry. Early entrants in biotechnology are trying to establish dominant positions, while later entrants work on technological advances that will give them a competitive niche.

New technologies also provide new production techniques. In manufacturing, sophisticated robots perform jobs without suffering fatigue, requiring vacations or weekends off, or demanding wage increases. Until the U.S. steel industry began modernizing its plants, its productivity lagged far behind that of the technologically superior Japanese plants.

New technologies also provide new ways to manage and communicate. Computerized management information systems (MIS) make information available when needed. Computers monitor productivity and note performance deficiencies. Telecommunications allow conferences to take place without requiring people to travel to the same location. Consider the following discussion of changes in the field of telecommunications. As you can see, technological advances create innovations in business. Strategies developed around the cutting edge of technological advances create a competitive advantage; strategies that ignore or lag behind competitors in considering technology lead to obsolescence and extinction. This issue is so important that we devote an entire chapter (Chapter 17) to the topic.

Technology changes telecommunications

Over a decade ago, American Telephone & Telegraph (AT&T) was forced to break up into smaller companies because Judge Harold Greene and the U.S. Department of Justice had decided that long-distance calling no longer qualified as a natural monopoly. Why? Microwave technology had helped long-distance telephony take to the air–go wireless like the radio before it–and this had opened up some very new possibilities about who could provide long-distance service.

Technology changed the nature of competition in the mid-1980s, and has been changing the telecommunications industry ever since. When companies moved to microwave technology, the telephone industry experienced excess capacity, so everyone has moved back to more traditional land-lined technologies such as fiber optics–again changing the structure of competition.

Currently technology is blending telephone and cable television. Coaxial cable, traditionally used as the medium for cable television, carries 900 times more information than conventional copper wire. As a consequence, most major telephone companies have been trying to partner with cable television companies to gain a better foothold with consumers. Although it is hard to see the future clearly, it appears that other technologies such as fiber optics, digital radio, direct broadcast satellite (DBS), and cellular communications are merging, thereby putting computers, television, and telecommunications in a position to either compete or cooperate. Add the Internet to this mix–with over 50 million current users–and the picture gets even fuzzier.

Companies are investing in low earth-orbiting satellite (LEO) systems as an alternative for telecommunications transmissions.
[Courtesy of Iridium, LTD.]

Companies such as Motorola, Loral, and TRW are investing in low earth-orbiting satellite (LEO) systems as an alternative for telecommunications transmissions. LEOs operate in a nongeostationary orbit, which is at a lower altitude than other satellites. As a result, the transmission time between two earth stations is shortened, which reduces or virtually eliminates the time delay present in current satellite systems. LEO systems can transmit voice and data directly or work with cellular networks as a hub for the satellites. Motorola's Iridium system consists of 66 LEOs, Loral's Globalstar system will have a 48-satellite constellation. TRW's Odyssey system will only have 12 satellites, but they will orbit at a higher altitude in order to cover the entire planet. Teledesic is putting forth the most aggressive proposal yet. Its system is being touted as a "global broad-band Internet-in-the-sky" system. The company is designing a mega-LEO constellation that has the potential to transform the entire satellite communications market. Investors in the project include Microsoft chairman Bill Gates, McCaw Cellular Communications' founder Craig McCaw, and Boeing's chairman Phil Condit.

These are just a sample of the changes on the horizon in telecommunications due to technological innovations. The possibilities seem endless, and the number of "on-ramps" to the information superhighway appears to be growing. We will talk more about these issues in Chapter 17.

Sources: Steve Arends, "Telecom's Future Is in the Stars," *Telephony,* June 2, 1997, pp. 212–219; Mark Sabet, "Trends and Turbulence on the Information Superhighway," *Business Forum,* Winter 1997, pp. 55–56; Ron Preston, "Telecommunications at the Crossroads: Convergence or Collision?" *Industry Forum,* July 1997, p. 25; Bill Cronin, "Ten Telco Trends for the Next Decade," *Rural Telecommunications,* March/April 1997, pp. 60–65; Andrew Kupfer, "GTE: Son of Internet," *Fortune,* June 23, 1997, pp. 120–122.

Demographics

demographics Measures of various characteristics of the people who comprise groups or other social units.

Demographics are measures of various characteristics of the people comprising groups or other social units. Work groups, organizations, countries, markets, or societies can be described statistically by referring to their members' age, gender, family size, income, education, occupation, and so forth.

Companies must consider workforce demographics in formulating their human resources strategies. Population growth influences the size and composition of the labor force. By 2005, the U.S. civilian labor force, growing at a rate of 1.3 percent annually, is expected to reach approximately 151 million. Fluctuations in the birthrate influence population trends somewhat. In past years, the number of younger workers (16 to 24 years of age) has declined, but now that children of the baby-boom generation are entering the workforce, this age group is expected to grow 16 percent by 2005. At the same time, baby boomers themselves are reaching retirement age, so the number of older workers (55 and above) will also rise to about 15 percent of the labor force. Eventually, declining participation in work of older persons will largely offset the increase in the number of persons in this population group.

Immigration is also a factor that significantly influences the U.S. population and labor force. Over the past decade, immigrants have accounted for approximately 40 percent of the increase in U.S. population growth, a trend that has an important impact on the labor force. Immigrants are frequently of working age but have different educational and occupational backgrounds from the rest of the labor force. By 2005, the labor force will be even more diverse than it is today. White males will constitute approximately 38 percent of the labor force, African-Americans 13 percent, Hispanics 16 percent, and Asians and others nearly 6 percent. Together these groups are expected to account for nearly 65 percent of the growth in the labor force by 2005.

Women continue to join the U.S. labor force in record numbers. In 1970, women made up only about one-third of the labor force. By 2005 women are expected to account for over 47 percent, a trend that provides companies with more talent from which to choose.[3]

A more diverse workforce has its advantages, but managers have to make certain they provide equality for women and minorities with respect to employment, advancement opportunities, and compensation. Strategic plans must be made for recruiting, retaining, training, motivating, and effectively utilizing people of diverse demographical backgrounds with the skills needed to achieve the company's mission. Large numbers of single-parent and two-income families with children led to the creation and success of KinderCare and other day care facilities. These demographic trends also led to policies such as parental leaves, part-time employment, flexible work schedules, job sharing, telecommuting, and child care assistance.

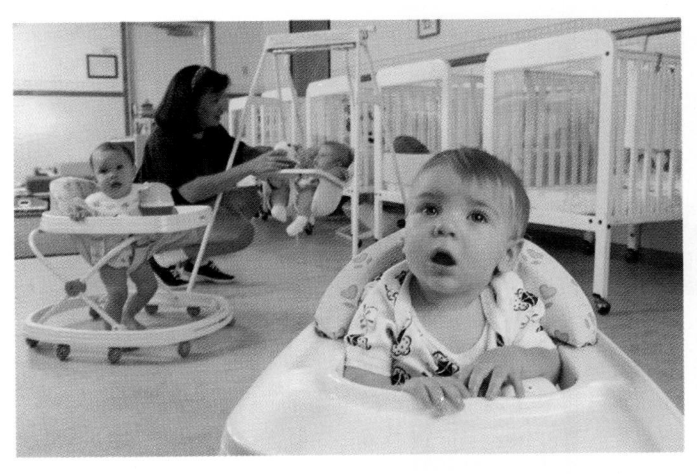

With ever-greater numbers of women entering the workforce, KinderCare centers such as this one in Plano, Texas, are becoming increasingly popular. *[Charles Thatcher]*

Social issues and the natural environment

Societal trends regarding how people think and behave have major implications for management of the labor force, corporate social actions, and strategic decisions about products and markets.

In the late 1970s and 1980s, it was unfashionable for women pursuing careers to have children; instead, they dedicated themselves to their work, postponing or deciding against having children. During the past decade, having children has become popular again. Today, companies that want to create or maintain a competitive advantage—or that merely hope to stay competitive—are introducing more supportive policies regarding maternal leave (and even paternal leave), flexible working hours, and child care.

A prominent issue in today's press pertains to the social costs of smoking. States such as Florida, Minnesota, and Texas have sued the tobacco companies to recoup billions of dollars in health care costs. In the summer of 1997, tobacco companies were ordered to pay $368.5 billion to settle the decades-long dispute over how to cut tobacco use. Currently there is legislation being proposed to toughen penalties on tobacco companies and other legal battles about whether the Food and Drug Administration (FDA) has the authority to regulate tobacco advertising. This particular issue shows how various elements in the macroenvironment can combine to influence an industry.[4]

Another issue of growing concern is the protection of our natural environment. This topic is so important in managerial decision making that we devote an entire chapter to it (Chapter 7).

The competitive environment

All organizations are affected by the general components of the macroenvironment we have just discussed. Each organization also functions in a closer, more immediate competitive environment. The competitive environment comprises the specific organizations with which the organization interacts. As shown in Figure 2.3, the competitive environment includes rivalry among current competitors, threat of new entrants, threat of substitutes, power of suppliers, and power of customers. This model was originally developed by Michael Porter, a Harvard professor and noted authority on strategic management. According to Porter, successful managers do more than simply react to the environment; they act in ways that actually shape or change the organization's environment. In strategic decision making, Porter's model is an excellent method for analyzing the competitive environment in order to adapt to or influence the nature of competition.

Competitors

Of the various components of the competitive environment, competitors within the industry must first deal with one another. When organizations compete for the same customers and try to win market share at the others' expense, all must react to and anticipate their competitors' actions.

The first question to consider is: Who is the competition? Sometimes answers are obvious. Coca-Cola and PepsiCo are competitors, as are the Big Three automakers: General Motors, Ford, and Chrysler. But sometimes organizations focus too exclusively on traditional rivalries

figure 2.3
The competitive environment

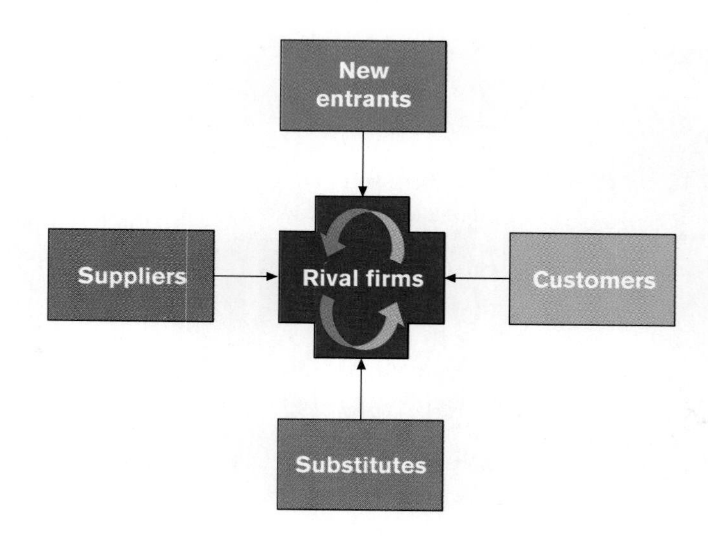

With the closing of many of its stores, Sears Roebuck faced near extinction. After making major managerial changes, this former giant is gradually regaining prominence. *[Mark Richards/DOT]*

and miss the emerging ones. Historically, Sears & Roebuck focused on its competition with J.C. Penney. However, Sears' real competitors are Kmart and Wal-Mart at the low end; Mervyn's in the middle; Nordstrom at the high end; and a variety of catalogers, such as Lands' End, L.L. Bean, and Eddie Bauer. Similarly, United Airlines, Delta, American, and U.S.Airways have focused their attention to a battle over long haul and international routes. In the process, they all but ignored smaller carriers such as Southwest, Alaska Air, and America West that have grown and succeeded in regional markets.[5]

Thus, as a first step in understanding their competitive environment, organizations must identify their competitors. Competitors may include (1) small domestic firms, especially their entry into tiny, premium markets; (2) overseas firms, especially their efforts to solidify positions in small niches (a traditional Japanese tactic); (3) big, new domestic companies exploring new markets; (4) strong regional competitors; and (5) unusual entries such as Internet shopping.

Once competitors have been identified, the next step is to analyze how they compete. Competitors use tactics like price reductions, new-product introductions, and advertising campaigns to gain advantage over their rivals. It's essential to understand what competitors are doing when honing your own strategy. Competition is most intense when there are many direct competitors (including foreign contenders), when industry growth is slow, and when the product or service cannot be differentiated in some way. New, high-growth industries offer enormous opportunities for profits. When an industry matures and growth slows, profits drop. Then, intense competition causes an industry shakeout: Weaker companies are eliminated, and the strong companies survive.[6]

Threat of new entrants

New entrants into an industry compete with established companies. If many factors prevent new companies from entering the industry, the threat to established firms is less serious. If there are few such **barriers to entry,** the threat of new entrants is more serious. Some major barriers to entry are government policy, capital requirements, brand identification, cost disadvantages, and distribution channels. The government can limit or prevent entry, as when the FDA forbids a new drug entrant. Some industries, such as trucking and liquor retailing, are regulated; more subtle government controls operate in fields such as mining and ski area development. Patents are also entry barriers. When a patent expires (like Polaroid's basic patents on instant photography), other companies (e.g., Kodak) can then enter the market.

barriers to entry Conditions that prevent new companies from entering an industry.

Other barriers are less formal but can have the same effect. Capital requirements may be so high that companies won't risk or try to raise such large amounts of money. Brand identification forces new entrants to spend heavily to overcome customer loyalty. The cost advantages established companies hold—due to large size, favorable locations, existing assets, and so forth—also can be formidable entry barriers.

Finally, existing competitors may have such tight distribution channels that new entrants have difficulty getting their products or services to customers. For example, established food products already have supermarket shelf space. New entrants must displace existing products with promotions, price breaks, intensive selling, and other tactics.

Threat of substitutes

Technological advances and economic efficiencies are among the ways that firms can develop substitutes for existing products. For example, although Southwest Airlines has developed strong rivalries with other airlines, it also competes—as a substitute—with bus companies such as Greyhound and rental car companies such as Avis. Southwest has gotten its cost base down to such a low point that it is now cheaper to fly from Los Angeles to Phoenix than it is to take a bus or rent a car. This particular example shows that substitute products or services can limit another industry's revenue potential. Companies in those industries are likely to suffer growth and earnings problems unless they improve quality or launch aggressive marketing campaigns.[7]

In addition to current substitutes, companies need to think about potential substitutes that may be viable in the near future. More and more people are buying books and music via the Internet. Companies such as Amazon.com that sell over the Internet represent a potential threat to retail stores. Traditional bookstores such as Barnes and Noble have invested heavily in Web technology to defuse the threat of this potential substitute. Table 2.1 shows a list of products and potential substitutes.[8]

Suppliers

Recall from our discussion of open systems that organizations must acquire resources from their environment and convert those resources into products or services to sell. Suppliers provide the resources needed for production and may come in the form of people (supplied by trade schools and universities), raw materials (supplied by producers, wholesalers, and distributors), information (supplied by researchers and consulting firms), and financial capital (supplied by banks and other sources). But suppliers are important to an organization for reasons beyond the resources they provide. Suppliers can raise their prices or provide poor quality goods and services. Labor unions can go on strike or demand higher wages. Workers may produce defective work. Powerful suppliers, then, can reduce an organization's profits, particularly if the organization cannot pass on price increases to its customers.

table 2.1
Potential Substitutes for Products

If the product is . . .	The substitute might be . . .
Cotton	Polyester
Coffee	Soft drinks
Fossil fuels	Solar fusion
Movie theater	Home video
Music CD	Radio, cassette, LP
Automobile	Train, bus, bicycle
Typewriter	Personal computer
Sugar	Nutrasweet
House	Apartment, condo, mobile home
Bricks	Aluminum siding
Trashy magazine	Internet
Local telephone	Cellular phone, pager

The recent UPS strike shows that the Teamsters union exerts a good deal of influence over how its members are treated.
[Agence France Presse/Corbis-Bettmann]

One particularly noteworthy set of suppliers to some industries is the international labor unions. Although unionization in the United States has dropped to about 10 percent of the private labor force, labor unions are still particularly powerful in industries such as steel, autos, and transportation. The recent UPS strike shows that the Teamsters union, in particular, exerts a good deal of influence over how its members are treated. Labor unions represent and protect the interests of their members with respect to hiring, wages, working conditions, job security, and due process appeals. Historically, the relationship between management and labor unions has been adversarial; however, both sides seem to realize that to increase productivity and competitiveness, management and labor work together in collaborative relationships. Troubled labor relations can create higher costs and productivity declines and eventually lead to layoffs.[9]

Organizations are at a disadvantage if they become overly dependent on any powerful supplier. A supplier is powerful if the buyer has few other sources of supply or if the supplier has many other buyers. For example, if computer companies can only go to Microsoft for software or to Intel for microchips, those suppliers can exert a great deal of pressure. In many cases, companies build up switching costs. **Switching costs** are fixed costs buyers face if they change suppliers. For example, once a buyer learns how to operate a supplier's equipment, such as computer software, the buyer faces both economic and psychological costs in changing to a new supplier.[10]

switching costs Fixed costs buyers face when they change suppliers.

Choosing the right supplier is an important strategic decision. Suppliers can affect manufacturing time, product quality, and inventory levels. The relationship between suppliers and the organization is changing in some companies. The close supplier relationship has become a new model for many organizations, such as Ford Motor, that are using a just-in-time manufacturing approach (discussed in Chapters 16 and 17).

Ford eliminates supplier surprise

Executives at Ford understand very well how good supplier relationships can enhance a company's competitive capability. In an industry moving toward more frequent model changes, shorter product life cycles, and smaller production runs, coordination with suppliers is critical for raising quality and lowering costs. To improve coordination with its network of 1,500 suppliers, Ford has undertaken a number of important initiatives.

To ensure consistently high quality, Ford gives its Q1 quality award to suppliers whose quality has been so dependable that Ford no longer has to inspect their incoming shipments. Suppliers trying to win the Q1 award go through a process of

correcting manufacturing inefficiencies and then inviting Ford teams in to visit them to see their progress. The program has been very successful, and Q1 has become the quality standard to which virtually all suppliers aspire. In the steel industry, Q1 awards have been given to Bethlehem Steel, Inland Steel, LTV, and USX.

In addition to setting quality standards for its suppliers, Ford has put in place a program called Direct Data Link (DDL) that provides suppliers with direct access to Ford's inventory control system. With DDL, suppliers have up-to-the minute data on supply requirements in each of Ford's 20 North American assembly plants, 61 manufacturing locations, and 10 parts and supply sites.

In the past, Ford employed a staff of about 100 people in Detroit to identify material shortages and notify suppliers of any problems. Now, thanks to DDL, each supplier is responsible for taking care of stock levels and shipments on its own. With DDL, suppliers even have the capability (using a security code) to update Ford's database when they send shipments. Because suppliers have better and more current information about Ford's needs, there are fewer surprises and emergencies. DDL enables suppliers to run their production schedules in parallel with Ford's, and in some cases suppliers such as Dana Corporation and O'Sullivan Corporation have even used DDL to design their own software systems that extract data and plan production cycles.

These efforts have helped reduce costs and upgrade quality for both Ford and its network of suppliers. In an environment where speed and quality are critical success factors, Ford has made great strides in creating a seamless buyer–supplier relationship.

Sources: John Burnell, "Henry Ford Would Be Proud," *Automatic I.D.* 13, no. 9 (August 1997), pp. 48–49; "Q1 Preferred Quality Award," *Management Accounting* 78, no. 9 (March 1997), p. 44; "Supply Chain Savings in EDI," *Purchasing* 121, no. 5 (October 3, 1996), p. 56; Joanne Cummings, "Another Bright Idea," *Network World,* November 23, 1993, pp. 31, 34, 36, 37; "Eliminating Redundant Quality Audits," *Quality,* January 1993, p. 16; Bryan Berry, "For Steelmakers, Quality Is Job Won," *Iron Age,* July 1992, pp. 24–27; Gary S. Vasilash, "Car Talk: What Every Auto Supplier Ought to Hear," *Production,* October 1992, pp. 34–37; and Drew Winter, "CAD/CAM Wars," *Ward's Auto World* 33, no. 6 (June 1997), p. 35.

Customers

final consumer Those who purchase products in their finished form.

intermediate consumer Customers who purchase raw materials or wholesale products before selling them to final customers.

customer service The speed and dependability with which an organization can deliver what customers want.

Customers purchase the products or services the organization offers. Without customers, a company won't survive. You are a **final consumer** when you buy a McDonald's hamburger or a pair of jeans from a retailer at the mall. **Intermediate consumers** buy raw materials or wholesale products and then sell to final consumers. Intermediate customers actually make more purchases than individual final consumers do. Examples of intermediate customers include retailers, who buy clothes from wholesalers and manufacturers' representatives before selling them to their customers, and industrial buyers, who buy raw materials (such as chemicals) before converting them into final products.

Like suppliers, customers are important to organizations for reasons other than the money they provide for goods and services. Customers can demand lower prices, higher quality, unique product specifications, or better service. They can also play competitors against one another, such as when a car customer (or a purchasing agent) collects different offers and negotiates for the best price.

Customer service means giving customers what they want or need, the way they want it, the first time. This usually depends on the speed and dependability with which an organization can deliver its products or services. Actions and attitudes that mean excellent customer service include:

- Speed of filling and delivering normal orders.
- Willingness to meet emergency needs.
- Merchandise delivered in good condition.
- Readiness to take back defective goods and resupply quickly.
- Availability of installation and repair services and parts.
- Service charges (that is, whether services are "free" or priced separately).[11]

In all businesses—services as well as manufacturing—strategies that emphasize good customer service provide a critical competitive advantage. The organization is at a disadvantage if it depends too heavily on powerful customers. Customers are powerful if they make large purchases or if they can easily find alternative places to buy. If you are the largest customer of a firm, and there are other firms from which you can buy, you have power over that firm, and you are likely to be able to negotiate with it successfully. Your firm's biggest customers—especially if they can buy from other sources—will have the greatest negotiating power over you.

Environmental analysis

If managers do not understand how the environment affects their organizations, or cannot identify opportunities and threats that are likely to be important, then their ability to make decisions and execute plans will be severely limited. For example, if little is known about customer likes and dislikes, organizations would have a difficult time designing new products, scheduling production, developing marketing plans, and the like. In short, timely and accurate environmental information is critical for running a business.

environmental uncertainty
Lack of information needed to understand or predict the future.

But information about the environment is not always readily available. **Environmental uncertainty** means that managers do not have enough information about the environment to understand or predict the future. Uncertainty arises from two related factors: (1) complexity and (2) dynamism. Environmental *complexity* refers to the number of issues to which a manager must attend as well as their interconnectedness. For example, industries that have many different firms that compete in vastly different ways tend to be more complex—and uncertain—than industries with only a few key competitors. Similarly, environmental *dynamism* refers to the degree of discontinuous change that occurs within the industry. For example, high-growth industries with products and technologies that change rapidly tend to be more uncertain than stable industries where change is less dramatic and more predictable.[12]

As environmental uncertainty increases, managers must develop techniques and methods for collecting, sorting through, and interpreting information about the environment. By analyzing environmental forces—both in the macro and competitive environments—managers can identify opportunities and threats that might impact the organization.

Environmental scanning

Perhaps the first step in coping with uncertainty in the environment is pinning down what might be of importance. It is frequently the case that organizations (and individuals) act out of ignorance, only to regret those actions in the future. IBM, for example, had the opportunity to purchase the technology behind xerography, but turned it down. Xerox saw the potential, and the rest is history. However, Xerox researchers later developed the technology for the original computer mouse, but not seeing the potential, the company missed an important market opportunity.

environmental scanning Searching for and sorting through information about the environment.

In order to understand and predict changes, opportunities, and threats, organizations such as Monsanto, Weyerhaeuser, and Union Carbide spend a good deal of time and money monitoring events in the environment. **Environmental scanning** means both searching out information that is unavailable to most people and also sorting through that information in order to interpret what is important and what is not. Managers can ask questions such as

- Who are our current competitors?
- Are there few or many entry barriers to our industry?
- What substitutes exist for our product or service?
- Is the company too dependent on powerful suppliers?
- Is the company too dependent on powerful customers?[13]

competitive intelligence Information that helps managers determine how to compete better.

Answers to these questions help managers develop **competitive intelligence,** the information necessary to decide how best to manage in the competitive environment they have identified.[14] Porter's competitive analysis, discussed earlier, can guide environmental scanning and help managers evaluate the competitive potential of different environments. Table 2.2 describes two extreme environments: an attractive environment, which gives a firm a competitive advantage, and an unattractive environment, which puts a firm at a competitive disadvantage.

Scenario development

scenario A narrative that describes a particular set of future conditions.

As managers attempt to determine the effect of environmental forces on their organizations, they frequently develop **scenarios** of the future. Scenarios represent alternative combinations of different factors into a total picture of the environment and the firm. For example, as Congress and the president try to work toward a balanced budget, and eventually reduce the federal debt, they have developed several different scenarios about what the economy is likely to do over the next decade or so. Frequently, organizations develop a *best-case scenario* (i.e., if events occur that are favorable to the firm), a *worst-case scenario* (i.e., if events are all unfavorable), and some middle-ground alternatives. The value of scenario development is that it helps managers develop contingency plans for what they might do given different outcomes.[15]

Forecasting

forecasting Method for predicting how variables will change the future.

Whereas environmental scanning is used to identify important factors and scenario development is used to develop alternative pictures of the future, **forecasting** is used to predict exactly how some variable or variables will change in the future. For example, in making capital investments, firms may try to forecast how interest rates will change. In deciding to expand or downsize a business, firms may try to forecast the demand for goods and services, or forecast the supply and demand of labor they would likely use. Available publications such as *Business Week*'s *Business Outlook* provide forecasts to businesses both large and small.

table 2.2 Attractive and unattractive environments

Environmental Factor	Unattractive	Attractive
Competitors	Many; low industry growth; equal size; commodity	Few; high industry growth; unequal size; differentiated
Threat of entry	High threat; few entry barriers	Low threat; many barriers
Substitutes	Many	Few
Suppliers	Few; high bargaining power	Many; low bargaining power
Customers	Few; high bargaining power	Many; low bargaining power

Although forecasts are designed to help executives make predictions about the future, their accuracy varies from application to application. Because they extrapolate from the past to project the future, forecasts tend to be most accurate when the future ends up looking a lot like the past. Of course, we don't need sophisticated forecasts in those instances. Forecasts are most useful when the future will look radically different than the past. Unfortunately, that is when forecasts tend not to be so accurate. The more things change, the less confidence we tend to have in our forecasts. The best advice for using forecasts might include the following:

- Use multiple forecasts and perhaps average their predictions.
- Remember that accuracy decreases the farther into the future you are trying to predict.
- Forecasts are no better than the data used to construct them.
- Use simple forecasts (rather than complicated ones) where possible.
- Important events often are surprises and represent a departure from predictions.[16]

Benchmarking

benchmarking The process of comparing the organization's practices and technologies with those of other companies.

In addition to trying to predict changes in the environment, firms can undertake intensive study of the best practices of various firms to understand their sources of competitive advantage. **Benchmarking** means identifying the best-in-class performance by a company in a given area, say product development or customer service, and then comparing your processes to theirs. To accomplish this, a benchmarking team would collect information on its own company's operations and those of the other firm in order to determine gaps. These gaps serve as a point of entry to learn the underlying causes of performance differences. Ultimately the team would map out a set of best practices that lead to world class performance. We will discuss benchmarking further in Chapter 4.[17]

From the Pages of BusinessWeek

Opening the Skies

Two decades after Congress voted to open the skies to greater competition, the government is planning to crack down on what it sees as anticompetitive behavior by the major carriers, and perhaps even passing new laws to protect startup airlines. The goals of the reform efforts are ambitious: Break the stronghold that major airlines have on the nation's busiest airports, bring more service to smaller cities, and attack allegedly predatory behavior–such as when an established carrier slashes fares and adds flights on a route to keep new airlines from making inroads. The Transportation Department plans to release a definition of predatory behavior in February, which could lead to stiffer enforcement. In Congress, at least five separate airline bills are expected this term.

Mostly, deregulation has worked: Since 1978, fares have dropped sharply. But lately, the majors have used a strong economy and worries about safety after the 1996 ValuJet crash to battle startups more fiercely. The big airlines have stopped competing with each other on some business routes and locked up a larger share of airport resources. At O'Hare Airport, American and United Airlines now fly about 87% of flights, up from 66% in 1986. "The practices have created a less and less competitive environment," says Craig E. Belmondo, president of Pro Air, a Detroit startup.

The solution? "We need to see expanded competition by allowing the smaller airlines to participate more freely in the market," says Senator Bill Frist (R-Tenn.), sponsor of one bill to provide low-rate loans to carriers that would fly to cities with limited service. Most of the other bills attack the big airlines more directly. Among the proposals are two bills, by Representative Charles E. Schumer (D-N.Y.) and Senator John McCain (R-Ariz.), that call for some takeoff and landing slots at four of the nation's busiest airports–in Chicago, Washington, and New York–to be taken from the majors and auctioned off to low-fare rivals, sources say.

The next move on airline competition will be the DOT's release of its definition of predatory behavior. The DOT will try to be more precise about when airlines break rules by driving rivals out of markets with fare cuts, intimidation, discounts for travel agents, or new flights. The key test: Is a larger airline deliberately sustaining losses to hurt a rival?

The airlines say predatory practices are not feasible in such a competitive sector. As for the proposed bills, they say reclaiming airport slots would force them to abandon their least profitable routes–often to the same cities the lawmakers aim to help. But the government is unlikely to back off. Business is screaming about rising fares, and the data show that when a low-fare carrier enters a busy market, rates are often halved and flight frequencies can triple. That's something to celebrate.

Discussion Questions

1. What are the pros and cons of regulation in an industry? What reasons do you suppose there were for deregulation in 1978, and what reasons are there for increased regulation today?
2. What will the short-term effects of regulation be on the consumers? What might the long-term effects be?
3. What other industries might have a similar competitive environment? How would regulation work in those industries?

Source: David Leonhardt "Prying Open the Open Skies," *Business Week:* February 9, 1998. ●

Responding to the environment

Organizations have a number of options for responding to the environment. In general, these can be grouped into three categories: (1) adapting to the environment, (2) influencing the environment, and (3) selecting a new environment.

Adapting to the environment: changing yourself

In order to cope with environmental uncertainty, organizations frequently make adjustments in their structures and work processes. In the case of uncertainty arising from environmental complexity, we can say that organizations tend to adapt by *decentralizing* decision making. For example, if a company faces a growing number of competitors in various markets, if different customers want different things, if the characteristics of different products keep increasing, and if production facilities are being built in different regions of the world, then it may be impossible for the chief executive (or a small group of top executives) to keep abreast of all activities and understand all the operational details of a business. In these cases, the top management team is likely to give authority to lower level managers to make decisions that benefit the firm. The term **empowerment** is frequently used today to talk about this type of decentralized authority. We will address empowerment and decision making in more detail in Chapters 3 and 9.

empowerment The process of sharing power with employees, thereby enhancing their confidence in their ability to perform their jobs and their belief that they are influential contributors to the organization.

In response to uncertainty caused by change (dynamism) in the environment, organizations tend to establish more flexible structures. In today's business world, it is commonplace for the term *bureaucracy* to take on a bad connotation. Most of us recognize that bureaucratic organizations tend to be formalized and very stable; frequently they are unable to adjust to change or exceptional circumstances that "don't fit the rules." And while bureaucratic organizations may be efficient and controlled if the environment is stable, they tend to be slow moving and plodding when products, technologies, customers, competitors, and the like start changing over time. In these cases, more *organic* structures tend to have the flexibility needed to adjust to change. Although we will discuss organic structures in more detail in Chapter 9, suffice it to say here that they are less formal than bureaucratic organizations, so decisions tend to be made more through interaction and mutual adjustment among individuals rather than via a set of predefined rules. Table 2.3 shows four different approaches that organizations can take in adapting to environmental uncertainty.

buffering Creating supplies of excess resources in case of unpredictable needs.

Adapting at the boundaries

From the standpoint of an open system, organizations create buffers on both the input and output sides of their boundaries with the environment. **Buffering** is one such approach used for adapting to uncertainty. On the input side, organizations establish relationships with employment agencies to hire part-time and temporary help during rush periods when labor demand is difficult to predict. The growth of contingent workers in the U.S. labor force is a good indication of the popularity of this approach to buffering input uncertainties. On the output side of the system, most organizations use some type of ending inventories that allow them to keep merchandise on hand in case a rush of customers decide to buy their products. Auto dealers are a particularly common example of this use of buffers, but we can see similar use of buffer inventories in fast food restaurants, book stores, clothing stores, and even real estate agencies.[18]

smoothing Leveling normal fluctuations at the boundaries of the environment.

In addition to buffering, organizations may try **smoothing** or leveling normal fluctuations at the boundaries of the environment. For example, during winter months (up north) when automobile sales drop off, it is not uncommon for dealers to cut the price of their in-stock vehicles in order to increase demand. At the end of each clothing season, retailers discount their merchandise to clear it out in order to make room for incoming inventories. These are each examples of smoothing environmental cycles in order to level off fluctuations in demand.

flexible processes Methods for adapting the technical core to changes in the environment.

Adapting at the core

While buffering and smoothing work to manage uncertainties at the boundaries of the organization, firms also can establish **flexible processes** that allow for adaptation in their technical core. For example, firms increasingly try to customize their products and services to meet the varied and changing demands of customers. Even in manufacturing, where it is difficult to change basic core processes, firms are adopting techniques of mass customization that help them create flexible factories. Instead of mass-producing large quantities of a "one-size-fits-all" product, mass customization means

table 2.3
Four approaches for managing uncertainty

	Stable	Dynamic
Complex	Decentralized Bureaucratic (Standardized skills)	Decentralized Organic (Mutual adjustment)
Simple	Centralized Bureaucratic (Standardized work processes)	Centralized Organic (Direct supervision)

that organizations can produce individually customized products at an equally low cost. Whereas Henry Ford used to claim that "you could have a Model T in any color you wanted, as long as it was black," auto companies now offer a wide array of colors and trim lines, with different options and accessories. The process of mass customization involves the use of a network of independent operating units that each performs a specific process or task such as making a dashboard assembly on an automobile. When an order comes in, different modules join forces to deliver the product or service as specified by the customer. We will discuss mass customization and flexible factories in more depth in Chapters 9.[19]

Influencing your environment

In addition to adapting or reacting to the environment, organizations can develop proactive responses aimed at changing the environment. Two general types of proactive responses include independent action and cooperative action.

independent strategies
Strategies that an organization acting on its own uses to change some aspect of its current environment.

Independent action

A company uses **independent strategies** when it acts on its own to change some aspect of its current environment.[20] Table 2.4 shows the definitions and uses of these strategies. For example, when Southwest Airlines enters a new market, they demonstrate competitive aggression by cutting fares so that other less-efficient airlines must follow them down. In contrast, Kellogg Company typically promotes the cereal industry as a whole, thereby demonstrating competitive pacification. Weyerhaeuser Company advertises its reforestation efforts (public relations). First Boston forgoes its Christmas party and donates thousands of dollars to the poor (voluntary action). Dow Chemical recently sued General Electric for hiring away some of its engineers (legal action). Dow Corning lobbied and recently won the right to put silicon implants back on the market (political action). Each of these examples shows how organizations—on their own—can have an impact on the environment.

table 2.4 Independent action

Strategy	Definition	Examples
Competitive aggression	Exploiting a distinctive competence or improving internal efficiency for competitive advantage.	Aggressive pricing; comparative advertising (e.g., Advil)
Competitive pacification	Independent action to improve relations with competitors.	Helping competitors find raw materials
Public relations	Establishing and maintaining favorable images in the minds of those making up the environment.	Sponsoring sporting events
Voluntary action	Voluntary commitment to various interest groups, causes, and social problems.	Ronald McDonald Houses
Legal action	Company engages in private legal battle with competitor on antitrust, deceptive advertising, or other grounds.	Blue Mountain Arts, Inc.'s lawsuit against Hallmark for allegedly copying its cards
Political action	Efforts to influence elected representatives to create a more favorable business environment or limit competition.	ARCO's corporate constituency programs; issue advertising; lobbying at state and national levels

Source: Reprinted from *Journal of Marketing,* published by the American Marketing Association. C. Zeithaml and V. Zeithaml, "Environmental Management: Revising the Marketing Perspective," Spring 1984.

table 2.5
Cooperative action

Strategy	Definition	Examples
Contracting	Negotiation of an agreement between the organization and another group to exchange goods, services, information, patents, and so on.	Contractual marketing systems
Cooptation	Absorbing new elements into the organization's leadership structure to avert threats to its stability or existence.	Consumer and labor representatives and bankers on boards of directors.
Coalition	Two or more groups coalesce and act jointly with respect to some set of issues for some period of time.	Industry associations; political initiatives of the Business Roundtable and the U.S. Chamber of Commerce

Source: Reprinted from *Journal of Marketing,* published by the American Marketing Association. C. Zeithaml and V. Zeithaml, "Environmental Management: Revising the Marketing Perspective," Spring 1984.

cooperative strategies
Strategies used by two or more organizations working together to manage the external environment.

Cooperative action In some situations, two or more organizations work together using cooperative strategies to influence the environment.[21] Table 2.5 shows several examples of **cooperative strategies.** An example of contracting occurs when suppliers and customers, or managers and labor unions, sign formal agreements about the terms and conditions of their future relationships. These contracts are explicit attempts to make their future relationship predictable. An example of cooptation might occur when universities invite wealthy alumni to join their boards of directors. Finally, an example of *coalition* formation might be when local businesses band together to curb the rise of employee health care costs and when organizations in the same industry form industry associations and special-interest groups. You may have seen cooperative advertising strategies, such as when dairy producers, beef producers, orange growers, and the like jointly pay for television commercials.

At a more organizational level, organizations establish strategic alliances, partnerships, joint ventures, and mergers with competitors to deal with environmental uncertainties. Cooperative strategies such as these make most sense when (1) taking joint action will reduce the organizations' costs and risks and (2) cooperation will increase their power (that is, their ability to successfully accomplish the changes they desire).

Goodyear associates help to build a playground along with United Way.
[Courtesy of The Goodyear Tire and Rubber Company]

table 2.6
Strategic maneuvering

Strategy	Definition	Examples
Domain selection	Entering industries or markets with limited competition or regulation and ample suppliers and customers; entering high-growth markets.	IBM's entry into the personal computer market; Miller's entry into the light-beer market
Diversification	Investing in different types of businesses; manufacturing different types of products; or geographic expansion to reduce dependence on single market or technology.	General Electric's purchase of RCA and NBC
Merger and acquisition	Combining two or more firms into a single enterprise; gaining possession of an ongoing enterprise.	RJR and Nabisco; Sperry and Burroughs (now Unisys); Boeing and McDonnell Douglas
Divestiture	Selling one or more businesses.	Kodak and Eastman Chemical

Source: Reprinted from *Journal of Marketing,* published by the American Marketing Association. C. Zeithaml and V. Zeithaml, "Environmental Management: Revising the Marketing Perspective," Spring 1984.

Changing the environment you are in

strategic maneuvering The organization's conscious efforts to change the boundaries of its task environment.

prospectors Companies that continuously change the boundaries of their task environments by seeking new products and markets, diversifying and merging, or acquiring new enterprises.

As we noted above, organizations can cope with environmental uncertainty by changing themselves (environmental adapatation), changing the environment, or changing the environment they are in. We refer to this last category as **strategic maneuvering.** By making a conscious effort to change the boundaries of its competitive environment, firms can maneuver around potential threats and capitalize on arising opportunities.[22] Table 2.6 defines and gives examples of several of these strategies, including domain selection, diversification, merger and acquisition, and divestiture.

Organizations engage in strategic maneuvering when they move into different environments. Some companies, called **prospectors,** are more likely than others to engage in strategic maneuvering.[23] Aggressive companies continuously change the boundaries of their competitive environments by seeking new products and markets, diversifying, and merging or acquiring new enterprises. In these and other ways, corporations put their competitors on the defensive and force them to react. **Defenders,** on the other hand, stay within a more limited, stable product domain.

Choosing a response approach

defenders Companies that stay within a stable product domain as a strategic maneuver.

Three general considerations help guide management's response to the environment. First, organizations should attempt to *change appropriate elements of the environment.* Environmental responses are most useful when aimed at elements of the environment that (1) cause the company problems; (2) provide it with opportunities; and (3) allow the company to change successfully. Thus, automobile companies faced with intense competition from Japanese automakers successfully lobbied (along with labor) for government-imposed ceilings on Japanese imports. And one charcoal producer, hoping to increase consumers' opportunities to use its product, launched a campaign to increase daylight saving time.

Second, organizations should *choose responses that focus on pertinent elements of the environment.* If a company wants to better manage its competitive environment, competitive aggression and pacification are viable options. Political action influences the legal environment, and contracting helps manage customers and suppliers.

Third, companies should *choose responses that offer the most benefit at the lowest cost.* Return-on-investment calculations should incorporate short-term financial considerations as well as long-term impact. Strategic managers who carefully consider these factors will more effectively guide their organizations to competitive advantage.

Key terms

Barriers to entry, p. 59
Benchmarking, p. 65
Buffereing, p. 67
Competitive environment, p. 52
Competitive intelligence, p. 64
Cooperative strategies, p. 69
Customer service, p. 62
Defenders, p. 70
Demographics, p. 57
Empowerment, p. 66
Environmental scanning, p. 64
Environmental uncertainty, p. 63
External environment, p. 52
Final consumer, p. 62
Flexible processes, p. 67
Forecasting, p. 64
Independent strategies, p. 68
Intermediate consumer, p. 62
Macroenvironment, p. 52
Prospectors, p. 70
Scenarios, p. 64
Smoothing, p. 67
Strategic maneuvering, p. 70
Switching costs, p. 61

Summary of learning objectives

Now that you have studied Chapter 2, you should know:

How environmental forces influence organizations, as well as how organizations can influence their environments.

Organizations are open systems that are affected by, and in turn affect, their external environments. Organizations receive financial, human, material, and information resources from the environment; transform these resources into finished goods and services; and then send these outputs back into the environment.

How to make a distinction between the macroenvironment and the competitive environment.

The macroenvironment is composed of international, legal and political, economic, technological, and social forces that influence strategic decisions. The competitive environment is composed of forces closer to the organization, such as current competitors, threat of new entrants, threat of substitutes, suppliers, and customers. Perhaps the simplest distinction between the macroenvironment and the competitive environment is in the amount of control that a firm can exert on external forces. Macroenvironmental forces such as the economy or social trends are much less controllable than forces in the competitive environment such as suppliers and customers.

Why organizations should attend to economic and social developments in the international environment.

Developments in other countries have a profound effect on the way U.S. companies compete. European unification, for example, is creating a formidable buying and selling bloc. The North American Free Trade Agreement opened up trade between the United States, Canada, and Mexico. Managed well, the EU and NAFTA represent opportunities for market growth, joint ventures, and the like. Managed poorly, these free trade agreements may give advantage to more competitive firms and nations.

How to analyze the competitive environment in order to formulate strategy.

Environments can range from favorable to unfavorable. To determine how favorable a competitive environment is, managers should consider the nature of the competitors, potential new entrants, threat of substitutes, suppliers, and customers. Analyzing how these five forces influence the organization provides an indication of potential threats and opportunities. Attractive environments tend to be those that have high industry growth, few competitors, products that can be differentiated, few potential entrants, many barriers to entry, few substitutes, many suppliers (none with much power), and many customers. After identifying and analyzing competitive forces, managers must formulate a strategy that minimizes the power that external forces have over the organization (a topic to be discussed more fully in Chapter 5).

How environmental management strategies can be used to shape external forces.

Responding effectively to the environment often involves devising proactive strategies to change the environment. Strategic maneuvering, for example, involves changing the boundaries of the competitive environment through domain selection, diversification, mergers, and the like. Independent strategies, on the other hand, do not require moving into a new environment but rather changing some aspect of the current environment through competitive aggression, public relations, legal action, and so on. Finally, cooperative strategies, such as contracting, cooptation, and coalition building, involve the working together of two or more organizations.

Discussion questions

1. This chapter's opening quote by Peter Drucker said, "The essence of a business is outside itself." What do you think this means? Do you agree?

2. What are the most important forces in the macroenvironment facing companies today?

3. Go back to the Boeing example in "Setting the Stage." What other organizations have faced or are facing similar circumstances in their external environments?

4. What are the main differences between the macroenvironment and the competitive environment?

5. What kinds of changes do companies make in response to environmental uncertainty?

6. We outlined several proactive responses organizations can make to the environment. What examples have you seen recently of an organization's responding effectively to its environment? Did the effectiveness of the response depend on whether the organization was facing a threat or an opportunity?

Concluding Case

Greyhound is looking like a dog

In the 1934 movie *It happened One Night,* Clark Gable romanced Claudette Colbert on a Greyhound bus, and moviegoers flocked to become passengers to share the glamour. Nowadays, Greyhound is more likely to be featured in a horror movie. Since the mid-1980s, the Dallas-based company has been fighting several monsters at once—fierce regional competition, substitutes in the airline and rental car businesses, labor strikes, economic downturns, a fickle customer base, a leveraged buyout, and at least one cliff-hanger in bankruptcy court.

In the modern era, bus companies face stiff competition from substitute forms of transportation. In particular, the airlines have reduced their cost structures to a point where they are stealing a big chunk of Greyhound's business. Southwest Airlines, for example, charges $31 for a one-way ticket from Phoenix to San Diego. Greyhound charges $34—that's $3 more to travel by bus. Unless you especially like the view in Death Valley, you would probably take the plane.

Even those travelers who do decide to go by bus are more frequently taking a local or regional carrier rather than traveling with Greyhound. Peter Pan, for example, is a small enterprise that has been successful serving small towns in the Northeast that are ignored by major bus companies and air carriers. The company started off "connecting the dots" between Springfield, Boston, and western Massachusetts, but in 1986 it bought the rights to Trailways' routes from New England to New York City. Now Peter Pan has gained a strong foothold in the lower-income, ethnic customer base of inner-city travel. This has been a mainstay of Greyhound's business, and Peter Pan is cutting into its market share.

In addition to problems with competitors and substitutes, Greyhound has had labor difficulties. In 1990, the Amalgamated Transit Union, which represented more than 6,000 drivers and 3,000 mechanics, struck Greyhound. To keep operations going, Greyhound took a hard line against the union and hired 2,000 strike replacements. After a bitter and sometimes violent three-year work stoppage, the union finally allowed its members to return to work. Meanwhile, Greyhound had filed for Chapter 11 bankruptcy protection. After emerging from bankruptcy in 1991, Greyhound embarked on a restructuring program designed to reduce operating expenses. CEO Frank Schmieder cut Greyhound's fleet by 50 percent to just under 2,000 buses and trimmed the workforce by about 20 percent.

But as management cut expenses, services on many routes were reduced. Overworked and unmotivated employees frequently allowed telephones to go unanswered during peak business hours, alienating would-be customers. To rectify the problem and streamline operations, Greyhound borrowed an idea from the airline industry and rolled out its first national computer reservation system in 1993. The system, known as Trips, had a toll-free telephone number that customers could use to make reservations nationwide. The computer system was a flop, requiring 45 seconds to respond to each key stroke and taking up to seven minutes to print out a ticket. Unhappy customers either had to jump out of line or miss the bus—literally. To stop the exodus of passengers, Greyhound began shutting down the system and slashing fares, operating far below cost in some regions. The company hired Bradley Harslem, former guru of American Airlines' Sabre reservation system, to revamp the system, and response time was cut from 45 seconds to just 2 seconds. Trips now handles more than 70 percent of Greyhound's traffic, connecting over 250 cities and providing the kind of information that will help the company identify which routes (Greyhound serves 2,600 destinations) are most profitable.

Critics say Greyhound management lacks the know-how to keep the buses running on time. *[Tim Rasmussen/Sygma]*

Other efforts by Schmieder to resuscitate Greyhound included a $184 million investment in new buses, bringing the average age of the fleet down from 11.5 years to 6.5 years. Greyhound tried an image-boosting promotion with the theme "I go simple, I go easy, I go Greyhound." But it may be a case of too little, too late. With strong competition and excellent substitutes, Greyhound's utilized capacity dropped way off historical levels of 80 percent to less than 50 percent. On-time performance slipped below 60 percent. It's hard to make money running a half-empty bus that arrives late.

In August 1994, Frank Schmieder was forced to resign as CEO and was replaced by Craig Lentzsch, a former Greyhound executive. Several other top executives have also been forced out, including Michael Doyle, Greyhound's chief financial officer. Greyhound's stock price has fallen by 90 percent since May 1993, and the company is once again on the brink of bankruptcy.

Questions

1. What factors in Porter's model of the competitive environment are operating in this example? How attractive is this industry?
2. What mistakes have Greyhound's executives made? What have they done right?
3. Imagine you were running Greyhound. What response(s) would you suggest given the company's environmental situation?
4. Do you see any similarities between Greyhound's situation and the situation facing Boeing in "Setting the Stage"?

Sources: "Greyhound Lines: Bused Again?" *The Economist,* November 12, 1994, pp. 81–82; Wendy Zeller, "Greyhound Is Limping Badly," *Business Week,* August 22, 1994, p. 32; Gregory E. David, "Greyhound Lines: Goodbye, Dog Days?" *Financial World,* July 5, 1994, p. 16; Alex Saunders, "Greyhound Utilizes Dynatech CPX Equipment to Integrate Protocols over Frame Relay," *Telecommunications,* September 1994, p. 68; Peter Fuhrman, "The Little Bus Company That Could," *Forbes,* August 25, 1986, p. 74; and Michael H. Cimini and Susan L. Behrmann, "Dispute Ends at Greyhound," *Monthly Labor Review,* July 1993, p. 56. ●

Video Case

The environment of business

Today more than ever, American businesses are feeling the heat from foreign competition. The combination of high tariffs at home and cheaper labor costs in other countries has made it increasingly difficult for American companies to beat the foreign competition's prices. The competition is fierce, but American businesses can meet the challenges both at home and abroad by emphasizing the quality of American products and services. And the key to developing a successful quality strategy is management. Managers must include quality in every aspect of their business. This requires a huge shift in most managing styles. But it's got to be done. If quality is not made top priority in American businesses, you bet the foreign competition will leave them in the dust.

One company that knows the realities of the global market is Trek. Trek was founded in 1976 by a small group of biking enthusiasts who wanted to combine American manufacturing technology with precision hand craftsmanship to build the highest quality bicycles in the world. At first, everything ran smoothly. But by the mid-80s, Trek began to run into trouble. Joyce Keehn, Sales Manager of International Accounts, said, "In the 80s, we sort of hit a brick wall, so to speak, in that we had high inventory, sales were down, we didn't have as many dealers as we should have had so we were sitting here with a lot of inventory and we were nearly bankrupt. And we had to relook at the situation while we were still running the business from a management standpoint as well as quality and getting our orders in and how we were dealing with the marketplace."

Trek had to develop a new game plan. The company decided to capitalize on its reputation as a leader in technology and quality craftsmanship. Keehn said, "When we look at our quality back in the 80s it wasn't what our U.S. dealers expected our quality to be, so we realized that if we wanted to increase our business domestically we had to increase our quality. And we began doing that for the U.S. market but an interesting thing that we found is that when we began to get into other markets like Germany and Japan their standards were much higher than what we were experiencing here in the states."

Trek's international response was phenomenal and growth was rapid. Today, Trek sells its bicycles in 55 countries with international sales accounting for 40 percent of its business. International competition strengthened Trek in domestic markets as well. As a result, Trek has grown 700 percent since 1988, making it the largest manufacturer of quality bicycles in the United States. In fact, in 1992, when bicycle sales in the United States were down 6 percent, Trek's sales were up 17 percent. The key to Trek's amazing comeback was the increased emphasis on technology and quality in every aspect of the company.

Trek empowered its employees with decision-making authority in several areas. It became a Trek policy that any employee can and should stop the assembly line if he or she detects the slightest problem with the product. Trek also organized employee group management teams. The focus of those teams has been to try to plan processes, work, and products as early as possible into the cycle, and by doing this planning, incorporate ideas into the quality system.

Trek management also opened up internal and external communication. Internally, all Trek employees know the president's door is always open if they have questions and concerns. Externally, an open communication policy with employees, dealers, and customers affects Trek's design and marketing decisions. Dealer advice meetings allow dealers the opportunity to provide feedback, and see the results of previous suggestions. Field quality audits are set up to field questions from Trek's sales representatives.

Trek also realized that producing the highest quality bicycle in the world would require more than a shift in management function. The manufacturing process itself would have to be completely regeared toward quality. At Trek this meant using the most innovative materials and technology available. Brad Wagner, engineer manager, said, "It's manufacturing's job to make sure that the product team's design is buildable. We have 10 of these manufacturing engineers. These guys design the fixtures and the processes. That's how each Trek gets the attention to detail, the flawless welds, and the detailed inspection that result in a great riding bike."

Trek engineers have become pioneers in the field of bicycle technology. They revolutionized the process in which bike frames are built, using stronger and lighter carbon fiber frames. Their most recent development is the carbon composite lug, which is used in the joints of the bicycle frame for increased, lightweight strength. Trek has also borrowed plasma welding techniques used in the aerospace industry to create a higher quality bike.

To discover and correct problems before they occur, Trek conducts extensive testing on every model. Every frame is inspected to ensure quality standards before it is allowed out of the factory. One such test is called the high fatigue test, which was developed using a Japanese industrial standard. In the test, weights are placed on a bike frame to simulate the weight of the rider. The frame is then put through a rigorous set of tests to check its durability.

Trek's emphasis on quality as a competitive strategy for success in the global market has helped it to not only survive but prosper. They are proof positive that quality must be integrated into every management process for American businesses to survive in a global market.

Critical Thinking Questions

1. Why was Trek unable to compete with foreign bicycle manufacturing based on price?

2. Trek employees can stop the assembly line if they spot a defect. What are the advantages and disadvantages of this policy?

3. What is the importance of Trek's "dealer advice meetings"?

Experiential Exercises

2.1 Demography and the future

Background information and objectives

What happened to Gerber Products? Why did it add new products beyond its baby food line? American Hospital Supply Company has grown at a phenomenal rate lately. Why? Part of the answer to these questions is that the baby boom became a baby bust. After a steady decline in the U.S. birthrate from the 1800s to 1940, a 20-year period of increased birthrate occurred in which the population grew from about two to four children per woman. This was followed by a decline in the 1960s and 1970s. The birthrate (among other variables) has an impact on total population size and affects age range proportions, which, in turn, affect basic demand patterns for certain goods and services.

Another significant feature of birthrate data is the number of families without children. Due to overall lifestyle, a two-paycheck family with no children results in different housing patterns, disposable income, and unique consumption patterns. A nation where the average family has two children will have a higher per capita income than a nation where the average family has three children. Disposable income would increase and be used for travel, entertainment, or a house at the beach. Although people would not eat more, they might eat more convenience foods or gourmet foods, or go to restaurants more often.

The workforce, meanwhile, also begins to take on a different composition. The post–World War II baby boom means more people competing for middle management positions in the 1980s. With fewer full-time students, thousands of teachers are also competing for jobs. A smaller group of young people, those growing up after the baby-boom generation, may see a perpetual barrier to success and prosperity. However, the scarcity of young people may place them in demand for jobs requiring youthful energy and fresh training. Demand for specialists may also change. For example, while there may be an oversupply of physicians, there may be less need for obstetricians and more need for specialists in geriatric care.

What some have come to call the "graying of America" could have significant impact on demand patterns for products and services, as well as both threats and opportunities for various segments of the economy in the future. Birthrate data and the population's age composition can give significant clues to the patterns that could emerge in the future, patterns that would affect businesses and their managers in predictable ways. This exercise seeks to stimulate your thinking about these patterns and their implications for you.

Instructions

1. Gather basic data on the population. Your library should have census data collected by the government. *The Statistical Abstract of the United States* provides convenient reference data.

2. Draw a series of bar charts showing trends for each decade from 1900 through 1990 (every 10 years) for the following:
   - *a.* Total population.
   - *b.* Number of men and women.
   - *c.* Children born per woman (births, rates, fertility).
   - *d.* Percent of population by the following age categories: 1–13; 14–21; 22–35; 36–65; over 65.

3. For each of the categories of economic activity in the Demography and the Future Worksheet, indicate what your data suggest. (Check whether the segment will be hurt or helped, and provide a brief explanation indicating which of your charts leads you to your conclusions.)

4. Comment on how these data are likely to affect you as a manager.

5. Bring your findings to class to discuss and compare.

Demography and the future worksheet

Economic segment	Helped	Hurt	Why? What chart supports it?
Advertising			
Autos			
Broadcasting			
Clothing			

Economic segment	Helped	Hurt	Why? What chart supports it?
Health care			
Housing			
Jewelry and watches			
Life insurance			
Liquor			
Movie theaters			
Restaurants			
Sports and recreation			
Tobacco			
Travel			

Source: Excerpted from Lawrence R. Jauch, Arthur G. Bedeian, Sally A. Coltrin, and William F. Glueck, *The Managerial Experience: Cases, Exercises, and Readings,* 4th ed.

2.2 Environmental factors

Objective

To establish an Environmental Threat and Opportunity Profile (ETOP) for a company by utilizing environmental scanning.

Instructions

1. Select a company in the industry of your choice.
2. Under each of the environmental categories in the Environmental Threat and Opportunity Worksheet, list each relevant factor and include a brief description of how it will impact the company.
3. Calculate the environmental threat and opportunity by doing the following:

a. Indicate the *impact* of each factor (from a +5 "strongly positive" to 0 "neutral" to –5 "strongly negative").

b. Rank the *importance* of each factor (from 0 "unimportant" to 10 "very important").

c. Multiply the impact by the importance and place the score in the third column.

d. Next to that score, indicate whether it is a potential opportunity or threat by placing either a + or – sign in front of the score.

e. Total the scores to establish the Environmental Threat and Opportunity Profile.

Environmental threat and opportunity worksheet

Economic factors
(e.g., inflationary trends, consumption, employment, investment, monetary and fiscal policies)

Political factors
(e.g., political power, different ideologies, interest groups, social stability, legislation, and regulation)

Social factors
(e.g., age distribution, geographic distribution, income distribution, mobility, education, family values, work and business attitudes)

Technological factors
(e.g., rate of technological change, future raw material availability, raw material cost, technological developments in related areas)

Competitive factors
(e.g., entry and exit of major competitors, major strategic changes by competitors)

Environmental threat and opportunity profile (ETOP)

Factors	Impact of factor*	Importance of factor‡	Potential opportunity (+) or threat (–)
Economic			
Political			
Social			
Technological			
Competitive			

*Impact: from +5 (strongly positive) to 0 (neutral) to –5 (strongly negative).
‡Importance of factor ranked from 0 (unimportant) to 10 (very important).

Source: Alan J. Rowe, Richard O. Mason, and Karl E. Dickel, *Strategic Management: A Methodical Approach,* 2nd ed., pp. 101–104. Reprinted by permission of Addison-Wesley Publishing Company, Inc.

Chapter Three
Managerial Decision Making

The business executive is by profession a decision maker. Uncertainty is his opponent. Overcoming it is his mission.

–John McDonald

Chapter Outline

Learning Objectives

After studying Chapter 3, you will know:

1. The kinds of decisions you will face as a manager.
2. How to make "rational" decisions.
3. The pitfalls you should avoid when making decisions.
4. The pros and cons of using a group to make decisions.
5. The procedures to use in leading a decision-making group.
6. How to encourage creative decisions.
7. The processes by which decisions are made in organizations.
8. How to make decisions in a crisis.

Setting the Stage

Using Consultants for Decision Making

Business consultants have received a lot of bad press of late. Andersen Consulting, formed in 1989 by partners of the Big Six accounting firm Arthur Andersen, was wracked by conflict as the consulting arm grew and became more powerful, and battled with the accounting arm. Clients have seen the rifts, and complained, and it became front-page *Wall Street Journal* news.

Another front-pager: The former chairman of Club Med filed a $70 million lawsuit against consulting firm Bain & Co. Serge Trigano alleges that he was fired after the consulting firm used proprietary information, compiled a secret report, and distributed it. Mr. Trigano, meanwhile, received only Bain's official consulting report, which was not nearly as critical. Trigano charges that Bain distributed the secret report and distorted the presentation to undermine him and get him fired. Moreover, the second report used information that Bain was paid, by management, to collect—and then that report went only to selected shareholders and not Mr. Trigano. Bain denied the charges vehemently.

A much-publicized book about consultants appeared in 1997. The title, *Dangerous Company,* suggests that consulting firms often do more harm than good. Figgie International almost went bankrupt after relying heavily on consultants; the board then ousted the top executives (Harry Figgie and his son) and filed lawsuits against the consultants. Of course, there are success stories as well, such as the oustanding job done by A. T. Kearney consultants working with CEO Arthur Martinez on the Sears turnaround. And, of course, most consulting jobs turn out to be somewhere in between.

Serge Trigano, former chairman of Club Med, filed a $70 million lawsuit against Bain & Co. for a secret report that got him fired. *[Daniel Giry/Sygma]*

An editorial writer (a consultant) points out, "Even the most progressive companies . . . waste money on consultants instead of using the experts already on the payroll." Why does this happen? Why are the consultants becoming so big, and so powerful, with such mixed results for their clients? Some argue that too many managers are abdicating their responsibilities, hiring consultants to tell them what to do and make decisions for them. And too many managers, critics say, lack pragmatic judgment: they uncritically accept faddish, off-the-shelf solutions, rather than pick and choose the best ideas, rigorously, in the context of their particular companies.

Source: T. Kamm and A.C. Copeta, " Ex-Club Med Chief Files $70 Million Suit against Bain & Co.," The Wall Street Journal, *September 4, 1997, pp. 1, 2; J. White and E. MacDonald, "At Arthur Andersen, Accountants Face Unlikely Adversary,"* The Wall Street Journal, *April 24, 1997, pp. 1, 4; C. Cantoni, "The Consulting Mystique,"* The Wall Street Journal, *March 11, 1997, p. 8; N. Nohria and J. Berkley, "Whatever Happened to the Take-Charge Manager?"* Harvard Business Review, *January–February, 1994, pp. 130–37; R. Lieber, Review of* Dangerous Company *by J. O'Shae and C. Madigan,* Fortune.

Some might disagree with the harsh conclusions in "Setting the Stage." It is inarguable, though, that consulting firms do huge business and have become incredibly powerful as they influence important management decisions in companies all over the world. Managers hire them because they face consequential decisions all the time, in which risks are high, doubts persist, and often there seem to be no "correct" answers. Any help in solving problems and making decisions is welcomed.

On the other hand, the best managers make decisions constantly, and make them well. At CNN, the president makes critical decisions every minute or two, all day long, while standing eye-to-eye with reporters, editors, and others. Executive producers may make a hundred decisions during a live one-hour show. And these instantaneous decisions have lasting impact. It is no task for the indecisive or squeamish. As CNN's vice chairman says, "Nobody is going to tell you what to do. It's up to you to figure out what to do, then do it. Always take the proactive path. Ask for advice, sure, but don't sit on your hands waiting for an order."[1]

Decisions. If you can't make them, you won't be an effective manager. This chapter discusses the kinds of decisions managers face, how they are made, and how they *should* be made.

Characteristics of managerial decisions

Managers face problems constantly. Some problems that require a decision are relatively simple; others seem overwhelming. Some demand immediate action, while others take months or even years to unfold.

Actually, managers often ignore problems. For several reasons, they avoid taking action.[2] First, managers can't be sure how much time, energy, or trouble lies ahead once they start working on a problem. Second, getting involved is risky; tackling a problem but failing to solve it successfully can hurt the manager's track record. Third, because problems can be so perplexing, it is easier to procrastinate or to get busy with less demanding activities.

It is important to understand why decision making can be so challenging. Figure 3.1 illustrates several characteristics of managerial decisions that contribute to their difficulty and pressure. Most managerial decisions lack structure and entail risk, uncertainty, and conflict.

figure 3.1
Characteristics of managerial decisions

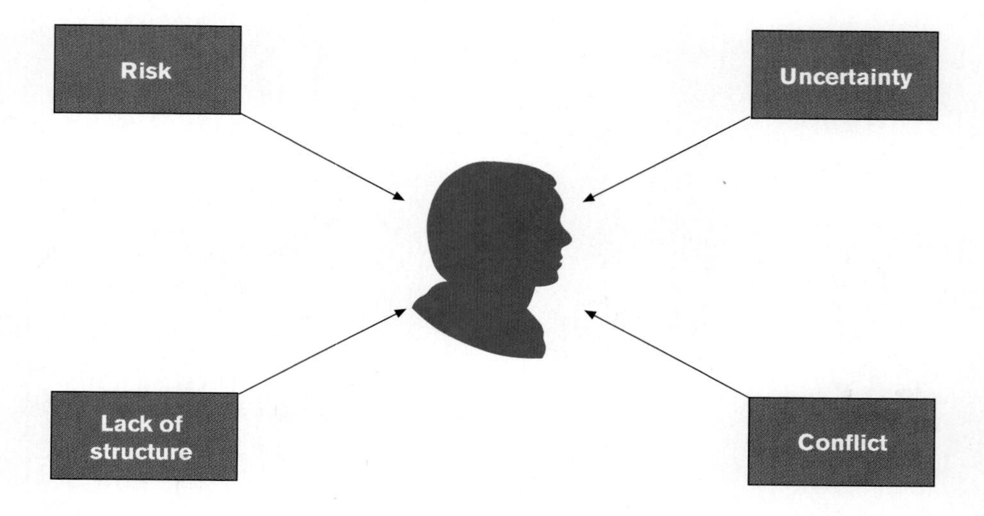

Lack of structure

Lack of structure is the usual state of affairs in managerial decision making.[3] Although some decisions are routine and clear-cut, for most there is no automatic procedure to follow. Problems are novel and unstructured, leaving the decision maker uncertain about how to proceed.

A well-known distinction illustrating this point is between programmed and nonprogrammed decisions. **Programmed decisions** have been encountered and made before. They have objectively correct answers and can be solved by using simple rules, policies, or numerical computations. If you face a programmed decision, there exists a clear procedure or structure for arriving at the right decision. For example, if you are a small-business owner and must decide the amounts for your employees' paychecks, you can use a calculator—and if the amounts are wrong, your employees will prove it to you. Table 3.1 gives some other examples.

programmed decisions Decisions encountered and made before, having objectively correct answers, and solvable by using simple rules, policies, or numerical computations.

If most important decisions were programmed, managerial life would be much easier. But managers typically face **nonprogrammed decisions**: new, novel, complex decisions having no certain outcomes. There are a variety of possible solutions, all of which have merits and drawbacks. The decision maker must create or impose a method for making the decision; there is no predetermined structure on which to rely. As Table 3.1 suggests, important, difficult decisions tend to be nonprogrammed, and they demand creative approaches.

nonprogrammed decisions New, novel, complex decisions having no proven answers.

Uncertainty and risk

If you have all the information you need, and can predict precisely the consequences of your actions, you are operating under a condition of **certainty.**[4] Managers are expressing their preference for certainty when they are not satisfied hearing about what *may have*

certainty The state that exists when decision makers have accurate and comprehensive information.

table 3.1
Types of decisions

	Programmed decisions	Nonprogrammed decisions
Type of problem	Frequent, repetitive, routine, much certainty regarding cause-and-effect relationships.	Novel, unstructured, much uncertainty regarding cause-and-effect relationships.
Procedure	Dependence on policies, rules, and definite procedures.	Necessity for creativity, intuition, tolerance for ambiguity, creative problem solving.
Examples	Business firm: Periodic reorders of inventory.	Business firm: Diversification into new products and markets.
	University: Necessary grade-point average for good academic standing.	University: Construction of new classroom facilities.
	Health care: Procedure for admitting patients.	Health care: Purchase of experimental equipment.
	Government: Merit system for promotion of state employees.	Government: Reorganization of state government agencies.

Source: J. Gibson, J. Ivancevich, and J. Donnelly, Jr., *Organizations,* 5th ed. (Plano, Tex.: BPI, 1985).

happened or *might* happen and insist on hearing what *did* or *will* happen.[5] But perfect certainty is rare. For important, nonprogrammed managerial decisions, uncertainty is the rule.

uncertainty The state that exists when decision makers have insufficient information.

Uncertainty means the manager has insufficient information to know the consequences of different actions. Decision makers may have strong opinions—they may feel sure of themselves—but they are still operating under conditions of uncertainty if they lack pertinent information and cannot estimate the likelihood of different results of their actions.

When you can estimate the likelihood of various consequences, but still do not know with certainty what will happen, you are facing **risk.** Risk exists when the probability of an action being successful is less than 100 percent. If the decision is the wrong one, you may lose money, time, reputation, or other important assets.

risk The state that exists when the probability of success is less than 100 percent.

Risk, like uncertainty, is a fact of life in managerial decision making. But this is not the same as *taking* a risk. Whereas it sometimes seems as though risk takers are admired, and that entrepreneurs and investors thrive on taking risks, the reality is that good decision makers prefer to *avoid* or *manage* risk. This means that, while they accept the fact that consequential decisions entail risk, they do everything they can to anticipate the risk, minimize it, and control it.

Conflict

Important decisions are even more difficult because of the conflict managers face. **Conflict,** which exists when the manager must consider opposing pressures from different sources, exists at two levels.

conflict Opposing pressures from different sources. Two levels of conflict are psychological conflict and conflict that arises among individuals or groups.

First, individual decision makers experience psychological conflict when several options are attractive, or when none of the options is attractive. For instance, a manager may have to decide whom to lay off, when she doesn't want to lay off anyone. Or she may have three promising job applicants for one position—but choosing one means she has to reject the other two.

Second, conflict arises between individuals or groups. The chief financial officer argues in favor of increasing long-term debt to finance an acquisition. The chief executive officer, however, prefers to minimize such debt and find the funds elsewhere. The marketing department wants more product lines to sell to its customers, and engineers want higher-quality products. But production people want to lower costs by having longer production runs of fewer products with no changes. Management wants to enforce some rigid work rules, while labor seeks looser rule enforcement. As you can see, few decisions are unanimous or uncompromised.

The stages of decision making

Faced with these challenges, how are good decisions made? The ideal decision-making process moves through six stages. At Xerox, which has institutionalized this process, the stages are intended to answer the following questions:[6] What do we want to change? What's preventing us from reaching the "desired state"? How *could* we make the change? What's the *best* way to do it? Are we following the plan? and How well did it work out?

More formally, as Figure 3.2 illustrates, decision makers should (1) identify and diagnose the problem, (2) generate alternative solutions, (3) evaluate alternatives, (4) make the choice, (5) implement the decision, and (6) evaluate the decision.

Identifying and diagnosing the problem

The first stage in the decision-making process is to recognize that a problem exists and must be solved. Typically, a manager realizes some discrepancy between the current state (the way things are) and a desired state (the way things ought to be). Such discrepancies—say, in organizational or departmental performance—may be detected by comparing current

figure 3.2
The stages of decision making

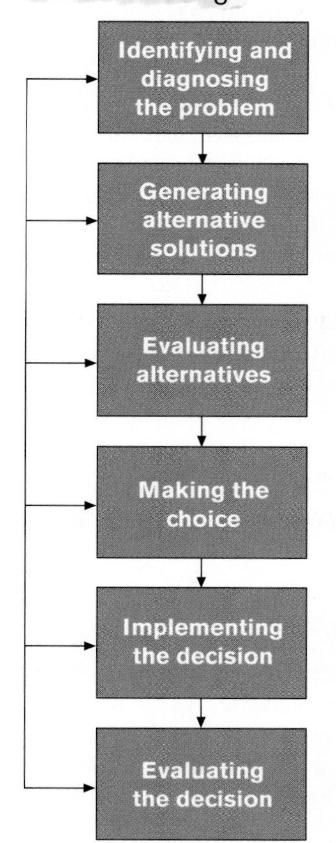

performance against (1) *past* performance, (2) the *current* performance of other organizations or departments, or (3) *future* expected performance as determined by plans and forecasts.[7]

Recognizing that a problem exists is only the beginning of this stage. The decision maker also must want to do something about it and must believe that the resources and abilities necessary for solving the problem exist.[8] Then the decision maker must dig in deeper and attempt to *diagnose* the true cause of the problem symptoms that surfaced.

For example, a sales manager knows that sales have dropped drastically. If he is leaving the company soon or believes the decreased sales volume is due to the economy (which he can't do anything about), he won't take further action. But if he does try to solve the problem, he should not automatically reprimand his sales staff, add new people, or increase the advertising budget. He must analyze *why* sales are down and then develop a solution appropriate to his analysis. Asking why, of yourself and others, is essential to understanding the real problem.

Useful questions to ask and answer in this stage include[9]

- Is there a difference between what is actually happening and what should be happening?
- How can you describe the deviation, as specifically as possible?
- What is/are the cause(s) of the deviation?
- What specific goals should be met?
- Which of these goals are absolutely critical to the success of the decision?

Generating alternative solutions

In the second stage, problem diagnosis is linked to the development of alternative courses of action aimed at solving the problem. Managers generate at least some alternative solutions based on past experiences.[10]

Solutions range from ready made to custom made.[11] Decision makers who search for **ready-made solutions** use ideas they have seen or tried before or follow the advice of others who have faced similar problems. **Custom-made solutions,** on the other hand, must be designed for specific problems. This technique requires combining ideas into new, creative solutions. For example, the Sony Walkman was created by combining two existing products: earphones and a tape player.[12] Potentially, custom-made solutions can be devised for any challenge.

Choosing a ready-made alternative is much easier than designing a custom-made solution. Therefore, most decision makers use the ready-made approach, sometimes even when the ready-made alternative is inappropriate. If this approach fails to deliver acceptable solutions or results, the harder work of devising a unique solution must begin. For important, irreversible decisions, custom-made alternatives should be developed because they are more likely to lead to higher-quality solutions.[13]

ready-made solutions
Ideas that have been seen or tried before, or follow the advice of others who have faced similar problems.

custom-made solutions
The combination of ideas into new, creative solutions.

Useful questions at this stage include[14]

- Is there a particular alternative to be evaluated?
- Are there others we should consider?
- Who can help us by providing ideas?
- How can we generate additional alternatives creatively?

We will discuss later in the chapter how to generate creative ideas.

Evaluating alternatives

The third stage involves determining the value or adequacy of the alternatives that were generated. Which solution will be the best?

Too often, alternatives are evaluated with little thought or logic. After Walter P. Chrysler died, Chrysler's lawyer sometimes contacted the ghost of Walter P. for advice. The lawyer would excuse himself from the meeting, go into Chrysler's office, close the door and drapes, turn off the lights, and conjure up Chrysler's spirit. Then the lawyer would return to the meeting and reveal his findings, which the Chrysler executives would use to make the final decision.[15]

Alternatives obviously should be evaluated more carefully than this. Fundamental to this process is to predict the consequences that will occur if the various options are put into effect.

Managers should consider several types of consequences. Obviously, they must attempt to predict the effects on financial or other performance measures. But there are other, less clear-cut consequences to address.[16] Decisions set a precedent; will this precedent be a help or a hindrance in the future? Also, the success or failure of the decision will go into the track records of those involved in making it.

Refer again to your original goals, defined in the first stage. Which goals does each alternative meet, and fail to meet? Which alternatives are most acceptable to you and to other important stakeholders? If several alternatives may solve the problem, which can be implemented at the lowest cost? If no alternative achieves all your goals, perhaps you can combine two or more of the best ones.

Key questions here are[17]

- Is our information about alternatives complete and current? If not, can we get more and better information?
- Does the alternative meet our primary objectives?
- What problems could we have if we implement the alternative?

contingency plans Alternative courses of action that can be implemented based on how the future unfolds.

Of course, results cannot be forecast with perfect accuracy. But sometimes decision makers can build in safeguards against an uncertain future by considering the potential consequences of several different scenarios. Then they generate **contingency plans**—alternative courses of action that can be implemented based on how the future unfolds.

For example, scenario planners making decisions about the future might consider four alternative views of the future state of the U.S. economy:[18] 1) An economic boom with 5 to 6 percent annual growth and the United States much stronger than its global competitors; 2) a moderately strong economy with 2 to 3 percent growth and the United States pulling out of a recession; 3) a pessimistic outlook with no growth, rising unemployment, and recession; or 4) a worse scenario with global depression, massive unemployment, and widespread social unrest.

Some scenarios will seem more likely than others, and some may seem highly improbable, Ultimately, one of the scenarios will prove to be more accurate than the others. The process of considering multiple scenarios raises important "what if?" questions for decision makers and highlights the need for preparedness and contingency plans.

As you read this, what economic scenario is unfolding? What are the important current events and trends? What scenarios could evolve six or eight years from now? How will *you* prepare?

From the Pages of BusinessWeek

New-Style Decision Making at AT&T

Michael Armstrong is the new CEO of AT&T. He is the first outsider to head the company in eight decades. He must push AT&T–long considered a telecom dinosaur–into the Digital Age.

Armstrong's strategy involves both fine-tuning some businesses and also taking bold measures. The centerpiece of AT&T's post-deregulation strategy was its entry into the crucial, $80 billion local phone market. When Armstrong came on board, the company had spent $3 billion trying to crack the market. Revenues were at $65 million. Most observers expected him to spend heavily.

Instead, he put a halt to the effort, pulling the plug on the former strategic centerpiece. This was three weeks into his tenure. "We're not a nonprofit organization" he said. He signaled clearly that old-style thinking would not cut it anymore.

Armstrong is working hard to break up AT&T's bureaucracy and place more emphasis in execution. "I'm demanding. If we're going to think through something, then get on with it. Don't study it to death. We'll never know everything we need to know. But we do know that if we don't make a decision in a timely way, we're in trouble."

Ready, fire, aim

On his second day on the job, when an executive made a request to experiment with a new idea, Armstrong merely said, with excitement, "Go do it." Two months into his tenure, he decided to sell off AT&T's underperforming paging unit. At the same time, the company acquired Teleport Communications Group–talks had been going on for years. John Zeglis, AT&T's president, says "Everything we do takes about a third of the time it used to take."

Armstrong discovered that three different committees were involved in similar top-level strategic decisions. But it was not clear who had final say. So he pared them down to just one group, that meets every Monday to discuss top strategic priorities.

In decision-making style, Armstrong's predecessor was described as a courtroom judge. Armstrong is called a coach. He asks questions, suggests alternatives, and tries to reach consensus. States an executive vice president, "The process is designed to allow the team to rally behind an idea."

It was rumored that Armstrong's contract was for three years. In fact, he has a six-year contract. He asks, "Can you imagine trying to turn AT&T around in three years?" After three months, he was off to a good start. How are he, and AT&T, doing now?

Discussion Questions

1. Discuss Michael Armstrong's approach to decision making using concepts in the chapter.
2. How is Michael Armstrong, and AT&T, doing now?

Source: P. Elstrom, with K. Kerwin, "New boss new plan," *Business Week,* February 2, 1998, 42–48.

Making the choice

maximize A decision realizing the best possible outcome.

satisfice To choose an option that is acceptable although not necessarily the best or perfect.

Once you have considered the possible consequences of your options, it is time to make your decision. Important concepts here are maximizing, satisficing, and optimizing.[19]

To **maximize** is to make the best possible decision. The maximizing decision realizes the greatest positive consequences and the fewest negative consequences. In other words, maximizing results in the greatest benefit at the lowest cost, with the largest expected total return. Maximizing requires searching thoroughly for a complete range of alternatives, carefully assessing each alternative, comparing one to another, and then choosing or creating the very best.

To **satisfice** is to choose the first option that is minimally acceptable or adequate; the choice appears to meet a targeted goal or criterion. When you satisfice, you compare your choice against your goal, not against other options. Satisficing means a search for alternatives stops at the first one that is okay. Commonly, people do not expend the time or energy to gather complete information. Instead, they make the expedient decision based on readily available information. Satisficing is sometimes a result of laziness; other times, there is no other option because time is short, information is unavailable, or other constraints make it impossible to maximize.

Let's say you are purchasing new equipment and your goal is to avoid spending too much money. You would be maximizing if you checked out all your options and their prices, and then bought the cheapest one that met your performance requirements. But you would be satisficing if you bought the first one you found that was within your budget and failed to look for less expensive options.

optimizing Achieving the best possible balance among several goals.

Optimizing means that you achieve the best possible balance among several goals. Perhaps, in purchasing equipment, you are interested in quality and durability as well as price. So, instead of buying the cheapest piece of equipment that works, you buy the one with the best combination of attributes, even though there may be options that are better on the price criterion and others that are better on the quality and durability criteria.

The same idea applies to achieving business goals: one marketing strategy could maximize sales, while a different strategy might maximize profit. An optimizing strategy is the one that achieves the best balance among multiple goals.

Implementing the decision

The decision-making process does not end once a choice is made. The chosen alternative must be implemented. Sometimes the people involved in making the choice must put it into effect. At other times, they delegate the responsibility for implementation to others, such as when a top management team changes a policy or operating procedures and has operational managers carry out the change.

Those who implement the decision must *understand* the choice and why it was made. They also must be *committed* to its successful implementation. These needs can be met by involving those people in the early stages of the decision process. At Steelcase, the world's largest manufacturer of office furniture, new product ideas are put through simultaneous design, engineering, and marketing scrutiny.[20] This is in contrast to an approach whereby designers design and the concept is later relayed to other departments for implementation. In the latter case, understanding and commitment of all departments are less likely to result.

Managers should plan implementation carefully. Adequate planning requires several steps:[21]

1. Determine how things will look when the decision is fully operational.
2. Chronologically order, perhaps with a flow diagram, the steps necessary to achieve a fully operational decision.
3. List the resources and activities required to implement each step.
4. Estimate the time needed for each step.
5. Assign responsibility for each step to specific individuals.

Decision makers should assume that things will *not* go smoothly during implementation. It is very useful to take a little extra time to *identify potential problems* and *identify potential opportunities*. Then, you can take actions to prevent problems and also be ready to seize on unexpected opportunities. Useful questions are

- What problems could this action cause?
- What can we do to prevent the problems?
- What unintended benefits or opportunities could arise?

- How can we make sure they happen?
- How can we be ready to act when the opportunities come?

The following example illustrates what happens when potential problems are not explicitly considered.

Worse off than before

Everybody had agreed on the proposed plan. The mayor had the support of both the citizens and the city council. Because the volume of traffic downtown and the resultant noise and air pollution had become intolerable, the speed limit was lowered to 20 miles per hour and concrete speed bumps were installed to prevent cars from exceeding it.

But the results were hardly what the planners anticipated. The lower speeds forced cars to travel in second rather than third gear, so they were noisier and produced more exhaust. Shopping trips that used to take only 20 minutes now took 30, so the number of cars in the downtown area at any given time increased markedly. A disaster? No–shopping downtown became so nerve-racking that fewer and fewer people went there. So the desired result was achieved after all? Not really, for even though the volume of traffic gradually went back to its original level, the noise and air pollution remained significant. To make matters worse, during the period of increased traffic, word had gotten around that once-a-week shopping expeditions to a nearby mall on the outskirts of a neighboring town were practical and saved time. More and more people started shopping that way. To the distress of the mayor, downtown businesses that had been flourishing now teetered on the verge of bankruptcy. Tax revenues sank drastically. The master plan turned out to be a major blunder, the consequences of which will burden this community for a long time to come.

Source: From D. Dorner, "Unforeseen Consequences," *Across the Board,* November–December, 1996, pp 25–28. Reprinted with permission of The Conference Board. ●

Always expect the unexpected. It is better not to learn about unexpected issues in the implementation stage but to do a thorough job thinking through the earlier stages in the decision-making process.

Many of the chapters in this book are concerned with implementation issues: how to implement strategy, allocate resources, organize for results, lead and motivate people, manage change, and so on. View the chapters from that perspective, and learn as much as you can about how to implement properly.

Evaluating the decision

The final stage in the decision-making process is evaluating the decision. This means collecting information on how well the decision is working. Quantifiable goals—a 20 percent increase in sales, a 95 percent reduction in accidents, 100 percent on-time deliveries—can be set before the solution to the problem is implemented. Then objective data can be gathered to accurately determine the success (or failure) of the decision.

Decision evaluation is useful whether the feedback is positive or negative. Feedback that suggests the decision is working implies that the decision should be continued and perhaps applied elsewhere in the organization. Negative feedback, indicating failure, means that either (1) implementation will require more time, resources, effort, or thought; or (2) the decision was a bad one.

If the decision appears inappropriate, it's back to the drawing board. Then the process cycles back to the first stage: (re)definition of the problem. The decision-making process begins anew, preferably with more information, new suggestions, and an approach that attempts to eliminate the mistakes made the first time around.

The best decision

How can managers tell whether they have made the best decision? One approach is to wait until the results are in. But what if the decision has been made but not yet implemented? While nothing can guarantee a "best" decision, managers should at least be confident that they followed proper *procedures* that will yield the best possible decision under the circumstances. This means that the decision makers were appropriately vigilant in making the decision. **Vigilance** occurs when the decision makers carefully and conscientiously execute all six stages of decision making, including making provisions for implementation and evaluation.[22]

vigilance A process in which a decision maker carefully executes all stages of decision making.

Even if managers reflect on these decision-making activities and conclude that they were executed conscientiously, they still will not know whether the decision will work; after all, nothing guarantees a good outcome. But they *will* know that they did their best to make the best possible decision.

Most of the causes of business failures described below are a result of inadequate vigilance. Consider them decision traps; if you find yourself thinking in the following ways, you may be making poor decisions.

Why businesses fail

Why do firms fail? According to *Inc.* magazine, the most common reason has nothing to do with products, market knowledge, or effort. What kills companies is poor decisions at the top. Once entrepreneurs decide to start a business, they put their hearts into it but fail to use their heads.

- *Is this a great product, or what?* If you love it, or it's clever, that doesn't mean it meets a market need.
- *What a business!* It's easy–and cheap–to start right away. This may be true, but if it's true for you, it is for competitors as well. You'd better find a way to be better than the others.
- *My forecasts are conservative.* You may think you can make your plan work because you have made cautious predictions. But you'd better have contingency plans in case your forecasts prove wrong. A rule of thumb is that start-ups take twice as long or need three times as much money as their founders predict. Sales projections are almost never met.
- *With this much money to work with, we can't miss.* It's tough to have to pinch pennies. But too much money may make for risky or poorly thought-out decisions, and you will lose control of costs.
- *Fortunately, our biggest customer is General Motors (or Xerox, or IBM).* Traditionally, many managers would have loved to be in such a position. Today, they'd better be ready in case they lose their biggest customer–it happens all the time.

- *My people aren't afraid of me. They tell me what they think all day long.* They may be telling you what they think you want to hear. You need honest, valid information, and trusted advisors. These things don't fall into your lap automatically; you have to work to get them.
- *Actually, our important numbers have never looked better.* Don't ignore signs of trouble; don't assume problems are temporary. Look constantly for trouble signs, and act on them immediately.

Source: B. G. Posner, "Why Companies Fail," *Inc.*, June 1993, pp. 102–6.

Barriers to effective decision making

Vigilance and full execution of the six-stage decision-making process are the exception rather than the rule in managerial decision making. But research shows that when managers use such rational processes, better decisions result.[23] Managers who make sure they engage in these processes are more effective.

Why don't people automatically invoke such rational processes? It is easy to neglect or improperly execute these processes. The problem may be improperly defined, or goals misidentified. Not enough solutions may be generated, or they may be evaluated incompletely. A satisficing rather than maximizing choice may be made. Implementation may be poorly planned or executed, or monitoring may be inadequate or nonexistent. And decisions are influenced by subjective psychological biases, time pressures, and social realities.

Psychological biases

Decision makers are far from objective in the way they gather, evaluate, and apply information toward making their choices. People have biases that interfere with objective rationality. The examples that follow represent only a few of the many documented subjective biases.[24]

illusion of control People's belief that they can influence events, even when they have no control over what will happen.

The **illusion of control** is a belief that one can influence events even when one has no control over what will happen. Gambling is one example: Some people believe they have the skill to beat the odds even though most people, most of the time, cannot. In business, such overconfidence can lead to failure because decision makers ignore risks and fail to objectively evaluate the odds of success. Relatedly, they may have an unrealistically positive

Professional gambling establishments count on people's willingness to try to beat the odds. This illusion of control is a major contributor to the high profits earned by most casinos.
[Jose Fuste Raga/The Stock Market]

view of themselves or their companies, believe they can do no wrong, or hold a general optimism about the future that can lead them to believe they are immune from risk and failure.[25]

framing effects A psychological bias influenced by the way in which a problem or decision alternative is phrased or presented.

discount the future Weight short-term costs and benefits more heavily than longer-term costs and benefits.

Framing effects refer to how problems or decision alternatives are phrased or perceived, and how these subjective influences can override objective facts. In one example, managers indicated a desire to invest more money in a course of action that was reported to have a 70 percent chance of profit than in one said to have a 30 percent chance of loss.[26] The choices were equivalent in their chances of success; it was the way the options were framed that determined the managers' choices. Thus, framing can exert an undue, irrational influence on people's decisions.

Often decision makers **discount the future.** That is, in their evaluation of alternatives, they weigh short-term costs and benefits more heavily than longer-term costs and benefits. Consider your own decision about whether or not to go for a dental checkup. The choice to go poses short-term financial costs, anxiety, and perhaps physical pain. The choice not to go will inflict even greater costs and more severe pain if dental problems worsen. How do you choose? Many people decide to avoid the short-term costs by not going for regular checkups but end up facing much greater pain in the long run.

The same bias applies to students who don't study, weight watchers who sneak dessert or skip an exercise routine, and working people who take the afternoon off to play golf when they really need to work. It can also affect managers who hesitate to invest funds in research and development programs that may not pay off until the future. In all these cases, the avoidance of short-term costs or the seeking of short-term rewards results in negative long-term consequences.

The Japanese have been lauded for their attention to long-run considerations. When U.S. companies sacrifice present value to invest for the future—such as when Weyerhaeuser incurs enormous costs for its reforestation efforts that won't lead to harvest until 60 years in the future—it seems the exception rather than the rule. Discounting the future is said to explain partly governmental budget deficits, environmental destruction, and the decaying urban infrastructure.[27]

Personality and decision making

Individuals differ in their approaches to decision making. One well-known measure that assesses how people differ from one another, the Myers-Briggs Type Indicator (MBTI), has implications for how people make decisions both individually and in groups.

The basis for the MBTI is that people have preferences for one way of doing things over another. This is not about skill or ability, but about what people would do and how they would do it given free choice to exercise their true preferences. If you were to complete the MBTI, your results would indicate your preferences with respect to four basic choices:

1. Which do you prefer: extraversion (E)–attending to the external world of action, people, activities, and things–or introversion (I)–attending to the internal world of reflection, thought, ideas, and concepts?
2. Do you prefer sensing (S)–absorbing detailed, factual information through all the senses, through direct experience–or intuiting (N)–seeing the big picture and learning through reading, discussing, and interpreting?
3. Do you prefer thinking (T)–making decisions based on rational, economic logic and objective, quantitative criteria–or feeling (F)–making decisions also in a logical way but invoking personal values and impact on other people?
4. Do you prefer judging (J)–living a structured, well-planned, organized life, and making decisions quickly in order to reach closure–or perceiving (P)–being flexible and

adaptable, going with the flow, and being comfortable with postponing decisions and keeping options open?

Think about your own preferences on these dimensions. What implications do these different types—especially S versus N and T versus F—have for decision making? Which of the types have the most relevance to which stages of the rational model? How might individuals differ in the way they go through the stages? And what are the implications for a group of people making decisions together? For example, what if everyone at the meeting is an E? Or everyone an I? Everyone a T, or everyone an F?

Source: S. K. Hirsh and J. M. Kummerow, *Introduction to Type in Organizations* (Oxford: Oxford Psychologists Press,1994); and D. Leonard and S. Straus, "Putting Your Company's Whole Brain to Work," *Harvard Business Review,* July–August, 1997, pp. 110–21. ●

Time pressures

In today's rapidly changing business environment, the premium is on acting quickly and keeping pace. The most conscientiously-made business decisions can become irrelevant and even disastrous if managers take too long to make them.

How can managers make decisions quickly? Some natural tendencies, at least for North Americans, might be to skimp on analysis (not be too vigilant), suppress conflict, and make decisions on your own without consulting other managers.[28] These strategies might speed up decision making, but they reduce decision *quality*.

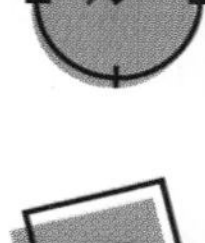

Can managers under time pressure make both timely and high-quality decisions? A recent study of decision-making processes in microcomputer firms—a high-tech, fast-paced industry—showed some important differences between fast-acting and slower-acting firms.[29] The fast-acting firms realized significant competitive advantages—and did not sacrifice the quality of their decisions.

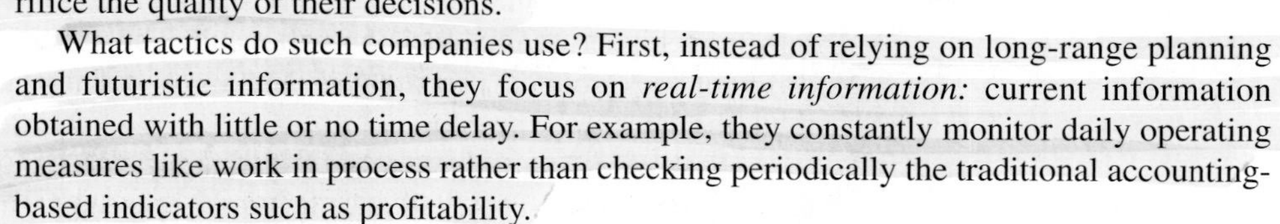

What tactics do such companies use? First, instead of relying on long-range planning and futuristic information, they focus on *real-time information:* current information obtained with little or no time delay. For example, they constantly monitor daily operating measures like work in process rather than checking periodically the traditional accounting-based indicators such as profitability.

Second, they *involve people more effectively and efficiently* in the decision-making process. They rely heavily on trusted experts, which yields both good advice and the confidence to act quickly despite uncertainty. They also take a realistic view of conflict: They value differing opinions, but they know that if disagreements are not resolved, the top executive must make the final choice in the end. Slow-moving firms, in contrast, are stymied by conflict. Like the fast-moving firms they seek consensus, but when disagreements persist they fail to come to a decision.

Social realities

As the description of decision making in the microcomputer industry implies, many decisions are made by a group rather than by an individual manager. In the slow-moving firms, interpersonal factors decrease decision-making effectiveness. Even the manager acting alone is accountable to the boss and to others and must consider the preferences and reactions of many people. Important managerial decisions are marked by conflict among interested parties. Therefore, many decisions are the result of intensive social interactions, bargaining, and politicking.

The remainder of this chapter focuses on the social context of decisions, including decision making in groups and the realities of decision making in organizations.

Decision making in groups

Ongoing work teams solve problems and make decisions continually. Sometimes a manager finds it necessary to convene a group of people for the purpose of making an important decision. Some advise that in today's complex business environment, significant problems should *always* be tackled by teams.[30] Managers therefore must understand how groups and teams operate and how to use them to improve decision making. For this discussion, we will use the term "groups." You will learn much more about how teams work later in the book.

The basic philosophy behind using a group to make decisions is captured by the adage "two heads are better than one." But is this statement really valid? Yes, it is—potentially.

If enough time is available, groups usually make higher-quality decisions than most individuals acting alone. However, groups often are inferior to the best individual.[31] How well the group performs depends on how effectively it capitalizes on the potential advantages and minimizes the potential problems of using a group. Table 3.2 summarizes these issues.

Potential advantages of using a group

If other people have something to contribute, using groups to make a decision offers at least five potential advantages.[32]

1. More *information* is available when several people are making the decision. If one member doesn't have all the facts or the pertinent expertise, another member might.

2. A greater number of *perspectives* on the issues, or different *approaches* to solving the problem, are available. The problem may be new to one group member but familiar to another. Or the group may need to consider other viewpoints—financial, legal, marketing, human resources, and so on—to achieve an optimal solution.

3. Group discussion provides an opportunity for *intellectual stimulation.* It can get people thinking and unleash their creativity to a far greater extent than would be possible with individual decision making.

These three potential advantages of using a group improve the chance that a more fully informed, higher-quality decision will result. Thus, managers should involve people with different backgrounds, perspectives, and access to information, not just their cronies who think the same way they do.

4. People who participate in a group discussion are more likely to *understand* why the decision was made. They will have heard the relevant arguments both for the chosen alternative and against the rejected alternatives.

5. Group discussion typically leads to a higher level of *commitment* to the decision. Buying into the proposed solution translates into high motivation to ensure that it is implemented successfully.

The last two advantages improve the chances that the decision will be executed effectively. Therefore, managers should involve the people who will be responsible for implementing the decision as early in the deliberations as possible.

table 3.2
Pros and cons of using a group to make decisions

Potential advantages	Potential disadvantages
1. Larger pool of information.	1. One person dominates.
2. More perspectives and approaches.	2. Satisficing.
3. Intellectual stimulation.	3. Groupthink.
4. People understand the decision.	4. Goal displacement.
5. People are committed to the decision.	

Potential problems in using a group

Things *can* go wrong when groups make decisions. Most of the potential problems concern the process through which group members interact with one another.[33]

1. Sometimes one group member *dominates* the discussion. When this occurs—such as when a strong leader makes his or her preferences clear—the result is the same as if the dominant individual made the decision alone. Individual dominance has two disadvantages. First, the dominant person does not necessarily have the most valid opinions, and may even have the most unsound ideas. Second, even if that person's preference leads to a good decision, convening as a group will have been a waste of everyone else's time.

2. *Satisficing* is more likely with groups. Most people don't like meetings and will do whatever they can to end them. This may include criticizing members who want to continue exploring new and better alternatives. The result is a satisficing rather than an optimizing or maximizing decision.

3. *Pressure to avoid disagreement* can lead to a phenomenon called *groupthink*. **Groupthink** occurs when people choose not to disagree or raise objections because they don't want to break up a positive team spirit. Some groups want to think as one, tolerate no dissension, and strive to remain cordial. Such groups are overconfident, complacent, and perhaps too willing to take risks. Pressure to go along with the group's preferred solution stifles creativity and the other behaviors characteristic of vigilant decision making.

groupthink A phenomenon that occurs in decision making when group members avoid disagreement as they strive for consensus.

4. *Goal displacement* often occurs in groups. The goal of group members should be to come up with the best possible solution to the problem. But when **goal displacement** occurs, new goals emerge to replace the original ones. It is common for two or more group members to have different opinions and present their conflicting cases. Attempts at rational persuasion become heated disagreement. The new goal becomes winning the argument. Saving face and defeating the other person's idea become more important than solving the problem.

goal displacement A condition that occurs when a decision-making group loses sight of its original goal and a new, possibly less important goal emerges.

Effective managers pay close attention to the group process; they manage it carefully. The following sections and later chapters provide suggestions for the effective management of group meetings.

Managing group decision making

Figure 3.3 illustrates the requirements for effectively managing group decision making: (1) an appropriate leadership style; (2) the constructive use of disagreement and conflict; and (3) the enhancement of creativity.

Leadership style

The leader of a decision-making body must attempt to minimize process-related problems. The leader should avoid dominating the discussion or allowing another individual to dominate. This means encouraging less vocal group members to air their opinions and suggestions and asking for dissenting viewpoints.

At the same time, the leader should not allow the group to pressure people into conforming. The leader should be alert to the dangers of groupthink and satisficing. Also, she or he should be attuned to indications that group members are losing sight of the primary objective: to come up with the best possible solution to the problem.

This implies two things. First, don't lose sight of the problem. Second, make a decision! Keep in mind the slow-moving microcomputer firms that were paralyzed when group members couldn't come to an agreement.

Constructive conflict

Total and consistent agreement among group members can be destructive. It can lead to groupthink, uncreative solutions, and a waste of the knowledge and diverse viewpoints that individuals bring to the group. Thus, a certain amount of *constructive* conflict should exist.

figure 3.3 Managing group decision making

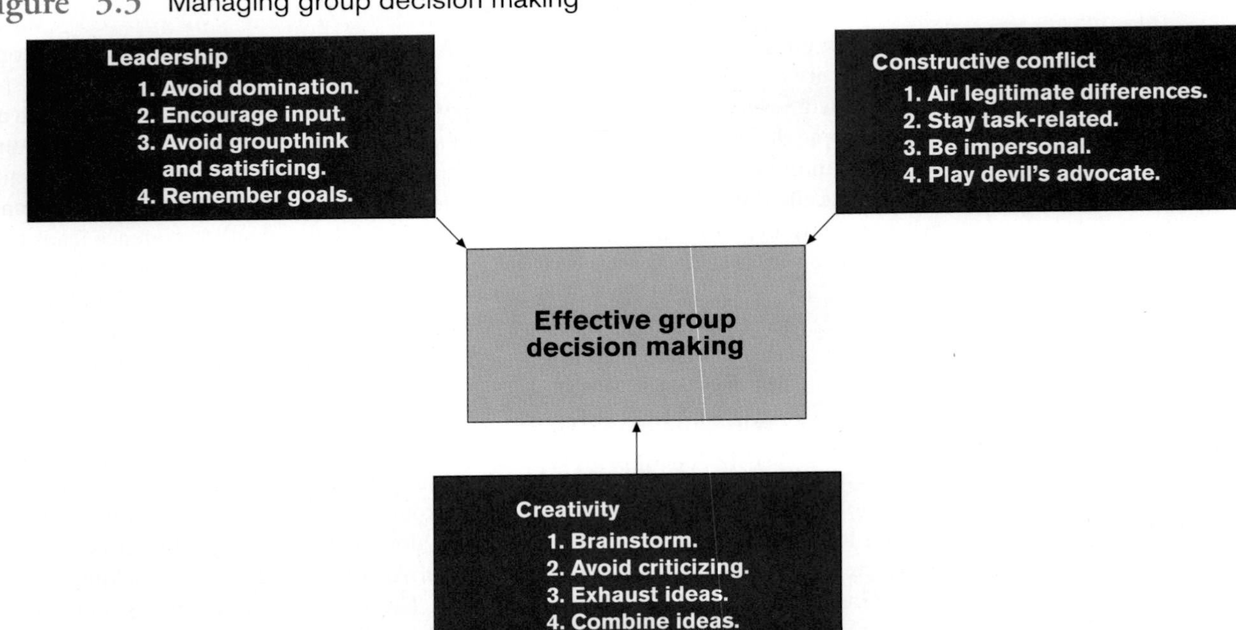
Leadership
1. Avoid domination.
2. Encourage input.
3. Avoid groupthink and satisficing.
4. Remember goals.
Constructive conflict
1. Air legitimate differences.
2. Stay task-related.
3. Be impersonal.
4. Play devil's advocate.
Effective group decision making
Creativity
1. Brainstorm.
2. Avoid criticizing.
3. Exhaust ideas.
4. Combine ideas.

Some companies, including Sun Microsystems, Xerox, Compaq, and United Parcel Service, take steps to ensure that conflict and debate are generated within their management teams.[34]

cognitive conflict Issue-based differences in perspectives or judgments.

affective conflict Emotional disagreement directed toward other people.

The most constructive type of conflict is **cognitive conflict,** or differences in perspectives or judgments about issues. In contrast, **affective conflict** is emotional and directed at other people. Affective conflict is likely to be destructive to the group because it can lead to anger, bitterness, goal displacement, and lower-quality decisions. Cognitive conflict, on the other hand, can air legitimate differences of opinion and develop better ideas and problem solutions. Conflict, then, should be task related rather than personal.[35]

Many management teams have too little conflict; their culture is one in which the boss dominates and crushes dissension, or in which people urge one another to be agreeable or not make waves. Such teams are losing the potential benefits of constructive conflict.

Constructive conflict can arise from public disagreement surfacing in an open, participative environment. Managers can increase the likelihood of constructive conflict by assembling teams of different types of people, by creating frequent interactions and active debates, and by encouraging multiple alternatives to be generated from a variety of perspectives.[36]

Conflict also can be generated formally through structured processes.[37] Two techniques that purposely program cognitive conflict into the decision-making process are devil's advocacy and the dialectic method.

devil's advocate A person who has the job of criticizing ideas to ensure that different viewpoints are fully explored.

A **devil's advocate** has the job of criticizing ideas. The group leader can formally assign people to play this role. Requiring people to present contrary arguments can lessen inhibitions about disagreeing and make the conflict less personal and emotional.

dialectic A structured debate comparing two conflicting courses of action.

An alternative to devil's advocacy is the dialectic. The **dialectic** goes a step beyond devil's advocacy by requiring a structured debate between two conflicting courses of action.[38] The philosophy of the dialectic stems from Plato and Aristotle, who advocated synthesizing the conflicting views of a thesis and an antithesis. Structured debates between plans and counterplans can be useful prior to making a strategic decision. For example, one team might present the case for acquiring a firm while another team advocates not making the acquisition.

It is important to remember that generating constructive conflict does not need to be done on such a formal basis, and is not solely the leader's responsibility. Any team member can introduce cognitive conflict by being honest with opinions; by not being afraid to disagree with others; by pushing the group to action if it is taking too long, or making the group slow down if necessary; and by advocating long-term considerations if the group is too focused on short-term results. Introducing constructive conflict might be seen as a legitimate and necessary responsibility of all group members interested in improving the group's decision-making effectiveness.

Encouraging creativity

As you've already learned, ready-made solutions to a problem can be inadequate or unavailable. In such cases, custom-made solutions are necessary. This means the group must be creative in generating ideas.

Some say we are in the midst of the next great business revolution: the "creative revolution."[39] Said to transcend the agricultural, industrial, and information revolutions, the most fundamental unit of value in the creativity revolution is ideas. Creativity is more than just an option; it is essential to survival. Allowing people to be creative may be one of the manager's most important and challenging responsibilities.

You might be saying to yourself, "I'm not creative." But even if you are not an artist or a musician, you do have potential to be creative in countless other ways. You are being creative if you (1) bring a new thing into being (*creation*); (2) join two previously unrelated things (*synthesis*); or (3) improve something or give it a new application (*modification*). You don't need to be a genius in school, either—Thomas Edison and Albert Einstein were not particularly good students. Nor does something need to change the world to be creative; the "little things" can always be done in new, creative ways that add value to the product and the customer.

How do you "get" creative?[40] Recognize the almost infinite "little" opportunities to be creative. Assume you can be creative if you give it a try. Obtain sufficient resources, including facilities, equipment, information, and funds. Escape from work once in a while. Read widely, and try new experiences. Talk to people, constantly, about the issues and ideas with which you are wrestling. And take a course or find a good book about creative thought processes; there are plenty available.

How do you "get" creativity out of other people?[41] Give creative efforts the credit they are due, and don't punish creative failures. If possible, relax pressure for short-term results. Stimulate and challenge people intellectually, and give people some creative freedom. Allow enough time to explore different ideas. Put together teams of people with different styles of thinking and behaving. Get your people in touch with customers, and let them bounce ideas around. Protect them from managers who demand immediate payoffs, who don't understand the importance of creative contributions, or who try to take credit for others' successes. And strive to be creative yourself—you'll set a good example.

brainstorming A process in which group members generate as many ideas about a problem as they can; criticism is withheld until all ideas have been proposed.

A commonly used technique is brainstorming. In **brainstorming,** group members generate as many ideas about a problem as they can. As the ideas are presented, they are posted so that everyone can read them, and people can use the ideas as building blocks. The group is encouraged to say anything that comes to mind, with one exception: No criticism of other people or their ideas is allowed. This rule was violated at the Walt Disney Company when, during a brainstorming session for the design of Euro Disneyland, two architects began shoving each other and almost came to blows.[42]

In the proper brainstorming environment—free of criticism—people are less inhibited and more likely to voice their unusual, creative, or even wild ideas. By the time people have exhausted their ideas, a long list of alternatives has been generated. Only then does the group turn to the evaluation stage. At that point, many different ideas can be considered, modified, or combined into a creative, custom-made solution to the problem.

Brainstorming in a face-to-face group setting is a vital way for product designers at IDEO to generate ideas.
[Courtesy of IDEO]

Although brainstorming is a common practice, research in the laboratory has shown that face-to-face groups generate fewer independent ideas than the same number of people working alone. This is because, 1) in a group, some people, worried about what others might think, are reluctant to express their ideas; 2) people don't always work as hard as if they are alone and accountable for results as individuals; and 3) listening to others takes time that can block people's productivity. But a recent study at IDEO, the largest product design consulting company in the world, makes clear the potential benefits of good brainstorming.[43]

Brainstorming at IDEO

IDEO, founded in 1978 by chief executive officer David Kelley, employs more than 150 product designers and has contributed to the development of over 3,000 products in over 40 industries.

Brainstorming is a vital part of the way they operate. A "brainstormer" at IDEO is a scheduled, face-to-face meeting called to generate ideas. For new projects, two to four brainstormers are called during the first few weeks, and then perhaps one every month.

The rules are (1) defer judgment, (2) build on the ideas of others, (3) have one conversation at a time, (4) stay focused on the topic, and (5) encourage wild ideas. These rules are posted on the wall, and enforced.

Several benefits of brainstorming accrue to IDEO. First, the company is better able to acquire, remember, and use potential solutions to design products. Second, brainstorming adds variety and fun to the job. Third, it helps designers acquire wisdom, to be both confident and humble, as they learn what they know and also what they don't know. Fourth, it encourages people to respect others and work to gain others' respect, so they go out of their way to contribute and to help one another. Fifth, it impresses clients ("We really wow 'em!"). Sixth, it provides income. Clients are billed for the brainstorming sessions. And whereas clients in all industries have complaints about their bills, complaints about these charges are rare because clients see the value.

And the design results? Examples are the original Apple computer mouse, Crest toothpaste tubes, bike helmets, an electric guitar, Nike sunglasses, part of the Jaminator toy guitar, an angioplasty device, fishing equipment, Smith ski goggles, and a combination beach chair and cooler. Steelcase has invested in IDEO to guarantee its help with future innovations, and IDEO now runs "Samsung University" to help that Korean company. IDEO has won more *Business Week* Design Excellent Awards, for several years running, than any other product design firm.

Sources: R. Sutton and A. Hargadon, "Brainstorming Groups in Context: Effectiveness in a Product Design Firm." *Administrative Science Quarterly* 41, (1996), pp. 685–718, and B. Nussbaum, "Winners: The Best Product Designs of the Year," *Business Week,* June 2, 1997, pp. 38–41.

Organizational decision making

Individuals and groups make decisions constantly and everywhere throughout organizations. To understand decision making in organizations, a manager must consider a number of additional concepts and processes, including (1) the constraints decision makers face, (2) organizational decision processes, (3) negotiations and politics, (4) decision making during a crisis, and (5) emergent strategies.

Constraints on decision makers

Organizations—or, more accurately, the people who make important decisions—cannot do whatever they wish. They face various constraints—financial, legal, market, human, and organizational—that inhibit certain actions. Capital or product markets may make an expensive new venture impossible. Legal restrictions may restrain the kinds of international business activities in which a firm can participate. Labor unions may successfully defeat a contract proposed by management, contracts may prevent certain managerial actions, and managers and investors may block a takeover attempt.

Suppose you have a great idea that will provide a revolutionary service for your bank's customers. You won't be able to put your idea into action immediately. You will have to sell it to the people who can give you the go-ahead and also to those whose help you will need to carry out the project. You might start by convincing your boss of your idea's merit. Next, the two of you may have to hash it out with a vice president. Then maybe the president has to be sold. At each stage, you must listen to these individuals' opinions and suggestions and often incorporate them into your original concept. Ultimately, you will have to derive a proposal acceptable to everyone.

In addition, ethical and legal considerations must be thought out carefully. You will have plenty of opportunity to think about ethical issues in Chapter 6. Decision makers must consider ethics and the preferences of many constituent groups—the realities of life in organizations.

Models of organizational decision processes

bounded rationality A less-than-perfect form of rationality in which decision makers cannot conduct a complete, rational analysis because decisions are complex and complete information is unavailable.

Just as with individuals and groups, organizational decision making historically was described with rational models like the one depicted earlier in Figure 3.2. But Nobel laureate Herbert Simon challenged the rational model and proposed an important alternative called *bounded rationality.* According to Simon's **bounded rationality,** decision makers cannot be truly rational because (1) they have imperfect, incomplete information about alternatives and consequences; (2) the problems they face are so complex; (3) human beings simply cannot process all the information to which they are exposed; (4) there is not enough time to process all relevant information fully; and (5) people, including managers within the same firm, have conflicting goals.

When these conditions hold—and they do, for most consequential managerial decisions—perfect rationality will give way to more biased, subjective, messier decision processes. For example, the **incremental model** of decision making occurs when decision makers make small decisions, take little steps, move cautiously, and move in piecemeal fashion toward a bigger solution. The classic example is the budget process, which traditionally begins with the budget from the previous period and makes incremental decisions from that starting point.

incremental model Model of organizational decision making in which major solutions arise through a series of smaller decisions.

The **coalitional model** of decision making arises when people disagree on goals or compete with one another for resources. The decision process becomes political, as groups of individuals band together and try collectively to influence the decision. Two or more coalitions form, each representing a different preference, and each tries to use power and negotiations to sway the decision.

coalitional model Model of organizational decision making in which groups with differing preferences use power and negotiations to influence decisions.

The **garbage can model** of decision making occurs when people aren't sure of their goals, or disagree about the goals, and likewise are unsure of or in disagreement about what to do. This occurs because some problems simply are so complex that they are not well understood, and also because decision makers move in and out of the decision process because they have so many other things to attend to as well. This model implies that some decisions are chaotic, and almost random. You can see that this is a dramatic departure from rationality in decision making.

garbage can model Model of organizational decision making depicting a chaotic process and seemly random decisions.

Every one of these processes occurs in every organization. Let's look more closely at a few of the practical realities of organizational life that make it impossible to achieve perfect rationality.

Negotiations and politics

As the coalitional model suggests, decision makers often need to negotiate, bargain, or compromise. Some decisions must be negotiated with parties outside the organization, such as local government, consumer groups, or environmental groups. Even inside the organization, decisions are negotiated among a number of people.

The fact that decisions often must be negotiated implies that they are political; that is, they galvanize the preferences of competing groups and individuals. The decision that is best on objective grounds may lose out because powerful individuals push through their preferred alternatives.

Consider a company that is pursuing a strategy of growth through acquisitions. Such activity constitutes a favorite power game of a powerful coalition of top executives. These executives may prefer to acquire another company even if their own company really needs to focus its efforts on strengthening its internal operations. Decisions on pay raises, promotions, and budgets also may be made (and criticized) on the basis of politics.

Organizational politics, in which people try to influence organizational decisions so that their own interests will be served and use power to pursue hidden agendas, reduces decision-making effectiveness.[44] One of the best ways to reduce such politics, and to make sure that constructive cognitive conflict does not degenerate into affective conflict, is to *create common goals* for members of the team. That is, make the decision-making process a collaborative, rather than a competitive, exercise by establishing a goal around which the group can rally. In one study, top management teams with stated goals like "build the biggest financial war chest" for an upcoming competitive battle, or "create *the* computer firm of the decade," or "build the best damn machine on the market" were less likely to have dysfunctional conflict and politics between members.[45]

Most managers accept political realities and consider them a basic challenge of organizational life.[46] For any important decision that you wish to influence, it is essential that you identify and marshal the support of powerful individuals or interest groups.

Decision making in a crisis

In crisis situations, managers must make decisions under a great deal of pressure.[47] A VIP customer threatens to cancel his contract if your company doesn't get his computers operating within the hour. A strike shuts down your plant. People are killed or injured in a crash of one of your airline's jets or in an explosion in one of your company's mines. What actions will you take? Whatever you decide, you must do it quickly.

You have no doubt heard of some of the most famous recent crises: the *Exxon Valdez;* bombings in Oklahoma City and the World Trade Center; Barings Bank's collapse; bankruptcy in Orange County, California; and five USAir crashes between 1989 and 1994. Union Carbide's gas leak in Bhopal, India, killed thousands of people; several people were killed in the cyanide poisonings of Johnson & Johnson's Tylenol. As outlined in Table 3.3, the two companies handled their crises in very different ways. To this day, J&J is known for its effective handling of the crisis, as outlined in the table.

Commonly a crisis makes effective decision making less likely. Psychological stress and lack of time cause decision makers to think in simplistic terms, to fail to consider an adequate number of alternatives, and to ignore the long-term implications of their actions.

Some crises can be prevented by clarifying the corporation's values and social responsibilities, and monitoring people's behavior and ethical conduct as described in later chapters. For example, at Barings Bank a single employee was allowed to conduct and oversee his own trades. The lack of control systems allowed the trader to increase his activity dramatically, use leverage to an extreme, escalate trade amounts, and greatly increase risk. The resulting crisis brought down the entire bank.

Your organization should be prepared for crises in advance. However, many Fortune 1000 firms have no crisis-management plan at all.[48] Table 3.4 lists some common rationalizations that prevent companies from preparing for and managing crises properly. Effective managers do not allow these evasions to prevent them from preparing carefully for crisis.

Crisis management experts have identified several lessons from crises such as the USAir deaths, the Orange County bankruptcy, and Intel's defective Pentium chip.[49] First, it is essential to detect the signals that a potential crisis is looming. Second, if a crisis arises, the world will learn all there is to know about your daily operations and crisis preparation

Companies handle crisis decision making in different ways. Union Carbide's mishandling of the gas leak in Bhopal, India, resulted in the perception that the company was negligent and uncaring. Even ten years after the tragic accident, people demonstrated vigorously against the company. *(AP/Wide World Photos)*

table 3.3
Two disasters

Union Carbide	Johnson & Johnson
Failed to identify as a crisis the public perception that the company was a negligent, uncaring killer.	Identified the crisis of public perception that Tylenol was unsafe and J&J was not in control.
No planning before reaction: CEO immediately went to India to inspect damage. All executives involved.	Planned before reacting: CEO picked one executive to head crisis team. Rest of company involved only on a strict need-to-know basis.
Set no goals.	Set goals to: Stop the killings. Find reasons for the killings. Provide assistance to the victims. Restore Tylenol's credibility.
Action: Damage control/stonewalling. Distanced itself. Misrepresented safety conditions. Did not inform spokespeople. Adopted bunker mentality.	Action: Gave complete information. Worked with authorities. Pulled Tylenol from shelves (first-year cost: $150 million). Used strong marketing program. Reissued Tylenol with tamper-proof packaging.
Chronic problems continued: Public confidence low. Costly litigation. No formal crisis plan resulted.	Crisis resolved: Public confidence high. Sales high again. Well-documented crisis management plan.

and response. You will be thoroughly investigated and publicized immediately. Third, the remedy for one problem can create others, so attention to implementation and monitoring is vital. Although many companies don't concern themselves with crisis management, it is imperative that it be on management's agenda.

An effective plan for crisis management (CM) should include the following elements:[50]

1. *Strategic actions* such as integrating CM into strategic planning and official policies.
2. *Technical and structural actions* such as creating a CM team and dedicating a budget to CM.
3. *Evaluation and diagnostic actions* such as conducting audits of threats and liabilities, conducting environmental impact audits, and establishing tracking systems for early warning signals.
4. *Communication actions* such as providing training for dealing with the media, local communities, and police and government officials.
5. *Psychological and cultural actions* such as showing a strong top management commitment to CM and providing training and psychological support services regarding the human and emotional impacts of crises.

Ultimately, it is imperative that management be able to answer the following questions:[51]

table 3.4
Mistaken assumptions: how *not* to handle crisis management

We don't have a crisis.
We can handle a crisis.
Crisis management is a luxury we can't afford.
If a major crisis happens, someone else will rescue us.
Accidents are just a cost of doing business.
Most crises are the fault of bad individuals; therefore, there's not much we can do to prevent them.
Only executives need to be aware of our crisis plans; why scare our employees or members of the community?
We are tough enough to react to a crisis in an objective and rational manner.
The most important thing in crisis management is to protect the good image of the organization through public relations and advertising campaigns.

Source: From C. M. Pearson and I. I. Mitroff, "From Crisis Prone to Crisis Prepared: A Framework for Crisis Management," *The Executive,* February 1993, pp. 48–59. Reprinted by permission of the Academy of Management.

- What kinds of crises could your company face?
- Can your company detect a crisis in its early stages?
- How will it manage a crisis if one occurs?
- How can it benefit from a crisis after it has passed?

The last question makes an important point: a crisis, managed effectively, can have *benefits.* Old as well as new problems can be resolved, new strategies and competitive advantages may appear, and positive change can emerge. And if someone steps in and manages the crisis well, a hero is born.

Emergent strategies

Emergent strategy The strategy that evolves from all the activities engaged in by people throughout the organization.

Soon you will learn more about how managers formulate strategies for their firms to pursue. Again, a rational model can describe this process in its ideal form. But once again, the reality of organizational decision making often differs. **Emergent strategy** is the strategy that the organization "ends up" pursuing, based not solely on what was originally planned and attempted, but also on what actually evolves from all the activities engaged in by people throughout the organization.

As shown in Figure 3.4, decision making and strategy emergence are dynamic processes through which people engage in discovery; make decisions; carry out those choices in sometimes tentative, trial-and-error ways; and discover new things and new ways by chance. Discovery is the process of systematically gathering facts and analyzing them. This forms the basis for decision making, which includes generating and selecting goals and courses of action. Action, then, is implementation and evaluation. Discovery continues unabated.

Thus, emergent strategies may start with planning from the top executives, but may also involve trial-and-error, experimenting, learning from mistakes, seizing unexpected opportunities, and so on. And these activities can occur at any organizational level, in any unit, at any location.

You may notice that all of those processes are constructive and useful. In the coming chapters, we will discuss in more depth the strategy formulation process and its implementation, as well as learning, adapting, and changing to thrive in changing circumstances.

figure 3.4
Emergent strategies

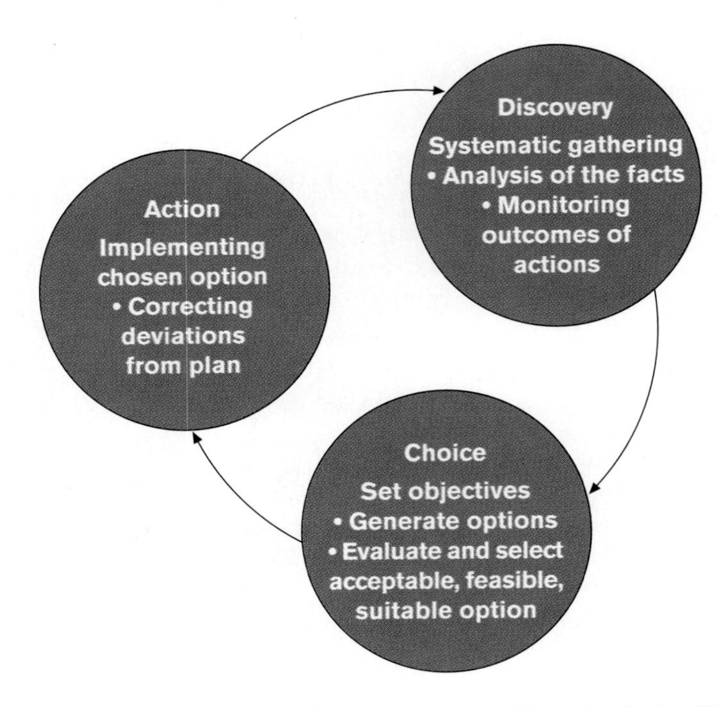

Adapted from: Ralph D. Stacey, *Strategic Management and Organizational Dynamics,* London: Pittman Publishing, 1993. p. 27.

Key terms

Affective conflict, p. 94
Bounded rationality, p. 97
Brainstorming, p. 95
Certainty, p. 81
Coalitional model, p. 98
Cognitive conflict, p. 94
Conflict, p. 82
Custom-made solutions, p. 83
Devil's advocate, p. 94
Dialectic, p. 94
Discount the future, p. 90
Emergent strategy, p. 101
Framing effects, p. 90
Garbage can model, p. 98
Goal displacement, p. 93
Groupthink, p. 93
Illusion of control, p. 89
Incremental model, p. 98
Maximize, p. 85
Nonprogrammed decisions, p. 81
Optimize, p. 86
Programmed decisions, p. 81
Ready-made solutions, p. 83
Risk, p. 82
Satisfice, p. 85
Uncertainty, p. 82
Vigilance, p. 88

Summary of learning objectives

Now that you have studied Chapter 3, you should know:

The kinds of decisions you will face as a manager.

Most important managerial decisions are ill structured and characterized by uncertainty, risk, and conflict. Yet managers are expected to make rational decisions in the face of these challenges.

How to make "rational" decisions.

The ideal decision-making process involves six stages. The first, identifying and diagnosing the problem, requires recognizing a discrepancy between the current state and a desired state and then delving below surface symptoms to uncover the underlying causes of the problem. The second stage, generating alternative solutions, requires adopting ready-made or designing custom-made solutions. The third, evaluating alternatives, means predicting the consequences of different alternatives, sometimes through building scenarios of the future. Fourth, a solution is chosen; the solution might maximize, satisfice, or optimize. Fifth, decision makers implement the decision; this stage requires more careful planning than it often receives. Finally, managers should evaluate how well the decision is working. This means gathering objective, valid information about the impact the decision is having. If the evidence suggests the problem is not getting solved, either a better decision or a better implementation plan must be developed.

The pitfalls you should avoid when making decisions.

Situational and human limitations lead most decision makers to satisfice rather than maximize. Psychological biases, time pressures, and the social realities of organizational life may prevent rational execution of the six decision-making stages. But vigilance and an understanding of how to manage decision-making groups and organizational constraints will improve the process and result in better decisions.

The pros and cons of using a group to make decisions.

Advantages include more information, perspectives, and approaches brought to bear on problem solving; intellectual stimulation; greater understanding by all of the final decision; and higher commitment to the decision once it is made. Potential dangers or disadvantages of using groups include individual domination of discussions, satisficing, groupthink, and goal displacement.

The procedures to use in leading a decision-making team.

Effective leaders in decision-making teams or groups avoid dominating the discussion; encourage people's input; avoid groupthink and satisficing; and stay focused on the group's goals. They encourage constructive conflict devil's advocacy, and the dialectic, posing opposite sides of an issue or solutions to a problem. They also encourage creativity through a variety of techniques.

How to encourage creative decisions.

When creative ideas are needed, leaders should set a good example by being creative themselves. They should recognize the almost infinite "little" opportunities for creativity and have confidence in their own creative abilities. They can inspire creativity in others by pushing for creative freedom, rewarding creativity, and not punishing creative failures. They should encourage interaction with customers, stimulate discussion, and protect people from managers who might squelch the creative processes. Brainstorming is one of the most popular techniques for generating creative ideas.

The processes by which decisions are made in organizations.

Decision making in organizations is often a highly complex process. Individuals and groups are constrained by a variety of factors and constituencies. In practice, decision makers are boundedly rational rather than purely rational. Some decisions are made on an incremental basis. Coalitions form to represent different preferences. The process is often chaotic, as depicted in the garbage can model. Politics enter the process, decisions are negotiated, crises arise, and strategies emerge and evolve.

How to make decisions in a crisis.

Crisis conditions make sound, effective decision making more difficult. However, it is possible for crises to be managed well. A strategy for crisis management can be developed beforehand, and the mechanisms put into readiness, so that if crises do arise, decision makers are prepared.

Discussion questions

1. Refer back to "Setting the Stage." What do you think of the boom in the consulting industry? Would you use consultants? If so, how?

2. Identify some risky decisions you have made. Why did you take the risks? How did they work out? Looking back, what did you learn?

3. Identify a decision you made that had important unintended consequences. Were the consequences good, bad, or both? Should you, and could you, have done anything differently in making the decision?

4. What do you think is your Myers-Briggs type? What are the personal implications?

5. Recall a recent decision that you had difficulty making. Describe it in terms of the characteristics of managerial decisions.

6. Do you think managers can use computer technology to improve the rationality of their decisions? Why (and how?) or why not?

7. Do you think that when managers make decisions they follow the decision-making steps as presented in this chapter? Which steps are apt to be overlooked or given inadequate attention? What can people do to make sure they do a more thorough job?

8. Discuss the potential advantages and disadvantages of using a group to make decisions. Give examples in your experience.

9. Suppose you are the CEO of a major corporation and one of your company's oil tanks has erupted, spilling thousands of gallons of oil into a river that empties into the ocean. What should you do to handle the crisis?

10. Look at the mistaken assumptions described in Table 3.4. Why do such assumptions arise, and what can be done to overcome these biases?

11. Identify some problems you want to solve. Brainstorm with others a variety of creative solutions.

Concluding Case

Bad decisions at Euro Disney

Two years after Walt Disney Co. opened its new park in France, Euro Disney was losing $1 million per day, despite over a million visitors per month. What had gone wrong?

Disney was overly ambitious, and had made serious strategic and financial miscalculations. It relied too heavily on debt, just as interest rates started to rise. It assumed a real estate boom would continue, allowing it to sell some properties to pay off its debts. It made mistakes in the park itself, including cost overruns, a no-alcohol policy (in a country where a glass of wine for lunch is standard), too few bathrooms, and a mistaken assumption that the French would not want breakfast at the hotel restaurants.

The Walt Disney Company made a host of bad decisions regarding its Euro Disney theme park in France. In the end, the park remained open, but observers say it will take extreme measures to make the project profitable. *[Sichov/SIPA]*

The company blamed its problems on a severe European recession, high interest rates, and the devaluation of several currencies against the French franc. But it had alienated the people with whom it needed to work. Disney thought it knew best, and persistently imposed its will on others. "They were always sure it would work because they were Disney," said one French construction-industry official. Disney's European executives felt they were always playing second fiddle to corporate executives.

Disney showed its overconfidence in many ways. Executives boasted they could predict future living patterns in Paris; they predicted people would move to the east near Euro Disney. They believed they could change European habits. For instance, Europeans are more reluctant than Americans to let their kids skip school, and prefer longer vacations to short breaks. Disney believed it could change this.

"There was a tendency to believe that everything they touched would be perfect," said a former Disney executive. Disney believed that what it could do in Florida, it could do in France. The perceived arrogance, and a critical press, demoralized the workforce, and initially kept visitors away.

The risky financing of Euro Disney was based on a highly optimistic scenario with little margin for error. When critics said the financial structure was far too clever for its own good, Disney's attitude was that cautious, old-world European thinking couldn't comprehend U.S.-style, free-market financing.

Eventually, the park had as many visitors as projected. But costs were way too high, and the economic environment had changed. To cover costs, park admission was set at $42.45, higher than in the United States. But Disney failed to see the warnings of a European depression. Said one executive, "Between the glamour and the pressure of opening and the intensity of the project itself, we didn't realize a major recession was coming."

Michael Eisner, chairman of Disney, vowed to make Euro Disney the company's most lavish project ever. He was obsessed with maintaining Disney's reputation for quality, but he went way over budget to do things that critics considered frivolous.

When things were at their bleakest, Disney threatened to close the park, but negotiated last-minute, favorable new financing arrangements. The crisis seemed solved, at least temporarily. Many observers maintained, however, that Euro Disney was not really in danger of shutting down—too much was at stake, for the company, its creditors, and the French government, which initially had provided road and rail networks to the park and $750 million in loans at below-market rates.

Prices have been dropped, and some costs have also been reduced by new management. Euro Disney has now recovered and is becoming financially healthy. But once again, Disney is angering Europeans. The animated films *Hercules* and *The Hunchback of Notre Dame* enraged people over the gross liberties taken in distorting the original stories. A leading newspaper read throughout Europe decried "a cartoon [*Hercules*] that distorts and abuses one of the founding myths of European culture" (Millar 1997, p. 9). Furthermore, "though sensitive to what is thought to be politically correct in the United States, it is wholly indifferent to where it lifts its raw material from, provided it makes money. And it does, in the billions" ("Disney's Lesson," p. 5). And another quote: "No studio has so comprehensively pillaged European culture in the service of its own focus-group-driven Hollywood money machine than Disney" (ibid.).

Questions

1. How many decisions can you count in this case? What others can you think of that needed to be made for such an ambitious undertaking?

2. What concepts from the chapter can you spot in this case? What mistakes do you see by Disney executives?

3. With the benefit of hindsight, what could Disney have done differently?

4. What do you think of the European reaction described in the last paragraph? What should Disney do?

Sources: P. Gumbel and R. Turner, "Fans Like Euro Disney, but Its Parent's Goofs Weigh the Park Down," *The Wall Street Journal,* March 10, 1994, pp. A1, A12; and P. Millar, "Lock up Your Legends" *The European,* September 3, 1997, pp. 8–12. Also, "Disney's Lesson," editorial; *The European,* September 3, 1997, p. 5. ●

Video Case

Decision making

In a global economy, sound business decisions depend on a number of important factors. The quality of managerial decisions can determine a company's success or failure. A recent study concluded that managers spend approximately 50 percent of their time dealing with the consequences of bad decision making.

In this video case study, two successful businesses—the Second City Theater in Chicago and Heavenly Ski Resort in Lake Tahoe—explore the following decision-making topics:

1. Managers make different decisions under different business conditions.

2. When managers take steps to explore and evaluate alternatives it leads to more effective decisions.

3. All managers need to be aware of the many factors that can affect the decision-making process.

Broadly defined, decision making is a process of choosing among alternative courses of action. In the business world, this process takes place under varying conditions of certainty and risk. Decision making is more likely to be effective when approached in a series of steps that explore and evaluate alternatives.

1. Identify the problem.
2. Generate alternative solutions.
3. Evaluate the alternatives.
4. Select the best alternative.

5. Implement the decision.
6. Evaluate the decision.

To evaluate a decision, managers must gather information that can shed light on its effectiveness. Although most managers would prefer to follow all of these decision-making steps, time and circumstances don't always allow it. This decision-making process can also be influenced by other important factors such as intuition, emotion, stress, confidence, and risk propensity.

Second City has grown from its roots as a small "mom and pop" theater to a large, internationally known corporate enterprise. Rather than investing all its resources into its immensely popular old-town Chicago improv theater, the Second City has decided to translate its expertise into other ventures, such as television, corporate training, and other theaters in Toronto, suburban Chicago, and Detroit.

Heavenly Ski Resort in Lake Tahoe accommodates nearly 750,000 skiers per year and competes as one of eight large Tahoe-area resorts. Like the Second City Theater, managers at Heavenly must make decisions affecting the growth of the company in less-than-ideal conditions.

Although following the six decision-making steps may lead to a sounder decision-making process, theory doesn't always play out in practice. Management may follow some steps, but perhaps not all of them, depending on the factors affecting the decision-making process. "Most of the managers are encouraged to make a decision right away and don't hold on to the problem. It's such a fast pace that I want them to just go on to the next thing and not hold the problem back. I've empowered them to pretty much make their own decisions," said Steve Jacobson, director of food and beverage at Heavenly.

Making people laugh takes a lot of hard work and courage, as well as creativity and insight. Decisions about artistic design don't always fit the mold of the decision-making model. Kelly Leonard, associate producer at Second City, said, "We did a show which was a parody of *Our Town,* and it was at times brilliant and at times not. It got great reviews, it was very intricate in its knowledge of *Our Town.* However, it demanded a certain understanding of the play and of the Second City form to really get all the jokes. What we found is that though critics loved it and many of us loved it here, the audience didn't understand it. We tried an advertising campaign to support it, which to that time we had not advertised much and it didn't work and people wouldn't come. So we had to switch over the show."

Both the Second City Theater and Heavenly Ski Resort face the challenge of providing entertainment to consumers. In their day-to-day operations, both companies experience the need to make decisions in varying conditions of certainty, uncertainty, and risk. Awareness of the nature of decision making, its important steps, and its influential factors may help managers minimize the time they spend responding to the consequences of poor decision making. This can enable managers to spend more time maximizing opportunities for growth.

Discussion Questions

1. Decision making is described in the video as a series of steps. Do you agree with the six steps as outlined in the video? What additional procedures might be added to the process?

2. There are situations where decision making requires input from many people, and times when decisions have to be made by an individual. Describe a situation that would require wide input, and one where an individual should make a decision without outside input. How do these situations differ?

3. Managerial decision making is affected by something called "risk propensity." What does this term mean? How can people "manage" their risk propensity?

Experiential Exercises

3.1 Competitive escalation: The dollar auction

Objective

To explore the effects of competition on decision making.

Instructions

Step 1: 5 Minutes. The instructor will play the role of auctioneer. In this auction, the instructor will auction off $1 bills (the instructor will inform you whether this money is real or imaginary). All members of the class may participate in the auction at the same time.

The rules for this auction are slightly different from those of a normal auction. In this version, *both the highest bidder and the next highest bidder will pay their last bids* even though the dollar is only awarded to the highest bidder. For example, if Bidder A bids 15 cents for the dollar and Bidder B bids 10 cents, and there is no further bidding, then A pays 15 cents for the dollar and receives the dollar, while B pays 10 cents and receives nothing. The auctioneer would lose 75 cents on the dollar just sold.

Bids must be made in multiples of 5 cents. The dollar will be sold when there is no further bidding. If two individuals bid the same amount at the same time, ties are resolved in favor of the bidder located physically closest to the auctioneer. *During each round, there is to be no talking except for making bids.*

Step 2: 15 Minutes. The instructor (auctioneer) will auction off five individual dollars to the class. Any student may bid in an effort to win the dollar. A record sheet of the bidding and winners can be kept in the worksheet that follows.

Discussion questions

1. Who made the most money in this exercise—one of the bidders or the auctioneer? Why?
2. As the auction proceeded, did bidders become more competitive or more cooperative? Why?
3. Did two bidders ever pay more for the money being auctioned than the value of the money itself? Explain how and why this happened.
4. Did you become involved in the bidding? Why?
   a. If you became involved, what were your motivations? Did you accomplish your objectives?
   b. If not, why didn't you become involved? What did you think were the goals and objectives of those who did become involved?
5. Did people say things to one another during the bidding to influence their actions? What was said, and how was it influential?

Dollar Auction Worksheet

	Amount paid by winning bidder	Amount paid by second bidder	Total paid for this dollar
First dollar			
Second dollar			
Third dollar			
Fourth dollar			
Fifth dollar			

Source: Excerpted from R. Lewicki, *Experiences in Management and Organizational Behavior* (New York: John Wiley and Sons, 1991), pp. 91–92, 27–28, and 225–227. Reprinted by permission of John Wiley and Sons, Inc.

3.2 Group problem-solving meeting at the community agency

Objective

Through role playing a meeting between a chairman and his subordinates, to understand the interactions in group decision making.

Instructions

1. Gather role sheets for each character and instructions for observers.
2. Set up a table in front of the room with five chairs around it arranged in such a way that participants can talk comfortably and have their faces visible to observers.
3. Read the introduction and cast of characters.
4. Five members from the class are selected to role play the five characters. All other members act as observers. The participants study the roles. All should play their roles without referring to the role sheets.
5. The observers read the instructions for observers.
6. When everyone is ready, John Cabot enters his office, joins the others at the table, and the scene begins. Allow 20 minutes to complete the meeting. The meeting is carried to the point of completion unless an argument develops and no progress is evident after 10 or 15 minutes of conflict.

Discussion Questions

1. Describe the group's behavior. What did each member say? Do?
2. Evaluate the effectiveness of the group's decision making.
3. Did any problems exist in leadership, power, motivation, communication, or perception?
4. How could the group's effectiveness be increased?

Introduction

The Community Agency is a role-play exercise of a meeting between the chairman of the board of a social service agency and four of his subordinates. Each character's role is designed to recreate the reality of a business meeting. Each character comes to the meeting with a unique perspective on a major problem facing the agency as well as some personal impressions of the other characters developed over several years of business and social associations.

The Cast of Characters

John Cabot, the Chairman, was the principal force behind the formation of the Community Agency, a multiservice agency. The agency employs 50 people, and during its 19 years of operations has enjoyed better client relations, a better service record, and a better reputation than other local agencies because of a reputation for high-quality service at a moderate cost to funding agencies. Recently, however, competitors have begun to overtake the Community Agency, resulting in declining contracts. John Cabot is expending every possible effort to keep his agency comfortably at the top.

Ron Smith, Director of the Agency, reports directly to Cabot. He has held this position since he helped Cabot establish the agency 19 years ago.

Joan Sweet, Head of Client Services, reports to Smith. She has been with the Agency 12 years, having worked before that for HEW as a contracting officer.

Tom Lynch, Head Community Liaison, reports to Joan Sweet. He came to the Community Agency at Sweet's request, having worked with Sweet previously at HEW.

Jane Cox, Head Case Worker, also works for Joan Sweet. Cox was promoted to this position two years ago. Prior to that time, Jane had gone through a year's training program after receiving an MSW from a large urban university.

Today's meeting

John Cabot has called the meeting with these four managers in order to solve some problems that have developed in meeting service schedules and contract requirements. Cabot must catch a plane to Washington in half an hour; he has an appointment to negotiate a key contract that means a great deal to the future of the Community Agency. He has only 20 minutes to meet with his managers and still catch the plane. Cabot feels that getting the Washington contract is absolutely crucial to the future of the agency.

Integrating Case

SSS Software In-Basket Exercise

One way to assess your own strengths and weaknesses in management skills is to engage in an actual managerial work experience. The following exercise gives you a realistic glimpse of the tasks faced regularly by practicing managers. Complete the exercise, and then compare your own decisions and actions with those of classmates.

SSS Software designs and develops customized software for businesses. It also integrates this software with the customer's existing systems and provides system maintenance. SSS Software has customers in the following industries: airlines, automotive, finance/banking, health/hospital, consumer products, electronics, and government. The company has also begun to generate important international clients. These include the European Airbus consortium and a consortium of banks and financial firms based in Kenya.

SSS Software has grown rapidly since its inception just over a decade ago. Its revenue, net income, and earnings per share have all been above the industry average for the past several years. However, competition in this technologically sophisticated field has grown very rapidly. Recently, it has become more difficult to compete for major contracts. Moreover, although SSS Software's revenue and net income continue to grow, the rate of growth declined during the last fiscal year.

SSS Software's 250 employees are divided into several operating divisions with employees at four levels: Nonmanagement, technical/professional, managerial, and executive. Nonmanagement employees take care of the clerical and facilities support functions. The technical/professional staff perform the core technical work for the firm. Most managerial employees are group managers who supervise a team of technical/professional employees working on a project for a particular customer. Staff who work in specialized areas such as finance, accounting, human resources, nursing, and law are also considered managerial employees. The executive level includes the 12 highest-ranking employees at SSS Software. There is an organization chart in Figure A that illustrates SSS Software's structure. There is also an Employee Classification Report that lists the number of employees at each level of the organization.

In this exercise, you will play the role of Chris Perillo, Vice President of Operations for Health and Financial Services. You learned last Wednesday, October 13, that your predecessor, Michael Grant, has resigned and gone to Universal Business Solutions, Inc. You were offered his former job, and you accepted it. Previously, you were the Group Manager for a team of 15 software developers assigned to work on the Airbus consortium project in the Airline Services Division. You spent all of Thursday, Friday, and most of the weekend finishing up parts of the project, briefing your successor, and preparing for an interim report you will deliver in Paris on October 21.

It is now 7 AM Monday and you are in your new office. You have arrived at work early so you can spend the next two hours reviewing material in your in-basket (including some memos and messages to Michael Grant), as well as your voice mail and e-mail. Your daily planning book indicates that you have no appointments today or tomorrow but will have to catch a plane for Paris early Wednesday morning. You have a full schedule for the remainder of the week and all of next week.

Assignment

During the next two hours, review all the material in your in-basket, as well as your voice mail and e-mail. Take only two hours. Use the response form below as a model, indicate how you want to respond to each item (that is, via letter/memo, e-mail, phone/voice mail, or personal meeting). If you decide not to respond to an item, check "no response" on the response form. All your responses must be written on the response forms. Write your precise, detailed response (do not merely jot down a few notes). For example, you might draft a memo or write out a message that you will deliver via phone/voice mail. You may also decide to meet with an individual (or individuals) during the limited time available on your calendar today or tomorrow. If so, prepare an agenda for a personal meeting and list your goals for the meeting. As you read through the items, you may occasionally observe some information that you think is relevant and want to remember (or attend to in the future) but that you decide not to include in any of your responses to employees. Write down such information on a sheet of paper titled "note to self."

Source: D. Whetten and K. Cameron, *Developing Management Skills,* 3e, New York: Harper Collins, 1995

figure A Partial organization chart of health and financial services devision

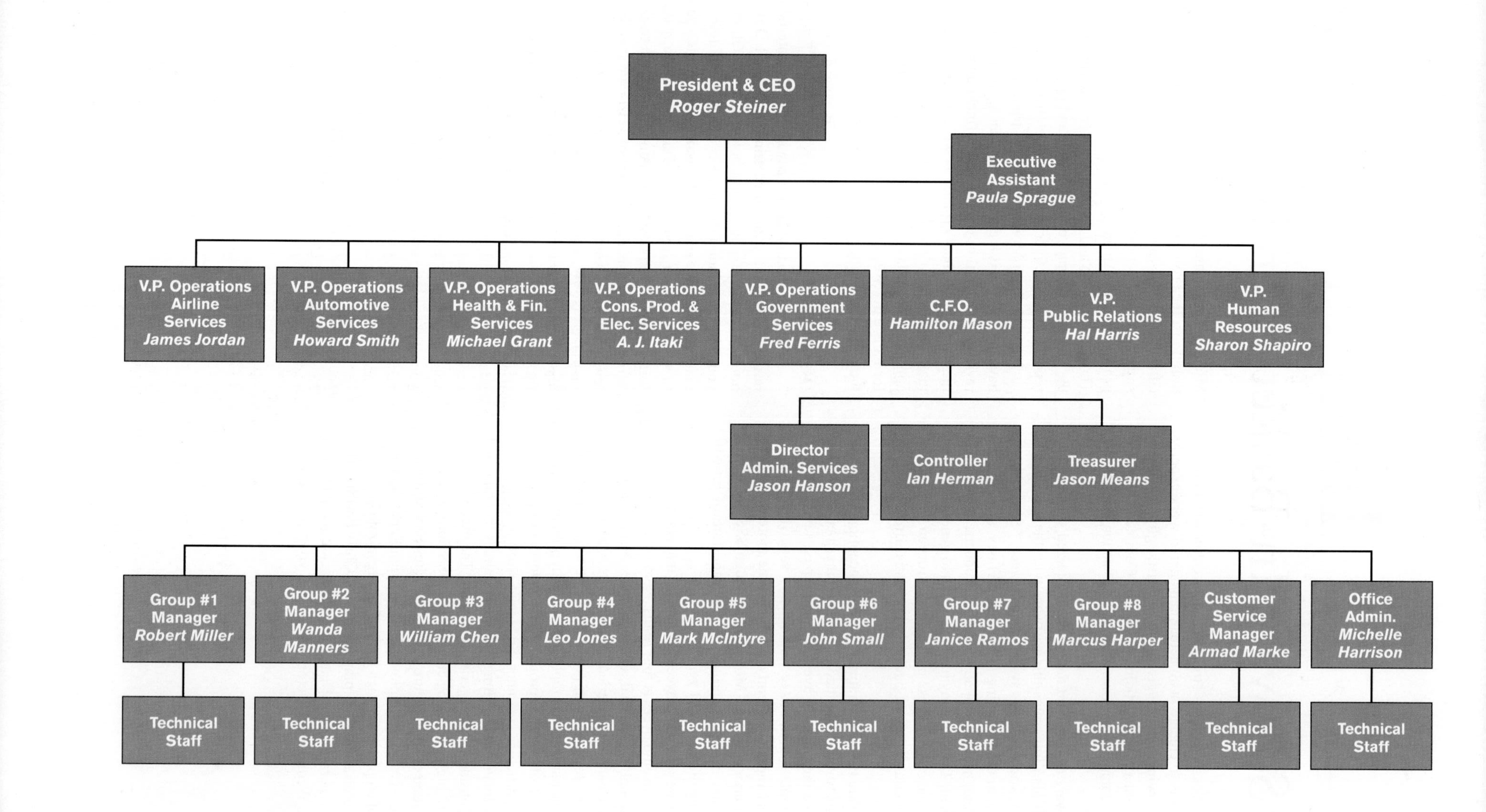

Sample Response Form

Relates To:

Memo # __________ E-Mail # __________ Voice mail #__________

Response form:

________ Letter/Memo ________ Meet with person (when, where)

________ E-Mail ________ Note to self

________ Phone call/Voice mail ________ No response

ITEM 1 Memo

TO: All Employees

FROM: Roger Steiner, Chief Executive Officer

DATE: October 15

I am pleased to announce that Chris Perillo has been appointed as Vice President of Operations for Health and Financial Services. Chris will immediately assume responsibility for all operations previously managed by Michael Grant. Chris will have end-to-end responsibility for the design, development, integration, and maintenance of custom software for the health and finance/banking industries. This responsibility includes all technical, financial, and staffing issues. Chris will also manage our program of software support and integration for the recently announced merger of three large health maintenance organizations (HMOs). Chris will be responsible for our recently announced project with a consortium of banks and financial firms operating in Kenya. This project represents an exciting opportunity for us, and Chris's background seems ideally suited to the task.

Chris comes to this position with an undergraduate degree in Computer Science from the California Institute of Technology and an M.B.A. from the University of Virginia. Chris began as a member of our technical/professional staff six years ago and has most recently served for three years as a Group Manager supporting domestic and international projects for our airlines industry group, including our recent work for the European Airbus consortium.

I am sure you all join me in offering congratulations to Chris for this promotion.

ITEM 2 Memo

TO: All Managers

FROM: Hal Harris, Vice President, Community and Public Relations

DATE: October 15

For your information, the following article appeared on the front page of the business section of Thursday's *Los Angeles Times*.

In a move that may create problems for SSS Software, Michael Grant and Janice Ramos have left SSS Software and moved to Universal Business Solutions Inc. Industry analysts see the move as another victory for Universal Business Solutions Inc. in their battle with SSS Software for share of the growing software development and integration business. Both Grant and Ramos had been with SSS Software for over 7 years. Grant was most recently Vice President of Operations for all SSS Software's work in two industries: health and hospitals, and finance and banking. Ramos brings to Universal Business Solutions Inc. her special expertise in the growing area of international software development and integration.

Hillary Collins, an industry analyst with Merrill Lynch, said "the loss of key staff to a competitor can often create serious problems for a firm such as SSS Software. Grant and Ramos have an insider's understanding of SSS Software's strategic and technical limitations. It will be interesting to see if they can exploit this knowledge to the advantage of Universal Business Solutions Inc."

ITEM 3 Memo

TO: Chris Perillo

FROM: Paula Sprague, Executive Assistance to Roger Steiner

DATE: October 15

Chris, I know that in your former position as a Group Manager in the Airline Services Division, you probably have met most of the group managers in the Health and Financial Services Division, but I thought you might like some more personal information about them. These people will be your direct reports on the management team.

Group #1: Bob Miller, 55-year-old white male, married (Anne) with two children and three grandchildren. Active in local Republican politics. Well regarded as a "hands-off" manager heading a high-performing team. Plays golf regularly with Mark McIntyre, John Small, and a couple of V.P.s from other divisions.

Group #2: Wanda Manners, 38-year-old white female, single with one school-age child. A fitness "nut," has run in several marathons. Some experience in Germany and Japan. Considered a hard-driving manager with a constant focus on the task at hand. Will be the first person to show up every morning.

Group #3: William Chen, 31-year-old male of Chinese descent, married (Harriet), two young children from his first marriage. Enjoys tennis and is quite good at it. A rising star in the company, he is highly respected by his peers as a "man of action" and a good friend.

Group #4: Leo Jones, 36-year-old white male, married (Janet), with an infant daughter. Recently returned from paternity leave. Has travelled extensively on projects, since he speaks three languages. Has liked hockey ever since the time he spent in Montreal. Considered a strong manager who gets the most out of his people.

Group #5: Mark McIntyre, 45-year-old white male, married (Mary Theresa) to an executive in the banking industry. No children. A lot of experience in Germany and Eastern Europe. Has been writing a mystery novel. Has always been a good "team player," but several members of his technical staff are not well respected and he hasn't addressed the problem.

Group #6: John Small, 38-year-old white male, recently divorced. Three children living with his wife. A gregarious individual who likes sports. He spent a lot of time in Mexico and Central America before he came to SSS Software. Recently has been doing mostly contract work with the federal government. An average manager, has had some trouble keeping his people on schedule.

Group #7: This position vacant since Janice Ramos left. Roger thinks we ought to fill this position quickly. Get in touch with me if you want information on any in-house candidates for any position.

Group #8: Marcus Harper, 42-year-old black male, married (Tamara) with two teenage children. Recently won an award in a local photography contest. Considered a strong manager who gets along with peers and works long hours.

Customer Services: Armand Marke, 38-year-old Armenian male, divorced. A basketball fan. Originally from Armenia. Previously a Group Manager. Worked hard to establish the Technical Services Phone Line, but now has pretty much left it alone.

Office Administrator: Michelle Harrison, 41-year-old white female, single. Grew up on a ranch and still rides horses whenever she can. A strict administrator.

There are a number of good folks here, but they don't function well as a management team. I think Michael played favorites, especially with Janice and Leo. There are a few cliques in this group and I'm not sure how effectively Michael dealt with them. I expect you will find it a challenge to build a cohesive team

ITEM 4 Memo

TO: Chris Perillo

FROM: Wanda Manners, Group 2 Manager

DATE: October 15, 1998

CONFIDENTIAL AND RESTRICTED

Although I know you are new to your job, I feel it is important that I let you know about some information I just obtained concerning the development work we recently completed for First National Investment. Our project involved the development of asset management software for managing their international funds. This was a very complex project due to the volatile exchange rates and the forecasting tools we needed to develop.

As part of this project, we had to integrate the software and reports with all their existing systems and reporting mechanisms. To do this we were given access to all of their existing software (much of which was developed by Universal Business Solutions Inc.). Of course, we signed an agreement acknowledging that the software to which we were given access was proprietary and that our access was solely for the purpose of our system integration work associated with the project.

Unfortunately, I have learned that some parts of the software we developed actually "borrow" heavily from complex application programs developed for First National Investment by Universal Business Solutions Inc. It seems obvious to me that one or more of the software developers from Group 5 (that is, Mark McIntyre's group) inappropriately "borrowed" algorithms developed by Universal Business Solutions Inc. I am sure that doing so saved us significant development time on some aspects of the project. It seems very unlikely that First National Investment or Universal Business Solutions Inc. will ever become aware of this issue.

Finally, First National Investment is successfully using the software we developed and is thrilled with the work we did. We brought the project in on time and under budget. Your probably know that they have invited us to bid on several other substantial projects.

I'm sorry to bring this delicate matter to your attention, but I thought you should know about it.

ITEM 5 Memo

TO: Chris Perillo

FROM: Paula Sprague, Executive Assistant to Roger Steiner

DATE: October 15

RE: Letter from C.A.R.E. Services (copies attached)

Roger asked me to work on this C.A.R.E. project and obviously wants some fast action. A lot of the staff are already booked solid for the next couple of weeks. I knew that Elise Soto and Chu Hung Woo have the expertise to do this system and when I checked with them, they were relatively free. I had them pencil in the next two weeks and wanted to let you know. Hopefully, it will take a "hot potato" out of your hands.

ITEM 5 Copy of Fax

C.A.R.E.
Child and Adolescent Rehabilitative and Educational Services
A United Way Member Agency
200 Main Street
Los Angeles, California 90230

DATE: October 11

Mr. Roger Steiner, CEO
SSS Software
13 Miller Way
Los Angeles, California 90224

Dear Roger,

This letter is a follow-up to our conversation after last night's board meeting. I appreciated your comments during the board meeting about the need for sophisticated computer systems in nonprofit organizations and I especially appreciate your generous offer of assistance to have SSS Software provide assistance to deal with the immediate problem with our accounting system. Since the board voted to fire the computer consultant, I am very worried about getting our reports done in time to meet the state funding cycle.

Thanks again for your offer of help during this crisis.

Sincerely yours,

Janice Polocizwic

Janice Polocizwic
Executive Director

ITEM 5C Copy of Letter

SSS SOFTWARE
13 Miller Way
Los Angeles, CA 90224

213-635-2000

DATE: October 12

Janice Polocizwic
Executive Director, C.A.R.E. Services
200 Main Street
Los Angeles, California 90230

Dear Janice,

I received your fax of October 11. I have asked Paula Sprague, my executive assistant, to line up people to work on your accounting system as soon as possible. Your can expect to hear from her shortly.

Sincerely,

Roger Steiner

Roger Steiner

cc: Paula Sprague, Executive Assistant

ITEM 6 Memo

TO: Michael Grant

FROM: Harry Withers, Group 6 Technical Staff

DATE: October 12

PERSONAL AND CONFIDENTIAL

Our team is having difficulty meeting the submission deadline of November 5 for the Halstrom project. Kim, Fred, Peter, Kyoto, Susan, Mala, and I have been working on the project for several weeks, but are experiencing some problems and may need additional time. I hesitate to write this letter, but the main problem is that our group manager, John Small, is involved in a relationship with Mala. Mala gets John's support for her ideas and brings them to the team as required components of the project. Needless to say, this has posed some problems for the group. Mala's background is especially valuable for this project, but Kim and Fred who have both worked very hard on the project, do not want to work with her. In addition, one member of the team has been unavailable recently because of child-care needs. Commitment to the project and team morale have plummeted. However, we'll do our best to get the project finished as soon as possible. Mala will be on vacation the next two weeks, so I'm expecting that some of us can complete it in her absence.

ITEM 7 Voice Mail

Hello, Michael. This is Jim Bishop of United Hospitals. I wanted to talk with you about the quality assurance project that you are working on for us. When Jose Martinez first started talking with us, I was impressed with his friendliness and expertise. But recently, he doesn't seem to be getting much accomplished and has seemed distant and on-edge in conversations. Today, I asked him about the schedule and he seemed very defensive and not entirely in control of his emotions. I am quite concerned about our project. Please give me a call at 213-951-1234.

ITEM 8 Voice Mail

Hi Michael. This is Armand. I wanted to talk with you about some issues with the Technical Services Phone Line. I've recently received some complaint letters from Phone Line customers whose complaints have included: long delays while waiting for a technician to answer the phone; technicians who are not knowledgeable enough to solve problems and, on occasion, rude service. Needless to say, I'm quite concerned about these complaints.

I believe that the overall quality of the phone line staff is very good, but we continue to be understaffed, even with the recent hires. The new technicians look strong, but are working on the help-line before being fully trained. Antolina, our best tech, often brings her child to work, which is adding to the craziness around here.

I think you should know that we're feeling a lot of stress here. I'll talk to you soon.

ITEM 9 Voice Mail

Hi Chris, it's Pat. Congratulations on your promotion. They definitely picked the right person. It's great news—for me, too. You've been a terrific mentor so far, so I'm expecting to learn a lot from you in your new position. How about lunch next week?

ITEM 10 Voice Mail

Chris, this is Bob Miller. Just thought you'd like to know that John's joke during our planning meeting has disturbed a few of the women in my group. Frankly I think the thing's being blown out of proportion, especially since we all know this is a good place for both men and women to work. Give me a call if you want to chat about this.

ITEM 11 Voice Mail

Hello. This is Lorraine Adams from Westside Hospital. I read in today's Los Angeles Times that you will be taking over from Michael Grant. We haven't met yet, but your division has recently finished two large million dollar projects for Westside. Michael Grant and I had some discussion about a small conversion of a piece of existing software to be compatible with the new systems. The original vendor had said that they would do the work, but has been stalling and I need to move quickly. Can you see if Harris Wilson, Chu Hung Woo, and Elise Soto are available to do this work as soon as possible? They were on the original project and work well with our people. You can call me at 213-555-3456.

Um . . . (long pause) I guess I should tell you that I got a call from Michael offering to do this work. But I think I should stick with SSS Software. Give me a call.

ITEM 12 Voice Mail

Hi Chris, This is Roosevelt Moore calling. I'm a member of your technical/professional staff. I used to report to Janice Ramos, but since she left the firm, I thought I'd bring my concerns directly to you. I'd like to arrange some time to talk with you about my experience since returning from six weeks of paternity leave. Some of my major responsibilities have been turned over to others. I seem to be out of the loop and wonder if my career is at risk. Also, I am afraid that I won't be supported or seriously considered for the opening created by Janice's departure. Frankly, I feel I'm being screwed for taking my leave. I'd like to talk with you this week.

ITEM 13 E-Mail

To: Michael Grant

From: Jose Martinez, Group 1 Technical Staff

Date: October 12

I would like to set up a meeting with you as soon as possible. I suspect that you will get a call from Jim Bishop of United Hospitals and want to be sure that you hear my side of the story first. I have been working on a customized system design for quality assurance for them using a variation of the J-3 product we developed several years ago. They had a number of special requirements and some quirks in their accounting systems, so I have had to put in especially long hours. I've worked hard to meet their demands, but they keep changing the ground rules. I keep thinking, this is just another J-3 I'm working on, but they have been interfering with an elegant design I have developed. It seems I'm not getting anywhere on this project. Then Mr. Bishop asked me if the system was running yet. I was worn out from dealing with the Controller, and I made a sarcastic comment to Mr. Bishop. He gave me a funny look and just walked out of the room.

I would like to talk with you about this situation at your earliest convenience.

ITEM 14 E-Mail

TO: Chris Perillo

FROM: John Small, Group 6 Manager

DATE: October 15

Welcome aboard, Chris. I look forward to meeting with you. I just wanted to put a bug in your ear about finding a replacement for Janice Ramos. One of my technical staff, Mala Abendano, has the ability and drive to make an excellent group manager. I have encouraged her to apply for the position. I'd be happy to talk with you further about this, at your convenience.

ITEM 15 E-Mail

TO: Chris Perillo

FROM: Paula Spague, Executive Assistant to Roger Steiner

DATE: October 15

Roger asked me to let you know about the large contract we have gotten in Kenya. It means that a team of four managers will be making a short trip to determine current needs. They will assign their technical staff the task of developing a system and software here over the next six months, and then the managers and possibly some team members will be spending about 10 months on site in Kenya to handle the implementation. Roger would appreciate an E-mail of your thoughts about the issues to be discussed at this meeting, additional considerations about sending people to Kenya, and about how you will put together an effective team to work on this project. The October 15 memo I sent to you will provide you with some information you'll need to start making these decisions.

ITEM 16 E-Mail

TO: Chris Perillo

FROM: Sharon Shapiro, V. P. of Human Resources

DATE: October 15

RE: Upcoming meeting

I want to update you on the rippling effect of John Small's sexual joke at last week's planning meeting. Quite a few woman have been very upset and have met informally to talk about it. They have decided to call a meeting of all the people concerned about this kind of behavior throughout the firm. I plan to attend, so I'll keep you posted.

Item 17 E-Mail

TO: All SSS-Software Managers
FROM: Sharon Shapiro, Vice President, Human Resources
DATE: October 14
RE: Promotions and External Hires

Year-to-date (January through September) promotions and external hires

	Race					Sex		
Level	White	Black	Asian	Hispanic	Native American	M	F	Total
Hires into Executive Level	0 (0%)	0 (0%)	0 (0%)	0 (0%)	0 (0%)	0 (0%)	0 (0%)	0
Promotions to Executive Level	0 (0%)	0 (0%)	0 (0%)	0 (0%)	0 (0%)	0 (0%)	0 (0%)	0
Hires into Management Level	2 (67%)	1 (33%)	0 (0%)	0 (0%)	0 (0%)	2 (67%)	1 (33%)	3
Promotions to Management Level	7 (88%)	0 (0%)	1 (12%)	0 (0%)	0 (0%)	7 (88%)	1 (12%)	8
Hires into Technical/ Professional Level	10 (36%)	6 (21%)	10 (36%)	2 (7%)	0 (0%)	14 (50%)	14 (50%)	28
Promotions to Technical/ Professional Level	0 (0%)	0 (0%)	0 (0%)	0 (0%)	0 (0%)	0 (0%)	0 (0%)	0
Hires into Non-Management Level	4 (20%)	10 (50%)	2 (10%)	4 (20%)	0 (0%)	6 (30%)	14 (70%)	20
Promotions to Non-Management Level	NA	NA	NA	NA	NA	NA	NA	NA

SSS Software employee (EEO) classification report as of June 30

	Race					Sex		
Level	White	Black	Asian	Hispanic	Native American	M	F	Total
Executive Level	11 (92%)	0 (0%)	1 (8%)	0 (0%)	0 (0%)	11 (92%)	1 (8%)	12
Management Level	43 (90%)	2 (4%)	2 (4%)	1 (2%)	0 (0%)	38 (79%)	10 (21%)	48
Technical/ Professional Level	58 (45%)	20 (15%)	37 (28%)	14 (11%)	1 (1%)	80 (62%)	50 (38%)	130
Non-Management Level	29 (48%)	22 (37%)	4 (7%)	4 (7%)	1 (2%)	12 (20%)	48 (80%)	60
Total	141 (56%)	44 (18%)	44 (18%)	19 (8%)	2 (1%)	141 (56%)	109 (44%)	250

Critical Incidents

Employee raiding

Litson Cotton Yarn Manufacturing Company, located in Murray, New Jersey, decided as a result of increasing labor costs to relocate its plant in Fairlee, a southern community of 4,200. Plant construction was started, and a human resources office was opened in the state employment office, located in Fairlee.

Because of ineffective HR practices in the other three textile mills located within a 50-mile radius of Fairlee, Litson was receiving applications from some of the most highly skilled and trained textile operators in the state. After receiving applications from approximately 500 people, employment was offered to 260 male and female applicants. These employees would be placed immediately on the payroll with instructions to await final installation of machinery, which was expected within the following six weeks.

The managers of the three other textile companies, faced with resignations from their most efficient and best-trained employees, approached the Litson managers with the complaint that their labor force was being "raided." They registered a strong protest to cease such practices and demanded an immediate cancellation of the employment of the 260 people hired by Litson.

Litson managers discussed the ethical and moral considerations involved in offering employment to the 260 people. Litson clearly faced a tight labor market in Fairlee, and management thought that if the 260 employees were discharged, the company would face cancellation of its plans and large construction losses. Litson management also felt obligated to the 260 employees who had resigned from their previous employment in favor of Litson.

The dilemma was compounded when the manager of one community plant reminded Litson that his plant was part of a nationwide chain supplied with cotton yarn from Litson. He implied that Litson's attempts to continue operations in Fairlee could result in cancellation of orders and the possible loss of approximately 18 percent market share. It was also suggested to Litson managers that actions taken by the nationwide textile chain could result in cancellation of orders from other textile companies. Litson's president held an urgent meeting of his top subordinates to (1) decide what to do about the situation in Fairlee, (2) formulate a written policy statement indicating Litson's position regarding employee raiding, and (3) develop a plan for implementing the policy.

Source: J. Champion and J. James, *Critical Incidents in Management: Decision and Policy Issues,* 6th ed. (Burr Ridge, IL: Richard D. Irwin, 1989).

Effective management

Dr. Sam Perkins, a graduate of the Harvard University College of Medicine, had a private practice in internal medicine for 12 years. Fourteen months ago, he was persuaded by the Massachusetts governor to give up private practice to be director of the State Division of Human Services.

After one year as director, Perkins recognized he had made little progress in reducing the considerable inefficiency in the division. Employee morale and effectiveness seemed even lower than when he had assumed the position. He realized his past training and experiences were of a clinical nature with little exposure to effective management techniques. Perkins decided to research literature on the subject of management available to him at a local university.

Perkins soon realized that management scholars are divided on the question of what constitutes effective management. Some believe people are born with certain identifiable personality traits that make them effective managers. Others believe a manager can learn to be effective by treating subordinates with a personal and considerate approach and by giving particular attention to their need for favorable working conditions. Still others emphasize the importance of developing a management style characterized by either authoritarian, democratic, or laissez-faire approaches. Perkins was further confused when he learned that a growing number of scholars advocate that effective management is contingent on the situation.

Since a state university was located nearby, Perkins contacted the dean of its college of business administration. The dean referred him to the director of the college's management center, Professor Joel McCann. Discussions between Perkins and McCann resulted in a tentative agreement that the management center would organize a series of management training sessions for the State Division of Human Services. Before agreeing on the price tag for the management conference, Perkins asked McCann to prepare a proposal reflecting his thoughts on the following questions:

1. How will the question of what constitutes effective management be answered during the conference?
2. What will be the specific subject content of the conference?
3. Who will the instructors be?
4. What will be the conference's duration?
5. How can the conference's effectiveness be evaluated?
6. What policies should the State Division of Human Services adopt regarding who the conference participants should be and how they should be selected? How can these policies be best implemented?

Source: J. Champion and J. James, *Critical Incidents in Management: Decision and Policy Issues,* 6th ed. (Burr Ridge, IL: Richard D. Irwin, 1989). ●

Part Two

Planning and Strategy

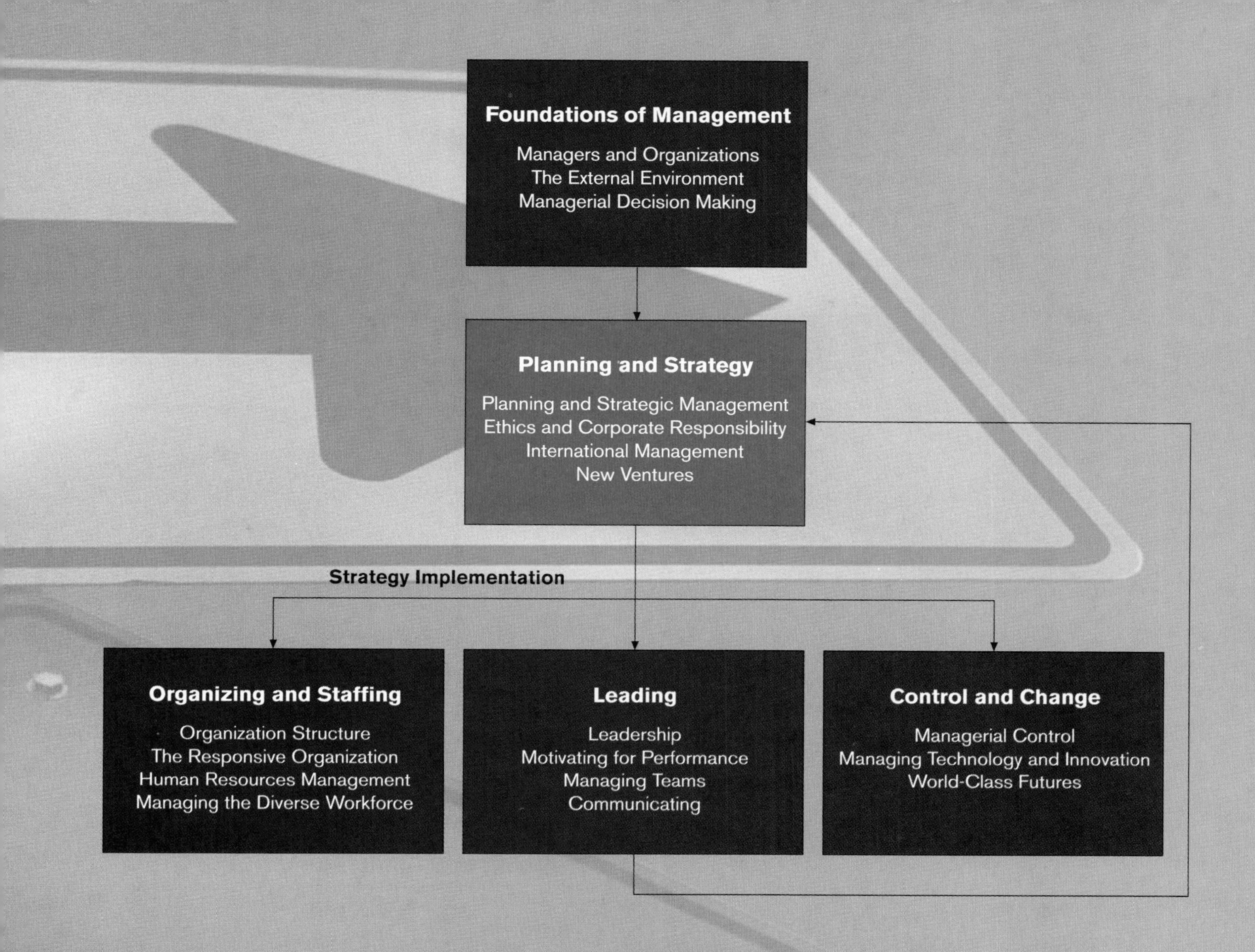

Part II introduces key concepts of planning and strategy. The topics emphasize the decisions made by top managers and their implications for the entire organization. Chapter 4 presents a summary of the planning process and an overview of how senior executives manage strategically. The next three chapters treat subjects that have recently emerged as vital considerations for modern managers. Chapter 5 examines the impact of ethical concerns and social and political factors on major decisions. Chapter 6 addresses the pressing reality of managing in a global competitive environment. Finally, Chapter 7 describes entrepreneurs and the new ventures they create. These chapters will provide you with a clear understanding of the strategic directions that effective organizations pursue.

Chapter Four
Planning and Strategic Management

Manage your destiny, or someone else will.

—Jack Welch, CEO, General Electric

Chapter Outline

Learning Objectives

After studying Chapter 4, you will know:

1. How to proceed through the basic steps in any planning process.
2. How strategic planning differs from tactical and operational planning.
3. Why it is important to analyze both the external environment and internal resources of the firm before formulating a strategy.
4. The choices available for corporate strategy.
5. How companies can achieve competitive advantage through business strategy.
6. How core competencies provide the foundation for business strategy.
7. The keys to effective strategy implementation.

Setting the Stage

Developing the Big Picture at Kodak

When George Fisher took over as CEO of Eastman Kodak in 1994, people expected him to revitalize the company the way he had at Motorola a few years before. At Motorola, Fisher had reduced costs, enhanced quality, and pioneered technology-driven products such as pagers and cellular telephones that had a clear advantage in the market. The challenges at Kodak were no less difficult. Prior to Fisher's arrival, Kodak executives had developed a diversification strategy that used cash from mature film businesses to pay for entry into new, faster-growing markets. In the 1980s, the company looked to everything from drugs to copiers, but none provided the growth engine Kodak needed.

In his first three years at Kodak, Fisher worked to get back to the basic competencies of Kodak in photographic technologies. Rather than continue its strategy of broad diversification, Kodak sold off $8.9 billion in noncore businesses such as chemicals and copiers. That helped reduce costs and lower the company's debt from $7.5 billion to $1.5 billion. But this was only part of the strategy. Fisher has devoted substantial energy to making Kodak more like Motorola, capable of producing new state-of-the-art digital imaging products every few months. Kodak is pouring approximately $500 million a year into research and product development, and company factories are churning out an impressive array of digital cameras, scanners, and other devices at a breakneck clip. Because of Kodak's product breadth, it is far ahead of any other company and sales of digital products continue to increase at about 25 percent a year. However, so far the payoff from Kodak's digital strategy has been elusive.

George Fisher, CEO of Eastman Kodak has been developing a strategy to make the company more innovative and competitive in digital photography. *[James Leynse/Saba]*

The problem is that competitors such as Hewlett-Packard, Fuji, Canon, and Epson are fast and flexible, and are more accustomed to the blistering pace of change in digital technology. They are rapidly producing competing products at lower prices. As a consequence, Kodak has had trouble developing any kind of technological leadership. Winning in the technology arena requires speed and flexibility and critics say that Kodak has a slow bureaucratic culture left over from an earlier manufacturing age. Although Fisher has been able to change the culture at the top, he has been less successful convincing middle and lower level managers. To shake things up, Kodak instituted a pay-for-performance system, but many observers fear that the old-line manufacturing culture continues to impede Kodak's efforts to implement its high-tech growth strategy.

In addition to culture and human resource issues in Kodak's strategy implementation, Fisher and other executives have been busy laying out a plan to significantly cut manufacturing costs and to accelerate Kodak's five-year plan to slash overhead and administrative costs. Fisher also acknowledges the need to cut payroll costs. Kodak's sales per employee are only about half those of Japanese competitor Fuji. Yet even now, Fisher is reluctant to lay off more employees. In response to Wall Street's demand that Kodak lay off 20,000 of Kodak's 94,800 employees, Fisher has been quoted as saying, "I don't know how many of these people have ever run a company." Fisher firmly believes that investing in people is part of the bigger picture in Kodak's long-term growth strategy.

Sources: Geoffrey Smith, "Can George Fisher Save Kodak?" Business Week, *October 20, 1997, pp. 116–28; Peter Johnston, "Kodak Sets Digital Imaging Strategy,"* Graphic Arts Monthly *67, no. 6 (June 1995), p. 81; and Riccardo A. Davis, "Kodak Rethinks Strategy."* Advertising Age *64, no. 20 (May 10, 1993), p. 48.*

Trying to sort out the plans of a company as large and complex as Eastman Kodak can be mind-boggling. Yet there are a few key ideas that are fundamental to the planning process that most companies—including Kodak—use to figure out how to succeed. In this chapter, we examine the most important concepts and processes involved in planning and strategic management. By learning these concepts, and reviewing the steps outlined below, you will be on your way to understanding the current approaches to the strategic management of today's organizations.

An overview of planning fundamentals

Planning is the conscious, systematic process of making decisions about goals and activities that an individual, group, work unit, or organization will pursue in the future. Planning is not an informal or haphazard response to a crisis; it is a purposeful effort, directed and controlled by managers, often drawing on the knowledge and experience of employees throughout the organization. Planning provides individuals and work units with a clear map to follow in their future activities; at the same time this map may allow for individual circumstances and changing conditions.

The importance of formal planning in organizations has grown dramatically. During the first half of this century, most planning was unstructured and fragmented, and formal planning was restricted to a few large corporations. Although management pioneers such as Alfred Sloan of General Motors instituted formal planning processes, planning became a widespread management function only during the last 30 years. While larger organizations adopted formal planning initially, even small firms operated by aggressive, opportunistic entrepreneurs now engage in formal planning.[1]

The basic planning process

situational analysis A process planners use, within time and resource constraints, to gather, interpret, and summarize all information relevant to the planning issue under consideration.

Because planning is a decision process, the important steps followed during formal planning are similar to the basic decision-making steps discussed in Chapter 4. Figure 4.1 shows these formal planning steps and their decision process counterparts.

Step one: situational analysis. As the contingency approach advocates, planning begins with a situational analysis. Within their time and resource constraints, planners should gather, interpret, and summarize all information relevant to the planning issue

figure 4.1
Decision-making stages (Chapter 3) and formal planning steps (Chapter 4)

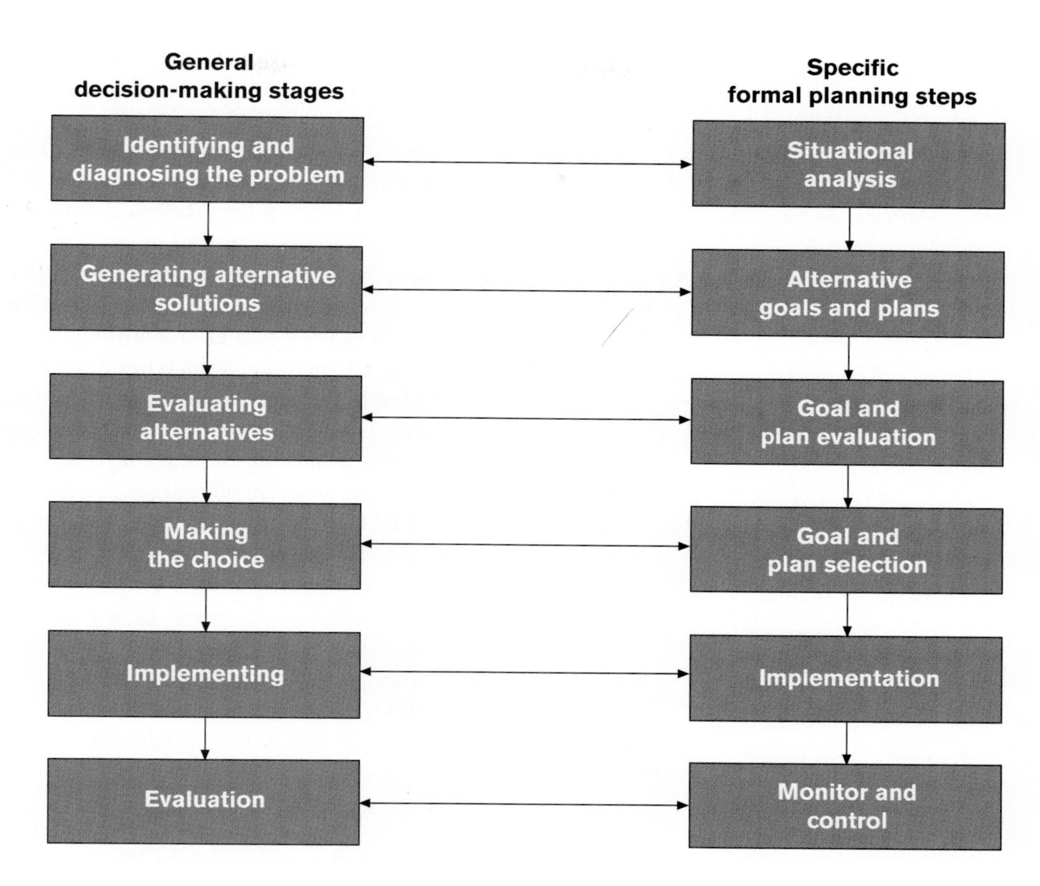

in question. A thorough situational analysis studies past events, examines current conditions, and attempts to forecast future trends. It focuses on the internal forces at work in the organization or work unit and, consistent with the open-systems approach, examines influences from the external environment. The outcome of this step is the identification and diagnosis of planning assumptions, issues, and problems.

A recent situational analysis conducted by a major medical center gathered extensive information from external groups such as consumers, physicians, government and regulatory agencies, insurance companies, and other hospitals. The analysis included information from all departments in these organizations. Historical trends in financial data and the use of various hospital services were examined, and projections were developed based on assumptions about the future. The situational analysis took 10 months, and the information was summarized in a 250-page planning document. To give you an idea of the importance of this step to the planning process, the remaining steps took only three months, and the final set of goals and plans was only 50 pages long!

Step two: alternative goals and plans. Based on the situational analysis, the planning process should generate alternative goals that may be pursued in the future and the alternative plans that may be used to achieve those goals. This step in the process should stress creativity and encourage managers and employees to assume a broad perspective about their jobs. Evaluation of the merits of these alternative goals and plans should be delayed until a range of alternatives has been developed.

goal A target or end that management desires to reach.

Goals are the targets or ends the manager wants to reach. Goals should be specific, challenging, and realistic. Jack Welch's goal of making General Electric first or at least second in all its markets is specific and challenging. When appropriate, goals should also be quantified and linked to a time frame. They should be acceptable to the managers and employees charged with achieving them, and they should be consistent both within and among work units.

plans The actions or means that managers intend to use to achieve organizational goals.

Plans are the actions or means the manager intends to use to achieve goals. At a minimum, this step should outline alternative actions that may lead to the attainment of each goal, the resources required to reach the goal through those means, and the obstacles that may develop. Aramark's plan to become the premier provider of corporate services outlines the company's activities designed to expand business in catering, food services, and uniform services, as well as health and education. This plan is focused on the company's goals of 10 percent annual growth in sales and profitability.[2]

In this chapter we will talk about various types of plans. Some plans, called *single-use plans,* are designed to achieve a set of goals that are not likely to be repeated in the future. For example, city planners might prepare for an upcoming sesquicentennial celebration by putting in place a plan for parades, festivities, speeches, and the like. Other plans, called *standing plans,* focus on ongoing activities designed to achieve an enduring set of goals. For example, many companies have standing plans for their efforts to recruit minorities and women. Frequently, standing plans become more permanent policies and rules for running the organization. Finally, *contingency plans* might be referred to as "what if" plans. They include sets of actions to be taken when a company's initial plans have not worked well or if events in the external environment require a sudden change. British Airway's original plan to penetrate the American marketplace through cooperative arrangements with U.S. Airways did not work out so well. The company is stepping back from that plan and is now pursuing agreements—as a contingency plan—with American Airlines.[3]

Step three: goal and plan evaluation. Next, decision makers must evaluate the advantages, disadvantages, and potential effects of each alternative goal and plan. Decision makers must prioritize those goals or even eliminate some from further consideration. At the same time, the manager needs to consider the implications of alternative plans designed to meet high-priority goals.

In some companies, special teams of managers with diverse backgrounds conduct this evaluation. During major planning efforts at Atlantic Richfield Company (ARCO), senior executives meet with planning groups from strategic planning, public and government affairs, operations, marketing, and other areas. Often the different perspectives and ideas such groups generate lead to a more balanced and comprehensive review of company goals and plans. This approach often identifies new alternatives or refines existing ones.

Step four: goal and plan selection. The planner is now in a position to select the most appropriate and feasible goals and plans. The evaluation process should identify the priorities and trade-offs among goals and plans and leave the final choice to the decision maker. Experienced judgment always plays an important role. However, as you will discover later in the chapter, relying on judgment alone may not be the best way to proceed.

scenario A narrative that describes a particular set of future conditions.

Typically, a formal planning process leads to a written set of goals and plans that are appropriate and feasible within a predicted set of circumstances. In some organizations, the alternative generation, evaluation, and selection steps generate planning **scenarios,** as discussed in Chapter 2. A different contingency plan is attached to each scenario. The manager pursues the goals and implements the plans associated with the most likely scenario. However, the work unit is prepared to switch to another set of plans if the situational contingencies change and another scenario becomes relevant. This approach helps avoid crises and allows greater flexibility and responsiveness.

Step five: implementation. Once managers have selected the goals and plans, they must implement the plans designed to achieve the goals. The best plans are useless unless they are implemented properly. Managers and employees must understand the plan, have the resources necessary to implement it, and be motivated to do so. If both managers and employees have participated in the previous steps of the planning process, the implementation phase probably will be more effective and efficient. Employees usually are better informed, more committed, and more highly motivated when a goal or plan is one that they helped develop.

Finally, successful implementation requires that the plan be linked to other systems in the organization, particularly the budget and reward systems. If the budget does not provide the manager with sufficient financial resources to execute the plan, the plan is probably doomed. Similarly, goal achievement must be linked to the organization's reward system. Many organizations use incentive programs to encourage employees to achieve goals and to implement plans properly. Commissions, salaries, promotions, bonuses, and other rewards are based on successful performance.

Step six: monitor and control. Although it is sometimes ignored, the final step in the formal planning process—monitor and control—is essential. Because planning is an ongoing, repetitive process, managers must continually monitor the actual performance of their work units according to the unit's goals and plans. Also, they must develop control systems that allow the organization to take corrective action when the plans are implemented improperly or when the situation changes. You will study control systems in greater detail later in this chapter and in Chapter 16.

Levels of planning

In Chapter 1, you learned about the three major types of managers: top-level (*strategic* managers), middle-level (*tactical* managers), and front-line (*operational* managers). Because planning is an important management function, managers at all three levels use it. However, the scope and activities of the planning process at each level of the organization often differ.

Strategic planning

Strategic planning involves making decisions about the organization's long-term goals and strategies. Strategic plans have a strong external orientation and cover major portions of the organization. Senior executives are responsible for the development and execution of the strategic plan, although they usually do not personally formulate or implement the entire plan.

strategic planning A set of procedures for making decisions about the organization's long-term goals and strategies.

strategic goals Major targets or end results relating to the organization's long-term survival, value, and growth.

strategy A pattern of actions and resource allocations designed to achieve the organization's goals.

Strategic goals are major targets or end results that relate to the long-term survival, value, and growth of the organization. Strategic managers—top-level managers—usually establish goals that reflect both effectiveness (providing appropriate outputs) and efficiency (a high ratio of outputs to inputs). Typical strategic goals include various measures of return to shareholders, profitability, quantity and quality of outputs, market share, productivity, and contribution to society.

A **strategy** is a pattern of actions and resource allocations designed to achieve the goals of the organization. The strategy an organization implements is an attempt to match the skills and resources of the organization to the opportunities found in the external environment; that is, every organization has certain strengths and weaknesses. The actions, or strategies, the organization implements should be directed toward building strengths in areas that satisfy the wants and needs of consumers and other key actors in the organization's external environment. Also, some organizations may implement strategies that change or influence the external environment, as discussed in Chapter 2.

Employees at Wal-Mart have been instructed to "think like a partner" to help keep costs down and also have received company stock.
[Jose Carrillo/PhotoEdit]

Tactical and operational planning

tactical planning A set of procedures for translating broad strategic goals and plans into specific goals and plans that are relevant to a distinct portion of the organization, such as a functional area like marketing.

operational planning The process of identifying the specific procedures and processes required at lower levels of the organization.

Once the organization's strategic goals and plans are identified, they become the basis of planning done by middle-level and frontline managers. Goals and plans become more specific and involve shorter periods of time as planning moves from the strategic level to the operational level. **Tactical planning** translates broad strategic goals and plans into specific goals and plans that are relevant to a definite portion of the organization, often a functional area like marketing or human resources. Tactical plans focus on the major actions that a unit must take to fulfill its part of the strategic plan. **Operational planning** identifies the specific procedures and processes required at lower levels of the organization. Frontline managers usually develop plans for very short periods of time and focus on routine tasks such as production runs, delivery schedules, and human resources requirements.

The organization's strategic, tactical, and operational goals and plans must be consistent and mutually supportive. Wal-Mart, for example, has built is growth strategy around the notion of everyday low prices. A key tactical planning issue has been finding ways to maintain control over costs. Sam Walton, the founder of Wal-Mart, believed that every employee should think like a partner if he or she were expected to keep costs down. To increase their commitment to strategic goals and enhance their sense of belonging, he called them "associates" and gave them company stock. The company has designed incentive systems around cost containment and profitability. In addition, to avoid high costs and head-to-head competition, Wal-Mart has focused on mid-sized towns in regional markets of the Midwest.

To fit the strategic goal of cost containment into its operating systems, Wal-Mart invested early in advanced distribution systems and merchandise-tracking systems. The company uses electronic data transfer (EDI) technology to make certain that products are on the shelves and inventory costs are kept to a minimum. While the up-front costs were significant, the company has a much more efficient process for handling supply chains and distribution channels. The result of careful alignment of strategic, tactical, and operational planning is that Wal-Mart has achieved a cost base that is significantly lower than competitors such as Sears and Kmart.[4]

Using this overview of planning as background, we will devote the remainder of this chapter to strategic issues, concepts, and processes. Strategic decision making is one of the most exciting and controversial topics in management today. In fact, many organizations currently are changing the ways they develop and execute their strategic plans.

From the Pages of BusinessWeek

Adrenaline Rush at Adidas

After Robert Louis-Dreyfus, CEO of Adidas, clinched a deal on Sept. 15 to buy French sports-equipment maker Salomon (for $1.3 billion), he celebrated with Salomon family members over champagne at Geneva's swank Hotel des Bergues. And if Louis-Dreyfus was feeling a little flushed, it probably wasn't from the champagne. In one deft strategic move, Louis-Dreyfus had broadened his sports company's product base and balanced its geographic reach. With better insulation against fickle swings in fashion and regional downturns, Adidas is a much stronger competitor in the $100 billion global sports-equipment market.

Adidas and archrival Nike Inc. are squaring off to see which will dominate the sporting-goods market in the next century. While Nike has expand aggressively outside its U.S. stronghold Adidas has outmaneuvered Nike in the rush to diversify from shoes and apparel. Adidas' diversification via Salomon vaults it past Reebok into the No. 2 spot worldwide. The combined company, to be called Adidas-Salomon, will have sales of about $3.4 billion annually. Salomon, which makes ski gear, golf clubs, and bike components, will boost Adidas in Asia and North America, where it is weak. And the combined company's reliance on the slow-growing European market will decline, since sales there will drop to 60% of the total, down from 66% for Adidas before the merger.

To be sure, Nike remains the industry leader and the company to beat. Its annual sales of $9.1 billion dwarf those of all rivals. It will outspend the new, bulked-up Adidas 2-to-1 on marketing and promotions, with annual outlays of about $1.1 billion. One of Nike's most valuable assets is the stable of superstar athletes who promote its Swoosh trademark, from golf phenom Tiger Woods to basketballer Michael Jordan. But Nike has had only limited success with its diversification strategy. Several years ago, the company bought Bauer, a Canadian maker of hockey skates and accessories. And that venture has done very little for the company's competitiveness. Shoes and clothing still make up 95% of Nike's sales.

Salomon's product line gives Adidas a new edge. The company makes finely engineered products that command premium prices and deliver higher margins than T-shirts or sneakers. They also attract attention from upscale consumers. For instance, two years ago, Salomon introduced thicker "bubble" shafts in its Taylor Made golf-club brand that give a player's swing more power. Sales have surged, and Taylor is the No. 2 brand in the U.S. What's more, Salomon's bindings are the industry standard for both downhill and cross-country skis. One-fourth of Adidas-Salomon's sales will come from such high-margin products, vs. just 5% for the stand-alone Adidas.

Although Adidas still won't be able to match Nike's marketing muscle, its spending will probably become more efficient. For instance, it may introduce Taylor Made golf bags and apparel, so spending on the brand will cover a wider range of products.

So far, Adidas hasn't been able to steal much market share from Nike. Instead, the fight between the titans is costing smaller players, say analysts. In Japan, where Nike is No. 1, local brands such as Asics have lost share. And in the U.S., Fila's order book for the next six months has dried up. Louis-Dreyfus knows all too well, however, that he must keep his eye on the ball–the one emblazoned with a Nike Swoosh.

Discussion Questions

1. What are the pros and cons of Adidas' purchase of French sports-equipment maker Salomon? What reasons do you suppose there were for Adidas to pursue this strategy?
2. What will the short-term effects of this strategic move be for the industry? What will the long-term effects be?
3. What course of action would you recommend to competitors in this industry to compete with the Nike and surging Adidas? What should Adidas do to protect their growing market share?

Source: David Woodruff and Mia Trinephi "An Adrenaline Rush at Adidas," *Business Week:* September 29, 1997. ●

Strategic planning: yesterday and today

From the 1960s through the mid-1980s, strategic planning often emphasized a top-down approach to goal setting and planning.[5] That is, senior managers and specialized strategic planning units developed goals and plans for the entire organization. Tactical and operational managers often received goals and plans from staff members, and their own planning activities were limited to specific procedures and budgets for their units.

During this period, individual companies and consulting firms innovated a variety of analytical techniques and planning approaches, many of which became corporate fads. These techniques often were used inappropriately and led to strategic decisions based on simplistic conclusions and evaluations. In many instances, senior managers spent more time with their planning staffs and consultants than with the managers who worked for them. Often a wide gap developed between strategic managers and tactical

McDonald's tactical planning efforts have resulted in a menu that now includes everything from the renowned Big Mac to pizza, tacos, and egg rolls.
[Michael Abramson]

and operational managers. Managers and employees throughout their organizations felt alienated and lost their commitment to the organization's success.

Today, however, senior executives increasingly are involving managers throughout the organization in the strategy formation process.[6] The problems just described and the rapidly changing environment of the 1980s and 1990s have forced executives to look to all levels of the organization for ideas and innovations to make their firms more competitive. Although the CEO and other top managers continue to furnish the strategic direction or "vision" of the organization, tactical and even operational managers often provide valuable inputs to the organization's strategic plan. In some cases, these managers also have substantial autonomy to formulate or change their own plans. This increases flexibility and responsiveness, critical requirements of success in the modern organization.

strategic management A process that involves managers from all parts of the organization in the formulation and implementation of strategic goals and strategies.

Because of this trend, a new term for the strategic planning process has emerged: *strategic management.* **Strategic management** involves managers from all parts of the organization in the formulation and implementation of strategic goals and strategies. It integrates strategic planning and management into a single process. Strategic planning becomes an ongoing activity in which all managers are encouraged to think strategically and to focus on long-term, externally oriented issues as well as short-term tactical and operational issues.

Figure 4.2 shows the six major components of the strategic management process: (1) establishment of mission, vision, and goals; (2) analysis of external opportunities and threats; (3) analysis of internal strengths and weaknesses; (4) SWOT analysis and strategy formulations; (5) strategy implementation; and (6) strategic control. Because this process is a planning and decision process, it is similar to the planning framework discussed earlier. Although organizations may use different terms or emphasize different parts of the process, the components and concepts described in this section are found either explicitly or implicitly in every organization.

Step 1: Establishment of mission, vision, and goals

mission An organization's basic purpose and scope of operations.

The first step in strategic planning is establishing a mission, vision, and goals for the organization. The **mission** is the basic purpose and values of the organization, as well as its scope of operations. It is a statement of the organization's reason to exist. The mission often is written in terms of the general clients it serves. Depending on the scope of the organization, the mission may be broad or narrow. For example, the mission of Kellogg Company is to be the world's leading producer of ready-to-eat cereal products and to

figure 4.2 The strategic management process

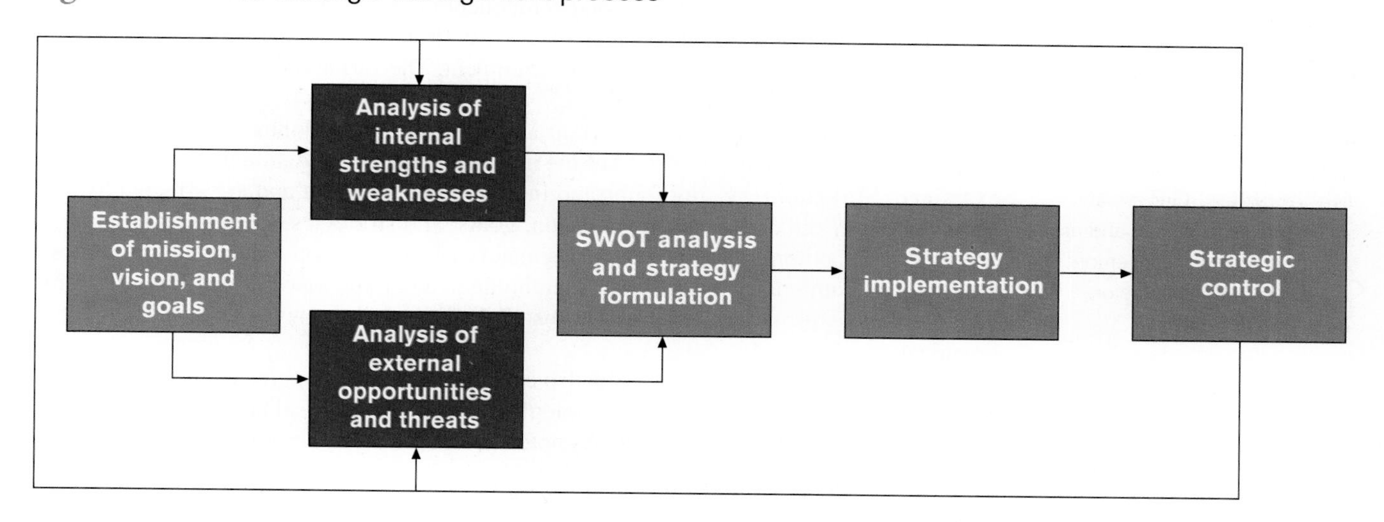

manufacture frozen pies and waffles, toaster pastries, soups, and other convenience foods. On the other hand, the local bar found next to most campuses has the implicit mission of selling large quantities of inexpensive beer to college students.

strategic vision The long-term direction and strategic intent of a company.

The **strategic vision** moves beyond the mission statement to provide a perspective on where the company is headed and what the organization can become. Although the terms *mission* and *vision* often are used interchangeably, the vision statement ideally clarifies the long-term direction of the company and its *strategic intent.* Shell Oil, for example, has a stated vision of becoming the "premier U.S. company." As described below, this vision conveys Shell's dedication to technology development, customer service, employee development, and community involvement.[7]

Shell Oil Company's Mission and Vision

Mission:

Shell Oil Company is in business to excel in the oil, gas, petrochemical, and related businesses in the United States and where we add value internationally. In doing so, our mission is to maximize long-term shareholder value by being the best at meeting the expectations of customers, employees, suppliers, and the public.

We are an independently managed company within the Royal Dutch/Shell Group that benefits from and contributes to the Group's worldwide knowledge and technology base.

Vision:

Our vision is to be the premier U.S. company with sustained world-class performance in all aspects of our business.

We will be a dynamic characterized by our integrity, customer focus, profitable growth, the value placed on people, and superior applications of technology. We will be the best at generating and applying new ideas and learning faster than other organizations.

Customers will prefer us because of our unsurpassed responsiveness and our ability to provide value. People will be proud to work for Shell because we consistently attain superior business results, offer fulfilling work, and provide the opportunity for individuals to achieve their full potential. The communities in which we operate will welcome us because of our sensitivity and involvement.

We, the people of Shell, are the key to achieving this vision and will be distinguished by our professionalism, energy, sense of urgency to improve, and our shared core values.

Strategic goals evolve from the mission and vision of the organization. The chief executive officer of the organization, with the input and approval of the board of directors, establishes the mission, vision, and major strategic goals. These three statements need to be communicated to everyone who has contact with the organization.

Step 2: Analysis of external opportunities and threats

The mission and vision drive the second component of the strategic management process, analysis of the external environment. Successful strategic management depends on an accurate and thorough evaluation of the environment. The various components of the environment were introduced in Chapter 2.

stakeholders Groups and individuals who affect and are affected by the achievement of the organization's mission, goals, and strategies.

Table 4.1 lists some of the important activities in an environmental analysis. The analysis begins with an examination of the industry. Next, organizational stakeholders are examined. **Stakeholders** are groups and individuals who affect and are affected by the achievement of the organization's mission, goals, and strategies. They include buyers, suppliers, competitors, government and regulatory agencies, unions and employee groups, the financial community, owners and shareholders, and trade associations. The environmental analysis provides a map of these stakeholders and the ways they influence the organization.[8]

The environmental analysis should also examine other forces in the environment, such as macroeconomic conditions and technological factors. One critical task in environmental analysis is forecasting future trends. As noted in Chapter 2, forecasting techniques range

table 4.1
Environmental Analysis

Industry and market analysis
- *Industry profile:* major product lines and significant market segments in the industry.
- *Industry growth:* growth rates for the entire industry, growth rates for key market segments, projected changes in patterns of growth, and the determinants of growth.
- *Industry forces:* threat of new industry entrants, threat of substitutes, economic power of buyers, economic power of suppliers, and internal industry rivalry (recall Chapter 2).

Competitor analysis
- *Competitor profile:* major competitors and their market shares.
- *Competitor analysis:* goals, strategies, strengths, and weaknesses of each major competitor.
- *Competitor advantages:* the degree to which industry competitors have differentiated their products or services or achieved cost leadership.

Political and regulatory analysis
- *Legislation and regulatory activities* and their effects on the industry.
- *Political activity:* the level of political activity that organizations and associations within the industry undertake (see Chapter 5).

Social analysis
- *Social issues:* current and potential social issues and their effects on the industry.
- *Social interest groups:* consumer, environmental, and similar activist groups that attempt to influence the industry (see Chapters 5 and 6).

Human resources analysis
- *Labor issues:* key labor needs, shortages, opportunities, and problems confronting the industry (see Chapters 10 and 11).

Macroeconomic analysis
- *Macroeconomic conditions:* economic factors that affect supply, demand, growth, competition, and profitability within the industry.

Technological analysis
- *Technological factors:* scientific or technical methods that affect the industry, particularly recent and potential innovations (see Chapter 17).

from simple judgment to complex mathematical models that examine systematic relationships among many variables. Even simple quantitative techniques outperform the intuitive assessments of experts. Judgment is susceptible to bias, and managers have a limited ability to process information. Managers should use subjective judgments as inputs to quantitative models or when they confront new situations.

The example of Compaq Computer Corporation shows the power of understanding the external environment, and correctly forecasting future trends in the industry.

Compaq really understands its market!

From its beginnings, Compaq Computer Corporation had achieved success in the PC business by understanding its marketplace. As the most successful start-up company in history, Compaq has bested competitors such as IBM, Hewlett-Packard, Packard Bell, and Apple to become the market leader in the PC industry.

In 1993, Compaq made its first move to adapt to environmental changes. While the company established its early reputation on uncompromising engineering and technological innovation, Compaq transformed itself from a performance-is-king

company with a high-priced line of products into an aggressive, branded, low-cost producer with multiple product lines. Many experts argued the strategy was too risky and predicted that Compaq was doomed. But Compaq executives realized that cost and quality were no longer strategic trade-offs as many had assumed; a company could and should pursue both fervently. Compaq also had correctly identified that the market was changing and it was time to segment its product lines to fit different kinds of customers. It was the first company to offer three kinds of desktop computers, and two kinds of notebook computers.

Then in 1996, Compaq made another bold move based on its projection that computers priced under $1,000 would soon become hugely popular. The company picked a Cyrix microprocessor to power its first low-end system (Cyrix is a rival of Intel). The Cyrix chip, which was specifically designed for less-expensive computers, cut Compaq's cost per machine by about $100. To keep other costs down, Compaq contracted with First International Computer Inc. to assemble the machines in Austin, Texas. As a result, Compaq was in an early position to sell less expensive machines and still maintain a healthy profit margin.

The gamble has paid off for Compaq. While other competitors have been blind-sided by these market changes (IBM, for example, has had to consolidate its home PC and business PC businesses into one unit), Compaq's revenues and profits are up about 50 percent.

Sources: Evan Ramsted, "As Cheaper PCs Trip Up Rivals, Compaq Scores," *The Wall Street Journal*, October 17, 1997, pp. B1, B4; and Stewart Alsop, "I Guess Compaq and Lotus Know What They're Doing After All," *Infoworld*, July 19, 1993, p. 4.

This Compaq example illustrates how organizations can develop a clear sense of market opportunities by analyzing the external environment. In the same way, executives can identify potential threats as well. Of course, what is an opportunity to one company may be a threat to another (as the comparison between Compaq and IBM shows).

Frequently, the difference between an opportunity and a threat depends upon how a company positions itself strategically. For example, Southwest Airline's original base of operations at Love Field (outside of Dallas, Texas) was originally seen as a problem for the company. Other major competitors were permitted to fly into the larger and state-of-the-art Dallas–Fort Worth Airport, but Southwest was not. However, given this apparent threat, Southwest built its strategy around point-to-point flights into smaller airports that catered to business travelers. Other airlines soon found that they could not compete with Southwest in its niche. So what was originally seen as a threat turned into an opportunity for Southwest.[9]

Step 3: analysis of internal strengths and weaknesses

At the same time external analysis is conducted, the strengths and weaknesses of major functional areas within the organization are assessed. Internal analysis provides strategic decision makers with an inventory of the organization's skills and resources as well as its overall and functional performance levels. Many of your other business courses will prepare you to conduct internal analysis. Table 4.2 lists some of the major components of the internal resource analysis.

Resources Inputs to a system that can enhance performance.

Resources and core competencies

Without question, strategic planning has been strongly influenced in recent year by a focus on internal resources. **Resources** are

table 4.2
Internal resource analysis

Financial analysis

Examines financial strengths and weaknesses through financial statements such as a balance sheet and an income statement and compares trends to historical and industry figures (see Chapter 18).

Human resources assessment

Examines strengths and weaknesses of all levels of management and employees and focuses on key human resources activities, including recruitment, selection, placement, training, labor (union) relationships, compensation, promotion, appraisal, quality of work life, and human resources planning (see Chapters 10 and 11).

Marketing audit

Examines strengths and weaknesses of major marketing activities and identifies markets, key market segments, and the competitive position (market share) of the organization within key markets.

Operations analysis

Examines the strengths and weaknesses of the manufacturing, production, or service delivery activities of the organization (see Chapters 9, 16, and 17).

Other internal resource analyses

Examine, as necessary and appropriate, the strengths and weaknesses of other organizational activities, such as research and development (product and process), management information systems, engineering, and purchasing.

inputs to production (recall systems theory) that can be accumulated over time to enhance the performance of a firm. Resources can take many forms, but tend to fall into two broad categories: (1) *tangible assets* such as real estate, production facilities, raw materials, and so on, and (2) *intangible assets* such as company reputation, culture, technical knowledge, patents, as well as accumulated learning and experience. The Walt Disney Company, for example, has developed its strategic plan on combinations of tangible assets (e.g., hotels and theme parks) as well as intangible assets (brand recognition, talented craftspeople, culture focused on customer service).[10]

Effective internal analysis provides a clearer understanding of how a company can compete through its resources. Resources are a source of competitive advantage only under certain circumstances. First, if the resource is instrumental for creating customer *value*—that is, if it increases the benefits customers derive from a product or service relative to the costs they incur—then the resource can lead to a competitive advantage. For example, Wal-Mart's computerized inventory control system mentioned above helps make certain that products are on the shelves and that inventory costs are minimized. In this case, Wal-Mart's information technology is clearly a valuable resource.

Second, resources are a source of advantage if they are *rare* and not equally available to all competitors. Even for extremely valuable resources, if all competitors have equal access, the resource cannot provide a source of competitive advantage. For example, when long-distance telephone service was deregulated, AT&T no longer had exclusive use of its telecommunications infrastructure. For companies such as Merck, DuPont, Dow Chemical, and others, patented formulas represent important resources that are both rare and valuable.

Third, if resources are *difficult to imitate,* they provide a source of competitive advantage. Xerox, for example, believed for many years that no one could duplicate its reprographic capabilities. Kodak and Canon soon proved Xerox wrong. McDonald's brand-name recognition, on the other hand, has been extremely difficult for competitors such as Burger King, Wendy's, and others to duplicate.[11]

Finally, resources can enhance a firm's competitive advantage when they are well *organized*. For example, as strategies are changed and organizations are restructured, many companies lay off long-time employees and lose as well their potentially valuable skills. To avoid this problem and maintain its flexibility, AT&T has developed its own internal employment agency—called Resource Link—to reassign "at-risk" employees to other jobs within the company rather than laying them off. Resource Link employs AT&T people full-time and contracts them out to various AT&T businesses on a part-time basis. Resource Link provides AT&T a great deal of flexibility, helps manage the flow of people throughout the organization, and ensures that the company makes the most of its valuable human resources.[12]

As shown in Figure 4.3, when resources that are valuable, rare, inimitable, and organized, they can be viewed as a company's core competencies. Simply stated, a **core competence** is something a company does especially well relative to its competitors. Honda, for example, has a core competence in small engine design and manufacturing; Sony has a core competence in miniaturization; Federal Express has a core competence in logistics and customer service. Typically, a core competence refers to a set of skills or expertise in some activity, rather than physical or financial assets. For example, among U.S. automobile manufacturers, General Motors has traditionally been viewed as having a core competence in marketing, while Ford has established quality as its number one strength. Recently Chrysler redefined its core competence around design and engineering.

core competencies The unique skills or knowledge an organization possesses that give it an edge over competitors.

Benchmarking Benchmarking is the process of assessing how well one company's basic functions and skills compare to those of some other company or set of companies. The goal of benchmarking is to thoroughly understand the "best practices" of other firms, and to undertake actions to achieve both better performance and lower costs. For example, Xerox Corporation, a pioneer in benchmarking, established a program to study 67 of its

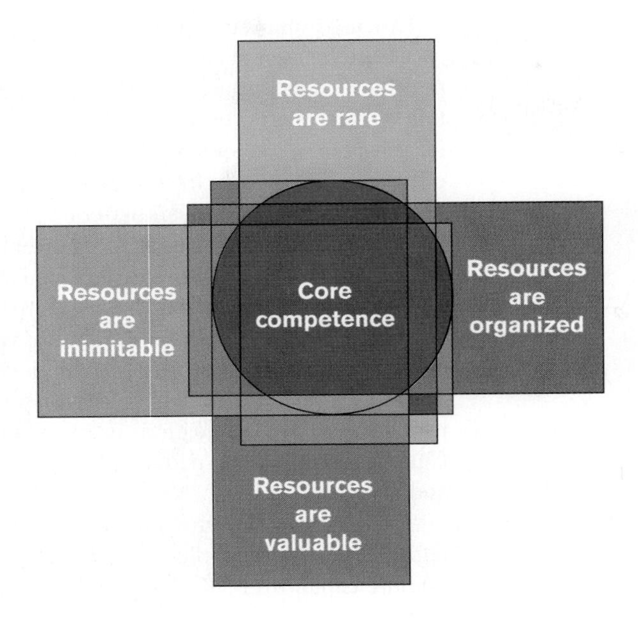

figure 4.3
Resources and core competence

key work processes against "world class" companies. Many of these companies were not in the copier business. For example, in an effort to improve its order fulfillment process, Xerox studied L. L. Bean, the clothing mail-order company. Benchmarking programs have helped Xerox and a myriad of other companies such as Ford, Corning, Hewlett-Packard, and Anheuser-Busch make great strides in eliminating inefficiencies and improving competitiveness. Perhaps the only downside of benchmarking is that it only helps a company perform as well as its competitors; strategic management ultimately is about surpassing those companies.[13]

SWOT analysis A comparison of strengths, weaknesses, opportunities, and threats that help executives formulate strategy.

Step 4: SWOT analysis and strategy formulation

After analyzing the external environment and internal resources, strategic decision makers have the information they need to formulate corporate, business, and functional strategies of the organization. A comparison of strengths, weaknesses, opportunities, and threats is normally referred to as a **SWOT analysis.** SWOT analysis helps executives summarize the major facts and forecasts derived from the external and internal analyses. From this, executives can derive a series of statements that identify the primary and secondary strategic issues confronting the organization. Strategy formulation builds on SWOT analysis to utilize strengths of the organization in order to capitalize on opportunities, counteract threats, and alleviate internal weaknesses. In short, strategy formulation moves from simply analysis to devising a coherent course of action.

corporate strategy The set of businesses, markets, or industries in which an organization competes and the distribution of resources among those entities.

concentration A strategy employed for an organization that operates a single business and competes in a single industry.

vertical integration The acquisition or development of new businesses that produce parts or components of the organization's product.

concentric diversification A strategy used to add new businesses that produce related products or are involved in related markets and activities.

conglomerate diversification A strategy used to add new businesses that produce unrelated products or are involved in unrelated markets and activities.

Corporate strategy

Corporate strategy identifies the set of businesses, markets, or industries in which the organization competes and the distribution of resources among those businesses. An organization has four basic corporate strategy alternatives, ranging from very specialized to highly diverse. A **concentration** strategy focuses on a single business competing in a single industry. In the food-retailing industry, Kroger, Safeway, and A&P all pursue concentration strategies. Frequently companies pursue concentration strategies to gain entry into an industry, when industry growth is good, or when the company has a narrow range of competencies.

A **vertical integration** strategy involves expanding the domain of the organization into supply channels or to distributors. At one time, Henry Ford had fully integrated his company from the ore mines needed to make steel all the way to the showrooms where his cars were sold. Vertical integration is generally used to eliminate uncertainties and reduce costs associated with suppliers or distributors. A strategy of **concentric diversification** involves moving into new businesses that are related to the company's original core business. William Marriott expanded his original restaurant business outside Washington, D.C., by moving into airline catering, hotels, and fast food. Each of these businesses within the hospitality industry is related in terms of the services they provide, the skills necessary for success, and the customers they attract. Often companies such as Marriott pursue a strategy of concentric diversification to take advantage of their strengths in one business to gain advantage in another. Because the businesses are related, the products, markets, technologies, or capabilities used in one business can be transferred to another.

In contrast to concentric diversification, **conglomerate diversification** is a corporate strategy that involves expansion into unrelated businesses. Union Pacific Corporation has diversified from its original base in railroads to such wide-ranging industries as oil and gas exploration, mining, microwave and fiber optic systems, hazardous waste disposal, trucking, and real estate. Typically, companies pursue a conglomerate diversification strategy to minimize risks due to market fluctuations in one industry. The corporate strategy of an organization is sometimes called its business portfolio. One of the most popular techniques for analyzing and communicating corporate strategy has been the BCG matrix.

The BCG matrix

Over the past 30 years, many U.S. corporations have purchased or developed new businesses. These corporations have changed from individual businesses competing in a single industry to broad collections of businesses competing in a variety of industries.

In response to senior executives' needs to understand and manage complex, modern organizations, the Boston Consulting Group (BCG) introduced the growth/share matrix. The BCG matrix is shown here. Each business in the corporation is plotted on the matrix based on the growth rate of its market and the relative strength of its competitive position in that market (market share). The business is represented by a circle whose size depends on the business's contribution to corporate revenues.

High-growth, weak-competitive-position businesses are called *question marks.* They require substantial investment to improve their position; otherwise, divestiture is recommended. High-growth, strong-competitive-position businesses are called *stars.* These businesses require heavy investment, but their strong position allows them to generate the needed revenues. Low-growth, strong-competitive-position businesses are called *cash cows.* These businesses generate revenues in excess of their investment needs and therefore fund other businesses. Finally, low-growth, weak-competitive-position businesses are called *dogs.* The remaining revenues from these businesses are realized, and then the businesses are divested.

Although the BCG matrix helps identify businesses that should be sold, it does not help managers of an individual business develop strategies to improve its competitiveness. Furthermore, the nicknames can lead to self-fulfilling prophecies. For example, a mature business may receive inadequate investment and be abandoned despite its potential for long-term profits and growth. This is particularly a problem for a business labeled a *dog.*

figure 4.3
Resources and core competence.

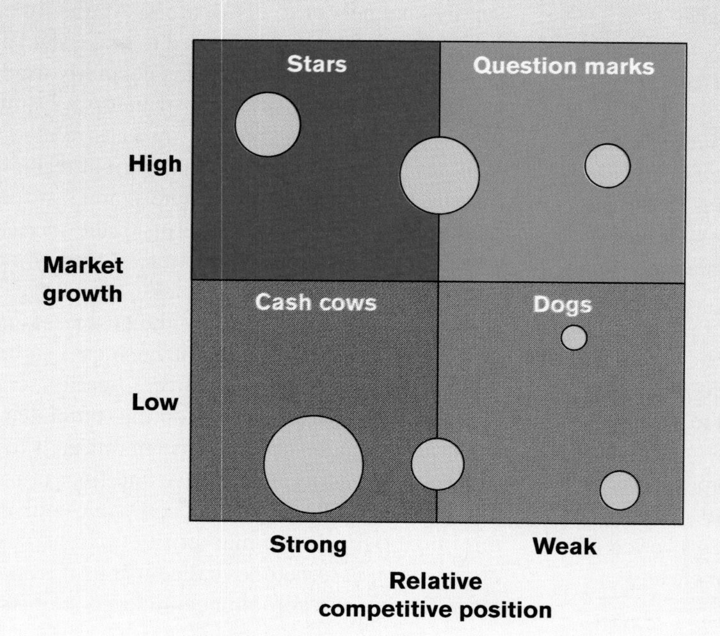

The BCG Matrix and similar tools can help both the corporation and the businesses if they are used as vehicles for discussion rather than as bases for major strategic decisions. The matrix should be applied with other techniques, and strategic managers must emphasize the development of long-term competitive advantages for all businesses. No single technique is a substitute for creativity, insight, or leadership.

Sources: P. Haspeslagh, "Portfolio Planning: Uses and Limits," *Harvard Business Review* 60, no. 1 (1982), pp. 58–67; R. Hamermesh, *Making Strategy Work* (New York: John Wiley & Sons, 1986); and R. A. Proctor, "Toward a New Model for Product Portfolio Analysis," *Management Decision* 28, no. 3 (1990), pp. 14–17.

Trends in corporate strategy In recent years, corporate America has been swept by a wave of mergers and acquisitions (such as Chrysler and Mercedes Benz, Boeing and McDonnell Douglas). Such mergers and acquisitions often influence the organization's corporate strategy, either by concentrating in one industry or by diversifying its portfolio.

The value of implementing a diversified corporate strategy depends on individual circumstances. Many critics have argued that unrelated diversification hurts a company more often than it helps them. In recent years, a number of diversified companies have sold their peripheral businesses so they could concentrate on a more focused portfolio. For example, Merck & Company sold its consumer products business to focus on the application of biotechnology in the pharmaceutical industry. Sears sold Allstate Insurance to concentrate more on the core business of retail merchandising. Kodak sold off Eastman Chemical to boost profitability and concentrate more on their imaging business.[14]

On the other hand, the diversification efforts of an organization competing in a slow-growth, mature, or threatened industry often are applauded. Many recent bank mergers, such as the creation of Citigroup from Travelers and Citicorp, were designed to yield greater efficiencies and increased market share in the banking industry.

Although the merits of diversification are an issue for continued study, most observers agree that organizations usually perform better if they implement a more concentric diversification strategy in which businesses are somehow related or similar to one another. Disney, for example, spent $19 billion to merge with ABC/Cap Cities. While the two companies are somewhat different, their businesses are complementary. Disney's success in movies and videos is matched by ABC's network TV as well as its production capabilities in Cap Cities. Though Disney has a cable channel (The Disney Channel), its ability to reach millions of viewers has been enhanced by ABC's presence in network television.[15]

business strategy The major actions by which a business competes in a particular industry or market.

Business strategy After the top management team and board make the corporate strategic decisions, executives must determine how they will compete in each business area. **Business strategy** defines the major actions by which an organization builds and strengthens its competitive position in the marketplace. A competitive advantage typically results from one of two generic business strategies introduced here and elaborated in Chapter 7.[16]

low-cost strategy A strategy an organization uses to build competitive advantage by being efficient and offering a standard, no-frills product.

First, organizations such as Wal-Mart and Southwest Airlines (mentioned earlier) pursue competitive advantage through **low-cost strategies.** Businesses using a low-cost strategy attempt to be efficient and offer a standard, no-frills product. They often are large and try to take advantage of economies of scale in production or distribution. In many cases, the large size allows them to sell their products and services at a lower price, which leads to higher market share, volume, and, ultimately, profits. To succeed, an organization using this strategy often must be the cost leader in its industry or market segment. However, even

a cost leader must offer a product that is acceptable to customers when compared to competitors' products. In the toy-retailing industry, Toys 'Я' Us has successfully used a low-cost strategy in the United States, emphasizing large stores and prices that are 10 to 15 percent lower than competitors'. The company is now using this strategy to penetrate overseas markets, including Japan.[17]

differentiation strategy A strategy an organization uses to build competitive advantage by being unique in its industry or market segment along one or more dimensions.

Second, an organization may pursue a **differentiation strategy.** With a differentiation strategy, a company attempts to be unique in its industry or market segment along some dimensions that customers value. This unique or differentiated position within the industry often is based on high product quality, excellent marketing and distribution, or superior service. Nordstom's commitment to quality and customer service in the retail apparel industry is an excellent example of a differentiation strategy. While perhaps not as fancy as competitors such as Saks Fifth Avenue and Neiman Marcus, Nordstrom's strategy focuses on providing a full assortment of clothing and accessories to customers and ensuring their personal attention. The company's personal shopper program has become a hit in all of the company's 84 stores. Customers can come in and enjoy a refreshing beverage in a private room while a tireless assistant brings them endless wardrobe options. Nordstrom's personal shoppers reinforce efficiency, speed, and individual service. Better still for the customer, there is absolutely no charge for the service. So in an otherwise impersonal and at times overwhelming department store, Nordstrom's differentiates itself by returning to the days when service was more genteel and individualized.[18]

functional strategies Strategies implemented by each functional area of the organization to support the organization's business strategy.

Functional strategy The final step in strategy formulation is to establish the major functional strategies. **Functional strategies** are implemented by each functional area of the organization to support the business strategy. The typical functional areas include production, human resources, marketing, research and development, finance, and distribution. For example, the human resource strategy at Starbucks Coffee supports the firm's strategy of differentiation through customer service.

Starbucks: inside the coffee cult

The phenomenal growth and success of Starbucks Coffee is in no small measure due to the way the company manages its people. By putting together a well-devised human resources plan, Starbucks has been able to instill a passion for customer service in its 20,000 employees, called "partners." To get the best possible employees, Starbucks hires young, enthusiastic, interpersonal people. The average age of a partner is 26, and about 85 percent have some education beyond high school.

Starbucks takes these "tattooed kids" (as *Fortune* magazine put it) and puts them through a rigorous training program to teach them the finer points of coffee and customer service. "Brewing the Perfect Cup of Coffee" is a course that must be completed by all partners within the first six weeks of employment. It teaches "baristas" how to "call" (yell out orders) and make drinks. There are a lot of rules—more than you might think—that have to be memorized. For example, milk must be steamed to at least 150 degrees, but never more than 170. Every espresso shot has to be pulled within 23 seconds or it is thrown out. Another program, called "Retail Skills," involves eight hours of lectures, demonstrations, and hands-on practice wiping oil from the coffee bin, opening a giant bag of beans (you never put your hand in there!), and cleaning the milk wand on the espresso machine. The training also shows partners how to fill one-pound sacks with coffee (never more, never less) and how to affix a sticker exactly one-half inch over the Starbucks logo.

Starbucks employees go through a rigorous training program to learn a lot of rules—more than you might think—just to pour a good cup of coffee. They're rewarded with a paycheck above industry standards.
[AP Photo/Don Ryan/Wide World Photos]

"Coffee Knowledge" covers the finer points of exotic blends (partners taste various coffees and learn to distinguish their characteristics). "Customer Service" teaches partners the finer points of interpersonal relations skills (e.g., maintain and enhance self-esteem, listen and acknowledge, ask for help). Pay is also part of Starbuck's human resources strategy. To make certain that it gets—and keeps—the best employees, Starbucks offers pay that is above the industry average ($6–8 per hour to start) for entry-level food service jobs. It also offers health insurance to all employees (even part-timers) as well as stock options.

The company also puts in place a number of mechanisms to make certain that employees can express their ideas and concerns. E-mail, suggestion cards, and regular forums help to increase the amount of upward feedback to managers. In return, employees are expected to adhere to a fairly rigid dress code (e.g., no tongue studs or visible tattoos).

The payoff from this human resources strategy is pretty impressive. Turnover at Starbucks is less than half the industry average (which stands at about 60 percent), and partners truly seem to feel a part of things. Company growth is quite impressive. Today there are more than 1,000 Starbucks in the United States, and profits have hit about $35 million. The company is expanding overseas and has a goal of 2,000 within only a few short years.

Sources: Howard Schultz and Dori Jones Yan, "Starbucks: Making Values Pay," *Fortune,* September 29, 1997 pp. 261–72; Alice Z. Cuneo, "Starbucks Breaks Largest Ad Blitz. *Advertising Age."* 68 no. 20. (May 19, 1997), pp. 3,84; Joan Voight, "Goodbye, Silverstein's First Starbucks Campaign Touts Frappuccino with Witty, New Yorker Feel," *Adweek* 38, no. 20 (May 19, 1997), p. 5; Ian McGugan, "Attack of the Killer Cappuccino," *Canadian Business* 69, no. 15 (December 1996), p. 149; and Jennifer Reese, "Starbucks: Inside the Coffee Cult," *Fortune* 134, no. 11 (Dec 9, 1996), pp. 190–200.

Functional strategies such as these described at Starbucks are typically put together by functional area executives with the input and approval of the executives responsible for business strategy. Senior strategic decision makers review the functional strategies to ensure that each major department is operating in a manner consistent with the business strategies of the organization.

Step 5: strategy implementation

As with any plan, formulating the appropriate strategy is not enough. Strategic managers also must ensure that the new strategies are implemented effectively and efficiently. Recently corporations and strategy consultants have been paying more attention to implementation. They realize that clever techniques and a good plan do not guarantee success. This greater appreciation is reflected in two major trends.

First, organizations are adopting a more comprehensive view of implementation. The strategy must be supported by decisions regarding the appropriate organization structure, technology, human resources, reward systems, information systems, organization culture, and leadership style. Just as the strategy of the organization must be matched to the external environment, it also must fit the multiple factors responsible for its implementation. The remainder of this text discusses these factors and the ways they can be used to implement strategy.

Second, many organizations are extending the more participative strategic management process to implementation. Managers at all levels are involved with strategy formulation and the identification and execution of the means to implement the new strategies. Senior executives still may orchestrate the overall implementation process, but they place much greater responsibility and authority in the hands of others in the organization.

Strategy implementation at Becton Dickinson

Implementing major strategic change requires a fundamental shift in top management's approach to organizing and managing. At Becton Dickinson (BD), the $2.5 billion medical technology company, executives have put in place a planning process designed to forge and then benefit from a partnership with employees throughout the organization. This partnership is designed to fulfill the three major requirements of strategy implementation: (1) competence–to have the business, technical, analytical, and interpersonal skills required to perform well; (2) coordination–to have the teamwork needed to respond to cost, quality, and innovation opportunities; and (3) commitment–to have high levels of motivation at all levels directed at achieving the new vision.

Executives at BD understand that deficiencies in any of these areas can undermine strategy implementation. In their view, the underlying obstacles to successful implementation often are deep-seated problems that are rarely discussed publicly, what they refer to as "iceberg issues." To help surface these issues, BD's implementation process facilitates open, fact-based communication among employees at all organizational levels. Since employees at lower levels are the ones most involved in actually implementing strategy, and the ones who best know where hidden icebergs lie, effective implementation depends on their involvement.

Defining strategic tasks. The first step in BD's implementation process is articulating in simple language what must be done in a particular business to create or sustain a competitive advantage. For example, BD's Diabetes Health Care business developed the following list:

- Maintain the core insulin syringe business by providing superior service and products.
- Sense new industry trends and develop new services or products to meet those trends.
- Achieve both of the above on a worldwide basis.

Defining strategic tasks helps employees understand how they each contribute to the organization, and can also redefine relationships between the parts of the organization.

Assessing the organization's capabilities. After defining strategic tasks, BD's management creates an employee task force composed of respected individuals from various parts of the organization to assess the organization's capacity to implement the strategic tasks. The task force interviews employees and managers to identify specific practices or organizational arrangements that help or hinder effective strategy implementation. Results of these interviews are summarized for top management.

Developing an implementation agenda. Once organizational capabilities are assessed, top management reaches consensus on (1) how they will change their management pattern; (2) how critical interdependencies will be managed; (3) what skills and which individuals are needed in key roles; and (4) what structural, measurement, information, and reward systems might ultimately support specified behavior. A philosophy statement–communicated in value terms–is the natural outcome of this process.

Implementation planning. Finally a plan is developed jointly between the top management team, the employee task force, and the rest of the organization to modify, refine, and implement the vision. As organizational changes are implemented, progress is monitored by the top management team. The employee task force is charged with providing feedback about how members of the organization are responding to the changes.

According to executives at BD, their implementation process works well because it addresses, in an integrated way, all the critical dimensions of aligning a business enterprise and its strategy.

Sources: This article is reprinted from Russell A. Eisenstat, "Implementing Strategy: Developing a Partnership for Change," *Planning Review,* September–October 1993, pp. 33–36, with permission from The Planning Forum, The International Society for Strategic Management and Planning. See, also, Raymond V. Gilmartin, "Integrating Strategy with the Management Process," *Business Forum* 16, no. 1. (Winter 1991), pp. 6–7; James R. Wessel, "The Strategic Human Resource Management Process in Practice," *Planning Review* 21, no. 5 (September/October 1993), pp. 37–38; and "A Bold Step," *Industry Week,* July 15, 1996, p. 58.

Step 6: strategic control

strategic control system
A system designed to support managers in evaluating the organization's progress regarding its strategy and, when discrepancies exist, taking corrective action.

The final component of the strategic management process is strategic control. A **strategic control system** is designed to support managers in evaluating the organization's progress with its strategy and, when discrepancies exist, in taking corrective action.[19] The system must encourage efficient operations that are consistent with the plan while allowing the flexibility to adapt to changing conditions. As with all control systems, the organization must develop performance indicators, an information system, and specific mechanisms to monitor progress.

Most strategic control systems include some type of budget to monitor and control major financial expenditures. The dual responsibilities of a control system—efficiency and flexibility—often seem contradictory with respect to budgets. The budget usually establishes limits on spending, but changing conditions or innovation may require different financial commitments during the budgetary period. To solve this dilemma, some companies have responded with two separate budgets: strategic and operational. For example, managers at Texas Instruments Incorporated control two budgets under the OST (objectives-strategies-tactics) system. The strategic budget is used to create and maintain long-term effectiveness, and the operational budget is tightly monitored to achieve short-term efficiency. The topic of control in general, and budget in particular, will be discussed in more detail in Chapter 16.

Key terms

Business strategy, p. 139
Concentration, p. 137
Concentric diversification, p. 137
Conglomerate diversification, p. 137
Core competencies, p. 136
Corporate strategy, p. 137
Differentiation strategy, p. 140
Functional strategies, p. 140
Goals, p. 125
Low-cost strategy, p. 139
Mission, p. 131
Operational planning, p. 128
Plans, p. 126
Resources, p. 135
Scenario, p. 126
Situational analysis, p. 124
Stakeholders, p. 132
Strategic control system, p. 143
Strategic goals, p. 127
Strategic management, p. 131
Strategic planning, p. 127
Strategic vision, p. 132
Strategy, p. 127
SWOT analysis, p. 137
Tactical planning, p. 128
Vertical integration, p. 137

Summary of learning objectives

Now that you have studied Chapter 4, you should know:

How to proceed through the basic steps in any planning process.

The planning process begins with a situation analysis of the external and internal forces affecting the organization. This will help identify and diagnose issues and problems, and may surface alternative goals and plans for the firm. Next the advantages and disadvantages of these goals and plans should be evaluated against one another. Once a set of goals and a plan have been selected, implementation involves communicating the plan to employees, allocating resources, and making certain that other systems such as rewards and budgets are supporting the plan. Finally, planning requires that control systems are put in place to monitor progress toward the goals.

How strategic planning differs from tactical and operational planning.

Strategic planning is different from operational planning in that it involves making long-term decisions about the entire organization. Tactical planning translates broad goals and strategies into specific actions to be taken within parts of the organization. Operational planning identifies the specific short-term procedures and processes required at lower levels of the organization.

Why it is important to analyze both the external environment and internal resources of the firm before formulating a strategy.

Strategic planning is designed to leverage the strengths of a firm while minimizing the effects of its weaknesses. It is difficult to know the potential advantage a firm may have unless external analysis is done well. For example, a company may have a talented marketing department or an efficient production system. However, there is no way to determine whether these internal characteristics are sources of competitive advantage until something is known about how well the competitors stack up in these areas.

The choices available for corporate strategy.

Corporate strategy identifies the breadth of a firm's competitive domain. Corporate strategy can be kept narrow, as in a concentration strategy, or can move to suppliers and buyers via vertical integration. Corporate strategy can also broaden a firm's domain via concentric (related) diversification or conglomerate (unrelated) diversification.

How companies can achieve competitive advantage through business strategy.

Companies gain competitive advantage in two primary ways. They can attempt to be unique in some way by pursuing a differentiation strategy, or they can focus on efficiency and price by pursuing a low-cost strategy.

How core competencies provide the foundation for business strategy.

A core competence is something a company does especially well relative to its competitors. When this competence, say in engineering or marketing, is in some area important to market success, it becomes the foundation for developing a competitive advantage.

The keys to effective strategy implementation.

Many good plans are doomed to failure because they are not implemented correctly. Strategy must be supported by structure, technology, human resources, rewards, information systems, culture, leadership, and so on. Ultimately the success of a plan depends on how well employees at low levels are able and willing to implement it. Participative management is one of the more popular approaches used by executives to gain employees' input and ensure their commitment to strategy implementation.

Discussion questions

1. This chapter opened with a quote by GE's Jack Welch: "Manage your destiny, or someone else will." What does this mean for strategic management? What does it mean when Welch adds, ". . . or someone else will"?

2. How do strategic, operational, and tactical planning differ? How might the three levels complement one another in an organization?

3. What accounts for the shift from strategic planning to strategic management? In which industries would you be most likely to observe these trends?

4. In your opinion, what are the core competencies of companies in the auto industry such as General Motors, Ford, and Chrysler? How do these competencies help them compete against foreign competitors such as Honda, Toyota, Nissan, Mercedes Benz, BMW, and others?

5. What are the key challenges in strategy implementation? In the example of Becton Dickinson, is each of these challenges addressed effectively?

Concluding Case

Planning for change at DuPont

Since John A. (Jack) Krol took over as CEO of DuPont, he has loosened up meetings and created a very different climate for planning and decision making. He has even been known to lead other executives in song—"You Are My Sunshine" is his favorite. Krol's idea is that the tone of meetings has to change in order to revamp DuPont from a slow-moving giant into a more vital growth machine. Competitors such as Monsanto are more agile and their successes are cause for concern.

To get things moving, Krol has modified the planning process. In the past, DuPont executives tended to keep planning centralized; only a small circle of advisers were let in on the discussions. Krol, by contrast, likes to involve a large number of executives in the decisions. He takes a good deal of time listening to what people have to say. This is not the quickest way to make planning decisions, but by getting everyone's input Krol believes he receives better advice and more commitment from people when changes are put in motion.

And DuPont *is* in motion. Here is Krol's formula: The plan is to accelerate DuPont's push into high-growth life sciences such as biotech agriculture and pharmaceuticals. The goal is to increase the company's percentage of sales in this area from 20 percent to 30 percent within three years. To achieve this operationally, DuPont has spent $3.2 billion to buy Protein Technologies and a portion of Pioneer Hi-Bred International (to research genetically enhanced crops). But Krol does not want to slight DuPont's core chemical and fiber businesses. The goal is to be number 1 or number 2 in core chemicals and fibers, and to solidify its position DuPont has spent over $3 billion to buy the white-pigment business outside North America and the polyester unit from ICI.

Although DuPont's corporate strategy is growth through diversification, the

With John Krol in charge, the planning process of DuPont is more informed and involves more people to generate the best ideas.
[Manuello Paganelli]

company is spinning off businesses that do not fit its overall strategic portfolio. For example, the low-margin medical-products division has not done well as part of DuPont and has been sold. Krol has also been putting together a deal to divest it of its hydrogen-peroxide operations. There has even been some talk about spinning off the $20 billion Conoco oil and gas unit.

Each of these changes fits into the company's overall plan to concentrate on faster-growing markets that build on the company's core competencies. For Jack Krol, the challenge is formulating and implementing a strategic plan that will make the company more flexible and dynamic in order to adapt to a changing environment.

Discussion Questions

1. Do you think Krol's approach to strategic planning is important to DuPont's success? Why or why not?

2. How is DuPont approaching its corporate strategy of diversification?

3. What do you think are DuPont's core competencies? How do these fit with the company's strategy?

Source: Amy Barrett, "At DuPont, Time to Both Reap and Sow," *Business Week,* September 29, 1997, pp. 107–8. Reprinted by special permission © 1997 by McGraw-Hill Companies. ●

Video Case

Planning and Strategic Management at Ford Motor Company

Ford Motor Company, like the other two major automobile manufacturers in the United States, experienced difficult times during the early 1980s. Ford and the others had seen their market share severely eroded by better-quality cars from international competitors. Ford was able to weather the competitive storm, and has seen its fortunes rebound, through effective strategic planning.

Donald Peterson was Ford's CEO during the company's recovery period. To create an atmosphere of trust among employees, and between employees and management, Peterson and his fellow managers at Ford emphasized the use of employee teams to solve corporate problems. This emphasis, according to Peterson, was based on the assumption that employees want to contribute, and want to do the right thing.

As the environment at Ford began to change for the better, the leadership initiated a process to establish a strategic vision for the company. Out of this process came a written statement of the company's mission, values, and guiding principles (MVGP) that would provide strategic focus for all the company's employees. The mission is a definition of the purpose of the company. The key values were defined as people, process, and profits. The guiding principles are the code of conduct for Ford's people as they conduct the company's business worldwide.

Reflecting on how he was able to steer Ford through the thicket of intense competition, employee skepticism, and consumer dissatisfaction characterizing the early part of the decade, Peterson said, "As we were working through the extraordinarily difficult early 1980s, when we were losing so much money, we had many gatherings of our employees, talking about our problems and talking about what we had to do to solve them. And it became very clear that there was a pattern in these conversations of a request from people in the company to understand clearly what it is we stand for—what is the basic, core culture of this company. We set about the process of letting the people think about that very question. And then they in turn selected a team of themselves to continue the process in a series of meetings with top Ford executives to work out what we call our mission, values, and guiding principles."

In a video presentation to all Ford employees in 1985, Peterson introduced the MVGP statement. He explained that he wanted the statement to be a "basic platform" upon which the board and all Ford employees would stand together. Peterson told the video audience that he hoped all employees would understand and embrace what the statement meant, what was behind it, and what it would take to live the values and guiding principles in day-to-day work.

As a result of the broad acceptance of the MVGP statement, Ford has made employee involvement and teamwork a way of life at the company. People at all levels of the organization have learned new skills to help them contribute to the continuous improvement of quality. The Taurus project team, for example, is legendary for its efficiency in the design, development, manufacture, and marketing of the Ford Taurus. The new employee spirit was captured by chip-and-scratch coordinator Leon Garner when he said, "I look at each car as if I'm buying it."

The MVGP statement led to a renewed emphasis on quality throughout the company. Terry Holcomb, statistical process control coordinator in the trim department at Ford's Atlanta assembly plant, noted, "There's always room for improvement. The day that there's no room for improvement I guess I'll quit." Holcomb's plant won Ford's internal Q1 (the "Q" stands for "quality") award in 1991. One improvement that Holcomb's plant made during 1990 was in the placement of the moonroof control relay. The relay had been located behind the glove box and had interfered with the smooth functioning of the glove box door. Using a "management by facts" approach, Holcomb's team determined the best way to fix the problem. Their improvement lowered the plant's TGW (things gone wrong) rate from 18 in the second quarter of 1990, to just 2 in the first quarter of 1991.

Bob Anderson, the Atlanta plant manager, said, "When management and the workforce settle on a common goal, with that goal being productivity and quality, you end up with [that] result. But you've got to have that common goal and everyone willing to get behind that common goal." Harold Poling, chairman of the board and chief executive officer, summarized the impact of the MVGP statement on Ford's operations: "I think that if our employees recommit themselves to the basics of the business, which were the things that helped us achieve our success in the 80s, quality, product, cost, and employee relations and relations with our dealers and suppliers, then we'll be successful in the years ahead. It's a team effort and that's what we had in the decade of the 80s. And I'm confident that with that same teamwork we'll be successful in the decade of the 90s."

Critical Thinking Questions

1. Ford is a complex organization with a highly diverse workforce and worldwide operations. Do you think it is possible that the statement of mission, vision, and guiding principles can be applied in all of the company's transactions? What are the limits of such a statement?

2. According to the video, Ford put together its MVGP statement through lengthy discussions with employees. Why do you think it was desirable for Ford executives to include employees in the drafting of the statement? Do you think this was the most *efficient* way to complete this project? Explain.

3. One of the reasons the automobile industry in America lost its competitive standing to foreign competition was that the internal organizational structure of each of the Big Three auto manufacturers had become stagnant. One lesson that has been learned by many companies in a variety of industries is that stagnation leads to competitive decline. Do you think a statement such as Ford's MVGP will help the company continue to change? Explain.

Experiential Exercises

4.1 Strategic planning

Objective

To study the strategic planning of a corporation recently in the news.

Instructions

Business Week magazine has frequent articles on the strategies of various corporations. Find a recent article on a corporation in an industry of interest to you. Read the article and answer the questions below.

Strategic planning worksheet

1. Has the firm clearly identified what business it is in and how it is different from its competitors? Explain.

____

____

____

____

____

____

2. What are the key assumptions about the future that have shaped the firm's new strategy?

3. What key strengths and weaknesses of the firm influenced the selection of the new strategy?

4. What specific objectives has the firm set in conjunction with the new strategy?

Source: R. R. McGrath, Jr., *Exercises in Management Fundamentals* (Englewood Cliffs, NJ: Prentice Hall, 1985), p. 15. Reprinted by permission of Prentice-Hall, Inc.

4.2 Formulating business strategy

Objectives

1. To illustrate the complex interrelationships central to business strategy formulation.

2. To demonstrate the use of SWOT (Strengths-Weaknesses-Opportunities-Threats) analysis in a business situation.

Instructions

1. Your instructor will divide the class into small groups and assign each group with a well-known organization for analysis.

2. Each group will

   a. Study the SWOT Introduction and the SWOT Worksheet to understand the work needed to complete the assignment.

   b. Obtain the needed information about the organization under study through library research, interviews, and so on.

   c. Complete the SWOT Worksheet.

   d. Prepare group responses to the discussion questions.

3. After the class reconvenes, group spokespersons present group findings.

Discussion questions

1. Why would most organizations not develop strategies for matches between opportunities and strengths?

2. Why would most organizations not develop strategies for matches between opportunities and weaknesses?

3. Why do most organizations want to deal from strength?

SWOT introduction

One of the more commonly used strategy tools is SWOT (Strengths-Weaknesses-Opportunities-Threats) analysis, which is accomplished in four steps:

Step 1: Analyze the organization's internal environment, identifying its strengths and weaknesses.

Step 2: Analyze the organization's external environment, identifying its opportunities and threats.

Step3: Match (1) strengths with opportunities, (2) weaknesses with threats, (3) strengths with threats, and (4) weaknesses with opportunities.

Step 4: Develop strategies for those matches that appear to be of greatest importance to the organization. Most organizations give top priority to strategies that involve the matching of strengths with opportunities and second priority to strategies that involve the matching of weaknesses with threats. The key is to exploit opportunities where the organization has a strength and to defend against threats where the organization has a weakness. ●

SWOT worksheet

Organization being analyzed: ______________________________

Internal Analysis	External Analysis
Strengths	**Opportunities**
Weaknesses	**Threats**

Strategies that match strengths with opportunities	Strategies that match weaknesses with threats

Chapter Five
Ethics and Corporate Responsibility

It is truly enough said that a corporation has no conscience; but a corporation of conscientious men is a corporation with a conscience.

—Henry David Thoreau

Chapter Outline

Learning Objectives

After studying Chapter 5, you will know:

1. How different ethical perspectives guide decision making.
2. How companies influence the ethics environment.
3. The options you have when confronting ethical issues.
4. The important issues surrounding corporate social responsibility.
5. How the political and social environment affects your firm's competitive position and legitimacy.
6. The strategies corporations use to manage the political and social environment.
7. The role of managers in our natural environment.

Setting the Stage

A Saint or a Fool?

When the Malden Mills factory in Lawrence, Massachusetts, suffered one of the biggest industrial fires in New England history, it had to shut down for several months. The workforce would be laid off, without work or paychecks, right? Wrong, according to Aaron Feuerstein, the owner, president, and CEO of Malden Mills. He continued providing full paychecks to more than 1,000 jobless employees for several months while the mill was rebuilt. Total wages and benefits—for which the company received no work in return—came to $15 million.

He's a saint, said many. He's a fool, said many others.

Who calls Mr. Feuerstein a saint, and why? As you might guess, his workforce, who adore him. Newspapers, magazines, and TV stations all over the country hailed him as a hero. President Clinton invited him to Washington for the State of the Union address. Columnists, unions, and religious leaders praised him for taking care of his people against his own best interests. His selfless example vividly stood out against many people's cynical outlook toward the unabashed profit-seeking of corporate America.

Others call Mr. Feuerstein a fool. They say he acted irrationally. They think he should have pocketed the insurance money and closed the business. Or, if he wanted to continue the business, he could have seized the opportunity and moved the company to another state or country with low labor costs. Real businessmen should be tougher and must not risk the survival of the business by paying out so much unnecessary money. At least one business school professor says that people should not look to Mr. Feuerstein as a role model.

Is he a saint or a fool? Or both, or neither?

Why did Mr. Feuerstein give $15 million to over 1,000 jobless people, when it was unnecessary and contrary to what so many businesspeople would do and advise? For one thing, at age 70+ he still loves what he does. For another, he is a hard-nosed businessman who sees strict business logic behind his actions.

If your company burned to the ground, would you pay 1,000 jobless employees for several months while your company was rebuilt? Aaron Feuerstein (above right) did. *[AP Photo/Gail Oskin/Wide World Photos]*

Early in his career, Mr. Feuerstein had seen many textile mills close in New England and move south, where labor costs were far lower. Many of those companies failed, in Mr. Feurstein's opinion, because they focused too much on costs and not enough on quality. Low costs are a temporary advantage, whereas quality lasts. And to achieve quality, your people are key. He wants skilled labor, and committed people, not cheap labor.

As *Fortune* magazine put it, "Here he has shown his real genius. Any idiot with a strong enough stomach can make quick money, sometimes a lot of it, by slashing costs and milking customers, employees, or a company's reputation." But the way to make money for a long time is to create superior value through superior employees. At Malden Mills, employees and customers are incredibly loyal, and productivity is fantastic. *Fortune* concludes, "No wonder Aaron Feuerstein loves those employees enough to risk $15 million to keep them available and motivated to help him rise from the literal ashes of last year's catastrophe. This isn't the work of a saint or a fool, it's the considered and historically successful policy of a genial manufacturing genius. Who might serve as a model for every man and woman in business." (p. 113)

Source: T. Teal, "Not a Fool, Not a Saint." Fortune, *November 11, 1996, pp. 111–13.*

Mr. Feuerstein was the head of his own company, and could do whatever he chose. But consequential actions are taken constantly by managers at all levels. Some are good ones, some are bad ones, some ethical and others unethical. They often are subjective, open to interpretation, and viewed differently by different people.

This chapter will help you understand the complex issues associated with business ethics and corporate social responsibility. Business is in the center of a controversy; although most agree that corporations should avoid illegal actions and decisions that significantly harm society, there is no agreement about the extent of their responsibility for the overall impact of their activities.

Ethics

The aim of ethics is to identify both the rules that should govern people's behavior and the "goods" that are worth seeking. All ethical decisions are guided by the underlying values of the individual. Values are principles of conduct such as caring, honesty, keeping of promises, pursuit of excellence, loyalty, fairness, integrity, respect for others, and responsible citizenship.[1]

Most people would agree that all these values are admirable guidelines for behavior. However, ethics becomes a more complicated issue when a situation dictates that one value overrule others. **Ethics** is the system of rules that governs the ordering of values.

ethics The system of rules governing the ordering of values.

An **ethical issue** is a situation, problem, or opportunity in which an individual must choose among several actions that must be evaluated as right or wrong.[2] Ethical issues arise in every facet of life; we concern ourselves here with business ethics in particular. **Business ethics** comprises the moral principles and standards that guide behavior in the world of business.[3]

ethical issue Situation, problem, or opportunity in which an individual must choose among several actions that must be evaluated as right or wrong.

business ethics The moral principles and standards that guide behavior in the world of business.

Ethical systems

Moral philosophy refers to the principles, rules, and values people use in deciding what is right or wrong. This is a simple definition, in the abstract, but often terribly complex and difficult when facing real choices. How do you decide what is right and wrong? Do you know what criteria you apply, and how you apply them?

moral philosophy Principles, rules, and values people use in deciding what is right or wrong.

Ethics scholars point to various major ethical systems as guides.[4] The first ethical system, **universalism,** states that individuals should uphold certain values, such as honesty, regardless of the immediate result. The important values are those society needs to function. For instance, people should always be honest because otherwise communication would break down.

universalism The ethical system upholding certain values regardless of immediate result.

But rarely are things so simple. Before we describe other ethical systems, consider the following example, and think about how you or others would resolve it. Remember, what you would do is not necessarily what others would do. And what people say, hope, or think they would do is often different from what they *really* would do, faced with the demands and pressures of the real situation.

An example

Suppose that Sam Colt, a sales representative, is preparing a sales presentation for his firm, Midwest Hardware, which manufactures nuts and bolts. Colt hopes to obtain a large sale from a construction firm that is building a bridge across the Missouri River near St. Louis. The bolts manufactured by Midwest Hardware have a 3 percent defect rate, which, although acceptable in the industry, makes them unsuitable for use in certain types of projects, such as those that might be subject to sudden, severe stress. The new bridge will be located near the New Madrid Fault line, the source of the United States' greatest earthquakes in 1811. The epicenter of that earthquake, which caused extensive damage and altered the flow of the Missouri, is less than two hundred miles from the new bridge site. Earthquake experts believe there is a 50 percent chance that an earthquake with a magnitude greater than 7 on the Richter scale will occur somewhere along the New Madrid Fault by the year 2000. Bridge construction in the area is not regulated by earthquake codes, however. If Colt wins the sale, he will earn a commission of $25,000 on top of his regular salary. But if he tells the contractors about the defect rate, Midwest may lose the sale to a competitor whose bolts are more reliable. Thus Colt's ethical issue is whether to point out to the bridge contractor that in the event of an earthquake, Midwest bolts could fail, possibly resulting in the collapse of the bridge and the death of anyone driving across it at the time.

Source: O. C. Farrell and J. Fraedrich, *Business Ethics: Ethical Decision Making and Cases,* 3rd ed. Copyright© 1997 by Houghton Mifflin Company. Used with permission.

Not everyone would behave the same in this scenario. Different individuals would apply different moral philosophies. Consider each of the following moral philosophies and to what actions they might lead in the above case.[5]

teleology Considers an act to be morally right or acceptable if it produces a desired result.

egoism An ethical system defining acceptable behavior as that which maximizes consequences for the individual.

Teleology

Teleology considers an act to be morally right or acceptable if it produces a desired result. The result can be anything desired by the person, including pleasure, personal growth, money, knowledge, or other self-interest. The key criterion is the consequences of the act, so teleology is sometimes referred to as consequentialism.

Two types of teleology are egoism and utilitarianism. **Egoism** defines acceptable behavior as that which maximizes consequences for the individual. "Doing the right thing," the focus of moral philosophy, is defined by egoism as "do the act that promotes the greatest good for oneself." If everyone follows this system, the well-being of society as a whole should increase. This notion is similar to Adam Smith's concept of the invisible hand in

In the movie "Amistad," what type of ethical system do you think was portrayed?
[©1997 Dream Works/ Wide World/Photo by Lorey Sebastian/Motion Picture & TV]

business. Smith argued that if every organization follows its own economic self-interest, the total wealth of society will be maximized.

utilitarianism An ethical system which states that the greatest good for the greatest number should be the overriding concern of decision makers.

Utilitarianism is also concerned with consequences, and as such is a teleological philosophy. But unlike egoism, utilitarianism seeks the greatest good for the greatest number of people. A utilitarian approach seeks to maximize total utility, achieving the greatest benefit for everyone affected by a decision.

In a utilitarian approach, what criteria determine morality? *Rule utilitarians* apply general principles and rules. Rule utilitarianism uses societal rules and customs to weigh the importance of conflicting values. *Act utilitarians* examine the actions themselves, and choose the one with the greatest utility (to the best of their determination). For example, rule utilitarianism might apply a principle that bribery is wrong, dictating that bribery never be used. Act utilitarianism might use bribery-is-wrong as a guiding principle, but might also find that bribery is acceptable under certain circumstances in which the total utility of resorting to bribery is seen as greater than the alternatives.

deontology focuses on rights of individuals.

Deontology

Deontology focuses on the rights of individuals. Attention to individual rights ensures that equal respect is given to all persons. In this way, actions that maximize utility for many parties will be rejected if they do serious injustice to just one party. Utilitarianism might allow such an action in the spirit of maximizing overall consequences. Utilitarianism concentrates more on ends, and deontology more on means.

Like utilitarianism, deontology can be divided into rule and act criteria. *Rule deontology* uses reason and logic to formulate rules such as "Do unto others as you would have them do unto you." *Act deontology* would use rules as guidelines, but would consider specific contexts, actions, and consequences before making a final choice.

What criteria do *you* use? You may or may not be able by this point to choose the perspective that you use or would use in making tough decisions. But it should be clear that ethical issues can and are evaluated from many different perspectives, that each perspective has a different basis for deciding right and wrong, and that people will disagree about what is and is not ethical because they are assessing ethics by their own, different, ethical standards.

Relativism

It is perhaps implicit to the discussion to this point that the individual makes ethical choices on a personal basis, applying personal perspectives. But this is not necessarily the case. **Relativism** defines ethical behavior based on the opinions and behaviors of relevant other people. This perspective acknowledges the existence of different ethical viewpoints, and turns to other people for advice, input, and opinions. Professional bodies provide guidelines to follow, and decision makers can convene a group to share perspectives and derive conclusions. Group consensus is sought; a positive consensus signifies that an action is right, ethical, and acceptable.

relativism bases ethical behavior on the opinions and behaviors of relevant other people.

virtue ethics A perspective that what is moral comes from what a mature person with "good" moral character would deem right.

The moral philosophies described above apply different types of rules and reasoning. **Virtue ethics** is a perspective that goes beyond the conventional rules of society by suggesting that what is moral must also come from what a mature person with "good" moral character would deem right. Society's rules provide a moral minimum, and then moral individuals can transcend rules by applying their personal virtues such as faith, honesty, and integrity.

Kohlberg's model of cognitive moral development classifies people into one of three categories based on their level of moral judgment.

Individuals differ in this regard. **Kohlberg's model of cognitive moral development** classifies people into one of three categories based on their level of moral judgment.[6] People in the *preconventional* stage make decisions based on concrete rewards and punishments and immediate self-interest. People in the *conventional* stage conform to the expectations of ethical behavior held by groups or institutions such as society, family, or peers. People in the *principled* stage take a broader perspective in which they see beyond authority, laws, and norms and follow their self-chosen ethical principles.[7] Some people forever reside in the preconventional stage, some move into the conventional stage, and some develop further yet into the principled stage. Over time, and through education and experience, people may change their values and ethical behavior.

Returning to the defective bolts example, egoism would result in keeping quiet about the bolts' defect rate. Utilitarianism would dictate a more thorough cost–benefit analysis and possibly the conclusion that the probability of a bridge collapse is so low compared to the utility of jobs, economic growth, and company growth that the defect rate is not worth mentioning. Deontology would likely create an obligation to tell because of the potential danger. The relativist perspective might prompt the salesperson to look at company policy and general industry practice, and to seek opinions from colleagues and perhaps trade journals and ethics codes. Whatever is then perceived to be a consensus or normal practice would dictate action. And finally, virtue ethics, applied by people in the principled stage of moral development, would likely lead to full disclosure about the product and risks, and perhaps suggestions for alternatives that would reduce the risk.[8]

These major ethical systems underlie personal moral choices and ethical decisions in business.

Business ethics

Questions of ethics in business have been prominent in the news in recent years. Insider trading, illegal campaign contributions, bribery, and other scandals have created a perception that business leaders use illegal means to gain competitive advantage, increase profits, or improve their personal positions. In a survey of 200 professionals, 35 percent admitted lying to customers and colleagues. In another recent survey, of 158 experienced businesspeople, 65 percent agreed that mid- to upper-level managers believe that profits are more important than product safety. Shareholders tend to ignore fraudulent financial reporting, believing it is routine, as long as profits and market share don't suffer.[9] By the way, you might find it interesting that surveys suggest that males are more likely to behave unethically than females, probably because of a stronger tendency to get carried away by the competition and to go along with the team.[10]

Neither young managers[11] nor consumers[12] believe top executives are doing a good job of establishing high ethical standards. Some even joke that *business ethics* has become a contradiction in terms.

Most business leaders believe they uphold ethical standards in business practices.[13] Nevertheless, many managers and their organizations are reexamining their personal business ethics. On a daily basis, they must deal with ethical dilemmas such as those described in Tables 5.1 and 5.2 on page 159.

Think about this: just how ethical are businesspeople? Opinions differ.

Differences of opinion

Are businesspeople ethical? The following statements are taken from a recent article in *Across the Board,* an influential magazine for American executives:

- Business "is a game with different rules from those that apply to the rest of society." (p. 17)
- "Most large firms . . . suffer from a surfeit of ethics. They have their high ethics . . . ethics as it is preached. Then they also have an ethics as it is practiced." (p. 18)
- MBA students "won't necessarily cheat or lie more than other people, but they . . . are more willing to accept the unethicalness of others, because they expect it as normal." (p. 18)

In today's business environment, managers face ethical dilemas daily. *[Kaluzny/Thatcher/Tony Stone Images]*

- "Is there something about large business organizations in particular that leads people astray? The answer seems to be: just about everything." (p. 18)
- "The essence of business is competition, making business still a game where winning matters more than how the game is played." (p. 21)
- "In most of the infamous cases of corporate wrongdoing—the exploding Pinto is a famous example—it was not just one person who did wrong but sometimes dozens." (p. 21)
- "Everyone agrees that lying is unethical, but misrepresentation during a purchase negotiation is widely considered not to be lying, because if all parties know that everyone is lying there is no deception and thus no sin." (p. 22)

On the other hand, this article generated outrage from many readers, who wrote in a subsequent issue of the magazine:

- "[I and others] would strongly debate the notion that business ethics is different from everyday ethics." (p. 48)
- "For every unethical or amoral manager, there is at least another manager trying to do the right thing for the right reasons." (p. 48)
- "People can make the difference. They can set the tone of ethical behavior . . . it's imperative. It will make the difference for the future. Because a sale is nice, but the future is the future." (p. 49)
- "There are certainly many companies—even hierarchical ones operating in highly competitive environments with enormous sums of money at stake—whose managers do behave responsibly, indeed sometimes even courageously." (p. 49)
- "Business will (must) act in such a way that its market approves. Thank goodness that today's societal market demands accountability and checks ethical behavior." (p. 50)
- "At the heart of business success . . . is customer or client trust and loyalty. This trust and loyalty is [sic] built by product or service credibility, reliability, and performance, which is [sic] reinforced by ethical standards and behavior. Attempting to define business interests and ethical interests as separate, or antithetical, ignores this fundamental fact of how business survives and prospers." (p. 50)

Sources: J. Krohe Jr., "Ethics Are Nice, but Business Is Business," *Across the Board,* April 1997, pp. 16–22; and D. Driscoll, M. Rion, M. Roth, D. Vogel, L. Pincus, and D. Orlov, "Who Says Ethics Are 'Nice'"? *Across the Board,* June 1997, pp. 47–50. Reprinted with permission of the Conference Board.

table 5.1
Some ethically questionable acts

- A bar owner runs an "All You Can Drink Special" but does not provide transportation home for intoxicated patrons because of the high cost.
- A manager fires several long-time employees because the business is undergoing financial difficulties.
- An executive collects frequent-flyer miles from company-paid business trips to use for her personal air travel.
- Instead of relying on the traditional "blind" bidding procedure, a building contractor negotiates an agreement with other major contractors so that all bids submitted will provide a reasonable profit.
- A supplier sends expensive Christmas gifts to purchasing agents in an attempt to influence their future purchase decisions.
- An owner of a small business obtains a free copy of a computer software program from a friend instead of paying the $500 licensing fee to the software manufacturer.
- A manufacturer of violence-oriented children's toys buys time on television cartoon programs to create demand for its product.

Source: S. Burton, M. Johnston, and E. Wilson, "An Experimental Assessment of Alternative Teaching Approaches for Introducing Business Ethics to Undergraduate Business Students," *Journal of Business Ethics,* July 1991, pp. 507–17. Reprinted with kind permission from Kluwer Academic Publishers.

The ethics environment

ethical climate of an organization refers to the processes by which decisions are evaluated and made on the basis of right and wrong.

Ethics are not shaped only by society and by individual development and virtue. They also may be influenced by the company's work environment. The **ethical climate** of an organization refers to the processes by which decisions are evaluated and made on the basis of right and wrong.[14]

table 5.2
Ethical decision making in the international context

What would you do in each of these true-life situations, and why?

- You are a sales representative for a construction company in the Middle East. Your company wants very much to land a particular project. The cousin of the minister who will award the contract informs you that the minister wants $20,000 in addition to the standard fees. If you do not make this payment, your competition certainly will–and will get the contract.
- You are international vice president of a multinational chemical corporation. Your company is the sole producer of an insecticide that will effectively combat a recent infestation of West African crops. The minister of agriculture in a small, developing African country has put in a large order for your product. Your insecticide is highly toxic and is banned in the United States. You inform the minister of the risks of using your product, but he insists on using it and claims it will be used "intelligently." The president of your company believes you should fill the order, but the decision ultimately is yours.
- You are a new marketing manager for a large automobile tire manufacturer. Your company's advertising agency has just presented plans for introducing a new tire into the Southeast Asia market. Your tire is a truly good product, but the proposed advertising is deceptive. For example, the "reduced price" was reduced from a hypothetical amount that was established only so it could be "reduced," and claims that the tire was tested under the "most adverse" conditions ignore the fact that it was not tested in prolonged tropical heat and humidity. Your superiors are not concerned about deceptive advertising, and they are counting on you to see that the tire does extremely well in the new market. Will you approve the ad plan?

Source: N. Adler, *International Dimensions of Organizational Behavior* 2nd ed. (Boston: Kent, 1997).

When people make decisions that are judged by ethical criteria, these questions always seem to get asked: why did she do it? Good motives or bad ones? His responsibility or someone else's? Who gets the credit, or the blame? So often, responsibility for unethical acts is placed squarely on the individual who commits them. But the environment has a profound influence, as well.

Consider the question of responsibility in the cases of illegal, unethical actions at Kidder Peabody and at Sears, Roebuck. A securities trader at Kidder Peabody allegedly created about $350 million in phony profits for the firm. By engaging in these illegalities, he made $9 million in salary and bonuses. (By playing it straight and honest, he would have made $2 or $3 million.)

How could the scandal have happened? Was it just a renegade trader? The trader's immediate boss claimed he could not monitor the records of all 750 traders in his department. Kidder's CEO said the same thing could have happened anywhere on Wall Street. Supporters said that in a company as big as GE (Kidder's parent corporation), there are bound to be some bad apples. And Kidder top executives, according to GE's Jack Welch, were open and candid and worked hard to get at the truth once the scandal was uncovered.[15] But the profits the trader claimed were outrageous; $5 million to $10 million per month on government bonds seemed impossible. Kidder executives consistently ignored, evaded, or answered incorrectly questions about his profits. Critics cannot understand why it took so long to uncover the misdeeds, and maintained that the trader could not have pulled it off if management had been paying attention.

In another example of mutual individual–company responsibility, Sears, Roebuck did not set out to defraud its automotive service customers in the early 1990s. Nor did employees necessarily intend to cheat consumers. But when the company instituted high-pressure, unrealistic quotas and incentives, people's judgment was affected. Management did not make clear the distinction between unnecessary service and legitimate preventive maintenance. Moreover, customers were often ignorant or oblivious. A vast gray area of repair options was exaggerated, overinterpreted, and misrepresented. The company may not have intended to deceive customers, but the result of the work environment was that consumers and attorneys general in more than 40 states accused the company of fraud. The total cost of the settlement was an estimated $60 million.[16]

As illustrated by the Kidder Peabody and Sears examples, unethical corporate behavior may be the responsibility of an unethical individual; but it often also reveals a company culture that is ethically lax.[17] Likewise, ethical individuals are likely to behave ethically, but all the more so in organizations that infuse a sense of ethics into their people.

Corporate ethical standards People often give in to what they perceive to be the pressures or preferences of powerful others. States Professor Arthur Brief of Tulane University, "If the boss says, 'Achieve a specific sales or profit target, period,' I think people will do their very best to achieve those directions even if it means sacrificing their own values. They may not like it, but they define it as part of the job."[18]

Because individuals have differing personal ethical codes, organizations must be explicit regarding their corporate ethical standards and expectations. Some companies advocate the "golden rule": Do unto others as you would have them do unto you. However, others argue that current or accepted business practice should govern behavior. Their motto is "Everyone else does it." A more extreme attitude is that organizations should seek every possible advantage without regard for traditional social laws and customs—a "might equals right" philosophy. Finally, some believe that ethics should be determined by intuition, that is, by doing whatever "feels right."

IBM uses a guideline for business conduct that asks employees to determine whether under the "full glare of examination by associates, friends, and family, they would remain comfortable with their decisions." One suggestion is to imagine how you would feel if you saw your decision and its consequences on the front page of the newspaper.[19] This "light of day" or "sunshine" ethical framework is extremely powerful.[20]

Such fear of exposure compels people more strongly in some cultures than in others. In Asia, anxiety about losing face often makes Asian executives resign immediately if they are caught in ethical transgressions, or if their companies are embarrassed by revelations in the press. By contrast, in the United States, exposed executives might respond with indignation, intransigence, stonewalling, and an everyone-else-does-it self-defense, or by not admitting wrongdoing and giving no sign that resignation ever crossed their minds. Partly because of legal tradition, the attitude often is: never explain, never apologize, do not resign, even if the entire world knows exactly what happened. Don't admit the mistake and accept the consequences.[21]

Danger signs In organizations, it is an ongoing challenge to maintain consistent ethical behavior by all employees. What are some danger signs that an organization may be allowing or even encouraging unethical behavior among its people? Many factors create a climate conducive to unethical behavior, including (1) excessive emphasis on short-term revenues over longer-term considerations; (2) failure to establish a written code of ethics; (3) a desire for simple, "quick fix" solutions to ethical problems; (4) an unwillingness to take an ethical stand that may impose financial costs; (5) consideration of ethics solely as a legal issue or a public relations tool; (6) lack of clear procedures for handling ethical problems; and (7) response to the demands of shareholders at the expense of other constituencies.[22]

Ethics codes One of the most visible signs of possible corporate commitment to ethical behavior is a written code of ethics. Corporate ethics or values statements are much more common today than they used to be. They became popular in the 1980s, and then tough new federal sentencing guidelines in 1991 increased fines for illegal activities and specified more lenient fines for those companies that had an ethics statement in place. Often, the statements are just for show, but when implemented well they can change a company's ethical climate for the better and truly encourage ethical behavior.

Ethics codes must be carefully written and tailored to individual companies' philosophies. Hewlett-Packard is dedicated to the dignity and worth of its employees. Aetna Life & Casualty believes that tending to the broader needs of society is essential to fulfilling its economic role. Johnson & Johnson has one of the most famous ethics codes (see Table 5.3). J&J consistently receives high rankings for community and social responsibility in *Fortune*'s annual survey of corporate reputations.

Most ethics codes address subjects such as employee conduct, community and environment, shareholders, customers, suppliers and contractors, political activity, and technology. Often the codes are drawn up by the organizations' legal departments and begin with research into other companies' codes. The Ethics Resource Center in Washington assists companies interested in establishing a corporate code of ethics.[23]

To make an ethics code effective, do the following:[24] (1) involve everyone, meaning every person who has to live with it, in writing the statement; (2) have a corporate statement, but also allow separate statements by different units throughout the organization; (3) keep it short and therefore easily understood and remembered; (4) don't make it too corny—make it something important, that people really believe in; and (5) set the tone at the top, having executives talk about and live up to the statement. When reality differs from the statement—as when a motto says people are our most precious asset or a product is the finest in the world, but in fact people are treated poorly or product quality is weak—the statement becomes a joke to employees rather than a guiding light.

Ethics programs As we have seen, unethical behavior is not always the sole responsibility of those who engage in it. This is true in a legal sense as well. Under new federal guidelines, a company's fines are based in part on whether it has taken actions to

table 5.3
Johnson & Johnson's ethics code

We believe our first responsibility is to the doctors, nurses, and patients, to mothers and all others who use our products and services. In meeting their needs everything we do must be of high quality. We must constantly strive to reduce our costs in order to maintain reasonable prices. Customers' orders must be serviced promptly and accurately. Our suppliers and distributors must have an opportunity to make a fair profit.

We are responsible to our employees: the men and women who work with us throughout the world. Everyone must be considered as an individual. We must respect their dignity and recognize their merit. They must have a sense of security in their jobs. Compensation must be fair and adequate, and working conditions clean, orderly, and safe. Employees must feel free to make suggestions and complaints. There must be equal opportunity for employment, development, and advancement for those qualified. We must provide competent management, and their actions must be just and ethical.

We are responsible to the communities in which we live and work and to the world community as well.

We must be good citizens—support good works and charities and bear our fair share of taxes. We must encourage civic improvements and better health and education.

We must maintain in good order the property we are privileged to use, protecting the environment and natural resources.

Our final responsibility is to our stockholders. Business must make a sound profit. We must experiment with new ideas. Research must be carried on, innovative programs developed, and mistakes paid for. New equipment must be purchased, new facilities provided, and new products launched. Reserves must be created to provide for adverse times.

When we operate according to these principles, the stockholders should realize a fair return.

Source: Reprinted with permission of Johnson & Johnson.

prevent the misconduct. Thus, responsibility is shared by those who fail to provide proper ethical leadership and controls.

compliance-based ethics programs Company mechanisms typically designed by corporate counsel to prevent, detect, and punish legal violations.

Ethics programs can range from compliance-based to integrity-based.[25] **Compliance-based ethics programs** are designed by corporate counsel to prevent, detect, and punish legal violations. Compliance-based programs increase surveillance and controls on people and impose punishments on wrongdoers. Program elements include establishing and communicating legal standards and procedures, assigning high-level managers to oversee compliance, auditing and monitoring compliance, reporting criminal misconduct, punishing wrongdoers, and taking steps to prevent offenses in the future.

Such programs should reduce illegal behavior and help the company stay out of court. But they do not create a moral commitment to ethical conduct; they merely ensure moral mediocrity. As Richard Breeden, former chairman of the SEC, said, "It is not an adequate ethical standard to aspire to get through the day without being indicted."[26]

integrity-based ethics programs Company mechanisms designed to instill in people a personal responsibility for ethical behavior.

Integrity-based ethics programs go beyond the mere avoidance of illegality; they are concerned with the law but also with instilling in people a personal responsibility for ethical behavior. With such a program, companies and people govern themselves through a set of guiding principles that they embrace.

For example, the Americans with Disabilities Act (ADA) attempts to protect the rights of persons with both visible and invisible (for example, psychiatric) disabilities. The law requires companies to change the physical work environment so it will allow people with disabilities to function on the job. Mere compliance would involve making the necessary

Integrity-based programs go beyond mere compliance with a law.
[David Young Wolff/Tony Stone Images]

changes to avoid legal problems. Integrity-based programs would go farther, by training people to understand and perhaps change attitudes toward people with disabilities, and sending clear signals that people with disabilities also have valued abilities. Helping people feel important to the company goes far beyond taking action to stay out of trouble with the law.

Integrity-based programs view ethics as a driving force in the enterprise. The company's ethics help define what it is and what it cares about. Programs based on integrity have the elements of compliance-based programs, but also an articulated set of values developed not by counsel but by managers throughout the organization. The elements of an integrity strategy include

1. The guiding values are shared and clearly understood by everyone.
2. Company leaders are personally committed to the values and willing to take action on them.
3. The values are considered in decision making and reflected in all important activities.
4. Information systems, reporting relationships, and performance appraisals support and reinforce the values. At some companies, like Levi Strauss, people's raises depend in part on the ethics of their decisions.
5. People at all levels have the skills and knowledge to make ethically sound decisions on a daily basis.

Companies with strong integrity-based programs include Martin Marietta, NovaCare (a provider of rehabilitation services to hospitals and nursing homes), and Wetherill Associates (a supplier of electrical parts to the automotive market). These companies believe that their programs contribute to competitiveness, higher morale, and sustainable relationships with key stakeholders.[27]

Ethical decision making

Good people sometimes commit unethical acts because they do not carefully think through the consequences and implications of their actions.[28] Corporate policies can help ensure ethical decision making. In addition, some guidelines for decision making may help individuals avoid inadvertent breaches of ethics.[29]

First, *define the issue clearly.* What is the context of the issue? Who are the affected stakeholders? Talk to various stakeholders to ensure that all the facts are considered. Often a decision maker omits this step, assuming she or he already understands the problem without stopping to consider all of its components.

Second, *identify the relevant values in the situation.* Any ethical dilemma involves multiple values: the various consequences of your choices, what you care about the most, and what others care about the most. Clearly stating these values focuses attention on the ethical component of the decision.

Third, *weigh the conflicting values and choose an option that balances them,* with greatest emphasis on the most important values. At this stage, the decision maker must decide which values are more important than others. Companies that have clearly defined their values through a code of ethics and other actions already have clarified the value priorities. In organizations in which values are unclear or inconsistent, balancing the values is a more difficult challenge.

Fourth, *implement the decision.* This step may require justifying the organization's actions. Because the short- and long-term ethical consequences already have been assessed, the decision maker can more effectively defend the decision to stakeholders.

What can you do if you see managers in your company behaving in ways that go against your ethical principles? Your options include the following, among others:[30] (1) Don't think about it; (2) go along with it to avoid conflict; (3) object, verbally or via memo; (4) quit; (5) privately or publicly blow the whistle—that is, inform others inside or outside the organization about what you have observed; or (6) negotiate and build a consensus for changing the unethical behavior. What are the advantages and disadvantages of each of these options? What other options can you think of? What do you think determines which option a person chooses?

Recalling Chapter 3, ethical dilemmas are ill-structured problems made under conditions of uncertainty. As such, there are no formulas, and no clear right or wrong answers. Mistakes will be made. But also recalling Chapter 3, the more you engage in vigilance and procedural rationality—and the better you understand your own moral philosophy and criteria—the better chance you have of making the most ethical decisions possible. Importantly, the stronger your intentions to behave in an ethical manner, consistently over time, the better chance you have of making decisions with which you and others can live. While mistakes still may be made—recalling also the likelihood of unintended consequences—good intentions, and vigilant decision processes, followed by actions that are consistent with ethical judgments, will reduce guilt and raise the overall level of positive consequences for decision makers, for organizations, and for society.

Corporate social responsibility

Should business be responsible for social concerns lying beyond its own economic well-being? Do social concerns affect a corporation's financial performance? The extent of business's responsibility for noneconomic concerns has been hotly debated. In the 1960s and 1970s, the political and social environment became more important to United States corporations as society turned its attention to issues like equal opportunity, pollution control, energy and natural resource conservation, and consumer and worker protection.[31] Public debate addressed these issues and how business should respond to them. This controversy focused on the concept of corporate social responsibility.

corporate social responsibility Obligation toward society assumed by business.

Corporate social responsibility is the obligation toward society assumed by business. The socially responsible business maximizes its positive effects on society and minimizes its negative effects.[32]

economic responsibilities are to produce goods and services that society wants at a price that perpetuates the business and satisfies its obligations to investors.

legal responsibilities To obey local, state, federal, and relevant international laws.

ethical responsibilities Meeting other social expectations, not written as law.

voluntary responsibilities Additional behaviors and activities that society finds desirable and that the values of the business dictate.

Social responsibilities can be categorized more specifically,[33] as shown in Figure 5.1. The **economic responsibilities** of business are to produce goods and services that society wants at a price that perpetuates the business and satisfies its obligations to investors. **Legal responsibilities** are, at the very least, to obey local, state, federal, and relevant international laws. **Ethical responsibilities** include meeting other societal expectations, not written as law. As such, ethics is one dimension of social responsibility. Finally, **voluntary responsibilities** are additional behaviors and activities that society finds desirable and that the values of the business dictate. Examples include supporting community projects and making charitable contributions.

To clarify these distinctions, consider economic and legal responsibilities to be those that society requires of business; ethical responsibilities to be expected from business; and voluntary responsibilities to be desired from business. Bear in mind, also, that any given issue—think, for example, of corporate actions as they affect our natural environment—can cut across all four categories of social responsibility.

Although criteria and standards for determining these responsibilities vary among organizations and countries, some efforts have been made to establish sets of global or universal ethical principles. For example, it is widely agreed that all people are morally obligated to adhere to core principles such as avoid harm to others, respect the autonomy of others, avoid lying, and honor agreements.[34] Appendix A shows the international ethics code created by the Caux Roundtable in Switzerland, collaborating with business leaders from Europe, Japan, and the United States.

figure 5.1
The pyramid of corporate social responsibility

Voluntary
responsibilities
Be a good corporate citizen.
Contribute resources
to the community;
improve quality of life.
Ethical
responsibilities
Be ethical.
Obligation to do what is right,
just, and fair. Avoid harm.
Legal
responsibilities
Obey the law.
Law is society's codification of right
and wrong. Play by the rules of the game.
Economic
responsibilities
Be profitable.
The foundation upon which all others rest.

Source: Archie B. Carroll, "The Pyramid of Corporate Responsibility: Toward the Moral Management of Organizational Stakeholders," adaptation of Figure 3, p. 42. Reprinted from *Business Horizons,* July/August 1991. Copyright 1991 by the Foundation for the School of Business at Indiana University. Used with permission.

Contrasting views

Two basic and contrasting views about which principles should guide managerial responsibility are common. The first, critical of the broad domain of corporate social responsibility described above, is that managers act as agents for shareholders and, as such, are obligated to maximize the present value of the firm. This tenet of capitalism is widely associated with the early writings of Adam Smith in *The Wealth of Nations,* and more recently by Milton Friedman, the Nobel Prize–winning economist of the University of Chicago. With his now-famous dictum "The social responsibility of business is to increase profits," Friedman contended that organizations may help improve the quality of life as long as such actions are directed at increasing profits.

These critics argue that in a capitalistic society, economic performance is an organization's primary social responsibility. If corporations do not serve shareholders first, they will fail to serve society. Society relies on the profit incentive to motivate organizations to create jobs and make investments. Without investments, economic growth is impossible. Also, if organizations do not directly pursue economic success in highly competitive national and international markets, the chance of failure increases significantly. Corporate decline and failure benefit no one (except possibly the competition).

business judgment rule allows management wide latitude in policy if the policy can be justified.

The duty to pursue profits is limited, however. The **business judgment rule** allows management wide latitude in policy if the policy can be justified. The goal of shareholder wealth is legally qualified by the American Law Institute's (ALI) Principles of Corporate Governance, which state that the corporation "may take into account ethical considerations that are reasonably regarded as appropriate to the responsible conduct of the business."[35]

Some people disagree with the qualifier "may".[36] They see ethical actions as not optional, but mandatory.[37] At the very least, managers must not act in contradiction to a minimal set of universal principles.[38] This is the second perspective, different from the profit maximization perspective: that managers should be motivated by principled moral reasoning. Followers of Friedman and *The Wealth of Nations* might sneer at such soft-headed propaganda, but it is argued that Adam Smith wrote about a different world from the one we are in now, driven in the 18th century by the self-interest of small owner-operated farms and craft shops trying to generate a living income for themselves and their families, a self-interest quite different from the top executives of modern corporations.[39] It is interesting to note that Adam Smith also wrote *A Theory of Moral Sentiments,* in which he argued that "sympathy," defined as a proper regard for others, was the basis of a civilized society.[40]

Advocates of corporate social responsibility argue that organizations have a wider range of responsibilities that extend beyond the production of goods and services at a profit. As members of society, organizations should actively and responsibly participate in the community and in the larger environment.

How would these perspectives apply to the following example?

American cigarettes overseas

Some people argue that U. S. tobacco companies should not promote tobacco abroad while they must warn Americans about the dangers of smoking. The tobacco companies disagree. The Chinese already manufacture and consume well over 1 trillion cigarettes annually (90 percent of Chinese males and 63 percent of Japanese males smoke), and the U.S. tobacco industry wants part of that market. U.S. tobacco companies argue that Asians complain about the menace of American cigarette conglomerates but do little in terms of requiring warning labels, prohibiting sales to minors, or banning smoking. Taiwan has a cigarette brand called "Long Life," and Japan's tepid health warning reads, "Please don't smoke too much." Smoking-related deaths have overtaken communicable diseases as Asia's top health risk.

Fewer than 10 percent of Asian women and adolescents smoke, and U. S. companies have promised not to court those markets. Nevertheless, R. J. R. sponsored three concerts featuring a popular Hong Kong rock star (admission was five empty Winston packs), and Philip Morris International advertises Virginia Slims, a brand aimed at women. A Taiwanese official complained that U. S. manufacturers hand out cigarettes to 12-year-olds at amusement parks. Critics claim that saturation marketing, depicting smoking as glamorous, rugged, and very Western, is designed to entice the enormous, untapped market of Asian women and teens.

In Europe, member countries of the European Union are working to ban tobacco advertising in sport, but U. K. Prime Minister Tony Blair voted to exclude Formula One auto racing from the ban. Formula One claims to be the third biggest sport worldwide in television audience, after the Olympic Games and the World Cup. And tobacco is easily the largest sponsor. Former racing great Jackie Stewart, whose team refuses tobacco ads because its sponsors (Ford and Hewlett-Packard) are nonsmoking companies, estimates his team is 25–30 percent poorer as a result.

Tobacco companies have no place else to advertise on television. Recent studies show that young male Formula One fans are four times more likely to become smokers. A ban would greatly reduce the sport's income, and some fear it would leave Europe and move elsewhere, in particular, East Asia. Others maintain the sport would not and could not leave Europe.

Antismoking activists maintain that an unbridled pursuit of profit is fueling an anti-American backlash and hostility toward other U. S. exports. Tobacco interests counter that taxes on their products go directly into the coffers of very poor countries.

Sources: M. Levin, "U.S. Tobacco Firms Push Eagerly into the Asian Market," *Marketing News,* January 21, 1991, pp. 2. 14; P. Schmeiser, "Pushing Cigarettes Overseas," *New York Times Magazine,* July 10, 1988, pp. 16 ff; and M. Jacques, "Can Formula One Give Up the Tobacco Habit?" *The European,* November 13–19, 1997, pp. 9–13. ●

Reconciliation

It used to be that these views were regarded as antagonistic, leading to opposing policies. But now, in a more "ethicized" business climate, policy divergence is not seen as necessary; the two views can converge.[41] As the contemporary British economist and management scholar Charles Handy put it, "Markets, for wealth and efficiency, need to be balanced by sympathy [as Adam Smith defined it], for civilization.[42] Even supporters of the wealth maximization view now often consider explicitly important legal, ethical, and social issues. "Strategic ethics" is seen as a tool that increases the firm's present value.

Earlier attention to corporate social responsibility focused on alleged wrongdoing and how to control it. More recently, attention has been on the possible competitive advantage of socially responsible actions, including financial success and consumer purchase decisions. For example, a recent study showed that corporate social responsibility enhances company reputations, which in turn makes them more attractive employers, and they attract more applicants.[43] Thus corporate social responsibility can provide competitive advantage by helping to attract and perhaps retain superior employees.

Moreover, recent evidence reveals that companies convicted of illegalities may pay unanticipated prices. Convictions for illegal activity hurt the stock price for only a few days, as investors quickly forget the past and look to the future. But these future expectations appear to underestimate the effects of the illegalities, as convictions have been shown to reduce companies' sales growth and accounting returns over a period of several years.[44]

Socially responsible actions can have other long-term advantages for organizations. Organizations can improve their images and avoid unnecessary and costly regulation if they are perceived as socially responsible. Honesty and fairness—including admitting mistakes; apologizing genuinely, quickly, and sincerely; and making up for the mistake—may pay great dividends to the conscience, to the personal reputation, to the public image of the company, and to the market response.[45] In addition, society's problems can offer business opportunities, and profits can be made from systematic and vigorous efforts to solve these problems. In other words, it pays to be good.[46]

Merck, for example, states in its internal management guide, "We are in the business of improving human life. All of our actions must be measured by our success in achieving this goal." And they mean it. For example, Merck developed a drug called Mectizan to cure "river blindness," a disease that infected over a million people. That's a big potential market, except that the victims could not afford the product. Merck hoped that someone else would help pay for the cure, but the company gave the drug away for free, and invested in costly distribution efforts to make sure the people who needed it were able to get it.[47]

Asked why Merck did this, then-CEO Roy Vagelos said to not do so would have been to violate the reason the company was in business and would demoralize its scientists. He also cited an earlier example: After World War II, Merck brought streptomycin to Japan to cure tuberculosis, which was devastating Japan. Merck made no money but did tremendous good. And today Merck has a tremendous reputation and presence in Japan.[48]

Corporate social responsiveness

corporate social responsiveness The process companies follow and the actions they take in the domain of corporate social responsibility.

How companies respond to the *corporate social responsibility* debate is called **corporate social responsiveness.**[49] The two are sometimes distinguished by the acronyms CSR1 and CSR2. Whereas CSR1 (corporate social responsibility) refers to principles, philosophies, and beliefs, CSR2 (corporate social responsiveness) refers to the processes companies follow and the actions they take. These processes and strategies are reactive, defensive, accommodative, and proactive. Table 5.4 summarizes these responses.

Both corporate social responsibility and corporate social responsiveness have their critics, in both academia and business.[50] Critics say these ideas came from outside the business world and are value laden, poorly defined, and vague. As such, to many they are not as meaningful as stakeholder management. Managers do not manage relationships with society, they say, but with stakeholders. As such, stakeholder management is much more directly relevant, real, and manageable.

Stakeholder management considers key stakeholders and the specific issues relevant to each. For any manager, stakeholders would include the company, employees, shareholders, customers, suppliers, and public stakeholders.[51] Company issues would include economic performance, organizational mission or purpose, the competitive environment, and corporate codes. Employee issues include compensation and rewards, health and assistance programs, leaves of absence, dismissals and appeals, terminations and layoffs, discrimination, family accommodation, safety, career planning, and others. Shareholder issues include shareholder rights, advocacy, communications, and complaints. Customer issues include communications, complaints, product safety, services, and others.

Hanna Anderson receives awards for its community commitment, including a program called Hannadowns that donates customers' outgrown clothing to local charities and disaster relief.
[Robbie McClaran]

table 5.4
Approaches to corporate social responsiveness

Rating	Posture or strategy	Performance
1. Reactive	Deny responsibility	Do less than required
2. Defensive	Admit responsibility but fight it	Do the least that is required
3. Accommodative	Accept responsibility	Do all that is required
4. Proactive	Anticipate responsibility	Do more than required

Source: M. B. E. Clarkson, "A Stakeholder Framework for Analyzing and Evaluating Corporate Social Performance," *Academy of Management Review* 20 (1995), pp. 92–117.

Supplier issues include relative power, treatment, and other issues. Public issues include public health and safety, energy conservation, public policy, environmental issues, involvement in public policy, social donations, and community relations.

Many of these managerially relevant issues are discussed in other parts of this book. Now we turn our attention to three issues in particular: strategic voluntarism, the political environment, and the natural environment.

How small companies contribute to their communities

Small companies everywhere are inventing ways to give back to their communities. Greyston Bakery heads a program of job creation for welfare families in the Bronx. Southern Kitchens Inc. of Minneapolis hires ex-convicts and others who are hard to employ.

Many companies begin their philanthropy by giving money. Over time, they begin more ambitious programs. Such initiatives have the *potential* to do a lot of good, but like anything else, they must be well-managed. Programs will fail if employees aren't interested, if the results are discouraging, or if they are simply run poorly.

But when programs work, it is immensely satisfying for employees, customers, and communities. Here are a few ideas:

- *Donate your product*–Laury Hammel of the Longfellow Clubs in Massachusetts donates the use of its health-club facilities to children with special needs. Saint Louis Bread Co. donates its unsold goods at the end of each day to homeless shelters. Harper/Connecting Point Computer Center of Portland, Maine, donates computers and training services to members of the community who can benefit most from them.
- *Involve your employees*–This magnifies the effect of anything you do. Rhino Records gives its people a week off with pay if they contribute 16 hours of personal time per year to community service. Many companies target certain charities and also give employees a chance to work for a cause of their own choosing.
- *Involve other companies*–Longfellow organized an environmental task force at the Chamber of Commerce, and got 50 local businesses to commit to 10 environmentally sound practices. Just Desserts, the San Francisco bakery, involved 35 other companies in adopting a local school in a low-income area.
- *Leverage your company's expertise*–Gilbert Tween Associates, an executive search firm, teaches nonprofit organizations how to recruit, select, and retain good

volunteers. Gardener's Supply in Vermont composts food scraps, provides the nutrient-rich compost to gardeners, and uses the compost to grow produce for a medical-center cafeteria.

- *Enlist suppliers and customers*—Yakima Products of California created an easy way for customers to mail the packaging materials back to the company, for free. The company then reuses and recycles the materials. Some firms are more likely to do business with suppliers having good records of social responsibility, all else equal. And many companies announce to customers that a percentage of their purchases will be donated to a charitable cause.

Source: Reprinted with permission of *Inc.* magazine, Goldhirsh Group. Inc., 38 Commercial Wharf, Boston, MA 02110. (http://www.inc.com) Excerpted from "Making Good," E. E. Spragins, May 1993. Reproduced by permission of the publisher via Copyright Clearance Center, Inc.

Strategic voluntarism

Community service by corporate executives traditionally was a matter of giving some time and money to civic organizations, and going to luncheons and charity balls. Such activities generated political connections, goodwill, and marketing benefits. The biggest charitable givers locally are those with the highest local visibility, such as banks, retailers, and insurance companies. States a banker, "Community service helps us cultivate customers. We will have no customers unless the community is vital."[52]

Companies today are engaging in philanthropic activities more strategically and actively than the traditional cocktail circuit, seeking more focus and impact. Bank of Boston's senior vice president for government and community affairs said, "We want to make a difference, not just play a part. We were giving to too many causes at too modest a level. It didn't make much difference . . . now we want to leverage our investments."[53] Bank of Boston and other strategic philanthropists strive to do things that matter, to get recognition for their contribution, and to support causes that both capitalize on and serve their businesses.

BankBoston sponsors a program for young people to learn the ins and outs of basic banking. *[Skjold/PhotoEdit]*

Thus, a book publisher sponsors literacy programs, and donates books and cash to a children's library at a hospital. Wellfleet Communications and AT&T donated technology, training, and engineering support to the New England Shelter for Homeless veterans, and thus developed demonstration sites while connecting homeless shelters nationwide. And Lotus assisted black communities with information technology projects, and offered internships to black programming trainees, as it entered the South African software market.[54]

Community service is increasingly an employee benefit, as well. Employees sometimes are given a say in their companies' philanthropic activities. Their communities benefit, and they develop pride in their company.

Volunteer work: Good or bad for your career?

Don't do too much volunteer community service, because it could harm your career.

This was the message of an article in *The Wall Street Journal.* A few years ago, many companies urged people to get involved in volunteer work. But in the 1990s, said the article, more companies want more than 40 hours of work per week out of you, and want your extra hours spent working for them, not others.

To some bosses, if you are doing a lot of volunteer work, you must not be spending enough time on your paid job. Said one consultant, "If I were a manager today and had an employee who was extraordinarily task-oriented and another who was a mediocre performer but a great citizen in the community, I'd promote the person getting the important things done in the company. Who's kidding whom? The very survival of the corporation is at stake."

Some companies, like Schnucks Supermarkets in St. Louis and General Mills in Minneapolis, consider community involvement in performance reviews and pay raises. But this is uncommon. Community service can help you meet business contacts, acquire leadership experience, and develop other skills. But some experts say it's not worth the risk if your company doesn't value outside activities.

However, volunteering is an essential part of the lives of most executives in the United States. They find it personally satisfying , and it gives them the opportunity to practice business skills. In other words, they extend their leadership beyond their companies to the larger problems of the world.

Executives say they volunteer because they believe in it and they have a sense of community responsibility. To get the most out of volunteer work, executives say you should choose activities wisely, based on your interests, goals, competencies, and situations. Don't overload yourself; turn down some invitations, perhaps passing them along to a colleague. Apply to this work the same business standards for rigorous, objective decision making. And manage your activities as a portfolio; this means occasionally adding new ones, divesting old ones, and devoting more time and energy to some than to others, in order to achieve the right balance for your goals.

What do you think? How should you make decisions about your own volunteer activities?

Sources: T. D. Schellhardt, "Fewer Good Deeds Go Unpunished in 90s Corporate Climate," *The Wall Street Journal,* October 6, 1993, p. B1; and J. A. Ross, "Community Service: More Rewarding Than You Think," *Harvard Business Review,* July–August 1997, p. 14.

The political environment

The explosive growth of regulation in the late 1960s and early 1970s imposed a vast body of laws and public policy on organizations. Through this regulation, government decision makers exerted increasing control over key areas of managerial decision making—areas where managers often did not want to lose control. While managers may use public policy to define their social responsibilities, they also may recognize the need to influence the laws and regulations that constitute public policy. Therefore, organizations attempt to influence the political environment to achieve two principal goals within their ethical structures: competitive advantage and corporate legitimacy.

Competitive advantage

In many cases, the corporate community sees government as an adversary. However, many progressive organizations realize that government may be the source of competitive advantages for an individual company or an entire industry.[55] For example, public policy may prevent or limit entry into an industry by new foreign or domestic competitors. Government may subsidize failing companies or provide tax breaks to some. Federal patents may be used to protect innovative products or production process technologies. Legislation may be passed to support industry prices, thereby guaranteeing profits or survival. Finally, regulation may favor competitors in one region of the country.

Specific examples of public policy beneficial to business are numerous. Government loan guarantees saved Chrysler Corporation from probable bankruptcy and gave it the opportunity to become a viable, profitable corporation. The utility industry entered into the nuclear power business only after the government provided insurance through the Price-Anderson Act. Since the Great Depression, farmers have been the beneficiaries of government aid and subsidies. Several airlines received help from the government or employed various regulatory and legal maneuvers to promote their survival.

Corporate legitimacy

corporate legitimacy A motive for organizational involvement in the public policy process. The assumption is that organizations are legitimate to the extent that their goals, purposes, and methods are consistent with those of society.

domain defense Activities intended to counter challenges to the organization's legitimacy.

The second motive for corporate involvement in the public process is to increase **corporate legitimacy.**[56] Corporations are legitimate to the extent that their goals, purposes, and methods are consistent with those of society. Because the broader social system is the source of corporate support and allows organizations to pursue their goals, corporations must be sensitive to the expectations and values society establishes. These expectations, in the form of social norms, laws, and regulations, act as controls on the company's behavior. Gross or frequent violations of these expectations will cause the corporation to lose its support and will limit its discretion.

Corporations sometimes face threats that challenge the legitimacy of their existence or their actions. They may be criticized for their efforts to gain competitive advantage, or questions regarding their social responsibility or ethical behavior may be raised. Activity intended to counter challenges to the organization's legitimacy is called **domain defense.**[57] It is designed to strengthen the corporation's right to exist and to operate freely. Domain defense is corporations, acting in their own self-interest, using socially responsible and ethical behavior to maintain and enhance their legitimacy.

From the Pages of BusinessWeek

Money and Olympic Ideals

The International Olympic Committee (IOC) has transformed a bankrupt, amateurishly managed operation into a tremendously successful global marketing machine. In 15 years, the Olympic movement's revenues have multiplied fortyfold, to an annual average of about $1 billion.

Critics say the raw pursuit of money is a betrayal of the Olympic ideal of amateur athletics for its own sake. Defenders say the powerful new Olympic "brand" has saved the Games. IOC President Juan Antonio Samaranch says in response to the criticism, "Society changes. So does sport and the Olympic movement. We have adapted our organization to a new reality."

Samaranch is a highly controversial leader. The president hand-picks most of the 112 IOC members, and most are named for life. Many are long-time communists, and many have close links to deposed or current dictators. Samaranch was a faithful supporter of Spanish dictator Francisco Franco. States one author, "It's an authoritarian club run by an old Francoist who doesn't believe democracy works." Samaranch says he must include officials named by governments even if he doesn't like their politics. He is proud of the record number of countries that now participate, and the unity he has forged.

Critics also allege bribery of committee members by host cities, and drug abuse cover-ups. The IOC says it does more about drugs than other sports organizations.

Samaranch is said to run the IOC in an authoritarian fashion, pushing relentlessly for greater control and even more money. The IOC releases no official financial statements. It says it will open its books in the near future, but doesn't say when.

Business Week concludes that the IOC is an increasingly powerful multinational "accountable only to itself. That makes it like no other multinational on the planet."

Discussion Questions

1. Discuss the International Olympic Committee, as described here, using concepts in this chapter.
2. Based on current news and your own research, how is the IOC operating now, and what are the current controversies and opinions?

Source: W. Echikson, "Making the games run on time" *Business Week,* February 9, 1998, pp. 58–59. ●

Strategies for influencing the political environment

public affairs department
A department that monitors key events and trends in the organization's political and social environments, analyzes their effects on the organization, recommends organizational responses, and implements political strategies.

Managers have an array of strategic options for dealing with the political environment. Many corporations have specialized units for managing these activities. The **public affairs department** of a corporation monitors key events and trends in the political and social environment, analyzes their effects on the organization, recommends the appropriate corporate responses, and implements political strategies. A successful public affairs program enhances an organization's credibility, facilitates a timely and appropriate response to issues, and has a positive financial impact (although this impact may be difficult to measure accurately).[58]

Depending on the needs of an industry or of an individual campaign, the public affairs department performs a variety of important activities:[59]

- *Issues management.* It identifies important social, political, economic, and technological developments and integrates this information into strategic planning.
- *Government relations (federal, state, and local).* It monitors legislative and regulatory developments, assesses their implications, and tries to affect the course of public policy.

- *Public relations.* It communicates information about the organization to the media.
- *International relations.* It promotes company interests in foreign capitals and in international forums.
- *Investor and stockholder relations.* It is often in charge of company communications with investors, brokerage houses, and other financial institutions.
- *Corporate contributions.* It frequently coordinates company contributions to the community.
- *Institutional advertising.* To heighten public awareness, it often engages in image building through nonproduct advertising.

Some specific strategies and vehicles used for managing the political environment are lobbying, PACs, corporate constituency programs, coalition building, stonewalling, and strategic retreat.[60]

Lobbying Lobbying is the most traditional form of influencing the political environment. Lobbying involves efforts by political professionals or company executives to establish communication channels with regulatory bodies, legislators, and their staffs. It is designed to monitor legislation, provide issues papers and other information on the anticipated effects of proposed legislation, convey the company's sentiments on legislative issues to elected officials and their staffs, and attempt to influence the decisions of legislators and key advisers.

Political action committees (PACs) In recent years, many businesses have created corporate **political action committees (PACs).** PACs make donations to candidates for political office. Under reforms in federal election laws passed after the Watergate scandal, companies are allowed to ask their employees and shareholders for contributions for political candidates, subject to a set of limitations.

political action committees (PACs) Political action groups that represent an organization and make donations to candidates for political office.

The PAC system has received much criticism. Some opponents complain that it gives large donors an unfair advantage both in an election and when their interests are brought before the elected legislator. Others claim PAC contributions are not an effective or efficient way for corporations to influence the legislative process. Because political candidates often accept contributions from many diverse and even opposing interests, the impact of any specific contribution is offset by other donations. As a result, the PAC contribution may be "protection money"—a corporation may donate funds to a candidate to ensure that it does not start at a disadvantage during the legislative process. Because of such criticisms, a number of reforms are now being discussed.

Corporate constituency programs In the 1980s, many organizations started political action programs called **corporate constituency programs.** Constituency programs encourage interested stakeholders to engage in grassroots political activity on behalf of the corporation. These actions may include writing a letter to a congressperson or local politician, signing a petition, marching in a demonstration, or expressing an opinion on a television or radio talk show. Some companies spend a great amount of time and money identifying interested stakeholders and educating them on the issues.

corporate constituency programs Organizational efforts to identify, educate, and motivate individuals to take political action that could benefit the organization.

Of the common political strategies, a comprehensive corporate constituency program probably requires the greatest commitment of organizational resources. However, many experts believe this strategy may have the most significant long-term potential to influence the political environment. Instead of providing money to politicians, constituency programs may deliver something even more valuable to elected officials: votes!

Small California wineries are subject to the same government regulations as large wineries, which makes it difficult for wineries such as the one pictured here to sell and distribute their products. *[David Ball/The Stock Market]*

coalition building Finding other organizations or groups of voters that share political interests on a particular legislative issue.

Coalition building

Many corporations and senior executives participate in cooperative efforts to manage the political and social environment. **Coalition building** involves efforts to find other organizations or groups of voters who share interest in a particular legislative issue, and attempt to influence the environment through combined effort and power.

stonewalling The use of public relations, legal action, and administrative processes to prevent or delay the introduction of legislation and regulation that may have an adverse impact on the organization.

Stonewalling

The final two political strategies—stonewalling and strategic retreat—are less opportunistic and proactive than the strategies just discussed, but they are viable options for managing the political and social environment. **Stonewalling** is the use of public relations, legal action, and administrative processes to delay legislation and regulation that may have an adverse impact on the organization. Legal suits or campaigns that improve the company's public image may help protect the organization against threat.

However, stonewalling has disadvantages. Although it may prevent certain problems, it rarely changes the conditions that led to the adverse law or regulation. The organization may constantly be in court or waging a continuous, losing battle for favorable public opinion. This strategy does not create opportunities for the company. Stonewalling often consumes considerable time and money that could be spent on activities leading to long-term positive outcomes. It also may undermine relations with key stakeholders, including customers.

strategic retreat Efforts to adapt products and processes to changes in the political and social environments while minimizing the negative effects of those changes.

Strategic retreat

In some situations, top management and public affairs executives decide the organization will be better served by accepting legislative or regulatory changes even if the changes may hurt the company. **Strategic retreat** involves an organization's efforts to adapt its products and processes to changes in the political and social environment while minimizing the negative effects of these changes. Senior managers may realize that the new law or regulation has support in most segments of society. Political action or stonewalling to oppose the change could have more negative consequences for the company, particularly in the long term, than would adapting to the environment or implementing more proactive strategies.[61]

Small business and government regulators

Large corporations may have public affairs departments, but what can small companies do about government regulations? Here are a few approaches:

Work around the legislation: For example, states have the right to regulate the sale and distribution of alcoholic beverages. Small California wineries must register in other states and are not allowed to sell directly to consumers, wine shops, restaurants, or hotels; they must sell through a distributor. Large wineries can afford this, but small ones cannot. One strategy for the small California winery, then, is to sell only in California and in states that have no licensing fees, like New York and New Jersey. Thus, they are regional–on the two separate coasts.

Work with the regulators: Regulators enforce the law, but they are also human beings. If small business owners explain their compliance problem, they may get helpful advice.

Change product strategies: Blockbuster products in the health care industry can take up to six or seven years to gain approval from the FDA. Small companies therefore cannot devote all their attention to developing big products with substantial market impact. They must have a development mix including small products for which it is easier to gain approval; they may not have great potential, but they can generate some cash flow and enhance financing opportunities. And instead of selling unapproved products to customers, which is illegal, firms can sell them to other companies that can afford to wait through the approval process.

Be a voice in the wilderness: When the Bell system was broken up and the Baby Bells were prohibited from getting into manufacturing and a variety of services, many small companies were hurt because they couldn't sell to the Bells. Small-business people wrote letters to the editor, testified before Congress, and took other actions to make their plight known. It wasn't just whining–they also made the case that small businesses thrive around large companies, not only for sales but also in joint ventures. The result was a relaxation of some of the regulations and a number of new business opportunities.

Source: Reprinted with permission of *Inc.* magazine, Goldhirsh Group. Inc., 38 Commercial Wharf, Boston, MA 02110. (http://www.inc.com) Excerpted from "How Can You Survive the Regulators?" J. Seglin, September 1994. Reproduced by permission of the publisher via Copyright Clearance Center, Inc.

The natural environment

Managers operating in today's world face a new and urgent imperative: to create a new relationship between business activity and our natural environment that will halt environmental damage and clean up the effects of past practices.[62] James Post, professor of management and public policy at Boston University, states, "[E]nvironmental issues will be . . . a force of such power as to literally transform the way managers manage their businesses and think about the relationship of the firm to its internal and external stakeholders."

The range of environmental issues is broad, and the impact huge. Effectively managing with the environment in mind requires attention to efficiency, effectiveness, and long-term goals. Environmental management must consider a mix of technical, ethical, social, and competitive issues.[63]

A McKinsey survey found that 92 percent of CEOs and board members stated the environment should be one of the top three management priorities; 85 percent said one of their major goals should be integrating environment into strategy, but only 37 percent said they do so successfully.[64] Richard A. Clarke, CEO of Pacific Gas and Electric

Company, put it this way: "A strong global economy is sustained only if it integrates economic, social, and environmental well-being."[65]

Business used to look at environmental issues as a no-win situation: You either help the environment and hurt your business, or help your business only at a cost to the environment. Fortunately, things have changed. "When Americans first demanded a cleanup of the environment during the early 1970s, corporations threw a tantrum. Their response ran the psychological gamut from denial to hostility, defiance, obstinacy, and fear. But today, when it comes to green issues, many U.S. companies have turned from rebellious underachievers to active problem solvers."[66]

A risk society

We live in a risk society. That is, the creation and distribution of wealth generate byproducts that can cause injury, loss, or danger to people and the environment. The fundamental sources of risk in modern society are the excessive production of hazards and ecologically unsustainable consumption of natural resources.[67] Risk has proliferated through population explosion, industrial pollution, environmental degradation, and poor risk management.[68]

Industrial pollution risks include air pollution, smog, global warming, ozone depletion, acid rain, toxic waste sites, nuclear hazards, obsolete weapons arsenals, industrial accidents, and hazardous products. Over 30,000 uncontrolled toxic waste sites have been documented in the United States alone, and the number is increasing by perhaps 2,500 per year. The situation is far worse in other parts of the world. The pattern, for toxic waste and many other risks, is one of accumulating risks and inadequate remedies. The institutions that create environmental and technological risk (corporations and government agencies) also are in charge of controlling and managing the risks.[69]

Ecocentric management

ecocentric management has as its goal the creation of sustainable economic development and improvement of quality of life worldwide for all organizational stakeholders.

design for environment (DFE) A tool for creating products that are easy to recover, reuse, or recycle.

Ecocentric management has as its goal the creation of sustainable economic development and improvement of quality of life worldwide for all organizational stakeholders.[70] Management decisions seek to minimize negative environmental impact through all aspects of the organization: its mission, inputs, throughputs, and outputs. Ecocentric management encourages low energy use, smaller resource quantities, environmentally appropriate production technologies, and products with ecofriendly packaging and recyclable materials. It minimizes waste and pollution and tries to renew natural resources.

As you can see, ecocentric management uses a complete open systems perspective, and each business function operates with the ecology in mind. An important example is **design for environment (DFE),** a tool for creating products that are easier to recover, reuse, or recycle. All environmental effects of a product are examined during the design phase. The analysis is cradle-to-grave: full assessment of all inputs, through a detailed analysis of how customers use and dispose of it.

In Germany, the "take-back" law passed in 1990 requires auto manufacturers to take responsibility for their products up through the very end of their useful lives. Thus, BMW designs its cars not just for assembly, but for disassembly as well. And Amory Lovins of the Rocky Mountain Institute is pushing hypercars that are 20 times more energy efficient, use lightweight composite materials, have very small engines, and are fully recyclable. You can read more specifics about this approach in Appendix B at the end of this chapter.

Proponents of ecocentric management state that corporations must do more than optimize production variables such as productivity, growth, and profits. They also must manage risk variables, including pollution, resources, waste, technological hazards, dangerous products, and public safety.[71] Profitability need not suffer, and in fact may in time be positively affected by ecocentric philosophies and practices. Some, but not all, research has indicated a positive relationship between corporate environmental performance and profitability.[72]

Monsanto, for example, intends to feed the world's exploding population and heal the environment at the same time. CEO Robert Shapiro is a crusader for this vision of the company and of sustainable development. He also believes in tough business logic. As he puts it, "If Monsanto and other companies can get environmentally better products that people want to market faster at lower costs, we will kick butt in the marketplace."[73]

The most admired company in Britain, British Petroleum, ranks No. 1 in the country in environmental responsibility. For example, BP spent about $80 million adding environmental safeguards to a facility in Scotland. CEO John Browne said, "Unlike in the U.S., there was no regulatory pressure at all to do that in Scotland, but we did it voluntarily. It's our way of saying to people, we're here to stay."[74]

Environmental agenda for the future

Business strategies and tactics for greening have up to now been primarily technical and operational, as in the pollution-prevention programs that have saved companies billions of dollars. Now, however, some executives are realizing how environmental opportunities can create revenue growth. In the past, companies were oblivious to their negative environmental impact; more recently, many have begun striving for low impact. Now, some strive for positive impact, and to sell solutions to the world's problems.

Environmental problems are traced to explosive population growth and rapid economic development. These issues are beyond the ability and mandate of a single company to solve. But corporations are the only organizations with the resources, technology, and global power to help create a sustainable world. And individual companies do not need to act alone. Webs of companies with a common ecological vision can combine their efforts into high-leverage, impactful action.[75] In Kalundborg, Denmark, such a collaborative alliance exists among an electric power generating plant, an oil refiner, a biotech production plant, a plasterboard factory, cement producers, heating utilities, a sulfuric acid producer, and local agriculture and horticulture. Chemicals, energy (for both heating and cooling), water, and organic materials flow between companies. Resources are conserved, "waste" materials generate revenues, and water, air, and ground pollution all are reduced.

Companies not only have the *ability* to solve environmental problems; they are coming to see and acquire the *motivation* as well. Many industries are now turning their attention to pursuing what some see as one of the biggest opportunities in the history of commerce.[76]

Key terms

Business ethics, p. 154
Business judgment rule, p. 166
Coalition building, p. 175
Compliance-based ethics programs, p. 162
Corporate constituency programs, p. 174
Corporate legitimacy, p. 173
Corporate social responsibility, p. 164
Corporate social responsiveness, p. 168
Deontology, p. 156
Design for environment (DFE), p. 177
Domain defense, p. 173
Ecocentric management, p.177
Economic responsibilities, p. 164
Egoism, p. 155
Ethical climate, p. 159
Ethical issue, p. 154
Ethical responsibilities, p. 164
Ethics, p. 154
Integrity-based ethics programs, p. 162
Kohlberg's model of cognitive moral development, p. 156
Legal responsibilities, p. 164
Moral philosophy, p. 154
Political action committees (PACs), p. 174
Public affairs department, p. 173
Relativism, p. 156
Stonewalling, p. 175
Strategic retreat, p. 175
Teleology, p. 155
Universalism, p. 154
Utilitarianism, p. 156
Virtue ethics, p. 156
Voluntary responsibilities, p. 164

Summary of learning objectives

Now that you have studied Chapter 5, you should know:

How different ethical perspectives guide decision making.

The purpose of ethics is to identify the rules that govern human behavior and the "goods" that are worth seeking. Ethical decisions are guided by the individual's values, or principles of conduct such as honesty, fairness, integrity, respect for others, and responsible citizenship. Different ethical systems include universalism; teleology, including egoism and utilitarianism; deontology, including rule deontology and act deontology; relativism; and virtue ethics. These philosophical systems, as practiced by different individuals according to their level of cognitive moral development and other factors, underlie the ethical stances of individuals and organizations.

How companies influence the ethics environment.

Different organizations apply different ethical perspectives and standards. Ethical codes sometimes are helpful, although they must be implemented properly. Ethics programs can range from compliance-based to integrity-based. An increasing number of organizations are adopting ethics codes. Such codes address employee conduct, community and environment, shareholders, customers, suppliers and contractors, political activity, and technology.

The options you have when confronting ethical issues.

Individuals have a variety of options when they witness unethical behavior. Their choice of action will depend on both their beliefs about the action's likely outcomes and their own moral judgment. When faced with ethical dilemmas, you should define the issue clearly, identify relevant values, weigh conflicting values and choose an appropriate option, and implement your decision.

The important issues surrounding corporate social responsibility.

Corporate social responsibility is the extension of the corporate role beyond economic pursuits. It includes not only economic but also legal, ethical, and voluntary responsibilities. Advocates believe managers should consider societal and human needs in their business decisions because corporations are members of society and carry a wide range of responsibilities. Critics of corporate responsibility believe managers' first responsibility is to increase profits for the shareholders who own the corporation. The two perspectives are potentially reconcilable. Whereas corporate social responsibility (CSR1) refers to principles, philosophies, and beliefs surrounding these issues, corporate social responsiveness (CSR2) is the processes companies actually use and the actions they take.

How the political and social environment affects your firm's competitive position and legitimacy.

Corporations have two goals within their ethical structures: competitive advantage and corporate legitimacy. Progressive organizations realize that the government can be an ally and a source of competitive advantage rather than just an adversary. Corporate legitimacy comes from goals, purposes, and methods that are consistent with those of society. Thus, organizations must be sensitive to the expectations and values of society.

The strategies corporations use to manage the political and social environment.

The public affairs department monitors the political and social environment, analyzes its impact on the organization, and implements political strategies. Strategies include lobbying, political action committees, corporate constituency programs, coalition building, stonewalling, and strategic retreat. Generally, strategies that adapt to or change the environment are most effective in the long run.

The role of managers in our natural environment.

Organizations have contributed risk to society and have some responsibility for reducing risk to the environment. They also have the capability to help solve environmental problems. Ecocentric management attempts to minimize negative environmental impact, create sustainable economic development, and improve the quality of life worldwide. Some companies now are moving beyond pollution prevention programs and zero-impact efforts to interorganizational alliances and strategic initiatives that pursue positive opportunities and revenue growth.

Discussion questions

1. Assess the example in Setting the Stage using concepts in the chapter and your personal opinion.

2. What kinds of questions concern ethical thinkers? Provide concrete examples and discuss.

3. Which of the acts in Table 5.1 are most unethical? Least unethical? Discuss.

4. What would you do in each of the scenarios described in Table 5.2, "Ethical Decision Making in the International Context"?

5. Identify and discuss illegal, unethical, and socially responsible business actions in the current news.

6. Does your school have a code of ethics? If so, what does it say? Is it effective? Why or why not?

7. You have a job you like at which you work 40 to 45 hours per week. How much off-the-job volunteer work would you do? What kinds of volunteer work? How will you react if your boss makes it clear he or she wants you to cut back on the outside activities and devote more hours to your job?

8. What are the arguments for and against the concept of corporate social responsibility? Where do you stand, and why? Give your opinions, specifically, with respect to the text discussions of American cigarettes overseas and the International Olympic Committee.

9. How can the political and social environment both constrain and help the corporation in its pursuit of competitive advantage? Give examples.

10. Under what conditions might stonewalling and strategic retreat be the most appropriate political strategies? Have you seen these tactics work?

11. A company in England slaughters 70,000 baby ostrich chicks each year for their meat. It told a teen magazine that it would stop if it received enough complaints. Analyze this policy, practice, and public statement using the concepts discussed in the chapter.

12. A Nike ad in the U.S. magazine *Seventeen* shows a picture of a girl, aged perhaps 8 or 9. The ad reads,

> If you let me play . . .
>
> I will like myself more.
>
> I will have more self-confidence.
>
> I will suffer less depression.
>
> I will be 60% less likely to get breast cancer.
>
> I will be more likely to leave a man who beats me.
>
> I will be less likely to get pregnant before I want to.
>
> I will learn what it means to be strong.
>
> If you let me play sports.

Assess this ad in terms of chapter concepts surrounding ethics and social responsibility. What questions would you ask in doing this analysis?

Concluding Case

Nike controversies

"A company that ignores its social responsibility is playing with fire," states one critic of Nike. Another condemns Nike for glorifying violence and bad taste, and for doing "nothing to promote values, especially among impressionable youngsters." International soccer barons fume that Nike is infecting futbol with the American disease of money-will-get-you-everything. Human rights groups accuse Nike contractors of operating their factories like prison camps, hiring 13-year-old children and treating workers "little better than slaves." Nike denies such charges, but also is changing its ways.

Nike has always prided itself on its radical, rebellious, anti-establishment image. Its brashness has paid off big-time in the United States. But Nike believes its domestic sales are topping out, and that its future lies in the international arena. Whereas domestic sales average $20 per American, Nike per capita sales are $4 in Japan, $3 in Germany, and under 3 cents in China. The company wants to generate more than half of its revenues overseas by the year 2000. But as its marketing efforts expand into the international arena, many of the company's decisions are decried as irresponsible.

A Nike ad in *Soccer America* magazine crowed, "Europe, Asia, and Latin America: Barricade your stadiums. Hide your trophies. Invest in some deodorant. As Asia and Latin America have been crushed, so shall Europe . . . the world has been warned." The deodorant line did not amuse, and Nike was seen by many as the ugly American crashing hallowed traditions.

The soccer market has been dominated by Adidas, but Nike wants it. In 1994, Nike had several Brazilian stars under individual contract. Phil Knight, Nike's chairman and "an otherwise proud American," as *The Wall Street Journal* put it, rooted for Brazil against the United States. When Brazil won, he decided to buy the team. One-and-a-half years and $200 million later, it was his. Nike announced it would take the Brazilians on a world tour, and *The Wall Street Journal* asked, "Was this carpetbagger from Beaverton [Oregon, Nike's headquarters location] trying to buy Brazil's passion and history and pass it off as its own ?"

A TV commercial featured a Manchester United player explaining how spitting at a fan and insulting a coach won him a Nike contract. A Nike advertising campaign at the Atlanta Olympic Games employed the slogan, "You don't win silver, you lose gold." Olympic committees from several countries were incensed; the slogan was said to denigrate the Olympic spirit of competition, and belittled all the athletes who failed to win gold.

In Vietnam, Nike pays its workers a daily wage less than the cost of three meals of rice, vegetables, and tofu. American businessman Thuyen Nguyen interviewed 35 Vietnamese workers and concluded that 32 had lost weight, and that they were subjected to humiliations including having stiffly-enforced limits of two drinks of water and one bathroom break in an eight-hour shift; being hit over the head for poor workmanship; being forced to kneel with their hands in the air for up to 25 minutes; having their mouths taped for talking; and being "sundried"—forced to stand in the hot sun for lengthy periods writing their mistakes over and over. Nike has since been criticized in *Doonesbury* for the factory conditions in Viet Nam, although even Nike critics concede that Nike is not the only, or the worst, corporate offender.

Nike has designs on untapped market share in the international arena, but must overcome controversies such as the accusation by human rights groups that their factories are like prison camps.
[Reuters/Keith B. Richburg/Archive Photos]

Many people would consider the Vietnam factory conditions as highly unethical. But even these are defended by some observers on ethical grounds. In a *Fortune* article titled "The Case for Sweatshops," David R. Henderson of the Hoover Institution and the Naval Postgraduate School argues that critics must not lose sight of what happens when low-wage child laborers lose their jobs. "They are worse off," Henderson writes. "You don't make someone better off by taking away the best of their bad options . . . sweatshops, in short, are a path from poverty to greater wealth." (p. 22)

In its global marketing, Nike has realized that its tactics are backfiring and hurting its global ambitions. Phil Knight says that Nike is now making an effort to get along. Nike's soccer chief stated, "We're not intentionally going to go out and offend. That would be counterproductive." In late 1997, Nike announced at its shareholder meeting that it would sever ties with four Indonesian factories for violating labor standards. Such violations are exceptions, though, said the chairman. "Good shoes are made in good factories. Good factories have good labor relations." Then, in mid-1998, Phil Knight publicly acknowledged how much damage the criticism had done to his company's image, and announced that it would raise the minimum wage for its workers and impose American air quality standards on its overseas plants.

Questions

1. Nike's success in the United States is inarguable. What about its strategies and tactics? What do you think of the decisions described above? Are they just poor business decisions that backfired? Or are they also irresponsible, unethical?

2. If some of Nike's decisions are unethical, which are the most unethical, and which least? How did you reach these judgments?

3. What do you think of the Nike response to the criticism?

4. What else, if any thing, should Nike do about the issues raised in the case?

Sources: "Nike Sanctions 3 Firms for Labor Abuses," *International Herald Tribune,* September 24, 1997, p. 19; B. Herbert, "Making Billions on the Backs of Hungry Women," *International Herald Tribune,* April 1, 1997, p. 9; R. Thurow, "In Global Push, Nike Finds Its Brash Ways Don't Always Pay Off," *The Wall Street Journal,* May 6, 1997, pp. 1, 6; and D. R. Henderson, "The Case for Sweatshops," *Fortune,* October 28, 1996, pp. 20, 22; E. J. Dionne, Jr. "Swoosh! Shaming Net Results," *International Herald Tribune,* May 15, 1998, p. 11. ●

Video Case

The high bid dilemma

Purpose

This exercise provides students with the opportunity to view the possibility of conflict of interest when dealing with an outside vendor.

A purchasing agent (PA) and his assistant are reviewing bids from seven companies to determine which company should receive a contract. The PA's assistant proposes that the bid should be awarded to Metaltech, the low bidder, which is located some 300 miles away. His boss, the PA agent, leans toward Spin Cast Systems, a nearby company, which has submitted a much higher bid. Both companies submitting bids have the ability to provide a quality product complete with delivery and support capabilities.

The PA attempts to persuade his assistant that the contract should be awarded to Spin Cast Systems despite its higher bid that will create a budgetary problem. He informs his assistant that he has used Spin Cast's services previously. Moreover, Greg Sommers, the president of Spin Cast, is his personal friend, his fraternity brother, and his sailing companion. The PA tells his assistant, "You take care of your suppliers and they'll take care of you." In fact, to show his assistant that Sommers is a "nice guy," the PA will ask Sommers to invite the assistant to a house party.

Critical Thinking Questions

1. Does the issue of a "conflict of interest" surface in this exercise? If so, how? If not, why not?

2. Will the purchasing assistant compromise his own ethics if he allows his boss to award the bid to Spin Cast Systems even though such an award will create a budget overrun and does not follow company regulations?

3. Does the purchasing agent's assistant have any possible options if his boss decides to award the bid to Spin Cast? ●

Video Case

Competition or revenge

Purpose

This exercise questions the ethics of an ex-employee competing with his former employer for the same client.

A group of salespeople are discussing the impact a former employee is having on their current sales. Jack Rebeck, who was recently fired from his position, is now soliciting former clients. In one instance he has been successful in underbidding his old firm. The members of the sales group are concerned with Rebeck's competing for the same client pool.

Because Rebeck has limited financial resources, George, one member of the sales group, suggests that the company underbid Rebeck on projects. Jean, another former colleague, suggests that the group spread stories within the industry about the reasons Rebeck was terminated by the company, and finally, Jeff, the last member of the sales group, believes that bad-mouthing and undermining Rebeck is fruitless and will not have an impact on the company's business.

Critical Thinking Questions

1. Is it ethical for an ex-employee to compete with a former company? If so, when? Under what circumstances?

2. Is it ethical for a company to attempt to undermine a former employee who is now a competitor?

3. If a company discusses the reason(s) an employee was terminated, does it violate employee confidentiality? ●

Video Case

Creative expense reporting

Purpose

This video raises the issues of padding the expense account by submitting unsubstantiated expense vouchers to a company for reimbursement.

Jim, a salesperson, enters Ken's workstation to discuss a problem. He apparently has lost the hotel room receipt for his last stay in New York. Ken tells him the cost of his larger suite. Jim also asks Ken about the cost of a taxi ride so that he can prepare his expense voucher. Ken informs him of the cost of his taxi ride.

Jim, after some deliberation, decides to pad both his hotel room and his taxi ride by settling on an "odd-dollar" amount that will appear more realistic to those reviewing the submission of his voucher. Finally, Jim informs Ken of his intention to pad the lunch and dinner bills to cover entertainment costs he incurred during the trip. Since Jim considers entertainment as a part of conducting business, no one would question an expense of a few extra dollars on the voucher.

Critical Thinking Questions

1. Should Ken tell his superiors that Jim has padded the expense voucher?

2. Is padding a business expense ever justified? If so, when? Why?

3. If he wanted to submit an accurate expense voucher, what options are available to Jim to secure the correct information?

Experiential Exercises

5.1 Measuring your ethical work behavior

Objectives

1. To explore a range of ethically perplexing situations.
2. To understand your own ethical attitudes.

Instructions

Make decisions in the situations described in the Ethical Behavior Worksheet. You will not have all the background information on each situation, and, instead, you should make whatever assumptions you feel you would make if you were actually confronted with the decision choices described. Select the decision choice that most closely represents the decision you feel you would make personally. You should choose decision choices even though you can envision other creative solutions that were not included in the exercise.

Ethical behavior worksheet

Situation 1. You are taking a very difficult chemistry course, which you must pass to maintain your scholarship and to avoid damaging your application for graduate school. Chemistry is not your strong suit, and, because of a just-below-failing average in the course, you will have to receive a grade of 90 or better on the final exam, which is two days away. A janitor, who is aware of your plight, informs you that he has found the master stencil for the chemistry final in a trash barrel and saved it. He will make it available to you for a price, which is high, but which you could afford. What would you do?

_______ (a) I would tell the janitor thanks, but no thanks.

_______ (b) I would report the janitor to the proper officials.

_______ (c) I would buy the exam and keep it to myself.

_______ (d) I would not buy the exam myself, but I would let some of my friends, who are also flunking the course, know that it is available.

Situation 2. You have been working on some financial projections manually for two days now. It seems that each time you think you have them completed your boss shows up with a new assumption or another "what-if" question. If you only had a copy of a spreadsheet software program for your personal computer, you could plug in the new assumptions and revise the estimates with ease. Then, a colleague offers to let you make a copy of some software that is copyrighted. What would you do?

_______ (a) I would accept my friend's generous offer and make a copy of the software.

_______ (b) I would decline to copy it and plug away manually on the numbers.

_______ (c) I would decide to go buy a copy of the software myself, for $300, and hope I would be reimbursed by the company in a month or two.

_______ (d) I would request another extension on an already overdue project date.

Situation 3. Your small manufacturing company is in serious financial difficulty. A large order of your products is ready to be delivered to a key customer when you discover that the product is simply not right. It will not meet all performance specifications, will cause problems for your customer, and will require rework in the field; but this, you know, will not become evident until after the customer has received and paid for the order. If you do not ship the order and receive the payment as expected, your business may be forced into bankruptcy. And if you delay the shipment or inform the customer of these problems, you may lose the order and also go bankrupt. What would you do?

_______ (a) I would not ship the order and place my firm in voluntary bankruptcy.

_______ (b) I would inform the customer and declare voluntary bankruptcy.

_______ (c) I would ship the order and inform the customer, after I received payment.

_______ (d) I would ship the order and not inform the customer.

Situation 4. You are the cofounder and president of a new venture, manufacturing products for the recreational market. Five months after launching the business, one of your suppliers informs you it can no longer supply you with a critical raw material since you are not a large-quantity user. Without the raw material, the business cannot continue. What would you do?

_______ (a) I would grossly overstate my requirements to another supplier to make the supplier think I am a much larger potential customer in order to secure the raw material from that supplier, even though this would mean the supplier will no longer be able to supply another, non-competing small manufacturer who may thus be forced out of business.

_______ (b) I would steal raw material from another firm (noncompeting) where I am aware of a sizable stockpile.

_______ (c) I would pay off the supplier, since I have reason to believe that the supplier could be "persuaded" to meet my needs with a sizable "under the table" payoff that my company could afford.

_______ (d) I would declare voluntary bankruptcy.

Situation 5. You are on a marketing trip for your new venture for the purpose of calling on the purchasing agent of a major prospective client. Your company is manufacturing an electronic system that you hope the purchasing agent will buy. During the course of your conversation, you notice on the cluttered desk of the purchasing agent several copies of a cost proposal for a system from one of your direct competitors. This purchasing agent has previously reported mislaying several of your own company's proposals and has asked for additional copies. The purchasing agent leaves the room momentarily to get you a cup of coffee, leaving you alone with your competitor's proposals less than an arm's length away. What would you do?

_______ (a) I would do nothing but await the man's return.

_______ (b) I would sneak a quick peek at the proposal, looking for bottom-line numbers.

_______ (c) I would put the copy of the proposal in my briefcase.

_______ (d) I would wait until the man returns and ask his permission to see the copy.

Source: Jeffrey A. Timmons, *New Venture Creation,* 3rd ed. (Burr Ridge, IL: Richard D. Irwin, 1994), pp. 285–86. ●

5.2 Social responsibility

Objectives

1. To have a look at a socially responsible undertaking of a firm.
2. To examine the pros and cons of firms taking on the role of trying to solve social ills.

Instructions

There are many arguments for and against firms taking a role in trying to alleviate community or social ills. Find an example of a business acting in a manner that is clearly socially responsible, such as providing job training programs for the unemployed or providing financial support for urban renewal. You may be able to find your own example of this locally, or in articles in business periodicals.

Ethical behavior worksheet

1. Briefly describe the firm and its program(s).

2. What is the rationale the firm uses to support this program?

3. What is the response from those affected by the program?

4. What is the response, if any, from those who oppose the program?

5. Do you think the company is benefiting from the program to the extent of the program's cost?

Source: R. R. McGrath Jr., *Exercises in Management Fundamentals* (Englewood Cliffs, NJ: Prentice Hall, 1985), p. 192. Reprinted by permission of Prentice-Hall, Inc.

5.3 Strategy for dealing with toxic waste in the river

Objectives

1. To examine your attitude toward managing in our natural environment.
2. To explore new strategies for dealing with a natural-environment challenge.

Instructions

1. Read the scenario below about discovery of a toxic effluent by a firm's chemist.
2. You are the manager and must decide how to respond to the discovery of the unsuspected toxic by-product.

Discovery of a toxic by-product

You are the plant manager of a small chemical plant north of St. Louis. For years your firm dumped its untreated effluents into the Mississippi as a matter of everyday business. Recently, Environmental Protection Agency standards have required you to install a treatment system to minimize the level of several specific contaminants. Your firm has abided by the ruling; only treated sewage is being dumped into the river. However, you have just received a report from your head chemist, who has discovered that a by-product of a new chemical being produced by the firm is highly toxic. Moreover, the present filtration system utterly fails to filter out the toxic substance. It is all headed downstream toward St. Louis.

Strategy worksheet

Now that you have this report, what do you plan to do? Consider your alternatives and develop a strategy. If part of your strategy is to get in touch with your boss at company headquarters in Chicago, state what recommendation you intend to make.

5.4 An environmental protection code of ethics

Objectives

1. To further clarify the role business plays in environmental pollution.
2. To identify codes of ethics that businesses adopt to minimize the potential adverse impact of their activities on the environment.

Instructions

1. Your instructor will divide the class into small groups and assign each group one or more environmental problems to investigate.
2. For each environmental problem assigned, the groups will complete the Environmental Code of Ethics Worksheet by investigating the things business does that affect the environment and developing "code of ethics" statements by which businesses can deal with the problems in a positive, socially responsible manner.
3. After the class reconvenes, group spokespersons present group findings.
4. The class may proceed to the development of an overall Environmental Code of Ethics for businesses.

The environmental code of ethics worksheet

In the space provided below, identify business activities that contribute to the environmental problem(s) assigned by your instructor and develop code of ethics statements that can be adopted to deal with the problem(s).

Environmental Pollution Problem: ______________________________

Business activity	Corresponding code of ethics statement

Appendix A

The Caux Round Table Business Principles of Ethics

Principle 1. the responsibilities of businesses: beyond shareholders toward stakeholders

The value of a business to society is the wealth and employment it creates and the marketable products and services it provides to consumers at a reasonable price commensurate with quality. To create such value, a business must maintain its own economic health and viability, but survival is not a sufficient goal.

Businesses have a role to play in improving the lives of all their customers, employees, and shareholders by sharing with them the wealth they have created. Suppliers and competitors as well should expect businesses to honor their obligations in a spirit of honesty and fairness. As responsible citizens of the local, national, regional, and global communities in which they operate, businesses share a part in shaping the future of those communities.

Principle 2. the economic and social impact of business: toward innovation, justice, and world community

Businesses established in foreign countries to develop, produce, or sell should also contribute to the social advancement of those countries by creating productive employment and helping to raise the purchasing power of their citizens. Businesses also should contribute to human rights, education, welfare, and vitalization of the countries in which they operate.

Businesses should contribute to economic and social development not only in the countries in which they operate, but also in the world community at large, through effective and prudent use of resources, free and fair competition, and emphasis upon innovation in technology, production, methods, marketing, and communications.

Principle 3. business behavior: beyond the letter of law toward a spirit of trust

While accepting the legitimacy of trade secrets, businesses should recognize that sincerity, candor, truthfulness, the keeping of promises, and transparency contribute not only to their own credibility and stability but also to the smoothness and efficiency of business transactions, particularly on the international level.

Principle 4. respect for rules

To avoid trade friction and to promote freer trade, equal conditions for competition, and fair and equitable treatment for all participants, businesses should respect international and domestic rules. In addition, they should recognize that some behavior, although legal, may still have adverse consequences.

Principle 5. support for multilateral trade

Businesses should support the multilateral trade systems of GATT/World Trade Organization and similar international agreements. They should cooperate in efforts to promote the progressive and judicious liberalization of trade, and to relax those domestic measures that unreasonably hinder global commerce, while giving due respect to national policy objectives.

Principle 6. respect for the environment

A business should protect and, where possible, improve the environment, promote sustainable development, and prevent the wasteful use of natural resources.

Principle 7. avoidance of illicit operations

A business should not participate in or condone bribery, money laundering, or other corrupt practices; indeed, it should seek cooperation with others to eliminate them. It should not trade in arms or other materials used for terrorist activities, drug traffic, or other organized crime.

Principle 8. customers

We believe in treating all customers with dignity, irrespective of whether they purchase our products and services directly from us or otherwise acquire them in the market. We therefore have a responsibility to:

- provide our customers with the highest quality products and services consistent with their requirements;
- treat our customers fairly in all respects of our business transactions, including a high level of service and remedies for their dissatisfaction;
- make every effort to ensure that the health and safety of our customers, as well as the quality of their environment, will be sustained or enhanced by our products and services;
- assure respect for human dignity in products offered, marketing, and advertising; and respect the integrity of the culture of our customers.

Principle 9. employees

We believe in the dignity of every employee and in taking employee interests seriously. We therefore have a responsibility to:

- provide jobs and compensation that improve worker's living conditions;

- provide work conditions that respect each employee's health and dignity;
- be honest in communications with employees and open in sharing information, limited only by legal and competitive restraint;
- listen to and, where possible, act on employee suggestions, ideas, requests, and complaints;
- engage in good faith negotiations when conflict arises;
- avoid discriminatory practices and guarantee equal treatment and opportunity in areas such as gender, age, race, and religion;
- promote in the business itself the employment of differently abled people in places of work where they can be genuinely useful;
- protect employees from avoidable injury and illness in the workplace;
- encourage and assist employees in developing relevant and transferable skills and knowledge; and
- be sensitive to serious unemployment problems frequently associated with business decisions, and work with the government, employee groups, other agencies and each other in addressing these dislocations.

Principle 10. owners/investors

We believe in honoring the trust our investors place in us. We therefore have a responsibility to:

- apply professional and diligent management in order to secure a fair and competitive return on our owners' investment;
- disclose relevant information to owners/investors subject only to legal requirements and competitive constraints;
- conserve, protect, and increase the owners/investors' assets; and
- respect owners/investors' requests, suggestions, complaints, and formal resolutions.

Principle 11. suppliers

Our relationship with suppliers and subcontractors must be based on mutual respect. We therefore have a responsibility to:

- seek fairness and truthfulness in all of our activities, including pricing, licensing, and rights to sell;
- ensure that business activities are free from coercion and unnecessary litigation;
- foster long-term stability in the supplier relationship in return for value, quality, competitiveness, and liability;
- share information with suppliers and integrate them into our planning processes;
- pay suppliers on time and in accordance with agreed terms of trade;
- seek, encourage, and prefer suppliers and subcontractors whose employment practices respect human dignity.

Principle 12. competitors

We believe that fair economic competition is one of the basic requirements for increasing the wealth of the nations and, ultimately, for making possible the just distribution of goods and services. We therefore have a responsibility to:

- foster open markets for trade and investments;
- promote competitive behavior that is socially and environmentally beneficial and demonstrates mutual respect among competitors;
- refrain from either seeking or participating in questionable payments of favors to secure competitive advantages;
- respect both tangible and intellectual property rights; and
- refuse to acquire commercial information by dishonest or unethical means, such as industrial espionage.

Principle 13. communities

We believe that as global corporate citizens, we can contribute to such forces of reform and human rights as are at work in the communities in which we operate. We therefore have a responsibility in those communities to:

- respect human rights and democratic institutions, and promote them wherever practicable;
- recognize government's legitimate obligation to the society at large and support public policies and practices that promote human development through harmonious relations between business and other segments;
- collaborate with those forces in the community dedicated to raising standards of health, education, workplace safety, and economic well-being;
- promote and stimulate sustainable development and play a leading role in preserving and enhancing the physical environment and conserving the earth's resources;
- support peace, security, diversity, and social integration;
- respect the integrity of local cultures; and
- be a good corporate citizen through charitable donations, educational and cultural contributions, and employee participation in community and civic affairs.

Source: Caux Round Table in Switzerland, "Principles for Business," special advertising supplement contributed as a public service by Canon, *Business Ethics,* May–June 1995, p. 35.

Appendix B
Managing in our natural environment

Business and the Environment: Conflicting Views

Some people believe everyone wins when business tackles environmental issues. Others disagree.

The win-win mentality Business used to look at environmental issues as a no-win situation: You either help the environment and hurt your business, or help your business only at a cost to the environment. Fortunately, things have changed. As stated in the chapter, "When Americans first demanded a cleanup of the environment during the early 1970s, corporations threw a tantrum. Their response ran the psychological gamut from denial to hostility, defiance, obstinacy, and fear. But today, when it comes to green issues, many U.S. companies have turned from rebellious underachievers to active problem solvers."[1]

The Earth Summit in Rio in 1992 helped increase awareness of environmental issues. States Livio DeSimone, CEO of 3M, "There has been an evolution of most groups—whether industry, governments, or nongovernmental organizations—toward a recognition that everyone plays a part in reaching a solution."[2]

Being "green" is potentially a catalyst for innovation, new market opportunities, and wealth creation. Advocates believe that this is truly a win-win situation; actions can be taken that benefit both business and the environment. For example, Procter & Gamble in a span of five years reduced disposable wastes by over 50 percent while increasing sales by 25 percent.[3] Only win-win companies will survive; they will come out ahead of those companies that have an us-versus-them, we-can't-afford-to-protect-the-environment mentality. Table 5.B.1 gives just a few examples of things U.S. corporations are doing to help solve environmental problems.

Is the easy part over? Companies have found a lot of easy-to-harvest, "low-hanging fruit"—that is, overly costly practices that were made environmentally friendlier and that saved money at the same time. Many big companies have made these easy changes, and reaped benefits from them. Many small companies still have such low-hanging fruit to harvest.[4]

The dissenting view The critics of environmentalism in business are vocal. Some economists maintain that not a single empirical analysis supports the "free lunch view" that spending money on environmental problems provides full payback to the firm.[5] Skepticism should continue, they say; the belief that everyone will come out a winner is naive.

What really upsets many businesspeople is the financial cost of complying with environmental regulations.[6] Consider a few examples:

- GM is spending $1.3 billion to comply with California requirements that 10 percent of the cars sold there be emission-free. European automakers spent $7 billion to install pollution-control equipment in all new cars during a five-year period.
- At Bayer, 20 percent of manufacturing costs are for the environment. This is approximately the same amount spent for labor.

table 5.B.1
What companies are doing to enhance the environment

- Ben & Jerry's Homemade feeds to pigs the sludge left over from the manufacture of ice cream; it also pours it on farmland as fertilizer.
- Texaco created a new division for the environment, health, and safety; the head of the division reports directly to the CEO.
- Kodak is recycling its disposable cameras and spending $46 million to cut methylene chloride emissions 70 percent.
- Monsanto has pledged to reduce toxic air emissions 90 percent from 1988 levels.
- Procter & Gamble is experimenting with recycling disposable diapers into drywall backing and selling Spic 'n Span Pine in containers made entirely from used pop bottles.
- ARCO and Pacific Gas & Electric have prominent environmentalists on their boards of directors.
- Nissan enlisted a group of ecologists, energy experts, and science writers to brainstorm about how an environmentally responsible car company might behave. Among the ideas: to produce automobiles that snap together into electrically powered trains for long trips and then detach for the dispersion to final destinations.
- BMW and Volkswagen have efforts under way to make cars entirely recyclable.

Sources: C. Garfield, *Second to None: How Our Smartest Companies Put People First* (Burr Ridge, IL: Business One–Irwin, 1992); C. Morrison, *Managing Environmental Affairs: Corporate Practices in the United States, Canada, and Europe* (New York: The Conference Board, 1991); A. Kleiner, "What Does It Mean to Be Green?" *Harvard Business Review,* July–August 1991, pp. 38–47; and E. Smith and V. Cahan, "The Greening of Corporate America," *Business Week,* April 23, 1990, pp. 96–103.

- The Clean Air Act alone is expected to cost U.S. petroleum refiners $37 billion, more than the book value of the entire industry.
- Executives expect environmental expenditures to double as a percentage of sales in the next few years.
- California's tough laws are a major reason manufacturers move to Arkansas or Nevada.

In industries like chemicals and petroleum, already plagued by fierce competition and declining profit margins, the ability to respond to environmental regulations may determine their very survival.[7]

Balance A more balanced view is that business must weigh the environmental benefits of an action against value destruction. The advice here is, don't obstruct progress, but pick your environmental initiatives carefully. J. Ladd Greeno of Arthur D. Little believes that compliance and remediation efforts will protect, but not increase, shareholder value.[8] And it is shareholder value, rather than compliance, emissions, or costs, that should be the focus of objective cost/benefit analyses. Such an approach is environmentally sound but also hardheaded in a business sense, and is the one approach that is truly sustainable over the long term.

Johan Piet maintains, "Only win-win companies will survive, but that does not mean that all win-win ideas will be successful."[9] In other words, rigorous analysis is essential. Thus, Polaroid maintains continuous improvement in environmental performance, but funds only projects that meet financial objectives.

Most people understand that business has the resources and the competence to bring about constructive change, and that this creates great opportunity—if well managed—for both business and the environment.

Why Manage with the Environment in Mind?

Business is turning its full attention to environmental issues for many reasons, including legal compliance, cost effectiveness, competitive advantage, public opinion, and long-term thinking.

Legal Compliance Table 5.B.2 shows just some of the most important U.S. environmental laws. Government regulations and liability for damages provide strong economic incentives to comply with environmental guidelines. Most industries already have made environmental protection regulation and liability an integral part of their business planning.[10] The U.S. Justice Department is handing out tough prison sentences to executives whose companies violate hazardous-waste requirements.

Many businesspeople consider the regulations to be too rigid, inflexible, and unfair. In response to this concern, regulatory reform may become more creative. The Aspen Institute Series on the Environment in the Twenty-First Century is trying to increase the cost-effectiveness of compliance measures through more flexibility in meeting standards and relying on market-based incentives. Such mechanisms, including tradable permits, pollution charges, and deposit refund systems, provide positive financial incentives for good environmental performance.[11]

table 5.B.2
Some U.S. environmental laws

Superfund [Comprehensive Environmental Response, Compensation, and Liability Act (CERCLA)]: Establishes potential liability for any person or organization responsible for creating an environmental health hazard. Individuals may be prosecuted, fined, or taxed to fund cleanup.

Clean Water Act [Federal Water Pollution Control Act]: Regulates all discharges into surface waters, and affects the construction and performance of sewer systems. The Safe Drinking Water Act similarly protects ground waters.

Clean Air Act: Regulates the emission into the air of any substance that affects air quality, including nitrous oxides, sulfur dioxide, and carbon dioxide.

Community Response and Right-to-Know Act: Mandates that all facilities producing, transporting, storing, using, or releasing hazardous substances provide full information to local and state authorities and maintain emergency-action plans.

Federal Hazardous Substances Act: Regulates hazards to health and safety associated with consumer products. The Consumer Product Safety Commission has the right to recall hazardous products.

Hazardous Materials Transportation Act: Regulates the packaging, marketing, and labeling of shipments of flammable, toxic, and radioactive materials.

Resource Conservation and Recovery Act: Extends to small-quantity generators the laws regulating generation, treatment, and disposal of solid and hazardous wastes.

Surface Mining Control and Reclamation Act: Establishes environmental standards for all surface-mining operations.

Toxic Substances Control Act: Addresses the manufacture, processing, distribution, use, and disposal of dangerous chemical substances and mixtures.

Source: Dennis C. Kinlaw, *Competitive and Green: Sustainable Performance in the Environmental Age* (Amsterdam: Pfeiffer & Co., 1993). Reprinted by permission of the author.

Cost effectiveness Environmentally conscious strategies can be cost effective. In the short run, company after company is realizing cost savings from repackaging, recycling, and other approaches. Union Carbide, for instance, faced costs of $30 a ton for disposal of solid wastes and $2,000 a ton for disposal of hazardous wastes. By recycling, reclaiming, or selling its waste, it avoided $8.5 million in costs *and* generated $3.5 million in income during a six-month period. Dow Chemical launched in 1996 a 10-year program to improve its environmental, health, and safety performance worldwide. Dow projects that the environmental improvements will save $1.8 billion over the 10-year period.[12]

Environmentally conscious strategies offer long-run cost advantages as well. Companies that are functioning barely within legal limits today may incur big costs—being forced to pay damages or upgrade technologies and practices—when laws change down the road.

A few of the other cost savings include fines, cleanups, and litigation; lower raw materials costs; reduced energy use; less-expensive waste handling and disposal; lower insurance rates; and possibly higher interest rates.

Competitive advantage Corporations gain a competitive advantage by channeling their environmental concerns into entrepreneurial opportunities and by producing higher-quality products that meet consumer demand. Business opportunities abound in pollution protection equipment and processes, waste cleanup, low-water-use plumbing, new light bulb technology, and marketing of environmentally safe products like biodegradable plastics. With new pools of venture capital, government funding, and specialized investment funds available, environmental technology is becoming a major sector of the venture-capital industry.[13]

In addition, companies that fail to innovate in this area will be at a competitive *disadvantage.* Environmental protection is not only a universal need; it is also a major export industry. U.S. trade has suffered as other countries—notably Germany—have taken the lead in patenting and exporting anti–air pollution and other environmental technologies. If the United States does not produce innovative, competitive new technologies, it will forsake a growth industry and see most of its domestic spending for environmental protection go to imports.[14]

In short, competitive advantage can be gained by maintaining market share with old customers, and by creating new products for new market opportunities. And, if you are an environmental leader, you may set the standards for future regulations—regulations that you are prepared to meet, while your competitors are not.

Public opinion The majority of the U.S. population believes business must clean up; few people think it is doing its job well. Gallup surveys show that more than 80 percent of U.S. consumers consider environmentalism in making purchases. An international survey of 22 countries found that majorities in 20 countries gave priority to environmental protection even at the risk of slowing economic growth. Consumers seem to have reached the point of routinely expecting companies to come up with environmentally friendly alternatives to current products and practices.[15]

Companies also receive pressure from local communities and from their own employees. Sometimes the pressure is informal and low key, but much pressure is exerted by environmental organizations, aroused citizen groups, societies and associations, international codes of conduct, and environmentally conscious investors.[16]

Another important reason for paying attention to environmental impact is TRI, the Toxic Release Inventory.[17] Starting in 1986, the EPA required all the plants of approximately 10,000 U.S. manufacturers to report annual releases of 317 toxic chemicals into the air, ground, and water. The substances include freon, PCBs, asbestos, and lead compounds. Hundreds of others are being added to the list. The releases are not necessarily illegal, but they provide the public with an annual environmental benchmark. TRI provides a powerful incentive to reduce emissions.

Finally, it is useful to remember that companies recover very slowly in public opinion from the impact of an environmental disaster. Adverse public opinion may affect sales as well as the firm's ability to attract and retain talented people. You can see why companies like P&G consider concern for the environment a new consumer need, making it a basic and critical business issue.

Long-term thinking Long-term thinking about resources helps business leaders understand the nature of their responsibilities with regard to environmental concerns. Economic arguments, sustainable growth, and the tragedy of the commons highlight the need for long-term thinking.

Economic arguments In Chapter 3, we discussed long-term versus short-term decision making. We stated that it is common for managers to succumb to short-term pressure for profits and to avoid spending now when the potential payoff is years down the road. In addition, some economists maintain that it is the responsibility of management to maximize returns for shareholders, implying the preeminence of the short-term profit goal.

But other economists argue that such a strategy caters to immediate profit maximization for stock speculators and neglects serious investors who are with the company for the long haul. Attention to environmental issues enhances the organization's long-term viability because the goal is the long-term creation of wealth for the patient, serious investors in the company[18]—not to mention the future state of our planet and the new generations who will inhabit it.

Sustainable growth Today many companies are moving beyond the law to be truly environmentalist in their philosophies and practices. Their aim is to jointly achieve the goals of economic growth and environmental quality in the long run by striving for sustainable growth. **Sustainable growth** is economic growth and development that meets the organization's present needs without harming the ability of future generations to meet their needs.[19] Sustainability is fully compatible with the natural ecosystems that generate and preserve life.

Some believe that the concept of sustainable growth offers[20] (1) a framework for organizations to use in communicating to all stakeholders, (2) a planning and strategy guide, and (3) a tool for evaluating and improving the ability to compete. The principle can begin at the highest organizational levels and be made explicit in performance appraisals and reward systems.

The tragedy of the commons In a classic article in *Science,* Garrett Hardin described a situation that applies to all business decisions and social concerns regarding scarce resources like clean water, air, and land.[21] Throughout human history, a commons was a tract of land shared by communities of people on which they grazed their animals. A commons has limited **carrying capacity,** or the ability to sustain a population, because it is a finite resource. For individual herders, short-term interest lies in adding as many animals to the commons as they can. But problems develop as more herders add more animals to graze the commons. This leads to tragedy: As each herder acts in his short-term interest, the long-run impact is the destruction of the commons. The only solution is to make choices according to long-run rather than short-run consequences.

In many ways, we are witnessing this **tragedy of the commons.** Carrying capacities are shrinking as precious resources, water chief among them, become scarcer. Inevitably, conflict arises—and solutions are urgently needed.

The Environmental Movement The 1990s have been labeled the "earth decade" when a "new environmentalism" with new features is emerging.[22] For example, proponents of the new environmentalism are asking companies to reduce their wastes, use resources prudently, market safe products, and take responsibility for past damages. These requests have been formalized in the *Valdez* principles (see Table 5.B.3).

The new environmentalism combines many diverse viewpoints, but initially it did not blend easily with traditional business values. Some of the key aspects of this philosophy are noted in the following discussion of the history of the movement.[23]

Conservation and environmentalism A strand of environmental philosophy that is not at odds with business management is **conservation.** The conservation movement is anthropocentric (human centered), technologically optimistic, and concerned chiefly with the efficient use of resources. The movement seeks to avoid waste, promote the rational and efficient use of natural resources, and maximize long-term yields, especially of renewable resources.

The **environmental movement,** in contrast, historically has posed dilemmas for business management. Following the lead of early thinkers like George Perkins Marsh (1801–1882), it has shown that the unintended negative effects of human economic activities on the environment often are greater than the benefits. For example, there are links between forest cutting and soil erosion and between the draining of marshes and lakes and the decline of animal life.

Other early environmentalists, such as John Muir (1838– 1914) and Aldo Leopold (1886–1948), argued that humans are not above nature but a part of it. Nature is not for humans to subdue but is sacred and should be preserved not simply for economic use but for its own sake—that is, for what people can learn from it.

Science and the Environment Rachel Carson's 1962 best-selling book *The Silent Spring* helped ignite the modern environmental movement by alerting the public to the dangers of unrestricted pesticide use.[24] Carson brought together the findings of toxicology, ecology, and epidemiology in a form accessible to the public. Blending scientific, moral, and political arguments, she connected environmental politics and values with scientific knowledge.

Barry Commoner's *Science and Survival* (1963) continued in this vein. Commoner expanded the scope of ecology to include everything in the physical, chemical, biological, social, political, economic, and philosophical worlds.[25] He argued that all these

table 5.B.3
The *Valdez* principles

- **Protection of the biosphere:** Minimize the release of pollutants that may cause environmental damage.
- **Sustainable use of natural resources:** Conserve nonrenewable resources through efficient use and careful planning.
- **Reduction and disposal of waste:** Minimize the creation of waste, especially hazardous waste, and dispose of such materials in a safe, responsible manner.
- **Wise use of energy:** Make every effort to use environmentally safe and sustainable energy sources to meet operating requirements.
- **Risk reduction:** Diminish environmental, health, and safety risks to employees.
- **Marketing of safe products and services:** Sell products that minimize adverse environmental impact and are safe for consumers.
- **Damage compensation:** Accept responsibility for any harm the company causes the environment; conduct bioremediation; and compensate affected parties.
- **Disclosure of environmental incidents:** Public dissemination of accidents relating to operations that harm the environment or pose health or safety risks.
- **Environmental directors:** Appoint at least one board member who is qualified to represent environmental interests; create a position for vice president for environmental affairs.
- **Assessment and annual audit:** Produce and publicize each year a self-evaluation of progress toward implementing the principles and meeting all applicable laws and regulations worldwide. Environmental audits will also be produced annually and distributed to the public.

Sources: *Chemical Week,* September 20, 1989, copyright permission granted by *Chemical Week* magazine. *CERES Coalition Handbook.*

elements fit together, and have to be understood as a whole. According to Commoner, the symptoms of environmental problems are in the biological world, but their source lies in economic and political organizations.

Economics and the environment Economists promote growth for many reasons: to restore the balance of payments, to make the nation more competitive, to create jobs, to reduce the deficit, to provide for the elderly and the sick, and to reduce poverty. Environmentalists criticize economics for its notions of efficiency and its emphasis on economic growth.[26] For example, environmentalists argue that economists do not adequately consider the unintended side effects of efficiency. Environmentalists hold that economists need to supplement estimates of the economic costs and benefits of growth with estimates of other factors that historically were not measured in economic terms.[27]

Economists and public policy analysts argue that the benefits of eliminating risk to the environment and to people must be balanced against the costs. Reducing risk involves determining how effective the proposed methods of reduction are likely to be and how much they will cost. There are many ways to consider cost factors. Analysts can perform cost effectiveness analyses, in which they attempt to figure out how to achieve a given goal with limited resources, or they can conduct more formal risk-benefit and cost-benefit analyses, in which they quantify both the benefits and the costs of risk reduction.[28]

The environmental movement is a worldwide phenomenon. The "Greens," pictured here demonstrating in LePuy, France, are a growing European political party.
[Maillac/REA–SABA]

Qualitative judgments in cost–benefit analysis Formal, quantitative approaches to balancing costs and benefits do not eliminate the need for qualitative judgments. For example, how does one assess the value of a magnificent vista obscured by air pollution? What is the loss to society if a given genetic strain of grass or animal species becomes extinct? How does one assess the lost opportunity costs of spending vast amounts of money on air pollution that could have been spent on productivity enhancement and global competitiveness?

Fairness cannot be ignored when doing cost-benefit analysis.[29] For example, the costs of air pollution reduction may have to be borne disproportionately by the poor in the form of higher gasoline and automobile prices. Intergenerational fairness also plays a role.[30] Future generations have no representatives in the current market and political processes. Therefore, to what extent should the current generation hold back on its own consumption for the sake of posterity? This question is particularly poignant because few people in the world today are well off. To ask the poor to reduce their life's chances for the sake of a generation yet to come is asking for a great sacrifice.

International perspectives Environmental problems present a different face in various countries and regions of the world. The United States and Great Britain lag behind Germany and Japan in mandated emissions standards.[31] In Europe the Dutch, the Germans, and the Danes are among the most environmentally conscious. Italy, Ireland, Spain, Portugal, and Greece are in the early stages of developing environmental policies. Poland, Hungary, the Czech Republic, and former East Germany are the most polluted of the world's industrialized nations.[32]

U.S. companies need to realize that there is a large growth market in Western Europe for environmentally "friendly" products. U.S. managers also need to be fully aware of the environmental movement in Western Europe. Environmentalists in Europe have been successful in halting many projects.[33] Along with events like Chernobyl, the Greens—a political party—have played an important role in stopping the further expansion of nuclear power. They also have had local successes in halting development. It is now impossible to plan a large-scale project in Western Europe without considering an adverse reaction by the Greens.

Industries that pollute or make polluting products will have to adjust to the new reality, and companies selling products in this part of the world must take into account a growing consumer consciousness about environmental protection. manufacturers may even be legally required to take products and packaging back from customers after use, to recycle or dispose of. In order to meet these requirements in Germany, and be prepared for similar demands in other countries, Hewlett-Packard redesigned its office-machine packaging worldwide.

What Managers Can Do

To be truly "green"—that is, a cutting-edge company with respect to environmental concerns—legal compliance is not enough. Progressive companies stay abreast *and* ahead of the laws by going beyond marginal compliance and anticipating future requirements and needs. But companies can go further still by experimenting continually with innovations that protect the environment. McDonald's, for example, conducted tests and pilot projects in composting food scraps and in offering refillable coffee mugs and starch-based (biodegradable) cutlery.[34]

Systems thinking The first thing managers can do to better understand environmental issues in their companies is to engage in systems thinking. Recalling the systems model discussed in Chapter 1, we can see that environmental considerations relate to the organization's inputs, processes, and outputs.[35] *Inputs* include raw materials and energy. Environmental pressures are causing prices of some raw materials, such as metals, to rise. This greatly increases the costs of production. Higher energy costs are causing firms to switch to more fuel-efficient sources.

Firms are considering new *processes* or methods of production that will reduce water pollution, air pollution, noise and vibration, and waste. They are incorporating technologies that sample and monitor (control) these by-products of business processes. Some chemical plants have a computerized system that flashes warnings when a maximum allowable pollution level is soon to be reached. Many companies keep only minimal stocks of hazardous materials, making serious accidents less likely.

Outputs have environmental impact, whether the products themselves or the waste or by-products of processes. To reduce the impact of its outputs, Herman Miller recycles or reuses nearly all waste from the manufacturing process. It sells fabric scraps to the auto industry, leather trim to luggage makers, and vinyl to stereo and auto manufacturers. It buys back its old furniture, refurbishes it, and resells it. Its corporatewide goal is to send zero waste to landfills. Environmental manager Paul Murray says, "There is never an acceptable level of waste at Miller. There are always new things we can learn."[36]

Strategic integration Systems thinking reveals that environmental issues permeate the firm, and therefore should be addressed in a comprehensive, integrative fashion. Perhaps the first step is to create the proper mindset. Does your firm see environmental concerns merely in terms of a business versus environment trade-off, or does it see in it a potential source of competitive advantage and an important part of a strategy for long-term survival and effectiveness? The latter attitude, of course, is more likely to set the stage for the following strategic actions.

These basic steps help to strategically integrate environmental considerations into the firm's ongoing activities:[37]

1. *Develop a mission statement and strong values supporting environmental advocacy.* Table 5.B.4 shows Procter & Gamble's environmental quality policy.

2. *Establish a framework for managing environmental initiatives.* J&J has an Environmental Responsibility Program consisting of two initiatives:[38] Environmental Regulatory Affairs ensures that regulations are followed worldwide, and uses external audit teams to conduct environmental audits. The Community Environmental Responsibility Program incudes emergency preparedness, strategy and planning, and the development of products and processes with neutral environmental impact.

3. *Engage in "green" process and product design.* The core concept of TQM is that products will cost more to fix after manufacture than if the defects are prevented in the first place. With respect to the environment, a similar concept is pollution prevention as opposed to "end-of-pipe" cleanup strategies. Such programs strive for zero emissions or at least continuous improvement toward that goal. Olin Corporation, the chemical company, announced a 70 percent reduction of reportable emissions through source reduction, recycling, treatment, and other pollution prevention techniques.[39]

table 5.B.4
Procter & Gamble's environmental quality policy

Procter & Gamble is committed to providing products of superior quality and value that best fill the needs of the world's consumers. As part of this, Procter & Gamble continually strives to improve the environmental quality of its products, packaging, and operations around the world. To carry out this commitment, it is Procter & Gamble's policy to:

- Ensure our products, packaging, and operations are safe for our employees, consumers, and the environment.
- Reduce or prevent the environmental impact of our products and packaging in their design, manufacture, distribution, use, and disposal whenever possible.
- Meet or exceed the requirements of all environmental laws and regulations.
- Continually assess our environmental technology and programs, and monitor programs toward environmental goals.
- Provide our consumers, customers, employees, communities, public interest groups, and others with relevant and appropriate factual information about the environmental quality of P&G products, packaging, and operations.
- Ensure every employee understands and is responsible and accountable for incorporating environmental quality considerations in daily business activities.
- Have operating policies, programs, and resources in place to implement our environmental quality policy.

Source: K. Dechant and B. Altman, "Environmental Leadership: From Compliance to Competitive Advantage," *The Academy of Management Executive,* August 1994, p. 10. Reprinted by permission.

4. *Establish environmentally focused stakeholder relationships.* Many firms work closely with the FDA and receive technical assistance to help convert to more energy-efficient facilities. And to defray costs as well as develop new ideas, small companies like WHYCO Chromium Company establish environmental management partnerships with firms like IBM and GM.[40]

5. *Provide internal and external education.* Engage employees in environmental actions. Dow's WRAP program has cut millions of pounds of hazardous and solid waste and emissions, and achieved annual cost savings of over $10 million, all through employee suggestions.[41] At the same time, inform the public of your firm's environmental initiatives. For example, eco-labeling can urge consumers to recycle and communicate the environmental friendliness of your product.

Life cycle analysis Increasingly, firms are paying attention to the pollution caused by their manufacturing processes in the context of the total environmental impact throughout the entire life cycle of their products. **Life-cycle analysis (LCA)** is a process of analyzing all inputs and outputs to determine the total environmental impact of the production and use of a product.[42] LCA quantifies the total use of resources, and the releases into the air, water, and land. For example, Xerox is using product life-cycle analysis in its design-for-environment tool kit in its efforts to make research and technology investment decisions to improve environmental performance.[43]

Green design considers the extraction of raw materials, product packaging, transportation, and disposal. Consider packaging alone. Goods make the journey from manufacturer to wholesaler to retailer to customer, and are then recycled back to the manufacturer. They may be packaged and repackaged several times, from bulk transport to large crates to cardboard boxes to individual consumer sizes. Repackaging not only creates waste—it costs *time.* The design of initial packaging in sizes and formats adaptable to the final customer can minimize the need for repackaging, cut waste, and realize many benefits.

Implementation How can companies implement "greening" strategies? A fundamental requirement for effective environmentalism is a commitment by top management. Specific actions could include commissioning an environmental audit in which an outside company checks for environmental hazards, drafting (or reviewing) the organization's environmental policy, communicating the policy and making it highly visible throughout the organization, having environmental professionals within the company report directly to the president or CEO, allocating sufficient resources to support the environmental effort, and building bridges between the organization and other companies, governments, environmentalists, and local communities.

Ultimately, it is essential to make employees accountable for any of their actions that have environmental impact.[44] Texaco, Du Pont, and other companies evaluate managers on their ideas for minimizing pollution and for new, environment-friendly products. Kodak ties some managers' compensation to the prevention of chemical spills; the company attributes to this policy a dramatic reduction in accidents.[45]

Companies can employ all areas of the organization to meet the challenges posed by pollution and environmental problems. A variety of companies have responded creatively to these challenges[46] and may serve as models for other organizations. The following sections describe more specific actions companies can take to address environmental issues.

Strategy Actions companies can take in the area of strategy include the following:

1. *Cut back on environmentally unsafe businesses.* Du Pont, the leading producer of CFCs, announced it would voluntarily pull out of this $750 million business by the year 2000.[47]

2. *Carry out R&D on environmentally safe activities.* Du Pont claims it is spending up to $1 billion on the best replacements for CFCs.

3. *Develop and expand environmental cleanup services.* Building on the expertise gained in cleaning up its own plants, Du Pont is forming a safety and environmental resources division to help industrial customers clean up their toxic wastes. The projected future revenues are $1 billion by the year 2000.[48]

4. *Compensate for environmentally risky projects.* Applied Energy Services, a power plant management firm, donated $2 million for tree planting in Guatemala to compensate for a coal-fired plant it was building in Connecticut. The trees were meant to offset emissions that might lead to global warming.

5. *Make your company accountable to others.* Danish health care and enzymes company Novo Nordisk has purposely asked for feedback from environmentalists, regulators, and other interested bodies from around Europe. Its reputation has been enhanced, its people have learned a lot, and new market opportunities have been identified.[49]

6. *Make every new product environmentally better than the last.* This is IBM's goal. IBM aims to use recyclable materials, reduce hazardous materials, reduce emissions, and use natural energy and resources in packaging.[50]

Public Affairs In the area of public affairs, companies can take a variety of actions:

1. *Attempt to gain environmental legitimacy and credibility.* Edgar Woolard, CEO of Du Pont, delivers speeches on corporate environmentalism. The cosponsors of Earth Day included Apple Computer, Hewlett-Packard, Shaklee, and the Chemical Manufacturers Association. McDonald's has made efforts to show that it is a proponent of recycling; it has tried to become a corporate environmental "educator."

2. *Try to avoid losses caused by insensitivity to environmental issues.* As a result of Exxon's apparent lack of concern after the *Valdez* oil spill, 41 percent of Americans polled said they would consider boycotting the company.[51]

3. *Collaborate with environmentalists.* Executives at Pacific Gas & Electric seek discussions and joint projects with any willing

environmental group. They have teamed up with environmental groups to study energy efficiency, and the company rented a computer model from the Environmental Defense Fund (EDF) that showed the relationship between conservation and electricity costs.

The Legal Area Actions companies can take in the legal area include the following:

1. *Try to avoid confrontation with state or federal pollution control agencies.* W. R. Grace faced expensive and time-consuming lawsuits as a result of its toxic dumps. Browning-Ferris, Waste Management Inc., and Louisiana-Pacific were charged with pollution control violations, damaging their reputations.

2. *Comply early.* Since compliance costs only increase over time, the first companies to act will have lower costs. This will enable them to increase their market share and profits and win competitive advantage. 3M's goal was to meet government requirements to replace or improve underground storage tanks by 1993 instead of 1998, the legally mandated year.

3. *Take advantage of innovative compliance programs.* Instead of source-by-source reduction, the EPA's bubble policy allows factories to reduce pollution at different sources by different amounts, provided the overall result is equivalent. Therefore, 3M has installed equipment on only certain production lines at its tape-manufacturing facility in Pennsylvania, thereby lowering its compliance costs.[52] Today, there is greater use of economic instruments like tradable pollution permits, charges, and taxes to encourage improvements.[53] *Joint implementation* (or *activities implemented jointly)* involves companies in industrialized nations working with businesses in developing countries to help them reduce greenhouse gas emissions. The company lending a hand then receives credit toward fulfilling its environmental obligations at home. The developing country receives investment, technology, and jobs; the company giving a lending hand receives environmental credits; and the world gets cleaner air.[54]

4. *Don't deal with fly-by-night subcontractors for waste disposal.* They are more likely to cut corners, break laws, and do a poor job. Moreover, the result for you could be bad publicity and legal problems.[55]

Operations The actions companies can take in the area of operations include the following:

1. *Promote new manufacturing technologies.* Louisville Gas and Electric took the lead in installing smokestack scrubbers, Consolidated Natural Gas has pioneered the use of clean-burning technologies, and Nucor developed state-of-the-art steel mills. Pacific Gas & Electric agreed to rely on combinations of smaller-scale generating facilities like windmills or cogeneration plants alongside aggressive conservation efforts. It has canceled plans to build large coal and nuclear power plants.

2. *Aim for zero waste or zero discharge.* This may be unachievable, but it is a useful target. It imposes discipline and encourages continuous improvement.

3. *Encourage technological advances that reduce pollution from products and manufacturing processes.* 3M's "Pollution Prevention Pays" program is based on the premise that it is too costly for companies to employ add-on technology and instead they should attempt to eliminate pollution at the source.[56] Add-on technology is expensive because it takes resources to remove the pollution; the pollution removal in turn generates new wastes, which requires more resources for their removal.

4. *Develop new product formulations.* One way to accomplish source reduction is to develop new product formulations. 3M's rapid fire-extinguishing agent for petroleum fires did not meet EPA requirements. Therefore, the company had to develop a new formulation. The new formulation was one-fortieth as toxic as the former, but it was equally effective and less expensive to produce.

5. *Eliminate manufacturing wastes.* With fewer wastes, add-on equipment becomes less necessary. 3M's philosophy is to invest in reducing the number of materials that can trigger regulation. For example, it replaced volatile solvents with water-based ones, thereby eliminating the need for costly air pollution control equipment. Amoco and Polaroid have implemented similar programs.

6. *Find alternative uses for wastes.* When Du Pont halted ocean dumping of acid iron salts, it discovered that the salts could be sold to water treatment plants at a profit.

7. *Insist that your suppliers have strong environmental performance.* IBM, British Telecom, Wal-Mart, British supermarkets, and many others do this. Scott Paper discovered that many of its environmental problems were "imported" through the supply chain. Initially focusing on pulp suppliers, the company sent questionnaires asking for figures on air, water, and land releases, energy consumption, and energy sources. Scott was astonished at the variance. For example, carbon dioxide emissions varied by a factor of 17 among different suppliers. Scott dropped the worst performers and announced that the best performers would in the future receive preference in its purchasing decisions.[57]

8. *Assemble products with the environment in mind.* Make them easy to snap apart, sort, and recycle, and avoid glues and screws.

Marketing Companies can also take actions in the marketing area:

1. *Cast products in an environment-friendly light.* Most Americans believe a company's environmental reputation influences what they buy.[58] Companies such as Procter & Gamble, Arco, Colgate-Palmolive, Lever Brothers, 3M, and Sunoco have tried to act on the basis of this finding. Wal-Mart has made efforts to provide customers with recycled or recyclable products.

2. *Avoid attacks by environmentalists for unsubstantiated or inappropriate claims.* British Petroleum claimed that a new brand of unleaded gasoline caused no pollution, a claim that it had to withdraw after suffering much embarrassment. The degradable-plastics controversy should serve as another warning to consumers about the perils of unsubstantiated or inappropriate claims. Companies should be honest with their employees and the public and educate them continuously.

3. *Differentiate your product via environmental services.* ICI takes back and disposes of customers' waste as a customer service.

Disposal is costly, but the service differentiates the firm's products. Teach customers how to use and dispose of products; for instance, farmers inadvertently abuse pesticides. Make education a part of a firm's after-sales service.

Accounting Actions companies can take in the accounting area include the following:

1. *Collect useful data.* The best current reporters of environmental information include Dow Europe, Danish Steel Works, BSO/Origin, 3M, and Monsanto. BSO/Origin has begun to explore a system for corporate environmental accounting.[59]

2. *Make polluters pay.* CIBA-GEIGY has a "polluter pays principle" throughout the firm, so managers have the incentive to combat pollution at the sources they can influence.[60]

3. *Demonstrate that antipollution programs pay off.* 3M's Pollution Prevention Pays program is based on the premise that only if the program pays will there be the motivation to carry it out. Environmental pressures have forced U.S. companies to spend large sums of money that otherwise could have been used for capital formation, new-product research and development, and process improvements. Thus, every company owes it not only to itself but also to the nation to be cost effective in its pollution reduction efforts.

4. *Use an advanced waste accounting system.* Do this in addition to standard management accounting, which can hinder investment in new technologies. Waste accounting makes sure all costs are identified and better decisions can be made.

5. *Adopt full cost accounting.* This approach, called for by Frank Popoff, Dow's chairman, ensures that the price of a product reflects its full environmental cost.[61]

6. *Show the overall impact of the pollution reduction program.* Companies have an obligation to account for the costs and benefits of their pollution reduction programs. 3M claims half a *billion* dollars in savings from pollution prevention efforts.[62]

Finance In the area of finance, companies can do the following:

1. *Gain the respect of the socially responsible investment community.* More than 50 funds in the United States and Europe take environmental criteria into account. A study by ICF Kaiser concluded that environmental improvements could lead to significant reduction in the perceived risk of a firm, with a possible 5 percent increase in stock.[63] Socially responsible rating services and investment funds try to help people invest with a "clean conscience."[64] Their motto is that people should be able to do well while they are doing good. They believe socially responsible investments are likely to be profitable because if the companies can deal creatively with pollution, safety, and employment problems, they will tend to be innovative in other areas.

2. *Recognize true liability.* Smith Barney, Kidder Peabody & Company, and other investment houses employ environmental analysts who search for companies' true environmental liability in evaluating their potential performance. Bankers look at environmental risks and environmental market opportunities when evaluating a company's credit rating.[65] The Securities and Exchange Commission in New York requires some companies to report certain environmental costs. The Swiss Bank Corp. has specialized Environmental Performance Rating Units to include environmental criteria in order to improve the quality of financial analysis.[66]

3. *Recognize business opportunities.* The prospects for solid-waste companies (for example, Waste Management, Laidlaw Industries, and Browning-Ferris) are favorable because of a scarcity of landfill in parts of the United States, and because cities like New York have no alternative ways to get rid of their garbage. The prospects for hazardous-waste companies look promising because the Departments of Defense and Energy will have to clean up toxic wastes they have created in various parts of the country.

Key terms

Carrying capacity The ability of a finite resource to sustain a population. p. 194

Conservation An environmental philosophy that seeks to avoid waste, promote the rational and efficient use of natural resources, and maximize long-term yields, especially of renewable resources. p. 194

Environmental Movement An environmental philosophy postulating that the unintended negative effects of human economic activities on the environment are often greater than the benefits, and that nature should be preserved. p. 194

Life-cycle analysis (LCA) A process of evaluating all inputs and outputs to determine the total environmental impact of the production and use of a product. p. 197

Sustainable growth Economic growth and development that meet the organization's present needs without harming the ability of future generations to meet their needs. p. 193

Tragedy of the commons A term describing the environmental destruction that results as individuals and businesses consume finite resources (i.e., the "commons") to serve their short-term interests without regard for the long-term consequences. p. 194

Discussion questions

1. To what extent can we rely on government to solve environmental problems? What are some of government's limitations? Take a stand on the role and usefulness of government regulations on business activities.

2. To what extent should managers today be responsible for cleaning up mistakes from years past that have hurt the environment?

3. How would you characterize the environmental movement in Western Europe? How does it differ from the United States. movement? What difference will this make to a multinational company that wants to produce and market goods in many countries?

4. What business opportunities can you see in meeting environmental challenges? Be specific.

5. You are appointed environmental manager of XYZ Company. Describe some actions you will take to address environmental challenges. Discuss obstacles you are likely to encounter in the company and how you will manage them.

6. Interview a businessperson about environmental regulations and report your findings to the class. How would you characterize his or her attitude? How constructive is his or her attitude?

7. Interview a businessperson about actions he or she has taken that have helped the environment. Report your findings to the class and discuss.

8. Identify and discuss some examples of the tragedy of the commons. How can the tragedies be avoided?

9. Discuss the status of recycling efforts in your community, your perspectives on it as a consumer, and what business opportunities could be available.

10. What companies currently come to mind as having the best and worst reputations with respect to the environment? Why do they have these reputations?

11. Choose one product and discuss its environmental impact through its entire life cycle.

12. What are you, your college or university, and your community doing about the environment? What would you recommend doing?

Video Case

Management and the natural environment

Environmental awareness is a growing concern among corporations in the United States, and in many foreign countries as well. In this video tape, the environmental protection practices of Mobil Oil Corporation are reviewed. The company is actively involved in a number of initiatives aimed at protecting and preserving the natural environment. Mobil tries to integrate environmental awareness into its entire operation, from exploration and drilling to its "downstream" businesses, including its retail dealerships.

While most people will agree that concern for the natural environment should be an important consideration for businesses, balancing the costs of environmental concern with the pressures to turn a profit is never easy. It is also difficult to determine what level of "pollution" is acceptable. Should companies strive for zero pollution? Doing so may be so costly as to prohibit business activity entirely.

Complex issues about appropriate levels of pollution, environmental cost accounting, and free market approaches to environmental control are in the early stages of discussion across the United States. Some states are now in the business of allocating **effluent securities.** Companies are allowed a fixed amount of securities that they use to pay for effluents they produce. Companies are allowed to trade these securities with other companies, enabling them to exceed their original allotment, but keeping total discharge within specified limits.

Purpose:

The purpose of this exercise is to provide you with an opportunity to explore the environmental practices of a company near you. Companies take a variety of approaches to involvement in the natural environment, from producing so-called *green* products to supporting environmental causes through charitable donations.

This exercise will help you understand the struggle managers must face when balancing the costs of environmental programs with their benefits.

Procedure:

Identify a manufacturing company in your area that you would be interested in learning about. You will contact a representative of that company to determine the extent of environmental initiatives the company undertakes. Gather information about state and federal environmental laws and guidelines with which the company must comply and the costs of compliance. After you have identified a representative of the company, proceed through the following steps:

1. Contact the representative and set up a meeting at a mutually convenient time to discuss the company's environmental practices.
2. Before going to the meeting, prepare a set of questions. Your questions should focus on determining three things: the types of environmental initiatives the company currently pursues; the state and federal regulations with which the company must comply; and the cost of complying with these regulations.
3. Arrive on time for the scheduled meeting. Proceed through your prepared questions. Tape-record the interview if your interviewee agrees. Take good notes whether or not taping is allowed. If the company representative offers to give you a tour of the company's environmental projects, go along if you have the time.
4. Use your notes to begin to compile a brief report on your findings for presentation to the class. Provide a chart that outlines environmental regulations to which the company is subject, and the procedures the company uses to comply with those regulations.
5. Now conduct library research to benchmark the company you studied against another company that has been recognized for environmental excellence. If you can't find any data in the library for benchmarking, as an alternative, think of some ways on your own that the company might go beyond its current environmental practices.
6. In your final report for the class, contrast the company's practices with those of the benchmark company or with those you have developed. Consider the costs and benefits of adopting these more extensive practices. Conclude with a recommendation for the company.
7. If possible, invite your interviewee to class on the day you are scheduled to report your findings and recommendations. If the person is able to attend, provide him or her with an opportunity to respond to your report.

Chapter Six
International Management

It was once said that the sun never sets on the British Empire. Today, the sun does set on the British Empire, but not on the scores of global empires, including those of IBM, Unilever, Volkswagen, and Hitachi.

—Lester Brown

Chapter Outline

The Global Environment
- European Unification
- The Pacific Rim
- North America
- The Rest of the World

Consequences of a Global Economy

Global Strategy
- Pressures for Global Integration
- Pressures for Local Responsiveness
- Choosing Global Strategy

Entry Mode
- Exporting
- Licensing
- Franchising
- Joint Ventures
- Wholly Owned Subsidiaries

Management across Borders
- Skills of the Global Manager
- Understanding Cultural Issues
- Ethical Issues in International Management

Learning Objectives

After studying Chapter 6, you will know:

1. Why the world economy is becoming more integrated than ever before.
2. What integration of the global economy means for individual companies and for their managers.
3. The strategies organizations use to compete in the global marketplace.
4. The various entry modes organizations use to enter overseas markets.
5. How companies can approach the task of staffing overseas operations.
6. The skills and knowledge managers need to manage globally.
7. Why cultural differences across countries influence management.

Setting the Stage

For Disney, It's a Small World After All

The Walt Disney Company has achieved an enviable level of success in the U.S. entertainment industry and is renowned for its creativity and long-term vision. For over half a century, familiar Disney characters, from Mickey Mouse and Donald Duck to Pocahontas and Hercules, have become icons of American pop culture. But can a company whose formula for success rests on cartoon characters, stories, and songs transfer its magic to other countries and cultures around the world? Well, yes, no, and maybe.

Disney expanded to Japan in 1962 and opened Tokyo Disneyland in 1983. From the first day, Disney had an enormous hit. Today Tokyo Disneyland is the single most successful tourist attraction in Japan and has hosted over 100 million visitors. And although Disney made some adaptations for Japanese culture, most experts believe that the principal reason Disney succeeded in Japan is that the original concept of Disneyland was authentically recreated.

In sharp contrast, Disney has had a tough go of things in Europe. Euro-Disney applied the same formula that worked in Japan to its $4 billion theme park near Paris, and the results were disappointing. Part of the problem was that Disneyland Paris was opened as Europe was heading into a recession and Euro-Disney made the mistake of treating all Europeans alike instead of recognizing differences across countries. As a result, Disneyland Paris drew far less than the 11 million visitors it needed each year to break even, and even those that did come did not act like typical Disney tourists. Penny-pinching Europeans did not spend as much on food or merchandise, and did not stay for extended vacations in the surrounding hotels as visitors do at the U.S. and Tokyo parks. To address these problems, Euro-Disney changed its management team, revamped its marketing, modified its food and service offerings, and dropped prices. The results are encouraging. Attendance has climbed to almost 13 million visitors a year, and profits in 1997 reached $38 million.

The empty streets of Euro Disney near Paris stood in sharp contrast to packed-in crowds at Disney World in Orlando, Florida and Disneyland in Tokyo, Japan. *[Figaro Magazine/Liaision International]*

Now Disney is looking at China. The Chinese people are attracted to Disney, some say because the warmth and humor of Disney characters play to the Confucian values of family that are paramount in Asia. However, when Disney recently produced a film entitled Kundun (about Tibet's spiritual leader, the Dalai Lama), China's communist government became furious. Disney has stuck with the project and, as a result, Beijing officials have put a freeze on all Disney projects and have forbidden any new ventures in the country. Although the outcome for Disney in China is not yet clear, what is clear from these contrasting stories is that managing across borders is neither easy nor predictable.

Sources: Joyce Barnathan, Matt Miller, and Dexter Roberts, "Has Disney Become the Forbidden Studio?" Business Week, *3538 (August 4, 1997), p. 51; "The Kingdom Inside a Republic,"* The Economist, *339, no.7961 (April 13, 1997), pp. 66–67; "Variations on a Theme Park,"* Marketing, *(May 2, 1996), p. 14; David Hulme, "Ex-Cop in Mickey Mouse Job,"* Asia Business, *30, no. 6 (1994), p. 70; Stewart Toy and Paul Dwyer, "Is Disney Headed for the Euro-Trash Heap?"* Business Week, *January 24, 1994, p. 52; and Harriot Lane Fox, "Disney Opts for Lead UK Man,"* Marketing, *Oct. 27, 1994, p. 4.*

As the story of Disney shows, today's managers must constantly make decisions about whether and how to pursue opportunities all over the globe. Of course, opportunities must be evaluated carefully. In many industries competition is now a global game in which the same competitors confront one another in a variety of markets around the world. In this chapter, we review the reasons for the globalization of competition, examine why international management differs from domestic management, consider how companies expand globally, and see how companies can develop individuals to manage across borders.

The global environment

In the new millennium, the global economy is becoming more integrated than ever before. Three spheres of economic influence—typically referred to as the triad of North America, Europe, and Asia—are most dominant. However, other developing countries and regions represent important areas for economic growth as well.

European unification

Europe is integrating economically to form the biggest market in the world. In concept, the European Union (EU) will allow goods, services, capital, and human resources to flow freely across national borders. Figure 6.1 shows a map of participating countries in the EU. The goal of unification is to strengthen Europe's position as the third economic superpower, right behind the United States and Japan. As a single entity, the EU has a population of 320 million and a gross national product of over $4 trillion.[1]

Under the Maastricht Treaty, member countries have agreed to adopt a common European currency by 1999. However, the pace of unification has been slower than anticipated. In part this has been due to a global recession, but there are other structural issues within Europe that need to be corrected for the EU to function effectively. In particular, Western Europeans on average work fewer hours, earn more pay, take longer vacations, and enjoy far more social entitlements than their counterparts in North America and Asia. To be competitive in a global economy, Europeans must increase their level of productivity. In the past, powerful trade unions have fiercely defended social benefits, and local governments have regulated the labor markets. Both these actions have encouraged companies such as Siemens and ABB Asea Brown Boveri Ltd. to move operations abroad. Now it appears that labor markets are being deregulated and there are more incentives to create jobs.[2]

Unification will create a more competitive Europe. The EU's share of the world's top 100 industrial firms is rising. The community is pursuing an active industrial policy to

figure 6.1 The nations of the European Union

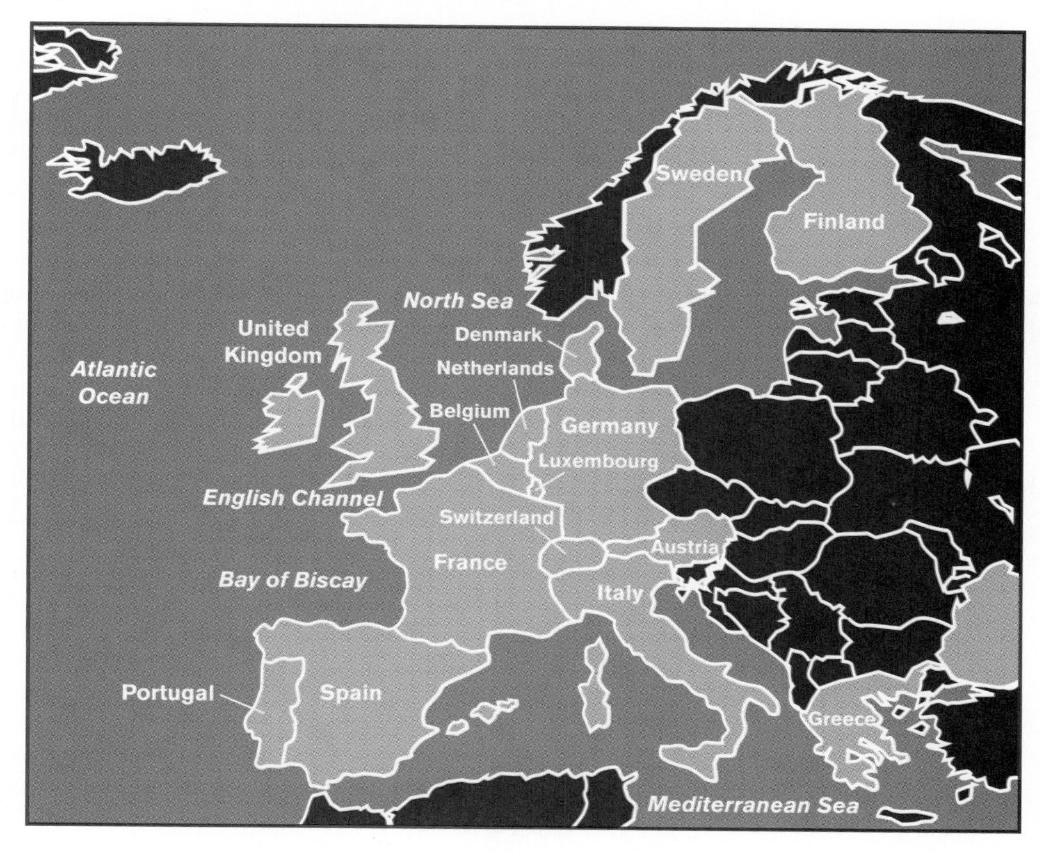

enhance its competitiveness in information technology. It is making fast gains in semiconductors and is restructuring in defense and aerospace.

The impact is hard to predict, but there are many possibilities. U.S. exports to Europe could be replaced by the goods of European producers; European exports could replace U.S. products in other markets; U.S. capital could flow into Europe to the detriment of capital formation and productivity growth in the United States. Another possibility is a "Fortress Europe" that restricts trade with countries outside EU walls.

Siemens Microelectronics Inc. of Cupertino, California, is one of more than 30 Siemens companies located in the United States.
[Courtesy of Siemens Microelectronics, Inc.]

The consensus among U.S. observers is that the United States must remain vigilant to ensure that a Fortress Europe does not close itself to U.S. goods and services. Management and labor must work cooperatively to achieve high levels of quality that will make U.S. products and services attractive to consumers in Europe and other markets across the world. The United States needs not only managers who will stay on top of worldwide developments and manage high-quality, efficient organizations but a well-educated, well-trained, and continually *retrained* labor force to remain competitive with the Europeans, the Japanese, and other formidable competitors.[3]

The Pacific Rim

Among the Pacific Rim countries, Japan dominated world attention during the 1980s and much of the 1990s. But Japan is hardly the only important global player from the Pacific region. China is developing and becoming more prosperous. Even Japan is concerned about the countries known as the "four tigers" or the "four dragons": South Korea, Taiwan, Singapore, and Hong Kong. Korea is foremost among them; its immediate goal is to become one of the world's 10 most technologically advanced nations by the year 2000. Already the four dragons, along with other Asian growth nations like Thailand, Malaysia, and the Philippines, account for more trade with the United States than Japan does.[4]

For the past several years, the 18 member countries of the Asia-Pacific Economic Cooperation (APEC) have been working to reduce trade barriers and establish general rules for investment and policies that encourage international commerce. Recent volatility in global financial markets has been directly linked to economic uncertainties in the Pacific Rim. The U.S. government has been working with APEC countries to stabilize the economic environment and facilitate more open-trade agreements. Although the United States has been trading with member countries such as Australia, Singapore, Malaysia, Japan, Indonesia, China, and South Korea, APEC holds much the same promise as NAFTA and the EU in facilitating and strengthening international business relationships. Member countries represent 40 percent of the world's population and 50 percent of the world's economic output.[5]

North America

North American Free Trade Agreement (NAFTA) An economic pact that combined the economies of the United States, Canada, and Mexico into the world's largest trading block.

The **North American Free Trade Agreement (NAFTA)** combined the economies of the United States, Canada, and Mexico into the world's largest trading bloc with more than 370 million customers and approximately $6.5 trillion in total GNP. Within the next 10 years, virtually all United States industrial exports into Mexico and Canada will be duty free. Although the United States has had a longer-standing agreement with Canada, Mexico has quickly emerged as the United States' third-largest trading partner as a result of NAFTA. U.S. industries that have benefited in the short run include capital-goods suppliers, manufacturers of consumer durables, grain producers and distributors, construction equipment manufacturers, the auto industry, as well as the financial industry, which now has privileged access into a previously protected market.

Despite the potential benefits of NAFTA, Mexico will need to bolster its infrastructure and take care of troubling environmental issues in order to support its economic growth. Mexico has recently established a comprehensive statute for environmental regulation to address issues such as air pollution, hazardous waste, water pollution, and noise pollution. Surprisingly, Mexico has very strict laws protecting natural resources, many of which were fashioned after U.S. laws. However, there has not been sufficient enforcement of those laws. Mexico has some way to go in developing a strong environmental services industry to handle environmental protection and cleanup. Both the United States and Mexico are committing up to $8 billion for environmental protection.[6]

The rest of the world

We can't begin to fully discuss all the important developments, markets, and competitors shaping the global environment. But we can convey the immense potential for other major developments and new competitive threats and opportunities. For example, globalization so far has left out three huge, high-potential regions of the world: the Middle East, Africa, and Latin America.[7] Together these regions comprise a major share of the world's natural resources and are among the fastest-growing economies. Their potential has not begun to be realized.[8]

Consequences of a global economy

The increasing integration of the global economy has had many consequences. First, over the last decade the volume of world trade has grown at a faster rate than the volume of world output. Over the past few decades, world output has grown by approximately 30 percent while world trade has grown by over 50 percent.[9] Years of emphasis on international commerce by major industrial countries, as well as recent liberalized trading brought about by NAFTA, EU, and APEC, have resulted in lowering the barriers to the free flow of goods, services, and capital among nation-states. The impact of these trends is staggering. For example, the General Agreement on Tariffs and Trade (GATT) alone is expected to add $330 billion to the world economy by allowing companies to sell and invest in markets that were closed to them before. Most experts expect competition to increase as trade is liberalized, and as is so often the case, the more efficient players will survive. To succeed in this industrial climate, managers need to study opportunities in existing markets, as well as work to enhance the competitiveness of their firms. Second, *foreign direct investment (FDI)* is playing an ever-increasing role in the global economy as companies of all sizes invest in overseas operations (see Figure 6.2). As shown in Table 6.1, foreign direct investments are matched closely on a regional basis by U.S. investments abroad. The major investments have been among the United States, Europe, and Japan. These figures support the idea of the economic triad mentioned earlier.[10]

figure 6.2
Direct investment positions on a historical-cost basis, 1982–95

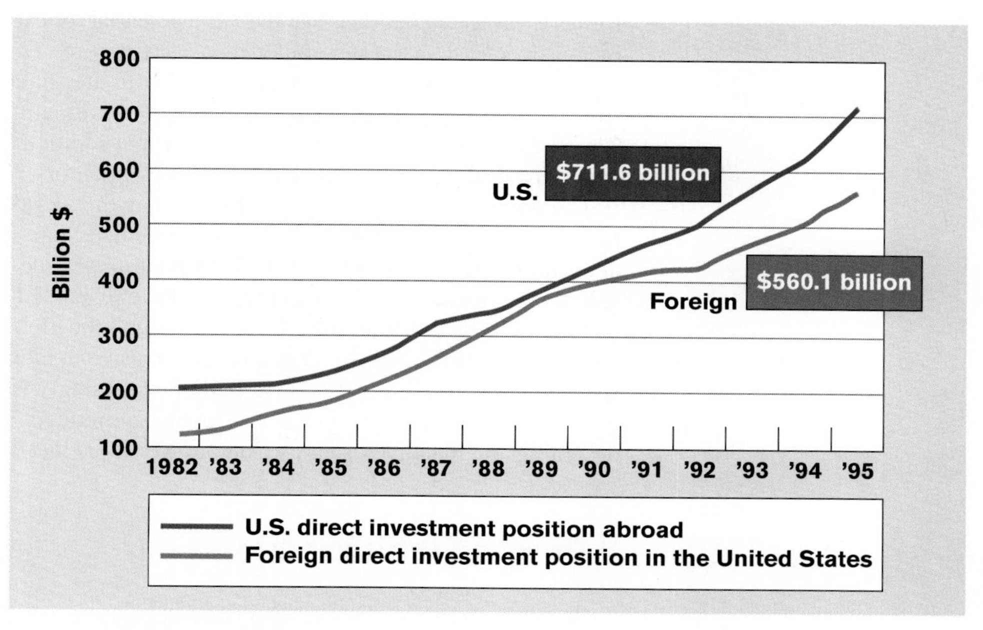

Source U.S. Department of Commerce, Bureau of Economic Analysis.

table 6.1
U.S. and foreign direct investments (1995)

	United States investment abroad	Foreign direct investment in United States
Canada	$ 81,387	$ 46,005
Europe	363,527	360,762
Latin America	122,765	22,716
Africa	347	936
Middle East	7,982	5,053
Asia and Pacific	125,968	124,615

Source: Jeffrey H. Lowe and Sylvia E. Bargas, "Direct Investment Positions on a Historical-Cost Basis," *Survey of Current Business,* July 1996, pp. 45–55.

A third consequence of an increasingly integrated global economy is that imports are penetrating deeper into the world's largest economies. For the first time, manufactured goods rather than raw materials account for more than half of Japan's imports.[11] The growth of imports is a natural by-product of the growth of world trade and the trend toward the manufacture of component parts, or even entire products, overseas before shipping them back home for final sale.

Finally, the growth of world trade, foreign direct investment, and imports implies that companies around the globe are finding their home markets under attack from foreign competitors. This is true in Japan, where Kodak has taken market share in the photographic film industry away from Fuji; in the United States, where Japanese automakers have captured market share from GM, Ford, and Chrysler; and in Western Europe, where the once-dominant Dutch company Philips N. V. has lost market share in the consumer electronics industry to Japan's JVC, Matsushita, and Sony.

What does all of this mean for the manager? Compared with only a few years ago, *opportunities are greater* because the movement toward free trade has opened up many formerly protected national markets. The potential for export, and for making direct investments overseas, is greater today than ever before. *The environment is more complex* because today's manager often has to deal with the challenges of doing business in countries with radically different cultures and of coordinating globally dispersed operations. *The environment is more competitive* because in addition to domestic competitors the manager must deal with cost-efficient overseas competitors.

Companies both large and small now view the world, rather than a single country, as their marketplace. As Table 6.2 shows, the United States has no monopoly on international business. Nearly half of the top 50 corporations in the world are based in countries outside the United States. Also, companies have dispersed their manufacturing, marketing, and research facilities to those locations around the globe where cost and skill conditions are most favorable. This trend is now so pervasive in industries such as automobiles, aerospace, and electronics that it is becoming increasingly irrelevant to talk about "American products" or "British products" or "Japanese products." Consider how Ford went about designing and manufacturing its Contour/Mystique line.

Ford's $6 billion world car

Its code name is CDW27. We know it better as the Ford Contour or Mercury Mystique. In Europe its called the Ford Mondeo. It took 11 years to develop and cost over $6 billion to launch, but CDW27 is more than a car; it is a platform for

Ford Motor Company's "global" car, the Ford Mondeo, has become a leader in the mid-sized segment of the European market. Its U.S. versions (Contour and Mystique) are doing well, too. *(Courtesy of Ford Motor Company)*

how Ford is competing globally. Most experts agree that national borders mean less and less in the world auto industry, and that building a world car—one that can be made and marketed around the world—can provide the ultimate in economies of scale.

To organize the design and manufacture of CDW27, Ford had four design studios in Italy, California, Germany, and Michigan work on the project. Engineers in Detroit designed the all-new 2.5-liter V-6 engine, the automatic transmission, and the heating and air-conditioning units. A team in Dunton, England, contributed the interior, the steering, the suspension, the electronics, the manual transmission, and the new four-cylinder engine. Employees in Cologne, Germany, did the basic structural engineering and also designed three sheet-metal bodies for the car tailored to different markets. In addition to design, renovations and retooling were done at nine factories, including engine parts in Wales, Cologne, Cleveland, and Chihuahua, Mexico. To ensure quality, Ford airlifted 150 engineers from England and Germany to mobile offices outside the production plant in Genk, Belgium. The executive in charge of CDW27, John Oldfield, was British and based in Cologne, Germany. But final responsibility for the program rested at Ford's world headquarters in Dearborn, Michigan.

With all the obstacles that had to be overcome, why did Ford create CDW27? Ford executives point to the economics of the project as a primary rationale. By designing and manufacturing the car for both Europe and the United States, Ford was able to allocate people and facilities to other projects. By using identical production tools at both Genk and Kansas City, Ford saved an estimated 25 percent on custom-built factory items. In the end, Ford saved $150 per car. Spread over 700,000 units, the total savings is $100 million a year. A second reason for CDW27 was that it was a learning experience. CDW27 is the nucleus for a decade's worth of products, all built from a common design and with great economies of scale. Ford's chairman, Alex Trotman, points out that for $6 billion the company got three new models, two new engines, two new transmissions, and nine new or revamped factories.

Sources: "Long-Term Update: Ford Contour SE," *Ward's Auto World* 32, no.2. (February 1996), p. 60; Wade A. Hoyt, "Chevrolet Lumina and Ford Contour: Going Head-to-Head against Popular Japanese Sedans," *Medical Economics* 72, no. 4. (February 27, 1995), pp. 44–53; Ken Korane, "Mercury Mystique: Look out, Imports," *Machine Design* 67, no. 6. (March 23, 1995), pp. 102–3; Jerry Flint, "Will It, or Won't It?" *Forbes,* February 28, 1994, p. 18; and "Enter the McFord," *The Economist,* July 23, 1994, p. 69.

table 6.2 The top 50 companies

Rank, 1995		Market value (billions of U.S. dollars)		Rank, 1995		Market value (billions of U.S. dollars)	
1	NTT	Japan	129.01	26	Mobil	U.S.	39.40
2	Royal Dutch/Shell	Neth./Britain	107.63	27	Glaxo Wellcome	Britain	39.38
3	General Electric	U.S.	98.24	28	British Telecomms.	Britain	38.93
4	Exxon	U.S.	88.65	29	British Petroleum	Britain	38.88
5	AT&T	U.S.	80.30	30	Pepsico	U.S.	38.71
6	Coca-Cola	U.S.	78.63	31	Allianz Holding	Germany	37.51
7	Toyota Motor	Japan	72.43	32	General Motors	U.S.	36.13
8	Mitsubishi Bank	Japan	68.75	33	Bank of Tokyo	Japan	36.06
9	Industrial Bank	Japan	68.34	34	AIG	U.S.	35.94
10	Fuji Bank	Japan	66.40	35	Unilever	Neth./Britain	35.89
11	Sumitomo Bank	Japan	65.31	36	DuPont	U.S.	35.74
12	Sanwa Bank	Japan	62.03	37	Nomura Securities	Japan	35.25
13	Philip Morris	U.S.	61.57	38	Motorola	U.S.	35.21
14	Roche Holding	Switzerland	60.50	30	HSBC Holdings	Britain	34.00
15	Dai-Ichi Kangyo Bank	Japan	58.99	40	Amoco	U.S.	33.94
16	Merck	U.S.	58.12	41	Bristol-Myers Squibb	U.S.	33.67
17	Wal-Mart Stores	U.S.	57.14	42	Hewlett-Packard	U.S.	33.64
18	IBM	U.S.	54.00	43	Matsushita Electric Indl.	Japan	32.46
19	Procter & Gamble	U.S.	49.40	44	GTE	U.S.	32.21
20	Microsoft	U.S.	49.15	45	Hitachi Ltd.	Japan	32.16
21	Intel	U.S.	46.36	46	Abbott Laboratories	U.S.	32.12
22	Johnson & Johnson	U.S.	42.66	47	Chevron	U.S.	32.02
23	Tokyo Electric Power	Japan	42.41	48	Singapore Telecomms.	Singapore	31.18
24	Sakura Bank	Japan	40.15	49	BellSouth	U.S	30.34
25	Nestle	Switzerland	39.47	50	Ford Motor	U.S.	29.96

Source: Adapted from *The Wall Street Journal, Business Week,* and other company documents.

So is the Ford Contour an "American product"? Not really—but neither is it a "British product," a "German product," a "Belgian product," a "French product," an "Italian product," a "Mexican product," and so on. You get the idea. Like an increasing number of the products we buy today, it is an international product.

Internationalization is not limited to large corporations like General Motors. An increasing number of medium-size and small firms also engage in international trade. Some companies have limited their involvement to exporting, while others have taken the process a step further by setting up production facilities overseas. Consider Lubricating Systems Inc. of Kent, Washington. The company manufactures lubricating fluids for machine tools. The company is hardly an industrial giant, yet approximately one-third of its total sales are generated by exports to countries such as Japan, Israel, and the United Arab Emirates. Moreover, Lubricating Systems is now setting up a joint venture with a German company to serve the European market. Even a tiny company such as SpringHill Greenhouses in

Lodi, Ohio, operates internationally. With only a half dozen employees, SpringHill works with wholesale growers in the Netherlands (for tulips and lilies) and Colombia (for roses) to get the best value for flowers. Then, working through global associations such as FTD and Teleflora, SpringHill networks with other florists to send and receive orders virtually anywhere around the world.[12]

Global strategy

One of the critical tasks an international manager faces is to identify the best strategy for competing in a global marketplace. To approach this issue, it is helpful to plot a company's position on an integration–responsiveness grid (see Figure 6.3). The vertical axis measures pressures for *global integration,* and the horizontal axis measures pressures for local responsiveness.

Pressures for global integration

Universal needs create strong pressure for a global strategy. Universal needs exist when the tastes and preferences of consumers in different countries with regard to a product are similar. Products that serve universal needs require little adaptation across national markets; thus, global integration is facilitated. This is the case in many industrial markets. Electronic products such as capacitors, resistors, and semiconductor chips are products that meet universal needs.

Competitive *pressures to reduce costs* may force a company to globally integrate manufacturing. This can be particularly important in industries in which price is the main competitive weapon and competition is intense (for example, hand-held calculators and semiconductor chips). It is also important in industries in which key international competitors are based in countries with low factor costs (e.g., low labor and energy costs).

The presence of competitors engaged in *global strategic coordination* is another factor that creates pressure for global integration. Reacting to global competitive threats calls for global strategic coordination, which creates pressure to centralize decisions regarding the competitive strategies of different national subsidiaries at corporate headquarters. Thus, once one multinational company in an industry adopts global strategic coordination, its competitors may be forced to respond in kind.

figure 6.3
Organizational models

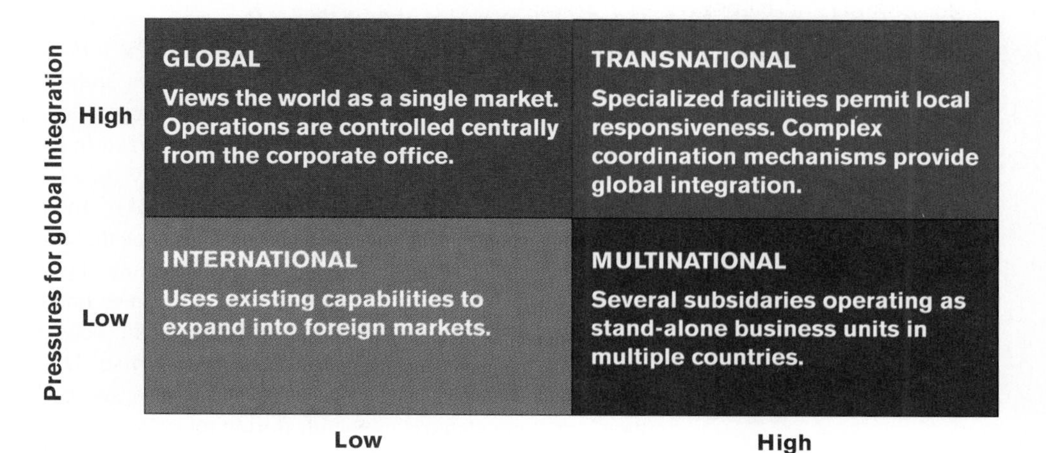

Sources: Christopher A. Bartlett and Sumantra Ghoshal, *Managing across Borders: The Transnational Solution* (Boston: Harvard Business School Press, 1991); and Sumantra Ghoshal and Nitin Nohria, "Horses for Courses: Organizational Forms for Multinational Corporations," *Sloan Management Review,* Winter 1993, pp. 23–35.

Pressures for local responsiveness

In some circumstances, companies must be able to adapt to different needs in different locations. Strong pressures for local responsiveness emerge when *consumer tastes and preferences differ significantly* among countries. In such cases, product and/or marketing messages have to be customized.

In the automobile industry, for example, demand by United States consumers for pickup trucks is strong. This is particularly true in the South and West, where many families have a pickup truck as a second or third car. In contrast, in Europe pickup trucks are viewed as utility vehicles and are purchased primarily by companies rather than by individuals. As a result, automakers must tailor their marketing messages to the differences in consumer demand.

Pressures for local responsiveness also emerge when there are *differences in traditional practices* among countries. For example, in Great Britain people drive on the left side of the road, creating a demand for right-hand-drive cars, whereas in neighboring France people drive on the right side of the road. Obviously automobiles must be customized to accommodate this difference in traditional practices.

Differences in distribution channels and sales practices among countries may also create pressures for local responsiveness. In the pharmaceutical industry, the Japanese distribution system differs radically from the U.S. system. Japanese doctors will respond unfavorably to an American-style, high-pressure sales force. Thus, pharmaceutical companies have to adopt different marketing practices in Japan (soft versus hard sell).

Finally, *economic and political demands* imposed by host country governments may necessitate a degree of local responsiveness. Most important, threats of protectionism, economic nationalism, and local content rules (rules requiring that a certain percentage of a product be manufactured locally) dictate that international companies manufacture locally.

Choosing a global strategy

Figure 6.3 shows the integration-responsiveness grid implying the existence of four approaches to international competition: the international model, the multinational model, the global model, and the transnational model. Each of these types of organizations differs in terms of its approach to strategy as well as the structure and systems that drive operations.

international organization model An organization model that is composed of a company's overseas subsidiaries and characterized by greater control by the parent company over the research function and local product and marketing strategies than is the case in the multinational model.

The international model

The **international organization model** is designed to help companies exploit their existing core capabilities to expand into foreign markets. The international model uses subsidiaries in each country in which the company does business, with ultimate control exercised by the parent company. In particular, while subsidiaries may have some latitude to adapt products to local conditions, core functions such as research and development tend to be centralized in the parent company. Consequently, subsidiary dependence on the parent company for new products, processes, and ideas requires a great deal of coordination and control by the parent company.

The advantage of this model is that it facilitates the transfer of skills and know-how from the parent company to subsidiaries around the globe. For example, IBM, Xerox, and Kodak all profited from the transfer of their core skills in technology and R&D overseas. The overseas successes of Kellogg, Coca-Cola, Heinz, and Procter & Gamble are based more on marketing know-how than on technological expertise. During the 1970s and 1980s, many Japanese companies, including Toyota and Honda, successfully penetrated U.S. markets with their core competencies in manufacturing relative to local competitors. Still others have based their competitive advantage on general management skills. These factors explain the growth of international hotel chains such as Hilton International, Intercontinental, and Sheraton.

One disadvantage of the international model is that it does not provide maximum latitude for responding to local conditions. In addition, it frequently does not provide the opportunity to achieve a low-cost position via scale economics.

Heinz is especially skilled at overseas marketing. This prominent billboard is displayed in Guangdong, China. *[Greg Girard/Contact Press Images]*

multinational organization model An organization model that consists of the subsidiaries in each country in which a company does business, with ultimate control exercised by the parent company.

The multinational model In contrast to the international model, the **multinational organization model** uses subsidiaries (i.e., independent companies) in each country in which the company does business, and provides a great deal of discretion to those subsidiaries to respond to local conditions. Each local subsidiary is a self-contained unit with all the functions required for operating in the host market. Thus, each subsidiary has its own manufacturing, marketing, research, and human resources functions. Because of this autonomy, each multinational subsidiary can customize its products and strategies according to the tastes and preferences of local consumers; the competitive conditions; and political, legal, and social structures.

The multinational model was widespread among many of the early European corporations such as Unilever and Royal Dutch Shell. One advantage of allowing local responsiveness is that there is less need for coordination and direction from corporate headquarters. Since each subsidiary is a self-contained unit, few transfers of goods and services occur among subsidiaries, thus alleviating problems with transfer pricing and the like.

A major disadvantage of the multinational form is higher manufacturing costs and duplication of effort. Although a multinational can transfer core skills among its international operations, it cannot realize scale economies from centralizing manufacturing facilities and offering a standardized product to the global marketplace. Moreover, since a multinational approach tends to decentralize strategy decisions (discussed further in Chapters 8 and 9), it is difficult to launch coordinated global attacks against competitors. This can be a significant disadvantage when competitors have this ability.

global organization model An organization model consisting of a company's overseas subsidiaries and characterized by centralized decision making and tight control by the parent company over most aspects of worldwide operations. Typically adopted by organizations that base their global competitive strategy on low cost.

The global model The **global organization model** is designed to enable a company to market a standardized product in the global marketplace and to manufacture that product in a limited number of locations where the mix of costs and skills is most favorable. The global model has been adopted by companies that view the world as one market and assume that there are no tangible differences among countries with regard to consumer tastes and preferences. Procter & Gamble, for example, has been successful in Europe against Unilever because it has approached the entire continent as a unified whole.

Companies that adopt the global model tend to become the low-cost players in any industry. These companies construct global-scale manufacturing facilities in a few selected low-cost locations so that they can realize scale economies. These scale economies come from spreading the fixed costs of investments in new-product development, plant and equipment, and the like over worldwide sales. By using centralized manufacturing facilities and global marketing strategies, Sony was able to push down its unit costs to the point where it became the low-cost player in the global television market. This enabled Sony to take market share away from Philips, RCA, and Zenith, all of which traditionally based manufacturing operations in each major national market (a characteristic of the multinational approach). Because operations are centralized, subsidiaries usually are limited to marketing and service functions.

On the downside, because a company pursuing a purely global approach tries to standardize its products and services, it may be less responsive to consumer tastes and demands in different countries. Attempts to lower costs through global product standardization may result in a product that fails to satisfy anyone. For example, while Procter & Gamble has been quite successful using a global approach, the company experienced problems when it tried to market Cheer in Japan. Unfortunately for P&G, the product did not "suds up" as promoted in Japan because the Japanese use a great deal of fabric softener, which suppresses suds. Moreover, the claim that Cheer worked in all water temperatures was irrelevant in Japan, where most washing is done in cold water.

Companies pursuing a pure global approach to strategy require increased coordination, and paperwork and additional staff. Moreover, such companies must decide how to price transfers of goods and services among parts of the company based in different countries. Transfer-pricing problems are difficult enough to resolve within just one country; in a global company, transfer pricing can be further complicated by volatile exchange rates.

The transnational model

In today's global economy, achieving a competitive advantage often requires the *simultaneous* pursuit of gains from local responsiveness, transfer of know-how, and cost economies.[13] This raises the question of whether it is possible to design an organization that enables a company to simultaneously reap all the benefits of global expansion. Recently a number of companies, including Unilever, Caterpillar, and Philips, have been experimenting with a new organization model—the transnational organization model—that is designed to do just that.

transnational organization model An organization model characterized by centralization of certain functions in locations that best achieve cost economies; basing of other functions in the company's national subsidiaries to facilitate greater local responsiveness; and fostering of communication among subsidiaries to permit transfer of technological expertise and skills.

In companies that adopt the **transnational organization model,** certain functions, particularly research, tend to be centralized at home. Other functions are also centralized, but not necessarily in the home country. To achieve cost economies, companies may base global-scale production plants for labor-intensive products in low-wage countries such as Mexico or Singapore and locate production plants that require a skilled work force in high-skill countries such as Germany or Japan.

Other functions, particularly marketing, service, and final-assembly functions, tend to be based in the national subsidiaries to facilitate greater local responsiveness. Thus, major components may be manufactured in centralized production plants to realize scale economies and then shipped to local plants, where the final product is assembled and customized to fit local needs.

Caterpillar Tractor is a transnational company.[14] The need to compete with low-cost competitors such as Komatsu has forced Caterpillar to look for greater cost economies by centralizing global production at locations where the factor cost/skill mix is most favorable. At the same time, variations in construction practices and government regulations across countries mean that Caterpillar must be responsive to local needs. On the integration-responsiveness grid in Figure 6.3, therefore, Caterpillar is situated toward the top right-hand corner.

To deal with these simultaneous demands, Caterpillar has designed its products to use many identical components and invested in a few large-scale component manufacturing facilities to fill global demand and realize scale economies. But while the company manufactures components centrally, it has assembly plants in each of its major markets. At these plants Caterpillar adds local product features, tailoring the finished product to local needs. Thus, Caterpillar is able to realize many of the benefits of global manufacturing while managing pressure for local responsiveness by differentiating its product among national markets.

Perhaps the most important distinguishing characteristic of the transnational organization is the fostering of communications among subsidiaries. National subsidiaries communicate better with one another so that they can transfer technological expertise and skills among themselves to their mutual benefit. At the same time, centralized manufacturing plants coordinate their production with local assembly plants, thereby facilitating the smooth operation of an integrated, worldwide production system.

Achieving such communications across subsidiaries requires elaborate formal mechanisms, such as transnational committees staffed by people from the various subsidiaries who are responsible for monitoring coordination among subsidiaries. Equally important is to transfer managers among subsidiaries on a regular basis. This enables international managers to establish a global network of personal contacts in different subsidiaries with whom they can share information as the need arises. Finally, achieving coordination among subsidiaries requires that the head office play a proactive role in coordinating their activities.

Entry mode

When considering global expansion, international managers must decide on the best means of entering an overseas market. There are five basic ways to expand overseas: exporting, licensing, franchising, entering into a joint venture with a host country company, and setting up a wholly owned subsidiary in the host country.[15] Table 6.3 compares the entry modes.

Exporting

Most manufacturing companies begin global expansion as exporters and later switch to one of the other modes for serving an overseas market. Advantages of exporting are that it (1) provides scale economies by avoiding the costs of manufacturing in other countries and (2) is consistent with a pure global strategy. By manufacturing the product in a centralized location and then exporting it to other national markets, the company may be able to realize substantial scale economies from its global sales volume.

table 6.3 Comparison of entry modes

	Exporting	Licensing	Franchising	Joint venture	Wholly owned subsidiary
Advantages	Scale economies	Lower development costs	Lower development costs	Local knowledge	Maintains control over technology
	Consistent with pure global strategy	Lower political risk	Lower political risk	Shared costs and risk	Maintains control over operations
				May be the only option	
Disadvantages	No low-cost sites	Loss of control over technology	Loss of control over quality	Loss of control over technology	High cost
	High transportation costs			Conflict between partners	High risk
	Tariff barriers				

On the other hand, exporting has a number of drawbacks. First, exporting from the company's home base may be inappropriate if other countries offer lower-cost locations for manufacturing the product. An alternative is to manufacture in a location where the mix of factor costs and skills is most favorable and then export from that location to other markets to achieve scale economies. Several U.S. electronics companies have moved some manufacturing operations to the Far East, where low-cost, high-skill labor is available, then export from that location to other countries, including the United States.

A second drawback of exporting is that high transportation costs can make it uneconomical, particularly in the case of bulk products. Chemical companies get around this by manufacturing their products on a regional basis, serving several countries in a region from one facility.

A third drawback is that host countries can impose (or threaten to impose) tariff barriers. As noted earlier, Japanese automakers reduced this risk by setting up manufacturing plants in the United States.

Licensing

International licensing is an arrangement whereby a licensee in another country buys the rights to manufacture a company's product in its own country for a negotiated fee (typically, royalty payments on the number of units sold). The licensee then puts up most of the capital necessary to get the overseas operation going. The advantage of licensing is that the company need not bear the costs and risks of opening up an overseas market.

On the other hand, a problem arises when a company licenses its technological expertise to overseas companies. Technological know-how is the basis of the competitive advantage of many multinational companies. But RCA Corporation lost control over its color TV technology by licensing it to a number of Japanese companies. The Japanese companies quickly assimilated RCA's technology and then used it to enter the U. S. market. Now the Japanese have a bigger share of the U.S. market than the RCA brand does.

Franchising

In many respects, franchising is similar to licensing. However, whereas licensing is a strategy pursued primarily by manufacturing companies, franchising is used primarily by service companies. McDonald's, Hilton International, and many other companies have expanded overseas by franchising.

In franchising, the company sells limited rights to use its brand name to franchisees in return for a lump-sum payment and a share of the franchisees' profits. However, unlike most licensing agreements, the franchisee has to agree to abide by strict rules as to how it does business. Thus, when McDonald's enters into a franchising agreement with an overseas company, it expects the franchisee to run its restaurants in a manner identical to those run under the McDonald's name elsewhere in the world.

Pizza, subs, burgers and chips: Franchising Europe

The fast-food revolution hit Europe in the early 1990s, and companies such as McDonald's (with over 2,000 units) and Burger King (with over 700 units) have led the way. Other companies such as Pizza Hut and Kentucky Fried Chicken are pouring tens of millions of dollars annually into expanding their number of franchises. Pizza Hut has over 350 units in the U.K. alone and is expanding at the rate of about 60 units per year. KFC International has even more ambitious growth plans and hopes to triple its number of European units over the next few years. In Germany alone, the company has plans to open 30–50 units per year. Blimpie predicts that it will have well over 500 units throughout Europe within 10 years.

American fast-food franchises have taken European markets by storm, as evidenced by this Kentucky Fried Chicken store in France.
[Courtesy of Kentucky Fried Chicken (KFC)]

Subway estimates that it will have at least 500 stores within five years. Applebee's, Chili's, Bennigan's, and Tony Roma's all have plans to open at least 20 units within the next five years. TGI Friday's plans to open 50 restaurants in the next 10 years. Pretty aggressive. How do they do it?

Franchising is the key to this breakneck pace of expansion. Franchising offers fast-food companies a relatively low-risk investment while facilitating a low-cost transfer of know-how, technology, training, and management skills to other parts of the world. Franchising has been especially successful for U.S.–based companies trying to expand into parts of Eastern Europe. Unification and the elimination of customs barriers have made it much easier for companies to open fast-food franchises and conduct business across borders. However, while an integrated Europe makes free-market transactions easier, there is no such thing as a homogeneous European market–U.S.–based operators have had to alter their concept of fast food for each region. KFC's first restaurant in Europe, for example, included a menu of sandwiches, salads, and desserts, while providing a more country French decor. Pizza Hut also has made extensive menu changes, from bigger salads to a broader dessert selection. McDonald's, which rightfully prides itself on providing a consistent and standardized fare, has made adjustments to accommodate local preferences. Here again is an advantage of franchising–local knowledge helps to fine-tune each company's product line and provide ways of integrating fast food into the European culture. No longer just fish 'n chips or croissants, fast-food franchises are changing the way Europeans eat.

Sources: Leonard N. Swartz, "Exploring Global Franchising Trends," *Franchising World,* March/April 1997, pp. 7–16; Don Nichols, "Foreign Intrigue," *Restaurant Business,* May 20, 1996, pp. 122–31; "Pizza Hut Boosts 21st Century Growth Plan," *Marketing,* July 28, 1994, p. 5; Stephanie Anderson Forest, "How Enrico Put the Spice Back in Pizza Hut," *Business Week,* March 11, 1996, pp. 72–73; "Corporate Strategies: KFC Goes after Pakistan's Yuppies," *Crossborder Monitor* 5, no. 36 (September 10, 1997), pp. 1, 9; Stephanie Bentley, "KFC to Shake Up Euro Operation," *Marketing Week,* February 23, 1996, p. 11; David Lennon, "Goodbye Fish and Chips," *Europe,* July–August 1994, pp. 43–44; and Danny Rogers, "Burger King Lifts British Beef Ban," *Marketing,* July 3, 1997, p. 2. ●

The advantages of franchising as an entry mode are similar to those of licensing. The most significant disadvantage concerns quality control. The company's brand name guarantees consistency in the company's product. Thus, a business traveler booking into a Hilton International hotel in Hong Kong can reasonably expect the same quality of room, food, and service that he or she would receive in New York. But if overseas franchisees are less concerned about quality than they should be, the impact can go beyond lost sales in the local market to a decline in the company's reputation worldwide. If a business traveler has an unpleasant experience at the Hilton in Hong Kong, she or he may decide never to go to another Hilton hotel—and urge colleagues to do likewise. To make matters worse, the geographical distance between the franchisor and its overseas franchisees makes poor quality difficult to detect.

Joint ventures

Establishing a joint venture (a formal business agreement discussed in more detail in Chapter 11) with a company in another country has long been a popular means for entering a new market. Joint ventures benefit a company through (1) the local partner's knowledge of the host country's competitive conditions, culture, language, political systems, and business systems; and (2) the sharing of development costs and/or risks with the local partner. In addition, many countries' political considerations make joint ventures the only feasible entry mode. As discussed below, many U.S. companies are finding this to be the case in China.

Good fortune in China

A number of U.S. companies are making inroads to China via joint ventures and other forms of partnerships. Several are summarized below:

- Eastman Kodak has established a joint venture with China Lucky Film Corporation in order to gain a stronger foothold in the country's $250 million market for film. Kodak's investment not only will help China Lucky's financial performance (which has been poor of late) but will allow Kodak to avoid the 60 percent duty on imported film. This venture remains caught in a national debate about whether China should bolster its domestic producers or allow foreign investment.
- Dow Chemical recently signed a letter of intent with China Petrochemical Corporation (Sinopec) and Tianjin Petrochemical Corporation to join in the development of a multibillion dollar ethylene-based complex near Beijing. The agreement calls for a 50/50 partnership.

Joint ventures enable companies like Chrysler to gain better access to foreign markets.
[Jeffrey Aaronsen/Network Aspen]

- Goodyear Tire and Rubber got a late start in China, but has become a key foreign player in the country's tire market because of its partnership with Dalian General Rubber Factory. Dalian was in dire financial condition and had no access to advanced technology. Goodyear provided money, technology, and management. In return, Goodyear got a small partner that could teach it how to operate in China.
- IBM launched International Information Products Corporation (IIPC), a joint venture with Great Wall Computer Group. IBM owns 51 percent of the venture.
- Maytag has invested approximately $70 million in a series of joint ventures in laundry and refrigeration with the Hefei Rongshida Group.

Sources: Norman C. Remich, Jr., "Maytag: A China Connection," *Appliance Manufacturer* 45, no. 2 (February 1997), pp. G16–G17; "IBM's Chinese PCs," *Crossborder Monitor* 5, no. 6 (February 12, 1997), pp. 1, 9; "Goodyear in China: Rolling Along," *Crossborder Monitor* 5, no. 17 (April 30, 1997), p. 8; Robert Warren, "Dow Signs with Sinopec at Tianjin," *Chemical Market Reporter* 251, no. 26 (June 30, 1997), pp. 3, 20; Dexter Robers and Joyce Barnathan, "Will Kodak Get Lucky in China?" *Business Week* 3537 (July 28, 1997), p. 48. ●

Despite the advantages of joint ventures such as these, they also have two possible disadvantages. First, as in the case of licensing, a company runs the risk of losing control over its technology to its venture partner. Second, because control is shared with the partner, the company may lose control over its subsidiaries. Indeed, conflict over who controls what within a joint venture is a primary reason many joint ventures fail.

Wholly owned subsidiaries

Establishing a wholly owned subsidiary, that is, an independent company owned by the parent corporation, is the most costly method of serving an overseas market. Companies that use this approach must bear the full costs and risks associated with setting up overseas operations (as opposed to joint ventures, in which the costs and risks are shared, or licensing, in which the licensee bears most of the costs and risks).

Nevertheless, setting up a wholly owned subsidiary offers two clear advantages. First, when a company's competitive advantage is based on technology, a wholly owned subsidiary normally will be the preferred entry mode because it reduces the risk of losing control over the technology. This was the case for 3M, who was the first to set up a wholly owned subsidiary in China.[16] Wholly owned subsidiaries tend to be the favored entry mode in the semiconductor, electronics, and pharmaceutical industries.

expatriates Parent-company nationals who are sent to work at a foreign subsidiary.

host-country nationals Natives of the country where an overseas subsidiary is located.

Second, a wholly owned subsidiary gives a company tight control over operations in other countries, which is necessary if it chooses to pursue a global strategy. Establishing a global manufacturing system requires world headquarters to have a high degree of control over the operations of national affiliates. Unlike licensees or joint venture partners, wholly owned subsidiaries usually accept centrally determined decisions about how to produce, how much to produce, and how to price output for transfer among operations.

Managing across borders

third-country nationals Natives of a country other than the home country or the host country of an overseas subsidiary.

When establishing operations overseas, headquarter executives have a choice among sending **expatriates** (individuals from the parent country), using **host-country nationals** (natives of the host country), or deploying **third-country nationals** (natives of a country other than the home country or the host country). While most corporations use some combination of all three types of employees, there are advantages and disadvantages of each. Colgate-Palmolive, for example, uses expatriates in an effort to shorten the delivery time of products-to-market, while AT&T uses expatriates to help transfer the company's culture. On the other hand, companies such as Chevron and Texas Instruments make more limited use of expatriates. Chevron typically sends a management team to review the skills of local employees, and sends expatriates only if their technical skills are needed. If expatriates are sent, it is expected that operational control will be passed over to local employees. Texas Instruments uses very few expatriates, but relies on phone, fax, and computers to facilitate communication. However, TI frequently sends people on extended travel so they meet their cohorts around the world.[17]

Colgate-Palmolive's global workforce

Colgate-Palmolive has been operating internationally for more than 50 years. Its products, such as Colgate toothpaste, Palmolive soap, Fab detergent, and Ajax cleanser, are household names in more than 170 countries. Since more than 70 percent of the company's $7 billion in sales comes from overseas markets, Colgate requires a certain type of manager who understands not only the particular niches and communities in which the company operates locally, but also the benefits of a global product line. And because about a quarter of its far-flung operations have been set up in the past five years (mostly in developing countries), the challenge to recruit, train, and retain global managers and employees has intensified.

The composition of Colgate's executive team gives the company a good start. Two of its last four CEOs have come from outside the United States, and all of the top executives speak at least two languages. Six of the 24 corporate officers are from countries outside the United States and 18 of them have resided in overseas locations during their careers.

But having a cadre of *globalite executives*—as Colgate-Palmolive calls them—is not enough. Fully two-thirds of the company's employees work outside the United States. And 60 percent of its expatriates are from places other than the United States. Given this, the company goes to great lengths to attract and develop individuals who want international careers anywhere in the world. One example of Colgate's commitment to recruiting and staffing globally is its Global Marketing Program. The program takes approximately 15 high-potential MBA graduates and rotates them through various departments for 18 to 24 months. Recruits gain experience in the global business development group and, after their stint in Colgate's headquarters, they are deployed overseas. The success of this program extends beyond its training value. The Global Marketing Program also serves as an excellent recruiting device—more than 15,000 candidates apply for the 15 slots each year.

Once on board, employees are provided an array of overseas assignments: long term, short term, and stopgap for addressing particular competency needs. The company has developed competency programs, performance/potential programs, and career-tracking programs to define the developmental needs of each person. While the programs vary based on the individual's interests and capabilities, they are all designed to provide exposure to the corporate—as well as local—culture. Ultimately, Colgate's objective is to generate an international core of managers who will be the future leaders of the company.

Sources: Judy Quinn, "Motivators of the Year," *Incentive,* January, 1996, pp. 26–30; Robert Agate, "Success(ion) Story," *CFO,* September 1996, pp. 89–90; Charlene Marmer Solomon, "Staff Selection Impacts Global Success," *Personnel Journal,* January 1994, pp. 88–101; and Dawn Anfuso, "Colgate Aligns HR with Its Global Vision," *Personnel Journal* 74, no. 1 (January 1995), p. 74.

Developing a valuable pool of expatriates—as Colgate has—is important. However, as shown in Figure 6.4, companies tend to make more use of host-country nationals over time. Local employees are more available, tend to have familiarity with the culture and language, and usually cost less because they do not have to be displaced. In addition, local governments often provide incentives to companies that create good jobs for their citizens (or they may place restrictions on the use of expatriates). For these reasons, executives at Allen Bradley, a division of Rockwell International, believe that building a strong local workforce is critical to their success overseas, and they transport key host-country nationals to the United States for skills training. The trend away from using expatriates in top management positions is especially apparent in companies that truly want to create a multinational culture. In Honeywell's European division, for example, many of the top executive positions are held by non-Americans.[18]

Over the years, U.S.–based companies, in particular, have tended to use more third-country nationals to work in a country different from their own, and different from the parent company's. When Eastman Kodak assembled a management team to devise a launch strategy for its Photo-CD line in Europe, the team members were based in London, but the leader was from Belgium. Because third-country nationals can soften the political tensions between the parent country and the host country, they often represent a convenient compromise.[19]

Skills of the global manager

It is estimated that by the year 2000, nearly 15 percent of all employee transfers will be to an international location. However, a recent survey of 1,500 senior executives showed that there is a critical shortage of U.S. managers equipped to run global businesses.[20] Indicative of this fact is the **failure rate** among expatriates (defined as those who come home early), which has been estimated to range from 25 to 50 percent. The average cost of each of these failed assignments ranges from $40,000 to $250,000.[21] Typically the causes for failure overseas extend beyond technical capability, and include personal and social issues as well. Interestingly, one of the biggest problems is a spouse's inability to adjust to his or her new surroundings. For both the expatriate and the spouse, adjustment requires flexibility, emotional stability, empathy for the culture, communication skills, resourcefulness, initiative, and diplomatic skills.[22]

failure rate The number of expatriate managers of an overseas operation that come home early.

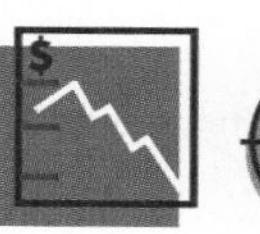

figure 6.4
Evolution of a foreign subsidiary

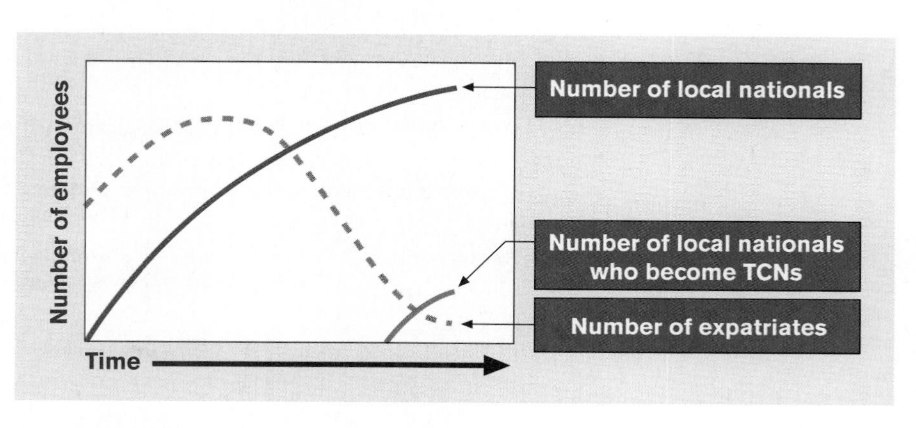

Source: Calvin Reynolds, "Strategic Employment of Third Country Nationals," *Human Resource Planning* v20, nl, 1997, pp. 33–93. Reprinted by permission of Organization Resources Counselors, Inc.

Interestingly, while many U.S. companies have hesitated to send women abroad—believing that women either do not want international assignments or that other cultures would not welcome women—their success rate has been estimated at 97 percent (far greater than for their male counterparts).[23] Ironically, for a country which had been viewed as not welcoming foreign women, in Japan U.S. women are first viewed as foreigners (*gaijin* in Japanese) and only second as women. And because it is unusual for women to be sent on foreign assignments, their distinctiveness and visibility tend to increase their chances for success.[24]

Companies, such as Levi-Strauss, Bechtel, Monsanto, Whirlpool, and Dow Chemical have worked to identify the characteristics of individuals that will predict their success abroad. Figure 6.5 shows a list of skills that can be used to identify candidates who are likely to succeed in a global environment. Interestingly, in addition to such things as cultural sensitivity, technical expertise, and business knowledge, an individual's success abroad may depend a great deal on his or her ability to learn from experience.[25]

figure 6.5
Identifying international executives

End-state dimensions	Sample items
1. Sensitivity to cultural differences	When working with people from other cultures, works hard to understand their perspective.
2. Business knowledge	Has a solid understanding of the company's products and services.
3. Courage to take a stand	Is willing to take a stand on issues.
4. Brings out the best in people	Has a special talent for dealing with people.
5. Acts with integrity	Can be depended on to tell the truth regardless of circumstances.
6. Is insightful	Is good at identifying the most important part of a complex problem.
7. Is committed to success	Clearly demonstrates commitment to seeing the organization succeed.
8. Takes risks	Takes personal as well as business risks.
Learning-oriented dimensions	**Sample items**
1. Uses feedback	Has changed as a result of feedback.
2. Is culturally adventurous	Enjoys the challenge of working in countries other than his/her own.
3. Seeks opportunities to learn	Takes advantage of opportunities to do new things.
4. Is open to criticism	Appears brittle—as if criticism might cause him/her to break.
5. Seeks feedback	Pursues feedback even when others are reluctant to give it.
6. Is flexible	Doesn't get so invested in things that he/she cannot change when something doesn't work.

Source: Gretchen M. Sprietzer, Morgan W. McCall, and Joan D. Mahoney, "Early Identification of International Executive Potential," *Journal of Applied Psychology* 82, no. 1 (1997), pp. 6–29.

table 6.4
How to prevent failed assignments

Structure assignments clearly: Develop clear reporting relationships and job responsibilities.
Create clear job objectives.
Develop performance measurements based on objectives.
Use effective, validated selection and screening criteria (both personal and technical attributes).
Prepare expatriates and families for assignments (briefings, training, support).
Create a vehicle for ongoing communication with expatriate.
Anticipate repatriation to facilitate reentry when they come back home.
Consider developing a mentor program that will help monitor and intervene in case of trouble.

Companies such as Amoco, Mercedes Benz, Hyatt, British Petroleum, and others with large international staffs have extensive training programs to prepare employees for international assignments. Table 6.4 suggests ways to improve their likelihood of success. Other organizations such as Coca-Cola, Motorola, Chevron, and Mattel have extended this training to include employees who may be located in the United States but who nevertheless deal in international markets. These programs focus on areas such as language, culture, and career development.

Understanding cultural issues

In many ways, cultural issues represent the most elusive aspect of international business. In an era when modern transportation and communication technologies have created a "global village," it is easy to forget how deep and enduring the differences among nations actually can be. The fact that people everywhere drink Coke, wear blue jeans, and drive Toyotas doesn't mean we are all becoming alike. Each country is unique for reasons rooted in history, culture, language, geography, social conditions, race, and religion. These differences complicate any international activities, and represent the fundamental issues that inform and guide how a company should conduct business across borders.

Ironically, while most of us would guess that the trick to working abroad is learning about the foreign culture, in reality our problems often stem from our being oblivious to our own cultural conditioning. Most of us pay no attention to how culture influences our everyday behavior, and because of this we tend to adapt poorly to situations that are unique or foreign to us. This is one reason why people traveling abroad frequently experience **culture shock**—the disorientation and stress associated with being in a foreign environment. Managers who ignore culture put their organizations at a great disadvantage in the global marketplace. Since each culture has its own norms, customs, and expectations for behavior, success in an international environment depends on one's ability to understand one's own and the other culture and to recognize that abrupt changes will be met with resistance.[26]

culture shock The disorientation and stress associated with being in a foreign environment.

A wealth of cross-cultural research has been conducted on the differences and similarities between various countries. Geert Hofstede, for example, has identified four dimensions along which managers in multinational corporations tend to view cultural differences:

- *Power distance:* the extent to which a society accepts the fact that power in organizations is distributed unequally.
- *Individualism/collectivism:* the extent to which people act on their own or as a part of a group.

- *Uncertainty avoidance:* the extent to which people in a society feel threatened by uncertain and ambiguous situations.
- *Masculinity/femininity:* the extent to which a society values quantity of life (e.g., accomplishment, money) over quality of life (e.g., compassion, beauty).

Figure 6.6 offers a graphic depiction of how 40 different nations differ on the dimensions of individualism/collectivism and power distance. Clearly, cultures such as the United

figure 6.6
The position of the 40 countries on the power distance and individualism scales

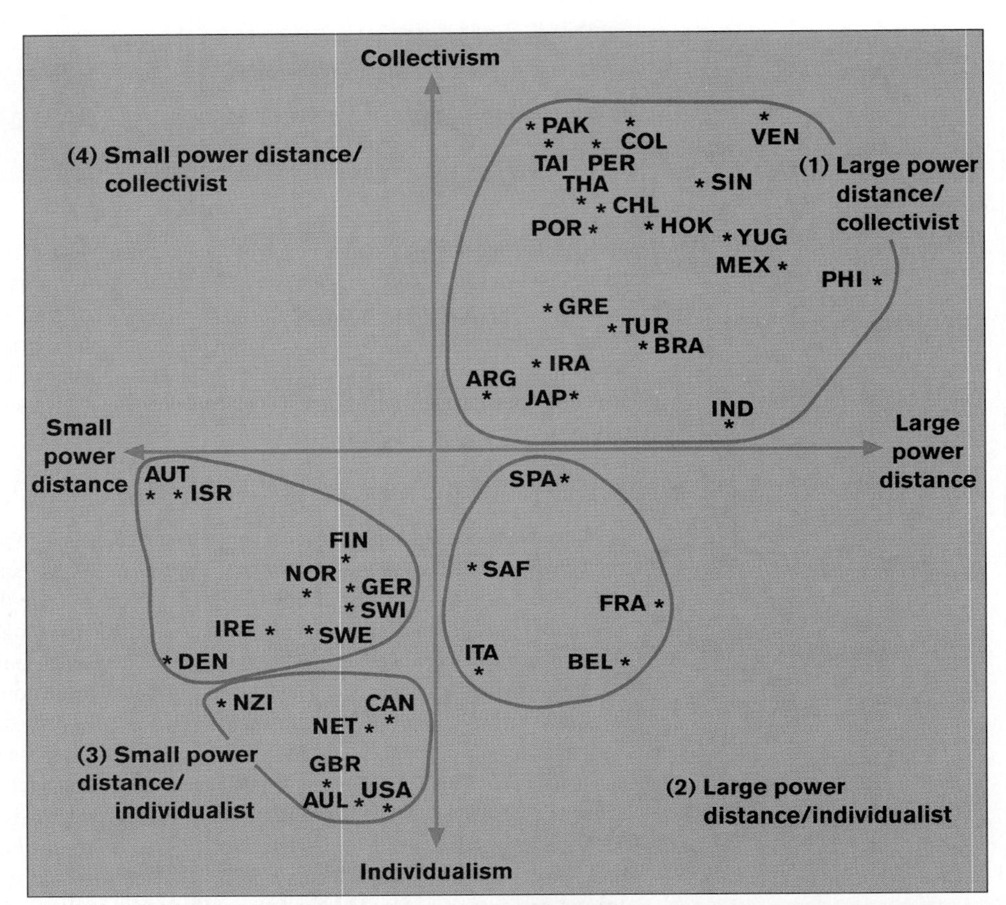

The 40 Countries
(Showing abbreviations used above)

ARG	Argentina	FRA	France	JAP	Japan	SIN	Singapore
AUL	Australia	GBR	Great Britain	MEX	Mexico	SPA	Spain
AUT	Austria	GER	Germany (West)	NET	Netherlands	SWE	Sweden
BEL	Belgium	GRE	Greece	NOR	Norway	SWI	Switzerland
BRA	Brazil	HOK	Hong Kong	NZL	New Zealand	TAI	Taiwan
CAN	Canada	IND	India	PAK	Pakistan	THA	Thailand
CHL	Chile	IRA	Iran	PER	Peru	TUR	Turkey
COL	Colombia	IR	Ireland	PHI	Philippines	USA	United States
DEN	Denmark	ISR	Israel	POR	Portugal	VEN	Venezuela
FIN	Finland	ITA	Italy	SAF	South Africa	YUG	Yugoslavia

Source: Geert Hofstede, "Motivation, Leadership, and Organization: Do American Theories Apply Abroad?" *Organizational Dynamics* 9, no. 1 (Summer 1980), pp. 42–63. Reprinted by permission.

States' that emphasize "rugged individualism" differ significantly from collectivistic cultures such as those of Pakistan, Taiwan, and Colombia. In order to be effective in cultures that exhibit a greater power distance, managers often must behave more autocratically, perhaps being less participative in decision making. Conversely, in Scandinavian cultures, in Sweden, for instance, where power distance is low, the very idea that management has the prerogative to make decisions on their own may be called into question. Here, managers tend to work more toward creating processes that reflect an "industrial democracy."

Cross-cultural management extends beyond U.S. employees going abroad. As the Mazda case exemplifies, international workers also have a difficult time adjusting to the United States.

Amazed at Mazda

The Japanese management team that went to Flat Rock, Michigan, to launch the first Mazda manufacturing plant on U.S. soil had been warned that working with American autoworkers would be different than managing their counterparts back in Japan. The rumor circulating among the Japanese expatriate community was that Americans lacked dedicated work habits.

Even so forewarned, the Mazda managers were amazed at what they found. By the first fall, the plant was closing in on its targeted first-year production numbers, the Americans having proved able workers and the start-up having gone as well as could be expected. Then November rolled around and production slowed to a crawl as half the plant's line workers and supervisors requested time off. Why so many? And why now? The answer: Deer season.

Welcome to America, land of the bottom line and the blaze-orange vest. The fact that Americans hunt was hardly new information to the Japanese. The idea that Americans would think nothing of sacrificing the operation of an automobile plant for the opening of deer season came as quite a shock.

Source: From "Welcome to America" by David Stamps. Reprinted with permission from the November 1996 issue of *Training Magazine*. Lakewood Publications, Minneapolis, MN.

Cultural differences can often affect management expectations and styles. *[Loren Santow/Tony Stone Images]*

This example from Mazda shows that culture shock works both ways. U.S.employees going abroad must adjust. But international workers must adjust as well. But despite the difficulties, there are a number of things that can be done to ease the adjustment of international workers coming to the United States. A few basic categories include the following:

- *Meetings:* Americans may dislike meetings, but they tend to have a fairly specific view of the purpose for them and how much time can be wasted. International workers, on the other hand, may have different preconceptions about how time is supposed to be spent in meetings and whether or not it is being wasted.
- *Work(aholic) schedules:* Workers from other countries can work long hours, but may be puzzled how U. S. workers can survive with only two or three weeks of vacation. Europeans in particular may balk at the idea of working on weekends.
- *E-mail:* Most of the world has not embraced e-mail and voice mail the way U.S. workers have. Most others would prefer to communicate face-to-face.
- *Fast-trackers:* Although U.S. companies may take a young MBA student and put him or her on the fast track to management, most other cultures (Germany and Japan in particular) still see no substitute for the wisdom gained through experience.
- *Feedback:* A manager's use of excessive positive feedback tends to be less prevalent in other cultures than in the United States.[27]

Ethical issues in international management

If managers are to function effectively in a foreign setting, they must understand how culture influences both how they are perceived as well as how others behave. One of the most sensitive issues in this regard is understanding how culture plays out in terms of ethical behavior.[28] Issues of right and wrong get blurred as we move from one culture to another, and actions that may be normal and customary in one setting may be unethical—even illegal—in another. The use of bribes, for example, is an accepted part of commercial transactions in many Asian, African, Latin American, and Middle Eastern cultures. In the United States, of course, such behavior is illegal, but what should a U.S. businessperson do when working abroad? Estimates are that bribery and corruption cost U.S. firms over $64 billion in lost business each year.[29]

Though most Americans prefer to conduct business in a way consistent with prevailing U.S. laws, many people feel that we should not impose our cultural values on others. As a consequence, opinions differ widely on what is acceptable behavior when confronted with certain ethical dilemmas. Figure 6.7 shows the results of a recent survey that asked managers about the ethicality of payments to foreign officials. Surprisingly, less than half of the respondents said that the bribes were never acceptable, and in many cases managers suggested that such behavior would be acceptable if it was the local custom. In reality, these particular views are somewhat naive—while giving and receiving business gifts may be acceptable, the Foreign Corrupt Practices Act (1977) strictly prohibits U.S. employees from providing payments to foreign officials. While small "grease payments" to lower-level figures are permissible under the act, if the dollar amount of the payments is significant and would influence the outcome of negotiations, the transaction would be illegal.

Without an understanding of local customs, ethical standards, and applicable laws, an expatriate might be woefully unprepared to work internationally. To safeguard against these and other ethical problems, companies such as Caterpillar Tractor, General Dynamics, and United Technologies have established codes of conduct for international business. The codes lay out precisely what kinds of actions are permissible, and provide procedures and support systems that individuals can use in ambiguous situations. Five steps for establishing and reinforcing these codes might include the following:

figure 6.7
Is this ethical?

Ethical dilemma: A company paid a $350,000 "consulting" fee to an official of a foreign country. In return, the official promised assistance in obtaining a contract that should produce a $10 million profit for the contracting company.

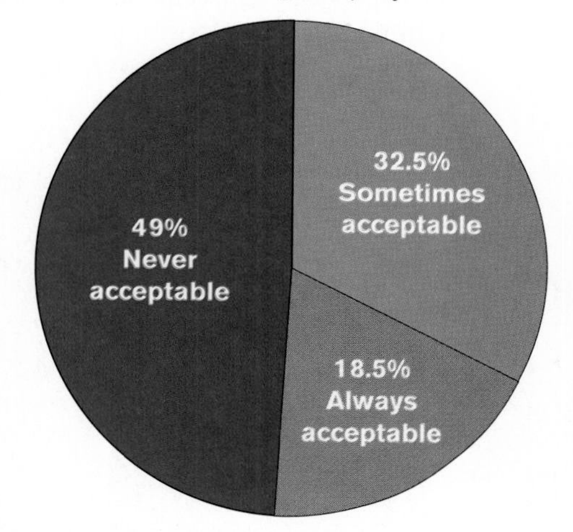

Percentage of respondents who said the payments were:

49.0% "never acceptable"
32.5% "sometimes acceptable"
18.5% "always acceptable"

Source: J. G. Longenecker, J. A. McKinney, and C. W. Moore, "The Ethical Issues of International Bribery: A Study of Attitudes among U.S. Business Professionals, *Journal of Business Ethics* 7 (1988), pp. 341–46. Reprinted with kind permission from Kluwer Academic Publishers.

- *Clearly articulate the company's values.* For example, Digital Equipment's Code of Business Conduct contains 27 pages of practices the company expects employees to use as well as suggestions for dealing with gray areas such as gifts given and received.
- *Train employees to apply the values.* Levi Strauss has a three-day ethics course (called the Principled Reasoning Approach) that teaches employees how to logically evaluate situations and figure out how ethical values translate into behavior.
- *Let business partners know the standards.* Levi Strauss has established a set of global sourcing and operating guidelines that address workplace issues for all of its partners. The terms of engagement detail everything from environmental requirements to health and safety issues.
- *Translate ethics into performance appraisal.* H. B. Fuller ties compensation to performance evaluation (which includes an ethical component). It also conducts audits of key people who are in positions that could be subjected to difficult moral decisions.[30]

Interestingly, despite some obvious differences across cultures, research suggests that there are actually a set of five core values that most people embrace regardless of nationality or religion: *compassion, fairness, honesty, responsibility,* and *respect for others.* These values lie at the heart of human rights issues and seem to transcend more superficial differences among Americans, Europeans, and Asians. Finding shared values such as these allows companies to build more effective partnerships and alliances, especially across cultures. It may be the case that as long as people understand that there is a set of core values, they can permit all kinds of differences in strategy and tactics.[31]

To a large extent, the challenge of managing across borders comes down to the philosophies and systems used to manage people. In moving from domestic to international management, managers need to develop a wide portfolio of behaviors along with the capacity to adjust their behavior for a particular situation. This adjustment, however, should not compromise the values, integrity, and strengths of their home country. When managers can transcend national borders, and move among different cultures, then they will finally be in a position to leverage the strategic capabilities of the organization and take advantage of the opportunities that our global economy has to offer.

Key terms

Culture shock, p. 223
Expatriates, p. 219
Failure rate, p. 221
Global organization model, p. 213
Host-country nationals, p. 219
International organization model, p. 212
Multinational organization model, p. 213
North American Free Trade Agreement (NAFTA), p. 206
Third-country nationals, p. 219
Transnational organization model, p. 214

Summary of learning objectives

Now that you have studied Chapter 6, you should know:

Why the world economy is becoming more integrated than ever before.

The gradual lowering of barriers to free trade is making the world economy more integrated. This means that the modern manager operates in an environment that offers more opportunities but is also more complex and competitive than that faced by the manager of a generation ago.

What integration of the global economy means for individual companies and for their managers.

In recent years, rapid growth in world trade, foreign direct investment, and imports has occurred. One consequence is that companies around the globe are now finding their home markets under attack from international competitors. The global competitive environment is becoming a much tougher place in which to do business. However, companies now have access to markets that were previously denied to them.

The strategies organizations use to compete in the global marketplace.

The international corporation builds on its existing core capabilities in R&D, marketing, manufacturing, and so on, to penetrate overseas markets. A multinational is a more complex form that usually has fully autonomous units operating in multiple countries. Subsidiaries are given latitude to address local issues such as consumer preferences, political pressures, or economic trends in different regions of the world. The global organization pulls control of overseas operations back into the headquarters and tends to approach the world market as a "unified whole" by combining activities in each country to maximize efficiency on a global scale. A transnational attempts to achieve both local responsiveness and global integration by utilizing a network structure that coordinates specialized facilities positioned around the world.

The various entry modes organizations use to enter overseas markets.

There are five ways to enter an overseas market: exporting, licensing, franchising, entering into a joint venture, and setting up a wholly owned subsidiary. Each mode has advantages and disadvantages.

How companies can approach the task of staffing overseas operations.

Most executives use a combination of expatriates, host-country nationals, or third-country nationals. Expatriates are sometimes used to quickly establish new country operations, transfer the company's culture, and bring in a specific technical skill. Host-country nationals have the advantages that they are familiar with local customs and culture, may cost less, and are viewed more favorably by local governments. Third-country nationals are often used as a compromise in politically touchy situations or when home-country expatriates are not available.

The skills and knowledge managers need to manage globally.

The causes for failure overseas extend beyond technical capability, and include personal and social issues as well. Success depends on a manager's core skills such as having a multidimensional perspective, having proficiency in line management and decision making; and having resourcefulness, cultural adaptability, sensitivity, team-building skills, and mental maturity. In addition, helpful augmented skills include computer literacy, negotiating skills, strategic vision, and ability to delegate.

Why cultural differences across countries influence management.

Culture influences our actions and perceptions as well as the actions and perceptions of others. Unfortunately, we are often unaware of how culture influences us, and this can cause problems. Today, managers must be able to change their behavior to match the needs and customs of local cultures. For example, in various cultures, employees expect a manager to be either more or less autocratic or participative. By recognizing their cultural differences, people can find it easier to work together collaboratively and benefit from the exchange.

Discussion questions

1. Why is the world economy becoming more integrated? What are the implications of this integration for international managers?

2. Imagine you were the CEO of a major company. What approach to global competition would you choose for your firm: international, multinational, global, or transnational? Why?

3. Why have franchises been so popular as a method of international expansion in the fast-food industry? Contrast this with high-tech manufacturing where joint ventures and partnerships have been more popular. What accounts for the differences across industries?

4. What are the pros and cons of using expatriates, host-country nationals, and third-country nationals to run overseas operations? If you were expanding your business, what approach would you use?

5. If you had entered into a joint venture with a foreign company, but knew that women were not treated fairly in that culture, would you consider sending a female expatriate to handle the startup? Why or why not?

6. What are the biggest cultural obstacles that we must overcome if we are to work effectively in Mexico? Are there different obstacles in France? Japan?

Concluding Case

Has Nike stubbed its toe in Asia?

Nike, the world's largest athletic-shoe maker, is well known for its use of Asian contractors to outsource manufacturing processes. According to Phil Night, the company's CEO, all contractors must follow applicable laws in their countries and must meet the requirements laid out in Nike's code of conduct. Despite the efforts to be a good global citizen, Nike has come under increasing scrutiny over the past few years about the labor practices used by its contractors in Asia.

In China, for example, human rights groups have complained that contractors (in two factories) employ children as young as 13, require them to work 72-hour weeks, and don't meet China's minimum-wage requirements. Nike executives have denied these allegations and have stated wages in those factories are nearly double the minimum wage. In addition, all workers are required to be at least 16 years old, the legal minimum. Nike did its own investigation of these issues, and because of this, some observers still don't buy its story.

In response to these concerns, Nike asked international accounting firm Ernst & Young to conduct ongoing audits of labor practices used by its contractors in Vietnam. According to the Ernst & Young report, the standard workweek in Vietnam is eight hours a day, six days a week, or 48 hours a week. The maximum allowable overtime is 200 hours per worker per year. Workers receive 150 percent of their regular wage for overtime hours. Employees generally make about $40 per month (average basic salary in Vietnam is $45 per month). Salary and overtime are typically paid on time. Health insurance and taxes are withheld properly, and safety regulations are generally followed appropriately. In those cases where Ernst & Young has found problems, Nike has taken immediate steps to correct the situation.

Most recently, Nike has investigated criticism over labor practices in four of its contractors' factories in Indonesia. While Nike has over 50 factories in Indonesia, four were found to be in violation of the company's code of conduct, which includes a provision that contractors pay the minimum wage set by the government. Indonesia increased the minimum wage by 11 percent in April 1997 but allowed companies to seek exemptions. The four contractors in question had received exemptions, but Nike said that under its policy, the contractors must pay the full minimum wage. To reinforce the importance of this policy, Phil Night announced the move at the company's annual shareholders' meeting. It was the first time Nike had fired contractors for noncompliance with the company's code of conduct.

Questions:

1. What strategic reasons does Nike have for partnering with foreign contractors? What other approaches might they take to globalization?

2. What responsibilities does Nike have in controlling the labor practices of its foreign partners?

3. Should labor practices, safety and health policies, and so forth, be the same for foreign contractors as they are for United States contractors?

Sources: "Nike Cancels Pacts with Indonesia Plants over Wage Policies," *The Wall Street Journal,* September 23, 1997, p. A6; and "Nike Releases Third-Party Audit of Vietnam Subcontracted Factory," *PR Newswire,* November 7, 1997. ●

Workers such as these work for Nike contractors. Recently those contractors have been investigated for labor violations.
[Reuters/Keith B. Richburg/Archive Photos]

Video Case

International management at Coca-Cola

Over the past several decades, many large corporations have developed international markets for their products and services. Today, it is commonplace to speak of a global economy, where goods and services flow across international borders and across vast oceans with few impediments. Although international trade has for centuries been a source of wealth creation for a few of the most developed countries, the modern global economy is distinguished by the number of countries now participating. American companies are finding great opportunities abroad for their products and services. At the same time, new competitors have entered the contest for global market share.

Coca-Cola is a well-established American company that has aggressively pursued foreign markets. One of the most attractive foreign markets is Japan. Although Coca-Cola has been bottling its flagship Coke since 1915, it was not widely available in Japanese markets until 1960. Today, Japan is the company's most important international market.

Originally, the license to distribute Coke in Japan was purchased by a Japanese businessman. This approach of partnering with a foreign businessperson wasn't common practice at the time. As it turned out, the partnering strategy was vital to Coke's success in the Japanese market, and was a precursor to the partnering strategy that is widely used today by large, multinational corporations. Over the years, Coke has applied the partnering approach with companies like Mitsui and Mitsubishi to build up its bottling and distribution operations across the country. Today, Coca-Cola Japan calls itself a "multilocal," rather than a multinational, company. Local expertise offered by the Japanese bottlers was essential in introducing the new products to Japan. Local expertise also allowed the company to circumvent the traditional mode of distribution of foreign products in Japan, bypassing wholesalers and selling directly to retailers.

Frank Kelly, Jr., senior vice president and marketing director, Coca-Cola (Japan) Co., Ltd., said, "When we introduced Coca-Cola we introduced the 'store door' delivery system. In the beginning, we had a very difficult time convincing the local population that this was the way to go. The second major hurdle was that, in the beginning, all of our products were sold for cash. In Japan, based on cultural experiences, bills were only paid once or twice per year." Because of these different expectations, the Japanese retailers would send Coke's drivers away and tell them to come back when they had returned to their senses and were ready to behave like "normal people."

Despite these difficulties, Coke persisted, and within a few years the company was able to convince the Japanese of the value of its style of doing business. Still, the company made a few concessions to Japanese traditions. For example, at the Fuji Bottling plant, most of the workers have a lifetime employment contract. This reflects the Japanese belief that long-term commitments result in more-productive workers. Inside the plant, decision making is based on consensus. Kelly says that Coca-Cola Japan operates as a "hybrid" company. "Here in Japan we do things such as assist our employees in purchasing a home with low interest loans. We have a number of social clubs within the company. What we have here is a lot of group activities. We do a lot of things as a team rather than as individuals."

Another key factor in the success of Coca-Cola Japan is that it creates and tailors new products to meet the tastes of local consumers. For example, the company has created an entirely new line of soft-drink products that are distributed only in Japan. Coke's advertising strategy in Japan also tries to cultivate its image as a good citizen, and to demonstrate the fact that its products have become a part of everyday life throughout Japan.

Over the years Coke has strengthened its position in Japan to a point where it now holds over 30 percent of the soft drink market share, and over 90 percent of the cola market. Its distribution system sells to over a million retailers, and it operates over 700,000 vending machines. Summarizing Coke's success in Japan, Kelly said, "I think that the most important thing that you have to learn as a foreigner in Japan is to develop, or to have, patience. Patience is very important because consensus building is a key to success here. So you have to be patient and you have to let things develop."

As Coke learned, doing business in international markets is a delicate balancing act. Companies must maintain the integrity of their products and leverage their knowledge of effective production processes, but they must also pay attention to the needs and demands of the foreign culture and of the foreign workers who operate their plants. Perhaps the key to Coke's success in Japan is that it never lost track of its need to be a good citizen.

Critical Thinking Questions

1. The lessons in this video case pertain to the Japanese market. With other foreign markets in Asia, Latin America, and elsewhere developing rapidly, do you think the keys to successful business in Japan apply in these markets? Explain your answer.

2. One of the keys to success for Coke in Japan is the adoption of traditional Japanese practices, such as lifetime employment, in its local plants. Why do you think this is important?

3. Coke entered the Japanese market by developing partnerships with local businesspeople. What are some other potential modes of entry to the Japanese market that Coke might have used instead? What do you think would have been the outcome of these alternative approaches?

4. Frank Kelly, Coke's senior vice president and marketing director in Japan, said that one of the most important things for doing business in Japan is patience. What did he mean?

Experiential Exercises

6.1 Understanding multinational corporations

Objective

To gain a more thorough picture of how a multinational corporation operates.

Instructions

Perhaps the best way to gain an understanding of multinational corporations is to study a specific organization and how it operates throughout the world. Select a multinational corporation and find several articles on that company and answer the questions on the Multinational Worksheet.

Multinational worksheet

1. What is the primary business of this organization?

2. To what extent does the company engage in multinational operations? For example, does it only market its products/services in other countries or does it have manufacturing facilities? What portion of the firm's operating income comes from overseas operations?

3. What percentage of the managers in international activities are American (or from the country the corporation considers home)? Are these managers given any special training prior to their international assignment?

4. What characteristics of the organization have contributed to its success or lack of success in the international marketplace?

Source: R. R. McGrath, Jr., *Exercises in Management Fundamentals* (Englewood Cliffs, NJ: Prentice Hall, 1985), p. 177. Reprinted by permission of Prentice-Hall, Inc.

6.2 Expatriates versus locals

Objectives

1. To help you understand the various advantages and disadvantages of using expatriates and locals as managers and professional staffers.

2. To broaden your understanding of the difficult human resources management problems the multinational enterprise faces.

Instructions

1. Working alone, read the Expatriates versus Locals Situation.

2. Go to the library and research the pros and cons of using expatriates versus locals.

3. Complete the Expatriates versus Locals Worksheet.

4. When the class reconvenes, your instructor can organize a debate on the expatriates versus locals issue.

Expatriates versus locals situation

Your company is planning to open a number of manufacturing and distribution centers in other countries to become a true multinational enterprise. There has been considerable controversy among top management as to how to staff the overseas operations. It's agreed that for nonmanagerial and nonprofessional staff positions, locals should be hired and trained whenever possible. However, for managerial and professional staff positions, there is considerable and sometimes emotional disagreement. You are to investigate the various advantages and disadvantages in using expatriates versus locals in overseas operations.

Expatriates versus locals worksheet

Advantages of using expatriates	Advantages of using locals

Chapter Seven
New Ventures

A man is known by the company he organizes.

—*Ambrose Bierce*

Chapter Outline

Learning Objectives

After studying Chapter 7, you will know:

1. The activities of entrepreneurship.
2. How to find and evaluate ideas for new business ventures.
3. What it takes to be a successful entrepreneur.
4. How to write a great business plan.
5. The important management skills, resources, and strategies needed to avoid failure and achieve success.
6. Key criteria for deciding whether your start-up should be global from the outset.
7. The process of spinning off new ventures.
8. How to foster intrapreneurship and an entrepreneurial orientation in large companies.

Setting the Stage

Humble Beginnings

All successful businesspeople started somewhere:

- Thomas First and Thomas Scott spent summers doing odd jobs on Nantucket Island, then started making and selling fruit juices off their 19-foot motorboat and out of an icehouse at Nantucket Harbor. At $1 per bottle, they sold 2,000 bottles in the first summer. They then expanded to Boston-area college football games. Then, to Georgetown and Washington, DC. A few years later, Nantucket Nectars sold 28 varieties of juice and had $30 million in sales.
- Abby Margalith was waiting tables, and her brother Ethan had just finished high school and needed a summer job. He borrowed a truck and hauled a few items, made some cash, and realized he had his summer job. Abby joined him in the moving business. Their first real moving truck was a 1944 weapons carrier they dug out of a mud slide. After painting "Starving Students" and their phone number on the side, they parked it at a Beverly Hills street corner. The phone rang off the hook. After a couple of years, Starving Students had 14 locations in five states, and sales had reached $15 million.
- One day, Dan Hoard cut off a pants leg and put it on his head. He and his buddy, Tom Bunnell, laughed so hard they said, "We have to sell this. We have to at least try." Thus was born Mambosoks. They made five more and gave them to Bunnell's wedding party in 1990, who did the polka in them at the reception. Next, in 1991, they contracted with a manufacturer to make 1,000 Mambosoks. Tom sold them to patrons of the bar where he worked. The partners expanded production, and by year two their sales reached $1 million. In response to Mambosoks knockoffs, they have diversified into dozens of other items, including the Mambohead Shirt, the Chubby Summer Snowboarding Shorts, and the three-foot Polar Dunce Cap. Soon Mambosoks was serving 1,000 accounts all over the world.
- Richard Thompson has pumped almost $30 million over four years into his firm, probably more by the time you read this. Microsoft started for less. Thompson's product? Pasta for dogs. While visiting Italy, he noticed Italians cooking pasta for their dogs. Americans don't cook for their dogs, but they do pay premium prices for pet foods. Thompson has patented his process, gambled a fortune, and not yet made a profit. But he believes in his idea and his company.
- Jason Olim was a student at Brown University when he got his entrepreneurial idea: selling hard-to-find CDs. He didn't have the money to open a real store, so he opened his on the Internet. He and his parents invested $20,000 for a Macintosh, a Unix server, software licenses, fees for engineers to help with programming problems, graphic designers, print advertisements, and a public relations contract. In its first month, his company, Cdnow, brought in

Abby Margalith and her brother started their Starving Students moving company with one 50-year-old truck. Today, their sales have reached $15 million.
[Rocky Thies]

$387 in revenues. Two years later, it was at $6 million. Olim expects that to triple in the next year, as he has arranged for private equity financing and a major marketing push, as well as reached agreement with Yahoo! that links any page with a music reference to the Cdnow homepage.

Sources: K. Burger, "A Drink with an Attitude, Forbes, February 10, 1997, pp. 112–113; T. Ehrenfeld, P. Hise, R. Mamis, and A. Murphy, "Where Great Ideas for New Businesses Come from," Inc., September 1993, pp. 54–62; J. C. Collins, "Sometimes a Great Notion," Inc., July 1993, pp. 90–91; D. Machan, "Ziti for Dogs." Forbes, February 24, 1997, pp. 94–98; and J. Akasie, "Imaging, No Inventory," Forbes, November 17, 1997, pp. 144–46.

entrepreneurship The act of forming a new organization of value.

Great opportunity is available to those who develop a vitally important skill: entrepreneurship. **Entrepreneurship** is the act of forming a new organization of value.[1] To be an entrepreneur is to initiate and build an organization, rather than being only a passive part of one[2]. It involves creating *new* systems, resources, or processes to produce *new* goods or services and/or to serve *new* markets.[3]

Some observers further describe entrepreneurship by how it differs from management generally and from small business management in particular. An entrepreneur *is* a manager, but engages in additional activities that not all managers do.[4] Whereas managers operate in a more formal management hierarchy, with more clearly defined authority and responsibility, entrepreneurs must get others involved and committed based on using networks of contacts more than formal authority. And whereas managers usually prefer to own assets, entrepreneurs often rent or use assets on a temporary basis. Some say that managers often are slower to act and tend to avoid risk, whereas entrepreneurs are quicker to act and actively manage risk.

small business A business having fewer than 100 employees, independently owned and operated, not dominant in its field, and not characterized by many innovative practices.

entrepreneurial venture A new business having growth and high profitability as primary objectives.

How does entrepreneurship differ from managing a small business?[5] A **small business** is often defined as having fewer than 100 employees, being independently owned and operated, not dominant in its field, and not characterized by many innovative practices. Small business owners tend not to manage particularly aggressively and they expect normal, moderate sales, profits, and growth. In contrast, an **entrepreneurial venture** has growth and high profitability as primary objectives. The entrepreneurs manage aggressively and invoke innovative strategies, practices, and products. They and their financial backers usually seek rapid growth, immediate and high profits, and sometimes a quick sellout with large capital gains.

Simply put, entrepreneurs generate new ideas and turn them into business ventures.[6] But entrepreneurship is not simple, and it is frequently misunderstood. Read Table 7.1 to start you thinking about the myths and realities of this important career option.

independent entrepreneur An individual who establishes a new organization without the benefit of corporate sponsorship.

spin-off A new company started by managers who create independent businesses that split from the parent corporation.

Here is another myth, not in the table: that being an entrepreneur is great because you can "get rich quick" and enjoy a lot of leisure time while your employees run the company. But the downsides can be brutal. As described by Tom Peters,[7] "You must have incredible mental toughness to survive—let alone thrive." During the start-up period, you are likely to have a lot of bad days. It's exhausting. Your product has to be outstanding. So do your marketing, selling, distribution, quality, and so forth. And, even if you don't have employees, you should expect "communications breakdowns" and other "people problems" with agents, vendors, distributors, family, subcontractors, lenders, whomever.

As you read this chapter, you will learn about the three primary sources of new venture creation: independent entrepreneurship, corporate spin-offs, and intrapreneurship. **Independent entrepreneurship** occurs when an individual establishes a new organization without the benefit of corporate support. In **spin-offs,** corporate managers become

table 7.1
Some myths about entrepreneurs

Myth #1: Entrepreneurs are born, not made.

Reality: The making of an entrepreneur occurs by accumulating the relevant skills, know-how, experiences, and contacts over a period of years and includes large doses of self-development.

Myth #2: Anyone can start a business.

Reality: The easiest part is starting up. What is hardest is surviving, sustaining, and building a venture so its founders can realize a harvest.

Myth #3: Entrepreneurs are gamblers.

Reality: Successful entrepreneurs take very careful, calculated risks. They do not deliberately take unnecessary risk, nor do they shy away from unavoidable risk.

Myth #4: Entrepreneurs want the whole show to themselves.

Reality: Solo entrepreneurs make a living, but it is extremely difficult to grow a higher-potential venture by working single-handedly. Higher-potential entrepreneurs build a team, an organization, and a company.

Myth #5: Entrepreneurs are their own bosses and completely independent.

Reality: Entrepreneurs have to serve many masters and constituencies, including partners, investors, customers, suppliers, creditors, employees, and families. Entrepreneurs can, however, make free choices of whether, when, and to what they respond.

Myth #6: Entrepreneurs experience a great deal of stress and pay a high price.

Reality: No doubt about it: being an entrepreneur is stressful and demanding. But there is no evidence that it is any more stressful than numerous other highly demanding professional roles, and entrepreneurs find their jobs very satisfying.

Myth #7: Entrepreneurs should be young and energetic.

Reality: These qualities may help, but age is no barrier. The average age of entrepreneurs starting high-potential businesses is in the mid-30s, and many start businesses in their 60s.

Myth #8: If an entrepreneur has enough start-up capital, he or she can't miss.

Reality: The opposite is often true. Too much money often creates euphoria, lack of discipline, and impulsive spending, leading to serious problems.

Myth #9: If an entrepreneur is talented, success will happen in a year or two.

Reality: An old maxim among venture capitalists says that the lemons ripen in two and a half years, but the pearls take seven or eight. Rarely is the new business established solidly in less than three or four years.

Source: J. Timmons, *New Venture Creation* (Burr Ridge, IL: Richard D. Irwin, 1994), pp. 23–24. Reprinted by permission.

intrapreneurs New venture creators working in big corporations.

entrepreneurs by splitting from the parent company and creating new businesses. **Intrapreneurs** are new venture creators working in big corporations; they are corporate entrepreneurs.[8]

Independent entrepreneurs

Our discussion of independent entrepreneurs will answer questions about why people start their own business, the role of the economic environment, what kind of business a person should start, what it takes to be successful, planning and decision making, and the hazards of entrepreneurship.

Why become an independent entrepreneur?

Bill Gross is only 38 years old and has started dozens of companies.[9] When he was a boy he devised homemade electric games and sold candy for a profit to friends. In college, he built and sold plans for a solar heating device, started a stereo equipment company, and sold a software product to Lotus. In 1991 he sold his educational software company for almost $100 million. And in 1996 he started Idealab!, which has hatched dozens of start-ups on the Internet. Even before achieving positive cash flow, he will go public with many of his Internet companies.

Why do Bill Gross and other entrepreneurs do what they do? Entrepreneurs start their own firms because of the challenge, the profit potential, and the enormous satisfaction they hope lies ahead.[10] People starting their own businesses are seeking a better quality of life than they might have at big companies. They seek independence and a feeling of being part of the action. They feel tremendous satisfaction in building something from nothing, seeing it succeed, and watching the market embrace their ideas and products.

Entrepreneurship can also be great fun. Some people love to make a splash, love the action. "Entrepreneurship is a subversive activity. It upsets the status quo, disrupts accepted ways of doing things, and alters traditional patterns of behavior. It is, at heart, a change process that undermines current market conditions by introducing something new or different in response to perceived needs. It is sometimes chaotic, often unpredictable."[11]

In addition, limited opportunities elsewhere can inspire people to become independent entrepreneurs. People start their own companies when they see their progress blocked at big corporations. When people are laid off, they often try to start businesses of their own. And when employed people believe there is no promotion in their future, or are frustrated by bureaucracy or other features of corporate life, they may quit and become entrepreneurs.

New immigrants may find existing paths to economic success closed to them.[12] Blocked from conventional means of advancement, these newcomers turn to the alternative paths entrepreneurship provides. For example, the Cuban community in Miami has produced many entrepreneurs, as has the Vietnamese community throughout the United States.

At present, timing is good for starting new companies. According to *Fortune,* "Now is a great time to start a new venture . . . we've entered a particularly fertile era for entrepreneurism . . . [This is] an age in which nimble and often smaller organizations will perform best. In this new environment, entrepreneurs will flourish as in no time since the onset of the Industrial Age."[13]

The role of the economic environment

Money is a critical resource for all new businesses. As the money supply and the supply of bank loans increase, a larger number of loan applicants can secure funds. The result is a rise in the rate of business formation. Conversely, as the supply of money and loans decreases, fewer aspiring business owners can find funding. The rate of business formation then declines.

Other economic factors contribute to an improved climate for business formation. Real economic growth and improved stock market performance lead to both improved prospects and increased sources of capital. In turn, the prospects and the capital increase the rate of business formation. However, the economy is a double-edged sword; the same factors have a long-term effect on business failure.[14] Under favorable conditions, many aspiring entrepreneurs find early success. But economic cycles dictate that favorable conditions will change. To succeed, entrepreneurs must have the foresight and talent to survive when the environment becomes more hostile.

Sometimes areas with weak economies but potential for growth are overlooked by entrepreneurs. But those who understand the potential can achieve business success. The inner city is an example.

Entrepreneurship in the inner city

Today's inner cities hold tremendous business opportunity. Retailers have fled the cities and located in the suburbs, and now the suburbs are saturated. Inner-city residents have to travel long distances for many of their shopping needs. The Tops supermarket chain is one company that is capitalizing on the inner-city vacuum. A well-run supermarket in a low-income neighborhood faces virtually no competition.

James Rouse is a for-profit developer who is revitalizing a blighted area in Baltimore. He organized the neighborhood into task forces to tackle issues of education, crime, family support, community spirit, and health care. He sees the plight of the central cities as a severe threat to our civilization, and feels that if the dreadful conditions are not changed our country will not be able to compete economically and our standard of living will drop precipitously. People who don't live in the inner cities don't know the extent of the threat; the cost of these conditions, according to Mr. Rouse, is about $750 billion a year. Mr. Rouse wants to show that it is both possible and economical to alleviate the conditions of poverty.

Philanthropic money seems to be more available to the inner city than money for business activities. Financing pools or government-backed loan guarantees can be made available to small businesses that invest in the inner city. Investment opportunities could be identified to attract nonminority businesses as partners for inner-city firms. In Miami, Tools for Change, an organization of the Black Economic Development Coalition, serves 650 clients a year. In one recent year, it incorporated 160 businesses and packaged 81 loans valued at over $10 million. And the Dade Community Foundation provides funding to organizations with applications showing how they intend to cross ethnic barriers or collaborate with neighboring groups.

Fortune calls these people and others like them social entrepreneurs. They pursue social objectives through private enterprise practices that earn money, create jobs, and save tax dollars.

Sources: M. Alpert, "The Ghetto's Hidden Wealth," *Fortune,* July 29, 1991, pp. 167–74; J. Huey, "Finding New Heros for a New Era," *Fortune,* January 25, 1993, pp. 62–69; and R. M. Kanter, *World Class: Thriving Locally in the Global Economy* (New York, Touchstone, 1995).

Business incubators Local government officials and educators are concerned about their role in promoting business formation in their regions. In particular, they have addressed the need to provide a nurturing environment for fledgling enterprises. That concern led to the growth of business incubators.

business incubators Protected environments for new, small businesses.

Business incubators, often located in industrial parks or abandoned factories, are protected environments for new, small businesses. Incubators offer benefits such as low rents and shared costs. The rents often are subsidized by a sponsoring agency. Shared staff costs, such as for receptionists and secretaries, avoid the expense of a full-time employee but still provide convenient access to services.

The incubator also provides professional service for its young business clientele. Usually the staff manager is an experienced businessperson or consultant. The manager's job is to serve as adviser to the new-business owners. Incubators often are associated with universities, which provide technical and business services for the new company.

The most amazing region for start-ups is Silicon Valley, a 50-mile-long corridor in California where 20 percent of the world's 100 biggest electronics and software companies were born.[15] A Valley company goes public about every five days. Local universities (particularly Stanford), great talent, pioneering successes, and then venture capitalists and a complete tech infrastructure characterized by a risk-taking culture have made the Valley an exceptional environment for incubating ideas and companies. Other regions, including Boston, North Carolina, and Austin, have tried to emulate the Valley's success. None has matched it, although Seattle is coming on strong.[16]

Other regions in the world are following suit.[17] Government money and tax breaks have helped Taiwan's Hsinchu Science–based industrial park flourish. In the Malaysia jungles, populated by rubber and palm-oil plantations, the Multimedia Supercorridor is planned to become Southeast Asia's Silicon Valley. Cyberjaya is the "intelligent city" at the center of the supercorridor. To entice corporations, the Malaysian government has dedicated a 15 × 50 kilometer zone, promised to leave two-thirds undeveloped, given tax exemptions, offered unlimited duty-free importation of multimedia equipment, allowed unrestricted numbers of foreign "knowledge workers" to enter the country, and promised not to censor the Internet. Sun Microsystems, Oracle, Microsoft, and Nippon Telegraph & Telephone Corp. were among the first to sign on.

From the Pages of BusinessWeek

The Best Entrepreneurs

Business Week annually profiles a handful of entrepreneurs it hails as "the best." Here are some of them:

Sky Dayton owned two coffeehouses in Los Angeles when he started an Internet service provider called EarthLink Network. Three years later, he had 600,000 customers and was fast creeping up on the Microsoft Network. At 26 years old, Dayton was setting his sights on the No. 2 position in the industry, behind America Online.

Anthony Mark Hawkins built a $40 million clothing business in only three years. He sells to over 1,000 stores including Sears and Nordstrom, has his own show on the Home Shopping Network, and expanded into home furnishings and fragrances. At 29 years old, Hawkins released his autobiography in 1998.

Dineh Mohajer founded Hard Candy by mixing mod nail-polish shades in her West Hollywood bungalow. The pastel look caught on with celebrities, and was soon sold in Bloomingdale's and Neiman Marcus. Sales quickly hit $20 million, when Mohajer was 25 years old.

Matthew Rizai is CEO of Engineering Animation, based in Ames, Iowa. In 1997, he sold $40 million in computer-animation to customers including Ford and Deere. More growth lies ahead from new interactive consumer software, such as a CD-ROM for Mattel with which kids can style Barbie's hair. In one year, earnings soared more than 200%, to over $5 million.

Irwin Simon took out a second mortgage to buy a kosher frozen-foods business. He now sells healthful and diverse brands that dominate some of the fastest-growing food categories including organic, sugar-free, and dairy-free products. In three years, sales grew from $15 to $65 million.

As *Business Week* concludes, "It looks so easy. All it seems to take is a worthy idea and a bit of good luck. But in a world where giant corporations dominate the landscape, becoming a standout entrepreneur is a whole lot tougher than that. [These entrepreneurs] had far more than great ideas. They also pushed ahead with impeccable timing, mind-numbing hard work, and the self-confidence to battle their way into the game."

Discussion Question

1. Whom would you nominate as "best entrepreneurs"? Choose someone well-known nationally (or internationally), and also someone local or whom you know personally. Describe why you would nominate these entrepreneurs.

Source: "The best entrepreneurs" *Business Week,* January 12, 1998, pp. 35–37.

What business should you start?

You need a good idea, and you need to find or create a good opportunity.

The idea

Many entrepreneurs and observers say that in contemplating your business, you must start with a great idea. A great product, an untapped market, and good timing are indeed essential ingredients in any recipe for success.

Personal inspiration is a great source of ideas, and a good ingredient to add to the recipe. Harrison Trask got his idea while flyfishing, gazing at a herd of grazing buffalo, and welling up with emotion for the American West. He quit his job as a shoe salesman to become independent, to be his own boss, like the old cowboys. He now sells buffalo-hide shoes. No one had been offering such a product, and there was a ready supply of low-cost hides (most of which ranchers discarded). He made a cold-call to L.L. Bean and got a good-sized order. Trask, whose company's revenues have grown to $12 million, says he is selling not just shoes but the tranquility of the Western outdoors.[18]

Many great organizations have been built based on a different kind of idea: the founder's desire to build a great organization, rather than to offer a particular product.[19] Bill Hewlett and Dave Packard decided to start a company first, and then figured out what to make. J. Willard Marriott knew he wanted to be in business for himself but didn't have a product in mind until he opened an A&W root beer stand. Masaru Ibuka had no specific product idea when he founded Sony in 1945. Sony's first product attempt, a rice cooker, didn't work, and its first product (a tape recorder) didn't sell. The company stayed alive by making and selling crude heating pads.

Many now-great companies had early failures. But the founders persisted; they believed in themselves, and in their dreams of building great organizations. Whereas conventional logic is to see the company as a vehicle for your products, this perspective sees the products as a vehicle for your company. Be prepared to kill or revise an idea, but never give up on your company—this has been a prescription for success for many great entrepreneurs and business leaders.

Think about Sony, Disney, Hewlett-Packard, Procter & Gamble, IBM, and Wal-Mart: their founders' greatest achievements—their greatest ideas—are their organizations.[20]

The opportunity

Entrepreneurs spot, create, and exploit opportunities in a variety of ways.[21] Jaye Muller spotted an opportunity while touring Europe on a concert tour. The German rock musician missed some important faxes while moving from hotel to hotel. He put his recording career on hold (he still records periodically) and hired some programmers to develop software that can compress faxes into files and send them to Internet e-mail addresses. The company has taken off, and Muller now says he wants to build a "monster telecommunications company."[22]

Java, the Internet programming language, was designed to be safe, and was widely perceived to be safe when it first appeared. But Shlomo Touboul saw it differently. When he talked about his plans to market a Java security product, people scoffed. Alone, he worked to develop a product that would protect companies from hostile programs embedded in the Java code. When some Princeton scientists subsequently found ways that hackers could exploit Java weak spots, Touboul was ready and far ahead of any would-be competitors.[23]

Shlomo Touboul foresaw the possibility that hackers would try to exploit Java's weaknesses. So he developed a product to protect the programs. *[Courtesy of Finjin Software]*

Always be on the lookout. Talk to consumers, business associates, and technical people. Monitor and evaluate products currently on the market. Think about how current needs can be filled in new ways, and how current products can be improved.

Think carefully about events and trends as they unfold. Consider, for example:[24]

- *Technological discoveries.* Start-ups in biotechnology, microcomputers, and electronics followed.
- *Demographic changes.* Medical and nursing organizations have sprung up to serve an aging population.
- *Lifestyle and taste changes.* Start-ups have capitalized on new clothing trends, desire for fast food, and public interest in sports.
- *Economic dislocations,* such as booms or failures. The oil boycott spawned new drilling firms. Steel industry collapse was accompanied by mini-mill start-ups.
- *Calamities* such as wars and natural disasters. Mt. St. Helen's eruption spawned new tourism companies. Andrew Higgins' business expanded from wooden boats for the Louisiana swamps to the design and mass production of the landing vehicles that carried infantry ashore in World War II.
- *Rule changes by government.* Environmental legislation created opportunities for new consulting firms and cleanup machinery firms. The Small Business Innovation Research Program underwrote new product innovation firms. Deregulation spawned new airlines and trucking companies.
- *Resource discoveries.* North Slope oil production spawned new construction firms in Alaska. When the price of gold rose, new companies in Colorado and Nevada started to reprocess the tailings of old mines.

The next frontiers The next frontiers for entrepreneurship—where do they lie? Throughout history, aspiring entrepreneurs have asked this question. Biotech, Eastern Europe, nanotechnology, oceanography . . . make your own list.

One fascinating and high-potential opportunity for entrepreneurs is outer space.[25] Historically, the space market was driven by the government, and was dominated by big players like Boeing and Lockheed Martin. But now, with huge demand for satellite launches and potential profits skyrocketing, it is more driven by commercial forces. Smaller, aggressive entrepreneurs are entering the field. A new firm called Spacehab builds pressurized containers for the space shuttle, far more cheaply than the government did. Spacehab was the first company to successfully risk its own capital to build something NASA did not specifically request. CEO Shelley Harrison formed the

Spacehab CEO Shelley Harrison and President Chet Lee saw a need and moved to fill it–building pressurized containers for the space shuttle (something it can do far more cheaply than the government did). *[Brian Smith]*

company when the big aerospace companies told him that they merely respond to government requests; they don't take the risk and then look for customers.

Kistler Aerospace is even more daring.[26] It is going head-to-head against Boeing and Lockheed Martin, with no technological or financial help from NASA, to build a reusable launch vehicle that would take satellites into space at a fraction of the current cost. A great and respected management team has helped them raise the money to start. The senior design team includes the former chief engineers for the Apollo spacecraft, the B-2 bomber, the space shuttle, and the space station. And the CEO is George Mueller, who ran the Apollo program and was a leader in the space shuttle concept and the Gemini, Saturn, and Skylab programs.

Other new ventures in space include satellites for automobile navigation, tracking trucking fleets, and monitoring flow rates and leaks in pipelines; testing designer drugs in the near-zero-gravity environment; and using remote sensing to monitor global warming, spot fish concentrations, and detect crop stress for precision farming. And think about this: Instead of the government funding, managing, and implementing Mars travel, one possibility is that it will offer a $20 billion prize to the winner of a private-company race to the red planet.[27]

side street effect As you head down a road, unexpected opportunities begin to appear.

Side streets There also exists a useful role for trial and error. Some entrepreneurs start their enterprises and then let the market decide whether it likes their ideas or not. This is risky, of course, and should be done only if you can afford the risks. But even if the original idea doesn't work, you may be able to capitalize on the **side street effect:**[28] As you head down a road, you come to unknown places, and unexpected opportunities begin to appear.

And, while you are looking, *prepare* so you are able to act quickly and effectively on the opportunity when it does present itself.

What does it take to be successful?

The following characteristics contribute to entrepreneurs' success:[29]

1. *Personal characteristics:* You are more likely to succeed as an entrepreneur if you exhibit certain characteristics and if you make good choices about which business to pursue.
2. *Commitment and determination:* They are decisive, tenacious, disciplined, willing to sacrifice, and able to immerse themselves totally in their enterprises.
3. *Leadership:* They are self-starters, team builders, superior learners, and teachers.
4. *Opportunity obsession:* They have an intimate knowledge of customers' needs, are market driven, and are obsessed with value creation and enhancement.

Trial and error can give rise to the side street effect where, like Dorothy in *The Wizard of Oz,* you head down a road and the unexpected begins to appear.
[MGM/Courtesy Kobal]

5. *Tolerance of risk, ambiguity, and uncertainty:* They are calculated risk takers, risk minimizers, tolerant of stress, and able to resolve problems.
6. *Creativity, self-reliance, and ability to adapt:* They are open-minded, restless with the status quo, able to learn quickly, highly adaptable, creative, skilled at conceptualizing, and attentive to details.
7. *Motivation to excel:* They have a clear results orientation, set high but realistic goals, have a strong drive to achieve, know their own weaknesses and strengths, and focus on what can be done rather than on the reasons things can't be done.

Many people assume there exists an "entrepreneurial personality."[30] Most academic research supports the characteristics discussed above. And new research suggests that there are four different personality profiles—not just one—that lead to entrepreneurial success, as described below.

The profiles of successful entrepreneurs

Do you wonder if you've "got what it takes" to be a successful entrepreneur? Maybe you don't fit the stereotype, or whatever image you might have in your mind. The good news is that there is no single personality type that predicts entrepreneurial success. Recent research indicates at least four personality profiles for success.

Personal achievers are the classic entrepreneurs who enjoy the hard work required to grow a company. They are self-starters who prefer making their own decisions and running things themselves. They have a high need for achievement, work with drive and tenacity, have a strong desire for feedback on their performance, and believe that one person can make a difference.

Empathic supersalespeople enjoy social interaction, are good listeners, are warm toward others, and use persuasion to get things done. They like to help others and adapt to the needs of others. They are good at empathizing–understanding and relating to the feelings of others. They believe that social processes are important in business, and believe in the importance of a strong, capable salesforce.

Real managers want an organization that is big enough to really manage. Sometimes they take over from personal achievers as firms grow. They are comfortable being in a position of authority and respect others in authority. They are competitive, loving to win and hating to lose. They are comfortable attracting attention and can be assertive and outspoken. They are decisive and secure in their work, feeling capable of managing in demanding situations.

Expert idea generators are inventors who go into business for themselves. They love ideas, love to innovate, love to find a better way. They are not enthusiastic about ideas lacking practical relevance.

Which profile best describes you? Can you think of entrepreneurs that fit each type?

Sources: J. B. Miner, "The Expanded Horizon for Achieving Entrepreneurial Success," *Organizational Dynamics,* Winter 1997, pp. 54–67; J. B. Miner, *The 4 Routes to Entrepreneurial Success.* (San Francisco: Berrett-Koehler, 1996).

Making good choices Success is a function not only of personal characteristics, but also of making good choices about the business you start. Figure 7.1 presents a model for conceptualizing entrepreneurial ventures and making the best possible choices. It depicts

figure 7.1
Entrepreneurial strategy matrix

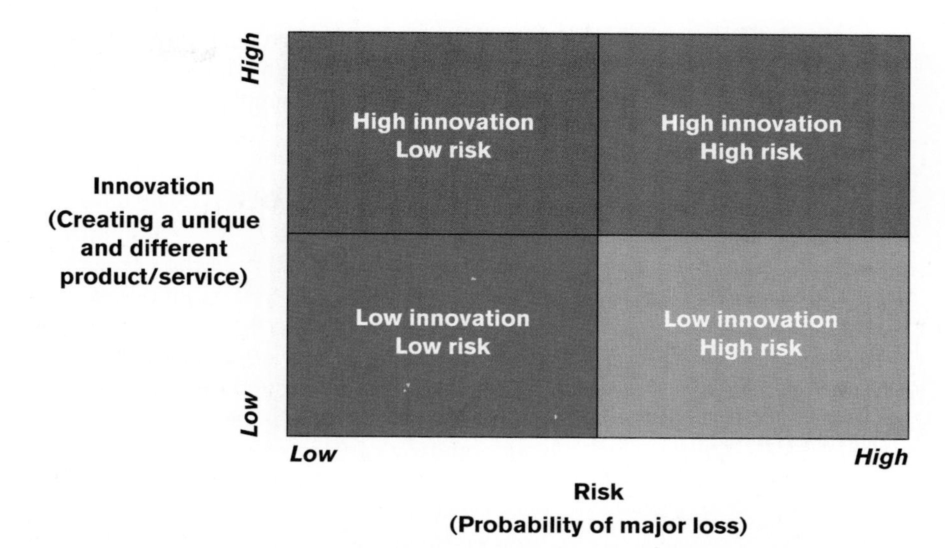

Source: From "Entrepreneurial Strategy Matrix: A Model of New and Ongoing Ventures," by Sonfield and Lussier. Reprinted from *Business Horizons,* May–June 1997. Copyright © 1997 by the Foundation for the School of Business at Indiana University. Used with permission.

ventures along two dimensions: innovation and risk. The new venture may involve high or low levels of *innovation,* or the creation of something new and different. It can also be characterized by low or high *risk.* Risk refers primarily to the probability of major financial loss. But it also is more than that; it is psychological, or risk as perceived by the entrepreneur, including risk to reputation and ego.[31]

The upper-left quadrant, high innovation/low risk, depicts ventures of truly novel ideas with little risk. As examples, the inventors of Lego building blocks and Velcro fasteners could build their products by hand, at little expense. Even some early electronics companies started in this situation. A pioneering product idea from Procter & Gamble might fit here if there are no current competitors and because, for a company of that size, the financial risks of new product investments can seem relatively small.

In the upper-right quadrant, high innovation/high risk, novel product ideas are accompanied by high risk because the financial investments are high and the competition is great. A new drug or a new automobile would likely fall in this category.

Most small business ventures are in the low innovation/high risk cell (lower right). These are fairly conventional entries in well-established fields. New restaurants, retail shops, or commercial outfits involve high investment for the small business entrepreneur and face direct competition from other similar businesses. Finally, the low innovation/low risk category includes ventures that require minimal investment and/or face minimal competition for strong market demand. Examples are some service businesses having low start-up costs and those involving entry into small towns if there is no competitor and demand is adequate.

How is this matrix useful? It helps entrepreneurs think about their ventures and decide whether they suit their particular objectives. It also helps identify effective and ineffective strategies. An entrepreneur might find one cell more appealing than others. The lower-left cell is likely to have relatively low payoffs and to provide more security. The higher risk/return tradeoffs are in other cells, especially the upper right. So an entrepreneur might place the new venture idea in the appropriate cell and determine whether that cell is the one in which he or she would prefer to operate. If it is, the venture is one that perhaps should be pursued, pending fuller analysis. If it is not, one can reject the idea or take action to move it toward a different cell.

The matrix also can help entrepreneurs remember a useful point: Successful companies do not always require a cutting-edge technology or an exciting new product. Even companies offering the most mundane products—the type that might reside in the lower left cell—can gain competitive advantage by doing basic things differently from and better than competitors, as the following examples show.

Masters of the ordinary

Every year, *Inc.* magazine publishes its list of the 500 fastest-growing companies in the United States. As you might guess, many companies on the list are high-tech enterprises. But the list also includes a baker, a candlemaker, a plumber, an antiques gallery, and an exterminator.

These are not hot growth industries. But they are industries. And knowing a lot about business and management, in any industry, provides a competitive edge. So your company can grow, even if your industry is not growing.

Larry Harmon of Demar Plumbing, Heating & Air-Conditioning strives to do business like Mary Kay, Walt Disney, Nordstrom's, and Federal Express. The way he sees it, people are not too enamored of plumbing–but would love a plumber who provides world-class customer service. He gives same-day service, trains his staff in customer relations, and makes his customers want to come back to him year after year.

Jim Jeffrey of Pest Control Technologies creates a professional image with white trucks and white uniforms for his employees, while his competitors work in blue jeans and T-shirts. Bear Barnes, a house painter, offers two-year guarantees and maintains a detailed database to target his market, track bids, and record every shade of paint on every house his company services.

Forbes's list of the richest people in America includes pig farmer Wendell Murphy, who started with one pen and turned it into the biggest hog-farming business in the country. He is now worth $1 billion. He applied computer technology to manage climate control and manure removal, and help make decisions surrounding when the sows should mate, how to breed, how to feed, and when to sell.

Other members of *Forbes*'s list include Monroe Carell, William and Kathryn Bartmann, and Whit Hudson. Monroe Carell is worth $600 million on the strength of his car-parking business. William and Kathryn Bartmann founded a debt-collecting business. Whit Hudson earned his fortune in the trash-collecting business, using computers to weigh the trash in his trucks.

In other words, many highly successful entrepreneurs are masters of the ordinary. They are in ordinary, dull (on the face of it) businesses, but they manage them extraordinarily well compared to their competitors.

Sources: A. Murphy, "Masters of the Ordinary," *Inc.*, October 1993, pp. 70–71; and M. Conlin, "Riding the Revolution," *Forbes*, October 13, 1997, pp. 99–104. ●

Planning

So you think you have spotted a business opportunity. And you have the personal potential to make it a success. Now what? Should you act on your idea? Where should you begin?

opportunity analysis A description of the product or service, an assessment of the opportunity, an assessment of the entrepreneur, specification of activities and resources needed to translate your idea into a viable business, and your source(s) of capital.

The business plan Your excitement and intuition may convince you that you are on to something. But they might not convince anyone else. You will need more thorough planning and analysis. This will help convince other people to get on board, and help you avoid costly mistakes.

The first formal planning step is to do an opportunity analysis. An **opportunity analysis** includes a description of the product or service, an assessment of the opportunity, an assessment of the entrepreneur (you), a specification of activities and resources needed to translate your idea into a viable business, and your source(s) of capital.[32] Table 7.2 shows the questions you should answer in an opportunity analysis.

The opportunity analysis, or opportunity assessment plan, focuses on the opportunity, not the entire venture. It provides the basis for making a decision on whether to act. Then, the **business plan** describes all the elements involved in starting the new venture.[33] The business plan describes the venture and its market, strategies, and future directions. It often includes functional plans including marketing, finance, manufacturing, and human resources.

business plan A formal planning step in starting a new business that focuses on the entire venture and describes all the elements involved in starting it.

Table 7.3 shows an outline for a typical business plan. The business plan (1) helps determine the viability of your enterprise; (2) guides you as you plan and organize; and (3) helps you obtain financing. It is read by potential investors, suppliers, customers, and others. Get help in writing up a sound plan!

Key planning elements Most business plans devote so much attention to financial projections that they neglect other important information—information that matters greatly to astute investors. In fact, financial projections are often way off base; new ventures are far too uncertain, with far too many unknowns, to allow accurate forecasts of revenues and profits. The projections tend to be overly optimistic. Investors know this and discount the figures. These inaccuracies and biases benefit no one.[34]

The numbers in the plan are important in that they indicate the key drivers of success and failure. But in addition to the numbers, the best plans convey—and make certain that the entrepreneurs have carefully thought through—five key factors: the people, the opportunity, the competition, the context, and risk and reward.[35]

The *people* should be energetic and have skills and expertise directly relevant to the venture. For many astute investors, the people are the most important variable, more important even than the idea. Venture capital firms often receive 2,000 business plans per year, and many believe that ideas are a dime a dozen and what counts is the ability to execute. Arthur Rock, a legendary venture capitalist who helped start Intel, Teledyne, and Apple, stated, "I invest in people, not ideas. If you can find good people, if they're wrong about the product, they'll make a switch."[36]

The *opportunity* should allow a competitive advantage that can be defended. Many options should exist for the management to expand the scale and scope of the business. Customers are the focus here: Who is the customer? How does the customer make decisions? How will the product be priced? How will the venture reach all customer segments? How much does it cost to acquire and support a customer, and to produce and deliver the product? How easy or difficult is it to retain a customer?

table 7.2
Opportunity analysis

What market need does my idea fill?
What personal observations have I experienced or recorded with regard to that market need?
What social condition underlies this market need?
What market research data can be marshaled to describe this market need?
What patents might be available to fulfill this need?
What competition exists in this market? How would I describe the behavior of this competition?
What does the international market look like?
What does the international competition look like?
Where is the money to be made in this activity?

Source: R. Hisrich and M. Peters, *Entrepreneurship: Starting, Developing, and Managing a New Enterprise* (Burr Ridge, IL: Richard D. Irwin, 1995), p. 33.

table 7.3 Outline of a business plan

I. Introductory Page
- A. Name and address of business
- B. Name(s) and address(es) of principals
- C. Nature of business
- D. Statement of financing needed
- E. Statement of confidentiality of report

II. Executive Summary—Three to four pages summarizing the complete business plan

III. Industry Analysis
- A. Future outlook and trends
- B. Analysis of competitors
- C. Market segmentation
- D. Industry forecasts

IV. Description of Venture
- A. Product(s)
- B. Service(s)
- C. Size of business
- D. Office equipment and personnel
- E. Background of entrepreneurs

V. Production Plan
- A. Manufacturing process (amount subcontracted)
- B. Physical plant
- C. Machinery and equipment
- D. Names of suppliers of raw materials

VI. Marketing Plan
- A. Pricing
- B. Distribution
- C. Promotion
- D. Product forecasts
- E. Controls

VII. Organizational Plan
- A. Form of ownership
- B. Identification of partners or principal shareholders
- C. Authority of principals
- D. Management-team background
- E. Roles and responsibilities of members of organization

VIII. Assessment of Risk
- A. Evaluate weakness of business
- B. New technologies
- C. Contingency plans

IX. Financial Plan
- A. Pro forma income statement
- B. Cash flow projections
- C. Pro forma balance sheet
- D. Break-even analysis
- E. Sources and applications of funds

X. Appendix (contains backup material)
- A. Letters
- B. Market research data
- C. Leases or contracts
- D. Price lists from suppliers

Source: R. Hisrich and M. Peters, *Entrepreneurship: Starting, Developing, and Managing a New Enterprise* (Burr Ridge, IL: Richard D. Irwin, 1994). Reprinted by permission.

It is also essential to fully consider the *competition.* The plan must identify current competitors and their strengths and weaknesses, predict how they will respond to the new venture, indicate how the new venture will respond to the competitors' responses, identify future potential competitors, and consider how to collaborate with actual or potential competitors. Thus, for example, Andrew Busey created ichat, the leading provider of software for chat rooms. But now America Online and Microsoft are competing directly with the young entrepreneur. He is responding by collaborating with IBM; the Lotus division will bundle ichat's software with its Internet-ready version of Notes.[37]

The environmental *context* should be a favorable one, from regulatory and economic perspectives. Such factors as tax policies, rules about raising capital, interest rates, inflation, and exchange rates will affect the viability of the new venture. The context can make it easier or harder to get backing and to succeed. Importantly, the plan should make clear that you know that the context inevitably will change, how the changes will affect the business, and how you will deal with the changes.

The *risk* must be understood and addressed as fully as possible. The future is always uncertain, and the elements described in the plan will change over time. Although you cannot predict the future, you must contemplate head-on the possibilities of key people leaving, interest rates changing, a key customer leaving, or a powerful competitor responding ferociously. Then describe what you will do to prevent, avoid, or cope with such possibilities. You should also speak to the end of the process: how to get money out of the business eventually. Will you go public? Will you sell or liquidate? What are the various possibilities for investors to realize their ultimate gains?[38]

Selling the plan Once you have written your plan, your goal is to get investors to agree. The elements of a great plan, described above, are essential. Also important is whom you decide to try to convince to back your plan.

Many entrepreneurs want passive investors who will give them money and let them do what they want. Doctors and dentists generally fit this image. Professional venture capitalists do not, as they demand more control and more of the returns. But when business goes wrong—and chances are, it will—nonprofessional investors are less helpful, and less likely to advance more (needed) money. Sophisticated investors have seen sinking ships before and know how to help. They are more likely to solve problems, provide more money, and also navigate financial and legal waters such as going public.[39]

Business deals should not be viewed as static, one-time documents negotiating one lump sum. Ideally, they are dynamic, and should be envisioned that way.[40] It can help to view the new venture as a series of experiments. Try the venture on a small scale, test the product with focus groups, build a prototype, conduct a regional rollout. You can reduce the initial risk, impress potential investors, learn about the product and customers, and get a better understanding of how much money is actually needed and in what stages.

View the plan as a way for you to figure out how to reduce risk and maximize reward, and to convince others that you understand the entire new venture process. Don't put together a plan built on naïveté or overconfidence, or that cleverly hides major flaws. You might not fool others, and you certainly would be fooling yourself.[41]

Nonfinancial Resources Nonfinancial resources—particularly other people—also are crucial to the success of a new business.

Networks The entrepreneur can realize efficiencies by using a *network* of suppliers and customers. For example, entrepreneurs often delegate work to a network of subcontractors. The subcontractors work only part-time for the entrepreneurs, but as full-time specialists at their jobs, they give the entrepreneur some of the advantages of specialization.[42]

Top Management Teams The top management team is another crucial resource. The board of directors improves the company's image, develops longer-term plans for expansion, supports day-to-day activities, and develops a network of information sources. Michael Dell, founder of Dell Computer at age 19, knows the importance of surrounding himself with talent. He hires managers who are far more experienced than he, and prominent and powerful board members. In 1995, at age 30, Michael Dell held the longest tenure of any chief executive in the industry.[43]

Advisory Boards Anita Brattina thought after two or three years of running her own marketing firm she would have lots of cash, no debt, and time to enjoy her independence.[44] Eight years later, she still worked 50 to 60 hours a week and was not making much money. So she got an advisory board. They taught her how to do cash-flow analysis, suggested some strategic changes, and encouraged her to cultivate relationships with a banker, an accountant, and an attorney. In addition, they helped her interview salespeople, develop a long-term marketing strategy, and reorganize operations. They also vetoed a number of her ideas. Sales are now up, after one year of listening to the board and implementing its ideas. She is confident that she is well on her way to the coveted goal of $1 million in sales.

Partners Often, two people go into business together as partners. Traditionally, partners are family members or friends. Nowadays, partnerships form between people from among the millions laid off, who meet each other and discover they have common interests and complementary skills. Partners can help one another access capital, spread the workload, share the risk, and furnish expertise.

Incompatible partners

Despite the potential advantages of finding a compatible partner, partnerships are not always marriages made in heaven.

- One partner in a plastics fabricator learned that his partners scheduled business meetings without telling him, took customers to lunch and didn't invite him, hired assistants for themselves but not for him, and finally forced him out. "If people's moral intentions are no good, the best legal document in the world is hooey," he says.
- "Mark" talked three of his friends into joining him in starting his own telecommunications company because he didn't want to try it alone. He learned quickly that while he wanted to put money into growing the business, his three partners wanted the company to pay for their cars and meetings in the Bahamas. The company collapsed. "I never thought a business relationship could overpower friendship, but this one did. Where money's involved, people change."
- An insurance broker, a lawyer, and a contractor bought a small mall. Only the insurance broker found the time to make decisions and take action; the others "just couldn't get to it." But they did find time to complain about everything the broker did. The broker quit in disgust.
- Patti and Michael Zacks owned a camera store in Providence, Rhode Island, for 13 years. Then they got a divorce. Michael opened a competing store just a few doors away. Now they fight for customers. Long-time customers much choose between them. Some go to one and park where the other can't see their cars. Patti is a good friend to the owners of the Italian Deli, but Michael is a good customer. Patti doesn't go there anymore because Michael does. The deli owners sometimes bring Patti lunch in her shop. Patti thinks Michael is being vindictive, but Michael insists running a camera business is what he knows, and he needs to be close to the children.

To be successful, partners need to acknowledge one another's talents, let each other do what they do best, communicate honestly, and listen to one another. And they must learn to trust each other by making and keeping agreements. If they must break an agreement, it is crucial that they give early notice and clean up after their mistakes.

Sources: R. A. Mamis, "Partner War," *Inc.*, June 1994, pp. 36–44; and H. Stout, "War of the Zackses: Divorce Splits Up Mom and Pop Store," *The Wall Street Journal*, November 13, 1997, pp. 1, 2.

The image of the family business is one of a business started by one founder and then passed down from generation to generation. Now, a different model is appearing: parents and children starting new companies as partners.[45] Linda Oldham quit her job to join her son Todd's business. Todd Oldham is a fashion designer who has appeared on MTV's *House of Style*. In similar fashion, Gregg Levin designed a plastic product called the Curve, which bends the visors of baseball caps into perfect curves. His father Barry is quitting his solo law practice to become his son's partner. In 1997, Perfect Curve Inc. had 250 accounts with 350 stores.

Americans under the age of 30 are more likely than any other age group to start or buy businesses. The children have ideas and stamina. The parents have experience and money. And for some parents, it offers a second career for downsized corporate executives.

Entrepreneurial hazards

Not all companies get off to a great start. Some die a quick death. Others, a slow, agonizing one. Even those that make honored lists, like the *Forbes* best small companies or *Inc.*'s hottest growth companies, don't always remain on the fast track. Some flame out. The child safety product company behind those "Baby on Board" car window signs tripled its sales in two years, almost tripled its stock (to about $33), and returned nearly 100 percent on equity over a five-year period. But in the last three years, it has lost $30 million and the stock has collapsed to about $5.[46]

In *Forbes*'s annual list of the 200 best small companies in America, in the past decade 42 percent have continued to grow impressively, but 56 percent hit trouble and went into negative growth. Only 2 percent hit the "middle ground" of continuing to grow, but slowly.[47] Perhaps, as the magazine suggests, hot growth companies hit a crucial point that can be exceedingly dangerous. "The faster they run, the harder they fall."[48] A common cause is growth into new products, or new geographic areas, that are poorly understood. Success can cause management to become overconfident or complacent. And growth can be so fast that the company goes out of control and isn't managed properly, resulting in lower quality goods and services.

The hazards of striking out on your own are many. First, you may start your own company and find out that you don't enjoy it. One person who quit a large company to start his own small one stated, "As an executive in a large company, the issues are strategic. You're implementing programs that affect thousands of people. In a small business, the issues are less complex . . . you worry about inventory every day, because you may not be in business next week if you have negative cash flow." His most unpleasant surprise: "How much you have to sell. You're always out selling . . . I didn't want to be a salesman. I wanted to be an executive."[49]

And survival is difficult. As *Fortune* put it, "Misjudgments are punished ruthlessly. When competition gets tougher, small businesses feel it first. Financing is hard to find, sometimes impossible . . . 'In small business there are no small mistakes'—it's a phrase that comes up time and again when you talk to the owners."[50] But, says *Fortune*, most are proud of this description of entrepreneurial hazards.

Failure can be devastating. "I remember thinking I was very comfortable financially, and the crystal chandelier hit the floor . . . I remember trying to find enough money to buy groceries. You never forget that."[51] So stated David Pomije, CEO and founder of Funco, a chain that buys and resells used and new Nintendo and Sega videogames. Fortunately, he has turned the corner; he now operates over 100 stores with sales of $50 million.

Failure can be traced to several hazards; the most common are mortality, the inability to delegate, misuse of funds, and poor planning and controls.

Mortality

One long-term measure of an entrepreneur's success is the fate of the venture after the founder's death. The organization can outlive the entrepreneur under one of two conditions: (1) if the company has gone public or (2) if the entrepreneur has planned an orderly family succession. Both conditions are relatively rare.

Entrepreneurs often fail to seek public capital because equity capital is scarce and expensive or because they want to maintain control. One entrepreneur's comment suggests how important the business is to a founder: "The satisfaction of starting and operating a successful business is one of life's most rewarding experiences, and the loss or sale of an enterprise can be a fate worse than death."[52] An entrepreneur who is funded with public equity risks losing the business if stockholders are not satisfied. To avoid this risk, the entrepreneur maintains private control over the business. But founding entrepreneurs often fail to plan for succession. When death occurs, estate tax problems and/or the lack of a skilled replacement for the founder can lead to business failure.

Management guru Peter Drucker offers the following advice to help family-managed businesses survive and prosper:[53] Family members working in the business must be at least as capable and hard-working as other employees; at least one key position should be filled by a nonfamily member; and someone outside the family and the business should help plan succession. Family members who are mediocre performers are resented by others; outsiders can be more objective and contribute expertise the family might not have; and issues of management succession are often the most difficult of all, causing serious conflict and possible breakup of the firm.

Inadequate delegation Although mortality contributes to some new venture failures, the founder's death usually cannot be blamed. Most new businesses collapse before their owners do. In these cases, the cause of the demise often can be traced to the entrepreneur's desire to personally control every aspect of the business.

Just as entrepreneurs resist loss of control of the company to either public investors or heirs, they often hesitate to delegate work to people within the business. This managerial flaw is not unique to the entrepreneurial company, but it is a critical problem. The entrepreneur's desire for control fosters a climate in which managers and workers depend too heavily on the entrepreneur's decisions. When this happens, opportunities are lost and the employees (and the organization) fail to develop. Once the organization reaches a certain size, the entrepreneur's attempt to exert personal control becomes dysfunctional. The company's competitive advantage may be lost, and the company ultimately may fail.

Misuse of funds Many unsuccessful entrepreneurs blame their failure on inadequate financial resources. Yet failure due to a lack of financial resources doesn't necessarily indicate a real lack of money; it could mean a failure to properly use the resources available. Entrepreneurs who fail to use their resources wisely usually make one of two mistakes: They apply financial resources to the wrong uses, or they maintain inadequate control over their resources.

One aspiring entrepreneur borrowed $100,000 and used $25,000 of that money to buy a dating service. He then used the remaining $75,000 to buy radio advertising for the business. A few months later, bankrupt and bitter, he blamed his failure on a lack of financial resources. But a more objective view might reveal that he did not use his resources wisely. In this case, he should not have spent $25,000 to purchase the business; he could have entered the business at a lower cost by starting his own operation. In addition, he should not have spent $75,000 on advertising without specific knowledge about how that advertising would affect his business. This entrepreneur failed because he applied his financial resources to the wrong uses.

Poor planning and controls Even when financial resources are applied correctly, improper control of money can cause business failures. Entrepreneurs, in part because they are very busy, often fail to use formal planning and control systems. Planning takes time from activities that entrepreneurs may find more enjoyable, such as selling, producing, and buying. Many entrepreneurs fail because they don't anticipate predictable problems such as cash flow shortages and the loss of key customers.

One common entrepreneurial malady is an aversion to record keeping. Expenses mount, but records do not keep pace. Pricing decisions are based on intuition without adequate reference to costs. As a result, the company earns inadequate margins to support growth. With accurate records, the entrepreneur could identify those areas where costs could be cut or prices increased. Without them, the entrepreneur can only guess. Guesses are nearly always inaccurate, and when made too often they guarantee failure. Such entrepreneurs learn too late that prevention is the best cure.

Even in high-growth companies, great numbers can mask brewing problems. Blinded by the light of growing sales, many entrepreneurs fail to maintain vigilance over other aspects of the business. In the absence of controls, the business veers out of control. As the chief financial officer of FTP Software puts it, "Success is the worst thing that can happen to a company. You start believing your own headlines. You get sloppy."[54]

It is important to keep asking critical questions: Is our success based on just one big customer? Is our product just a fad that can fade away? Can other companies easily enter our domain and hurt our business? Are we losing a technology lead? Do we really understand the numbers, know where they come from, and have any hidden causes for concern?

Other advice on how to keep on growing:[55] Run scared; assume that the customer is never satisfied. Advertise like crazy. Remember product, product, product; keep it unique. Hire the best possible people and motivate them like crazy. Keep setting higher and higher goals. And be fast in everything that you do—especially in the eyes of the customer.

Global start-ups

Most people, particularly Americans, have an image of new ventures beginning domestically and then slowly, over time, evolving toward international operations. But a new model is beginning to appear, and it will become increasingly important in the future. A **global start-up** is a new venture that is international from the very beginning.[56]

global start-up A new venture that is international from the very beginning.

The costs of doing business internationally have decreased dramatically, reducing the competitive advantage of large, established organizations and presenting outstanding opportunity to new ventures. Global start-ups have the potential to be a powerful economic engine and to provide great success to entrepreneurs.

If you are contemplating a start-up, you should ask the following questions to determine whether you should begin with a domestic or a global outlook:[57] First, where are the best people? The United States has great software designers; Italy is known for fine leathers; Japan, for its manufacturing quality. Are the world-class people you need to make the venture a great success located in the neighborhood, or on the other side of the world?

Second, where is the financing easiest and most suitable? Some entrepreneurs maintain that courting European investors is more productive than approaching U.S. venture capitalists, who have made the investment process less intuitive and more institutionalized and bureaucratic. Third, where are the targeted customers? If a big percentage are abroad, it may be illogical to limit operations domestically.

Fourth, when global operators learn about your venture, will they go head-to-head with you? If so, how quickly? Instead of having to defend your domestic markets, you might be better served by going on the offensive internationally. Fifth, if you postpone going international, will your domestic inertia cripple your longer-term prospects? Strategies and tactics that succeed domestically will not necessarily work internationally, and can interfere when you try to adopt new approaches. Why not learn now about going global, rather than later when you could be too slow and too late?

So, you've decided to begin globally rather than just domestically? You'd better know the critical success factors for global start-ups.[58] You should think globally from day one, and be able to communicate your global vision to everyone else associated with the venture. The founders and top management team must have international experience, and with your staff you should develop deep cultural and cross-cultural understanding.[59] You and your team should have in place a network of trusted financiers, suppliers, distributors, and other business associates. You must have a product (good or service) that provides a clear advantage to customers, in order to overcome the advantages already held by indigenous competitors. It also helps to have other, more intangible assets, such as unique knowledge that competitors lack. You should continue innovating, extending your product line over time in order to maintain or build your lead over competitors. And you should coordinate closely every aspect of the organization worldwide via teamwork, extensive travel, personal communications, a sophisticated communications infrastructure, and constant transfer of knowledge among widely dispersed locations.[60]

Entrepreneur's creed

When asked what are the most critical concepts and skills for running a business, here's what entrepreneurs have to say. When the statements are considered together, they might be considered a creed.

- Do what gives you energy–have fun.
- Figure out how to make it work.
- Say "can do" rather than "cannot" or "maybe."
- Tenacity and creativity will triumph.
- Be dissatisfied with the way things are–and look for improvement.
- Do things differently.
- Make opportunity and results–not money–your obsession.
- Take pride in your accomplishments–it's contagious.
- Sweat the details that are critical to success.
- Play for the long haul–it is rarely possible to get rich quickly.

Source: Abridged from J. Timmons, *New Venture Creation* (Burr Ridge, IL: Richard D. Irwin, 1994), p. 202. Reprinted by permission.

Spin-offs

The independent entrepreneur is the initiating agent of the new business, but many established organizations also play an important role in new venture creation. These organizations give most entrepreneurs their initial professional experience and contacts.[61] In some cases, aspiring entrepreneurs remain with their employers and act as intrapreneurs. But often, the entrepreneurs leave their employers and become owners of a spin-off—a division of a company that splits from its parent company to become an independent company that offers a product similar to those of the owners' former employers.

Why spin-offs occur

Spin-offs occur frequently and may take place with the original employer's approval. The approved spin-off occurs when the established company senses an opportunity but does not pursue the opportunity with internal resources. However, the company recognizes that it might still profit from the idea by selling the patents to a new entity or by investing in a new enterprise.

Employer approval is not necessary to create a spin-off. Often spin-offs occur when entrepreneurs disagree with their former employers. An entrepreneur may sense an opportunity that the employer considers unprofitable. Or both the entrepreneur and the employer may see an opportunity for gain, but the employer has other, more attractive opportunities.

Often, spin-offs occur when employees feel stifled by the corporate environment. Thomas Watson (left) and Ross Perot are two well-known examples of people who quit corporate jobs and became immensely successful founders of new companies.
[Courtesy International Business Machines Corporation]

Stories abound about the flight of the entrepreneur from the stifling handcuffs of the corporation. Thomas Watson left National Cash Register to become the founder of IBM. Ross Perot quit IBM to start EDS. And there are countless success stories of people whose names you've never heard.

The spin-off process

Figure 7.2 summarizes the stages of the spin-off process. Factors such as the stage of the product life cycle and the type of industry contribute to the frequency of spin-offs. The entrepreneur's ability to attract capital and build a team determines the ultimate destiny of the new venture. If the spin-off successfully wards off competition, both the company's survival and the entrepreneur's wealth are ensured.

figure 7.2
Stages of the spin-off process

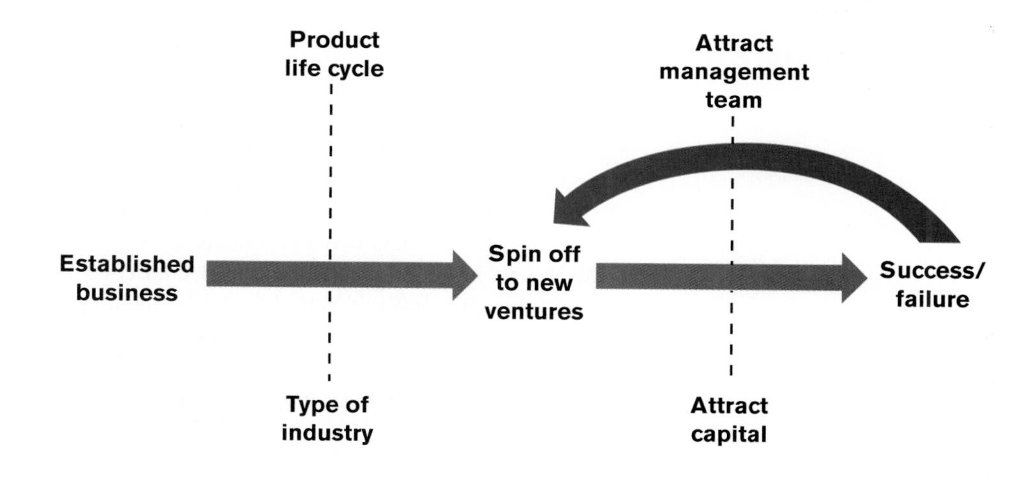

Early stage Spin-offs occur most often at the early stages of the product life cycle. When an industry is first formed, real demand often outstrips supply, promising excellent opportunities. At the same time, the absence of product standards provides the opportunity for a variety of competitive approaches to the market.

The computer industry offers many examples of spin-off activity in a new industry. Early on, Amdahl was created by an IBM executive. Data General grew out of Digital Equipment Corporation. Countless software companies spun off from the major hardware producers and their customers. Silicon Valley grew exponentially as one company grew into two, two branched into four or more, and so on.

Industry types New industries are not the only source of spin-offs. Mature industries that are fragmented or undergoing change and declining industries also generate significant spin-off activity.

A *fragmented industry* has few barriers to entry and therefore has many competitors. Such an industry offers great opportunity for spin-offs. In the restaurant industry, for example, a talented chef can make more money by owning a bistro than by working for another owner. Thus, good restaurants—and stores, consulting firms, travel agencies, and so on—often spin off new competitors.

In a *mature industry* undergoing change, new competitors may have an advantage over established competitors. For example, the cable industry is mature. Established cable companies were slow to respond to the demands of networked computers. Cabletron was started by two entrepreneurs (one a sales representative for an established company) to provide cables for computer networks. In a few years, the company became a dominant producer.[62]

A different logic explains spin-offs in *declining industries.* Established organizations, frustrated by stagnant conditions in their industry, often seek opportunity in newer industries. A company can fund new opportunities by selling its older businesses. The original companies encourage management or employees to purchase aging plants through employee stock ownership plans (ESOPs). Unburdened by corporate overhead and neglect, the new owners are able to revitalize the business while the former owners invest the funds from the buyout elsewhere.

Regardless of the situation, the spin-off entrepreneur faces key challenges. Specifically, the entrepreneur needs to build a management team and raise sufficient capital.

Attracting management teams and capital Unlike the entrepreneur of classical folklore, today's entrepreneur who is involved in a spin-off usually is a highly educated professional. Many spin-off entrepreneurs have undergraduate or graduate training in science. But as a specialist, the entrepreneur in the spin-off has limited knowledge of some business functions. Moreover, the entrepreneur's time usually is spent pursuing his or her specialty. Therefore, the entrepreneur must build a strong management team.

Consider the two research biologists who helped form Electro-Biology, Inc. They discovered a new method for healing bone fractures by using electronic processes. Although each was a highly skilled researcher, neither had a working knowledge of finance, marketing, and medical law. However, they quickly recognized their weaknesses and found specialists to supervise each area. The company prospered, while the biologists returned to the lab to search for new (and better) products.

The search for capital is the greatest challenge for spin-off owners. For company-sponsored spin-offs, favorable purchase terms and long-term loans provide some of this capital. But like managers in all ventures, spin-off managers need to be creative in their pursuit and use of capital. Although the company was not a spin-off, Performance Inc.'s owner Garry Snook provides an excellent example of the creative use of capital. Snook minimized his need for capital by convincing a supplier to rent him unused factory space. Similarly, he lowered the cost of retail space by renting ski equipment supply stores during their off season.

Change in industry structure

Once the entrepreneur builds a management team and obtains capital, the spin-off faces the hazards of competition and change. A change in industry structure may be the most critical hazard for the spin-off business. While this change is most likely to arise in the early stages of an industry's evolution, it can occur at any time. During its early stages, the industry has a wide variety of product types, production methods, and distribution methods. As the personal computer industry developed, some companies offered stand-alone units, while others offered modular units. Various companies offered different software packages. In the production area, some companies produced the majority of their components, while others assembled purchased goods. In the marketing area, companies sold through catalogs, established their own retail outlets, sold through specialty stores, or sold through department stores. Department stores sold the machines as toys, electronic goods, or business machines. Confusion reigned!

However, a pattern emerged from the chaos. The modular unit became the market leader and was distributed primarily through retail specialists. PC-DOS captured the operating system market, and a narrow band of software applications became the standard fare for initial sales. This emerging pattern changed the structure of the industry. Competitors that initially chose a different product design, a different software system, or a different distribution network faced a competitive disadvantage. Those companies could only change, or fail. Changes in industry structure are common hazards in entrepreneurial environments, and the spin-off entrepreneur, like all entrepreneurs, should be prepared to face them.

Intrapreneurship

Today's large corporations are more than passive bystanders in the entrepreneurial explosion. Even established companies try to find and pursue new and profitable ideas—and they need intrapreneurs to do so. If you work in a company, and are considering preparing a new business venture, Table 7.4 can help you decide whether the new idea is worth pursuing.

Building support for your idea

A manager who has a new idea to capitalize on a market opportunity will need to get others in the organization to buy in or sign on. In other words, you need to build a network of allies who support and will help implement the idea.

If you need to build support for a project idea, the first step involves *clearing the investment* with your immediate boss or bosses.[63] At this stage, you explain the idea and seek approval to look for wider support.

Higher executives often want evidence that the project is backed by your peers before committing to it. This involves *making cheerleaders*—people who will support the manager before formal approval from higher levels. Managers at General Electric refer to this strategy as "loading the gun"—lining up ammunition.

Next, *horse trading* begins. You can offer promises of payoffs from the project in return for support, time, money, and other resources that peers and others contribute.

Finally, you should *get the blessing* of relevant higher-level officials. This usually involves a formal presentation. You will need to guarantee the project's technical and political feasibility. Higher management's endorsement of the project and promises of resources help convert potential supporters into an enthusiastic team. At this point, you can go back to your boss and make specific plans for going ahead with the project.

Along the way, expect resistance and frustration—and use passion and persistence, as well as business logic, to persuade others to get on board.[64]

table 7.4
Checklist for choosing ideas

Fit with your skills and experience

Do you believe in the product or service?

Does the need it fits mean something to you personally?

Do you like and understand the potential customers?

Do you have experience in this type of business?

Do the basic success factors of this business fit your skills?

Are the tasks of the enterprise ones you could enjoy doing yourself?

Are the people the enterprise will employ ones you will enjoy working with and supervising?

Has the idea begun to take over your imagination and spare time?

Fit with the market

Is there a real customer need?

Can you get a price that gives you good margins?

Would customers believe in the product coming from your company?

Does the product or service you propose produce a clearly perceivable customer benefit that is significantly better than that offered by competing ways to satisfy the same basic need?

Is there a cost-effective way to get the message and the product to the customers?

Fit with the company

Is there a reason to believe your company could be very good at the business?

Does it fit the company culture?

Does it look profitable (high margin/low investment)?

Will it lead to larger markets and growth?

What to do when your idea is rejected

As an intrapreneur, you will frequently find that your idea has been rejected. There are a few things you can do.

1. Give up and select a new idea.
2. Listen carefully, understand what is wrong, improve your idea and your presentation, and try again.
3. Find someone else to whom you can present your idea by considering
   - *a.* Who will benefit most if it works? Can they be a sponsor?
   - *b.* Who are potential customers? Will they demand the product?
   - *c.* How can you get to the people who really care about intrapreneurial ideas?

Source: G. Pinchot III, *Intrapreneuring*. Copyright © 1985 by Gifford Pinchot III. Reprinted by permission of HarperCollins Publishers, Inc.

Building intrapreneurship

skunkworks A project team designated to produce a new, innovative product.

Can corporations foster intrapreneurship? If so, how? Two common approaches used to stimulate intrapreneurial activity are skunkworks and bootlegging. **Skunkworks** are project teams designated to produce a new product. A team is formed with a specific goal within a specified time frame. A respected person is chosen to be manager of the skunkworks. In this approach to corporate innovation, risk takers are not punished for taking risks and failing—their former jobs are held for them. The risk takers also have the opportunity to earn large rewards.

bootlegging Informal efforts by managers and employees to create new products and new processes.

Bootlegging refers to informal efforts by managers and employees to create new products and new processes. "Informal" can mean "secretive," such as when a bootlegger believes the company will frown on these activities. But the intrapreneurial organization should tolerate and even encourage bootlegging.

Decentralization, which you will read more about in Chapter 8, is another way to encourage intrapreneurship. Although decentralization is not an attractive option for all companies, the decentralized company is a natural laboratory for new ideas. The decentralized company, in which individuals and units have a high degree of autonomy and discretion, can allocate capital to fund new ideas. The internal capital allocation process can mimic the private venture capital market. Ideas compete in an open arena for capital funding. The competition fuels the engines of innovation.

Merck, desiring entrepreneurial thinking and behavior in R&D, explicitly rejects budgets for planning and control. New product teams don't *get* a budget. They must persuade people to join their team and commit *their* resources. This creates a survival-of-the-fittest process, mirroring the competition in the real world.[65]

Organizing new corporate ventures

For large-scale innovation, strategic alliances—cooperation among different organizations—can be a useful route. By engaging in joint efforts, organizations can minimize their investment and risk. You will learn more about strategic alliances in Chapter 9.

However, innovation often takes place on a small scale. Aspiring intrapreneurs might need access to small amounts of capital. At Teleflex, intrapreneurs can apply for grants of $1,000 to $200,000. At Kodak, innovation offices located throughout the company help intrapreneurs find sponsors within the organization. Also, committees will provide seed money for new ideas.[66]

Technical assistance can be as valuable to the intrapreneur as money. In recognition of this fact, Raytheon maintains a new-products center (NPC). The job of an NPC is to develop products for internal clients. Scientists in the NPC work for a variety of internal clients, providing a cross-fertilization of ideas among divisions. The flow of product ideas goes both ways: Clients ask the NPC to develop certain products, while the NPC advises its internal clients about opportunities they might miss.

The encouragement of intrapreneurship gives these large companies two advantages: First, their policies encourage aspiring entrepreneurs within the company to pursue their ideas. Second, they help the companies attract people interested in intrapreneurial pursuits. Companies that institutionalize innovation are, like great Broadway musicals, assured a long run. Innovation is so important to an organization—and so central to the process of change—that an entire chapter (Chapter 17) is devoted to it in Part V of the text.

Hazards in intrapreneurship

Organizations that encourage intrapreneurship face an obvious risk: The effort can fail. One author noted, "There is considerable history of internal venture development by large firms, and it does not encourage optimism."[67] However, this risk can be managed. In fact, failing to foster intrapreneurship may represent a subtler but greater risk than encouraging it. The organization that resists intrapreneurial initiative may lose its ability to adapt when conditions dictate change.

The most dangerous risk in intrapreneurship is the risk of overreliance on a single project. Many companies fail while awaiting the completion of one large, innovative project.[68] The successful intrapreneurial organization avoids overcommitment to a single project and relies on its entrepreneurial spirit to produce at least one winner from among several projects.

Organizations also court failure when they spread their intrapreneurial efforts over too many projects.[69] If there are many intrapreneurial projects, all their efforts may be too small in scale. Managers will consider the projects unattractive because of their small size. Or, those recruited to manage the projects may have difficulty building power and status within the organization.

The hazards in intrapreneurship, then, are related to scale. One large project is a threat, as are too many underfunded projects. But a carefully managed approach to this strategically important process will upgrade an organization's chances for long-term survival.

Entrepreneurial orientation

Earlier in this chapter, we described the characteristics of individual entrepreneurs. Now, we do the same for companies: we describe how companies that are highly entrepreneurial differ from those that are not.

entrepreneurial orientation
The tendency of an organization to engage in activities designed to identify and capitalize successfully on opportunities to launch new ventures by entering new or established markets with new or existing goods or services.

Entrepreneurial orientation is the tendency of an organization to engage in activities designed to identify and capitalize successfully on opportunities to launch new ventures by entering new or established markets with new or existing goods or services.[70] The extent to which an organization has a strong entrepreneurial orientation is determined by five tendencies: to allow independent action, innovate, take risks, be proactive, and be competitively aggressive.

To *allow independent action* is to grant to individuals and teams the freedom to exercise their creativity, champion promising ideas, and carry them through to completion. *Innovativeness* requires the firm to support new ideas, experimentation, and creative processes that can lead to new products or processes; it requires a willingness to depart from existing practices and venture beyond the status quo. *Risk taking* comes from a willingness to commit significant resources, and perhaps borrow heavily, to venture into the unknown. The tendency to take risks can be assessed by considering whether people are bold or cautious, whether they require high levels of certainty before taking or allowing action, and whether they tend to follow tried-and-true paths.

To be *proactive* is to act in anticipation of future problems and opportunities. A proactive firm shapes the environment and changes the competitive landscape; other firms merely react. Proactive firms are forward thinking and fast to act, and are leaders rather than followers. Similarly, some individuals are more likely to be proactive, to shape and create their own environments, than others who more passively cope with and adapt to the situations in which they find themselves.[71] Proactive firms encourage and allow individuals and teams to *be* proactive.

Finally, *competitive aggressiveness* is the tendency of the firm to directly and intensely challenge competitors in order to achieve entry or improve its position. In other words, it is a competitive tendency to outperform one's rivals in the marketplace. This might take the form of striking fast to beat competitors to the punch, to tackle them head-to-head, and to analyze and target competitors' weaknesses. Michael Dell provides a good example: he can state clearly how each of his competitors—IBM, Packard Bell, Apple, Gateway, Compaq—is vulnerable and poised to fail.[72]

What makes a firm "entrepreneurial" is its engagement in an effective combination of independent action, innovativeness, risk taking, proactiveness, and competitive aggressiveness.[73] The relationship between these factors and the performance of the firm is a complicated one, depending on many things. Nevertheless, you can imagine how the opposite profile—too many constraints on action, business-as-usual, extreme caution, passivity, and a lack of competitive fire—will undermine entrepreneurial activities. And without entrepreneurship, how would firms survive and thrive in a constantly-changing competitive environment?

3M: A prototype

3M is a prototype of an entrepreneurial organization. It manages 60,000 products. The company respects doers and innovators more than hierarchy and autocratic bosses. People say and do what they believe is right. Management teams in all businesses have substantial freedom, and they pass freedom along to others. In 1949, Chairman William McKnight exhorted his managers to delegate responsibility, encourage people to exercise their own initiative, and be tolerant of mistakes. McKnight's phrases became well known:[74]

- "Listen to anyone with an original idea, no matter how absurd it might sound at first."
- "Encourage, don't nitpick. Let people run with an idea."
- "Hire good people, and leave them alone."
- "Encourage experimental doodling."
- "Give it a try—and quick!"

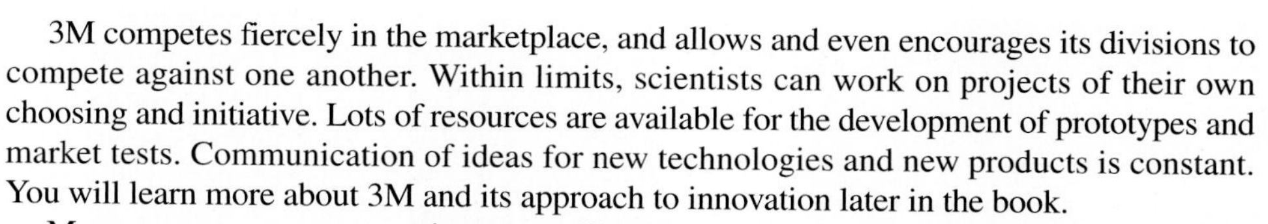

3M competes fiercely in the marketplace, and allows and even encourages its divisions to compete against one another. Within limits, scientists can work on projects of their own choosing and initiative. Lots of resources are available for the development of prototypes and market tests. Communication of ideas for new technologies and new products is constant. You will learn more about 3M and its approach to innovation later in the book.

Management can create environments like this in order to foster more entrepreneurship. If your bosses are not doing this, consider trying some entrepreneurial experiments on your own.[75] Seek out others with an entrepreneurial bent. What can you learn from them, and what can you teach others? Sometimes it takes individuals and teams of experimenters to show the possibilities to those at the top. Ask yourself, and ask others: Between the bureaucrats and the entrepreneurs, who is having more effect? And who is having more fun?

Key terms

Bootlegging, p. 259
Business incubators, p. 239
Business plan, p. 247
Entrepreneurial orientation, p. 260
Entrepreneurial venture, p. 236
Entrepreneurship, p. 236
Global start-up, p. 253
Independent entrepreneurship, p. 236
Intrapreneurs, p. 237
Opportunity analysis, p. 246
Side street effect, p. 243
Skunkworks, p. 258
Small business, p. 236
Spin-off, pp. 236

Summary of learning objectives

Now that you have studied Chapter 7, you should know:

The activities of entrepreneurship.

Entrepreneurship is the act of forming a new organization. The independent entrepreneur is the individual who establishes a new organization. Spin-offs are businesses founded by innovators who leave their organizations to start firms producing and selling similar products. Intrapreneurs are new venture creators who work within the boundaries of their established companies.

How to find and evaluate ideas for new business ventures.

You should always be on the lookout for new ideas, talking to other people and monitoring current products, the business environment, and other indicators of opportunity. Trial and error and preparation play important roles. Ideas should be carefully assessed via opportunity analysis and a thorough business plan.

What it takes to be a successful entrepreneur.

Successful entrepreneurs are determined, effective leaders; obsessed with the opportunity; tolerant of risk, ambiguity, and uncertainty; creative; self-reliant; adaptable; and motivated to excel. Recent research shows four very different kinds of profiles of successful entrepreneurs: personal achievers, empathic supersalespeople, real managers, and expert idea generators.

How to write a great business plan.

The business plan helps you determine the viability of your enterprise and convince others to provide financing. It describes the venture and its future, provides financial projections, and includes plans for marketing, manufacturing, and other business functions. The plan should describe at length the people involved in the venture, a full assessment of the opportunity (including customers and competitors), the environmental context (including regulatory and economic perspectives), and the risk (including future risks and how you intend to deal with them).

The important management skills, resources, and strategies needed to avoid failure and achieve success.

Successful entrepreneurs also understand how to plan their new venture, obtain financial resources, and develop a network of other people including suppliers, customers, partners, and boards of directors. Through effective use of their skills, resources, and appropriate strategy, they avoid major causes of failure including failure to plan for succession, inadequate delegation, poor financial controls, and inappropriate allocation of financial resources.

Key criteria for deciding whether your start-up should be global from the outset.

Traditionally, new ventures start on a small scale and then expand, occasionally internationally. Now a new model is appearing: the global start-up, which is international from the very beginning. Whether to begin domestically or globally is an important question, answered by determining where the best people are located, where financing is available and most suitable, where the targeted customers are, and how global competitors will react to you.

The process of spinning off new ventures.

A spin-off occurs when an employee with a new-product idea quits his or her employer and starts an independent business offering a product similar to those of the former parent company. Typically, spin-offs occur in new industries, but they are also found in mature or declining industries that are fragmented or undergoing change. To be successful, the spin-off must attract a strong management team and adapt to changes in the structure of the industry.

How to foster intrapreneurship and an entrepreneurial orientation in large corporations.

Intrapreneurs work within established companies to develop new goods or services that allow the corporation to reap the benefits of innovation. To facilitate intrapreneurship, organizations use skunkworks—project teams designated to develop a new product—and allow bootlegging—informal efforts to create new products and processes. Businesses also may work together through strategic alliances to create new ventures. Whatever the approach, the organization must select its projects carefully and fund them appropriately. Ultimately, a true entrepreneurial orientation in a firm comes from encouraging independent actions, innovativeness, risk taking, proactiveness, and competitive aggressiveness.

Discussion questions

1. What is your level of personal interest in becoming an independent entrepreneur? Why did you rate yourself as you did?

2. How would you assess your capability of being a successful entrepreneur? What are your strengths and weaknesses? How would you increase your capability?

3. Which of the four entrepreneurial "personalities" describes you most accurately? Which least? What are the implications for your entrepreneurial strategies?

4. Identify and discuss new ventures that fit each of the four cells in the entrepreneurial strategy matrix.

5. Brainstorm a list of ideas for new business ventures. From where did the ideas come? Which ones are most and least viable, and why?

6. Identify some businesses that have recently opened in your area. What are their chances of survival, and why? How would you advise the owners or managers of those businesses to enhance their success?

7. Assume you are writing a story about what it's really like to be an entrepreneur. To whom would you talk, and what questions would you ask?

8. Conduct interviews with two entrepreneurs, asking whatever questions most interest you. Share your findings with the class. How do the interviews differ from one another, and what do they have in common?

9. Read Table 7.1, some myths about entrepreneurs. Which myths did you believe? Do you still? Why or why not? Interview two entrepreneurs by asking each myth as a true-or-false question. Then ask them to elaborate on their answers. What did they say? What do you conclude?

10. With your classmates, form small teams of skunkworks. Your charge is to identify an innovation that you think would benefit your school, college, or university, and to outline an action plan for bringing your idea to reality.

11. Identify some bootlegging activities in which you have engaged or have seen others engage. What resulted from the activities? Were the efforts successful? Why or why not?

12. Identify a business that recently folded. What were the causes of the failure? What could have been done differently to prevent the failure?

Concluding Case

America Online

Stephen M. Case was a consumer marketer for PepsiCo Inc. in 1982. When he discovered online services that year, he naturally wanted something user-friendly. That's not what he found. Case believed online services had a huge potential market if they simply could be easier to use, so in 1985 he cofounded America Online. His marketing strategy was to pursue niches instead of the mass approach used by competitors such as Prodigy, the joint venture of IBM and Sears, Roebuck. "The others are like *Time* magazine or *USA Today,*" he said. "We see ourselves as a series of specialized magazines catering to specific interests."

America Online became profitable within two years of start-up. It reached 180,000 subscribers by mid-1992, and by the end of 1994, the company was claiming 1.25 million subscribers. Despite its astonishing growth, entrepreneurial thinking has remained with the company. In November 1994, America Online announced a competition allowing entrepreneurs to apply for The AOL Greenhouse, an initiative giving them a chance to launch their business ideas using the online service, the Internet, and other interactive media.

"Entrepreneurs are often the most creative force in any new medium. In fact, we know that members of our online community have some of the best ideas for expanding our service . . . We hope to identify and support the best, most creative infopreneurs and help them offer their content and ideas to over 1.25 million AOL members and to the entire Internet community," said a spokesperson for the company.

America Online wanted to recruit individuals and organizations who understand market segments and are able to deliver what those customers want. Winning applicants would be independent contractors with knowledge of online media and especially a great idea. In return, AOL promised seed equity, production support, and online promotion. Winners would gain access to AOL members and participation in Internet initiatives. Significantly, the company said that winners were expected to think about alternative sources of revenue and financing

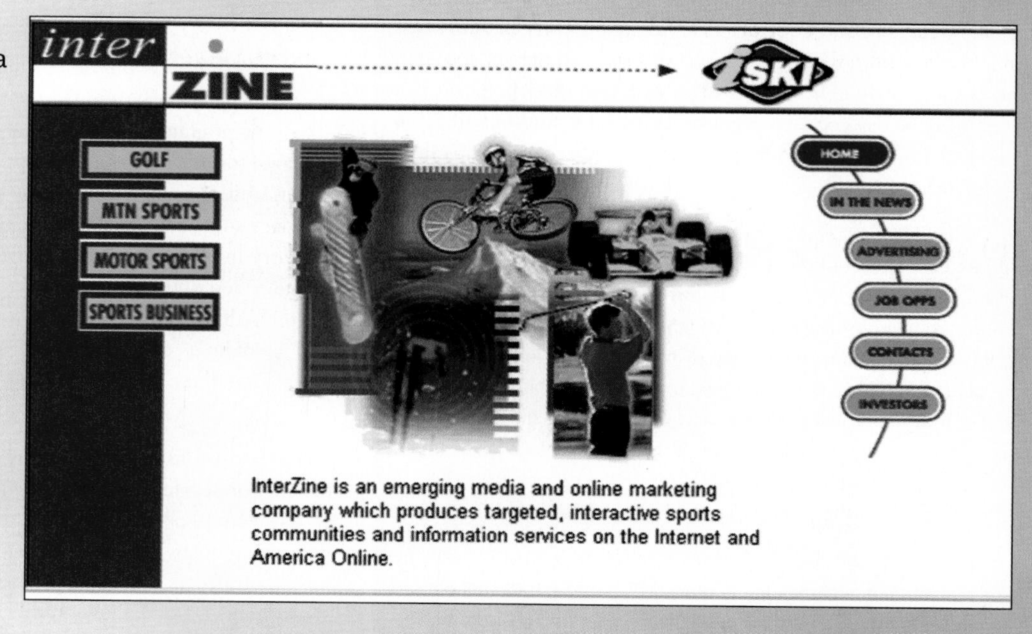

InterZine Productions, the sports on-line media company, was one of the first companies backed by the AOL Greenhouse initiative for entrepreneurs. *[Courtesy of Greenhouse Networks]*

InterZine Productions, the sports online media company, was one of the first companies backed by the program. Its popular sites include iGOLF, iSKI, and the Sports Business Daily. InterZine's products have attracted advertising support from over 100 companies including AT&T, Lexus, Taylor Made Golf, American Express, Microsoft, and Cadillac.

Greenhouse is now a full-fledged business unit of AOL, helping entrepreneurs develop Internet ventures using the company's online production support, marketing expertise, and equity funding. But it is seeking to move away from small-scale ideas and sites and allocate more funds to fewer, bigger projects. Meanwhile, Netscape and YAHOO! are looking to come out with new services in 12 defined categories to compete with AOL.

Questions

1. How many infopreneurial proposals can you generate for possible submission to these potential partners?

2. Pick the best idea(s) and determine how to proceed.

Sources: America Online; *PC Week,* December 5, 1994; *Business Week,* June 21, 1993; *Business Week,* September 14, 1992, "LightSpeed Zips to Greenhouse," *Hollywood Reporter,* March 10, 1997, p. 4+; and "America Online at the Crossroads," *Interactive Consumers,* March 1997, p. 1+.

Video Case

Managing new ventures: Investigate a new venture idea

Purpose

To introduce you to the basic procedures that entrepreneurs use to determine the viability of new product or service ideas.

Procedure

View the McGraw-Hill videotape that features the start-up story of the children's food company My Own Meals, Inc. Note in particular the five steps needed for managing new ventures: Problem Recognition, Information Search, Alternative Evaluation, Purchase Decision, and Postpurchase Behavior. Over the next two weeks develop a product or service idea and conduct the research necessary on each of the five steps to determine whether it is a viable business concept. Keep track of your findings in a log book, and be prepared to discuss what you have learned in class. Below is a guide for each step of your research:

1. *Problem recognition:* Identify problems that could be solved through the introduction of a new product or service. Think about ordinary problems in your day-to-day life that could be made easier if a product or service were available. Make a list of these ideas. Ask your friends how much they would be willing to pay for the product or service and list that next to the idea. Recall that, in the video, Mary Ann Jackson created My Own Meals, Inc., out of her recognition of the problem that there were no nutritious meals for children that could be served quickly from the microwave oven. Identify one idea that you intend to investigate further.

2. *Information search:* Decide whether it is feasible to bring your product or service idea to market. Several issues that should be addressed include the potential market for the product or service and the cost of each product or service unit. Identify resources you can use to find reasonable answers to these questions. Be aware that new start-up ventures often can't find certainty on some issues, but must make reasonable assumptions based on available data. Note how the video emphasizes the need for objective data as it discusses in detail the statistics about the percentage of homes with microwave ovens, the percentage of working mothers with school-age children, and the percentage of children who eat less-nutritious foods—such as McDonald's. Gather objective data about the potential market for your product or service idea.

3. *Alternative evaluation:* One of the major issues entrepreneurs must address is competition. Most products and services are able to be produced and delivered by many competitors, and it is essential for new-venture start-ups to know who their competitors are or, if there currently are none, who they are likely to be if the business succeeds. My Own Meals, Inc., created a new product category in which there were no existing competitors. However, as the video stated, the concept was quickly copied by some major food producers. Determine how your product or service will maintain its distinctiveness from existing or potential competition. Determine your advertising strategy.

4. *Purchase decision:* Identify several factors that will be important to consumers in making a purchase decision about your product or service. Note in the videotape how My Own Meal's shelf-stable packaging affects the purchase decision. Also note that the company essentially created a new product category and how that affects the purchase decision. Finally, be aware that some things beyond your control can affect the purchase decision.

For example, in the video, the grocer's decision about where to place My Own Meals on the shelves affects buyer behavior.

5. *Postpurchase behavior:* Customer satisfaction is the ultimate goal of any company. Without customers, there is no business. Therefore, all companies must be concerned about whether their customers are satisfied with the products or services they provide. With the information about your product or service that you have already developed, determine ways in which customer postpurchase behavior could be evaluated. Identify some key factors that should be evaluated, and also identify some tools or techniques that could be used to measure those factors.

Experiential Exercises

7.1 Take an entrepreneur to dinner

Objectives

1. To get to know what an entrepreneur does, how she or he got started, and what it took to succeed.
2. To interview a particular entrepreneur in depth about her or his career and experiences.
3. To acquire a feeling for whether you might find an entrepreneurial career rewarding.

Instructions

1. Identify an entrepreneur in your area you would like to interview.
2. Contact the person you have selected and make an appointment. Be sure to explain why you want the appointment and to give a realistic estimate of how much time you will need.
3. Identify specific questions you would like to have answered and the general areas about which you would like information. (See suggested interview below.) Using a combination of open-ended questions, such as general questions about how the entrepreneur got started, what happened next, and so forth, and closed-ended questions, such as specific questions about what his or her goals were, if he or she had to find partners, and so forth, will help to keep the interview focused and yet allow for unexpected comments and insights.
4. Conduct the interview. If *both* you and the person you are interviewing are comfortable, using a small tape recorder during the interview can be of great help to you later. Remember, too, that you most likely will learn more if you are an "interested listener."
5. Evaluate what you have learned. Write down the information you have gathered in some form that will be helpful to you later on. Be as specific as you can. Jotting down direct quotes is more effective than statements such as "highly motivated individual." And be sure to make a note of what you did not find out.
6. Write a thank-you note. This is more than a courtesy; it will also help the entrepreneur to remember you favorably should you want to follow up on the interview.

Suggested interview

Questions for Gathering Information

- *Would you tell me about yourself before you started your first venture?*

  Were your parents, relatives, or close friends entrepreneurial? How so?

  Did you have any other role models?

  What was your education/military experience? In hindsight, was it helpful? In what specific ways?

  What was your previous work experience? Was it helpful? What particular "chunks of experience" were especially valuable or irrelevant?

  In particular, did you have any sales or marketing experience? How important was it or a lack of it to starting your company?

- *How did you start your venture?*

  How did you spot the opportunity? How did it surface?

What were your goals? What were your lifestyle or other personal requirements? How did you fit these together?

How did you evaluate the opportunity in terms of the critical elements for success? The competition? The market?

Did you find or have partners? What kind of planning did you do? What kind of financing did you have?

Did you have a start-up business plan of any kind? Please tell me about it.

How much time did it take from conception to the first day of business? How many hours a day did you spend working on it?

How much capital did it take? How long did it take to reach a positive cash flow and break-even sales volume? If you did not have enough money at the time, what were some ways in which you "bootstrapped" the venture (i.e., bartering, borrowing, and the like). Tell me about the pressures and crises during that early survival period.

What outside help did you get? Did you have experienced advisors? Lawyers? Accountants? Tax experts? Patent experts? How did you develop these networks and how long did it take?

What was your family situation at the time?

What did you perceive to be your own strengths? Weaknesses?

What did you perceive to be the strengths of your venture? Weaknesses?

What was your most triumphant moment? Your worst moment?

Did you want to have partners or do it solo? Why?

- *Once you got going, then:*

What were the most difficult gaps to fill and problems to solve as you began to grow rapidly?

When you looked for key people as partners, advisors, or managers, were there any personal attributes or attitudes you were especially seeking because you knew they would fit with you and were important to success? How did you find them?

Are there any attributes among partners and advisors that you would definitely try to avoid?

Have things become more predictable? Or less?

Do you spend more/same/less time with your business now than in the early years?

Do you feel more managerial and less entrepreneurial now?

In terms of the future, do you plan to harvest? To maintain? To expand?

Do you plan ever to retire? Would you explain?

Have your goals changed? Have you met them?

Has your family situation changed?

Questions for Concluding (choose one)

- What do you consider your most valuable asset—the thing that enabled you to "make it"?
- If you had it to do over again, would you do it again, in the same way?
- Looking back, what do you feel are the most critical concepts, skills, attitudes, and know-how you needed to get your company started and grown to where it is today? What will be needed for the next five years? To what extent can any of these be learned?
- Some people say there is a lot of stress being an entrepreneur. What have you experienced? How would you say it compares with other "hot seat" jobs, such as the head of a big company or a partner in a large law, consulting, or accounting firm?
- What are the things that you find personally rewarding and satisfying as an entrepreneur? What have been the rewards, risks, and trade-offs?
- Who should try to be an entrepreneur? Can you give me any ideas there?
- What advice would you give an aspiring entrepreneur? Could you suggest the three most important "lessons" you have learned? How can I learn them while minimizing the tuition?

Source: Jeffry A. Timmons, *New Venture Creation,* 3rd ed. (Burr Ridge, IL: Richard D. Irwin, Inc., 1994), p. 33.

7.2 Starting a new business

Objectives

1. To introduce you to the complexities of going into business for yourself.

2. To provide hands-on experience in making new-business decisions.

Instructions

1. Your instructor will divide the class into teams and assign each team the task of investigating the start-up of one of the following businesses:
   a. Submarine sandwich shop
   b. Day care service
   c. Bookstore
   d. Gasoline service station
   e. Other

2. Each team should research the information necessary to complete the New-Business Start-Up Worksheet. The following agencies or organizations might be of assistance:
   a. Small Business Administration
   b. Local county/city administration agencies
   c. Local chamber of commerce
   d. Local small-business development corporation
   e. U.S. Department of Commerce
   f. Farmer's Home Administration
   g. Local realtors
   h. Local businesspeople in the same or a similar business
   i. Banks and S&Ls

3. Each team presents its findings to the class.

New-business start-up worksheet

1. *Product* ____________________

   What customer need will we satisfy? ____________________

   How can our product be unique? ____________________

2. *Customer* ____________________

   Who are our customers? What are their profiles? ____________________

   Where do they live/work/play? ____________________

   What are their buying habits? ____________________

   What are their needs? ____________________

3. *Competition* ____________________

   Who/where is the competition? ____________________

   What are their strengths and weaknesses? ____________________

   How might they respond to us? ____________________

4. *Suppliers* ____________________

   Who/where are our suppliers? ____________________

   What are their business practices? ____________________

   What relationships can we expect? ____________________

5. *Location* ____________________
   Where are our customers/competitors/suppliers? ____________________
   What are the location costs? ____________________
   What are the legal limitations to location? ____________________
6. *Physical Facilities/Equipment* ____________________
   Rent/own/build/refurbish facilities? ____________________
   Rent/lease/purchase equipment? ____________________
   Maintenance? ____________________
7. *Human Resources* ____________________
   Availability? ____________________
   Training? ____________________
   Costs? ____________________
8. *Legal/Regulatory Environment* ____________________
   Licenses/permits/certifications? ____________________
   Government agencies? ____________________
   Liability? ____________________
9. *Cultural/Social Environment* ____________________
   Cultural issues? ____________________
   Social issues? ____________________
10. *International Environment* ____________________
    International issues? ____________________
11. *Other* ____________________

Chapter Appendix

Information for entrepreneurs

If you are interested in starting or managing a small business, you have access to many sources of information.

The **Small Business Administration (SBA)** is an agency of the federal government charged with promoting the growth of small businesses. It provides financial, educational, and lobbying services. The SBA defines a small business as a business that has fewer than 500 employees or lacks dominant market power.

The SBA's most visible services are its direct loans and loan guarantees. Under the direct loan program, the SBA acts as a lender of last resort to small businesses. In recent years, these loans generally have been used for special target populations. Under the loan guarantee program, the SBA protects the lender in the event the loan holder defaults. Each loan program is designed to improve the environment for small business by expanding the sources of capital. Many states offer similar lending programs to encourage investment in certain industries or geographic areas.

The SBA sponsors and delivers training programs and provides a wide range of booklets and brochures on small-business management. Many SBA training programs are delivered through community colleges and universities. Some of these programs, such as the Small Business Institute and Small Business Development Centers, involve students and faculty in special consulting projects designed to help specific clients. In addition to its college-based programs, the SBA uses SCORE (Service Corps of Retired Executives) to provide services for struggling new businesses. Most of these services are free; for others, a small fee is charged.

Several publications are produced specifically for the entrepreneurial audience. *Inc.* publishes articles about the management problems of growing businesses. *Venture Capital Journal* caters to entrepreneurs and the venture capital industry at large. Pratt's *Guide to Venture Capital* is a "must-have" for any entrepreneur; it covers not only the how-to's of starting a business and obtaining venture capital but also profiles every major venture capital organization in the country.

Still other sources of help are available. Private groups, universities, and government agencies supply technical and managerial assistance to entrepreneurs. For example, several organizations in various parts of the country offer the services of a board of directors for an evening. One such program, the MIT Forum, is offered by volunteers in cities nationwide. At each meeting of the Forum, a business presents its plan to an audience and preselected panelists provide feedback on the plan. Then the audience reacts to both the plan and the panelists. Most presenters find they obtain more advice than they could purchase on the open market.

In addition, several major accounting firms have groups specifically geared to the needs of smaller, emerging companies. Most publish guides to new-business formation and management as a service to their current and prospective clientele. These companies can provide professional consulting and financial services and also make critical introductions within the financial community. One screened introduction can save months of effort and thousands of dollars in lost opportunities.

Small-business ownership or management can provide a challenging and rewarding career. The interested student should start looking in the local community for sources of ideas and assistance. Planning can't begin too soon! ●

Integrating Case

University Medical Center

Stan Ferguson, executive director of University Medical Center (UMC), sat back from his report-cluttered desk and contemplated the current and future competitive environment of his institution. Recently he had been hired to formulate and implement a strategic plan that would guide UMC through the turbulent conditions facing the health care industry in the 1990s.

Industry Overview

As the chief officer of a large, not-for-profit teaching and research hospital, Ferguson was aware of the many complex changes affecting the health care industry. Federal and state governments were trying to cap health care spending. Hospitals were hit with $55 billion in proposed cuts in federal health programs from 1986 to 1990, after absorbing $40 billion in cuts over the previous five years. Private health insurers and employers also were clamping down, forcing health care providers to compete with one another and to seek new ways to cut costs and deliver their services.

As government and private insurance spending growth slowed, many hospitals were losing business. Nonessential surgery often was delayed, and minor procedures were performed in doctors' offices and outpatient clinics. Patients often left the hospital sooner to stay under the medicare reimbursement ceiling. Hospital occupancy rates fell from 75 percent in 1980 to 65 percent in 1985 and below 60 percent by 1990. Many experts argued that the U.S. hospital industry simply suffered from excess capacity, with at least 25 percent too many beds.

Many not-for-profit hospitals were experiencing the worst problems. Dozens were being purchased at bargain prices by for-profit hospital chains such as Hospital Corporation of America (HCA) and Humana. Many industry observers believed the for-profit hospitals were likely to be the strongest survivors of the industry shakeout. Traditionally, these hospitals had kept their costs low. However, even the for-profit hospitals were feeling the pressure.

Competitive pressure came not only from the for-profit hospitals but from health maintenance organizations (HMOs) and a variety of outpatient and nursing facilities. For a single fee paid in advance, usually by an employer or an insurance company, an HMO contracts to provide its members with complete health care, from routine physical exams to major surgery. Employers like HMOs and often encourage their workers to join.

The emphasis on HMOs and other forms of group practice was also changing traditional referral patterns. Not only were hospital admissions dropping, but fewer were coming through primary care physicians. In an effort to "lock up" new referral patterns, hospital management companies and those not-for-profits that could afford it were starting or buying HMOs, getting into the health insurance business, and building freestanding emergency and surgical centers (often called "docs-in-a-box"). However, the not-for-profit hospital often operates at a disadvantage in its efforts to open an HMO or similar facility. The initial costs are high, and the competition, particularly in certain areas, can be frantic.

Some hospitals have begun to specialize to a greater degree, emphasizing profitable services that give them a distinctive competence in the marketplace. For example, some hospitals stress psychiatric care and alcohol and drug treatment programs. This area of growth is supported by government, consumer, church, and law enforcement groups, not to mention all professional sports and entertainment. Several hospitals around the country have provided unique services tailored to the needs and preferences of women. Many of these programs have been successful.

Alternatively, because many patients are leaving the hospital sooner, some health care institutions were diversifying into nursing homes and home health care programs. The changing demographics in the aging of America favor nursing homes. One trend was for

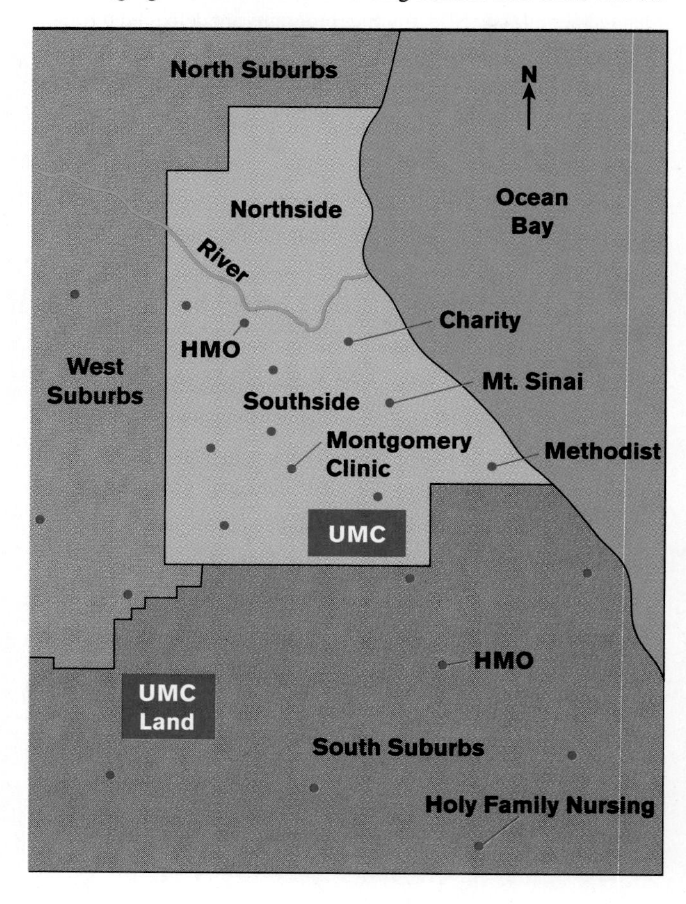

greater luxury in nursing homes, thus giving retirees and established patients with adequate incomes an attractive option over either hospital or home care. Providing home health care through the delivery of equipment, supplies, and services was another alternative, but this diversification alternative, like others, entailed high start-up costs.

Hospital supply companies, which sell sutures, solutions, and syringes to hospitals, were feeling the pressure as well. In response, suppliers have diversified into other businesses, often competing directly with hospitals, and have engaged in mergers to strengthen their competitive positions. Many pharmaceutical companies also faced potential problems as hospitals turned away from high-priced brand name drugs and toward generic drugs to cut costs. Also, manufacturers of expensive diagnostic equipment were feeling the squeeze.

Finally, physicians, the ultimate supplier of health care services, were beginning to feel the effects of the new environment. Large physician surpluses arose by 1990. This situation encouraged the formation of large group practices and clinics, which created additional competition for hospitals. Ironically, the individuals who controlled hospital usage, the physicians, became serious competitors. Hospitals sought to improve this relationship by constructing medical office buildings adjacent to hospitals and engaging in a variety of joint ventures (e.g., surgery and radiology centers) with physicians.

Despite all these economic, regulatory, and competitive shocks, Stan Ferguson knew that the health care system remained under attack. Critics claimed that hospitals still were not addressing the problem. Although national health expenditures were declining in current dollars, national health spending in real terms (dollars deflated by the consumer price index) had accelerated since 1980. Others suggested hospitals were covering their inefficiency and overcapacity with slick marketing programs designed to attract customers. Ferguson realized that the competitive pressures from both outside and within the industry were likely to worsen before they improved.

UMC Location, Background, and Facilities

UMC was located on the southern edge of a major city on the East Coast (see the map). The city was divided into Northside and Southside by a major river, which also divided the city's downtown area. The primary service area for UMC was the Southside and the suburbs located to the south and west of the city. The Southside included most of the city's major industrial plants, two major universities, several high-crime areas, and many of the city's oldest and poorest neighborhoods. The western suburbs consisted primarily of moderate-income families and the affluent southern suburbs of single professionals and high-income families. The secondary service area included the Northside and the northern suburbs.

UMC was founded in 1920 by a teaching hospital affiliated with the medical and nursing schools of a well-respected private university. Since that time, UMC had grown in both size and prestige and often was rated one of the better health care facilities in the country. Today UMC consists of six interconnected buildings with a variety of services and a total of 933 beds.

UMC was not affiliated with an HMO or nursing home, and it did not operate any satellite units or nursing facilities. It was involved in a home health care program in a limited way. Some of the large employers and insurance companies in the area had discussed the possibility of developing a prepaid program, but these talks were still in the planning stages. UMC also owned an undeveloped, 10-acre tract of land in the southern suburbs, and several ideas had been proposed for its use. Ferguson realized that UMC should consider some of the options more seriously in the near future.

UMC Patient Care

Approximately 85 percent of all patients admitted came from the primary service area, a slight increase over the past few years. The remaining 15 percent were admitted to take advantage of services not available in other locations. Of all patients admitted, 7 percent of private patients came from the Southside, 30 percent from the western suburbs, and 47 percent from the southern suburbs. The remaining private patients came from the secondary service area. The Southside contributed 79 percent of the staff patients, and 16 percent of the staff patients came from the western and southern suburbs. Ninety-eight percent of the ambulatory care clinic patients and emergency ward patients came from the primary service area. Eighty-seven percent of the clinic patients and 60 percent of the emergency ward patients came from the Southside.

The number of beds had not changed in the past 10 years, but inpatient activity had changed dramatically over the last year. The number of beds devoted to staff patients had increased, although overall admissions to the institution were down slightly. Pediatric patients were holding steady, medicine and surgery patients were down slightly, but serious drops in volume were reported for ob-gyn patients. Newborn inpatient activity had declined 28 percent in the past four years. Psychiatric inpatient activity was up 24 percent, partially because of a new substance abuse program. Overall, private inpatient days declined 9 percent, and staff inpatient days were down 3 percent. The average length of stay for all patients declined sharply, causing a lower occupancy rate. Overall, occupancy at UMC had declined from 74 percent to 69 percent.

Visits to the emergency ward and ambulatory care clinic were increasing, but at a decreasing rate. These trends were attributed to the Southside community's greater use of HMOs and other freestanding clinics. Although UMC continued to be the largest provider of ambulatory care in its primary service area, Ferguson was concerned that this trend was responsible for some recent declines in inpatient admissions and would threaten the institution's ability to attract patients for its inpatient care and related teaching programs. The ambulatory care clinic was the primary source of staff inpatients, followed by the emergency ward.

UMC Medical Staff, Personnel, and Finances

The full-time medical staff had increased from 210 to 240 physicians (14 percent) in the past five years, while the part-time staff had increased from 307 to 379 physicians (23 percent). However, the staff had lost several of its better-known and respected physicians to other hospitals and a number of the younger staff to HMOs and other facilities. UMC relied heavily on a group of older, full-time physicians for a disproportionate share of private patient admissions. Obviously, this concerned Ferguson.

The number of other personnel employed by the hospital had held steady, including the nursing staff. The only real increases had been in the ambulatory care clinic and the emergency ward. Unemployment in the area had made recruiting unskilled employees to cover normal turnover relatively easy. A recruitment program was used to identify and attract qualified nurses, an essential activity given the nationwide shortage.

The changes confronted by UMC and the rest of the health care industry had an adverse impact on the financial picture of the institution. Although total income had increased from $162 million to approximately $169 million during the last five years, total expenses had increased from $166 million to $172 million. Endowment income, which stood at about $2 million, failed to cover the deficit.

Service Area Characteristics

Demographic data contained a number of trends that, if continued, would have a significant impact on the volume and types of demand for UMC patient care programs. The population of the Southside had declined 5 percent over the past five years to 496,000, a trend that could reduce the number of patients using the clinic and the emergency ward. This trend eventually could have serious implications for the demand for staff services, because the residents of the Southside were older, poorer, and less healthy. On the other hand, the population of the more affluent southern suburbs had increased 15 percent over the past five years to 250,000 and that of the western suburbs had increased approximately 7 percent to 300,000.

Competition

The UMC service area map indicates the location of other health care facilities in UMC's service area. Competition within the UMC service area had increased dramatically. Several area hospitals had constructed major additions in the past five years, thereby increasing the number of inpatient beds for the service area. Given the decline in occupancy rates for most hospitals, the entire region suffered from excess capacity. Despite UMC's history of drawing patients from the suburbs, many health care experts believed its competitive position in the suburbs was under serious attack. Suburban hospitals were newer, more convenient, and attracting both new physicians and more affluent patients.

The area was experiencing a birthrate decline of 20 percent. This decline was lower than the drop in demand for obstetric services at UMC, indicating a loss of market share. Fewer suburban women were using UMC. The demand for ambulatory care had increased greatly within the service area, although this increase was being met by several alternative channels of health care delivery. Three hospitals in the suburbs had opened outpatient clinics, all with surgical units. Two of these clinics were operating in the western suburbs and one in the southern suburbs. A major HMO in the southern suburbs was attracting an increasing number of patients, particularly among younger singles and families. A variety of freestanding primary care clinics had opened throughout the area, although most did not have a formal affiliation with a hospital.

Among the Southside hospitals, UMC was the second largest. Mt. Sinai had slightly over 1,000 beds. With the exception of the Montgomery Clinic, these hospitals were experiencing the same problem as UMC, but most were in much worse financial condition. A relatively large, although not very successful HMO operated in the center of the city, and several freestanding clinics had opened in different neighborhoods.

Charity Hospital, perhaps the most aggressive hospital in the Southside, was planning an HMO facility. Montgomery Clinic was considered a hospital for the "rich and famous," specializing primarily in expensive and sophisticated procedures. This hospital had no financial problems and was considered among the five best hospitals in the country (if not the world). However, it had no outpatient or emergency facilities, and it devoted limited space to obstetrics and pediatrics.

Methodist Hospital, located near the southeastern boundary of the Southside, represented a special problem. Three years ago, Methodist had undertaken an expansion and renovation program that placed a tremendous strain on the financial condition of the hospital. Although the hospital had an excellent physical plant, it suffered from management problems, a difficult union, and a restless medical staff. Ferguson knew that the for-profit hospital management companies considered Methodist an attractive target, and one was beginning negotiations for a management contract or purchase.

Two nursing care facilities operated in the Southside. Three nursing homes were located in the suburbs, and a fourth, owned by a national chain, was a possibility. All essentially were filled, but the cost and quality of care varied greatly. Only one nursing home—Holy Family, in the extreme southern suburbs—was considered well above average in quality of care. It was also more expensive than the others, but it had a long waiting list.

The Future

Ferguson knew that UMC was in a difficult position, but he now had a greater appreciation for some of the essential competitive issues facing the institution. He was anxious to develop a strategic plan for the institution. Once he fully understood the sources of competitive pressure, he could develop a coherent and integrated strategy with which to respond.

Questions

1. Using Porter's competitive forces model (described in Chapter 4), conduct an analysis of the health care industry.

2. Based on your analysis of the health care industry, what strategies would you recommend for UMC? How would you recommend that UMC gain a competitive advantage in its market?

3. What are the important social and political issues confronting UMC? What should UMC do to deal with these issues?

Case Incidents

Whistle-blowing

Albert Higgenbotham, a 48-year-old middle manager for United Fibers, Inc., discovered that the company's owners were cheating the government out of several thousand dollars in taxes annually. Albert believed he had an obligation to do something about the situation, but he also had a sense of loyalty to the firm and to his superiors. He also desired to keep his job. Thus far, Albert had not done anything except worry.

Needing to talk with someone helpful and "safe," Albert thought of his brother, Richard, who worked at the same company as a quality assurance manager. One Tuesday after work, Albert drove over to his brother's house and accepted a seat on the patio and a beer. Wanting to ease into the discussion of his concerns, Albert mentioned an item printed in that day's newspaper entitled "Pentagon Whistle-Blower Wins Promotion and Legal Fees." Albert had read the article carefully and had learned that years earlier, whistle-blower Ernest Fitzgerald had blown the whistle on a $2 billion cost overun on the giant C-5A military transport plane project. Because of his action, Fitzgerald was fired from the Air Force. The brothers exchanged views and agreed that it had taken great personal courage for Fitzgerald to blow the whistle, be ousted from his job, then struggle through the long and expensive battle to obtain a reinstatement order from the Civil Service Commission and back pay, and win a legal suit for recovery of $200,000 in legal costs he had sustained. The brothers agreed that volunteering for those experiences bordered on the heroic. They speculated that Fitzgerald had expected better treatment than he received.

While trying to work up to presenting his problem to Richard, Albert referred to several other examples of ethical puzzles and whistle-blowing in business organizations he had read about. He mentioned the B. F. Goodrich Company employee who allegedly was pressured by superiors to misrepresent test results on a new brake designed for military planes. Albert also recalled a senior design engineer for Ford Motor Company who, after objecting to the hazardous design features of the Ford Pinto's gas tank and windshield, was demoted and terminated and then sued the company. After relating these examples of conflict between employees' personal values and company goals and practices, Albert shifted the conversation to his ethical problem, described it fully to Richard, and asked for his brother's thoughts.

Richard responded by describing his own ethical predicament to a dismayed Albert:

Our company has been selling defective parachute cord to the federal government for the past six months. When my chief quality control inspector first discovered the parachute cord flaws and informed me, I immediately informed my superior. He suggested that my data must be erroneous and instructed me to run the tests again. I did. The results of the second round of tests were similar to the earlier ones. Learning the results, my superior told me that the statistical incidence of cord failure was acceptable to our company, that the parachute cord we were selling to the government was being stockpiled anyway, and that it probably would never be used. He suggested that I not worry unnecessarily. I have continued to worry a lot. It looks like you and I are in the same boat, brother. Do you think we should blow the whistle? If we do blow the whistle, what will be the consequences? What should we do?

Albert had no ready answers to Richard's questions. Indeed, Albert had come expecting to ask similar questions, and he was dismayed to find Richard with similar problems. Albert felt pulled in three directions. First were his personal values, his own interests, and his sense of professional integrity. Second was a sense of loyalty to the company and to its owners. Third was a moral obligation to prevent serious injuries and injustice to the public. The pressures of these unresolved forces tugging at him were beginning to make Albert's stomach ache.

At work, Albert had discreetly inquired about company policy regarding actions an employee should take in the situation he and Richard were in. No such policy existed. Albert needed to decide about blowing the whistle. Also, he needed a list of prudent guiding steps he could take that might make it unnecessary to blow the whistle. Finally, before acting he needed a comparison of desirable and undesirable consequences likely to be generated by his whistle-blowing.

It wasn't easy to know the right thing to do, nor was it easy to know if it was worth doing or not. Albert did know that he and his brother needed relief from the uncertainty and indecision.

Source: J. Champion and J. James, *Critical Incidents in Management: Decision and Policy Issues,* 6th ed. (Homewood, IL: Richard D. Irwin, 1989). ●

Part Three

Organizing and Staffing

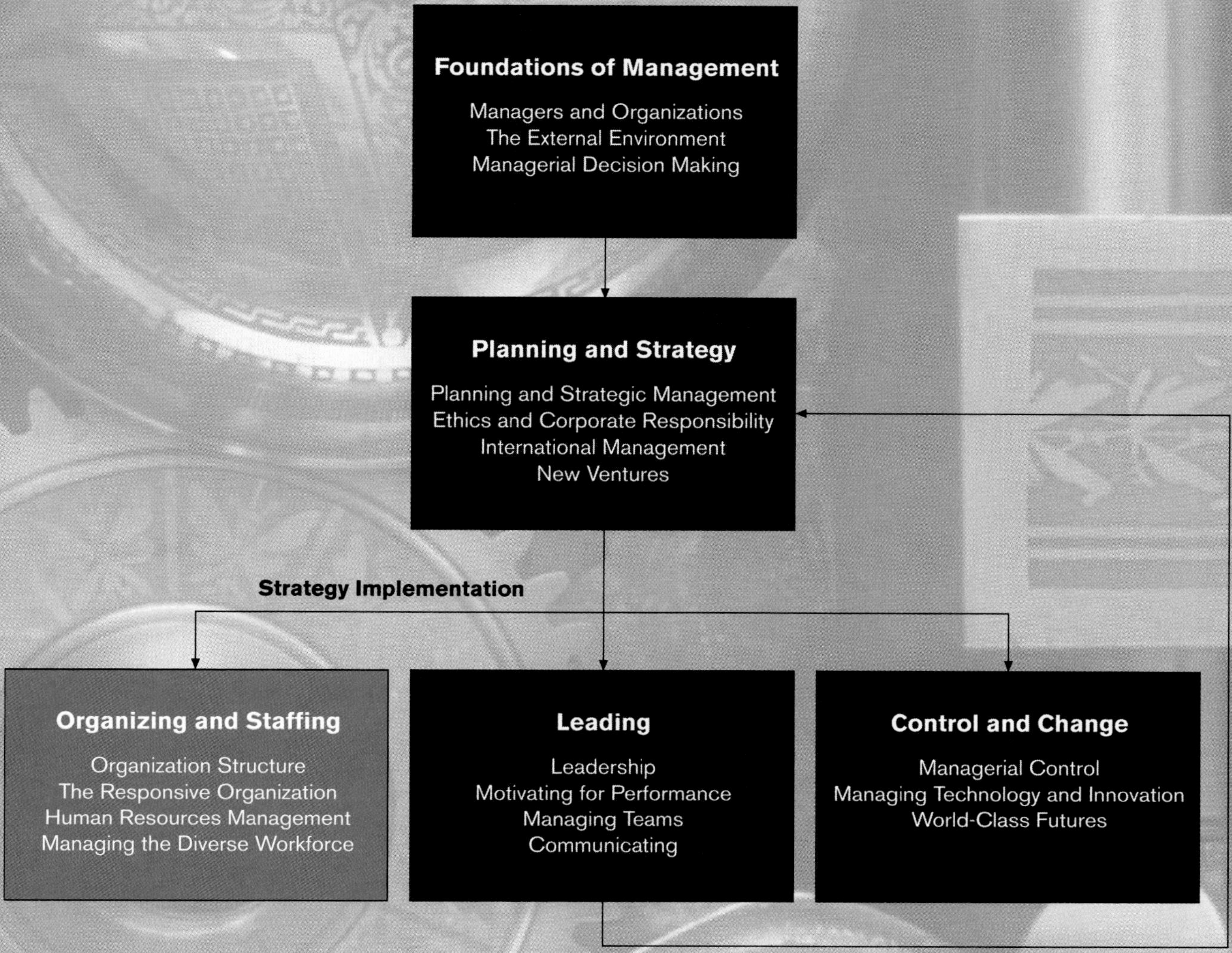

Foundations of Management

Managers and Organizations
The External Environment
Managerial Decision Making

Planning and Strategy

Planning and Strategic Management
Ethics and Corporate Responsibility
International Management
New Ventures

Strategy Implementation

Organizing and Staffing

Organization Structure
The Responsive Organization
Human Resources Management
Managing the Diverse Workforce

Leading

Leadership
Motivating for Performance
Managing Teams
Communicating

Control and Change

Managerial Control
Managing Technology and Innovation
World-Class Futures

Now that you know about planning and strategy, the remaining three parts correspond to the other three functions of management: organizing, leading, and controlling. Parts III, IV, and V discuss issues pertaining to *implementing* strategic plans. In Part III, we describe how to organize and staff for maximum effectiveness. Chapter 8 introduces you to different organization structures and explains how to group and delegate tasks. Chapter 9 builds on those basic concepts by describing more complex organization designs. This chapter discusses how firms can adapt quickly to rapidly changing environments and how "corporate America" is restructuring. Chapter 10 addresses the management of human resources. Its focus is on staffing the firm with capable employees and the issues surrounding employee reward systems. Finally, Chapter 11 discusses the challenge of managing today's workforce, one composed of diverse groups of people. Chapters 12 and 13 set the stage for Part IV, which further elaborates on how to manage people.

Chapter Eight

Organization Structure

Take my assets—but leave me my organization and in five years I'll have it all back.

—*Alfred P. Sloan, Jr.*

Chapter Outline

Learning Objectives

After studying Chapter 8, you will know:

1. How differentiation and integration influence your organization's structure.
2. How authority operates.
3. The roles of the board of directors and the chief executive officer.
4. How span of control affects structure and managerial effectiveness.
5. How to delegate work effectively.
6. The difference between centralized and decentralized organizations.
7. How to allocate jobs to work units.
8. How to manage the unique challenges of the matrix organization.
9. The nature of important integrative mechanisms.

Setting the Stage

Struggling with Structure

It's not always easy to tell how companies are organized. Especially the big ones are truly complex beasts. And just when you think you understand things, the companies change their structures for reasons that aren't always clear to outsiders. Almost daily we can find examples of well-known companies that are tweaking—or maybe overhauling—their organizations. Consider just a few different examples:

- Microsoft has been reorganizing to take advantage of the Internet. After resisting the idea for some time, Bill Gates recently created a new division in Microsoft completely devoted to the Internet. The new division, which will be responsible for Microsoft's Explorer Internet browser, works in conjunction with two other units: one focused on consumers and one focused on business systems and desktops. Gates believes that the new structure will help the company focus on key opportunities that take its Windows business forward while becoming a more dominant player on the Internet.
- Ford Motors, meanwhile, has been trying to find the right structure for managing its different automotive products. In 1996, Ford created five management teams it referred to rather creatively as the "youthful," "family," "sporting," "expressive," and "tough" brand groups. The monikers didn't work out very well and in 1997 the company scrapped the descriptive labels and reorganized around three main brand groups: the car group, the multipurpose-vehicle group (sport utility vehicles), and the truck group. A different manager was put in charge of each of the groups.
- Royal Dutch/Shell, the Anglo-Dutch oil and chemicals giant, recently put in place a newly reorganized structure that abolishes its former complex matrix of regional, functional, and business-sector organization. In its place, the company has made things simpler by establishing just four overall global businesses: exploration and production, oil products, gas and coal, and chemicals. Each of these businesses, in turn, guides a number of operating companies.

Bill Gates has created a new vision at Microsoft completely devoted to its Internet Explorer. *[Reuters/Clay McLachlan/Archive Photos]*

- Sears has been trying to change its structure to push more decisions down to individual stores. Instead of making key decisions at the very top of the organization, Sears's CEO, Arthur C. Martinez, has tried over the past few years to give more autonomy to local managers so that they can provide better customer service. This a very different approach to organizing for Sears, and one that has had both pluses and minuses.
- Finally, recall the Boeing and McDonnell Douglas merger from Chapter 2? The two companies have been working tirelessly to reorganize operations to become the world's largest aerospace company. Phil Condit, chairman and CEO of Boeing, has promised that there will be very few layoffs, but the combined organization has 220,000 employees. As a consequence, the top management team has been working to restructure business units to "blend" McDonnell Douglas into the rest of the company.

Sources: Richard Tedesco, "Microsoft Reorganizes, Targets Internet Business," Broadcasting & Cable *126, no. 29 (February 26, 1996), p. 53; Mary Connelly, "Ford Division Revamps Brand Structure, Adds Managers,"* Advertising Age, *July 28,*

1997, p. 2; Jennifer Seinhauer, "Time to Call a Sears Repairman: A Turnaround Is Sidetracked by Its Own Oversell," New York Times, *January 15, 1997, pp. D1, D3; Paul Proctor, "Merged Boeing Details New Corporate Structure,"* Aviation Week & Space Technology *147 no. 6 (August 11, 1997), pp. 31–33; Patricia L. Layman, "Shell Reorganizes to Better Focus Its Portfolio on Global Markets,"* Chemical and Engineering News *74, no. 31 (July 29, 1996), pp. 25–28.*

Each of these different approaches to organizing has different strengths and weaknesses. But truthfully, the examples in "Setting the Stage" probably don't provide enough information to help you understand why these organizations have done what they did, or to decide which approach is best. Instead, they are meant to highlight a few important issues that we want to cover in this chapter about how organizations are structured. These issues may say a lot about your own company or the one for which you may work some day. They also may influence in part how satisfied and successful you will be there.

In this chapter, we focus on the vertical and horizontal dimensions of organization structure. We begin this chapter by covering basic principles of *differentiation* and *integration.* Next, we discuss the vertical structure, which includes issues of *authority,* hierarchy, delegation, and decentralization. We continue on to describe the horizontal structure which includes functional, divisional, and matrix forms. Finally, we illustrate the ways that organizations can integrate their structures: coordination by standardization, coordination by plan, and coordination by mutual adjustment.

In the next chapter, we continue on with the topic organization structure, but take a different perspective. In that chapter we will focus on the flexibility and responsiveness of an organization; that is, how capable it is of changing its form and adapting to strategy, technology, the environment, and so on.

Fundamentals of organizing

organization chart The reporting structure and division of labor in an organization.

To get going, let's start simple. We often begin to describe a firm's structure by looking at its organization chart. The **organization chart** depicts the positions in the firm and how they are arranged. The chart provides a picture of the reporting structure (who reports to whom) and the various activities that are carried out by different individuals. Most companies have official organization charts drawn up to give people this information.

Figure 8.1 shows the traditional organization chart. Note the various kinds of information that are conveyed in a very simple way:[1]

1. The boxes represent different work.
2. The titles in the boxes show the work performed by each unit.
3. Reporting and authority relationships are indicated by solid lines showing superior–subordinate connections.
4. Levels of management are indicated by the number of horizontal layers in the chart. All persons or units that are of the same rank and report to the same person are on one level.

differentiation An aspect of the organization's internal environment created by job specialization and the division of labor.

Although the organization chart presents some clearly important structural features, there are other design issues related to structure that—while not so obvious—are no less important. Two fundamental concepts around which organizations are structured are differentiation and integration. **Differentiation** means that the organization is comprised of

figure 8.1
A conventional organizational chart

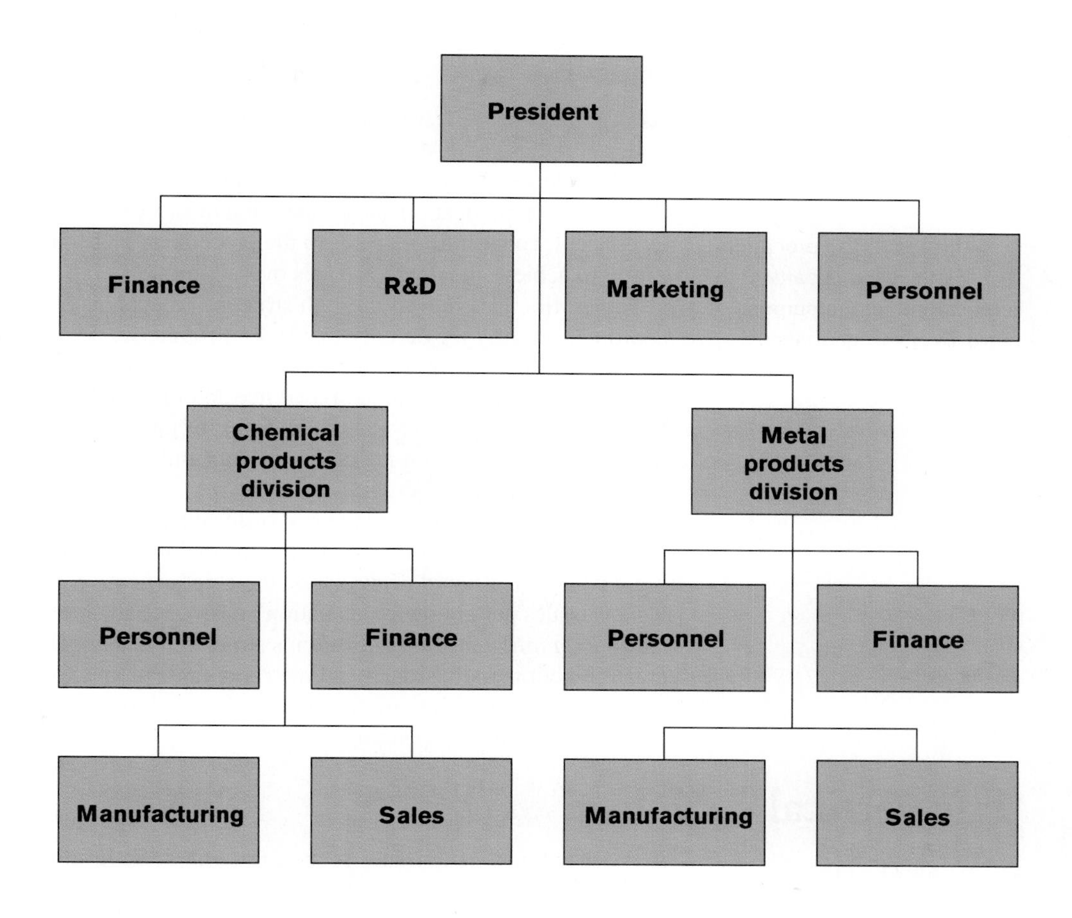

many different units that work on different kinds of tasks, using different skills and work methods. **Integration,** on the other hand, means that these differentiated units are put back together so that work is coordinated into an overall product.

integration The degree to which differentiated work units work together and coordinate their efforts.

Differentiation

Several related concepts underlie the idea of structural differentiation. For example, differentiation is created through division of labor and job specialization. **Division of labor** means that the work of the organization is subdivided into smaller tasks. Various individuals and units throughout the organization perform different tasks.[2] **Specialization,** in turn, refers to the fact that different people or groups often perform specific parts of the entire task. The two concepts are, of course, closely related. Secretaries and accountants specialize in, and perform, different jobs; similarly, marketing, finance, and human resources tasks are divided among those respective departments. The numerous tasks that must be carried out in an organization make specialization and division of labor necessities. Otherwise the complexity of the overall work of the organization would be too much for any individual.

division of labor The assignment of different tasks to different people or groups.

specialization A process in which different individuals and units perform different tasks.

Differentiation is high when there are many subunits and many kinds of specialists who think differently. Harvard professors Lawrence and Lorsch found that organizations in complex, dynamic environments (plastics firms, in their study) developed a high degree of differentiation in order to cope with the complex challenges. Companies in simple, stable environments (container companies) had low levels of differentiation. Companies in intermediate environments (food companies) had intermediate differentiation.[3]

Integration

As organizations differentiate their structures, managers must simultaneously consider issues of integration. All the specialized tasks in an organization cannot be performed completely independently. Because the different units are part of the larger organization, some degree of communication and cooperation must exist among them. Integration and its related concept, **coordination,** refer to the procedures that link the various parts of the organization to achieve the organization's overall mission.

coordination The procedures that link the various parts of the organization for the purpose of achieving the organization's overall mission.

Integration is achieved through structural mechanisms that enhance collaboration and coordination. Any job activity that links different work units performs an integrative function. Remember, the more highly differentiated your firm, the greater the need for integration among the different units. Lawrence and Lorsch found that highly differentiated firms were successful if they also had high levels of integration. Organizations are more likely to fail if they exist in complex environments and are highly differentiated, but fail to adequately integrate their activities.[4]

These concepts permeate the rest of the chapter. First we will discuss *vertical differentiation* within organization structure. This includes issues pertaining to authority within an organization, the board of directors, the chief executive officer, and hierarchical levels, as well as issues pertaining to delegation and decentralization. Next, we will discuss *horizontal differentiation* in an organization's structure including issues of departmentalization that create functional, divisional, and matrix organizations. Finally, we will discuss issues pertaining to structural integration including coordination, organizational roles, interdependence, and boundary spanning.

The vertical structure

In order to understand issues such as reporting relationships, authority, responsibility, and the like, we need to begin with the vertical dimension of a firm's structure.

Authority in organizations

Fundamental to the functioning of every organization is **authority**: the legitimate right to make decisions and to tell other people what to do. For example, a boss has the authority to give an order to a subordinate.

authority The legitimate right to make decisions and to tell other people what to do.

Authority resides in *positions* rather than in people. Thus, the job of vice president of a particular division has authority over that division, regardless of how many people come and go in that position and who presently holds it.

Authority resides in *positions* rather than people.
[Matthew Borkoski/Folio]

In private business enterprises, the owners have ultimate authority. In most small, simply structured companies, the owner also acts as manager. Sometimes the owner hires another person to manage the business and its employees. The owner gives this manager some authority to oversee the operations, but the manager is accountable to—that is, reports and defers to—the owner. Thus, the owner still has the ultimate authority.

Traditionally authority has been the primary means of running an organization. An order that a boss gives to a lower-level employee is usually carried out. As this occurs throughout the organization day after day, the organization can move forward toward achieving its goals.[5]

We will discuss the authority structure of organizations from the top down, beginning with the board of directors.

The board of directors. In corporations, the owners are the stockholders. But because there are numerous stockholders, and these individuals generally lack timely information, few are directly involved in managing the organization. Stockholders elect a board of directors to oversee the organization.The board, led by the chair, makes major decisions affecting the organization, subject to corporate charter and bylaw provisions. Boards perform at least three major sets of duties: (1) selecting, assessing, rewarding, and perhaps replacing the CEO; (2) determining the firm's strategic direction and reviewing financial performance; and (3) assuring ethical, socially responsible, and legal conduct.[6]

Some top executives are likely to sit on the board (they are called *inside directors*). Outside members of the board tend to be executives at other companies. The trend in recent years has been toward reducing the number of insiders and increasing the number of outsiders. Today, most companies have a majority of outside directors. Boards made up of strong, independent outsiders are more likely to provide different information and perspectives and to prevent big mistakes. Table 8.1 shows the results of a recent *Business Week* poll of the best and worst boards. Successful boards tend to be those that are active, critical participants in determining company strategies. Campbell Soup's board, for example, took control over selecting a new CEO and routinely conducts performance evaluations on board members to make certain they are active contributors.[7]

The chief executive officer. The authority officially vested in the board of directors is assigned to a chief executive officer, who occupies the top of the organizational pyramid. The chief executive is personally accountable to the board and to the owners for the organization's performance.

It is estimated that in 15 percent of Fortune 500 corporations, one person holds all three positions of CEO, chair of the board of directors, and president.[8] More commonly, however, one person holds two of those positions, with the CEO serving also as either the chair of the board or the president of the organization. When the CEO is president, the chair may be honorary and may do little more than conduct meetings. In other cases, the chair may be the CEO and the president is second in command.

The top management team. Increasingly, CEOs share their authority with other key members of the top management team. Top management teams are typically comprised of the CEO, president, chief operating officer, chief financial officer, and other key executives. Rather than make critical decisions on their own, CEOs at companies such as Shell, Honeywell, and Merck regularly meet with their top management teams to make decisions as a unit.[9]

Hierarchical levels

In Chapter 1, we discussed the three broad levels of the organizational pyramid, commonly called the **hierarchy.** The CEO occupies the top position and is the senior member of top management. The top managerial level also includes presidents and vice presidents.

hierarchy The authority levels of the organizational pyramid.

table 8.1
The best and the worst boards of directors

Business Week rank	Details
The best boards of directors	
1. Campbell Soup	Board involvement in recent CEO change rewrites the book on how to do it.
2. General Electric	Won most votes in poll for best board; outside directors own lots of GE stock.
3. Compaq Computer	Model board with nonexecutive chair has delivered big results for investors.
4. Microsoft	Small board wins praise from investors who don't worry about CEO succession.
5. IBM	Turnaround by board-recruited CEO keeps major shareholders happy.
6. Chrysler	Leader in many governance practices, though many directors on too many boards.
7. General Motors	Among first to publish guidelines; only weakness: overextended directors.
8. Intel	Board gains high marks from investors; directors own lots of stock.
9. Colgate Palmolive	All directors own significant stock; only one insider on board: the CEO.
10. Texas Instruments	Pays half of retainer in stock; outsiders average more than $400K of stock.
***Business Week* rank**	**Details**
The worst boards of directors	
1. Disney	Investors decry board for conflicts; many directors own little if any stock.
2. AT&T	Investors scorn board for failing to control succession, not ousting CEO.
3. H. J. Heinz	Longtime CEO dominates insider-filled board; resists investor call for change.
4. Archer Daniels Midland	Board changes fail to satisfy investors, who say directors lack independence.
5. Dow Jones	Investors disenchanted with performance; weakest attendance record of any board.
6. Dillard's	Board loaded with insiders; lack an outsider with retail expertise or CEO.
7. Rollins International	Board dominated by family members and insiders; lacks nominating panel.
8. Occidental Petroleum	Investors outraged over $95 million payout to CEO by cozy, aging board.
9. Ogden	Board has three consultants and a lawyer who do business with company.
10. Maxxam	Tiny board with little business experience dominated by CEO.

Source: John A. Byrne, Ronald Grover, and Richard A. Melcher, "The Best and Worst Boards," *Business Week,* December 8, 1997, pp. 90–98. Reprinted by special permission.

These are the strategic managers in charge of the entire organization. The second broad level is middle management. At this level, managers are in charge of plants or departments. The lowest level is made up of lower management and workers. It includes office managers, sales managers, supervisors, and other first-line managers, as well as the employees who report directly to them. This level is also called the *operational level* of the organization.

An authority structure is the glue that holds these levels together. Generally (but not always), people at higher levels have the authority to make decisions and to tell lower-level people what to do. For example, middle managers can give orders to first-line supervisors; first-line supervisors, in turn, direct operative-level workers.

subunits Subdivisions of an organization.

In the 1980s, a powerful trend for U.S. businesses was to reduce the number of hierarchical layers. General Electric used to have 29 levels; today, following a major reorganization, it has only 5. Most executives today believe that fewer layers create a more efficient, fast-acting, and cost-effective organization. This also holds true for the **subunits** of major corporations. A study of 234 branches of a financial services company found that branches with fewer layers tended to have higher operating efficiency than branches with more layers.[10]

Span of control

span of control The number of subordinates who report directly to an executive or supervisor.

The number of people under a manager is an important feature of an organization's structure. The number of subordinates who report directly to an executive or supervisor is called the **span of control.** The implications of differences in the span of control for the shape of an organization are straightforward. Holding size constant, narrow spans build a *tall* organization that has many reporting levels. Wide spans create a *flat* organization with fewer reporting levels. The span of control can be too narrow or too wide. The optimal span of control maximizes effectiveness because it is (1) narrow enough to permit managers to maintain control over subordinates, but (2) not so narrow that it leads to overcontrol and an excessive number of managers who oversee a small number of subordinates.

What is the optimal number of subordinates? Five, according to Napoleon.[11] Some managers today still consider five a good number. At one Japanese bank, in contrast, several hundred branch managers report to the same boss.

Actually, the optimal span of control depends on a number of factors. The span should be wider when (1) the work is clearly defined and unambiguous, (2) subordinates are highly trained and have access to information, (3) the manager is highly capable and supportive, (4) jobs are similar and performance measures are comparable, and (5) subordinates prefer autonomy to close supervisory control. If the opposite conditions exist, a narrow span of control may be more appropriate.[12]

Delegation

delegation The assignment of new or additional responsibilities to a subordinate.

As we look at organizations, and recognize that authority is spread out over various levels and spans of control, the issue of delegation becomes paramount. Specifically, **delegation** is the assignment of authority and responsibility to a subordinate at a lower level. It requires that the subordinate report back to his or her boss as to how effectively the assignment was carried out. Delegation is perhaps the most fundamental feature of management, because it entails getting work done through others. Thus, delegation is important at all hierarchical levels. The process can occur between any two individuals in any type of structure with regard to any task.

Some managers are comfortable delegating to subordinates; others are not. Consider the differences between the two office managers and the ways they gave out the same assignment in the following example.

Are these both examples of delegation?

Manager A: "Call Tom Burton at Nittany Office Equipment. Ask him to give you the price list on an upgrade for our personal computers. I want to move up to a Pentium 233 or 266 with 64 megs of RAM and at least a five gigabyte hard drive. Ask them to give you a demonstration of Windows NT and Office 97. I want to be able to establish a LAN for the entire group. Invite Cochran and Snow to the demonstration and let them try it out. Have them write up a summary of their needs and the potential applications they see for the new systems. Then prepare me a report with the costs and specifications of the upgrade for the entire department. Oh yes, be sure to ask for information on service costs."

Manager B: "I'd like to do something about our personal computer system. I've been getting some complaints that the current systems are too slow, can't run current software, and don't allow for networking. Could you evaluate our options and give me a recommendation on what we should do? Our budget is probably around $3,500 per person, but I'd like to stay under that if we can. Feel free to talk to some of the managers to get their input, but we need to have this done as soon as possible."

Responsibility, authority, and accountability. When delegating work, it is helpful to keep in mind the important distinctions among the concepts of authority, responsibility, and accountability.

responsibility The assignment of a task that an employee is supposed to carry out.

Responsibility means that a person is assigned a task that he or she is supposed to carry out. When delegating work responsibilities, the manager should also delegate to the subordinate enough authority to get the job done. *Authority,* recall, means that the person has the power and the right to make decisions, give orders, draw upon resources, and do whatever else is necessary to fulfill the responsibility. Ironically, it is quite common for people to have more responsibility than authority; they must perform as best they can through informal influence tactics instead of relying purely on authority. More will be said about informal power and how to use it in Chapter 12.

accountability The expectation that employees perform a job, take corrective action when necessary, and report upward on the status and quality of their performance.

As the manager delegates responsibilities, subordinates are held accountable for achieving results. **Accountability** means that the subordinate's manager has the right to expect the subordinate to perform the job, and the right to take corrective action in the event the subordinate fails to do so. The subordinate must report upward on the status and quality of his or her performance of the task.

On the other hand, the ultimate responsibility—accountability to higher-ups—lies with the manager doing the delegating. Managers remain responsible and accountable not only for their own actions but for the actions of their subordinates. Thus, managers should not resort to delegation to others as a means of escaping their own responsibilities. In many cases, however, managers refuse to accept responsibility for subordinates' actions. Managers often "pass the buck" or take other evasive action to ensure they are not held accountable for mistakes.[13]

Advantages of delegation. Delegating work offers important advantages. The manager saves time by giving some of his or her own responsibilities to someone else. Then the manager is free to devote energy to important, higher-level activities like planning, setting objectives, and monitoring performance.

Delegation essentially gives the subordinate a more important job. The subordinate acquires an opportunity to develop new skills and to demonstrate potential for additional responsibilities and perhaps promotion. In essence, the subordinate receives a vital form of on-the-job training that could pay off in the future.

The organization also receives payoffs. Allowing managers to devote more time to important managerial functions while lower-level employees carry out assignments means that jobs are done in a more efficient and cost-effective manner.

How should managers delegate? To achieve the advantages discussed above, delegation must be done properly. As Figure 8.2 shows, effective delegation proceeds through several steps.[14]

The first step in the delegation process, defining the goal, requires that the manager have a clear understanding of the outcome he or she wants. Then the manager should select a person who is capable of performing the task.

The person who gets the assignment should be given the authority, time, and resources needed to successfully carry out the task. Throughout the delegation process, the manager and the subordinate must work together and communicate about the project. The manager should know the subordinate's ideas at the beginning and should inquire about progress or problems at periodic meetings and review sessions. Thus, even though the subordinate performs the assignment, the manager is available and aware of its current status.

figure 8.2
The steps in effective delegation

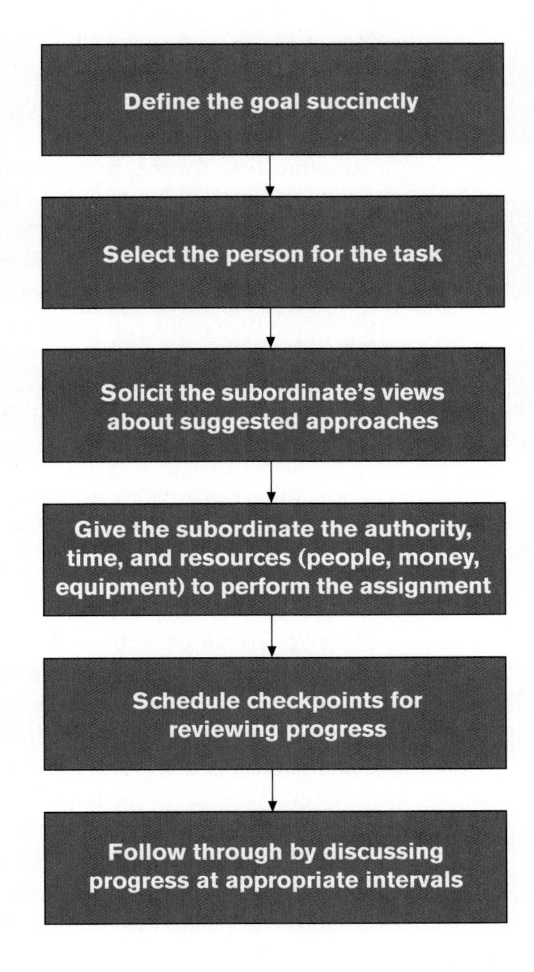

Some tasks, such as disciplining subordinates and conducting performance reviews, should not be delegated. But when managers err, it usually is because they delegated too little rather than too much. The manager who wants to learn how to delegate more effectively should remember this distinction: If you are not delegating, you are merely *doing* things; but the more you delegate, the more you are truly *building* and *managing* an organization.[15]

Decentralization

centralized organization An organization in which high-level executives make most decisions and pass them down to lower levels for implementation.

decentralized organization An organization in which lower-level managers make important decisions.

The delegation of responsibility and authority *decentralizes* decision making. In a centralized **organization,** important decisions usually are made at the top. In **decentralized organizations,** more decisions are made at lower levels. Ideally, decision making occurs at the level of the people who are most directly affected and have the most intimate knowledge about the problem. This is particularly important when the business environment is fast-changing and decisions must be made quickly and well.

For example, in the example of Sears in "Setting the Stage," CEO Arthur C. Martinez pushed more decisions down to individual store managers so that they could react more quickly and effectively to customer needs. Harley-Davidson is going through a similar change.

Harley-Davidson: Re-born to be wild?

In the 1980s, Harley-Davidson faced tough competition from Honda, Suzuki, and Yamaha. The company was able to survive under the direction of a very strong hierarchical, centralized leadership group. The key structural concerns at that time were reining in control, getting a firm grasp on manufacturing costs, and producing a quality product at a reasonable price.

Today, that approach alone probably won't work. According to CEO Richard F. Teerlink, the days of controlling leaders and dependent followers are long gone. Over the past three years, Harley-Davidson has been making the transition to a flatter, more empowered organization that decentralizes decision making. In order to support individual growth and excellence, Teerlink has been recreating Harley-Davidson to replace hierarchy with collaborative leadership. As a consequence of pushing down authority, managers are finding that trust replaces fear-based power. Ultimately the goal is to establish a much more innovative organization that taps into the creativity and resourcefulness of its employees. This is believed to be the type of organization needed to address today's complex business challenges.

Source: Clyde Fessler, "Rotating Leadership at Harley-Davidson: From Hierarchy to Interdependence," *Strategy & Leadership* 25, no. 4 (July/August 1997), pp. 42–43.

Most American executives today understand the advantages of pushing decision-making authority down to the point of the action. The level that deals directly with problems and opportunities has the most relevant information and can best foresee the consequences of decisions. They also see how the decentralized approach allows people to take more timely action.[16] At Nucor Steel, for example, plant managers are responsible for virtually every aspect of the business. Each of the 21 plants does its own purchasing, sets its own production quotas, and sells its own products. Many of these functions are often centralized at other companies, but there are only 23 people at Nucor's headquarters. Nucor executives know it would cost less to centralize these functions but believes that decentralization makes the company more responsive to the marketplace.[17]

The horizontal structure

Up to this point, we've talked primarily about vertical aspects of organization structure. Issues of authority, span of control, delegation, and decentralization are important in that they give us an idea of how managers and employees relate to one another at different levels. At the same time, separating vertical differentiation from horizontal differentiation is a bit artificial since the elements work simultaneously.

As the tasks of organizations become increasingly complex, the organization inevitably must be subdivided—that is, *departmentalized*—into smaller units or departments. One of the first places this can be seen is in the distinction between line and staff departments. **Line departments** are those that have responsibility for the principle activities of the firm. Line units deal directly with the organization's primary goods or services; they make things, sell things, or provide customer service. At General Motors, for example, line departments would include such areas as product design, fabrication, assembly, distribution, and the like. Line managers typically have much authority and power in the organization. They have the ultimate responsibility for making major operating decisions. They also are accountable for the "bottom-line" results of their decisions.

line departments Units that deal directly with the organization's primary goods and services.

Staff departments are those that provide specialized or professional skills that support line departments. These would include research, legal, accounting, public relations, and human resources departments. Each of these specialized units often has its own vice president. And some are vested with a great deal of authority, as when accounting or finance groups approve and monitor budgetary activities. But while staff units formerly focused on monitoring and controlling performance, today most staff units are moving toward a new role focused on strategic support and expert advice.[18]

staff departments Units that support line departments.

As organizations divide work into different units, we can detect patterns in the way departments are clustered and arranged. The three basic approaches to **departmentalization** include functional, divisional, and matrix. We will talk about each and highlight some of their similarities and differences.

departmentalization Subdividing an organization into smaller subunits.

The functional organization

In a **functional organization,** jobs (and departments) are specialized and grouped according to *business functions* and the skills they require: production, marketing, human resources, research and development, finance, accounting, and so forth. At perhaps the most basic level, we can think about a functional structure being organized around a firm's value chain. A **value chain** depicts the relationships among separate activities that are performed to create a product or service. Figure 8.3(*a*) shows a generic value chain and Figure 8.3(*b*) shows how it might be translated into an organization's functional structure.[19]

functional organization Departmentalization around specialized activities, such as production, marketing, human resources, etc.

value chain Sequence of activities that flow from raw materials to the delivery of a product or service.

Functional departmentalization is common in both large and small organizations. Large companies may organize along several different functional groupings, including groupings unique to their business. For example, Carmike Cinema has vice presidents of finance, real estate, operations, advertising, information systems, technical, and concessions and a vice president who is the head film buyer.

The traditional functional approach to departmentalization has a number of potential advantages for an organization:[20]

1. *Economies of scale can be realized.* When people with similar skills are grouped, more efficient equipment can be purchased, and discounts for large purchases can be used.
2. *Monitoring of the environment* is more effective. Each functional group is more closely attuned to developments in its own field and therefore can adapt more readily.
3. *Performance standards* are better maintained. People with similar training and interests may develop a shared concern for performance in their jobs.

figure 8.3 Generic value chain and functional structure

a. Generic value chain

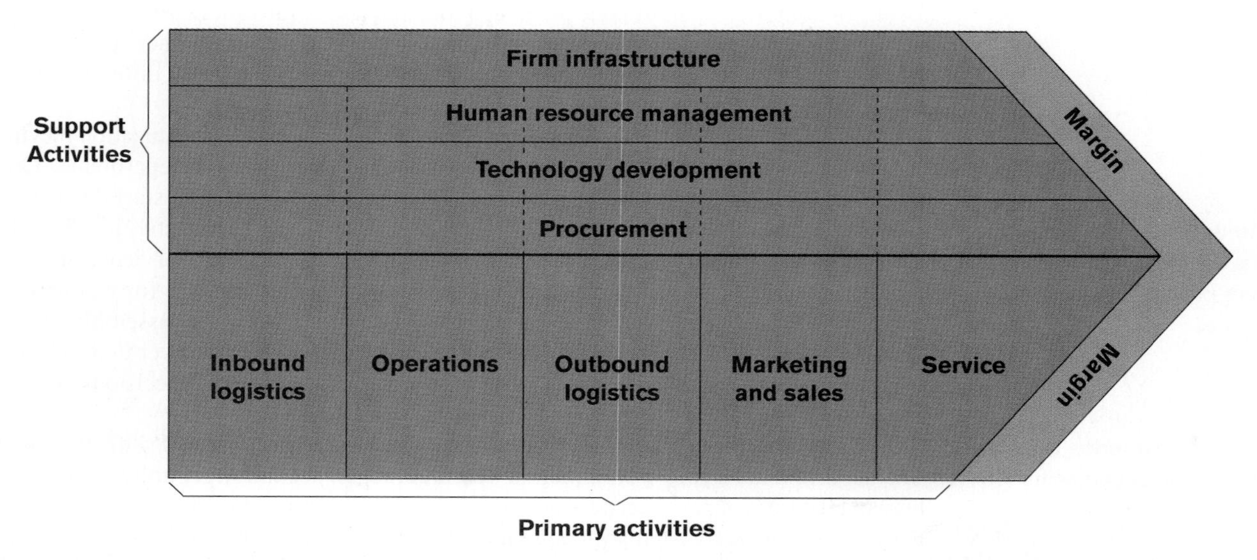

Source: Michael Porter, *Competitive Advantage: Creating and Sustaining Superior Performance* (New York: Free Press, 1985).

b. Functional structure

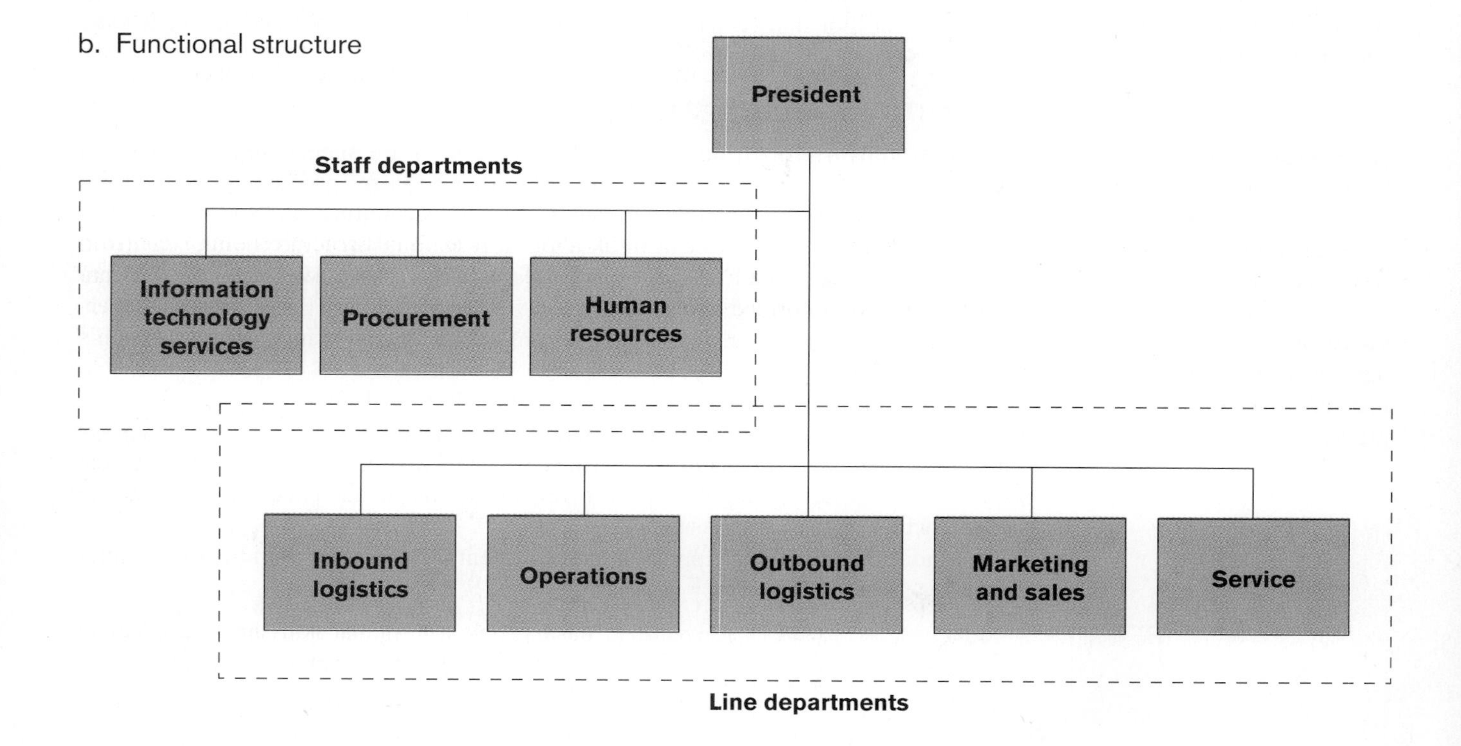

4. People have greater opportunity for *specialized training* and *in-depth skill development.*
5. Technical specialists are relatively *free of administrative work.*
6. *Decision making* and *lines of communication* are simple and clearly understood.

The functional form has disadvantages as well as advantages. People may care more about their own function than about the company as a whole, and their attention to functional tasks may make them lose focus on overall product quality and customer satisfaction. Managers develop functional expertise but do not acquire knowledge of the other areas of the business; they become specialists, but not generalists. Between functions, conflicts arise, and communication and coordination fall off. In short, while functional differentiation may exist, *functional integration* may not.

As a consequence, the functional structure may be most appropriate in rather simple, stable environments. If the organization becomes fragmented (or *dis*-integrated), it may be difficult to develop and bring new products to market, and difficult to respond quickly to customer demands and other changes. Particularly when companies are growing and business environments changing, the need arises to integrate work areas more effectively so that the organization can be more flexible and responsive. Other forms of departmentalization can be more flexible and responsive than the functional structure.

For a time, some observers believed that the functional structure was disappearing—that in today's complex, rapidly changing business environment, the functional form had to give way to alternative forms discussed later. But in the 1980s, pressures to reduce costs brought a resurgence of the more cost-effective functional structure.[21]

Nonetheless, recent demands for total quality, customer service, innovation, and speed have made clear the shortcomings of the functional form for some firms. Functional organizations are highly differentiated and create barriers to coordination across functions. Cross-functional coordination is essential for total quality, customer service, innovations, and speed. The functional organization will not disappear, in part because functional specialists will always be needed, but functional managers will make fewer decisions. The more important units will be cross-functional teams that have integrative responsibilities for products, processes, or customers.[22]

The divisional organization

divisional organization Departmentalization that groups units around products, customers, or geographic regions.

The discussion of a functional structure's weaknesses leads us to the **divisional structure.** As organizations grow and become increasingly diversified, they find that functional departments have difficulty managing a wide variety of products, customers, and geographic regions. In this case, organizations may restructure in order to group all functions into a single division, and duplicate each of the functions across all of the divisions. Division A has its own operations and marketing department, Division B has its own operations and marketing department, and so on. In this regard, separate divisions may act almost as separate businesses or profit centers and work autonomously to accomplish the goals of the entire enterprise. Table 8.2 presents examples of how the same tasks would be organized under functional and product structures.

There are several ways to create a divisional structure. It can be created around products, customers, or geographic regions. Each of these is described below.

Product divisions. In the product organization, all functions that contribute to a given product are organized under one manager. Figure 8.4 shows a product structure. In the product organization, managers in charge of functions for a particular product report to a product manager. Johnson & Johnson is one example of this form. J&J has 168 independent divisions in 33 groups, each responsible for a handful of products worldwide.

table 8.2
Examples of functional and product organization

Functional organization	Product organization
A typing pool.	Each typist is assigned to one boss.
A central purchasing department.	Each division has its own purchasing unit.
Separate companywide marketing, production, design, and engineering departments.	Each product group has experts in marketing, design, production, and engineering.
A central-city health department.	The school district and the prison have their own health units.
Plantwide inspection, maintenance, and supply departments.	Production Team Y does its own inspection, maintenance, and supply.
A university statistics department teaches statistics for the entire university.	Each department hires statisticians to teach its own students.

Source: George Strauss and Leonard R. Sayles, *Strauss and Sayles's Behavioral Strategies for Managers,* © 1980, p. 221. Reprinted by permission of Prentice-Hall, Inc., Englewood Cliffs, New Jersey.

Another example is 3M, at which a new product or product line typically becomes an independent division once it reaches a certain size.

The product approach to departmentalization offers a number of advantages:[23]

1. *Information needs are managed more easily.* Less information is required, because people work closely on one product and need not worry about other products.
2. *People have a full-time commitment to a particular product line.* They develop a greater awareness of how their jobs fit into the broader scheme.

figure 8.4
Product divisions

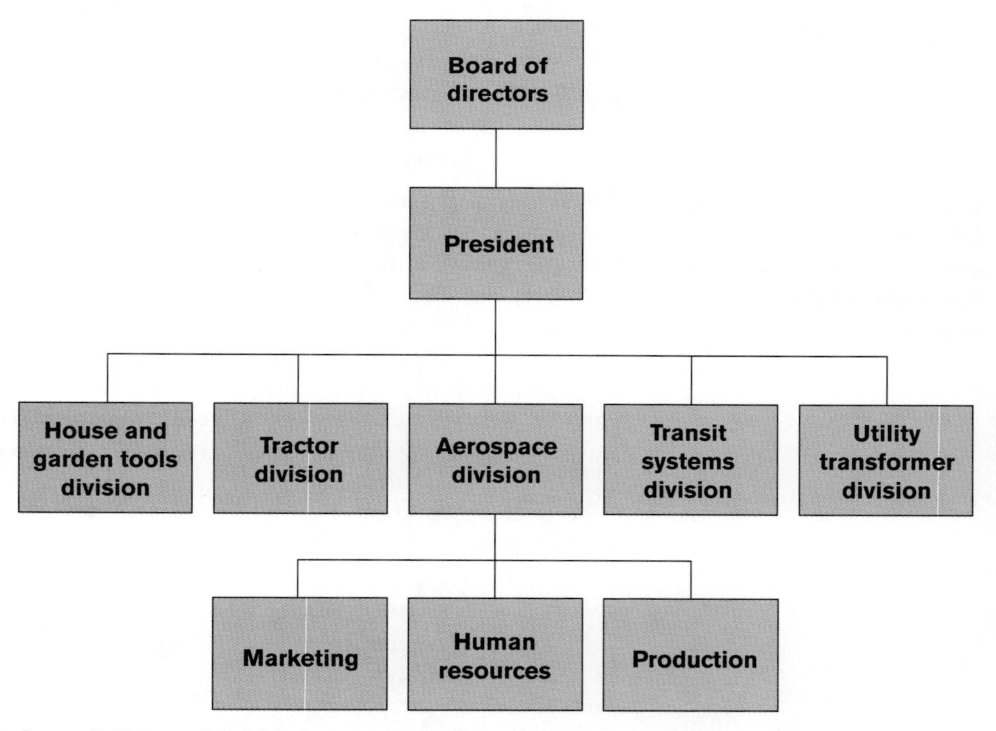

Source: D. Robey and C. Sales, *Designing Organizations,* 4th ed. (Burr Ridge, IL: Richard D. Irwin, 1994), p. 188. Reprinted by permission.

3. *Task responsibilities are clear.* When things go wrong in a functional organization, functional managers can "pass the buck" ("that other department is messing up, making it harder for us to do our jobs"). In a product structure, managers are more independent and accountable because they usually have the resources they need to perform their tasks. Also, the performances of different divisions can be compared by contrasting their profits and other measures.
4. *People receive broader training.* General managers develop a wide variety of skills, and they learn to be judged by results. Many top executives received crucial early experience in product structures.

Because the product structure is more flexible than the functional structure, it is best suited for unstable environments, when an ability to rapidly adapt to change is important. But the product structure also has disadvantages. It is difficult to coordinate across product lines and divisions. And, although managers learn to become generalists, they may not acquire the depth of functional expertise that develops in the functional structure.

Furthermore, functions are not centralized at headquarters where they can be done for all product lines or divisions. Such duplication of effort is expensive. Also, decision making is decentralized in this structure, so top management can lose some control over decisions made in the divisions. Proper management of all the issues surrounding decentralization and delegation, as discussed earlier, is essential for this structure to be effective.

Customer and geographical divisions. Some companies build divisions around groups of customers or around geographical distinctions. Universities, for example, often have *customer* divisions. Different faculty and administrators may be put in charge of undergraduate, master's, doctoral, executive and part-time programs. These distinctions depend on the mix of students the university serves. Similarly, a hospital may organize its services around child, adult, psychiatric, and emergency cases. Bank loan departments commonly allocate assignments based on whether customers are requesting consumer, mortgage, small-business, corporate, or agricultural loans.

In contrast to customers, divisions can be structured around geographic regions. Sears, for example, was a pioneer in creating *geographic divisions.* Geographical distinctions include district, territory, region, and country. In companies like the industrial wholesaler diagrammed in Figure 8.5, different managers are in charge of the Southwest, Pacific, Midwest, Northeast, and Southeast regions. Seagram International is one of many companies that assign managers to Europe, the Far East, and Latin America.

figure 8.5
Geographical organization

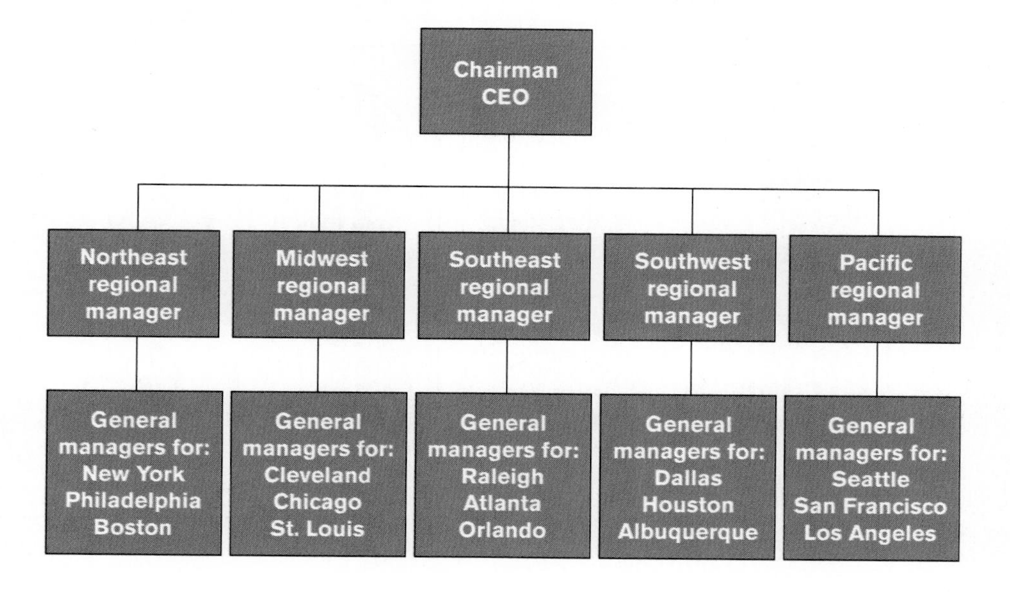

NASA successfully used the matrix organization to organize and implement the launch of the Mercury astronauts in the late 1950s.
[Courtesy of NASA]

matrix organization An organization composed of dual reporting relationships in which some managers report to two superiors, a functional manager, and a product manager.

unity-of-command principle A structure in which each worker reports to one boss, who in turn reports to one boss.

The primary advantage of both the product and customer/regional approaches to departmentalization is the ability to focus on customer needs and provide faster, better service. But again, duplication of activities across many customer groups and geographic areas is expensive.

The matrix organization

A **matrix organization** is a hybrid form of organization in which functional and divisional forms overlap. Managers and staff personnel report to two bosses—a functional manager and a divisional manager. Thus, matrix organizations have a dual rather than a single line of command. Figure 8.6 illustrates the basic matrix structure.

The matrix form originated in the aerospace industry, first with TRW in 1959 and then with NASA. Applications now occur in hospitals and health care agencies, entrepreneurial organizations, government laboratories, financial institutions, and multinational corporations.[24] Companies that have used or presently use the matrix form include IBM, Boeing, General Electric, Dow Chemical, Xerox, Shell Oil, Texas Instruments, Bechtel, Phillips Petroleum, and Dow Corning.

Pros and cons of the matrix form.

Like other organization structures, matrix has both strengths and weaknesses. Table 8.3 summarizes the advantages of using a matrix structure. The major potential advantage is a higher degree of flexibility and adaptability.

Table 8.4 summarizes the potential shortcomings of the matrix form. Many of the disadvantages stem from the matrix's inherent violation of the **unity-of-command principle,** which states that a person should have only one boss. Reporting to two superiors can create confusion and a difficult interpersonal situation.

figure 8.6
Matrix organizational structure

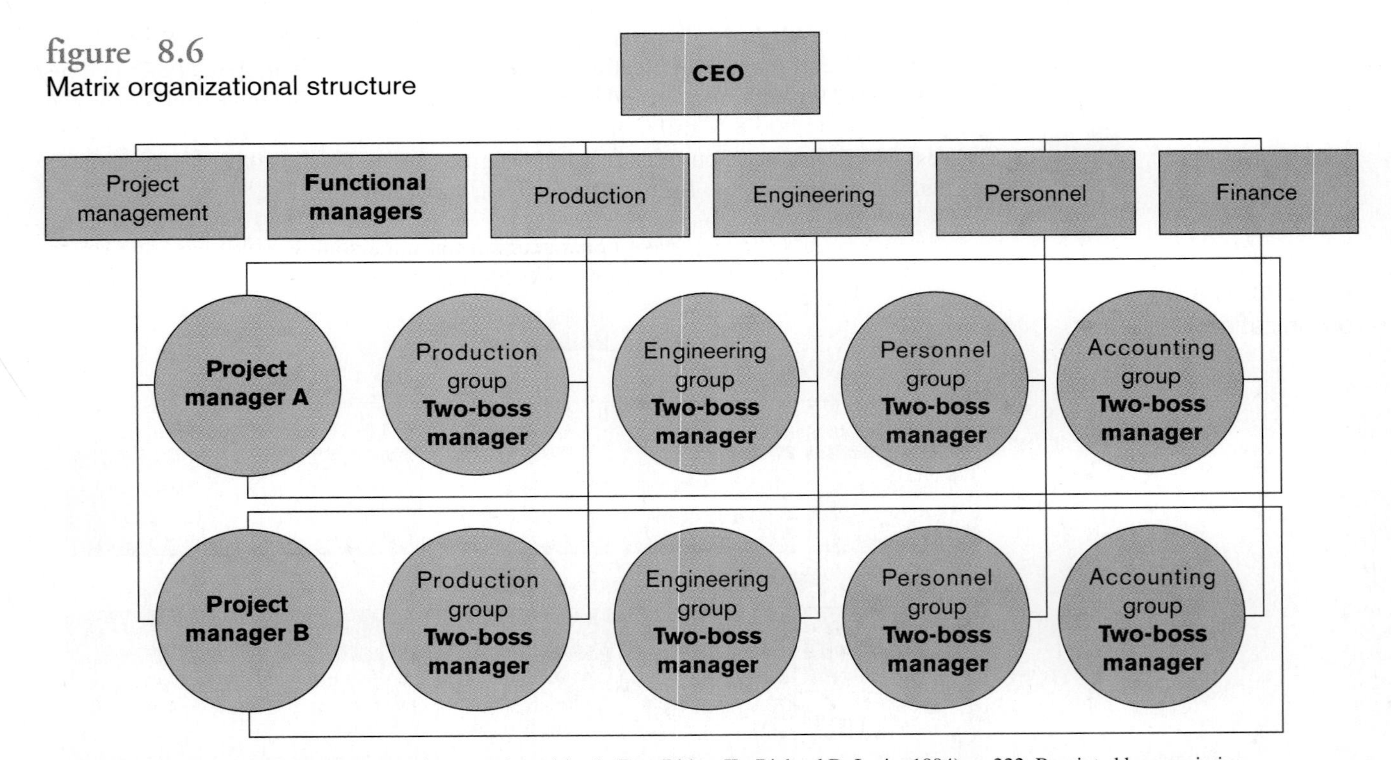

Source: D. Robey and C. Sales, *Designing Organizations,* 4th ed. (Burr Ridge, IL: Richard D. Irwin, 1994), p. 222. Reprinted by permission.

table 8.3
Advantages of the matrix design

- Decision making is decentralized to a level where information is processed properly and relevant knowledge is applied.
- Extensive communications networks help process large amounts of information.
- With decisions delegated to appropriate levels, higher management levels are not overloaded with operational decisions.
- Resource utilization is efficient, because key resources are shared across several important programs or products at the same time.
- Employees learn the collaborative skills needed to function in an environment characterized by frequent meetings and more informal interactions.
- Dual career ladders are elaborated as more career options become available on both sides of the organization.

Source: H. Kolodny, "Managing in a Matrix," *Business Horizons,* March–April 1981, pp. 17–24.

Matrix survival skills. To a large degree, problems can be avoided if the key managers in the matrix learn the behavioral skills demanded in the matrix structure.[25] These skills vary depending on the job in the four-person diamond structure shown in Figure 8.7.

The *top executive,* who heads the matrix, must learn to balance power and emphasis between the product and functional orientations. *Product or program managers* and *functional managers* must learn to collaborate and manage their conflicts constructively. Finally, the *two-boss managers* or employees at the bottom of the diamond must learn how to be responsible to two superiors. This means prioritizing multiple demands and sometimes even reconciling conflicting orders. Some people function poorly under this ambiguous, conflictual circumstance; sometimes this signals the end of their careers with the company. Others learn to be proactive, communicate effectively with both superiors, rise above the difficulties, and manage these work relationships constructively.

The matrix form today. The matrix organization was popular in the 1970s and lost favor in the 1980s when many companies had difficulty implementing it. But in the 1990s it came back strong. Reasons for this resurgence included pressures to consolidate costs and be faster to market, creating a need for better coordination across functions in the business units, and a need for coordination across countries for firms with global business strategies. Many of the challenges created by the matrix are particularly acute in an international context.[26]

The structure of the matrix hasn't changed, but our understanding of it has. The key to managing today's matrix is not the formal structure itself but the realization that the matrix is a *process.* Companies that have had trouble adopting the matrix form may have been correct in creating such a multidimensional structure to cope with environmental complexity, but they needed to go further than try to construct a flexible organization simply by changing the structure. The formal structure is merely the organization's anatomy. Executives must also attend to its physiology—the relationships that allow information to

table 8.4
Disadvantages of the matrix design

- Confusion can arise because people do not have a single superior to whom they feel primary responsibility.
- The design encourages managers who share subordinates to jockey for power.
- The mistaken belief can arise that matrix management is the same thing as group decision making–in other words, everyone must be consulted for every decision.
- Too much democracy can lead to not enough action.

Source: H. Kolodny, "Managing in a Matrix," *Business Horizons,* March–April 1981, pp. 17–24.

figure 8.7
The matrix diamond

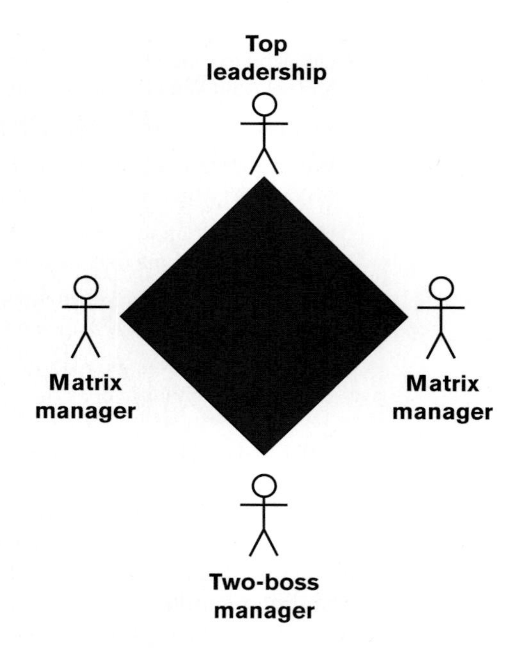

Source: Reprinted, by permission of the publisher, from *Organizational Dynamics* (Summer 1977) © 1977, American Management Association, New York. http://www.amanet.org. All rights reserved.

flow through the organization—and its psychology—the norms, values, and attitudes that shape how people think and behave.[27] We will address these issues in the next chapter and in Part IV of the text, which focuses on how to lead and manage people. The issues also arise again in Chapter 16 on control and culture.

Organizational integration

Although we have covered both the vertical and horizontal dimensions of organizational structure we have really only focused on structural *differentiation.* At the outset we noted that as organizations differentiate their structures, they also need to be concerned about *integration* and *coordination.* Because of specialization and the division of labor, different groups of managers and employees develop different orientations. Depending on whether employees are in a functional department or in a divisional group, are line or staff, and so on, they will think and act in ways that are geared toward their particular work units. In short, people working in separate functions, divisions, and business units literally tend to forget about one another. When this happens, it is difficult for managers to combine all their activities into an integrated whole.

There are a variety of approaches available to managers to help them make certain that interdependent units and individuals will work together to achieve a common purpose. Coordination methods include standardization, plans, and mutual adjustment.[28]

Coordination by standardization

When organizations coordinate activities by establishing routines and standard operating procedures that remain in place over time, we say that work has been standardized. **Standardization** constrains actions and integrates various units by regulating what people do. People oftentimes know how to act—and know how to interact—because there are standard operating procedures that spell out what they should do. Employee manuals and policies, for example, may explain what actions a manager should take to discipline an employee or deal with an unhappy customer.

Standardization
Establishing common rules and procedures that apply uniformly to everyone.

Would you believe all of these people worked on putting this textbook together, not including the authors who wrote it!

Organizations also may rely on rules and regulations to govern how people interact (we call this *formalization*). Simple policies regarding attendance, dress, and decorum, for example, may help eliminate a good deal of uncertainty at work. But an important assumption underlying both standardization and formalization is that the rules and procedures should apply to most (if not all) situations. These approaches, therefore, are most appropriate in situations that are relatively stable and unchanging. In some cases, when the work environment requires flexibility, coordination by standardization may not be very effective. Who hasn't experienced a time when rules and procedures—frequently associated with a slow bureaucracy—prevented timely action to address a problem? In these instances, we often refer to rules and regulations as "red tape."[29]

Coordination by plan

Coordination by plan Interdependent units are required to meet deadlines and objectives that contribute to a common goal.

If it is difficult to lay out the exact rules and procedures by which work should be integrated, organizations may provide more latitude by establishing goals and schedules for interdependent units. **Coordination by plan** does not require the same high degree of stability and routinization required for coordination by standardization. Interdependent units are free to modify and adapt their actions, as long as they meet the deadlines and targets required for working with others.

In writing this textbook, for example, we (the authors) sat down with the publication team that included the editors, the marketing staff, the production group, and support staff. Together we ironed out a schedule for developing this book that covered approximately a two-year period. That development plan included dates and "deliverables" that specified what was to be accomplished and forwarded to the others in the organization. The plan allowed for a good deal of flexibility on each sub-unit's part, and the overall approach allowed us to work together effectively.

Coordination by mutual adjustment

Coordination by mutual adjustment Units interact with one another to make accommodations so as to achieve flexible coordination.

Ironically, the simplest and most flexible approach to coordination may just be to have interdependent parties to talk to one another. **Coordination by mutual adjustment** involves feedback and discussions to jointly figure out how to approach problems and devise solutions that are agreeable to everyone. The popularity of teams today is in part due to the fact that they allow for flexible coordination; teams can operate under the principle of mutual adjustment.

But the flexibility of mutual adjustment as a coordination device does not come without some cost. "Hashing out" every issue takes a good deal of time and may not be the most expedient approach for organizing work. Imagine how long it would take to accomplish even the most basic tasks if sub-units had to talk through every situation. At the same time, mutual adjustment can be very effective when problems are novel and cannot be programmed in advance with rules, procedures, or plans. Particularly in crisis situations where rules and procedures don't apply, mutual adjustment is likely to be the most effective approach to coordination.

From the Pages of BusinessWeek

"Can Deutsche Measure Up?"

From Rolf E. Breuer's office atop the Frankfurt headquarters of giant Deutsche Bank, you can survey the offices of just about every big lender in Germany, not to mention those of several other rivals. That's a handy perspective: Breuer, Deutsche Bank's CEO since last May, has been widely rumored to be looking to buy some of these very banks. But as Breuer talks about his strategy, you get the sense that he's not in a buying mood just yet.

"Our answer is to get our machine on the street and drive it at full horsepower," he says. Breuer, 60, is test driving a new strategy that he hopes will rev up growth in the increasingly competitive world of Eurobanking. In late January 1997, he announced a reorganization and a wide-ranging restructuring of investment banking and other businesses. The goal: to slash bureaucracy, increase top managers' accountability, and boost Deutsche's pretax return on equity from about 17 percent to 25 percent by the year 2000. Analysts also expect Breuer to slash his workforce by as much as 9 percent–or 8,000 jobs–within three years.

But is that enough? Analysts doubt that Breuer's reorganization will achieve 25 percent pretax returns. A source close to the bank says Breuer would have to close 500 of Deutsche's 2,400 domestic branches and cut 10,000 jobs to really cut into the bank's bureaucracy. Still, Deutsche's stock has risen since Breuer's bombshell announcement, mainly because–despite Breuer's denials–investors see the restructuring as an interim step.

Breuer is simplifying Deutsche's convoluted structure by reorganizing it into five global lines of business: asset management, middle-market corporate banking, retail banking, back-office operations, and wholesale and investment banking. The biggest departure, though, is Breuer's attack on his bureaucracy. He cut the bank's management board from 10 members to eight. He is shaking up a lower level board of operating executives and is effectively giving each of his business units a CEO responsible for achieving financial goals. The bank's structure "has to be lean, direct, and responsive," Breuer says. "We have to identify the people who do a fabulous deal and reward them."

Still, Breuer tacitly acknowledges that Deutsche's biggest diversification of the last decade–investment banking–isn't working. Deutsche Morgan Grenfell lost $55 million in investment banking, global fixed income, and global equities in 1997. Now, Breuer is reining in the unit. He's combining it with corporate lending and will probably drop the venerable Morgan Grenfell name for many businesses. The idea is to cut costs and gain focus, especially in Germany, where Deutsche corporate bankers often tangled with DMG investment bankers over business.

While Breuer attempts to get investment banking under control, he is also under the gun to boost profits from traditional lending. Deutsche has been paring its retail banking network in Germany for five years, but further cost-cutting is planned. Corporate lending also could use a shake-up, says J.P. Morgan analyst Stuart Graham.

Changes such as Breuer is seeking won't come easily. "German banks have lived for many years in a relatively stable environment," says Antonio Borges, head of INSEAD, the business school in Fontainebleau, France. "Now they have to adapt very quickly to a new European environment." The question now is whether Breuer has taken that lesson adequately to heart.

Discussion Questions:

1. What approach to structure has Breurer taken for Deutsche Bank?
2. Why do you think it was important to cut the management board and change the board of operating executives?
3. What integrative mechanisms do you think would be helpful for reining in costs and reducing bureaucracy?

Source: Thane Peterson and Stanley Reed, "Can Deutsche Measure Up?" *Business Week:* February 16, 1998. ●

Looking ahead

The organization chart, differentiation, integration, authority, delegation, coordination, and the like convey fundamental information about an organization's structure. However, the information so far has provided only a snapshot. The real organization is more like a motion picture—it moves! More flexible and innovative—even virtual—forms of organizations are evolving.

No organization is merely a set of static work relationships. Because organizations are composed of people, they are hotbeds of social relationships. Networks of individuals cutting across departmental boundaries interact with one another. Various friendship groups or cliques band together to form *coalitions*—members of the organization who jointly support a particular issue and try to ensure that their viewpoints determine the outcome of policy decisions.[30]

Thus, the formal organization structure does not describe all about how the company really works. Even if you know departments and authority relationships, there is still much to understand. How do things really get done? Who influences whom, and how? Which managers are the most powerful? How effective is the top leadership? Which groups are most and which are least effective? What is the nature of communication patterns throughout the organization? These issues are discussed throughout the rest of the book.

Now you are familiar with the basic organizing concepts discussed in this chapter. In the next chapter, we will discuss the current challenges of designing the modern organization with which the modern executive constantly grapples.

Key terms

Summary of learning objectives

Now that you have studied Chapter 8, you should know:

How differentiation and integration influence your organization's structure.

Differentiation means that organizations have many parts. Specialization means that various individuals and units throughout the organization perform different tasks. The assignment of tasks to different people or groups is often referred to as the division of labor. But the specialized tasks in an organization cannot all be performed independently of one another. Coordination links the various tasks in order to achieve the organization's overall mission. When there are many different specialized tasks and work units, the organization is highly differentiated; the more differentiated the organization, the more integration or coordination is required.

How authority operates.

Authority is the legitimate right to make decisions and tell other people what to do. Authority is exercised throughout the hierarchy, as bosses have the authority to give orders to subordinates. Through the day-to-day operation of authority, the organization proceeds toward achieving its goals. Owners or stockholders have ultimate authority.

The roles of the board of directors and the chief executive officer.

Boards of directors report to stockholders. The board of directors controls or advises management, considers the firm's legal and other interests, and protects stockholders' rights. The chief executive officer reports to the board and is accountable for the organization's performance.

How span of control affects structure and managerial effectiveness.

Span of control is the number of people who report directly to a manager. Narrow spans create tall organizations, and wide spans create flat ones. No single span of control is always appropriate; the optimal span is determined by characteristics of the work, the subordinates, the manager, and the organization.

How to delegate work effectively.

Delegation is the assignment of tasks and responsibilities. Delegation has many potential advantages for the manager, the subordinate, and the organization. But to be effective, the process must be managed carefully. The manager should define the goal, select the person, solicit opinions, provide resources, schedule checkpoints, and discuss progress periodically.

The difference between centralized and decentralized organizations.

In centralized organizations, most important decisions are made by top managers. In decentralized organizations, many decisions are delegated to lower levels.

How to allocate jobs to work units.

Jobs can be departmentalized on the basis of function, product, customers, or geography. Most organizations use several different types of departmentalization.

How to manage the unique challenges of the matrix organization.

The matrix is a complex structure with a dual authority structure. A well-managed matrix enables organizations to adapt to change. But it can also create confusion and interpersonal difficulties. People in all positions in the matrix—top executives, product and function managers, and two-boss managers—must acquire unique survival skills.

The nature of important integrating mechanisms.

Managers can coordinate interdependent units through standardization, plans, and mutual adjustment. Standardization occurs when routines and standard operating procedures are put in place. They are typically accompanied by formalized rules. Coordination by plan is more flexible and allows more freedom in how tasks are carried out, but keeps interdependent units focused on schedules and joint goals. Mutual adjustment involves feedback and discussions among related parties to accommodate each others' needs. It is at once the most flexible and simple to administer, but it is time consuming.

Discussion questions

1. Using the concepts in the chapter, discuss the advantages and disadvantages of the organization structure approaches described in "Setting the Stage."

2. What are some advantages and disadvantages of being in the CEO position?

3. Would you like to sit on a board of directors? Why or why not? If you did serve on a board, what kind of organization would you prefer? As a board member, in what kinds of activities do you think you would most actively engage?

4. Interview a member of a board of directors and discuss the member's perspectives on his or her role.

5. Pick a job you have held and describe it in terms of span of control, delegation, responsibility, authority, and accountability.

6. Why do you think managers have difficulty delegating? What can be done to overcome these difficulties?

7. Consider an organization in which you have worked, draw its organization chart, and describe it using terms in this chapter. How did you like working there, and why?

8. Would you rather work in a functional or divisional organization? Why?

9. If you learned that a company had a matrix structure, would you be more or less interested in working there? Explain your answer. How would you prepare yourself to work effectively in a matrix?

10. Brainstorm a list of methods for integrating interdependent work units. Discuss the activities that need to be undertaken and the pros and cons of each approach.

Concluding Case

Mobil restructures . . . and restructures

Like top executives of other very large companies, Lucio A. Noto, CEO of Mobil Corporation, has the complex task of creating an organization structure that simultaneously makes the most efficient use of company assets, aligns activities with customer interests, and coordinates an entire portfolio of products into an integrated whole.

Before 1997, Mobil had been organized into three main business units that primarily represented a functional structure: (1) exploration and production, (2) chemicals, and (3) refining and marketing. However, in an attempt to capitalize on new business opportunities that promised the best growth for the company, Noto realigned his management team and restructured the company into 11 divisional business groups. The 11 business groups reflected specific markets and regions, and fall into four general categories:

To compete in today's environment, Lucio Noto has realigned Mobil's structure twice within a short period of time.
[The Gamma Liaison Network]

- **North American Business.** Though North America is viewed as a single region, it was divided into two separate organizations—one for "upstream" activities (North American Exploration and Production) and one for "downstream" activities (North American Marketing; and Refining and Marketing).
- **Integrated Regional Businesses.** Apart from North America, businesses in four other regions combined Mobil's exploration, production, marketing, and refining. These integrated regional businesses included (1) Africa and the Middle East, (2) Asia and Pacific, (3) Europe, and (4) South America.
- **Worldwide Business Groups.** While integrated regional businesses combine functional operations within certain parts of the world, Mobil has certain products and processes that transcend regional markets. To address customers, competitors, and opportunities around the globe, Worldwide Business Groups were created for (1) Chemicals, (2) Liquefied Natural Gas and Independent Power Projects, (3) New Exploration, Producing Ventures, and Exploration, (4) Supply, Trading, and Transportation, and (5) Technology.
- **Business Councils.** In addition to the regional business units and worldwide business groups, two business councils were created to oversee global strategy and performance for Mobil's marketing and refining, exploration and producing, and chemical activities. The two councils were: (1) the Downstream Council, and (2) the Upstream Coordination Council.

According to Noto, the reorganization of Mobil was to better the focus the company's entrepreneurial talents on seizing new business opportunities while at the same time maintaining its commitment to technology and functional excellence in its upstream and downstream activities. But now—less than a year after this reorganization—Noto has realigned Mobil's structure again (following the election of Eugene A. Renna as President and Chief Operating Officer). The latest incarnation of the company has seven major business groups:

- **International Exploration and Producing.** M. W. Scoggins will oversee Mobil's exploration and producing activities outside the Americas. Scoggins also will lead the coordination of Mobil's global drilling, exploration and new venture activities and he will continue to chair the company's upstream business council.
- **American Exploration and Producing.** Louis W. Allstadt will oversee Mobil's exploration and producing activities in the United States, Canada, and Latin America, as well as new ventures in those regions.
- **Global Midstream.** Thomas C. DeLoach will head this new organization to focus on global supply and trading, and leveraging Mobil's strategic business activities and opportunities in natural gas. The Midstream portfolio will include supply, trading and transportation, liquefied natural gas/independent power projects, liquefied petroleum gas, Middle East ventures, and the Qatar affiliate. DeLoach will also continue to coordinate Mobil's motorsports affiliations.
- **International Marketing and Refining.** Stephen D. Pryor will oversee Mobil's marketing and refining activities in Europe, Africa, Asia-Pacific, and Latin America, as well as the Middle East lubricants business. In his new assignment, Pryor also will coordinate Mobil's global lubricants activities. He will continue as chairman of the company's downstream business council.
- **North America Marketing and Refining.** Brain R. Baker will continue to oversee all of Mobil's marketing and refining in the United States and Mexico.
- **Chemicals.** Raymond J. McGowan will continue to focus on petrochemicals, films, and chemical products on a global basis.
- **Technology.** Michael P. Ramage will head this business group to focus on research, technical services, capital projects and technology sales and licensing.

According to COO Renna, "We think now is a good time to return to a more functional structure, which permits us to better drive shareholder value. This structure will promote growth for the corporation, and provide a heightened focus on making certain we keep our organization efficient and effective."

For a closer look at Mobil's organization chart and more news and information about the company, interested readers can check out the company's web pages www.mobil.com/structure/orgchart.html and *www.mobil.com/news.*

Questions

1. Why do you think that Noto has changed the structure so many times in recent years?

2. Do you support the latest version, a previous version, or something else? Why?

3. What challenges is Mobil likely to face with this approach to structure?

Sources: John S. DeMott, "The Key Issue: Managing Bigness," *Worldbusiness* 2, no. 5 (September/October 1996), pp. 30–33; Andrew Wood, "Mobil Shifts to Business Groups: McGowan to Head Chemicals," *Chemical Week* 158, no. 23 (June 12, 1996), p. 9; "Mobil's Realignment Reflects Growth Objective," *National Petroleum News* 88, no. 7 (July 1996), p. 24; "Restoring 'Functional Excellence' Through Best Practices," *Oil and Gas Investor,* 1996, pp. 8–9; "Mobil Realigns Structure," *Chemical Marketing Reporter* 249, no. 24 (June 10, 1996), p.111; "Mobil Announces Organizational Realignment," *Business Wire* (February 11, 1998). ●

Experiential Exercises

8.1 The Business School Organization Chart

Objectives

1. To clarify the factors that determine organization structure.
2. To provide insight into the workings of an organization.
3. To examine the working relationships within an organization.

Instructions

1. Draw an organization chart for your school of business. Be sure to identify all the staff and line positions in the school. Specify the chain of command and the levels of administration. Note the different spans of control. Are there

any advisory groups, task forces, or committees to consider?

2. Review the chapter material on organization structure to help identify both strong and weak points in your school's organization. Now draw another organization chart for the school, incorporating any changes that you believe would improve the quality of the school. Support the second chart with a list of recommended changes and reasons for their inclusion.

Discussion Questions

1. Is your business school well organized? Why or why not?
2. Is your school's organization organic or mechanistic? In what ways?
3. In what ways is the school's structure designed to suit the needs of students, faculty, staff, the administration, and the business community?

8.2 Mechanistic and Organic Structures

Objectives

1. To think about your own preferences when it comes to working in a particular organizational structure.
2. To examine aspects of organizations using as an example *this class* you are a member of.

Instructions

1. Complete the Mechanistic and Organic Worksheet below.
2. Meet in groups of four to six persons. Share your data from parts 1 and 2 of the worksheet. Discuss the reasons for your responses, and analyze the factors that probably encouraged your instructor to choose the type of structure that now exists.

Mechanistic and Organic Worksheet

1. Indicate your general preference for working in one of these two organizational structures by circling the appropriate response:

Mechanistic	1	2	3	4	5	6	7	8	9	10	**Organic**

2. Indicate your perception of the form of organization that is used in *this class* by circling the appropriate response for each item:

A. **Task-role definition**											
Rigid	1	2	3	4	5	6	7	8	9	10	**Flexible**
B. **Communication**											
Vertical	1	2	3	4	5	6	7	8	9	10	**Multidirectional**
C. **Decision making**											
Centralized	1	2	3	4	5	6	7	8	9	10	**Decentralized**
D. **Sensitivity to the environment**											
Closed	1	2	3	4	5	6	7	8	9	10	**Open**

Source: Keith Davis and John. W. Newstrom, *Human Behavior at Work,* 9th ed. (New York: McGraw-Hill, 1993), p. 358. Reprinted by permission of McGraw-Hill, Inc. ●

Chapter Nine

The Responsive Organization

Bureaucracy defends the status quo long past the time when the quo has lost its status.

—Laurence J. Peter

Chapter Outline

Today's Imperatives

Organizing for Optimal Size

The Case for Big

The Case for Small

Organizing for Environmental Response

Organizing to Manage Information

Organizing for Customer Responsiveness

Organizing for Technological Response

Types of Technology Configurations

Organizing for Flexible Manufacturing

Organizing for Speed: Time-Based Competition

Organizing for Strategic Response

Organizing around Core Competencies

The Network Organization

Strategic Alliances

The Learning Organization

The High-Involvement Organization

Final Thoughts about Responsive Organizations

Learning Objectives

After studying Chapter 9, you will know:

1. The market imperatives a firm must meet to survive.
2. The potential advantages of creating an organic form of organization.
3. How a firm can "be" both small and big.
4. How to manage information-processing demands.
5. How firms organize to meet customer requirements.
6. How firms organize around different types of technology.
7. The new types of dynamic organizational concepts and forms that are being used for strategic responsiveness.

Setting the Stage

Two Vastly Different Companies

Consider two very different, successful companies:

- ABB Asea Brown Boveri, based in Zurich, is a huge industrial firm. It is broken down into eight major business segments, 65 business areas, 1,300 independent companies, and about 5,000 autonomous profit centers of about 50 people each. The profit centers are further broken down into 10-person teams. Each profit center performs multiple business functions, has its own balance sheet and profit-and-loss statement, and directly serves its own customers. Every employee is part of a team that is itself a small business.
- Paul Farrow started Walden Paddlers in 1992. In a very short period of time, he has designed, produced, and marketed a line of eight different high-tech kayaks made from 100 percent recycled plastic. The kayaks tend to cost less than the competition's—and perform better. The company has been so successful that in 1997 it won the Outstanding Recycling Innovation Award by the National Recycling Coalition (NRC).

Paul Farrow shows off the 1997 NRC (National Recycling Coalition) Outstanding Product Innovation Award for having the world's only line of boats (kayaks) made of recycled plastics. *[Courtesy of Walden Paddlers, Inc.]*

Interestingly, Walden Paddlers originally had only one employee: Paul Farrow, himself. Now there are eight full-time employees. While their sales have grown, the company has stayed extremely small. Why? Farrow originally figured that building a company to design, manufacture, and market kayaks would take forever and cost over $1 million, which he did not have. So he looked for partners. He became a customer to a talented molder who would take on custom work from the outside—and the molder was a serious whitewater kayaker. Then he found a talented designer with the same passion. And then he contacted successful retailers and gave them demonstration kayaks for 30 days, allowing them to paddle them, take them apart, or sell them. All the people involved are talented, share a passion for the product, and have personal or business reasons to trust one another. And they share the costs, as well as the profits, of Paul Farrow's business dream. You can find out more about this organization by visiting their website:

http://members.aol.com/waldenpad/about.htm.

Sources: Mark Dolliver, "What's New Portfolio," Adweek, *January 22, 1996, pp. 31–32; E. O. Welles, "Virtual Realities,"* Inc., *August 1993, pp. 50–58; "The ABB of Management,"* Economist *338, no. 7947 (January 6, 1996), p. 56; James Bredin, "Europe's Best Practices,"* Industry Week *244 no. 18 (October 2, 1995), pp. 66–70; G. E. Schares, "Percy Barnevik's Global Crusade,"* Business Week, *1993 Special Issue, pp. 204–11.*

As you can see from the two examples on page 303, there are different routes to success. One organization is huge, the other small. One is organized around teams, the other is an eight-person firm that contracts with other firms in what is called a network organization. Today's companies are taking many other approaches to organizing as well. In this chapter, you will learn about these developments and their impact on organizations.

Chapter 8 described the formal structure of organizations. The ideas we discussed there are traditional and basic, and fundamental to understanding organizations. But a firm's formal structure is only part of the story. There are other subtle aspects of organizing that really distinguish how firms operate for maximum effectiveness. Organizations are not static structures, but complex systems in which many people do many different things at the same time. The overall behavior of organizations does not just pop out of a chart, but emerges out of other processes, systems, and relationships among interrelated parties. In today's modern firm, new approaches to organizing are emerging. The emphasis in this chapter is not on the formal organization, but on organizing for *action.*[1]

Today's imperatives

The formal structure is put in place to *control* people, decisions, and actions. But in today's fast-changing business environment, *responsiveness*—quickness, agility, the ability to adapt to changing demands—is more vital than ever to a firm's survival.[2]

Progressive companies place a premium on being able to act, and act fast. They want to act in accord with customer needs and other outside pressures. They want to take actions to correct past mistakes, and also to prepare for an uncertain future. They want to be able to respond to threats and opportunities. To do these things, they try to operate organically, manage size effectively, process huge amounts of information, and adopt new forms of organization.

Many years after Max Weber wrote about the concept of bureaucracy, two British management scholars (Burns and Stalker) described what they called the **mechanistic organization.**[3] The common mechanistic structure they described was similar to Weber's bureaucracy. But they went on to suggest that in the modern corporation, the mechanistic structure is not the only option. The **organic structure** (introduced in Chapter 2) stands in stark contrast to the mechanistic organization.[4] It is much less rigid and, in fact, emphasizes flexibility. The organic structure can be described as follows:

mechanistic organization A form of organization that seeks to maximize internal efficiency.

organic structure An organizational form that emphasizes flexibility.

1. Jobholders have broader responsibilities that change as the need arises.
2. Communication occurs through advice and information rather than through orders and instructions.
3. Decision making and influence are more decentralized and informal.
4. Expertise is highly valued.
5. Jobholders rely more heavily on judgment than on rules.
6. Obedience to authority is less important than commitment to the organization's goals.
7. Employees depend more on one another and relate more informally and personally.

Figure 9.1 compares the mechanistic and organic structures in terms of who interacts with whom in the work unit.[5] People in the organic organization work more as teammates than as subordinates who take orders from the boss, thus breaking away from the traditional bureaucratic form.[6]

We rely on the ideas underlying the organic structure as a foundation for discussing the newer forms of organization described in this chapter. The more organic a firm is, the more responsive it will be to changing competitive demands and market realities. For the

figure 9.1
Mechanistic versus organic work units

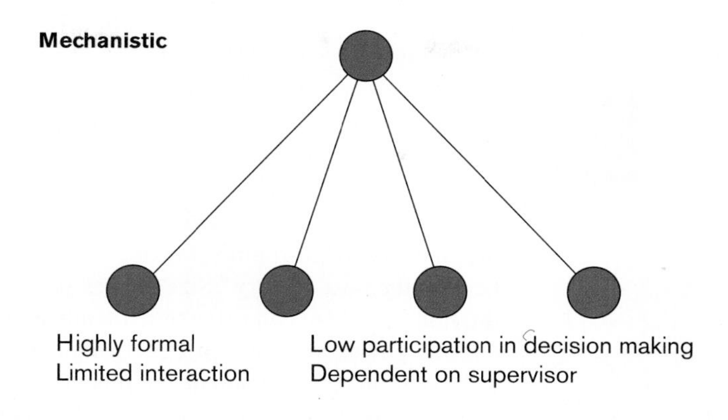

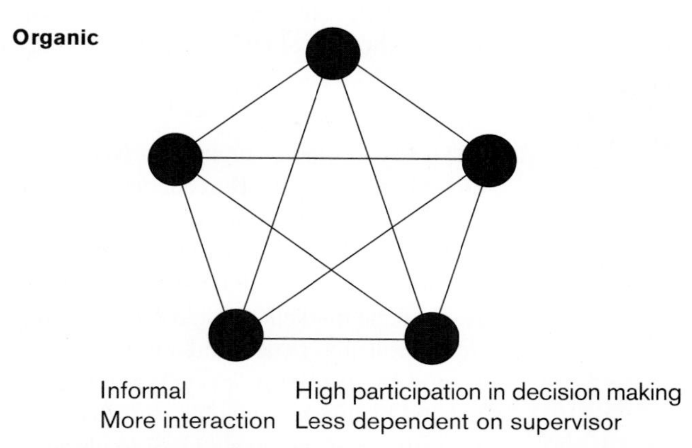

Source: Adapted from D. Nadler, J. Hackman, and E. E. Lawler III, *Managing Organizational Behavior* (Boston: Little, Brown, 1979).

remainder of this chapter, we summarize some of the most important issues that require organizations to adopt organic structures. These include organizing for optimal size, organizing for environmental response, organizing for technological response, and organizing for strategic response.

Organizing for optimal size

One of the most important characteristics of an organization is its size. Large organizations are typically less organic and more bureaucratic. For example, at Hewlett-Packard, before the recent reduction of its stifling bureaucracy, it took over 90 people on nine committees more than seven months to decide what to name some new software.[7]

In large organizations, jobs become more specialized. More distinct groups of specialists get created because large organizations can add a new specialty at lower proportional expense. The complexity these numerous specialties create makes the organization harder to control. Therefore, management has traditionally added more levels to keep spans of control from becoming too large.[8] To cope with complexity, large companies tend to become more bureaucratic. Rules, procedures, and paperwork are introduced.

Thus, with size comes greater complexity, and complexity brings a need for increased control. In response, organizations adopt bureaucratic strategies of control. The conventional wisdom is that bureaucratization increases efficiency but decreases a company's ability to innovate. So is large size a good thing or a bad thing? Let's see.

The case for big

Bigger was better after World War II, when foreign competition was limited and growth seemed limitless. To meet high demand for its products, U.S. industry embraced high-volume, low-cost manufacturing methods. IBM, GM, and Sears all grew into behemoths during these decades.

Alfred Chandler, distinguished professor emeritus at Harvard, believes that big companies have been the engine of economic growth throughout this century and will continue to be over the next century.[9] Size creates *scale economies,* that is, lower costs per unit of production. And size can offer specific advantages like lowered operating costs, greater purchasing power, and easier access to capital. For example, Intel spends more than $1 billion each year on research and development, far more than its rivals can afford.[10] Size also creates **economies of scope;** materials and processes employed in one product can be used to make other, related products. With such advantages, huge companies with lots of money may be the best at taking on large foreign rivals in huge global markets.

economies of scope Economies in which materials and processes employed in one product can be used to make other, related products.

The case for small

But a huge, complex organization can find it hard to manage relationships with customers and among its own units. Bureaucracy can run rampant. Too much success can breed complacency, and the resulting inertia hinders change. Experts suggest that this is a surefire formula for being "left in the dust" by hungry competitors. Moreover, some economies of scale are declining; for instance, small firms now can purchase tremendous computing power at low cost, and reach niche markets through cable TV and target marketing rather than mass media.[11]

As consumers demand a more diverse array of high quality, customized products supported by excellent service, giant companies have begun to stumble. A new term has entered business vocabulary: *dis*economies of scale, or the *costs* of being too big. "Small is beautiful" has become a favorite phrase of entrepreneurial business managers.

Smaller companies can move fast, can provide quality goods and services to targeted market niches, and can inspire greater involvement from their people. Nimble, small firms frequently outmaneuver big bureaucracies. They introduce new and better products, and they steal market share. The premium now is on flexibility and responsiveness—the unique potential strengths of the small firm. For example, Ultra Pac Inc. produces recyclable plastic food containers.[12] It has only 300 employees, but competes against Mobil Corp. and Tenneco Inc. The smaller company turns out 500 different kinds of packaging and ships within three days of an order, in contrast to over a week at the larger companies.

Arthur Young, one of the former Big Eight accounting firms, used to give great service to small business. But after Young merged with Ernst & Whinney to form Ernst & Young, the firm began losing clients because of poor service. In particular, smaller clients felt they had no contact with partners and had no personal relationships. In accounting, as elsewhere, big companies are losing clients to smaller competitors.[13]

Small within big

Small *is* beautiful for unleashing energy and speed. But in buying and selling, size offers market power. The challenge then is to be both big and small to capitalize on the advantages of each. IBM is trying to do both in order to regain its past glory. It is working together on major projects with Siemens, Motorola, and a variety of other partners. At the same time it is creating smaller, more flexible business units.[14]

Motorola is a large company that has successfully maintained a "small-within-big" mentality. Although it is difficult to stay small when sales double every five years, Motorola is widely considered among the best-managed companies in the world. To avoid the problems of growth, Motorola decentralizes decision making and organizes around small, adaptive, team-based work units.[15]

Downsizing is the planned elimination of jobs. The fact that layoffs are planned doesn't mean people aren't frightened and angry when they lose their jobs, as evidenced by these placard-carrying ex-employees.
[Tom McKitterick/Impact Visuals]

downsizing The planned elimination of positions or jobs.

rightsizing A successful effort to achieve an appropriate size at which the company performs most effectively.

survivor's syndrome Loss of productivity and morale in employees who remain after a downsizing.

Downsizing As large companies attempt to regain the responsiveness of small, they often face the dilemma of downsizing. **Downsizing** (or **rightsizing**) is the planned elimination of positions or jobs. Common approaches to downsizing include eliminating functions, hierarchical levels, or units.[16] It is hard to pick up a newspaper without seeing announcements of another company downsizing; likewise, it is hard to name a major corporation that has not downsized in recent years. The list includes IBM, Citicorp, AT&T, Kodak, Goodyear, Exxon, Xerox, TRW, General Motors, and so on. Microsoft is one notable exception in that it has carefully controlled its size even as revenues have mushroomed. Its approach to head-count growth is "n-minus-one": if a task requires five extra people, Microsoft allocates four. As it turns out, the work gets done, and the company has not become bloated to the point of needing to downsize.[17]

Historically, layoffs tended to affect manufacturing firms, and operative level workers in particular. But given that the most recent cycle of downsizing has focused on delayering and eliminating bureaucratic structures, "white collar" middle managers have been those chiefly affected.

What can be done to manage downsizing effectively—to help make it a more effective "rightsizing"? First of all, firms should avoid excessive (cyclical) hiring to help reduce the need to engage in major or multiple downsizings. But beyond that, firms must avoid common mistakes such as making slow, small, frequent layoffs; implementing voluntary early retirement programs that entice the best people to leave; or laying off so many people that the company's work can no longer be performed.[18] Instead, firms can engage in a number of positive practices to ease the pain of downsizing:

- Choose positions to be eliminated based on careful analysis and strategic thinking.
- Train people to cope with the new situation.
- Identify and protect talented people.
- Give special attention and help to those who have lost their jobs.
- Communicate constantly with people about the process.
- Emphasize a positive future and people's new roles in attaining it.[19]

Interestingly, the people who lose their jobs because of downsizing are not the only ones deeply affected. Those who survive the process—who keep their jobs—tend to exhibit what has become known as **survivor's syndrome.**[20] They struggle with heavier workloads, wonder who will be next to go, try to figure out how to survive, lose commitment to the company and faith in their bosses, and become narrow-minded, self-absorbed, and risk averse. As a consequence, morale and productivity usually drop.

You will learn more about some of these ideas in later chapters on human resources management, leadership, motivation, communication, and managing change.

From the Pages of BusinessWeek

Digital Brokers on the Net

Bruce Yoxsimer owned a travel agency for 13 years before events forced him into a bold, new strategy. The seven-employee company in Palo Alto, California, was doing nicely. Annual bookings came to nearly $4 million. But when the airlines capped commissions on ticket sales in 1994, the agency's largest source of revenue was suddenly under siege. To adapt, Yoxsimer took a farsighted approach: He set up shop all over again–this time on the World Wide Web.

Yoxsimer teamed up with a pair of software experts to launch the Internet Travel Network (www.itn.net). In 1995, it became one of the first companies to book trips over the Web. Despite the far greater sales volume of competing airline Web sites, the company has secured a place in the Web ticketing business by being there early and building a name. With just 50 employees, it is processing up to 1,000 reservations a day, a rate that is growing by about 10 percent a month, thanks to word-of-mouth referrals, advertising, and Internet search engines–not to mention businesses that have signed ITN as their exclusive on-line agent.

ITN is a sterling example of how rapidly the Web is forcing change on small businesses. From real estate, travel, and insurance agents to car dealers and recruitment firms, many businesses are finding fresh opportunities on the Web. Virtually all, though, will have to change how they do business. That may mean providing a level of customer service that a computer cannot deliver. Or teaming up with an Internet partner. Or converting the business to a Web site. As the new digital brokers gobble up market share, giving customers more options than ever, middlemen of all stripes need to develop survival strategies.

However, those who broker products and information without adding value beware. If your business merely sells access to a database–such as airline schedules, real estate listings, insurance rates, and stock exchanges–watch out. Realistically, you won't be able to beat the Web at its own game: Offering fast access to databases and interactive information tailored to individual consumers. Even businesses that do add some value will have to rethink their business models, says Jeffrey F. Rayport, an assistant professor at the Harvard business school. "It's a wholesale conversion to a better, faster, cheaper, more flexible way of doing business," he says.

As Yoxsimer's success shows, the Web is a superbly efficient way to sell airline tickets. About 1 percent of domestic tickets are now sold on-line, according to the American Society of Travel Agents, and Forrester Research Inc. forecasts that volume will quadruple to nearly $5 billion in sales by 2000. That's why Phil Davidoff, 57, owner and co-founder of 28-year-old Bel-air/Empress Travel, a small agency in Bowie, Maryland, has deemphasized airline ticket sales. He says that commission caps may have started the free-fall, but on-line competition–which emboldened the airlines to slash commissions–accelerated the plunge. In the past three years, airline ticket commissions dropped from 62 percent of his revenues to less than 30 percent. In response, Davidoff is now doing what computers can't–getting to know customers so well that he can advise them on cruises that he books. Other agencies are focusing on specialties such as adventure trips, senior citizen travel, or eco-tourism.

It appears that digital brokers are rapidly changing the face of some businesses. They surface wherever there's a demand for convenient–and often more efficient–services. But if you don't want to go the way of the milkman or become an on-line broker yourself, what choice remains? Everyone is learning to adapt, and being responsive to customer needs has never been more important.

Source: Evan I. Schwartz, "How Middlemen Can Come Out On Top," *Business Week:* February 9, 1998.

Discussion Questions

1. How does network brokering lead to better customer responsiveness?
2. What other businesses might be good prospects for on-line brokering?
3. What types of organizational adaptation would be required to compete with networking businesses? ●

Organizing for environmental response

Apart from organizing for optimal size, organizations also have to adapt to external environments. In a sense, this is the crux of creating a responsive organization. In Chapter 2, we introduced various approaches organizations might take to respond to the environment. They included *adapting* to the environment, *influencing* the environment, and *selecting* a new environment. In this section, we want to delve more deeply into how organizations organize for environmental response.

Organizing to manage information

Today's environments tend to be complex, dynamic, and (therefore) uncertain. Huge amounts of information flow from the external environment to the organization and back to the environment. To cope, organizations must acquire, process, and respond to that information. Doing so has direct implications for how firms organize. To function effectively, organizations need to develop structures for processing information.

Figure 9.2 shows two general strategies that can help managers cope with high uncertainty and heavy information demands. First, management can act to reduce the need for information. Second, it can increase its capacity to handle more information.[21]

Option one: Reducing the need for information

Managers can reduce the need for information in two ways: (a) creating slack resources and (b) creating self-contained tasks. *Slack resources* are simply extra resources on which the organization can rely "in a pinch" so that if they get caught off guard, they can still adjust. Inventory, for example, is a type of slack resource that provides extra stock on hand in case it is needed. With extra inventory, an organization does not have to have as much information about sales demand, lead-time, and the like. Employees can also be a type of slack resource. Recall Walden Paddlers in "Setting the Stage" has only eight full-time employees.

figure 9.2
Managing high information-processing demands

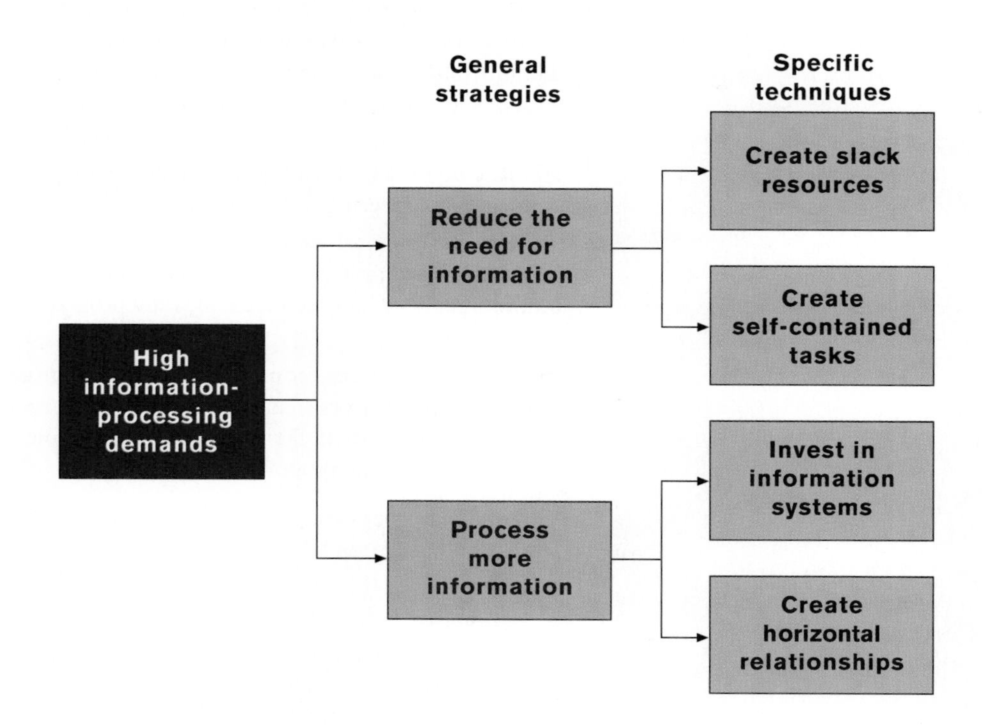

However, the company has contacts with a crew of 14 part-time employees who come aboard during busy seasons. These part-timers represent a type of slack resource for Walden Paddlers in that the company does not have to perfectly forecast sales peaks, but can rely on supplementary workers to handle irregularities.[22]

Like slack resources, creating *self-contained tasks* allow organizations to reduce the need for some information. *Creating self-contained tasks* refers to changing from a functional organization to a product or project organization and giving each unit the resources it needs to perform its task. Information-processing problems are reduced because each unit has its own full complement of specialties instead of functional specialties having to share their expertise among a number of different product teams. Communications then flow within each team rather than among a complex array of interdependent groups.

Option two: Increasing information processing capability. Instead of reducing the need for information, organizations may take the approach of increasing its information processing capability. They can *invest in information systems,* which usually means employing or expanding computer systems. And they can create horizontal relationships to foster coordination across different units. Such horizontal relationships are effective because they increase integration (recall Chapter 8), which Lawrence and Lorsch suggest is necessary for managing complex environments. As uncertainty increases, the following horizontal processes may be used, ranging from the simplest to the most complex:[23]

1. *Direct contact* (mutual adjustment) among managers who share a problem. In a university, for example, a residence hall adviser might call a meeting to resolve differences between two feuding students who live in adjacent rooms.
2. *Liaison roles,* or specialized jobs to handle communications between two departments. A fraternity representative is a liaison between the fraternity and the interfraternity council, the university, or the local community.
3. *Task forces,* or groups of representatives from different departments, brought together temporarily to solve a common problem. For example, students, faculty, and administrators may be members of a task force charged with bringing distinguished speakers to campus for a current-events seminar.
4. *Teams,* or permanent interdepartmental decision-making groups. An executive council made up of department heads might meet regularly to make decisions affecting a college of engineering or liberal arts.
5 *Product, program, or project managers* who direct interdisciplinary groups with a common task to perform. In a college of business administration, a faculty administrator might head an executive education program composed of professors from several disciplines.
6. *Matrix organizations,* composed of dual relationships in which some managers report to two superiors (recall Chapter 8). Your instructors, for example, may report to department heads in their respective disciplines and also to a director of undergraduate or graduate programs.

Several of these processes are discussed further in Chapter 14, where we examine managing teams and intergroup relations.

Organizing for customer responsiveness

Although it is valuable to discuss environmental uncertainty in general, at this point we hope to move to a more concrete set of circumstances. From Chapter 2 recall that the environment is composed of many different parts (e.g., government, suppliers, competitors, and the like). Perhaps no other aspect of the environment has had a more profound impact on

figure 9.3
The strategic triangle

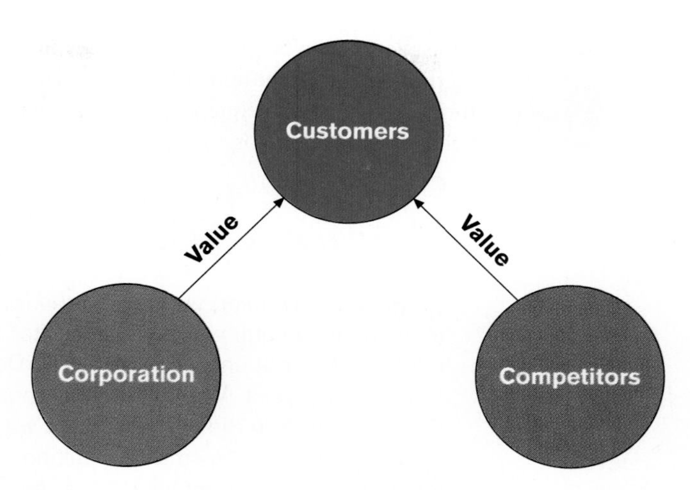

Source: From K. Ohmae et al., *The Mind of the Strategist* Reprinted with permission from the McGraw-Hill Companies.

organizing in recent years than a focus on *customers.* Dr. Kenichi Ohmae points out that any business unit must take into account three key players: the *company* itself, the *competition,* and the *customer.* These components form what Ohmae refers to as the *strategic triangle* as shown in Figure 9.3. Managers need to balance the strategic triangle, and successful organizations use their strengths to create value by meeting customer requirements better than competitors do.[24]

As discussed throughout this book, customers want quality goods and service, low cost, innovative products, and speed. Traditional thinking considered these basic customer wants as a set of potential trade-offs. For instance, customers wanted high quality or low costs passed along in the form of low prices. But world-class companies today know that the "trade-off" mentality no longer applies. Customers want it *all,* and they are learning that somewhere an organization exists that will provide it all.

But if all companies seek to satisfy customers, how can a company realize a competitive advantage? World-class companies have learned that most any advantage is temporary, for competitors will strive to catch up. Simply stated—though obviously not simply done—a company attains and retains competitive advantage by continuing to improve. This concept—*kaizen,* or continuous improvement—is an integral part of Japanese operations strategy. Motorola, a winner of the Malcolm Baldrige National Quality Award, operates with the philosophy that "the company that is satisfied with its progress will soon find that its customers are not."

As organizations focus on responding to customer needs, they soon find that traditional meaning of customer expands to include "internal customers." The word *customer* now refers to the *next process,* or *wherever the work goes next.*[25] This highlights the idea of interdependence among related functions and means that all functions of the organization—not just marketing people—have to be concerned with customer satisfaction. All recipients of a person's work, whether co-worker, boss, subordinate, or external party, come to be viewed as the customer.

total quality management
An integrative approach to management that supports the attainment of customer satisfaction through a wide variety of tools and techniques that result in high-quality goods and services.

Total quality management (TQM)

Total quality management is a way of managing in which everyone is committed to continuous improvement of their part of the operation. In business, success depends on having quality products. As described in Chapter 1 and throughout the book, TQM is a comprehensive approach to improving product quality and thereby customer satisfaction.[26] It is characterized by a strong orientation toward customers (external and internal) and has become an umbrella theme for organizing work. TQM reorients managers toward involving people across departments in improving

all aspects of the business. Continuous improvement requires integrative mechanisms that facilitate group problem solving, information sharing, and cooperation across business functions. As a consequence, the walls that separate stages and functions of work tend to come down, and the organization operates more in a team-oriented manner.[27]

W. Edwards Deming

W. Edwards Deming was one of the founders of the quality management movement. He first went to Japan after World War II as one of a number of U.S. advisers. But not until the 1980s did Deming become known in the United States.

America's post–World War II economic power bred widespread complacency. Deming's work in the United States was confined to a teaching position at New York University and a small consulting practice. Then, in 1980, he appeared on a television documentary titled "If Japan Can, Why Can't We?" Since then, his work has been embraced by major U.S. companies, including Ford Motor Company, AT&T, General Motors, and Procter & Gamble.

Deming advocates a "holistic" approach to management that demands intimate understanding of "the process"–the delicate interaction of materials, machines, and people that determines productivity, quality, and competitive advantage. Starting with a statistical analysis, which he likens to a surgeon's diagnosis before operating on a patient, the Deming approach expands into 14 management principles that revolve around casting the manager as a coordinator and coach, teamwork, relations with suppliers, and multidisciplinary problem solving.

Deming's famous "14 points" of quality are shown in the accompanying table.

Deming's 14 points

1. *Create constancy of purpose.* Strive for long-term improvement more than short-term profits.
2. *Adopt the new philosophy.* Accept as gospel the need for total quality, with no tolerance for delays and mistakes.
3. *Cease dependence on mass inspection.* Build quality into the process, and identify and correct problems early rather than late.
4. *End the practice of awarding business on price tag alone.* Don't purchase from the cheapest supplier. Build long-term supplier relationships based on loyalty and trust.
5. *Improve constantly and forever the system of production and service.* At every stage of the process, strive to continually improve and satisfy internal as well as external customers.
6. *Institute training and retraining.* This includes continual updating and training in statistical methods and thinking.
7. *Institute leadership.* Remove barriers that prevent employees from performing effectively, and continually provide the resources needed for effectiveness.
8. *Drive out fear.* People must believe it is safe to report problems or mistakes or to ask for help.
9. *Break down barriers among departments.* Promote teamwork and communications across departments, and provide a common organizational vision.
10. *Eliminate slogans, exhortations, and arbitrary targets.* Supply methods, not just buzzwords.
11. *Eliminate numerical quotas.* Quotas place a limit on improvement and are contrary to the idea of *continuous* improvement.
12. *Remove barriers to pride in workmanship.* Allow autonomy and spontaneity. Regular performance reviews should be abandoned.
13. *Institute a vigorous program of education and retraining.* This is similar to Point 6, but is meant to highlight a philosophy that people are assets, not commodities.
14. *Take action to accomplish the transformation.* Provide access to top management, an organization structure, and information that allows the other 13 points to be adhered to on a daily basis.

Sources: H. Rowen, "Bringing American Ideas Home from Japan," *Washington Post,* July 25, 1991, p. A17; and A. Gabor, "The Man Who Changed the World of Quality," *International Management*, March 1988, pp. 42–46.

The Baldrige criteria and TQM in the United States As you know, the Baldrige Award is the prestigious award given to U.S. companies that achieve quality excellence. The award is granted on the basis of the seven criteria highlighted below. Included are brief descriptions of the strengths of companies that have applied for the Baldrige Award, and some guidelines for further improvement:

1. *Leadership.* Senior managers in the best companies are committed to quality, have communicated quality values throughout their companies, and have instilled a strong customer orientation. They need to make certain that they balance financial performance with operational issues as well.
2. *Information and analysis.* The very best TQM companies have excellent information systems. Companies need to make certain that information is well organized to support quality management.
3. *Strategic quality planning.* The best TQM companies have written quality plans and quality goals (often stretch goals). In addition, companies need to make certain that they communicate these plans to people so that everyone knows how their activities and objectives relate to the overall plans.
4. *Human resource development and management.* Teams focus on quality improvement projects, all employees receive basic quality training, and plenty of resources are devoted to safety. Beyond this, companies have to make certain that teams are managed effectively, and that management truly empowers these teams to make decisions. The performance evaluation system should be aligned with the quality management system.
5. *Management of process quality.* Most companies use statistical process control, have quality programs in conjunction with their suppliers, have greatly improved the development of new goods and services, and have developed measures of the service production process. Areas for improvement include limited new-product development activity (particularly services), slow and inadequate feedback from customers, and the lack of quality systems audits.
6. *Quality and operational results.* The best Baldrige companies demonstrate the quality of their products and their sustained year-to-year improvement with objective data.
7. *Customer focus and satisfaction.* The better Baldrige companies use surveys and focus groups to assess customer satisfaction, train their customer service representatives well, establish service standards, give more authority to service representatives to solve customer problems, and work hard to provide easy access and quick response times to customers. In addition, companies have to clearly understand customer needs and expectations. Customer data needs to be used in new-product development, and companies need to pay attention to lost customers, new customers, and competitors' customers.[28]

As you can see, total quality requires a thorough, extensive, integrated approach to organizing. Looking carefully at the strengths and improvement needs of good U.S. companies on the Baldrige criteria, you can see that quality comes from the issues and practices discussed throughout this course.

ISO 9000 A series of quality standards developed by a committee working under the International Organization for Standardization to improve total quality in all businesses for the benefit of both producers and consumers.

ISO 9000. The influence of total quality management on the organizing process has become even more acute with the emergence of ISO 9000. **ISO 9000** is a series of quality standards developed by a committee working under the International Organization for Standardization.[29] The purpose of the standards is to improve total quality in all businesses for the benefit of producers and consumers alike. ISO 9000 was originally designed for manufacturing; however, most of the standards can also be readily applied to services operations.

Companies like Ford emphasize the importance of quality. *[Courtesy of Ford Motor Company]*

U.S. companies first became interested in ISO 9000 because overseas customers, particularly the European Community (EC), embraced it. Companies that comply with the quality guidelines of ISO 9000 can apply for official certification; some countries and companies demand certification as an acknowledgment of compliance before they will do business. Now, some U.S. customers as well are making the same demand.[30]

Reengineering Extending from TQM and a focus on organizing around customer needs, organizations have also embraced the notion of reegineering (introduced in Chapter 1). The principal idea of reengineering is to revolutionize key organizational systems and processes to answer the question: "If you were the customer, how would you like us to operate?" The answer to this question forms a vision for how the organization should run, and then decisions are made and actions are taken to make the organization operate like the vision.[31] Processes such as product development, order fulfillment, customer service, inventory management, billing, production, and the like are redesigned from scratch just as if the organization were brand new and just starting out.

For example: Procter & Gamble learned that the average family buying its products rather than private-label or low-priced brands pay an extra $725 per year. That figure, P&G realized, was far too high, and a signal that the company's high prices could drive the company to extinction. Other data also signaled the need for P&G to change. Market shares of famous brands such as Comet, Mr. Clean, and Ivory had been dropping for 25 years. P&G was making 55 price changes *daily* on about 80 brands, and inaccurate billings were common. Its plants were inefficient, and the company had the highest overhead in the business. It was clear that it had to cut prices, and to do that it had to cut costs.

In response, P&G reengineered. The company tore down and rebuilt nearly every activity that contributed to its high costs. It redesigned the way it develops, manufactures, distributes, prices, markets, and sells products. The reengineering was difficult, time-consuming, and expensive. But now, after the changes, price changes are rare, factories are far more efficient, inventory is way down, and sales and profits are up. And P&G brands are now priced comparably to store brands. P&G may have reinvented itself as a leader in the industry once again, and created for itself a long-term competitive advantage that others are scrambling to match.[32]

As you can see, reengineering is not about making minor organizational changes here and there. It is about completely overhauling the operation, in revolutionary ways, in order to achieve the greatest possible benefits to the customer and to the organization.

Organizing for technological response

technology The systematic application of scientific knowledge to a new product, process, or service.

Broadly speaking, **technology** can be viewed as the methods, processes, systems, and skills used to transform resources (inputs) into products (outputs). Although we will discuss technology—and innovation—more fully in Chapter 17, in this chapter we want to highlight some of the important influences technology has on organizational design.

Types of technology configurations

Research by Joan Woodward laid the foundation for understanding technology and structure. According to Woodward, there are three basic technologies that characterize how work is done: small batch, large batch, and continuous process technologies. These three classifications are equally useful for describing either service or manufacturing technologies. Each differs in terms of volume produced and variety of products/services offered. Each also has a different influence on organizing.[33]

small batches Technologies that produce goods and services in low volume.

Small batch technologies

When goods or services are provided in very low volume or **small batches,** a company that does such work is called a *job shop.* An example is John Thomas, a specialty printer in Lansing, Michigan, that manufactures printed material for the florist and garden industry. A service example is the doctor's office, which provides a high variety of low-volume, customized services.

In a small batch organization, structure tends to be very organic. There tend not to be a lot of rules and formal procedures, and decision making tends to be decentralized. The emphasis is on mutual adjustment among people.

large batch Technologies that produce goods and services in high volume.

Large batch technologies

As volume increases, product variety usually decreases. Companies with higher volumes and lower varieties than a job shop tend to be characterized as **large batch** or mass production technologies. Examples of large batch technologies include auto assembly operations of General Motors, Ford, and Chrysler. In the service sector, McDonald's and Burger King might be good examples. Their production runs tend to be more standardized and all customers receive similar (if not identical) products. Machines tend to replace people in the physical execution of work. People run the machines.

With a large batch technology, structure tends to be more mechanistic. There tend not to be many more rules and formal procedures; and decision making tends to be centralized with higher spans of control. Communication tends to be more formal where hierarchical authority is more prominent.

continuous process A process that is highly automated and has a continuous production flow.

Continuous process technologies

At the very-high-volume end of the scale are companies that use **continuous process** technologies, technologies that do not stop and start. Domino Sugar and Standard Oil, for example, use continuous process technologies where there are a very limited number of products to be produced. People are completely removed from the work itself. It is entirely done by machines and/or computers. In some cases, it may be that people run the computers that run the machines.

Ironically, with continuous process technology, structure can return to a more organic form since less monitoring and supervision are needed. Communication tends to be more informal where fewer rules and regulations are established.

Organizing for flexible manufacturing

mass customization The production of varied, individually customized products at the low cost of standardized, mass-produced products.

Although issues of volume and variety often have been seen as tradeoffs in a technological sense, today organizations are trying to produce both high-volume and high-variety products at the same time. This is referred to as **mass customization.**[34] Automobiles, clothes, computers, and other products are increasingly being manufactured to match each customer's taste, specifications, and budget. While this seemed like only a fantasy a few years ago, mass customization is quickly becoming more prevalent among leading firms. Levi's has been testing mass customization in its women's line. Companies like Motorola, Bell Atlantic, and Hallmark are achieving great success with mass customization. Dow Jones, Amdahl, Mitsubishi, and Mazda are struggling with it, but expect positive results ultimately.

How do companies organize to pull off this kind of customization at such low cost? They organize around a dynamic network of relatively independent operating units.[35] Each unit performs a specific process or task—called a *module*—like making a component, performing a credit check, or performing a particular welding method. Some modules may be performed by outside suppliers or vendors. Different modules join forces to make the good or provide a service. How and when the various modules interact with one another are dictated by the unique requests of each customer. The manager's responsibility is to make it easier and less costly for modules to come together, complete their tasks, and then recombine to meet the next customer demand. The ultimate goal of mass customization is a never-ending campaign to expand the number of ways a company can satisfy customers.

There are a variety of other ways that organizations are attempting to gain more flexibility in their manufacturing operations.

Levis has been successful in using mass customization to better serve its female customers. *[Ryder Photography]*

computer-integrated manufacturing The use of computer-aided design and computer-aided manufacturing to sequence and optimize a number of production processes.

Computer-integrated manufacturing

Computer-integrated manufacturing (CIM) encompasses a host of computerized production efforts linked together. Two examples are computer-aided design and computer-aided manufacturing, which offer the ultimate in computerized process technologies. For example, a manufacturer's engineering function may contain a large variety of software applications used in both electronic and mechanical design. Using CIM, different design team members can work on the network from remote sites, often their homes. These systems provide maximum process flexibility with lowest costs of production. They produce high-variety and high-volume products at the same time.

CIM potentially affords greater control and predictability of production processes, reduced waste, faster throughput times, and higher quality.[36] But a company cannot "buy" its way out of competitive trouble simply by investing in superior hardware (technology) alone. It must also ensure that it has strategic and "people" strengths, and a well-designed plan for implementing the technological changes.

flexible factories Manufacturing plants that have short production runs, are organized around products, and use decentralized scheduling.

Flexible factories

As the name implies, **flexible factories** provide more production options and a greater variety of products. They differ from traditional factories in three primary ways: lot size, flow patterns, and scheduling.[37]

First, the traditional factory has long production runs, generating high volumes of a standardized product. Flexible factories have much shorter production runs, with many different products. Second, traditional factories move parts down the line from one location in the production sequence to the next. Flexible factories are organized around products, in work cells or teams, so that people work closely together and parts move shorter distances with shorter or no delays. Third, traditional factories use centralized scheduling, which is time-consuming, inaccurate, and slow to adapt to changes. Flexible factories use local or decentralized scheduling, in which decisions are made on the shop floor by the people doing the work.

lean manufacturing An operation that strives to achieve the highest possible productivity and total quality, cost effectively, by eliminating unnecessary steps in the production process and continually strives for improvement.

Lean manufacturing

Lean manufacturing means an operation that is both efficient and effective; it strives to achieve the highest possible productivity and total quality, cost effectively, by eliminating unnecessary steps in the production process and continually striving for improvement.[38] Rejects are unacceptable, and staff, overhead, and inventory are considered wasteful. In a lean operation, the emphasis is on quality, speed, and flexibility more than on cost, efficiency, and hierarchy. But with a well-managed lean production process—like the operations at Toyota and Chrysler—a company can develop, produce, and distribute products with half or less of the human effort, space, tools, time, and overall cost.[39]

For the lean approach to result in more effective operations, the following conditions must be met:[40]

- People are broadly trained rather than specialized.
- Communication is informal and horizontal among line workers.
- Equipment is general-purpose.
- Work is organized in teams, or *cells,* that produce a group of similar products.
- Supplier relationships are long-term and cooperative.
- Product development is concurrent, not sequential, and done by cross-functional teams.

In recent years, many companies have tried to become more lean by cutting overhead costs, laying off operative-level workers, eliminating layers of management, and utilizing capital equipment more efficiently. But if the move to lean manufacturing is simply a harsh, haphazard cost-cutting approach, the result will be chaos, overworked people, and low morale.

Organizing for speed: Time-based competition

Companies worldwide have devoted so much energy to improving product quality that high quality is now the standard attained by all top competitors. Competition has driven quality to such heights that quality products no longer are enough to distinguish one company from another. *Time* is emerging as the key competitive advantage that can separate market leaders from also-rans.[41]

Companies today must learn what the customer needs and meet those needs as quickly as possible. **Time-based competition (TBC)** refers to strategies aimed at reducing the total time it takes to deliver the product or service. There are several key organizational elements to TBC: logistics, just-in-time (JIT), and simultaneous engineering. JIT production systems reduce the time it takes to manufacture products. Logistics speeds the delivery of products to customers. Both are essential steps toward bringing products to customers in the shortest time possible. In today's world, speed is essential.

time-based competition (TBC) Strategies aimed at reducing the total time it takes to deliver a product or service.

Logistics

Logistics is the movement of resources into the organization (inbound) and products from the organization to its customers (outbound).[42] As an extension of the organization's technology configuration, organizing the logistics function is often critical to an organization's responsiveness and competitive advantage.

logistics The movement of the right goods in the right amount to the right place at the right time.

Logistics is a great mass of parts, materials, and products moving via trucks, trains, planes, and ships. An average box of breakfast cereal spends 104 days getting from the factory to the supermarket, moving through the warehouses of wholesalers, distributors, brokers, and others! If the grocery industry streamlined logistics, it could save an estimated $30 billion annually.[43] Depending on the product, the duplication and inefficiency in distribution can cost far more than making the product itself.

By contrast, Saturn's distribution system is world-class. GM selected Ryder—the biggest logistics management firm in the United States—to perform most of its distribution for Saturn. Suppliers, factories, and dealers are linked so tightly and efficiently that Saturn barely has any parts inventory.[44]

Just-in-time operations

An additional element of TBC involves **just-in-time (JIT)** operations. JIT calls for subassemblies and components to be manufactured in very small lots and delivered to the next stage in the process precisely at the time needed, or

just-in-time (JIT) A system that calls for subassemblies and components to be manufactured in very small lots and delivered to the next stage of the production process just as they are needed.

GM selected Ryder–the biggest logistics management firm in the United States–to perform most of its distribution for Saturn.
[Courtesy of Ryder Systems, Inc.]

"just in time." A customer order triggers a factory order and the production process. The supplying work centers do not produce the next lot of product until the consuming work center requires it. Even external suppliers deliver to the company just-in-time.

Just-in-time is a companywide philosophy oriented toward eliminating waste throughout all operations and improving materials throughout. In this way, excess inventory is eliminated and costs are reduced. The ultimate goal of JIT is to better serve the customer by providing higher levels of quality and service.[45]

JIT represents a number of key production concepts. The system, which originated in Japan's Toyota Motor Corporation, includes the following concepts:

- *Elimination of waste.* Eliminate all waste from the production process, including waste of time, people, machinery, space, and materials.
- *Perfect quality.* Produce perfect parts even when lot sizes are reduced, and produce the product exactly when it is needed in the exact quantities that are needed.
- *Reduced cycle times.* Accomplish the entire manufacturing process more rapidly. Reduce setup times for equipment, move parts only short distances (machinery is placed in closer proximity), and eliminate all delays. The goal is to reduce action to the time spent working on the parts. For most manufacturers today, the percentage of time parts are worked on is about 5 percent of the total production time. JIT seeks to eliminate the other 95 percent, that is, to reduce to zero the time spent not working on the parts.
- *Employee involvement.* In JIT, employee involvement is central to success. The workers are responsible for production decisions. Managers and supervisors are coaches. Top management pledges that there will never be layoffs due to improved productivity.
- *Value-added manufacturing.* Do only those things (actions, work, etc.) that add value to the finished product. If it doesn't add value, don't do it. For example, inspection does not add value to the finished product, so make the product correctly the first time and inspection will not be necessary.
- *Discovery of problems and prevention of recurrence.* Foolproofing, or failsafing, is a key component of JIT. To prevent problems from arising, their cause(s) must be known and acted on. Thus, in JIT operations, people try to find the "weak link in the chain" by forcing problem areas to the surface so that preventive measures may be determined and implemented.

Many believe that only a fraction of JIT's potential has been realized. JIT has been applied extensively to manufacturing, but not yet to other processes such as service, distribution, and new-product development. Another potential benefit may come from applying JIT to information processes in offices.[46]

simultaneous engineering A design approach in which all relevant functions cooperate jointly and continually in a maximum effort aimed at producing high-quality products that meet customers' needs.

Simultaneous engineering

JIT is a vital component of TBC, but JIT concentrates on reducing time in only one function: manufacturing. TBC attempts to deliver speed in *all* functions—product development, manufacturing, logistics, and customer service. Customers will not be impressed if you manufacture quickly, but it takes weeks for them to receive their products or get a problem solved.

Many companies are turning to simultaneous engineering as the cornerstone of their TBC strategy. **Simultaneous engineering**—also an important component of total quality management—is a major departure from the old development process in which tasks were assigned to various functions in sequence. When R&D completed its part of the project, the work was "passed over the wall" to engineering, which completed its task and passed it over the wall to manufacturing, and so on. This process was highly inefficient, and errors took a long time to correct.

In contrast, simultaneous engineering incorporates the issues and perspectives of all the functions—and customers and suppliers—from the beginning of the process. This team-based approach results in a higher-quality product that is designed for efficient manufacturing *and* customer needs.[47] The team approach offers many advantages that speed up the process. The Impact, General Motors' new electric car, is a good example.

The Electric Car

With new state and federal regulations dictating stricter clean-air and fuel-efficiency standards, General Motors decided electric car technology was of major importance for its future. According to Kenneth R. Baker, GM's electric car project leader, the competitive advantage of GM's electric car, called the Impact, was that it would allow the company "to recapture the reputation for international automotive leadership."

GM's traditional approach to producing a new-concept car was to use an inefficient army of engineers. Each functional group within the company, such as marketing and manufacturing, was involved in the development process sequentially throughout the project. GM's bureaucratic structure and protocol created delays and stifled potential.

To combat these problems in the development of the Impact, GM hand-picked 200 individuals from the functional areas and included production workers in the formation of the project team. The team worked together simultaneously to develop the car. The team's goal was to develop an electric car from scratch by breaking away from conventional thinking, imagining the impossible, and then forming a plan to make it happen.

Impact's design team successfully tackled every challenge from the ground up. The Impact had a 0–60 mph acceleration time of 7.9 seconds (beating a Nissan 300ZX sports car in a drag race); a 124-mile battery charge, which is acceptable for most commuting; exotic styling; and an assembly design that dramatically cut the number of total components to simplify manufacturing. Furthermore, the team approach accelerated the development process so that the Impact project had the very realistic goal of producing a production car from scratch in four years, versus the eight years it took to develop GM's Saturn.

GM has now backed off of the project, believing the product will not be profitable. But others in the United States are picking up the slack. Venture capitalists, the electric-utility industry, scientists, and environmentalists are working together to create the electric-car industry. And Robert Stempel, former GM chairman, is pursuing his own electric-car venture. He believes he has all the technology he needs to make the concept a marketable reality.

However these groups proceed, speed will be of the essence. It's not as if the Japanese and the Europeans are oblivious to the idea.

Sources: William J. Cook, "The Soul of a New Machine," *U.S. News and World Report,* September 2, 1991, pp. 80–82; D. Woodruff, "GM: All Charged Up over the Electric Car," *Business Week,* October 21, 1991, pp. 106–8; P. Frame, "Former GM Chief Throws the Switch on EV Project," *Raleigh News and Observer,* January 27, 1994, pp. 1D, 2D; and O. Suris, "Californians Collide with Folks in Detroit over the Electric Car," *The Wall Street Journal,* January 24, 1994, pp. A1, A5. ●

Some managers resist the idea of simultaneous engineering. Why should marketing, product planning and design, and R&D "allow" manufacturing to get involved in "their" work?[48] The answer is: because the decisions made during the early, product-concept stage determine most of the manufacturing cost and quality. Furthermore, manufacturing can offer ideas about the product because of its experience with the prior generation of the product and with direct customer feedback. Also, the other functions must know early on what manufacturing can and cannot do. Finally, when manufacturing is in from the start, it is a full and true partner and will be more committed to decisions it helped make.

Organizing for strategic response

As our discussions thus far have focused on organizing in ways that improve responsiveness, they have been, in a sense, about competitive advantage and strategy. Organizational size, environmental adaptation, technology decisions, and the like are all elements of strategic management, as you know. And they all influence the design of organizations.

At the same time, there are issues directly pertaining to other aspects of strategy that influence how an organization is structured and managed. These include core competencies, network organizations, strategic alliances, learning organizations, and high-involvement organizations.

Organizing around core competencies

A recent, different, and important perspective on strategy, organization, and competition hinges on the concept of *core competence.*[49] Companies compete not just with their products, but also on the basis of their core strengths and expertise.

As you learned in Chapter 4, a core competence is the capability—knowledge, expertise, skill—that underlies a company's ability to be a leader in providing a range of specific goods or services. A core competence gives value to customers, makes the company's products different from (and better than) competitors', and can be used in creating new products. Think of core competencies as the roots of competitiveness, and products as the fruits.

What are some concrete examples of core competencies? And how can they be used to make firms more responsive and competitive?

Core competencies: Examples

Sharp and Toshiba committed years ago to being the world's best creators of flat-screen displays. They wanted to monopolize the markets for flat screens, although they didn't yet know all the potential product applications. A business case could not be made for each application; in fact, all applications couldn't even be envisioned. But the companies knew that this would be an important technology of the future.

The applications began with calculators. Over time, flat-screen displays were needed in pocket diaries, laptop computers, miniature televisions, LCD projection televisions, and video telephones. By committing early to a *competence,* these companies were ready for new and future *products* and *markets.*

As another example, SKF is the world's largest manufacturer of roller bearings. Are roller bearings its core competence? No, this would limit its products and market access. SKF's core competencies are antifriction, precision engineering, and making perfectly spherical devices. Perhaps they could manufacture other products, for example, the round, high-precision rolling heads that go inside a VCR, or the tiny balls in roller-ball pens.

Some other examples of companies with special competencies, which feed many specific products, are Hewlett-Packard (measurement, computing, communications); Sony (miniaturization); Rubbermaid (low-tech plastics); Lotus (enterprise computing or "groupware"); 3M (adhesives and advanced materials); EDS (systems integration); and Motorola (wireless communications).

Sources: G. Hamel and C. K. Prahalad, *Competing for the Future* (Boston: Harvard Business School Press, 1994); M. Loeb, "How to Grow a New Product Every Day," *Fortune,* November 14, 1994, pp. 269–70; L. Hays, S. Lipin, and W. Bulkeley, "Software Landscape Shifts as IBM Makes Hostile Bid for Lotus," *The Wall Street Journal,* June 6, 1995, pp. A1, A10.

Successfully developing a world-class core competence opens the door to a variety of future opportunities; failure means being foreclosed from many markets. Thus, a well-understood, well-developed core competence can enhance a company's responsiveness and competitiveness. Strategically, this means that companies should commit to excellence and leadership in competencies before they commit to winning market share for specific products. Organizationally, this means that the corporation should be viewed as a portfolio of competencies, not just a portfolio of specific businesses. Companies should strive for core competence leadership, not just product leadership.

Managers who want to strengthen their firms' competitiveness via core competencies need to focus on several related issues:

- Identify existing core competencies.
- Acquire or build core competencies that will be important for the future.
- Keep investing in competencies so the firm remains world-class and better than competitors.
- Extend competencies to find new applications and opportunities for the markets of tomorrow.[50]

The network organization

The notion of core competencies takes us right into a discussion of network organizations. Remember Walden Paddlers in "Setting the Stage"? In contrast to the traditional, hierarchical firm performing all the business functions, the network organization is a collection of independent, mostly single-function firms. As depicted in Figure 9.4, the **network organization** describes not one organization but the web of interrelationships among many firms. Network organizations are flexible arrangements among designers, suppliers, producers, distributors, and customers where each firm is able to pursue its own distinctive competence. The network as a whole, then, can display the technical specialization of the functional structure, the market responsiveness of the product structure, and the balance and flexibility of the matrix.[51]

network organization A collection of independent, mostly single-function firms.

The **dynamic network**—also called the *modular* or *virtual* corporation—is comprised of temporary arrangements among members that can be assembled and reassembled to meet a changing competitive environment. The members of the network are held together by contracts that stipulate results expected (market mechanisms) rather than by hierarchy and authority. Poorly performing firms can be removed and replaced.

dynamic network Temporary arrangements among partners that can be assembled and reassembled to adapt to the environment.

Such arrangements are common in the electronics, toy, and apparel industries, each of which creates and sells trendy products at a fast pace.[52] For example, Reebok owns no plants; it designs and markets, but does not produce. Nike owns only one small factory that makes sneaker parts. Other examples include the Bombay Company, Louis Galoob Toys, Brooks Brothers, and the Registry (which markets the services of independent software engineers, programmers, and technical writers).[53] In biotechnology, smaller firms do research and manufacture, and the drug giants market the products.[54]

figure 9.4
A dynamic network

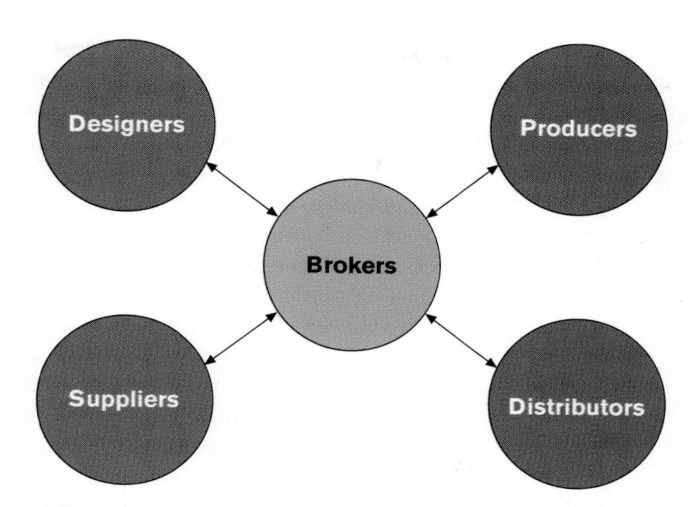

Source: R. Miles and C. Snow, "Organizations: New Concepts for New Forms," *California Management Review,* Spring 1986, p. 65. Copyright © 1986 by The Regents of the University of California. Reprinted from the *California Management Review*, Vol. 28, No. 3. By permission of The Regents.

Successful networks potentially offer flexibility, innovation, quick responses to threats and opportunities, and reduced costs and risk. But for these arrangements to be successful, several things must occur.

- The firm must choose the right specialty. This must be something (product or service) that the market needs and for which the firm is better at providing than other firms.
- The firm must choose collaborators that also are excellent at what they do and that provide complementary strengths.
- The firm must make certain that all parties fully understand the strategic goals of the partnership.
- Each party must be able to trust one another with strategic information and also trust that each collaborator will deliver quality products, even if the business grows quickly and makes heavy demands.[55]

broker Persons who assemble and coordinate participants in a network.

The role of managers shifts in a network from that of command and control to more like a **broker.** Broker/managers serve several important boundary roles that aid network integration and coordination:

- *Designer role.* The broker serves as a network architect who envisions a set of groups or firms whose collective expertise could be focused on a particular product or service.
- *Process engineering role.* The broker serves as a *network co-operator* who takes the initiative to lay out the flow of resources and relationships and makes certain that everyone shares the same goals, standards, payments, and the like.
- *Nurturing role.* The broker serves as a network developer that nurtures and enhances the network (like team building) to make certain the relationships are healthy and mutually beneficial.[56]

Strategic alliances

As discussed earlier, the modern organization has a variety of links with other organizations. These links are more complex than the standard relationships with traditional stakeholders like suppliers and clients. Today even fierce *competitors* are working together at unprecedented levels to achieve their strategic goals.[57] For example, IBM, Apple, and Intel have some cooperative arrangements; and GM, Ford, and Chrysler have been doing joint research and development to boost fuel efficiency and reduce exhaust emissions.[58]

strategic alliance A formal relationship created among independent organizations with the purpose of joint pursuit of mutual goals.

A **strategic alliance** is a formal relationship created with the purpose of joint pursuit of mutual goals. In a strategic alliance, individual organizations share administrative authority, form social links, and accept joint ownership. Such alliances are blurring firms' boundaries. They occur between companies and their competitors, governments, and universities. Such partnering often crosses national and cultural boundaries.[59] Companies form strategic alliances to develop new technologies, enter new markets, and reduce manufacturing costs. Alliances are often the fastest, most efficient way to achieve objectives. Moreover, strategic alliances can pay off not only through the immediate deal, but through creating additional, unforeseen opportunities and opening new doors to the future.[60]

Managers typically devote plenty of time to screening potential partners in financial terms.[61] But for the alliance to work, managers must also foster and develop the human relationships in the partnership. Asian companies seem to be the most comfortable with the nonfinancial, "people" side of alliances; European companies the next so; and U.S. companies the least. So, U.S. companies may need to pay extra attention to the human side of alliances.[62] Table 9.1 shows some recommendations for how to do this. In fact, most of the ideas apply not only to strategic alliances but to any type of relationship.

The learning organization

learning organization An organization skilled at creating, acquiring, and transferring knowledge, and at modifying its behavior to reflect new knowledge and insights.

Being responsive requires continually changing and learning new ways to act. Some experts have stated that the only sustainable advantage is learning faster than the competition. This has led to a new term that is now part of the vocabulary of most managers: the learning organization.[63] A **learning organization** is "an organization skilled at creating, acquiring, and transferring knowledge, and at modifying its behavior to reflect new knowledge and insights."[64]

GE, Corning, and Honda are good examples of learning organizations. Such organizations are skilled at solving problems, experimenting with new approaches, learning from their own experiences, learning from other organizations, and spreading knowledge quickly and efficiently.

table 9.1 How I's can become we's

The best alliances are true partnerships that meet these criteria:

1. *Individual excellence:* both partners add value, and their motives are positive (pursue opportunity) rather than negative (mask weaknesses).
2. *Importance:* both partners want the relationship to work because it helps them meet long-term strategic objectives.
3. *Interdependence:* the partners need each other; each helps the other reach its goal.
4. *Investment:* the partners devote financial and other resources to the relationship.
5. *Information:* the partners communicate openly about goals, technical data, problems, and changing situations.
6. *Integration:* the partners develop shared ways of operating; they teach each other and learn from each other.
7. *Institutionalization:* the relationship has formal status with clear responsibilities.
8. *Integrity:* both partners are trustworthy and honorable.

Source: R. M. Kanter, "Collaborative Advantage: The Art of Alliances," *Harvard Business Review,* July–August 1994, pp. 96–108.

How do firms become true learning organizations? There are a few important ingredients:[65]

1. Their people must engage in disciplined thinking and attention to details, making decisions based on data and evidence rather than guesswork and assumptions.
2. They search constantly for new knowledge, looking for expanding horizons and opportunities rather than quick fixes to current problems.
3. They carefully review both successes and failures, looking for lessons and deeper understanding.
4. Learning organizations *benchmark*—they identify and implement the best business practices of other organizations, stealing ideas shamelessly.
5. They share ideas throughout the organization via reports, information systems, informal discussions, site visits, education, and training.

The high-involvement organization

Participative management is becoming increasingly popular as a way to create a competitive advantage. Particularly in high-technology companies facing stiff international competition, such as Microsystems and Compaq Computer, the aim is to generate high levels of commitment and involvement as employees and managers work together to achieve organizational goals.[66]

high-involvement organization A type of organization in which top management ensures that there is consensus about the direction in which the business is heading.

In the **high-involvement organization,** top management ensures that there is a consensus about the direction in which the business is heading. The leader seeks input from his or her top management team and from lower levels of the company. Task forces, study groups, and other techniques are used to foster participation in decisions that affect the entire organization. Also fundamental to the high-involvement organization is continual feedback to participants regarding how they are doing compared to the competition and how effectively they are meeting the strategic agenda.

Structurally, this usually means that even lower-level employees have a direct relationship with a customer or supplier and thus they receive feedback and are held accountable for a product or service delivery. The organizational form is a flat, decentralized structure built around customer, product, or service.[67] Employee involvement is particularly powerful when the environment changes rapidly, work is creative, complex activities require coordination, and firms need major breakthroughs in innovation and speed[68]—in other words, when companies need to be more responsive.

Final thoughts about responsive organizations

As organizations strive to maximize responsiveness, they have to balance their needs for efficiency and effectiveness. We have pointed out throughout this chapter (and the one before) that *any* approach to organizing has its strengths and limitations. And we have noted that advantages gained by a firm through innovative structures and systems are likely to be short-lived. Competitors catch up.

Today's advantages are tomorrow's "table stakes;" requirements that need to be met if a firm expects to be a major player in an industry. Increasingly we hear executives such as GE's Jack Welch or Kodak's George Fisher say that their goal is to create a *boundaryless organization* capable of doing anything, anytime, anywhere around the world. This is, of course, a lofty goal and one that requires organizations to transcend the limits of their existing structures, technologies, and systems.[69]

Key terms

Broker, p. 323
Computer-integrated manufacturing (CIM), p. 317
Continuous process, p. 315
Downsizing, p. 307
Dynamic network, p. 322
Economies of scope, p. 306
Flexible factories, p. 317
High-involvement organization, p. 325
ISO 9000, p. 313
Just-in-time (JIT), p. 318
Large batch, p.315
Lean manufacturing, p. 317
Learning organization, p. 324
Logistics, p. 318
Mass customization, p. 316
Mechanistic organization, p. 304
Network organization, p. 322
Organic structure, p. 304
Rightsizing, p. 307
Simultaneous engineering, p. 319
Small batches, p. 315
Strategic alliance, p. 324
Survivor's syndrome, p. 307
Technology, p. 315
Time-based competition, p. 318
Total quality management, p. 311

Summary of learning objectives

Now that you have studied Chapter 9, you should know:

The market imperatives your firm must meet to survive.

Organizations have a formal structure to help control what goes on within them. But to survive today, firms need more than control—they need responsiveness. They must act quickly and adapt to fast-changing demands.

The potential advantages of creating an organic form of organization.

The organic form emphasizes flexibility. Organic organizations are decentralized, informal, and dependent on the judgment and expertise of people with broad responsibilities. The organic form is not a single formal structure, but a concept that underlies all the new forms discussed in this chapter.

How your firm can "be" both small and big.

Historically, large organizations have had important advantages over small. Today, small size has advantages, including the ability to act quickly, respond to customer demands, and serve small niches. The ideal firm today combines the advantages of both: It creates many small, flexible units, while the corporate level adds value by taking advantage of its size and power.

How to manage information-processing demands.

Integrative mechanisms help coordinate the efforts of differentiated subunits. Slack resources and self-contained tasks reduce the need to process information. Information systems and horizontal relationships help the organization process information.

How firms organize to meet customer requirements.

Firms have embraced principles of continuous improvement and total quality management to respond to customer needs. Baldrige criteria and ISO 9000 standards help firms organize to meet better quality specifications. Extending these, reengineering efforts are directed at completely overhauling processes to provide world-class customer service.

How firms organize around different types of technology.

Organizations tend to move from organic structures to mechanistic structures and back to organic structures as they transition from small batch to large batch and continuous process technologies.To organize for flexible manufacturing, organizations pursue mass customization via computer-integrated manufacturing and lean manufacturing. To organize for time-based competition, firms emphasize their logistics operations, just-in-time operations, and simultaneous engineering.

The new types of dynamic organizational concepts and forms that are being used for strategic responsiveness.

New and emerging organizational concepts and forms include core competencies, network organizations, strategic alliances, learning organizations, and high-involvement organizations.

Discussion questions

1. Discuss evidence you have seen of the imperatives for change, flexibility, and responsiveness faced by today's firms.

2. Describe large, bureaucratic organizations with which you have had contact that have not responded flexibly to customer demands. Also describe examples of satisfactory responsiveness. What do you think accounts for the differences between the responsive and nonresponsive organizations?

3. Considering the potential advantages of large and small size, would you describe the "feel" of your college or university as big, small, or small-within-big? Why? What might make it feel different?

4. What is a core competence? Generate some examples of companies with distinctive competencies, identifying what those competencies are. Brainstorm some creative new products and markets to which these competencies could be applied.

5. If you were going into business for yourself, what would be your core competencies? What competencies do you have now, and what competencies are you going to develop? Describe what your role would be in a network organization, and the competencies and roles of other firms you would want in your network.

6. Identify some recently formed alliances between competitors. What are the goals of the alliance? What brought them together? What have they done to ensure success? How are they doing now?

7. What skills will you need to work effectively in (1) a network organization; (2) a learning organization; and (3) a high-involvement organization? Be specific, generating long lists. Would you enjoy working in these environments? Why or why not? What can you do to prepare yourself for these eventualities?

Concluding Case

Franco's immaculate confection

How did Franco Harris, the former Pittsburgh Steeler football star, create a $10 million donut bakery with just 10 people? It was no piece of cake. The institutional baked goods industry is highly competitive, and fragmented and offers little opportunity for growth. In fact, overall sales in the industry have been declining for over the past decade. And yet, Super Bakery®, Inc., has been quietly gaining market share since the early 1990s and continues to post annual revenue increases with strong profits.

What makes Super Bakery so interesting is how the company is organized. Formed in 1990, the company has achieved national presence by operating as a virtual corporation. Instead of creating a large, sprawling, multifunctional organization to administer the business, Super Bakery focused on the

Franco Harris' Super Bakery, Inc., beats the odds and successfully entered the highly competitive institutional baked goods industry. It now has an annual growth rate of around 20 to 30 percent with profits that are twice the industry average. *[Norbert Schmidt/Sports Illustrated]*

key drivers of customer value and developed skills and competencies in these areas alone and has outsourced the rest.

Super Bakery handles strategic planning, marketing, R&D, and finance/accounting internally. However, Super Bakery does not manufacture its own product. A network of outside bakers does that. And yet, because Super Bakery formulates its own recipes, purchases its ingredients, and produces its own bakery fortifier, Nutri Dough®, it maintains firm control over product quality. Franco Harris even hired a master baker to develop new products. The contracted bakeries simply follow Super Bakery's standard operating procedures for manufacturing each item.

Beyond product considerations, Super Bakery also analyzed which service elements were most important to customers before deciding to contract out certain functions. It turns out that managing orders effectively has one of the biggest influences on customer satisfaction. So while selling, production, warehousing, and shipping activities have been contracted, Super Bakery management has retained control over the planning and tracking of these activities in the order management process.

Super Bakery's major challenge has been to coordinate and control the various functional activities performed outside the company by brokers and contractors. Outside brokers, manufacturers, and trucking companies can make or break Super Bakery because they stand between the company and its customers. Many of their concerns can be addressed by clarifying performance standards with contractors in painstaking detail. In addition, the company has developed a performance reporting system that provides a balance of nonfinancial and financial measures. The nonfinancial measures track customer satisfaction and the financial measures track the cost of filling orders and serving customers. To keep track of these measures, Super Bakery created a relational database that stores and processes the information. The technology infrastructure helps to provide a constant stream of feedback between Super Bakery and its partners.

Questions

1. How does this story differ from the two you read about in "Setting the Stage"? How are they similar?

2. What are the strengths and weaknesses of Super Bakery's organizational structure?

3. What are the biggest challenges of managers in running a business such as this?

Sources: T. R. V. Davis and B. L. Darling, "Update on Super Bakery, Inc.," *Organization Dynamics,* Autumn 1996, pp. 86–87; T. R. V. Davis and B. L. Darling, "How Virtual Corporations Manage the Performance of Contractors: The Super Bakery Case," *Organization Dynamics,* Summer 1995, pp. 70–75; and T. R. V. Davis and B. L. Darling, "ABC in a Virtual Corporation," *Management Accounting,* October 1996, pp. 18–26.

Video Case

The responsive organization

In the past, a corporation was structured much like the military, with a formal chain of command and division of labor. Over time, many companies came to realize that the bureaucratic structure of the traditional corporation can often cause breakdowns in communication and lower efficiency.

Manufacturers of products in relatively unchanging environments often take a mechanistic approach to production. In such environments, employees strictly adhere to their job descriptions. However, companies that depend on their ability to continuously introduce new innovations usually take a more organic approach, giving employees more room to make decisions and communicate outside the chain of command. Some companies may choose to radically modify or reengineer their structure.

Big Apple Bagels and St. Louis Bread Company are two rapidly growing businesses that share a similar market. However, each organization is structured quite differently. Whatever the structure, for an organization to be successful, it must be responsive to its customers. This operating principle means more than just making sure the right kind of cheese gets put on a turkey sandwich.

Many companies are finding that changing the way in which they are organized improves their responsiveness. They may choose to simplify their structure and reduce the layers of management, thus reducing the layers in the chain of command. Another option is to widen the spans of control. The traditional organization has a tall structure and a narrow span of control, which means managers have few subordinates who report directly to them. A company with a flat organizational structure has a wide span of control with fewer reporting levels.

Many companies are empowering their employees and allowing them to make decisions rather than insisting that they report to various levels of management. When Paul Stolzer opened the first Big Apple Bagel store in 1985, he had no idea that in seven years his small store would grow into a franchise that boasts 75 stores with more opening all the time. Stolzer said, "The stores have changed quite extensively over the years. We are actually a fourth or fifth generation store right now. Initially the stores were set up as strictly bagel bakeries with a predominant product being bagels and cream cheese. We've progressed to a more aggressive stature, adding a few more dimensions to our operation in that we have dine-in facilities, a more extensive sandwich menu, and a very, very strong coffee program."

One thing that hasn't changed in Big Apple Bagels' open-door policy. From top management to line workers, communication channels are open. Jim Lentz, director of training said, "At Big Apple Bagels we have an open door policy between the franchisee and the franchisor, and between the ultimate consumer and the franchisor in that we encourage people to come up with suggestions, new products, new ideas."

In 1987, Ken Rosenthal opened his first St. Louis Bread Company store in Kirkwood, Missouri, with used baking equipment. Today, St. Louis Bread company operates over 50 stores in the St. Louis area, with stores opening in other midwestern markets as well. The growth happened quickly, forcing the company to change its organizational structure. Originally, it was a small store with 17 employees. When it became a large chain, employing over 1,000 people, a more traditional organizational structure was needed.

When a company is growing, it may need to use some of the concepts of reengineering. Reengineering entails the radical redesign of business processes to achieve major gains in cost, service, or time. For example, by mid-1992, St. Louis Bread was growing at a frantic pace. The partners had reached a point where the controls and information systems they had in place were inadequate for a larger operation. New equipment was purchased to automate processes on the line, and $30,000 point-of-purchase cash registers were installed to track everything from sales per hour to sales per stock keeping unit to sales by stores.

Doron Berger said, "The organization at St. Louis Bread Company is probably not atypical of many organizations. While we have a hierarchical structure in terms of someone is ultimately accountable for the results of the business. We do fight vigorously to maintain a flat organization. In other words, there aren't a lot of layers between the president CEO and the people who are on the front lines. I think we have succeeded because of the effort we have put into that."

In November of 1983, Au Bon Pain, the dominant bakery/cafe chain in the country acquired St. Louis Bread Company. David Hutkin said, "Our organizational structure had not changed dramatically. It really hasn't changed since the acquisition.

A company like Big Apple Bagels is considered to be a boundaryless organization. In such an organization, the corporate structure is more horizontal than vertical. Boundaryless businesses are typically organized around core customer-oriented processes, such as communication, customer contact, and managing quality. In order to enjoy the benefits a horizontal organization offers, four boundaries must be overcome: authority, task, political, identity.

Even a relatively boundaryless company has an authority boundary. Some people lead, others follow. To overcome problems that may arise, managers must learn how to lead and still remain open to criticism. Their "subordinates" need to be trained and encouraged not only to follow but also to challenge their superiors if there is an issue worth considering.

The task boundary arises out of the "it's not my job" mentality. A task boundary can be overcome by clearly defining who does what when employees from different departments divide up work.

The political boundary derives from the differences in political agendas that often separate employees and can cause conflict. This is closely related to identity boundary, which emerges due to an employee tendency to identify with those individuals or groups with whom they have shared experiences, or with whom they share fundamental values.

Critical Thinking Questions

1. If companies today are working so hard to break down boundaries, why is it that there are boundaries in the first place?

2. What are some new technologies that will help managers keep lines of communication open to employees? To customers?

3. The video mentions that St. Louis Bread Company had to use a more traditional organizational structure when it grew rapidly. Why do you think that was necessary? What do you think the company gains by adopting such a structure? What does it lose?

Experiential Exercises

9.1 Decentralization: Pros and Cons

Objective

To explore the reasons for, as well as the pros and cons of, decentralizing.

Instructions

Below in the Decentralization Worksheet are some observations on decentralization. As you review each of the statements, provide an example that illustrates why this statement is important and related problems and benefits of the situation or condition indicated in the statement.

Decentralization Worksheet

A large number of factors determine the extent to which a manager should decentralize. Clearly, anything that increases a manager's workload creates a pressure for decentralization since there is only a finite level of work that can be accomplished by a single person. As with many facets of management, there are advantages and disadvantages to decentralization.

1. The greater the diversity of products, the greater the decentralization.

2. The larger the size of the organization, the more the decentralization.

3. The more rapidly changing the organization's environment, the more decentralization.

4. Developing adequate, timely controls is the essence of decentralizing.

5. Managers should delegate those decisions that involve large amounts of time but minimal erosions of their power and control.

6. Decentralizing involves delegating authority, and therefore, the principles of delegation apply to decentralization. (List the principles of delegation before you start your discussion).

____

____

____

____

____

____

Source: R. R. McGrath, Jr., *Exercises in Management Fundamentals* (Englewood Cliffs, N.J.: Prentice-Hall, 1985) pp. 59–60. Reprinted by permission of Prentice-Hall, Inc.

9.2 The University Culture

Objectives

1. To measure the culture at your university.
2. To study the nature of organization culture.
3. To understand how a culture can be changed.

Instructions

1. Working alone, complete and score the University Culture Survey.
2. In small groups, exchange survey scores and develop responses to the discussion questions.
3. Group spokespersons report group findings to the class.

Discussion Questions

1. In what respects did students agree or disagree on survey test items?
2. What might account for differences in students' experiences and attitudes with respect to the university culture?
3. How can the survey results be put to constructive use? ●

Chapter Ten

Human Resources Management

You can get capital and erect buildings, but it takes people to build a business.

—Thomas J. Watson, Founder, IBM

Chapter Outline

Strategic Human Resources Management

- The HR Planning Process

Staffing the Organizations

- Recruitment
- Selection
- Workforce Reductions

Developing the Workforce

- Training and Development

Performance Appraisal

Designing Reward Systems

- Pay Decisions
- Incentive Systems and Variable Pay
- Employee Benefits
- Legal Issues in Compensation and Benefits
- Health and Safety

Labor Relations

- Labor Laws
- Unionization
- Collective Bargaining
- What Does the Future Hold?

Learning Objectives

After studying Chapter 10, you will know:

1. How companies use human resources management to gain competitive advantage.
2. Why companies recruit both internally and externally for new hires.
3. The various methods available for selecting new employees.
4. Why companies spend so much on training and development.
5. How to determine who should appraise an employee's performance.
6. How to analyze the fundamental aspects of a reward system.
7. How unions influence human resources management.
8. How the legal system influences human resources management.

Setting the Stage

Windows of Opportunity at Microsoft

If you think about it for just a minute, it's pretty easy to see why Microsoft believes that people are its most important asset. Unlike other companies in the computer industry that sell hardware, Microsoft focuses on software. And as Bill Gates, the company's CEO, put it, software is "packaged intelligence." The programs, algorithms, and applications that make Microsoft the preeminent force in software development come from the minds of some pretty smart people. Not surprisingly then, Microsoft does a darned good job of recruiting and hiring the very best talent in the industry.

Microsoft wants people who understand current technology, but who ask questions, and who have the potential to continually grow and change. In other words, the company looks for "learners" rather than "knowers." Microsoft wants its people to be able to think flexibly so they can create change in the industry.

Like most organizations, Microsoft relies on a variety of tools to reach potential candidates. Advertisements in newspapers and on the Internet help drum up applicants, as do activities at colleges and job fairs. The company receives about 12,000 résumés each month from job applicants, and each résumé is logged into a computer database from which recruiters can perform keyword searches for particular skills, abilities, and backgrounds.

Selecting employees is an interesting process as well. Instead of emphasizing traditional selection tests, reference checks, drug tests, and the like, Microsoft conducts some very intensive interview sessions. These interviews are primarily concerned with understanding how potential employees think and learn. For example, an interviewer may ask an applicant how much water flows through the Mississippi River on a daily basis, or why manhole covers are round. The interviews are not looking for correct answers so much as they want to see how the applicant goes about framing and solving the problem.

"How much water flows through the Mississippi River?" is a question you might be asked at an interview for a position at Microsoft. *[AP/The Vicksburg Post/Andrew Kent Miller/Wide World Photos]*

Do these hiring approaches work? Evidently so. Turnover for Microsoft employees is only about 7 percent a year, a rate far below the industry average.

Sources: Ron Lieber, "Wired for Hiring: Microsoft's Slick Recruiting Machine," Fortune, *February 5, 1996, pp. 123–24; George Taninecz, "In Search of Creative Sparks,"* Industry Week, *December 4, 1995, pp. 43–47; Stuart J. Johnson, "Microsoft Scrambles to Find the Brightest,"* Computerworld, *February 20, 1995, p. 32; Randall E. Stross, "Microsoft's Big Advantage—Hiring Only the Supersmart,"* Fortune, *November 25, 1996, pp. 159–62.*

human resources management (HRM) Formal systems for the management of people within the organization. Divided into three major areas: staffing, rewarding, and designing work.

Human resources management (HRM), historically known as personnel management, deals with formal systems for managing people at work. We begin this chapter by describing HRM as it relates to strategic management. The quote by Thomas Watson, founder of IBM, summarizes our view of the importance of people to any organization. We also discuss more of the "nuts and bolts" of HRM: staffing, training, performance appraisal, rewards, and labor relations. Throughout the chapter, we discuss legal issues that influence each aspect of HRM. In the next chapter, we expand this focus to address related issues of managing a diverse workforce.

Strategic human resources management

HRM has assumed a vital strategic role in recent years as organizations attempt to compete through people. Recall from Chapter 4, "Planning and Strategic Management," that firms can create a competitive advantage when they possess or develop resources that are valuable, rare, inimitable, and organized. We can use these same criteria to talk about the strategic impact of human resources.

1. **Creates value.** People can increase value through their efforts to decrease costs or provide something unique to customers, or some combination of the two. Empowerment programs, total quality initiatives, and continuous improvement efforts at companies such as Corning, Xerox, and Saturn are intentionally designed to increase the value that employees have on the bottom line.
2. **Is rare.** People are a source of competitive advantage when their skills, knowledge, and abilities are not equally available to all competitors. As the opening Microsoft example demonstrates, top companies invest a great deal to hire and train the best and the brightest employees in order to gain advantage over their competitors. Recently, Dow Chemical went to court to stop General Electric from hiring away its engineers. This case shows that some companies recognize both the value and rareness of certain employees.
3. **Is difficult to imitate.** People are a source of competitive advantage when their capabilities and contributions cannot be copied by others. Disney, Southwest Airlines, and Mirage Resorts are each known for creating unique cultures that get the most from employees (through teamwork) and are difficult to imitate.
4. **Is organized.** People are a source of competitive advantage when the talents can be combined together and rapidly deployed to work on new assignments at a moment's notice. Teamwork and cooperation are two pervasive methods for ensuring an organized workforce. But companies such as Spyglass (a software company) and AT&T have invested in information technology to help allocate and track employee assignments to temporary projects.

These four criteria highlight the importance of people and show the closeness of HRM to strategic management. In a recent survey by *USA Today* and Deloitte & Touche, nearly 80 percent of corporate executives said the importance of HRM in their firms has grown substantially over the past 10 years, and two-thirds said that HR expenditures are now viewed as a strategic investment rather than simply a cost to be minimized.[1] Because employee skills, knowledge, and abilities are among the most distinctive and renewable resources upon which a company can draw, their strategic management is more important than ever. Increasingly organizations are recognizing that their success depends on what people know; that is, their knowledge and skills. The term **human capital** (or more broadly, *intellectual capital*) is often used today to describe the strategic value of employee skills and knowledge.

human capital The knowledge, skills, and abilities of employees that have economic value.

But while concepts such as sustainable competitive advantage and human capital are certainly important, they remain only ideas for action. On a day-to-day basis, HR managers have many concerns regarding their workers and the entire personnel puzzle. These concerns include managing layoffs; addressing employee loyalty issues; managing diversity; creating a well-trained, highly motivated workforce; containing health care costs; and the like. Balancing these issues is a difficult task, and the best approach is likely to vary depending on the circumstances of the organization. A steel producer facing a cutback in business may need human resources activities to assist with layoffs, whereas a semiconductor company may need more staff to produce enough microchips to meet the demands of the burgeoning personal computer market. The emphasis on different HR activities depends on whether the organization is growing, declining, or standing still. This leads to the practical issues involved in HR planning.

The HR planning process

"Get me the right kind and the right number of people at the right time." It sounds simple enough, but meeting the organization's staffing needs requires strategic human resources planning: an activity with a strategic purpose derived from the organization's plans.

The HR planning process occurs in three stages: planning, programming, and evaluating. First, HR managers need to know the organization's business plans to ensure that the right number and types of people are available—where the company is headed, in what businesses it plans to be, what future growth is expected, and so forth. Few things are more damaging to morale than having to lay off recently hired college graduates because of inadequate planning for future needs. Second, the organization conducts programming of specific human resources activities, such as recruitment, training, or layoffs. In this stage, the company's plans are implemented. Third, human resources activities are evaluated to determine whether they are producing the results needed to contribute to the organization's business plans. Figure 10.1 illustrates the components of the human resources planning process. In this chapter, we focus on human resources planning and programming. Many of the other factors listed in Figure 10.1 are discussed in future chapters.

figure 10.1 An overview of the HR planning process

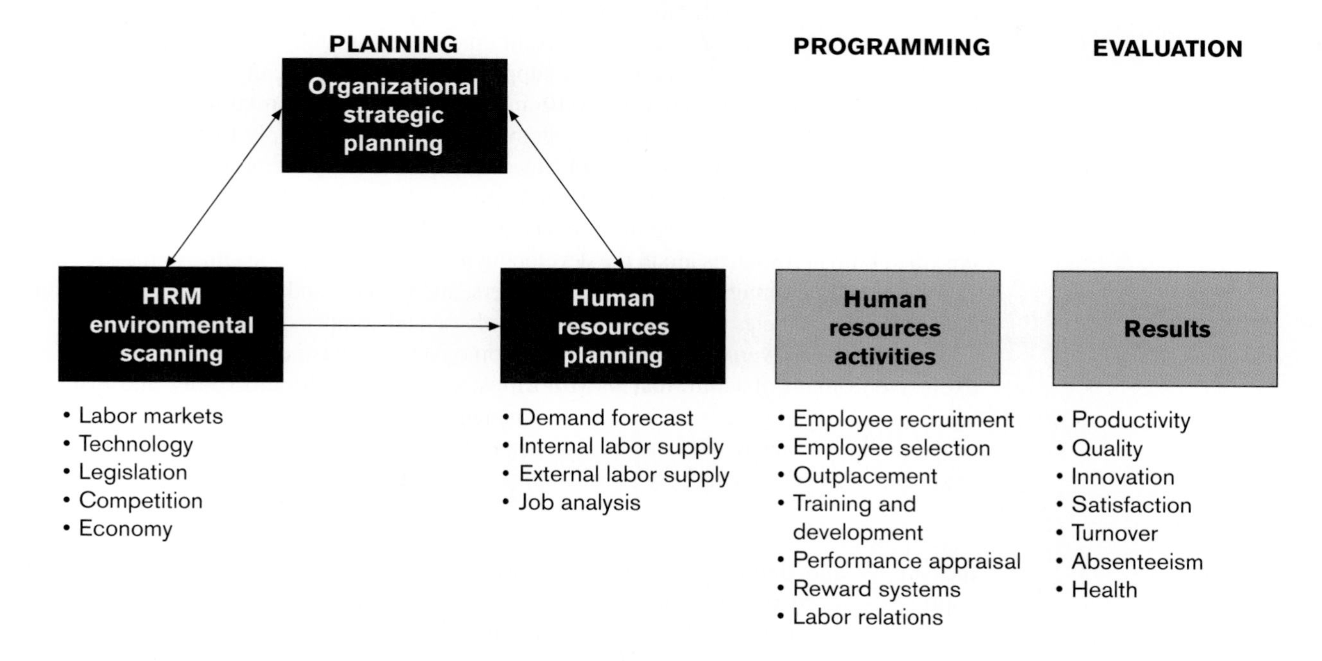

One of Marriott's HRM programs involves training and employing people with disabilities. Here, Laurie Axtell (left) coaches Jill Durbin. *[© 1991 Dennis Brack/Black Star]*

Demand forecasts Perhaps the most difficult part of human resources planning is conducting *demand* forecasts; that is, determining how many and what type of people are needed. Demand forecasts for people needs are derived from organizational plans. For example, suppose a pharmaceutical company such as Merck develops a new drug to cure baldness (one of your textbook authors hopes this is true). Merck's managers estimate the future size of this market based on demographic projections. Based on current sales and projected future sales growth, managers estimate the plant capacity needed to meet future demand, the sales force required, the support staff needed, and so forth. At this point, the number of labor-hours required to operate a plant, sell the product, distribute it, service customers, and so forth can be calculated. These estimates are used to determine the demand for different types of workers.

Labor supply forecasts In concert with demand forecasts, the *supply of labor* must also be forecast; that is, estimates of how many and what types of employees the organization actually will have. In performing a supply analysis, the organization estimates the number and quality of its current employees as well as the available external supply of workers. To estimate internal supply, the company typically relies on past experiences with turnover, terminations, retirements, or promotions and transfers. A computerized human resources information system assists greatly in supply forecasting.

Externally, organizations have to look at workforce trends to make projections. Worldwide, there is a growing gap between the world's supply of labor and the demand for labor.[2] Most of the well-paid jobs are generated in the cities of the industrialized world, but many skilled and unskilled human resources are in the developing nations. This gap is leading to massive relocation (including immigrants, temporary workers, and retirees) and a reduction of protectionist immigration policies (as countries come to rely on and compete for foreign workers).

Forecasts of a diverse workforce have become fact. The business world is no longer the exclusive domain of white males. Minorities, women, immigrants, older and disabled workers, and other groups have made the management of diversity a fundamental activity of the modern manager. Because of the importance of managing the "new workforce," the next chapter is devoted entirely to this topic.

Reconciling supply and demand Once managers have a good idea of both the supply and demand for various types of employees, they can start developing approaches for reconciling the two. In some cases, organizations find that they need more people than they currently have (i.e., a labor deficit). In such cases, organizations can hire new employees, promote current employees to new positions, or train other employees to move in from other areas in the organization. In other cases, organizations may find that they have more people than they need (i.e., a labor surplus). If this is detected far enough in advance, organizations can use attrition—the normal turnover of employees—to reduce the surplus. In other instances, the organization may lay off employees or transfer them to other areas. Each of these options is discussed in more detail below.

job analysis A tool for determining what is done on a given job and what should be done on that job.

Job analysis While supply and demand forecasting are fairly "macro" activities that are conducted at an organizational level, HR planning also has a "micro" side called *job analysis.* **Job analysis** does two things.[3] First, it tells the HR manager about the job itself: the essential tasks, duties, and responsibilities involved in performing the job. This information is called a *job description.* Second, job analysis describes the skills, knowledge, abilities, and other characteristics needed to perform the job. This is called the *job specification.*

Job analysis provides the information that virtually every human resources activity requires. It assists with the essential HR programs: recruitment, training, selection, appraisal, and reward systems. For example, a thorough job analysis helps organizations successfully defend themselves in lawsuits involving employment practices.[4] Ultimately, job analysis helps to increase the value added by employees to the organization since it clarifies what is really required to perform effectively.

From the Pages of BusinessWeek

Hiring the Right Stuff

The problem isn't numbers–we see an endless stream of job applicants at my family-owned factory. It's quality that's hard to find. Mostly, the job seekers we get are a sorry lot. Few are older than 20, and many look like they haven't changed clothes in a week. Chances are only one of the five folks who show up in a given week will pass our reading and technical-skills tests. Of those who succeed, about half will fail the drug screen. If a person manages to get hired at Emerald Packaging Inc., our plastic-package manufacturing company, he or she has only a 30 percent chance of lasting a year.

We have lived with this for a long time. When we were just looking for people to do production work, packing plastic bags in boxes, the relatively limited abilities of those we hired didn't matter. No longer. Our printing presses are getting too sophisticated, and the quality demanded by customers is now too exacting to put up with ragtag recruits. We have to find people who can think and care about quality, or we won't make the grade. Hiring off the street, in other words, just won't cut it.

Tuition payments. So how's a company like ours to find the skills it needs? For entry-level employees, we're teaming up with agencies that get applicants for us, approving only those who pass muster. Many of these groups are nontraditional employment agencies such as refugee support groups, churches, or welfare-to-work transition programs. But for our highly skilled jobs such as mechanics, bookkeepers, and machine operators, more and more, we're training internal candidates and paying tuition so people can go to school and pick up new skills. Sniffs one longtime manager: "It seems like we're becoming an educational institution." He's not far off. Since last June, we have put half of our 85 plant employees through 40 hours or more of training. Thanks to $25,000 supplied by the state of California Employment Training Panel, we have paid employees to teach production skills to their junior counterparts. We also offered a weeklong course on printing for our newer press operators, a 60-hour course on quality control for our more senior press operators, and another weeklong course for our employees who make bags. This is the first time most of our employees have received any formal training beyond what they got when they first arrived–in some cases, more than 20 years ago.

The payoff has been immediate. Simply by teaching our press operators some basic troubleshooting skills and making our quality standards clear, we have improved our print quality markedly. Spot inspections by managers have turned up far fewer flawed print jobs; complaints by customers are down by 50 percent. In our bag-making unit, waste has fallen about 25 percent since the course–a potential savings of over $100,000 for the year. Also important, morale on the shop floor has improved because the workers see they may get a chance to move into better jobs.

Recruiting outside to fill the highly skilled top jobs is a lot harder, though. Silicon Valley, only a short drive from our factory, has swept up most of the engineers and mechanics who might consider working for us. But even if we did find a willing engineer, we'd still be stuck with the training.

College material. So instead, we have decided to upgrade the skills of some of our best white-collar and more senior hourly employees by sending them back to school. We have already sent one of our younger office employees to school to learn accounting, expecting that she'll succeed our current controller, who is about to retire. Recently, we agreed to pay the tuition of our top maintenance man so he can earn an engineering degree going to a local college after work. He agreed, in return, to remain with us for five years after he finishes his degree.

Despite our recent successes, I suspect we'll always struggle to find good new employees. We're a growing company in a tough labor market. Worse yet, factory work is not most people's idea of a good job, even if the pay and benefits are decent. My aim is to balance the fight for quality hires by upgrading the skills of those who already work for us. Our early success with training–both internal and external–gives me some optimism. Which is more than I feel most days while I watch the latest job candidate shuffle past my office door.

Source: Kevin Kelly, "Hiring the Right Stuff," *Business Week:* February 9, 1998.

Discussion Questions

1. What are the keys to getting and keeping talented employees?
2. What is going on in the labor market that makes this difficult?
3. What other suggestions do you have for Mr. Kelly, the author of this article? ●

Staffing the organization

Once HR planning is completed, managers can focus on staffing the organization. The staffing function consists of three related activities: recruitment, selection, and outplacement.

Recruitment

recruitment The development of a pool of applicants for jobs in the organization.

Recruitment activities help to increase the pool of candidates that might be selected for a job. Recruitment may be internal to the organization (considering current employees for promotions and transfers) or external. Each approach has advantages and disadvantages.[5]

Internal recruiting

Advantages of internal recruiting are that employers know their employees, and employees know their organization. External candidates who are unfamiliar with the organization may find they don't like working there. Also, the opportunity to move up within the organization may encourage employees to remain with the company, work hard, and succeed. Recruiting from outside the company can be demoralizing to employees. Many companies, such as Sears Roebuck and Eli Lilly, prefer internal over external recruiting for these reasons.

Internal staffing has some drawbacks. If existing employees lack skills or talent, internal recruitment yields a limited applicant pool, leading to poor selection decisions. Also, an internal recruitment policy can inhibit a company that wants to change the nature or goals of the business by bringing in outside candidates. In changing from a rapidly growing, entrepreneurial organization to a mature business with more stable growth, Dell Computer went outside the organization to hire managers who better fit those needs.

Many companies that rely heavily on internal recruiting use a job-posting system. A *job-posting system* is a mechanism for advertising open positions, typically on a bulletin board. Texas Instruments uses job-posting. Employees complete a request form indicating interest in a posted job. The posted job description includes a list of duties and the minimum skills and experience required.

External recruiting External recruiting brings in "new blood" to a company and can inspire innovation. Among the most frequently used sources of outside applicants are newspaper advertisements, employee referrals, and college campus recruiting.

Newspaper advertisements are the most popular recruiting source for many occupations, because they are inexpensive and can generate a large number of responses. Employee referral is another frequently used source of applicants;[6] some companies actively encourage employees to refer their friends by offering cash rewards. The advantages of campus recruiting include a large pool of people from which to draw, applicants with up-to-date training, and a source of innovative ideas.[7]

It is becoming increasingly common for organizations such as Cisco Systems to use the Internet to advertise job openings and to gather applicant information. E-Span, for example, is an online service that lists professional and managerial positions. Federal Job Opportunity Board is a similar service that lists openings in the federal government.

The popularity of various recruiting methods notwithstanding, Figure 10.2 shows how 201 HR executives rated the effectiveness of nine different recruiting sources.

figure 10.2
Effectiveness of recruitment sources

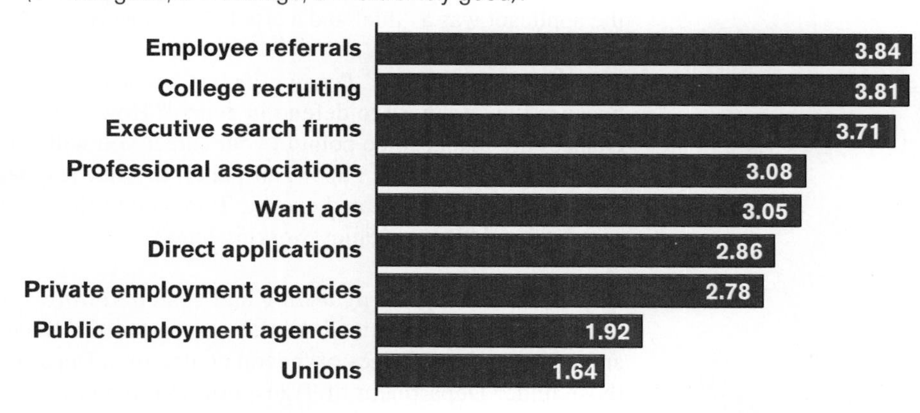

Source: David E. Terpstra, "The Search for Effective Methods," *HRFocus,* May 1996, pp. 16–17. Reprinted by permission of the publisher, from *HRFocus,* May 1996, © 1996. American Management Association, New York. http://www.amanet.org. All rights reserved. Arthur Sherman, George Bohlander, and Scott Snell, *Managing Human Resources,* 11th ed. (Cincinnati, OH: Southwestern Publishing, 1998).

Selection

selection Choosing from among qualified applicants to hire into an organization.

Selection builds on recruiting and involves decisions about whom to hire. As important as these decisions are, they are—unfortunately—at times made in very careless or cavalier ways. In this section we describe a number of selection instruments to which you may soon be exposed in your own careers.

Application and résumés

Application blanks and résumés provide basic information to prospective employers. In order to make a first cut through candidates, employers review the profiles and backgrounds of various job applicants. Applications and résumés typically include information about the applicant's name, educational background, citizenship, work experiences, certifications, and the like. While providing important information, applications and résumés tend not to be extremely useful for making final selection decisions.

Interviews

Interviews are the most popular selection tool, and every company uses some type of interview. However, employment interviewers must be careful about what they ask and how they ask it. Questions that are not job related are prohibited. In an unstructured (or nondirective) interview, the interviewer asks different interviewees different questions. The interviewer may also use probes; that is, ask follow-up questions to learn more about the candidate.[8]

structured interview Selection technique that involves asking each applicant the same questions and comparing their responses to a standardized set of answers.

In a **structured interview,** the interviewer conducts the same interview with each applicant. There are two basic types of structured interview. The first approach—called the *situational interview*—focuses on hypothetical situations. Zale Corporation, a major jewelry chain, uses this type of structured interview to select sales clerks. A sample question is: "A customer comes into the store to pick up a watch he had left for repair. The watch is not back yet from the repair shop, and the customer becomes angry. How would you handle the situation?" The second approach—called the *behavioral description interview*—explores what candidates have actually done in the past. In selecting college students for an officer training program, the U.S. army asks the following question to assess a candidate's ability to influence others: "What was the best idea you ever sold to a supervisor, teacher, peer, or subordinate?"

Reference checks

Reference checks are another commonly used screening device. Virtually all organizations use either a reference or an employment and education record check.[9] Although reference checking makes sense, reference information is becoming increasingly difficult to obtain as a result of several highly publicized lawsuits. In one case, an applicant sued a former boss on the grounds that the boss told prospective employers the applicant was a "thief and a crook." The jury awarded the applicant $80,000.

Personality tests

Personality tests are less popular for employee selection, largely because they are hard to defend in court.[10] However, they are regaining popularity, and chances are that at some point in your career you will complete some personality tests. A number of well-known paper-and-pencil inventories measure personality traits such as sociability, adjustment, and energy. Typical questions are "Do you like to socialize with people?" and "Do you enjoy working hard?"

Drug testing

Drug testing and *genetic testing* are among the most controversial screening instruments.[11] Since the passage of the Drug-Free Workplace Act of 1988, applicants and employees of federal contractors, Department of Defense contractors, and those under Department of Transportation regulations are subject to testing for illegal drugs. Urinalysis is the most common method of testing for the presence of drugs. A genetic test tries to identify the likelihood of contracting a disease (such as emphysema) based on genetic makeup. While genetic screening is far less common than drug testing, its popularity may increase as the technique is perfected.

Cognitive ability tests *Cognitive ability tests* are among the oldest employment selection devices. These tests measure a range of intellectual abilities, including verbal comprehension (vocabulary, reading) and numerical aptitude (mathematical calculations). About 20 percent of U.S. companies use cognitive ability tests for selection purposes.[12] Figure 10.3 shows some examples of cognitive ability test questions.

Performance tests *Performance tests* are procedures in which the test taker performs a sample of the job. Most companies use some type of performance test, typically for secretarial and clerical positions.[13] The most widely used performance test is the typing test. However, performance tests have been developed for almost every occupation, including managerial positions. Assessment centers are the most notable offshoot of the managerial performance test.

figure 10.3 Sample measures of cognitive ability

Verbal

1. What is the meaning of the word surreptitious?
   a. covert
   b. winding
   c. lively
   d. sweet

2. How is the noun clause used in the following sentence: "I hope that I can learn this game."
   a. subject
   b. predicate nominative
   c. direct object
   d. object of the preposition

Quantitative

3. Divide 50 by .5 and add 5. What is the result?
   a. 25
   b. 30
   c. 95
   d. 105

4. What is the value of 144^2?
   a. 12
   b. 72
   c. 288
   d. 20736

Reasoning

5. ____ is to boat as snow is to ____
   a. sail, ski
   b. water, winter
   c. water, ski
   d. engine, water

6. Two women played 5 games of chess. Each woman won the same number of games, yet there were no ties. How can this be so?
   a. There was a forfeit.
   b. One player cheated.
   c. They played different people.
   d. One game was still in progress.

Mechanical

7. If gear A and gear C are both turning counter-clockwise, what is happening to gear B?
   a. It is turning counter-clockwise.
   b. It is turning clockwise.
   c. It remains stationary.
   d. The whole system will jam.

A B C

Answers: 1a, 2c, 3d, 4d, 5c, 6c, 7b.

Source: Arthur Sherman, George Bohlander, and Scott Snell, *Managing Human Resources,* 11th ed. Copyright © 1998. Reprinted by permission of South-Western College Publishing, a division of International Thomson Publishing, Inc., Cincinnati, Ohio 45227.

assessment center A managerial performance test in which candidates participate in a variety of exercises and situations.

Assessment centers originated during World War II. A typical **assessment center** consists of 10 to 12 candidates who participate in a variety of exercises or situations; some of the exercises involve group interactions, and others are performed individually. Each exercise taps a number of critical managerial dimensions, such as leadership, decision-making skills, and communication ability. Assessors, generally line managers from the organization, observe and record information about the candidates' performance in each exercise. AT&T was the first organization to use assessment centers. Since then, a number of large organizations have used or currently are using the assessment center technique, including Bristol-Myers, the FBI, and Sears.

Integrity tests *Integrity tests* are used to assess a job candidate's honesty. Two forms of integrity tests are polygraphs and paper-and-pencil honesty tests. Polygraphs, or lie detector tests, have been banned for most employment purposes.[14] Paper-and-pencil honesty tests are more recent instruments for measuring integrity. These tests include questions such as whether a person has ever thought about stealing and whether he or she believes other people steal ("What percentage of people take more than $1 from their employer?"). Payless ShoeSource, based in Topeka, Kansas, has used an honesty test to reduce employee theft. Within only a year of implementing the program, inventory losses dropped by 20 percent, to less than 1 percent of sales. Despite compelling evidence such as this, the accuracy of these tests is still debatable.[15]

reliability The consistency of test scores over time and across alternative measurements.

validity The degree to which a selection test predicts or correlates with job performance.

Reliability and validity Regardless of the method used to select employees, two crucial issues that need to be addressed are a test's reliability and validity. **Reliability** refers to the consistency of test scores over time and across alternative measurements. For example, if three different interviewers talked to the same job candidate, but drew very different conclusions about the candidate's abilities, we might suspect that there were problems with the reliability of one or more of the selection tests or interview procedures.

Validity moves beyond reliability to assess the accuracy of the selection test. The most common form of validity, *criterion-related validity,* refers to the degree to which a test actually predicts or correlates with job performance. Figure 10.4 shows scatterplots of the correlations between two different tests and job performance. Each of the dots on the scatterplots corresponds to an individual's test score relative to his or her job performance. Dots in the bottom-left corner of each scatterplot show individuals who scored poorly on the test and performed poorly on the job. Individuals in the top-right corner are those who scored well on the selection test and also performed well on the job. By plotting many individual scores, the points begin to reveal a pattern in the relationship between test scores and job performance. This pattern can be captured statistically with a correlation coefficient (i.e., a validity coefficient) that ranges from −1.0 (a perfect negative correlation) to 1.0 (a perfect positive correlation). In reality, most validity coefficients fall somewhere in between these extremes. In Figure 10.4, for example, Test A has a validity coefficient of zero (0.0), indicating that there is no relationship between test scores and job success. Test B, however, has a validity coefficient of .75, indicating that high test scores tend to be strongly predictive of good performance. Managers would not want to use Test A—it is not valid—but would be wise to use Test B for selecting employees since it has high criterion-related validity.

Another form of validity, *content validity,* concerns the degree to which selection tests measure a representative sample of the knowledge, skills, and abilities required for the job. The best-known example of a content-valid test is a typing test for secretaries, because typing is a task a secretary almost always performs. However, to be completely content valid, the selection process should also measure other skills the secretary would be likely to perform, such as answering the telephone, duplicating and faxing documents, and dealing with the public. Content validity is more subjective (less statistical) than evaluations of criterion-related validity, but is no less important, particularly when defending employment decisions in court.

figure 10.4
Correlation scatter plots

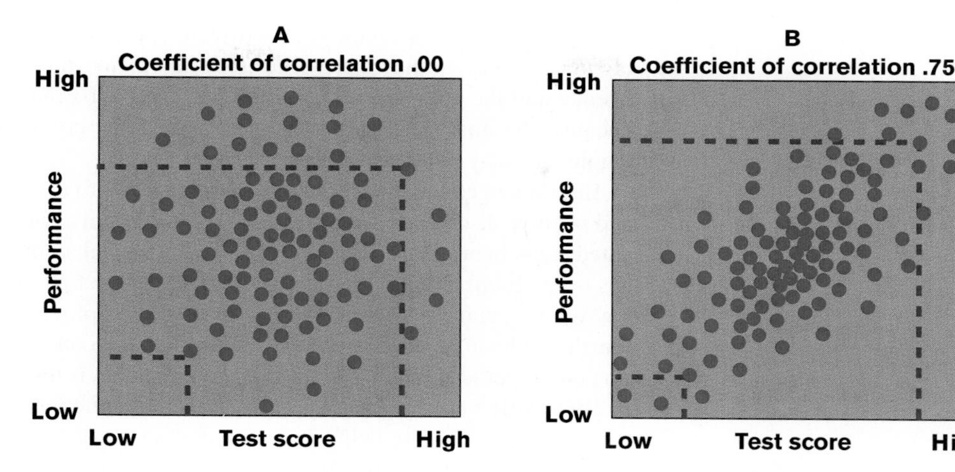

Workforce reductions

Unfortunately, staffing decisions do not simply focus on hiring employees. As organizations evolve and markets change, the demand for certain employees rises and falls. Also, some employees simply do not perform at a level required to justify continued employment. For these reasons, managers must make sometimes difficult decisions to terminate their employment.

Layoffs

As a result of the massive restructuring of American industry brought about by mergers and acquisitions, divestiture, and increased competition, organizations have been *downsizing*—laying off large numbers of managerial and other employees. Dismissing any employee is tough, but when a company lays off a substantial portion of its workforce, the results can rock the foundations of the organization.[16] The victims of restructuring face all the difficulties of being let go—loss of self-esteem, demoralizing job searches, and the stigma of being out of work. **Outplacement** is the process of helping people who have been dismissed from the company to regain employment elsewhere. This can help to some extent, but the impact of layoffs goes even further than the employees who leave. For many of the employees who remain with the company, disenchantment, distrust, and lethargy overshadow the comfort of still having a job. In many respects, how management deals with dismissals will affect the productivity and satisfaction of those who remain. A well-thought-out dismissal process eases tensions and helps remaining employees adjust to the new work situation.

outplacement The process of helping people who have been dismissed from the company to regain employment elsewhere.

Organizations with strong performance evaluation systems benefit because the survivors are less likely to believe the decision was arbitrary. Further, if care is taken during the actual layoff process—that is, if workers are offered severance pay and help in finding a new job—remaining workers will be comforted. Companies should also avoid stringing out layoffs, that is, dismissing a few workers at a time.

Termination

People sometimes "get fired" for poor performance or other reasons. Should an employer have the right to fire a worker? In 1884, a Tennessee court ruled: "All may dismiss their employee(s) at will for good cause, for no cause, or even for cause morally wrong." The concept that an employee may be fired for any reason is known as *employment-at-will* or *termination-at-will* and was upheld in a 1908 Supreme Court ruling.[17] The logic is that if the employee may quit at any time, the employer is free to dismiss at any time.

Since the mid-1970s, courts in most states have made exceptions to this doctrine. For example, public policy is a policy or ruling designed to protect the public from harm. One exception to the employment-at-will concept under public policy is employee whistle-blowing. For example, if a worker reports an environmental violation to the regulatory agency and the company fires him or her, the courts may argue that the firing was unfair because the employee acted for the good of the community. Another example is that employees may not be fired for serving jury duty.

Employers can avoid the pitfalls associated with dismissal by developing progressive and positive disciplinary procedures.[18] By *progressive,* we mean that a manager takes graduated steps in attempting to correct a workplace behavior. For example, an employee who has been absent receives a verbal reprimand for the first offense. A second offense invokes a written reprimand. A third offense results in employee counseling and probation, and a fourth results in a paid-leave day to think over the consequences of future rule infractions. The employer is signaling to the employee that this is the "last straw." Arbitrators are more likely to side with the employer that fires someone when they believe the company has made sincere efforts to help the person correct his or her behavior.

termination interview A discussion between a manager and an employee about the employee's dismissal.

The **termination interview,** in which the manager discusses the company's position with the employee, is a stressful situation for both parties. The manager needs to determine beforehand what severance package to offer the employee. The trend in recent mass layoffs is to offer increased benefits. For example, when Stroh Brewery Company closed a facility in Detroit, workers received individualized career counseling, job search skills workshops, financial planning services, a research library, and telephone and secretarial services.[19] It is customary to have a third party, such as a representative from the HRM department, present as a witness to the interview. Table 10.1 summarizes guidelines for conducting a termination interview.

Legal issues and equal employment opportunity

In 1964, Congress passed the Civil Rights Act, which prohibits discrimination in employment based on race, sex, color, national origin, and religion. Title VII of the act specifically forbids discrimination

table 10.1
Advice on termination

Do's	Don'ts
• Give as much warning as possible for mass layoffs. • Sit down one on one with the individual, in a private office. • Complete a termination session within 15 minutes. • Provide written explanations of severance benefits. • Provide outplacement services away from company headquarters. • Be sure the employee hears about his or her termination from a manager, not a colleague. • Express appreciation for what the employee has contributed, if appropriate.	• Don't leave room for confusion when firing. Tell the individual in the first sentence that he or she is terminated. • Don't allow time for debate during a termination session. • Don't make personal comments when firing someone; keep the conversation professional. • Don't rush a fired employee offsite unless security is an issue. • Don't fire people on significant dates, like the 25th anniversary of their employment or the day their mother died. • Don't fire employees when they are on vacation or have just returned.

Source: S. Alexander, "Firms Get Plenty of Practice at Layoffs, but They Often Bungle the Firing Process," *The Wall Street Journal,* November 14, 1991, p. 31.

in employment decisions such as recruitment, hiring, discharge, layoff, discipline, promotion, compensation, and access to training.[20] In 1972, the act was amended to allow the Equal Employment Opportunity Commission (EEOC) to take employers to court. The amendments also expanded the scope of the act to cover private and public employers with 15 or more employees, labor organizations, and public and private employment agencies.

Nevertheless, employment discrimination remains a controversial and costly issue for both organizations and individuals. Opponents of the 1991 Civil Rights Act argued that the act would force companies to hire based on mandated quotas rather than on the most qualified candidates. But the new bill provides protection for many groups. The 1991 Civil Rights Act also provides for punitive damages to workers who sue under the Americans with Disabilities Act. The latter act, passed in 1990, prohibits employment discrimination against people with disabilities. Recovering alcoholics or drug abusers, cancer patients in remission, and AIDS victims are covered by this legislation.

Thousands of court cases have challenged employment decisions and practices. Today, one common reason employers are sued is *adverse impact,* in which an apparently neutral employment practice adversely affects a *group* of individuals protected by the Civil Rights Act.[21] Discrimination issues provide a means for both minority groups as well as individuals to seek Title VII protection from employment discrimination. Today, the "Uniform Guidelines on Employee Selection Procedures" deal specifically with how to develop employment practices that comply with the law.[22]

Many other important staffing laws affect employment practices. The *Rehabilitation Act* of 1973 and the *Americans with Disabilities Act* of 1990 prohibit discrimination against persons with physical and mental disabilities. The *Age Discrimination in Employment Act (ADEA)* of 1967 and amendments in 1978 and 1986 prohibit discrimination against people age 40 and over. The *Immigration Act* of 1990 was designed to allow immigrants into the country based on what they can contribute to the economy. This legislation nearly tripled the cap on immigrant visas to 140,000 but limited nonimmigrant or temporary visas to 90,000 (the latter category previously was unrestricted). This new law complicates the hiring process for non-U.S. professionals under temporary visas such as investment bankers, scientists, and engineers. Finally, the *Worker Adjustment and Retraining Notification Act* of 1989, commonly known as the *WARN Act* or *Plant Closing Bill,* requires covered employers to give affected employees 60 days' written notice of plant closings or mass layoffs. Table 10.2 summarizes many of these major equal employment laws.

Developing the workforce

The skills and performance of employees and managers must be upgraded continually. Meeting this requirement involves training and development activities and appraising performance for the purposes of giving feedback and motivating people to perform at their best.

Training and development

Annual spending by employers on formal training is over $54 billion. Add informal educational and development experiences to that and the number balloons to $200 billion—slightly more than annual public and private spending on elementary and secondary education.[23]

General Motors has invested more than $2 billion over the past decade on education and training, making it the largest privately funded educational institution in the United States. IBM's annual training cost of $1.5 billion exceeds Harvard University's annual operating expenses of $951.7 million. Although these amounts sound like a lot of money (they are),

table 10.2 U.S. equal employment laws

Act	Major provisions	Enforcement and remedies
Equal Pay Act (1963)	Prohibits gender-based pay discrimination between two jobs substantially similar in skill, effort, responsibility, and working conditions.	Fines up to $10,000, imprisonment up to 6 months, or both; enforced by Equal Employment Opportunity Commission (EEOC); private actions for double damages up to 3 years' wages, liquidated damages, reinstatement, or promotion.
Title VII of Civil Rights Act (1964)	Prohibits discrimination based on race, sex, color, religion, or national origin in employment decisions: hiring, pay, working conditions, promotion, discipline, or discharge.	Enforced by EEOC; private actions, back pay, front pay, reinstatement, restoration of seniority and pension benefits, attorneys' fees and costs.
Executive Orders 11246 and 11375 (1965)	Requires equal opportunity clauses in federal contracts; prohibits employment discrimination by federal contractors based on race, color, religion, sex, or national origin.	Established Office of Federal Contract Compliance Programs (OFCCP) to investigate violations; empowered to terminate violator's federal contracts.
Age Discrimination in Employment Act (1967)	Prohibits employment discrimination based on age for persons over 40 years; restricts mandatory retirement.	EEOC enforcement; private actions for reinstatement, back pay, front pay, restoration of seniority and pension benefits; double unpaid wages for willful violations; attorneys' fees and costs.
Vocational Rehabilitation Act (1973)	Requires affirmative action by all federal contractors for persons with disabilities; defines disabilities as physical or mental impairments that substantially limit life activities.	Federal contractors must consider hiring disabled persons capable of performance after reasonable accommodations.
Americans with Disabilities Act (1990)	Extends affirmative action provisions of Vocational Rehabilitation Act to private employers; requires workplace modifications to facilitate disabled employees; prohibits discrimination against disabled.	EEOC enforcement; private actions for Title VII remedies.
Civil Rights Act (1991)	Clarifies Title VII requirements: disparate treatment impact suits, business necessity, job relatedness; shifts burden of proof to employer; permits punitive damages and jury trials.	Punitive damages limited to sliding scale only in intentional discrimination based on sex, religion, and disabilities.
Family and Medical Leave Act (1991)	Requires 12 weeks' unpaid leave for medical or family needs: paternity, family member illness.	Private actions for lost wages and other expenses, reinstatement.

the American Society for Training and Development (ASTD) argues that as a percentage of total payroll, the average organizational investment in training is too small.[24] This is of great concern given that jobs today are requiring more education, but the education level of U.S. workers is not keeping pace.

Mirage Resorts is a good example of one company's commitment to training and development and the impact that it can have on competitive advantage.

Is this a Mirage?

How does Mirage Resorts, Inc., compete in Las Vegas, where 25 million visitors can choose among 89 casino hotels? According to Arte Nathan, the company's vice president of human resources, the key is investing in employee development and training. Before The Mirage opened, Nathan conducted interviews with more than 200 companies in a variety of industries that had opened in the previous 10 years. The vast majority of them regretted not having done more training prior to opening. Accordingly, The Mirage put together a strong training program, spending approximately $3.5 million for preopening training at The Mirage and almost $3 million at Treasure Island. Interestingly, now that the hotel is open, Nathan still has no fixed limit on the training budget. If employees make a good case for a program, Nathan approves the training.

The effectiveness of this approach is almost self-evident. Mirage enjoys a 98 percent occupancy rate and the vast majority of their visitors are repeat patrons. Furthermore, employee turnover is only 13.5 percent compared with a 40 percent average in Las Vegas, and 70 percent nationwide. In recognition of their excellence in human resources management, Mirage Resorts received *Personnel Journal*'s Optimas Award for Competitive Advantage.

Source: Reprinted from Dawn Anfuso, "HR Helps The Mirage Thrive in Crowded Vegas," *Personnel Journal*, January 1994, p. 72. ●

training Teaching lower-level employees how to perform their present jobs.

development Teaching managers and professional employees broad skills needed for their present and future jobs.

needs assessment An analysis identifying the jobs, people, and departments for which training is necessary.

orientation training Training designed to introduce new employees to the company and familiarize them with policies, procedures, culture, and the like.

team training Training that provides employees with the skills and perspectives they need to work in collaboration with others.

Overview of the training process

Although we use the general term *training* here, training is sometimes distinguished from development. **Training** usually refers to teaching lower-level employees how to perform their present jobs, while **development** involves teaching managers and professional employees broader skills needed for their present and future jobs. *Phase one* of training should include a **needs assessment.** An analysis should be conducted to identify the jobs, people, and departments for which training is necessary. Job analysis and performance measurements are useful for this purpose.

Phase two involves the design of training programs. Based on needs assessment, training objectives and content can be established. *Phase three* involves decisions about the training methods to be used. A basic decision for selecting a training method is whether to provide on-the-job or off-the-job training. Examples of training methods include lectures, role playing, programmed learning, case discussion, business simulation, behavior modeling (watching a videotape and imitating what is observed), assigned readings, conferences, job rotation, vestibule training (practice in a simulated job environment), and apprenticeship training. Finally, *phase four* of training should evaluate the program's effectiveness in terms of employee reactions, learning, behavior transferred to the job, and bottom-line results.

Types of training

Companies invest in training to enhance individual performance and organizational productivity. Table 10.3 shows the variety of subjects covered in company training programs. In addition to these, several topics are particularly noteworthy.

Orientation training is typically used to familiarize new employees with their new jobs, work units, and the organization in general. Done well, orientation training has a number of reputed benefits including lower employee turnover, increased moral, better productivity, lower recruiting and training costs, and the like.

Team training has taken on more importance as organizations reorganize to facilitate individuals working together. Team training teaches employees the skills they need to work

table 10.3 General types of training

Types of training	Percent providing*	Number of employees 100–499	500–999	1,000–2,499	2,500–9,999	10,000 or more
Basic computer skills	93	92	95	93	96	95
Management skills/development	86	85	89	90	95	95
Technical skills/knowledge	85	85	88	86	90	92
Supervisory skills	85	83	89	89	94	93
Communication skills	85	83	90	89	93	93
Customer relations/service	82	81	82	85	86	86
New methods/procedures	80	80	81	81	85	85
Executive development	75	74	72	75	85	86
Personal growth	71	69	72	73	82	84
Clerical/secretarial skills	68	67	75	70	74	76
Employee/labor relations	66	66	67	64	74	80
Customer education	65	67	61	56	59	65
Wellness	58	57	61	64	66	72
Sales	55	55	53	50	59	60
Remedial/basic education	43	41	45	45	55	61

*Percent of all organizations that provide these types of training

Source: "1995 Industry Report," *Training* 32, no. 10 (October 1995), pp. 37–82.

diversity training Programs that focus on identifying and reducing hidden biases against people with differences and developing the skills needed to effectively manage a diversified workforce.

together and also facilitates their interaction. Coca-Cola's Fountain Manufacturing Operation recently developed a team training program that focused on technical, interpersonal, and team interaction skills.[25]

Diversity training is now offered in over 50 percent of all U.S. organizations. The programs focus on building awareness of diversity issues as well as providing the skills employees need to work with others who are different from them. This topic is so important that the next chapter is devoted solely to managing diversity.

Performance appraisal

performance appraisal Assessment of an employee's job performance.

Performance appraisal (PA) is the assessment of an employee's job performance. Performance appraisal has two basic purposes. First, appraisal serves an *administrative* purpose. It provides information for making salary, promotion, and layoff decisions, as well as providing documentation that can justify these decisions in court. Second, and perhaps more importantly, performance appraisal serves a *developmental* purpose. The information can be used to diagnose training needs, career planning, and the like. Feedback and coaching based on appraisal information provide the basis for improving day-to-day performance.

What do you appraise? Performance measures fall into one of three basic categories: traits, behaviors, and results. *Trait appraisals* involve subjective judgments about employee performance. They contain dimensions such as initiative, leadership, and attitude, and ask raters to indicate how much of each trait the employee possesses. Because trait scales tend to be ambiguous (as well as subjective), they often lead to personal bias and may not be suitable for obtaining useful feedback. So while this approach is extremely common—trait scales are easy to develop and implement—they unfortunately are often not valid.

Behavioral appraisals, while still subjective, focus more on observable aspects of performance. They were actually developed in response to the problems of trait appraisals. These scales focus on specific, prescribed behaviors, which can help ensure that all parties understand what the ratings are really measuring. Because they are less ambiguous, they also can help provide useful feedback. Figure 10.5 contains an example of a behaviorally anchored rating scale (BARS) for evaluating quality.

management by objectives (MBO) A process in which objectives set by a subordinate and supervisor must be reached within a given time period.

Results appraisals tend to be more objective and can focus on production data such as sales volume (for a salesperson), units produced (for a line worker), or profits (for a manager). One approach to results appraisals—called **management by objectives (MBO)—** involves a subordinate and a supervisor agreeing on specific performance goals (objectives). They then develop a plan that describes the time frame and criteria for determining whether the objectives have been reached. The aim is to agree on a set of objectives that are clear, specific, and reachable. For example, an objective for a salesperson might be to increase sales 25 percent during the following year. An objective for a computer programmer might be to complete two projects within the next six months. MBO has several advantages and can be useful when managers want to empower employees to adapt their behavior as they

figure 10.5 Example of BARS used for evaluating quality

Performance Dimension: Total Quality Management. This area of performance concerns the extent to which a person is aware of, endorses, and develops proactive procedures to enhance product quality, ensure early disclosure of discrepancies, and integrate quality assessments with cost and schedule performance measurement reports to maximize client's satisfaction with overall performance.

OUTSTANDING	7	**Uses measures of quality and well-defined processes to achieve project goals.** **Defines quality from the client's perspective.**
	6	**Look for/identifies ways to continually improve the process.**
	5	**Clearly communicates quality management to others.** **Develops a plan that defines how the team will participate in quality.** **Appreciates TQM as an investment.**
AVERAGE	4	**Has measures of quality that define tolerance levels.**
	3	**Views quality as costly.** **Legislates quality.**
	2	**Focuses his/her concerns only on outputs and deliverables, ignoring the underlying processes.**
POOR	1	**Blames others for absence of quality.** **Gives lip service only to quality concerns.**

Source: Landy, Jacobs, and Associates. Used with permission.

deem necessary in order to achieve desired results. Although MBO helps focus employees on reaching specific goals and encourages planning and development, it often focuses too much on short-term achievement and ignores long-term goals.

None of these performance appraisal systems are easy to conduct properly; and all have drawbacks that must be guarded against. In choosing an appraisal method, the following guidelines may prove helpful:

1. Always take legal considerations into account.
2. Base performance standards on job analysis.
3. Communicate performance standards to employees.
4. Evaluate employees on specific performance-related behaviors rather than on a single global or overall measure.
5. Document the PA process carefully.
6. If possible, use more than one rater (discussed below).
7. Develop a formal appeal process.[26]

Who should do the appraisal? Just as there are multiple methods for gathering performance appraisal information, there are several different sources who can provide PA information. *Managers* and *supervisors* are the traditional source of appraisal information since they are often in the best position to observe an employee's performance. However, companies such as Coors, General Foods, and Digital are turning to peers and team members to provide input to the performance appraisal. *Peers* and *team members* often see different dimensions of performance, and are often best at identifying leadership potential and interpersonal skills.

One increasingly popular source of appraisal is the person's subordinates. Appraisal by *subordinates* has been used by companies such as Xerox and IBM to give superiors feedback on how their employees view them. However, since this process gives employees power over their bosses, it is normally only used for developmental purposes.

Internal and external customers are also used as sources of performance appraisal information, particularly for companies such as Ford and Honda that are focused on total quality management. External customers have been used for some time to appraise restaurant employees, but internal customers can include anyone inside the organization who depends upon an employee's work output. Finally, it is usually a good idea for employees to evaluate their own performance. Although *self-appraisals* may be biased upward, the process of self-evaluation helps increase the employee's involvement in the review process, and is a starting point for establishing future goals.

Since each source of PA information has some limitations, and different people may see different aspects of performance, companies such as Westinghouse and Eastman Kodak have taken to using multiple-rater approaches that involve more than one source for appraisal information. By combining different sources—in a process referred to as **360 degree appraisal**—it is possible to obtain a more complete assessment of an employee's performance.

360 degree appraisal
Process of using multiple sources of appraisal to gain a comprehensive perspective of one's performance.

How do you give employees feedback? Giving PA feedback can be a stressful task for both managers and subordinates. The purposes of PA conflict to some degree. Providing growth and development requires understanding and support; however, the manager must be impersonal and be able to make tough decisions. Employees want to know how they are doing, but typically they are uncomfortable about getting feedback. Finally, the organization's need to make HR decisions conflicts with the individual employee's need to maintain a positive image.[27] These conflicts often make the PA interview difficult; therefore, managers should conduct such interviews thoughtfully.

There is no one "best" way to do a PA interview. The most difficult interviews are those with employees who are performing poorly. Here is a useful PA interview format to use when an employee is performing below acceptable standards:

1. Summarize the employee's specific performance. Describe the performance in behavioral or outcome terms, such as sales or absenteeism. Don't say the employee has a poor attitude; rather, explain which employee behaviors indicate a poor attitude.
2. Describe the expectations and standards, and be specific.
3. Determine the causes for the low performance; get the employee's input.
4. Discuss solutions to the problem, and have the employee play a major role in the process.
5. Agree to a solution. As a supervisor, you have input into the solution. Raise issues and questions, but also provide support.
6. Agree to a timetable for improvement.
7. Document the meeting.

Follow-up meetings may be needed. Here are some guidelines for giving feedback to an average employee:

1. Summarize the employee's performance, and be specific.
2. Explain why the employee's work is important to the organization.
3. Thank the employee for doing the job.
4. Raise any relevant issues, such as areas for improvement.
5. Express confidence in the employee's future good performance.

Designing reward systems

Reward systems are another major set of HRM activities. Most of this section will be devoted to monetary rewards such as pay and fringe benefits. Although traditionally pay has been of primary interest, benefits have received increased attention in recent years. Benefits make up a far greater percentage of the total payroll than in past decades.[28] The typical employer today pays nearly 40 percent of payroll costs in benefits. Accordingly, employers are trying to find ways to reduce these costs. Another reason for the growing interest in benefits is increased complexity. Many new types of benefits are now available, and tax laws affect myriad fringe benefits, such as health insurance and pension plans.

Pay decisions

Reward systems can serve the strategic purposes of attracting, motivating, and retaining people. The wages paid to employees are based on a complex set of forces. Beyond the body of laws governing compensation, a number of basic decisions must be made in choosing the appropriate pay plan. Figure 10.6 illustrates some of the factors that influence the wage mix.

Three types of decisions are crucial for designing an effective pay plan: pay level, pay structure, and individual pay.

Pay level refers to the choice of whether to be a high-, average-, or low-paying company. Compensation is a major cost for any organization, so low wages can be justified on a short-term financial basis. But being the high-wage employer—the highest-paying company in the region—ensures that the company will attract many applicants. Being a wage leader may be important during times of low unemployment or intense competition.

The *pay structure* decision is the choice of how to price different jobs within the organization. Jobs that are similar in worth usually are grouped together into job families. A

figure 10.6
Factors affecting the wage mix

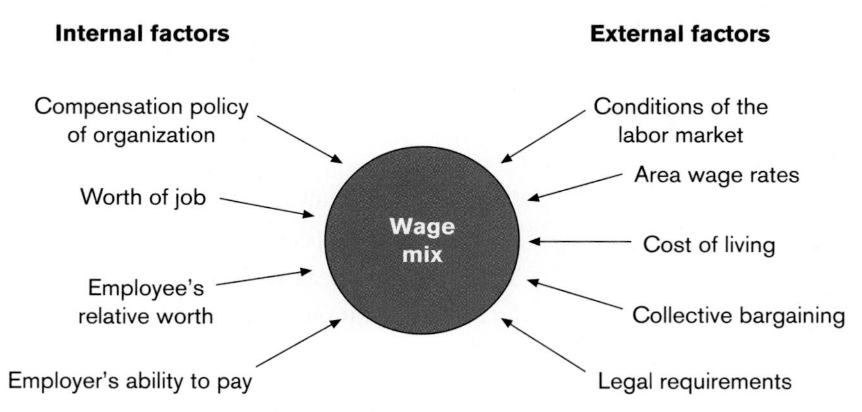

Source: Arthur Sherman, George Bohlander, and Scott Snell, *Managing Human Resources,* 11th ed. Copyright © 1998. Reprinted by permission of South-Western College Publishing, a division of International Thomson Publishing, Inc., Cincinnati, Ohio 45227.

pay grade, with a floor and ceiling, is established for each job family. Figure 10.7 illustrates a hypothetical pay structure.

Finally, *individual pay decisions* concern different pay rates for jobs of similar worth within the same family. Differences in pay within job families are decided in two ways. First, some jobs are occupied by individuals with more seniority than others. Second, some people may be better performers, therefore deserving of a higher level of pay.

Incentive systems and variable pay

A number of incentive systems have been devised to encourage and motivate employees to be more productive.[29] (See Chapter 13 for more discussion of rewarding performance.)

figure 10.7
Pay structure

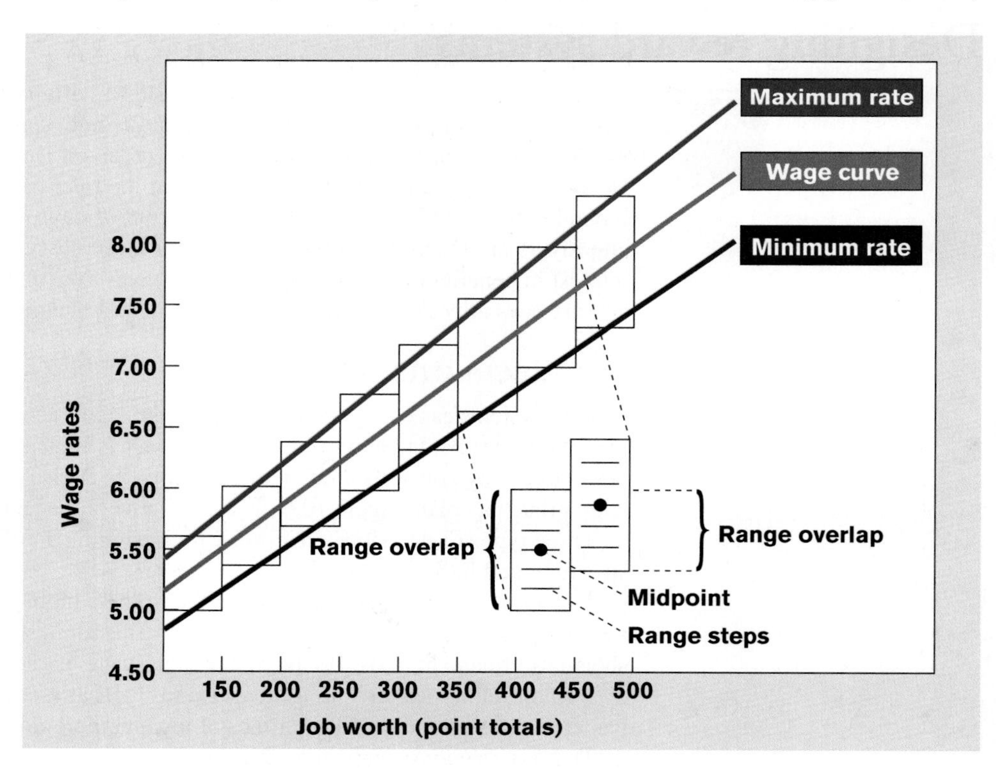

Source: *Effective Personal Management*, 3rd ed., by Randall S. Schuler, Nicholas J. Bentell and Stuart A. Youngblood. Copyright © 1989 by West Publishing Company.

Individual incentive plans are the most common type of incentive plan. An individual incentive system consists of an objective standard against which a worker's performance is compared. Pay is determined by the employee's performance. Individual incentive plans frequently are used in sales jobs. If effectively designed, individual incentive plans can be highly motivating.

There are several types of group incentive plans in which pay is based on group performance. *Gainsharing plans* concentrate on saving money.[30] The best known is the Scanlon plan, which is based on a function of the ratio between labor costs and sales value of production. An additional feature of the Scanlon plan is the use of employee committees to evaluate workers' suggestions for improving productivity.

Profit-sharing plans give employee incentives based on unit, department, plant, or company productivity. Nucor Steel, one of the nation's most profitable steel companies, relies heavily on a group-oriented profit-sharing plan. The entire company—4,000 employees—is broken down into bonus groups. For instance, each mill consists of groups of 25 to 35 employees who perform a complete task (e.g., melting and casting the steel or rolling the steel). Each group has a production standard and is paid for the amount of production over the specified level.[31]

When objective performance measures are not available but the company still wants to base pay on performance, it uses a *merit pay system.* Individuals' pay raises and bonuses are based on the judgmental merit rating they receive from their boss. Lincoln Electric Company has a particularly effective merit pay plan.[32]

Employee benefits

Like pay systems, employee benefit plans are subject to regulation. Employee benefits are divided into those required by law and those optional for an employer.

The three basic required benefits are workers' compensation, social security, and unemployment insurance. *Workers' compensation* provides financial support to employees suffering a work-related injury or illness. *Social security,* as established in the Social Security Act of 1935, provides financial support to retirees; in subsequent amendments, the act was expanded to cover disabled employees. The funds come from payments made by employers, employees, and self-employed workers. *Unemployment insurance* provides financial support to employees who are laid off for reasons they cannot control. Companies that have terminated fewer employees pay less into the unemployment insurance fund; thus, organizations have an incentive to keep terminations at a minimum.

A large number of benefits are not required to be employer provided. The most common are pension plans and medical and hospital insurance. Other optional employee benefits include dental insurance, life insurance, and vacation time. Because of the wide variety of possible benefits and the considerable differences in employee preferences and needs, companies often use **cafeteria** or **flexible benefit programs.** In this type of program, employees are given credits that they "spend" on benefits they desire. FinPac Corporation, a small computer software company, provides each employee with a required amount of life and disability insurance. Then employees use their credits toward individualized packages of additional benefits, including medical and dental insurance, dependent care, extra life insurance, or cash.

cafeteria benefit program
Employee benefit programs in which employees choose from a menu of options to create a benefit package tailored to their needs.

flexible benefit programs
Benefit programs in which employees are given credits to spend on benefits that fit their unique needs.

Legal issues in compensation and benefits

A number of laws affect employee compensation and benefits.[33] *The Fair Labor Standards Act (FLSA)* of 1938 set minimum wages, maximum hours, child labor standards, and overtime pay provisions. The Department of Labor monitors and enforces the FLSA. *Nonexempt* employees are entitled to premium pay for overtime (e.g., time-and-one-half). *Exempt* employees (e.g., executives, administrators, and professionals) are not subject to the overtime and minimum wage provisions.

The *Equal Pay Act (EPA)* of 1963, now enforced by the EEOC, prohibits unequal pay for men and women who perform equal work. Equal work means jobs that require equal skill, effort, and responsibility and are performed under similar working conditions. The law does permit exceptions where the difference in pay is due to a seniority system, a merit system, an incentive system based on quantity or quality of production, or any other factor other than sex, such as market demand. Although equal pay for equal work may sound like common sense, many employers have fallen victim to this law by rationalizing that men, traditionally the "breadwinners," deserve more pay than women or by giving equal jobs different titles (senior assistant versus office manager) as the sole basis for pay differences.

comparable worth Principle of equal pay for different jobs of equal worth.

One controversy concerns male and female pay differences within the same company. **Comparable worth** doctrine implies that women who perform *different* jobs of *equal* worth as men should be paid the same wage.[34] In contrast to the equal-pay-for-equal-work notion, comparable worth suggests that the jobs need *not* be the same to require the same pay. For example, nurses (predominantly female) were found to be paid considerably less than skilled craftworkers (predominantly male), even though the two jobs were found to be of equal value or worth.[35] Under the Equal Pay Act, this would not constitute pay discrimination because the jobs are very different. But under the comparable-worth concept, these findings would indicate discrimination because the jobs are of equal worth.

To date, no federal law requires comparable worth, and the Supreme Court has made no decisive rulings about it. However, some states have considered developing comparable-worth laws, and others already have implemented comparable-worth changes, raising the wages of female-dominated jobs. For example, Minnesota passed a comparable-worth law for public-sector employees after finding that women on average were paid 25 percent less than men. Several other states have comparable-worth laws for public-sector employees, including Iowa, Idaho, New Mexico, Washington, and South Dakota.[36]

Some laws influence mostly benefit practices. The *Pregnancy Discrimination Act* of 1978 states that pregnancy is a disability and qualifies a woman to receive the same benefits that she would with any other disability. The *Employee Retirement Income Security Act (ERISA)* of 1974 protects private pension programs from mismanagement. ERISA requires that retirement benefits be paid to those who vest or earn a right to draw benefits and ensures retirement benefits for employees whose companies go bankrupt or who otherwise cannot meet their pension obligations.

Health and safety

The *Occupational Safety and Health Act (OSHA)* of 1970 requires employers to pursue workplace safety. Employers must maintain records of injuries and deaths caused by workplace accidents and submit to on-site inspections. Large-scale industrial accidents, such as the Union Carbide gas leak in Bhopal, India, and nuclear power plant accidents worldwide, have focused attention on the importance of workplace safety.

One of many examples of the importance of this issue is the coal-mining industry. Coal miners spend their workdays in three-foot-high spaces wading in mud and water. Nearly every coal miner can name a friend or family member who has been killed, maimed, or stricken with black lung disease. "You die quick or you die slow," reports one mine worker. However, according to the federal Mine Safety and Health Administration, mines are safer now, and catastrophic cave-ins are largely a thing of the past.[37]

Labor relations

labor relations The system of relations between workers and management.

Labor relations is the system of relations between workers and management. Labor unions recruit members, collect dues, and ensure that employees are treated fairly with respect to wages, working conditions, and other issues. When workers organize for the purpose of negotiating with management to improve their wages, hours, or working conditions, two processes are involved: unionization and collective bargaining. These processes have evolved over a 50-year period in the United States to provide important employee rights.[38]

Labor laws

Try to imagine what life would be like with unemployment at 25 percent. Pretty grim, you would say. Legislators in 1935 felt that way too. Therefore, organized labor received its Magna Carta with the passage of the National Labor Relations Act.

The *National Labor Relations Act* (also called the *Wagner Act* after its legislative sponsor) ushered in an era of rapid unionization by (1) declaring labor organizations legal, (2) establishing five unfair employer labor practices, and (3) creating the National Labor Relations Board (NLRB). Today, the NLRB conducts unionization elections, hears unfair labor practices complaints, and issues injunctions against offending employers. The Wagner Act greatly assisted the growth of unions by enabling workers to use the law and the courts to legally organize and collectively bargain for better wages, hours, and working conditions.

Public policy began on the side of organized labor in 1935, but over the next 25 years the pendulum swung toward the side of management. The *Labor-Management Relations Act,* or *Taft-Hartley Act* (1947), protected employers' free-speech rights, defined unfair labor practices by unions, and permitted workers to decertify (reject) a union as their representative.

Finally, the *Labor-Management Reporting and Disclosure Act,* or *Landrum-Griffin Act* (1959) swung the public policy pendulum midway between organized labor and management. By declaring a bill of rights for union members, establishing control over union dues increases, and imposing reporting requirements for unions, Landrum-Griffin was designed to curb abuses by union leadership and rid unions of corruption.

Unionization

How do workers join unions? Through a union organizer or local union representative, workers learn what benefits they may receive by joining.[39] The union representative distributes authorization cards that permit workers to indicate whether or not they want an election to be held to certify the union to represent them. The National Labor Relations Board will conduct a certification election if at least 30 percent of the employees sign authorization cards. Management has several choices at this stage: to recognize the union without an election, to consent to an election, or to contest the number of cards signed and resist an election.

If an election is warranted, an NLRB representative will conduct the election by secret ballot. A simple majority of those voting determines the winner. Thus, apathetic workers who do not show up to vote in effect support the union. If the union wins the election, it is certified as the bargaining unit representative.

During the campaign preceding the election, efforts are made by both management and the union to persuade the workers how to vote. Most workers, though, are somewhat resistant to campaign efforts, having made up their minds well before the NLRB appears on the scene. If the union wins the election, management and the union are legally required to bargain in good faith to obtain a collective bargaining agreement or contract.

Why do workers vote for a union? Four factors play a significant role (see Figure 10.8).[40] First, economic factors are important, especially for workers in low-paying jobs; unions attempt to raise the average wage rate for their members. Second, job dissatisfaction encourages workers to seek out a union. Poor supervisory practices, favoritism, lack of communication, and perceived unfair or arbitrary discipline and discharge are specific triggers of job dissatisfaction. Third, the belief that the union can obtain desired

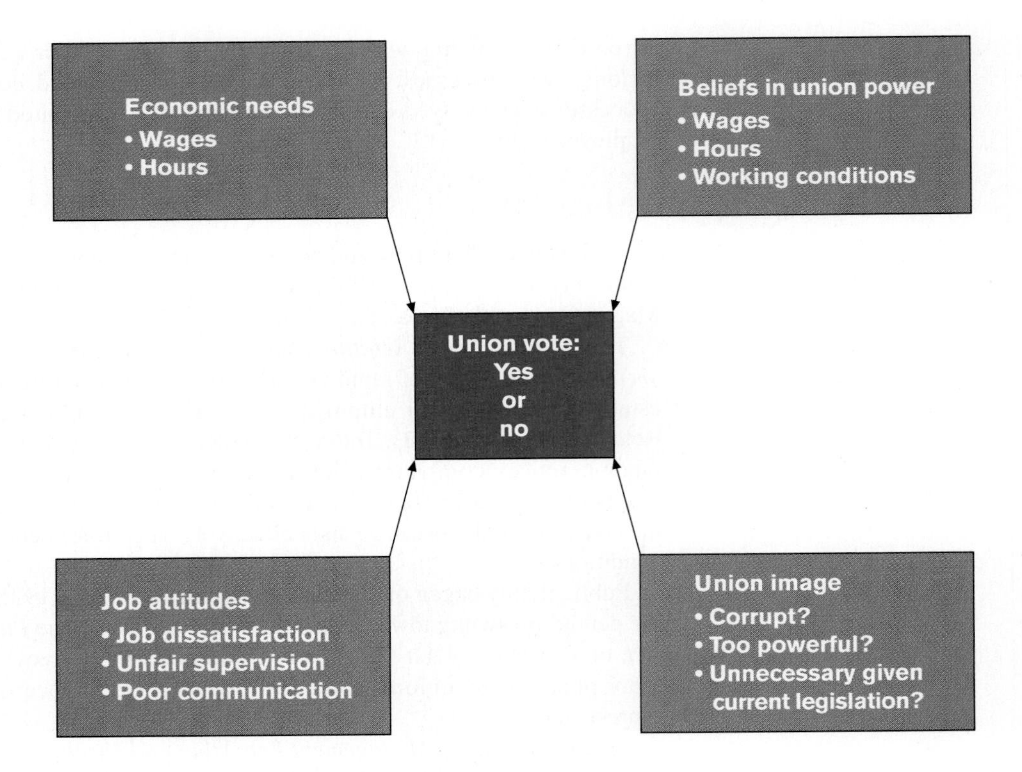

figure 10.8
Determinants of union voting behavior

benefits can generate a pro-union vote. Finally, the image of the union can determine whether a dissatisfied worker will seek out the union. Headline stories of union corruption and dishonesty can discourage workers from unionization.

Collective bargaining

In the United States, management and unions engage in a periodic ritual (typically every three years) of negotiating an agreement over wages, hours, and working conditions. Two types of disputes can arise during this process. First, before an agreement is reached, the workers may go on strike to compel agreement on their terms. Such an action is known as an *economic strike* and is permitted by law. Once the agreement is signed, however, management and the union can still disagree over *interpretation* of the agreement. Usually they settle their disputes through arbitration. **Arbitration** is the use of a neutral third party, typically jointly selected, to resolve the dispute. The United States uses arbitration while an agreement is in effect to avoid *wildcat strikes* (in which workers walk off the job in violation of the contract) or unplanned work stoppages.

arbitration The use of a neutral third party to resolve a labor dispute.

union shop An organization with a union and union security clause specifying that workers must join the union after a set period of time.

right to work Legislation that allows employees to work without having to join a union.

What does a collective bargaining agreement contain? In a **union shop,** a union security clause specifies that workers must join the union after a set period of time. **Right-to-work** states, through restrictive legislation, do not permit union shops; that is, workers have the right to work without being forced to join a union. The southern United States has many right-to-work states. The wage component of the contract spells out rates of pay, including premium pay for overtime and paid holidays. Individual rights usually are specified in terms of the use of seniority to determine pay increases, job bidding, and order of layoffs.

A feature of any contract is the grievance procedure. Unions perform a vital service for their membership in this regard by giving workers a voice in what goes on during both contract negotiations and administration through the grievance procedure.[41] In about 50 percent of discharge cases that go to arbitration, the arbitrator overturns management's

UAW Local 696 President Joe Hasenjager talks with striking workers outside the General Motors corporate plant in Dayton, Ohio.
[AP/Pat Sullivan/Wide World photos]

decision and reinstates the worker.[42] Unions have a legal duty of fair representation, which means they must represent all workers in the bargaining unit and ensure that workers' rights are protected.

What does the future hold?

In recent years, union membership has declined to less than 12 percent of the U.S. labor force as a consequence of changing laws concerning employee rights, global competition, decreased demand for the products of traditionally unionized industries, the rise of the service economy (which is difficult to unionize), and changing expectations of the new workforce.[43] Coupled with recent campaign fund raising scandals among union officials, and the prospects for organized labor in the United States is questionable.

Some people applaud unions' apparent decline. Others hope for an eventual reemergence based on the potential power of management–union cooperation to help U.S. businesses regain their competitive position in the global economy.[44] Unions may play a different role in the future, one that is less adversarial and more cooperative with management. Unions are adapting to changing workforce demographics; they are paying more attention to women, older workers, and people who work at home. Elimination of inefficient work rules, the introduction of profit sharing, and a guarantee of no layoffs were seen as a big step toward a fundamentally different, cooperative long-term relationship. Sometimes, as in the case of the recent UPS strike, labor–management relations can be highly destructive. In other cases, management and labor have worked to forge better relationships. Things are constantly changing, as illustrated by recent union efforts to buy United Airlines. In general, constructive change within a company or industry cannot occur without the positive transformation of labor–management relations.

Key terms

360 degree appraisal, p. 350
Arbitration, p. 356
Assessment center, p. 342
Cafeteria programs, p. 353
Comparable worth, p. 354
Development, p. 347
Diversity training, p. 348
Flexible benefit programs, p. 353
Human capital, p. 334
Human resources management (HRM), p. 334
Job analysis, p. 337
Labor relations, p. 354
Management by objectives (MBO), p. 349
Needs assessment, p. 347
Orientation training, p. 347
Outplacement, p. 343
Performance appraisal (PA), p. 348
Recruitment, p. 338
Reliability, p. 342
Right-to-work, p. 356
Selection, p. 340
Structured interview, p. 340
Team training, p. 347
Termination interview, p. 344
Training, p. 347
Union shop, p. 356
Validity, p. 342

Summary of learning objectives

Now that you have studied Chapter 10, you should know:

How companies use human resources management to gain competitive advantage.

To succeed, companies must align their human resources to their strategy. Effective planning is necessary to make certain that the right number and kind of employees are available to implement a company's strategic plan. For example, in the "Setting the Stage" case of Microsoft, it is clear that innovation in the software industry depends on hiring the most competent people and training them to perform well on the job. Other companies that compete on cost, quality, service, and so on should also use their staffing, training, appraisal, and reward systems to elicit and reinforce the kinds of behaviors that underlie their strategies.

Why companies recruit both internally and externally for new hires.

Some companies prefer to recruit internally to make certain that employees are familiar with organizational policies and values. AT&T's Resource Link is an example of a company trying very hard to make certain that available work goes to internal candidates before looking externally. In other instances, companies prefer to recruit externally to find individuals with new ideas and fresh perspectives.

The various methods available for selecting new employees.

There are a myriad of selection techniques from which to choose. Interviews and reference checks are most common. Personality tests and cognitive ability tests measure an individual's aptitude and potential to do well on the job. Other selection techniques include assessment centers and integrity tests. Regardless of the approach used, any test should be able to demonstrate reliability (consistency across time and different interview situations) and validity (accuracy in predicting job performance).

Why companies spend so much on training and development.

People cannot depend on a set of skills for all of their working lives. In today's changing, competitive world, old skills quickly become obsolete and new ones become essential for success. Refreshing or updating an individual's skills requires a great deal of continuous training. Companies such as Mirage Resorts understand that gaining a competitive edge in quality of service depends on having the most talented, flexible workers in the industry.

How to determine who should appraise an employee's performance.

Many companies are using multiple sources of appraisal since different people see different sides of an employee's performance. Typically, a superior is expected to evaluate an employee, but peers and team members are often in a good position to see aspects of performance that a superior misses. Even an employee's subordinates are being asked more often today to give their input in order to get yet another perspective on the evaluation. Particularly in companies concerned about quality, internal and external customers are also surveyed. Finally, employees should evaluate their own performance, if only to get them thinking about their own performance, as well as to engage them in the appraisal process.

How to analyze the fundamental aspects of a reward system.

Reward systems are broken down into three basic components: pay level, pay structure, and individual pay determination. To achieve an advantage over competitors, executives may want to generally pay a higher wage to their company's employees, but this decision must be weighed against the need to control costs (pay-level decisions are often tied to strategic concerns such as these). To achieve internal equity (paying people what they are worth relative to their peers within the company), managers must look at the pay structure, making certain that pay differentials are based on knowledge, effort, responsibility, working conditions, seniority, and so on. Individual pay determination is often based on merit or the different contributions of individuals. In these cases it is important to make certain that men and women receive equal pay for equal work, and managers may wish to base pay decisions on the idea of comparable worth (equal pay for equal contribution).

How unions influence human resources management.

Labor relations involve the interactions between workers and management. One mechanism by which this relationship is conducted is unions. Unions seek to present a collective voice for workers, to make their needs and wishes known to management. Unions negotiate agreements with management regarding a range of issues such as wages, hours, working conditions, job security, and health care. One important tool that unions can use is the grievance procedure established through collective bargaining. This gives employees a way to seek redress for wrongful action on the part of management. In this way, unions make certain that the rights of all employees are protected.

How the legal system influences human resources management.

The legal system influences managers by placing constraints on the ways potential and actual employees are treated. Equal opportunity laws ensure that companies do not discriminate in their hiring and training practices. The Fair Labor Standards Act and the Equal Pay Act ensure that people earn fair compensation for the contribution they make to the organization. The Occupational Safety and Health Act (OSHA) ensures that employees have a safe and healthy work environment. Labor laws seek to protect the rights of both employees and managers so that their relationship can be productive and agreeable.

Discussion questions

1. How will changes in the labor force affect HRM practices for the year 2005?

2. Describe the major regulations governing HRM practices.

3. Define job analysis. Why is job analysis relevant to each of the six key HRM activities discussed in the chapter (i.e., planning, staffing, training, performance appraisal, reward systems, labor relations)?

4. What are the various methods for recruiting employees? Why are some better than others? In what sense are they better?

5. What is a "test"? Give some examples of tests used by employers.

6. What purpose does performance appraisal serve? Why are there so many different methods of appraisal?

7. What are some key ideas to remember when conducting a performance interview?

8. How would you define an effective reward system? What role do benefits serve in a reward system?

9. Why do workers join unions? What implications would this have for the organization that wishes to remain nonunion?

10. Discuss the advantages and disadvantages of collective bargaining for the employer and the employee.

Concluding Case

Continental airlines sets a new heading

Yikes! This was a company in trouble. In 1994, Continental Airlines filed for bankruptcy (for a second time), lost $613 million, and was ranked dead last in industry indicators such as on-time performance among the major carriers. So bleak was their situation that Continental's mechanics used to routinely rip the logos off their uniforms so if they ran errands after work, no one would know they worked for the company. The result of these efforts was a demoralized workforce and a corporate reputation that put Continental near the top of *Fortune*'s list of "least admired" companies. According to Ned Walker, vice president of communications for the company, "You could not get any worse than Continental in 1994."

However, as the saying goes, that was then and this is now. Since Gordon Bethune arrived as their new CEO, Continental has made a 180-degree turnaround. Ironically, Bethune used Continental's unenviable position as a launching pad for his "From Worst to First" campaign. In order to refocus Continental and streamline operations, Bethune eliminated more than 7,000 jobs and dismissed 50 of his vice presidents. This sent a clear signal that major changes were underway.

Bethune; Ken Carig, vice president of human resources; and the new management team put together a plan, called *Go Forward,* that HR would have a major role in implementing. The plan has four major parts: (1) *Fly to Win,* making the routes Continental flies most profitable; (2) *Fund the Future,* eliminating unnecessary expenditures; (3) *Make Reliability a Reality,* boosting the company's image; and (4) *Working Together,* the part most focused on human resources.

The first step was to involve employees in decision making. For example, when Bethune announced that there would be layoffs, employees were given input into the process. To ensure effective communication, a toll-free number was established to allow employees to convey their concerns to top management. With more than 60 calls per day coming in, a committee was created to respond to problems within 48 hours. Moreover, Bethune invited workers to call his voice mail, and he called them back.

Performance appraisals were also changed to emphasize customer service rather than traditional cost-based measures. Consequently, the focus shifted toward achievement and facilitation of on-time flights. To emphasize the importance of this goal, Bethune and Carig devised an incentive system that paid each employee $65 per month when the airline finished in the top half of the Department of Transportation's rankings. If they achieved the number one ranking, each employee would receive $100. In addition, employees were provided information they needed to achieve these goals. Automated systems were put in place to help the staff track problems, and supervisors were able to show workers how their daily actions affected performance indicators. To encourage perfect attendance, Bethune drew the names of seven workers from a list of thousands to receive new Ford Explorers at the company's expense. Continental plans to continue this reward for perfect attendance every six months. To top it all off, once profits started to come in, the company paid employees a postponed wage increase that was not due until 1996.

Continental Airlines President Greg Brenneman talks with the media after awarding approximately $36 million in profit-sharing checks for 1997 with Houston-based employees.
[AP/Tom Uhlman/Wide World Photos]

Today employees are paying more attention to their work and there has been a sharp improvement in morale. By focusing on the workers and rewarding them for displaying the behaviors and actions that are needed for the company's success, Bethune is guiding the company in the right direction. Faced with the challenge to turn around Continental Airlines, Gordon Bethune has gained the confidence of his workers by following through on his promises, as has the entire company rallying around the future success of Continental. Indeed, all indications are that the company is back on track. Within just one year, Continential achieved the number one ranking in on-time performance and was highly ranked in baggage handling. Customer complaints are down more than 60 percent and Continental was recently awarded the distinction as the number one airline in customer satisfaction among the major U.S. carriers for long-distance flights. Moreover, sick leave and on-the-job injuries have decreased, and applications for employment at Continental are back up again. Perhaps most impressive is that Continental recorded an all-time record annual profit in 1995, and in 1996 Continental's stock price rose over 370 percent. These achievements helped the company win *Workforce Magazine*'s 1997 Optimas Award for Service Excellence.

Questions

1. How do you think human resource management practices have helped Continental?

2. What other changes might you suggest to improve morale, productivity, customer service, and the like?

3. What challenges to you think lie ahead for Continental Airlines?

4. Will this approach work in the long run for Continental?

Sources: Gillian Flynn, "A Flight Plan for Success," *Workforce,* July 1997, pp. 72–78; Wendy Zellner, "Back to 'Coffee, tea, or milk?'" *Business Week,* July 3, 1995, pp. 52–56; Scott McCartney, "Back on Course: Piloted by Bethune, Continental Air Lifts Its Workers' Morale," *The Wall Street Journal,* May 15, 1996, pp. A1, A8; Wendy Zellner, "The Right Place, the Right Time," *Business Week,* May 27, 1996, pp. 74–76; and "America's Most Admired Companies," *Fortune,* March 4, 1996, pp. 90–98.

Video Case

Human resources management

What is it about a company that allows it to attract the best employees? The first thing that usually comes to mind for most people is salary. Salary can be an effective lure to top talent, but benefits are also important when a candidate considers a position with a company. In most organizations, benefits make up a significant part of the total compensation paid to an employee. These benefits can include a variety of health insurance plans, retirement options, and life insurance choices. Employee benefits also include sick days, vacation days, holidays, and personal days. Typically, the human resources department of an organization administers benefit plans. The size of the human resources department can vary considerably depending on the size of the company, but one thing all human resources departments have in common despite their size is the need to manage large amounts of data that can be regularly updated and organized.

Efficient management of human resources data is crucial to containing costs and to providing the best possible service to employees. The computerized database is one tool HR departments commonly use to manage employee benefit information. Information systems that use databases organize data into fields. Each field contains specific information such as name, address, health insurance options, or available vacation days. Several fields make up a record. Generally, there is one record per employee. The database can be sorted by fields so that specific information on an individual employee can be extracted and analyzed alongside data from other individuals. This allows an organization to track information on a group of employees, such as total vacation days available.

Databases can be used by both large and small organizations since they can exist on large mainframes or personal computers. Two organizations that have found unique ways of using information systems for human resources management are Hewitt Associates and USX Corporation.

Hewitt Associates manages defined benefit programs such as 401(k) or other retirement plans for large companies. The company uses sophisticated technology and a customer-service orientation to excel in its industry. Account representative Laurie Caputo explained Hewitt's approach to customer service: "Whenever a call comes through to me as a representative on the phone, I feel the most important thing that I can impart to a person is personalized service and my complete attention during that call. I also want to provide accurate information. I consider myself an extension of their benefits office and the client, so it's very important that when they talk to us they get the sense that we care about them and that we are really part of their team."

Giving the right answers, performing transactions quickly and accurately, and providing professional counsel—for Laurie Caputo, these are the keys to keeping benefit plan participants and clients satisfied. Laurie is an account representative in Hewitt Associates' benefit center, a modern communications facility that lets participants find information on defined benefit, defined contribution, and flexible benefits programs. Through an interactive voice response system and a staff of account representatives, participants can get information, make transactions, and enter personal data. Brenda Sural, Hewitt's voice response system consultant, said, "Voice response provides an automated method of communicating with the plan. For the participants it's great because it provides a convenient and confidential method of getting information. When we sit down with a client to define a voice response system, we'll look very carefully at any printed material that they give to employees as well as study their plan features so we can customize a voice response system that's unique to them."

The voice response system is designed for ease of use by callers who are not necessarily familiar with the technology. A plan participant calls the voice response system and gets a professionally recorded message, which is actually a digitized audio file that is retrieved based on the caller's input. The system is linked to a mainframe database, and before any information is provided, the caller must pass security. When a caller enters the voice response system, they are first asked for their employer ID number and a four- to six-digit personal identification number. The computer treats the voice response unit as an input device, such as a computer terminal. The caller uses a Touch-Tone phone to answer the questions and navigate through the system. When a more personal touch is needed, participants can be connected to an account representative.

When a call reaches an account representative, that representative's screen displays how far into the voice response system the caller had journeyed. Thus, if the caller had already passed security, the representative would have the caller's name and account information already displayed on the screen. Account representatives' computer terminals are linked directly to Hewitt Associates' mainframe. A graphical user interface makes it easy for them to perform transactions, and offers the capability of running two different applications simultaneously, a function known as *multitasking*. One use of multitasking is the online help feature. When an account representative needs more information, the help feature provides information for whatever application is on the screen. The representative doesn't have to search through a list of choices. The system also uses a real-time database, meaning that any information that is retrieved is up to date. Any updates made to the participant's records by the account representative occur instantly, and a letter confirming the change is automatically sent the same day.

Hewitt Associates uses information technology to provide cost-effective solutions to defined benefits management for large corporations. The use of sophisticated voice response systems and databases and a focus on customer service enable Hewitt to save its clients money while making a profit. As the next example shows, some companies are using technology to let employees help themselves to important human resources data.

USX, one of the largest steel companies in the United States, also turned to computer technology to help its employees better plan their retirement investments. Bob McMaster, manager of USX's benefits information management system, said, "Basically we were looking for a better way to communicate information and benefits to the employees. With the changing environment people are retiring at an earlier age. We wanted them to have the ability to see what the effects on an earlier pension would be."

To address this concern, USX installed an interactive retirement planning application in multimedia kiosks throughout the company. At each kiosk, employees enter their Social Security number and a personal identification number to retrieve their retirement plan data directly from a host computer. A graphical interface and audio prompting make navigation easy. Employees can input personal savings information, and obtain 401(k) and Social Security projections along with their company pension plan. After projecting through retirement, the employee can print out the results and go back and review their assumptions. McMaster said, "The employees realize that this is truly a benefit for them. We have had 85 percent of our employees actually use the system at the kiosk. Many people, of course, return time and again to update their information."

According to McMaster, the benefits from an information systems approach to human resources management can include

- Cost savings.
- Better service for employees.
- Instant access to personnel data.
- Easy updating.

In summary, databases provide a useful tool for organizing and managing employee benefit and personal data. Fields in a database are used to group similar types of data such as last name, ZIP code, or telephone numbers. Sorting data by fields allows a human resources department to track specific types of data that can be useful in budgeting and controlling costs. A well-organized database can be instantly accessed and updated. Whether an organization uses a mainframe or personal computers, a database offers an efficient way for a human resources department to manage personnel data. As human resources management costs rise with the increasing price and number of benefit options, information systems that are well implemented can offer a way to contain costs and provide better employee service.

Critical thinking questions

1. Most of us have had some experience with voice response technology in registering for school, contacting a local government office, or elsewhere. What have you found to be some of the limitations of such a system? How could these limitations be overcome with enhanced or additional technology?

2. People that call Hewitt Associates can speak with an account representative if their questions aren't answered by the voice response system. Do you think Hewitt should do away with this option? Explain your answer.

3. Employee benefit plans have become more complex, allowing companies the flexibility of tailoring plans to meet individual needs. What are the advantages of this increasing complexity? What are some of the disadvantages? How did USX Corporation respond to the complexity of benefit plans?

4. USX Corporation allows employees to retrieve their retirement plan and determine what payments they can expect when they retire. Explain some potential pitfalls of the approach taken by USX.

Video Case

Compensation Issue

Purpose

This exercise discusses the possible problems that can occur when employees discuss their pay levels among themselves, and presents some of the possible issues of pay discrimination.

After Brenda, an African-American woman, and Sandy, a white woman, exchange pleasantries early on Friday morning, Brenda reveals to Sandy that she has just learned that another employee, June, who works in bookkeeping, receives $.30 an hour more pay. Brenda is upset by this information because both she and June began their employment with the company at the same time and they both perform similar functions.

Brenda believes that the company has "discriminated" against her because she is an African-American woman. She tells Sandy that she will hire an attorney to sue the company. Sandy suggests that the difference in pay, even for performing the same job functions, may be a result of other considerations. For example, even though both women were hired at the same time, June may have had previous experience that allows the company to pay her a slightly higher salary. Brenda counters Sandy's argument by saying that a similar job within the same company should mean that each employee receives the same salary.

Critical thinking questions

1. Is it ethical for employees to compare salaries when working for the same company? If so, why? If not, why not?

2. Do you believe that Brenda has been discriminated against by her company? If so, what type of discrimination?

3. Are there times when people working in the same company, hired at the same time, and doing the same work should be paid different salaries? Explain your answer.

Experiential Exercises

10.1 The "legal" interview

Objectives

1. To introduce you to the complexities of employment law.

2. To identify interview practices that might lead to discrimination in employment.

Instructions

1. Working alone, review the text material on interviewing and discrimination in employment.

2. In small groups, complete the "Legal" Interview Worksheet.

3. After the class reconvenes, group spokespersons present group findings.

"Legal" interview worksheet

The employment interview is one of the most critical steps in the employment selection process. It may also be an occasion for discriminating against individual employment candidates. The following (on page 364) represent questions that interviewers often ask job applicants. Identify the legality of each question by circling *L* (legal) or *I* (illegal) and briefly explain your decision.

Interview question	Legality	Explanation
1. Could you provide us with a photo for our files?	L I	
2. Have you ever used another name (previous married name or alias)?	L I	
3. What was your maiden name?	L I	
4. What was your wife's maiden name?	L I	
5. What was your mother's maiden name?	L I	
6. What is your current address?	L I	
7. What was your previous address?	L I	
8. What is your social security number?	L I	
9. Where was your place of birth?	L I	
10. Where were your parents born?	L I	
11. What is your national origin?	L I	
12. Are you a naturalized citizen?	L I	
13. What languages do you speak?	L I	
14. What is your religious/church affiliation?	L I	
15. What is your racial classification?	L I	
16. How many dependents do you have?	L I	
17. What are the ages of your dependent children?	L I	
18. What is your marital status?	L I	
19. How old are you?	L I	
20. Do you have proof of your age (birth certificate or baptismal record)?	L I	
21. Whom do we notify in case of an emergency?	L I	
22. What is your height and weight?	L I	
23 Have you ever been arrested?	L I	
24. Do you own your own car?	L I	
25. Do you own your own house?	L I	
26. Do you have any charge accounts?	L I	
27. Have you ever had your salary garnished?	L I	
28. To what organizations do you belong?	L I	
29. Are you available to work on Saturdays and Sundays?	L I	
30. Do you have any form of disability?	L I	

10.2 The pay raise

Objectives

1. To further your understanding of salary administration.
2. To examine the many facets of performance criteria, performance criteria weighting, performance evaluation, and rewards.

Instructions

1. Working in small groups, complete the Pay Raise Worksheet.
2. After the class reconvenes, group spokespersons present group findings.

Pay raise worksheet

April Knepper is the new supervisor of an assembly team. It is time for her to make pay raise allocations for her subordinates. She has been budgeted $30,000 to allocate among her seven subordinates as pay raises. There have been some ugly grievances in other work teams over past allocations, so April has been advised to base the allocations on objective criteria that can be quantified, weighted, and computed in numerical terms. After she makes her allocations, April must be prepared to justify her decisions. All of the evaluative criteria available to April are summarized as follows:

					Supervisory ratings			
Employee	EEO status	Seniority	Output rating*	Absent rate	Skills	Initiative	Attitude	Personal
David Bruce	Caucasian Male	15 yrs.	0.58	0.5%	Good	Poor	Poor	Nearing retirement. Wife just passed away. Having adjustment problems.
Eric Cattalini	Caucasian Male	12 yrs.	0.86	2.0	Excellent	Good	Excellent	Going to night school to finish his BA degree.
Chua Li	Asian Male	7 yrs.	0.80	3.5	Good	Excellent	Excellent	Legally deaf.
Marilee Miller	Black Female	1 yr.	0.50	10.0	Poor	Poor	Poor	Single parent with three children.
Victor Munoz	Hispanic Male	3 yrs.	0.62	2.5	Poor	Average	Good	Has six dependents. Speaks little English.
Derek Thompson	Caucasian Male	11 yrs.	0.64	8.0	Excellent	Average	Average	Married to rich wife. Personal problems.
Sarah Vickers	Caucasian Female	8 yrs.	0.76	7.0	Good	Poor	Poor	Women's activist. Wants to create a union.

*Output rating determined by production rate less errors and quality problem.

Chapter Eleven

Managing the Diverse Workforce

"e pluribus unum"

Chapter Outline

Diversity: A Brief History
Diversity Today
The Size of the Workforce
The Workers of the Future
The Age of the Workforce
Future Jobs and Workforce Qualifications
Managing Diversity versus Affirmative Action
Competitive Advantage through Diversity
Challenges of a Diverse Workforce
Multicultural Organizations
How Organizations Can Cultivate a Diverse Workforce
Top Management Leadership and Commitment
Organizational Assessment
Attracting Employees
Diversity Training
Retaining Employees

Learning Objectives

After studying Chapter 11, you will know:

1. How changes in the U.S. workforce make diversity a critical organizational and managerial issue.
2. The distinction between affirmative action and managing diversity.
3. How companies can gain a competitive edge by effectively managing diversity.
4. What challenges a company is likely to encounter with a diverse workforce.
5. How an organization can take steps to cultivate diversity.

Setting the Stage

Getting in Touch at Deloitte & Touche

Since the mid-1980s, Deloitte & Touche's new hires were approximately 50 percent women. Because it takes a minimum of 10 years to become a partner, the professional services firm based in Wilton, Connecticut, was anticipating that women would be candidates for admission to the partnership in significant numbers by the early 1990s. But something unexpected happened. In 1992, instead of seeing an increase in the percentage of women among candidates for partner, Deloitte & Touche saw a *decline.* In fact, talented women were leaving the firm and this represented a significant drain of capable people. They could not afford to lose valued potential partners.

To address the problem, Chairman & CEO J. Michael Cook formed and chaired the Task Force on the Retention and Advancement of Women to identify the reasons why women were leaving the firm and, therefore, were not advancing to the partnership at the same percentage as men. The task force conducted an extensive information-gathering initiative, interviewing women and men at all levels of the firm, including contacting women who had left the firm. The task force uncovered three main areas of concerns impacting women at the firm: (1) a culture and work environment that was male dominated, (2) perceived obstacles to career opportunities, such as a lack of role models, mentors, and networking opportunities, and (3) the difficulty of balancing career and personal lives.

Deloitte & Touche is basking in its new reputation as a women-friendly firm: It now has the most female employees among the major CPA firms.
[Courtesy of Deloitte & Touche, © 1995 All rights reserved]

To tackle these issues, Deloitte & Touche initially focused on changing its culture. The firm's 5,000 partners and managers were required to attend a two-day gender awareness workshop that explored gender stereotypes and the differences between men and women at a cost to the firm of approximately $3 million. The firm made a renewed commitment to flexible work arrangements and added parental leave benefits.

To maximize accountability of the initiative and enhance long-term success, Mike Cook approached Lynn Martin, former Secretary of Labor and creator of the Glass Ceiling Commission under the Bush Administration, to chair an external Advisory Council on the Advancement of Women. The council's mission is to provide oversight and challenge for the initiative for the retention and advancement of women.

The results of the initiative are impressive. The percentage of women at all levels has risen, and for the first time in the history of the firm, turnover rates for senior managers (the level before partner admission) have been lower for women than for men. In addition, in 1995 the firm admitted its highest percentage of new partners who were women (21 percent). Deloitte & Touche is basking in its new reputation as a women-friendly firm: In 1997, it was the first of the major professional services firms to achieve 10 percent women partners. The firm's overall progress gives them a laudable reputation with their clients. Apart from strictly diversity concerns, the business reasons for making these changes are coming home very quickly. For its efforts, Deloitte & Touche received the 1995 Catalyst Award, *Personnel Journal* 1996 Optimas Award for Competitive Advantage, and has been listed both in *Working Mother* magazine's list of "100 Best Companies for Working Mothers" (1994–97).

Source: "Firm's Diversity Efforts Even the Playing Field," Personnel Journal, *January 1996, p.56.*

managing diversity
Managing a culturally diverse workforce by recognizing the characteristics common to specific groups of employees while dealing with such employees as individuals and supporting, nurturing, and utilizing their differences to the organization's advantage.

As the Deloitte & Touche case illustrates, building a more diverse workforce is one of corporate America's biggest challenges. **Managing diversity** involves such things as recruiting, training, promoting, and utilizing to full advantage individuals with different backgrounds, beliefs, capabilities, and cultures. Managing diversity is more than just hiring minorities and women. It means understanding and appreciating employee differences to build a more effective and profitable organization.

In this chapter, we examine the meaning of diversity and the management skills and organizational processes involved in effectively managing the diverse workforce. We also explore the social and demographic changes and economic and employment shifts that are creating this changing U.S. workforce.

Diversity: A brief history

Managing diversity is not a new or futuristic management issue. From the late 1800s to the early 1900s, groups that immigrated to the United States were from Italy, Poland, Ireland, and Russia. Members of these groups were considered outsiders because they did not speak English and had different customs and work styles. They struggled, often violently, to gain acceptance in industries such as steel, coal, automobile manufacturing, insurance, and finance. In the 1800s, it was considered poor business practice for white-Protestant–dominated insurance companies to hire Irish, Italians, Catholics, or Jews.

By the 1960s, the struggle for acceptance by the various white ethnic and religious groups had succeeded. Once the white male members of the various ethnic and religious groups were successfully assimilated into the workforce, the stage was set for the next struggle of "outsiders": cultural and racial minorities and women. Today more than half of the U.S. workforce consists of people other than white, U.S.-born males, and this trend is expected to continue. Two-thirds of all global migration is into the United States.

The traditional American image of diversity has been one of assimilation. The United States was considered the "melting pot" of the world, a country in which ethnic and racial differences were blended into an American purée. In real life, many ethnic and most racial groups retained their identities—but they did not express them at work. Employees often abandoned most of their ethnic and cultural distinctions while at work to keep their jobs and get ahead. Many Europeans came to the United States, Americanized their names, perfected their English, and tried to enter the mainstream as quickly as possible.

Today's immigrants are willing to be part of an integrated team, but they no longer are willing to sacrifice their cultural identities to get ahead. Nor will they have to do so. Companies are finding that they should be more accommodating of differences, and that doing so pays off in business. Companies are also beginning to realize that their customers have become increasingly diverse and that retaining a diversified workforce can provide a competitive advantage in the marketplace.

Diversity today

Today *diversity* refers to far more than skin color and gender. It is a broad term used to refer to all kinds of differences, summarized in Figure 11.1. These differences include religious affiliation, age, disability status, military experience, sexual orientation, economic class, educational level, and lifestyle in addition to gender, race, ethnicity, and nationality.

Although members of different groups (white males, people born during the Depression, homosexuals, Vietnam veterans, Hispanics, Asians, women, blacks, etc.) share within their groups many common values, attitudes, and perceptions, there is also much diversity within each of these categories. Every group is made up of individuals who are unique in personality, education, and life experiences. There may be more differences among, say, three Asians from Thailand, Hong Kong, and Korea than among a Caucasian,

figure 11.1
Components of a diversified workforce

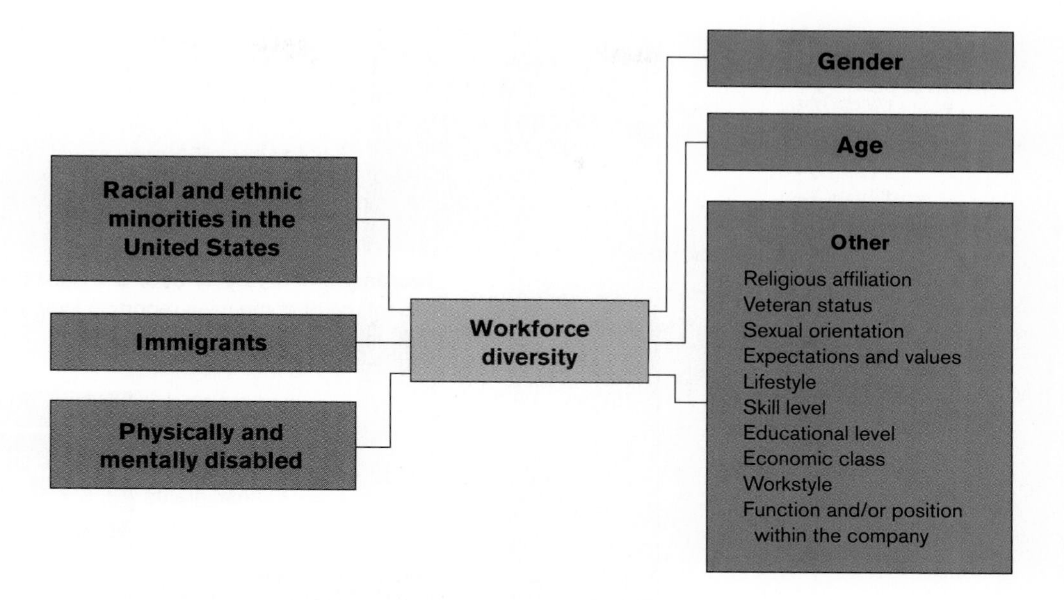

an African-American, and an Asian, all born in Chicago. And not all white males share the same personal or professional goals and values or behave alike.

Thus, managing diversity may seem a contradiction within itself. It means being acutely aware of characteristics *common* to a group of employees, while also managing these employees as *individuals*. Managing diversity means not just tolerating or accommodating all sorts of differences but supporting, nurturing, and utilizing these differences to the organization's advantage. U.S. businesses will not have a choice of whether or not to have a diverse workforce; if they want to survive, they must learn to manage a diverse workforce sooner or better than their competitors.

A good start toward effectively managing diversity is to understand that different groups value different things. A brief preview of some of the trends and issues addressed in this chapter is given in Figure 11.2.

The size of the workforce

The U.S. civilian labor force is expected to reach 151 million by 2005 (from 125 million in 1990). Though a 21 percent growth rate over 15 years may seem high, it is actually much lower than the 33 percent increase for the period 1975–90. The numbers show a slowing in both the number of people joining the labor force and the rate of labor force growth, which is now projected at 1.3 percent per year.[1] Changes in fertility, death, and immigration rates could increase the population, but probably not until later in the 21st century.

During most of its history, the United States has experienced a surplus of workers. But this situation is quickly changing. Using even modest economic growth projections, the number of jobs that will be created is expected to equal or exceed the growth in the labor force by the year 2005.[2] Employers today have to compete for the best candidates from a relatively smaller and more diverse labor pool. To compete effectively, employers have to know who these new workers are—and they must be prepared to meet those workers' needs.

The workers of the future

Until recently, white, American-born males dominated the U.S. workforce. Businesses catered to their needs. However, while this group still constitutes the largest percentage of workers—at about 38 percent of the workforce—it only accounts for 15 percent of the net growth (those entering minus those leaving). The remaining 85 percent of workforce growth is accounted for by U.S.-born white females, immigrants, and minorities.

figure 11.2
The diverse workforce

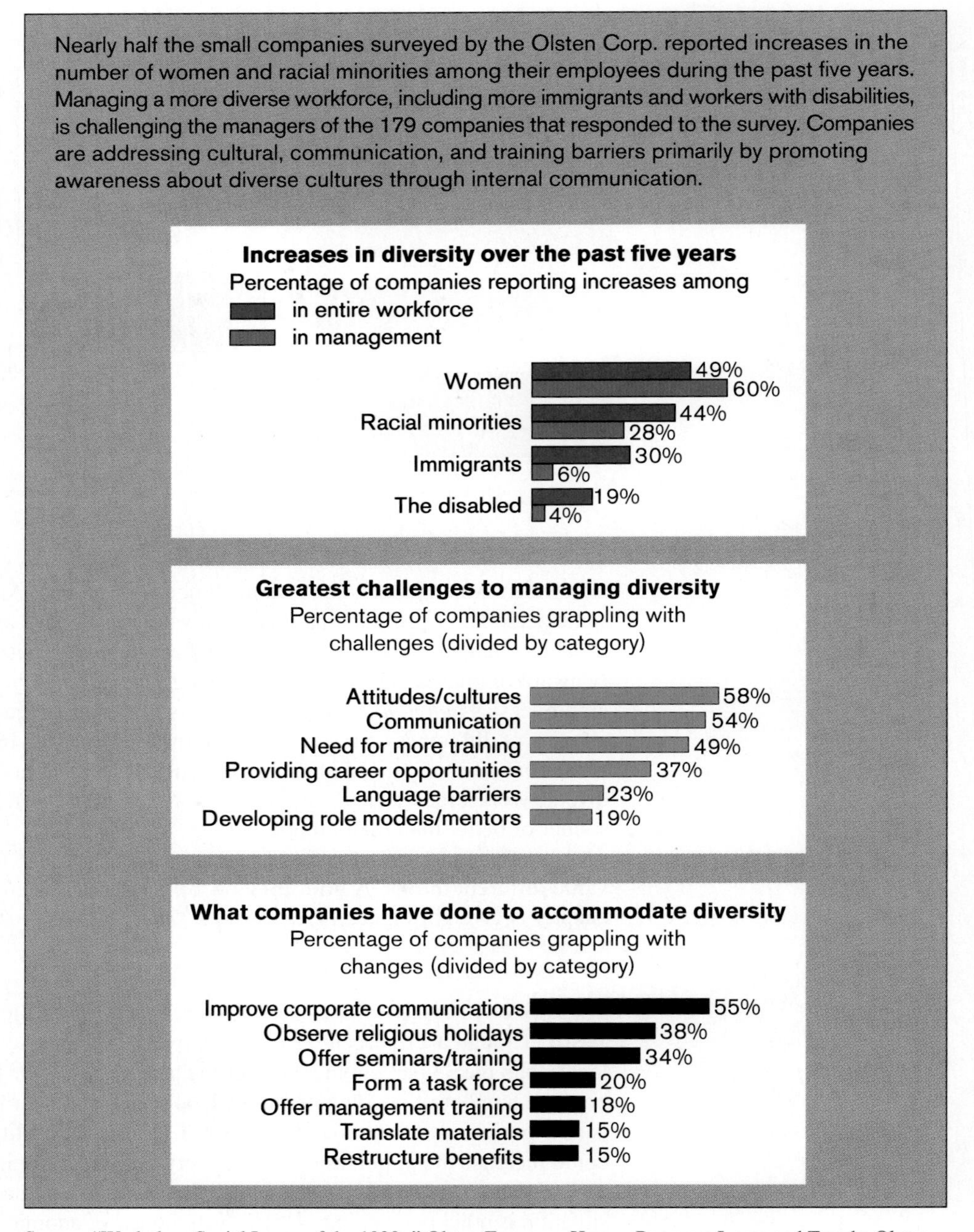
Nearly half the small companies surveyed by the Olsten Corp. reported increases in the number of women and racial minorities among their employees during the past five years. Managing a more diverse workforce, including more immigrants and workers with disabilities, is challenging the managers of the 179 companies that responded to the survey. Companies are addressing cultural, communication, and training barriers primarily by promoting awareness about diverse cultures through internal communication.
Increases in diversity over the past five years
Percentage of companies reporting increases among
in entire workforce
in management
Women
49%
60%
Racial minorities
44%
28%
Immigrants
30%
6%
The disabled
19%
4%
Greatest challenges to managing diversity
Percentage of companies grappling with challenges (divided by category)
Attitudes/cultures 58%
Communication 54%
Need for more training 49%
Providing career opportunities 37%
Language barriers 23%
Developing role models/mentors 19%
What companies have done to accommodate diversity
Percentage of companies grappling with changes (divided by category)
Improve corporate communications 55%
Observe religious holidays 38%
Offer seminars/training 34%
Form a task force 20%
Offer management training 18%
Translate materials 15%
Restructure benefits 15%

Source: "Workplace Social Issues of the 1990s," Olsten Forum on Human Resource Issues and Trends; Olsten Corp., Westbury, NY, 1992. Reprinted by permission.

Gender issues One of the most important developments in the U.S. labor market has been the growing number of women working outside the home. Social changes during the late 1960s and early 1970s, coupled with financial necessity, caused women to enter the workforce and redefine their role to include paid employment. Consider these figures:

- Women currently make up about 47 percent of the workforce.
- Over 60 percent of all women work outside the home.
- Women account for 62 percent of labor force growth.

- Over 40 percent of today's workforce consists of families in which both spouses are working.
- Women with children under age six make up the fastest-growing segment of the workforce.[3]

For many women, as well as their spouses, balancing work life with family responsibilities and parenting presents an enormous challenge. Although men's roles in our society have been changing, women still adopt the bulk of family responsibilities, including homemaking, child care, and care of elderly parents. As employers search for new workers from a shrinking supply and try to retain experienced employees, women will be in a position to make demands and companies will be forced to make it easier to balance work and family commitments.

The average full-time working female earns much less than the average working male—only about 75 percent as much as men in the same job (recall the discussion in Chapter 10 about equal pay and comparable worth). Fortunately, the median earnings of young women (ages 16 to 24) are 95 percent those of young men. At the level of vice president, the average female earns over 40 percent less than a male in the same job. However, this situation is getting somewhat better. Over the past decade, average total compensation for women executives has more than doubled to $187,000. (However, this is still much less than the $289,000 average for men.)[4]

glass ceiling An invisible barrier that makes it difficult for certain groups, such as minorities and women, to move beyond a certain level in the organizational hierarchy

Some of the discrepancy in compensation is the consequence of both the level and type of jobs women receive. As women—along with minorities—move up the corporate ladder, they encounter a "glass ceiling." The **glass ceiling** is an invisible barrier that makes it difficult for women and minorities to move beyond a certain level in the corporate hierarchy. In 1981, for example, only 1 percent of executives in Fortune 500 companies were women, and by 1991 this number had increased to only 3 percent. But the situation is improving, albeit too slowly. Today, the percentage of women who hold the title of executive vice president has jumped to almost 11 percent. Across all management levels, the picture is even more encouraging; the percentage of women managers has increased from 27 percent in 1981 to 43 percent today. In addition, evidence suggests that women no longer have to choose between careers and families. In 1982, only 49 percent of women executives were married and only 39 percent had children. Today, nearly 70 percent of women executives are married and 63 percent have children.[5] Table 11.1 shows a list of some very successful women in business today.

The glass ceiling is so named because it symbolizes an invisible barrier that makes it difficult for women and minorities to move beyond a certain point on the corporate ladder. *[Norman Sugimoto]*

table 11.1 The A-list: Women with the best shot at the top spot

Who will be the woman to be named CEO of a major American corporation? These are the 17 names *Working Woman* heard most often when they asked that question of business leaders and executive recruiters.

Jill Barad, 44	President and COO, Mattel	Marketing fast-tracker, from Max Factor to Mattel, from Hot Wheels to Barbie. (Recently promoted to CEO.) (See chapter 1.)
Brenda Barnes, 42	COO, Pepsi-Cola North American	A star marketer via Wilson Sporting Goods, Frito-Lay, and Pepsi.
Patricia Barron, 53	President, Xerox Engineering Systems	McKinsey consultant, then international ad marketing posts at Xerox.
Roxanne Decyk, 43	VP, corporate planning, Amoco	Led International Harvester's rebirth as Navistar and climbed sales ladder at Amoco.
Angela Dunlap, 39	President, marketing, MCI Telecommunications	Product-manager job at Hallmark led to string of marketing jobs at MCI.
Ann Fudge, 44	President, Maxwell House Coffee; EVP Kraft Foods	Followed marketing track from General Electric to General Mills to General Foods (since acquired by Kraft).
Ellen Hancock, 52	EVP and COO, National Semiconductor	Stepped off staff ladder at IBM to take operations job. Now runs National Semiconductor's product development.
Katherine Hudson, 52	CEO, W. H. Brady	Long stint at Kodak, capped by post overseeing instant photography. Now Brady's boss.
Lois Juliber, 47	President, Colgate-North America	General Mills brand manager. Colgate's chief techie and Asia hand.
Karen Katen, 46	President, U.S. Pharmaceuticals, Pfizer	Marketing and more marketing at Pfizer.
Judy Lewent, 46	CFO, Merck	Finance posts at Pfizer, Bankers Trust, and E. F. Hutton, Merck's money master since '80.
Alice Lusk, 48	Former corporate VP and group executive of health care and insurance, EDS	Nabbed Blue Cross contract, built GM's info infrastructure. Company grew from $750 million to $3 billion in her 20-year tenure.
Ellen Marram, 49	President, Seagram Beverage Group, EVP, The Seagram Company Ltd.	Came from Nabisco via '81 merger with Standard Brands. Launched SnackWells, then went to Seagram.
Gail McGovern, 44	EVP, business-markets division, AT&T	Programmed computers before the break-up; now programs Ma Bell's strategy.
Judith Rogala, 54	EVP, business-services division, Office Depot	Jumped from flight attendant to airline labor-relations exec to senior VP spot at Federal Express before taking flight for Office Depot.
Judith Sprieser, 42	CFA and senior VP, Sara Lee	Finance tracker, banking and accounting in Chicago, treasurer of Nalco Chemical, then head of Sara Lee's Mexican operations.
Carolyn Ticknor, 48	VP and general manager, Laser Jet Solutions Group, Hewlett-Packard	HP lifer has done it all: operations, R&D, division management.

Source: First appeared in *Working Woman* in April 1996. Written by Nancy Chambers. Reprinted with permission of MacDonald Communications Corporation. Copyright © 1997 by MacDonald Corporation. For subscriptions call 1-800-234-9675.

From the Pages of BusinessWeek

Sex on the Job

A few months back, Garry G. Mathiason, senior partner with Littler, Mendelson, Fastiff, Tichy & Mathiason, the nation's largest employment law firm, got a call from a very sheepish general counsel for a major company. The president of the company, the counsel said, "is planning to have a consensual affair with one of his employees," but before he does, "he wants to draft a written agreement" stating that the affair is voluntary–to reduce the chance that the woman might file a sexual-harassment suit if they broke up. "You won't believe it, " Mathiason assured the nervous counsel. "But we've already drafted a standard form" for just such cases.

Stunning. Welcome to the minefield that is office romance in the Nervous Nineties. Presidents, CEOs, and other top corporate execs have already discovered that an old-fashioned fling between boss and subordinate can be a fatal distraction. In fact, says Mathiason, "in the last three years, I've been involved in more terminations of CEOs due to claims of sex harassment" than for anything else.

That's a stunning change. In the old days, a top exec who requested some intimate overtime risked, at most, a slap in the face and the loss of a good secretary. These days the object of the boss's unwanted affection is likely to respond with a sexual-harassment suit. And as Mathiason's client feared, even when a relationship begins with mutual consent, after the breakup, the plaintiff lawyers appear. Elizabeth J. du Fresne, a senior partner at Miami law firm Steel, Hector & Davis, says she settles 10 or 15 such cases a year for over $500,000, and a few that top $1 million–double or triple the number of cases five years ago. Says Susan Meisinger, senior vice president at the Society for Human Resource Management: "Romance in the office ain't cheap."

As a result, more companies have adopted policies to minimize the liability. "Businesses that always closed their eyes to office romance . . . are having to think about it," says du Fresne. So far, however, less than 30 percent of companies have a clear policy on relationships between senior execs and their subordinates, according to a January survey by Human Resource Management.

So what's the best policy? The options range from voluntary disclosure to rigid rules with strict penalties. Intel Corp., for example, is among the companies that explicitly and severely limit office dating between superiors and subordinates. Intel's "nonfraternization guideline," for instance, forbids managers from dating any employee they supervise and warns violators that they may face termination.

But such iron-clad prohibitions "merely drive the relationships underground," says Freada Klein, founder of a Cambridge (Massachusetts) employee-relations consulting firm. She favors the more flexible policy adopted by companies such as General Motors Corp. There, managers are encouraged to report romantic involvements with subordinates. Usually, GM reacts by "creating a different reporting relationship to protect everyone," says a GM spokesman.

Given today's intense business climate, in which men and women are thrown together for days on end in meetings or on trips, "no company is going to stop Cupid at the front door," says Eric Greenberg, director of management studies at the American Management Association. "People meet at work. They date," says Gordon E. Eubanks Jr., chief executive of software-maker Symantec Corp.

The good news is that most relationships don't lead to trouble. In a Human Resource Management Survey, 55 percent of the 617 respondents said romances in their companies resulted in marriage. There are many famous examples: Microsoft CEO William H. Gates III met wife Melinda French while she was a product manager at the company. General Motors Chairman John F. Smith Jr. met his wife Lydia when she was briefly assigned to be his secretary in the late

The Score

A new survey of 2,800 human resources professionals shows that sex at the office is a constant–and a sometimes troublesome one.

1. Has the number of workplace romances at your organization increased, stayed the same, or decreased in the past five years?
   - Increased: 12%
   - Stayed same: 48%
   - Decreased: 12%
   - Don't know: 26%
2. In the past five years, have any of the following occurred as a result of a romance between employees?
   - Complaints of favoritism from co-workers: 28%
   - Claims of sexual harassment: 24%
   - Decreased productivity by those involved: 24%
   - Complaints of retaliation after it ended: 17%
   - Decreased morale of co-workers: 16%
3. Does your organization have a written policy about workplace romance?
   - Yes: 13%
   - No, but we have an unwritten policy: 14%
   - No: 72%
4. What do your policies prohibit?
   - Romance between superior and subordinate: 70%
   - Public displays of affection: 37%
   - Dating someone in the same department: 19%
   - Dating a customer/client: 13%
   - All dating among employees: 4%

Data: Society for Human Resource Management

1980s. French quit when she had a baby, and to avoid problems, Lydia Smith left her GM job shortly after meeting her future husband.

Still, when relationships don't end at the altar, "it can get very complicated afterwards," warns Ellen Bravo, co-director of 9to5, National Association of Working Women. Her group receives 15,000 calls a year from nonexecutive women, many complaining about a relationship with a superior. Silicon Valley buzzed for years about charges brought against Oracle Chairman Lawrence J. Ellison by an employee who alleged that he fired her when their affair fizzled. Ellison eventually prevailed in court, but it didn't help the corporate image.

Morale problems. Even if an affair doesn't cause legal problems, it can hurt morale. In 1996, Edward R. McCracken, then chairman and CEO of Silicon Graphics Inc., began dating a much younger woman who worked in human resources. McCracken has said the relationship was proper and above board. But the affair upset other employees, says one former SGI employee: "It's hard to be credible about sexual harassment when the chairman of the company dates somebody who works for him, even indirectly."

Source: William C. Symonds, Steve Hamm, Gail DeGeorge, "Sex on the Job," *Business Week:* February 16, 1998.

Discussion Questions

1. What are the reasons for and against allowing employees to date one another?
2. What are your views on what companies should do?
3. Are there current events in the press that relate to this situation? ●

sexual harassment Conduct of a sexual nature that has negative consequences for employment.

One persistent concern regarding men and women is the problem of **sexual harassment.** In 1995 alone, 15,549 sexual harassment complaints were filed with the Equal Employment Opportunity Commission (EEOC), and they fell into two different categories. The first, *quid pro quo harassment,* occurs when "submission to or rejection of sexual conduct is used as a basis for employment decisions." The second type of harassment, *hostile environment,* occurs when unwelcome sexual conduct "has the purpose or effect of unreasonably interfering with job performance or creating an intimidating, hostile, or offensive working environment." Table 11.2 shows the basic components of an effective sexual harassment policy. Companies such as Avon, Corning, and Metro-Goldwyn-Mayer have found that a strong commitment to diversity leads to fewer problems with sexual harassment.[6]

Before moving on, it is important to note that gender issues and the changing nature of work do not apply just to women. In some ways, the changing status of women has given men the opportunity to redefine their roles, expectations, and lifestyles. Some men are deciding that there is more to life than corporate success and are choosing to scale back work hours and commitments to spend time with their families. Worker values are shifting toward personal time, quality of life, self-fulfillment, and family. Workers today, both men and women, are looking to achieve a balance between career and family.

Minorities and immigrants

In addition to gender issues, the importance and scope of diversity are evident in the growth of racial minorities and immigrants in the workforce. Consider these facts:

- Minorities and immigrants hold approximately one out of every four jobs in the United States.
- Nonwhites make up 35 percent of the growth rate in the workforce, and will compose 27 percent of the total work population in 2005.
- The growth rate for African-Americans is 20 percent while the growth rate for Hispanics is 75 percent.

table 11.2
Basic components of an effective sexual harassment policy

1. Development a comprehensive organizationwide policy on sexual harassment and present it to all current and new employees. Stress that sexual harassment will not be tolerated under any circumstances. Emphasis is best achieved when the policy is publicized and supported by top management
2. Hold training sessions with supervisors to explain Title VII requirements, their role in providing an environment free of sexual harassment, and proper investigative procedures when charges occur.
3. Establish a formal complaint procedure in which employees can discuss problems without fear of retaliation. The complaint procedure should spell out how charges will be investigated and resolved.
4. Act immediately when employees complain of sexual harassment. Communicate widely that investigations will be conducted objectively and with appreciation for the sensitivity of the issue.
5. When an investigation supports employee charges, discipline the offender at once. For extremely serious offenses, discipline should include penalties up to and including discharge. Discipline should be applied consistently across similar cases and among managers and hourly employees alike.
6. Follow up on all cases to ensure a satisfactory resolution of the problem.

Source: Arthur Sherman, George Bohlander, and Scott Snell, *Managing Human Resources,* 11th ed. Copyright © 1998. Reprinted by permission of South-Western Publishing, a division of International Thomson Publishing, Inc., Cincinnati, Ohio 45227.

- English has become the second language for much of the population in California, Texas, and Florida.
- By 2020, most of California's entry-level workers will be Hispanic.
- Current projections indicate that Hispanics will surpass African-Americans as the largest racial minority in the next 20 to 25 years.
- Since 1970, 83 percent of immigrants to the United States have come from Asia and Latin America. Today, more than 30 percent of New York City's residents are non-U.S.-born, Miami is two-thirds Hispanic, Detroit is 79 percent African-American, and San Francisco is 33 percent Asian.[7]

These numbers indicate that the term "minority," as it is typically used, may quickly become outdated. Particularly in urban areas where white males do not predominate, managing diversity means more than eliminating discrimination; it means capitalizing on the wide variety of skills available in the labor market. Organizations that do not take full advantage of the skills and capabilities of minorities and immigrants are severely limiting their potential talent pool.

Even so, the evidence shows some troubling disparities in employment. Compared to white males who in 1996 had an unemployment rate of 4.3 percent, the unemployment rate for African-American males over 20 years old was 10.9 percent. In that same year, the weekly earnings of white males was around $580 compared to $417 for African-Americans and $344 for Hispanics.[8]

To address these problems, many organizations are working to do a better job of providing opportunities to minorities. Dunn and Bradstreet, for example, sponsors summer internship programs for minority M.B.A students. Lockheed Martin has partnered the American Management Association's Operation Enterprise to establish two-week paid summer internship programs for high school and college students. These internship programs help both students and organizations learn about one another and, ideally, turn into full-time employment opportunities. Figure 11.3 shows that minorities are finding it somewhat easier to move into management positions.

figure 11.3
Percentage of minority managers

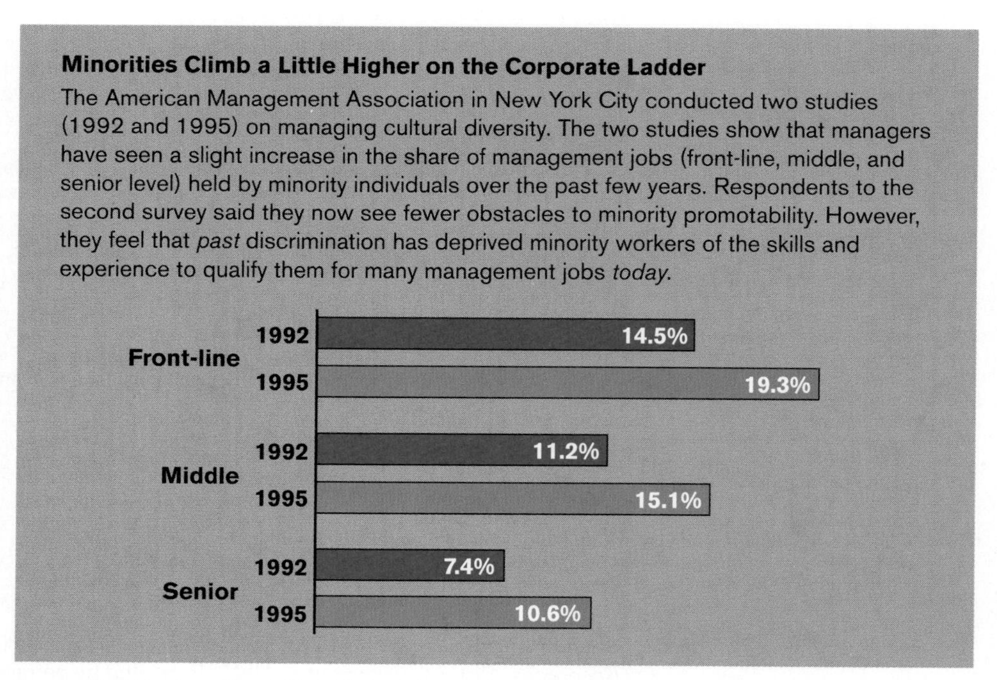

Source: Shari Candron, "Don't Make Texico's $175 Million Mistake," *Workforce,* March 1997, pp. 58–66.

Mentally and physically disabled The largest unemployed minority population in the United States is people with disabilities. Over the past decade, only about 10 percent of severely disabled adults have been employed. Meanwhile fully two-thirds of disabled adults without jobs say they want to work.[9]

The Americans with Disabilities Act (ADA), introduced in Chapter 10, defines a disability as a physical or mental impairment that substantially limits one or more major life activities. Examples of such physical or mental impairments include those resulting from conditions such as orthopedic, visual, speech, and hearing impairments; cerebral palsy; epilepsy; muscular dystrophy; multiple sclerosis; HIV infections; cancer; heart disease; diabetes; mental retardation; emotional illness; specific learning disabilities; drug abuse; and alcoholism.[10]

Because most disabilities are acquired, many people will become disabled in some way as they grow older. As the baby-boom generation ages, attitudes toward many disabilities may change. Mary Ann Breslin, executive director of Disability Rights Education and Defense Fund, Inc., states:

> Fifty or 100 years ago, wearing glasses was not acceptable, but today wearing corrective lenses is taken for granted, because it is a technology so ingrained in our culture. Glasses are orthopedic devices that are no different than an artificial limb or wheelchair or back brace.[11]

Individuals with disabilities have found themselves isolated from job opportunities largely because they have lacked access to educational and workplace environments. In addition, the attitudes of many employers and those of the disabled themselves have been barriers to employment. Today laws and technology are providing access to education and jobs. For most businesses, the mentally and physically disabled represent a largely unexplored labor market. Frequently, employers have found disabled employees are more dependable than typical employees, miss fewer days of work, and exhibit lower turnover.

One recent test of the limits of the ADA's applicability is Casey Martin's lawsuit against the Professional Golf Association (PGA). Because he has a degenerative condition of the muscle and bone in his right leg, Martin cannot walk an entire round of golf (which is required under PGA rules). In order that he might compete, Martin has sued the PGA under the ADA for the right to use a golf cart in tournaments.

The age of the workforce

The baby-boom generation (born between 1946 and 1964) is aging, which will cause the average age of the workforce to increase to around 40 by the year 2005. The number of people age 50 to 65 will increase at more than twice the rate of the overall population, and by 2005 over 15 percent of the workforce will be 55 years of age or older. At the same time, the number of younger workers (ages 16 to 24) is expected to drop to 16 percent in 2005.[12]

As a result of these trends, the Bureau of Labor Statistics projects that entry-level workers will be in short supply, and fewer new workers will enter the labor force than will be lost through retirement.[13] Many older employees are opting for early retirement even though there is no longer a mandatory retirement age and life expectancies have increased. Companies therefore need to retain and hire older, experienced workers. Figure 11.4 shows the perceived benefits and liabilities of employing older workers.

Retirement-age workers can be encouraged to remain in or reenter the workforce on a flexible or part-time basis, whether for economic reasons, desire for social interaction, or the need to be productive. The examples below show how creative companies are rethinking their retirement policies and solving their skilled-labor shortage by finding ways to attract and retain people over 55. These companies save on turnover and training costs and capitalize on the experience of their older employees.

Not yet ready for the rocker

Here are some examples of how leading organizations attract and retain older workers.

- Days Inns of America has been particularly successful at recruiting and keeping persons over age 65. Employees from this age group compose more than 25 percent of Days Inns' 650-person reservation staff. Evidence shows that older workers remain on the job longer than younger workers–annual turnover for this group is less than 2 percent versus 70 percent for younger workers (the reduction in turnover has reduced the center's recruitment and training costs by over 40 percent). Although older workers tend to be paid more than younger workers, this is because of their having been on the job longer. Performance measures show that older workers take more time talking with prospective customers and are more successful booking reservations.
- The Environmental Protection Agency (EPA) discovered the value of older workers back in 1976 when it pioneered one of the first programs for older workers. Through its Senior Environmental Employment (SEE) program, enrollees are assigned to a diverse set of jobs, ranging from messengers to accountants. These full- and part-time employees have been involved in every aspect of EPA's efforts to improve the environment. Work options implemented for all employees have especially benefited older workers by providing flextime, job sharing, part-time employment, and training for changing technologies.
- Eastman Kodak has concentrated on using redeployed mature employees in its project management division (PMD). Kodak has found that mature employees with the right skills can make excellent additions to the project management teams as either controls engineers or project managers. To take advantage of this opportunity, Kodak has established special selection criteria for people in project management, modified its job-posting process, and developed special training programs for new people in project management.
- Travelers Insurance was one of the first companies to establish a retiree job bank. After discovering that 90 percent of its older employees were interested in working part-time after retirement, the company established an in-house temporary agency using retirees to fill in during peak periods, absences, and vacations. After managers requested more retirees than Travelers could provide, the company opened up the program to retirees from other companies.

Sources: Robert J. Nemes, "The Golden Years and Project Management," *American Association of Cost Engineers Transactions* (1994 Transactions, HF5.1–HF5.3); Susan Street, "EPA's Seasoned Resource," *Public Manager* 22, no. 1 (Spring 1993), p. 26; William McNaught, "Are Older Workers Good Buys? A Case Study of Days Inns of America," *Sloan Management Review,* Spring 1993, pp. 53–63. ●

Future jobs and workforce qualifications

U.S. Department of Labor projections indicate that the United States will be a predominantly service-oriented economy by the year 2005 and that manufacturing will represent only 12 to 15 percent of all jobs. People without high school diplomas will be at an increasing disadvantage, because their employment opportunities will be confined to the lowest-paying service jobs. Even the lower-skilled occupations of the future will require workers who can communicate well and read and comprehend instructions, and have a working knowledge of basic mathematics. For example, the job of assembly-line worker traditionally was considered a low-skilled occupation. Today many of these workers are learning statistical process control techniques, which require a solid foundation in mathematics.

figure 11.4 Perceived benefits and liabilities of employing older workers

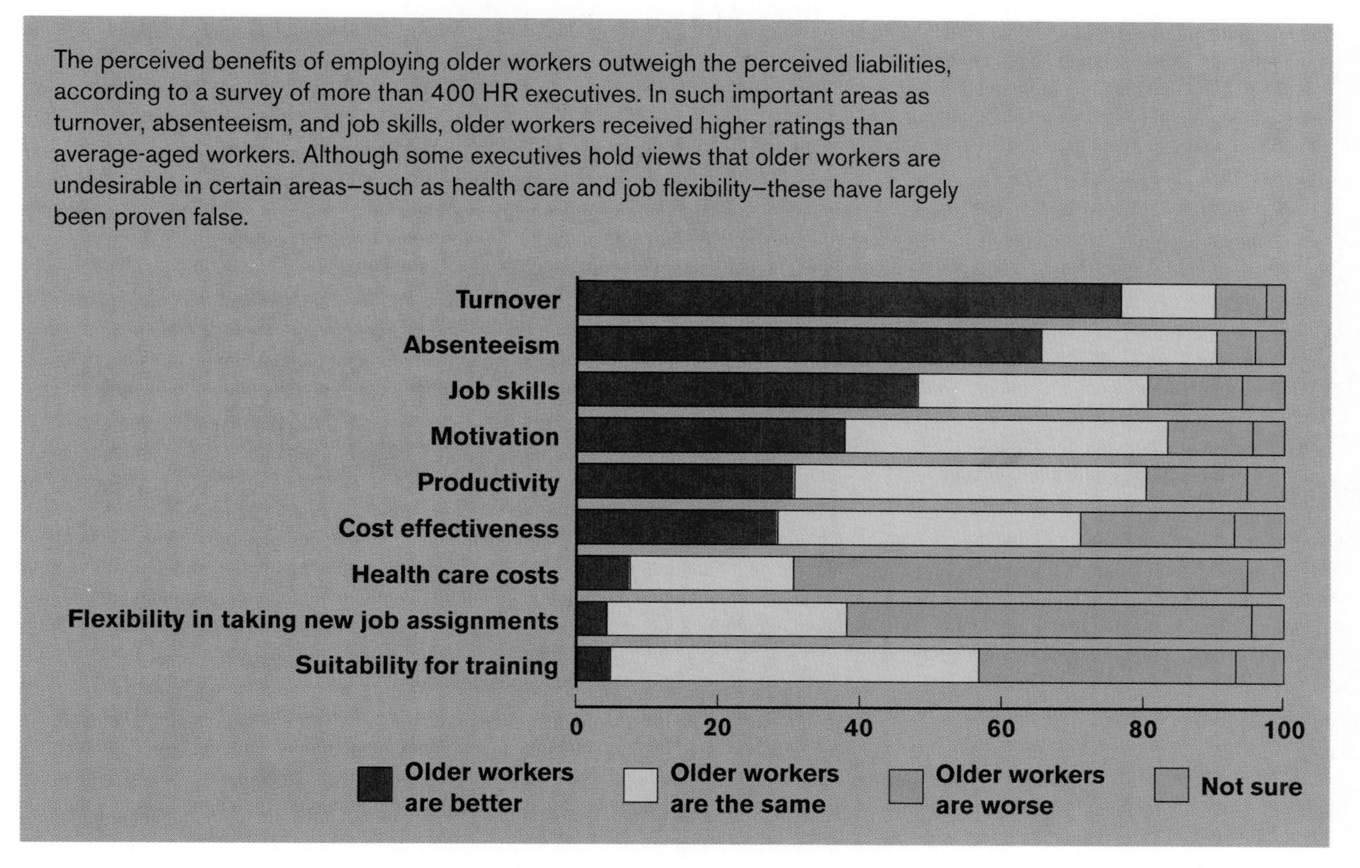
The perceived benefits of employing older workers outweigh the perceived liabilities, according to a survey of more than 400 HR executives. In such important areas as turnover, absenteeism, and job skills, older workers received higher ratings than average-aged workers. Although some executives hold views that older workers are undesirable in certain areas–such as health care and job flexibility–these have largely been proven false.
Turnover
Absenteeism
Job skills
Motivation
Productivity
Cost effectiveness
Health care costs
Flexibility in taking new job assignments
Suitability for training
0
20
40
60
80
100
Older workers are better
Older workers are the same
Older workers are worse
Not sure

Source: The Conference Board, "Availability of a Quality Workforce," *Personnel Journal,* October 1995, p. 60.

There is a growing gap between the knowledge and skills jobs require and those many employees and applicants possess. Skill deficiencies are particularly acute among minority workers and many immigrant populations. Illiteracy is often the underlying problem. It is estimated that 90 million Americans (about 47 percent of the adult population) have only limited reading and writing abilities needed to handle the minimal demands of job performance. The U.S. Department of Labor estimates that illiteracy costs U.S. businesses $225 billion a year in lost productivity. A recent survey of Fortune 1000 CEOs found that 90 percent recognized the problems of illiteracy, yet just 38 percent acknowledged that it was a problem for their workers (see Figure 11.5).[14]

Employers are combating this basic-skills gap in a number of ways. One approach is in-house basic-skills training programs. Ford, for example, offers reading courses at 25 of its plants. Domino's uses a videodisc program to teach reading and math. Other strategies include partnerships with public schools; community colleges; and local, state, and federal agencies. Many companies, including Esprit de Corp. and Hasbro, Inc., teach their employees English as a second language or offer second-language training to managers and employees to communicate that languages other than English are valued. Hasbro invites employees' families and friends to the classes to help reinforce the learning off the job.[15]

figure 11.5
CEOs' perception of illiteracy in corporate America

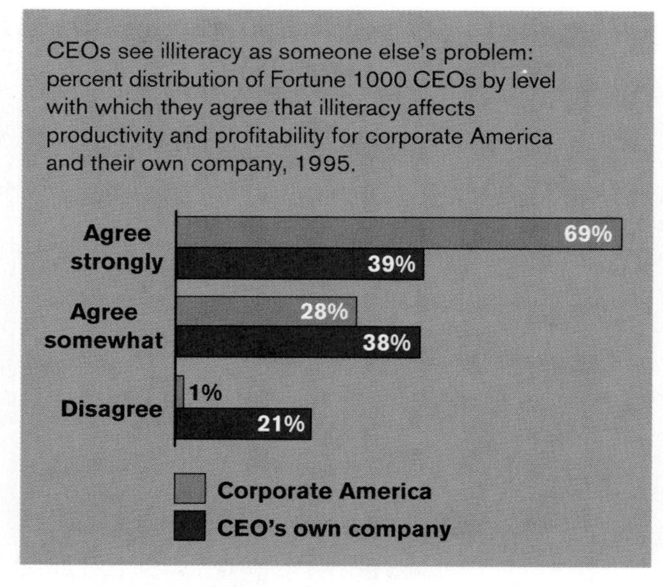
CEOs see illiteracy as someone else's problem: percent distribution of Fortune 1000 CEOs by level with which they agree that illiteracy affects productivity and profitability for corporate America and their own company, 1995.
Agree strongly
69%
39%
Agree somewhat
28%
38%
Disagree
1%
21%
Corporate America
CEO's own company

Source: Coors Literacy Survey.

Managing diversity versus affirmative action

Affirmative action (discussed in Chapter 10) was instituted to curb discrimination and correct the past exclusion of women and minorities from U.S. organizations. While a good deal of progress has been made in hiring women and minorities, Table 11.3 reveals that in most industries these groups continue to be disproportionately clustered at the bottom of corporate hierarchies (recall our earlier discussion of the *glass ceiling*).

In reality, a legislated approach tends to result in fragmented efforts that do not achieve the integrative goals of managing diversity. Employment discrimination still persists in organizations, and even after nearly three decades of government legislation, equal employment opportunity (EEO) and affirmative action laws have not adequately improved the upward mobility of women and minorities.

In fact, critics argue that the laws result in *de facto* employment quotas and those companies that conscientiously pursue affirmative action have had claims of preferential treatment and reverse discrimination leveled against them. Reverse discrimination exists when qualified white males are passed over for employment opportunities in favor of members of protected classes. For these reasons, several members of Congress have recently argued that the EEO and affirmative action laws should be dramatically changed or eliminated altogether.

In contrast to EEO and affirmative action programs, managing diversity means moving beyond legislated mandates to embrace a proactive business philosophy that values differences. Managing diversity involves organizations making changes in their systems, structures, and management practices in order to eliminate barriers that may keep people from reaching their full potential. The goal is not to treat all people the same but to treat people as individuals, recognizing that each employee has different needs and will need different things to succeed. This approach implies that different people in the workplace sometimes should be treated equally but differently.

Competitive advantage through diversity

For many organizations, the original impetus to diversify their workforces was social responsibility and legal necessity (recall Chapters 5 and 10). Morally, ethically, and legally, it is simply the right thing to do. Today many organizations are also

table 11.3
Where women and minorities are now

Percentage of managers who are women		Percentage of managers who are minorities	
Industry	**Percentage**	**Industry**	**Percentage**
Finance, insurance, real estate	41.4%	Retail trade	13.0%
Services	38.9	Transportation, communications, and public utilities	12.0
Retail trade	38.5	Services	11.0
Transportation, communications, and public utilities	25.6	Finance, insurance, and real estate	11.0
Wholesale trade	20.9	Agriculture	1.3
Manufacturing	15.9	Wholesale trade	0.9
Agriculture	14.5	Manufacturing	0.8
Construction	10.4	Mining	0.7
Mining	9.8	Construction	0.6

Source: Federal Glass Ceiling Commission.

approaching diversity from a more practical, business-oriented perspective. Increasingly, diversity can be a powerful tool for building competitive advantage. A recent study by the Department of Labor's Glass Ceiling Institute showed that the stock performance of firms that were high performers on diversity-related goals were 2.5 times higher than other firms. Conversely, announcements of damage awards from discrimination lawsuits has frequently had a negative effect on stock returns. Texaco, for example, agreed to pay $175 million to resolve a racial discrimination case, but the negative publicity from the case resulted in a severe stock price drop that will take years to restore.[16]

There are many advantages—and some obvious challenges—to managing a diverse workforce. Some of these are summarized in Table 11.4 and discussed below.

Ability to attract and retain motivated employees For companies facing changing demographics and business needs, diversity just makes good sense. Companies with a reputation for providing opportunities for diverse employees will have a competitive advantage in the labor market and will be sought out by the most qualified employees. In addition, when employees believe their differences are not merely tolerated but valued, they may become more loyal, productive, and committed.

table 11.4
The diverse workforce: advantages and challenges

Advantages	Challenges
• Fulfills social responsibility	• Lower cohesiveness
• Helps attract, retain, and motivate employees	• Communication problems
• Gains greater knowledge of diversified marketplace	• Mistrust and tension
• Promotes creativity, innovation, and problem solving	• Stereotyping
• Enhances organizational flexibility	

Better perspective of a differentiated market Companies such as Avon, Prudential, Eastman Kodak, and Toys "Я" Us are committed to diversity because as the composition of the American workforce changes, so does the customer base of these companies. Just as women and minorities may prefer to work for an employer that values diversity, they may prefer to patronize such organizations.

Many Asian-Americans, African-Americans, Mexican-Americans, and women have entered the middle class and now control consumer dollars. A multicultural workforce can provide a company with greater knowledge of the preferences and consuming habits of this diversified marketplace. This knowledge can assist companies in designing products and developing marketing campaigns to meet those consumers' needs. In addition, for at least some products and services, a multicultural sales force may help an organization sell to diverse groups. A diverse workforce can also give a company a competitive edge in a global economy by facilitating understanding of other customs, cultures, and marketplace needs.

Ability to leverage creativity and innovation in problem solving Work team diversity promotes creativity and innovation, because people from different backgrounds hold different perspectives on issues. Diverse groups have a broader base of experience from which to approach a problem; when effectively managed, they invent more options and create more solutions than homogeneous groups do. In addition, diverse work groups are freer to deviate from traditional approaches and practices. The presence of diversity can also help minimize "groupthink" (recall Chapter 3).[17]

Enhancement of organizational flexibility A diverse workforce can enhance organizational flexibility, because successfully managing diversity requires a corporate culture that tolerates many different styles and approaches. Less restrictive policies and procedures and less standardized operating methods enable organizations to become more flexible and thus better able to respond quickly to environmental changes (recall Chapters 2 and 9). Executives at Kodak and Prudential are so convinced of the competitive potential of a diverse workforce that they recently tied a portion of management compensation to success in recruiting and promoting minorities and women.[18]

Challenges of a diverse workforce

A diverse workforce also poses many challenges. Many of these challenges, summarized in Table 11.4, can be turned into advantages if the workforce is managed effectively.

Lower cohesiveness Diversity can create a lack of cohesiveness. Cohesiveness refers to how tightly knit the group is and the degree to which group members perceive, interpret, and act on their environment in similar or mutually agreed-upon ways. Because of their lack of similarity in language, culture, and/or experience, diverse groups typically are less cohesive than homogeneous groups. Often mistrust, miscommunication, stress, and attitudinal differences reduce cohesiveness, which in turn can diminish productivity. Group cohesiveness will be discussed in greater detail in Chapter 14.

Communication problems Perhaps the most common negative effect of diversity is communication problems. These difficulties include misunderstandings, inaccuracies, inefficiencies, and slowness. Speed is lost when not all group members are fluent in the same language or when additional time is required to explain things.

Diversity also increases errors and misunderstandings. Group members may assume they interpret things similarly when in fact they do not, or they may disagree because of their different frames of reference.[19]

Mistrust and tension People prefer to associate with others who are like themselves. This tendency often leads to mistrust and misunderstanding of those who are different because of a lack of contact and low familiarity. It also causes stress and tension, and reaching agreement on problems can be difficult.

Stereotyping We learn to see the world in a certain way based on our backgrounds and experiences. Our interests, values, and cultures act as filters and distort, block, and select what we see and hear. We see and hear what we expect to see and hear. Group members often inappropriately stereotype their "different" colleagues rather than accurately perceiving and evaluating those individuals' contributions, capabilities, aspirations, and motivations.

Such stereotypes in turn affect how people are treated. Employees stereotyped as unmotivated or emotional will be given less-stress-provoking (and perhaps less-important) jobs than their co-workers. Those job assignments will create frustrated employees, perhaps resulting in lower commitment, higher turnover, and underused skills.[20]

Multicultural organizations

To capitalize on the benefits and minimize the costs of a diverse workforce, organizations need to examine their assumptions about people and cultures. At a basic level, it is possible to categorize organizations according to their prevailing assumptions. Table 11.5 shows some of the most fundamental assumptions and describes how they influence management. Based on these assumptions, we can classify organizations as one of three types.

monolithic organization
An organization that has a low degree of structural integration–employing few women, minorities, or other groups that differ from the majority–and thus has a highly homogeneous employee population.

Some organizations are **monolithic.** This type of organization has very little *cultural integration;* in other words, it employs few women, minorities, or any other groups that differ from the majority. The organization is highly homogeneous in terms of its employee population. In monolithic organizations, if groups other than the norm are employed, they are found primarily in low-status jobs. Minority group members must adopt the norms of the majority to survive. This fact, coupled with small numbers, keeps conflicts among groups low. Discrimination and prejudice typically prevail, informal integration is almost nonexistent, and minority group members do not identify strongly with the company.

plural organization
An organization that has a relatively diverse employee population and makes an effort to involve employees from different gender, racial, or cultural backgrounds.

Most large U.S. organizations made the transition from monolithic to *plural* organizations in the 1960s and 1970s because of changing demographics as well as societal forces such as the civil rights and women's movements. **Plural organizations** have a more diverse employee population and take steps to involve persons from different gender, racial, or cultural backgrounds. These organizations use an affirmative action approach to managing diversity: They actively try to hire and train a diverse workforce, and to ensure against any discrimination against minority group members. They typically have much more integration than monolithic organizations; but like monolithic organizations, they often have minority group members clustered at certain levels or in particular functions within the organization.

Because of greater cultural integration, affirmative action programs, and training programs, the plural organization has some acceptance of minority group members into the informal network, much less discrimination, and less prejudice. Improved employment opportunities create greater identification with the organization among minority group members. Often the resentment of majority group members, coupled with the increased number of women and minorities, creates more conflict than in the monolithic organization.

multicultural organization
An organization that values cultural diversity and seeks to utilize and encourage it.

The plural organization fails to address the cultural aspects of integration. In contrast, in **multicultural organizations** diversity not only exists but is valued. These organizations fully integrate gender, racial, and minority group members both formally and informally. The multicultural organization is marked by an absence of prejudice and discrimination and by low levels of intergroup conflict. Such an organization creates a *synergistic* environment in which all members contribute to their maximum potential and the advantages of diversity can be fully realized.

table 11.5
Diversity assumptions and their implications for management

Common and misleading assumptions		Less common and more appropriate assumptions	
Homogeneity	*Melting pot myth:* We are all the same.	**Heterogeneity**	*Image of cultural pluralism:* We are not all the same; groups within society differ across cultures.
Similarity	*Similarity myth:* "They" are all just like me.	**Similarity and difference**	*They are not just like me:* Many people differ from me culturally. Most people exhibit both cultural similarities and differences when compared to me.
Parochialism	*Only-one-way myth:* Our way is the only way. We do not recognize any other way of living or working.	**Equifinality**	*Our way is not the only way:* There are many culturally distinct ways of reaching the same goal, of working, and of living one's life.
Ethnocentrism	*One-best-way myth:* Our way is the best way. All other approaches are inferior versions of our way.	**Culture contingency**	*Our way is one possible way:* There are many different and equally good ways to reach the same goal. The best way depends on the culture of the people involved.

Source: From "Diversity Assumptions and Their Implications for Management" by Nancy J. Adler, *Handbook of Organization,* 1996. Reprinted courtesy of Marcel Dekker, Inc. NY.

How organizations can cultivate a diverse workforce

An organization's plans for becoming multicultural and making the most of its diverse workforce should include (1) securing top management leadership and commitment, (2) assessing the workforce, (3) attracting employees, (4) developing employees, and (5) retaining employees.

Top management leadership and commitment

Obtaining top management leadership and commitment is critical for diversity programs to succeed. One way to communicate this commitment to all employees—as well as to the external environment—is to incorporate the organization's attitudes toward diversity into the corporate mission statement and into strategic plans and objectives. Managerial compensation can be directly linked to accomplishing diversity objectives. Adequate funding must be allocated to the diversity effort to ensure its success. Also, top management can set an example for other organization members by participating in diversity programs and making participation mandatory for all managers.

Some organizations have established corporate offices or committees to coordinate the companywide diversity effort and provide feedback to top management. Digital Equipment Corporation has a "director of valuing differences," Honeywell has a "director of workforce diversity," and Avon has a "director of multicultural planning and design." Other companies prefer to incorporate diversity management into the function of director of affirmative action or EEO.[21]

At Honeywell, disabled employees formed a council to discuss their needs and institute an accessibility program that went beyond federal regulations for accommodations of disabilities.
[David Young-Wolff/Tony Stone Images]

The work of managing diversity cannot be done by top management or diversity directors alone. Many companies rely on minority advisory groups or task forces to monitor organizational policies, practices, and attitudes; assess their impact on the diverse groups within the organization; and provide feedback and suggestions to top management.

For example, Digital Equipment Corporation uses Core Groups, in which employees from different backgrounds form small groups to address stereotypes and other relevant issues. At Equitable Life Assurance Society, Business Resource Groups meet regularly with the CEO to discuss issues pertaining to women, African-Americans, and Hispanics and make recommendations for improvement. U.S. West has a 33-member Pluralism Council that advises senior management on how to more effectively manage and utilize the company's diverse workforce. At Honeywell, disabled employees formed a council to discuss their needs. They proposed and accepted an accessibility program that went beyond federal regulations for accommodations of disabilities.

As you can see, progressive companies are moving from asking managers what they think minority employees need to asking the employees themselves what they need.

Organizational assessment

The next step in managing diversity is to establish an ongoing assessment of the organization's workforce, culture, policies, and practices in areas such as recruitment, promotions, benefits, and compensation. In addition, the demographics of the labor pool and the customer base should be evaluated. The objective is to identify problem areas and make recommendations where changes are needed.

For example, many women and Asians are at a disadvantage when aggressiveness is a valued part of the organization's culture. After analysis, management might decide that the organizational values need to be changed so that other styles of interacting are equally acceptable. Corporate values and norms should be identified and critically evaluated regarding their necessity and their impact on the diverse workforce.

Attracting employees

Companies can attract a diverse, qualified workforce through using effective recruiting practices, accommodating employees' work and family needs, and offering alternative work arrangements.

Recruitment A company's image can be a strong recruiting tool. Companies with reputations for hiring and promoting all types of people will have a competitive advantage. Xerox gives prospective minority employees reprints of an article that rates the company as one of the best places for African-Americans to work. Hewlett-Packard ensures that its female candidates are familiar with its high rating by *Working Woman* magazine. Many employers are implementing policies to attract more women, ensure that women's talents are used to full advantage, and avoid losing their most capable female employees.

Many minorities and economically disadvantaged people are physically isolated from job opportunities. Companies can bring information about job opportunities to the source of labor, or they can transport the labor to the jobs. Polycast Technology in Stamford, Connecticut, contracts with a private van company to transport workers from the Bronx in New York City to jobs in Stamford. Days Inn recruits homeless workers in Atlanta and houses them in a motel within walking distance of their jobs. Burger King has done a lot to recruit and hire immigrants in its fast-food restaurants.

Burger King makes the most of immigrants

Burger King Corporation has enjoyed a good deal of success in recruiting and hiring immigrants to work in its restaurants and retail operations. The Miami-based chain has discovered that newcomers to the United States are often attracted to fast-food jobs because entry-level positions require little skill, and flexible work hours allow them to hold down two jobs or go to school. In addition, since there is high turnover among employees, individuals with initiative and ambition are provided opportunities for rapid promotion.

To facilitate the hiring of foreign-born workers, Burger King has adopted several of its basic human resource systems. For example, employment applications are available in Spanish as well as English, an accommodation that is especially helpful in certain parts of the United States. In addition, several company videos are dubbed in Spanish. During the actual job interview, if an applicant speaks Spanish, he or she can be interviewed in that language. In addition, prospective employees can bring a family member or a friend to act as interpreter during the interview. To help applicants answer questions about employment eligibility and documentation, Burger King provides a toll-free number, staffed by people who speak Spanish. The company has contracted with an outside agency to ensure that all application forms are filled out correctly and that the company is in compliance with the law.

As part of its management training programs, Burger King teaches managers to be conscious of concerns immigrants may have, and their uneasiness with new surroundings. For example, many foreign-born workers simply don't understand the options they have regarding benefits. While the term *medical insurance* may be clear to U.S.-born workers, many immigrants may not understand what it means. This is also true of workers' compensation. When foreign-born employees are injured, they often hesitate to report the injury for fear of being fired. To enable its managers to handle these situations, Burger King has extensive training programs that address these specific concerns. Although there is no language requirement at Burger King, managers take cultural sensitivity seminars so that they can work well in a bilingual setting.

Each of these efforts has helped Burger King take advantage of an important and growing sector of the workforce. With immigrants making up as much as 40 percent of the annual growth in the U.S. labor force, Burger King and other companies are learning how to manage diversity successfully.

Source: Charlene Marmer Solomon, "Managing Today's Immigrants," *Personnel Journal,* February 1993, pp. 57–65.

Accommodating work and family needs

More job seekers are putting family needs first. Corporate work and family policies are now one of the most important recruiting tools.

Employers that have become involved in child care report decreased turnover and absenteeism and improved morale. In addition to providing child care, many companies now assist with care for elderly dependents, offer time off to care for sick family members, provide parental leaves of absence, and offer a variety of benefits that can be tailored to individual family needs. Some companies are accommodating the needs and concerns of dual-career couples by limiting relocation requirements or providing job search assistance to relocated spouses.

Alternative work arrangements

Another way companies accommodate diversity is to offer flexible work schedules and arrangements. The 11-branch New Haven region of People Bank based in Bridgeport, Connecticut, was having difficulty recruiting part-time tellers. The region's employee relations specialist initiated the Working Parent Program, which allowed part-timers to schedule their hours to coincide with their children's: home by 3 P.M., with summers and school holidays off. Staffing problems were solved by being flexible, using part-timers to cover peak hours, and hiring college students to fill in during holidays and summers.[22]

Other creative work arrangements include compressed workweeks (for example, four 10-hour days) and job sharing, in which two part-time workers share one full-time job. Another option to accommodate working mothers and the disabled is teleworking (working from home) or telecommuting (working from home via computer hookup to the main worksite). This option has been slow to catch on, but those organizations that have tried it report favorable results.

Diversity training

As you learned in Chapter 10, employees can be developed in a variety of ways. *Diversity training programs* attempt to identify and reduce hidden biases and develop the skills needed to effectively manage a diversified workforce. Traditionally, most management training has been based on the assumption that "managing" means managing a homogeneous, often white-male, full-time workforce. But gender, race, culture, and other differences create an additional layer of complexity.[23]

More than 50 percent of all U.S. organizations sponsor some sort of diversity training. Typically, diversity training has two components: awareness building and skill building.

Awareness building

Awareness building is designed to increase awareness of the meaning and importance of valuing diversity.[24] Its aim is not to teach specific skills but to sensitize employees to the assumptions they make about others and how these assumptions affect their behaviors, decisions, and judgment.

To build awareness, people are taught to become familiar with myths, stereotypes, and cultural differences as well as the organizational barriers that inhibit the full contributions of all employees. They develop a better understanding of corporate culture, requirements for success, and career choices that affect opportunities for advancement.

In most companies, the "rules" for success are ambiguous, unwritten, and perhaps inconsistent with written policy. A common problem for women and minorities is that they are unaware of many of the rules that are obvious to people in the mainstream. Valuing diversity means teaching the unwritten "rules" or cultural values to those who need to know them and changing the rules when necessary to benefit employees and hence the organization. It also requires inviting "outsiders" in and giving them access to information and meaningful relationships with people in power.

Skill building *Skill building* is designed to allow all employees and managers to develop the skills they need to deal effectively with one another and with customers in a diverse environment. Most of the skills taught are interpersonal, such as active listening, coaching, and giving feedback. Hewlett-Packard and Wisconsin Power and Light provide both awareness and skill building. These companies attempt to transfer the training to the job by asking managers to develop personal action plans before they leave the program. For example, a manager may recognize from training that his record of retaining African-American sales representatives is poor and plans to spend more time coaching these salespeople.[25]

Experiential exercises and videotapes often are used in the training programs to help expose stereotypes and encourage employees to discuss fears, biases, and problems. One widely used training tool is a series of seven 30-minute videotapes titled *Valuing Diversity,* produced by Copeland-Griggs with funding from 50 corporations, including Hewlett-Packard, Xerox, U.S. West, and Procter & Gamble. Table 11.6 provides a set of guidelines for designing effective diversity training.

Retaining employees

As replacing qualified and experienced workers becomes more difficult and costly, retaining good workers will become much more important. Aetna estimates its annual turnover expense at more than $100 million—largely money spent on training new employees and the costs of their lower productivity during the learning period.[26] The Deloitte & Touche example at the beginning of the chapter told of that firm's problem retaining minorities and women. Because top executives moved quickly, the firm not only ameliorated its problems but created a more positive environment for all employees. A number of policies and

table 11.6
Guidelines for diversity training

1. **Position training in your broad diversity strategy.** Training is one important element of managing diversity, but on its own it will probably fail. Culture change means altering underlying assumptions and systems that guide organizational behavior. Training programs must be internally consistent with, and complement, other initiatives focused on culture change.
2. **Do a thorough needs analysis.** Do not start training prematurely. As with any training program, eagerness to "do something" may backfire unless you have assessed what specific aspects of diversity need attention first. Focus groups help identify what employees view as priority issues.
3. **Distinguish between education and training.** Education helps build awareness and understanding but does not teach usable skills. Training involves activities that enhance skills in areas such as coaching, conducting performance appraisals, and adapting communications styles. Education and training are both important but they're not the same.
4. **Use a participative design process.** Tap a multitude of parties to ensure that the content and tone of the program are suitable to everyone involved. Outsider consultants often provide fresh perspectives, and have credibility. Insiders have specific company knowledge, sensitivity to local issues, and long-standing relationships with company members. Balance these various sources.
5. **Test the training thoroughly before rollout.** Given the sensitivity, even volatility, of diversity issues, use diversity councils and advocacy groups to pilot the programs. Build in ample feedback time to allow these groups to address sensitive concerns, and refine the training.
6. **Incorporate diversity programs into the core training curriculum.** One-time programs do not have a lasting impact. Blend the program's content into other training programs such as performance appraisal, coaching, and so on.

Source: Reprinted with permission from January 1993 issue of *Training* magazine. Copyright 1993. Lakewood Publications, Minneapolis, MN. All rights reserved. Not for resale.

strategies described below can be used to increase retention of all employees, especially those who are "different" from the norm.

Support groups Companies can help form minority networks and other support groups to promote information exchange and social support. Support groups provide emotional and career support for members who traditionally have not been included in the majority's informal groups. They also can help diverse employees understand work norms and the corporate culture.

At Apple headquarters in Cupertino, California, support groups include a Jewish cultural group, a gay/lesbian group, an African-American group, and a technical women's group. Avon encourages employees to organize into African-American, Hispanic, and Asian networks by granting them official recognition and providing a senior manager to provide advice. These groups help new employees adjust and provide direct feedback to management on problems that concern the groups. Avon once had a women's network, but that group disbanded years ago. With women holding 79 percent of management positions, female employees at Avon believed the group was no longer necessary.

Mentoring Many people have been puzzled at the inability of women and minorities to move up beyond a certain point on the corporate ladder (the glass ceiling). To help these groups enter the informal network that provides exposure to top management and access to information about organizational politics, many companies have implemented formal mentoring programs. **Mentors** are higher-level managers who help ensure that high-potential people are introduced to top management and socialized into the norms and values of the organization.

mentors Higher level managers who help ensure that high-potential people are introduced to top management and socialized into the norms and values of the organization.

Career development and promotions Because they are hitting a glass ceiling, many of the most talented women and minority group members are leaving their organizations in search of better opportunities elsewhere (including starting their own companies; see Chapter 7). In response, companies can give such employees the same key developmental jobs that traditionally have led to higher-level positions for their white male counterparts. For example, Mobil Oil has a special committee of executives that selects women and minorities with high potential for high-paying and critical line positions. Honeywell has established a team to evaluate the career progress of women, minorities, and employees with disabilities and to devise ways to move them up through the ranks.

Systems accommodation Organizations can support diversity by recognizing cultural and religious holidays, differing modes of dress, and dietary restrictions, as well as accommodating the needs of individuals with disabilities. One important disabling condition is AIDS. Under the ADA, organizations must accommodate AIDS sufferers as it would persons with any other disability, permitting and even encouraging them to continue working for as long as they are able and, if warranted, allowing flexible scheduling. AIDS sufferers also are eligible for corporate health and disability benefits.[27]

Accountability For diversity efforts to succeed, managers must be held accountable for workforce development. Organizations must ensure that their performance appraisal and reward systems reinforce the importance of effective diversity management. Baxter Health Care, Coca-Cola, and Merck (as well as Prudential and Kodak mentioned earlier) all tie compensation to managers' performance in diversity efforts.[28]

For 25 years, U.S. corporations were striving to integrate their workforces because of regulatory and social responsibility pressures. Today globalization, changing demographics, and the expansion of ethnic markets at home have made managing a diverse workforce a bottom-line issue. Labor shortages are causing companies to compete with one another in hiring, developing, and retaining women, minorities, and others who differ from the norm in age, appearance, physical ability, and lifestyle. Companies now realize that to remain competitive in the coming years, they will have to make managing diversity a strategic priority.

Key terms

Glass ceiling, p. 371
Managing diversity, p. 368
Mentors, p. 389
Monolithic organizations, p. 383
Multicultural organizations, p. 383
Plural organizations, p. 383
Sexual harassment, p. 375

Summary of learning objectives

Now that you have studied Chapter 11, you should know:

How changes in the U.S. workforce are making diversity a critical organizational and managerial issue.

The labor force is getting older, more ethnic, with a higher proportion of women. And while the absolute number of workers is increasing, the growth in jobs is outpacing the numerical growth of workers. In addition, the jobs that are being created frequently require higher skills than the typical worker can provide—thus, we are seeing a growing skills gap. To be competitive, organizations can no longer take the traditional approach of depending on white males to form the core of the workforce. Today, managers must look broadly to make use of talent wherever it can be found. As the labor market changes, organizations that can recruit, develop, motivate, and retain a diverse workforce will have a competitive advantage.

The distinction between affirmative action and managing diversity.

Affirmative action is designed to correct past exclusion of women and minorities from U.S. organizations. But despite the accomplishments of affirmative action, it has not resulted in eliminating barriers that prevent individuals from reaching their full potential. Managing diversity goes beyond hiring people who are different from the norm and seems to support, nurture, and use employee difference to the organization's advantage.

How companies can gain a competitive edge by effectively managing diversity.

Managing diversity is a bottomline issue. If managers are effective at managing diversity, they will have an easier time attracting, retaining, and motivating the best employees. They will be more effective at marketing to diverse consumer groups in the United States and globally. They will enjoy a workforce that is more creative, more innovative, and better able to solve problems. In addition, they are likely to increase the flexibility and responsiveness of the organization to environmental change.

What challenges a company is likely to encounter with a diverse workforce.

The challenges for managers created by a diverse workforce include decreased group cohesiveness, communication problems, mistrust and tension, and stereotyping. These challenges can be turned into advantages by training and effective management.

How an organization can take steps to cultivate diversity.

To be successful, organizational efforts to manage diversity must have top management support and commitment. Organizations should first undertake a thorough assessment of their cultures, policies, and practices, as well as the demographics of their labor pools and customer bases. Only after this diagnosis has been completed is the company in position to initiate programs designed to attract, develop, motivate, and retain a diverse workforce.

Discussion questions

1. What opportunities do you see as a result of changes in our nation's workforce?

2. Is prejudice declining in our society? In our organizations? Why or why not?

3. What distinctions can you make between affirmative action and managing diversity?

4. How can we overcome obstacles to diversity such as mistrust and tension, stereotyping, and communication problems?

5. How can organizations meet the special needs of different groups (e.g., work and family issues) without appearing to show favoritism to those particular sets of employees?

6. How can diversity give a company a competitive edge? Can diversity really make a difference in the bottom line? How?

Concluding Case

Prudential

In 1988, executives at The Prudential surveyed African-American employees to determine why so many were leaving the company. Turnover had been a serious problem, and Prudential executives wanted to find the underlying causes. After reviewing the results of the survey, management realized that the problem was widespread and affected more than just African-American employees. Most of the complaints about the organization's inability to meet employee needs went beyond its African-American associates and extended to issues that were also shared by females, other minority groups, and white males. In response to these concerns, Charles Thomas, then Vice President of Human Resources, and his team devised a managing-diversity program that would "reach organizational objectives by maximizing the contribution of every segment of the employee population." The goals of the program were to extend beyond employee relations by focusing squarely on business goals. Today, organizational diversity is viewed by Prudential's management as vital for enhancing productivity and improving customer relationships.

How did they accomplish such a turnaround? The original program consisted of a two-day workshop that all 12,000 mid- to upper-level managers attended to broaden understanding and establish an agenda for action. Each of the managers was required to develop a personal action plan stating in which activities and behaviors they would engage to demonstrate their commitment to organization diversity. Activities included improving communication skills, actively recruiting the talents of their diverse associates, and strengthening work teams. The program has been expanded to all of the company's 99,000 employees and has integrated a diversity component into existing training programs from new hire orientation programs to team-building workshops to management skills training.

But Prudential's commitment to diversity doesn't stop with training. All senior-level managers are now required to complete business-unit action plans and submit annual progress reports stating how they have addressed diversity issues as part of their strategic planning process. Business-unit actions include developing alternative work schedules, revising performance appraisals to include diversity dimensions, and identifying emerging client markets. Further, the company holds all managers financially accountable for their stated efforts to improve their organizational climates for diversity, and this has encouraged managers to work even harder to coach and provide feedback to employees who are different from themselves. To evaluate these efforts, special diversity councils have been established to monitor and make recommendations for improvement. African-American executives, for example, have formed a forum to help Prudential measure employee attitudes toward its diversity efforts and implement change. Other groups have also formed for similar purposes, including an association of gay and lesbian employees and one for individuals who are hearing disabled. Additionally, a division of the Corporate Human Resources Department, Prudential Diversity Consultants, has been formed to spearhead and support diversity efforts companywide.

Prudential's examination of employees' needs resulted in a managing-diversity program to "reach organizational objectives by maximizing the contributions of every segment of employee population."
[Myrleen Ferguson/PhotoEdit]

Obviously, diversity initiatives have gone far beyond the status of mere programs at Prudential. But what's interesting is that the company does not measure its success using traditional affirmative-action guidelines. While Prudential is doing much better at promoting minorities and women to upper-management positions, their sensitivity to diversity goes beyond race and gender to include sexual orientation, religion, age, managerial level, work styles, employee rank, and other differences. Efforts to acknowledge diversity issues and to promote positive responses to them have become institutionalized in the company's core values. For Prudential, it is simply the best way to conduct business.

Questions

1. What is your assessment of Prudential's diversity program? What suggestions do you have for improving the program?

2. How does the situation at Prudential compare to Deloitte & Touche in "Setting the Stage"?

3. Has diversity become a "way of life" at Prudential? Why or why not?

Source: "Successful Companies Realize That Diversity Is a Long-Term Process, Not a Program," *Personnel Journal,* April 1993, p. 54. 

Video Case

Valuing diversity

The modern workplace is fast becoming a microcosm of the American population. Minority groups that previously have not had access to management and leadership positions in organizations are now a significant proportion of the overall workforce. Organizations must be able to take advantage of this broader talent pool, ensuring that all people have the opportunity to contribute to the extent of their potential.

Not all organizations have evolved to a point where they are able to see beyond a person's gender or ethnic status and to appreciate people for what they are able to contribute. Eliminating barriers to merit-based advancement is a central part of valuing diversity in the modern workplace.

Purpose

To heighten your awareness of the issues that companies are facing as the workplace becomes more diverse, and to understand the issues faced by individuals who work there.

Procedure

In this exercise, you will identify and interview a corporate diversity officer, and you will identify and interview a person employed in a business or nonprofit organization whose ethnic or gender status differs from your own to learn about the issues he or she faces in the workplace.

1. *Identify and interview a corporate diversity officer:* Many organizations today have designated a staff position to handle diversity issues for the firm. You should identify a person who serves this function in a medium to large organization. Contact this person and arrange a one-hour information interview. Besides developing your own set of questions for the diversity officer, your interview should cover the following issues:
   - What type of diversity training program does the company have?
   - What are the major diversity issues the company faces?
   - What are the major problems faced by women and minorities in the organization?
   - Does the company recruit in a way that increases its diversity?
   - Does the company have an active affirmative action program?
2. *Identify and interview a person of different gender or ethnicity:* Identify and interview a person of managerial rank or better in a medium to large company who is different in gender or ethnicity from you. This person should *not* be directly involved in the organization's diversity function, and preferably should be in a line position. Arrange a one-hour information interview with this person to learn more about the challenges he or she perceives are directly related to his or her gender or ethnicity. This could be a sensitive issue for some people, so you may have to guarantee anonymity to the person you are interviewing. What you want to learn from this interview is how the individual believes her or his career has been affected because of gender or ethnicity. Several issues to explore include:
   - Has the person ever been passed up for career advancement based on gender or ethnic status?
   - Has the person ever felt that he or she has been given special consideration based on gender or ethnic status?
   - What kinds of organizational barriers does the person feel as a function of her or his gender or ethnic status?
   - What strategies does the person use to overcome these barriers?
3. *Report your findings to the class:* After conducting your two informal interviews, be prepared to discuss your findings with the class. You should be able to summarize the types of diversity training programs the organization you identified is using, and describe the effect of this training on the organization. You should also be able to summarize your interview with the individual of different gender or ethnic status. What are the key issues as this person sees them? Has this person benefited from or been harmed by corporate diversity programs? ●

Video Case

A very friendly fellow

Purpose

This exercise demonstrates the problems of sexual harassment on the job.

Bill and Shelly are having a conversation in the hallway. Shelly feels a certain degree of discomfort because Bill is standing very close to her. Ginny, another worker, meets them in the hallway, and Bill begins talking about the good time he had at a night club. He tells Shelly and Ginny that they should meet him and his friends after work at the Steak and Cap. Although Shelly, upset by his invitation, tells him she is busy and cannot make it, Ginny sees his invitation as a friendly social gesture from a co-worker.

When Shelly tells Ginny that she has to talk with her about a work project, Bill decides to return to his office. Shelly informs Ginny that Bill will not leave her alone. She believes that he has been making sexual advances toward her and that she will be unable to work with him. The problem is that he can not seem to keep his hands off of her. He "touches" her by massaging her neck or by squeezing her arm even though she has repeatedly told Bill to stop.

Critical Thinking Questions

1. What should Shelly do when she meets Bill at work?

2. What impact will Bill's "advances" have on their ability to work together on a new project?

3. Does Shelly have responsibility to report Bill's actions to the personnel office? ●

Experiential Exercises

11.1 Being different

Objectives

1. To increase your awareness of the feeling of "being different."
2. To better understand the context of "being different."

Instructions

1. Working alone, complete the Being Different Worksheet.
2. In small groups, compare worksheets and prepare answers to the discussion questions.
3. After the class reconvenes, group spokespersons present group findings.

Discussion questions

1. Were there students who experienced being different in situations that surprised you?
2. How would you define "being different"?
3. How can this exercise be used to good advantage?

Being different worksheet

Think back to a recent situation in which you experienced "being different," and answer the following questions:

1. Describe the situation in which you experienced "being different."

____

____

____

____

____

____

____

2. Explain how you felt.

3. What did you do as a result of "being different"? (That is, in what way was your behavior changed by the feeling of "being different"?)

4. What did others in the situation do? How do you think they felt about the situation?

5. How did the situation turn out in the end?

6. As a result of that event, how will you probably behave differently in the future? In what way has the situation changed you?

11.2 He works, she works

Instructions

1. Complete the He Works, She Works Worksheet. In the appropriate spaces, write what you think the stereotyped responses would be. Do not spend too much time considering any one item. Rather, respond quickly and let your first impression or thought guide your answer.

2. Compare your individual responses with those of other class members or participants. It is interesting to identify and discuss the most frequently used stereotypes.

He works, she works worksheet

The family picture is on *his* desk: *He's a solid, responsible family man.*

His desk is cluttered: ____________________

The family picture is on *her* desk: *Her family will come before her career.*

Her desk is cluttered: ____________________

The family picture is on *his* desk: *He's a solid, responsible family man.*

He's talking with co-workers: ______________________________

He's not at his desk: ______________________________

He's not in the office: ______________________________

He's having lunch with the boss: ______________________________

The boss criticized *him:* ______________________________

He got an unfair deal: ______________________________

He's getting married: ______________________________

He's going on a business trip: ______________________________

He's leaving for a better job: ______________________________

The family picture is on *her* desk: *Her family will come before her career.*

She's talking with co-workers: ______________________________

She's not at her desk: ______________________________

She's not in the office: ______________________________

She's having lunch with the boss: ______________________________

The boss criticized *her:* ______________________________

She got an unfair deal: ______________________________

She's getting married: ______________________________

She's going on a business trip: ______________________________

She's leaving for a better job: ______________________________

Source: F. Luthans, *Organizational Behavior,* (New York: McGraw-Hill, 1989), pp. 224–25. ●

Integrating Case

The merger of Federal Express and the Flying Tigers Line

It was January 1990. Thomas R. Oliver, senior vice president of International Operations for Federal Express Corporation, was on his way to meet with the members of his "Tigerclaws" Committee. The operational merger of Flying Tigers with Federal Express was supposed to have been concluded last August. Yet anticipated and unanticipated problems kept surfacing. International operations were draining financial resources, and there were other problems that had to be immediately resolved.

Several days ago, Mr. Oliver had met with Mr. Fred Smith, the company founder and CEO, and had been assigned the job of heading a special task force whose purpose was to direct the Flying Tigers' merger efforts and resolve the resulting problems. Mr. Oliver requested, and got, representatives of senior executives from every department of the company to form what he named the Tigerclaws Committee (see exhibit "The Tigerclaws Committee"). This committee had the power to cut across departmental bureaucratic lines. It had the resources of all the departments behind it to reach fast-track solutions to any problems in existence. Even with such commitments, Mr. Oliver realized what a formidable task he and his committee were facing.

The Tigerclaws Committee

Departments that are represented
Memphis SuperHub
Business Application
Airfreight Systems
Q.A. Audits
Planning and Administration
International Clearance
Communications
Ramp Plans/Program
Hub Operations
Personnel Services
International Operations
Central Support Services
Customer Support
COSMOS/Pulsar System Division
COO/Quality Improvement

Express and Freight Forwarding Industries

In 1990, sending documents or packages by priority mail was viewed as a necessary convenience, rather than a luxury. The domestic market was led by Federal Express Corporation with 53 percent of the market, followed by United Parcel Service at 19 percent. The U.S. Postal Service had 3 to 4 percent of the market.[1] The overnight letter traffic was characterized by slow growth because of the increased use of facsimile machines.

The increasing competition between express delivery services and the traditional air freight industry was changing the face of international cargo transportation. Many independent freight carriers complained that big couriers and integrated carriers were poaching on their market niches. Others ignored the competition, believing that the more personalized relationships provided by the traditional air freight companies would keep clients coming back. Still, such companies as Federal Express were having a big effect on the air freight industry. Express couriers were building their nondocument business by 25 to 30 percent a year.

Express Services in the United States

Federal Express, United Parcel Service (UPS), Airborne Express, and the U.S. Postal Service were quickly introducing services that promised to translate the fundamentals of speed and information into a powerful competitive edge. They were stressing good service at lower costs. For example, UPS had started offering discounts to its bigger customers and shippers that shipped over 250 pieces weekly. In addition, UPS was building an $80 million computer and telecommunications center to provide support for all operations worldwide. Airborne's chief advantage was that it operated its own airport and had begun operating a "commerce park" around its hub in Wilmington, Ohio.

Europe

The international document and parcel express delivery business was one of the fastest-growing sectors in Europe. Although the express business would become more important in the single European market, none of the four principal players in Europe was European. DHL, Federal Express, and UPS were United States companies while TNT was Australian. Europe was not expected to produce a challenger because the "Big Four" were buying smaller rivals at such a fast pace that the odds seemed to be heavily against a comparable competitor emerging.[2]

Pacific Rim

The Asia-Pacific air express market was expanding by 20 to 30 percent annually, and the world's major air express and air freight companies had launched massive infrastructure buildups to take advantage of this growth. Industry leader DHL strengthened its access to air service by agreeing to eventually sell 57.5 percent of the equity of its international operation to Japan Air Lines, Lufthansa, and Nissho Iwai trading company. TNT Skypak's strength was in providing niche services, and its ability to tap into the emerging Asian–East European route with its European air hub. Two new U.S. entrants, Federal Express and UPS, were engaged in an undeclared price war. Willing to lose millions of dollars annually to carve out a greater market share, Federal Express already had captured about 10 percent of Pacific express business and 15 percent of freight. UPS's strategy was to control costs and to offer no-frills service at low rates. All four companies were seeking to expand the proportion of parcels, which would yield about twice the profits of the express documents business.[3]

Major Airlines

Since the common adaptation of wide-body jets, major international airlines had extra cargo space in their planes. Japan Air Lines and Lufthansa were two of the worldwide players, with most national airlines providing regional services.

Airlines were expanding and automating their cargo services to meet the challenges presented by fast-growing integrated carriers. Two strategies were being employed: (1) the development of new products to fill the gap between the demand for next-day service and traditional air cargo service and (2) computerization of internal passenger and cargo operations.[4]

The Merging Organizations: Federal Express Corporation

Frederick W. Smith, founder of Federal Express Corporation, went to Yale University, where he was awarded a now infamous "C" on an economics paper that outlined his idea for an overnight delivery service.[5] After college and military service, Smith began selling corporate jets in Little Rock, Arkansas. In 1973, he tapped his $4 million inheritance, rounded up $70 million in venture capital, and launched Federal Express, testing his college paper's thesis. The company turned profitable after three years.

Federal Express always had taken pride in its people-oriented approach and its emphasis on service to its customers. Mr. Smith believed that, in the service industry, it is the employees that make the business.[6] The philosophy of Smith and his managing staff was manifested in many ways, including: (1) extensive orientation programs, (2) training and communications programs, (3) promotion of employees from within, and (4) a tuition reimbursement program. Federal Express's "open door policy" for the expression of employee concerns also illustrated the commitment of top management to resolve problems.[7]

As to services, Federal Express stressed the importance of on-time delivery and established a 100 percent on-time delivery goal. It has achieved a record 95 percent on-time delivery. In 1990, Federal Express was one of the five U.S. firms to win the Malcolm Baldrige National Quality Award. This award was given by the U.S. government to promote quality awareness and to recognize the quality achievements of U.S. companies.

Frederick W. Smith had a vision for the overnight express delivery business. Although Federal Express was the No. 1 express firm in the United States, Mr. Smith firmly believed that globalization was the future for the express business.[8] From 1986 to 1988, Federal struggled to become a major player in international deliveries. The company ran head-on into entrenched overseas rivals, such as DHL, and onerous foreign regulations.[9]

Frustrated with the legal processes in negotiating for landing rights that were restricted by bilateral aviation treaties,[10] Mr. Smith reversed his promise to build only from within and started on a series of acquisitions. From 1987 to 1988, Federal purchased 15 minor delivery companies, mostly in Europe. In December 1988, Mr. Smith announced the merger of Tiger International, Inc., best known for its Flying Tigers airfreight service. On paper, the merger of Federal Express and Tiger International seemed to be a marriage made in heaven. As one Federal Express executive pointed out: "If we lay a route map of Flying Tigers over that of Federal Express, there is almost a perfect match. There are only one or two minor overlaps. The Flying Tigers' routes are all over the world, with highest concentration in the Pacific Rim countries, while Federal Express's routes are mostly in domestic U.S.A." As a result of the merger, Federal Express's world routes were completed. For example, the acquisition of Flying Tigers brought with it the unrestricted cargo landing rights at three Japanese airports that Federal Express had been unsuccessful in acquiring for the last three years.[11]

One high-level Federal Express employee commented that the merger brought other benefits besides routes. He said: "We got a level of expertise with the people we brought in and a number of years of experiences in the company in handling air freight . . . You have to look at this acquisition also as a defensive move. If we hadn't bought Flying Tigers, UPS might have bought Flying Tigers."

The Merging Organizations: Tiger International, Inc.

Tiger International, Inc., better known for The Flying Tigers Line, Inc., freight service, or Flying Tigers, was founded 40 years ago by Robert Prescott. Over the years, the company became modestly profitable. But in 1977, Smith won his crusade for air-cargo deregulation over the strident objection of Prescott. Heightened competition, troubled acquisitions, and steep labor costs led to big losses at Tigers. In 1986, Stephen M. Wolf, the former chairman of Republic Airline Inc., came on board at Tigers and managed to get all employees, including those represented by unions, to accept wage cuts. As Tigers rebounded financially, it was ripe to be taken over by one of the major delivery service companies. In 1988, Federal Express announced the acquisition of Tigers to the pleasure of some and dismay of others. At the announcement, some Tigers' employees shouted, "TGIF—Thank God It's Federal" or "It's purple [Federal Express] not brown [UPS]—thank goodness." In contrast, Robert Sigafoos, who wrote a corporate history of Federal Express, commented, "Prescott must be turning over in his grave."[12]

Flying Tigers always had a distinctive culture, one that partly developed from the military image of its founders. Tigers' employees stressed "Tiger Spirit" or teamwork. Since Mr. Wolf took over as the chairman and CEO at an extremely difficult time, the general orientation of Flying Tigers was to keep the company flying.

The Merger

Federal Express announced the acquisition of Flying Tigers in December 1988. However, because of government regulations, the actual operational merging of the two companies did not occur until August 1989.

One top-level Federal Express executive, with considerable expertise in mergers, described the process in the following way: "I think that after any merger you go through three phases. You come in and you have euphoria. Everybody's happy. The second phase is the transition phase. In that phase, the primary qualification that every employee must have is sadomasochistic tendencies, because you kill yourself going through it . . . And then you start coming out of that into the regeneration and regrowth phase, where you clean up all this hazy area without knowing exactly what you are going to do or thinking this works and trying it out . . . In the meantime, going through all that turmoil creates a number of problems . . . People's morale starts to dip. People start to question all the leadership. You start to see the company reorganizing, you know, trying to figure out, well, what's the best thing to do here or there or whatever and, all of a sudden, all of the confidence that ever existed in the whole world starts to diminish."

Although the two companies were supposed to now become one, problems from the merger kept surfacing. Some of these problems were to be anticipated with the merger of two companies of these sizes. However, many problems were not anticipated and had become very costly to the company.

Human Resources Management Problems

There were union questions. Federal Express traditionally had been a nonunion shop, while the Flying Tigers' employees were predominately unionized. During the merger, the National Mediation Board could not determine a majority among the pilots at Federal Express and Flying Tigers. The board requires a majority to decide the union status at any firm. Because a majority could not be determined, the mediation board decided to allow the temporary mix of union and nonunion employees until the fall of 1989, when elections would determine if there would be union representation. The ruling had created ambiguities in employee status and raised some important financial and legal issues for Federal Express, unions, and employees.[13]

An executive in the international division described Federal Express's feelings on unions: "They [Flying Tigers] had a lot of unions. Tigers was a traditional company . . . and we [Federal Express] don't dislike unions . . . Our feelings about unions is [sic] that if you get a union, you deserve it, because you have not managed your business well. We would like to think that we could keep that old family [feeling]. We realize that we can't keep the old family. It's very difficult to keep the family spirit corporatewide [after a merger]."

Tiger people had a variety of attitudes to job offers after the merger. The employees of Federal Express believed that Federal Express was a great place to work, mainly because of its people-oriented policies. Because of this belief, most of the managers thought that the Flying Tigers' employees would "welcome the merger with open arms." A communications official said: "We tried to position Federal Express as a great place to work, a wonderful place to be—cutting edge technology, a great aircraft fleet, a great employee group, good management—all those types of things."

Flying Tigers had a rich and long history. Tiger employees prided themselves on their team spirit and their willingness to take pay cuts for the good of The Flying Tiger Line, Inc., during the lean years. Employees proudly displayed items with the Tiger logo on them.

A long-time Tiger employee and member of one of the pre-merger Tiger committees remarked on the job offers: "For the employees, it [the merger] was a spectrum, we've got all of them on a line. Up in front, we've got those employees for whom the merger was the best thing that ever happened to them. In the back, you've got the employees where it was the worst thing that ever happened—because of personal things, they decided to leave the company. And then there's the group of employees in the middle, which really composed the majority of Flying Tigers' employees, that it really didn't matter one way or the other since they never moved. All they did was change their uniforms from Friday to Monday. They're basically doing the same jobs in the same locations." A member of his family and many friends refused to accept a job with Federal Express. He explained their refusal, by saying: "Because [Federal Express was] taking the name away. You were taking the history of the Flying Tiger line away . . . because we were a small company, we were like a close-knit family." Another middle-level former Tiger said,

"Although a lot of merger information was provided to people at headquarters in L.A., people at other locations, like Boston, received less information." She said that some Tigers refused the job offer for the following reason: "They left, I think, just because of the attitude that . . . you're taking Flying Tigers away and I don't want to go with you." Some Tigers hoped that Federal Express would permit them to keep the Flying Tiger name or change the company name to Federal Tigers.

There were cultural differences. A Federal Express executive on the Tigerclaws Committee commented on cultural differences by saying: "The difference was astounding. Absolutely astounding. Federal Express's employees, typically, they seem to be younger, we're all in uniforms, enthusiastic about the company. You can walk around Federal Express and everybody can tell you what the corporate philosophy is . . . I remember standing in the Los Angeles airport facility . . . it's typical Federal Express. And you go over to the Tiger facility and here are all of these much older guys standing around. None of them in any type of uniform, clothes were all over the mat, there was [sic] no apparent standards, whatsoever. You know, kicking some of the packages, tossing them, throwing. It was just . . . just terrible. I couldn't believe it. But that was part of the way they did business. They referred to a lot of the cargo that they carried as big, ugly freight. And to us . . . we go around thinking every customer's package is the most important thing we carry."

A former Tiger employee shared her perspective on the differences: "Most of the employees that you dealt with you had known for a lot of years. We used to work together side by side very closely for 20 years. And this company, Federal Express, isn't even 20 years old. You walk into a meeting or classroom or something . . . Federal Express people are introducing themselves to other Federal Express people. Tiger people found that really hard to believe—that you didn't know everybody at Federal Express."

During the announcement of the merger, Mr. Smith made a job offer to all the employees of Flying Tigers. Almost 90 percent of the 6,600 former Tiger employees took the offer. In a two-week period, from July 15 to 31, over 4,000 new jobs were to be created and Tiger employees transferred to these jobs. Many employees had to be relocated, because the old Tiger hub in Columbus, Ohio, was phased out, and primarily only freight and maintenance personnel were kept at the hub in Los Angeles. Some job placements were troublesome, because the human resources department had difficulty obtaining job descriptions and pay scales from Flying Tigers. During the haste, there were quite a number of mismatches of jobs and employees.

One of Federal Express's personnel officers remarked: "I was concerned about being able to meet employee's expectations. A lot of times people coming in from outside of Federal Express have this—I mean it's a great place, but they have this picture that it's a fairy tale place, and that there aren't any real problems and that everybody gets his own way. So I was concerned about the expectations that people brought, both positive and negative. How are we going to make people feel real good about the company?"

To help former Flying Tigers' employees determine whether to accept Federal Express's job offers, Federal Express provided the employees with detailed information about the company. Videotapes introducing Federal Express and explaining the benefits of working for the company were mailed to the homes of Tiger employees. Additionally, many Tiger employees were flown into Federal Express's headquarters in Memphis and given the "grand tour." "Express Teams," groups of four to five employees, visited Flying Tigers' locations and gave them previews of what it was like to work for Federal Express.

Regarding expectations, one long-time Tiger remarked: "There's still a lot of unhappy people in Memphis that came out of L.A., because I think they expected an awful lot. They had the option of saying no to a job and being out on the street looking for something else, or they could come to Memphis and have Federal Express be their employer. And there are a lot of people that still take offense at the fact that Federal Express bought Flying Tigers. But those people have an attitude that they have to deal with." Another former Tiger remarked: "And I honestly thought that by going from a small company to a large company, I was just going to be another number. But . . . it's also their attention to people. All of the hype and promotion they did before T-day [merger day] to Flying Tiger people that they were people oriented . . . we really didn't [know] what that meant and what it would mean to us individually until we became employees."

Summary

Since 1985, Federal Express's international business had lost approximately $74 million and given company executives a lifetime supply of headaches.[14] To improve Federal Express's competitive position with its overseas rivals and overcome the foreign regulations regarding landing rights, Frederick Smith announced in December 1988 the acquisition of Tiger International, Inc. Although the combined companies would have $2.1 billion in debt, Flying Tigers was expected to provide Federal Express with desperately needed international delivery routes. The Tiger acquisition would allow Federal Express to use its own planes for overseas package delivery where Federal Express used to contract other carriers. In addition, Tigers' sizable long-range fleet could be used to achieve dominance in the international heavy-freight business that Federal Express had yet to crack.

Suppose you had been in Thomas Oliver's shoes and were the head of the Tigerclaws Committee. What were the major problems and opportunities facing Federal Express? What should be the priorities of the Tigerclaws Committee? How would you solve or reduce the problems and exploit the opportunities?

Source: A case study by Howard S. Tu, Fogelman College of Business and Economics, Memphis State University; and Sherry E. Sullivan, Bowling Green State University.

Case Incidents

Questionable purchasing practices

Motton Electronics was widely respected in the industry as being fair, dependable, and progressive. Cy Bennett, founder of the company, was chair of the board and majority stockholder. One of the company's progressive practices was to employ professional managers as members of top management. Each carefully selected manager received an excellent salary for performing his or her job. None of the top management group served on the board.

One month ago, Bennett reported to the board that he had facts proving that the director of purchasing for the company, Russell Hale, was giving preferential treatment to certain vendors and, in turn, was receiving merchandise and money. After the chair presented the evidence, the board formally condemned such purchasing practices by unanimous vote.

Immediately following this action, a vocal board member asserted that he believed the chief executive officer was responsible for all employee behavior on the job, that such administrative negligence should not be tolerated, and that the board needed a policy on the issue. This statement triggered an extensive discussion among the directors on topics such as shared responsibility for subordinates' actions, relevant duties of the board of directors, and related policy implications.

The meeting ended with a motion, unanimously supported, that Bennett (1) decide on appropriate measures regarding the errant director of purchasing and (2) develop and implement a policy on shared responsibility.

Bennett believed his prompt action on these matters would be critical to managerial performance, to the firm's profitability, and to the value of his majority block of company stock.

Source: J. Champion and J. Hames, *Critical Incidents in Management: Decision and Policy Issues,* 6th ed. (Burr Ridge, IL: Richard D. Irwin, 1989).

Workforce reduction policy

Five years ago Wireweave, Inc., moved to a rural area 25 miles outside a large southern city. The company, formerly situated in a midwestern industrial city, chose this location primarily because of the lower wage rates paid in the community, a nonunion tradition in the region, and a favorable tax situation.

Wireweave, a manufacturer of wire products, has two major high-volume product lines: aluminum wire screen and dish racks. The dish racks are supplied to several appliance manufacturers for use in automatic dishwashers.

Because of intense industry competition, Wireweave's management realized several years ago that if Wireweave was to continue manufacturing aluminum wire screen and dish racks—and even stay in business—it would have to procure up-to-date equipment, become more automated and computerized, and even use robots for some of the hottest and dustiest jobs. After a two-year evaluation of production needs and an analysis of technologically advanced manufacturing equipment (including robots), Wireweave purchased equipment that would modernize production and replace 65 employees, representing about 33 percent of the total labor force. Significant labor costs would be saved by this employment reduction. As a result, Steve Jackson, president of Wireweave, expected the company to regain its competitiveness and profitability.

The following spring, shortly after installing the new equipment, Jackson called in Muriel Fincher, human resources director, and told her that the company could no longer afford to employ the unneeded workers. He requested that she decide on an acceptable plan for reducing company employment by 65 persons, and the sooner the better in terms of company profitability. Jackson also asked that she recommend a specific operating policy covering future workforce reductions.

Fincher had successfully handled some tough challenges as human resources director, but the latest assignments from Jackson were the most difficult ones she had faced. As Fincher considered relevant options and constraints, her deliberations were dominated by three factors: (1) the company's economic and ethical responsibilities to terminated employees, (2) the potential moral problems for employees who would be retained, and (3) the pressure from Jackson for prompt decision and action.

Source: J. Champion and J. James, *Critical Incidents in Management: Decision and Policy Issues*, 6th ed. (Burr Ridge, IL: Richard D. Irwin. 1989). ●

Part Four
Leading

Now that you know about organizing and staffing, Part IV further elaborates on managing people by discussing the third function of management: leading. Effective managers know how to lead others toward unit and organizational success. Chapter 12 explores the essential components of leadership, including the use of power in the organization. Chapter 13 focuses on motivating people, with implications for enhancing performance. Chapter 14 examines work teams, including the management of task forces and relationships between groups. Finally, Chapter 15 addresses a vital management activity: communication. Here, you will learn how to maximize your effectiveness in communicating with other people throughout the organization.

Chapter Twelve
Leadership

Every soldier has a right to competent command.

—Julius Caesar

Chapter Outline

Learning Objectives

After studying Chapter 12, you will know:

1. What it means to be a leader.
2. How a good vision helps you be a better leader.
3. How to understand and use power.
4. The personal traits and skills of effective leaders.
5. The behaviors that will make you a better leader.
6. What it means to be a charismatic and transformational leader.
7. How to further your own leadership development.

Setting the Stage

A Few Good Leaders

Lou Gerstner took on the leadership at IBM when no one else wanted the job. The company had been clobbered by the PC revolution. Industry analysts had written off the mainframe, and IBM's stock had collapsed. Gerstner achieved initial fame by proclaiming, "The last thing IBM needs right now is a vision"—referrring to a fashionable management practice. But then he came up with his vision: to lead big companies into the networked world as the information company for corporate America. He led the overhaul and revival of the mainframe, charged into PCs, and improved services. As IBM revises companies' technology strategies, builds and runs their systems, and ties together companies and entire industries with IBM hardware and software, IBM may once again become indispensable. At the very least, the company many considered washed up is a player once again.

Franco Bernabe became chief executive of ENI, Italy's state oil company, in 1992. At the time, ENI was a financing machine for politicians, losing money and rife with scandals and corruption. By 1997, Bernabe's leadership had turned ENI into a modern, publicly traded corporation. Moreover, it was free from the control of powerful politicians and industrial clans. Bernabe is described as intellectual, realistic, and opportunistic. He focuses single-mindedly on improving shareholder value, something revolutionary in Europe and certainly for a company like ENI in an industry so crucial to the national interest. Hailed as one of a new generation of leaders in Italy, Bernabe wants ENI to become one of the great companies of the world.

Lou Gerstner said, "The last thing IBM needs right now is a vision," but then he gave them one.
[Michael Mella/Sygma]

Probably the most revered leader in Europe is Percy Barnevik, formerly CEO of ABB and now chair of Investor. Under Barnevik, ABB became a world leader in the power and engineering sector, rivaling GE and having 5,000 profit centers and over 200,000 employees. Barnevik was a pioneer in organizing the company, creating independent profit centers, lean corporate staff, and a fierce entrepreneurial spirit. Now, he faces a different challenge with Investor, the holding company controlled by the Wallenberg family of Sweden. Investor controls almost half of the capitalization of the Swedish stock market, including telecom giant Ericsson, highly profitable drugmaker Astra, Electrolux, and Saab. Investor's stockholders were thrilled with the announcement that Barnevik was taking over. Barnevik was known to be "a guy who doesn't wait around for things," "a person with a vision that works," and someone who is a charismatic leader.

Honda's president and CEO Nobuhiko Kawamoto took over when the car company had started falling apart in the early 90s. But seemingly in no time—two years—Honda zoomed ahead of its competitors and realized the best year in its history. "The traditions that guided this company for 40 years weren't functioning properly. Our focus on the customer was vague, and I said, it must be clear." At first, he involved himself closely in operations. Then, he stepped back to look at the larger strategic context. "The world condition is very difficult. I have to look for weak points that might cause fatal defects."

Sources: B. Morris, "Big Blue," Fortune, April 14, 1997, pp. 40–51; C. P. Wallace, "Percy Barnevik's Next Act," Fortune, May 26, 1997, pp. 70–72; J. Guyon, "The Power of One: ENI's Franco Bernabe," Fortune, May 12, 1997, pp. 80–83; and A. Taylor III, "The Man Who Put Honda Back on Track," Fortune, September 9, 1996, pp. 28–36.

People get excited about the topic of leadership. They want to know: What makes a great leader? Executives at all levels in all industries are interested in this question. They believe the answer will bring improved organizational performance and personal career success. They hope to acquire the skills that will transform an "average" manager into a true leader like the ones described in Setting the Stage.

Fortunately, leadership can be taught—and learned. According to one source, "Leadership seems to be the marshaling of skills possessed by a majority but used by a minority. But it's something that can be learned by anyone, taught to everyone, denied to no one."[1]

What is leadership? To start with, a leader is one who influences others to attain goals. The greater the number of followers, the greater the influence. And the more successful the attainment of worthy goals, the more evident the leadership. But we must explore beyond this bare definition to capture the excitement and intrigue that devoted followers and students of leadership feel when they see a great leader in action, and to understand what organizational leaders really do or what it really takes to gain entry into *Fortune*'s Hall of Fame for U.S. Business Leadership.

Outstanding leaders have vision. They move people and organizations in directions they otherwise would not go. They may launch enterprises, build organization cultures, win wars, or otherwise change the course of events.[2] They are strategists who seize opportunities others overlook, but "they are also passionately concerned with detail–all the small, fundamental realities that can make or mar the grandest of plans."[3]

Vision

"The leader's job is to create a vision," states Robert L. Swiggett, former chair of Kollmorgen Corporation.[4] Until a few years ago, vision was not a word one heard managers utter. But today, having a vision for the future and communicating that vision to others are known to be essential components of great leadership. "If there is no vision, there is no business," maintains entrepreneur Mark Leslie.[5] Joe Nevin, an MIS director, described leaders as "painters of the vision and architects of the journey."[6] Practicing businesspeople are not alone in this belief; leadership scholars have brought vision to a position of prominence in academic thinking as well.

vision A mental image of a possible and desirable future state of the organization.

A **vision** is a mental image of a possible and desirable future state of the organization. It expresses the leader's ambitions for the organization.[7] The best visions are both ideal and unique.[8] If a vision conveys an *ideal,* it communicates a standard of excellence and a clear choice of positive values. If the vision is also *unique,* it communicates and inspires pride in being different from other organizations. The choice of language is important; the words should imply a combination of realism and optimism, an action orientation, and resolution and confidence that the vision will be attained.[9]

Great leaders imagine an ideal future for their organizations that goes beyond the ordinary and beyond what others may have thought possible. They strive to realize significant achievements that others have not. In short, as the following examples show, leaders must be forward looking and clarify the directions in which they want their organizations and even entire industries to move.

Visions in action

Here are some examples of leaders and their visions:

- Peter Joyce founded Small Potatoes Inc. (SPI), a biotech company with a patented technology that makes pea-sized potatoes. These micro-tubers are then used to seed potatoes. The advantages over conventional seed potato techniques include year-round production, production in any climate, low cost, a pathogen-free environment, and easy transformation through gene splicing. Joyce intends to dominate the world market for seed potatoes; develop new varieties that are resistant to disease and insects, eliminating the need for pesticides and insecticides; and help address the world hunger crisis.
- Ted Turner's vision for CNN was to create the first truly "global information company," the "global network of record" (his terms), seen in every nation on the planet, broadcast in most major languages. He sees CNN and its people as world citizens who just happen to be based in the United States.
- Percy Barnevik, introduced in "Setting the Stage," wanted ABB to sell power equipment internationally. Not just some power equipment–all of it. And not just in certain countries, but everywhere. He envisioned a company with no national boundaries but that understands and capitalizes on local differences.
- Phil Turner was facilities manager at Raychem Corporation, fixing toilets and air conditioners. But rather than believing that the workers in the facilities were performing menial jobs and making only trivial contributions to the organization, Turner viewed their work as a mission–to make people feel good, "to lift people's spirits through beauty, cleanliness, and functionality, enthusiasm, good cheer, and excellence."

Sources: H. P. Sims Jr. and C. Manz, *Company of Heroes* (New York: John Wiley & Sons, 1996); J. Kouzes and B. Posner, *The Leadership Challenge* (San Francisco: Jossey-Bass, 1995); G. E. Schares, "Percy Barnevik's Global Crusade," *Business Week*, January 11, 1994, pp. 204–11; and T. Peters, *Liberation Management* (New York: Alfred A. Knopf, 1992).

Ted Turner's vision for CNN includes creating the first truly "global information company." *[Corbis-Bettmann]*

As you can see, visions can be small or large and can exist throughout all organizational levels as well as at the very top. The important points are that (1) a vision is necessary for effective leadership; (2) a person or team can develop a vision for any job, work unit, or organization; and (3) many people, including managers who do not develop into strong leaders, do not develop a clear vision—instead, they focus on performing or surviving on a day-by-day basis.

Put another way, leaders must know what they want.[10] And other people must understand what that is. The leader must be able to articulate the vision, clearly and often. Other people throughout the organization should understand the vision and be able to state it clearly themselves. That's a start. But the vision still means nothing until the leader and followers take action to turn the vision into reality.[11]

Two metaphors reinforce the important concept of vision.[12] The first is the jigsaw puzzle. It is much easier to put a puzzle together if you have the picture on the box cover in front of you. Without the picture, or vision, the lack of direction is likely to result in frustration and failure. The second metaphor is the slide projector. Imagine a projector that is out of focus. If you had to watch blurred images for a long period of time, you would get confused, impatient, and disoriented. You would stop following the presentation and lose respect for the presenter. It is the leader's job to focus the projector. That is what communicating a vision is all about: making it clear where you are heading.

Not just any vision will do, either for the leader or for the company. Whereas vision is very important for success, visions can be inappropriate, and even fail, for a variety of reasons.[13] First, an inappropriate vision may reflect merely the leader's personal needs. Such a vision can be unethical, or may fail because of lack of acceptance by the market or by those who must implement it.

Second (and related to the first), an inappropriate vision may ignore stakeholder needs. You learned about assessing stakeholders in earlier chapters. Third, the leader must stay abreast of environmental changes. Although effective leaders maintain confidence and persevere despite obstacles, the time may come when the facts dictate that the vision must change. You will learn more about change and how to manage it later in the text.

Leading and managing

Effective managers are not necessarily true leaders. Many administrators, supervisors, and even top executives execute their responsibilities without being great leaders. But these positions afford opportunity for leadership. The ability to lead effectively, then, will set the excellent managers apart from the average ones.

Managers must deal with the ongoing, day-to-day complexities of organizations. True leadership includes effectively orchestrating important change.[14] While managing requires planning and budgeting routines, leading includes setting the direction (creating a vision) for the firm. Management requires structuring the organization, staffing it with capable people, and monitoring activities; leadership goes beyond these functions by inspiring people to attain the vision. Great leaders keep people focused on moving the organization toward its ideal future, motivating them to overcome whatever obstacles lie in the way.

Many observers believe that U.S. business lost its competitive advantage because of a lack of strong leadership.[15] While many managers focus on superficial activities and worry about short-term profits and stock prices, too few have emerged as leaders who foster innovation and attainment of long-term goals. And whereas many managers are overly concerned with "fitting in" and not rocking the boat, those who emerge as leaders are more concerned with making important decisions that may break with tradition but are humane, moral, and right. The leader puts a premium on substance rather than on style.

It is important to be clear here about several things. First, management and leadership are both vitally important. To highlight the need for more leadership is not to minimize the importance of management or managers. It is to say that leadership involves unique processes that are distinguishable from basic management processes.[16] Moreover, just because they involve different processes does not mean that they require different, separate people. The same individual can exemplify effective managerial processes, leadership processes, both, or neither.

supervisory leadership Behavior that provides guidance, support, and corrective feedback for the day-to-day activities of work unit members.

strategic leadership Behavior that gives purpose and meaning to organizations.

Some people still will dislike the idea of distinguishing between management and leadership, maintaining it is artificial or derogatory toward the managers and management processes that make organizations run. Perhaps a better or more useful distinction is between supervisory and strategic leadership.[17] **Supervisory leadership** is behavior that provides guidance, support, and corrective feedback for the day-to-day activities of work unit members. **Strategic leadership** gives purpose and meaning to organizations. And in the modern business environment, in which people throughout the organization should think strategically and behave like complete businesspeople, strategic leadership needs to be an activity performed by people throughout the organization, not just by a few people at the very top.

Leading and following

Organizations succeed or fail not only because of how well they are led but because of how well followers follow. Just as managers are not necessarily good leaders, people are not always good followers. The most effective followers are capable of independent thinking and at the same time are actively committed to organizational goals.[18] Robert Townsend, former president and CEO of Avis Rent-a-Car who led a legendary turnaround at Avis, says that the most important characteristic of a follower may be the willingness to tell the truth.[19] Great leaders do the same.[20]

As a manager, you will be asked to play *both* roles. As you lead the people who report to you, you will report to your boss. You will be a member of some teams and committees, and you may chair others. While the leadership roles get the glamour and therefore are the roles that many people covet, followers must perform their responsibilities conscientiously as well.

Effective followers are distinguished from ineffective ones by their enthusiasm and commitment to the organization and to a person or purpose—an idea, a product—other than themselves or their own interests. They master skills that are useful to their organizations, and they hold performance standards that are higher than required. Effective followers may not get the glory, but they know their contributions to the organization are valuable. And as they make those contributions, they study leaders in preparation for their own leadership roles.[21]

Power and leadership

power The ability to influence others.

Central to effective leadership is **power**—the ability to influence other people. In organizations, this often means the ability to get things done or accomplish one's goals despite resistance from others.

Sources of power

One of the earliest and still most useful approaches to understanding power suggests that leaders have five important potential sources of power in organizations.[22] Figure 12.1 shows these power sources.

Legitimate power

The leader with *legitimate power* has the right, or the authority, to tell others what to do; employees are obligated to comply with legitimate orders. For example, a supervisor tells an employee to remove a safety hazard, and the employee removes the hazard because he has to obey the authority of his boss. In contrast, when a staff person lacks the authority to give an order to a line manager, the staff person has no

figure 12.1
Sources of power

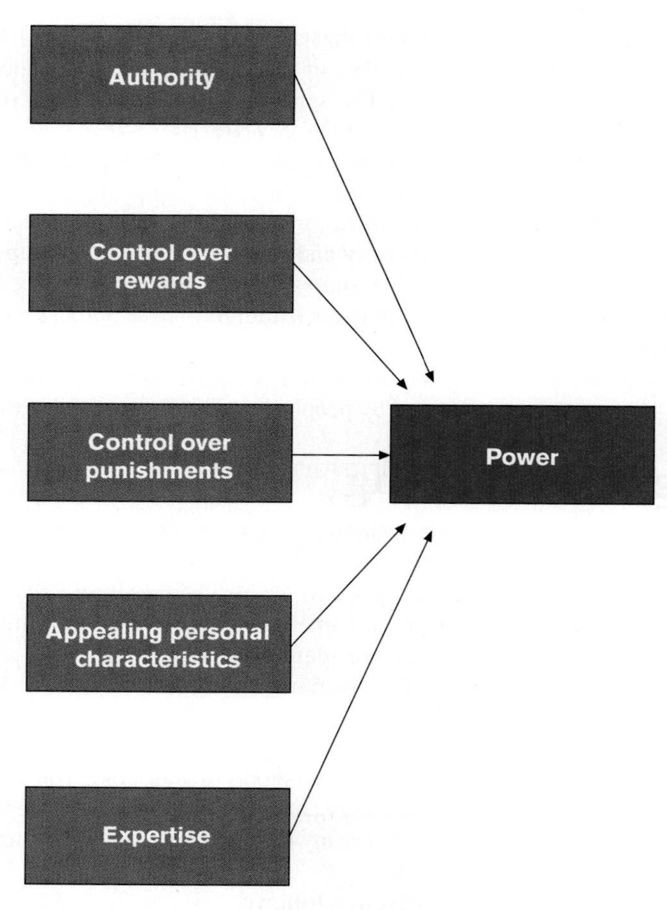

Source: Adapted from J. R. P. French and B. Raven, "The Bases of Social Power," in *Studies in Social Power,* ed. D. Cartwright (Ann Arbor, MI: Institute for Social Research, 1959).

legitimate power over the manager. And, as you might guess, managers have more legitimate power over their direct reports than they do over their peers, bosses, and others inside or outside their organizations.[23]

Reward power The leader who has *reward power* influences others because she or he controls valued rewards; people comply with the leader's wishes in order to receive those rewards. For example, a manager works hard to achieve her performance goals to get a positive performance review and a big pay raise from her boss. On the other hand, if company policy dictates that everyone receive the same salary increase, a leader's reward power decreases because he or she is unable to give higher raises.

Coercive power The leader with *coercive power* has control over punishments; people comply to avoid those punishments. For instance, a manager implements an absenteeism policy that administers disciplinary actions to offending employees. A manager has less coercive power if, say, a union contract prohibits him or her from punishing employees harshly. In general, lower-level managers have less coercive and reward power than do middle- and higher-level managers.[24]

Referent power The leader with *referent power* has personal characteristics that appeal to others; people comply because of admiration, a desire for approval, personal liking, or a desire to be like the leader. For example, young, ambitious managers emulate the work habits and personal style of a successful, charismatic executive. An executive who is incompetent, disliked, and commands little respect has little referent power.

Expert power The leader who has *expert power* has certain expertise or knowledge; people comply because they believe in, can learn from, or can otherwise gain from that expertise. For example, a sales manager gives her salespeople some tips on closing a deal. The salespeople then alter their sales techniques because they respect the manager's expertise. On the other hand, this manager may lack expert power in other areas, such as finance; thus, her salespeople may ignore her advice concerning financial matters.

People who are in a position that gives them the right to tell others what to do, who can reward and punish, who are well liked and admired, and who have expertise on which other people can draw will be powerful members of the organization. All these sources of power are potentially important. Although it is easy to assume that the most powerful bosses are those who have high legitimate power and control major rewards and punishments, it is important not to underestimate the more "personal" sources like expert and referent power. These personal sources of power are the ones most closely related to people's motivation to perform to their managers' expectations.[25]

Traditional approaches to understanding leadership

Three traditional approaches to studying leadership are the trait approach, the behavioral approach, and the situational approach.

Leadership traits

trait approach A leadership perspective that focuses on individual leaders and attempts to determine the personal characteristics that great leaders share.

The **trait approach** is the oldest leadership perspective and was dominant for several decades. This approach seems logical for studying leadership: It focuses on individual leaders and attempts to determine the personal characteristics (traits) that great leaders share. What set Winston Churchill, Alexander the Great, Gandhi, Napoleon, and Martin Luther King apart from the crowd? The trait approach assumes the existence of a leadership personality and assumes that leaders are born, not made.

From 1904 to 1948, over 100 leadership trait studies were conducted.[26] At the end of that period, management scholars concluded that no particular set of traits is necessary for a person to become a successful leader. Enthusiasm for the trait approach diminished, but some research on traits continued. By the mid-1970s, a more balanced view emerged: Although no traits ensure leadership success, certain characteristics are potentially useful. The perspective of the 1990s is that some personality characteristics—many of which a person need not be born with but can strive to acquire—do distinguish effective leaders from other people:[27]

1. **Drive.** *Drive* refers to a set of characteristics that reflect a high level of effort. Drive includes high need for achievement, constant striving for improvement, ambition, energy, tenacity (persistence in the face of obstacles), and initiative. In several countries, the achievement needs of top executives have been shown to be related to the growth rates of their organizations.[28] But need for achievement can be a drawback if leaders focus on personal achievement and get so personally involved with the work that they do not delegate enough authority and responsibility. And whereas need for achievement has been shown to predict organizational effectiveness in entrepreneurial firms, it does not for division heads in larger and more bureaucratic firms.[29]
2. **Leadership motivation.** Great leaders not only have drive; they *want to lead.* They have a high need for power, preferring to be in leadership rather than follower positions. A high power need induces people to attempt to influence others, and sustains interest and satisfaction in the process of leadership. When the power need is exer-

cised in moral and socially-constructive ways, rather than to the detriment of others, leaders will inspire more trust, respect, and commitment to their vision.

3. **Integrity.** *Integrity* is the correspondence between actions and words. Honesty and credibility, in addition to being desirable characteristics in their own right, are especially important for leaders because these traits inspire trust in others.
4. **Self-confidence.** *Self-confidence* is important for a number of reasons. The leadership role is challenging, and setbacks are inevitable. Self-confidence allows a leader to overcome obstacles, make decisions despite uncertainty, and instill confidence in others.
5. **Knowledge of the business.** Effective leaders have a high level of *knowledge* about their industries, companies, and technical matters. Leaders must have the intelligence to interpret vast quantities of information. Advanced degrees are useful in a career, but ultimately less important than acquired expertise in matters relevant to the organization.[30]

Finally, there is one personal skill that may be the most important: the ability to perceive the needs and goals of others and to adjust one's personal leadership approach accordingly.[31] Leadership means being able to assess others, evaluate the situation, and select or change behavior to more effectively respond to the demands of the circumstances.[32] This quality is the cornerstone of the situational approaches to leadership, which we will discuss shortly.

From the Pages of BusinessWeek

New Leader at Delta Air Lines

When Delta Air Lines' new CEO, Leo Mullin, was being interviewed for the job, he asked the interviewer, "Is anything or anyone sacred?" The board chose Mullin because they believed he would shake up the status quo.

Mullin is an industry outsider; he previously was vice chairman of a utility company and was a banker before that. Rivals question the hiring of someone not in the industry and who had never been a chief executive. Mullin responds, "My fundamental goal is to build a great organization that happens to be an airline."

But first, problems loomed. Mullin's predecessor was praised for his aggressive cost-cutting, but the cuts hurt both employee morale and customer service. In 1996, 61 percent of employees said they could not trust management, and 57 percent said service had declined. And problems grew between passengers and employees.

Mullin has taken quick action. He has given managers more say over day-to-day decisions, reached out to disgruntled employees, and made a $1.42 billion purchase of 10 aircraft. He got rid of the Chief Financial Officer, citing a lack of strategic vision. He made a positive symbolic gesture by agreeing to pay the expenses of the pilot's union representative to the board, and meets regularly with small groups of employees to identify problems and generate solutions. And he is moving to reinvent Delta's information systems, expanding Latin America operations, and lobbying hard in Washington over the long-running negotiations over landing rights in Japan, France, and Britain.

Mullin, says an admirer, can "look beyond the immediate situations that confront a company and help develop decisions as to what the company could become." *Business Week* describes him as studious and energetic, and states, "Mullin knows how to ask the right questions. So far, his answers look pretty good, too."

Source: D. Greising, "A break in the clouds for Delta." *Business Week,* December 22, 1997, pp. 63–64.

Leadership behaviors

behavioral approach A leadership perspective that attempts to identify what good leaders do—that is, what behaviors they exhibit.

The **behavioral approach** to leadership attempts to identify what good leaders do. Should leaders focus on getting the job done or on keeping their followers happy? Should they make decisions autocratically or democratically? In the behavioral approach, personal characteristics are considered less important than the actual behaviors leaders exhibit.

Three general categories of leadership behavior have received particular attention: behaviors related to task performance, group maintenance, and employee participation in decision making.

task performance behaviors Actions taken to ensure that the work group or organization reaches its goals.

Task performance

Leadership requires getting the job done. **Task performance behaviors** are the leader's efforts to ensure that the work unit or organization reaches its goals. This dimension is variously referred to as *concern for production, directive leadership, initiating structure,* or *closeness of supervision.* It includes a focus on work speed, quality and accuracy, quantity of output, and following the rules.[33]

group maintenance behaviors Actions taken to ensure the satisfaction of group members, develop and maintain harmonious work relationships, and preserve the social stability of the group.

Group maintenance

In exhibiting **group maintenance behaviors,** leaders take action to ensure the satisfaction of group members, develop and maintain harmonious work relationships, and preserve the social stability of the group. This dimension is sometimes referred to as *concern for people, supportive leadership,* or *consideration.* It includes a focus on people's feelings and comfort, appreciation of them, and stress reduction.[34]

What *specific* behaviors do performance- and maintenance-oriented leadership imply? To help answer this question, assume you are asked to rate your boss on these two dimensions. If a leadership study were conducted in your organization, you would be asked to fill out a questionnaire similar to the one in Table 12.1. The behaviors indicated in the first set of questions represent performance-oriented leadership; those indicated in the second set represent maintenance-oriented leadership.

Leader-Member Exchange (LMX) theory Highlights the importance of leader behaviors not just toward the group as a whole but toward individuals on a personal basis.

One theory of leadership, **Leader-Member Exchange (LMX) theory,**[35] highlights the importance of leader behaviors not just toward the group as a whole but toward individuals on a personal basis. The focus is primarily on the leader behaviors historically considered group maintenance.[36] According to LMX theory, and supported by research evidence, maintenance behaviors such as trust, open communication, mutual respect, mutual obligation, and mutual loyalty form the cornerstone of relationships that are satisfying and perhaps more productive.

Remember, though, the potential for cross-cultural differences. Maintenance behaviors are important everywhere, but the specific behaviors can differ from one culture to another. For example, in the United States, maintenance behaviors include dealing with people face-to-face; in Japan, written memos are preferred over giving directions face-to-face, thus avoiding confrontation and permitting face-saving in the event of disagreement.[37]

participation-in-decision-making Dimension of the range of leadership behaviors—autocratic to democratic—that managers perform in involving their employees in making decisions.

autocratic leadership A form of leadership in which the leader makes decisions on his or her own and then announces those decisions to the group.

democratic leadership A form of leadership in which the leader solicits input from subordinates.

Participation in decision making

How should a leader make decisions? More specifically, to what extent should leaders involve their people in making decisions?[38] The **participation-in-decision-making** dimension of leadership behavior can range from autocratic to democratic. **Autocratic leadership** makes decisions on their own and then announce them to the group. **Democratic leadership** solicits input from others. Democratic leadership seeks information, opinions, and preferences, sometimes to the point of meeting with the group, leading discussions, and using consensus or majority vote to make the final choice.

The effects of leader behavior

How the leader behaves influences people's attitudes and performance. Studies of these effects focus on autocratic versus democratic decision styles or on performance- versus maintenance-oriented behaviors.

table 12.1
Questions assessing task performance and group maintenance leadership

Task performance leadership

1. Is your superior strict about observing regulations?
2. To what extent does your superior give you instructions and orders?
3. Is your superior strict about the amount of work you do?
4. Does your superior urge you to complete your work by a specified time?
5. Does your superior try to make you work to your maximum capacity?
6. When you do an inadequate job, does your superior focus on the inadequate way the job is done?
7. Does your superior ask you for reports about the progress of your work?
8. How precisely does your superior work out plans for goal achievement each month?

Group maintenance leadership

1. Can you talk freely with your superior about your work?
2. Does your superior generally support you?
3. Is your superior concerned about your personal problems?
4. Do you think your superior trusts you?
5. Does your superior give you recognition when you do your job well?
6. When a problem arises in your workplace, does your superior ask your opinion about how to solve it?
7. Is your superior concerned about your future benefits, such as promotions and pay raises?
8. Does your superior treat you fairly?

Source: Reprinted from J. Misumi and M. Peterson, "The Performance-Maintenance (PM) Theory of Leadership: Review of a Japanese Research Program," *Administrative Science Quarterly* 30, no. 2 (June 1985), by permission of *Administrative Science Quarterly*, © 1985 by Cornell University.

laissez-faire A leadership philosophy characterized by an absence of managerial decision making.

Decision styles The classic study comparing autocratic and democratic styles found that a democratic approach resulted in the most positive attitudes, whereas an autocratic approach resulted in somewhat higher performance.[39] A **laissez-faire** style, in which the leader essentially made no decisions, led to more negative attitudes and lower performance. These results seem logical and probably represent the prevalent beliefs among managers about the general effects of these decision-making approaches.

However, more valid conclusions have been drawn since the early research. Whether a decision should be made autocratically or democratically depends on characteristics of the leader, the followers, and the situation.[40] Thus, a situational approach to leader decision styles, discussed later in the chapter, is appropriate.

Performance and maintenance behaviors The performance and maintenance dimensions of leadership are independent of each other. In other words, a leader can behave in ways that emphasize one, both, or neither of these dimensions. Some research indicates that the ideal combination is to engage in both types of leader behaviors.

In the well-known Ohio State studies, a team of Ohio State University researchers investigated the effects of leader behavior in a truck manufacturing plant of International Harvester.[41] Generally, supervisors who were high on *maintenance behaviors* (which the researchers termed *consideration*) had fewer grievances and less turnover in their work units than supervisors who were low on this dimension. The opposite held for *task performance behaviors* (which the team called *initiating structure*). Supervisors high on this dimension had more grievances and higher turnover rates.

When maintenance and performance leadership behaviors were considered together, the results were more complex. But one conclusion was clear: When a leader must be high on performance-oriented behaviors, he or she should *also* be maintenance oriented. Otherwise the leader will have employees with high rates of turnover and grievances.

At about the same time the Ohio State studies were being conducted, an equally famous research program at the University of Michigan was studying the impact of the same leader behaviors on groups' job performance.[42] Among other things, the researchers concluded that the most effective managers engaged in what they called *task-oriented behavior:* planning, scheduling, coordinating, providing resources, and setting performance goals. Effective managers also exhibited more *relationship-oriented behavior:* demonstrating trust and confidence, acting friendly and considerate, showing appreciation, keeping people informed, and so on. As you can see, these dimensions of leader behavior are essentially the task performance and group maintenance dimensions.

After the Ohio State and Michigan findings were published, it became popular to talk about the ideal leader as one who is always both performance and maintenance oriented. The best-known leadership training model to follow this style is Blake and Mouton's Leadership Grid®.[43] In grid training, managers are rated on their performance-oriented behavior (called *concern for production*) and maintenance-oriented behavior (*concern for people*). Then their scores are plotted on the grid shown in Figure 12.2. The highest score is a 9 on both dimensions.

figure 12.2 The Leadership Grid®

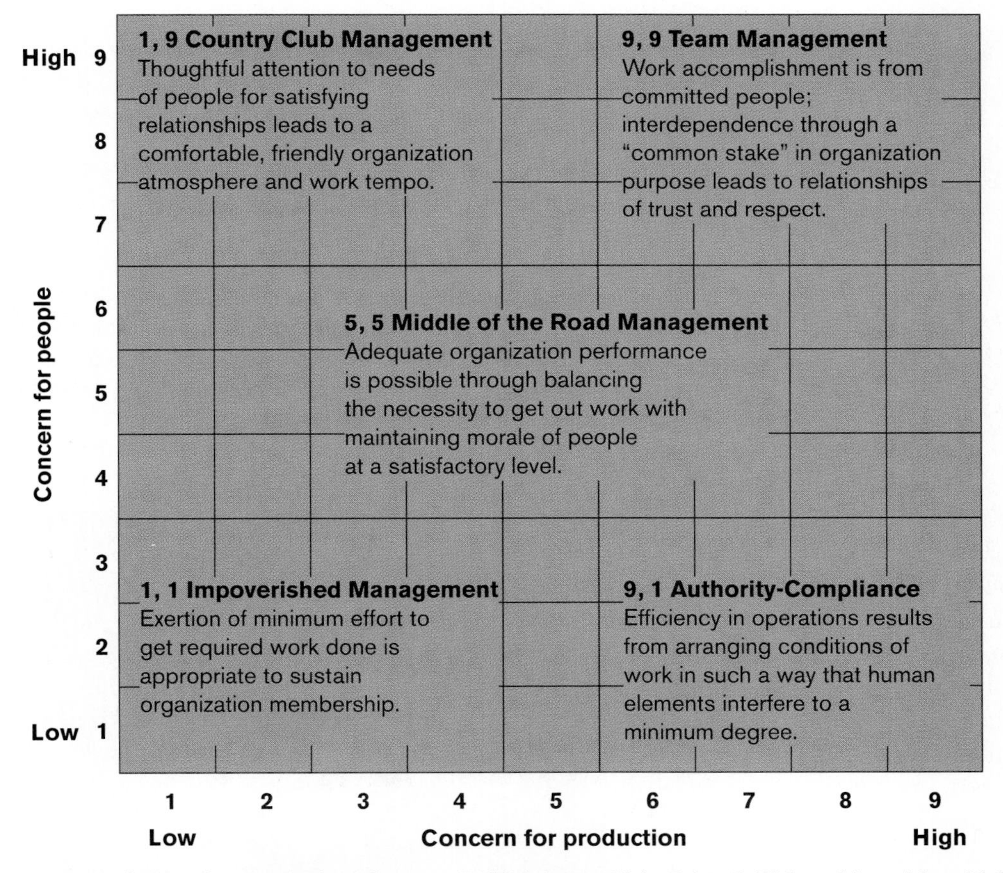

Source The Leadership Grid® Figure from *Leadership Dilemmas—Grid Solutions,* p. 29, by Robert R. Blake and Anne Adams McCanse.

As the figure shows, joint scores can fall at any point on the grid. Managers who did not score a 9,9—for example, those who were high on concern for people but low on concern for production—would then receive training on how to become a 9,9 leader.

For a long time, grid training was warmly received by U.S. business and industry. Later, however, it was criticized for embracing a simplistic, one-best-way style of leadership and ignoring the possibility that 9,9 is not best under all circumstances. For example, even 1,1 could be appropriate if employees know their jobs (and therefore don't need to receive directions). Also, they may enjoy their jobs and their co-workers enough that whether or not the boss shows personal concern for them is not very important. Nonetheless, if the manager is uncertain how to behave, it probably is best to exhibit behaviors that are related to both task performance and group maintenance.[44]

As the following example shows, a wide range of effective leadership styles exists. Organizations that understand the need for diverse leadership styles will have a competitive advantage in the modern business environment over those that believe there is only "one best way."

Men and women leaders: (How) do they differ?

On the average, men and women are equally effective as leaders. However, the situation may make a difference: male leaders are more effective in military settings, and women are more effective in educational, social service, and government organizations. Why this is so is not completely clear.

Think about it for a moment: Do women and men behave differently in leadership roles? Is there a "male" leadership style, and, if so, does it differ from the "female" style?

According to an article in *Harvard Business Review,* the first female executives had to behave like men to get to the top. But today, women are moving into top management by drawing on unique skills and attitudes that men are less likely to possess. Men, says author Judy Rosener, are more likely to rely on their formal authority and on rewards and punishments (legitimate, reward, and coercive powers), whereas women tend to use their charisma, interpersonal skills, hard work, and personal contacts. In Rosener's study, women leaders claimed to encourage participation, share power and information, and enhance other people's self-worth.

Men are said to be more effective in military settings while women work better in educational, social service, and government organizations. Illinois Senator Carol Moseley Braun's effectiveness would seem to bear out this hypothesis—so why are most politicians male? *[AP/Wide World Photos]*

Now consider some reactions to this article in a subsequent issue in *HBR:*

- Cynthia Fuchs Epstein, distinguished professor of the City University of New York, believes that too many articles have focused on identifying differences in how the sexes behave. Men should not be embarrassed about adopting the humanitarian styles described by the women leaders, and the "qualities of toughness and drive . . . should be prized in women who wish to express them when they are appropriate. The category is 'people,' not 'men and women.'"
- Monique R. Siegel of MRS Management Related Services AG in Zurich, Switzerland, wrote, "Haven't we all been told again and again that in a man's world we have to adjust to the male rules of the game? It is high time that we discard this myth–and Judy Rosener has done so . . . [T]op women succeed because they are women, not in spite of it . . . Our strength lies in not being like men, but–and this is good news–men's strength may very well lie in not being 'like a man' anymore."
- Management professor Jeffrey A. Sonnenfeld states that the female leadership style described by Rosener also characterizes the strengths of many prominent male corporate leaders, including Thomas J. Watson, Jr., of IBM; Ken Olsen of Digital Equipment; John McElwee of John Hancock; Edwin Land of Polaroid; and Jim Casey of United Parcel Service. Sonnenfeld also criticized the study on a number of methodological grounds.
- The letters to the editor concluded with one from Carol R. Goldberg, president and CEO of The Avcar Group, Ltd., of Boston, who agreed that the participative style comes more naturally to women. However, she wrote, "the Japanese, a very male-oriented culture, seem to have perfected the art of participatory management as a critical feature of their highly productive corporations . . . [We need to build] cultures that affirm diversity of styles in managers."

Source: J. B. Rosener, "Ways Women Lead," *Harvard Business Review* 68 (May–June 1990), pp. 103–11; "Debate: Ways Men and Women Lead," *Harvard Business Review* 69 (January–February 1991), pp. 150–60; and A. Eagly, S. Karom, and M. Makhijani, "Gender and the Effectiveness of Leaders: A Meta-Analysis," *Psychological Bulletin*, 1995, pp. 125–45.

Situational approaches to leadership

situational approach Leadership perspective proposing that universally important traits and behaviors do not exist, and that effective leadership behavior varies from situation to situation.

According to proponents of the **situational approach** to leadership, universally important traits and behaviors don't exist. They believe effective leader behaviors vary from situation to situation. *The leader should first analyze the situation and then decide what to do.* In other words, look before you lead.

Democracy versus dictatorship

A head nurse in a hospital described her leadership style:

> My leadership style is a mix of all styles. In this environment I normally let people participate . . .
>
> I very much like the participatory idea, but in a code blue situation where a patient is dying I automatically become very autocratic: "You do this; you do that; you, out of the room; you all better be quiet; you, get Dr. Mansfield." The staff tell me that's the only time they see me like that. In an emergency like that, you don't have time to vote, talk a lot, or yell at each other. It's time for someone to set up the order.

I remember one time, one person saying, "Wait a minute, I want to do this." He wanted to do the mouth-to-mouth resuscitation. I knew the person behind him did it better, so I said, "No, he does it." This fellow told me later that I hurt him so badly to yell that in front of all the staff and doctors. It was like he wasn't good enough. So I explained it to him: that's the way it is. A life was on the line. I couldn't give you warm fuzzies. I couldn't make you look good because you didn't have the skills to give the very best to that patient who wasn't breathing anymore.

If anyone ever tells me that they're a democratic type of leader, I don't want them. In an emergency, if you're a democratic leader, I wouldn't want you leading the team. There come times when you can't stop, vote, or have participation on what's to be done. If you're doing that all the time, then you aren't a leader.

Source: J. Wall, *Bosses* (Lexington, MA: Lexington Books, 1986), pp. 103–4.

This head nurse has her own intuitive situational approach to leadership. She knows the potential advantages of the participatory approach to decision making, but she also knows that in some circumstances she must make decisions on her own.

The first situational model of leadership was proposed in 1958 by Tannenbaum and Schmidt. In their classic *Harvard Business Review* article, these authors described how managers should consider three factors before deciding how to lead: forces in the manager, forces in the subordinate, and forces in the situation.[45] Forces in the manager include the manager's personal values, inclinations, feelings of security, and confidence in subordinates. Forces in the subordinate include the employee's knowledge and experience, readiness to assume responsibility for decision making, interest in the task or problem, and understanding and acceptance of the organization's goals. Forces in the situation include the type of leadership style the organization values, the degree to which the group works as a unit effectively, the problem itself and the type of information needed to solve it, and the amount of time the leader has to make the decision.

Consider which of these forces make an autocratic style most appropriate and which dictate a democratic, participative style. By engaging in this exercise, you are constructing a situational theory of leadership.

Although the Tannenbaum and Schmidt article was published almost a half-century ago, most of its arguments remain valid. Since that time, other situational models have emerged. We will focus here on two of them: the Vroom-Yetton-Jago model for decision making, and path-goal theory. The others are summarized in the appendix to this chapter.

Vroom-Yetton-Jago model
A situational model of leadership that focuses on how leaders go about making decisions.

The Vroom-Yetton-Jago Model

This situational model follows in the tradition of Tannenbaum and Schmidt. Developed initially by Vroom and Yetton[46] and revised by Vroom and Jago,[47] the **Vroom-Yetton-Jago model** emphasizes the participative dimension of leadership: how leaders go about making decisions. The model uses the basic situational approach of assessing the situation before determining the best leadership style.

Figure 12.3 shows the questions used to analyze problem situations. Each question is based on an important attribute of the problem the leader faces and should be answered with a yes or a no.

The Vroom-Yetton-Jago model is a decision tree. You answer the questions one at a time, sometimes skipping some questions as you follow the appropriate branch. Eventually, you reach one of 10 possible endpoints. For each endpoint, the model states which of the five decision styles (labeled AI through GII) is most appropriate. Several different decision styles may work, but the style recommended is the one in the feasible set that takes the least amount of time.

figure 12.3 The Vroom-Yetton-Jago model

State the Problem

QR	**Quality requirement:**	How important is the quality of this decision?
CR	**Commitment requirement:**	How important is subordinate commitment to the decision?
LI	**Leader's information:**	Do you have sufficient information to make a high-quality decision?
ST	**Problem structure:**	Is the problem well structured?
CP	**Commitment probability:**	If you were to make the decision by yourself, is it reasonably certain that your subordinates would be committed to it?
GC	**Goal congruence:**	Do subordinates share the organization goals to be attained by solving this problem?
CO	**Subordinate conflict:**	Is conflict among subordinates over preferred solutions likely?
SI	**Subordinate information:**	Do subordinates have sufficient information to make a high-quality decision?

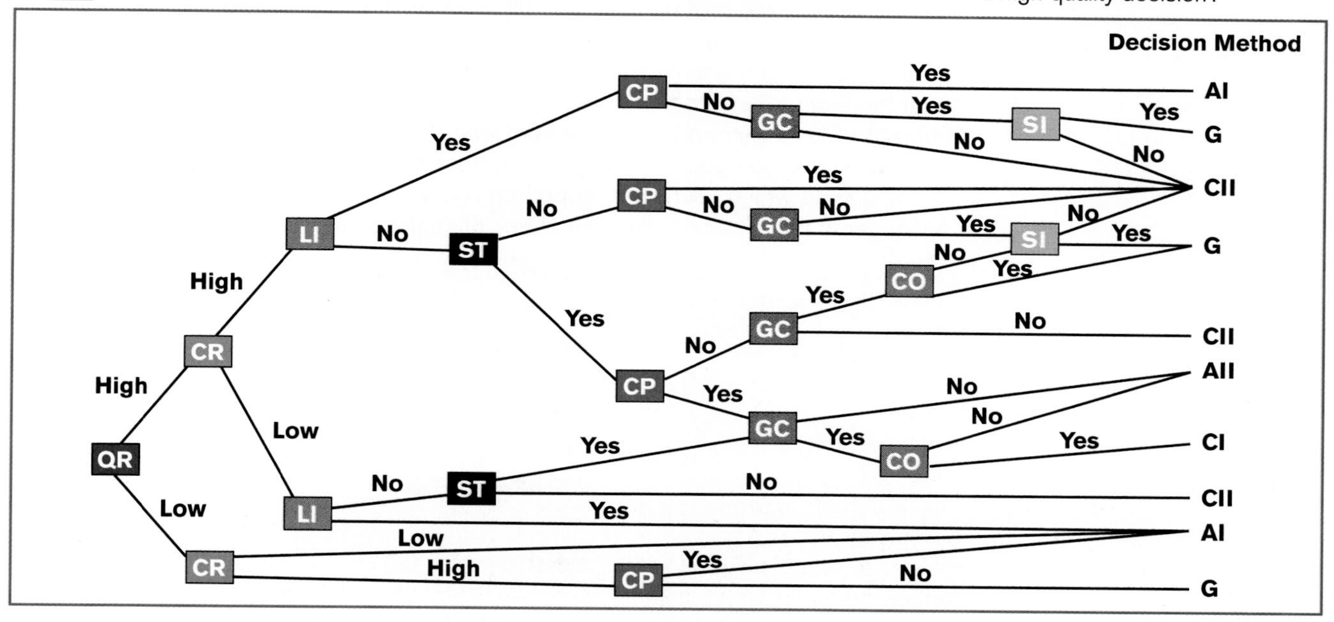

Source: Reprinted from Victor H. Vroom and Arthur G. Jago, *The New Leadership: Managing Participation in Organizations* (Englewood Cliffs, NJ: Prentice Hall, 1988). Copyright 1987 by V. H. Vroom and A. G. Jago. Used with permission of the authors.

Table 12.2 defines the types of leader decision styles. The five styles indicate that there are several shades of participation, not just autocratic or democratic.

The following example presents a managerial decision for you to work through the model tree.

Applying the Vroom-Yetton-Jago model

Imagine yourself in this situation. You are the head of a research and development laboratory in the nuclear reactor division of a large corporation. Often it is not clear whether a particular piece of research is potentially of commercial interest or merely of "academic" interest to the researchers. In your judgment, one major area of research has advanced well beyond the level at which operating divisions pertinent to the area could possibly assimilate or use the data being generated.

Recently two new areas with potentially high returns for commercial development have been proposed by one of the operating divisions. The team working in the area referred to in the previous paragraph is ideally qualified to research the new areas. Unfortunately, both areas are relatively devoid of scientific interest, while the project in which the team is currently engaged is of great scientific interest to all members.

At the moment, this is, or is close to being, your best research team. The team is very cohesive, has a high level of morale, and has been very productive. You are concerned not only that they would not want to switch their effort to the new areas but also that forcing them to concentrate on these two new projects could adversely affect their morale, their good working relations, and their future productivity both as individuals and as a team.

You have to respond to the operating division within the next two weeks indicating what resources, if any, can be devoted to working on these projects. It would be possible for the team to work on more than one project, but each project would need the combined skills of all the members of the team, so no fragmentation of the team is technically feasible. This fact, coupled with the fact that the team is very cohesive, means that a solution that satisfied any team member would very probably go a long way to satisfying everyone on the team.

How would you go about making this decision? Using Figure 12.3 and Table 12.2, decide which leadership approach you should apply if you were the manager in this situation. You can check the solution at the end of this section.

Source: V. Vroom and A. Jago, *The New Leadership: Managing Participation in Organizations* (Englewood Cliffs, NJ. Prentice Hall, 1988). ●

table 12.2
Types of management decision styles

AI	You solve the problem or make the decision yourself, using information available to you at that time.
AII	You obtain the necessary information from your subordinate(s), then decide on the solution to the problem yourself. You may or may not tell your subordinates what the problem is in getting the information from them. The role played by your subordinates in making the decision is clearly one of providing the necessary information to you, rather than generating or evaluating alternative solutions.
CI	You share the problem with relevant subordinates individually, getting their ideas and suggestions without bringing them together as a group. Then you make the decision that may or may not reflect your subordinates' influence.
CII	You share the problem with your subordinates as a group, collectively obtaining their ideas and suggestions. Then you make the decision that may or may not reflect your subordinates' influence.
G	You share a problem with your subordinates as a group. Together you generate and evaluate alternatives and attempt to reach agreement (consensus) on a solution. Your role is much like that of chairman. You do not try to influence the group to adopt "your" solution, and you are willing to accept and implement any solution that has the support of the entire group.

Source: Reprinted from *Leadership and Decision Making* by Victor H. Vroom and Philip W. Yetton by permission of the University of Pittsburgh Press. © 1973 by University of Pittsburgh Press.

Of course, not every managerial decision warrants this complicated analysis. Actually, the revised version of the model is more complex yet![48] But the model becomes less complex after one works through it a couple of times. Also, using the model for major decisions ensures that the manager considers the important situational factors and alerts the leader to the most appropriate style to use.[49]

Answer to Vroom-Yetton-Jago problem: Answers to questions are QR high, CR high, LI: yes, CP no, GC no. The preferred decision style is CII.

path-goal theory A theory that concerns how leaders influence subordinates' perceptions of their work goals and the paths they follow toward attainment of those goals.

Path-goal theory

Perhaps the most generally useful situational model of leadership effectiveness is path-goal theory. Developed by Robert House, **path-goal theory** gets its name from its concern with how leaders influence followers' perceptions of their work goals and the paths they follow toward goal attainment.[50]

The key situational factors in path-goal theory are (1) personal characteristics of followers and (2) environmental pressures and demands with which followers must cope to attain their work goals. These factors determine which leadership behaviors are most appropriate.

The four pertinent leadership behaviors are (1) *directive leadership,* a form of task performance–oriented behavior; (2) *supportive leadership,* a form of group maintenance–oriented behavior; (3) *participative leadership,* or decision style; and (4) *achievement-oriented leadership,* or behaviors geared toward motivating people, such as setting challenging goals and rewarding good performance.

These situational factors and leader behaviors are merged in Figure 12.4. As you can see, appropriate leader behaviors—as determined by characteristics of followers and the work environment—lead to effective performance.

The theory also specifies *which* follower and environmental features are important. There are three key follower characteristics. *Authoritarianism* is the degree to which individuals respect, admire, and defer to authority. *Locus of control* is the extent to which individuals see the environment as responsive to their own behavior. People with an *internal* locus of control believe that what happens to them is their own doing; people with an *external* locus of control believe that it is just luck or fate. Finally, *ability* is people's beliefs about their own abilities to do their assigned jobs.

Path-goal theory states that these personal characteristics determine the appropriateness of various leadership styles. For example, the theory makes the following propositions:

- A directive leadership style is more appropriate for highly authoritarian people, because such people respect authority.
- A participative leadership style is more appropriate for people who have an internal locus of control, because these individuals prefer to have more influence over their own lives.
- A directive style is more appropriate when subordinates' ability is low. The directive style helps people understand what has to be done.

Appropriate leadership style is also determined by three important environmental factors: people's tasks, the formal authority system of the organization, and the primary work group.

- Directive leadership is inappropriate if tasks already are well structured.
- If the task and the authority or rule system are dissatisfying, directive leadership will create greater dissatisfaction.
- If the task or authority system is dissatisfying, supportive leadership is especially appropriate, because it offers one positive source of gratification in an otherwise negative situation.
- If the primary work group provides social support to its members, supportive leadership is less important.

figure 12.4 The path-goal framework

Path-goal theory offers many more propositions. In general, the theory suggests that the functions of the leader are to (1) make the path to work goals easier to travel by providing coaching and direction; (2) reduce frustrating barriers to goal attainment; and (3) increase opportunities for personal satisfaction by increasing payoffs to people for achieving performance goals.

How best to do these things depends on your people and on the work situation. Again: Analyze, then adapt your style accordingly.

substitutes for leadership Factors in the workplace that can exert the same influence on employees that leaders would provide.

Substitutes for leadership

Sometimes leaders don't have to lead—or, situations constrain their ability to lead effectively. The situation may be one in which leadership is unnecessary or has little impact. **Substitutes for leadership** can provide the same influence on people that leaders otherwise would have.

Certain follower, task, and organizational factors are substitutes for task performance–oriented and group maintenance–oriented leader behaviors.[51] For example, group maintenance behaviors are less important and will have less impact if people already have a closely knit group, they have a professional orientation, the job is intrinsically satisfying, or there is great physical distance between leader and followers. Physicians who are strongly concerned with professional conduct, enjoy their work, and work independently do not need social support from hospital administrators.

Task performance leadership is less important and will have less positive effect if people have a lot of experience and ability, feedback is supplied to them directly from the task or by computer, or the rules and procedures are rigid. If these factors are operating, the leader does not have to tell people what to do or how well they are performing.

The concept of substitutes for leadership does more than indicate when a leader's attempts at influence will and will not work. It provides useful and practical prescriptions for how to manage more efficiently. If the manager can develop the work situation to the point where a number of these substitutes for leadership are operating, less time will need to be spent in direct attempts to influence people. The leader will be free to spend more time on other important activities.

Contemporary perspectives on leadership

So far, you have learned the major classic approaches to understanding leadership. Now we will discuss a number of new developments that are revolutionizing our understanding of this important aspect of management. These developments include charismatic leadership, transformational leadership, and post-heroic leadership.

Do you believe Princess Diana was a charismatic leader? Why or why not?
[Reuters/J.M.Ribeiro/Archive Photos]

Charismatic leadership

Like many great leaders, Ronald Reagan had charisma. Lee Iacocca, Thomas Watson, Alfred Sloan, and Steve Jobs are good examples of charismatic leaders in industry.

What *is* charisma, and how does one acquire it? Charisma is a rather evasive concept; it is easy to spot but hard to define. According to one definition, "Charisma packs an emotional wallop for followers above and beyond ordinary esteem, affection, admiration, and trust . . . The charismatic is an idolized hero, a messiah and a savior . . .[52] As you can see from this quotation, many people, particularly North Americans, value charisma in their leaders. But some people associate it with the negative charisma of Hitler.[53]

charismatic leader A person who is dominant, self-confident, convinced of the moral righteousness of his or her beliefs, and able to arouse a sense of excitement and adventure in subordinates.

Charismatic leaders are dominant and exceptionally self-confident and have a strong conviction in the moral righteousness of their beliefs.[54] They strive to create an aura of competence and success and communicate high expectations for and confidence in followers.

The charismatic leader articulates ideological goals. Martin Luther King had a dream for a better world, and John F. Kennedy spoke of landing a human on the moon. In other words, such leaders have a vision. The charismatic leader also arouses a sense of excitement and adventure. He or she is an eloquent speaker who exhibits superior verbal skills, which helps communicate the vision and motivate followers. Walt Disney was able to mesmerize people with his storytelling, had enormous creative talent, and instilled in his organization strong values of good taste, risk taking, and innovation.[55]

Leaders who possess these characteristics or do these things inspire in their followers trust, confidence, acceptance, obedience, emotional involvement, affection, admiration, and higher performance. Evidence for the positive effects of charismatic leadership has been found in a wide variety of groups, organizations, and management levels, and in countries including India, Singapore, The Netherlands, China, Japan, and Canada.[56]

transformational leader A leader who transforms a vision into reality and motivates people to transcend their personal interests for the good of the group.

Transformational leadership

Charisma contributes to transformational leadership. **Transformational leaders** change things from what could be to what is; that is, they translate a vision into reality. They get people to transcend their personal interests for the sake of the group. They generate excitement and revitalize organizations. At Hewlett-Packard, the ability to generate excitement is an explicit criterion for selecting managers.

The transformational process moves beyond the more traditional *transactional* approach to leadership.[57] The concept of **transactional leaders** views management as a series of business transactions in which leaders use their legitimate, reward, and coercive powers to give commands and exchange rewards for services rendered. Unlike transformational leadership, transactional leadership is dispassionate; it does not excite, transform, empower, or inspire people to focus on the interests of the group or organization.

transactional leaders Management through business transactions in which leaders use their legitimate, reward, and coercive powers to give commands and exchange rewards for services rendered.

Generating excitement. Transformational leaders generate excitement in three primary ways.[58] First, they are *charismatic,* as described earlier. Second, they give their followers *individualized attention.* Transformational leaders delegate challenging work to deserving people, increase people's responsibilities, keep lines of communication open, and provide one-on-one mentoring to develop their people. They do not treat everyone alike, because not everyone *is* alike.

Third, transformational leaders are *intellectually stimulating.* They arouse in their followers an awareness of problems and potential solutions. They articulate the organization's opportunities, threats, strengths, and weaknesses. They stir the imagination and generate insights. Therefore, problems are recognized and high-quality solutions are identified and implemented with the full commitment of followers.

Skills and Strategies. At least four skills or strategies contribute to transformational leadership.[59] First, transformational leaders *have a vision*—a goal, an agenda, or a results-orientation that grabs people's attention. Second, they *communicate their vision;* through words, manner, or symbolism, they relate a compelling image of the ultimate goal. Third, transformational leaders *build trust* by being consistent, dependable, and persistent. They position themselves clearly by choosing a direction and staying with it, thus projecting integrity. Finally, they have a *positive self-regard.* They do not feel self-important or complacent; rather, they recognize their personal strengths, compensate for their weaknesses, nurture and continually develop their talents, and know how to learn from failure. They strive for success rather than merely trying to avoid failure.

Transformational leadership has been identified in industry, the military, and politics.[60] Examples of transformational leaders include Henry Ford, who achieved his vision of an affordable, mass-produced automobile; General George Patton, who transformed the Third Army; Lee Iacocca, who carried Chrysler from bankruptcy to success; and Jan Carlzon, who turned Scandinavian Air System (SAS) from an $8 million loss to a $71 million profit (on sales of $2 billion) in a little over a year.[61] As with studies of charisma, transformational leadership and its positive impact on follower satisfaction and performance have been demonstrated in countries the world over, including Egypt, Germany, China, England, and Japan.[62]

Transforming leaders. Importantly, transformational leadership is not the exclusive domain of presidents and chief executives. Ford Motor Company, in collaboration with the University of Michigan School of Business, has put thousands of middle managers through a program designed to stimulate transformational leadership.[63] In this way, the traditional role of middle managers was to be transformed. The training included analysis of the changing business environment, company strategy, and personal reflection and discussion about the need to change. Participants assessed their own leadership styles and developed a specific change initiative to implement after the training—a change that would make a needed and lasting difference.

Over the next six months, the managers implemented change on the job. Almost half of the initiatives resulted in transformational changes in the organization or work unit; 54 percent of the changes were smaller, more incremental, or more personal. Whether managers made small or transformational changes depended on their attitude going into the training, their level of self-esteem, and the amount of support they received from others on the job for their efforts. Thus, some managers did not respond as hoped. But almost half embraced the training, became more transformational in orientation, and tackled significant transformational changes for the company.[64]

Post-heroic leadership

A common view of leaders is that they are heroes. Phenomenally talented, they step forward in difficult times and save the day. But in these complex times, it is foolhardy to assume that a great top executive can solve all problems by himself or herself.[65] No one person can deal with all of today's rapid-fire changes, competitive threats, and escalating customer demands.

Therefore, it is a big mistake to cruise along assuming Arnold Schwarzenegger will intervene and make things right. Implicit in this way of thinking is the belief that a single leader can save the firm. But effective leadership must permeate the organization, not reside in one or two superstars at the top.

The leader's job becomes one of spreading leadership abilities throughout the firm:[66] Make people responsible for their own performance. Create an environment in which each person can figure out what needs to be done and then do it well. Point the way and clear the path so people can succeed. Give them the credit they deserve. Make heroes out of *them.*

To do this, you can paint a clear picture of great performance, and engage individuals—their hearts, minds, and hands—in making the business better. This requires the leader to coach and develop individual capability and competence, and to challenge every individual to continually improve his or he abilities and make greater contributions.

Thus, the leader must be willing to visualize greatness, and take action to achieve it—and expect the same from everyone else in the organization. *Everyone* needs to think like a complete businessperson—like an entrepreneur, recalling Chapter 7. And everyone must be willing and able to take action on behalf of the business.

Metaphors for leadership

As noted above, our traditional view of leadership is of heroes who come to the fore in times of crisis. But a newer view is that the leader continually engages in subtler, more important tasks like building organizations in which people continually expand their capabilities. In other words, leaders encourage and facilitate continual learning. Three metaphors help describe the leader's role in helping people learn: leaders as designers, stewards, and teachers.

John Johnson, founder and CEO of Johnson Publishing, which includes Ebony magazine, personifies the leader as steward–someone who exercises responsible care over the organization that is entrusted to him.
[Chicago Tribune photo by Nancy Stone]

The leader as *designer:* What is the most important role in leading an ocean liner? The captain, who gives the orders? The navigator, who sets the direction? The engineer, who provides energy to make the ship move forward? Perhaps the most important role is that of designer. Even with orders, direction, and energy, the ship won't reach its destination if it doesn't *work.* The designer creates an organization that works. This role begins with establishing the vision, values, and mission of the organization, and creating an environment where people can do their jobs successfully and work together effectively toward achieving goals.

The leader as *steward:* A steward is a leader who exercises responsible care over the organization that is entrusted to him or her. Good leaders have a deep sense of purpose and destiny, and become stewards of their vision. They communicate the overarching explanation of why they do what they do, how their organization needs to grow, and how its development is part of a greater purpose. They convince people that their organization is a vehicle for bringing learning and change into society. They bring personal and universal meaning into the organization, and into people's work.

The leader as *teacher:* A teacher helps people achieve a richer and more accurate view of the world. Retired Herman Miller CEO Max de Pree said, "The first responsibility of a leader is defining reality." The leader as teacher helps people understand the forces shaping change, helps them learn, and inspires them to seek the truth.

Source: From *The Fifth Discipline* by Peter M. Senge. Copyright © 1990 by Peter M. Senge. Used by permission of Doubleday, a division of Bantam Doubleday Dell Publishing Group, Inc. and Random House UK Ltd. ●

A note on courage

To be a good leader, you need the courage to create a vision of greatness for your unit; identify and manage allies, adversaries, and fencesitters; and to execute your vision often against opposition. This does not mean you should commit career suicide by alienating too many powerful people; it does mean taking reasonable risks, with the good of the firm at heart, in order to produce constructive change.

Specifically, some acts of courage required to fulfill your vision will include:[67] (1) seeing things as they are and facing them head-on, making no excuses and harboring no wishful illusions; (2) saying what needs to be said to those who need to hear it; and (3) putting up with, and persisting despite, resistance, criticism, abuse, and setbacks. Courage includes stating the realities, even when they are harsh, and publicly stating what you will do to help and what you want from others. This means laying the cards on the table honestly: Here is what I want from you . . . What do you want from me?[68]

Developing your leadership skills

As with other things, you must work at *developing* your leadership abilities. Great musicians and great athletes don't become great on natural gifts alone. They also pay their dues by practicing, learning, and sacrificing. In interview studies, leaders in a variety of fields, asked how they become the best leader possible, offered the following comments:[69]

- "I've observed methods and skills of my bosses that I respected."
- "By taking risks, trying, and learning from my mistakes."

- "Reading autobiographies of leaders I admire to try to understand how they think."
- "Lots of practice."
- "By making mistakes myself and trying a different approach."
- "By purposely engaging with others to get things done."
- "By being put in positions of responsibility that other people counted on."

How do you go about developing your leadership abilities? In general, start by getting out of your "comfort zone." That is, don't seek out and remain in easy, nonchallenging situations; enter, create, and face situations that require you to adapt and change. This is the best way to learn, and it is the way great executives learn.[70]

More specifically, here are some developmental experiences you should seek:[71]

- *Assignments:* building something from nothing; fixing or turning around a failing operation; taking on project or task force responsibilities; accepting international assignments.
- *Other people:* having exposure to positive role models; increasing visibility to others; working with people of diverse backgrounds.
- *Hardships:* overcoming ideas that fail and deals that collapse; confronting others' performance problems; breaking out of a career rut.
- *Other events:* formal courses; challenging job experiences; supervision of others; experiences outside work.

These experiences do not guarantee that you will develop into an effective leader. But without them, your development will surely be constrained. Seek these experiences; expect mistakes and don't beat yourself up over them; and take time to learn from your experiences.

Key terms

Summary of learning objectives

Now that you have studied Chapter 12, you should know:

What it means to be a leader.

A leader is one who influences others to attain goals. Leaders orchestrate change, set direction, and motivate people to overcome obstacles and move the organization toward its ideal future.

How a good vision helps you be a better leader.

Outstanding leaders have vision. A vision is a mental image that goes beyond the ordinary and perhaps beyond what others thought possible. The vision provides the direction in which the leader wants the organization to move.

How to understand and use power.

Having power and using it appropriately are essential attributes of an effective leader. Managers have five potential sources of power: legitimate, reward, coercive, referent, and expert. These power sources are potentially available to managers at all organizational levels and should be used appropriately.

The personal traits and skills of effective leaders.

The old idea that leaders have certain traits or skills fell into disfavor but lately has been resurrected. Important leader characteristics include drive, leadership motivation, integrity, self-confidence, and knowledge of the business. Perhaps the most important skill is the ability to accurately perceive the situation and then change behavior accordingly.

The behaviors that will make you a better leader.

Important leader behaviors include task performance, group maintenance, and participation in decision making. Exhibiting more rather than fewer of these behaviors will enhance your effectiveness in the long run. The Vroom-Yetton-Jago model helps a leader decide how much participation to use in making decisions. Path-goal theory assesses characteristics of the followers, the leader, and the situation; it then indicates the appropriateness of directive, supportive, participative, or achievement-oriented leadership behaviors.

What it means to be a charismatic and transformational leader.

To have charisma is to be dominant and self-confident, to have a strong conviction of the righteousness of your beliefs, to create an aura of competence and success, and to communicate high expectations for and confidence in your followers. Charisma is one component of transformational leadership. Transformational leaders change things from what could be to what is; that is, they translate a vision into reality. They do this through charisma, individualized attention to followers, intellectual stimulation, formation and communication of their vision, building of trust, and positive self-regard.

How to further your own leadership development.

You can develop your own leadership skills not only by understanding what effective leadership is all about, but also by seeking challenging developmental experiences. Such important life experiences come about from taking challenging assignments, through exposure in working with other people, by overcoming hardships and failures, by taking formal courses, and by other actions.

Discussion questions

1. What elements from the chapter do you see in the four leaders described in "Setting the Stage"?

2. Is there a difference between effective management and effective leadership? Explain your views and learn from others' views.

3. Identify someone you think is an effective leader. What traits and skills does this individual possess that make him or her effective?

4. Do you think most managers can be transformational leaders? Why or why not?

5. In your own words, define courage. What is the role of courage in leadership? Give examples of acts of leadership you consider courageous.

6. Do you think men and women differ in their leadership styles? If so, how? Do men and/or women prefer different styles in their bosses? What evidence do you have for your answers?

7. Who are your heroes? Try to identify some traditional heroes and also some that are "post-heroic." What makes them heroes, and what can you learn from them in general? What can you learn from them about leadership in particular?

8. Assess yourself as a leader based on what you have read in this chapter. What are your strengths and weaknesses?

9. Identify the developmental experiences you have had that may have strengthened your ability to lead. What did those experiences teach you? Also identify some developmental experiences you need to acquire, and how you will seek them. Be specific.

10. Consider a couple of decisions you are facing that could involve other people. Use the Vroom-Yetton-Jago decision tree to decide what approach to use to make the decisions.

11. Consider an organization of which you are a leader or a member. What could great transformational leadership accomplish in the organization?

12. Consider a job you hold or have held in the past. Consider how your boss managed you. How would you describe him or her as a leader? What substitutes for leadership would you have enjoyed being put into place?

Concluding Case

Leadership at Fidelity Investments

In the early 1990s, Fidelity Investments was arguably the world's dominant financial services company. The family-owned mutual fund had ridden the 15-year bull market and brilliant fund managers to spectacular growth and a powerful brand name. But by the mid-90s, its funds were lagging the market and its fund managers were quitting left and right.

In 1997, CEO Ned Johnson III removed the head of investment management and replaced him with Robert Pozen, Fidelity's top lawyer. Pozen then named three deputies, including Johnson's 35-year-old daughter, Abigail, who apparently is being groomed to take over the company. And Johnson named James Curvey as chief operating officer, a position previously unfilled for 10 years.

The leadership team at Fidelity has the task of returning the company to its former greatness. *[John Abbott]*

Another change with which it must deal is a change in its core customer. The core customer is no longer the retail investor, who wanted tremendous growth, but the businesses that invest in Fidelity retirement accounts. And market share, after years of tremendous growth, has stabilized as competitors have made it clear to business clients that Fidelity's best-known funds were riskier than appropriate for retirement plans.

Fidelity's culture has changed as well. When the legendary Peter Lynch was running Fidelity's flagship Magellan fund, he believed in picking good stocks more than in trying to time the market. He was willing to listen to any analyst's ideas. He was flexible, and he encouraged others to be creative. When Lynch left, Jeff Vinik was named to head Magellan. His philosophy was quite different from Lynch's, as he tried to catch market trends and did not pay attention to other analysts. Magellan's returns dropped below the market, and Fidelity's competitors made the most of that news. Vinik is now gone.

Many would consider the management shake-up at Fidelity to be big news. These are significant leadership changes. Despite its lackluster performance and a lot of bad press, Fidelity is still the biggest mutual fund company in the world, still feared by the others. But major moves in companies like Fidelity set off alarms: they signal that the company has problems it can't ignore. So Fidelity held no press conference, told a reporter for *Fortune* that the changes were merely evolutionary, and implied they were no big deal.

According to *Fortune,* Fidelity in the early 90s had a "corrosive" culture in which many fund managers cared less about the huge portfolios entrusted to them than about their personal trading accounts. This has since subsided. For the *Fortune* article, every top executive interviewed denied that the company had any real problems, or that it was changing in any way. Fidelity denies performance downturns, despite the evidence of risky investments turning sour that seems clear to everyone else. And they showed their annoyance at having to answer questions. Whereas Curvey answered most of the reporter's questions on Johnson's behalf, Johnson did say that no one cares about customers more than Fidelity.

Back to Pozen: after 10 days on the job, he told *Fortune,* "I know what needs to be done, and I know I'm the right man to do the job." In his early days, Pozen convinced two reliable fund managers to stay, when there were rumors that they were leaving like so many others. He has less investment experience than the fund managers who report to him, but he insists, "This job requires a manager, not an investment professional."

Questions

1. To many observers, Fidelity has stumbled from its former greatness. Is the Fidelity situation a failure of leadership? Discuss.

2. What could have been done to prevent the problems at Fidelity?

3. What does Pozen face at Fidelity? What should he do?

Source: D. Whitford and J. Nocera, "Has Fidelity Lost It?" *Fortune,* June 9, 1997, pp. 42–51. ●

Video Case

Leadership and motivation at Bernard Welding Equipment Company

Leadership is a concept that is frequently discussed, but whose meaning is unclear. What distinguishes a manager from a leader? What is power? How can a manager develop leadership skills and use power in a manner that will motivate and inspire employees to go beyond their job description? In the workplace, leadership can be defined as the application of personal attributes and abilities, such as insight, energy, and knowledge, to create a shared vision of the future. A manager must deal with the pressures of the moment, and is responsible for organizing and controlling the workforce. The means by which a manager creates lasting meaning or purpose for employees defines the manager's "leadership style."

Bernard Welding Equipment Company has garnered a large share of the world's welding accessories business. The company's success may be attributed to the application of a new style of leadership, and a quality management approach to every stage of its operation. Reflecting on the important role of leadership at Bernard, company president Pat Cunningham said, "The leader of a company becomes the personality of the company. Very often, in the old days, he was an autocratic person. If you view old-time manufacturing, you've got one guy in the corner office barking out orders and people running around doing his bidding day in and day out. Well, in today's environment, where people are much more informed and communications can happen much more rapidly, that style of management is no longer effective."

Jim Therrien, Bernard's vice president of operations, noted in the video that his company began a continuous quality improvement journey in the early 1990s. The first step in the journey involved reviewing and refining the company's mission. Therrien explained the role of leadership in the mission review process: "The only constant in life is change, and the same is true in business. People who can capture change and run with it will be tremendously successful. Those that don't won't be in tune with the ever-changing markets and will be left behind. If management is efficiently climbing the ladder, then leadership is making sure the ladder is against the right wall. Our right wall is the customer need. Starting with that, and backing into the plant and moving through the organization gives you the wherewithal and the master plan to effect the kinds of changes that we've had at Bernard. As people become part of a team, they feel like they're accomplishing something. When people are in that mode, it's very easy to lead them in the right direction. And the right direction is always based on what the customer need is. And when you're filling those customer needs, there are fewer of those complaint calls, there are fewer people coming down on people and more people being up with people and helping to move things in the proper direction."

After reviewing the mission, the second stage of Bernard's continuous improvement process was to examine its manufacturing operations. The company's assembly line was improved through the participative leadership style. Training for both the managers and the workforce was key to the change. Managers needed to learn how to delegate and empower their workforce, and the workers needed to learn how to accept their new responsibilities.

Production supervisor Kathy Yates is enthusiastic about the changes in the workforce that resulted from Bernard's new participative leadership style: "In the past when we had problems on the assembly line the operators would come to me and ask, 'What should we do?' We're doing things a lot differently now. When problems arise on the assembly line we get together as a group, we talk it out, and we decide what the best solution is to that problem. We didn't do that in the past. We're more of a team effort now and it really shows up in the results. Our production is up, our quality is up, the morale of the people is up. It really has paid off."

Bernard's continuous improvement process has also focused on reducing costs. Using employee-driven quality improvement teams, the company changed its practice of maintaining a supply of precut, assembled cables for its welding guns because it incurred unnecessarily high inventory costs. Bernard now uses a delayed, differentiated quick response system. With this new approach, the cable needed to fill each order is cut to the customer's specifications from the spools of cable as needed. Reduced inventory lowers costs and benefits the customer through lower prices and quicker turnaround times.

Workers on the shop floor have embraced their new decision-making authority. Randy Warren, manufacturing engineer, noted another example of employee-led cost reduction: "We've been able to reduce set-up time across 65 percent of our head volume. A good example is our head forming process. A process that used to take a good set-up person 30 to 40 minutes to accomplish can now be done by the operator in less than a minute. We recognize that our most important resource is our people out there. By empowering the people to make decisions on their own we've been able to generate a lot of input right at the floor level where the process takes place. These are the experts in the manufacture of our products. They see things that we can't anticipate on the tooling side or on the process side."

Bernard's new participatory leadership style has motivated the employees to reach new levels of quality and customer satisfaction, as Kathy Yates elaborated: "We find that, on a daily basis, when problems come up, we get together as a team and we solve them. I have found that [the line workers] are the experts; they are the ones who are out there building this product day after day after day. They know more about the product than I do. So, when problems arise, we get together, we sit down, we talk it out, we brainstorm it, whatever it takes to come up with a solution. I think this has really helped the quality of our product. I think people are dedicated to their work areas, and they feel an ownership. They're very concerned about what they're putting out and how they're doing it. They feel that they've got to make the highest-quality product."

Therrien explained how his own leadership style has changed in the continuous quality improvement culture: "As I've transitioned from managing to leading in this organization, and I think the same holds true for most managers here, I've learned to listen better than I've ever listened before. I only thought I was listening. People have a lot to say. You don't always want to hear it. But when you sit quietly, and gather data from many directions, then the decisions that you make are better decisions because they're based on more information. When you have everyone in one room, then you are going to hear from all sides, and you will gather information in the same manner that it goes through the organization. Most large organizations are vertically structured, and most of the information that the customer needs, and the product, go through horizontally. Once you have your people in tune with that, the product and the information flow move horizontally, you will be able to look down on it and see where the bottlenecks are. Then you can bring your resources to bear to help the people do a better job."

Cunningham summarized the new leadership style being practiced at Bernard: "One of the benefits of the longer-term view that we've taken of improving the managerial capability of our people is their ability to make better decisions on improving productivity in a given product line. I can recall, some years ago, in sitting in meetings with our people, they looked to me and a couple of others to answer the key questions and communicate the direction of the company, to solve all of the problems, to take just about everything that needed to be decided and decide it. That doesn't make sense. For the CEO of a business or the top manager of a fairly sizable organization to think that he has the knowledge and capability to make all of the minute decisions that need to be made on a daily basis is kind of foolhardy. That may have been appropriate in a very small business 50 years ago, but it surely isn't appropriate in today's environment. We now bring customers and distributors right into our factories and sit them down with employees and let them communicate, let them get a better understanding of exactly what's going on in our business and what the needs of our customers are right from the horse's mouth. We provide each of our employees with access to all of our financial information regularly on exactly how this company is doing. Our employees actually have access to every piece of financial data that I have. And I'm proud to say that I think it's helped them become more informed employees, who are willing to recognize faster when change needs to be made. I think that our growth in our industry in the last couple of years, in terms of sales, earnings, and profit margins, and all the other places where you can measure the financial performance of a company, has outstripped all of our competitors as best we can judge that. And in many cases we can judge that very accurately. We think we do a better job, and the numbers are starting to prove that we do."

Critical Thinking Questions

1. Continuous quality improvement processes, like the approach being used at Bernard, call for authority and power to be pushed down from the management to employee level. Why do you think this is an important part of continuous improvement?

2. Bernard president Pat Cunningham stated that all employees have access to every bit of financial data pertinent to the company's performance. What are the possible advantages of sharing these data? What are the possible disadvantages?

3. Jim Therrien, vice president of operations, said that he has learned to listen better to employees. What role do you think listening should play in leadership? What steps can you take to become a more effective listener in your life?

Experiential Exercises

12.1 Power and influence

Objective

To explore the nature of power and influence, and your attitudes toward different kinds of power and influence.

Instructions

Read the introductions, "A. Power" and "B. Influence," to the Power and Influence Worksheet, and complete those sections of the worksheet. Then read and complete "C. Power and Influence."

Power and influence worksheet

A. Power

A number of people have made statements about power and winning (e.g., P. T. Barnum, Mao Tse-tung, Leo Durocher, Lord Action, Vince Lombardi). Some of them are listed in the table that follows. Indicate how you feel about each of the statements by circling number 1 if you strongly disagree, number 5 if you strongly agree, and so on.

	Strongly Disagree	Disagree	Neutral	Agree	Strongly Agree
Winning is everything.	1	2	3	4	5
Nice guys finish last.	1	2	3	4	5
There can only be one winner.	1	2	3	4	5
There's a sucker born every minute.	1	2	3	4	5
You can't completely trust anyone.	1	2	3	4	5
All power rests at the end of the gun.	1	2	3	4	5
Power seekers are greedy and can't be trusted.	1	2	3	4	5
Power corrupts; absolute power corrupts absolutely.	1	2	3	4	5
You get as much power as you pay for.	1	2	3	4	5

B. Influence

During the past week or so you have come in contact with many people. Some have influenced you positively (turned you on), some negatively (turned you off). Try to recall recent experiences with employers, peers, teachers, parents, clergy, and the like who may have influenced you in some way. Then try to think about how and why they influenced you as they did.

1. On the following table, list the names of all those who influenced you during the past week or so according to the kind of power that person used. The same person's name may appear under more than one type of social power if that person used multiple power bases. Also, indicate whether the influence was positive (+) or negative (–).

Social power base	Names and whether (+) or (–)
Legitimate authority	______________________
Reward	______________________
Coercive	______________________
Referent	______________________
Expert	______________________

2. After examining your list, check (✓) the questions below.

	Yes	No
a. Was there one person who had + marks appearing under several social power bases?	_____	_____
b. Was there one person who had – marks appearing under several social power bases?	_____	_____
c. Did you find that most of the people with + marks tended to fall under the same power bases?	_____	_____
d. Did you find that most of the people with – marks tended to fall under the same power bases?	_____	_____

3. From your answers to the last two questions, list which social power bases you found to be positive (+) and which you found to be negative (–).

+	–
_____	_____
_____	_____
_____	_____
_____	_____
_____	_____

Do you think you personally prefer to use those power bases you listed under + when you try to influence people? Do you actually use them?

C. Power and influence

From the table in Part B, find the one person whom you think had the strongest positive influence on you (Person 1), and the one who had the strongest negative influence (Person 2). These are most likely the persons whose names appear most frequently.

In the following table, place a 1 on the line for each statement that best indicates how you think Person 1 would respond to that statement. Put a 2 on the line for each statement that reflects how you think Person 2 would respond to that item.

	Strongly Disagree	Disagree	Neutral	Agree	Strongly Agree
Winning is everything.	_____	_____	_____	_____	_____
Nice guys finish last.	_____	_____	_____	_____	_____
There can only be one winner.	_____	_____	_____	_____	_____
There's a sucker born every minute.	_____	_____	_____	_____	_____
You can't completely trust anyone.	_____	_____	_____	_____	_____
All power rests at the end of the gun.	_____	_____	_____	_____	_____
Power seekers are greedy and can't be trusted.	_____	_____	_____	_____	_____
Power corrupts; absolute power corrupts absolutely.	_____	_____	_____	_____	_____
You get as much power as you pay for.	_____	_____	_____	_____	_____

Now compare your responses in Part A to those in Part C. Do you more closely resemble Person 1 or Person 2? Do you prefer to use the kinds of power that person uses? Which kinds of power do you use most frequently? Which do you use least frequently? When do you feel you have the greatest power? When do you have the least power? How do these answers compare to what you found in Part B3?

Excerpted from Lawrence R. Jauch, Arthur G. Bedian, Sally A. Coltin, and William F. Glueck, *The Managerial Experience: Cases, Exercises, and Readings,* 4th ed.

12.2 Evaluating your leadership style

Objectives

1. To examine your personal style of leadership.
2. To study the nature of the leadership process.
3. To identify ways to improve or modify your leadership style.

Instructions

1. Working alone, complete and score the Leadership Style Survey.
2. In small groups, exchange scores, compute average scores, and develop responses to the discussion questions.
3. After the class reconvenes, group spokespersons present group findings.

Discussion Questions

1. In what ways did your experience or lack of experience influence your responses to the survey?
2. In what ways did student scores and student responses to survey test items agree? In what ways did they disagree?
3. What do you think accounts for differences in student leadership attitudes?
4. How can students make constructive use of the survey results?

Leadership style survey

This survey describes various aspects of leadership behavior. To measure your leadership style, respond to each statement according to the way you would act (or think you would act) if you were a work group leader.

	Always	Frequently	Occasionally	Seldom	Never
1. I would allow team members the freedom to do their jobs in their own way.	5	4	3	2	1
2. I would make important decisions on my own initiative without consulting the workers.	5	4	3	2	1
3. I would allow the team members to make their own decisions.	5	4	3	2	1
4. I would not try to socialize with the workers.	5	4	3	2	1
5. I would allow team members to do their jobs as they see fit.	5	4	3	2	1
6. I would consider myself to be the group's spokesperson.	5	4	3	2	1
7. I would be warm, friendly, and approachable.	5	4	3	2	1
8. I would be sure that the workers understand and follow all the rules and regulations.	5	4	3	2	1
9. I would demonstrate a real concern for the workers' welfare.	5	4	3	2	1

	Always	Frequently	Occasionally	Seldom	Never
10. I would be the one to decide what is to be done and how it is to be done.	5	4	3	2	1
11. I would delegate authority to the workers.	5	4	3	2	1
12. I would urge the workers to meet production quotas.	5	4	3	2	1
13. I would trust the workers to use good judgment in decision making.	5	4	3	2	1
14. I would assign specific tasks to specific people.	5	4	3	2	1
15. I would let the workers establish their own work pace.	5	4	3	2	1
16. I would not feel that I have to explain my decisions to workers.	5	4	3	2	1
17. I would try to make each worker feel that his or her contribution is important.	5	4	3	2	1
18. I would establish the work schedules.	5	4	3	2	1
19. I would encourage workers to get involved in setting work goals.	5	4	3	2	1
20. I would be action oriented and results oriented.	5	4	3	2	1
21. I would get the workers involved in making decisions.	5	4	3	2	1
22. I would outline needed changes and monitor action closely.	5	4	3	2	1
23. I would help the group achieve consensus on important changes.	5	4	3	2	1
24. I would supervise closely to ensure that standards are met.	5	4	3	2	1
25. I would consistently reinforce good work.	5	4	3	2	1
26. I would nip problems in the bud.	5	4	3	2	1
27. I would consult the group before making decisions.	5	4	3	2	1

Chapter Appendix

Classic contingency models of leadership

The chapter described some situational or contingency models of leadership; here are two more, presented here in the interest of conserving chapter space.

Fiedler's Contingency Model

Fiedler's contingency model of leadership effectiveness states that effectiveness depends on two factors: the personal style of the leader and the degree to which the situation gives the leader power, control, and influence over the situation.[71] Figure 12.A.1 illustrates the contingency model. The upper half of the figure shows the situational analysis, and the lower half indicates the appropriate style. In the upper portion, three questions are used to analyze the situation:

1. Are leader–member relations good or poor? (To what extent is the leader accepted and supported by group members?)

2. Is the task structured or unstructured? (To what extent do group members know what their goals are and how to accomplish them?)

3. Is the leader's position power strong or weak (high or low)? (To what extent does the leader have the authority to reward and punish?)

These three sequential questions create a decision tree in which a situation is classified into one of eight categories. The lower the category number, the more favorable the situation is for the leader; the higher the number, the less favorable the situation. Originally, Fiedler called this variable "situational favorableness" but now calls it "situational control." Situation 1 is the best: Relations are good, task structure is high, and power is high. In the least favorable situation (8), in which the leader has very little situational control, relations are poor, tasks lack structure, and the leader's power is weak.

Different situations dictate different leadership styles. Fiedler measured leadership styles with an instrument assessing the leader's *least preferred coworker* (LPC), that is, the attitude toward the follower the leader liked the least. This was considered an indication more generally of leaders' attitudes toward people. If a leader can single out the person she likes the least, but her attitude is not all that negative, she received a high score on

figure 12.A.1 Fiedler's analysis of situations in which the task- or relationship-motivated leader is more effective

Leader–member relations	Good				Poor			
Task structure	Structured		Unstructured		Structured		Unstructured	
Leader position power	High	Low	High	Low	High	Low	High	Low
	1	2	3	4	5	6	7	8
Favorable for leader → Unfavorable for leader								
Type of leader most effective in the solution	Task-motivated	Task-motivated	Task-motivated	Relationship-motivated	Relationship-motivated	Relationship-motivated	Relationship-motivated	Task-motivated

Source: D. Organ and T. Bateman, *Organizational Behavior,* 4th ed. (Burr Ridge, IL: Richard D. Irwin, 1990).

the LPC scale. Leaders with more negative attitudes toward others would receive low LPC scores.

Based on the LPC score, Fiedler considered two leadership styles. **Task-motivated leadership** places primary emphasis on completing the task and is more likely exhibited by leaders with low LPC scores. **Relationship-motivated leadership** emphasizes maintaining good interpersonal relationships and is more likely from high-LPC leaders. These leadership styles correspond to task performance and group maintenance leader behaviors, respectively.

The lower part of Figure 12.A.1 indicates which style is situationally appropriate. For situations 1, 2, 3, and 8, a task-motivated leadership style is more effective. For situations 4 through 7, relationship-motivated leadership is more appropriate.

Fiedler's theory was not always supported by research. It is better supported if three broad rather than eight specific levels of situational control are assumed: low, medium, and high. It was quite controversial in academic circles; among other arguable things, it assumed that leaders cannot change their styles but must be assigned to situations that suit their styles. However, the model has withstood the test of time and still receives attention. Most important, it initiated and continues to emphasize the importance of finding a fit between the situation and the leader's style.

Hersey and Blanchard's Situational Theory

Hersey and Blanchard developed an important situational model that added another factor the leader should take into account before deciding whether task performance or maintenance behaviors are more important. Originally called the *life cycle theory of leadership,* their **situational theory** highlights the maturity of the followers as the key situational factor.[72] **Job maturity** is the level of the follower's skills and technical knowledge relative to the task being performed; **psychological maturity** is the follower's self-confidence and self-respect. High-maturity followers have both the ability and the confidence to do a good job.

The theory proposes a simple, linear relationship between a follower's maturity and the degree of task performance behaviors a leader should use. The more mature the followers, the less the leader needs to organize and explain tasks. The required amount of maintenance behaviors is a bit more complex. As in Fiedler's model, the relationship is curvilinear: Maintenance behaviors are not important with followers of low or high levels of maturity but are important for followers of moderate maturity. For low-maturity followers, the emphasis should be on performance-related leadership; for moderate-maturity followers, performance leadership is somewhat less important and maintenance behaviors become more important; and for high-maturity followers, neither dimension of leadership behavior is important.

Little academic research has been done on this situational theory, but the model is extremely popular in management training seminars. Regardless of its scientific validity, Hersey and Blanchard's model provides a reminder that it is important to treat different people differently. Moreover, it suggests the importance of treating the same individual differently from time to time as he or she changes jobs or acquires more maturity in her or his particular job.[73]

Appendix key terms

Fiedler's contingency model of leadership effectiveness A situational approach to leadership postulating that effectiveness depends on the personal style of the leader and the degree to which the situation gives the leader power, control, and influence over the situation. p. 436

Hersey and Blanchard's situational theory A life cycle of leadership developed by Hersey and Blanchard postulating that a manager should consider an employee's psychological and job maturity before deciding whether task performance or maintenance behaviors are more important. p. 437

Job maturity The level of the employee's skills and technical knowledge relative to the task being performed. p. 437

Psychological maturity An employee's self-confidence and self-respect. p. 437

Relationship-motivated leadership Leadership that places primary emphasis on maintaining good interpersonal relationships. p. 437

Task-motivated leadership Leadership that places primary emphasis on completing a task, p. 437

Chapter Thirteen

Motivating for Performance

The worst mistake a boss can make is not to say well done.

—John Ashcroft

The reward of a thing well done is to have done it.

—Ralph Waldo Emerson

Chapter Outline

Learning Objectives

After studying Chapter 13, you will know:

1 The kinds of behaviors managers need to motivate in people.
2. How to set challenging, motivating goals.
3. How to reward good performance.
4. The key beliefs that affect people's motivation.
5. The ways in which people's individual needs affect their behavior.
6. How to create a motivating, empowering job.
7. How people assess fairness and respond to unfair treatment.
8. The causes and consequences of a satisfied workforce.

Setting the Stage

Motivation at Lincoln Electric

Harvard Business School publishes 35,000 cases worldwide. The case purchased most often is about Lincoln Electric Company of Cleveland. Lincoln Electric produces industrial electric motors and is the world's largest manufacturer of arc welding products.

The attraction of the case is Lincoln's success at motivating workers by tying pay to performance. All of its 2,300 workers—most of whom are factory workers, and many without college degrees—participate in the company's incentive plan. All but two share in the annual bonus—the president and the chair. The two top executives are paid based on a percentage of sales; if sales go down, they take the first pay cut.

A committee evaluates each job to determine a fair hourly base rate. Lincoln also has a piecework rate, with which workers earn money based on how much they produce. All jobs in the company have pay ranges (hourly or salary) so that individuals who perform at their highest capability can move up to the top of the range for their particular job.

Every six months, the CEO personally reviews 2,300 merit ratings. Everyone is rated in four performance categories: output, quality, dependability (ability to work without supervision), and cooperation and ideas. Over the 50-plus years in which the system has been in place, the average year-end bonus has been 95.5 percent of base. In other words, employees commonly double their annual income by virtue of the annual bonus.

Lincoln has been number one in its business worldwide for the entire life of the incentive system. The quality of its products is quite high. The company has never faced a strike. It has no debt. Lincoln offers Incentive Management Seminars, free of charge, as a service to industry.

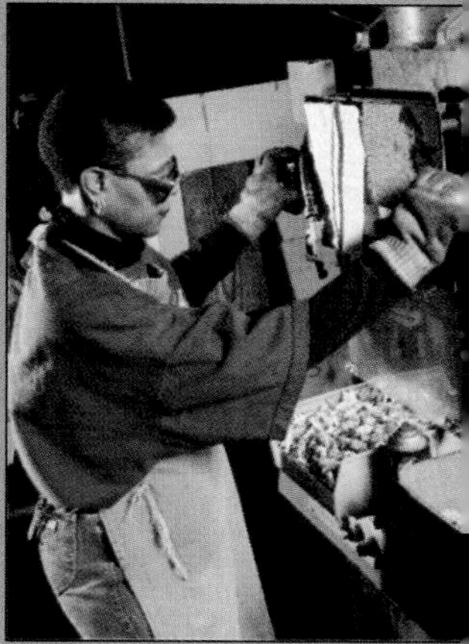

Lincoln Electric Company's merit pay plan allows most workers to double their base salary via their annual bonus.
[Courtesy of The Lincoln Electric Company, Cleveland, Ohio]

Lincoln Electric has outlasted giants like Westinghouse to dominate a fiercely competitive industry. Managers attribute their company's success to a philosophy: a strong belief in the power of unfettered capitalism. The incentive system supports the philosophy with measurable goals that provide evidence of progress. Moreover, the company attracts people who believe strongly in individual accountability and the power of pure meritocracy.

However, what works in the United States was unsuccessful overseas. And even in Ohio, a lot of new hires quit when they realize they don't fit in well with the Lincoln system. In one recent year, from 27,000 applicants the company selected 2,000 for hire. Within 90 days, over 1,000 quit. Overall, however, the turnover rate is low.

Sources: R. S. Sabo, "Linking Merit Pay with Performance at Lincoln Electric," in The Quest for Competitiveness, *ed. Y. K. Shetty and V. M. Buehler (New York: Quorum Books, 1991); C. Bartlett and S. Ghoshal, "Changing the Role of Top Management: Beyond Strategy to Purpose,"* Harvard Business Review, *November–December 1994, pp. 79–88; and R. M. Hodgetts, "A Conversation with Donald F. Hastings of The Lincoln Electric Company,"* Organizational Dynamics, *Winter 1997, pp. 68–74.*

Lincoln Electric has come up with a powerful solution to the age-old question tackled in this chapter: How can a manager motivate people to work hard and perform at their best levels? The case also points out that what motivates some people can "demotivate" others.

A sales manager in another company had a different approach to this question. Each month, the person with the worst sales performance took home a live goat for the weekend. The manager hoped the goat-of-the-month employee would be so embarrassed that he or she would work harder the next month to increase sales.[1]

This sales manager may get high marks for creativity. But if he is graded by results, as he grades his salespeople, he will fail. He may succeed in motivating a few of his people to increase sales, but others will be motivated to quit the company.

Motivating for performance

Understanding why people do the things they do on the job is not an easy task for the manager. *Predicting* their response to management's latest productivity program is harder yet. Fortunately, enough is known about motivation to give the thoughtful manager practical, effective techniques for increasing people's effort and performance.

motivation Forces that energize, direct, and sustain a person's efforts.

Motivation refers to forces that energize, direct, and sustain a person's efforts. All behavior, except involuntary reflexes like eye blinks (which have little to do with management), is motivated. A highly motivated person will work hard toward achieving performance goals. With adequate ability and understanding of the job, such a person will be highly productive.

To be effective motivators, managers must know what behaviors they want to motivate people to exhibit. Although productive people appear to do a seemingly limitless number of things, most of the important activities can be grouped into five general categories.[2] The company must motivate people to (1) *join the organization*; (2) *remain in the organization*; and (3) *come to work regularly*. Of course, they also want people to (4) *perform*—that is, once employees are at work, they should work hard to achieve high *output* (productivity) and high *quality*. Finally, managers want employees to (5) *exhibit good citizenship*. Good citizens of the organization are committed, satisfied employees who perform above and beyond the call of duty by doing extra things that can help the company. The importance of citizenship behaviors may be less obvious than productivity, but these behaviors help the organization function smoothly. They also make managers' lives easier.

Many ideas have been proposed to help managers motivate people to engage in these constructive behaviors. The most useful of these ideas are described in the following pages. We start with the most fundamental *processes* that influence the motivation of all people. These processes—described by goal setting, reinforcement, and expectancy theories—suggest basic and powerful actions for managers to take. Then we discuss the *content* of what people want and need from work, how individuals differ from one another, and how understanding people's needs leads to powerful prescriptions about designing motivating jobs and empowering people to perform at the highest possible levels. Finally, we discuss the most important beliefs and perceptions about fairness that people hold toward work, and the implications for managers.

Setting goals

Providing work-related goals for people is an extremely effective way to stimulate motivation. In fact, it is perhaps the most important, valid, and useful single approach to motivating performance. Therefore, we discuss it first.

goal-setting theory A motivation theory that states people have conscious goals that energize them and direct their thoughts and behaviors toward one end.

Goal-setting theory states that people have conscious goals that energize them and direct their thoughts and behaviors toward one end.[3] Thus, a person who wants to be a CPA has a goal that guides his or her selection of schools, courses, professional exam preparation, and job interview strategies. An individual whose goal is to become a self-employed entrepreneur will be motivated toward different, more personally appropriate actions.

Goals that motivate

What kinds of goals most effectively motivate people? How can managers set motivating goals for the people who report to them?

First, goals should be *acceptable* to employees. This means, among other things, that they should not conflict with people's personal values and that people have reasons to pursue the goals. Allowing people to participate in setting their work goals—as opposed to having the boss set goals for them—is often a great way to generate goals that people accept and pursue willingly.

Second, acceptable, maximally motivating goals should be *challenging but attainable.* In other words, they should be high enough to inspire better performance but not so high that people can never reach them. One team of consultants to an international corporation created more than 40 programs aimed at increasing quality. The company announced it did not expect significant quality improvement until the *fourth year* of the program. Such a goal obviously is not nearly demanding enough.[4]

Third, goals should be *specific, quantifiable,* and *measurable.* Ideal goals do not merely exhort employees to improve performance, start doing their best, increase productivity, or decrease the length of time that customers must wait to receive service. Goals should be more like Caterpillar Tractor's guaranteed parts delivery within 24 hours. Such deadlines, and measurable performance goals, are specific, quantifiable goals that employees are motivated to achieve.

Limitations of goal setting

Goal setting is an extraordinarily powerful management technique. But like anything else, even specific, challenging, attainable goals work better under some conditions than others. Individual performance goals can be dysfunctional if people work in a group and cooperation among team members is essential to team performance.[5] Individualized goals can create competition and reduce cooperation. If cooperation is essential, performance goals should be established *for the team.*

It is important that a single productivity goal not be established if there are other important dimensions of performance.[6] For instance, productivity goals will likely enhance productivity, but they may also cause employees to neglect other things like tackling new projects or developing creative solutions to job-related problems. The manager who wants to motivate creativity should establish creativity goals along with productivity goals. Even the prestigious Baldrige award for quality has been criticized as generating such zealous pursuit that companies focus single-mindedly on winning the award at the expense of other key elements of business success.[7]

Stretch goals

Many managers set goals that are simply not high enough; they do not make high performance demands on their people. They fail to recognize how much more motivation and performance they could generate if they communicated higher expectations.

By implementing stretch goals, Boeing cut the time needed to build an airplane from 18 to 8 months.
[Courtesy of The Boeing Company]

Top firms today set "stretch goals"–targets that are exceptionally demanding, and that some people would never even think of. But, impossible though they may seem to some, they are in fact attainable. Stretch goals represent a major shift away from mediocrity and toward tremendous achievement.

3M was famous for its amazing innovation prowess, consistently meeting its goal of generating 25 percent of revenues from new products introduced in the last five years. But then it surpassed itself again by increasing its goal, to 30 percent and four years. Boeing's stretch goals were to cut the cost of manufacturing an airplane 25 percent by 1998, and then it reduced the time needed to build one from 18 months to eight months. States Boeing's CEO, "We're doing things we didn't think were possible."

Some legendary business leaders drove themselves and their people via stretch goals. In the 1950s, when the label "Made in Japan" conveyed to Americans that the product was cheap junk, Sony's Akio Morita set out to change the world's perception of Japanese quality. At the time, he had fewer than 1,000 employees, with no significant overseas presence. Yet he succeeded. And in the United States, Sam Walton started out in 1945 by wanting to make his store in Newport the best variety store in Arkansas. Later, in 1977, he declared that Wal-Mart would double in size and become a $1 billion company within four years. Even in 1990, when Wal-Mart seemed to be everywhere, he set the target of doubling the number of stores and achieving sales volume of $125 billion. At that time, the largest retailer in the world had reached $30 billion.

Sources: J. Collins and J. Porras, *Built to Last.* (London: Century Business, 1996); R. H. Schaffer, "Demand Better Results—And Get Them," *Harvard Business Review,* March–April 1991, pp. 142–49; S. Tully, "Why to Go for Stretch Targets," *Fortune,* November 4, 1994, pp. 145–58; and K. Thompson, W. Hochwarter, and N. Mathys, "Stretch Targets: What Makes Them Effective?" *Academy of Management Executive* 11 (1997), pp. 48–60.

Reinforcing Performance

law of effect A theory formulated by Edward Thorndike in 1911 stating that

Goals are universal motivators. So are the processes of reinforcement described in this section. In 1911, psychologist Edward Thorndike formulated the **law of effect:** Behavior that is followed by positive consequences probably will be repeated.[8] This powerful law of behavior laid the foundation for countless investigations into the effects of the positive

behavior that is followed by positive consequences will likely be repeated.

reinforcers Positive consequences that motivate behavior.

organizational behavior modification (OB Mod) The application of reinforcement theory in organizational settings.

positive reinforcement Applying valued consequences that increase the likelihood that a person will repeat the behavior that led to it.

negative reinforcement Removing or withholding an undesirable consequence.

punishment Administering an aversive consequence.

extinction Withdrawing or failing to provide a reinforcing consequence.

consequences, called **reinforcers,** that motivate behavior. **Organizational behavior modification** attempts to influence people's behavior by systematically managing work conditions and the consequences of people's actions.

Four key consequences of behavior either encourage or discourage people's behavior (see Figure 13.1):

1. **Positive reinforcement**—applying a valued consequence that increases the likelihood that the person will repeat the behavior that led to it. Examples of positive reinforcers include compliments, letters of commendation, favorable performance evaluations, and pay raises. Equally important, *jobs* can be positively reinforcing. Performing well on interesting, challenging, or *enriched* jobs (discussed later in this chapter) is much more reinforcing, and therefore motivating, then performing well on jobs that are routine and monotonous.

2. **Negative reinforcement**—removing or withholding an undesirable consequence. For example, a manager takes an employee (or a school takes a student) off probation because of improved performance. A few years ago, Nordstrom, the prominent retailer, received a great deal of negative publicity about its overreliance on negative reinforcement as a motivational tool. Frequent threatening memos admonished people to achieve every one of their many performance goals: "If any of these areas are not met to our expectations, you will be terminated." Another memo reminded employees that calling in sick once every three months is "a lot" and enough to "question your dedication."[9] Negative reinforcement in these examples occurs when people perform well and avoid punishment.

3. **Punishment**—administering an aversive consequence. Examples include criticizing or shouting at an employee, assigning an unappealing task, and sending a worker home without pay. Negative reinforcement can involve the *threat* of punishment, but not delivering it when employees perform satisfactorily. Punishment is the actual delivery of the aversive consequence. Managers use punishment when they think it is warranted or when they believe others expect them to. When administering punishment, they usually concern themselves with following company policy and procedure, and with employees' emotions, perceptions of fairness, learning, and morale.[10]

4. **Extinction**—withdrawing or failing to provide a reinforcing consequence. When this occurs, motivation is reduced and the behavior is *extinguished,* or eliminated. Examples include not giving a compliment for a job well done, forgetting to say thanks for a favor, or setting impossible performance goals so that the person never experiences success.

The first two consequences, positive and negative reinforcement, are positive for the person receiving them: The person either gains something or avoids something negative. Therefore, the person who experiences these consequences will be motivated to behave in the ways that led to the reinforcement. The last two consequences, punishment and extinction, are negative outcomes for the person receiving them: Motivation to repeat the behavior that led to the undesirable results will be reduced.

figure 13.1
The consequences of behavior

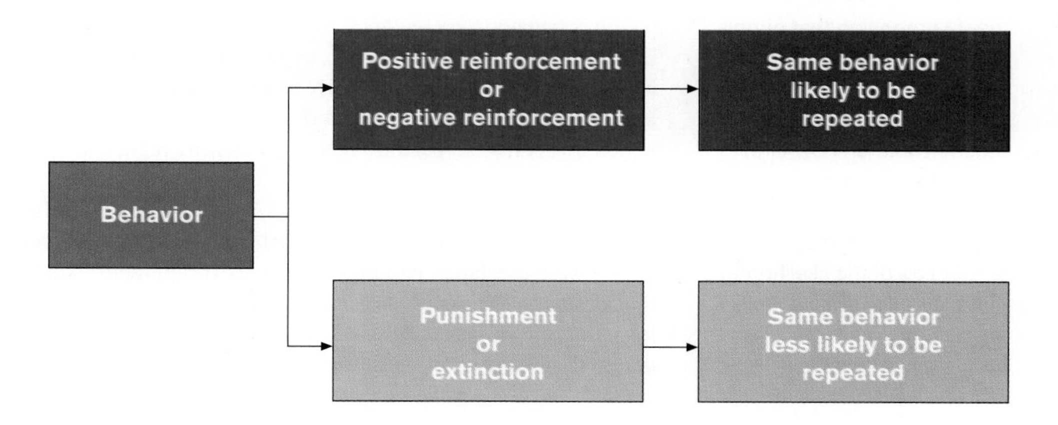

table 13.1
The greatest management principle in the world

"The things that get rewarded get done" is what one author calls The Greatest Management Principle in the World. With this in mind, Michael LeBoeuf offers 10 prescriptions for effectively motivating high performance. Companies, and individual managers, should reward the following:

1. *Solid solutions* instead of quick fixes.
2. *Risk taking* instead of risk avoiding.
3. *Applied creativity* instead of mindless conformity.
4. *Decisive action* instead of paralysis by analysis.
5. *Smart work* instead of busywork.
6. *Simplification* instead of needless complication.
7. *Quietly effective behavior* instead of squeaky wheels.
8. *Quality work* instead of fast work.
9. *Loyalty* instead of turnover.
10. *Working together* instead of working against.

Source: Reprinted by permission of The Putman Publishing Group from *The Greatest Management Principle in the World* by Michael LeBoeuf. Copyright © 1985 by Michael LeBoeuf.

Sometimes organizations and managers reinforce the wrong behaviors.[11] The company that bases performance reviews on short-term results is reinforcing a short-run perspective in decision making. At the same time, it is discouraging behaviors that will pay off only in the long run. Programs that punish employees for absenteeism beyond a certain limit may actually encourage them to be absent. People may use up all their allowable absences and fail to come to work regularly until they reach the point where their next absence will result in punishment. Managers must identify which kinds of behaviors they reinforce and which they discourage (see Table 13.1).

The creative use of reinforcers is particularly necessary during times when money is tight and companies cannot rely on pay raises to motivate people.[12] Promotions too are less available, as managers in today's flatter organizations can expect promotions much less often than in the past. Innovative managers therefore turn to nonmonetary rewards, including intellectual challenge, greater responsibility, autonomy, recognition, flexible benefits, and greater influence over decisions. These and other rewards for high-performing employees, when creatively devised and applied, can continue to motivate when pay and other traditional reinforcers are scarce.[13]

Performance-related beliefs

expectancy theory A theory proposing that people will behave based on their perceived likelihood that their effort will lead to a certain outcome and on how highly they value that outcome.

expectancy Employees' perception of the likelihood that their efforts will enable them to attain their performance goals.

Reinforcement theory describes the processes by which factors in the work environment affect people's behavior. Expectancy theory adds to that some of the cognitive processes that go on in people's heads. According to **expectancy theory,** the person's work *efforts* lead to some level of *performance.*[14] Then performance results in one or more *outcomes* for the person (see Figure 13.2). People develop two important beliefs linking these three events: expectancy, which links effort to performance, and instrumentality, which links performance to outcomes.

The effort-to-performance link The first belief, **expectancy,** is people's perceived likelihood that their efforts will enable them to successfully attain their performance goals. An expectancy can be high (up to 100 percent), such as when a student is confident that if she studies hard she can get a good grade on the final. An expectancy can also be low (down to a 0 percent likelihood), such as when a suitor is convinced that his dream date will never go out with him.

figure 13.2
Basic concepts of expectancy theory

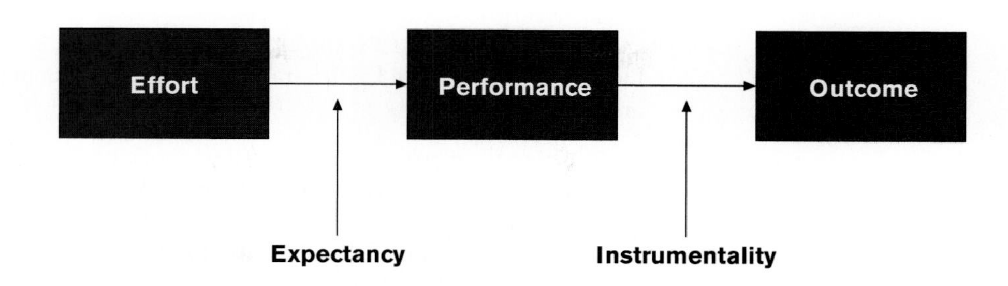

All else equal, high expectancies create higher motivation than do low expectancies. In the preceding examples, the student is more likely to study for the exam than the suitor is to pursue the dream date, even though both want their respective outcomes.

Expectancies can vary among individuals, even in the same situation. For example, a sales manager might initiate a competition in which the top salesperson wins a free trip to Hawaii. In such cases, the few top people, who have performed well in the past, will be more motivated by the contest than will the historically average and below-average performers. The top people will have higher expectancies—stronger beliefs that their efforts can help them turn in the top performance.

outcome A consequence a person receives for his or her performance.

The performance-to-outcome link The example about the sales contest illustrates how performance results in some kind of **outcome,** or consequence, for the person. Actually, it often results in several outcomes. For example, turning in the best sales performance could lead to (1) a competitive victory, (2) the free trip to Hawaii, (3) feelings of achievement, (4) recognition from the boss, (5) prestige throughout the company, and (6) resentment from other salespeople.

But how certain is it that performance will result in all those outcomes? Will winning the contest really lead to resentment? For that matter, will it really lead to increased prestige?

instrumentality The perceived likelihood that performance will be followed by a particular outcome.

valence The value an outcome holds for the person contemplating it.

These questions address the second key belief described by expectancy theory: instrumentality. **Instrumentality** is the perceived likelihood that performance will be followed by a particular outcome. Like expectancies, instrumentalities can be high (up to 100 percent) or low (approaching 0 percent).

Also, each outcome has an associated valence. **Valence** is the value the outcome holds for the person contemplating it. Valences can be positive (up to 1.0, in the theory's mathematical formulation), like the Hawaiian vacation, or negative (down to -1.0), like the other salespeople's resentment.

Impact on motivation For motivation to be high, expectancy, instrumentalities, and total valence of all outcomes must all be high. A person will not be highly motivated if any of the following conditions exist:

1. He believes he can't perform well enough to achieve the positive outcomes that he knows the company provides to good performers (high valence and high instrumentality but low expectancy).
2. He knows he can do the job, and is fairly certain what the ultimate outcomes will be (a promotion and a transfer). However, he doesn't want those outcomes or believes other, negative outcomes outweigh the positive (high expectancy and high instrumentality but low valence).
3. He knows he can do the job, and wants several important outcomes (a favorable performance review, a raise, and a promotion). But he believes that no matter how well he performs, the outcomes will not be forthcoming (high expectancy and positive valences but low instrumentality).

Managerial implications of expectancy theory Expectancy theory helps the manager zero in on key leverage points for influencing motivation. Three implications are crucial:

1. *Increase expectancies.* Provide a work environment that facilitates good performance, and set realistically attainable performance goals. Provide training, support, and encouragement so that people are confident they can perform at the levels expected of them. Recall from the last chapter that charismatic leaders excel at boosting their followers' confidence.
2. *Identify positively valent outcomes.* Understand what people want to get out of work. Think about what their jobs provide them and what is not, but could be, provided. Consider how people may differ in the valences they assign to outcomes. Know the need theories of motivation, described in the next section, and their implications for identifying important outcomes.
3. *Make performance instrumental toward positive outcomes.* Make sure that good performance is followed by personal recognition and praise, favorable performance reviews, pay increases, and other positive results. Also, make sure that working hard and doing things well will have as few negative results as possible. Finally, ensure that poor performance has fewer positive and more negative outcomes than good performance.

Understanding people's needs

So far we have focused on processes underlying motivation. The manager who appropriately applies goal-setting, reinforcement, and expectancy theories is creating essential motivating elements in the work environment. But characteristics of the person also affect motivation. The following *content theories* indicate the kinds of needs that people want to satisfy. People have different needs energizing and motivating them toward different goals and reinforcers. The extent to which and the ways in which a person's needs are met or not met at work affect his or her behavior on the job.

The most important content theories describing people's needs are Maslow's need hierarchy, ERG theory, and McClelland's needs.

Maslow's need hierarchy

need hierarchy A conception of human needs organizing needs into five major types, and postulating that people satisfy them one at a time from bottom to top.

Abraham Maslow organized five major types of human needs into a hierarchy, as shown in Figure 13.3[15] The **need hierarchy** illustrates Maslow's conception of people satisfying their needs in a specified order, from bottom to top. The needs, in ascending order, are

1. *Physiological* (food, water, sex, and shelter).
2. *Safety or security* (protection against threat and deprivation).
3. *Social* (friendship, affection, belonging, and love).
4. *Ego* (independence, achievement, freedom, status, recognition, and self-esteem).
5. *Self-actualization* (realizing one's full potential; becoming everything one is capable of being).

According to Maslow, people are motivated to satisfy the lower needs before they try to satisfy the higher needs. Also, once a need is satisfied it is no longer a powerful motivator. For example, labor unions negotiate for higher wages, benefits, safety standards, and job security. These bargaining issues relate directly to the satisfaction of Maslow's lower-level needs. Only after the physiological and safety needs are reasonably satisfied do the higher level needs—social, ego, and self-actualization—become dominant concerns.

Maslow's hierarchy, however, is a simplistic and not altogether accurate theory of human motivation.[16] For example, not everyone progresses through the five needs in hierarchical

figure 13.3
Maslow's need hierarchy

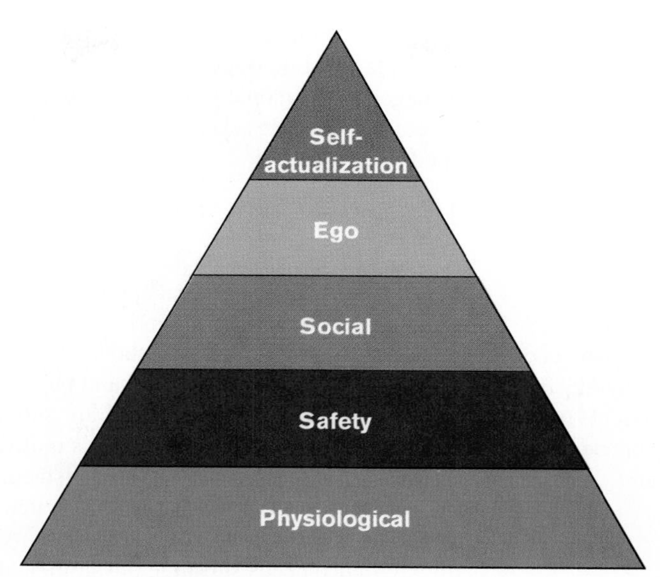

Source: D. Organ and T. Bateman, *Organizational Behavior* (Burr Ridge, IL: Richard D. Irwin, 1991).

order. But Maslow made three important contributions. First, he identified important need categories, which can help managers create effective positive reinforcers. Second, it is helpful to think of two general levels of needs, in which lower-level needs must be satisfied before higher-level needs become important. Third, Maslow sensitized managers to the importance of personal growth and self-actualization.

Self-actualization is the best-known concept arising from this theory. According to Maslow, the average person is only 10 percent self-actualized. In other words, most of us are living our lives and working at our jobs with a large untapped reservoir of potential. The implication is clear: Create a work environment that provides training, resources, autonomy, responsibilities, and challenging assignments. This type of organization culture gives people a chance to use their skills and abilities in creative ways and allows them to achieve more of their full potential.

So treat people not merely as a cost to be controlled but an asset to be developed. Many companies, including AT&T, Procter & Gamble, Du Pont, General Electric, Levi Strauss, and Coast Gas of Watsonville, California, are embarking on programs that provide personal growth experiences for their people.[17] Andersen Consulting's brochure promises that "after training with us, you could work for anyone, anywhere—or you could work for yourself."[18]

Andersen Consulting's brochure promises that "after training with us, you could work for anyone, anywhere–or you could work for yourself." *[John Abbott]*

Organizations gain by making full use of their human resources. Employees also gain by capitalizing on opportunities to meet their higher-order needs on the job. At Du Pont, managers set personal growth goals along with performance goals. "In the past," says one executive, "[people asked] what job am I getting next? Now, it's more, how can I be developed as a person?"[19]

ERG theory

A theory of human needs that is more advanced than Maslow's is Alderfer's ERG theory.[20] Maslow's theory has general applicability, but Alderfer aims his theory expressly at understanding people's needs at work.

ERG theory A human needs theory developed by Alderfer postulating that people have three basic sets of needs which can operate simultaneously.

ERG theory postulates three sets of needs: existence, relatedness, and growth. *Existence* needs are all material and physiological desires. *Relatedness* needs involve relationships with other people and are satisfied through the process of mutually sharing thoughts and feelings. *Growth* needs motivate people to productively or creatively change themselves or their environment. Satisfaction of the growth needs comes from fully utilizing personal capacities and developing new capacities.

What similarities do you see between Alderfer's and Maslow's needs? Roughly speaking, existence needs subsume physiological and security needs, relatedness needs are similar to social and esteem needs, and growth needs correspond to self-actualization.

ERG theory proposes that several different needs can be operating at once. Thus, whereas Maslow would say that self-actualization is important to people only after other sets of needs are satisfied, Alderfer maintains that people—particularly working people in our post-industrial society—can be motivated to satisfy both existence and growth needs at the same time.

Maslow's theory is better known to American managers than Alderfer's, but ERG theory has more scientific support.[21] Both have practical value in that they remind managers of the types of reinforcers or rewards that can be used to motivate people. Regardless of whether the manager prefers the Maslow or Alderfer version of the need hierarchy, he or she can motivate people by helping them satisfy their needs, and particularly by offering opportunities for self-actualization and growth.

McClelland's needs

David McClelland also identified a number of basic needs that guide people. The most important needs for managers, according to McClelland, are the needs for achievement, affiliation, and power.[22]

The need for *achievement* is characterized by a strong orientation toward accomplishment and an obsession with success and goal attainment. Most American managers and entrepreneurs have high levels of this need and like to see it in their employees.

The need for *affiliation* reflects a strong desire to be liked by other people. Individuals who have high levels of this need are more oriented toward getting along with others and may be less concerned with performing at high levels.

The need for *power* is a desire to influence or control other people. This need can be a negative force—termed *personalized power*—if it is expressed through the aggressive manipulation and exploitation of others. People high on the personalized-power need want power purely for the pursuit of their own goals. But the need for power also can be a positive motive—called *socialized power*—because it can be channeled toward the constructive improvement of organizations and societies.

Low need for affiliation and moderate to high need for power are associated with managerial success for both higher- and lower-level managers.[23] Recall from Chapter 12 that high power and achievement needs are traits that relate to effective leadership. One reason the need for affiliation is not important for management and leadership success is that people high on this need have difficulty making tough but necessary decisions that will make some people unhappy.

Need theories: International perspectives

How do the need theories apply abroad?[24] Whereas managers in the United States care most strongly about achievement, esteem, and self-actualization, managers in Greece and Japan are motivated more by security. Social needs are most important in Sweden, Norway, and Denmark. "Doing your own thing"—the phrase from the 1960s that describes an American culture oriented toward self-actualization—is not even translatable into Chinese. "Achievement" too is difficult to translate into most other languages. Researchers in France, Japan, and Sweden would have been unlikely to even conceive of McClelland's achievement motive, because people of those countries are more group than individual oriented.

Clearly, achievement, growth, and self-actualization are profoundly important in the United States (and in other Anglo-American countries like Canada and Great Britain). But these needs are not universally important. Every manager must remember that need hierarchies vary from country to country and that people may not be motivated by the same needs.

Designing motivating jobs

extrinsic reinforcers Reinforces given to a person by the boss, the company, or some other person.

intrinsic reward Reward a worker derives directly from performing the job itself.

Our earlier discussion of goal setting, reinforcement, and expectancy theories focused on **extrinsic reinforcers**—rewards given to high-performing people by the boss, the company, or some other person. In this section, we will discuss a different type of reinforcer. An **intrinsic reward** is reward the person derives directly from performing the job itself. An interesting project, an intriguing subject that is fun to study, a completed sale, and the discovery of the perfect solution to a difficult problem all can give people the feeling that they have done something well. This is the essence of the motivation that comes from intrinsic rewards.

Intrinsic rewards are essential to the motivation underlying creativity.[25] A challenging problem, a chance to create something new, and work that is exciting in and of itself can provide intrinsic motivation that inspires people to devote time and energy to the task. So do managers who allow people some freedom to pursue the tasks that interest them most. The opposite situations result in routine, habitual behaviors, which interfere with creativity.[26] A study in manufacturing facilities found that employees initiated more applications for patents, made more novel and useful suggestions, and were rated by their managers as more creative when their jobs were challenging and their managers did not control their activities closely.[27] On the other hand, some jobs and organizations create environments that quash creativity and motivation.[28]

The classic example of a demotivating job is the highly specialized assembly line job; each worker performs one boring operation before passing the work along to the next worker. Such specialization, or the "mechanistic" approach to job design, was the prevailing practice through most of the 20th century.[29]

But jobs that are too simple and routine result in employee dissatisfaction, absenteeism, and turnover. Increasingly, jobs are being designed in the following ways to increase intrinsic rewards and therefore motivation.

Job rotation, enlargement, and enrichment

job rotation Changing from one routine task to another to alleviate boredom.

With **job rotation,** workers who spend all their time in routine tasks can instead move from one job to another. Rather than dishing out the pasta in a cafeteria line all day, a person might work the pasta, then the salads, then the vegetables, drinks, or desserts. Job rotation is intended to alleviate boredom by giving people different things to do.

As you may guess, however, the person may just be changing from one boring job to another. But job rotation can benefit everyone when done properly, with career interests and the input of workers and managers in mind. At G.S.I. Transcomm Data Systems of Pittsburgh, people often voice their preferences and rotate laterally to new assignments.

Examples include an operations manager who moved into sales management, a programmer who moved into service for long-time customers, and a receptionist who moved into sales.[30] The result of the rotation policy often is a reenergized worker who stays with the company.

job enlargement Giving people additional tasks at the same time to alleviate boredom.

Job enlargement is similar to job rotation in that people are given different tasks to do. But whereas job rotation involves doing one set of tasks at one time and leaving those tasks for a different set at a different time, job enlargement means that the worker is given additional tasks at the same time. Thus, an assembly worker's job is enlarged if he or she is given two tasks rather than one to perform. In a recent study of job enlargement in a financial services organization, enlarged jobs led to higher job satisfaction, better error detection by clerks, and improved customer service.[31]

job enrichment Changing a task to make it inherently more rewarding, motivating, and satisfying.

With job enlargement, the person's additional tasks are at the same level of responsibility. More fundamental changes occur when jobs are enriched. **Job enrichment** means that jobs are restructured or redesigned by adding higher levels of responsibility. This includes giving people not only more tasks but higher-level ones, such as when decisions are delegated downward and authority is decentralized. Efforts to redesign jobs by enriching them are now common in American industry. Herzberg's two-factor theory was the first approach to job enrichment, followed by the Hackman and Oldham model.

Herzberg's two-factor theory

two-factor theory Herzberg's theory describing two factors affecting people's work motivation and satisfaction.

hygiene factors Characteristics of the workplace, such as company policies, working conditions, pay, and supervision, that make a job more satisfying.

motivators Factors that make a job more motivating, such as additional job responsibilities, opportunities for personal growth and recognition, and feelings of achievement.

Frederick Herzberg's **two-factor theory** distinguished between two broad categories of factors that affect people working on their jobs.[32] The first category, **hygiene factors,** are *characteristics of the workplace:* company policies, working conditions, pay, co-workers, supervision, and so forth. These factors can make people unhappy if they are poorly managed. If they are well-managed, and viewed as positive by employees, the employees will no longer be dissatisfied. However, no matter how good these factors are, they will not make people truly satisfied or motivated to do a good job.

According to Herzberg, the key to true job satisfaction and motivation to perform lies in the second category: the motivators. The **motivators** design the *job itself,* that is, what people *do* at work. Motivators are the nature of the work itself, the actual job responsibilities, opportunity for personal growth and recognition, and the feelings of achievement the job provides. When these factors are present, jobs are presumed to be both satisfying and motivating for most workers.

Herzberg's theory has been criticized by many scholars, and for that reason we will not go into more detail about his original theory. But Herzberg was a pioneer in the area of job design and still is a respected name among American managers. Furthermore, even if the specifics of his theory do not hold up to scientific scrutiny, he made several very important contributions. First, Herzberg's theory highlights the important distinction between extrinsic rewards (from hygiene factors) and intrinsic rewards (from motivators). Second, it reminds managers not to count solely on extrinsic rewards to motivate workers but to focus on intrinsic rewards as well. Third, it set the stage for later theories, such as the Hackman and Oldham model, that explain more precisely how managers can enrich people's jobs.

Motivator, hygiene, or distractor?

In the early 1900s, cigar makers paid people to read stories to employees working boring jobs. In the textile industry during the same period, managers allowed kittens to play on the floor, also to help workers fight boredom.

In the 1990s, bored employees wear Walkmans. People who wear them say doing so helps them get through a dull work day by keeping their minds off stress factors and making the time go faster. They also say the music—or the soaps—are not a distraction and have no effect on their job performance.

Some employers prohibit the Walkmans, maintaining they interfere with concentration and communication. But others see benefits. A Banc One executive sees people developing rhythmic work patterns, and believes the Walkmans improve concentration and quality. A study of assembly-line workers in a medical-equipment factory found that headphones had no impact on job performance, and that people wearing them reported higher job satisfaction.

Other people bored at work spend time in chatrooms, engage in other nonwork-related Internet activities, and play computer games. At a nuclear power plant, employees became hooked to the multi-user game Doom. The information technology manager claimed that safety wasn't compromised directly, but the Doom files are huge and can slow down the PC network. The manager, interviewed for a magazine article, requested anonymity.

Some employees do these things during work, some during lunch, some while on the telephone. PG&E believes that perhaps 60 to 70 percent of Web site visits by its employees are unrelated to business. Many companies are cracking down. Kraft Foods installed a system preventing employees from visiting World Wide Web sites unrelated to their jobs, the chief information officer saying, "We're here for business purposes, not for individual entertainment." Meanwhile, employees everywhere are finding ways to resist management's attempts to monitor and control. Don's Boss Page on the Web offers features like "Stealth Surfing: secret tips and tricks from the pros on how to look busy at work while you're cruising the Internet."

Some managers claim that these activities rob the company of productivity, others claim no effect, and still others maintain that people need a break once in a while. Many executives engage in the same activities, whereas some executives insist on firing anyone caught doing these things when they are supposed to be working.

What do you think? What do these activities have to do with job design, motivation, and job satisfaction? If you were a manager, how would you handle policy on this issue, and what would you do with people engaging in these activities?

Source: C. Powell, "When Workers Wear Walkmans on the Job," *The Wall Street Journal,* July 11, 1994, pp. B1, B8; J. Stuller, "Games Workers Play," *Across the Board,* July–August 1997, pp. 16–22; and C. Harmon, "Goofing Off at Work: First You Log on," *International Herald Tribune,* September 23, 1997, pp. 1, 10.

The Hackman and Oldham model of job design

Following Herzberg's work, Hackman and Oldham proposed a more complete model of job design.[33] Figure 13.4 illustrates their model. As you can see, well-designed jobs lead to high motivation, high-quality performance, high satisfaction, and low absenteeism and turnover. These outcomes occur when people experience three critical psychological states: (1) They believe they are doing something meaningful because their work is important to other people; (2) they feel personally responsible for how the work turns out; and (3) they learn how well they performed their jobs.

These psychological states occur when people are working on enriched jobs, that is, jobs that offer the following five core job dimensions:

1. *Skill variety*—different job activities involving several skills and talents. For example, at Ashton Photo in Salem, Oregon, employees decide what skills they need and grade themselves on their performance. Rewards are also based on ability to teach others new skills.[34]
2. *Task identity*—the completion of a whole, identifiable piece of work. People at Prospect Associates of Rockville, Maryland, market their ideas, and create new

figure 13.4
The Hackman and Oldham model of job enrichment

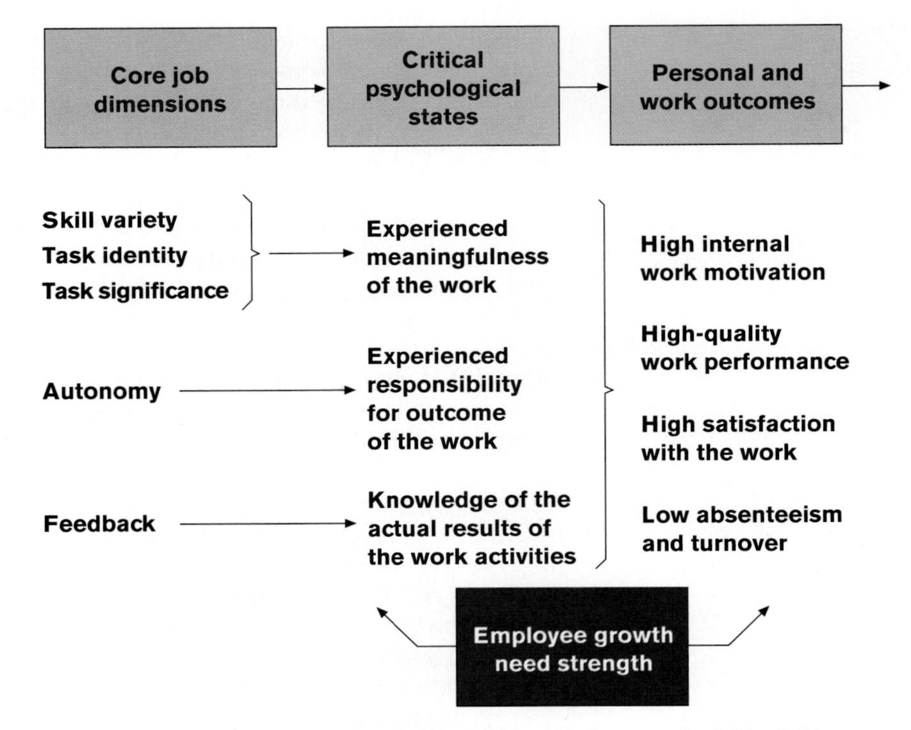

Source: From "A New Strategy for Job Enrichment" by J. Richard Hackman, et. al., *California Management Review*. Copyright © 1975 by the Regents of the University of California. Reprinted from the *California Management Review,* vol. 17, no. 4. By permission of The Regents.

business.[35] At State Farm Insurance, agents are independent contractors who sell and service State Farm products exclusively. They have built and invested in their own businesses. Agent retention and productivity are far better than industry norms.[36]

3. *Task significance*—an important, positive impact on the lives of others. At Giro Sports Design, manufacturer of bicycle helmets, employees know their product saves lives.[37] Odwall is a maker of fruit and vegetable juices; its employees are

Task identity is the completion of a whole, identifiable piece of work. At State Farm Insurance, agents are independent contractors who sell and service only State Farm products. Agent retention and productivity exceed industry norms.
[Courtesy of State Farm Insurance Companies]

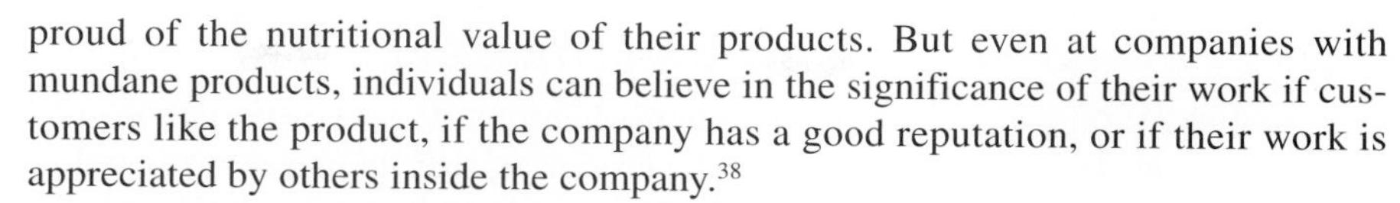

proud of the nutritional value of their products. But even at companies with mundane products, individuals can believe in the significance of their work if customers like the product, if the company has a good reputation, or if their work is appreciated by others inside the company.[38]

4. *Autonomy*—independence and discretion in making decisions. At Action Instruments of San Diego, employees are urged to "make it happen": discover problems and solve them.[39] At Childress Buick in Phoenix, lot salespeople can finalize deals; they don't have to check with the sales manager.[40] In a research hospital, a department administrator told her people to do the kinds of research they wanted as long as it was within budget (and legal!). With no other guidelines—that is, complete autonomy—productivity increased sixfold in a year.[41]
5. *Feedback*—information about job performance. Many companies post charts or provide computerized data indicating productivity, number of rejects, and other data. Aspect Communications, in San Jose, ties everyone's bonuses to measures of customer satisfaction.[42] Employees pay constant attention to the customer feedback on their performance. At Great Plains Software, programmers are expected to spend time with customers.[43] This way, they learn what customers think of their products, and what kind of impact they are having.

The most effective job enrichment increases all five core dimensions.

growth need strength The degree to which individuals want personal and psychological development.

A person's growth need strength will help determine just how effective a job enrichment program might be. **Growth need strength** is the degree to which individuals want personal and psychological development. Job enrichment would be more successful for people with high growth need strength. But very few people will respond negatively.[44]

Opel, General Motors' German subsidiary, operates a plant in Eisenach, which is one of the most productive plants among all European automobile manufacturers.[45] Opel—in revolutionizing its approach to combatting the world's highest labor costs—considers employee motivation a key to its excellence and has built into its operations the characteristics of motivating tasks. Employees have full responsibility over large segments of the production line including quality control, ordering supplies, and equipment maintenance; make decisions about work procedures; and can try innovative approaches to assembly, work flow, materials, and so on. Any employee can stop the production line whenever he deems it necessary. People seek advice and help from one another and give frank feedback to one another. Tapping people's ingenuity, listening to ideas, and allowing them some freedom and control over their work has generated incredible increases in productivity.[46]

The success of Opel's (GM) Eisenback facility is largely due to employee job enrichment.
[Courtesy of General Motors Corporation/GM Media Archives]

Empowerment

empowerment The process of sharing power with employees, thereby enhancing their confidence in their ability to perform their jobs and their belief that they are influential contributors to the organization.

Today one frequently hears managers talk about "empowering" their people. **Empowerment** is the process of sharing power with employees, thereby enhancing their confidence in their ability to perform their jobs and their belief that they are influential contributors to the organization. Empowerment results in changes in employees' beliefs—from feeling powerless to believing strongly in their own personal effectiveness. The result is that people take more initiative and persevere in achieving their goals and their leader's vision even in the face of obstacles.[47]

Specifically, empowerment encourages the following beliefs among employees:[48] First, they perceive *meaning* in their work, meaning that their job fits their values and attitudes. Second, they feel *competent,* or capable of performing their jobs with skill. Third, they have a sense of *self-determination,* of having some choice over the tasks, methods, and pace of their work. Fourth, they have an *impact*—that is, they have some influence over important strategic, administrative, or operating decisions or outcomes on the job. Table 13.2 shows some quotes comparing times when people felt empowered with times that they felt powerless.

table 13.2 Managers and empowerment

Powerless times	Powerful times
• I had no input into a hiring decision of someone who was to report directly to me. I didn't even get to speak to the candidate. • People picked me apart while I was making a presentation, and the champion of the project didn't support me. • I was told I couldn't ask questions because I lacked the appropriate educational level. • They treated us like mushrooms. They fed us and kept us in the dark. • I interviewed job candidates and then got no feedback on the results. • I worked extremely hard–long hours and late nights–on an urgent project, and then my manager took full credit for it. • My suggestions, whether good or bad, were either not solicited or, worse, ignored. • The project was reassigned without my knowledge or input. • I couldn't get answers to my questions.	• I was able to make a large financial decision on my own. I got to write a check for $200,000 without being questioned. • I was asked to take on a project for which I didn't have the experience. I was told, "I know you'll be successful." • After having received a memo that said, "Cut travel," I made my case about why it was necessary to travel for business reasons; and I was told to go ahead. • I was five years old, and my dad said, "You'll make a great mechanic one day." He planted the seed. Now I'm an engineer. • I wanted to put a new program into effect, but we'd reached the funding limit so my project was rejected. I went to a meeting with the president and asked him to take another look at the project. He did, turned to the VP, and said, "Fund it." • I got lots of helpful and useful suggestions without being criticized. • All the financial data were shared with me.

Source: J. Kouzes and B. Posner, *The Leadership Challenge,* (2e), San Francisco: Jossey-Bass, 1995, p. 183.

To foster empowerment, management must create an environment in which everyone feels they have real influence over performance standards and business effectiveness within their areas of responsibility.[49] An empowering work environment provides people with *information* neccessary for them to perform at their best, *knowledge* about how to use the information and how to do their work, *power* to make decisions that give them control over their work, and the *rewards* they deserve and earn for the contributions they make.[50] Such an environment reduces costs, because fewer people are needed to supervise, monitor, and coordinate. It improves quality and service, because high performance is inspired at the source, the people who do the work. It also allows quick action, because people on the spot see problems, solutions, and opportunities for innovation on which they are "empowered" to act.

What actions can leaders take to empower their people and generate these positive outcomes? Empowering people means allowing them to participate in decision making, expressing confidence in their ability to perform at high levels, designing their jobs so they have greater freedom, setting meaningful and challenging goals, applauding outstanding performance, and encouraging people to take personal responsibility for their work. It also means providing people access to information, and to other resources, and providing social and sometimes emotional support.[51] More specific actions include increasing signature authority at all levels; reducing the number of rules and approval steps; assigning nonroutine jobs; allowing independent judgment, flexibility, and creativity; defining jobs more broadly as projects rather than tasks; and providing more freedom of access to resources and people throughout the organization (and outside the organization!).[52]

Significantly, empowerment does not mean allowing people to decide trivial things like what color to paint the lunchroom. For empowerment to make a difference, people must have an impact on things about which they care, such as quality and productivity.[53] Companies including Lord Corporation in Dayton, Ohio (which produces engine mounts for aircraft), Herman Miller (the Michigan-based furniture manufacturer), Johnsonville Foods, and Goodyear have all been highly successful and received great acclaim for their empowerment programs.[54]

You should not be surprised when empowerment causes some problems, at least in the short term. This is the case with virtually any change, including changes for the better. People might make mistakes at first, especially until they have had adequate training. And since more training is needed, costs are higher. Also, because people acquire new skills and make greater contributions, they may demand higher wages. But if they are well-trained and truly empowered, they will deserve them—and both they and the company will benefit.

Achieving fairness

Ultimately, one of the most important issues in motivation surrounds how people view their contributions to the organization and what they receive from the organization. Ideally, they will view their relationship with their employer as a well-balanced, mutually beneficial exchange. As people work and realize the outcomes or consequences of their actions, they develop beliefs about how just those outcomes are. Basically, they assess how fairly the organization treats them.

The starting point for understanding how people interpret their contributions and outcomes is equity theory.[55] **Equity theory** proposes that when people assess how fairly they are treated, they consider two key factors: outcomes and inputs. *Outcomes,* as in expectancy theory, refer to the various things the person receives on the job: recognition, pay, benefits, satisfaction, security, job assignments, punishments, and so forth. *Inputs* refer to the contributions the person makes to the organization: effort, time, talent, performance, extra commitment, good citizenship, and so forth. People have a general expectation that the outcomes they receive will reflect, or be proportionate to, the inputs they provide—a fair day's pay (and other outcomes) for a fair day's work (broadly defined by how people view all their contributions).

equity theory A theory stating that people assess how fairly they have been treated according to two key factors: outcomes and inputs.

But this comparison of outcomes to inputs is not the whole story. People also pay attention to the outcomes and inputs others receive. At salary review time, for example, most people—from executives on down—try to pick up clues that will tell them who got the high raises. As described in the following section, they compare ratios, restore equity if necessary, and derive more or less satisfaction based on how fairly they believe they have been treated.

Assessing equity

Equity theory suggests that people compare the ratio of their own outcomes to inputs against the outcome-to-input ratio of some comparison person. The comparison person can be a fellow student, a co-worker, a boss, or an average industry pay scale. Stated more succinctly, people compare

$$\text{Their own } \frac{\text{Outcomes}}{\text{Inputs}} \text{ versus Others' } \frac{\text{Outcomes}}{\text{Inputs}}$$

If the ratios are equivalent, people believe the relationship is equitable, or fair. Equity causes people to be satisfied with their treatment. But the person who believes his or her ratio is lower than another's will feel inequitably treated. Inequity causes dissatisfaction and leads to an attempt to restore balance to the relationship.

There are many examples of inequity and the negative feelings it creates. As a student, perhaps you have been in the following situation. You stay up all night and get a C on the exam. Meanwhile another student studies a couple of hours, goes out for the rest of the evening, gets a good night's sleep, and gets a B on the exam. You perceive your inputs (time spent studying) as much greater than the other student's, but your outcomes are lower. You are displeased at the unfairness of the situation.

In business, the same thing happens with pay raises. One manager puts in 60-hour weeks, has a degree from a prestigious university, and believes she is destined for the top. When her archrival—whom she perceives as less deserving ("she never comes into the office on weekends, and all she does when she is here is butter up the boss")—gets the higher raise or the promotion, she experiences severe feelings of inequity.

Assessments of equity are not made objectively. They are subjective perceptions or beliefs. In the preceding example, the person who got the higher raise probably felt she deserved it. Even if she admits she doesn't put in long workweeks, she may convince herself she doesn't need to because she's so talented. The student who got the higher grade may believe it was a fair, equitable result because (1) she kept up all semester, while the other student did not, and (2) she's smart (ability and experience, not just effort, can be seen as inputs).

Restoring equity

People who feel inequitably treated and dissatisfied are motivated to do something to restore equity. They have a number of options which they carry out by actually doing something to change the ratios, or by reevaluating the situation and deciding it is equitable after all.

The equity equation shown earlier indicates a person's options for restoring equity. People who feel inequitably treated can *reduce their inputs* by giving less effort, performing at lower levels, or even quitting ("Well, if that's the way things work around here, there's no way I'm going to work that hard [or stick around]"). Or they can attempt to *increase their outcomes* ("My boss [or teacher] is going to hear about this. I deserve more; there must be some way I can get more").

Other ways of restoring equity focus on changing the other person's ratio. A person can *decrease others' outcomes.* For example, an employee may sabotage work to create problems for his company or his boss. A person can also change her perceptions of inputs or outcomes ("That promotion isn't as great a deal as he thinks. The pay is not that much better, and the headaches will be unbelievable"). It is also possible to *increase others' inputs,* particularly by changing perceptions ("The more I think about it, the more he deserved it. He's worked hard all year, he's competent, and it's about time he got a break").

Thus, a person can restore equity in a number of ways by behaviorally or perceptually changing inputs and outcomes.

Fair process

Inevitably, managers make decisions that have outcomes more favorable for some than for others. Those with favorable outcomes will be pleased; those with worse outcomes, all else equal, will be more displeased. But managers desiring to put salve on the wounds—say, of people they like or respect or want to keep and motivate—still can take actions to reduce the dissatisfaction. The key is for people to believe that managers provide **procedural justice**—using fair process in decision making and making sure others know that the process was as fair as possible.

procedural justice Using fair process in decision making and making sure others know that the process was as fair as possible.

Even if people believe that their *outcome* was inequitable, and unfair, they are more likely to view justice as having been served if the *process* was fair. For example, someone receiving a low pay raise, or someone overlooked for promotion or for a juicy assignment, might question the fairness of the decision. If the manager explains how she went about making the decision, and the logic behind the decision, and if the decision was made in an unbiased way, it is more likely to be understood and accepted. If not fully accepted, at least the employee will have had a fair hearing, a chance to voice complaints, ask questions, and receive in return the time and good faith effort from the boss. And most compelling of all, if employees make decisions together with the manager, and attention is paid to fair process, in the end an individual may not get that for which he or she hoped, but will at least understand that the procedures used were as fair as possible.

For example, at an elevator plant in the United States, an army of consultants arrived one day, unexplained and annoying.[56] The rumor mill kicked in; employees thought the plant was to be shut down, or that some of them would be laid off. Three months later, management unveiled its new plan, involving a new method of manufacturing based on teams. When employees sat in silence, management and the consultants (who finally were introduced to employees at this meeting) were pleased at the presumably positive reaction. But as the changes were implemented, management did not adequately answer questions about the purpose of the changes, employees resisted, conflicts arose, and the formerly popular plant manager lost the trust of his people. Costs skyrocketed, and quality plummeted.

Concerned, management called for an employee survey. Employees were skeptical that the survey results would lead to any positive changes and were worried that management would be angry that people had voiced their honest opinions. But management reacted by saying, "We were wrong, we screwed up, we didn't use the right process." They went on to share with employees critical business information, the limited options available, and the dire consequences if the company didn't change. Employees saw the dilemma, came to view the business problem as theirs as well as management's, but were scared that some of them would lose their jobs. Management retained the right to lay people off if business conditions grew worse, but also made several promises: no layoffs as a result of changes made; cross-training programs for employees; no replacements of departing people until conditions improved; a chance for employees to serve in new roles, as consultants on quality issues; and sharing of sales and cost data on a regular basis.

The news was bad, but people understood it and began to share responsibility with management. This was the beginning of the restoration of trust and commitment, and of steady improvements in performance.[57]

From the Pages of BusinessWeek

An Uncertain Future

Federal-Mogul Corporation, a collection of union-dominated auto-parts operations, had targeted Fel-Pro Inc. for takeover. Fel-Pro management had decided it was too small to do the things it wanted to do, so it entered negotiations with 12 suitors. Federal-Mogul emerged as the preferred winner, but Fel-Pro's Co-Chairman, Kenneth Lehman, laid out a final ultimatum: A guarantee that the company-owned summer camp for employees' children be continued. Federal-Mogul's chairman, Richard Snell, worried about what to do if some of his other 13,000 employees might want the same thing, Snell responded, "Go figure it out."

Fel-Pro also offered profit-sharing for all employees, above-market wages, an on-site fitness center, and scholarships for college tuition for employees' children. The company had created a work environment fostering teamwork, growing profits, margins at 40 percent above industry norms, frequent suggestions for operational improvements from people at all levels, and low employee turnover.

Can this family-friendly, high-performance environment continue now that Fel-Pro is not family-owned? Snell addressed Fel-Pro workers after the acquisition and won warm applause when he said he believed that Fel-Pro's benefits contributed to its success, and praised the company's values. And he committed to maintaining current programs for the short term, but made no long-term guarantees other than to say that Federal-Mogul might draw on Fel-Pro's ideas as it restructures.

People at Fel-Pro are uncertain about the future. One said, "It's like losing an uncle. It's been like family here. Now I don't know." Elliot Lehman, Kenneth's father and co-chairman emeritus, said after Snells's meeting with the workers, "I thought Snell did a great job. But a wonderful guy like Snell has 14 layers of bureaucracy beneath him. So, I'm praying."

Discussion Questions

1. What do you think are the equity and fairness issues here?
2. What decisions should be made, and what processes should be used?

Source: R.A. Melcher, "Warm and fuzzy, meet rough and tumble." *Business Week,* January 26, 1998, p. 36.

Job satisfaction

If people feel fairly treated from the outcomes they receive, or the processes used, they will be satisfied. A satisfied worker is not necessarily more productive than a dissatisfied one; sometimes people are happy with their jobs because they don't have to work hard! But job dissatisfaction, aggregated across many individuals, creates a workforce that is more likely to exhibit (1) higher turnover; (2) higher absenteeism; (3) lower corporate citizenship; (4) more grievances and lawsuits; (5) strikes; (6) stealing, sabotage, and vandalism; and (7) poorer mental and physical health (which can mean higher job stress, higher insurance costs, and more lawsuits).[58] All of these consequences of dissatisfaction, either directly or indirectly, are costly to organizations.

Quality of work life

quality of work life (QWL) programs Programs designed to create a workplace that enhances employee well-being.

Quality of work life (QWL) programs create a workplace that enhances employee well-being and satisfaction. The general goal of QWL programs is to satisfy the full range of employee needs. QWL has eight categories.[59]

1. Adequate and fair compensation.
2. A safe and healthy environment.

3. Jobs that develop human capacities.
4. A chance for personal growth and security.
5. A social environment that fosters personal identity, freedom from prejudice, a sense of community, and upward mobility.
6. Constitutionalism, or the rights of personal privacy, dissent, and due process.
7. A work role that minimizes infringement on personal leisure and family needs.
8. Socially responsible organizational actions.

Organizations differ drastically in their attention to QWL. Critics claim that QWL programs don't necessarily inspire employees to work harder if the company does not tie rewards directly to individual performance. Advocates of QWL claim that it improves organizational effectiveness and productivity. The term *productivity,* as applied by QWL programs, means much more than each person's quantity of work output.[60] It also includes turnover, absenteeism, accidents, theft, sabotage, creativity, innovation, and especially the quality of work.

Psychological contracts

psychological contract A set of perceptions of what employees owe their employers, and what their employers owe them.

The relationship between individuals and employing organizations typically is formalized by a written contract. But in employees' minds there also exists a **psychological contract**—a set of perceptions of what they owe their employers, and what their employers owe them.[61] This contract, whether it is seen as being upheld or violated—and whether the parties trust one another or not—has important implications for employee satisfaction and motivation and the effectiveness of the organization.

In today's world, the relationship between employer and employee is not the stable, secure one of decades past. It is more accurately described as "no guarantees." People who perceive their psychological contract as secure and comfortable are likely to be surprised and angered when business conditions and company policies change. Extending the equity theory ratio, people compare[62]

$$\frac{\text{Benefits provided by the organization}}{\text{Benefits promised by the organization}} \quad \text{versus} \quad \frac{\text{Contributions provided by the employee}}{\text{Contributions promised by the employee}}$$

To strengthen market share and boost competitiveness, Xerox employees were asked to become more involved in responding to customers. *[Courtesy of Xerox Corporation]*

Historically, in many companies this relationship has been stable and predictable. Now, mergers and layoffs and other disruptions have thrown asunder the "old deal." As a McGraw-Hill executive put it, "The 'used-to-be's' must give way to the realities of 'What is and what will be.'"[64] The fundamental "used-to-be" of traditionally managed organizations was that employees were expected to be loyal and employers would provide secure employment. Today, the implicit contract goes something like this:[65] If people stay, do their own job plus someone else's (who has been downsized), and do additional things like participating in task forces, the company will try to provide a job (if it can), provide gestures that it cares, and keep providing more or less the same pay (with periodic small increases). The likely result of this not-very-satisfying arrangement: uninspired people and a business trying to survive. This may sound like a cynical view, but a lot of people would agree with it.

But a better deal is possible, for both employers and employees.[66] You could work for a company that provides the following deal: If you develop the skills we need, apply them in ways that help the company succeed, and behave consistently with our values, then we will provide for you a challenging work environment, support for your development, and full, fair rewards for your contributions. The result of such a "contract" is much more likely to be a mutually beneficial, high-performing, successful organization.

Ideally now, all parties will understand and believe that the psychological contract must be a dynamic relationship characterized by an active, ongoing renegotiation requiring flexibility from all parties.[63] Some companies, like Hewlett Packard and Cummins Engine, have introduced changes in employment conditions successfully due to good treatment of and relationships with employees. These companies and others have been successful by involving people in the process, explaining, and making expectations clear and agreeable.[67] When Xerox lost market share to the Japanese and asked for greater employee involvement to increase customer responsiveness and competitiveness, CEO David Kearns made it clear to all the need for everyone to change. When Ameritech began downsizing through early retirement, it allowed employees to choose, within one year, the date of their retirement. Donnelley, in dramatically changing its corporate culture, asked veteran employees to act like new recruits, submitting resumes, going through interviews, going through new employee orientation, and signing a new employment contract stressing teamwork, innovation, and customer service. These are good examples of mutual adaptability to the demands of the new business world, made workable by an emphasis on fair process and agreeable psychological contracts.[68]

Key terms

Empowerment, p. 454
Equity theory, p. 455
ERG theory, p. 448
Expectancy, p. 444
Expectancy theory, p. 444
Extinction, p. 443
Extrinsic reinforcers, p. 449
Goal-setting theory, p. 441
Growth need strength. p. 453
Hygiene factors, p. 450
Instrumentality, p. 445
Intrinsic reward, p. 449
Job enlargement, p. 450
Job enrichment, p. 450
Job rotation, p. 449
Law of effect, p. 442
Motivation, p. 440
Motivators, p. 450
Need hierarchy, p. 446
Negative reinforcement, p. 443
Organizational behavior modification (OB Mod), p. 443
Outcome, p. 445
Positive reinforcement, p. 443
Procedural justice, p. 457
Psychological contract, p. 459
Punishment, p. 443
Quality of work life program (QWL), p. 458
Reinforcers, p. 443
Herzberg's two-factor theory, p. 450
Valence, p. 445

Summary of learning objectives

Now that you have studied Chapter 13, you should know:

The kinds of behaviors managers need to motivate in people.

All important work behaviors are motivated. Managers need to motivate employees to join and remain in the organization and to exhibit high attendance, job performance, and citizenship.

How to set challenging, motivating goals.

Goal setting is a powerful motivator. Specific, quantifiable, and challenging but attainable goals motivate high effort and performance. Goal setting can be used for teams as well as for individuals. Care should be taken that single goals are not set to the exclusion of other important dimensions of performance.

How to reward good performance.

Organizational behavior modification programs influence behavior at work by arranging consequences for people's actions. Most programs use positive reinforcement as a consequence, but other important consequences are negative reinforcement, punishment, and extinction. Care must be taken to reinforce appropriate, not inappropriate, behavior. Innovative managers use a wide variety of rewards for good performance.

The key beliefs that affect people's motivation.

Expectancy theory describes three important work-related beliefs. That is, motivation is a function of people's (1) expectancies, or effort–performance links; (2) instrumentalities, or performance-outcome links; and (3) the valences people attach to the outcomes of performance. Equity theory also addresses important beliefs about fairness.

The ways in which people's individual needs affect their behavior.

Maslow's five most important needs are physiological, safety, social, ego, and self-actualization. Alderfer's ERG theory describes three sets of needs: existence, relatedness, and growth. McClelland emphasizes three different needs: achievement, affiliation, and power. Because people are inclined to satisfy their various needs, these theories help to suggest to managers the kinds of rewards that motivate people.

How to create a motivating, empowering job.

One approach to satisfying needs and motivating people is to create intrinsic motivation through the improved design of jobs. Jobs can be enriched by building in more skill variety, task identity, task significance, autonomy, and feedback. Empowerment is the most recent development in the creation of motivating jobs. Empowerment includes the perceptions of meaning, competence, self-determination, and impact, and comes from an environment in which people have necessary information, knowledge, power, and rewards.

How people assess fairness and respond to unfair treatment.

Equity theory states that people compare their inputs and outcomes to the inputs and outcomes of others. Perceptions of equity (fair treatment) are satisfying; feelings of inequity (unfairness) are dissatisfying and motivate people to change their behavior or their perceptions to restore equity. In addition to fairness of outcomes, as described in equity theory, fairness is also appraised and managed through processes of procedural justice.

The causes and consequences of a satisfied work force.

A satisfied workforce has many advantages for the firm, including lower absenteeism and turnover; fewer grievances, lawsuits, and strikes; lower health costs; and higher-quality products. One general approach to generating higher satisfaction for people is to implement a quality of work life program. QWL seeks to provide a safe and healthy environment, opportunity for personal growth, a positive social environment, fair treatment, and other improvements in people's work life. These and other benefits from the organization, exchanged for contributions from employees, create a psychological contract. Over time, how the psychological contract is upheld or violated, and changed unfairly or fairly, will influence people's satisfaction and motivation.

Discussion questions

1. Referring to "Setting the Stage," how would you like to work in a system like Lincoln Electric's, and why?

2. Why do you think it is so difficult for managers to empower their people?

3. Think of a job you hold currently or have held in the past. How would you describe the psychological contract? How does (did) this affect your attitudes and behaviors on the job?

4. If a famous executive or sports figure were to give a passionate motivational speech, trying to persuade people to work harder, what do you think the impact would be? Why?

5. Give some examples of situations in which you wanted to do a great job but were prevented from doing so. What was the impact on you, and what would this suggest to you in your efforts to motivate other people to perform?

6. Discuss the similarities and differences between setting goals for other people and setting goals for yourself. When does goal-setting fail, and when does it succeed?

7. Identify four examples of people inadvertently reinforcing the wrong behaviors or punishing or extinguishing good behaviors.

8. Assess yourself on McClelland's three needs. On which need are you highest, and on which are you lowest? What are the implications for you as a manager?

9. Identify a job you have worked and appraise it on Hackman and Oldham's five core job dimensions. Also describe the degree to which it made you feel empowered. As a class, choose one job and discuss together how it could be changed to be more motivating and empowering.

10. Using expectancy theory, analyze how you have made and will make personal choices, such as a major area of study, a career to pursue, or job interviews to seek.

11. Describe a time that you felt unfairly treated and why. How did you respond to the inequity? What other options might you have had?

12. Provide examples of how outcomes perceived as unfair can decrease motivation. Then discuss how procedural justice, or fair process, can help overcome the negative effects.

13. What are the implications for your career of, and how will you prepare for, the psychological contracts described at the end of the chapter?

Concluding Case

Motivating with merit pay

You learned in Chapter 10 about merit pay—the practice of tying pay raises to performance. And you read about a well-known example, Lincoln Electric, at the beginning of this chapter. Let's examine in more depth the impact of merit pay on motivation and performance.

In principle, merit pay should "work"—it should reinforce high performance, extinguish low performance, increase instrumentalities, satisfy needs, achieve equity, and so forth. In practice, most observers contend that it does not motivate. And yet, companies keep using it.

The reasons it doesn't work have to do with implementation, and practices that violate the principles. Often, performance measures are not valid or accurate. The budget is usually small, without much flexibility. Managers are reluctant to give small raises that are insulting or lower than the cost-of-living increase. And they don't want to make enemies, or be accused of favoring their friends. The result is that the pay raise for the highest-rated performers is not different enough from the average or the lowest-rated to motivate people to strive for high, or better, performance the next time around.

At the top of the organization, more companies have moved to a system in which CEO pay is tied to performance. This is in reaction to media attacks and public outrage about exorbitant pay for executives of failing companies, and the "golden parachutes" awarded to poor-performing executives who are forced to leave. It is also a response to the Clinton administration's $1 million compensation cap on CEO pay deductions unless tied to company performance. Now corporate compensation committees are getting more and more creative in finding ways to tie CEO pay to company performance, and promise more and more millions in stock options. With stock prices soaring, CEO paychecks are astronomical and the media and public continue the outcry. In the United States, CEOs make far more money proportionately, compared to employees, than in other countries.

Critics compare stratospheric CEO pay to the multimillions paid to baseball players and other professional athletes. Is this the right system? Is it really necessary? A San Diego–based pay critic says, "If all these incentives really worked, what that means is that these CEOs are fundamentally lazy slobs who need these incentives to do a good job." Another says, "These guys are already working as hard as they can . . . They can't work harder for more money. They give their best. They have a lot of pride." An economist at the University of Southern California states that CEOs are obsessed with their compensation: Whereas "it's hard to get [them] focused on a $200 million acquisition . . . if you want to make a change in their pay packages, they're all ears." Monetary incentives, he says, are the central motivator of CEO behavior. But will $4 million in potential stock motivate more than $2 million?

Questions

1. Do you believe, philosophically, in merit pay? Why or why not?

2. Can merit pay be implemented so it is more effective? How?

3. What do you think of the effectiveness of high compensation levels for CEOs in the United States? Analyze in terms of the perspectives on motivation described in the chapter.

4. If you were an employee of a major corporation, what would be your opinion of high CEO pay? Would it affect your own motivation? Why and how, or why not?

Is money a motivator? It can be, but frequently isn't. Why? *[Gary Kaemmer/The Image Bank]*

Sources: M. Budman, "Is There Merit in Merit Pay?" *Across the Board,* June 1997, pp. 33–36; and M. Budman, "Does It Really Pay to Pay for Performance?" *Across the Board,* March 1997, pp. 16–23. ●

Video Case

Employee motivation at Tellabs, Inc.

It's important to understand the reasons why effective managers must be concerned with employee motivation. After identifying some of the factors contributing to motivation, this video looks at how Tellabs, Inc., has successfully applied motivation theory.

Tellabs is based in the Chicago area, but is internationally known for its telecommunications products and services. However, recently the company gained fame when its stock increased 1,683 percent over a five-year period, making Tellabs the best performing stock at that time on the New York Stock Exchange, the American Stock Exchange, and Nasdaq. Tellabs was founded in 1975 by a group of engineers brainstorming at a kitchen table, and grew from 20 employees with annual sales of $312,000 to 2,600 employees with annual sales of $494 million in 1994. Tellabs currently designs, manufactures, markets, and services voice and data transport and network access systems.

One of the principal reasons for Tellabs' remarkable success has been its ability to motivate its workforce. In simple terms, employee motivation refers to an employee's willingness to perform in his or her job. Effective managers must be concerned with motivating employees toward common goals that will improve the success of the company. At Tellabs, a motivated workforce has enhanced the quality of its products and services.

Tellabs' manager of quality, Joe Taylor, explains what's behind the company's motivated workers: "In the past 10 years, we've found that to improve our quality we had to invest in our employees through training programs. Specifically, they have the tools and the resources now to make a difference within our processes in the factory and provide us with process improvements."

A motivated workforce contributes to increased quality in goods and services, greater efficiency in work processes, and improved customer service. Grace Pastiak said, "When I look at the improvements that Tellabs has made since implementing just-in-time and Total Quality Commitment, by far the biggest gain has been exciting employees to do their best and giving them the opportunity to implement their own ideas."

At its core, motivation results from an individual's desire to satisfy personal needs or goals. Every person has a set of needs or goals that influences his or her behavior. Abraham Maslow postulated that needs can be placed in a hierarchy and that as each need level in the hierarchy is satisfied, the person will concentrate on meeting needs at the next level.

Frederick Herzberg conducted a study in the 1960s that concluded that factors pertaining to the work itself, such as achievement, recognition, and responsibility, tended to actually motivate employees. Other factors, such as supervision, pay, and company policies, might improve job satisfaction, but not necessarily employee motivation.

A third approach to motivation, developed by Douglas McGregor, involves two opposing theories about the nature of human behavior. Theory X holds that some employees are lazy or unwilling to work unless motivated by negative factors such as threats and constant supervision. Theory Y holds that employees want to work and do a good job and are motivated best by incentives, responsibility, and ownership of their work.

Maslow's hierarchy, Herzberg's factors, and McGregor's theories suggest that it is in a company's best interest to offer employees adequate rewards and to appeal to their pride of workmanship. At Tellabs, many employees say that the entrepreneurial atmosphere nurtured by managers makes them feel good about themselves. So Tellabs clearly takes a Theory Y approach.

Effective managers help create a work environment that encourages, supports, and sustains improvement in work performance. At Tellabs, managers have implemented job rotation systems and a cadre of high performance teams to help enrich jobs and create an innovative working environment. Another innovation at Tellabs to ensure a high level of employee motivation is high performance teams.

Some companies may use a combination of motivation theories. In 1992, Tellabs presented its corporate goals, known as Strategic Initiatives, to its employees. The corporate mission statement emphasized the company's goals for quality, customer satisfaction, profits, growth, its people, and its corporate integrity.

Tellabs' total compensation plan includes an Employee Stock Option Plan and retirement investments, such as 401(k). Also employees receive an annual bonus based on the company's productivity.

At Tellabs, employee motivation and performance are enhanced by an atmosphere in which employees are openly told they are valued and trusted. Managers encourage calculated risk taking and innovation. They empower workers through cross-functional teams so that they are able to identify problems and develop effective solutions.

Tellabs' Career Development System trains internal candidates for key management positions, while its competitive compensation plan shares the wealth, contributes to employee satisfaction, and encourages peak performance.

Critical Thinking Questions

1. McGregor's Theory X and Theory Y have totally different views of the typical worker. Which of the two theories do you think managers should adopt? Explain. Describe how adopting Theory X would affect a manager's behavior toward employees. Do the same for Theory Y.

2. What are some of the potential pitfalls of using employee empowerment as a motivational device in the workplace?

3. Herzberg's theory says workplace factors lead to employee motivation. What are some workplace factors not mentioned in the video that could affect employee motivation?

Experiential Exercises

13.1 Job satisfaction and job performance: A debate exercise

Objective

The objective of this exercise is to explore the relationship between job satisfaction and job performance. At the conclusion of the exercise, each student should have developed her or his own opinion regarding the relationship between these two variables.

Instructions

This in-class exercise takes the form of a nontraditional four-way debate. Students will be divided by the instructor into four debating teams, each having four or five members. The remaining students will then be divided into judging teams consisting of three to six members each. The debate itself will focus on the relationship between job satisfaction and job performance

Debating Positions

Each debating team will be assigned one of the following four positions:

1. There is a direct positive relationship between job satisfaction and job performance. The higher an employee's job satisfaction, the higher will be her or his job performance and vice versa.
2. Job satisfaction is related to job performance in only the following way: A slight amount of job dissatisfaction is a prerequisite to high job performance. Thus, employees who are somewhat dissatisfied with their jobs will have higher productivity than those who are very dissatisfied or those who are completely satisfied with their jobs.
3. Job performance ultimately causes an employee's job satisfaction (high or low). If employees achieve high job performance, they will receive high rewards and this, in turn, will result in high job satisfaction. If employees perform poorly on their jobs, resulting rewards will be low as will the employees' job satisfaction.
4. This position will be provided by the instructor.

The debate consists of two rounds. In round one each team first states its position and then tries to convince the judges, through the use of examples and other evidence, that its position is fully legitimate. During round two of the debate, each debating team counters the position of the other teams, that is, team one criticizes teams two, three, and four; team two criticizes teams one, three, and four; and so on. The group being countered may not rebut the criticisms made by the other teams during the debate unless specifically told to do so by the instructor. They just simply listen.

Round two, the last round of the debate, ends when team four has finished criticizing the positions of the other three teams. All debaters will be given a 10-minute recess between rounds one and two in order to finalize their criticisms of the other teams.

The judging teams' role during the debate is to "search for the truth," not select a "winner." They are to listen to all of the different arguments presented during the debate and, after it has ended, discuss the different positions among themselves until a consensus is reached regarding the "true" relationship between job satisfaction and job performance. There are no constraints placed on the judges; they are free to disagree with all of the positions presented, to agree with parts of two or more of them, and so forth. After their deliberations are complete (usually about 10 minutes), each judging team presents its conclusions to the class. Judges should hold preliminary discussions of the four positions during the intermission between rounds one and two.

Source: R. Bruce McAfee and Paul J. Champagne, *Job Satisfaction & Job Performance: A Debate Exercise* (St. Paul, MN: West Publishing, 1987), pp. 56-57. Reprinted by permission.

13.2 What do students want from their jobs?

Objectives

1. To demonstrate individual differences in job expectations.
2. To illustrate individual differences in need and motivational structures.
3. To examine and compare intrinsic rewards.

Instructions

1. Working alone, complete the What I Want from My Job Survey.
2. In small groups, compare and analyze differences in the survey results and prepare group responses to the discussion questions.
3. After the class reconvenes, group spokespersons present group findings.

Discussion Questions

1. Which job rewards are extrinsic, and which are intrinsic?
2. Were more response differences found in intrinsic or in extrinsic rewards?
3. In what ways do you think blue-collar workers' responses would differ from those of college students?

What I want from my job survey

Determine what you want from a job by circling the level of importance of each of the following job rewards.

	Very Important	Moderately Important	Indifferent	Moderately Unimportant	Very Unimportant
1. Advancement opportunities	5	4	3	2	1
2. Appropriate company policies	5	4	3	2	1
3. Authority	5	4	3	2	1
4. Autonomy and freedom on the job	5	4	3	2	1
5. Challenging work	5	4	3	2	1
6. Company reputation	5	4	3	2	1
7. Fringe benefits	5	4	3	2	1
8. Geographic location	5	4	3	2	1
9. Good co-workers	5	4	3	2	1
10. Good supervision	5	4	3	2	1
11. Job security	5	4	3	2	1
12. Money	5	4	3	2	1
13. Opportunity for self-development	5	4	3	2	1
14. Pleasant office and working conditions	5	4	3	2	1
15. Performance feedback	5	4	3	2	1
16. Prestigious job title	5	4	3	2	1

	Very Important	Moderately Important	Indifferent	Moderately Unimportant	Very Unimportant
17. Recognition for doing a good job	5	4	3	2	1
18. Responsibility	5	4	3	2	1
19. Sense of achievement	5	4	3	2	1
20. Training programs	5	4	3	2	1
21. Type of work	5	4	3	2	1
22. Working with people	5	4	3	2	1

Chapter Fourteen
Managing Teams

No one can whistle a symphony. It takes an orchestra to play it.

—Halford E. Luccock

Chapter Outline

Learning Objectives

After studying Chapter 14, you will know:

1. How teams contribute to your organization's effectiveness.
2. What makes the new team environment different from the old.
3. How groups become teams.
4. Why groups sometimes fail.
5. How to build an effective team.
6. How to manage your team's relationships with other teams.
7. How to manage conflict.

Setting the Stage

Great Teamwork

Thermos bottles and lunch boxes were not enough; Thermos needed a great new product, and CEO Monte Peterson hoped to create one in the $1-billion-a-year barbecue grill market. Peterson created a project team to invent a product that would meet all of people's cookout needs. He selected six middle managers from different functions including engineering, manufacturing, marketing, and finance. He emphasized his commitment to the project and the importance of the project to the entire corporation. The team began by spending a month traveling the country to find out what people really wanted in their grills. They visited families, met with focus groups, and videotaped cookouts. They learned the importance to consumers of appearance, safety, and the environment. They also learned that consumers hated electric grills because they don't provide a cookout taste, but also that they hated messy charcoal. Ultimately, the team defined its product as a new grill that looked like a piece of furniture, did not require charcoal fluid, was safe enough to use in condos and apartment buildings, and cooked food that tasted good. While engineering worked on the technology, marketing worked on differentiating the new product, and design and manufacturing worked together on the design. The result was a completely new type of electric grill that gave food that all-important cookout taste. The product is a huge hit, growth is way up, and the company's functional bureaucracy is gone. Thermos is now using flexible, multidisciplinary teams in all its product lines.

Opel Eisenach, one of the best auto plants in Europe (described in the previous chapter), operates with about 200 six- to eight-person teams. Each team, or manufacturing "cell," has full responsibility for the work within the cell. Teams have decision-making authority and are responsible for quality and faultless workmanship. Flexibility is key. Each team member is trained to handle every work station in the cell. Team members also are exchanged temporarily between teams, further enhancing flexibility. Everyone comes to understand the entire production system. This helps in problem solving, productivity, and morale. Recall from the previous chapter that employee motivation was the cornerstone of the plant's success. The team concept may be the cornerstone of motivation. Manfred Kaiser, a *Betriebsrat* (worker's council) member, says, "Teamwork is a good thing and creates family ties. It integrates outsiders and ultimately leads to a harmonious work unit" [p. 83].

This Thermos team created a new type of outdoor grill that was so successful the company now uses teams in all of its product lines.
[© James Schnepf]

Disney Animation, both in its beginning and now, provides another example of what great teams can do. In 1934, Snow White and the Seven Dwarfs was an amazing technical achievement, a collaborative effort of brilliantly talented people, driven by a vision in which they believed and about which they cared deeply. Under Walt Disney's leadership, each individual found the right niche, performance standards demanded perfection, and people had the creative freedom to contribute as they knew best ("Don't look to me for the answers," he would say, "All I want you to use me for is approval."). They developed one brilliant product after another. Unfortunately, by the mid-1980s, the company had lost all that, with the low-water mark being the release of *The Black Cauldron,* arguably the worst film ever made. Fortunately, when Michael Eisner became CEO he and his executive team battled to save the feature-animation department. They reorganized the department into project teams, working on several films simultaneously, instead of having everyone working on the same film. The project teams are inspired to compete intramurally against one another, and are competing successfully against the standards set by the great products of Disney's illustrious past.

Sources: B. Dumaine, "Payoff from the New Management," Fortune, *December 13, 1993, pp. 103–10; A. Haasen, "Opel Eisenach GMBH—Creating a High-Productivity Workplace,"* Organizational Dynamics, *Spring 1996, pp. 80–85; and W. Bennis,* Organizing Genius; *(Reading, MA: Addison-Wesley, 1997).*

The 1990s have witnessed great excitement in the business community about the potential of work teams to dramatically change and improve the ways companies do business. For example, in the Thermos case opening Setting the Stage, a group of people from different functions became a team that was so successful in meeting its charge that it paved the way for a complete overhaul of the organization's structure. More generally, almost all middle-sized and large companies use teams to produce goods and services, to manage projects, and to make decisions and run the company.[1] *Fortune* hailed well-designed teams as potentially "the productivity breakthrough of the 1990s."[2] Stated the CEO of Texas Instruments, "No matter what your business, these teams are the wave of the future."[3]

For you, this has two vital implications. First, you *will* be working in and perhaps managing teams. Second, the *ability* to work in and lead teams is valuable to your employer and important to your career.

The contributions of teams

It is no wonder that team-based approaches to work are generating such excitement. Used appropriately, teams can be powerfully effective as a:

- *Building block for organization structure.* Organizations like Semco and Kollmorgen, manufacturer of printed circuits and electro-optic devices, are structured entirely around teams. A team-oriented structure is also in place at Kyocera Corporation, which was voted the best-managed company in Japan.
- *Force for productivity.* Shenandoah Life Insurance Company credited its new team organization with a 50 percent increase in the handling of applications and customer service requests, with fewer people.[4]

- *Force for quality.* Quality rose 50 percent in a Northern Telecom facility, and Federal Express reduced billing errors and lost packages by 13 percent. Boeing's engineering teams built its new 777 passenger jet with far fewer design errors than in earlier programs,[5] and for the first time in Boeing's history parts from different suppliers needed very little reworking. As a result, Boeing received the fastest flight certification ever for a new commercial aircraft.[6]

- *Force for cost reduction.* Honeywell's teams saved over $11 million after reducing production times and shipping over 99 percent of orders on time.[7] Boeing management claims that it could not have developed the 777 without cross-functional teams; it would have been prohibitively expensive.[8]

- *Force for speed.* 3M, Chrysler, and many other companies are using teams to create new products quicker. Teams at Bell Atlantic are trying to make the company a high-speed force on the information highway.[9] Lenders have cut home mortgage improvement times from weeks to hours, and life insurance companies have cut time to issue new policies from six weeks to one day.[10]
- *Force for change.* At Bell Atlantic Corporation, a formerly monopolistic bureaucracy became more entrepreneurial in part through the creation of client service groups (CSGs).[11] At KPMG Netherlands, a strategic integration team of 12 partners, with 100 other professionals divided into 14 task forces, led strategic and cultural changes by studying future trends and scenarios, defining core competencies, and dealing with organizational challenges.[12]

- *Force for innovation.* The auto industry relies on project teams to develop new vehicles, with Chrysler leading the way in the United States and Ford achieving great success with its Taurus project.[13] At 3M, work teams turned around one division by tripling the number of new products.[14] 3M's innovative success stories are numerous and legendary, emerging through the use of teams that are small entrepreneurial businesses within the larger corporation.

Benefits of groups

Before discussing how to develop such high-performance teams, let us talk briefly about groups more generally. Groups form because they are useful. In organizations, groups serve numerous functions (see Table 14.1). Some of these functions benefit the organization directly; others benefit primarily the group's members.[15]

The organization benefits because groups have greater *total resources* (skills, talents, information, energy) than individuals do. Therefore, they can perform jobs that can't be done by individuals working alone. They also have a greater *diversity of resources,* which enables groups to perform complex tasks. Also, groups can aid decision making, as you

table 14.1
Functions served by groups in organizations

For the organization	For the individual
1. Accomplish tasks that could not be done by individuals working alone.	1. Aid in learning about the organization and its environment.
2. Bring multiple skills and talents to bear on complex tasks.	2. Aid in learning about oneself.
3. Provide a vehicle for decision making that permits multiple and conflicting views to be aired and considered.	3. Provide help in gaining new skills.
4. Provide an efficient means for organizational control of individual behavior.	4. Obtain valued rewards that are not accessible through individual initiative.
5. Facilitate changes in organizational policies or procedures.	5. Directly satisfy important personal needs, especially needs for social acceptance.
6. Increase organizational stability by transmitting shared beliefs and values to new members.	

Source: D. Nadler, J. R. Hackman, and E. E. Lawler III, *Managing Organizational Behavior* (Boston: Little, Brown, 1979), p. 102.

learned in Chapter 3. They help socialize new members, control individuals' behavior, and facilitate organizational performance, innovation, and change.

Groups also provide many benefits for their members. The group is a very useful learning mechanism. Members learn about the company and themselves, and they acquire new skills and performance strategies. The group can satisfy important personal needs, such as affiliation and esteem. Other needs are met as group members receive tangible organizational rewards that they could not have achieved working alone.

Group members can provide one another with feedback; identify opportunities for growth and development; and train, coach, and mentor.[16] A marketing representative can learn about financial modeling from a colleague on a new product development team, and the financial expert can learn about consumer marketing. Experience working together in a group, and developing strong team problem-solving capabilities, is a vital supplement to specific job skills or functional expertise. And the skills are transferable to new positions.

The new team environment

The words "group" and "team" often are used interchangeably.[17] Modern managers sometimes use the word *teams* to the point that it has become cliche; they talk about teams while skeptics perceive no real teamwork. Thus, making a distinction between groups and teams can be useful. A *working group* is a collection of people who work in the same area or have been drawn together to undertake a task but do not necessarily come together as a unit and achieve significant performance improvements. A real **team** is formed of people (usually a small number) with complementary skills who trust one another and are committed to a common purpose, common performance goals, and a common approach for which they hold themselves mutually accountable.[18] A real team is committed to working together successfully to achieve high performance.

team A small number of people with complementary skills who are committed to a common purpose, set of performance goals, and approach for which they hold themselves mutually accountable.

Organizations have been using groups for a long time. But things are different today.[19] Real teams are being more fully integrated into the organizational structure, and their authority is increasing. Managers realize more than ever that teams can provide competitive advantage and greatly improve organizational performance. They know the potential for the whole is far greater than the sum of its individual parts.

Thus, teams today are used in many different ways, and to far greater effect, than in the past. Table 14.2 highlights just a few of the differences between the traditional work environment and how true teams work today. As you can see, people are far more involved, they are better trained, cooperation is higher, and the culture is one of learning as well as producing.

Types of teams

There may be hundreds of groups and teams in your organization. Very generally, teams can be divided into four primary types.[20] **Work teams** make or do things such as manufacture, assemble, sell, or provide service. These typically are well-defined, a clear part of the formal organizational structure, and composed of full-time, stable membership. These are what most people think of when they think of teams in organizations.[21]

work teams Teams that make or do things like manufacture, assemble, sell, or provide.

Project and development teams work on long-term projects, often over a period of years. They have specific assignments, such as research or new-product development, and members usually must contribute expert knowledge and judgment. These teams work toward a one-time product, disbanding once their work is completed. Then, new teams are formed for new projects.

project and development teams Teams that work on long-term projects but disband once the work is completed.

Parallel teams operate separately from the regular work structure of the firm on a temporary basis. Members often come from different units or jobs and are asked to do work that is not normally done by the standard structure. Their charge is to recommend solutions to specific problems. They usually do not have authority to act, however. Examples include task forces and quality or safety teams formed to study a particular problem that has come up.

parallel teams Teams that operate separately from the regular work structure, and exist temporarily.

table 14.2
The new team environment

Traditional environment	Team environment
Managers determine and plan the work.	Managers and team members jointly determine and plan the work.
Jobs are narrowly defined.	Jobs require broad skills and knowledge.
Cross-training is viewed as inefficient.	Cross-training is the norm.
Most information is "management property."	Most information is freely shared at all levels.
Training for nonmanagers focuses on technical skills.	Continuous learning requires interpersonal, administrative, and technical training for all.
Risk taking is discouraged and punished.	Measured risk taking is encouraged and supported.
People work alone.	People work together.
Rewards are based on individual performance.	Rewards are based on individual performance and contributions to team performance.
Managers determine "best methods."	Everyone works to continuously improve methods and processes.

Source: From *Leading Teams* by J. Zenger and Associates. Reprinted by permission.

Management teams Teams that coordinate and provide direction to the subunits under their jurisdiction and integrate work among subunits.

Management teams coordinate and provide direction to the subunits under their jurisdiction and integrate work among subunits.[22] The management team is based on authority stemming from hierarchical rank and is responsible for the overall performance of the business unit. Managers responsible for different subunits form a team together, and at the top of the organization resides the executive management team that establishes strategic direction and manages the firm's overall performance.

Self-managed teams

There exist today many different types of work teams with many different labels. The terms can be confusing, and sometimes are used interchangeably out of a lack of awareness of actual differences. Figure 14.1 shows the different types according to how much autonomy they have.[23] To the left, teams are more traditional with little decision-making authority, being under the control of direct supervision. To the right is more autonomy, decision-making power, and self-direction.

figure 14.1 Team autonomy continuum

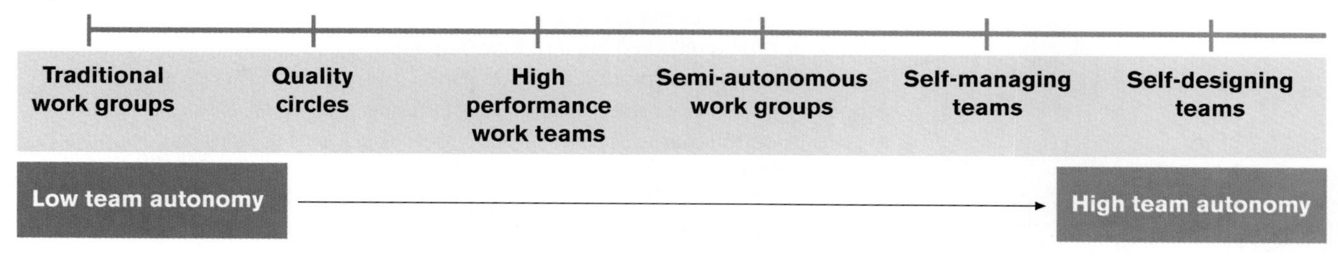

Source: R. Banker, J. Field, R. Schroeder, and K. Sinha, "Impact of Work Teams on Manufacturing Performance: A Longitudinal Field Study," *Academy of Management Journal* 39 (1996), pp. 867–90.

The popularity of teams is on the increase. This Herman Miller work team is jubilant about their accomplishments. *[Courtesy of Herman Miller, Inc.]*

self-managed teams Autonomous work groups in which workers are trained to do all or most of the jobs in a unit, have no immediate supervisor, and make decisions previously made by first-line supervisors.

The trend today is toward **self-managed teams**, in which workers are trained to do all or most of the jobs in the unit, they have no immediate supervisor, and they make decisions previously made by first-line supervisors.[24] Self-managed teams are most frequently found in manufacturing. Compared to traditionally managed teams, self-managed teams appear to be more productive, have lower costs, provide better customer service, provide higher quality, have better safety records, and be more satisfying for members.

Some self-managed teams

- Josten, manufacturer of a variety of products, introduced self-managed teams to increase speed and productivity in the making of class rings. Training was an essential first step. People were taught how to conduct effective meetings and how to solve problems. Everyone attended a World Class Manufacturing Seminar and a variety of workshops on empowerment, feedback, leadership, and the like. The company established the Josten's Learning Center Computer Lab for all to use. Results have been outstanding.

- Otis Engineering's plant in Dallas makes safety equipment for surface and subsurface oil wells. Before instituting self-managed teams, the company did a thorough job of communicating the philosophy behind them, as well as articulating the new roles of team coaches and members. Since Otis has moved to self-managed teams, its products that used to take four months to build are now completed in 10 days. This *despite* an emphasis on quality above efficiency! The firm's vice president for manufacturing believes empowered teams are the only option for survival.
- At Texas Instrument's facility in Sherman, Texas, peers conduct performance appraisals of one another. The purpose is to create a focus on team-oriented performance rather than individual productivity. Everyone on each team

receives feedback on interpersonal and administrative as well as technical skills. The teams have decided all these skills are essential to team success. The peer appraisals are used to provide constructive feedback, not for compensation decisions. Compensation is based on knowledge, skills, and team performance.

- A TRW plant in Kansas had been using teams for five years when volume fell and layoffs became necessary. Management, instead of deciding whom to let go, asked the teams to make those decisions. Teams had to discuss among themselves which of their teammates to lay off. Whereas traditional criteria for layoffs historically have been tenure and seniority, these self-managing teams decided to consider each individual's value to the team and the organization, and laid off those judged least valuable.

Source: D. Yeatts, M. Hipskind, and D. Barnes, "Lessons Learned from Self-Managed Work Teams," *Business Horizons,* July–August 1994, pp. 11–18; and E. E. Lawler III, *From the Ground Up* (San Francisco: Jossey-Bass, 1996). ●

traditional work groups Groups that have no managerial responsibilities.

quality circles Voluntary groups of people drawn from various production teams who make suggestions about quality.

semiautonomous work groups Groups that make decisions about managing and carrying out major production activities, but still get outside support for quality control and maintenance.

autonomous work groups Groups that control decisions about and execution of a complete range of tasks–acquiring raw materials, performing operations, quality control, maintenance, and shipping.

self-designing teams Teams with control over the design of the team, as well as the responsibilities of autonomous work groups.

Referring to Figure 14.1, **traditional work groups** have no managerial responsibilities. The first-line manager plans, organizes, staffs, directs, and controls them, and other groups provide support activities including quality control and maintenance. **Quality circles** are voluntary groups of people drawn from various production teams who make suggestions about quality but have no authority to make decisions or execute. **Semiautonomous work groups** make decisions about managing and carrying out major production activities, but still get outside support for quality control and maintenance. **Autonomous work groups,** or *self-managing teams,* control decisions about and execution of a complete range of tasks—acquiring raw materials, performing operations, quality control, maintenance, and shipping. They are fully responsible for an entire product or an entire part of a production process. **Self-designing teams** do all that and go one step further–they also have control over the design of the team. They decide themselves whom to hire, whom to fire, and what tasks the team will perform.

This Hon Industry safety team addresses issues such as member training, housekeeping, safe workplace design, procedures, and personal fitness. Here, team members exercise before starting their shift.
[Courtesy of Hon Industries]

Movement from left to right on the continuum corresponds with more and more worker participation. Toward the right, the participation is not trivial and not merely advisory. It has real substance, including not just suggestions but action and impact. When companies have introduced teams that reach the point of being truly self-managed, results have included lower costs and greater levels of team productivity, quality, and customer satisfaction.[25] Overall, semiautonomous and autonomous teams are known to improve the organization's financial and overall performance, at least in North America.[26]

Such results are inspiring U.S.-based multinational firms to use self-managed teams in their foreign facilities. For example, Goodyear Tire & Rubber has initiated self-managed work teams in Europe, Latin America, and Asia; Sara Lee in Puerto Rico and Mexico; and Texas Instruments in Malaysia. These companies are learning—and other companies should be forewarned—of the different ways that different cultures might respond to self-managed teams, and to customize implementation according to cultural values.[27]

How groups become teams

As a manager, you will want your group to become an effective team. To accomplish this, it will help you to understand how groups can become true teams, and why groups sometimes fail to become teams. Groups become true teams via basic group activities, the passage of time, and team development activities.

Group activities

Assume you are the leader of a newly formed group. What will you face as you attempt to develop your group into a high-performing team? If groups are to develop successfully, they will engage in various activities, including:[28]

- *Forming*—group members attempt to lay the ground rules for what types of behavior are acceptable.
- *Storming*—hostilities and conflict arise, and people jockey for positions of power and status.
- *Norming*—group members agree on their shared goals, and norms and closer relationships develop.
- *Performing*—the group channels its energies into performing its task.

Groups that deteriorate move to a *declining* stage, and temporary groups add an *adjourning* or terminating stage. Groups terminate when they complete their task or when they disband due to failure or loss of interest.

transnational teams
Work groups composed of multinational members whose activities span multiple countries.

A recent study investigated the group development activities of **transnational teams,** defined as work groups composed of multinational members whose activities span multiple countries.[29] Such teams differ from other work teams not only by being multicultural, but also by often being geographically dispersed, being psychologically distant, and working on highly complex projects having considerable impact on company objectives. In the beginning, such teams need to use *advocacy skills*—building the team's legitimacy, linking the team's mission to the corporate strategy, networking to obtain resources, and "bureaucracy busting" to eliminate old routines and facilitate experimentation. As the teams evolve, they use more *catalytic skills,* including working with external constituents, differentiating individual roles and responsibilities, building commitment, and rewarding members for their contributions. Eventually, mature teams invoke *integrative skills* such as emphasizing accomplishment and excellence, coordinating and problem solving, and measuring progress and results.

The passage of time

A key aspect of development is the passage of time. Groups pass through critical periods, or times when they are particularly open to formative experiences.[30] The first such critical period is in the forming stage, at the first meeting, when rules, norms, and roles are established that set long-lasting precedents. A second critical period is the midway point between the initial meeting and a deadline (e.g., completing a project or making a presentation). At this point, the group has enough experience to understand its work; it comes to realize that time is becoming a scarce resource and it must "get on with it," and there is enough time left to change its approach if necessary.

In the initial meeting, the group should establish desired norms, roles, and other determinants of effectiveness considered throughout this chapter. At the second critical period (the midpoint), groups should renew or open lines of communication with outside constituencies. The group can use fresh information from its external environment to revise its approach to performing its task and ensure that it meets the needs of customers and clients. Without these activities, groups may get off on the wrong foot from the beginning, and members may never revise their behavior in the appropriate direction.[31]

A developmental sequence: From group to team

As a manager or group member, you should expect the group to engage in all of the activities discussed above at various times. But groups are not always successful. They do not always engage in the developmental activities that turn them into effective, high-performing teams.

A useful developmental sequence is depicted in Figure 14.2. The figure shows the various activities as the leadership of the group moves from traditional supervision, through a more participative approach, to true team leadership.[32]

It is important to understand a couple of things about this model. Groups do not necessarily keep progressing from one "stage" to the next; they may remain permanently in the supervisory level, or become more participative but never make it to true team leadership. Therefore, progress on these dimensions must be a conscious goal of the leader and the members, and all should strive to meet these goals. Your group can meet these goals, and become a true team, by engaging in the activities in the figure.

Why groups sometimes fail

Team building does not necessarily progress smoothly through such a sequence, culminating in a well-oiled team and superb performance. Some groups never do work out. Such groups can be frustrating for managers and members, who may feel they are a waste of time, and that the difficulties outweigh the benefits. Says a top consultant: "Teams are the Ferraris of work design. They're high performance but high maintenance and expensive."[33]

It is not easy to build high-performance teams. "Teams" is often just a word used by management to describe merely putting people into groups. "Teams" sometimes are launched with little or no training or support systems. For example, managers as well as group members need new skills to make the group work. These skills include learning the art of diplomacy, tackling "people issues" head on, and walking the fine line between encouraging autonomy and rewarding team innovations without letting the team get too independent and out of control.[34] Giving up some control is very difficult for managers from traditional systems; they have to realize they will gain control in the long run by virtue of creating stronger, better-performing units.

Teams should be truly empowered, as discussed in Chapter 13. The benefits of teams are reduced when they are not allowed to make important decisions—in other words, when

figure 14.2
Stepping up to team leadership

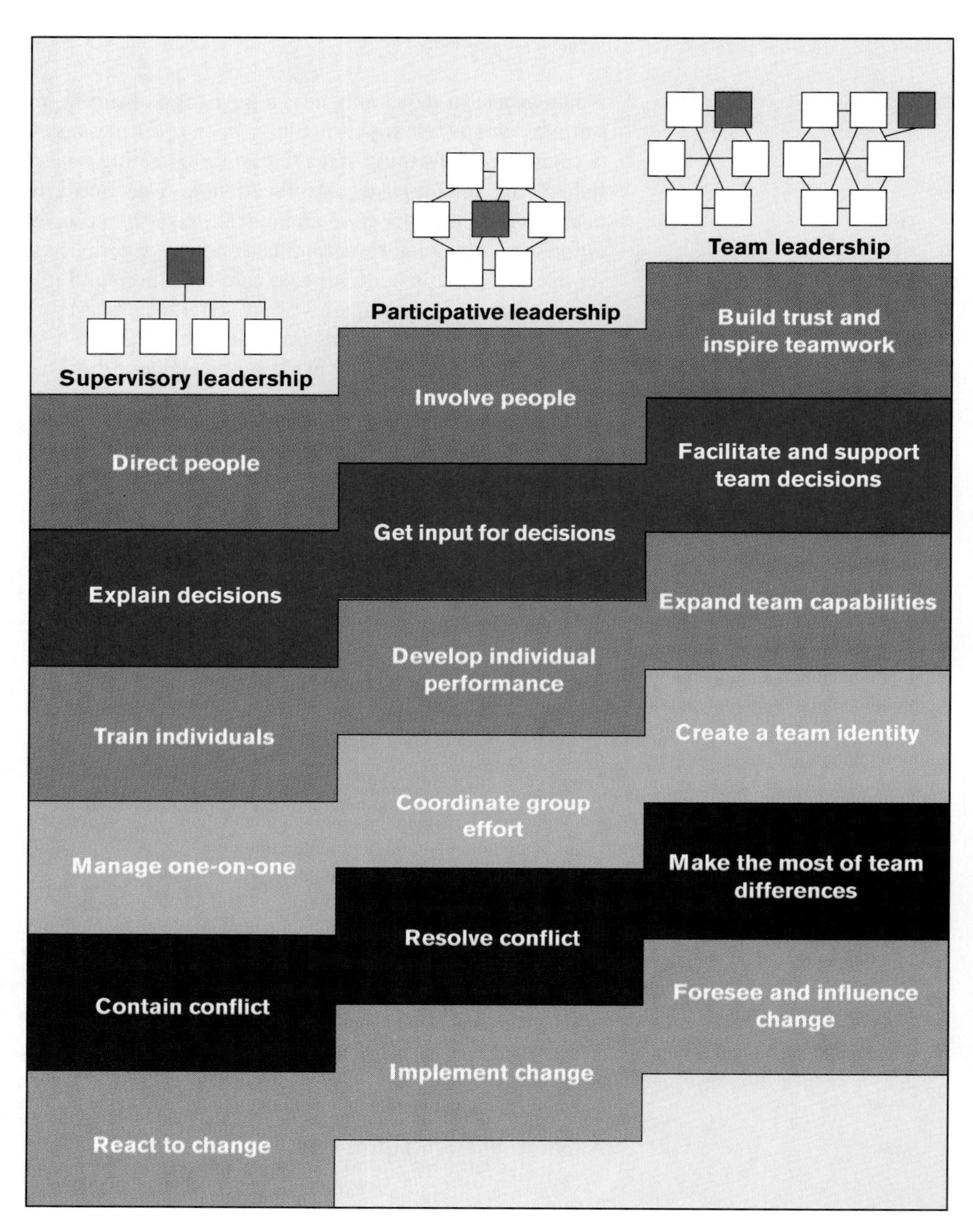

Source: From *Leading Times* by J. Zenger and Associates. Reprinted by permission.

management doesn't trust them with important responsibilities. If teams must acquire permission for every innovative idea, they will revert to making safe, traditional decisions.[35] Thus, management must truly support teams by giving them some freedom and rewarding their contributions.

Failure lies in not knowing and doing what makes teams successful. To be successful you must apply clear thinking and appropriate practices.[36] That is what the rest of the chapter is about.

Building effective teams

All the considerations just described form the building blocks of an effective work team. But what does it really mean for a team to be effective? What, precisely, can a manager do to design a truly effective team? Team effectiveness is defined by three criteria.[37]

First, the *productive output* of the team meets or exceeds the standards of quantity and quality; the team's output is acceptable to those customers, inside or outside the organization, who receive the team's products or services. As examples, Procter & Gamble's business teams are effective at reducing costs and at developing new products.[38] Clarence L. "Kelly" Johnson's group designed, built, and flew the first U.S. tactical jet fighter, XP80, in 143 days.[39] Tom West's legendary Eclipse Group at Data General worked overtime for a year and a half to create the 32-bit superminicomputer that heralded the next generation of minicomputers.[40]

Second, team members realize *satisfaction* of their personal needs. P&G's team members enjoy the opportunity to creatively participate. Johnson and West gave their teams the freedom to innovate and stretch their skills. Team members were enthusiastic and realized great pride and satisfaction in their work.

Third, team members remain *committed* to working together again; that is, the group doesn't burn out and disintegrate after a grueling project. Looking back, the members are glad they were involved. In other words, effective teams remain viable and have good prospects for repeated success in the future.[41]

A performance focus

The key element of effective teamwork is a commitment to a common purpose.[42] The best teams are ones that have been given an important performance challenge by management, and then have come to a common understanding and appreciation of their purpose. Without such understanding and commitment, a group will be just a bunch of individuals.

The best teams also work hard at developing a common understanding of how they will work together to achieve their purpose.[43] They discuss and agree upon such things as how tasks and roles will be allocated and how they will make decisions. The team should develop norms for examining its performance strategies and be amenable to changing when appropriate. With a clear, strong, motivating purpose, and effective performance strategies, people will pull together into a powerful force that has a chance to achieve extraordinary things.

The team's general purpose should be translated into specific, measurable performance goals.[44] You learned in Chapter 13 about how goals motivate individual performance. Team-based performance goals help define and distinguish the team's product, encourage communication within the team, energize and motivate team members, provide feedback on progress, signal team victories (and defeats), and ensure that the team focuses clearly on results.

The best team-based measurement systems will inform top management of the team's performance and will help the team understand its own processes and gauge its own progress.[45] Ideally, the team will play the lead role in designing its own measurement system. This is a great indicator of whether the team is truly "empowered."

Teams, like individuals, need feedback on their performance. Feedback from customers is critical. Some customers for the team's products are inside the organization. Teams should be responsible for satisfying them, and should be given or should seek performance feedback. Better yet, wherever possible, teams should interact directly with external customers who make the ultimate buy decisions about their products and services. This will be the most honest, and most crucial and useful, performance feedback of all.[46]

Motivating teamwork

social loafing working less hard and being less productive when in a group.

social facilitation effect working harder when in a group than when working alone.

Sometimes individuals work less hard and are less productive when they are members of a group. Such **social loafing** occurs when individuals believe that their contributions are not important, others will do the work for them, their lack of effort will go undetected, or they will be the lone sucker who works hard while others don't. On the other hand, sometimes individuals work harder when they are members of a group than if they are working alone. This **social facilitation effect** occurs because individuals usually are more motivated when others are present, they are concerned with what others think of them, and they want to maintain a positive self-image.

A social facilitation effect is maintained, and a social loafing effect can be avoided, when group members know each other, they can observe and communicate with one another, clear performance goals exist, the task is meaningful to the people working on it, they believe that their efforts matter and others would not take advantage of them, and there is a culture that supports teamwork.[47] Thus, ideally it will be clear that everyone works hard, contributes in concrete ways to the team's work, and is accountable to other team members. Accountability to one another, rather than just to "the boss," is an essential aspect of good teamwork. Accountability inspires mutual commitment and trust.[48] Trust in your teammates—and their trust in you—may be the ultimate key to effectiveness.

Team effort is also generated by designing the team's task to be motivating. Techniques for creating motivating tasks appear in the guidelines for job enrichment discussed in Chapter 13. Tasks are motivating when they use a variety of member skills and provide high task variety, identity, significance, autonomy, and performance feedback.

Ultimately, teamwork is best motivated by tying rewards to team performance.[49] If team performance can be measured validly, team-based rewards can be given accordingly. It is not easy to move from a system of rewards based on individual performance to one based on team performance. Importantly, it also may not be appropriate, unless people are truly interdependent and must collaborate to attain true team goals.[50] Sometimes team-based rewards can be added to existing rewards already based on individual performance. In the case of a financial services firm, year 1 of a new team system included pay increases based 15 percent on team performance, increasing to 50 percent by year 3.[51]

If team performance is difficult to measure validly, then desired behaviors, activities, and processes that indicate good teamwork can be rewarded. Individuals within teams can be given differential rewards based on teamwork indicated by active participation, cooperation, leadership, and other contributions to the team.

If team members are to be rewarded differentially, such decisions are better *not* left to the boss.[52] They should be made by the team itself, via peer ratings or multi-rater evaluation systems. Team members are in a better position to observe, know, and make valid reward allocations. Finally, the more teams the organization has, and the more of a full-team orientation that exists, the more valid and effective it will be to handle rewards via gainsharing and other organizationwide incentives.

Member contributions

Team members should be selected and trained so they become effective contributors to the team. Teams often hire their new members.[53] Miller Brewing Company and Eastman Chemical teams select members on the basis of tests designed to predict how well they will contribute to team success in an empowered environment. At Hannaford Brothers Company, a retail supermarket and food distributor in New York, new employees become "team certified" and then join their teams. At Texas Instruments, Human Resources screens applicants; then team members interview them and make selection decisions.

Some companies are developing computer systems combining PC networks with databases and video-conferencing to help teams identify and find the right new people.

Selecting new team members is a complicated process, but one for which there is a high payoff.
[Courtesy of Hewlett-Packard Company]

Generally, the skills required by the team include technical or functional expertise, problem-solving and decision-making skills, and interpersonal skills. Some managers and teams mistakenly overemphasize some skills, particularly technical or functional, and underemphasize the others. It is vitally important that all three types of skills are represented, and developed, among team members.

Development Dimensions International provides people with 300 hours of training, mostly about how to work in teams, but also technical cross-training. K Shoes, Ltd., trains team members in teamwork, overall business knowledge, supplier partnership development, and retail management. Kodak provides 150 hours of first-year training on team effectiveness, including teaching people to cross-train others, and 120 more hours subsequently on the same team skills plus business and financial skills.[54]

Norms

norms Shared beliefs about how people should think and behave.

Norms are shared beliefs about how people should think and behave. Recall from Chapter 8 that shared beliefs form the basis for the organization culture.

From the organization's standpoint, norms can be positive or negative. In some teams, everyone works hard; in other groups, employees are antimanagement and do as little work as possible. A norm could dictate that employees speak favorably of the company in public, or criticize it. Another norm could support being open and honest and respecting the opinions of others, or avoiding confronting important issues and gossiping behind people's backs. Team members may show concern about poor safety practices, drug and alcohol abuse, and employee theft, or they may not care about these issues (or they may even condone such practices). Health consciousness is the norm among executives at some companies, but smoking is the norm at tobacco companies.

A professor described his consulting experiences at two companies that exhibited different norms in their management teams.[55] At Federal Express Corporation, a young manager interrupted the professor's talk by proclaiming that a recent decision by top management ran counter to the professor's point about corporate planning. He was challenging top management to defend their decision. A hot debate ensued, and after an hour everyone went to lunch without a trace of hard feelings. But at another corporation, the professor opened a meeting by asking a group of top managers to describe the company's culture. There was silence. He asked again. More silence. Then someone passed him an unsigned note that read, "Dummy, can't you see that we can't speak our minds? Ask for the input anonymously, in writing." As you can see, norms are important, and can vary greatly from one group to another.

Roles

roles Different sets of expectations for how different individuals should behave.

task specialist An individual who has more advanced job-related skills and abilities than other group members possess.

Roles are different sets of expectations for how different individuals should behave. Whereas norms apply generally to all team members, different roles exist for different members within the norm structure.

Two important sets of roles must be performed.[56] **Task specialist** roles are filled by individuals who have more job-related skills and abilities than do other members. These employees have more decision-making responsibilities and provide instructions and advice. They keep the team moving toward task accomplishment. Team maintenance specialists develop and maintain harmony within the team. They boost morale, give support, provide humor, soothe hurt feelings, and generally exhibit a concern with members' well-being.

Note the similarity between these roles and the important task performance and group maintenance leadership behaviors you learned about in Chapter 12. As suggested in that chapter, some of these roles will be more important than others at different times and under different circumstances. But these behaviors need not be carried out only by one or two leaders; any member of the team can carry out these roles at any time. Over time, both types of roles can be performed by different individuals to maintain an effectively functioning work team.

If the team has a formal leader, the leader's role is to keep the team's purpose, goals, and approach relevant and meaningful; build commitment and confidence; strengthen the mix and level of team members' skills; manage relationships with outsiders; remove obstacles to the team's performance; create opportunities for the team and its members; and do real work, not just supervise.[57]

Self-managed teams report to a management representative, sometimes called the coach. For example, at Wilson Sporting Goods Company, coaches facilitate and provide support and direction to teams, and hourly associates share leadership responsibilities with the coaches.[58] In true self-managed teams, the coach is not a true member of the team.[59] This is because the group is supposed to make its own decisions, and because the relative power of the management representative can have a dampening effect on the team's openness and autonomy.

The role of the coach, then, is to help the team understand its role in the organization, and to act as a resource for the team. The coach can provide information, resources, and opinions that team members do not or cannot acquire on their own. And the coach should be an advocate for the team in the rest of the organization.

Cohesiveness

cohesiveness The degree to which a group is attractive to its members, members are motivated to remain in the group, and members influence one another.

One of the most important properties of a work team is cohesiveness.[60] **Cohesiveness** refers to how attractive the team is to its members, how motivated members are to remain in the team, and the degree to which team members influence one another. In general, it refers to how tightly knit the team is.

The importance of cohesiveness

Cohesiveness is important for two primary reasons. First, it contributes to *member satisfaction.* In a cohesive team, members communicate and get along well with one another. They feel good about being a part of the team. Even if their jobs are unfulfilling or the organization is oppressive, people gain some satisfaction from enjoying their co-workers.

Second, cohesiveness has a major impact on *performance.* A recent study of the creation of manufacturing teams led to a conclusion that performance improvements in both quality and productivity occurred in the most cohesive unit, whereas conflict within another team prevented any quality or productivity improvements.[61] Sports fans read about this all the time. When teams are winning, players talk about the team being close, getting along well, and knowing one another's games. In contrast, losing is attributed to infighting and divisiveness. Generally, cohesiveness clearly can and does have a positive effect on performance.[62]

But this interpretation is simplistic; exceptions to this intuitive relationship occur. Tightly knit work groups can be disruptive to the organization, such as when they sabotage the assembly line, get their boss fired, or enforce low performance norms.

When does high cohesiveness lead to good performance, and when does it result in poor performance? This depends on (1) the task and (2) whether the group has high or low performance norms.

The task If the task is to make a decision or solve a problem, cohesiveness can lead to poor performance. Groupthink (discussed in Chapter 3) occurs when a tightly knit group is so cooperative that agreeing with one another's opinions and refraining from criticizing others' ideas become norms. The following example illustrates this tendency.

The Abilene paradox

The July afternoon in Coleman, Texas (population 5,607), was particularly hot—104 degrees as measured by the Walgreen's Rexall Ex-Lax temperature gauge. In addition, the wind was blowing fine-grained West Texas topsoil through the house. But the afternoon was still tolerable—even potentially enjoyable. There was a fan going on the back porch; there was cold lemonade; and finally, there was entertainment. Dominoes. Perfect for the conditions. The game required little more physical exertion than an occasional mumbled comment, "Shuffle 'em," and an unhurried movement of the arm to place the spots in the appropriate perspective on the table. All in all, it had the makings of an agreeable Sunday afternoon in Coleman—that is, it was until my father-in-law suddenly said, "Let's get in the car and go to Abilene and have dinner at the cafeteria."

I thought, "What, go to Abilene? Fifty-three miles? In this dust storm and heat? And in an unairconditioned 1958 Buick?"

But my wife chimed in with, "Sounds like a great idea. I'd like to go. How about you, Jerry?" Since my own preferences were obviously out of step with the rest, I replied, "Sounds good to me," and added, "I just hope your mother wants to go."

"Of course I want to go," said my mother-in-law. "I haven't been to Abilene in a long time."

So into the car and off to Abilene we went. My predictions were fulfilled. The heat was brutal. We were coated with a fine layer of dust that was cemented with perspiration by the time we arrived. The food in the cafeteria provided first-rate testimonial material for antacid commercials.

Some four hours and 106 miles later we returned to Coleman, hot and exhausted. We sat in front of the fan for a long time in silence. Then, both to be sociable and to break the silence, I said, "It was a great trip, wasn't it?"

No one spoke.

Finally, my mother-in-law said, with some irritation, "Well, to tell the truth, I really didn't enjoy it much and would rather have stayed here. I just went along because the three of you were so enthusiastic about going. I wouldn't have gone if you all hadn't pressured me into it."

I couldn't believe it. "What do you mean 'you all'?" I said. "Don't put me in the 'you all' group. I was delighted to be doing what we were doing. I didn't want to go. I only went to satisfy the rest of you. You're the culprits."

My wife looked shocked. "Don't call me a culprit. You and Daddy and Mama were the ones who wanted to go. I just went along to be sociable and keep you happy. I would have had to be crazy to want to go out in heat like that."

Her father entered the conversation abruptly. "Hell!" he said.

He proceeded to expand on what was already absolutely clear. "Listen, I never wanted to go to Abilene. I just thought you might be bored. You visit so seldom I wanted to be sure you enjoyed it. I would have preferred to play another game of dominoes and eat the leftovers in the icebox."

After the outburst of recrimination, we all sat back in silence. Here we were, four reasonably sensible people who, of our own volition, had just taken a 106-mile trip across a godforsaken desert in furnacelike temperatures through a cloudlike dust storm to eat unpalatable food at a hole-in-the-wall cafeteria in Abilene, when none of us had really wanted to go. In fact, to be more accurate, we'd done just the opposite of what we wanted to do. The whole situation simply didn't make sense.

Source: Reprinted by permission of the publisher, from *Organizational Dynamics,* Summer 1974.

In the Abilene example, the group was exhibiting groupthink. Disagreement, which is more likely to occur in noncohesive groups, could have led to a better decision: to stay in Coleman. For a cohesive group to make good decisions, it should establish a norm of constructive disagreement. It could also create the role of devil's advocate, as suggested in Chapter 3.

Cohesiveness can enhance performance, particularly if the task is to produce some tangible output. In day-to-day work groups for which decision making is not the primary task, the effect of cohesiveness on performance can be positive. But that depends on the group's performance norms.[63]

Performance norms Some groups are better than others at ensuring that their members behave the way the group prefers. Cohesive groups are more effective than noncohesive groups at norm enforcement. But the next question is: Do they have norms of high or low performance?

As Figure 14.3 shows, the highest performance occurs when a cohesive team has high performance norms. But if a highly cohesive group has low performance norms, that group will have the worst performance. In the group's eyes, however, it will have succeeded in achieving

figure 14.3
Cohesiveness, performance norms, and group performance

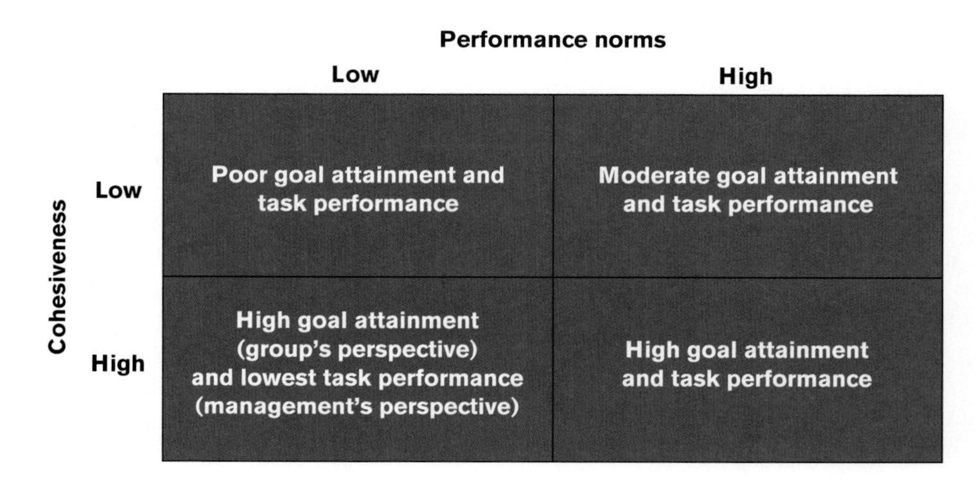

its goal of poor performance. Noncohesive groups with high performance norms will be effective from the company's standpoint. However, they won't be as productive as they would be if they were more cohesive. Noncohesive groups with low performance norms perform poorly, but they will not ruin things for management as effectively as cohesive groups can.

Building cohesiveness and high performance norms

As Figure 14.3 suggests, managers should build teams that are cohesive and have high performance norms. The following actions can help create such teams:[64]

1. *Recruit members with similar attitudes, values, and backgrounds.* Similar individuals are more likely to get along with one another. Don't do this, though, if the team's task requires heterogeneous skills and inputs. For example, a homogeneous committee or board might make relatively poor decisions, because it will lack different information and viewpoints and may succumb to groupthink.
2. *Maintain high entrance and socialization standards.* Teams and organizations that are difficult to get into have more prestige. Individuals who survive a difficult interview, selection, or training process will be proud of their accomplishment and feel more attachment to the team.
3. *Keep the team small* (but large enough to get the job done). The larger the group, the less important members may feel. Small teams make individuals feel like large contributors.
4. *Help the team succeed, and publicize its successes.* Be a path-goal leader who facilitates success; the experience of winning brings teams closer together. Then, if you inform superiors of your team's successes, members will believe they are part of an important, prestigious unit. Teams that get into a good performance track continue to perform well as time goes on; groups that don't often enter a downward spiral in which problems compound over time.[65]
5. *Be a participative leader.* Participation in decisions gets team members more involved with one another and striving toward goal accomplishment. Too much autocratic decision making can alienate the group from management.
6. *Present a challenge from outside the team.* Competition with other groups makes team members band together to defeat the enemy (witness what happens to school spirit before the big game against an archrival). Some of the greatest teams in business and in science have been completely focused on winning a competition.[66] But don't *you* become the outside threat. If team members dislike you as a boss, they will become more cohesive—but their performance norms will be against you, not with you.
7. *Tie rewards to team performance.* To a large degree, teams are motivated just as individuals are—they do the things that are rewarded. Make sure that high-performing teams get the rewards they deserve and that poorly performing groups get relatively few rewards. You read about this earlier. Bear in mind that not just monetary rewards, but also recognition for good work, are powerful motivators. Recognize and celebrate team accomplishments. The team will become more cohesive and perform better to reap their rewards. Performance goals will be high, the organization will benefit from higher team motivation and productivity, and the individual needs of team members will be better satisfied. Ideally, being a member of a high-performing team, recognized as such throughout the organization, will become a badge of honor.[67]

But keep in mind that strong cohesiveness encouraging "agreeableness" can be dysfunctional. For problem solving and decision making, the team should establish norms promoting an open, constructive atmosphere including honest disagreement over issues without personal conflict and animosity.[68] Thus, the team can avoid groupthink and a trip to Abilene.

Managing lateral relationships

Teams are open systems (recall Chapter 1). They are not closed systems functioning in a vacuum; they are interdependent with other teams. For example, at Miller Brewing Company, major team responsibilities include coordinating with other teams and policy groups. At Texas Instruments, teams are responsible for interfacing with other teams to eliminate production bottlenecks and implement new processes, and also for working with suppliers on quality issues.[69] Thus, activities crucial to the team are those that entail dealing with people *outside* the group.

Managing outward

Several vital roles link teams to their external environments, that is, to other individuals and groups both inside and outside the organization. You learned about *boundary-spanning roles* in Chapter 8. A specific type of a boundary spanner is the gatekeeper, a team member who stays abreast of current information in scientific and other fields and informs the group of important developments. Information useful to the group can also include information about resources, trends, and political support throughout the corporation or the industry.[70]

The team's strategy dictates the team's mix of internally versus externally focused roles and how the mix changes over time. General team strategies include informing, parading, and probing.[71] The **informing** strategy entails concentrating first on the internal team process to achieve a state of performance readiness. Then the team informs outsiders of its intentions. **Parading** means the team's strategy is to simultaneously emphasize internal team building and achieve external visibility. **Probing** involves a focus on external relations. This strategy requires team members to interact frequently with outsiders; diagnose the needs of customers, clients, and higher-ups; and experiment with solutions.

informing A team strategy that entails concentrating first on the internal team process to achieve a state of performance readiness, then informing outsiders of its intentions.

parading A team strategy that entails simultaneously emphasizing internal team building and achieving external visibility.

probing A team strategy that requires team members to interact frequently with outsiders, diagnose their needs, and experiment with solutions.

The appropriate balance between an internal and external strategic focus and between internal and external roles depends on how much the team needs information, support, and resources from outside. When teams have a high degree of dependence on outsiders, probing is the best strategy. Parading teams perform at an intermediate level, and informing teams are likely to fail. They are too isolated from the outside groups on which they depend.

Informing or parading strategies may be more effective for teams that are less dependent on outside groups, for example, established teams working on routine tasks in stable external environments. But for most important work teams of the future—task forces, new-product teams, and strategic decision-making teams tackling unstructured problems in a rapidly changing external environment—effective performance in roles that involve interfacing with the outside will be vital.

Lateral role relationships

Managing relationships with managers of other groups and teams means engaging in a dynamic give-and-take that ensures proper coordination throughout the management system. To many managers, this process often seems like a chaotic free-for-all. It is useful to identify the different types of lateral role relationships and take a strategic approach to building constructive relationships.

Different teams, like different individuals, have roles to perform. As teams carry out their roles, several distinct patterns of working relationships develop.[72]

1. *Work flow relationships* emerge as materials are passed from one group to another. A group commonly receives work from one unit, processes it, and sends it to the next unit in the process. Your group, then, will come before some groups and after others in the process.

2. *Service relationships* exist when top management centralizes an activity to which a large number of other units must gain access. Common examples are computing services, libraries, and clerical staff. Such units must service other people's requests.
3. *Advisory relationships* are created when teams with problems call on centralized sources of expert knowledge. For example, staff in the human resources or legal department advise work teams.
4. *Audit relationships* develop when people not directly in the chain of command evaluate the methods and performances of other teams. Financial auditors check the books, and technical auditors assess the methods and technical quality of the work.
5. *Stabilization relationships* involve auditing before the fact. In other words, teams sometimes must obtain clearance from others—for example, for large purchases—before they take action.
6. *Liaison relationships* involve intermediaries between teams. Managers often are called upon to mediate conflict between two organizational units. Public relations people, sales managers, purchasing agents, and others who work across organizational boundaries serve in liaison roles as they maintain communications between the organization and the outside world.

By assessing each working relationship with another unit ("From whom do we receive and to whom do we send work? What permissions do we control, and to whom must we go for authorizations?"), teams can better understand whom to contact and when, where, why, and how to do so. Coordination throughout the working system improves, problems are avoided or short-circuited before they get too serious, and performance improves.[73]

Intergroup conflict

The complex maze of interdependencies throughout organizations provides boundless opportunity for conflict to arise among groups and teams. Some conflict is constructive for the organization, as we discussed in Chapter 3. But many things cause great potential for destructive conflict: the sheer number and variety of contacts; ambiguities in jurisdiction and responsibility; differences in goals; intergroup competition for scarce resources; different perspectives held by members of different units; varying time horizons in which some units attend to long-term considerations and others focus on short-term needs; and other factors.

Tensions and anxieties are likely to arise in demographically diverse teams, or teams from different parts of the organization, or teams composed of contrasting personalities. These tensions need not be destructive influences. In fact, they can be an important source of information, new perspectives, and vitality. The team must learn not only to accept differences and conflict but to use them to advantage. The group must be willing and able to confront disagreement in direct, honest, sincere ways.[74]

Managing conflict

Teams inevitably face conflicts and must decide how to manage them. The aim should be to make the conflict productive, that is, for those involved to believe they have benefited rather than lost from the conflict.[75] People believe they have benefited from a conflict when (1) a new solution is implemented, the problem is solved, and it is unlikely to emerge again; and (2) work relationships have been strengthened and people believe they can work together productively in the future.

How can conflict be managed? A recent study of human resource (HR) managers and the conflicts with which they deal provides some insight.[76] HR managers deal with every type of conflict imaginable: interpersonal difficulties from minor irritations to jealousy to fights; operations issues including union issues, work assignments, overtime, and sick leave; discipline over infractions ranging from drug use and theft to sleeping on the job; sexual harassment and racial bias; pay and promotion issues; and feuds or strategic conflicts among divisions or individuals at the highest organizational levels.

In the study, the HR managers successfully settled most of the disputes. These managers typically follow a four-stage strategy. They *investigate* by interviewing the disputants and others and gathering more information. They *decide* how to resolve the dispute, often in conjunction with the disputants' bosses. They *take action* by explaining their decisions and the reasoning, and advise or train the disputants to avoid future such incidents. And they *follow up* by documenting the conflict and the resolution, and monitoring the results by checking back with the disputants and their bosses. Throughout, the objectives of the HR people are to be fully informed so they understand the conflict, to be active and assertive in trying to resolve it, to be as objective, neutral, and impartial as humanly possible, and to be flexible by modifying their approaches according to the situation.[77]

Here are some other recommendations for more effective conflict management.[78] Don't allow dysfunctional conflict to build, or hope or assume that it will go away. Address it before it escalates. Try to resolve it; and if the first efforts don't work, try others. And remember the earlier discussion (Chapter 13) of procedural justice. Even if disputants are not happy with your decisions, there are benefits to providing fair treatment, making a good faith effort, giving them a voice in the proceedings, and so on. Remember, too, that you may be able to ask HR specialists to help with difficult conflicts.

avoidance A reaction to conflict that involves either ignoring the problem by doing nothing at all, or by de-emphasizing the disagreement.

accommodation A style of dealing with conflict involving cooperation on behalf of the other party but not being assertive about one's own interests.

compromise A style of dealing with conflict involving moderate attention to both parties' concerns.

forcing A style of dealing with conflict involving competitiveness, strong focus on one's own goals and little or no concern for the other person's goals.

collaboration A style of dealing with conflict involving emphasizing both cooperation and assertiveness in order to maximize both parties' satisfaction.

Conflict styles

Intergroup conflict can be managed through structural solutions such as the integrating roles discussed in Chapter 8. But a group or an individual in a conflict situation has several additional options regarding the style used in interactions with others.[79] These personal styles of dealing with conflict, shown in Figure 14.4, are distinguished based on how much people strive to satisfy their own concerns (the assertiveness dimension) and to what degree they focus on satisfying the other party's concerns (the cooperativeness dimension). For example, a common reaction to conflict is **avoidance.** In this situation, people do nothing to satisfy themselves or others. They either ignore the problem by doing nothing at all or address it by merely smoothing over or deemphasizing the disagreement. This, of course, fails to solve the problem or clear the air.

Accommodation means cooperating on behalf of the other party but not being assertive about one's own interests. **Compromise** involves moderate attention to both parties' concerns, being neither highly cooperative nor highly assertive. This style therefore results in satisficing but not maximizing solutions. **Forcing** is a highly competitive response in which people focus strictly on their own wishes and are unwilling to recognize the other person's concerns. Finally, **collaboration** emphasizes both cooperation and assertiveness. The goal is to maximize satisfaction for both parties.

Different approaches are necessary at different times.[80] For example, competition or forcing can be healthy if it promotes positive motivation and even necessary when cutting costs or dealing with other scarce resources. Compromise may be useful when people are under time pressure, when they need to achieve a temporary solution, or when collaboration fails. People should accommodate when they learn they are wrong or to minimize loss when they are outmatched. Even avoiding may be appropriate if the issue is trivial or others should solve the conflict.

But when the conflict concerns important issues, when both sets of concerns are valid and important, when a creative solution is needed, and when commitment to the solution is vital to implementation, collaboration is the ideal approach. Collaboration can be achieved by airing feelings and opinions, addressing all concerns, and avoiding

figure 14.4
Conflict management strategies

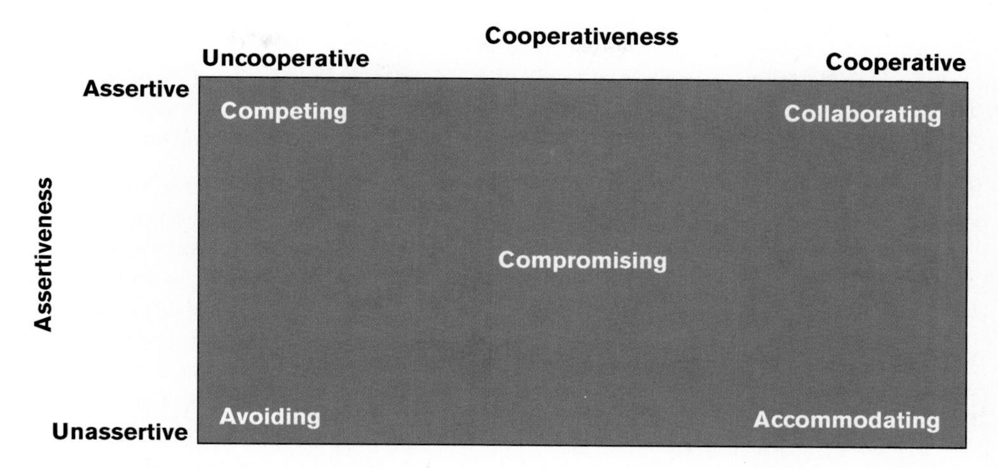

Source: K. Thomas, "Conflict and Conflict Management." In *Handbook of Industrial and Organizational Psychology,* ed. M. D. Dunnette. Copyright © 1976 John Wiley & Sons. Reprinted by permission of John Wiley & Sons, Inc.

superordinate goals Higher-level goals taking priority over specific individual or group goals.

goal displacement by not letting personal attacks interfere with problem solving. An important technique is to invoke **superordinate goals**—higher-level organizational goals toward which all teams should be striving and that ultimately need to take precedence over unit preferences. Collaboration offers the best chance of reaching mutually satisfactory solutions based on the ideas and interests of all parties and of maintaining and strengthening work relationships.

Key terms

Accommodation, p. 488
Autonomous work groups, p. 475
Avoidance, p. 488
Cohesiveness, p. 482
Collaboration, p. 488
Compromise, p. 488
Forcing, p. 488
Informing, p.486
Management teams, p. 473
Norms, p. 481
Parading, p. 486
Parallel teams, p. 472
Probing, p. 486
Project and development teams, p. 472
Quality circles, p. 475
Roles, p. 482
Self-designing teams, p. 475
Self-managed teams, p. 474
Semiautonomous work group, p. 475
Social facilitation effect, p. 480
Social loafing, p. 480
Superordinate goals, p. 489
Task specialist, p. 482
Team, p. 472
Traditional work groups, p. 475
Transnational teams, p. 476
Work teams, p. 472

Summary of learning objectives

Now that you have studied Chapter 14, you should know:

How teams can contribute to your organization's effectiveness.

Teams are building blocks for organization structure and forces for productivity, quality, cost savings, speed, change, and innovation. They have the potential to provide many benefits for both the organization and individual members.

What makes the new team environment different from the old.

Compared to traditional work groups that were closely supervised, today's teams have more authority and often are self-managed. Teams now are used in many more ways, for many more purposes, than in the past. Generally, types of teams include work teams, project and development teams, and parallel teams. More specifically, types of work teams range from traditional groups with low autonomy to self-designing teams with high autonomy.

How groups become teams.

Groups carry on a variety of important developmental activities including forming, storming, norming, and performing. For a group to become a team, it should move beyond traditional supervisory leadership, become more participative, and ultimately enjoy team leadership. A true team has members who complement one another; who are committed to a common purpose, performance goals, and approach; and who hold themselves accountable to one another.

Why teams sometimes fail.

Teams do not always work well. Some companies underestimate the difficulties of moving to a team-based approach. Teams require training, empowerment, and a well-managed transition to make them work. Groups may fail to become effective teams unless managers and team members commit to the idea, understand what makes teams work, and implement appropriate practices.

How to build an effective team.

Create a team with a high-performance focus by establishing a common purpose; by translating the purpose into measurable team goals; by designing the team's task so it is intrinsically motivating; by designing a team-based performance measurement system, and by providing team rewards.

Work to develop a common understanding of how the team will perform its task. Make it clear that everyone has to work hard and contribute in concrete ways. Establish mutual accountability and build trust among members. Examine the team's strategies periodically and be willing to adapt.

Make sure members contribute fully by selecting them appropriately, training them, and checking that all important roles are carried out. Take a variety of steps to establish team cohesiveness and high performance norms.

And don't just manage inwardly. Manage the team's relations with outsiders, too.

How to manage your team's relationships with other teams.

Perform important roles like boundary spanning, gatekeeping, informing, parading, and probing. Identify the types of lateral role relationships you have with outsiders. This can help coordinate efforts throughout the work system.

How to manage conflict.

Conflict arises because of the sheer number of contacts, ambiguities, goal differences, competition for scarce resources, and different perspectives and time horizons. Depending on the situation, five basic interpersonal approaches to managing conflict can be used: avoidance, accommodation, compromise, forcing, and collaboration. Superordinate goals offer a focus on higher-level organizational goals that can help generate a collaborative relationship.

Discussion questions

1. Why do you think some people resist the idea of working in teams? How would you deal with their resistance?

2 Consider a job you have held, and review Table 14.2 about the traditional and new team environment. Which environment best describes your job? Assess your job on each of the dimensions described in the table.

3. Assess your job as in question 2, using Figure 14.2, "Stepping Up to Team Leadership." Which leadership "stage" characterized your job environment?

4. Identify some things from a previous job that could have been done differently to move your work group closer toward the "team leadership" depicted in Figure 14.2.

5. Experts say that teams are a means, not an end. What do you think they mean? What do you think happens in a company that creates teams just for the sake of having teams because it's a fad or just because it sounds good? How can this pitfall be avoided?

6. Choose a sports team with which you are familiar. Assess its effectiveness and discuss the factors that contribute to its level of effectiveness.

7. Assess the effectiveness, as in question 6, of a student group with which you have been affiliated. Could anything have been done to make it more effective?

8. Consider the various roles that members have to perform for a team to be effective. Which roles would play to your strengths and which to your weaknesses? How can you become a better team member?

9. Can you think of any personal examples of the Abilene Paradox? Explain what happened and why.

10. What do you think are your own most commonly used approaches to handling conflict? Least common? What can you do to expand your repertoire and become more effective at conflict management?

11. Generate real examples of how superordinate goals have helped to resolve a conflict. Identify some current conflicts and provide some specific ideas for how superordinate goals could be used to help.

12. Have you ever been part of a group that was "self-managed"? What was good about it, and what not so good? Why do many managers resist this idea? Why do some people love the idea of being a member of such a team, while others don't?

13. How might self-managed teams operate differently in different cultures? What are the advantages, disadvantages, and implications of homogeneous versus highly diverse self-managed teams?

Concluding Case

Teams and GM's Saturn

GM's Saturn plant at Spring Hill, Tennessee, was designed when teamwork and empowerment had become the rage at GM. Saturn was to epitomize those concepts. Hourly workers got involved in virtually every decision, down to minor details. Managers and union workers went on Outward Bound–type training courses where they ran obstacle courses together and dealt with tasks that required teamwork and trust.

The organization chart was a series of interlocking circles, rather than the old GM pyramid. Each group ran its own show, and was to produce to schedule, perform to budget, create a quality product, and account for inventory control, repairs, absenteeism, scrap, and record-keeping. Moreover, teams were expected to communicate and cooperate with other teams.

Consensus and teamwork were the bywords. The Saturn plant hired exceptionally motivated workers, provided intensive training, and gave employees more say in their work. Also, it paid them salary plus performance bonuses—just as it paid executives. Even more radical was the company's bold experiment in organization structure. GM replaced its traditional line–staff hierarchy with management–union committees, as the table shows.

GM's Saturn Plant is designed around work teams and employee empowerment.
[© 1995 Kevin Horan]

The first Saturn cars went on sale in selected markets in October 1990. Production at that time was far below expectations, in part because of the Gulf War and the recession and partly because of production glitches. For example, workers took longer than expected to learn to inspect their own work, and they were so determined to ensure high quality that they stopped production frequently. Such problems, executives maintained, were to be expected in starting up such a complex operation.

Saturn is run by teams. At the most basic level, automobiles are built by the work units—teams of 6 to 15 workers, who in many respects manage themselves. Team members decide who does which job, when to order supplies, and how to control costs. Furthermore, each team maintains its own equipment, does its own inspections,

GM's traditional hierarchy	The Saturn structure
Plant manager	Strategic advisory committee (long-range planning)
Production manager General superintendent	Manufacturing advisory committee (oversees Saturn complex)
Production superintendent (5 per shift)	Business unit (coordinates plant-level operations)
General supervisor (15 per shift)	Work unit module
Supervisor/foreman (90 per shift)	Work units

sets relief and vacation schedules for its members, and tracks business data like production and freight schedules.

At the next level are work unit modules, groups of three to six work units led by a company adviser. Each module acts as a liaison between its work units and various company experts such as engineers, marketing specialists, and personnel representatives. In addition, these groups serve as a conduit of information to and from the business unit, which manages the entire plant. That group, composed of company representatives, elected workers, and various specialists, coordinates plant-level operations. Above that group are two specialty committees—one that decides on changes in salaries and benefits and one that handles long-range planning for the company.

The Spring Hill plant is currently investing tens of millions of dollars to update the plant to build parts for a new car model. The car itself, the Innovate, is being built at the GM plant in Wilmington, Delaware. The Wilmington plant had been scheduled to close, but the United Auto Workers agreed that its 2,600 workers at the plant will work in teams as they do at Spring Hill, Tennessee.

Questions

1. What did General Motors gain by being a leader in using this team-dominated structure?

2. What are the possible disadvantages?

3. How would you like working at Saturn?

4. How is Saturn doing today? How do you think the people working there respond to changes made by GM, such as the investment for building new parts? What do current reports say about morale, team effectiveness, quality, and productivity at the plant?

5. What do you forecast for the Wilmington plant? How can GM ensure success there?

Sources: "Saturn May Update Spring Hill Plant for a New Car Model," *USA Today,* January 14, 1997, p. 8B; M. Edid, "How Power Will Be Balanced on Saturn's Shop Floor," in *Inside Management: A Selection of Readings from Business Week,* ed. D. R. Hampton (New York: McGraw-Hall, 1986), pp. 154–56; A. Taylor III, "Back to the Future at Saturn," *Fortune,* August 1, 1988, pp. 83–89; M. Maynard, "Enthusiasm Drives Saturn Workers," *USA Today,* August 31, 1990, p. 2B; S. C. Gwynne, "The Right Stuff," *Time,* October 29, 1990, pp. 74–84; J. B. Treece, "Are the Planets Lining Up for Saturn?" *Business Week,* April 8, 1991, pp. 32–34; P. Ingrassia and J. White, *Comeback: The Fall and Rise of the American Automobile Industry* (New York: Simon & Schuster, 1994); E. Hitchner, *In the Rings of Saturn* (New York: Oxford University Press, 1994); and "GM Confirms Plan for a Midsize Saturn, Available by 1999," *The Wall Street Journal,* August 7, 1996, p. C18. ●

Video Case

Quality teamwork at the University of Michigan Hospitals

Foreign competition is increasing in almost every industry, and so are operating costs. Many industries have found that quality management is the solution to both of these challenges. As a result, a quality movement is sweeping across America. Teamwork is a significant part of this movement. Originally embraced by manufacturing industries, quality management and teamwork are now being used in many service industries as well. Service businesses appreciate the positive effect these practices have on employee morale, productivity, and customer satisfaction.

The University of Michigan Hospitals adopted quality management as a way to attract and keep top people in the health care profession. John Forsyth, executive director of the University of

Michigan Hospitals, explained, "The three reasons the University of Michigan has become involved in total quality are: number one, to become the provider of choice; number two, to become preeminent in education in the medical sciences; and number three, to become the employer of choice. The key here is to have a diverse and motivated workforce, and we believe total quality will empower people to that end."

The development of problem-solving teams composed of both managers and employees is one highly effective aspect of a quality program. Team problem-solving techniques are proving to be a simple, effective catalyst to organizational creativity, quality improvement, and higher quality of work life. But team building in the United States requires a major culture change. Working in groups is somewhat unnatural to Americans who are instilled with a philosophy of individual achievement beginning in elementary school and continuing throughout their academic and business careers. Larry Warren, an administrator at the University of Michigan Hospitals, expressed his personal reservations about changing to a team-oriented culture: "To suggest that we change the way we do business to one of a team approach, to everything that we do and do in the future, stressed me out a little bit."

For teamwork to be effective, new work relationships must be based on trust. One important way to establish this trust is through extensive training and team skills. Ellen Gaucher, senior associate hospital director, said, "We were very concerned about pushing people too hard. We thought they might think this was just another thing administration had up their sleeve for making them work harder. So we got involved with developing a training program that we thought would be the hook for us, would get them excited about total quality. And it has worked very well."

When a quality team is initially selected, it should include decision makers from several key groups: employees, peers, senior managers, customers, suppliers, and staff support. The common characteristics of any team member are interest in the team and the ability to make decisions and commitments on behalf of the team. Joan Robinson, director of ambulatory care nursing, said, "Our nurses are next to the action. They know what our problems are, and they have been schooled on a scientific process of how to address problems. The total quality approach gives us some of the answers in terms of tools that they can use, and working with other people to solve problems, both clinical and some of the problems in the systems of how we get things done here."

Leadership is crucial for a team approach to be effective. The biggest part of a team leader's job is to keep the team together while its members solve the problem. This means developing critical-thinking skills in other team members by asking open-ended questions, or by providing business information so decisions can be made. A team leader must know when to intervene and when to stand back. The leader must avoid the temptation to jump in with solutions, allowing the team to solve the problem with which it has been charged.

When a company develops a quality management program, it's important to implement it slowly and in stages. Widespread team mania at the start-up of a quality program can be dangerous. Leadership by example, employee involvement, and team-building pilot projects make the transition to team problem-solving easier. After training began at the University of Michigan Hospitals, for example, management looked for an area of the hospital to pilot the new team approach. The admitting/discharge unit was selected because of its convoluted system. After examining the problem, the quality team came up with a solution: use a computer link between admitting and housekeeping. Mary Decker Staples, associate hospital administrator, said, "It was successful enough that when we initiated measuring how long it was taking us to admit patients, we were averaging two hours after the patient was ready to go up to the room to actually get to the room. Last year the average was 24 minutes—a 65 percent reduction in the amount of time it takes to admit a patient."

This early success with the team approach built momentum for the future. Employees gained confidence that the approach was effective. Sally Ellis, clinical nurse, remarked, "I think the pilot program that we had with the admissions/discharge team has definitely helped. Some of the things that have come out after it are that we've all had an understanding now of what people do. It takes away some of the myths or perceptions of why something didn't happen. I think that prior to this it was easy to blame someone else why something didn't get done or why a patient didn't get out of here on time."

Once a pilot program has been implemented and employees begin to get excited about the new approach, quality teams can effectively solve all kinds of problems. At the University of Michigan Hospitals, another team tackled problems in accounts receivable. It found that the accounting department was receiving 200 to 300 calls a day—a volume so large that staff members were able to answer less than 50 percent of all calls. The quality team developed more effective means of bookkeeping, which freed up the staff so they were able to handle more calls. Pamela Chapelle, assistant manager of financial services, said, "For June, the number of calls that we answered was 74 percent. We have never, in the four years that I've been in this department, answered 74 percent of the calls that have come in."

Another quality team helped open up communication between departments for more effective patient care. A pharmacy team was reviewing the administration of drugs by the medical staff when it found that one drug could be administered on an eight-hour basis instead of the current six-hour basis. The team organized educational sessions with the medical and pharmacy staffs. Michael Ryan, assistant directory of pharmacy, said, "What we find now is that 97 percent of prescribing is being done on an eight-hour basis. This has resulted in savings of labor for staff that have to compound and administer the extra dose as well as the expense of the drug, which is a savings of about $30,000 per year."

The key element in effective team problem solving is employee empowerment. Teams cannot be effective if management changes or ignores the team's final recommendations. In a team situation, management must give employees wide latitude in how they go about achieving the company's goals. This requires turning the organization chart upside down, recognizing that management is there to aid the worker in overcoming problems that arise. True employee empowerment enables an employee to achieve his or her highest potential, which benefits the company and the customer.

The success of quality teams at the University of Michigan Hospitals has been recognized throughout the health care profession. In 1990, Witt and Associates, Inc., and the Health Care Forum awarded the University of Michigan Hospitals the Commitment to Quality Award. The award was established in 1987 to recognize health care professionals committed to quality health care services. The success of the teamwork approach at the University of Michigan Hospitals has convinced many managers that it is a worthwhile endeavor. Staples said, "I think one of the biggest advantages and positive aspects of total quality is our opportunity to use the knowledge that people who are working at the front line have about what works and what doesn't work. So often we as managers sit back thinking we know what's going on. And when you begin to ask employees what's going on, you get a very different picture of the process."

The employees at the University of Michigan Hospitals have embraced the philosophy of quality management, and the use of teams for solving problems, increasing work effort, and developing good employee attitudes. Not only do teams solve problems more effectively, but they allow the employees to focus on improving the processes that affect them. The result? Smoother working relationships, streamlined procedures, and reduced costs.

Critical Thinking Questions

1. Producing quality services through the use of teamwork has proven an effective approach for the University of Michigan Hospitals. Why do you think team problem solving has proven to be so effective? How do teams differ from committees or task forces?

2. As discussed briefly in the video, some employees will initially resist organizational transformation to a team approach. Why do you think employees would resist this change? What are some techniques a manager might use to help overcome this resistance?

3. Teams are very effective in solving problems related to the process flow of an organization. Try to think of some organizational problems or issues that are not likely to be resolved using a team approach. Explain why you think so.

Experiential Exercises

14.1 Prisoners' dilemma: An intergroup competition

Instructions

1. The instructor explains what will take place in this exercise and assigns people to groups. Two types of teams are formed and named Red and Blue (with no more than eight per group) and are not to communicate with the other team in any way, verbally or nonverbally, except when told to do so by the instructor. Groups are given time to study the Prisoner's Dilemma Tally Sheet.

2. (3 min.) Round 1. Each team has three minutes to make a team decision. Write your decisions when the instructor says time is up.

3. (2 min.) The choices of the teams are announced for Round 1. The scores are entered on the Tally Sheet.

4. (4–5 min.) Round 2 is conducted in the same manner as Round 1.

5. (6 min.) Round 3 is announced as a special round, for which the payoff points are doubled. Each team is instructed to send one representative to chairs in the center of the room. After representatives have conferred for three minutes, they return to their teams. Teams then have three minutes, as before, in which to make their decisions. When recording their scores, they should be reminded that points indicated by the payoff schedule are doubled for this round only.

6. (8–10 min.) Rounds 4, 5, and 6 are conducted in the same manner as the first three rounds.

7. (6 min.) Round 7 is announced as a special round, in which the payoff points are "squared" (multiplied by themselves: e.g., a score of 4 would be $4^2 = 16$). A minus sign would be retained: e.g., $-(3)^2 = -9$. Team representatives meet for three minutes; then the teams meet for three minutes. At the instructor's signal, the teams write their choices; then the two choices are announced.

8. (6 min.) Round 8 is handled exactly as Round 7 was. Payoff points are squared.

9. (10–20 min.) The point total for each team is announced, and the sum of the two team totals is calculated and compared to the maximum positive or negative outcomes (+108 or -108 points). A discussion on win–lose situations, competition, and so on will be conducted.

Prisoners' dilemma tally sheet

Instructions: For 10 successive rounds, the Red team will choose either an A or a B and the Blue team will choose either an X or a Y. The score each team receives in a round is determined by the pattern made by the choices of both teams, according to the schedule below.

Payoff Schedule:

AX—Both teams win 3 points.
AY—Red team loses 6 points; Blue team wins 6 points.
BX—Red team wins 6 points; Blue team loses 6 points.
BY—Both teams lose 3 points.

Scorecard:

Round	Minutes	Choice		Cumulative points	
		Red team	Blue team	Red team	Blue team
1	3				
2	3				
3*	3 (reps.) 3 (teams)				
4	3				
5	3				
6*	3 (reps.) 3 (teams)				
7**	3 (reps.) 3 (teams)				
8**	3 (reps.) 3 (teams)				

*Payoff points are doubled for this round. **Payoff points are squared for this round. (Retain the minus sign.)

Source: Dorothy Hai, "Prisoner's Dilemma," in *Organizational Behavior: Experiences and Cases* (St. Paul, Minn.: West, 1986), pp. 125–127. Reprinted by permission.

14.2 The traveler's check scam group exercise

Instructions

1. (3 minutes) Group selects an observer. The observer remains silent during the group problem-solving process, recording the activities of the group on the Observer's Report Form.

2. (15 minutes) Group members read the following problem and proceed to solve it.

The case of Mickey the Dip

Mickey the Dip, an expert pickpocket and forger, liked to work the Los Angeles International Airport on busy days. His technique was to pick the pockets of prosperous-looking victims just before they boarded planes to the East Coast. This gave Mickey five hours to use stolen credit cards before the owners could report their losses.

One morning Mickey snatched a fat wallet from a traveler and left the airport to examine his loot. To his surprise he found no credit cards but instead $500 in traveler's checks. After 20 minutes of practice, Mickey could sign a perfect imitation of the victim's signature. He then proceeded to a large department store where all suits were being sold for 75 percent of the regular price. Mickey purchased a suit for $225 and paid for it with $300 in stolen traveler's checks. After the clerk who served him went to lunch, he bought another suit for $150 and paid for it with the remaining $200 of stolen traveler's checks. Later, Mickey switched the labels on the two suits and, using the receipt from the $225 suit, returned the $150 suit at a centralized return desk for a refund. The refund clerk took the suit and gave Mickey eleven $20 bills, which he stuffed into his pocket and disappeared.

When the department store deposited the traveler's checks, they were returned as forgeries. Assuming the store normally sold suits at twice their wholesale price and used 10 percent of sales as an overhead cost figure, what was the cash value of the loss suffered by the store as a result of Mickey's caper? Do not consider taxes in your computations.

3. (2 minutes) When the group has a solution to the problem upon which all members agree, it will be written on a note and handed to the instructor.

4. (5 minutes) The observer briefs the group on the problem-solving processes observed during the exercise.

5. (25 minutes) The small group discusses the following topics:

   a. Did the group decide on a problem solution process before it attempted to solve the problem? If so, what was it?

   b. Was the solution of the problem hindered in any way by the lack of an appropriate agreed-upon group problem-solving process? Explain.

   c. Who were the leaders of the group during the exercise? What did they do? Critique their leadership activities.

   d. What communications patterns were used by the group during the exercise? Who participated the most? Who participated the least? Describe individual behaviors.

   e. Did the group solve the problem? How many members of the group discovered the correct answer on their own?

   f. Was using the group to solve this problem better than assigning the problem to one person? Explain the rationale for your answer.

The traveler's check scam exercise observer's report

1. What happened during the first few minutes the group met after members finished reading the problem? (List behaviors of specific group members.)

2. Identify the group role played by each group member during the exercise. Give examples of the behavior of each.

3. Were there any conflicts within or among group members during the exercise? Explain the nature of the conflicts and the behavior of the individual(s) involved.

4. How were decisions made in the group? Give specific examples.

5. How could the group improve its problem-solving skills?

Source: Peter P. Dawson, *Fundamentals of Organizational Behavior* (Englewood Cliffs, NJ: Prentice Hall, 1985), pp. 419–22. (c) 1985. Reprinted by permission of Prentice-Hall, Inc., Englewood Cliffs, N.J.

Chapter Fifteen
Communicating

Electronic engineers have yet to devise a better interoffice communications system than the water cooler.

—Leo Ellis

Chapter Outline

Interpersonal Communication
- One-Way versus Two-Way Communication
- Communication Pitfalls
- Mixed Signals and Misperception
- Oral and Written Channels
- Electronic Media
- Communications Networks
- Media Richness
- Efficiency and Effectiveness

Improving Communication Skills
- Improving Sender Skills
- Nonverbal Skills
- Improving Receiver Skills
- Effective Supervision

Organizational Communication
- Downward Communication
- Upward Communication
- Horizontal Communication
- Formal and Informal Communication
- Boundarylessness

Learning Objectives

After studying Chapter 15, you will know:

1. The important advantages of two-way communication.
2. Communications problems to avoid.
3. When and how to use the various communications channels.
4. Ways to become a better "sender" and "receiver" of information.
5. How to improve downward, upward, and horizontal communications.
6. How to work with the company grapevine.
7. The advantages and characteristics of the boundaryless organization.

Setting the Stage

Dialogue Instead of Debate

A steel mill in the Midwest had endured 30 years of labor–management animosity. Most recently, intensive downsizing had wrecked the company. The largest plant had shrunk to 1,000 people, from a peak of 5,000.

People called each other names, threw chairs, stormed out of meetings, and staged work slowdowns. Neither management nor labor trusted the other, and both sides doubted that reconciliation was possible. But tough competition from mini-mills forced them to try to cooperate. So they agreed to try a participative total quality improvement process, and formed joint problem-solving committees.

In the initial meetings, consultants helped the groups to communicate more constructively. Instead of placing blame and resurrecting old conflicts, people tried to step away from the past and really think about the present and the future. They began talking honestly about concerns, and openly considered other viewpoints.

The process was not an easy one; it took time, effort, and courage. But eventually, for the first time, both managers and union personnel began to talk about the business as theirs. They came to recognize that they all were part of the same organization, and they began to think together rather than separately.

According to the union president, the old antagonism is a thing of the past. "That's gone. Now we're looking at the future." The CEO describes it this way: "The process became a method of exchanging thoughts and realizing that none of us have the answer, but together we might have a better answer."

As this example illustrates, there may be no more crucial process in organizations than talking. Similar examples abound. At KPMG Netherlands, chairman Ruud Koedikj knew his firm was extremely successful but faced limited growth opportunities in the segments it served. He knew the firm had to move into new growth areas, but wasn't sure where they were or how to identify them. So he met with all 300 partners, described how he saw the firm's history, current business realities, and future challenges. He then asked how they could go about changing as a firm, and asked for their perspectives. Instead of announcing a new strategy, he engaged the partners in dialogue, thereby building trust and credibility. The partners responded by releasing 100 people from daily responsibilities so they could devote 60 percent of their time, over several months, to work on the strategic challenges faced by the firm.

After 30 years of labor–management conflict, this steel mill entered into a participative total quality improvement process and people finally began working together.
[Jeff Cormin/Tony Stone Images]

Organizations learn, and make progress, when people articulate their perceptions, understandings, and beliefs; listen to one another; and jointly construct new understanding and meanings. Perhaps the most fundamental element of individual learning , and of organizational learning, is the conversation.

Source: Used with permission of the publisher, from Organizational Dynamics, *Autumn 1993, copyright © 1993. American Management Association, New York. All rights reserved. Also, N. M. Dixon, "The Hallways of Learning,"* Organizational Dynamics, *Spring 1997, pp. 23–34; and R. Heifetz and D. Laurie, "The Work of Leadership,"* Harvard Business Review, *January–February 1996, pp. 124–34.*

discussion A type of discourse in which each person attempts to win a debate by having his or her view accepted by the group.

dialogue A discourse in which members explore complex issues from many viewpoints in order to come to a common deeper understanding.

Two types of discourse work together to help a group become a team and an organization become a more effective organization. The two types—and their impact—are illustrated in "Setting the Stage." **Discussion** is like a ping-pong match, with people hitting the ball back and forth.[1] Each person is trying to win a debate, in the sense of having his or her view accepted by the group. Discussions can be polite, and useful, but they can also work at cross-purposes and become destructive.

Dialogue, on the other hand, has the goal of going beyond one person's understanding. The goal is not to "win," but for the team to come to a common, deep understanding. Dialogue explores complex issues from many viewpoints. It requires a commitment to the truth, honesty about people's own beliefs, and true listening and open-mindedness toward others' beliefs. Free exploration of ideas helps individuals, and the group as a unit, to think and learn.[2]

Every group and organization should have both. The most common danger is plenty of discussion and argument, but not much in the way of real dialogue.

Discussion and dialogue are examples of how people communicate. Effective communication is a fundamental aspect of job performance and managerial effectiveness.[3] In this chapter, we will present important communication concepts and some practical guidelines for improving your effectiveness. We will discuss both interpersonal and organizational communication

Interpersonal communication

communication The transmission of information and meaning from one party to another through the use of shared symbols.

Communication is the transmission of information and meaning from one party to another through the use of shared symbols. Figure 15.1 shows a general model of the communication process.

The *sender* initiates the process by conveying information to the *receiver*—the person for whom the message is intended. The sender has a *meaning* he or she wishes to communicate and *encodes* the meaning into symbols (e.g., the words chosen for the message). Then the sender *transmits,* or sends, the message through some *channel,* such as a verbal or written medium.

The receiver *decodes* the message (e.g., reads it) and attempts to *interpret* the sender's meaning. The receiver may provide *feedback* to the sender by encoding a message in response to the sender's message.

figure 15.1 A model of the communication process

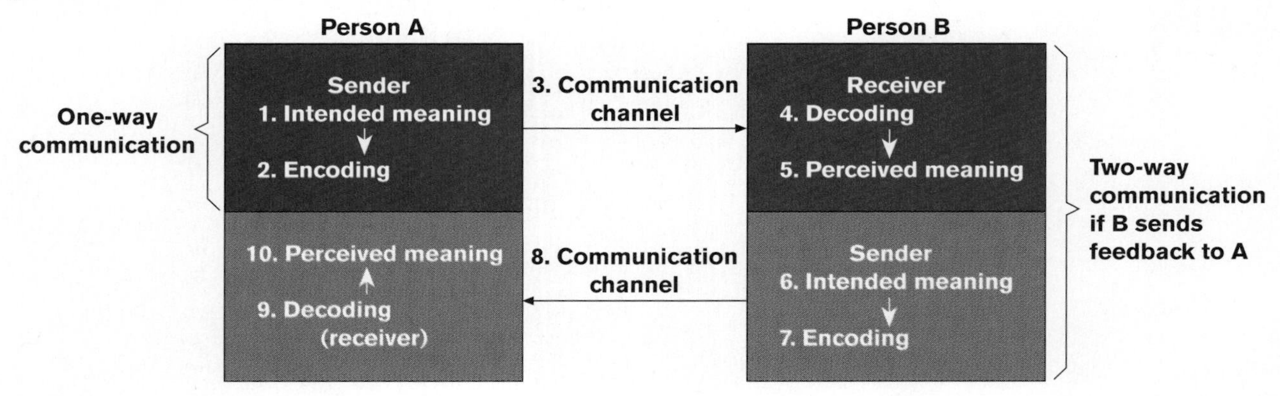

The communication process often is hampered by *noise,* or interference in the system, that blocks perfect understanding. Noise could be anything that interferes with accurate conversation: ringing telephones, thoughts about other things, or simple fatigue or stress.

The model in Figure 15.1 is more than a theoretical treatment of the communication process: It points out the key ways in which communications can break down. Mistakes can be made at each stage of the model. A manager who is alert to potential problems can perform each step carefully to ensure more effective communication. The model also helps explain the differences between one-way and two-way communication, communications pitfalls, misperception, and the various communication channels.

One-way versus two-way communication

one-way communication
A process in which information flows in only one direction—from the sender to the receiver, with no feedback loop.

two-way communication
A process in which information flows in two directions—the receiver provides feedback and the sender is receptive to the feedback.

In **one-way communication,** only the top half of the model in Figure 15.1 is operating. Information flows in only one direction—from the sender to the receiver, with no feedback loop. A manager sends a memo to a subordinate without asking for an immediate response. A boss gives an order over the phone. A father scolds his son and then storms out of the room.

When receivers do respond to senders, completing the Figure 15.1 model, **two-way communication** has occurred. One-way communication in situations like those just described can become two-way if the manager follows up her memo with a phone call and asks the receiver if he has any questions, the boss on the telephone listens to alternative suggestions for carrying out her order, and the father calms down and listens to his son's side of the story.

True two-way communication means not only that the receiver provides feedback but also that the sender is receptive to the feedback. In these constructive exchanges, information is shared between both parties rather than delivered from one person to the other.

One-way communication is much more common than it should be because it is faster and easier for the sender. The busy executive finds it easier to dash off a memo than to discuss the issue with the subordinate. Also, he doesn't have to deal with questions or be challenged by someone who disagrees.

Two-way communication is more difficult and time-consuming than one-way communication. However, it is more accurate; fewer mistakes occur and fewer problems arise. Receivers have a chance to ask questions, share concerns, make suggestions or modifications, and consequently understand more precisely what is being communicated and what they should do with the information.[4]

Communication pitfalls

The sender's intended message does not always "get across" to the receiver. Here is a fact that conveys the ambiguities of communicating and possibilities for misinterpretation: For the 500 most commonly used words in the English language, there are over 14,000 definitions.[5]

Errors can occur in all stages of the communication process. In the encoding stage, words can be misused, decimal points typed in the wrong places, facts left out, or ambiguous phrases inserted. In the transmission stage, a memo gets lost on a cluttered desk, the words on an overhead transparency are too small to read from the back of the room, or words are spoken with ambiguous inflections.

Decoding problems arise when the receiver doesn't listen carefully or reads too quickly and overlooks a key point. And, of course, receivers can misinterpret the message, as a reader draws the wrong conclusion from an unclear memo, a listener takes a general statement by the boss too personally, or a sideways glance is taken the wrong way.

perception The process of receiving and interpreting information.

filtering The process of withholding, ignoring, or distorting information.

More generally, people's perceptual and filtering processes create misinterpretations. **Perception** is the process of receiving and interpreting information. As you know, such processes are not perfectly objective. They are subjective, as people's self-interested motives and attitudes toward the sender and toward the message create biased interpretations.

Filtering is the process of withholding, ignoring, or distorting information. Senders do this, for example, when they tell the boss what they think the boss wants to hear, or give unwarranted compliments rather than honest criticism. Receivers can also filter information; they may fail to recognize an important message, or attend to some aspects of the message but not others.

Filtering and subjective perception pervade one interesting aspect of the communications dynamic: how men and women differ in their communicating styles. In the workplace, choices made at different stages of the model—choices in which senders and receivers filter and perceive different things—"affect judgments of competence and confidence, as wall as who gets heard, who gets credit, and what gets done."[6] According to Deborah Tannen, a popular writer and respected communications scholar at Georgetown, men speak in ways to establish power, gain personal credit, and minimize the appearance of uncertainty. They have trouble admitting fault or weakness, ask fewer questions, and ritually disagree with others. In contrast, women are more likely to speak in ways to establish rapport, to downplay their accomplishments (assuming they will get the credit they deserve), to help others save face, and to be more indirect in telling others what to do. Women, says Tannen, are more likely to say "we" in situations where men say "I."[7]

A manager at a magazine who tended to phrase the assignments she gave her reporters as questions—"How would you like to do the X project with Y?" and "I was thinking of putting you on the X project, is that okay?"—was criticized by her male boss, who told her she did not portray the proper demeanor with her staff.[8] Another, the owner of a retail operation, told one of her store managers to do something by saying, "The bookkeeper needs help with the billing. How would you feel about helping her out?" He said fine, but didn't do it. Whereas the boss thought he meant he would do it, he said he meant he would think about how he would feel about helping. He decided he had better things to do.[9]

Because of such filtering and perceptual differences, you cannot assume the other person means what you think he means, or understands the meanings you intend. Managers need to excel at reading interactions, and adjusting their communication styles and perceptions to the people with whom they interact.[10] The very human tendencies to filter and perceive subjectively underly many of the ineffective communications, and the need to engage in more effective communication practices, that you will read about through the rest of this chapter.

Mixed signals and misperception

A common thread underlying the discussion so far is that people's perceptions can undermine attempts to communicate. People do not pay attention to everything going on around them. They inadvertently send mixed signals that can undermine their intended messages. Different people attend to different things, and people interpret the same thing in different ways. All of this creates problems in communication.

If the communication is between people from different cultures, these problems are magnified.[11] Communication "breakdowns" often occur when business transactions take place between people from different countries. Chapter 6 introduced you to the importance of these cultural issues. Table 15.1 offers suggestions for communicating effectively with someone who speaks a different language.

The following examples further highlight the operation of mixed signals and misperceptions. A bank CEO knew that to be competitive he had to downsize his organization, and the employees who remained would have to commit to customer service, become more

table 15.1
What do I do if they do not speak my language?

Verbal behavior

- *Clear, slow speech.* Enunciate each word. Do not use colloquial expressions.
- *Repetition.* Repeat each important idea using different words to explain the same concept.
- *Simple sentences.* Avoid compound, long sentences.
- *Active verbs.* Avoid passive verbs.

Nonverbal behavior

- *Visual restatements.* Use as many visual restatements as possible, such as pictures, graphs, tables, and slides.
- *Gestures.* Use more facial and appropriate hand gestures to emphasize the meaning of words.
- *Demonstrations.* Act out as many themes as possible.
- *Pauses.* Pause more frequently.
- *Summaries.* Hand out written summaries of your verbal presentation.

Accurate Interpretation

- *Silence.* When there is a silence, wait. Do not jump in to fill the silence. The other person is probably just thinking more slowly in the nonnative language or translating.
- *Intelligence.* Do not equate poor grammar and mispronunciation with lack of intelligence; it is usually a sign of nonnative language use.
- *Differences.* If unsure, assume difference, not similarity.

Comprehension

- *Understanding.* Do not just assume that they understand; assume that they do not understand.
- *Checking comprehension.* Have colleagues repeat their understanding of the material back to you. Do not simply ask if they understand or not. Let them explain what they understand to you.

Design

- *Breaks.* Take more frequent breaks. Second language comprehension is exhausting.
- *Small modules.* Divide the material to be presented into smaller modules.
- *Longer time frame.* Allocate more time for each module than you usually need for presenting the same material to native speakers of your language.

Motivation

- *Encouragement.* Verbally and nonverbally encourage and reinforce speaking by nonnative language participants.
- *Drawing out.* Explicitly draw out marginal and passive participants.
- *Reinforcement.* Do not embarrass novice speakers.

Source: N. Adler, *International Dimensions of Organizational Behavior,* 3rd ed. (Cincinnati: Southwestern, 1997).

empowered, and really *earn* customer loyalty.[12] Knowing that his employees would have doubts and concerns about the coming reorganization, he decided to make a promise to them that he would do his best to guarantee employment, growth, and training.

What signals did the CEO communicate to his people by his promises? One positive signal was that he cared about his people. But he also signaled that *he* would take care of *them,* thus undermining his goal of giving them more responsibility and empowering them. The employees wanted management to take responsibility for the market challenge that *they* needed to face—to handle things for them when *they* needed to learn the new ways of doing business. Inadvertently, the CEO spoke to their backward-looking need for security when he had meant to make them see that the bank's future depended on *their* efforts.

Another CEO of another firm talked repeatedly about the importance of empowerment throughout the organization.[13] But during one meeting, when a young manager brought up a problem that the home office was not handling for him as he had requested, the CEO thanked the manager, told him to whom to talk, and assured him that he would pave the way. Many executives in attendance even praised the CEO for empowering the manager.

But the CEO could have given a better, much more empowering response. The CEO could have taken the opportunity to ask the manager how the organization could be redesigned so that he and other people like him felt they had the freedom to take the initiative and get results on their own. Promising to help one person on one issue, by invoking CEO power, does not communicate to people the goal of their true and permanent empowerment to make positive things happen on their own.[14]

Consider how many problems could be avoided—and how much more effective communication could be—if people took the time to (1) ensure that the receivers attend to the message they are sending; (2) consider the other party's frame of reference and attempt to convey the message from that perceptual viewpoint; (3) take concrete steps to minimize perceptual errors and improper signals, in both sending and receiving; and (4) send *consistent* messages. You should make an effort to predict people's interpretations of your messages and think in terms of how they could *misinterpret* your messages. It helps to say not only what you mean but also what you *don't* mean. Every time you say. "I am not saying *X*, I am saying *Y*," you eliminate a possible misinterpretation.[15]

Oral and written channels

Communication can be sent through a variety of channels (step 3 and 8 in the Figure 15.1 model) including oral, written, and electronic. Each channel has advantages and disadvantages.

Oral communication includes face-to-face discussion, telephone conversations, and formal presentations and speeches. Advantages are that questions can be asked and answered; feedback is immediate and direct; the receiver(s) can sense the sender's sincerity (or lack thereof); and oral communication is more persuasive and sometimes less expensive than written. However, oral communication also has disadvantages: It can lead to spontaneous, ill-considered statements (and regret), and there is no permanent record of it (unless an effort is made to record it).

Written communication includes memos, letters, reports, computer files, and other written documents. Advantages to using written messages are that the message can be revised several times, it is a permanent record that can be saved, the message stays the same even if relayed through many people, and the receiver has more time to analyze the message. Disadvantages are that the sender has no control over where, when, or if the message is read; the sender does not receive immediate feedback; the receiver may not understand parts of the message; and the message must be longer to contain enough information to answer anticipated questions.[16]

You should weigh these considerations when deciding whether to communicate orally or in writing. Also, sometimes use both channels, such as when following up a meeting with a confirming memo or writing a letter to prepare someone for your phone call.

Electronic media

A special category of communication channels is electronic media. Managers use computers not only to gather and distribute quantitative data but to "talk" with others via electronic mail (e-mail). For people who don't have direct access to each other via computer, facsimile (fax) machines can transmit messages in seconds through telephone lines all over the world. Other means of electronic communication include *teleconferencing,* in which groups of people in different locations interact over telephone lines (*audioconferencing*) and perhaps also see one another on television monitors as they participate in group discussions (*videoconferencing*).

Advantages *Advantages* of electronic communication technology are numerous and dramatic. You can learn in other courses and books about how to use these technologies to start and grow a successful business. Within firms, the advantages of electronic communication include the sharing of more information, and speed and efficiency in delivering routine messages to large numbers of people across vast geographic areas. It's also cheap: A message that costs $16 for overnight delivery, or $3 through snail mail, costs about 9 cents via e-mail.[17] Also, it can reduce time spent traveling to and interacting in group meetings. One study indicated that e-mail at a large office equipment corporation reduced time spent on the phone by 80 percent, interoffice mail by 94 percent, photocopying by 60 percent, and paper memos by 50 percent.[18] A Xerox Webmaster estimates that, with 75,000 hits per month, the 3,000 people who used the site in a six-month period saved 32 years of effort by getting information from the site rather than tracking it down themselves.[19]

Disadvantages *Disadvantages* of electronic communication include the difficulty of solving complex problems, which require more extended, face-to-face interaction, and the inability to pick up subtle, nonverbal, or inflectional clues about what the communicator is thinking or conveying. E-mail is most appropriate, then, for routine messages that do not require the exchange of large quantities of complex information. It is less suitable for confidential information, resolving conflicts, or negotiating.[20]

One inevitable consequence of electronic mail is "flaming": hurling insults, sending "nastygrams," venting frustration, snitching on co-workers to the boss, and otherwise breaching bureaucratic protocol.[21] E-mail liberates people to type and send things they would not say to a person's face. The lack of nonverbal cues can result in "kidding" remarks being taken seriously; this can cause resentment and regret. It is not unheard of for confidential messages, including details about people's personal lives and insulting, embarrassing remarks, to become public knowledge through electronic leaks.

Other downsides to electronic mail are important to know.[22] Different people and sometimes different working units latch onto different channels as their medium of choice. For example, an engineering division might use e-mail most; but a design group might rely primarily on voice mail or printed faxes, and neglect e-mail.[23] Another disadvantage is that e-mail messages sometimes are monitored or seen inadvertently by those for whom they are not intended. Deleting messages does not destroy them; they are saved elsewhere. Recipients can forward them to others, unbeknownst to or without the permission of the original sender. And they can be used in court cases to indict individuals or companies. E-mail messages are private property—but the private property of the system's owner, not of the sender.[24]

From the Pages of BusinessWeek

Computers and Speech

IBM recently beat most competitors to market with its new product ViaVoice Gold, an affordable speech program that transforms spoken sentences into text. Now powerful speech-recognition technology is bursting into the marketplace as machines learn how to recognize and understand "natural language" spoken by humans. The new generation of speech technology will have a profound impact on how we work and live.

Speech may be the ultimate bridge between people and machines. Companies are working on voice-controlled Web-browsing programs (imagine not having to click for hours on end, but just telling the computer what to do), programs that talk and respond to call-in customers (no more press-one/press-two phone menus), and other speech-recognition software products that do for you (rather, with you) such thing as trade stocks and options, check auto ads, get airline reservations, and retrieve voice-mail, e-mail, and faxes from a unified mailbox. General Magic's Serengeti service will read all your messages to you while you drive your car. Bill Gates calls speech "not just the future of Windows, but the future of computing itself."

Many companies hire temps in their call centers at busy times of year, such as Christmas. Speech recognition software is now available to do the same work at lower cost. AT&T claims that speech-recognition software from Bell Labs, used in managing collect and credit-card calls, has saved several hundred million dollars over six years.

Business Week concludes its cover article on speech recognition technology by stating, "speech is the most promising means for making information universally accessible. And it's the only one that is direct, spontaneous, and intuitive for all people. We can't guess what kinds of dialogs will evolve among humans and machines in the next century. But it's certain we'll all soon be spending a lot more time chatting with computers."

Source: N. Gross, P. Judge, O. Port, and S. Wildstrom, "Let's Talk!" *Business Week*, February 23, 1998, pp. 45–53.

The virtual office Many entrepreneurs conduct business via open "offices" on the Internet, working off their computers from wherever they happen to be. Similarly, major companies like IBM, AT&T, Xerox, GE, MCI, and Chiat/Day are slashing office space and giving people laptops or powerful notebook computers, telecommunications software,

Advances in information technology have made people more mobile, creating the new virtual office.
[Tony Freeman/PhotoEdit]

While the trend toward home offices is growing, companies are keeping a watchful eye on productivity and morale. To look at the man pictured here, the home or virtual office seems like the ultimate in the good life. *[Reed Rahn]*

virtual office A mobile office in which people can work anywhere, as long as they have the tools to communicate with customers and colleagues.

voice mail, and other communications technologies so they can work virtually anywhere, anytime. Based on the philosophy that management's focus should be on what people do, not where they are, the **virtual office** is a mobile office in which people can work anywhere—their home, car, airport, customers' offices—as long as they have the tools to communicate with customers and colleagues.[25] One observer calls the virtual office "the most radical redefinition of the workplace since the Industrial Revolution."[26]

In the short run, at least, the benefits appear substantial. Compaq Computer has reduced sales costs and administrative expenses from 22 percent of revenue to 12 percent. Perkin-Elmer, which makes scientific equipment, was able to close 35 branch offices. AT&T says mobile offices allow salespeople to spend 15 to 20 percent more time with customers.[27] And most people like the flexibility it gives them.

But what will be the longer-term impact on productivity and morale? Some people hate being forced to work at home. Some valuable people have quit. Some send faxes, e-mail, and voice mail in the middle of the night—and others receive them. Some work around the clock and still feel they are not doing enough. The long hours of being constantly close to the technical tools of work can cause burnout. And some companies are learning that direct supervision at the office is necessary to maintain the quality of work, especially when employees are inexperienced and need guidance. One company president says, "As soon as I separate my supervisors from the people they're supposed to be developing, I make if difficult for effective coaching to occur."[28]

At the moment, it appears that most people are pleased to have changed to mobile offices, and that they believe they are being more productive. But questions have arisen, and some companies are being careful with the new idea. AT&T no longer makes mobile offices mandatory. And many companies experiment with the idea and give people options as they try to win people's approval of the new tools.

Managing the electronic load

Electronic communication media seems essential these days, and people wonder how they ever worked without it. At the same time, the sheer volume of communication can be overwhelming.[29] In major corporations, more than one million e-mails per day are sent. Fax machines, mobile phones, voice mail, the Internet, the World Wide Web, and other systems seem to conspire to overload people with messages and information. The advent of self-directed and cross-functional teams

Julie of Netscapes begins checking her constant stream of e-mails from home *before* she even gets to work.
[Ed Kashi]

necessitates and inspires tremendous volumes of communications. Requests, FYI copies of everything under the sun, information from shared databases, and so on from co-workers, customers, vendors, trade and industry sources . . . Many managers routinely get 50 to 100 e-mails per day, some up to 500. And coming back from vacation can be tortuous. Andy Grove, chairman of Intel, is said to have four or five people who do nothing but handle his schedule, and half of their time is spent on e-mail.[30]

A few rules of thumb can help you in your electronic communications.[31] Use a medium that you know your audience uses. For messages delivered to many people, use a medium everyone understands is priority. Better yet, use multiple channels. If the message is important, make its importance clear. If you are requesting action, make that clear as well. Don't overrely on electronic media; other channels, including old-fashioned face-to-face conversation, are better for some purposes.

For the problem of information overload, the challenge is to separate the truly important from the routine. Effective managers find time to think about bigger business issues, and don't get too bogged down in responding to every message that seems urgent but may be trivial. Essential here is to think strategically about your goals, identify the things that are most important, and prioritize your time around those goals. This is easier said than done, of course, but it is essential, and it helps. And then, by the way, you can apply technological solutions: software that, based on the most important information needs you identify for yourself, can help protect you from the electronic information quagmire.[32]

Some companies are recognizing the downsides of electronic media overuse. They discourage people from sending too many unnecessary e-mails. Smith Kline Beecham, the Philadelphia-based pharmaceutical firm, charges business units fees based on the number and length of e-mail messages. Computer Associates shuts down the e-mail system every day for two hours. Many firms, and individuals and teams, set aside time every day, free from e-mails and phones, to work on their primary tasks. They often report this to be the most productive time of the day.[33]

Communications networks

The volume of communication an individual receives depends in part on his or her position in decision-making structures (see Figure 15.2).[34] Independent, decentralized decision makers have the lowest communications needs. Local store managers or local banks may make their own decisions without conferring with other stores, branches, or headquarters. More centralized decision makers need and are exposed to greater volumes of communication. Just as generals need information from battlefields, intelligence, and other sources in order

figure 15.2
Three communications networks

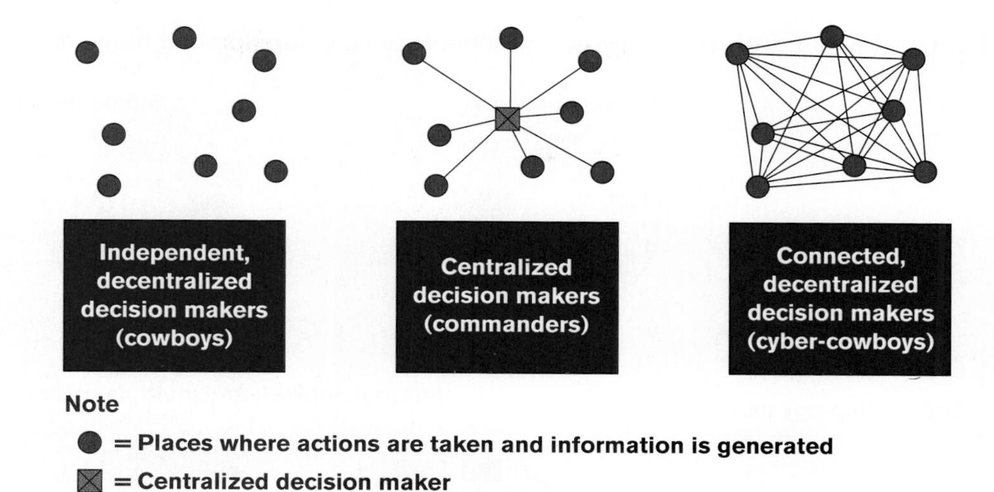

Source: Reprinted from "Is Empowerment Just a Fad? Control, Decision Making and IT," by J. Malone, *Sloan Management Review,* Winter 1997, pp. 23–35, by permission of publisher.

to make decisions, managers can make better decisions if they receive relevant information from different sites and from people both inside and outside the firm. And some decentralized decision makers are so interconnected that they require even more information than centralized ones. They make independent decisions, but their decisions must be based on vast amounts of information from remotes sites available through electronic or other networks. As shown in the figure, information needs to be brought to all the decentralized decision makers, not just a single centralized one. Given the dramatic increase in the need for communications, and the distances that information must travel, effective information sharing and good decisions would not be possible without information technologies.

Such complex networks of communications are exaggerated even further when we consider interorganization collaborations, discussed in previous chapters (and illustrated in Figure 15.3).[35] And firms today commonly are in a number of external networks, simultaneously and in succession. Even greater attention must be paid not only to the strategic decisions surrounding the partnerships, but also to having an adequate information technology infrastructure, through which people communicate and cooperate effectively.

Media richness

media richness The degree to which a communication channel conveys information.

As suggested above, some communication channels convey more information than others. The amount of information a medium conveys is called **media richness.** The more information or cues a medium sends to the receiver, the "richer" the medium is. The richest media are more personal than technological, provide quick feedback, allow lots of descriptive language, and send different types of cues. Thus, face-to-face communication is the richest medium because it offers a variety of cues in addition to words: tone of voice, facial expression, body language, and other nonverbal signals. It also allows more descriptive language than, say, a memo does. In addition, it affords more opportunity for the receiver to give feedback to and ask questions of the sender, turning one-way into two-way communication.

The telephone is less rich than face-to-face communication, electronic mail is less rich yet, and memos are the least rich medium. In general, you should send difficult and unusual messages through richer media, transmit simple and routine messages through less rich media like memos, and use multiple media for important messages that you want to ensure people attend

figure 15.3 Levels of complexity in technology collaboration and networks

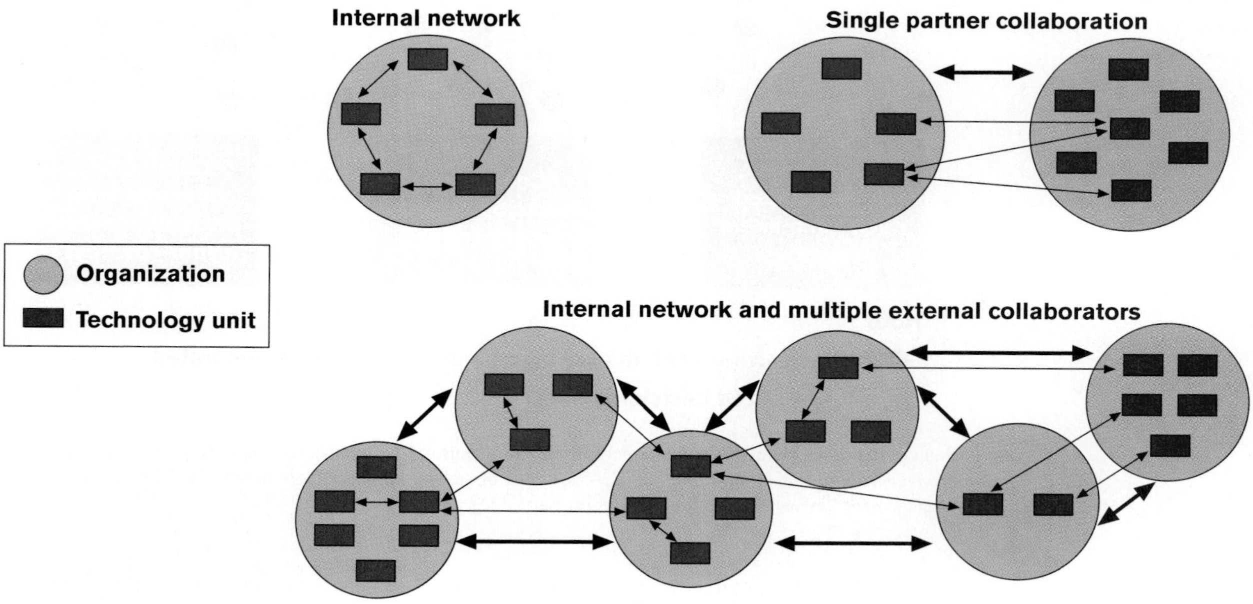

Internal network

Single partner collaboration

Organization

Technology unit

Internal network and multiple external collaborators

Source: From "Challenges in Managing Technology in Transnational Multipartner Networks," by J. Medcof. Reprinted from *Business Horizons,* January–February 1996. Copyright © 1996 by the Foundation for the School of Business at Indiana University. Used with permission.

to and understand.[36] You should also consider factors such as which medium your receiver prefers, the preferred communication style in your organization, and cost.[37] Table 15.2 gives some sample situations for choosing channels based on the message and the audience.

Efficiency and effectiveness

Some managers believe they should choose only one channel to communicate a message because doing so is more efficient.[38] But for important or complex messages, multiple channels may be appropriate. Consider how Citicorp communicated its new flexible benefits plan to 56,000 employees: through software, workbooks, videos, seminars and other teaching tools, a telephone hotline, and hundreds of trained human resources people who traveled to different sites to explain the benefits in person. The total cost was several million dollars, but Citicorp understood that different people were more likely to attend to and understand messages from different channels—and it wanted *all* its employees to fully understand the new benefits program.[39] In this case, by spending time and money to make sure everyone understood the plan, costly problems were avoided. Citicorp's communication efforts were both efficient and effective.

Some managers overrely on certain "efficient" channels and neglect the most important and richest channel of all: one-on-one conversations between supervisor and employee. Imagine a pizza chain communicating an important change to all employees and distributing a video starring the CEO.[40] You know who works in pizza restaurants; how will they respond? With rapt attention, total involvement, enthusiastic commitment to the announced change? Doubtful. Or how about the distribution of a printed publication? Employees often won't believe what they read, or understand it—that is, if they read it at all. Before important communications, put yourself in the shoes of the receiver and choose your approach accordingly. And for important communications, the sooner and more often they can be discussed face-to-face, one-on-one, or in small groups, the more effective they will be.[41]

table 15.2
Sample situations of media choice

Situation 1: A midsize construction firm wants to announce a new employee benefit program.

Poor choice: Memo **Better choice:** Small group meetings

Rationale: The memo does not offer the feedback potential necessary to explain what may be seen as obscure information. Moreover, with these employees there is a possibility of literacy problems. A group meeting will allow for an oral explanation after which participants can more easily ask questions about any of the complex materials.

Situation 2: A manager wishes to confirm a meeting time with 10 employees.

Poor choice: Phone **Better choice:** Voice mail or e-mail

Rationale: For a simple message like this, there is no need to use a rich medium when a lean one will do the job.

Situation 3: Increase enthusiasm in midsize insurance company for a program that asks employees from different departments to work on the same project team.

Poor choice: E-mail, voice mail **Better choice:** Face-to-face, telephone

Rationale: In situations requiring persuasion the sender must be able to quickly adapt the message to the receiver in order to counter objections. This is not a feature of either e-mail or v-mail. Face-to-face communication offers the sender the greatest flexibility. The phone is the next best alternative.

Situation 4: A group of engineers who are geographically dispersed want to exchange design ideas with one another.

Poor choice: Teleconference **Better choice:** Fax, computer conference

Rationale: A teleconference is apt to overly accentuate the status and personality differences among the engineers. Fax or computer conferencing would allow the quality of the ideas to be the central focus of interaction. Moreover, quick feedback is still possible with these media.

Situation 5: Describe a straightforward but somewhat detailed and updated version of a voice mail system to 1,000 employees who are geographically dispersed.

Poor choice: Newsletter **Better choice:** Videotape

Rationale: If employees are already persuaded of the updated system's merit, you can probably use the newsletter. But a videotape graphically conveys information that requires demonstration, and will educate people about procedures.

Source: From *Communicating for Managerial Effectiveness* by P. G. Clampitt. Copyright © 1991 by Sage Publications, Inc. Reprinted by permission of Sage Publications, Inc.

Improving communication skills

In recent years, employers have been dismayed by college graduates' poor communication skills. A demonstrated ability to communicate effectively makes a job candidate more attractive and distinguishes him or her from others. You can do many things to improve your communication skills, both as a sender and as a receiver.

Improving sender skills

Senders can improve their skills in making persuasive presentations, writing, language use, and sending nonverbal messages.

Presentational and persuasion skills As a manager, you will be called on frequently to "state your case" on a variety of issues. You will have information and perhaps an opinion or proposal to present to others. Typically, your goal will be to "sell" your idea. In other words, your challenge will be to persuade others to go along with your personal recommendation. As a leader, some of your toughest challenges will arise when people do not want to do what has to be done. Leaders have to be persuasive to get people "on board."[42]

In some organizations, as often in life, how you say things may count for more than what you say. If this is the case in your organization, you might strive for style and entertainment in your presentations. But as a manager, you should establish a communication culture that emphasizes accuracy, integrity, fairness, and objectivity rather than mere showmanship and image projection.[43]

Knowing a few fundamental principles of persuasion will help you convince others to adopt your viewpoint.[44] As the *sender* you must have credibility. This means that your audience must know about your expertise and believe you are trustworthy. Issues concerning your *message* include whether to voice opposing arguments and the order in which to present your arguments. How you solve these issues depends on characteristics of the *audience.* You should present only your side of the argument when the audience is friendly and unaware of opposing arguments. But if the audience is initially hostile to your position and aware of counterarguments, you should bring up and refute the opposing view. Also, when you present both arguments, you probably will be more effective if you present your viewpoint last.

It is generally effective to be *redundant.* This is not to say that you should stand in front of your audience and repeat yourself over and over again. It means you should state your viewpoint in a variety of ways and at different times with different audiences. Great leaders convey their visions by seizing every opportunity to talk about them and communicate them tirelessly until their followers "buy into" the message.

The most powerful and persuasive messages are simple and informative, are told with stories and anecdotes, and convey excitement.[45] GE's Jack Welch has had tremendous success with his simple message to all employees of speed, simplicity, and self-confidence. Lawrence Bossidy of AlliedSignal took a similar approach by talking frequently about the three P's: performance (meeting the numbers), portfolio (getting the right product mix), and people (attracting and motivating employees).[46] And the credible communicator backs up the message with actions consistent with the words.

Writing skills Effective writing is more than correct spelling, punctuation, and grammar (although these help!). Good writing above all requires clear, logical thinking.[47] The act of writing can be a powerful aid to thinking, because you have to think about what you really want to say and what the logic is behind your message.[48]

You want people to find your memos and reports readable and interesting. Strive for clarity, organization, readability, and brevity.[49] Brevity is much appreciated by readers who are overloaded with documents, including wordy memos. Use a dictionary and a thesaurus, and avoid fancy words. Charles Krauthammer, the newspaper columnist, praises brevity in a column titled "Make it Snappy."[50] He notes that Ian Wilmut, the scientist who cloned the sheep Dolly, announced his findings to the scientific community in a three-page journal article. Two of the greatest speeches in American history fit on part of one wall at the Lincoln memorial. The Truman doctrine, which set the course of American foreign policy for half a century, took only 18 minutes to deliver. Watson and Crick's article announcing the discovery of the structure of DNA was just over one page.

Your first draft rarely is as good as it could be. If you have time, revise it. Take the reader into consideration. Go through your entire letter, memo, or report and delete all unnecessary words, sentences, and paragraphs. Use specific, concrete words rather than abstract phrases. Instead of saying, "A period of unfavorable weather set in," say, "It rained every day for a week."

Be critical of your own writing. If you want to improve, start by reading *The Elements of Style* by William Strunk and E. B. White and the most recent edition of *The Little, Brown Handbook.*[51]

Language Word choice can enhance or interfere with communication effectiveness. For example, jargon is actually a form of shorthand and can make communication more effective when both the sender and the receiver know the buzzwords. But when the receiver is unfamiliar with the jargon, misunderstandings result. When people from different functional areas or disciplines communicate with one another, misunderstandings often occur because of "language" barriers. As in writing, simplicity usually helps.

Therefore, whether speaking or writing, you should consider the receiver's background and adjust your language accordingly. When you are receiving, don't assume that your understanding is the same as the speaker's intentions. Japanese use the simple word *hai* (yes) to convey that they understand what is being said; it does not necessarily mean that they agree. Asian businesspeople rarely use the direct "no," using more subtle or tangential ways of disagreeing.[52]

When conducting business overseas, try to learn something about the other country's language and customs. Americans are less likely to do this than people from some other cultures; most Americans do not consider a foreign language necessary for doing business abroad, and a significant majority of U.S. firms do not require employees sent abroad to know the local language.[53] But those who do will have a big edge over their competitors who do not.[54] Making the effort to learn the local language builds rapport, sets a proper tone for doing business, aids in adjustment to culture shock, and especially can help you "get inside" the other culture.[55] You will learn more about how people think, feel, and behave, both in their lives and in their business dealings.

Language barriers

Many employers in the United States are wrestling with these questions: Should they hire people with limited English skills? If they do, what should they do about the language barrier?

In the past, many employers hired only people who spoke English. Those that did hire immigrants did not need to communicate with them much because jobs were simple. And if a message had to be conveyed, someone would find an interpreter.

Today, however, immigrants make up a rapidly rising share of the workforce. Moreover, jobs are more complex; even the lowest-level jobs often require people to read blueprints, operate computers, and participate actively in meetings.

Some companies are responding with formal policies and programs. Motorola is spending about $30 million to provide language training to its workers. Pace Foods of San Antonio translates handbooks into Spanish and provides Spanish-speaking interpreters at staff meetings. But different problems arise when people communicate informally among themselves in their native languages.

For example, the day after Florida passed a referendum making English the official state language, an Anglo manager for Publix Supermarkets fired a cashier when she spoke Spanish to a co-worker (the company claims she was fired simply for talking on the job). A nurse is suing a hospital for prohibiting Filipino nurses from speaking Tagalog in front of patients and even among themselves at lunch or on the phone. The Equal Employment Opportunity Commission has ruled that English-only policies are discriminatory except when business reasons make them necessary.

Here's another twist: Bosses may exploit bilingual employees even while forbidding them to speak their native languages. For instance, Spanish is banned among workers, but the same workers are asked to translate when managers need them to do so (say, with a non–English-speaking customer). Contel Corporation was sued for penalizing bilingual employees by pulling them away from the work on which their productivity was evaluated in order to translate for customers. And some bilingual workers are now demanding that they be paid extra for their language skills. At higher organizational levels, bilingual skills are often prized.

This issue is not merely a matter of convenience, preference, or customers. In extreme cases, it can be a matter of life and death. Airline pilots, copilots, and first officers sometimes speak different languages and have only a rudimentary knowledge of their partner's languages. In Korea, few ground controllers speak English, so American pilots are required by law to be paired with a Korean first officer. But what if a crisis arises, and the American and Korean have trouble understanding each other? The problem goes beyond language to cultural norms. Korea's rigid hierarchical, authoritarian culture means that those of lower rank or younger age hesitate to volunteer information, ask questions, or make suggestions.

English is just one of the major languages of world trade, and it is the mother tongue of just 5 percent of the world's population. Businesspeople from other countries are tired of native English speakers assuming it is their responsibility to make the effort and speak English.

On the other hand, English is the second language of choice in most countries, and many observers believe that English eventually will become the world's first language. One observer, particularly critical of Japan's difficulties in communicating with people of other nationalities, says, "The Japanese will need to replace their own language with English as it becomes the language of the rest of the world."

Sources: R. L. Harmon, "Behind Every Buzzword Lurks a Great Idea," *Across the Board,* April 1996, pp. 23–27; J. Solomon, "Firms Grapple with Language Barriers," *The Wall Street Journal,* November 7, 1989, pp. B1, B5; S. Glain, "Language Barrier Proves Dangerous in Korea's Skies," *The Wall Street Journal,* October 4, 1994, pp. B1, B16; and G. Ferraro, "The Need for Linguistic Proficiency in Global Business," *Business Horizons,* May–June 1996, pp. 36–46. ●

Nonverbal skills

As you know, people send and interpret signals other than those that are spoken or written. Nonverbal messages can support or undermine the stated message. And often, nonverbal cues make a greater impact than other signals. For example, without doubt, in employees' eyes the actions of managers often speak louder than the words they choose.

In conversation, except when you intend to convey a negative message, you should give nonverbal signals that express warmth, respect, concern, a feeling of equality, and a willingness to listen. Negative nonverbal signals show coolness, disrespect, lack of interest, and a feeling of superiority.[56] The following suggestions can help you send positive nonverbal signals.

First, use *time* appropriately. Avoid keeping your employees waiting to see you. Devote sufficient time to your meetings with them, and communicate frequently with them to signal your interest in their concerns. Second, make your *office arrangement* conducive to open communication. A seating arrangement that avoids separation of people helps establish a warm, cooperative atmosphere (in contrast, an arrangement in which you sit behind your desk and your subordinate sits before you creates a more intimidating, authoritative environment).[57] Third, remember your *body language.* Research indicates that facial expression and tone of voice can account for 90 percent of the communication between two people.[58] Several nonverbal body signals convey a positive attitude toward the other person: assuming a position close to the person; gesturing frequently; maintaining eye contact; smiling; having an open body orientation, such as facing the other person directly; uncrossing arms; and leaning forward to convey interest in what the other person is saying.

Silence is an interesting nonverbal situation. The average American is said to spend about twice as many hours per day in conversation as the average Japanese.[59] North Americans tend to talk to fill silences. Japanese allow long silences to develop, believing they can get to know people better. Japanese believe that two people with good rapport will know each other's thoughts. The need to use words implies a lack of understanding.

Nonverbal signals in different countries

Here are just a few nonverbal mistakes that Americans might make in other countries.[60] Nodding the head up and down in Bulgaria means no. The American thumb-and-first-finger circular A-OK gesture is vulgar in Brazil, Singapore, Russia, and Paraguay. The head is sacred in Buddhist cultures, so you must never touch someone's head. In Muslim cultures, never touch or eat with the left hand, which is thought unclean. Crossing your ankle over your knee is rude in Indonesia, Thailand, and Syria. Don't point your finger toward yourself in Germany or Switzerland—it insults the other person.

You also need to correctly interpret the nonverbal signals of others. Chinese scratch their ears and cheeks to show happiness. Greeks puff air after they receive a compliment. Hondurans touch their fingers below their eyes to show disbelief or caution. Japanese indicate embarrassment or "no" by sucking in air and hissing through their teeth. Vietnamese look to the ground with their heads down to show respect. Compared to Americans, Russians use fewer facial expressions, and Scandinavians fewer hand gestures, whereas people in Mediterranean and Latin cultures may gesture and touch more. Brazilians are more likely than Americans to interrupt, Arabs to speak loudly, and Asians to respect silence.

Knowing the meaning of body signals in other cultures is imperative to the success of doing business outside of the United States.

[Robert E. Daemmrich/Tony Stone Images]

Improving receiver skills

Once you become effective at sending oral, written, and nonverbal messages, you are halfway home toward becoming a complete communicator. However, you must also develop adequate receiving capabilities. Receivers need good listening, reading, and observational skills.

Listening A recent survey to determine the most important basic skills needed to function in today's demanding work environment indicated that the most pronounced need among managers is better listening skills.[61] Although it is easy to assume that good listening is easy and natural to most people, in fact it is difficult and not nearly as common as needed.

reflection Process by which a person attempts to repeat and clarify what he or she believes the other person is saying.

A basic technique called *reflection* will help a manager listen effectively.[62] **Reflection** is a process by which a person attempts to repeat and clarify what he or she believes the other person is saying. This technique places a greater emphasis on listening than on talking. When both parties actively engage in reflection, they get into each other's frame of reference rather than listening and responding from their own. The result is more accurate two-way communication.

The best-known corporate effort to heighten managers' listening skills was based on an advertising theme—"We understand how important it is to listen"—that reflected a basic philosophy and way of doing business.[63] The company's senior management development specialists created listening training seminars for company personnel, drawing from a study of the 100 best and 100 worst listeners in the freshman class at the University of Minnesota. Table 15.3 summarizes these effective listening techniques.

Listening begins with personal contact. Staying in the office, keeping the door closed, and eating lunch at the desk are sometimes necessary to get pressing work done, but that is no way to stay on top of what's going on. Better to walk the halls at least 30 minutes per day, initiate conversations and go to lunch even with people outside your area, have coffee in a popular gathering place, and maybe even move your desk onto the factory floor.[64]

When a manager takes time to really listen to and get to know people, they think, "She's showing an interest in me" or "He's letting me know that I matter" or "She values my ideas and contributions." Trust develops. Such activities, and listening and learning from others, are even more important for innovation than for routine work. Successful change and innovation come through lots of human contact.

Reading Illiteracy is a significant problem in the United States. Even if illiteracy is not a problem in your organization, reading mistakes are common and costly. As a receiver, for your own benefit, read memos as soon as possible, before it's too late to respond. You may skim most of your reading materials, but read important memos, documents, and passages slowly and carefully. Note important points for later referral. Consider taking courses to increase your reading speed and comprehension skills. Finally, don't limit your reading to items about your particular job skill or technical expertise; read materials that fall outside of your immediate concerns. You never know when a creative idea that will help you in your work will be inspired by a novel, a biography, a sports story, or an article about a problem in another business or industry.

Observing Effective communicators are also capable of observing and interpreting nonverbal communications. (As Yogi Berra said, "You can see a lot by observing.") For example, by reading nonverbal cues a presenter can determine how her talk is going and adjust her approach if necessary. Some companies train their sales forces to interpret the nonverbal signals of potential customers. People can also decode nonverbal signals to determine whether a sender is being truthful or deceitful. Deceitful communicators maintain less eye contact, make either more or fewer body movements than usual, and smile either too much or too little. Verbally, they offer fewer specifics than do truthful senders.[65]

table 15.3
Ten keys to effective listening

1. *Find an area of interest.* Even if you decide the topic is dull, ask yourself, "What is the speaker saying that I can use?"
2. *Judge content, not delivery.* Don't get caught up in the speaker's personality, mannerisms, speaking voice, or clothing. Instead, try to learn what the speaker knows.
3. *Hold your fire.* Rather than getting immediately excited by what the speaker seems to be saying, withhold evaluation until you understand the speaker's message.
4. *Listen for ideas.* Don't get bogged down in all the facts and details; focus on central ideas.
5. *Be flexible.* Have several systems for note taking, and use the system best suited to the speaker's style. Don't take too many notes or try to force everything said by a disorganized speaker into a formal outline.
6. *Resist distraction.* Close the door, shut off the radio, move closer to the person talking, or ask him or her to speak louder. Don't look out the window or at papers on your desk.
7. *Exercise your mind.* Some people tune out when the material gets difficult. Develop an appetite for a good mental challenge.
8. *Keep your mind open.* Many people get overly emotional when they hear words referring to their most deeply held convictions, for example, *union, subsidy, import, Republican* or *Democrat,* and *big business.* Try not to let your emotions interfere with comprehension.
9. *Capitalize on thought speed.* Take advantage of the fact that most people talk at a rate of about 125 words per minute, but most of us think at about four times that rate. Use those extra 400 words per minute to think about what the speaker is saying rather than turning your thoughts to something else.
10. *Work at listening.* Spend some energy. Don't just pretend you're paying attention. Show interest. Good listening is hard work, but the benefits outweigh the costs.

Source: Ralph G. Nichols, "Listening Is a 10-Part Skill," *Nation's Business* 45 (July 1957), pp. 56–60. Cited in R. C. Huseman, C. M. Logue, and D. L. Freshley, eds., *Readings in Interpersonal and Organizational Communication* (Boston: Allyn & Bacon, 1977).

A vital source of useful observations comes from personally visiting plants and other locations to get a first-hand view of operations.[66] Many corporate executives rely heavily on reports from the field and don't travel to remote locations to observe first-hand what is going on. Just as people can learn more from getting out into the field and talking to customers, they can learn about their own company by visiting a plant. Reports often are not current or thorough, rarely reflect intangibles or valid assessments of things like a plant's revenue-generating potential or new capabilities, and don't indicate explicit courses of action. Even great reports are no substitute for actually seeing things happen in practice. Frequent visits to the field, and careful observation, can help a manager develop deep understanding of current operations, future prospects, and ideas for how to fully exploit capabilities.[67]

Of course, you must *accurately interpret* what you observe. A Canadian conducting business with a high-ranking official in Kuwait was surprised that the meeting was held in an open office and was interrupted constantly.[68] He interpreted the lack of a big, private office and secretary to screen out unwanted visitors to mean that the Kuwaiti was of low rank and uninterested in doing business, and he lost interest in the deal. The Canadian observed the facts accurately, but his perceptual biases and lack of awareness regarding how norms differ across cultures caused him to misinterpret what he saw.

The Japanese are particularly skilled at interpreting every nuance of voice and gesture, putting most Westerners at a disadvantage.[69] When conducting business in Asian or other countries, local guides can be invaluable not only to interpret language but to "decode" behavior at meetings, subtle hints and nonverbal cues, who the key people are, and how the decision-making process operates.

Effective supervision

Many studies have compared good and poor supervisors' communications skills.[70] Supervisors who receive higher evaluations exhibit several key characteristics. First, they *communicate more information.* For example, they give advance notice of impending changes, explain the reasons behind policies and regulations, and enjoy conversing with their subordinates. Second, effective supervisors *prefer asking and persuading* to telling and demanding (but are capable of using both styles if necessary). Third, they are *sensitive to people's feelings and needs.* For example, they are careful to reprimand privately rather than publicly. Finally, they are *willing, empathic listeners.* They respond with understanding to all questions from employees and give fair consideration to, and are willing to take appropriate action on, complaints and suggestions.

Thus, effective managers are more "communication minded" than ineffective managers. People who lack confidence in their communication skills, both oral and written, tend to avoid communication situations altogether. This tendency would be a severe handicap for any manager who wanted to enhance his or her unit's performance.[71]

Organizational communication

Being a skilled communicator is essential to being a good manager and team leader. But communication must also be managed throughout the organization. Every minute of every day, countless bits of information are transmitted through an organization. We will discuss downward, upward, horizontal, and informal communication in organizations.

Downward communication

downward communication
Information that flows from higher to lower levels in the organization's hierarchy.

Downward communication refers to the flow of information from higher to lower levels in the organization's hierarchy. Examples include a manager giving an assignment to a secretary, a supervisor making an announcement to his subordinates, and a company president delivering a talk to his management team.

People must receive the information they need to perform their jobs and become (and remain) loyal members of the organization. But they often lack adequate information.[72] One problem is *information overload:* They are bombarded with so much information that they fail to absorb everything. Much of the information is not very important, but its volume causes a lot of relevant information to be lost.

A second problem is a *lack of openness* between managers and employees. Managers may believe "No news is good news," "If only they knew what I know, they wouldn't be upset about this decision," "I don't have time to keep them informed of everything they want to know," or "It's none of their business, anyway." In other words, some managers withhold information even if sharing it is extremely important.

Most managers probably do not give their subordinates enough important information. Employees often are dismayed at how poorly informed their bosses keep them. This is especially true during a crisis or a major change. Generally, people want—and deserve—to know about things that affect them and their work. The manager should consider the consequences of *not* sharing a piece of information and make sure that relevant information is delivered.

A third problem is *filtering,* introduced earlier in the chapter. When messages are passed from one person to another, some information is left out. When a message passes through

figure 15.4
Information loss in downward communication

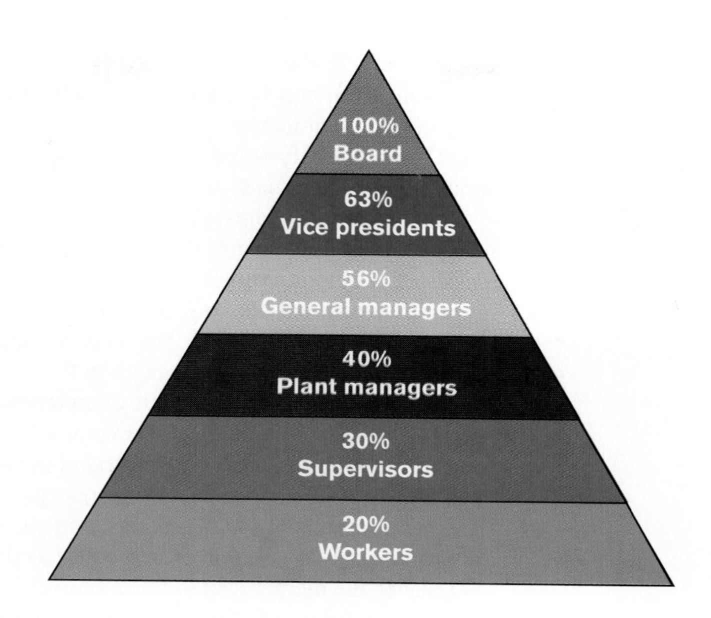

many people, each transmission may cause further information losses. The message can also be distorted as people add their own words or interpretations.

Filtering poses serious problems in organizations. As messages are communicated downward through many organizational levels, much information is lost. The data in Figure 15.4 suggest that by the time messages reach the people for whom they are intended, the receivers may actually get very little useful information.

The fewer the number of authority levels through which communications must pass, the less information will be lost or distorted. Recall from earlier chapters that companies are reducing the number of hierarchical layers. You can now see that the flatter organization offers another advantage: fewer problems caused by filtering of information as it cascades through many layers.

Coaching Some of the most important downward communications occur when managers give performance feedback to their direct reports. We have discussed earlier the importance of giving feedback and positive reinforcement when it is deserved. It is also important to explicitly discuss poor performance and areas that can be improved.

coaching Dialogue with a goal of helping another be more effective and achieve his or her full potential on the job.

Coaching is dialogue with a goal of helping another be more effective and achieve his or her full potential on the job.[73] When people have performance problems, or exhibit behaviors that need to be changed, coaching is often the best way to help the person change and succeed. And coaching is not just for poor performers; as even the greatest athletes know, it is for anyone who is good and aspires to excellence. Although coaches for executives sometimes are hired from the outside,[74] it often is incumbent upon managers to be coaches themselves.

Companies including Coca-Cola and Polaroid use coaching as an essential part of their executive development process, and one California utility has gone so far as to replace all of its executive training with coaching.[75] When done well, coaching is true dialogue between two committed people engaged in joint problem solving. Thus, it is far more than an occasion for highlighting poor performance, delivering reprimands, or giving advice. Good coaching requires achieving real understanding of the problem, the person, and the situation; jointly generating ideas for what to do; and encouraging the person to change. Good coaches ask a lot of questions, listen well, provide input, and also encourage others to think for themselves. Effective coaching requires honesty, calmness, and supportiveness—all aided by a sincere desire to help. The ultimate and longest-lasting form of help is to help people think through and solve their own problems.

Downward communication in difficult times Adequate downward communication can be particularly valuable during difficult times. During corporate mergers and acquisition, employees are anxious as they wonder how the merger will affect them. Ideally—and ethically—top management communicates with employees about the change as early as possible.

But some argue against that approach, maintaining that informing employees about the reorganization might cause them to quit too early. Then too, top management often cloisters itself, prompting rumors and anxiety. CEOs and other senior execs are surrounded by lawyers, investment bankers, and so on—people who are paid merely to make the deal happen, not to make it work. Yet with the people who are affected by the deal, you must increase, not decrease, communication.[76]

In a merger of two Fortune 500 companies, two plants received very different information.[77] All employees at both plants received the initial letter from the CEO announcing the merger. But after that, one plant was kept in the dark while the other was continually filled in about what was happening. Top management gave employees information about layoffs, transfers, promotions and demotions, and changes in pay, jobs, and benefits.

Which plant do you think fared better as the difficult transitional months unfolded? In both plants, the merger decreased employees' job satisfaction and commitment to the organization and increased their belief that the company was untrustworthy, dishonest, and uncaring. In the plant whose employees got little information, these problems persisted for a long time. But in the plant where employees received complete information, the situation stabilized and attitudes improved toward their normal levels. Full communication not only helped employees survive an anxious period; it served a symbolic value by signaling care and concern for employees. Without such communications, employee reactions to a merger or acquisition may be so negative as to undermine the corporate strategy.

open-book management Practice of sharing with employees at all levels of the organization vital information previously meant for management's eyes only.

Open-book management Executives often are proud of their newsletters, staff meetings, videos, and other vehicles of downward communication. More often than not, the information provided concerns company sports teams, birthdays, and new copy machines. But today a more unconventional philosophy is gathering steam. **Open-book management** is the practice of sharing with employees at all levels of the organization vital information previously meant for management's eyes only (see Table 15.4). This includes financial goals, income statements, budgets, sales, forecasts, and other relevant data about company performance and prospects.

These practices are controversial, as many managers prefer to keep such information to themselves. Sharing strategic plans and financial information with employees could lead to leaks to competitors or to employee dissatisfaction with their compensation. But the companies that share this information claim favorable impact on motivation and productivity. Cecil Ursprung, president and CEO of Reflexite Corporation in New Britain, Connecticut, says, "Why would you tell 5 percent of the team what the score was and not the other 95 percent?"[78]

Father of scientific management Frederick Taylor early in the 20th century would have considered opening the books to all employees "idiotic."[79] Almost everyone else would have also, including top executives, middle managers, union leaders, and employees. But then Springfield ReManufacturing Corporation, which was on the brink of collapse, tried it.[80] The company turned around dramatically, achieving profitability and a small measure of fame as it publicized its success in *Inc.* magazine and elsewhere. Other small companies joined the movement. Now, bigger companies like Amoco Canada, R. R. Donnelley, Wabash National, Baxter Healthcare, and AES Corporation are doing it as well. AES, a global power producer listed on the New York Stock Exchange, shares so much financial data with its employees that every one of them has been declared an insider for stock-trading purposes.

Opening the books, done properly, is a complete communications system that makes sense to people on the shop floor just as it does to the top executives. As Table 15.4 shows,

table 15.4
Principles of open-book management

1. Turn the management of a business into a game that employees can win.
2. Open the books and share financial and operating information with employees.
3. Teach employees to understand the financial statements of the company.
4. Show employees how their work influences financial results.
5. Link nonfinancial measures to financial results.
6. Target priority areas and empower employees to make improvements.
7. Review results together and keep employees accountable.
8. Post results and celebrate successes.
9. Distribute bonus awards based on employee contributions to financial outcomes.
10. Share the ownership of the company with employees.

Source: T. R. V. Davis, "Open-Book Management: Its Promise and Pitfalls," *Organizational Dynamics,* Winter 1997, pp. 7–20.

it is not merely the provision of data; people are trained so they understand what the data mean. They are then held accountable for the results of their unit. And they are rewarded for the success of the business, usually through sizable bonus plans and often stock ownership.

The system involves thorough and complete communication so that everything is clear to everyone. People see the numbers that determine success and failure; they learn how their own work is important to the business as a whole; and they know how they will be rewarded if the unit achieves its goals.[81]

This is dramatically different from the traditional closed-book approach in which people may or may not have a clue about how the company is doing, may or may not believe the things that management tells them, and may or may not believe that their personal performance makes a difference. You can see, then, the potential impact on motivation of communications that help people understand why it is important for them, and everyone, to care about business results. It can motivate people to figure out how they can contribute in different ways, to learn new skills, and to work harder and smarter to improve performance.

Upward communication

upward communication Information that flows from lower to higher levels in the organization's hierarchy.

Upward communication travels from lower to higher ranks in the hierarchy. Adequate upward communication is important for several reasons.[82] First, managers learn what's going on. Management gains a more accurate picture of subordinates' work, accomplishments, problems, plans, and attitudes. Management also gains subordinates' ideas. Second, employees gain from the opportunity to communicate upward. People can relieve some of their frustrations, achieve a stronger sense of participation in the enterprise, and improve morale. Third, effective upward communication facilitates downward communication as good listening becomes a two-way street.

The problems common in upward communication are similar to those for downward communication. Managers, like their subordinates, are bombarded with information and may neglect or miss information from below. Furthermore, some employees are not always open with their bosses; in other words, filtering occurs upward as well as downward. People tend to share only good news with their bosses and suppress bad news, because they (1) want to appear competent; (2) mistrust their boss and fear that if he or she finds out about something they have done they will be punished; (3) fear the boss will punish the messenger, even if the reported problem is not that person's fault; or (4) believe they are helping their boss if they shield him or her from problems. For these and other reasons, managers may not learn about important problems.

Managing upward communication Generating useful information from below requires doing two things. First, managers should *facilitate* upward communication. For example, they could have an open-door policy and encourage people to use it, have lunch or coffee with employees, pass out surveys that ask specific questions of people, or institute a program for productivity suggestions. These mechanisms are just a few possibilities that will make upward communication easier.

But managers must also *motivate* people to provide valid information. Useful upward communication must be reinforced and not punished. The person who tries to talk to the manager about a problem must not be brushed off consistently. An announced open-door policy must truly be open-door. Also, people must trust their supervisor and know that the manager will not hold a grudge if they deliver negative information.

Upward communication systems need not be formal; they can also be informal. The manager interested in improving upward communications can ask for employee advice, make informal visits to plants, really think about and respond to employee suggestions, and distribute summaries of new ideas and practices inspired by employee suggestions and actions.[83] For example, many executives practice MBWA (management by wandering around). The term, coined by Ed Carlson of United Airlines, refers simply to getting out of the office, walking around, and talking frequently and informally with employees.[84]

GE uses town meetings in which employees from multiple hierarchical levels meet off-site for dialogue and debate about business and organizational issues. For one or two days prior to the meeting, participants work in small groups generating ideas for improving the business. Then the entire community, bound together by a common boss or customer or business process, debates the ideas and reaches decisions.[85]

Horizontal communication

horizontal communication Information shared among people on the same hierarchical level.

Much information needs to be shared among people on the same hierarchical level. Such **horizontal communication** can take place among people in the same work team. Other important communication must occur between people in different departments. For example, a purchasing agent discusses a problem with a production engineer and a task force of department heads meets to discuss a particular concern.

Horizontal communication has several important functions.[86] First, it allows sharing of information, coordination, and problem solving among units. Second, it helps solve conflicts. Third, by allowing interaction among peers, it provides social and emotional support to people. All these factors contribute to morale and effectiveness.

Managing horizontal communication The need for horizontal communication is similar to the need for integration, discussed in Chapter 8. Particularly in complex environments, in which decisions in one unit affect another, information must be shared horizontally. In Chapters 8 and 9, we discussed numerous techniques for enhancing horizontal communication and integration: direct contact among managers, integrative roles, task forces, project teams, and so forth. Management information systems are another mechanism for making information available to all areas of the organization.

As examples of good horizontal communications, Motorola holds an annual conference for sharing best learnings across functional and business groups throughout the company. NASA co-locates scientists from different disciplines. Hewlett-Packard uses common databases for different product groups to share information and ideas.[87]

GE offers a great example of how to use productive horizontal communications as a competitive weapon.[88] GE consists of 14 divisions, including plastics, major appliances, medical systems, financial services, and NBC. CEO Jack Welch uses the term "integrated diversity" to describe how GE coordinates its 14 different businesses.

GE's businesses could operate completely independently. But each is supposed to help the others. They transfer technical resources, people, information, ideas, and money among themselves. GE accomplishes this high level of communication and cooperation through easy access between divisions and to the CEO; a culture of openness, honesty, trust, and mutual obligation; and quarterly meetings in which all the top executives get together informally to share information and ideas. The same kinds of things are done at lower levels as well.

Formal and informal communication

Organizational communications differ in formality. *Formal communications* are official, organization-sanctioned episodes of information transmission. They can move upward, downward, or horizontally and often involve paperwork, are prearranged, and are necessary for performing some task.

Informal communication is more unofficial. Gossip and rumors run wild on the corporate grapevine; employees complain about their boss; people talk about their favorite sports teams; they whisper secrets about their co-workers; work teams tell newcomers about how they operate.

grapevine Informal communication network.

The **grapevine** is the social network of informal communications that helps people interpret the organization, translates management's formal messages into "employee language," and conveys information that the formal system leaves unsaid. On the other hand, the grapevine can be destructive when irrelevant or erroneous gossip and rumors proliferate and harm operations.[89]

Managing informal communication

Most of the suggestions for improving personal skills and organizational communication—writing, speaking, listening, facilitating and reinforcing upward communication, and so on—typically are applied to improving formal communication. But they can help improve informal communication as well. Additional considerations also apply to managing informal communication effectively.

Rumors start over any number of topics, including who's leaving, who's getting a promotion, salaries, job security, and costly mistakes. Rumors can destroy people's faith and trust in the company—and in each other. But the grapevine cannot be eliminated. Therefore, managers need to *work with* the grapevine.

The grapevine can be managed in several ways.[90] First, if the manager hears a story that could get out of hand, he or she should *talk to the key people* involved to get the facts and their perspectives.

Second, suggestions for *preventing* rumors from starting include:[91] explain things that are important but have not been explained; dispel uncertainties by providing facts; and work to establish open communications and trust over time.

Third, *neutralize* rumors once they have started:[92] disregard the rumor if it is ridiculous (has no credence with others); openly confirm any parts that are true; make public comments (no-comment is seen as a confirmation of the rumor); deny the rumor, if the denial is based in truth (don't make false denials); make sure communications about the issue are consistent; select a spokesperson of appropriate rank and knowledge; and hold town meetings if needed.

Boundarylessness

boundaryless organization Organization in which there are no barriers to information flow.

Many executives and management scholars today consider free access to information in all directions to be an organizational imperative. Jack Welch of GE is the leading advocate and practitioner of what he has termed "boundarylessness." A **boundaryless organization** is one in which there are no barriers to information flow. Instead of boundaries separating people, jobs, processes, and places, ideas, information, decisions, and actions move to where they are most needed.[93] This does not imply a random free-for-all of unlimited communication and information overload. It implies information available *as needed* moving quickly and easily enough so that the organization functions far better as a whole than as separate parts.[94]

GE's successful Workout program shows the benefits of open dialogue across boundaries.
[Courtesy of GE]

Steve Kerr is GE's chief learning officer. When he teaches managers, he says, "I bet every one of you goes home at night with stuff in your head that would help the company . . . and you don't tell your boss" because "it's awkward or risky. Imagine if you could just unleash the power of the collective knowledge right in this room; imagine the good it would do."[95] Kerr uses the metaphor of the organization as a house having three kinds of boundaries: the floors and ceilings, the walls that separate the rooms, and the outside walls. These barriers[96] correspond in organizations to the boundaries between different organizational levels, different units and departments, and the organization and its external stakeholders—for example, suppliers and customers. GE adds a fourth wall: global boundaries separating domestic from global operations.

GE's famous Workout program is a series of meetings for members of a business across multiple hierarchical levels, characterized by extremely frank, tough discussions that break down vertical boundaries. Workout has involved over 222,000 GE people; in any given week over 20,000 are participating in a Workout program.[97] Workout is also done with customers and suppliers, breaking down outside boundaries.

GE uses plenty of other techniques to break down boundaries, as well. It relentlessly benchmarks competitors and companies in other industries to learn best practices all over the world. GE places different functions together physically, such as engineering and manufacturing. It shares services across units. And it sometimes shares physical locations with its customers.

GE takes a useful approach to helping people across the organization teach and learn from one another. The appliance group in Louisville, for example, may have implemented a great innovation.[98] A team from Louisville would then travel to the GE training center in Crotonville, New York. Teams from other businesses go also and receive from the Louisville team a 15-minute overview, just a teaser, describing briefly the situation. Then, small groups of managers fire questions at the Louisville managers to try to figure out what the team has learned and executed. Teams from the other businesses then work to crack the problem. When they think they've got it, they present to the Louisville group. When they don't quite get it right, Louisville tells them the key questions they failed to ask, and the teams proceed to learn what actually was done.

At the beginning of the chapter, we talked about the importance of open dialogue. Boundaryless organizations intentionally create dialogue across boundaries, turning barriers into permeable membranes. As the GE people put it, people from different parts of the organization need to learn "how to talk."[99] They must also learn "how to walk." That is, dialogue is essential, but must be followed by commensurate action.

Key terms

Boundaryless organization, p. 523
Coaching, p. 519
Communication, p. 500
Dialogue, p. 500
Discussion, p. 500
Downward communication, p. 518
Filtering, p. 502
Grapevine, p. 523
Horizontal communication, p. 522
Media richness, p. 509
One-way communication, p. 501
Open-book management, p. 520
Perception, p. 502
Reflection, p. 516
Two-way communication, p. 501
Upward communication, p. 521
Virtual office, p. 506

Summary of learning objectives

Now that you have studied Chapter 15, you should know:

Communications problems to avoid.

The communication process involves a sender who conveys information to a receiver. Problems in communication can occur in all stages: encoding, transmission, decoding, and interpreting. Noise in the system further complicates communication, creating more distortion. Moreover, feedback may be unavailable or misleading. Subjective perceptions and filtering add to the possibility for error.

The important advantages of two-way communication.

One-way communication flows from the sender to the receiver, with no feedback loop. In two-way communication, each person is both a sender and a receiver as both parities provide and react to information. One-way communication is faster and easier but less accurate than two-way; two-way communication is slower and more difficult, but is more accurate and results in better performance.

When and how to use the various communications channels.

Communications are sent through oral, written, and nonverbal channels. All have important advantages and disadvantages that should be considered before choosing a channel. Electronic media have a huge impact on interpersonal and organizational communications and make possible the virtual office. Key advantages of electronic media are speed, cost, and efficiency, but the downsides are also significant, including information overload. Media richness, or how much and what sort of information a channel conveys, is one factor to consider as you decide which channels to use and how to use them both efficiently and effectively.

Ways to become a better "sender" and "receiver" of information.

Practice writing, be critical of yourself, and revise. Train yourself as a speaker. Use language carefully and well, and work to overcome cross-cultural language differences. Be alert to the nonverbal signals that you send, including your use of time as perceived by other people. Know the common bad listening habits, and work to overcome them. Read widely, and engage in careful, first-hand observation and interpretation.

How to improve downward, upward, and horizontal communications.

Actively manage communications in all directions. In general, implement the guidelines discussed in the first part of the chapter; practice dialogue more than discussion; and engage in two-way communication more than one-way. Make information available to others, and make sure it is presented both efficiently and effectively. Useful approaches to downward communication include coaching, special communications during difficult periods, and open-book management. You should also both facilitate and motivate people to communicate upward. Many mechanisms exist for enhancing horizontal communications.

How to work with the company grapevine.

The informal flow of information can contribute as much as formal communication can to organizational effectiveness and morale. Managers must understand that the grapevine cannot be eliminated, and should be actively managed. Many of the suggestions for managing formal communications apply also to managing the grapevine. Moreover, managers can take steps to prevent rumors or neutralize the ones that do arise.

The advantages and characteristics of the boundaryless organization.

Boundaries—psychological if not physical—exist between different organizational levels, units, and organizations and external stakeholders. The ideal boundaryless organization is one in which there are no barriers to information flow. Ideas, information, decisions, and actions move to where they are most needed. Information is available as needed, freely accessible, so the organization as a whole functions far better than as separate parts.

Discussion questions

1. Think of an occasion when you faced a miscommunication problem. What do you think caused the problem? How do you think it should have been handled better?

2. Have you ever *not* given someone information or opinions that perhaps you should have? Why? Was it the right thing to do? Why or why not? What would cause you to be glad that you provided (or withheld) negative or difficult information? What would cause you to regret providing/withholding it?

3. Think back to "discussions" and "dialogues" you have heard. Talk about the differences between a discussion and a dialogue. How can a discussion be turned into a constructive dialogue?

4. Share with the class some of your experiences—both good and bad—with electronic media.

5. Report examples of "mixed signals" you have received (or sent). How can you reduce the potential for misunderstanding and misperception as you communicate with others?

6. What makes you want to say to someone, "You're not listening!"?

7. What do you think about the practice of "open-book management"? What would you think about it if you were running your own company?

8. Discuss rumors you have heard: what they were about, how they got started, how accurate they were, and how people reacted to them. What lessons can you learn from these episodes?

9. Refer to the section on "The Virtual Office." What do you think will be the long-term impact of the mobile office on job satisfaction and performance? If you were a manager, how would you maximize the benefits and minimize the drawbacks? If you worked in this environment, how would you manage yourself to maximize your performance and avoid burnout?

10. Have you ever made or seen mistakes due to people not speaking a common language well? How do you or will you deal with others who do not speak the same language as you?

11. Have you ever tried to coach someone? What did you do well, and what mistakes did you make? How can you become a better coach?

12. Have you ever been coached by someone? What did he or she do well, and what mistakes were made? How was it for you to be on the receiving end of the coaching, and how did you respond? What is required to be successful as the "receiver" of someone else's coaching attempts?

13. Refer to the box called "Language barriers." Discuss your reactions to the various examples and issues raised in the box.

Concluding Case

Would you open your books?

Imagine that you own and manage a small or mid-sized company. You pick the industry; you pick the location. Imagine, the firm is all yours.

You read in *Inc.* or *Fast Company* or *Harvard Business Review* about the latest management innovation: open-book management. You read about the original success story: Jack Stack bought Springfield ReManufacturing from International Harvester in 1983. It was collapsing after being rocked by a highly leveraged buyout. It had a first-year operating loss of about $60,000, over 100 employees who needed to be paid, and a debt-to-equity ratio of 89:1. Jack Stack opened the books, trained his people, and persuaded them to view the business as a game they could learn to play and win. The company returned to profitability, and is now written up in magazines and books as a brilliant model of how to do it.

You learn also of a number of companies that realized great results through opening the books, and understand the reasons why from taking a management course. And then you learn that Springfield ReManufacturing now holds seminars to teach other companies how to practice open-book management. You go to one, and you participate in exercises, simulations, and games to learn more about it. You are impressed, and are inclined to give it a try.

But there are downsides, as you learn when you get home and read another article. Your company has been around for a while, and the operating norms are pretty well established. How will people respond to this idea of opening the books? Will they understand? What will they think of the numbers? Will they want higher pay? Do they want a more active role in the company affairs? Do they even want to know the numbers?

Importantly, you will need to train them. You will need to commit to a lengthy, time-consuming learning period. Some of your managers and accountants, who had been privy to the confidential information, might not like the idea. They might fear they will lose power and status, or they might not trust the workers

Opening the books to employees worked for Springheld Remanufacturing. Would it work for your company?
[Ken Reid/FPG International]

with the information. Possibly some confidential information will leak to competitors.

There are a few other issues as well. Changes in accounting and financial systems and statements will be required, performance measures will have to be established that link with financial statements, and a system of rewards linked to performance must be established. The system must be understood by everyone and, above all, be seen as fair.

You see the advantages; the HBR article concludes by saying, "The power of open-book management lies not in the short term but in the long term, in its ability to change how people think and act, day in and day out . . . The people who work for open-book companies give their employers a powerful competitive edge . . ."

You are not naive about the potential downsides, or the implementation challenges. Not everyone will like the idea—including your friends, who own *their* own companies.

Questions

1. You have the sole authority to make this decision for your company. Yes or no: Would you implement an open-book system?
2. If the answer is no, what would you do and say if some of your people came to you and proposed it?
3. If you are undecided, would you convene a meeting to discuss the idea? If so, how would you handle the meeting?
4. If your answer is yes, how would you proceed?

Sources: J. Case, "Opening the Books," *Harvard Business Review*, March–April 1997, pp. 118–127; and R. T. V. Davis, "Open-Book Management: Its Promise and Pitfalls," *Organizational Dynamics*, Winter 1997, pp. 7–20.

Video Case

Communication

Communication and information technology are advancing at a rapid pace. AT&T has revealed its vision for revolutionizing workplace communication in a futuristic video. The impact of these advances will have a tremendous effect on the role of communication management in business.

The process of communication in organizations has been studied by management scholars for almost 100 years. The accumulation of knowledge in this important area of management is extensive. Yet, it is questionable whether much of it will apply as the new communications technologies take over the workplace. After viewing the AT&T video, complete the following exercise.

Purpose:

To stimulate your thinking about current communication technologies, their direction, and the challenges they pose for managers.

Procedure:

Identify one currently popular tool for communications in the workplace that was not widely available 20 years ago. Your task will be to examine how this device became popular in the workplace, its uses, and the new problems that it has created. Some examples of communication tools that have entered the workplace in the last 20 years are fax machines, cellular telephones, computer networks, pagers, and voice mail. After you have identified the communication tool that interests you, write a briefing for class presentation that covers the following issues:

1. When was the device invented? Oftentimes new inventions take many years to disseminate and become widely used. Try to track down when the tool was invented. Next, give a brief history of how the device came to its current rate of usage.

2. How is the device currently being used in the workplace? Describe the primary and secondary uses of the device. What are its primary functions? Is it a money saver? A time saver? Has the device displaced any human workers? How do managers use the device to improve productivity, quality, and competitiveness?

3. What new workplace problems have been created by the device? Often, new tools for the workplace are created to solve specific problems. Usually, the solution of those problems leads to new problems or issues. For example, the invention of the automobile was to solve the problem of travel, and it has led to the new problems of congestion and air pollution.

4. What new communication tools do you think lie on the horizon? To finish your class presentation, describe what new communication tools you think will be available in the workplace in 20 years. Be creative. Remember that, 20 years ago, not many people would have been able to envision the communication tools that we now take for granted.

Experiential Exercises

15.1 Nonverbal communication

Objective

To become more conscious of nonverbal messages.

Instructions

Below is a list of nonverbal communication "methods." Pick a day on which you will attempt to keep track of these methods. Think back at the end of the day to three people with whom you communicated in some way. Record how you responded to these people in terms of their nonverbal communication methods. Identify those that had the greatest and least effect on your behavior.

Nonverbal communication worksheet

Medium	What was the message?	How did you respond?	Which affected your behavior most and least?
How they shook hands			
Their posture			

Medium	What was the message?	How did you respond?	Which affected your behavior most and least?
Their facial expressions			
Their appearance			
Their voice tones			
Their smiles			
The expressions in their eyes			
Their confidence			
The way they moved			
The way they stood			
How close they stood to you			
How they smelled			
Symbols or gestures they used			
How loudly they spoke			

15.2 Listening skills survey

Objectives

1. To measure your skills as a listener.
2. To gain insight into the factors that determine good listening habits.
3. To demonstrate how you can become a better listener.

Instructions

1. Working alone, complete the Listening Skills Survey.
2. In small groups, compare scores, discuss survey test items, and prepare responses to the discussion questions.
3. After the class reconvenes, group spokespersons present group findings.

Discussion Questions

1. In what ways did students' responses on the survey agree or disagree?
2. What do you think accounts for the differences?
3. How can the results of this survey be put to practical use?

Listening skills survey

To measure your listening skills, complete the following survey by circling the degree to which you agree with each statement.

	Strongly agree	Agree	Neither agree nor disagree	Disagree	Strongly disagree
1. I tend to be patient with the speaker, making sure she or he is finished speaking before I respond in any fashion.	5	4	3	2	1
2. When listening I don't doodle or fiddle with papers and things that might distract me from the speaker.	5	4	3	2	1
3. I attempt to understand the speaker's point of view.	5	4	3	2	1
4. I try not to put the speaker on the defensive by arguing or criticizing.	5	4	3	2	1
5. When I listen, I focus on the speaker's feelings.	5	4	3	2	1
6. I let a speaker's annoying mannerisms distract me.	5	4	3	2	1
7. While the speaker is talking, I watch carefully for facial expressions and other types of body language.	5	4	3	2	1
8. I never talk when the other person is trying to say something.	5	4	3	2	1
9. During a conversation, a period of silence seems awkward to me.	5	4	3	2	1
10. I want people to just give me the facts and allow me to make up my own mind.	5	4	3	2	1
11. When the speaker is finished, I respond to his or her feelings.	5	4	3	2	1

	Strongly agree	Agree	Neither agree nor disagree	Disagree	Strongly disagree
12. I don't evaluate the speaker's words until she or he is finished talking.	5	4	3	2	1
13. I formulate my response while the speaker is still talking.	5	4	3	2	1
14. I never pretend that I'm listening when I'm not.	5	4	3	2	1
15. I can focus on message content even if the delivery is poor.	5	4	3	2	1
16. I encourage the speaker with frequent nods, smiles, and other forms of body language.	5	4	3	2	1
17. Sometimes I can predict what someone is going to say before she or he says it.	5	4	3	2	1
18. Even if a speaker makes me angry, I hold my temper.	5	4	3	2	1
19. I maintain good eye contact with the speaker.	5	4	3	2	1
20. I try to focus on the speaker's message, not his or her delivery.	5	4	3	2	1
21. If I am confused by a statement someone makes, I never respond until I have asked for and received adequate clarification.	5	4	3	2	1

Integrating Case

Frank Perriman's appointment

Indefatigable Mutual Insurance is a large, national company with more than 10,000 employees in the 50 states and Canada. Its basic organization has been as shown in the organization chart. Each divisional vice president has access to the president if so desired, but most communications between the field and home office are with the functional vice presidents, who set policy and monitor performance in their respective functional areas. Two senior vice presidents have acted as staff to the president in their areas of expertise—one in actuarial and statistical matters and the other in investments and finance. In general, Indefatigable has been a highly centralized, regionally dispersed organization.

Frank Perriman has had exceptional success at Indefatigable. After experience primarily in sales, Frank was appointed vice president of the Middle Division at age 35—the youngest such appointment in the company's history. One annual report contained an individual picture of Perriman (the only divisional vice president so honored) with a caption describing him as an example of what could happen to young people at Indefatigable. However, most executives were old.

After eight years as division vice president, Perriman was promoted to senior vice president (thus making three senior vice presidents) and transferred to the home office. The president sent the bulletins shown on page 533.

At the time Perriman thought he had no problem. After all, he had been given a significant promotion. Nonetheless, he was concerned because he feared resentment from others and was unclear about what the president wanted. Perriman had recently attended an executive program in which they had discussed a case titled "The Dashman Company," which told about a new vice president who failed to exert any impact on the organization (see the Dashman Company case on page 533). Accordingly, he decided to see Professor Eagleson, who had conducted various management training programs for the company.

During the conversation, Eagleson pointed out that there was a disparity in the managerial styles of the various division vice presidents. For example, when conducting a training program for managers in the Northern Division, he had the divisional functional managers draw an organization chart (illustrated on page 534). When sitting in the Northern Division's vice president's office one day, a divisional functional manager had come in with a problem about how to treat a certain policyholder. The vice president had asked the manager to read the relevant home office regulation on the matter and then directed the functional manager to adhere exactly to the home office rule.

By chance, Professor Eagleson had once been sitting in Perriman's office when a similar event occurred. After listening to the divisional manager and reading the home office regulation, Perriman had advised the manager that the regulation didn't exactly apply, so they were free to handle the matter as they deemed best. If headquarters would later complain to the manager, Perriman promised to say the action was his responsibility. When the Middle Division divisional managers had drawn the organization chart in their training session, it was as pictured on page 535. In general, Eagleson felt that the Northern Division's vice president's behavior was more typical of the division vice presidents than Perriman's.

Organizational chart

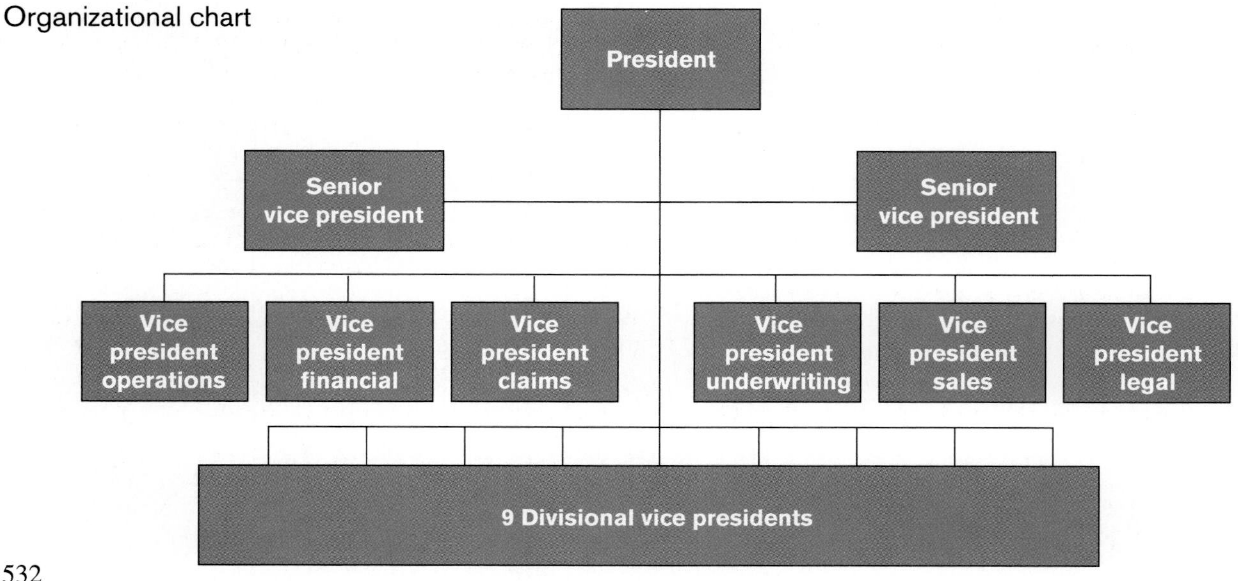

HOME OFFICE ADMINISTRATION
June 29
ORGANIZATIONAL BULLETIN—GENERAL No. 349

Effective August 1, Mr. Frank Perriman, Vice President and Division Manager, Middle Division, will transfer to the President's staff at the home office.

Perriman will be responsible to the President for achieving division performance in accordance with company policies and objectives.

Mr. Perriman will assist Division Managers in obtaining well-coordinated efforts by all departments and will establish and use measurements of results for each Division.

Divisional Vice Presidents will report to and be responsible to Mr. Perriman.

Thomas Achison
President

HOME OFFICE ADMINISTRATION
July 14
ORGANIZATIONAL BULLETIN—GENERAL No. 351

Effective July 14, the Board of Directors made the following election: Mr. Frank Perriman—Senior Vice President

Thomas Achison
President

Dashman Company

The Dashman Company was a large concern making many types of equipment for the armed forces of the United States. It had over 20 plants, located in the central part of the country, whose purchasing procedures had never been completely coordinated. In fact, the head office of the company had encouraged each of the plant managers to operate with their staffs as separate independent units in most matters. Late in 1940, when it began to appear that the company would face increasing difficulty in securing certain essential raw materials, Mr. Manson, the company's president, appointed an experienced purchasing executive, Mr. Post, as vice president in charge of purchasing, a position especially created for him. Mr. Manson gave Mr. Post wide latitude in organizing his job, and he assigned Mr. Larson as Mr. Post's assistant. Mr. Larson had served the company in a variety of capacities for many years and knew most of the plant executives personally. Mr. Post's appointment was announced through the formal channels usual in the company, including a notice in the house organ published by the company.

One of Mr. Post's first decisions was to begin immediately to centralize the company's purchasing procedure. As a first step he decided that he would require each of the executives who handled purchasing in the individual plants to clear with the head office all purchase contracts which they made in excess of $10,000. He felt that if the head office was to do any coordinating in a way that would be helpful to each plant and to the company as a whole, he must be notified that the contracts were being prepared at least a week before they were to be signed. He talked his proposal over with Mr. Manson, who presented it to his board of directors. They approved the plan.

Although the company made purchases throughout the year, the beginning of its peak buying season was only three weeks away at the time this new plan was adopted. Mr. Post prepared a letter to be sent to the 20 purchasing executives of the company. The letter follows:

Dear__________________:
The board of directors of our company has recently authorized a change in our purchasing procedures. Hereafter, each of the purchasing executives in the several plants of the company will notify the vice president in charge of purchasing of all contracts in excess of $10,000 they are negotiating at least a week in advance of the date on which they are to be signed. I am sure that you will understand that this step is necessary to coordinate the purchasing requirements of the company in these times when we are facing increasing difficulty in securing essential supplies. This procedure should give us in the central office the information we need to see that each plant secures the optimum supply of materials. In this way the interests of each plant and of the company as a whole will best be served.

Yours very truly,

Mr. Post showed the letter to Mr. Larson and invited his comments. Mr. Larson thought the letter an excellent one but suggested that, since Mr. Post had not met more than a few of the purchasing executives, he might like to visit all of them and take the matter up with each of them personally. Mr. Post dismissed the idea at once because, as he said, he had so many things to do at the head office that he could not get away for a trip. Consequently he had the letters sent out over his signature.

During the two following weeks replies came in from all except a few plants. Although a few executives wrote at greater length, the following reply was typical:

Dear Mr. Post:
Your recent communication in regard to notifying the head office a week in advance of our intention to sign contracts has been received. This suggestion seems a most practical one. We want to assure you that you can count on our cooperation.

Yours very truly,

During the next six weeks the head office received no notices from any plant that contracts were being negotiated. Executives in other departments who made frequent trips to the plants reported that the plants were busy, and the usual routines for that time of year were being followed.

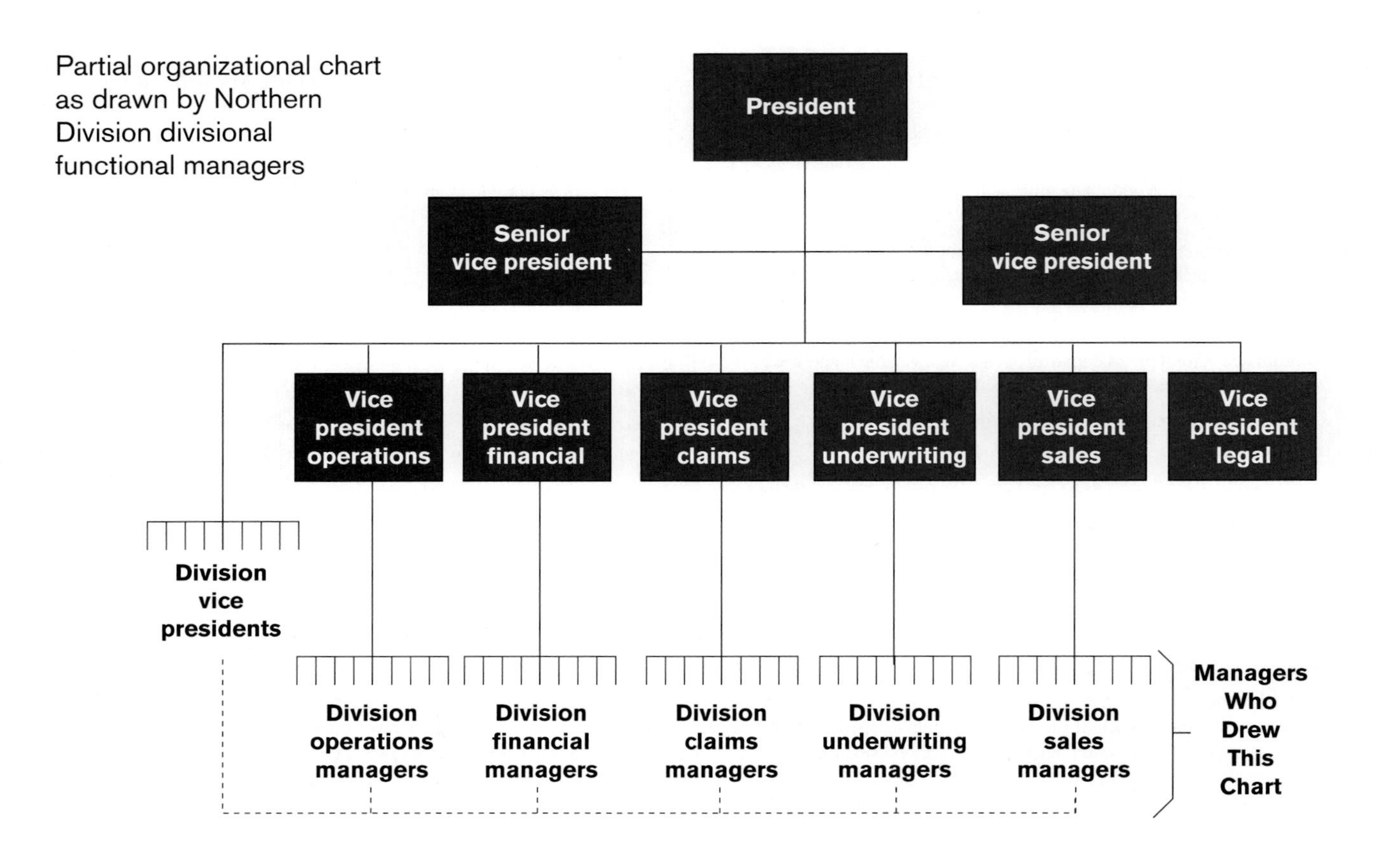

When Perriman asked Eagleson what he thought the president expected of the new position, the professor said he wasn't sure. Nonetheless, he mentioned that when he recently had seen the president about the company training programs, the executive had expressed concern about his age, next year's 100th anniversary celebration of the firm, and the company's expense position. He had remarked on the way to lunch that the only thing wrong with the company was that the field personnel "just didn't follow home office rules." The president indicated that the company was losing money on automobile insurance policies, especially because sales was selling to less desirable risks—contrary to the company's long-standing strategy of preferred risks. Perhaps, the president concluded, the field staff should be reduced and sales curtailed.

Pondering these points, Perriman wondered if one of his first steps as a senior vice president should be to pick a fight with one of the home office functional vice presidents to impress the division vice presidents with his willingness to battle on their behalf.

Questions

1. Discuss any problems Perriman might have in establishing authority and influence in his new post.

2. What factors should aid Perriman?

3. How do you think the divisional vice presidents will react to this appointment? Why?

4. How do you think the functional vice presidents will react to this appointment? Why?

5. How do you think Achison should have proceeded?

6. How do you interpret the differences in the organization charts as drawn by the division functional managers in the Northern Division compared with the Middle Division?

7. What do the president's remarks to Professor Eagleson suggest about his intentions for Perriman as the new senior vice president?

8. What recommendations would you offer Perriman now? Why?

Source: R. Weber, M. Morgan, and P. Brown, *Management,* 3rd ed. (Burr Ridge, IL: Richard D. Irwin, 1985), pp. 253–57.

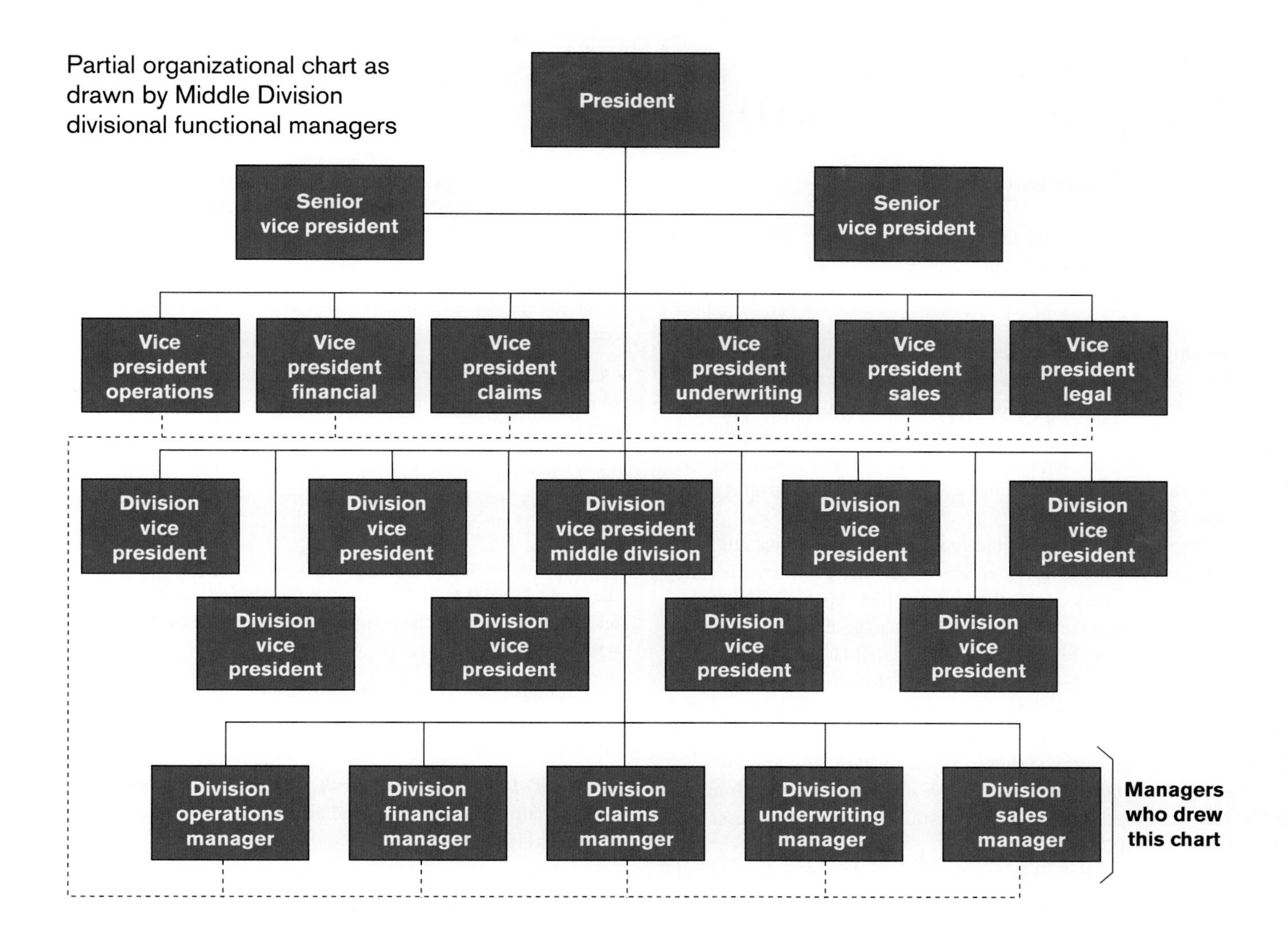
Partial organizational chart as drawn by Middle Division divisional functional managers
President
Senior vice president
Senior vice president
Vice president operations
Vice president financial
Vice president claims
Vice president underwriting
Vice president sales
Vice president legal
Division vice president
Division vice president
Division vice president middle division
Division vice president
Division vice president
Division vice president
Division vice president
Division vice president
Division vice president
Division operations manager
Division financial manager
Division claims mamnger
Division underwriting manager
Division sales manager
Managers who drew this chart

Case Incidents

Suggestion system policy

OFFICE OF THE PRESIDENT
Memorandum
Date: Friday, November 18
From: Bob Adams, president
To: John Sullens, vice president for human resources

Employee suggestion systems have been around for a long time. The positive financial impact of suggestion systems is significant in some organizations, according to my reading. For example, the National Association of Suggestions Systems estimates that 80 percent of the 500 largest U.S. corporations have such programs and that employee suggestions save the nation's companies more than $500 million a year.

The negative aspect of the suggestion system is that employees may become disgruntled about how the company runs the system. You may recall that two United Airlines employees charged in court that United stole their suggestion for a reduced-fare plan for employees of all airlines, that United successfully implemented the plan, and that United cheated them out of hundreds of thousands of dollars that they had coming under the company's suggestion system. They cited a provision of United Airlines' suggestion system rules that stated, "An employee is entitled to 10 percent of a typical year's profits resulting from an idea submitted through the suggestion system and successfully implemented."

During the trial, expert witnesses testified that in a typical year of operations under the reduced-fare plan, United earned $3 million attributable to the plan, of which 10 percent, or $300,000, rightfully belongs to the two employees who submitted the suggestion. The jury found that the company acted in bad faith by failing to pay off under the suggestion system and assessed $1.8 million in damages against the airline, which a judge later reduced to $368,000.

We can't afford to risk such financial peril! It's crucial, therefore, that you promptly review our suggestion system rules and policies and that you give me recommendations on the following issues. Include advantages and disadvantages associated with your policy recommendations.

1. *Calculation of award amount.* Should we offer a flat amount of money for each accepted suggestion, or should the award be based on a percentage of the savings (earnings) during some period? What percentage? What period?

2. *Maximum award.* Should we have a maximum limit on the payoff for any single suggestion (perhaps $10,000), or should it be open ended?

3. *Time of award payment.* Should we pay the award in full when the suggestion is accepted or as the savings (earnings) are realized annually?

4. *Joint award allocation.* When two or more employees combine on a suggestion, how should we allocate the award among them?

5. *Originality.* Should we pay off for suggestions that help us, even if they aren't original with the employee(s) making the suggestion?

6. *Impetus award.* Are you in favor of an "impetus award" in the range of $100 to $500 to recognize a suggestion that hastens an action initiated by the company before receipt of the suggestion?

7. *Written rules.* Do you think we need to spell out in writing every aspect of our suggestion system, or will an informal approach be more conducive to employee participation?

8. *Proof of knowledge.* Should we require all employees to sign a form stating that they have read and understand the suggestion system's rules (if we decide to write them up)?

9. *Another limitation.* Should an employee be limited to suggestions relating only to his or her area of the organization?

10. *An exclusion.* Should our marketing function and financial policy (including product and service pricing) be excluded from the suggestion system?

11. *Evaluation.* Do you have any suggestions on a procedure for evaluating suggestions?

12. *Abandonment.* Maybe dropping the suggestion system would be easier. What do you think?

We are reviewing all aspects of our suggestion system policy. Our attorney recommends abandonment. Let me hear from you as soon as possible. Treat this as a priority item.

Source: J. M. Champion and J. H. James, *Critical Incidents in Management: Decision and Policy Issues,* 6th ed. (Burr Ridge, IL: Richard D. Irwin, 1989).

Quality circle consequence

John Stevens, plant manager of the Fairlead Plant of Lockstead Corporation, which manufactures structural components for aircraft wings and bodies, became interested in using quality circles to improve performance in his plant. *Quality circles* was the name used to describe joint labor–supervision participation teams operating at the shop-floor level at Lockstead. Other companies called quality circles by names such as "productivity groups," "people involvement programs," and "departmental teams." Whatever the name, the purpose of quality circles was to improve the quality of manufacturing performance.

The subject of quality circles was a hot topic in the press. Stevens had seen books on Japanese management and productivity successes, which featured the use of quality circles. All these books featured the slogan "None of us is as smart as all of us."

Other books related quality circles to productivity gains. Articles on quality circles appeared often in trade journals and in business magazines, including *Business Week.*

Stevens also had a pamphlet from a management consulting firm announcing a "new and improved" training course for quality circle leaders, scheduled consecutively in Birmingham, Alabama; Williamsburg, Virginia; and Orlando, Florida. Another consultant offered "a program that will teach your managers and supervisors how to increase productivity and efficiency without making costly investments . . . by focusing on techniques germane to the quality circle process." Stevens was impressed enough to attend an advanced management seminar at a large midwestern university. A large part of the program concentrated on quality circles.

Professor Albert Mennon particularly impressed Stevens with his lectures on group discussion, team problem solving, and group decision making. Mennon convinced Stevens that employees meeting in quality circle teams with adequate leaders could effectively consider problems and formulate quality decisions that would be acceptable to employees. The staff conducting this state-of-the-art seminar covered five areas: (1) how to train quality circle members in the six-step problem sequence; (2) a description of what leaders and facilitators should do during the quality circle sessions; (3) planning and writing a policy guide; (4) developing an implementation plan; and (5) measuring quality circle progress and success.

Both the company and its employees were expected to benefit from a successfully implemented quality circle program. The list of payoffs included increased job satisfaction, productivity improvement, efficiency gains, and improved performance and labor relations. Moreover, it was expected that a reduction would occur in areas such a grievance loads, absenteeism, and costs.

Returning to his plant after the seminar, Stevens decided to practice some of the principles he had learned. He called together the 25 employees of Department B and told them that production standards established several years ago were too low in view of the recent installation of automated equipment. He gave the workers the opportunity to discuss the mitigating circumstances and to decide among themselves, as a group, what their standards should be. On leaving the room, he believed that the workers would establish much higher standards than he would have dared propose.

After an hour of discussion, the group summoned Stevens and notified him that, contrary to his opinion, they had decided the standards already were too high and, since they had been given the authority to establish their own standards, they were making a reduction of 10 percent. Stevens knew these standards were far too low to provide a fair profit on the owner's investment. Yet he believed his refusal to accept the group decision would be disastrous. Stevens thought of telephoning Professor Mennon for consultation on the quality circle dilemma, but he chose to act on his own.

Several options filled Steven's mind: (1) He could accept the blame for the quality circle experiment having gone awry and tell them to begin anew; (2) he could establish incentive pay adjustment linkages between the quality circle's decisions and productivity improvement; (3) he might even operate at a loss for a short while to prove that the original quality circle decision had been unacceptable; or (4) he might abandon the participative team program. Stevens needed a decision, an operational policy for the quality circle program, and an implementation plan.

Source: J. H. Champion and J. H. James, *Critical Incidents in Management: Decision and Policy Issues,* 6th ed. (Burr Ridge, IL: Richard D. Irwin, 1989). ●

Part Five
Control and Change

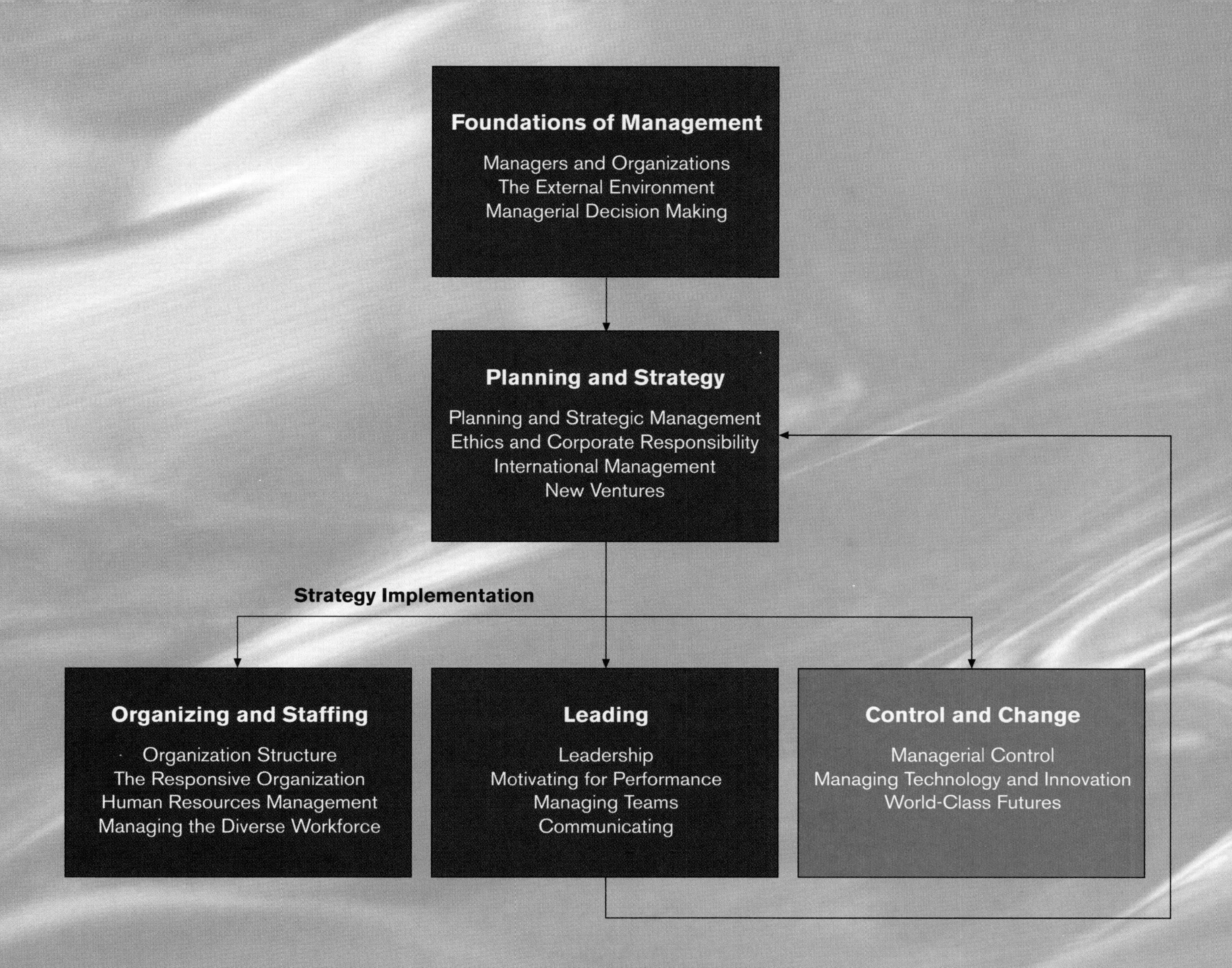

In Parts I through IV, you learned about the foundations of management, planning and strategy, and how to implement plans by organizing, staffing, and leading. Part V concludes with three chapters about controlling and changing what the organization and its people are doing. Chapter 16 describes managerial control, including issues related to culture as well as techniques for ensuring that intended activities are carried out and goals are accomplished.

The last two chapters focus on change and renewal. Chapter 17 discusses technology and innovation, including a strategic approach to new technologies and the creation of a culture for innovation. Chapter 18 examines an ongoing challenge for the modern executive: Becoming world class through the management of change. In that chapter, we describe the nature of this challenge and how managers can deal with it. Some of the topics you learned about in earlier chapters play central roles in the change process; Chapter 18 should remind you how your understanding of them will continually benefit your managerial career.

Chapter Sixteen
Managerial Control

More than at any time in the past, companies will not be able to hold themselves together with the traditional methods of control: hierarchy, systems, budgets, and the like . . . The bonding glue will increasingly become ideological.

—Collins & Porras[1]

Use your good judgment in all situations. There will be no additional rules.

—Nordstrom's employee manual

Chapter Outline

Learning Objectives

After studying Chapter 16, you will know:

1. Why companies develop control systems for employees.
2. How to design a basic bureaucratic control system.
3. The purposes for using budgets as a control device.
4. How to intrepret financial ratios and other financial controls.
5. The procedures for implementing effective control systems.
6. The different ways that market control mechanisms are used by organizations
7. How clan control can be approached in an empowered organization.

Setting the Stage

Couldn't Bausch & Lomb See Straight?

Bausch & Lomb enjoyed a great run of success during the 1980s and early 1990s. Rapid growth in high-margin contact lenses and the Ray-Ban Wayfarer sunglass line—popularized in movies such as *The Blues Brothers* and *Risky Business*—tripled sales and earnings to $1.5 billion and $150 million, respectively. Shareholders were rewarded with a fivefold increase in value and CEO Dan Gill's compensation soared to over $6.5 million.

Achieving double-digit growth was Gill's overriding goal and he was unrelenting in its pursuit. The culture at B&L became a mirror image of Gill: tenacious, demanding, and very numbers-oriented. Harold Johnson, the former head of the contact-lens unit, recalls, "Each year, the top executives would agree on what numbers they wanted to make. There was little tolerance for shortfalls. Once you signed up for your number, you were expected to reach it."

That's where things began to unravel. During the mid-1990s, growth slowed in the United States and Europe as competition intensified. But despite the slow-down, Gill's unyielding growth targets remained. To cope, operating managers pushed inventory on distributors in order to make their revenue targets. In one case, Johnson required 30 of B&L's U.S. distributors to take immense stocks of old Optima lenses—up to two years' worth—or face cancellation of their distributor agreements. All but two agreed—those two were terminated—and Johnson booked an extra $23 million in sales. Eventually, most of the unwanted inventory had made its way back to B&L, as the distributors refused to pay. These actions became the core of both an SEC investigation and a shareholder class action suit that accused the company of misleading investors by falsely inflating sales and earnings. Although Gill denied that such distributor loading took place, others viewed it as all too typical. A similar occurrence was uncovered in the Ray-Ban division. And in B&L's Hong Kong operations, managers pretended to book huge sales to Southeast Asian distributors, but never shipped the product. Instead, the goods were moved to an outside warehouse from which B&L sales managers attempted to persuade distributors to buy the excess.

With their Wayfarer sunglasses line in movies like *Risky Business* and *Men in Black*, Bausch and Lomb tripled sales in the 1980s and 1990s.
[Tommy Lee Jones, Will Smith, Linda Fiorentino/© 1997 Columbia/Motion Picture & TV Archives]

Even after B&L's headquarters was tipped off by declining revenues and soaring receivables, there was no let-up on the pressure for sales results: 1994 sales were targeted to rise to $176 million from $151 million. But with bulging distribution channels, the sales came in at only $85.8 million coupled with a $61.7 million loss. Internal auditors belatedly discovered significant irregularities—including half a million pairs of sunglasses stashed in a Hong Kong warehouse!

Isolated problems? Some think so. According to Kenneth Wolfe, head of B&L's audit committee, "Unfortunately, when you have operations scattered throughout the world, people do things they shouldn't. But I don't think there's a larger problem." Gill denied accountability: "It's generally accepted that day-to-day operations of a company are overseen by the chief operating officer. I don't mean to pass the buck, but . . . as chairman, I'd have only a general understanding of what happened." In December 1995, B&L announced Gill's retirement.

Source: Joseph C. Picken and Gregory G. Dess, "Out of (Strategic) Control," Organizational Dynamics *26, no. 1 (Summer 1997), pp. 25–48.*

How does a respected company like Bausch & Lomb get so out of control? Left on their own, people may knowingly or unknowingly act in ways that they perceive to be beneficial to them individually but that may work to the detriment of the organization as a whole. This is what happened at Bausch and Lomb. Without some means of regulating what people do, the organization can literally fall apart. In this regard, control is one of the fundamental forces that keeps the organization together.

control The process of measuring progress toward planned performance and applying corrective measures to ensure that performance is in line with managers' objectives.

Control is typically defined as any process that directs the activities of individuals toward the achievement of organizational goals. Some managers don't want to admit it (see Table 16.1), but control problems—the lack of controls or the wrong kinds of controls—frequently cause irreparable damage to organizations. Ineffective control systems result in problems ranging from employee theft to financial losses from unauthorized foreign exchange speculation. Employees simply wasting time costs U.S. employers over $100 billion a year![2]

table 16.1

The leadership symptoms of an out-of-control company

David Ferrari, president of Argus Management Corporation, maintains that many businesses are in big trouble without the CEO even knowing it. The symptoms:

- **Misplaced confidence**–believing that everything they do is right and they cannot make mistakes.
- **Blame deflection**–if they admit they are in trouble, they blame everything but themselves.
- **Avoidance**–doing "busy work" that is easy to handle rather than tackling the big, companywide issues.
- **An eye to the past**–justifying current practices by saying, "We've always done it that way."
- **Blind optimism**–refusing to believe bad numbers and believing that things will take care of themselves.
- **Setting a poor example**–spending lavishly on perks for themselves rather than living up to the same stringent standards expected of others.
- **Isolation**–other people–subordinates, directors, outsiders–don't send warning signals or stand up to the CEO to convince him or her that things are perilously out of control.

Source: Reprinted with permission from *Inc.* magazine, July 1990. Copyright © 1990 by Goldhirsh Group, Inc., 38 Commercial Wharf, Boston, MA 02110.

Control has been called one of the Siamese twins of management. The other twin is planning. Some means of control are necessary because once managers form plans and strategies, they must ensure the plans are carried out. This means making sure that other people are doing what needs to be done and not doing inappropriate things. If plans are not carried out properly, management must take steps to correct the problem. This is the primary control function of management. Ensuring creativity, enhancing quality, reducing costs—managers must figure out ways to control what occurs in their organizations.

Not surprisingly, effective planning facilitates control, and control facilitates planning. Planning lays out a framework for the future, and in this sense, provides a blueprint for control. Control systems, in turn, regulate the allocation and utilization of resources, and in so doing, facilitate the process of planning. In today's complex organizational environment, both functions have become more difficult to implement at the same time they have become more important in every department of the organization. Managers today must control their people, inventories, quality, and costs, to mention just a few of their responsibilities.

bureaucratic control The use of rules, regulations, and authority to guide performance.

market control Control based on the use of financial and economic information.

clan control Control based on the norms, values, shared goals, and trust among group members.

According to William Ouchi of the University of California at Los Angeles, managers can apply three broad strategies for achieving organizational control: bureaucratic control, market control, and clan control.[3] **Bureaucratic control** is the use of rules, regulations, and formal authority to guide performance. It includes such things as budgets, statistical reports, performance appraisals, and the like to regulate behavior and results. **Market control** involves the use of pricing mechanisms to regulate activities in organizations as though they were economic transactions. Business units may be treated as profit centers and trade resources (services or products) with one another via such mechanisms. Managers who run these units may be evaluated on the basis of profit and loss. **Clan control,** unlike the first two types, does not assume that the interests of the organization and individuals naturally diverge. Instead, clan control is based on the idea that employees may share the values, expectations and goals of the organization and act in accordance with them. When members of an organization have common values and goals—and trust one another—formal controls may be less necessary. Clan control is based on many of the interpersonal processes described in Chapter 12 on leadership and Chapter 14 on groups and teams (e.g., group norms and cohesiveness).

Table 16.2 summarizes the main features of bureaucratic, market, and culture controls. We use this framework as a foundation for our discussions throughout the chapter.

table 16.2
Characteristics of controls

System control	Features and requirements
Bureaucratic control	Uses formal rules, standards, hierarchy, legitimate authority. Works best where tasks are certain and workers are independent.
Market control	Uses prices, competition, profit centers, exchange relationships. Works best where tangible output can be identified and market can be established between parties.
Clan control	Involves culture, shared values, beliefs, expectations, and trust. Works best where there is "no one best way" to do a job and where employees are empowered to make decisions.

Sources: W. G. Ouchi, "A Conceptual Framework for the Design of Organizational Control Mechanisms," *Management Science* 25 (1979), pp. 833–48; W. G. Ouchi, "Markets, Bureaucracies, and Clans," *Administrative Science Quarterly* 25 (1980), pp. 129–41; and Richard D. Robey and C. A. Sales, *Designing Organizations* (Burr Ridge, IL: Richard D. Irwin, 1994).

Bureaucratic control systems

Bureaucratic (or formal) control systems are designed to measure progress toward planned performance and, if necessary, to apply corrective measures to ensure that performance is in line with managers' objectives. Control systems detect and correct significant variations, or discrepancies, in the results obtained from planned activities.

The control cycle

Figure 16.1 shows a typical control system with four major steps: (1) setting performance standards, (2) measuring performance, (3) comparing performance against the standards and determining deviations, and (4) taking corrective action.

standard Expected performance for a given goal; a target that establishes a desired performance level, motivates performance, and serves as a benchmark against which actual performance is assessed.

Step 1: Setting performance standards

Every organization has goals, including profitability, innovation, satisfaction of constituencies, and so on. A **standard** is the level of expected performance for a given goal. Standards are performance targets that establish desired performance levels, motivate performance, and serve as benchmarks against which to assess actual performance. Standards can be set for any activity—financial activities, operating activities, legal compliance, charitable contributions, and so on.[4]

We have discussed setting performance standards in other parts of the text. For example, employee goal setting for motivation is built around the concept of specific, measurable performance standards. Such standards should be challenging and typically should aim for improvement over past performance. Thus, useful performance targets for control purposes would include increasing market share by 20 percent, cutting costs by 15 percent, answering all customer complaints within 24 hours, achieving a return on investment of 8 percent, or producing 800,000 units in a year. Job requirements and objective data can provide guidance in setting standards. For example, to keep sales expenses under control, expense standards can be based on salespersons' need to travel and on the number of nights on the road. A small number of experienced people could keep track of their actual expenses to provide data for future standard setting.[5]

figure 16.1
The control process

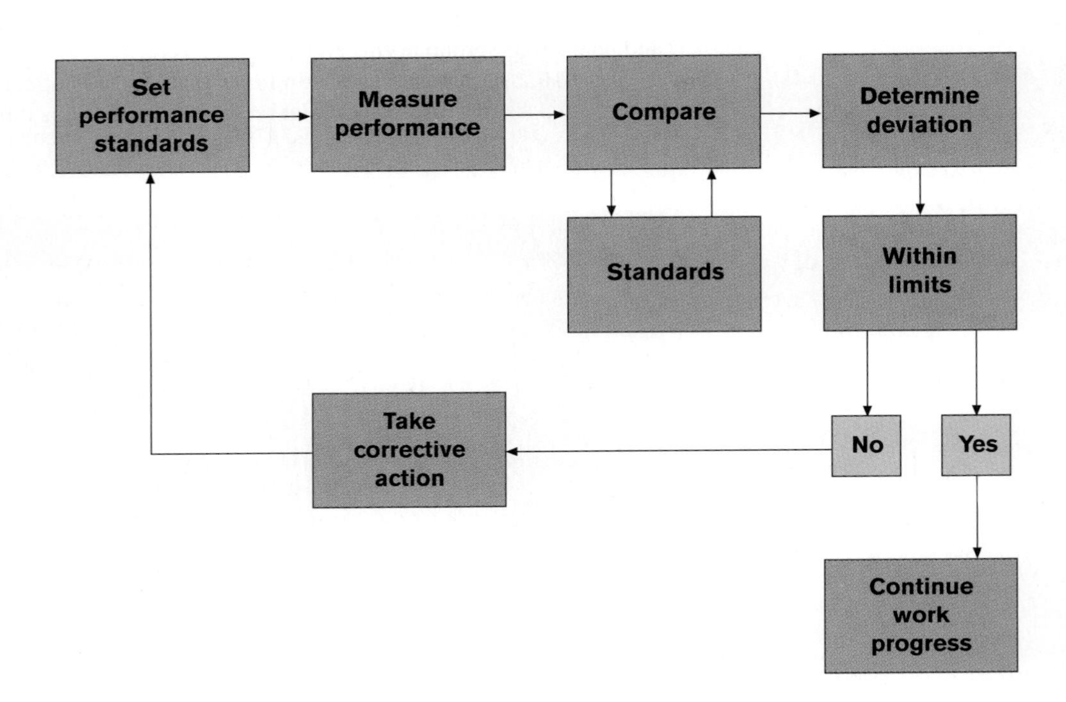

Performance standards can be set with respect to (1) quantity, (2) quality, (3) time used, and (4) cost. For example, production activities include volume of output (quantity), defects (quality), on-time availability of finished goods (time use), and dollar expenditures for raw materials and direct labor (cost). Many important aspects of performance, such as customer service, can be measured by the same standards—for example, adequate supply and availability of products, quality of service, speed of delivery, and so forth.

One word of caution: the Bausch & Lomb example in "Setting the Stage" shows the downside of establishing performance targets and standards that aren't supported by other elements of the entire control system. Each piece of the system is important and dependent on the others. Otherwise the system can get terribly out of balance.

Step 2: measuring performance The second step in the control process is to measure performance levels. For example, managers can count units produced, days absent, papers filed, samples distributed, and dollars earned. Performance data commonly are obtained from three sources: written reports, oral reports, and personal observations.

Written reports include computer printouts. Thanks to computers' increasing capabilities and decreasing costs, both large and small companies can gather huge amounts of performance data.

One common example of *oral reports* occurs when a salesperson contacts his or her immediate manager at the close of each business day to report the accomplishments, problems, or customers' reactions during the day. The manager can ask questions to gain additional information or clear up any misunderstandings. When necessary, tentative corrective actions can be worked out during the discussion.

Personal observation involves going to the area of activities and watching what is occurring. The manager can observe work methods, employees' nonverbal signals, and the general operation. Personal observation gives an intimate picture of what is going on. But it also has some disadvantages. It does not provide accurate quantitative data; the information usually is general and subjective. Also, employees can misconstrue personal observation as mistrust or a lack of confidence. Nevertheless, many managers believe there is no good substitute for firsthand observation. As you learned in earlier chapters, personal contact can increase leadership visibility and upward communication. It also provides valuable information about performance to supplement written and oral reports.

Step 3: comparing performance with the standard The third step in the control process is comparing performance with the standard. In this process, the manager evaluates the performance. For some activities relatively small deviations from the standard are acceptable, while in others a slight deviation may be serious. Managers who perform the controlling work therefore must carefully analyze and evaluate the results.

The managerial **principle of exception** states that control is enhanced by concentrating on the exceptions, or significant deviations, from the expected result or standard. In comparing performance with the standard, managers need to direct their attention to the exception. For example, controlling the quality of components produced on an assembly line might show that only five pieces per 1,000 fall out of line. These five components are the exceptions and should be investigated further. [6]

principle of exception A managerial principle stating that control is enhanced by concentrating on the exceptions or significant deviations from the expected result or standard.

With the principle of exception, only exceptional cases require corrective action. The manager should not be concerned with performance that equals or closely approximates the expected results. This principle is important in controlling. Managers can save much time and effort if they apply the principle of exception.

Step 4: taking corrective action The last step in the control process is to take action to correct significant deviations. This step ensures that operations are adjusted where necessary to achieve the initially planned results. Where significant variances are discovered, the manager should take immediate and vigorous action. Effective control cannot tolerate needless delays, excuses, or exceptions.

Typically the corrective action is initiated by those who have authority over the actual performance. For example, United Parcel Service (UPS) uses tight controls over its drivers. Every day, management compares each driver's performance (number of miles, deliveries, and pickups) with a computerized projection of what performance should have been. When drivers fail to meet standards, a supervisor rides with them and provides suggestions for improvement. Drivers who do not improve are warned, then suspended, and finally dismissed.[7]

An alternative approach is for the corrective action to be taken not by higher-ups but by the operator at the point of the problem. In computer-controlled production technology, two basic types of control are feasible: specialist control and operator control. With *specialist control,* operators of computer-numerical-control (CNC) machines must notify engineering specialists of malfunctions. With this traditional division of labor, the specialist takes corrective action. With *operator control,* multiskilled operators can rectify their own problems as they occur. Not only is this strategy more efficient, because deviations are controlled closer to their source; operators benefit by virtue of a more enriched job.[8]

The appropriate corrective action depends on the nature of the problem. The corrective action may involve a change in a procedure or method, a disciplinary action, a new way to check the accuracy of manufactured parts, or a major organizational modification. Or it may simply be an inexpensive investment in employee training. At Corning, the source of major quality and production problems was traced to minute drafting errors by the engineering group. One of the solutions was quite simple: An engineer was sent to a proofreading class.[9]

feedforward control The control process used before operations begin, including policies, procedures, and rules designed to ensure that planned activities are carried out properly.

concurrent control The control process used while plans are being carried out, including directing, monitoring, and fine-tuning activities as they are performed.

feedback control Control that focuses on the use of information about previous results to correct deviations from the acceptable standard.

Approaches to bureaucratic control

The three approaches to bureaucratic control are feedforward, concurrent, and feedback.[10] **Feedforward control** takes place before operations begin and includes policies, procedures, and rules designed to ensure that planned activities are carried out properly. Examples include inspection of raw materials and proper selection and training of employees. **Concurrent control** takes place while plans are being carried out. It includes directing, monitoring, and fine-tuning activities as they occur. **Feedback control** focuses on the use of information about results to correct deviations from the acceptable standard after they arise.

Feedforward control

Feedforward control (sometimes called *preliminary* control) is future oriented; its aim is to prevent problems before they arise. Instead of waiting for results and comparing them with goals, a manager can exert control by limiting activities in advance. For example, companies have policies defining the scope within which decisions are made. A company may dictate that managers adhere to clear ethical and legal guidelines when making decisions. Formal rules and procedures also prescribe people's actions before they occur. Stating that a financial officer must approve expenditures over $1,000 or that only components that pass all safety tests can be used in a product specifies in advance which actions can and cannot be taken. To prevent loan defaults, banks may require extensive loan documentation, reviews, and approvals by bank officers before authorizing a loan.

Control and quality at GE Aircraft Engines

In recent years, much has been said about "the quality revolution" as if no one had ever taken a rational approach to quality control in the past. Nothing could be further from the truth at General Electric Aircraft Engines, where quality and safety have always been fundamental requirements and major competitive strengths. But while emphasis on quality has been constant, GE's approach to controlling quality has changed in recent years.

In the past GE Aircraft Engines was a classic quality control organization; an independent internal group audited the work of the rest of the organization by inspecting products, both hardware and other deliverables, to detect defects. Since quality at 30,000 feet is critical, Aircraft Engines did a lot of inspections, often 200 or 300 percent inspections of critical characteristics. By the time the product reached the customer, it was safe and met stringent specifications for performance.

But the cost of quality and the lead times needed to deliver it were heavy burdens. To stay competitive, GE redesigned its quality initiatives to focus on speed or cycle time as well as traditional quality metrics. To achieve this goal, quality control has shifted from defect detection (a feedback system) to defect prevention (a feedforward system). To achieve continuous reduction of process variation, customers and suppliers are integrated with a team of designers, project engineers, purchasing agents, and manufacturing employees. Design for manufacturability has become a whole new approach to enhancing quality and customer value. The essence of quality is "doing it right the first time."

Along with control system changes designed to enhance quality, GE has also focused on the cultural aspects of change associated with continuous improvement–teamwork and empowerment are viewed as vital elements of total quality management. As a result of the culture changes, quality control is no longer the province of a backroom quality department; it has become an "up-front" responsibility of each supplier, manager, and employee within the organization.

Source: Adapted from Al Parker, "The Changing Role of Quality at GE Aircraft Engines," *Quality,* September 1993, pp. 18–21. Reprinted by permission.

Concurrent control Concurrent control, which takes place while plans are carried out, is the heart of any control system. On the production floor, all efforts are directed toward producing the correct quantity and quality of the right products in the specified amount of time. In an airline terminal, the baggage must get to the right airplanes before flights depart. In factories, materials must be available when and where needed, and breakdowns in the production process must be repaired immediately. Concurrent control

While General Electric Aircraft Engines has always emphasized quality, most recently the company has focused on speed and cycle time as well as traditional quality metrics. This shift reflects the importance to this company of *controlling* quality.
[Courtesy of GE Aircraft Engines]

also is in operation when supervisors watch employees to ensure they work efficiently and avoid mistakes. Advances in information technology have created powerful concurrent controls. Computerized systems give managers immediate access to data from the most remote corners of their companies. For example, managers can continuously update budgets based on an ongoing flow of performance data. In production facilities, monitoring systems that track errors per hour, machine speeds, and other measures allow managers to continuously correct small production problems before they become disasters.[11]

Feedback control

Feedback control implies that performance data were gathered and analyzed and the results returned to someone (or something) in the process to make corrections. When supervisors monitor behavior, they are exercising concurrent control. When they point out and correct improper performance, they are using feedback as a means of control.

Timing is an important aspect of feedback control. Long time lags often occur between performance and feedback, such as when actual spending is compared against the quarterly budget or when some aspect of performance is compared to the projection made a year ago. If feedback on performance is not timely, managers cannot quickly identify and eliminate the problem and prevent more serious harm.

Some feedback processes are under real-time (concurrent) control, such as a computer-controlled robot on an assembly line. Such units have sensing units, which continually determine whether they are in the correct position to perform their functions. If not, a built-in control device makes immediate corrections.

You may notice a connection between the three types of control and two important models described elsewhere in the text. First, feedforward, concurrent, and feedback controls focus on the inputs, transformation processes, and outputs, respectively, of the systems model described in Chapter 1. Second, they also correspond to the A-B-C model of motivation described in Chapter 13. Preliminary control sets antecedents that dictate how people should behave. Concurrent control monitors behavior as it takes place. Feedback control occurs after the fact, and the corrective action can include rewards and punishments for proper and improper performance.

Management audits

management audits An evaluation of the effectiveness and efficiency of various systems within an organization.

Over the years, **management audits** have developed as a means for evaluating the effectiveness and efficiency of various systems within an organization, from social responsibility to accounting control.[12] Management audits may be external or internal. Managers conduct external audits of other companies and internal audits of their own company. Some of the same tools and approaches are used for both types of audits.

external audit An evaluation conducted by one organization, such as a CPA firm, on another.

External audits

An **external audit** occurs when one organization evaluates another organization. Typically an external body such as a CPA firm conducts financial audits of an organization (accounting audits are discussed later). But any company can also conduct external audits of competitors or other companies for strategic decision-making purposes. This type of analysis (1) investigates other organizations for possible merger or acquisition; (2) determines the soundness of a company that will be used as a major supplier; or (3) discovers the strengths and weaknesses of a competitor to maintain or better exploit the competitive advantage of the investigating organization. Publicly available data usually are used for these evaluations.[13]

External audits were used in feedback control in the discovery and investigation of the savings and loan scandals. They also are useful for preliminary control because they can prevent problems from occurring. If a company gathers adequate, accurate information about acquisition candidates, it is more likely to acquire the most appropriate companies and avoid unsound acquisitions.

internal audit A periodic assessment of a company's own planning, organizing, leading, and controlling processes.

Internal audits

Internal audits assesses (1) what the company has done for itself and (2) what it has done for its customers or other recipients of its goods or services. The company can be evaluated on a number of factors, including financial stability, production efficiency, sales effectiveness, human resources development, earnings growth, public relations, civic responsibility, or other criteria of organizational effectiveness. The audit reviews the company's past, present, and future.[14]

To perform a management audit, a list of desired qualifications is drawn up and weights are attached to each qualification. Among the more common undesirable practices uncovered by a management audit are the performance of unnecessary work; duplication of work; poor inventory control; uneconomical use of equipment and machines; procedures that are more costly than necessary; and wasted resources. Square D, the electrical equipment manufacturer, discovered it could throw away four manuals with 760 rules and regulations in favor of 11 policy statements. At Heinz, a quality program aimed mostly at eliminating waste and rework is estimated to save $250 million over three years. Oryx, the world's largest independent oil and gas producer, now takes six weeks instead of seven months to produce the annual budget and has cut in half the average time and cost of finding new oil and gas reserves.[15]

Budgetary control

budgeting The process of investigating what is being done and comparing the results with the corresponding budget data to verify accomplishments or remedy differences. Also called budgetary controlling.

Budgetary control is one of the most widely recognized and commonly used methods of managerial control. It ties together feedforward control, concurrent control, and feedback control, depending on the point at which it is applied. *Budgetary control* is the process of finding out what's being done and comparing the results with the corresponding budget data to verify accomplishments or to remedy differences. Budgetary control commonly is called **budgeting.**

Fundamental budgetary considerations

In private industry, budgetary control begins with an estimate of sales and expected income. Table 16.3 shows a budget with

table 16.3 A sales-expense budget

	January		February		March	
	Expectancy	Actual	Expectancy	Actual	Expectancy	Actual
Sales	$1,200,000		$1,350,000		$1,400,000	
Expenses						
General overhead	310,000		310,000		310,000	
Selling	242,000		275,000		288,000	
Producing	327,000		430,500		456,800	
Research	118,400		118,400		115,000	
Office	90,000		91,200		91,500	
Advertising	32,500		27,000		25,800	
Estimated gross profit	80,100		97,900		112,900	

estimates for sales and expenses for the first three months of the year. There is space to enter the actual accomplishments to expedite comparison between expected and actual results. Note that the total expenses plus estimated gross profit equal the total sales expectancy.

Budgeting information is supplied to the entire enterprise or to any of its units; it is not confined to financial matters. Units other than dollars typically can be used. For example, industry uses budgeting of production in physical units and of labor by different skills.

A primary consideration of budgeting is the length of the budget period. All budgets are prepared for a definite time period. Many budgets are for one, three, or six months or for one year. The length of time selected depends on the primary purpose of the budgeting. The period chosen should include the enterprise's complete normal cycle of activity. For example, seasonal variations should be included both for production and for sales. The budget period commonly coincides with other control devices, such as managerial reports, balance sheets, and statements of profit and loss. In addition, the extent to which reasonable forecasts can be made should be considered in selecting the length of the budget period.

Budgetary control proceeds through several stages. *Establishing expectancies* starts with the broad plan for the company and the estimate of sales, and it ends with budget approval and publication. The *budgetary operations* stage, then, deals with finding out what is being accomplished and comparing the results with expectancies. The last stage, as in any control process, involves taking corrective action when necessary.

Although practices differ widely, a member of top management often serves as the chief coordinator for formulating and using the budget. Usually the treasurer, controller, or chief accountant has these duties. He or she needs to be less concerned with the details than with resolving conflicting interests, recommending adjustments when needed, and giving official sanction to the budgetary procedures.

Types of budgets

There are many types of budgets. Some of the more common types are as follows:

- *Sales budget.* Usually data for the sales budget are prepared by month, sales area, and product.
- *Production budget.* The production budget commonly is expressed in physical units. Required information for preparing this budget includes types and capacities of machines, economic quantities to produce, and availability of materials.
- *Cost production budget.* The information in the cost production budget sometimes is included in production budgets. Comparing production cost with sales price shows whether or not profit margins are adequate.
- *Cash budget.* The cash budget is essential to every business. It should be prepared after all other budget estimates are completed. The cash budget shows the anticipated receipts and expenditures, the amount of working capital available, the extent to which outside financing may be required, and the periods and amounts of cash available.
- *Master budget.* The master budget includes all major activities of the business. It brings together and coordinates all the activities of the other budgets and can be thought of as a "budget of budgets."

Accounting records must be inspected periodically to ensure they were properly prepared and are correct. **Accounting audits,** which verify accounting reports and statements, are essential to the control process. This audit is performed by members of an outside firm of public accountants. Knowing that accounting records are accurate, true, and in keeping with generally accepted accounting practices (GAAP) creates confidence that a reliable base exists for sound overall controlling purposes.

accounting audits
Procedures used to verify accounting reports and statements.

Activity-based costing It is now widely recognized that traditional methods of cost accounting may be inappropriate in today's business environment because they are based on outdated methods of rigid hierarchical organization. Instead of assuming that organizations are bureaucratic "machines" that can be separated into component functions such as human resources, purchasing, or maintenance, companies such as Chrysler, Hewlett-Packard, and GE have begun using **activity-based costing (ABC)** to allocate costs across business processes.

activity-based costing A method of cost accounting designed to identify streams of activity, and then to allocate costs across particular business processes according to the amount of time employees devote to particular activities.

ABC starts with the assumption that organizations are collections of people performing many different but related activities to satisfy customer needs. The ABC system is designed to identify those streams of activity, and then to allocate costs across particular business processes. The basic procedure works as follows (see Figure 16.2): First, employees are asked to break down what they do each day in order to define their *basic activities*. For example, employees in Dana Corporation's material control department engage in a number of activities ranging from processing sales orders and sourcing parts to requesting engineering changes and solving problems. These activities form the basis for ABC. Second, managers look at total expenses computed by traditional accounting—such as fixed costs, supplies, salaries, fringe benefits, and so on—and spread total amounts over the activities according to the amount of time spent on each activity. At Dana, customer service employees spend nearly 25 percent of their time processing sales orders and only about 3 percent on scheduling parts. So 25 percent of the total cost ($144,846) goes to order processing and 3 percent ($15,390) goes to scheduling parts. As can be seen in Figure 16.2, both the traditional and ABC systems reach the same bottom line. However, because the ABC method allocates costs across business processes, it provides a more accurate picture of how costs should be charged to products and services.[16]

Perhaps more important than the accuracy of ABC, the system highlights where wasted activities are occurring or if activities cost too much relative to the benefits they provide to customers. By providing this type of information, ABC has quickly become a valuable method for streamlining business processes. The example on page 552 from GE Medical shows how.

figure 16.2
How Dana discovers what its true costs are

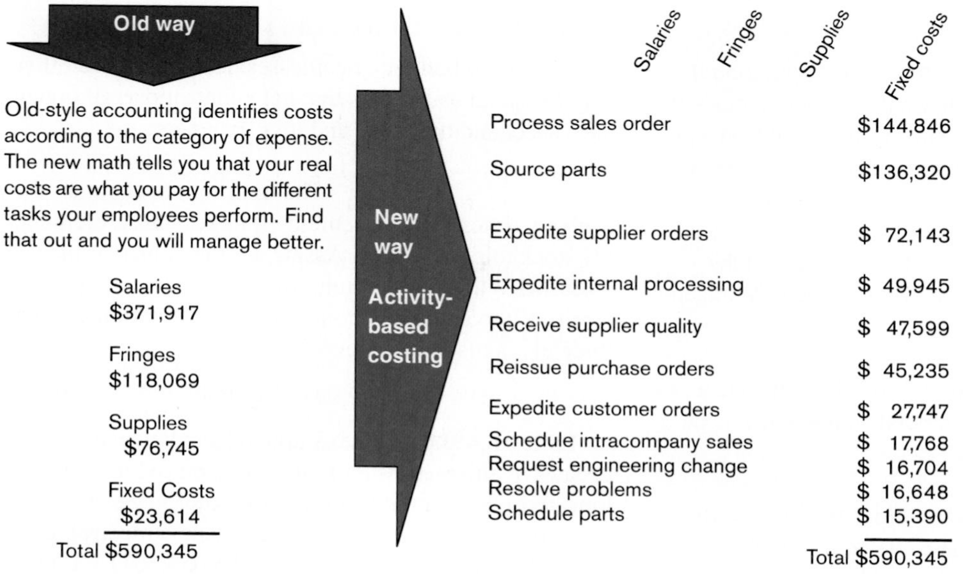

Old way

Old-style accounting identifies costs according to the category of expense. The new math tells you that your real costs are what you pay for the different tasks your employees perform. Find that out and you will manage better.

Old way	
Salaries	$371,917
Fringes	$118,069
Supplies	$76,745
Fixed Costs	$23,614
Total	$590,345

New way — Activity-based costing

(Salaries, Fringes, Supplies, Fixed costs)

Process sales order	$144,846
Source parts	$136,320
Expedite supplier orders	$ 72,143
Expedite internal processing	$ 49,945
Receive supplier quality	$ 47,599
Reissue purchase orders	$ 45,235
Expedite customer orders	$ 27,747
Schedule intracompany sales	$ 17,768
Request engineering change	$ 16,704
Resolve problems	$ 16,648
Schedule parts	$ 15,390
Total	$590,345

Source: Courtesy Dana Corp.

The ABCs of GE Medical

At General Electric Medical Systems, activity-based costing (ABC) has been particularly helpful for streamlining business processes. Case in point: Field engineers, the people who service the huge imaging machines GE manufactures, used to lug around on each service call a trunk full of manuals that weighed nearly 200 pounds. While on the job, these technicians frequently had to make several trips to their cars to check procedures or get information to help diagnose problems. If they had not updated their manuals, which they were supposed to do periodically, they had to call the office for information. All in all, the field engineers estimated they spent as much as 15 percent of their time during service calls shuttling back and forth to their cars. ABC provided some insights to this problem. By allocating expenses over each activity field engineers undertook, it was possible to isolate the costs of wasted activities. As the people in the field saw it, the remedy to their problem was to issue laptop computers with CD-ROM readers that would allow them to carry all reference information right to the job site. But with 2,500 field engineers in the United States alone, switching to laptops was a major capital expenditure. However, once the ABC activity analysis was completed, the decision was easy.

Switching to laptops has helped GE Medical raise productivity 9 percent–the equivalent of a \$25 million increase in sales with no increase in cost. One unexpected benefit: The field engineers' cars are 200 pounds lighter, which improves their gas mileage. Eventually GE believes that use of laptops will help technicians channel service information back to the manufacturing units so that design improvements can be approached with an eye toward servicing costs. When this connection occurs, ABC will be helping to improve the design process for million-dollar pieces of medical equipment.

Source: Terence P. Pare, "A New Tool for Managing Costs," *Fortune,* June 14, 1993, pp. 124–29.

Financial controls

balance sheet A report that shows the financial picture of a company at a given time and itemizes assets, liabilities, and stockholders' equity.

assets The values of the various items the corporation owns.

liabilities The amounts a corporation owes to various creditors.

stockholders' equity The amount accruing to the corporation's owners.

In addition to budgets, businesses commonly use other statements for financial control. Two financial statements that help control overall organizational performance are the balance sheet and the profit and loss statement.

The balance sheet

The **balance sheet** shows the financial picture of a company at a given time. This statement itemizes three elements: (1) assets, (2) liabilities, and (3) stockholders' equity. **Assets** are the values of the various items the corporation owns. **Liabilities** are the amounts the corporation owes to various creditors. **Stockholders' equity** is the amount accruing to the corporation's owners. The relationships among these three elements is as follows:

Assets = Liabilities + Stockholders' equity

Table 16.4 shows an example of a balance sheet. During the year, the company grew because it enlarged its building and acquired more machinery and equipment by means of long-term debt in the form of a first mortgage. Additional stock was sold to help finance the expansion. At the same time, accounts receivable were increased and work in process reduced. Observe that Total assets (\$3,053,367) = Total liabilities (\$677,204 + \$618,600) + Stockholders' equity (\$700,000 + \$981,943 + \$75,620).

table 16.4
A comparative balance sheet

Comparative Balance Sheet For the Years Ending December 31	This year	Last year
Assets		
Current assets:		
Cash	$ 161,870	$ 119,200
U.S. Treasury bills	250,400	30,760
Accounts receivable	825,595	458,762
Inventories:		
Work in process and finished products	429,250	770,800
Raw materials and supplies	251,340	231,010
Total current assets	1,918,455	1,610,532
Other assets:		
Land	157,570	155,250
Building	740,135	91,784
Machinery and equipment	172,688	63,673
Furniture and fixtures	132,494	57,110
Total other assets before depreciation	1,202,887	367,817
Less: Accumulated depreciation and amortization	67,975	63,786
Total other assets	1,134,912	304,031
Total assets	$3,053,367	$1,914,563
Liabilities and stockholders' equity		
Current liabilities:		
Accounts payable	$ 287,564	$ 441,685
Payrolls and withholdings from employees	44,055	49,580
Commissions and sundry accruals	83,260	41,362
Federal taxes on income	176,340	50,770
Current installment on long-term debt	85,985	38,624
Total current liabilities	667,204	622,021
Long-term liabilities:		
15-year, 9 percent loan, payable in each of the years1988 to 2001	210,000	225,000
5 percent first mortgage	408,600	
Registered 9 percent notes payable		275,000
Total long-term liabilities	618,600	500,000
Stockholders' equity:		
Common stock: authorized 1,000,000 shares, outstanding last year 492,000 shares, outstanding this year 700,000 shares at $1 par value	700,000	492,000
Capital surplus	981,943	248,836
Earned surplus	75,620	51,706
Total liabilities and stockholders' equity	$3,053,367	$1,914,563

Summarizing balance sheet items over a long period of time uncovers important trends and gives a manager further insight into overall performance and areas in which adjustments need to be made.

profit and loss statement An itemized financial statement of the income and expenses of a company's operations.

The profit and loss statement

The **profit and loss statement** is an itemized financial statement of the income and expenses of the company's operations. Table 16.5 shows a comparative statement of profit and loss for two consecutive years. In this illustration, the operating revenue of the enterprise has increased. Expense also has increased, but at a lower rate, resulting in a higher net income. Some managers draw up tentative profit and loss statements and use them as goals. Then performance is measured against these goals or standards. From comparative statements of this type, a manager can identify trouble areas and correct them.

Controlling by profit and loss is most commonly used for the entire enterprise and, in the case of a diversified corporation, its divisions. However, if controlling is by departments, as in a decentralized organization in which department managers have control over both revenue and expense, a profit and loss statement is used for each department. Each department's output is measured, and a cost, including overhead, is charged to each department's operation. Expected net income is the standard for measuring a department's performance.

Financial ratios

An effective approach for checking on the overall performance of an enterprise is to use key financial ratios. Ratios help indicate possible strengths and weaknesses in the company's operations. Key ratios are calculated from selected items on the profit and loss statement and the balance sheet. We will briefly discuss three categories of financial ratios: liquidity, leverage, and profitability.

current ratio A liquidity ratio which indicates the extent to which short-term assets can decline and still be adequate to pay short-term liabilities.

- **Liquidity ratios.** *Liquidity ratios* indicate the company's ability to pay short-term debts. The most common liquidity ratio is *current assets to current liabilities,* called the **current ratio** or *net working capital ratio.* This ratio indicates the extent to which

table 16.5
A comparative statement of profit and loss

Comparative Statement of Profit and Loss For the Years Ending June 30	This year	Last year	Increase or decrease
Income:			
Net sales	$ 253,218	$ 257,636	$ 4,418*
Dividends from investments	480	430	50
Other	1,741	1,773	32
Total	255,439	259,839	4,400*
Deductions:			
Cost of goods sold	180,481	178,866	1,615
Selling and administrative expenses	39,218	34,019	5,199
Interest expense	2,483	2,604	121*
Other	1,941	1,139	802
Total	224,123	216,628	7,495
Income before taxes	31,316	43,211	11,895*
Provision for taxes	3,300	9,500	6,200*
Net income	$ 28,016	$ 33,711	$ 5,695*

*Decrease.

current assets can decline and still be adequate to pay current liabilities. Some analysts set a ratio of 2 to 1, or 2.00, as the desirable minimum.

- **Leverage ratios.** *Leverage ratios* show the relative amount of funds in the business supplied by creditors and shareholders. An important example is the **debt-equity ratio,** which indicates the company's ability to meet its long-term financial obligations. If this ratio is less than 1.5, the amount of debt is not considered excessive.
- **Profitability ratios.** *Profitability ratios* indicate management's ability to generate a financial return on sales or investment. For example, **return on investment (ROI)** is a ratio of profit to capital used, or a rate of return from capital.

debt-equity ratio A leverage ratio which indicates the company's ability to meet its long-term financial obligations.

return on investment (ROI) A ratio of profit to capital used, or a rate of return from capital.

management myopia Focusing on short-term earnings and profits at the expense of longer-term strategic obligations.

Using financial ratios

Although ratios provide both performance standards and indicators of what has occurred, exclusive reliance on financial ratios can have negative consequences as well. Because ratios usually are expressed in compressed time horizons (monthly, quarterly, or yearly), they often cause **management myopia**—managers focus on short-term earnings and profits at the expense of their longer-term strategic obligations.[17] Control systems using long-term (e.g., three-to-six-year) performance targets can reduce management myopia and focus attention farther into the future.

A second negative outcome of ratios is that they relegate other important considerations to a secondary position. Research and development, management development, progressive human resources practices, and other considerations may receive insufficient attention. Therefore, the use of ratios should be supplemented with other control measures. Organizations can hold managers accountable for market share, number of patents granted, sales of new products, human resources development, and other performance indicators.

The downside of bureaucratic control

So far, you have learned about control from a mechanical viewpoint. But organizations are not strictly mechanical; they are composed of people. While control systems are used to constrain people's behavior and make their future behavior predictable, people are not machines that automatically fall into line as the designers of control systems intend. In fact, control systems can lead to dysfunctional behavior. A control system cannot be effective without consideration of how people will react to it. For effective control of employee behavior, managers should consider three types of potential responses to control: rigid bureaucratic behavior, tactical behavior, and resistance.[18]

Rigid bureaucratic behavior

Often people act in ways that will help them look good on the control system's measures. This tendency can be useful, because it causes people to focus on the behaviors management requires. But it can result in rigid, inflexible behavior geared toward doing *only* what the system requires.

Rigid bureaucratic behavior occurs when control systems prompt employees to stay out of trouble by following the rules. Unfortunately, such systems often lead to poor customer service and make the entire organization slow to act (recall the discussion of bureaucracy in Chapter 10).

We have perhaps all been victimized at some time by rigid bureaucratic behavior. Reflect for a moment on this now classic story of a "nightmare" at a hospital:

> At midnight, a patient with eye pains enters an emergency room at a hospital. At the reception area, he is classified as a nonemergency case and referred to the hospital's eye clinic. Trouble is, the eye clinic doesn't open until the next morning. When he arrives at the clinic, the nurse asks for his referral slip, but the emergency room doctor had forgotten to give it to him. The patient has to return to the emergency room and wait for another physician to screen him. The physician refers him back to the eye clinic and to a social worker to arrange payment. Finally, a third doctor looks into his eye, sees a small piece of metal, and removes it—a 30-second procedure.[19]

Stories such as these have, of course, given bureaucracy a bad name. Some managers will not even use the term *bureaucratic control* because of its potentially negative connotation. That is unfortunate because the control system itself is not the problem. The problems occur when the systems are no longer viewed as tools for running the business, but as rules for dictating rigid behavior.

Tactical behavior Control systems will be ineffective if employees engage in tactics aimed at "beating the system." The most common type of tactical behavior is to manipulate information or report false performance data. People may produce two kinds of invalid data: about what *has* been done and about what *can* be done. False reporting about the past is less common, because it is easier to identify someone who misreports what happened than someone who gives an erroneous prediction or estimate of what might happen.[20] Still, managers sometimes change their accounting systems to "smooth out" the numbers. Also, people may intentionally feed false information into a management information system to cover up errors or poor performance.[21]

More commonly, people falsify their predictions or requests for the future. When asked to give budgetary estimates, employees usually ask for larger amounts than they need. On the other hand, they sometimes submit unrealistically *low* estimates when they believe a low estimate will help them get a budget or a project approved. Budget-setting sessions can become tugs-of-war between subordinates trying to get slack in the budget and superiors attempting to minimize slack. Similar tactics are exhibited when managers negotiate unrealistically low performance standards so that subordinates will have little trouble meeting them; when salespeople project low forecasts so they will look good by exceeding them; and when workers slow down the work pace when time-study analysts are setting work pace standards.[22] In these and other cases, such as the Bausch & Lomb example in "Setting the Stage," people are concerned only with their own performance figures rather than with the overall performance of their departments or companies.

Resistance to control Often people strongly resist control systems. This occurs for several reasons.[23] First, comprehensive control systems increase the accuracy of performance data and make employees more accountable for their actions. Control systems uncover mistakes, threaten people's job security and status, and decrease people's autonomy.

Second, control systems can change expertise and power structures. For example, management information systems can make the costing, purchasing, and production decisions previously made by managers. Thus, individuals fear a loss of expertise, power, and decision-making authority.

Third, control systems can change the social structure of the organization. They can create competition and disrupt social groups and friendships. People may end up competing against those with whom they formerly had comfortable, cooperative relationships. Because people's social needs are so important, they will resist control systems that reduce social need satisfaction.

Fourth, control systems may be seen as an invasion of privacy. The following illustration shows that some control systems are controversial, particularly when their accuracy is suspect or when they are viewed as unnecessary.

Drug testing: a controversial control system

Employee drug use is a serious problem. Possible consequences of employee drug use include injuries, illness, absenteeism, breakage, theft, and reduced productivity. A recent report by the U.S. Department of Health and Human Services reveals that nearly 10 percent of persons under the age of 50 admitted to taking illicit drugs on a regular basis. It is estimated that in the United States the use of illegal drugs by employees costs industry $25 billion a year. The magnitude of the problem has challenged managers to find ways to discourage or prevent employee drug use. One common approach is to implement a drug-testing program.

Approximately three-fourths of all large companies have drug-testing programs, though a study by the Substance Abuse & Mental Health Services Adminstration indicates that testing is more likely for blue-collar employees than for white-collar employees. Companies test for cause (e.g., an accident or excessive absenteeism), randomly, on all employees, or on all applicants. The most common test is a urinalysis; the employee supplies a urine sample that is chemically tested for traces of drugs in his or her system.

Some people have strongly resisted drug testing. Many object to it on philosophical and constitutional grounds. They claim the tests intrude on their personal lives, particularly because the tests reveal drug use during personal time, the effects of which may have worn off. They also claim the tests violate the right to privacy and constitute unreasonable search and seizure. People also object because the urinalysis tests are not 100 percent accurate. "False positive" test results—which indicate illegal drugs when there are none in the person's system—can be triggered by some foods and legal over-the-counter drugs.

Employees have responded to this control system in ways beyond verbal protest. Many have challenged the programs by filing lawsuits. Others take the tests but try not to get caught with drugs in their systems. They change the timing or substance of their drug use, submit friends' urine samples as their own, or put substances in their own samples that will make the drugs less detectable. Also, clean urine samples can be purchased. When drug testing first became popular in the mid-1980s, people sold samples on the streets. Now they can even be purchased by mail order.

Employers have responded by tightening the control system. A common technique is to have someone watch employees submit their samples to make sure no one cheats. Some companies use expensive and accurate chemical tests, and some even use undercover agents and drug-sniffing dogs. At least one company is now marketing an alternative approach: a video game that tests eye-hand coordination to assess fitness for work duty.

Sources: M. Boles, "Blue-Collar Workers Face More Drug Tests," *Workforce* 76, no. 8 (August 1997), p. 22; M. Ligos, "Are Your Reps High?" *Sales & Marketing Management* 149, no. 11 (October 1997), pp. 80–86; J. Hamilton, "A Video Game That Tells if Employees Are Fit for Work," *Business Week,* June 3, 1991, p. 36; H. Hayghe, "Anti-Drug Programs in the Workplace: Are They Here to Stay?", *Monthly Labor Review* 114 (April 1991), pp. 26–29; and M. Crant and T. Bateman, "Employee Responses to Drug-Testing Programs," *Employee Responsibilities and Rights Journal,* 1989. ●

Designing effective control systems

Effective control systems maximize the potential benefits and minimize dysfunctional behaviors. To achieve this, management needs to design control systems that (1) are based on valid performance standards, (2) communicate adequate information to employees, (3) are acceptable to employees, (4) use multiple approaches, and (5) recognize the relationship between empowerment and control.

Establish valid performance standards An effective control system must be based on valid and accurate performance standards. The most effective standards, as discussed earlier, tend to be expressed in quantitative terms; they are objective rather than subjective. Also, the measures should not be capable of being easily sabotaged or faked. Moreover, the system must incorporate all important aspects of performance. As you learned earlier, unmeasured behaviors are neglected. But management must also defend against another problem: too many measures that create overcontrol and employee resistance. To make many controls tolerable, managers can devote attention to a few key areas while setting "satisfactory" performance standards in others. Or they can establish simple priorities. The purchasing agent may have to meet targets in the following sequence: quality, availability, cost, inventory level. Finally, managers can set tolerance ranges. For example, in financial budgeting optimistic, expected, and minimum levels sometimes are specified.[24]

Many companies' budgets set cost targets only.[25] This causes managers to control spending, but also to neglect earnings. At Emerson Electric, profit rather than cost is the key measure. If an unanticipated opportunity to increase market share arises, managers can spend what they need to go after it. The phrase "it's not in the budget" is less likely to stifle people at Emerson than at most other companies.

This principle applies to nonfinancial aspects of performance as well. At Motorola, the recruiting department used to be measured by how much money it spent for each new hire. Now it is measured by how well its recruits subsequently perform.[26]

Provide adequate information Management must adequately communicate to employees the importance and nature of the control system. Then people must receive feedback about their performance. Feedback motivates people and provides information that enables them to correct their own deviations from performance standards. Allowing people to initiate their own corrective action encourages self-control and reduces the need for outside supervision.

Information should be as accessible as possible, particularly when people must make decisions quickly and frequently. For example, a national food company with its own truck fleet had a difficult problem. The company wanted drivers to go through customer sales records every night, insert new prices from headquarters every morning, and still make their rounds—an impossible set of demands. To solve this control problem, the company installed microcomputers in more than 1,000 delivery trucks. Now drivers use their PCs for daily two-way communication with headquarters. Each night drivers send information about the stores, and each morning headquarters sends prices and recommended stock mixes.[27]

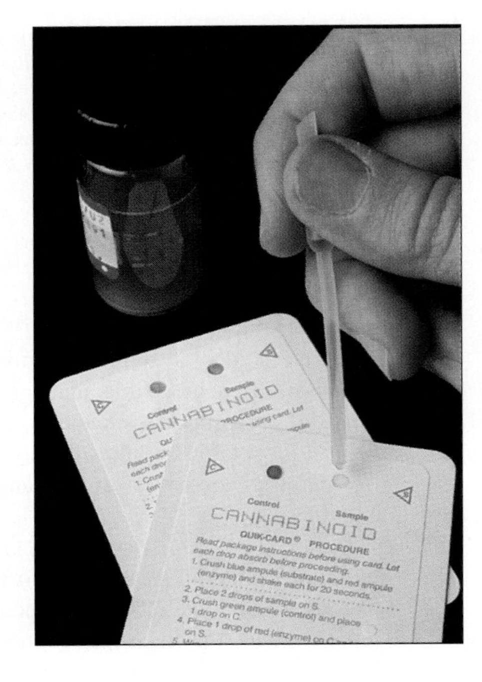

Many people favor employee drug testing as a control measure, but some change their minds when they are asked to personally submit a urine speciman.
[Charles Gupton/The Stock Market]

In general, a manager designing a control system should evaluate the information system in terms of the following questions:

1. Does it provide people with data relevant to the decisions they need to make?
2. Does it provide the right amount of information to decision makers throughout the organization?
3. Does it provide enough information to each part of the organization about how other related parts of the organization are functioning?[28]

Ensure acceptability to employees Employees are less likely to resist a control system and exhibit dysfunctional behaviors if they accept the system. They are more likely to accept systems that have useful performance standards but are not overcontrolling. One Food Lion (a supermarket chain) store manager said to a *Fortune* reporter about standards he considered unreasonable, "I put in more and more and more time—a hundred hours a week—but no matter . . . I could never satisfy the supervisors . . . They wanted 100 percent conditions, seven days a week, 24 hours a day. And there's no . . . way you could do it."[29] Employees will find systems more acceptable if they believe the standards are possible to achieve.

The control system should emphasize positive behavior rather than focus on controlling negative behavior alone. As noted earlier, companies like Emerson look at profits rather than costs. Jean-Marie Descarpentries of Franco-British CMB Packaging clearly prefers to highlight the positive: He has the heads of 94 profit centers project their best possible performance if everything goes perfectly. He wants his managers to "dream the impossible dream." Then he avoids penalizing people who just miss their lofty goals by assessing them based on how they performed this year versus last year and against the performances of the best managers in the industry.[30]

One of the best ways to establish reasonable standards and thus gain employee acceptance of the control system is to set standards participatively. As we discussed in Chapter 4, participation in decision making secures people's understanding and acceptance and results in better decisions. Allowing employees to participate in control system decisions that directly affect their jobs will help overcome resistance and foster acceptance of the system.

Use multiple approaches Multiple controls are necessary. For example, casinos exercise control over card dealers by (1) requiring them to have a card dealer's license before being hired; (2) using various forms of direct scrutiny, including up to three levels of direct supervision, closed-circuit cameras, and observation through one-way mirrors; and (3) requiring detailed paperwork to audit transfers of cash and cash equivalents.[31] As you learned earlier in this chapter, control systems generally should include both financial and nonfinancial performance targets and incorporate aspects of preliminary, concurrent, and feedback control.

The other controls: markets and clans

Although the concept of control has always been a central feature of organizations, the principles and philosophies underlying its use are changing. In the past, control has been almost exclusively focused on bureaucratic (and market) mechanisms. Generations of managers have been taught that they could maximize productivity by regulating what employees did on the job—through standard operating procedures, rules, regulations, and close supervision. To increase output on an assembly line, for example, managers in the past tried to identify the "one best way" to approach the work and then to monitor employee activities to make certain that they followed standard operating procedures. In short, they controlled work by dividing and simplifying tasks, a process we referred to in Chapter 1 as scientific management.

Although formal bureaucratic control systems are perhaps the most pervasive in organizations (and the most talked about in management textbooks), they are not always the most effective. *Market controls* and *clan controls* may both represent more flexible, though no less potent, approaches to regulating performance.

Market control

In contrast to bureaucratic controls, market controls involve the use of economic forces—and the pricing mechanisms that accompany them—to regulate performance. The system works like this: In cases where output from an individual, department, or business unit has value to other people, a price can be negotiated for its exchange. As a market for these transactions becomes established, two effects occur:

- Price becomes an indicator of the value of the product or service.
- Price competition has the effect of controlling productivity and performance.

The basic principles that underlie market controls can actually operate at the corporate level, the business unit (or department) level, and the individual level. Figure 16.3 shows a few different ways that market controls are used in an organization.

Market controls at the corporate level

In large diversified companies, market controls are often used to regulate independent business units. Particularly in large conglomerate firms that act as holding companies, business units are typically treated as profit centers that compete with one another. Top executives may place very few bureaucratic controls on business unit managers, but use profit and loss data for

figure 16.3 Examples of market control

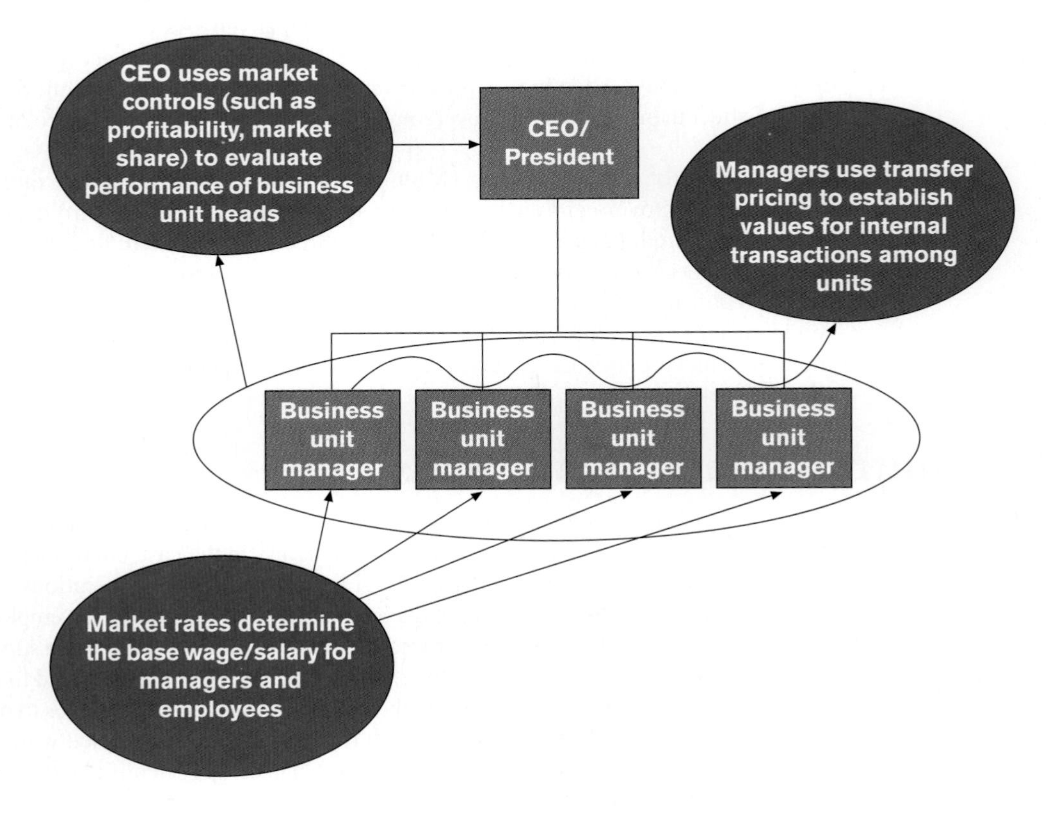

evaluating performance. So while decision making and power are decentralized to the business units, market controls ensure that business unit performance is in line with corporate objectives.

Use of market control mechanisms in this way has been criticized by those who insist that economic measures do not adequately reflect the complete value of an organization. Employees often suffer as diversified companies are repeatedly bought and sold based on market controls.

Market controls at the business unit level

Market control can also be used within business units to regulate exchanges among departments and functions. Transfer pricing is one method that organizations use to try to reflect market forces for internal transations. A **transfer price** is the price charged by one unit in the organization for a product or service that it supplies to another unit of the same organization. For example, in automobile manufacturing, a transfer price may be affixed to components and subassemblies before they are shipped to subsequent business units for final assembly. Ideally the transfer price reflects the price that the receiving business unit would have to pay for that product or service in the marketplace.

transfer price Price charged by one unit for a product or service provided to another unit within the organization.

As organizations have more options to outsource products and services to external partners, market controls such as transfer prices provide natural incentives to keep costs down, and quality up. Consider the situation where training and development activities can be done internally by the human resources department or outsourced to a consulting firm. If the human resources department cannot supply quality training at a reasonable price, then there may be no reason for that department to exist inside the firm. Organizations such as Continental Airlines, IBM, and Corning have placed strict market controls on their human resources functions in order to manage costs and performance.[32]

Market controls at the individual level

Market controls are also used at the individual level. For example, in situations where organizations are trying to hire employees, the supply and demand for particular skills influence the wages employees can expect to receive and the rate organizations are likely to pay. Employees or job candidates that have more valuable skills tend to be paid a higher wage. Of course, wages don't always reflect market rates—sometimes they are set (perhaps arbitrarily) based on internal resource considerations—but the market rate is often the best indicator of an employee's potential worth to a firm.

Market-based controls such as these are important in that they provide a natural incentive for employees to enhance their skills and offer them to potential firms. Even after individuals gain employment, market-based wages are important as controls in that persons with higher economic value may be promoted faster to higher positions in the organization.

Market controls are often used by boards of directors to manage CEOs of major corporations. Ironically, CEOs are usually seen as the ones controlling everyone else in the company, but the fact is that the CEO is accountable to the board of directors, and the board must devise ways to ensure that the CEO acts in their interest. Believe it or not, CEOs often do not want to accept the associated risk required to achieve higher profits for the owners, and consequently may act in ways that make them look good personally (such as making the company bigger or more diversified) but that don't translate into higher profits for the firm.

To attach some strings to the actions of CEOs, boards typically use at least two types of incentives on top of base salary: First, some type of bonus is tied to short-term profit targets such as return on equity. In large U.S. companies, fully 79 percent of the pay of CEOs is now at risk, meaning it's variable depending on the performance of the company. In addition to short-term incentives, boards also use some type of long-term incentives linked to the firm's share price, usually through stock options. More than half of a CEO's pay typically depends on delivering superior performance over time. According to Pearl Meyer, an executive pay consultant in New York, the typical CEO pay package is 21 percent salary, 27 percent short-term (annual) incentives, 16 percent long-term incentives, and 36 percent stock-based pay (mostly options, which usually cannot be exercised for three years).[33]

Clan control: the role of empowerment and culture

Increasingly, managers are discovering that control systems based solely on bureaucratic and market mechanisms are insufficient for directing today's workforce. There are several reasons for this.

- *Employees' jobs have changed.* The nature of work is evolving. Employees working with computers, for example, have more variability in their jobs, and much of their work is intellectual, and therefore invisible. Because of this, there is no one best way to perform a task, and programming or standardizing jobs becomes extremely difficult. Close supervision is also unrealistic since it is nearly impossible to supervise activities like reasoning and problem solving.
- *The nature of management has changed.* The role of managers is evolving, too. It used to be the case that managers knew more about the job than employees did. Today, it is typical for employees to know more about their jobs than anyone else. We refer to this as the shift from touch labor to knowledge work.[34] When real expertise in organizations exists at the very lowest levels, hierarchical control becomes impractical.
- *The employment relationship has changed.* The social contract at work is being renegotiated. It used to be that employees were most concerned about issues such as pay, job security, the hours of work, and the like. Today, however, more and more employees want to be more fully engaged in their work, taking part in decision making, deriving solutions to unique problems, and receiving assignments that are challenging and involving. They want to use their brains.

For these three reasons, the concept of *empowerment* has not only become more and more popular in organizations, but it has become a necessary aspect of a manager's repertoire of control. With no "one best way" to approach a job, and no way to scrutinize what employees do every day, managers must empower employees to make decisions and trust that they will act in the best interests of the firm. But this does not mean giving up control. Instead it means that managers need to make better use of clan control, as opposed to authoritarian control.[35] As we noted at the beginning of this chapter, *clan control* involves creating relationships built on mutual respect, and encouraging each individual to take responsibility for his or her actions. Employees work within a guiding framework of values, and they are expected to use good judgment. At Nordstrom, the fashion retailer, for example, instead of a thick manual laying out company policies, employees are simply given a five-by-eight-inch card that reads: "Use good judgment in all situations. There will be no additional rules."[36] The emphasis in an empowered organization is on satisfying customers, not on pleasing the boss. Mistakes are tolerated, as the unavoidable by-product of dealing with change and uncertainty, and viewed as opportunities to learn. And team members learn together. Table 16.6 provides a set of guidelines for managing in an empowered world.

Understanding culture's role in control

Organization culture is the foundation of clan control. **Organization culture** is the set of important assumptions about the organization and its goals and practices that members of the company share.[37] It is a system of shared values about what is important and beliefs about how the world works. In this way, a company's culture provides a framework that organizes and directs people's behavior on the job. That's the essence of control.

organization culture The set of important assumptions about the organization and its goals and practices that members of the company share.

Cultures can be strong or weak; strong cultures can have great influence on how people think and behave. A strong culture is one in which everyone understands and believes in the firm's goals, priorities, and practices. A strong culture can be a real advantage to the

At Nordstrom, the fashion retailer, employees are simply given a five-by-eight-inch card with one rule on it.
[Courtesy of Nordstrom, Inc.]

organization if the behaviors it encourages and facilitates are appropriate ones. At several points in this textbook, we have alluded to strong cultures at companies such as Southwest Airlines, Starbuck's Coffee, or the Walt Disney Company that encourage extraordinary devotion to customer service. Employees in these companies don't need rule books to dictate how they act; their actions are rooted in their companies' cultures.

On the other hand, a strong culture that encourages the wrong behaviors can severely hinder the company's efforts to bring about appropriate changes. IBM, for example, is

table 16.6
Management control in an empowered setting

1. *Put control where the operation is.* Layers of hierarchy, close supervision, and checks and balances are quickly disappearing and being replaced with self-guided teams. For centuries even the British Empire–as large as it was–never had more than six levels of management including the Queen.

2. *Use "real time" rather than after-the-fact controls.* Issues and problems must be solved at the source by the people doing the actual work. Managers become a resource to help out the team.

3. *Rebuild the assumptions underlying management control to build on trust rather than distrust.* Today's "high-flex" organizations are based on empowerment, not obedience. Information must facilitate decision making, not police it.

4. *Move to control based on peer norms.* Clan control is a powerful thing. Workers in Japan, for example, have been known to commit suicide rather than disappoint or lose face within their team. Although this is extreme, it underlines the power of peer influence. The Japanese have a far more homogeneous culture and set of values than we do. In North America, we must build peer norms systematically and put much less emphasis on managing by the numbers.

5. *Rebuild the incentive systems to reinforce responsiveness and teamwork.* The twin goals of adding value to the customer and team performance must become the dominant raison d'être of the measurement systems.

Source: Gerald H. B. Ross, "Revolution in Management Control," *Management Accounting*, November 1990, pp. 23–27. Reprinted by permission.

frequently discussed as an organization that had a very strong culture that served it well for several decades. But the uniformity and conformity established by IBM's culture was ill-suited for creating a more dynamic and flexible organization needed today. One of Lou Gerstner's first tasks after taking over as CEO was to transform the culture to focus on creativity, innovation, and radical thinking. One symbolic gesture in that regard was relaxing IBM's traditional dress code of white shirts and blue pin-striped suits. The dress code itself was not important. But it represented the stodgy old IBM that Gerstner wanted to change.

In contrast to strong cultures, weak cultures have the following characteristics: Different people hold different values, there is confusion about corporate goals, and it is not clear from one day to the next what principles should guide decisions. As you can guess, such a culture fosters confusion, conflict, and poor performance. Most managers would agree that they want to create a strong culture that encourages and supports goals and useful behaviors that will make the company more effective.[38]

Diagnosing culture Let's say that you want to understand a company's culture. Perhaps you are thinking about working there and you want a good "fit," or perhaps you are working there right now and you want to expand your repertoire of clan control. How would you go about making the diagnosis? A variety of things will give you useful clues about culture:

- *Corporate mission statements and official goals* are a starting point, as they will tell you the firm's desired public image. But you still need to figure out whether the public statements truly reflect how the firm conducts business.
- *Business practices* can be observed. How a company responds to problems, makes strategic decisions, and treats employees and customers tells a lot about what top management really values.
- *Symbols, rites, and ceremonies* give further clues about culture. For instance, status symbols can give you a feel for how rigid the hierarchy is and for the nature of relationships between lower and higher levels. Who is hired and fired—and why—and the activities that are rewarded indicate the firm's real values.
- *The stories people tell* carry a lot of information about their company's culture. Every company has its myths, legends, and true stories about important past decisions and actions that convey the company's main values. Traditionally, Frito-Lay tells service stories, J&J tells quality stories, and 3M tells innovation stories. The stories often feature the company's heroes: persons once or still active possessed of the qualities and characteristics that the culture especially values, who act as models for others about how to behave.

From the Pages of BusinessWeek

Grabbing Hold of Coke

In 1954, Roberto C. Goizueta answered a help-wanted advertisement for a chemical engineer in a Havana newspaper and went to work for The Coca-Cola Co. Twenty-six years later, the Cuban-born executive was named president and elected chairman and chief executive of one of the world's great enterprises. But Goizueta could hardly afford to rest on his laurels. He recognized that the company had no strategic vision, and creativity was stifled by a blind adherence to tradition and a refusal to take risks. Worst of all, Coke's stock had fallen by half, and the company was barely turning a profit. So Goizueta set in motion a series of initiatives that would set the course for Coca-Cola for the next 17 years.

"The Spanish Inquisition"

Goizueta began zeroing in on the areas where he saw weaknesses in the company. It was all a buildup to the battery of pointed, provocative, and sometimes hostile questions that rained down on Coke's top worldwide executives during a reign of interlocutory terror that became known as "the Spanish Inquisition." To those who had only heard about, but not yet witnessed, the impatient and sometimes even abusive side of Goizueta, the experience was a shock. To those who endured the trial, it was the first concrete sign that their world was about to change forever. Financial results would count above all. And managers would be held responsible for whatever happened on their watch.

At the start of the Spanish Inquisition, Goizueta was shocked to learn how little Coke's managers knew about the financial end of the business–ironically, a criticism that could have been leveled against him just a few months earlier. "None of our operating executives can read a balance sheet," he grumbled. By the time it was finished, he had taken them to school and issued one of the most far-reaching imperatives of his tenure. From that point on, Goizueta warned at one of the closing budget sessions, the corporation would charge its operating units a set percentage for the capital they used. Performance, he declared, would be judged on "economic profit," the unit's operating profit after a deduction for the cost of capital.

Future Shock

The change of approach was desperately needed. To have a lasting impact on the numbers and on Coke's corporate culture, Goizueta realized, he needed to overhaul the way Coca-Cola did business, from the top down. It would be a long and difficult battle to mold Coke into a world-class company at every level. But his job, as he saw it, was to jolt Coke into the future–to shake up the managers and make them understand. The Spanish Inquisition had set the right tone, creating a healthy understanding of the need for change. But without an overarching vision, the revamping would not mean anything. The next step was to establish the guiding principles that would carry Coca-Cola through the 1980s, and a blueprint for how to implement those principles.

Two measures would set the process in place. First, Goizueta would create a mission statement for the company. Then, he would gather his top management from around the world and make them sign on, face to face, to his program. Goizueta wanted the mission statement to combine a broad vision of Coca-Cola Co. for the next decade with a set of specific strategic steps. He spent weeks bouncing ideas off board members, executives, and consultants–to the point that people scratched their heads at Goizueta's obsession with such a seemingly pie-in-the-sky project.

"Our Challenge," the statement opened, will be to enhance and protect the Coca-Cola trademark, giving shareholders an above-average return and entering new businesses only if they can perform at a rate substantially above inflation. "Our Business," Goizueta wrote, will continue to concentrate in soft drinks, emphasize leadership in other segments, and most likely expand into "industries in which we are not today." Only market segments with inherent real growth would be attractive. "Increasing annual earnings per share and effecting increased return on equity are still the name of the game," Goizueta wrote.

The statement concluded with a broad-based section about "Our Wisdom," a set of guiding principles that Goizueta believed would make Coke a leading company as it entered the final decade of the 20th century. As they worked their way into the 1990s, Goizueta wrote, Coke's employees must consider "the long-term consequences of current actions," sacrifice short-term gains when necessary, adapt to changes in consumer tastes and needs, and become a welcome part of every country in which Coke does business. Finally, every Coke employee must exhibit "the capacity to control what is controllable and the wisdom not to bother [with] what is not."

"No Sacred Cows"

Executives were exposed to the plan at a conference in Palm Springs. The broad outlines of the Goizueta era were laid out, loud and clear. Goizueta announced that a period of rapid change was about to take place at Coca-Cola. "Those who don't adapt will be left behind or out–no matter what level they are," he warned. Goizueta cautioned everyone not to mistake the mission statement for corporate puffery. "Don't take it lightly," he said. Nothing at Coke was so sacred it could not be sacrificed for the greater good of the company, and he laid waste to some of Coke's most cherished myths. People needed to take bold risks to survive. Concocting soda-pop formulas and processing orange juice did not amount to world-class technical strength. And the culture of complacency must change. "The only company that continues to enjoy success is the company that keeps struggling to achieve it," Goizueta said.

Though known even within Coke as a halting and uninspiring speaker, Goizueta had galvanized his executives. He built on that by visiting, one by one, with every one of his top managers. "Now we've got a compact," he would say, after they told him they agreed with his plans. Ultimately, Goizueta shared quiet words with the managers at the end of the conference. Many were apprehensive, uncertain about the future. As he finished, the chief executive turned to a colleague. "Well," Goizueta said, "we're off to a start."

Epilogue

So what happened? From the time he became chief executive until his death in 1997, Coke's sales more than quadrupled, from $4 billion to $18 billion. Its market capitalization ballooned from $4.3 billion to $180 billion, a staggering 3,500% increase. The blueprint for that record–one of Corporate America's very best–was largely drawn up during those first few months that Goizueta was in office.

Source: David Greising, "I'd Like to Buy the World a Coke," *Business Week:* April 13, 1998.

Questions

1. What approaches to control did Goizueta use to manage Coke?
2. Do you agree with the approach he took to managing culture change? What aspects were most intriguing to you?
3. What other control mechanisms do you believe would have been useful for Coke's managers and employees? ●

Managing culture to reinforce clan control Most companies today know that improving quality, adopting a customer orientation, and other moves necessary to being competitive are so essential that they require deep-rooted cultural changes.[39]

Top management can take several approaches to managing culture. First, corporate leadership should espouse lofty ideals and visions for the company that will inspire the organization's members. (We first spoke of vision in Chapter 4 on strategy, and we discussed it more fully in Chapter 12 on leadership.) The vision—whether it concerns quality, integrity, innovation, or whatever—should be articulated over and over until it becomes a tangible presence throughout the organization.

Second, executives must give constant attention to the mundane details of daily affairs such as communicating regularly, being visible and active throughout the company, and setting examples. The CEO should not only talk about the vision; he or she should embody it day in and day out. This makes the CEO's pronouncements credible, creates a personal example others can emulate, and builds trust that the organization's progress toward the vision will continue over the long run.

Important here are the moments of truth when hard choices must be made. Imagine top management trumpeting a culture that emphasizes quality and then discovering that a part used in a batch of assembled products is defective. The decision whether to replace the part at great expense in the interest of quality or to ship the defective part just to save time and money will go a long way toward either reinforcing or destroying a quality-oriented culture.

All along, it is essential that the CEO and other executives celebrate and reward those who exemplify the new values. Another key to managing culture involves hiring, socializing newcomers, and promoting based on the new corporate values. In this way, the new culture will begin to permeate the organization. While this may seem a time-consuming approach to building a new culture, executives must recognize that it can take years to replace a long-time culture of traditional values with one that embodies the competitive values needed in the future.

The resiliency and time investment of clan control are a "double-edged sword." Clan control takes a long time to develop, and an even longer time to change. This gives an organization stability and direction during periods of upheaval in the environment or the organization (e.g., during changes in the top management). And yet if managers want to establish a new culture—a new form of clan control—they must help employees unlearn the old values and embrace the new. We will talk about this transition process more in the final chapter of this book (Chapter 18, "World Class Futures").

Key terms

Accounting audits, p. 550
Activity-based costing (ABC), p. 551
Assets, p. 552
Balance sheet, p. 552
Budgeting, p. 549
Bureaucratic control, p. 543
Clan control, p. 543
Concurrent control, p. 546
Control, p. 542
Current ratio, p. 554
Debt-equity ratio, p. 555
External audit, p. 548
Feedback control, p. 546
Feedforward control, p. 546
Internal audit, p. 549
Liabilities, p. 552
Management audits, p. 548
Management myopia, p. 555
Market control, p. 543
Operator control, p. 546
Organization culture, p. 562
Principle of exception, p. 545
Profit and loss statement, p. 554
Return on investment (ROI), p. 555
Specialist control, p. 546
Standard, p. 544
Stockholders' equity, p. 552
Transfer price, p. 561

Summary of learning objectives

Now that you have studied Chapter 16, you should know:

Why companies develop control systems for employees.

Left to their own devices, employees may act in ways that do not benefit the organization. Control systems are designed to eliminate idiosyncratic behavior and keep employees directed toward achieving the goals of the firm. Control systems are a steering mechanism for guiding resources, for helping each individual act in behalf of the organization.

How to design a basic bureaucratic control system.

The design of a basic control system involves four steps: (1) setting performance standards; (2) measuring performance; (3) comparing performance with the standards; and (4) eliminating unfavorable deviations by taking corrective action. Performance standards should be valid, and should cover issues such as quantity, quality, time, and cost. Once performance is compared with the standards, the principle of exception suggests that the manager needs to direct attention to the exceptional cases that have significant deviations. Then the manager takes the action most likely to solve the problem.

The purposes for using budgets as a control device.

Budgets combine the benefits of feedforward, concurrent, and feedback controls. They are used as an initial guide for allocating resources, a reference point for using funds, and a feedback mechanism for comparing actual levels of sales and expenses to their expected levels. Recently, companies have modified their budgeting processes to allocate costs over basic processes (such as customer service) rather than to functions or departments. By changing the way they prepare budgets, many companies have discovered ways to eliminate waste and improve business processes.

How to interpret financial ratios and other financial controls.

The basic financial statements are the balance sheet and the profit and loss statement. The balance sheet compares the value of company assets to the obligations it owes to owners and creditors. The profit and loss statement shows company income relative to costs incurred. In addition to these statements, companies look at liquidity ratios (whether the company can pay its short-term debts), leverage ratios (the extent to which the company is funding operations by going into debt), and profitability ratios (profit relative to investment). These ratios provide a goal for managers as well as a standard against which to evaluate performance.

The procedures for implementing effective control systems.

To maximize the effectiveness of controls, managers should (1) design control systems based on valid performance standards, (2) ensure that employees are provided with adequate information about their performance, (3) encourage employees to participate in the control system's design, (4) see that multiple approaches are used (such as bureaucratic, market, and clan control), and (5) recognize the relationship between empowerment and control.

The different ways that market control mechanisms are used by organizations.

Market controls can be used at the level of the corporation, the business unit or department, or the individual. At the corporate level business units are evaluated against one another based on profitability. At times less profitable businesses are sold while more profitable businesses receive more resources. Within business units, transfer pricing may be used to approximate market mechanisms to control transactions among departments. At the individual level, market mechanisms control the wage rate of employees and can be used to evaluate the performance of individual managers.

How clan control can be approached in an empowered organization.

Increasingly, it is not practical to approach control from a centralized, mechanistic viewpoint. In today's organizations, it is difficult to program "one best way" to approach work, and it is often difficult to monitor performance. To be responsive to customers, companies must harness the expertise of employees and give them the freedom to act on their own initiative. To maintain control while empowering employees, companies should (1) use self-guided teams, (2) allow decision making at the source of the problems, (3) build trust and mutual respect, (4) base control on a guiding framework of norms, and (5) use incentive systems that encourage teamwork.

Discussion questions

1. Can you think of an instance where an organization did not use some form of control? What happened?

2. How are leadership and control different? How are planning and control different? How are structure and control different?

3. Of the four steps in the control process, which is the most important?

4. What are the pros and cons of bureaucratic controls such as rules, procedures, supervision, and the like?

5. How effective is organizational culture as a control mechanism? What are its strengths? Its limitations? When would a manager rely on clan control the most?

6. Does empowerment imply the loss of control? Why or why not?

Concluding Case

Owens-Corning asks, "Who needs managers?"

In March 1994, the Owens-Corning Insulation Division went online with FAST—the Field Automation Sales Team System—a sales-force automation system that does away with bureaucracy and empowers salespeople to make more decisions on their own. The laptop computers cost $5,000 apiece, and training on the portable systems will cost over $300,000. But despite the cost, FAST promises to give salespeople information once available only to top managers, and at the same time provide managers with the ability to monitor sales-force activities more closely than ever before.

FAST contains three types of software: (1) generic tools—word processing, fax transmission, and so on; (2) product information—customer specifications, pricing information; and (3) customer information—account information, buying history, products ordered, preferred payment terms. Updating will be almost automatic by hooking up to Owens-Corning central computers via modem.

Improvement in information technology, including laptop computers, have made it possible for off-site employees to have access to more information more often.
[Gary Buss/PFG International]

On the manager's end of things, FAST provides up-to-date sales statistics and marketplace trends. Managers know which customers are buying what products, how well a promotion is doing as it's happening, and whether a salesperson is running into trouble in a territory. This information gives managers the ability to see things as they happen, and change tactics and strategies in "real time."

Clearly, information technology is changing both the salespeople's and their managers' jobs. By providing employees with comprehensive information, FAST empowers them to act on their own initiatives. At the same time, the technology also increases each manager's span of control because it enables him or her to monitor performance so much more effectively. The net effect is that Owens-Corning now has only half the managers that it did in 1986—having eliminated a whole layer of senior management—and it has steadily trimmed support staff as well. In preautomation days, these managers and support staff were the ones who dealt with customer complaints, watched for problem orders, and resolved irritating issues. Today, systems such as FAST empower people at the scene of the action to become "real managers of their own business and their own territories."

But is there a downside to sales-force automation? Well, yes. Other companies such as PepsiCo, Johnson & Johnson, and Procter & Gamble have used similar systems—not always with unbridled enthusiasm on the part of employees. Electronic call reports, inherent in sales-force automation systems, are viewed by some salespeople as creating needless "administrivia." Since the best employees spend a good deal of time with their customers, they learn a great deal about their preferences, interests, and buying demands. Much of this critical information they keep in their heads, so there's little benefit to constantly typing information into their laptops. Furthermore, many salespeople have become unhappy about what they refer to as "the sales-force automation police"—managers who constantly monitor every activity they undertake and intimidate employees by "remote control." Effective field managers are often the ones who can create a climate of trust between themselves and their employees, but electronic monitoring threatens to destroy that trust, and jeopardize quality relationships in the process. The control freaks have gotten so out of hand, some say, that Senator Paul Simon has actually developed a workplace privacy bill that will regulate all aspects of business conduct. Will it include sales-force automation systems?

Questions

1. What are the pros and cons of a system such as FAST for controlling salespeople?

2. As the automated system empowers salespeople, does it take away power from managers?

3. How would you judge control exerted via FAST as against control achieved through the company culture? Is there a conflict?

4. Do managers have a right to monitor detailed activities of the sales force?

Sources: Tony Seideman, "Who Needs Managers?" *Sales and Marketing Management,* June 1994, pp. 14–17; Jack Falvey, "On Guard!" *Sales and Marketing Management,* January 1994, p. 41; "Groupware for the Virtual Office," *Network World,* August 29, 1994, p. 42. ●

Video Exercise

Organizational Control

Managerial control is the process of measuring progress toward planned performance and, if necessary, taking corrective action. Typically, managerial control includes the use of financial controls, quality controls, and human resource controls. To ensure that planned activities occur in each of these critical areas, managers must set performance standards, measure performance, compare performance with the standard, and take corrective action if it's needed. Emphasizing the need for measurable goals, First National Bank of Chicago Senior Vice President Richard J. Gilgan said, "You can't manage what you don't understand, and you don't understand what you don't measure. So measurement is critical to understanding where our performance is improving or not improving, where we have problems, and we can then go back and identify the root causes of those problems."All managers are involved in controlling one or more of the three critical areas identified in the videotape: financial, quality, and human resources. Techniques and examples are discussed for each.

Financial Controls

Financial controls are implemented by a company so that it can measure and control activities that yield quantitative data such as sales (in dollars), inventory (in units), and productivity per worker. Budgeting is the most common type of financial control. Every company develops budgets that compare past, present, and anticipated future performance. Budgets allow managers to plan for and track the success of their business. Some of the work processes that are controlled through budgeting include sales and income forecasts; production budgets for input, output, and capacity of machinery; and cash budgets that measure anticipated receipts and expenses so a company can determine its working capital needs.

As an example of financial control through the use of budgets, consider the potato chip sales of Nalley Fine Foods. Sales of potato chips generate revenue for the company. All the materials that go into producing the chips are expenses or costs. Besides the cost of materials, there are other costs that must be accounted for, such as direct labor costs, machinery costs, and additional overhead such as management and administrative expenses, marketing costs, and distribution expenses. A simple budget for potato chip sales for Nalley Fine Foods might look something like the following:

Sales
– Expenses
Profit

A more detailed budget would provide a line item for each expense, and would probably include a line item by customer for sales. With such detail, Nalley managers could determine ways to reduce costs or improve sales. Even with the extra detail, however, in essence the budget is summarized by the simple equation:

Sales – Expenses = Profit.

Other types of financial controls that businesses typically use are the balance sheet, profit and loss statement, and financial ratios. These measures give managers a clear picture of how their business is performing from a financial perspective.

Quality Controls

The emphasis of the quality control function is to eliminate manufacturing defects, to improve customer service, and to institute procedures that emphasize doing things right the first time. Effective quality controls can often lead to cost reductions and higher rates of customer satisfaction. Motorola, for example, has made quality control a central piece of its overall operations. Their famous "Six Sigma" quality program strives to attain a defect rate of no more than 3.4 per million. To attain this remarkably low defect rate, Motorola has made statistical quality control techniques a part of every employee's job. Former Motorola CEO Robert Galvin, the man who brought the quality approach to the company, said, "Quality saves money, and makes products appealing and attractive. Anything that's wrong is costing you money. If you get the process exactly right, it's going to be cheaper and it's going to be better."

Quality management is a process that continually improves performance at every level of the organization. Management takes responsibility for the quality of what's produced, and develops cooperative systems with employees to create solutions to organizational problems. The complete changeover to a quality management approach may take time, but the benefits can be worth it. A successful quality management approach creates a work environment where all workers can achieve high performance and participate in all levels of decision making.

Human Resource Controls

The human resources of an organization are a vital key to its success. To effectively manage the use of human resources, management needs a control system that includes two basic components: valid and acceptable performance standards, and adequate information communicated between employees and management. Setting appropriate standards incorporates all important aspects of performance, and strikes a balance between too few controls and too many. Employee participation in decisions that directly affect their jobs is one way of ensuring reasonable, acceptable standards. Feedback from employees is necessary to accomplish this. The workforce also gains important information about accepted performance through feedback from management.

Listening to the staff enables empathy, trust, and esteem to grow within an organization. One way a manager can demonstrate listening skills is to get out on the floor and actively participate in the work that is being done. This has been called "management by walking around" or MBWA. As one hospital administrator put it, "If you want to improve service in an organization, you have to make the front-line people feel as if they're valued. And if they're well treated, they'll pass it on."

By establishing valid and acceptable standards, and by providing adequate information and feedback to employees, a companywide commitment is fostered. The primary goal of the managerial controlling function is to measure actual performance, and to implement corrective action, so that performance meets expected plans. This goal is achieved through the four steps of the control process:

- Setting standards.
- Measuring performance.
- Comparing performance with standards.
- Taking corrective action.

The understanding of managerial control gives management insight into questions like "What can be done to increase sales revenue?" or "What can be done to increase this organization's efficiency?" The answers to these questions are the starting points for feedback or corrective action processes in organizational control.

Critical Thinking Questions

1. The videotape identified the three primary types of organizational control as financial, quality, and human resources. Describe instances in which controlling one of these areas may influence organizational performance in another. How should managers deal with this interaction?

2. Managerial control requires establishing clear performance standards. Why do you think it's necessary to have measurable standards? Can you think of some types of organizational performance that might be difficult to measure?

3. Quality control is becoming an increasingly important element of the overall performance of organizations. Even business schools are concerned about the quality of services they provide. Think of some quality control measures that a business school could use to determine its performance. Do you think your business school is performing at an optimal level on these measures? How could it improve?

Experiential Exercises

16.1 Safety Program

Objective

To understand some of the specific activities that fall under the management functions *planning, organizing, controlling and staffing,* and *directing.*

Instructions

After reading the following case, briefly describe the kinds of steps you would take as production manager in trying to solve your safety problem. Be sure to specifically relate your answer to the activities of *planning, organizing, controlling and staffing,* and *directing.*

Managing the Vamp Co. Safety Program

If there are specific things that a manager does, how are they done? What does it "look like" when one manages? The following describes a typical situation in which a manager performs managerial functions:

As production manager of the Vamp Stamping Company, you've become quite concerned over the metal stamping shop's safety record. Accidents that resulted in operators' missing time on the job have increased quite rapidly in the past year. These more serious accidents have jumped from 3 percent of all accidents reported to a current level of 10 percent.

Since you're concerned about your workers' safety as well as the company's ability to meet its customers' orders, you want to reduce this downtime accident rate to its previous level or lower within the next six months.

You call the accident trend to the attention of your production supervisors, pointing out the seriousness of the situation and their continuing responsibility to enforce the gloves and safety goggles rules. Effective immediately, every supervisor will review his or her accident reports for the past year, file a report summarizing these accidents with you, and state their intended actions to correct recurring causes of the accidents. They will make out weekly safety reports as well as meet with you every Friday to discuss what is being done and any problems they are running into.

You request the union steward's cooperation in helping the safety supervisor set up a short program on shop safety practices.

Since the machine operators are having the accidents, you encourage your supervisors to talk to their workers and find out what they think can be done to reduce the downtime accident rate to its previous level.

While the program is going on, you review the weekly reports, looking for patterns that will tell you how effective the program is and where the trouble spots are. If a supervisor's operators are not decreasing their accident rate, you discuss the matter in considerable detail with the supervisor and his or her key workers.

16.2 Preliminary, Concurrent, and Feedback Control

Objectives

1. To demonstrate the need for control procedures.
2. To gain experience in determining when to use preliminary, concurrent, and feedback controls.

Instructions

1. Read the text materials on preliminary, concurrent, and feedback control.
2. Read the Control Problem Situation and be prepared to resolve those control problems in a group setting.

3. Your instructor will divide the class into small groups. Each group completes the Preliminary, Concurrent, and Feedback Control Worksheet by achieving consensus on the types of control that should be applied in each situation. The group also develops responses to the discussion questions.

4. After the class reconvenes, group spokespersons present group findings.

Discussion Questions

1. For which control(s) was it easier to determine application? For which was it harder?

2. Would this exercise be better assigned to groups or to individuals?

Control Problem Situation

Your management consulting team has just been hired by Technocron International, a rapidly growing producer of electronic surveillance devices that are sold to commercial and government end users. Some sales are made through direct selling and some through industrial resellers. Direct-sale profits are being hurt by what seem to be exorbitant expenses paid to a few of the salespeople, especially those who fly all over the world in patterns that suggest little planning and control. There is trouble among the resellers because standard contracts have not been established and each reseller has an entirely different contractual relationship. Repayment schedules also vary widely from customer to customer. Also, profits are reduced by the need to specialize most orders, making mass production almost impossible. However, no effort has been made to create interchangeable components. There are also tremendous inventory problems. Some raw materials and parts are bought in such small quantities that new orders are being placed almost daily. Other orders are so large that there is hardly room to store everything. Many of these purchased components are later found to be defective and unusable, causing production delays. Engineering changes are made that make large numbers of old components still in storage obsolete. Some delays result from designs that are very difficult to assemble, and assemblers complain that their corrective suggestions are ignored by engineering. To save money, untrained workers are hired and assigned to experienced "worker-buddies" who are expected to train them on the job. However, many of the new people are too poorly educated to understand their assignments, and their worker-buddies wind up doing a great deal of their work. This, along with the low pay and lack of consideration from engineering, is causing a great deal of worker unrest and talk of forming a union. Last week alone there were nine new worker grievances filed, and the U.S. Equal Employment Opportunity Commission has just announced intentions to investigate two charges of discrimination on the part of the company. There is also a serious cash flow problem, as a number of long-term debts are coming due at the same time. The cash flow problem could be relieved somewhat if some of the accounts payable could be collected.

The CEO manages corporate matters through five functional divisions: operations, engineering, marketing, finance, and human resources management and general administration.

Preliminary, Concurrent, and Feedback Control Worksheet

Technocron International is in need of a variety of controls. Complete the following matrix by noting the preliminary, concurrent, and feedback controls that are needed in each of the five functional divisions.

Divisions	Preliminary Controls	Concurrent Controls	Feedback Controls
HRM and general administration			
Operations			
Engineering			
Marketing			
Finance			

Chapter Seventeen

Managing Technology and Innovation

A wise man will make more opportunities than he finds.

—Francis Bacon

Chapter Outline

Learning Objectives

After studying Chapter 17, you will know:

1. The processes involved in the development of new technologies.
2. How technologies proceed through a life cycle.
3. How to manage technology for competitive advantage.
4. How to assess technology needs.
5. Where new technologies originate and the best strategies for acquiring them.
6. How people play a role in managing technology.
7. How to develop an innovative organization.
8. The key characteristics of successful development projects.

Setting the Stage

Detroit's Impossible Dream

Two years ago, Bradford B. Bates of Ford Motor Company predicted he wouldn't live to see cars powered by the space-age devices that are his passion—fuel cells—because that would be three decades in the future. Now Bates, who's 60 and a key fuel-cell researcher at Ford, says he expects to be able to purchase an electric car powered by the devices "before I give up driving." Indeed, he's now striving to fulfill Ford's promise to put a fuel-cell car on the road by 2004. Suddenly the fuel cell, once found only on NASA spacecraft, has become Detroit's pet project.

Fuel-cell cars appear to be the perfect antidote to today's ozone-depleting, smog-making, internal combustion vehicles. Through a chemical reaction between hydrogen and oxygen, fuel cells generate the juice to power an electric motor—and the only emission out the tailpipe is a trickle of water! The technology is even ahead of current electric cars, with their limited-range batteries and long recharging times. With fuel cells, drivers would "recharge" by filling up at the same service station they've always used. That's because new technology can extract hydrogen gas from liquid fuels. And we're not talking about old fossil fuels; the new technology can extract hydrogen from methanol and ethanol, a corn-based fuel. As a result, even Detroiters are predicting what was once unthinkable: the demise of the internal combustion engine. "Fuel cells have strong potential to be the best long-term solution," says General Motors Vice Chairman Harry J. Pearce. "Our fuel-cell test vehicle gets 80 miles per gallon and has a driving range of 300 miles."

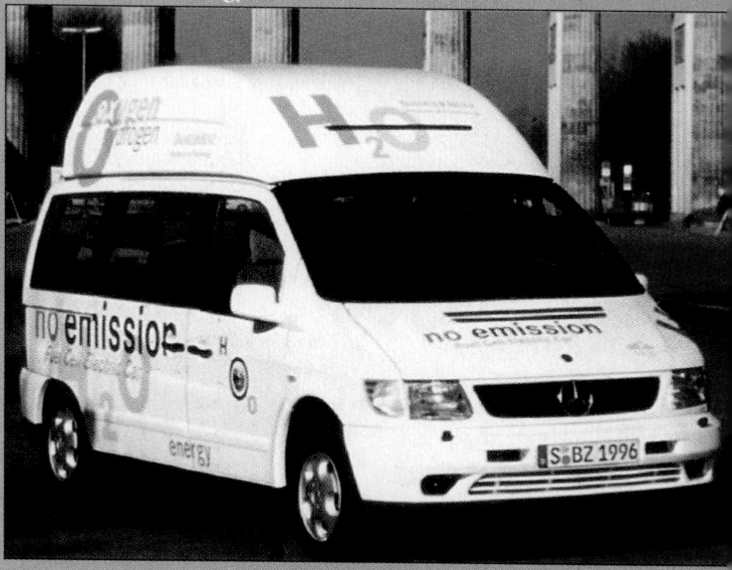

Toyota and Mercedes-Benz are also aggressively pursuing the technology. Toyota President Hiroshi Okuda pledged that his company would be the first to market with such a car. Mercedes executives, meanwhile, predict that their company will sell 40,000 fuel-cell cars by 2006. To avoid being left in the dust, Ford is investing $420 million to join with Mercedes and fuel-cell supplier Ballard Power Systems Inc. in Vancouver, British Columbia. Chrysler Corporation has hooked up with GM's Delphi unit, an auto-parts supplier, and expects to be cranking out 200,000 fuel-cell cars by 2010.

Fuel cell cars could be the answer to pollution-causing, gas-guzzling cars of today. Do you think you'll be driving this type of car in your lifetime?
[Reuters/Archive Photos]

Cost—not surprisingly—is the biggest roadblock. An electric car needs about 80 kilowatts of power for acceptable performance and today, using fuel cells, the kilowatt cost stands at roughly $250. At that rate Ford's Chairman, Alexander Trotman, estimates that a Ford Taurus outfitted with fuel-cell technology (and supporting paraphernalia) would have a sticker price of about $200,000. But things are looking up—10 years ago a fuel-cell vehicle would have cost $20 million. Experts predict that within 10 years, the fuel cells will cost no more that a traditional engine.

Source: Keith Naughton, "Detroit's Impossible Dream?" Business Week *(March 2, 1998), pp. 66–67.*

As with other aspects of managing today's organizations, technological innovation is daunting in its complexity and pace of change. And as you have no doubt figured out, it is therefore vital for competitive advantage. Not long ago, new products took years to plan and develop, were standardized and mass produced, and were pushed onto the market through extensive selling and promotional campaigns. With sales lives for these products measured in decades, production processes used equipment dedicated to making only those standardized products and achieved savings through economies of scale. But today's customers often demand products that have yet to be designed. Product development is now a race to become the first to introduce innovative products—products whose lives often are measured in months as they are quickly replaced by other, even more technologically sophisticated products.

Managing today's technology requires that managers understand how technologies emerge, develop, and affect the ways organizations compete and the ways people work. In this chapter, we discuss how technology can affect an organization's competitiveness and how to integrate technology into the organization's competitive strategy. Then we assess the technological needs of the organization and the means by which these needs can be met.

Technology and innovation

technology The systematic application of scientific knowledge to a new product, process, or service.

innovation A change in technology; a departure from previous ways of doing things.

In Chapter 9 ("The Responsive Organization") we defined **technology** as the methods, processes, systems, and skills used to transform resources into products. More broadly speaking we can think about technology as the commercialization of science; the systematic application of scientific knowledge to a new product, process, or service. In this sense, technology is embedded in every product, service, and procedure used or produced.[1]

If we find a better product, process, or procedure to accomplish our task, we have an innovation. **Innovation** is a change in technology—a departure from previous ways of doing things. Two fundamental types of innovation are product and process innovation.[2] *Process innovations* are changes that affect the methods of producing outputs. In Chapter 9 we discussed flexible manufacturing practices such as just-in-time, massed customization, simultaneous engineering, and the like. Each of these innovations has changed the way products are manufactured and distributed. In contrast, *product innovations* are changes in the actual outputs (products and services) themselves.[3]

There are definable and predictable patterns in the way technologies emerge, develop, and are replaced. Critical forces converge to create new technologies, which then follow well-defined, life-cycle patterns. Understanding the forces driving technological development and the patterns they follow can help a manager anticipate, monitor, and manage technologies more effectively.

- First, there must be a *need,* or *demand,* for the technology. Without this need driving the process, there is no reason for technological innovation to occur.
- Second, meeting the need must be theoretically possible, and the *knowledge* to do so must be available from basic science.
- Third, we must be able to *convert* the scientific knowledge into practice, in both engineering and economic terms. If we can theoretically do something, but doing it is economically impractical, the technology cannot be expected to emerge.
- Fourth, the *funding, skilled labor, time, space,* and *other resources* needed to develop the technology must be available.
- Finally, *entrepreneurial initiative* is needed to identify and pull all the necessary elements together.

The technology life cycle

technology life cycle A predictable pattern followed by a technological innovation starting from its inception and development to market saturation and replacement.

Technological innovations typically follow a relatively predictable pattern called the **technology life cycle.** Figure 17.1 depicts the pattern. The cycle begins with the recognition of a need and a perception of a means by which the need can be satisfied through applied science or knowledge. The knowledge and ideas are brought together and developed, culminating in a new technological innovation. Early progress can be slow in these formative years as competitors experiment a great deal with product design and operational characteristics to meet consumer needs. Here is where the rate of product innovation tends to be highest. For example, during the early years of the auto industry, companies tried a wide range of machines including electric- and steam-driven cars to determine which product would be most effective. Eventually the internal combustion engine emerged as the dominant design, and the number of product innovations leveled off. Of, course, the example of fuel-cell technology described in "Setting the Stage" is an excellent example of how technological innovations continue to transform the auto industry.

Once early problems are resolved and a dominant design emerges, improvements come more from process innovations to refine the technology.[4] It is at this point that companies can gain an advantage by pursuing process efficiencies and cost competitiveness. In the auto example, as companies settled on a product standard, they began leveraging the benefits of mass production and vertical integration to improve productivity. These process innovations were instrumental in lowering production costs and bringing the price of automobiles in line with consumer budgets.

Eventually the new technology begins to reach the upper limits of both its performance capabilities and the spread of its usage. Development slows and becomes increasingly costly, and the market becomes saturated (i.e., there are few new customers). The technology can remain in this mature stage for some time—as in the case of autos—or be quickly replaced by another technology offering superior performance or economic advantage. As we shall see later in the chapter, U.S. auto companies are working right now on new aerospace technologies that will transform the automobile industry. The evolution of life cycles can take decades or even centuries, as in the case of iron and steelmaking technologies. A dramatic example of a rapidly evolving technology can be found in speech-recognition software.

figure 17.1
The technology life cycle

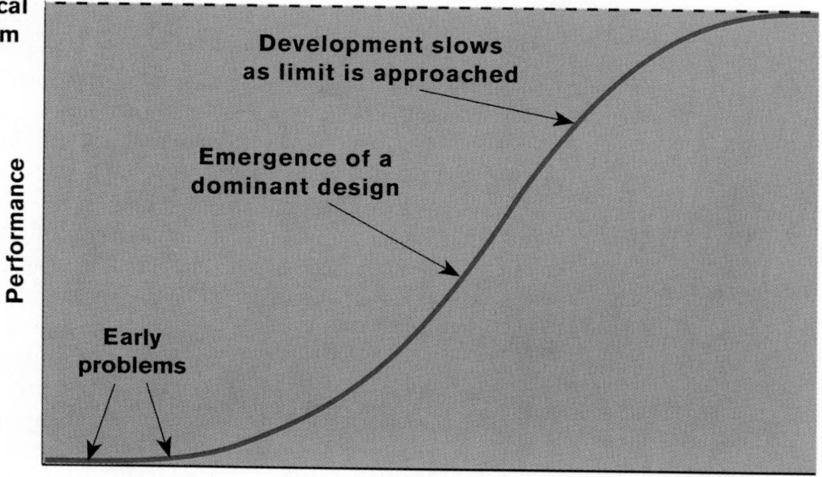

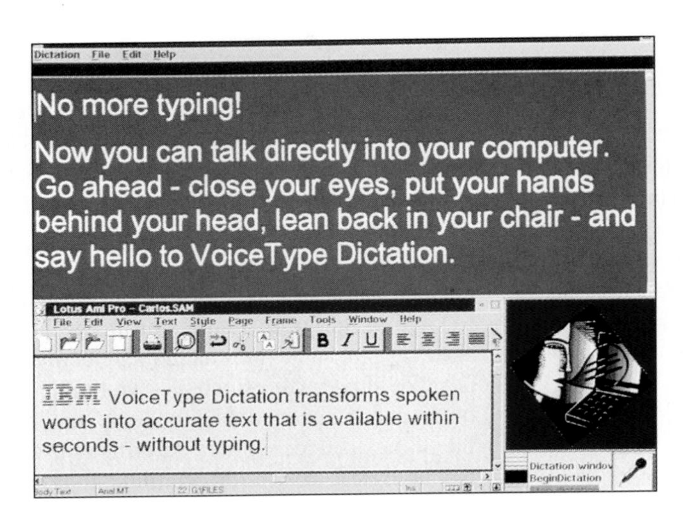

Voice-recognition technology is revolutionizing communications. What business might take advantage of this innovation?
[Courtesy of International Business Machines]

"Good morning, Dave." "Good morning, Hal."

In the Stanley Kubrick movie *2001: A Space Odyssey,* astronauts on the way to Jupiter simply talked to their computer HAL to give it instructions and ask questions. But the idea of a computer carrying on conversations with people seemed like pure science fiction back in the 1960s. Actually, AT&T's Bell Labs created the first crude speech recognizer back in 1952. And researchers at IBM's T. J. Watson Research Center have been trying to teach computers to talk with humans since the 1960s (rumor has it that Kubrick came up with the name H-A-L by transposing one letter back from I-B-M).

Now after decades of painstaking research, powerful speech-recognition technology is bursting into the marketplace. You first read about voice recognition technology in our communication chapter (Chapter 15). In addition to its relevance in that context, we should also focus on its relevance to managing technology and innovation. The plummeting cost of computing and a competitive frenzy among speech researchers is fueling the long-overdue phenomenon. For years, phone companies have used limited speech-recognition technology in directory-assistance services. Now companies such as Charles Schwab, UPS, American Express, and United Air Lines are testing programs that liberate call-in customers from tedious, "press-one, press-two," phone menus. But this is kid stuff compared to what's coming out now.

IBM beat most everyone to the market in 1997 with ViaVoice Gold, a program that transforms spoken sentences into text on a computer screen and lets users open Windows programs by voice command. Microsoft is spending millions to blend speech-recognition into its Windows software. CEO Bill Gates put it this way, "Speech is not just the future of Windows, but the future of computing itself." The error rate of speech recognition is decreasing at 30–40 percent a year. IBM's ViaVoice Gold system can recognize what people say with more than 95 percent accuracy.

As speech recognition becomes cheaper and more pervasive, it will be designed into hundreds of different kinds of products, from computers and cars to consumer electronics and household appliances to telephones and toys. When this happens, companies that sell speech enhanced products—rather than those that developed the speech software—hold most of the cards.

Source: Neil Gross, Paul Judge, Otis Port, and Stephen Wildstrom, "Let's Talk!" *Business Week,* (February 23, 1998), pp. 61–72.

As this example of speech-recognition software shows, a technology life cycle typically is made up of many individual *product* life cycles. Each of these products is an incremental improvement over its predecessors. In this way, technological development involves significant innovations, often representing entirely new technologies, followed by a large number of small incremental innovations. Ongoing development of a technology increases the benefits gained through its use, makes the technology easier to use, and allows more applications. In the process, the use of the technology expands to new adopters.

The diffusion of technological innovations

The spread in the use of a new technology over time follows an S-shaped pattern (see Figure 17.2). This pattern, first observed in 1903, has been verified with many new technologies and ideas in a wide variety of industries and settings.[5] The adopters of a new technology fall into five groups.

The first group, representing approximately 2.5 percent of adopters, are the *innovators*. Typically innovators are adventurous, but some might consider them headstrong or even extreme.

The next 13.5 percent of adopters are *early adopters*. This group is critical to the success of a new technology, because its members include well-respected opinion leaders. Early adopters often are the people or organizations to whom others look for leadership, ideas, and up-to-date technological information. The next group, representing 34 percent of adopters, is the *early majority*. These adopters are more deliberate and take longer to decide to use something new. Often they are important members of a community or industry, but typically not the leaders.

Representing the next 34 percent are the late *majority*. Members of this group are more skeptical of technological change and approach innovation with great caution, often adopting only out of economic necessity or increasing social pressure.

The final 16 percent are *laggards*. Often isolated and highly conservative in their views, laggards are extremely suspicious of innovation and change.

Much of the speed with which an innovation spreads depends on five attributes.[6] An innovation will spread quickly if it

1. Has a great advantage over its predecessor.
2. Is compatible with existing systems, procedures, infrastructures, and ways of thinking.

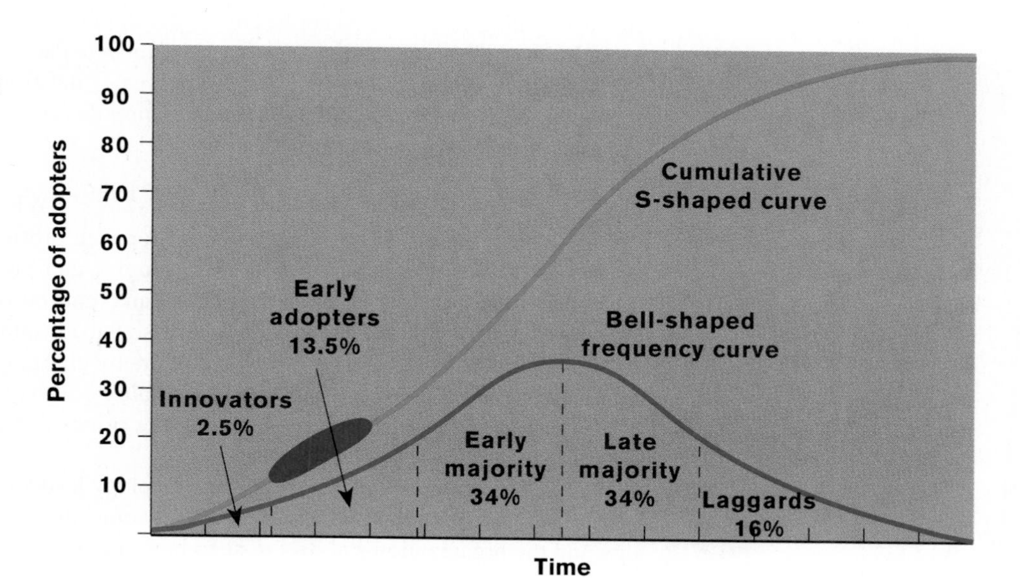

figure 17.2
Technology dissemination pattern and adopter categories

3. Has less rather than greater complexity.
4. Can be easily tried or tested without significant cost or commitment.
5. Can be easily observed and copied.

Designing products with these technological considerations in mind can make a critical difference in their success.

Technological innovation in a competitive environment

Discussions about technology life cycles and diffusion patterns may imply that technological change occurs naturally or automatically. Just the opposite; change is neither easy nor natural in organizations (we discuss change more fully in the next chapter). Decisions about technology and innovation are very strategic and need to be approached in a systematic way.

In Chapter 4, we discussed two generic strategies a company can use to position itself in the market: low cost and differentiation. With *low-cost* leadership, the company maintains an advantage because it has a lower cost than its competitors. With a *differentiation* strategy, the advantage comes from having a unique product or service for which customers are willing to pay a premium price.[7] Technological innovations can support either of these strategies: They can be used to gain cost advantage through pioneering lower-cost product designs and creating low-cost ways to perform needed operations or they can support differentiation by pioneering unique products or services that increase buyer value and thus command premium prices.

In some cases, a new technology can completely change the rules of competition within an industry.[8] Leading companies that respond ineffectively to technological opportunities can falter while new companies emerge as the dominant competitors. The stories of how Microsoft and Intel grew from the opportunities provided by IBM are now well known.

But industries are seldom transformed overnight. Typically, signals of a new technology's impact are visible well in advance, leaving time for companies and people to respond. For example, most any competitor in the telecommunications industry fully understands the potential value of cellular technology. Often the key issue is not *whether* to adopt a new technology but *when* to adopt it and how to integrate the change with the organization's operating practices and strategies.

Technology leadership

The adage "timing is everything" is applied to many things, ranging from financial investments to telling jokes. It also applies to the development and exploitation of new technologies. Industry leaders such as Xerox, 3M, Hewlett-Packard, and Merck built and now maintain their competitive positions through early development and application of new technologies. However, technology leadership imposes costs and risks, and it is not the best approach for every organization (see Table 17.1).[9]

Advantages of technology leadership

What makes innovators and technology leadership attractive is the potential for high profits and first-mover advantages. Being the first to market with new technologies can provide significant competitive advantage. If technology leadership increases an organization's efficiency relative to competitors, it achieves a cost advantage. It can use the advantage to either reap greater profits than competitors or attract more customers by charging lower prices. Similarly, if a company is first to market with a new technology, it may be able to charge a premium price because it faces no competition. Higher prices and greater profits can defray the costs of developing new technologies.

This one-time advantage of being the technology leader can be turned into a sustainable advantage. Sustainability of a lead depends on competitors' ability to duplicate the technology and the organization's ability to keep building on the lead quickly enough to outpace

table 17.1
Advantages and disadvantages of technology leadership

Advantages	Disadvantages
First mover advantage	Greater risks
Little or no competition	Cost of technology development
Greater efficiency	Costs of market development and customer education
Higher profit margins	Infrastructure costs
Sustainable advantage	Costs of learning and eliminating defects
Reputation for innovation	Possible cannibalization of existing products
Establishment of entry barriers	
Occupying of best market niches	
Opportunities to learn	

competitors. It can do this in several ways. The reputation for being an innovator can create an ongoing advantage and even spill over to the company's other products. For example, 3M's reputation for innovation and quality differentiates some of its standard products such as adhesive tape and allows the product to command a premium price. A competitor may be able to copy the product but not the reputation. Patents and other institutional barriers also can be used to block competitors and maintain leadership. Polaroid has successfully kept industry giant Kodak out of the instant-photography market for years through a series of patents. In 1991, Kodak agreed to pay Polaroid $925 million in compensation for patent infringement.[10]

The first mover can also preempt competitors by occupying the best market niches. If it can establish high switching costs (recall Chapter 2) for repeat customers, these positions can be difficult for competitors to capture. Microsoft has dominated the software market for computers with its Windows operating system despite assaults by other manufacturers. This is because of the large library of software that is packaged with Windows. Although other companies can offer more advanced software, their products are not as attractive because they are not bundled as the Windows-based systems are (this advantage is now being tested in court).

Technology leadership can provide a significant learning advantage. While competitors may be able to copy or adopt a new technology, ongoing learning by the technology leader can keep the company ahead by generating minor improvements that are difficult to imitate. Many Japanese manufacturers use several small incremental improvements generated with their *kaizen* programs (recall Chapter 9) to continuously upgrade the quality of their products and processes.[11] All these minor improvements cannot be easily copied by competitors, and collectively they can provide a significant advantage.

Apple Computers felt that their hand-held computer "Newton" would be a hit. Did Apple try too hard to "be the leader?" Are there other possible explanations as to the "failure" of Newton? Do *you* consider Newton a failure?
[© Davies & Starr Inc./Liaison International.]

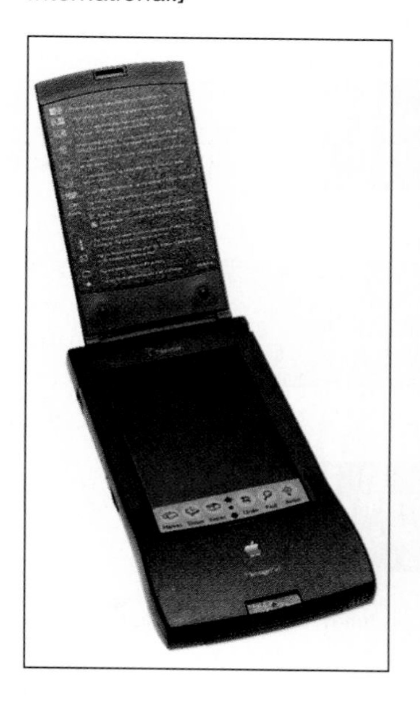

Disadvantages of technology leadership However, being the first to develop or adopt a new technology does not always lead to immediate advantage and high profits. While such potential may exist, technology leadership imposes high costs and risks that followers are not required to bear. Being the leader thus can be more costly than being the follower. These costs include educating buyers unfamiliar with the new technology, building an infrastructure to support the technology, and developing complementary products to achieve the technology's full potential. Also, regulatory approval may be needed. For example, the cost of producing a new drug, including testing and the expense of obtaining FDA approval, is estimated at around $200 million.[12] While followers do not get the benefits of being first to market, they can copy the drug for a fraction of this cost once the original patents expire.

Being a pioneer carries other risks. If raw materials and equipment are new or have unique specifications, a ready supply at a reasonable cost may not be available. Or the technology may not be fully developed and may have problems yet to be resolved. In addition, the unproved market for the technology creates uncertainty in demand. Finally, the new technology may have an adverse impact on existing structures or business. It may cannibalize current products or make existing investments obsolete.

Technology followership

Not all organizations are equally prepared to be technology leaders, nor would leadership benefit each organization equally. Much of the difference in choosing to be a technology leader or follower depends on how a company positions itself to compete, the benefits gained through the use of a technology, and the characteristics of the organization.

Interestingly, technology followership also can be used to support both low-cost and differentiation strategies. If the follower learns from the leader's experience, it can avoid the costs and risks of technology leadership, thereby establishing a low-cost position. Manufacturers of IBM-compatible computers have been successful with this type of followership strategy. IBM's personal computer market share within the United States has been challenged largely because of low-cost technology followers such as Dell and Gateway. Followership can also support differentiation. By learning from the leader, the follower can adapt the products or delivery systems to more closely fit buyers' needs.

Adoption timing is dependent on the organization's strategic needs and technology skills as well as the potential benefits of the new technology. As discussed earlier, technologies do not emerge in their final state; rather, they undergo *development over time* (see Figure 17.3). Development makes the technology easier to use and more adaptable to various strategies. At the same time, *complementary products and technologies* may be developed and introduced that make the main technology more useful. For example, software and printer technologies traditionally lag computer hardware technology, thereby limiting the usefulness of hardware technology breakthroughs.

These complementary products and technologies combine with the *gradual diffusion* of the technology to form a shifting competitive impact from the technology.[13] The appropriate time for an organization to adopt technological innovations is when the costs and risks of switching to the technology are outweighed by the benefits. This point differs among organizations and depends largely on the company's characteristics and strategies.

figure 17.3
Dynamic forces of a technology's competitive impact

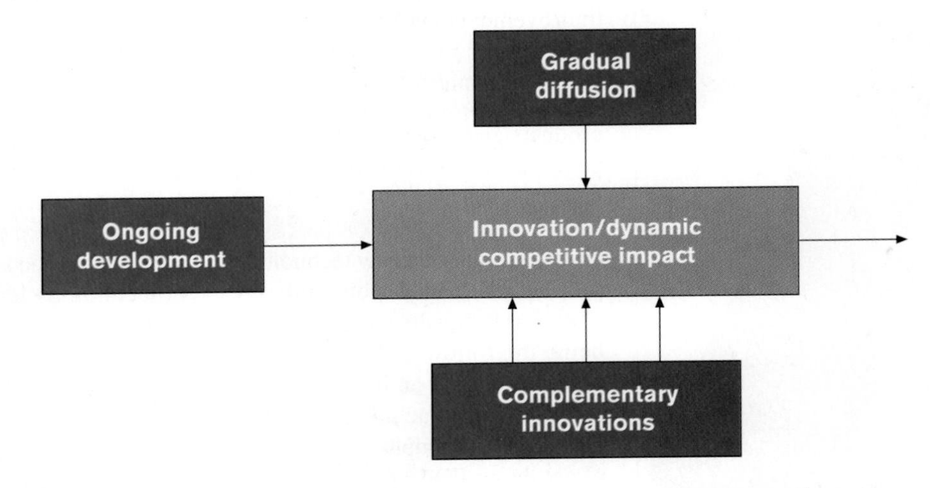

Source: D. M. Schroeder, "A Dynamic Perspective on the Impact of Process Innovation upon Competitive Strategies," *Strategic Management Journal* 11 (January 1990), pp. 25–42.

Assessing technology needs

A decade ago, the major U.S. steel companies suffered from significant cost disadvantages relative to non-U.S. producers. These high costs were due largely to poor productivity resulting from aging plants and obsolete equipment. U.S. companies lagged their European and Japanese counterparts in adopting new, productivity-enhancing process technologies such as the basic oxygen furnace and the continuous-casting process. Had the U.S. companies accurately assessed and adopted these technologies in a timely manner, the massive layoffs (about 60 percent) of the industry's workforce could have been avoided.[14]

Assessing the technology needs of the organization involves measuring current technologies as well as external trends affecting the industry.

Measuring current technologies

technology audit Process of clarifying the key technologies upon which an organization depends.

Before organizations can devise strategies for developing and exploiting technological innovation, they must gain a clear understanding of their current technology base. A **technology audit** helps to clarify the key technologies upon which the organization depends. The most important dimension of a new technology is its competitive value. Arthur D. Little, Inc., has developed a technique for measuring competitive value that categorizes technologies as emerging, pacing, key, and base.[15]

- *Emerging technologies* are still under development and thus are unproved. They may, however, significantly alter the rules of competition in the more distant future.
- *Pacing technologies* have yet to prove their full value but have the potential to alter the rules of competition by providing significant advantage.
- *Key technologies* have proven effective, but they also provide a strategic advantage because not everyone uses them. Knowledge and dissemination of these technologies are limited and they continue to provide some first-mover advantages.
- *Base technologies* are those that are commonplace in the industry; everyone must have them to be able to operate. Thus, they provide little competitive advantage.

Technologies can evolve rapidly through these categories. For example, electronic word processing was considered an emerging technology in the late 1970s. By the early 1980s, it could be considered pacing. While promising advantages, the technology's cost and capabilities restricted its usefulness to a limited number of applications. With continued improvements and more powerful computer chips, electronic word processing quickly became a key technology. Its costs dropped, its usage spread, and it demonstrated the capacity to enhance productivity. By the late 1980s, it was considered a base technology in most applications. Word processing technology is now so widely used that it is viewed as a routine activity in almost every office.

Assessing external technological trends

Just as with any planning, decisions about technology must balance internal capabilities (strengths and weaknesses) with external opportunities and threats. There are several techniques that organizations use to better understand how technology is changing within an industry.

Benchmarking

As mentioned in Chapter 4, *benchmarking* is the process of comparing the organization's practices and technologies with those of other companies. The ability to benchmark technologies against those of competitors can vary among industries. While competitors understandably are reluctant to share their secrets, information trading for benchmarking is not uncommon and can prove highly valuable. For example, Harley

Davidson's recovery of its reputation for manufacturing quality motorcycles began only after company executives toured Honda's plant and witnessed firsthand the weaknesses of Harley's manufacturing technologies and the vast potential for improvement. In fact, Japanese companies often are willing to show U.S. competitors their operations because they believe the U.S. companies won't use the information!

It is important to benchmark against potential competitors in other nations. There may be key or pacing technologies in use that can easily be imported and offer significant advantage. Also, overseas firms may be more willing to share their knowledge if they are not direct competitors and if they are anxious to exchange information for the benefit of both companies.

Scanning Whereas benchmarking focuses on what is being done currently, *scanning* focuses on what can be done and what is being developed. In other words, benchmarking examines key and perhaps some pacing technologies, while scanning seeks out pacing and emerging technologies—those just being introduced and still in their development.

Scanning typically involves a number of tactics, many of them the same as those used in benchmarking. However, scanning places greater emphasis on identifying and monitoring the sources of new technologies for an industry. It may also dictate that executives read more cutting-edge research journals and attend research conferences and seminars. The extent to which scanning is done depends largely on how close to the cutting edge of technology the organization needs to operate.

Framing decisions about technological innovation

Once an organization has done a thorough job of analyzing its current technological position, it can begin to make decisions about how to proceed into the future to either develop or exploit emerging technological innovations. Decisions about technological innovations must balance many interrelated factors. The most effective approach to technology depends not only on the technology's potential to support the organization's strategic needs, but also on the organization's skills and capabilities to successfully exploit the technology. The organization's competitive strategy, the technical abilities of its employees to deal with the new technology, the fit of the technology with the company's operations, and the company's ability to deal with the risks and ambiguities of adopting a new technology all must be timed to coincide with the dynamic forces of a developing technology. This does not always mean waiting for the technology to develop. Often it requires changing the capabilities and strategies of the organization to match the needs of the technology. This could include hiring new people, training existing employees, changing internal policies and procedures, and changing strategies. These considerations are discussed below.[16]

Anticipated market receptiveness

The first consideration that needs to be addressed when developing a strategy around technological innovation is market potential. In many cases, innovations are stimulated by external demand for new products and services. For example, current work to develop low earth-orbiting satellites (LEOs) for wireless communications is motivated by a clear understanding of its worldwide market potential. Telecommunications companies such as Motorola (discussed later in the chapter), TRW, and Loral are diligently working to develop innovative technologies in this arena.[17]

In assessing market receptiveness, executives need to make two determinations. In the short run, there should be an immediate application that demonstrates the value of the new technology. In the long run, there needs to be a set of applications that show the technology is the proven means to satisfy a market need. For example, despite the recent dominant use of audio cassette players, the shift to digital encoding has resulted in compact disc (CD) technology becoming perceived as the legitimate approach to high-quality audio. LPs and 8-tracks (does anyone remember these?) are virtually nonexistent today.

Technological feasibility

In addition to market receptiveness, organizations must also consider the feasibility of technological innovations. Visions can stay unrealized for a long time. Technical obstacles may represent barriers to progress. Companies such as Intel and Cyrix face continual hurdles in developing newer and faster computer chips.

What's the Buzz in Microprocessing?

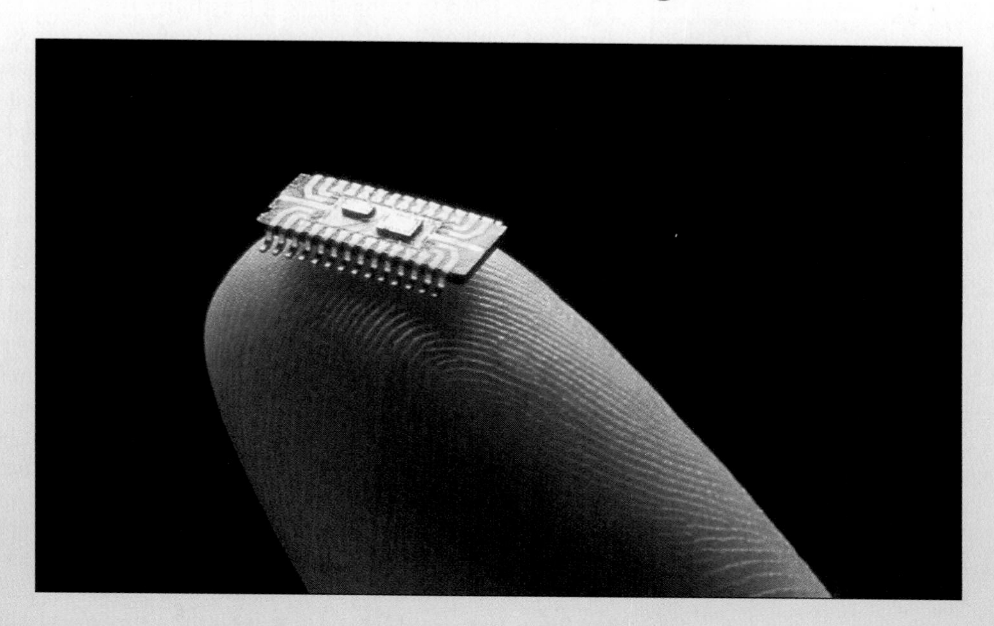

Technological innovations in microprocessing may soon be slowed by the limits of physics.
[Jeff Titcomb/Liaison International]

Microprocessors are the brains of virtually all electronic devices these days; not just personal computers. These marvels of miniaturization pack millions of tiny transistors–electrical on/off switches that calculate the ones and zeros of computer instructions–into silicon wafers. By one estimate, there are 200 quadrillion transistors in use each day, or about 40 million for every man, woman, and child on the planet.

Since Intel brought the first microprocessor to market in 1971, chip makers have made dramatic advances in computing. The number of transistors on a chip, and its resulting performance, has doubled nearly every 18 to 24 months; upholding what has become known as Moore's Law (Gordon Moore is the cofounder of Intel).

But the future of microprocessor technology is being called into question by the combined forces of physics and economics. Can chip makers continue etching smaller, faster components onto silicon chips the size of postage stamps? The wires that run between transistors right now are 400 times thinner than a human hair. Can they be made skinnier yet? Yes, but the task of continually doubling the speed of electrons passing wires of near-zero width will be tricky–and maybe impossible–at some point. Even if it's technically feasible, can companies afford the massive investments needed to do so?

Source: "Computing's Outer Limits," *Popular Science* 252, no. 3 (March 1998), p. 64.

Other industries face similar technological hurdles. In the oil industry, for example, technological barriers prevent exploration and drilling in the deepest parts of the ocean. In medicine, scientists and doctors work continuously to identify the causes and cures for diseases such as cancer and AIDS. In aviation and aeronautics, researchers are working to develop technologies that allow pilots to "see" through clouds. Each of these potentially valuable innovations is slowed by the technical limits of currently available technologies.[18]

Economic viability

Closely related to technological feasibility is economic viability. Apart from whether a firm can "pull off" a technological innovation, executives must consider whether there is a good financial incentive for doing so. For example, the use of solar fusion to generate electricity has been technically feasible for years. However, its cost remains prohibitively higher than the cost of fossil fuels. Similarly, the use of fuel-cell technology for automobiles is almost technically feasible, but its costs are still way too high (recall the $200,000 Ford Taurus in "Setting the Stage").[19]

The issue of economic viability takes us back to our earlier discussion of adoption timing. Earlier adopters may have first-mover advantages, but there are costs associated with this strategic approach. The development costs of a particular technological innovation may be quite high such as in pharmaceuticals, chemicals, software, and the like. Patents and copyrights often help organizations recoup the costs of their investments in technological innovations. Without such protection, the investments in research and development might not be justifiable.

An exception to the "economic viability" rule might be the now-classic story of Merck and the drug Mectizan. Mectizan is the commercial name for a drug called ivermectin developed by Merck scientists to cure river blindness (onchocerciasis). The success rate of the drug has been astoundingly high, but governments in the third-world countries where it is needed cannot afford it. Seeing no economic viability, Merck executives decided to commercialize the drug anyway and donate it to those who need it. Merck has gotten help from 13 organizations including the World Health Organization (WHO), The United Nations Development Programme, and The Carter Center (in 1996 alone, 16 million people in 31 countries in Africa, the Middle East, and Latin America were given treatment).[20]

Anticipated competency development

It has been repeatedly stated in this text that organizations should (and do) build their strategies based on core competencies. This advice applies to technology and innovation strategies as well. Frequently, we can view technological innovations that are the tangible product of intangible—or tacit—knowledge and capabilities that make up a firm's core competence. The Merck and Intel examples above illustrate instances where core competencies in research and development lead to new technological innovations.

In contrast, the fuel-cell example in "Setting the Stage" illustrates a situation where Ford and other automakers must develop new competencies in order to commercialize the new technologies. Recall from Chapter 4 ("Planning and Strategic Management") that Kodak faces a similar situation in digital photography. To gain technological leadership, the company has to bolster its competencies in digital imaging, and this has not been easy to do. Here's a quick recap of that scenario.

Flashback: Another look at Kodak's digital strategy

Eastman Kodak has invested approximately $500 million per year to increase its competencies in digital imaging. The company's research and product development group is rapidly producing an impressive array of digital cameras, scanners, and other devices. And because of Kodak's product breadth, it is far ahead of its competitors in sales (revenues from digital products are increasing at about 25 percent a year). However, so far Kodak's digital strategy has not paid off financially. Competitors such as Hewlett-Packard, Fuji, Canon, and Epson are fast and flexible, and are more accustomed to the blistering pace of change in digital technology. Their capabilities in this arena allow them to rapidly produce competing products at lower prices. As a consequence, Kodak has had trouble gaining technological leadership.

Sources: Geoffrey Smith, "Can George Fisher Save Kodak?" *Business Week,* October 20, 1997, pp. 116–28; Peter Johnston, "Kodak Sets Digital Imaging Strategy," *Graphic Arts Monthly* 67, no. 6 (June 1995), p. 81; Riccardo A. Davis, "Kodak Rethinks Strategy," *Advertising Age* 64, no. 20 (May 10, 1993), p. 48. ●

The upshot from this is that while certain technologies may have tremendous market applicability, firms must have (or develop) the internal competencies needed to execute their technology strategy. Without the skills needed to implement an innovation, even promising technological advances may prove disastrous.

Organizational suitability

The final issues that tend to be addressed when deciding on technological innovations have to do with the culture of the organization, the interests of managers, and the expectations of stakeholders. Companies such as 3M and Sony who are seen as proactive "technology-push" innovators tend to have cultures that are more outward-looking and opportunistic. Executives accord considerable priority to developing and exploiting technological expertise, and decision makers tend to have bold intuitive visions of the future. Typically there are technology champions (discussed below) who articulate competitively aggressive, first-mover technological strategies. In many cases, executives are more concerned about the opportunity costs of not taking action than they are about the potential to fail.

By contrast, *defender* firms such as Rolls Royce tend to adopt a more circumspect posture toward innovation. Their strategies are focused more on deepening their capability base through complementary technologies that extend rather than replace their current ones. Strategic decisions are likely to be based on careful analysis and experience in the industry setting. A hybrid *analyzer* firm like Matsushita tends to allow others to demonstrate solid demand in new arenas before it responds. As we noted above, these types of firms tend to adopt an early-follower strategy to grab a dominant position more from their strengths in marketing and manufacturing than through technological innovation.[21]

Every company has different capabilities to deal with new technology. As discussed previously, early adopters have characteristics different from late adopters. Early adopters of new technologies tend to be larger, more profitable, and more specialized. Therefore, they are in an economic position to absorb the risks associated with early adoption while profiting more from its advantages. In addition, the people involved in early adoption are more highly educated, have a greater ability to deal with abstraction, can more effectively cope with uncertainty, and have strong problem-solving capabilities. Thus, early adopters can more effectively manage the difficulties and uncertainty of a less fully developed technology.[22]

From the Pages of BusinessWeek

Ericsson's Big Leap

When Sven-Christer Nilsson was summoned to L.M. Ericsson's Stockholm headquarters for an early-morning chat with CEO Lars Ramqvist in January 1998, he had an inkling of what to expect. Yet when Ramqvist leaned over the boardroom suite's burled wood coffee table that day and asked him whether he'd take the job as the company's new CEO, Nilsson played it cool—and ultimately took a week to get back to Ramqvist with his answer.

Nilsson needs that kind of self-assurance as Ericsson's new boss. Not only will the youthful 53-year-old take over Sweden's largest company, but he will also face the crucial task of preserving Ericsson's technological edge in mobile phones, where it vies with Motorola Inc. and Nokia Group for global leadership. With the telecommunications and computer industries converging, Ericsson is in a race to develop advanced networks to help the world's phone companies provide the next generation of multimedia services, from videoconferences to speedy Net surfing over cellular phones.

To reach its goals, Ericsson is already prowling the globe for acquisition deals in data communications—the company's "weakest point," Ramqvist told *Business Week* in a recent interview. The likely target is a company in the U.S., Nilsson adds, because that's where telecom and computers are converging most quickly. Ericsson has begun collaborating on some projects with data-communications companies such as Cisco Systems Inc. and Bay Networks Inc. Cisco would be an attractive partner, but a smaller, less costly company still on its way up is a more likely target, Ramqvist notes. Data-networking companies such as 3Com Corp. and Bay Networks would be easier for Ericsson to swallow.

Nilsson knows that filling Ramqvist's shoes will be a tough assignment. Ramqvist was a "strong person" as CEO and may be a hard act to follow, observes a senior exec from a rival company, adding that Ericsson's large size makes it "harder to generate growth and innovation." Indeed, while Ramqvist was CEO, Ericsson's stock jumped fifteenfold, and the company earned a record $2.2 billion in pretax profits in 1997. The profit surge was fueled by mobile handset sales—up some 87% last year—as Ericsson's heavy R&D investment in establishing the Europe-wide GSM mobile-phone standard has paid off.

Behind Ericsson's success is its youthful and flexible culture. Half of its 100,000 employees are under 30, and around 1,000 jobs a month are shifting to the fast-growing mobile business from Ericsson's troubled fixed-line phone unit, where margins have been squeezed by new rivals. The division has shed a fifth of its workforce and plans to lose an additional 10,000 in the coming two years.

It also looks as if Ericsson's bet on the next mobile multimedia phone may pay off. On Jan. 29, Europe's mobile-phone industry voted to adopt a standard drawing heavily from the one Ericsson had spent more than eight years and millions of dollars to develop. These phones will receive data nearly seven times faster than traditional fixed lines. Over time, analysts expect more users will shift to the high-speed mobile phones, abandoning traditional fixed-line phones. Says Douglas Smith, European technology analyst for Salomon Smith Barney in London: "Ericsson has a very significant head start."

Will Ericsson's new CEO keep up the pace? Nilsson, who spent several weeks last summer on a 10-meter sailboat in the Bay of Biscay, knows something about navigating amid shifting winds. For 3 1/2 days, the boat and its crew were buffeted by gales. "It was hilarious. I never felt unsafe," recalls Nilsson, who enjoyed the thrill of surfing the whitecaps in a small boat. Considering the wild fluctuations of the telecom industry, Ericsson may have found the right captain.

Source: Julia Flynn and Peter Elstrom, "Ericsson's Big Leap," *Business Week:* February 16, 1998.

Questions

1. What is Ericsson's main strategy appear to be for acquiring new technology to maintain its leadership position?
2. What roles is Nilsson likely to play in order to facilitate technology innovation?
3. What strengths does Ericsson have as an organization to help its position as a technology leader? ●

Sourcing and acquiring new technologies

Developing new technology may conjure up visions of scientists and product developers working in R&D laboratories. In reality, new technology comes from many different sources, including suppliers, manufacturers, users, other industries, universities, the government, and overseas companies. While every source of innovation should be explored, each industry usually has specific sources for most of its new technologies. For example, because of the limited size of most farming operations, innovations in farming most often come from manufacturers, suppliers, and government extension services. Seed manufacturers develop and market new, superior hybrids; chemical producers improve pesticides and herbicides; and equipment manufacturers design improved farm equipment. Land-grant universities develop new farming techniques, and extension agents spread their usage.

In many industries, however, the primary sources of new technology are the organizations that use the technology. For instance, over three-fourths of scientific innovations are developed by the users of the scientific instruments being improved and may subsequently be licensed or sold to manufacturers or suppliers.[23]

make-or-buy decision The question an organization asks itself about whether to acquire new technology from an outside source or develop it itself.

Essentially, the question of how to acquire new technology is a **make-or-buy decision.** In other words, should the organization develop the technology itself or acquire it from an outside source? However, the decision is not that simple. There are many alternatives, and each has advantages and disadvantages. Some of the more common options are discussed in the following paragraphs.

Internal development Developing a new technology within the company has the potential advantage of keeping the technology proprietary (exclusive to the organization). This provides an important advantage over competitors.

Purchase Most technology already is available in products or processes that can be openly purchased. For example, a bank that needs sophisticated information-processing equipment need not develop the technology itself. It can simply purchase the technology from manufacturers or suppliers. In most situations, this is the simplest, easiest, and most cost-effective way to acquire new technology.

Contracted development If the technology is not available and a company lacks the resources or time to develop it internally, it may choose to contract the development from outside sources. Possible contractors include other companies, independent research laboratories, and university and government institutions.

Licensing Certain technologies that are not easily purchased as part of a product can be licensed for a fee. Pioneers of the VHS format for videocassette recorders held the critical patents, but they freely licensed the technology and the right to use it to competing manufacturers of video equipment. This practice helped make VHS the dominant format (over Beta) by providing other manufacturers with easy access to the technology, thereby creating an industry standard.

Technology trading Technology trading is another way to gain access to new technologies. Ironically, this tactic sometimes is used between rival companies. For example, U.S. steel producers that use the minimill concept freely trade a great deal of know-how among one another. In some cases, this activity extends to training without charge a competitor's employees on new process improvements.[24] While not all industries are amenable to technology sharing, trading is becoming increasingly common because of the high cost of developing advanced technologies independently.

Research partnerships and joint ventures Research partnerships are arrangements designed to jointly pursue specific new-technology development. Typically, each member enters the partnership with different skills or resources needed for successful new-technology development. An effective combination is an established company and a start-up.[25] Joint ventures are similar in most respects to research partnerships, but they tend to have greater permanence and their outcomes result in entirely new companies.

Acquisition of an owner of the technology If a company lacks the needed technology but wishes to acquire proprietary ownership of it, one option is to purchase the company that owns the technology. This transaction can take a number of forms, ranging from an outright purchase of the entire company to a minority interest sufficient to gain access to the technology. General Motors discovered that its need to modernize its information technologies was so extensive that it purchased EDS, a world leader in information services.

Choosing among these alternatives can be simplified by asking the following basic questions:

1. Is it important (and possible) in terms of competitive advantage that the technology remain proprietary?
2. Are the time, skills, and resources for internal development available?
3. Is the technology readily available outside the company?

As Figure 17.4 illustrates, the answers to these questions guide the manager to the most appropriate technology acquisition option.

The illustration of GTE below shows that developing and exploiting technological innovations may require a combination of approaches.

figure 17.4
Technology acquisition options

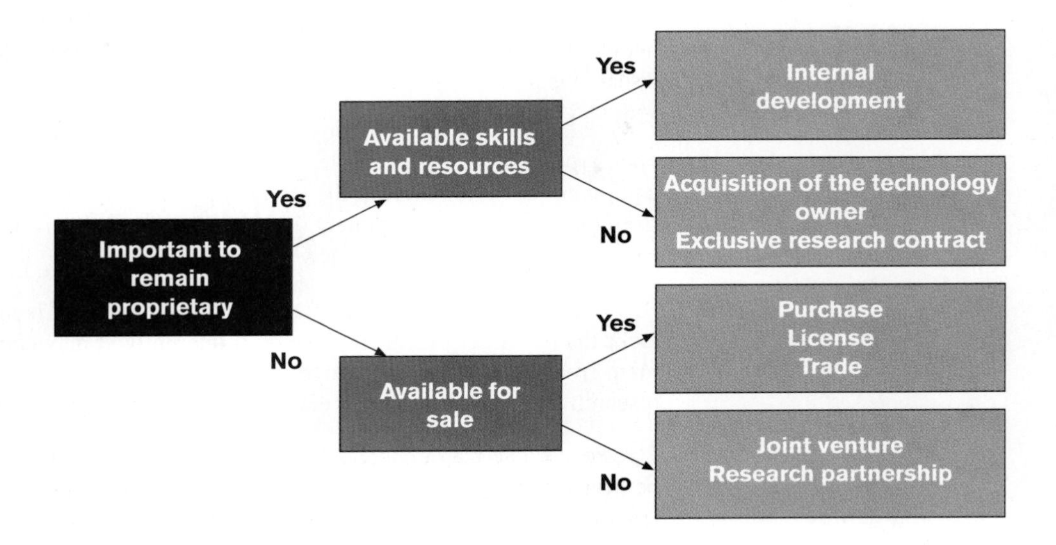

Gee–No, GTE: Creating technological innovation

GTE has lived in the shadow of AT&T for years. The company was pieced together from a hodgepodge of rural phone companies that AT&T didn't want and for many years had no regional identity, no real power base, and no center. But GTE may have a plan that is nothing less than a new model for the future of the telecommunications business. From nowhere, the company has emerged as possibly the savviest company in the industry, staking out a strong position in every important sector–local, wireless, online services, and long distance. GTE is betting that telecom will change from a business that is all about voice to one that is mostly about data.

GTE's plan is to marry the efficiency of data networks (like the Internet) with the reliability of the telephone system. Currently, the Internet jams up when its traffic gets heavy. GTE plans to overcome these problems by building and managing its own private data network that can handle data transfer, like the Internet does, but at higher speeds and with greater security.

GTE is investing billions to build a private, 13,000-mile-long, Internet-like data network. The company is spending $616 million to buy BBN, the company that developed the Internet for the Defense Department back in the 1960s (the same company that invented the modem, sent the first e-mail message, and selected the @ symbol as the signpost of the networked era). GTE also paid $485 million for a big piece of a new nationwide fiber network that will be completed late next year by a company called Qwest. GTE has also signed a partnership agreement with Cisco Systems, the leading maker of hardware and software for data networks. Partly because of expenditures for Cisco gear, GTE's capital spending will rise by $2.5 billion over the next five years. But the expense is worth it, according to GTE Chairman Charles Lee. If traffic over data networks grows as predicted, GTE expects that by 2001 its revenues from data services will be $5 billion annually. That's 10 times what they are today.

Source: Condensed from Andrew Kupfer, "Son of Internet," *Fortune,* June 23, 1997, pp 120–22. ●

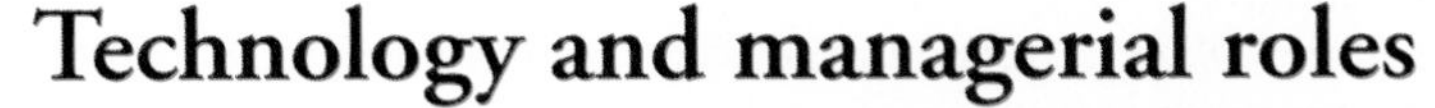

Technology and managerial roles

chief technology officer (CTO) Executive in charge of technology strategy and development.

In organizations, technology traditionally has been the responsibility of vice presidents for research and development (R&D). These executives are directly responsible for corporate and divisional R&D laboratories. Typically their jobs have a functional orientation. But increasingly companies are creating the position of **chief technology officer (CTO).** The CTO is a senior position at the corporate level with broad, integrative responsibilities.[26] CTOs coordinate the technological efforts of the various business units, act as a voice for technology in the top management team, supervise new-technology development, and assess the technological implications of major strategic initiatives such as acquisitions, new ventures, and strategic alliances.

CTOs also perform an important boundary role: They work directly with outside organizations. For example, they work with universities for funding research to stay abreast of technical developments and with regulatory agencies to ensure compliance with regulations, identify trends, and influence the regulatory process.

Other people play a variety of critical roles in developing new technology. Recall from Chapter 7 that it is the *entrepreneur* who, in an effort to exploit untried technologies, invents new products or finds new ways to produce old products. The entrepreneur opens up new possibilities that change the competitive structure of entire industries.[27] For example, Steven Jobs started Apple Computer in his garage and launched the multibillion-dollar personal computer industry.

technical innovator A person who develops a new technology or has the key skills to install and operate the technology.

product champion A person who promotes a new technology throughout the organization in an effort to obtain acceptance and support for it.

executive champion An executive who supports a new technology and protects the product champion of the innovation.

Key roles in acquiring and developing new technologies are the technical innovator, product champion, and executive champion.[28] The **technical innovator** develops the new technology or has the key skills needed to instill and operate the technology. This person possesses the requisite technical skills, but he or she may not have the managerial skills needed to push the idea forward and secure acceptance within the organization. This is where the product champion gets involved. Introducing new technology into an organization requires that someone promote the idea. The **product champion**—often at the risk of his or her position and prestige—promotes the idea throughout the organization, searching for support and acceptance. The champion can be a high-level manager, but often this is not the case. If the champion lacks the power and financial resources to make the required changes independently, she or he must convince people who have such authority to support the innovation. In other words, product champions must get sponsorship.

Sponsorship comes from the **executive champion,** who has the status, authority, and financial resources to support the project and protect the product champion. Without this support and protection, the product champion, and thus the new technology, could not succeed. Resources needed to develop the innovation would be unavailable, and without protection the champion would not be allowed to continue promoting the change.

Organizing for innovation

Organizing for innovation requires a balance between unleashing people's creative energies and capabilities and controlling the results to meet market needs in a timely manner.

Unleashing creativity

As discussed in Chapter 7 (New Ventures), 3M has a strong orientation toward *intrapreneurship,* and derives about one-third of its revenues from new products.[29] 3M, along with other companies such as Merck, Hewlett-Packard, and Rubbermaid, have well-established histories of producing many successful new technologies and products. What sets these and other continuous innovators apart? The one thing these companies have in common is an organization culture that encourages innovation.

Consider the 3M legend from the early 1920s of inventor Francis G. Okie. Okie dreamed up the idea of using sandpaper instead of razor blades for shaving. The aim was to reduce the risk of nicks and avoid sharp instruments. The idea failed, but rather than being punished for the failure, Okie was encouraged to champion other ideas, which included 3M's first blockbuster success: waterproof sandpaper. A culture that permits failure is crucial for fostering the creative thinking and risk taking required for innovation.

As strange as it may seem, *celebrating* failure can be vital to the innovation process.[30] Failure is the essence of learning, growing, and succeeding. Innovative companies have many balls in the air at all times, with many people trying many new ideas. A majority of the ideas will fail—but it is only through this process that the few big "hits" will emerge that make a company an innovative star.

3M uses the simple set of rules listed in Table 17.2 to help foster innovation. These rules can be—and are—copied by other companies. But 3M has an advantage in that it has followed these rules since its inception and ingrained them in its culture. This culture is shared and passed on in part through stories. One such legend is about the 3M engineer who was fired because he refused to stop working on a project that his boss thought was wasting resources. Despite being fired, the engineer came to work as usual, finished the project, and demonstrated the value of his innovation. The engineer eventually was promoted to head a new division created to manufacture and market the innovation.

table 17.2
3M's rules for an innovative culture

- **Set goals for innovation.** By corporate decree, 25 to 30 percent of annual sales must come from new products that are five years old or less.
- **Commit to research and development.** 3M invests in R&D at almost double the rate of the average U.S. company. One R&D goal is to cut in half the time it takes to introduce new products.
- **Inspire intrapreneurship.** Champions are encouraged to run with new ideas, and they get a chance to manage their products as if they were running their own businesses. 3Mers are allowed to spend 15 percent of their time pursuing personal research interests unrelated to current company projects.
- **Facilitate, don't obstruct.** Divisions are kept small and allowed to operate with a great deal of independence but have constant access to information and technical resources. Researchers with good ideas are awarded $50,000 Genesis grants to develop their brainstorms into new products.
- **Focus on the customer.** 3M's definition of quality is to demonstrate that the product can do what the customer–not some arbitrary standard–dictates.
- **Tolerate failure.** 3Mers know that if their ideas fail, they will still be encouraged to pursue other innovative ideas. Management knows that mistakes will be made, and that destructive criticism kills initiative.

Sources: Company reports; R. Mitchell, "Masters of Innovation: How 3M Keeps Its New Products Coming," *Business Week,* April 10, 1989, pp. 58–63; T. Katauskas, "Follow-Through: 3M's Formula for Success," *R&D,* November 1990; and Thomas J. Martin, "Ten Commandments for Managing Creative People," *Fortune,* January 16, 1995, pp. 135–36.

Bureaucracy Busting

Bureaucracy is an enemy of innovation. While bureaucracy is useful to maintain orderliness and gain efficiencies, it also can work directly against innovativeness. Developing radically different technologies requires a more fluid and flexible (organic) structure that does not restrict thought and action. However, such a structure can be chaotic and disruptive to normal operations. Consequently, companies often establish special temporary project structures that are isolated from the rest of the organization and allowed to operate under different rules. These units go by many names, including "skunkworks" (recall Chapter 7), "greenhouses," and "reserves."

In Japan, *angura* is an "underground research" policy that allows scientists to spend up to 20 percent of their time pursuing projects about which only the immediate supervisor knows.[31] When Apple developed the Macintosh, Steve Jobs took a small group of young engineers and programmers and set up operations apart from the remainder of the plant. They started from scratch, trying to completely rethink the personal computer. A pirate's flag was flown over their operation to demonstrate that they were not part of the regular bureaucratic operating structure and defied conventional rules. The result was a very successful new product.

Other structural arrangements also facilitate innovation.[32] *Flat structures* reduce bureaucracy and allow flexibility and innovation. *Granting autonomy* to divisions, including giving them spending authority and other necessary resources, does the same. It is particularly important to break down differentiation based on functional area, as typified by the traditional, vertical hierarchy (Chapter 8). Instead, the organization should create a *horizontal orientation* in which communications flow across functions. The best way to do this is to establish *cross-functional teams.* The aim should be to destroy the traditional boundaries between design, engineering, manufacturing/operations, purchasing, marketing, and other functions. Motorola's IRIDIUM project illustrates many of these principles.

Motorola's IRIDIUM project is out of this world

Innovations are commonplace at Motorola, and the company's latest brainstorm is called the IRIDIUM system—the creation of a network of low-level, earth-orbiting satellites (LEOs) that provide wireless communications to anyone, anytime, anywhere in the world. Subscribers to IRIDIUM will use a pocket-sized handset similar to today's portable cellular phones, but will be able to transmit voice, data, fax, and paging services to any location on the planet.

To get the project off the ground, Motorola created a new strategic business unit called Satellite Communications Division (SATCOM). Durrell Hillis heads the unit and, from the beginning, he and other executives recognized that the organization needed to be a fluid structure of boundary-busting self-managed teams. Each of the teams is cross-functional and organized around work processes such as financing, regulatory, design, technical, and launch. The teams span both organizational and geographic boundaries. Indeed, many of the project's suppliers sit on the various teams.

SATCOM has no organizational chart, and Hillis deliberately discourages formal structure and hierarchical titles because they destroy trust and empowerment among team members. Leadership roles shift as the work of the team progresses. Teams form, disband, and reform around new tasks as needed. To date, the critical management tasks have been those associated with integrating the teams toward one shared goal. To make certain that everyone has up-to-date information and the ability to share knowledge, a software template has been developed to allow anyone in the business unit to enter a topic and, in return, receive a listing of the teams working in that area. In addition, to develop a common language, common tools, and shared guidelines, team members have gone through training together. To encourage "real-time" development, the training is delivered on a just-in-time basis, providing small work-bytes as needed.

Sources: Theodore B. Kinni, "A Ma Bell for the Space Age," *Industry Week,* March 21, 1994, pp. 71–72; Theodore B. Kinni, "Boundary-Busting Teamwork," *Industry Week,* March 21, 1994, pp. 72–74; Charles F. Mason, "IRIDIUM Forges Ahead with Its Grand PCN Plan," *Telephony,* November 1, 1993; Michael Krantz, "Gates and McCaw Blast Off," *Mediaweek* 4, no. 13 (March 28, 1994), p. 12; Charles F. Mason, "Scientific-Atlanta Wins IRIDIUM Deal," *Telephony* 226, no. 6 (February 1994), p. 10; "IRIDIUM: A Closer Look," *Telecommunications* 27, no. 12 (December 1993), p. 27.

Implementing development projects

development project A focused organizational effort to create a new product or process via technological advances.

A powerful tool for managing technology and innovations is the **development project.**[33] A development project is a focused organizational effort to create a new product or process via technological advances. For example, in 1987 Eastman Kodak launched a development project to create the FunSaver Camera. The concept was simple: to package film in an inexpensive plastic camera body so that after the pictures were taken, the consumer could simply drop the whole assembly with a photo finisher. While the FunSaver utilized existing design knowledge, it was developed on a unique computer-aided design and manufacturing (CAD/CAM) system. Two years earlier, Hewlett-Packard had initiated a development project of its own to design a new class of low-cost computer printers based on ink-jet technology. HP's Deskjet Printer was one of the company's first attempts to integrate manufacturing, marketing, and R&D. The development project allowed the company to achieve an unprecedented advantage in both cost and speed.

In general, development projects fall into one of four categories: (1) *research or advanced development projects* designed to invent new science for application in a specific project;

(2) *breakthrough development projects* designed to create the first generation of a product or process; (3) *platform development projects* that establish the basic architecture for a whole set of follow-on projects; and (4) *derivative development projects* that are narrower in scope and are designed to provide incremental improvements to an existing product or process.[34]

Development projects such as these typically feature a special cross-functional team that works together on an overall concept or idea. Like most cross-functional teams, their success depends on how well individuals work together to pursue a common vision. And in the case of development projects, teams must frequently interact with suppliers and customers—making the complexity of their task that much greater. Because of their urgency and strategic importance, most development projects are conducted under intense time and budget pressures, thus presenting a real-time test of the company's ability to innovate.

Managers should recognize that development projects have multiple benefits. Not only are they useful for creating new products and processes, but they frequently cultivate skills and knowledge that can be used for future endeavors. In other words, the capabilities that companies derive from a development project frequently can be turned into a source of competitive advantage. For example, in 1986 when Ford created a development project to design an air-conditioning compressor to outperform its Japanese rival, executives also discovered they had laid the foundation for new processes that Ford could use in future projects. Their new capability in integrated design and manufacturing helped Ford reduce the costs and lead times for other product developments. Thus, *organizational learning* had become an equally important criterion for evaluating the success of the project.

For development projects to achieve their fullest benefit, they should: build on core competencies (recall Chapters 4 and 9); have a guiding vision about what must be accomplished and why (Chapter 12); have a committed team (Chapters 12 and 14); instill a philosophy of continuous improvement (Chapter 9); and generate integrated, coordinated efforts across all units (Chapters 8 and 9).

Technology, job design, and human resources

Adopting a new technology typically requires changes in the way jobs are designed. Often the way the task is redefined fits people to the demands of the technology to maximize the technology's operation. But this often fails to maximize total productivity, because it ignores the human part of the equation. The social relationships and human aspects of the task may suffer, lowering overall productivity.

Hewlett-Packard undertook a development project that resulted in the inkjet printer, a product that gave the company an unprecedented advantage in both cost and speed.
[Courtesy of Hewlett-Packard Company]

sociotechnical systems
An approach to job design that attempts to redesign tasks to optimize operation of a new technology while preserving employees' interpersonal relationships and other human aspects of the work.

The **sociotechnical systems** approach to work redesign specifically addresses this problem. This approach redesigns tasks in a manner that jointly optimizes the social and technical efficiency of work. Beginning with studies on the introduction of new coal-mining technologies in 1949, the sociotechnical systems approach to work design focused on small, self-regulating work groups.[35] Later it was found that such work arrangements could operate effectively only in an environment in which bureaucracy was limited. Today's trends in bureaucracy "bashing," lean and flat organizations, work teams, and an empowered workforce are logical extensions of the sociotechnical philosophy of work design. At the same time, the technologies of the information age—in which people at all organizational levels have access to vast amounts of information—make these leaner and less bureaucratic organizations possible.

Managers face several choices regarding how to apply a new technology. Technology can be used to limit the tasks and responsibilities of workers and "deskill" the workforce, thus turning workers into servants of the technology.

Alternatively, managers can select and train workers to master the technology, using it to achieve great accomplishments and improve the quality of their lives.[36] Technology, when managed effectively, can empower workers as it improves the competitiveness of organizations.

However, as managers make decisions about how to design jobs and manage employees, they also need to consider other human resource systems that complement the introduction of new technology. Table 17.3, for example, shows how compensation systems can be changed to facilitate the implementation of advanced manufacturing technology. In the contemporary setting, use of group incentives, salary, and skill-based pay systems helps reinforce collective effort (recall the use of cross-functional teams), professionalism, empowerment, and flexibility required for knowledge work. If a company's pay system is

table 17.3
Compensation practices in traditional and advanced manufacturing firms

Type of compensation practice	Traditional factory	Integrated manufacturing
Performance contingent	Focus on *individual incentives* reflects division of labor and separation of stages and functions.	Extensive use of *group incentives* to encourage teamwork, cooperation, and joint problem solving.
Job contingent	Use of *hourly wage* assumes that the differences in employee contribution are captured in job classifications and that performance is largely determined by the production system.	Use of *salary* assumes that employees' contributions transcend the job per se to substantially affect output. The distinctions between classes of employment are diminished.
Person contingent	*Seniority pay* rewards experience as a surrogate for knowledge and skill in a stable environment and rewards loyalty to reduce uncertainty within the system.	*Skill-based* pay rewards continuous learning and the value-added derived from increased flexibility in a dynamic environment.

Source: Scott A. Snell and James W. Dean, Jr., "Strategic Compensation for Integrated Manufacturing: The Moderating Effects of Jobs and Organizational Inertia," *Academy of Management Journal* 37, no. 5 (1994), pp. 1109–40.

not aligned with the new technologies, it may not reward behavior that is needed to make the changes work. Worse yet, existing reward systems may actually reinforce old behaviors that run counter to what is needed for the new technology.

Taken as a whole, these ideas provide a set of guidelines for managing the strategic and organizational issues associated with technology and innovation. In Chapter 18, we expand this discussion to focus on how organizations can reshape themselves to adapt to a dynamic marketplace. Managing change and organizational learning are central elements of what it takes to become a world-class organization.

Key terms

Chief technology officer (CTO), p. 591
Development project, p. 594
Executive champion, p. 592
Innovation, p. 576
Make-or-buy decision, p. 589
Product champion, p. 592
Sociotechnical systems, p. 596
Technical innovator, p. 592
Technology, p. 576
Technology audit, p. 583
Technology life cycle, p. 577

Summary of learning objectives

Now that you have studied Chapter 17, you should know:

The processes involved in the development of new technologies.

Forces that compel the emergence of a new technology include (1) a need for the technology, (2) the requisite scientific knowledge, (3) technical convertibility of this knowledge, (4) the capital resources to fund development, and (5) the entrepreneurial insight and initiative to pull the components together.

How technologies proceed through a life cycle.

New technologies follow a predictable life cycle. First, a workable idea about how to meet a market need is developed into some product innovation. Early progress can be slow as competitors experiment with product designs. Eventually a dominant design emerges as the market accepts the technology, and further refinements to the technology occur from process innovations. As the technology begins to approach both the theoretical limits to its performance potential and market saturation, growth slows and the technology matures. At this point the technology can remain stable or be replaced by a new technology.

How to manage technology for competitive advantage.

Adopters of new technologies are categorized according to the timing of their adoption: innovators, early adopters, the early majority, the late majority, and laggards. Technology leadership has many first-mover advantages, but also poses significant disadvantages. The same may be said for followership. After that, technology that helps improve efficiency will support a low-cost strategy, while technologies that help make products more distinctive or unique will support a differentiation strategy. Determining an appropriate technology strategy depends on the degree to which the technology supports the organization's competitive requirements and, if a technology leadership strategy is chosen, the company's ability, in terms of skills, resources, and commitment, to deal with the risks and uncertainties of leadership.

How to assess technology needs.

Assessing the technology needs of a company begins by benchmarking, or comparing, the technologies it employs with those of both competitors and noncompetitors. Benchmarking should be done on a global basis to understand practices used worldwide. Technology scanning helps identify emerging technologies and those still under development in an effort to project their eventual competitive impact.

Where new technologies originate and the best strategies for acquiring them.

New technologies can be acquired or developed. Options include internal development, purchase, contracted development, licensing, trading, research partnerships and joint ventures, and acquisition. The approach used depends on the existing availability of the technology, the skills, resources, and time available, and importance of keeping the technology proprietary.

How people play a role in managing technology.

People play many different roles in managing technology. For example, the chief technology officer (CTO) is the person with broad, integrative responsibility for technological innovation. In addition, the entrepreneur is the person who recognizes the competitive potential of the technology and finds new ways to exploit opportunities. The technical innovator has the key skills needed to develop or install and operate the technology. The product champion is the person who promotes the new idea(s) in order to gain support throughout the organization. The executive champion is the person with status and resources to support the project.

How to develop an innovative organization.

Organizing for innovation involves unleashing the creative energies of employees while directing their efforts toward meeting market needs in a timely manner. Culture, structure, development projects, and job design are critical for building an innovative organization.

The key characteristics of successful development projects.

For development projects to achieve their fullest benefit, they should (1) build on core competencies; (2) have a guiding vision about what must be accomplished and why; (3) have a committed team; (4) instill a philosophy of continuous improvement; and (5) generate integrated, coordinated efforts across all teams and units.

Discussion questions

1. At the beginning of this chapter there is a quote by Francis Bacon that reads, "A wise man will make more opportunities than he finds." What does this have to do with technology and innovation? What does it have to do with competitive advantage?

2. What examples of technological innovation can you identify? What forces led to the commercialization of the science behind these technologies? Did the capability exist before the market demand, or was the demand there before the technology was available?

3. Thomas Edison once said that most innovations are 10 percent inspiration and 90 percent perspiration. How does this match with what you know about technology life cycles?

4. Why would a company choose to follow rather than lead technological innovations? Is the potential advantage of technological leadership greater when innovations are occurring rapidly, or is it better in this case to follow?

5. If you were in the grocery business, who would you benchmark for technological innovations? Would the companies be inside or outside your industry? Why?

6. How would you see the executive champion, the chief technology officer, and the product champion working together? Could the roles all be played by the same individual? Why or why not?

Concluding Case

Asea Brown Boveri (ABB)

Percy Barnevik surprised the business community in 1987 by announcing the creation of one of the world's largest crossborder mergers. Barnevik combined ASEA, a Swedish engineering group, with Brown Boveri , a Swiss competitor, and created a $30 billion giant with a portfolio covering global markets for electric power generation and transmission equipment, high speed trains, automation and robotics, and environmental control systems. Because of the mix of businesses that make up this conglomerate, the success of ABB depends upon its technological leadership. Top management actively supports that notion, and its dedication can be seen explicitly in ABB's mission:

> Our technological competence determines the quality, performance, and cost of our products, and thereby establishes our competitiveness in the marketplace. Technological innovation is essential to secure ABB's future. ABB's objective is to maintain or achieve leadership in technologies of key importance to our core.

ABB allocates a substantial amount of resources to R&D, technology-based joint ventures, and license agreements. For example, in 1995 and 1996, the expenditures for research and development reached $2.6 billion, amounting to about 8 percent of revenues. In its highly decentralized structure, ABB's corporate research activities deal with longer-range basic research projects, and 90 percent of all R&D is decentralized to companies that are centers of excellence and operate close to customers.

ABB's management is serious about developing the technical competencies it needs for future competitiveness. According to Harold M. Stillman, Vice President of Technology and Innovation, "If we want to be technological leaders—and we deem that necessary for success in our business—then we must have a clear sense of our technological position and not delude ourselves." To assure its technology position, ABB has formalized a technology competitiveness audit—called Business Technology Evaluation (BTE)—to inform managers on the adequacy of its technical resources. BTE helps managers identify areas of present or potential weakness and opportunities for innovation.

According to Harold M. Stillman, ABB's Vice President of Technology and Innovation, "If we want to be technological leaders–and we deem that necessary for success in our business–then we must have a clear sense of our technological position and not delude ourselves." *[Courtesy of Harold M. Stillman/ABB Brown Boveri Ltd.]*

Objectives of BTE Projects

BTE is a systematic process to assess the role of R&D and product/process technology in enhancing a business area's competitive position and market/financial success. BTE lays the groundwork for selecting the product or process technology areas suited to support a business. This translates into four specific objectives:

1. *Identification of breakout opportunities.* BTE should try to identify new technology applications that may lead to innovative product offerings.

2. *Achievement of cost reduction.* BTE should determine whether there are new product or process technologies in sight that could enable the business units to manufacture at a substantially lower cost.

3. *Identification of, and defense against, technology threats.* The commercial success of current products can be threatened by new products based on superior technology leading to better quality.

4. *Review and filling of gaps in capacity.* Review key aspects of a business unit's technology development process to ensure that it meets time, cost, performance, and quality targets.

Responsibility for the BTE Projects

Assessing and assuring the technological strength of the ABB Group is a major responsibility of the senior corporate technology officer (CTO). At ABB, the BTE process is managed by a small corporate technology evaluation team whose principal responsibilities are assessing, evaluating, and auditing the technical resources, strengths, needs, and innovation opportunities of ABB businesses. The team ranks ABB businesses in terms of their needs and helps them establish plans to implement BTE projects. The team also provides leadership for BTE projects and takes responsibility on behalf of the firm's CTO to assure the quality and timeliness of the activity. Finally, the BTE team makes recommendations about appropriate top management programs to fill technical gaps and to otherwise assure technological competitiveness of ABB businesses.

A Three-Stage Process

While each BTE is customized to the individual business unit (ABB is a loosely connected set of companies), the corporate team has developed a three stage framework that guides all BTE projects:

- *Project stage one.* Every BTE project starts by determining the critical questions and issues that need to be answered by the analysis. The focus of project stage one is an efficient, structured information collection effort required to begin to answer the critical BTE issues developed at the outset. At the end of stage one, an evaluation workshop is held to review and aggregate the technology information collected.
- *Project stage two.* At this stage the information collected is used in several types of analyses that are geared toward evaluating a business's current situation. In the *market assessment,* the focus is on identifying the key market characteristics such as segmentation, growth, size, customer

needs, buying behavior and potential demand forecast, and in determining the key success factors of the business. The *technology assessment* focuses on evaluating the performance and other characteristics of the relevant technologies, as well as on technological trends. The *competitive assessment* compares a business's products, processes, cost, and efficiency with other firms through such techniques as benchmarking, cost structure analysis, and product teardowns. Finally, the *capability assessment* is geared toward evaluating a business's infrastructure capabilities relative to its competitors.

- *Project stage three.* The final stage of the BTE project is used to develop recommendations. The individual analyses of stage two are integrated into an overall scenario or set of alternatives for the business under investigation. The outcome of a BTE is a strategic concept of how the business wants to improve overall performance.

BTE projects in one business often have linkages with similar projects in other businesses. Because of this, the direct support and guidance of ABB business-unit managers—and senior corporate executives—are vital to the success of BTE projects. To facilitate their contribution, BTE projects are directed by a steering committee with senior managers as members. The steering committee guides the core BTE team mainly through review sessions at the end of each of the three BTE project stages. The core teams are comprised of four to nine professionals drawn from relevant business units as well as R&D, marketing, and manufacturing, as well as experts from outside the company. At each review session, the team is expected to demonstrate to the steering committee that it has discovered something new, enlightening, or nonobvious that should reshape everyone's thinking about the issue being addressed.

The value of BTE is that it provides a thorough and objective picture of perhaps ABB's most important competency. There are no long-term certainties at ABB except that its business will be based on exploiting its technological competencies. BTE is seen as a method that helps ABB assure itself that it is making the right investments in technology.

Questions

1. What similarities do you find between the BTE projects that ABB conducts and the techniques discussed in this chapter?

2. How does ABB organize its BTE projects? What recommendations would you ask Mr. Barnevik to consider in organizing for BTE?

3. After BTE, what should the next step be for ABB in order to assure its leadership in technological innovations?

Source: Harold M. Stillman, "How ABB Decides on the Right Technology Investments," *Research Technology Management*, November–December 1997, pp. 14–22.

Video Case

The nature of business featuring Motorola

Almost everyone could rattle off a long list of businesses that are considered successful. They come in all sizes, shapes, and levels of advancement. You probably encounter many products and services of well known businesses each day. Yet a deeper understanding of how these businesses work is sometimes more difficult to obtain. Many companies enjoy a sudden boom of success only to fade into obscurity after a brief time. Others are able to prepare for the future and position themselves to adapt to changes in technology. Foresight, and the ability to adapt to change are what gives an organization the edge over its competition in the present and in the future.

In 1928 Paul Galvin started a small company to manufacture a battery eliminator for radios. The battery eliminator enabled consumers to operate radios directly from household current, rather than from the cumbersome battery supplied with most early radios. Galvin's next invention was a radio for automobiles. It was the concept of marrying sound and motion that provided Galvin with a name for his company—Motorola. Today Motorola is recognized as one of the world leaders in the communications industry.

From day one Paul Galvin knew that the key to success was recognizing customers' needs. Finding ways to fill these needs at Motorola involves a commitment to total customer satisfaction, constant renewal of knowledge and skills, and the ability to see the future. On a trip to Europe in the 1930s, for example, Galvin became convinced that a war of major proportions was about to develop. From this observation, Galvin foresaw a need for mobile communications. Back at home, Motorola began work on what was to become the handy-talkie, a hand-held, two-way radio that set the pace for the company's future.

At the time of Galvin's death in 1959, Motorola was the leader in military, space, and commercial communications. The company had also built its first semiconductor facility, and was a growing force in consumer electronics. Bob Galvin, Paul's son, took Motorola into international markets in the 1960s and the company began to shift its focus away from consumer electronics. Motorola's television business was sold in the mid 1970s as the company again shifted focus and moved more into electronics and communications. By 1990 Motorola had become the premiere, worldwide supplier of cellular telephones. Changing with the times is a way of life at Motorola.

E. David Metz of Motorola's Semiconductor Products Sector, said: "Our factories today, if they're going to be competitive, have to be sensitive to and respond to the opportunities to make and produce a product that people will want to buy tomorrow. They may get tired of today's model and the people who are making those new products may have to learn to use new tools or use older tools in a new way."

It's important for any organization to be able to measure success. This is often easiest to gauge by looking at some of the indicators of business success. Like all businesses, Motorola is concerned with financial performance. However, it goes much further than that. Motorola uses the following indicators of business success:

- Achieving financial performance.
- Meeting customer needs and values.
- Building quality products and services.
- Encouraging innovation and creativity.
- Gaining employee commitment.

Managers study indicators such as sales revenues, net profits, and return on investments. They also look at how these indicators change over time. Meeting customer needs and values is also a way to measure performance. Since Motorola is in the communication business, knowing the communication needs of its customers and filling those needs is of great importance. Quality is another defining indicator of a company's success. Since 1928 Motorola has had to reinvent itself every decade, although the company's commitment to quality and to its employees remains legendary.

Due to its large size and varied areas of specialized technology, Motorola is divided into a number of business sectors. Each is responsible for a different arm of Motorola communication technology. These sectors are:

- Semiconductor Products.
- Cellular Subscribers.
- Cellular Networks and Space.
- Land Mobile Products.
- Messaging, Information, and Media.
- Automotive, Component, Computer, and Energy Sector.

Companywide the culture at Motorola is definitely one where quality is the norm. Motorola is recognized worldwide for producing products that never fail. In addition to this, Motorola is consistently listed as one of the best companies to work for in the United States.

Increasingly, today's businesses must focus on the quality and value of their products and services. Most customers just won't tolerate low quality. Companies like Motorola have made quality the foundation for their future. They have formalized plans and programs for promoting and ensuring a quality focus. For example, Motorola University was established in 1981 to provide training that secures these quality ideals companywide. This training emphasizes the organization's goals while providing learning environments where employees can keep abreast of the changes in communication technology. At a company like Motorola, where the international marketplace is an important one, flexibility is a requirement for employees and the organization as a whole.

Roger Bertelson, Managing Director in Malaysia said: "Our workforce is going have to accept the fact that they need to be flexible. They are going to have to be a more educated workforce and they are going to have to be more adaptable to change. Because a changing environment is part of manufacturing as it is today."

Another indicator of success is the encouragement of innovation and creativity. With new technologies being developed all the time, the only way a business can stay on top and compete is to be creative and innovative. Employee commitment is yet another prime indicator of success. The dedication of its employees enables Motorola to continue to produce top quality, leading edge products and technology. When quality is of the essence, highly motivated employees are a must. Just listen to the comments of some of Motorola's valuable employees:

> "Commitment at Motorola, and I'll speak for the cellular construction group, is honestly the middle name."

> "People here are all self-starters and they always take the initiative to do their own job and try to fulfill their duties and responsibilities."

> "My belief is that if the people are good at what they do then they will respond to being given increasingly more difficult tasks to perform."

> "I must exceed customer expectations. I want to leave the customer delighted with our services."

> "I find that this company conducts its business in an honorable fashion and that is something that I can always be proud of."

Success in business depends on many factors. The ability to recognize or even predict customer needs is a solid place to start. The next step is to deliver a quality product or service to the customer. But most challenging of all, the company must be able to make changes and adapt to changes in technology and customer needs to remain competitive for the long run.

Measuring success by looking at the key indicators can help a business stay on the right track.

Motorola has enjoyed success because it has a business structure in place that was built on adaptation and reorganization. The company and its products are different than they were 10, 20, or 30 years ago. By having to reinvent itself every decade, Motorola is able to move with the many changes and advancements in communication technologies. Motorola expects to adapt and time and time again it has proven to be up to the challenge.

Critical Thinking Questions

1. What is the purpose of Motorola University? In what ways do you think Motorola University provides training that differs from a regular university? Why do you think so many companies have developed their own universities?

2. Managers must study the key indicators of success in order to determine the health of a business. Why do you think these indicators need to be studied both in the present and over time? Are there any indicators of success that you think are important that were not mentioned in this video? Explain.

3. The videotape states that businesses must be able to foresee the future in order to be successful. How do you think it's possible for a business to do this? What tools might a business use to "foresee the future?"

Experiential Exercises

17.1 Planning for Innovation

Objectives

1. To brainstorm innovative ideas for a company that has become stagnant.
2. To explore what are the elements of a good innovation plan.

Instructions

1. Read the Mason, Inc., scenario below.
2. Individually or in small groups, offer a plan for encouraging innovation at Mason, Inc. Discuss staffing, rewards, organizational structure, work design, and any other facets of organizational behavior that apply.
3. In small groups, or with the entire class, share the plans you developed.

Mason, Inc., Scenario

Mason, Inc., is a Fortune 500 company that designs, develops, and manufactures personal grooming products. From 1950 to 1980 it was a leader in introducing new, profitable products into the marketplace. Its Research and Development Division grew from 20 to 150 professionals during that time. Since 1980, however, the company has relied on its past successes and has failed to introduce any significant innovative product into the marketplace. Top management wants to reestablish Mason's reputation as the number-one innovator in the industry.

Discussion Questions

1. What elements do these plans have in common?
2. How well do the plans follow the innovation process?
3. Do the plans incorporate provisions for fulfilling the various roles required for innovation?
4. What are the strengths and weaknesses of each plan?
5. What should be the components of an effective plan?

Source: J. Gordon, *A Diagnostic Approach to Organizational Behavior* (Englewood Cliffs, N.J.: Prentice-Hall, 1983), p. 654. Reprinted by permission of Prentice-Hall, Inc., Englewood Cliffs, N.J.

17.2 Innovation for the Future

Objective

To look ahead to the 21st century.

Instructions

Choose a partner. Together, develop an innovative product or service that will be popular in the year 2025. As you develop your product or service, ask yourselves the following questions:

1. What trends lead you to believe that this product or service will be successful?
2. What current technologies, services, or products will be replaced by your idea?

Present your idea to the class for discussion.

Chapter Eighteen
World-Class Futures

The world hates change, yet that is the only thing that has brought progress.

—Charles Kettering

My interest is in the future because I am going to spend the rest of my life there.

—Charles Kettering

Chapter Outline

Becoming World Class
- Sustainable, Great Futures
- The Tyranny of the *"Or"*
- The Genius of the *"And"*

Managing Change
- Motivating People to Change
- Harmonizing Multiple Changes
- Leading Change

Shaping the Future
- Exercising Foresight
- Learning Continuously
- Pursuing Growth
- Seizing Advantage
- Creating the Future
- Shaping Your Own Future

Learning Objectives

After studying Chapter 18, you will know:

1. What it takes to be world class.
2. How to manage change effectively.
3. How to best prepare for the future.

Setting the Stage

The Need to Change

- "Want a tough job? Try leading an organization through major change . . . Almost without exception, executives claim it's the hardest work they've ever done."—T. A. Stewart, *Fortune.*
- "Even if your company's financials are terrific, you might want to . . . build support for improving your own performance before you're attacked . . . We're starting almost from scratch in reshaping the way the whole enterprise runs."—Lawrence Bossidy, Allied Signal.
- "In terms of channeling the energies of all our people and unleashing our potential productivity, we're halfway home at best. And that's not bad. I know a lot of companies in the United States that may think they've come more than halfway, but I don't know very many that actually have come even that far."—Michael Walsh, Tenneco.
- "People always ask, 'Is the change over? Can we stop now?' You've got to tell them, 'No, it's just begun.'"—Jack Welch, General Electric.
- "These days, no one knows when a competitive and healthy conglomerate will fail. In such times we must work with a crisis mentality."—Koo Bon Moo, chairman of Korea's LG Group.
- "The issues are always the same . . . but each plant deals with them in a different way. We don't have cookbooks because there isn't a cookbook. We're on a journey that never ends. And the day we think we've got it made, that's the day we'd better start worrying about going out of business."—Rich Teerlink, CEO, Harley-Davidson.
- "Only the paranoid survive."—Andrew Grove, Chairman, Intel.
- "The capacity to change is a key success factor. You have to constantly reinvent yourself."—Edgardo Pappacena, partner, Arthur Andersen.
- "You know how it is in the music business. Fickle! Here today, gone today!"—Chris Rock, comedian.

The CEOs pictured here—Larry Bossidy of Allied Signal, Bill Weiss of Ameritech, Mike Walsh of Tenneco, and Jack Welsh of GE—realize the importance of channeling their employees' energies in the direction of the cutting edge of change. *[John Abbott]*

Sources: M. Gunther, "This Gang Controls Your Kids' Brains," Fortune, *October 27, 1997, pp. 104–10; A. Grove,* Only the Paranoid Survive *Currency/Doubleday, 1996; T. A. Stewart, "How to Lead a Revolution,"* Fortune, *November 28, 1994, pp. 48–61; L. Kraar,* Fortune, *December 8, 1997, pp. 64–68; S. Sherman, "A Master Class in Radical Change,"* Fortune, *December 13, 1993, pp. 82–90; G. Imperato, "Harley Shifts Gears,"* Fast Company, *June–July 1997, pp. 194–213; J. McCune, Management's Brave New World,"* Management Review, *October 1997, pp. 11–14.*

These executives—and Chris Rock—are all talking about the same things: the difficulties and challenges of creating change, and the need to improve constantly in order to achieve world-class excellence and competitive advantage for the future.

This chapter discusses managing change. Today's managers deal with and lead far-reaching changes in their organizations as they respond to the pressures to become world class. We will examine why people resist change, and how the change process can best be managed. And we'll discuss ideas about how to prepare for an uncertain future.

Becoming world class

Managers today want, or *should* want, their organizations to become world class.[1] To some people, striving for world-class excellence seems a lofty, impossible, unnecessary goal. But it is a goal that is essential to survival and success in today's intensely competitive business world.

Being world-class requires applying the best and latest knowledge and ideas, and having the ability to operate at the highest standards of any place anywhere.[2] Thus, becoming world class does not mean merely improving. It means becoming one of the very best in the world at what you do. Some have estimated that for most companies, becoming world class requires increasing quality by 100 to 1,000 times, decreasing costs by 30 percent to 50 percent, increasing productivity by two to four times, decreasing order-to-delivery time by a factor of 5 to 10, and decreasing new-product development times by 30 percent to 60 percent. And even if your firm realizes these dramatic improvements, it still will have to keep on getting better![3]

World-class companies create high-value products and earn superior profits over the long run. They demolish the obsolete methods, systems, and cultures of the past that have impeded their competitive progress, and apply more effective and competitive organizational strategies, structures, processes, and management of human resources. The result is an organization capable of competing successfully on a global basis.[4]

Sustainable, great futures

Two Stanford professors, James Collins and Jerry Porras, studied 18 corporations that had achieved and maintained greatness for half a century or more.[5] The companies include Sony, American Express, Ford, Motorola, Merck, Marriott, Johnson & Johnson, Disney, 3M, Hewlett-Packard, Citicorp, Wal-Mart, and others. Over the years, these companies have been widely admired, been considered the premier institutions in their industries, and made a real *impact* on the world. Although every company goes through periodic downturns—and these were no exceptions, over their long histories—these companies consistently prevailed across the decades. They turn in extraordinary performance *over the long run,* rather than fleeting greatness. This study is reported in the book called *Built to Last*—which is what these great organizations were and are.

The researchers sought to identify the essential characteristics of enduringly great companies. What characteristics did they discover? Among other things, these great companies have strong core values in which they believe deeply, and they express and live the values consistently. They are driven by goals—not just incremental improvements or business-as-usual goals, but stretch goals (recall Chapter 13). They change continuously, driving for progress via adaptability, experimentation, trial and error, opportunistic thinking, and fast action. And they focus not on beating the competition; they focus primarily on beating themselves. They continually ask, "How can we improve ourselves to do better tomorrow than we did today?"

But underneath the action and the changes, the core values and vision remain steadfast and uncompromised. Table 18.1 displays the core values of several of the companies that were "built to last." Note that the values are not all the same. In fact, there was no set of common values that consistently predicted success. Instead, the critical factor is that the great companies *have* core values, *know* what they are and what they mean, and *live* by them—year after year after year.

table 18.1
Core ideologies in built-to-last companies

3M	Innovation; "Thou shalt not kill a new product idea"
	Absolute integrity
	Respect for individual initiative and personal growth
	Tolerance for honest mistakes
	Product quality and reliability
	"Our real business is solving problems"
American Express	Heroic customer service
	Worldwide reliability of services
	Encouragement of individual initiative
Boeing	Being on the leading edge of aeronautics; being pioneers
	Tackling huge challenges and risks
	Product safety and quality
	Integrity and ethical business
	To "eat, breathe, and sleep the world of aeronautics"
Sony	To experience the sheer joy that comes from the advancement, application, and innovation of technology that benefits the general public
	To elevate the Japanese culture and national status
	Being pioneers–not following others, but doing the impossible
	Respecting and encouraging each individual's ability and creativity
Wal-Mart	"We exist to provide value to our customers"–to make their lives better via lower prices and greater selection; all else is secondary
	Swim up-stream, buck conventional wisdom
	Be in partnership with employees
	Work with passion, commitment, and enthusiasm
	Run lean
	Pursue ever-higher goals
Walt Disney	No cynicism allowed
	Fanatical attention to consistency and detail
	Continuous progress via creativity, dreams, and imagination
	Fanatical control and preservation of Disney's "magic" image
	"To bring happiness to millions" and to celebrate, nurture, and promulgate "wholesome American values"

Source: From *Built to Last* by James C. Collins and Jerry I. Porras. Copyright © 1994 by James C. Collins and Jerry I. Porras. Reprinted by permission of HarperCollins Publishers, Inc.

The tyranny of the *"or"*

tyranny of the "or" The belief that things must be either A or B, and cannot be both; that only one goal and not another can be attained.

Many companies, and individuals, are plagued by what the authors of *Built to Last* call the "tyranny of the *or*." This refers to the belief that things must be either A or B, and cannot be both. The authors provide many common examples:[6] beliefs that you must choose either change or stability; be conservative or bold; have control and consistency or creative freedom; do well in the short-term or invest for the future; plan methodically or be opportunistic; create shareholder wealth or do good for the world; be pragmatic or idealistic. Such beliefs—that only one goal but not another can be attained—often are invalid and certainly are constraining—unnecessarily so.

The genius of the *"and"*

the genius of the "and" The ability to pursue multiple goals at once.

In contrast to the "tyranny of the *or,*" the "genius of the *and*" is the ability to pursue multiple goals at once. We have discussed earlier in the book the importance of delivering multiple competitive values to customers; performing all the management functions; reconciling hard-nosed business logic with ethics; leading and empowering; and others. Authors Collins and Porras add their own list,[7] which includes:

- Purpose beyond profit *and* pragmatic pursuit of profit.
- Relatively fixed core values *and* vigorous change and movement.
- Conservatism with the core values *and* bold business moves.
- Clear vision and direction *and* experimentation.
- Stretch goals *and* incremental progress.
- Control based on values *and* operational freedom.
- Long-term thinking and investment *and* demand for short-term results.
- Visionary, futuristic thinking *and* daily, nuts-and-bolts execution.

You have learned about all of these things throughout this course and should not lose sight of any of them—either in your mind or in your actions. To achieve them all requires the continuous and effective management of change.

Managing change

Every manager needs a clear understanding of how to manage change effectively. Organizational change is managed effectively when[8]

1. The organization is moved from its current state to some planned future state that will exist after the change.
2. The functioning of the organization in the future state meets expectations; that is, the change works as planned.
3. The transition is accomplished without excessive cost to the organization.
4. The transition is accomplished without excessive cost to individual organizational members.

People are the key to successful change. For an organization to be great, or even just to survive, people have to care about its fate, and know how they can contribute. But typically, leadership lies with only a few people at the top. Too few take on the burden of change. The number of people who care deeply, and who make innovative contributions, is too small. People throughout the organization need to take a greater interest and a more active role in helping the business as a whole. They have to believe they can make a difference. And they have to identify with the entire organization, not just with their unit and close colleagues.

These important attitudes and feelings are common in start-ups and very small organizations. Too often they are lost with growth and over time. In large, traditional corporations, they are all too rare. There needs to be a permanent rekindling of individual creativity and responsibility, a true change in the behavior of people throughout the organization. The essential task is to motivate people fully to keep changing in response to new business challenges.

Motivating people to change

People must be *motivated* to change. But often they resist changing. For example, if your boss were to tell you; "We have to become world-class;" what would be your reaction?

Resistance to becoming world class

Many people settle for mediocrity rather than aspire to world-class status. They resist the idea of striving mightily for excellence; they say things such as the following:

- "Those world-class performance numbers are ridiculous! I don't believe them, they are impossible! Maybe in some industries, some companies . . . but ours is unique . . ."
- "Sure, maybe some companies achieve those numbers, but there's no hurry . . . We're doing all right. Sales were up 5 percent this year, costs were down 2 percent. And we've got to keep cutting corners . . ."
- "We can't afford to be world class like those big global companies, we don't have the money or staff . . ."
- "Our workforce prevents us from being world class. You can't find anyone who is willing to work today. Our schools are doing a lousy job. Where's some old-fashioned street smarts, discipline, and work ethic?"
- "Yeah, we all know we have to change things around here. But who's going to tell our senior management? They're isolated in their headquarters, and only seem to care about short-term financial measures that satisfy Wall Street."
- "We don't believe this stuff about global markets and competitors. We don't need to expand internationally. One of our local competitors tried that a few years ago and lost its shirt."
- "It's not a level playing field . . . the others have unfair advantages . . ."

Excuses and rationalizations don't cut it. To survive and prosper today, organizations need to launch an assault on achieving world-class excellence.

Source: From *21st Century Manufacturing: Creating Winning Business Performance* by Thomas G. Gunn. Copyright © 1992 by Thomas G. Gunn. Reprinted by permission of HarperCollins Publishers, Inc.

If management is to overcome such reactions, and successfully implement positive change, it is important to understand why people often resist change. Figure 18.1 shows the common reasons for resistance. Some reasons are general and arise in most change efforts. Other reasons for resistance relate to the specific nature of a particular change.

General reasons for resistance Several reasons for resistance arise regardless of the actual content of the change.[9]

- *Inertia.* Usually people don't want to disturb the status quo. The old ways of doing things are comfortable and easy, so people don't want to shake things up and try something new. For example, it is easier to keep living in the same apartment or house than to move to another.
- *Timing.* People often resist change because of poor timing. Maybe you would like to move to a different place to live, but do you want to move this week? Even if a place were available, you probably couldn't take the time. If managers or employees are unusually busy or under stress, or if relations between management and workers are strained, the timing is wrong for introducing new proposals. Where possible, managers should introduce change when people are receptive.
- *Surprise.* One key aspect of timing and receptivity is surprise. If the change is sudden, unexpected, or extreme, resistance may be the initial—almost reflexive—reaction. Suppose your university announced an increase in tuition, effective at the beginning of next term. Resistance would be high. At the very least, you would want to know about this change far enough in advance to give you time to prepare for it.

figure 18.1
Reasons for resistance to change

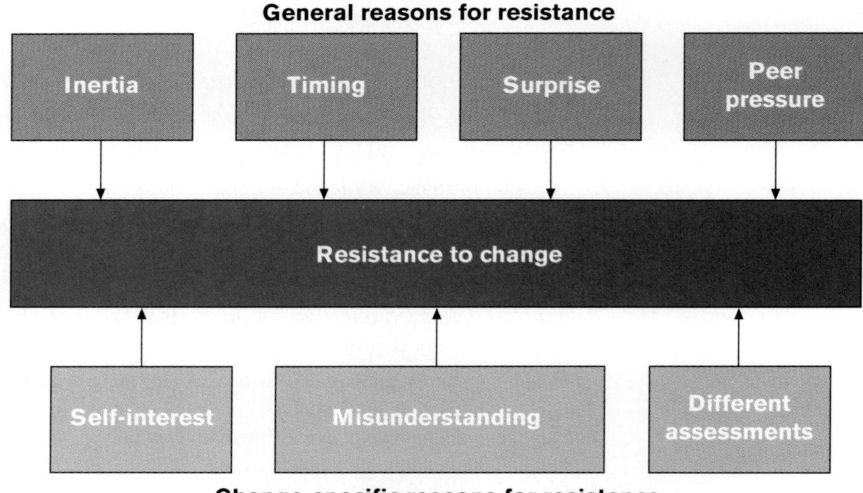

• *Peer pressure.* Sometimes work teams resist new ideas. Even if individual members do not strongly oppose a change suggested by management, the team may band together in opposition. If a group is highly cohesive and has antimanagement norms (recall Chapter 14), peer pressure will cause individuals to resist even reasonable changes.

Change-specific reasons for resistance Other causes of resistance arise from the specific nature of a proposed change. Change-specific reasons for resistance stem from what people perceive as the personal consequences of the change.[10]

• *Self-interest.* Most people care less about the organization's best interest than they do about their own best interests. They will resist a change if they think it will cause them to lose something of value.

What could people fear to lose? At worst, their jobs, if management is considering closing down a plant. A merger or reorganization, or technological change, could create the same fear. Despite assurances that no one will be laid off or fired, people might fear a cut in pay or loss of power and status under the new arrangement.

• *Misunderstanding.* Even when management proposes a change that will benefit everyone, people may resist because they don't fully understand its purpose. One company met resistance to the idea of introducing flexible working hours, a system in which workers have some say regarding the hours they work. This system can benefit employees, but a false rumor circulated among plant employees that people would have to work evenings, weekends, or whenever their supervisors wanted. The employees' union demanded that management drop the flexible-hours idea. The president was caught completely off guard by this unexpected resistance, and complied with the union's demand.

• *Different assessments.* Employees receive different—and usually less—information than management receives. Even within top management ranks, some executives know more than others do. Such discrepancies cause people to develop different assessments of proposed changes. Some may be aware that the benefits outweigh the costs, while others may see only the costs and not perceive the advantages. This is a common problem when management announces a change, say, in work procedures and doesn't explain to employees why the change is needed. Management expects advantages in terms of increased efficiency, but workers may see the change as another arbitrary, ill-informed management rule that causes headaches for those who must carry it out.

It is important to recognize that employees' assessments can be more accurate than management's; they may know a change won't work even if management doesn't. In this case, resistance to change is beneficial for the organization. Thus, even though management typically considers resistance a challenge to be overcome, it may actually represent an important signal that a proposed change requires further, more open-minded scrutiny.

A general model for managing resistance

Figure 18.2 shows that motivating people to change often requires three basic stages: unfreezing, moving to institute the change, and refreezing.[11]

unfreezing Realizing that current practices are inappropriate and that new behavior must be enacted.

In the **unfreezing** stage, management realizes that its current practices are no longer appropriate and the company must break out of (unfreeze) its present mold by doing things differently. Unfreezing often results from an assessment of the company's adjustment to its present environment and its readiness for the future. The diagnosis should be thorough and unbiased. If management concludes that the fit between the company and its present or anticipated environment is poor, change is needed.

Particularly in turnaround situations, top management must take steps to unfreeze the old organization culture. People must come to recognize that some of the past ways of thinking, feeling, and doing things are obsolete.[12] Perhaps the most effective way to do this is to communicate to people the negative consequences of the old ways by comparing the organization's performance to its competitors'. As discussed in Chapter 15, management can share with employees data about costs, quality, and profits.[13] However, care must be taken not to arouse people's defensiveness by pinning the blame directly and entirely on them.[14]

performance gap The difference between actual performance and the desired performance.

An important contributor to unfreezing is the recognition of a performance gap, which can be a precipitator of major change. A **performance gap** is the difference between actual performance and the performance that should or could exist.[15] A gap typically implies poor performance; for example, sales, profits, stock price, or other financial indicators are down. This situation attracts management's attention, and management introduces changes to try to correct things. When Arthur C. Martinez launched at Sears what is arguably the greatest turnaround in American corporate history,[16] what really caught the attention of top executives were hard data comparing Sears' performance against Wal-Mart and the comment from a customer that "What I think about Sears is that it is a bunch of old, gray-haired men in dark suits sitting in a boardroom choosing bad merchandise."[17]

Another, very important form of performance gap can exist. This type of gap can occur when performance is good but someone realizes that it could be better. Thus, the gap is between what is and what *could be*. This is where entrepreneurs seize opportunities and where companies that engage in strategic maneuvering gain a competitive edge. It is where innovators with ideas look for opportunities for application. Whereas many change efforts begin with the negative, it often is more valuable to identify strengths and potential and then develop new modes of operating from that positive perspective.[18]

As an impetus for change, a performance gap can apply to the organization as a whole; it also applies to departments, groups, and individuals. If a department or work group is not performing as well as others in the company, or if it sees an opportunity that it can exploit, that unit will be motivated to change. Similarly, an individual may receive negative performance

figure 18.2
Implementing change

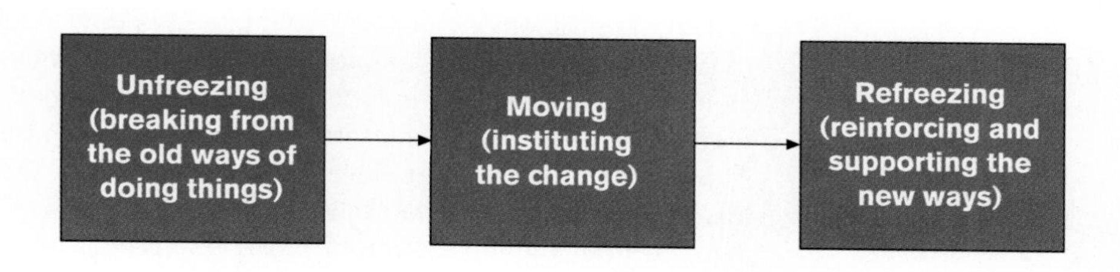

feedback or see a personal opportunity on which to capitalize. Under these circumstances, unfreezing begins, and people can be more motivated to change than if no such gap exists.

moving Instituting the change.

Moving to institute the change begins with establishing a vision of where the company is heading. You learned about vision in the leadership and other sections of the course. The vision can be realized through strategic, structural, cultural, and individual change. Strategic ideas are discussed throughout the book. Changes in structure may involve moving to the divisional, matrix, or some other appropriate form (discussed in Chapters 8 and 9). Cultural changes (Chapter 9) are institutionalized through effective leadership (Chapters 12 through 15). Individuals will change as new people join the company (Chapters 10 and 11) and as people throughout the organization adopt the leader's new vision for the future.

refreezing Strengthening the new behaviors that support the change.

Finally, **refreezing** means strengthening the new behaviors that support the change. The changes must be diffused and stabilized throughout the company. Refreezing involves implementing control systems that support the change (Chapter 16), applying corrective action when necessary, and reinforcing behaviors and performance (Chapter 13) that support the agenda. Management should consistently support and reward all evidence of movement in the right direction.[19]

In today's organizations, refreezing is not always the best third step, if it creates new behaviors that are as rigid as the old ones. The ideal new culture is one of continuous change. Refreezing is appropriate when it permanently installs behaviors that maintain essential core values, such as a focus on important business results and those maintained by the companies that are "built to last." But refreezing should not create new rigidities that might become dysfunctional as the business environment continues to change.[20] The behaviors that should be refrozen are those that promote continued adaptability, flexibility, experimentation, assessment of results, and continuous improvement. In other words, lock in key values, capabilities, and strategic mission, but not necessarily specific management practices and procedures.

From the Pages of BusinessWeek

A Hollywood Performance Gap: Will it Unfreeze?

Sony-Columbia, Time Warner, Walt Disney, and other TV producers have realized huge profits by exporting reruns of domestic hits to the huge European market. And they expected to keep doing so. They assumed that U.S. pop culture is eminently exportable–which it was, for a time.

They now know otherwise; the competitive landscape has changed dramatically. And Hollywood now must change its ways. If they want to succeed in the future as they have in the past, they must invest more to adapt to local markets.

In the past, reruns of TV sitcoms and shows like "Dallas," "Dynasty," and "Bonanza" have been huge hits in Europe and immensely profitable for the Hollywood producers. And currently, "Baywatch" and "Santa Barbara" are big hits in Europe. But recently the appeal of U.S. products has dropped. German viewers rejected "Who's the Boss" because its living room set had stairs leading to the second floor (few German homes are built this way) and because they didn't like the "American" ring of the telephone.

But the problem is not just local taste–it is now local competition. An explosion of European producers has created a major competitive threat. They produce their own TV shows that play to local tastes, and the market is eating them up. States a French actress, "Our characters eat cheese, not hamburgers."

MTV attracts far fewer viewers than two clones, Germany's Viva and France's MCM. Most French cable networks carried CNN–until France's TF1 launched its own 24-hour all-news station. Now, "CNN will never be more than an ex-pat station," says one industry observer. And states another, NBC's Super Channel "doesn't get big enough audiences to even bother measuring."

As the European TV industry grows, its executives are hoping to squeeze Hollywood into smaller and smaller segments of European airtime. And, says a French producer, "We need to crack the American market."

Source: W. Echikson, D. Woodruff, M. Larner, and A. Robinson, "Move over, Hollywood!" *Business Week*, December 15, 1997, 24–27.

Specific approaches to enlist cooperation As discussed earlier, management must enlist the cooperation of its people to implement a change. But how can managers get people to cooperate? How, specifically, can they manage their employees' resistance to change?

Most managers underestimate the variety of ways they can influence people during a period of change.[21] Several effective approaches to managing resistance and enlisting cooperation are available, as described in Table 18.2:

1. **Education and communication.** Management should educate people about upcoming changes before they occur. It should communicate not only the *nature* of the change but its *logic*. This process can include one-on-one discussions, presentations to groups, or

table 18.2 Methods for dealing with resistance to change

Approach	Commonly used in situations	Advantages	Drawbacks
Education and communication	Where there is a lack of information or inaccurate information and analysis.	Once persuaded, people will often help with the implementation of the change.	Can be very time-consuming if lots of people are involved.
Participation and involvement	Where the initiators do not have all the information they need to design the change, and where others have considerable power to resist.	People who participate will be committed to implementing change, and any relevant information they have will be integrated into the change plan.	Can be very time-consuming if participators design an inappropriate change.
Facilitation and support	Where people are resisting because of adjustment problems.	No other approach works as well with adjustment problems.	Can be time-consuming and expensive, and still fail.
Negotiation and agreement	Where someone or some group will clearly lose out in a change, and where that group has considerable power to resist.	Sometimes it is a relatively easy way to avoid major resistance.	Can be too expensive in many cases if it alerts others to negotiate for compliance.
Manipulation and cooptation	Where other tactics will not work, or are too expensive.	It can be a relatively quick and inexpensive solution to resistance problems.	Can lead to future problems if people feel manipulated.
Explicit and implicit coercion	Where speed is essential, and the change initiators possess considerable power.	It is speedy and can overcome any kind of resistance.	Can be risky if it leaves people angry at the initiators.

Source: Reprinted by permission of the *Harvard Business Review*. An exhibit from "Choosing Strategies for Change" by John P. Kotter and Leonard A. Schlesinger (March–April 1979).

reports and memos. When Arthur Martinez launched the Sears revival, he began by communicating clearly that he was not going to be the same kind of leader the company had had throughout its history, leading it by the early 1990s to the brink of bankruptcy. Previous top executives were ceremonial, remote, not personally involved in the details of the business. Martinez personally facilitated meetings, conveying that he was in the fight with everyone; was not going to sit in his office, criticize, and make proclamations; and "was going to be on the ground with them involved in the steps we had to take to get this business put back together."[22]

2. **Participation and involvement.** It is important to listen to the people who are affected by the change. They should be involved in the change's design and implementation. When feasible, management should use their advice. Often it will be useful, and it may lead to consideration of important issues previously overlooked. At Sears, Martinez said, "I *really* wanted to hear what [his people] had to say . . . there was no way I . . . could have all the answers. Their input and constructive thinking processes were critical to get us moving again."[23] He went deep into the management ranks to develop a clear corporate strategy, and formed teams of executives and employees to scour the country to find concrete ideas for making Sears a better place to work, shop, and invest.[24]

As you learned in Chapter 3, people who are involved in decisions understand them more fully and are more committed to them. People's understanding and commitment are important ingredients in the successful implementation of a change. Participation also provides an excellent opportunity for education and communication.

3. **Facilitation and support.** Management should make the change as easy as possible for employees and be supportive of their efforts. Facilitation involves providing the training and other resources people need to carry out the change and perform their jobs under the new circumstances. This step often includes decentralizing authority and empowering people, that is, giving them the power to make the decisions and changes needed to improve their performance.

Offering support involves listening patiently to problems, being understanding if performance drops temporarily or the change is not perfected immediately, and generally being on the employees' side and showing consideration during a difficult period.

4. **Negotiation and rewards.** When necessary, management can offer concrete incentives for cooperation with the change. Perhaps job enrichment is acceptable only with a higher wage rate, or a work rule change is resisted until management agrees to a concession on some other rule (say, regarding taking breaks). Even among higher-level managers, one executive might agree to another's idea for a policy change only in return for support on some other issue of more personal importance. Rewards such as bonuses, wages and salaries, recognition, job assignments, and perks can be examined and perhaps restructured to reinforce the direction of the change.[25]

5. **Manipulation and cooptation.** Sometimes managers use more subtle, covert tactics to implement change. One form of manipulation is cooptation, which involves giving a resisting individual a desirable role in the change process. The leader of a resisting group often is coopted. For example, management might invite a union leader to be a member of an executive committee or ask a key member of an outside organization to join the company's board of directors. As a person becomes involved in the change, he or she may become less resistant to the actions of the coopting group or organization.

6. **Coercion.** Some managers apply punishment or the threat of punishment to those who resist change. With this approach, managers use force to make people comply with their wishes. For example, a boss might insist that subordinates cooperate with the change and threaten them with job loss, denial of a promotion, or an unattractive work assignment.

Each approach to overcoming resistance has advantages and drawbacks, and, like many of the other situational or contingency management approaches described in the text, each is useful in different situations. Table 18.2 summarizes the advantages, drawbacks, and appropriate circumstances for these approaches to managing resistance to change. As the table implies, managers should not use just one or two general approaches, regardless of the circumstances. Effective change managers are familiar with the various approaches and know how to apply them according to the situation.

Throughout the process, change leaders need to build in stability. Recall from the companies that were "built to last," they all have essential core characteristics of which they don't lose sight. In the midst of change, turmoil, and uncertainty, people need anchors onto which they can latch. This means keeping some things constant and visible, such as the organization's values and mission. It can help further to maintain the visibility of key people, continue key assignments and projects, and make announcements about which organizational components will not change. Such anchors will reduce anxiety and help overcome resistance.

Harmonizing multiple changes

total organization change Introducting and sustaining multiple policies, practices, and procedures across multiple units and levels.

There are no "silver bullets," or single-shot methods of changing organizations for success. Single shots rarely hit a challenging target. Usually, many issues need simultaneous attention, and any single, small changes will be absorbed by the prevailing culture and disappear. **Total organization change** involves introducing and sustaining multiple policies, practices, and procedures across multiple units and levels.[26] Such change affects the thinking and behavior of everyone in the organization, can enhance the organization's culture and success, and can be sustained over time.

A survey at a Harvard Business School conference found that the average attendee's company had five major change efforts going on at once.[27] The most common change programs were the things you have studied in this course: continuous improvement, TQM, time-based competition, and creation of a learning organization, a team-based organization, a network organization, core competencies, and strategic alliances. The problem is, these efforts usually are simultaneous but not coordinated. The result for the people involved is confusion, frustration, low morale, and low motivation.

Because companies introduce new changes constantly, many people complain about their companies' "flavor-of-the-month" approach to change. That is, employees often see many change efforts as just the company's jumping on board the latest bandwagon or fad. The more these change fads come and go, the more cynical people become, and the more difficult it is to get them committed to making the change a success.[28]

In this context, it helps tremendously to avoid fads. If a change initiative is nothing more than a passing fad, why should people invest their energy and time in it? Before initiating change, management should ask:[29] Will it really make a difference in results? Will it help provide employees with information, knowledge, power, and rewards to become more fully involved in making the business succeed and thrive? Does it really help people add value throughout their work? Does it help us focus better on customers and the things they value?

Management also needs to "connect the dots"—that is, integrate the various efforts into a coherent picture that people can see, understand, and get behind.[30] You connect the dots by understanding each change program and what its goals are, by identifying similarities among the programs and identifying their differences, and by dropping programs that don't meet priority goals with a clear results orientation. Most important, you do it by communicating to everyone concerned the common themes among the various programs: their common rationales, objectives, and methods. You show them how the various parts fit the strategic big picture, and how the changes will make things better for the company and its people. You must communicate these things thoroughly, honestly, and frequently.[31]

Leading change

Successful change requires managers to actively lead it. The essential activities of leading change are summarized in Figure 18.3.

figure 18.3
Leading change

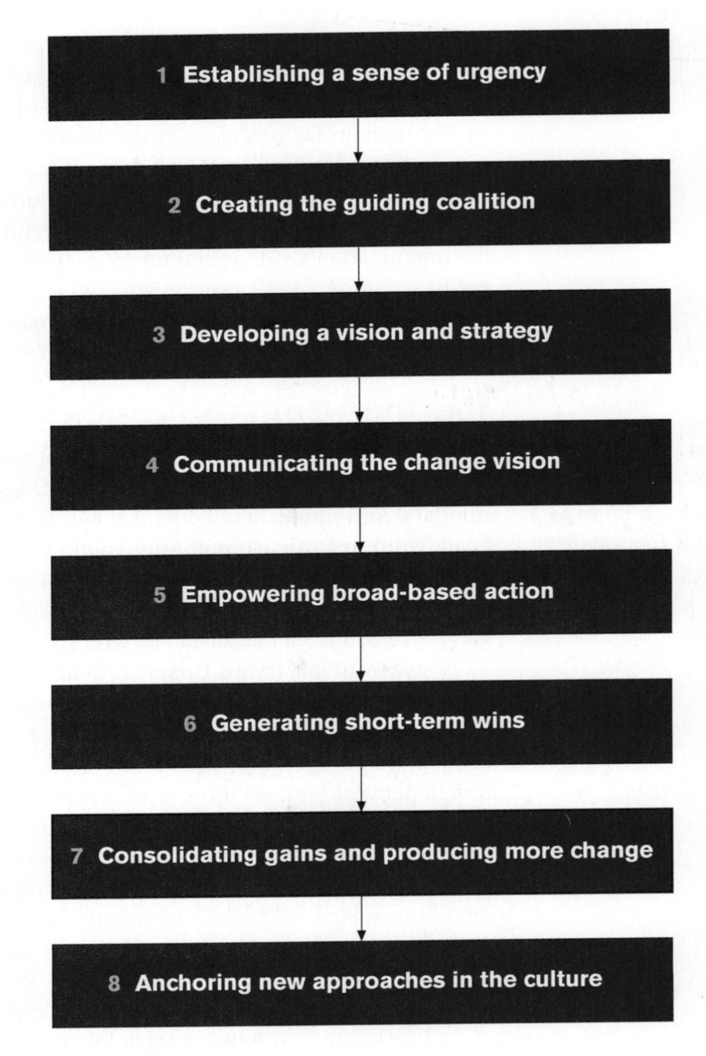

Source: J. Kotter, *Leading Change* (Boston: Harvard Business School Press, 1996).

A crucial responsibility for change leaders is to *establish a sense of urgency.*[32] This requires examining current realities and pressures in the marketplace and the competitive arena, identifying both crises and opportunities, and being frank and honest about them. This is an important component, in part because so many large companies have grown complacent, like Sears before its turnaround in the mid-1990s. At Sears, when Arthur Martinez took over, he stated publicly that they would have a comprehensive plan by Christmas, just 100 days away.

Figure 18.4 shows some of the common reasons for complacency. To stop complacency and create urgency, the manager can talk candidly about weaknesses compared to competitors, making a point of backing up statements with data. Other tactics include setting stretch goals, putting employees in direct contact with unhappy customers and shareholders, distributing worrisome information to all employees instead of merely engaging in management "happy talk," eliminating excessive perks, and highlighting to everyone the future opportunities that exist but that the organization so far has not pursued.

Ultimately, urgency is driven by compelling business reasons for change. Survival, competition, and winning in the marketplace are compelling; they provide a sense of

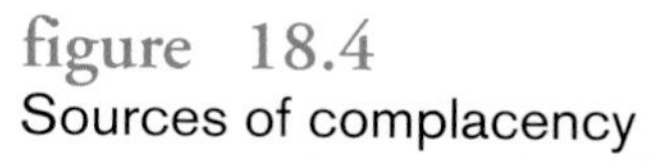
figure 18.4
Sources of complacency

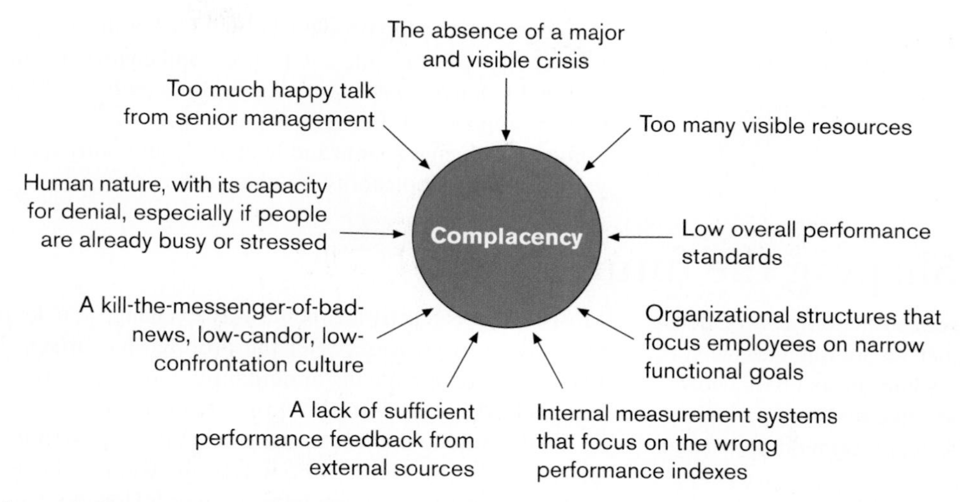

Source: J. Kotter, *Leading Change* (Boston: Harvard Business School Press, 1996).

direction and energy around change. Change becomes not a hobby, a luxury, or something nice to do, but a business necessity.[33]

To *create a guiding coalition* means putting together a group with enough power to lead the change. Change efforts fail when a sufficiently powerful coalition is not formed.[34] Major organization change requires leadership from top management, working as a team. But over time, the support must gradually expand outward and downward throughout the organization. Middle managers and supervisors are essential. Groups at all levels are the glue that can hold change efforts together, the medium for communicating about the changes, and the means for enacting new behaviors.[35]

Developing a vision and strategy, as discussed in earlier chapters, will direct the change effort. This process involves determining the idealized, expected state of affairs after the change is implemented. Because confusion is common during a major organizational change, the clearest possible image of the future state must be developed and conveyed to everyone.[36] This image, or vision, will be a target or guideline that can clarify expectations, dispel rumors, and mobilize people's energies. The portrait of the future also should communicate how the transition will occur, why the change is being implemented, and how people will be affected by the change. The power of a compelling vision is one of the most important aspects of change, and should not be underestimated or underutilized.

Communicating the change vision requires using every possible channel and opportunity to talk up and reinforce the vision and required new behaviors. Review Chapter 15 to recall how to communicate for maximum effectiveness. It is said that aspiring change leaders undercommunicate the vision by a factor of 10, or even 100 or 1,000, seriously undermining the chances of success.[37]

Empowering broad-based action means getting rid of obstacles to success, including systems and structures that constrain rather than facilitate. At Sears, Arthur Martinez got rid of the manual of rules and procedures that was 29,000 pages long, replacing it with a slim folder with a one-page letter from him and the broad outlines of shared beliefs, principles, and ethical codes.[38] Encourage risk taking and experimentation, and empower people by providing information, knowledge, authority, and rewards, as described in Chapter 13.

Generate short-term wins. Don't wait for the ultimate grand realization of the vision. Plan for and create small victories that indicate to everyone that progress is being made. Recognize and reward the people who made the wins possible, doing it as visibly as you can so people notice and the positive message permeates the organization.

Make sure you *consolidate gains and produce more change.* With the well-earned credibility of previous successes, keep changing things in ways that support the vision. Hire, promote, and develop people who will further the vision. Reinvigorate the organization and your change efforts with new projects and change agents.

Finally, *anchor new approaches in the culture.*[39] Highlight positive results, communicate the connections between the new behaviors and the improved results, and keep developing new change agents and leaders. Continually increase the number of people joining you in taking responsibilty for change.[40]

Shaping the future

reactive change A response that occurs when events in the environment have already affected the firm's performance; problem-driven change.

proactive change A response that is initiated before a performance gap has occurred.

Most change is reactive. A better way to change is to be proactive. **Reactive** change means responding to pressure, after the problem has arisen. It also implies being a follower. **Proactive** change means anticipating and preparing for an uncertain future. It implies being a leader and *creating* the future you want.

On the road to the future, there are drivers, passengers, and road kill. Put another way: On the road to the future, who will be the windshield, and who will be the bug?[41]

Needless to say, it's best to be a driver.[42] How do you become a driver? By being proactive more than merely reactive. By exercising foresight, learning continuously, pursuing growth, seizing advantage, and creating futures.

Exercising foresight

If you think only about the present, or wallow in the uncertainties of the future, your future is just a roll of the dice. It is far better to exercise foresight, set an agenda for the future, and pursue it with everything you've got.

So, contemplate and envision the future.

Envisioning the future

Nissan's vision for its future is that it must provide the five *A*s: any volume, anytime, anybody, anywhere, anything.

Dow Jones' strategic goal is providing "business and financial news and information however, wherever, and whenever customers want to receive it."

And Motorola asks, "How do you use your Motorola pager?" Answers: "Anytime," "For anything," and "Anywhere I want."

At Taco Bell, the anywhere, anytime vision is for great-tasting food, delivered fast, customized yet low-priced. Taco Bell had 9,000 points of access (POAs) in 1993, including not only restaurants but also carts, kiosks, vans, and express units in high school and college cafeterias, airports, malls, gas stations, convenience stores, and the Moscow subway station. Its goal is to have 200,000 POAs by the turn of the century.

Oticon, the Danish hearing aid manufacturer, leveraged an approach it calls the "Human Link"—combining the expertise of scientists, physicians, hearing care professionals, and users—to create hearing aids that are molded and tuned to the precise needs of each customer's needs and preferences. Now it is introducing a new generation of digital hearing aids. Its Digifocus hearing aids "learn." They can process over 100 sound differentiating parameters, tuned and adapted to each individual, and adjust automatically to different sound environments. The vision is a product and service that can sense, respond, and adapt continually to customer experiences.

Sources: J. Pine, B. Victor, and A. Boynton, "Making Mass Customization Work," *Harvard Business Review,* September–October 1993, pp. 108–22; J. Slocum, Jr., M. McGill, and D. Lei, "The New Learning Strategy: Anytime, Anything, Anywhere," *Organizational Dynamics,* Autumn 1994, pp. 33–47; B. Victor and A. Boynton, *Invented Here.* (Boston: Harvard Business School Press, 1998).

Taco Bell's "anywhere, anytime" vision has led to a goal of creating 200,000 points of access by the turn of the century.
[Courtesy of Taco Bell Corporation]

If you and your bosses think you know what you need to do to succeed in the future, you probably need a dose of humility—it is impossible to know the future with certainty. But this does not need to be a reactive, defeatist view. It can be highly proactive, in a subtle but vitally important way. Managers may acknowledge that they don't know exactly what customers will want in the future, and what products they will have to deliver. But they *can* know that they have, or can acquire, the *capabilities* to deliver.[43] Thus, the focus is on identifying and building core competencies, as discussed in earlier chapters, and on improving continuously in the activities that will enable your firm to succeed in the future.

Learning continuously

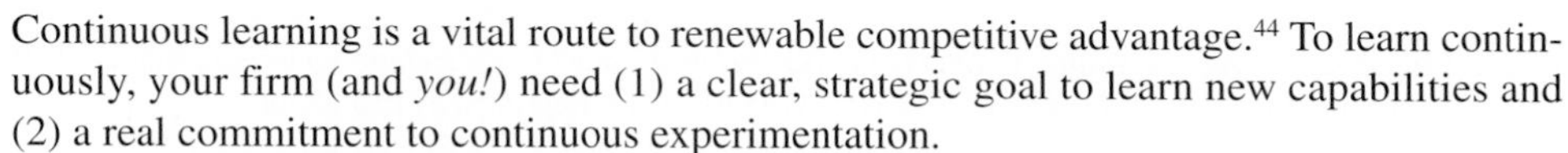

Continuous learning is a vital route to renewable competitive advantage.[44] To learn continuously, your firm (and *you!*) need (1) a clear, strategic goal to learn new capabilities and (2) a real commitment to continuous experimentation.

Continuous improvement is a key to excellence. Companies and individuals striving for world-class excellence must improve constantly. Continuous improvement, a concept introduced in Chapter 17 and made legendary by Toyota Motor Company, is a relentless drive to be better in every way: to find faster, more-efficient, low-cost methods to develop new, high-quality products. When Toyota became so successful at making low-cost, defect-free cars, it set the quality standard.[45]

In an environment of continuous improvement, everyone engages in exploration, discovery, and action, continually learns what is effective and what is not, and adjusts and improves accordingly. Figure 18.5 elaborates. With this philosophy, and the appropriate approaches, your company *can* have it all: low cost, high quality, flexibility, responsiveness, innovation, and speed. This process also generates learning on a more individual level, generating personal growth and development.

As described in other chapters, experimentation means trying new things in the spirit of continuous improvement, investing in research and long-term development projects, encouraging risks, and tolerating failures. Companies like J&J, 3M, and Bally Engineering practice self-obsolescence. That is, they try to make their own products obsolete. Why? Because the products will become obsolete sooner or later, and it's better to replace them with their own new products than to have competitors beat them to it. Home Depot will even close a thriving store and open two smaller ones in an effort to keep improving customers' shopping experiences.[46]

figure 18.5 Learning cycle: explore, discover, act

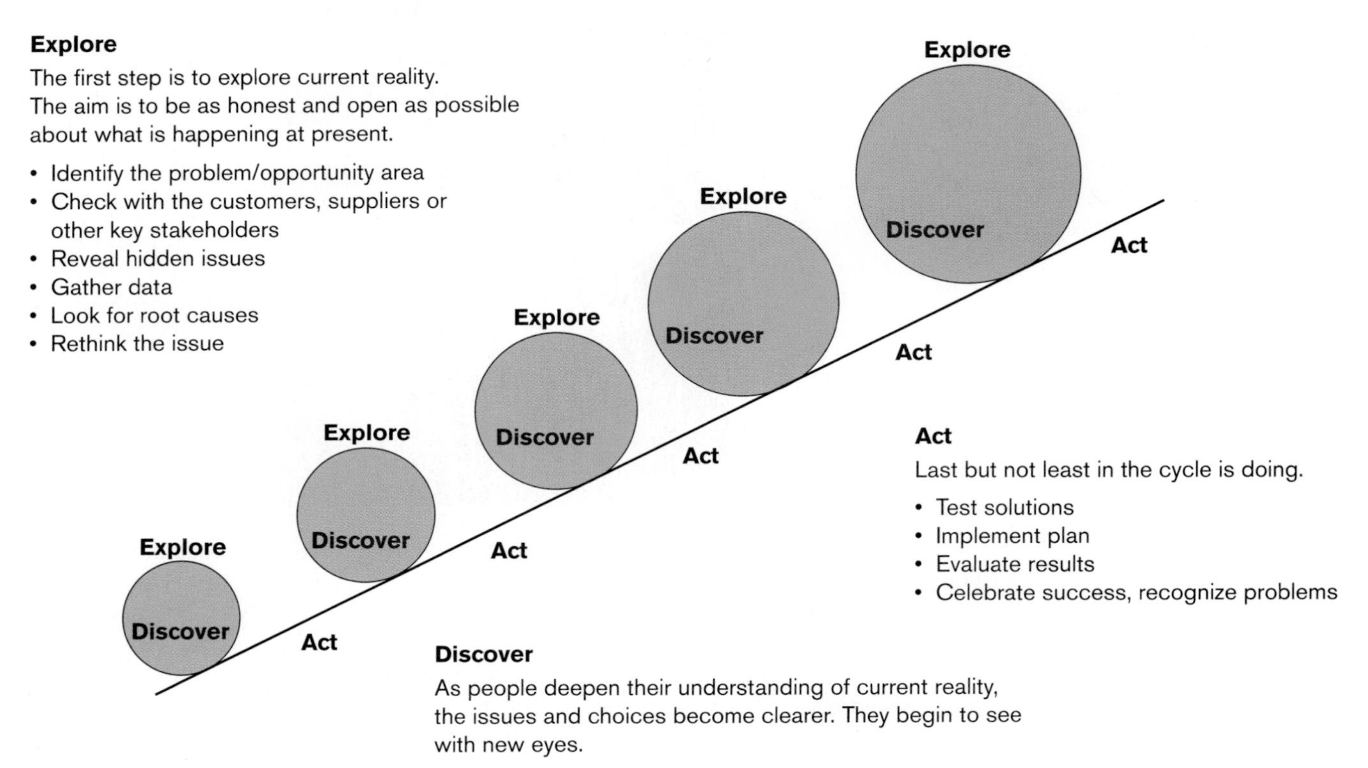

Explore
The first step is to explore current reality.
The aim is to be as honest and open as possible about what is happening at present.
• Identify the problem/opportunity area
• Check with the customers, suppliers or other key stakeholders
• Reveal hidden issues
• Gather data
• Look for root causes
• Rethink the issue
Explore
Discover
Act
Explore
Discover
Act
Explore
Discover
Act
Explore
Discover
Act
Explore
Discover
Act
Act
Last but not least in the cycle is doing.
• Test solutions
• Implement plan
• Evaluate results
• Celebrate success, recognize problems
Discover
As people deepen their understanding of current reality, the issues and choices become clearer. They begin to see with new eyes.
• Identify possible solutions
• Plan
• Anticipate problems

Source: From *Leaning into the Future: Changing the Way People Change Organizations* by George Binney and Colin Williams; published by Nicholas Brealey Publishing Ltd., Tel: (0171) 430-0224, Fax: (0171) 404-8311. Reprinted by permission.

Similarly, Sony and Mitsubishi use "systematic abandonment" of their products.[47] When they introduce a new product, they establish a "sunset date" at which they will drop the product. Thus, they create a deadline for introducing a future product that will replace the brand new product, and begin those development efforts immediately. Their goal is to create three new products for every one they phase out: an incrementally improved product, a new product spin-off, and an entirely new innovation.

Pursuing growth

Cutting costs can be vitally important, but can only get you so far. You also must grow. "You can't save your way to prosperity. That alone won't get you there," says Wayne Calloway, CEO of PepsiCo.[48] Downsizing, reengineering, and other approaches to cost cutting sooner or later will reach their limits. You must also, then, be able to go for growth by increasing revenues. This requires focusing on things such as technology, investment, product development, and creation of new markets.

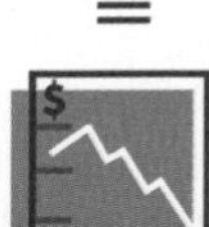

In other words, you can raise profits by shrinking expenses (the denominator in financial ratios), and also by increasing revenues (the numerator).[49] Cutting costs is relatively easy. Increasing revenues is more difficult. Unfortunately, the numerator has not received nearly the emphasis it deserves. States an influential management expert, "We've produced a generation of denominator managers in the U.S."[50]

How many companies pictured at this electronics convention do you think practice "systematic abandonment?" How many products represented will be spun-off or dropped by the time you read this?
[Courtesy of Softbank COMDEX]

At Sears, Martinez started slashing costs immediately. This step was essential to survival. But he then turned his attention to growth. "The real enduring success in this business has to do with revenue growth and market share growth."[51] Martinez put his retailing instincts to work, and along with the help of people throughout Sears attained dramatic increases in sales, operating profit margins, and earnings. Sears had its first billion-dollar week in December 1995.

Strategic growth

- Union Carbide has a low-cost strategy, but it achieves low cost *and growth* through its competitive advantage in technology. Two decades ago it developed a low-cost process for making polyethylene, the most widely used basic plastic. And *it has constantly improved the process ever since* in order to increase its lead.
- Bausch & Lomb sold its weak businesses and used the money to modernize technology in its remaining businesses. It also scoured the globe asking consumers and health care professionals for expansion ideas. Its contact lenses and solutions grew into a general eye care business, and the company entered a number of other health-related growth businesses as well. Bausch & Lomb is now *entering emerging markets;* it *created* and dominates the Chinese contact lens market, and is expanding into India and Poland.
- CEO Harry Merlo of Louisiana-Pacific has devised new products to *substitute for old standards,* and is satisfying new customers and markets. He developed waferwood and took business away from plywood, and he developed a new board that is replacing Sheetrock because it is more soundproof, holds nails better, breaks less easily, and is produced more efficiently.
- Dell Computer and Price/Costco thrive via a strategy of *high quality bought easily and inexpensively.* Price/Costco is a chain of warehouse club stores. Its competitors offer some 50,000 items, whereas Price/Costco offers only 3,500 items. But it succeeds by *operational excellence* that customers love because it saves them hassle *and* money *and* offers an enjoyable shopping experience. Price/Costco rigorously evaluates and chooses and then sells only the best brand in each product category. This allows it to buy large quantities and negotiate better prices than

Price/Costco is a chain of warehouse club stores that sells only the best brand in each product category.
[David Perry/Price/Costco]

competitors. Customers enjoy lower prices, and they don't have to spend time making decisions about which brand of coffee or appliance to buy. New items, a value-of-the-week atmosphere, and the smell of baking bread and pastries add to the pleasure of shopping.

- PepsiCo's growth is due in large part to its corporate culture. CEO Wayne Calloway wants managers to *look out on the competitive horizon* rather than on the trivial, the bureaucratic, and traditional markets. He believes growth keeps his people energized, vibrant, and ready for the future. He encourages risk taking, and wants his managers to *completely reconceive their businesses.* Calloway states, "It's that whole mindset that says, 'I don't have to keep on with what I'm doing. I can change the game.'" PepsiCo's sales have grown at an annual compound rate of 17 percent since 1984.
- Shaw Industries, a manufacturer of carpet, grew because it was able to *capitalize on discontinuities.* A discontinuity is an abrupt change in society, economics, policy, or technology that transforms industries. Discontinuities create powerful opportunities for those companies that act fast. Shaw Industries is a manufacturer of carpet. Two technological breakthroughs in the 1980s created the potential to transform the industry. Seeing the opportunity and acting faster than anyone else, Shaw executives took on $200 million in debt to install new manufacturing equipment and information systems. The company achieved far lower product costs than its competitors and halved the delivery time to retailers. The competition was crippled. Many gave up and sold out to Shaw. Shaw's market share rose from 5 percent to 35 percent.

Sources: M. Magnet, "Let's Go for Growth," *Fortune,* March 7, 1994, pp. 60–72; M. Treacy and F. Wiersema, "How Market Leaders Keep Their Edge," *Fortune,* February 6, 1995, pp. 88–98; S. Goldstein, "Exploit Discontinuities to Grow," *Strategy & Leadership,* September/October 1996, pp. 12–17.

A *Fortune* article concludes, "Without doubt, it's easier to get a dollar of profit growth by cutting costs than by raising revenues. But investors, the final arbiters of value, well know that those two dollars are very unlike in terms of the future they presage."[52] In other words, cost cutting is a start, but additionally essential to long-term great success are revenue growth and a proactive eye to the future.

Seizing advantage

In the period from 1986 to 1996, 17 companies in the Fortune 1000 grew total shareholder return by 35 percent or more per year.[53] How did they do it? They invented totally new industries, or completely reinvented existing industries. Harley-Davidson turned around by selling not just motorcycles, but nostalgia. Amgen broke the rules of the biotech industry by focusing not on what customers wanted, but on great science. Starbuck's took a commodity and began selling it in trendy stores. CarMax, Auto-By-Tel, AutoNation USA, and Driver's Mart are the companies reinventing the auto industry.[54]

To create new markets or transform industries—these are perhaps the ultimate forms of proactive change.[55] Competing for the future thus involves creating and dominating emerging opportunities. Consider:

Instead of . . .	Why not . . . ?
• fitting the firm to the environment	• change the environment to fit the firm
• preserving old advantages	• create new advantages
• locking in old markets	• create new markets
• investing in fixed assets	• invest in evolving/emerging opportunities

You need to create advantages. The challenge is not to maintain your position in the current competitive arena, but to create new competitive arenas, transform your industry, and imagine a future that others don't see. Creating advantage is better than playing catch-up through downsizing and reengineering. At best, such restructuring buys time; it cannot get you out ahead of the pack and buy world-class excellence.[56]

So, which should you and your firm do?

- Take the path of greatest familiarity, or the path of greatest opportunity, wherever that may lead?
- Be only a good benchmarker, or a pathbreaker?
- Focus just on product time to market, or on time to global preeminence?
- Be a product leader, or also a core competence leader?
- Place priority on short-term financial returns, or on making a real, long-term impact?
- Look to the past, or live for the future?
- Do only what seems doable, or what is difficult and worthwhile?
- Change what is, or create what isn't?
- Solve problems, or create entirely new opportunities?

Creating the future

adapters Companies that take the current industry structure, and its future evolution, as givens.

shapers Companies that try to change the structure of their industries, creating a future competitive landscape of their own design.

Companies can try different strategic postures to prepare to compete in an uncertain future. **Adapters** take the current industry structure, and its future evolution, as givens. They choose where and how to compete. This posture is taken by most companies in fairly predictable environments, by conducting standard strategic analysis and choosing how to compete.

In contrast, **shapers** try to change the structure of their industries, creating a future competitive landscape of their own design.[57] For example, Federal Express entered the mail-and-package delivery industry with a strategy of delivering overnight. FedEx almost went bankrupt in its first two years, but ultimately reshaped the industry. Its bet paid off hugely, forcing others like United Parcel Service to adapt.

To get ahead of the pack, create the future.

Creating futures

- Motorola sees a world in which telephone numbers will be assigned not to places but to people; small hand-held devices allow communication between people no matter where they may be; and people send video images and data, not just voice signals. To realize this world, Motorola knows it must strengthen its competencies in digital compression, flat screen displays, and battery technology.

- General Magic, a consortium including Motorola, Philips, AT&T, and others, envisions a world in which people use hand-held devices to visit a "virtual downtown" of travel agents, banks, libraries, and so on. "Information agents" in cyberspace make reservations, review financial data, or retrieve magazine articles. Has this world yet become a reality? Maybe not, but it never will, without the vision to create it. But vision and foresight, of course, must also be followed by creation.

- Dreamworks SKG was created by Steven Spielberg, Jeffrey Katzenberg, and David Geffen. Spielberg directed *ET* and *Jurassic Park,* among other great films. Katzenberg was responsible for the great recent animated films from the Disney Co. Geffen is the music executive and producer associated with Nirvana, Guns N' Roses, the Eagles, Tom Cruise movies, and Cats. Now they have joined forces to create what *Time* magazine calls the "prototype plugged-in multimedia company of the new millennium."

- Mondex International is a consortium of financial services providers and technology companies attempting to establish universal electronic-cash standards. It is spending big money on product development, infrastructure, and pilot experiments to gain quick customer acceptance.

- Netscape shaped Internet browser standards. In Netscape's case, the company did not have to rely on the usual big-bet spending that typifies industry re-shaping. Its leadership team was so highly respected in the industry that others just assumed Netscape's approach *must* be right.

Jeffrey Katzenberg, Steven Spielburg, and David Geffen joined forces to create Dreamworks SKG. The company has been billed as the "prototype plugged-in multimedia company of the new millennium," according to *Time* magazine. *[AP/Wide World Photos]*

Source: G. Hamel and C. K. Prahalad, *Competing for the Future* (Boston: Harvard Business School Press, 1994); R. Corliss, "Hey, Let's Put On a Show!" *Time,* March 27, 1995, pp. 54–60; and H. Courtney, J. Kirkland, and P. Viguerie, "Strategy under Uncertainty," *Harvard Business Review,* November–December 1997, pp. 66–79.

Creating the future is not for the faint-hearted; it requires high-stakes bets.[58] Eastman Kodak is spending $500 million per year to develop digital photography products. The company *hopes* it will change fundamentally the way people create, view, and store pictures. But Hewlett-Packard is pursuing its own, competing vision for reshaping the industry, centered around photo processing done in the home rather than in shops. Which will win? Or will they both? Or neither?

The Microsoft Network (MSN) aimed to become the standard for conducting transactions between networked computers. Microsoft bet big—not only with developmental costs, but in terms of attention, exposure, and credibility—that it could create the proprietary network and shape the evolution of electronic commerce. But it became clear that open networks would prevail, and Microsoft refocused its MSN concept around the Internet. Thus Microsoft's shaping posture failed, but it responded quickly by becoming an adapter. It adapted successfully because it closely monitored the evolution of the market (for example, growth in the numbers of MSN and Internet subscribers), was willing to cut its losses, and learned useful lessons from the experience. For example, its engineers had acquired useful new learning about general programming and product development.

Figure 18.6 illustrates the vast opportunity to create new markets. Articulated needs are those that customers acknowledge and try to satisfy. Unarticulated needs are those that customers have not yet experienced. Served customers are those to whom your company is now selling, and unserved customers are untapped markets.

Business-as-usual concentrates on the lower-left quadrant. The leaders who recreate the game are constantly trying to create new opportunities in the other three quadrants.[59]

Shaping your own future

If you are an organizational leader, and your organization operates in traditional ways, your key goal should be to create a revolution, genetically reengineering your company before it becomes a dinosaur of the modern era.[60] What should be the goals of the revolution? You've been learning about them throughout this course.

figure 18.6
Vast opportunity

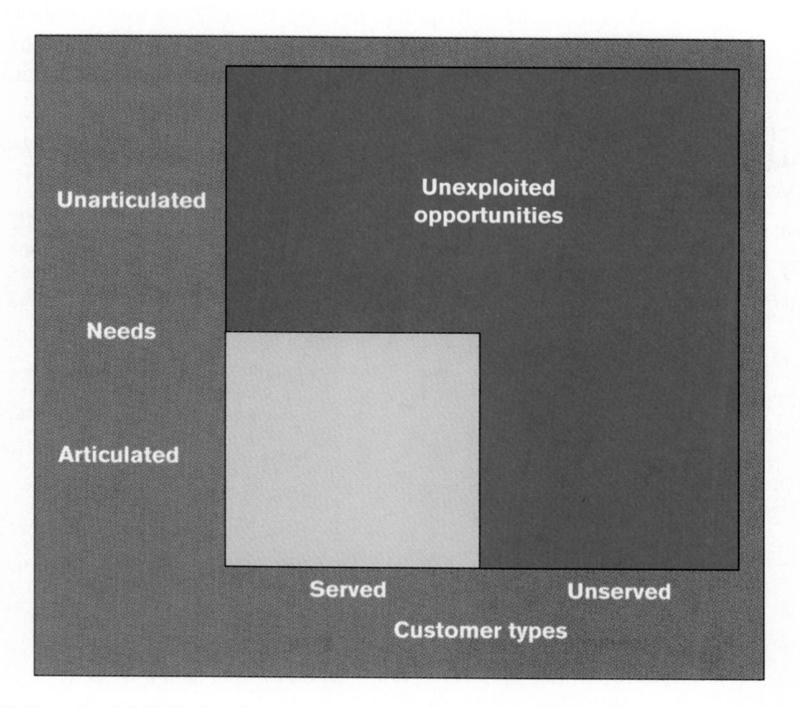

Source: G. Hamel and C. K. Prahalad, *Competing for the Future* (Boston: Harvard Business School Press, 1994).

But maybe you are not going to lead a revolution. Maybe you just want a successful career and a good life. You still must be able to deal with an economic environment that is increasingly competitive and fast-moving.[61] Creating the future you want for yourself requires setting high personal standards. Don't settle for mediocrity; don't assume that "good" is necessarily good enough—for yourself or for your employer. Try to avoid companies and industries that are less competitive than the world norm.[62]

Table 18.3 helps you think about how you can continually add value to your employer and also to yourself, as you upgrade your skills, your ability to contribute, your security with your current employer, and your ability to find alternative employment if necessary.

More advice, from the leading authors on career management:[63] Consciously and actively manage your own career. Develop marketable skills, and keep developing more. Make career choices based on personal growth, development, and learning opportunities. Look for positions that stretch you, and for bosses who develop their protégés. Seek out environments that provide training and opportunity to experiment and innovate. And know yourself: Assess your strengths and weaknesses, your true interests and ethical standards. If you are not already thinking in these terms and taking commensurate action, you should start now.

Additionally: Become indispensable to your organization. Be happy and enthusiastic in your job, and committed to doing great work, but don't be blindly loyal to one company. Be prepared to leave if necessary. View your job as an opportunity to prove what you can do and increase what you can do, not as a comfortable niche for the long term.[64] Go on your own if it meets your skills and temperament.

This points out the need to maintain your options. More and more, contemporary careers can involve leaving behind the large organization and going entrepreneurial, becoming self-employed in the "post-corporate world."[65] In such a career, independent individuals are free to make their own choices. They can flexibly and quickly respond to demands and opportunities. Developing start-up ventures, consulting, accepting temporary employment, doing project work for one organization and then another, working in professional partnerships, being a constant deal-maker—these can be the elements of a successful career. Ideally, this self-employed model can help provide a balanced approach to working and to living life at home and with family, because people have more control over their work activities and schedules.

This can sound like the ideal world. It also has downsides. The independence can be frightening, the future unpredictable. It can isolate "road warriors" who are always on the

table 18.3
Adding Value, Personally

Go beyond your job description:
- volunteer for projects.
- identify problems.
- initiate solutions.

Seek out others and share ideas and advice.

Offer your opinions and respect those of others.

Take an inventory of your skills every few months.

Learn something new every week.

Discover new ways to make a contribution.

Engage in active thought and deliberate action.

Take risks based on what you know and believe.

Recognize, research, and pursue opportunity.

Differentiate yourself.

Source: Compiled from C. Hakim, *We Are All Self-Employed,* (San Francisco: Berrett-Koehler, 1994).

go, working from their cars and airports, and interfere with social and family life.[66] Effective self-management is needed to keep things in perspective and in control.

Into the future Commit to lifelong learning. Lifelong learning includes being willing to seek new challenges and to reflect honestly on successes and failures.[67] Lifelong learning requires occasionally taking risks; moving outside of your "comfort zone;" honestly assessing the reasons behind your successes and failures; aggressively asking for and listening to other people's information and opinions; and being open to new ideas.

Honored as one of the best management books of the year in Europe, *Leaning into the Future* gets its title from a combination of the words "leading" and "learning."[68] The two perspectives, on the surface, appear very different. But they also are powerful when pursued in complementary ways. Figure 18.7 captures the synergies of combining both leading and learning. Success in the future will come from shaping the future *and* adapting to the world;

figure 18.7 Leaning into the future

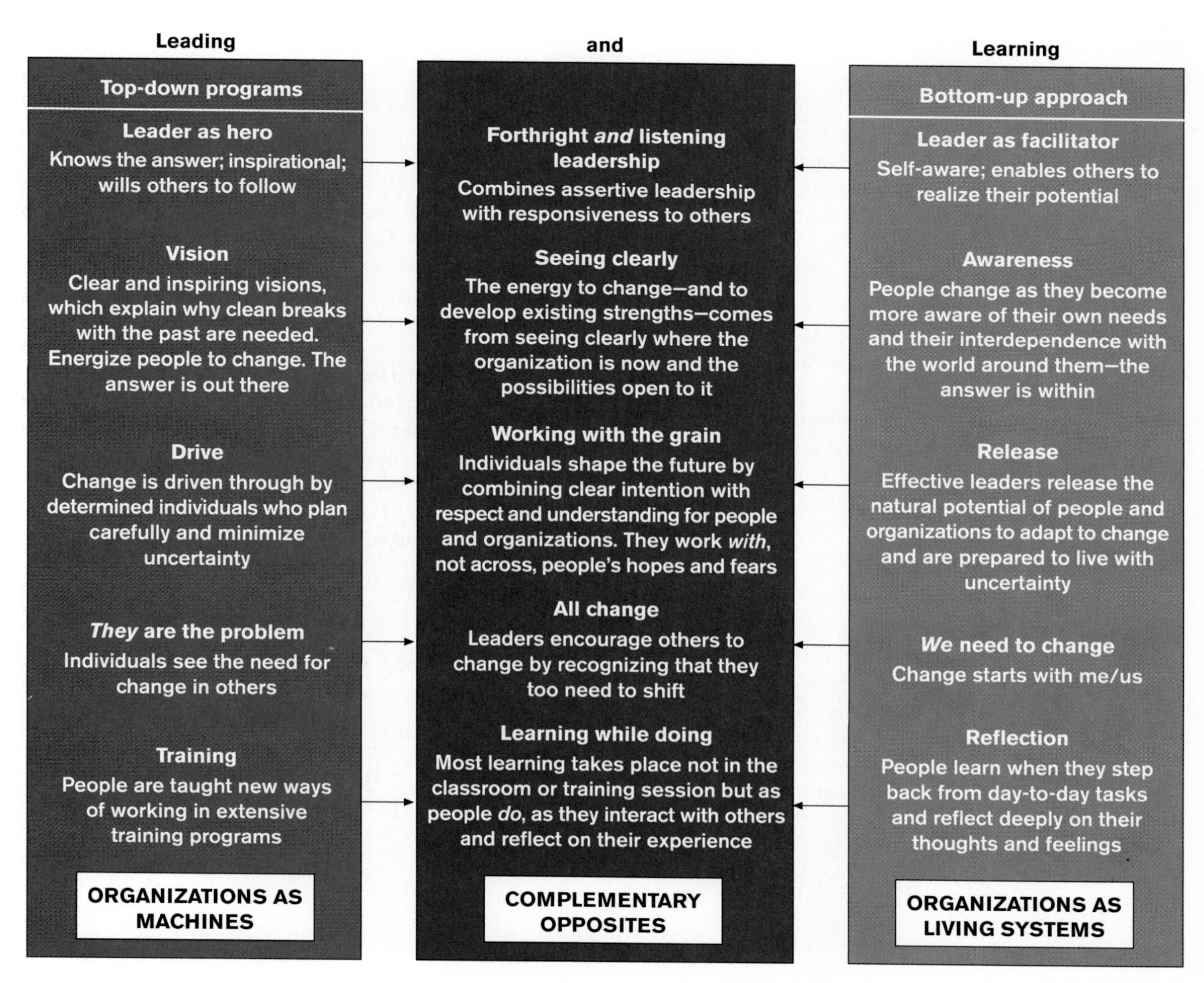

Source: From *Leaning into the Future: Changing the Way People Change Organizations* by George Binney and Colin Williams; published by Nicholas Brealey Publishing Ltd., Tel: (0171) 430-0224, Fax: (0171) 404-8311. Reprinted by permission.

being clear about what you want to change *and* being responsive to others' perspectives; passionately pursuing your vision *and* understanding current realities; leading *and* learning.

This is another example of an important concept from the beginning of the chapter. For yourself, as well as for your organization, recognize and live the genius of the *and.*

Key terms

Adapters, p. 623
Genius of the "and," p. 608
Moving, p. 612
Performance gap, p. 611
Proactive change, p. 618
Reactive change, p. 618
Refreezing, p. 612
Shapers, p. 623
Total organization change, p. 615
Tyranny of the "or," p. 607
Unfreezing, p. 611

Summary of learning objectives

Now that you have studied Chapter 18, you should know:

What it takes to be world class.

You need to strive for world-class excellence, which means using the very best and latest knowledge and ideas to operate at the highest standards of any place anywhere. Sustainable greatness comes from, among other things, having strong core values, living those values constantly, striving for continuous improvement, experimenting, and always trying to do better tomorrow than today. It is essential to not fall prey to the tyranny of the *or,* that is, the belief that one important goal can be attained only at the expense of the other. The genius of the *and* is that multiple important goals can be achieved simultaneously and synergistically.

How to manage change effectively.

Effective change management occurs when the organization moves from its current state to a desired future state without excessive cost to the organization or its people. People resist change for a variety of reasons, including inertia, poor timing, surprise, peer pressure, self-interest, misunderstanding, and different information about (and assessments of) the change.

Motivating people to change requires a general process of unfreezing, moving, and refreezing, with the caveat that appropriate and not inappropriate behaviors be "refrozen." More specific techniques to motivate people to change include education and communication, participation and involvement, facilitation and support, negotiation and rewards, manipulation and cooptation, and coercion. Each approach has strengths, weaknesses, and appropriate uses, and multiple approaches can be used. More generally, it is important to harmonize the multiple changes that are occurring throughout the organization.

Effective change requires active leadership, including creating a sense of urgency, forming a guiding coalition, developing a vision and strategy, communicating the change vision, empowering broad-based action, generating short-term wins, consolidating gains and producing more change, and anchoring the new approaches in the culture.

How to best prepare for the future.

Preparing for an uncertain future requires a proactive approach. Being proactive includes exercising foresight, learning continuously, pursuing growth, seizing advantages, and creating the future. You can proactively shape your own future by actively managing your career and your personal development, and becoming an active leader and a lifelong learner.

Discussion questions

1. Review the quotes on page 609, in "Resistance to Becoming World Class." Why do some people resist the goal of becoming world class? What lies behind the quotes? How can this resistance be overcome?

2. Generate specific examples of world-class business that you have seen as a consumer. Also, generate examples of poor business practice. Why and how do some companies inspire world-class practices, while others fail?

3. How can you make the concept of continuous improvement useful to you in your personal life and your career?

4. Generate and discuss examples of problems and opportunities that have inspired change, both in businesses and in you, personally.

5. Choose some specific types of changes you would like to see happen in groups or organizations with which you are familiar. Imagine that you were to try to bring about these changes. What sources of resistance should you anticipate? How would you manage the resistance?

6. How would you "exercise foresight" with regard to your personal life and career?

7. Develop a specific plan for becoming a "continuous learner."

8. Consider a business with which you are familiar and discuss some ideas for how it should pursue a growth strategy. What are some pros and cons to your ideas? How might the best ideas be implemented?

9. In your own words, what does the idea of "creating the future" mean to you? How can you put this concept to good use? Again, generate some specific ideas that you can really use.

Concluding Case

The future of the automobile industry

How many great brand names can you identify among the European automakers? BMW, Mercedes Benz, Volkswagen . . . The impressive list goes on, their success great and global, their reputations and their futures secure. Or so it seems. But some observers say that in Europe the car industry is in crisis, and that some venerable brands will end up in the graveyard.

The market appears to be saturated. Global competition is intense. Environmental regulations are more stringent. Even as cars are becoming more luxurious, prices are falling. Manufacturing overcapacity in Europe stands at seven million cars a year. Not only is this position untenable, but it's getting worse; the major manufacturers are rushing to build more, each believing that it will survive while others will not.

The French manufacturers are struggling in markets outside of France; it is rumored that Renault and Peugeot will merge. In Italy, Fiat's new models are doing well, but its famed Alfa-Romeo brand is hurting. In England, Rover (owned by BMW) needs new models and Ford's factory suffers from low productivity. In Germany, Mercedes is doing well but Volkswagen's margins and profits are poor despite increased sales.

Forecasters predict flat sales at best in 1998 and 1999, and a sharp decline by 2000. But the head of General Motors International dismisses the forecast as mere crystal-ball gazing into an unknowable future.

BMW and Porsche have responded by offering new models that can cruise the autobahn at 280 kilometres (168 miles) per hour, while environmentalists protest. At the other extreme, Mercedes has launched the Smart,

Competition in the automobile industry is extremely intense. There is likely to be a shakeout among major companies as developing countries begin to manufacture their own brands. In the end, only world class competitors—those who compete on cost, quality, speed and innovation—will survive. *[Courtsy of Mercedes Benz]*

a downmarket compact for in-town driving. Designed in collaboration with Swatch, the Swiss watchmaker, the Smart was described by the German press as having room for two people and two beer crates. It is described elsewhere as the clearest indication that the industry is trying to rethink itself.

The established companies now must compete with vehicles from Poland and the Czech Republic, where labor costs can be only one-eighth as high as some in the West. And even these countries have high labor costs compared to other countries soon to enter the global auto industry, such as Indonesia, India, and China.

According to Jurgen Hubbert, chairman of Mercedes-Benz cars, "Nothing is rosy. The only way to survive in the future is by being competitive, by being swifter and better. Competition will only get tougher."

Discussion questions

1. What is the relevance of this description of Europe to the U.S. auto industry?

2. Put yourself in the following positions and describe the best ways to help your company, and yourself, better prepare for and compete in the future:

- A top executive in an auto manufacturer.
- A middle manager in the same company.
- A member of a production team in a manufacturing plant in the same company.
- A local car dealer.
- A supplier to a local auto plant.
- A restaurant owner with a customer base made up of auto plant employees.
- A political leader of a community heavily dependent on the auto plant.

3. Imagine that you are a small-business owner in a small community. A group of local community and business leaders approaches you to join them in their efforts to woo a foreign manufacturer to build an auto plant in your community. They say it's the only way to ensure a thriving future for the community.

Another group resists the idea, maintaining that the community is doing fine now, bringing in such a dominant player would cause problems, and there are other alternatives to ensuring a strong future.

What do you think? What will you do?

Source: M. Porter and D. Brierley, "Has the Car Reached the End of the Road?" *The European*, September 18, 1997, cover story, pp. 8–13.

Video Case

Managing organizational change at ABTCO

Most modern observers of economic and social trends agree that the global economy has been experiencing an accelerating pace of change. New technologies, new competitive pressures, and new organizational structures have created an environment in which organizations are also changing rapidly. But change is disconcerting for most people, and it's even more disconcerting for employees when entire organizations are faced with change. There are many reasons for employee resistance to change. Fortunately, resistance to change can be overcome by using various techniques for managing change. Many techniques are designed to give employees a stake in the outcomes of change.

Managing change requires that managers have a sense of the depth of the intervention they are making. Depth of intervention is defined as the degree of change that the intervention is intended to bring about. Team building and empowerment are examples of moderate depth intervention. The greater the depth of the intervention, the greater the amount of resistance.

The culture and structure of a company significantly affect the kinds of changes that can occur. To reshape the internal culture of a company, managers can adjust such elements as the internal reward system, educational and training opportunities, or the hiring and socialization processes. Through training and development, managers can encourage more interaction among employees, which helps them become more attuned to the culture and helps them feel a part of the change process. These important techniques for managing organizational change were effectively applied at Abitibi-Price Building Products Company.

Michigan-based Abitibi-Price, one of the largest building products and newsprint businesses in North America, found itself in serious financial trouble in the early 1990s. Sales were weak, especially in the newsprint division, and annual earnings had declined steadily from a high of $188.2 million in 1987 to a loss of $75.9 million in 1990. Employees were anxious over reports of weak sales and of the bleak outlook in their industry. Their company was for sale, and there were concerns about who the new employer would be, or whether anyone would buy the company to keep it afloat. The survival of their company was very much on the minds of the workers.

At the time Abitibi-Price was experiencing its problems, George Brophy, CEO of a Wisconsin-based building-products firm, was experiencing his own. He had been diagnosed with stomach cancer, and faced a struggle for his personal survival. Brophy successfully battled his cancer, and upon doing so sought a new challenge. He left his company in Wisconsin and joined forces with Kohlberg & Company, a leading merchant banking firm, to buy Abitibi-Price. This buyout rescued the company from certain doom.

Brophy and his partners instituted swift changes at the building-products company. The first order of business was to put together a new management team. Drawing on the contacts he had made in his 27 years in the building-products industry, Brophy assembled a very experienced management team. Selecting a name for the new company was Brophy's next challenge. ABTCO (pronounced A-B-T-co) was selected because of its similarity to the well-known Abitibi. Stationery, signage, packaging, and advertising all had to be changed. But, more importantly, a new image had to be established.

When the new management team took over, ABTCO's product line included engineered wood for paneling and siding, and also plastic products for molding, architectural trim, and shutters. The new management team noted that, over the previous five years, the price of lumber had increased by over 20 percent for new home buyers. Therefore, the team decided to shift the company's focus to its plastic, simulated wood products. ABTCO's simulated wood products would enable builders to save $4,000 to $8,000 on an average home, while remodelers could save up to $2,000 on an average bathroom. Over the next two to three years, ABTCO anticipated that 40 percent of its sales would be for new construction, which they expected to increase at about 10 percent per year. The rest of the business would come from repair and remodeling.

ABTCO's new management team was pleasantly surprised to discover little employee resistance to its change initiatives. This lack of resistance was primarily due to employee participation and empowerment being a major part of the company's change process. According to Vice President of Marketing William J. Adams, "Our management style was one where a lower-level employee could pick up the telephone and call the vice president of his division. We interfaced with each other on a regular basis. We have teams that worked together on different projects just because we all happened to be involved. In the past, we had walls where marketing was over here, and manufacturing was over there, and the two were constantly doing battle. That never gets results, it only causes friction."

Under the change initiatives, managers began showing a new level of confidence in employees, giving them more discretion and flexibility in the workplace. This, in turn, gave managers the opportunity to focus more on customer needs and service, and increase the company's emphasis on quality. Top managers began meeting with customers, and customer response was overwhelmingly positive. CEO Brophy said, "It demonstrates that we are interested in the customer. Every top executive in this company has to visit at least 15 of our top customers each year."

Changes were also evident on the shop floor, in terms of both process and quality improvements. James P. Kinzler, operations manager, noting the improvement in the process of bringing new products to market, said, "What we've seen is we've been able to get new products to market very rapidly under the new ownership. We've been empowered at the plant level to make decisions here and keep things moving in the right direction." Tim Keeney, quality development manager, said, "I think the new ownership has taken a look at new markets. In the past we were tied to a do-it-yourselfer or home-center type market. The new owners have helped expand that to where we are competing directly with wood, which is something we hadn't done before. The volumes with the wood market are much higher than what we had been restricted to previously, so the possibility for growth coupled with the willingness to take some risks is a big change."

ABTCO's turnaround has been successful. Revenues are expected to increase 15 percent annually, and the company's stock price doubled in the first eight months of the new management's regime. ABTCO and CEO Brophy both came back from near disaster by managing and accepting change. Brophy summarized the change process at ABTCO by stating, "Everybody chipped in here. We had people giving concessions, we had people who were doing new jobs, we had new management that we brought in. It was a classic team effort."

Critical thinking questions

1. ABTCO's new management team broke through resistance to change through employee participation and empowerment. Explain why this approach is effective in managing change.

2. Most of the measures of the effectiveness of the change intervention reported in this video concern sales, profits, and revenue projections. What are some other measures managers might use to determine the effectiveness of a major change initiative? Can you think of some nonquantitative measures?

3. Resistance to change is a very common phenomenon that managers experience. Discuss the reasons for resisting change cited in the video. Do you think there are some other reasons people might resist change? How can these be overcome?

Experiential Exercises

18.1 A force-field analysis

Objective

To introduce you to force-field analysis of organizations and challenges facing them.

Instructions

Read about force-field analysis below, and come up with an organizational problem of your own to analyze.

Force-field analysis

A force-field analysis is one way to assess what is happening in an organization. This concept reflects the forces, driving and restraining, at work at a particular time. It helps to assess organizational strengths and to select forces to add or remove in order to create change. The theory of change suggested by Kurt Lewin, who developed the force-field analysis, is that while driving forces may be more easily affected, shifting them could increase opposition (tension and/or conflict) within the organization and add restraining forces. Therefore, it may be more effective to remove restraining forces to create change.

The use of the force-field analysis will demonstrate the range of forces pressing on an organization at a particular time. This analysis can increase the organization's optimism that it is possible to strategize and plan for change.

Example—Trying to increase student participation in student government.

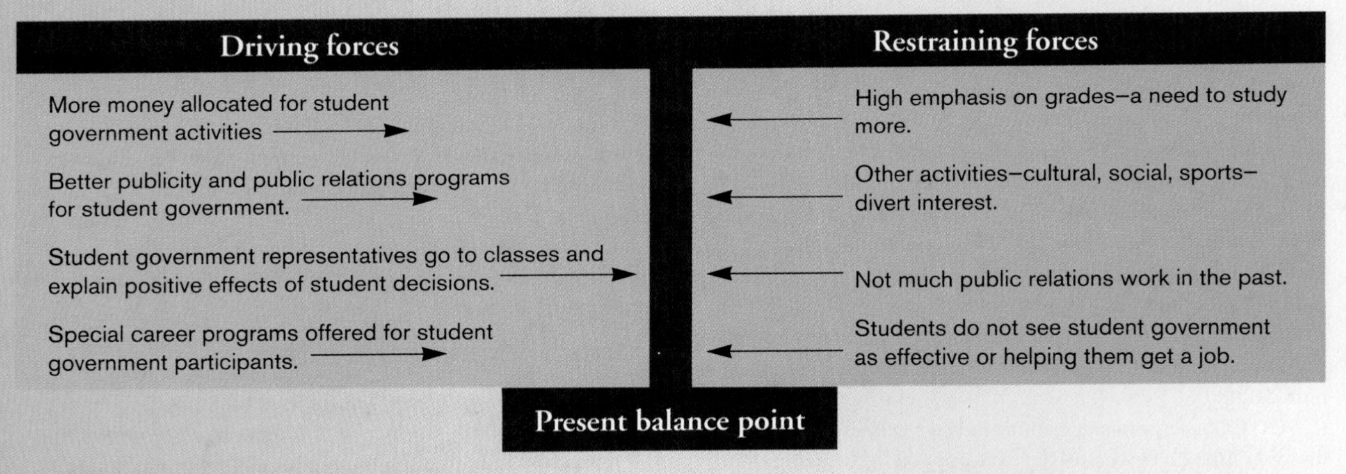

Driving forces
Restraining forces
More money allocated for student government activities
Better publicity and public relations programs for student government.
Student government representatives go to classes and explain positive effects of student decisions.
Special career programs offered for student government participants.
High emphasis on grades–a need to study more.
Other activities–cultural, social, sports–divert interest.
Not much public relations work in the past.
Students do not see student government as effective or helping them get a job.
Present balance point

Force-field analysis worksheet

1. (10–15 min.) Complete the Problem Analysis section and fill in the model.
2. (20 min.) In groups of 3–4, discuss the driving and restraining forces in each person's problem.
3. (10 min.) Class discussion
   a. Why is it useful to break a problem situation up into driving and restraining forces?
   b. Would the model be used any differently whether applied to an individual or organizational problem?

Problem analysis

1. **Describe the problem in a few words.**

____
____
____
____
____
____

2. **A list of forces *driving* toward change would include:**

   a. ____
   b. ____
   c. ____
   d. ____
   e. ____
   f. ____

3. **A list of forces *restraining* change would include:**

   a. ____
   b. ____
   c. ____
   d. ____
   e. ____
   f. ____

4. **Put the driving and restraining forces of the problem on the force-field analysis below, according to their degree of impact on change.**

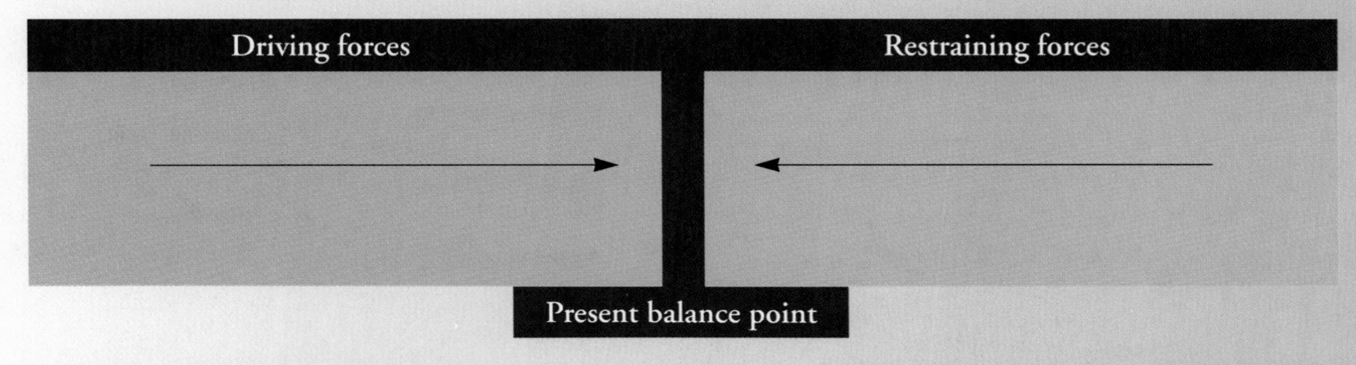

Source: Dorothy Hai, "Force-Field Analysis" in *Organizational Behavior: Experiences and Cases* (St. Paul, MN: West, 1986), pp. 259–61. Reprinted by permission.

18.2 Sears versus Kmart

Objective

To analyze operations at two well-known retail firms, with a view to making recommendations for changes that will improve profitability, sales, and customer service.

Instructions

Your group, Fastalk Consultants, is known as the shrewdest, most insightful, and most overpaid management consulting firm in the country. You have been hired by the president of Sears to make recommendations for improving the motivation and performance of personnel in their operations. Let us assume that the key job activity in store operations is dealing with customers.

Recently, the president of Sears has come to suspect that his company's competitor, Kmart, is making heavy inroads into Sears' market. He has also hired a market research firm to investigate and compare the relative merits of products and prices in the two establishments, and has asked the market research firm to assess the advertising campaigns of the two organizations. Hence, you will not need to be concerned with marketing issues, except as they may have an impact on employee behavior. The president wants you to look into the organization of the two stores to determine the strengths and weaknesses of each.

The president has established an unusual contract with you. He wants you to make your recommendations based upon your observations *as a customer.* He does not want you to do a complete diagnosis with interviews, surveys, or behind-the-scenes observations. He wants your report in two parts.

Sears versus Kmart worksheet

1. Given his organization's goals of profitability, sales volume, and fast and courteous service, he wants an analysis that will compare and contrast Sears and Kmart in terms of the following concepts:

Organizational Goals

Conflict? ______________________

Clarity? ______________________

Environment

Stable/Changing? ______________________

Simple/Complex? ______________________

Certain/Uncertain? ______________________

Size

Large? ______________________

Medium? ______________________

Small? ______________________

Personnel

Knowledgeable? ______________________

Well Trained? ______________________

Jobs

Variety? ______________________

Wholeness? ______________________

Interaction? ______________________

Freedom? ______________________

Time of Work? ______________________

Location of Work? ______________________

Horizontal Division of Labor

Formalized Policies? ______________________

Departmentalization? ______________________

Standardization of Rules? ______________________

Vertical Division of Labor

Number of Levels? ______________________

Span of Control? ______________________

Centralization? ______________________

Communication?

Direction? ______________________

Openness? ______

Leadership Style

Task Oriented? ______

People Oriented? ______

Employee Motivation

Type? ______

Intrinsic/Extrinsic? ______

Rewards? ______

Support? ______

Coordination? ______

Decision Making? ______

How do Sears and Kmart differ in these aspects? Which company has the best approach?

______

______

2. Given the corporate goals listed under part 1, what specific changes might Sears' management make in the following areas to achieve these goals (profitability, sales volume, fast and courteous service)?

- Job design and work flow

______

______

- Organization structure (at the individual store level)

______

______

- Employee incentives

______

______

- Leadership

______

______

- Employee selection

______

______

3. Having completed your contract with the president of Sears, prepare a report for presentation to class. This should include specific recommendations you have considered in part 2 above.

Source: Excerpted from Lawrence R. Jauch, Arthur G. Bedeian, Sally A. Coltrin, and William F. Glueck, *The Managerial Experience: Cases, Exercises, and Readings,* 4th ed.

Integrating Case

Xerox Corporation looks to the future and sees only quality

Company Background

The organization now known as Xerox Corporation was incorporated on April 18, 1906, under the name Haloid Company. In 1958, the name was changed to Haloid Xerox Incorporated, and the present name was selected three years later.

Originally, Xerox dominated the market for document processing. But by 1970, the Japanese were rapidly overtaking the industry with lower-cost products. Xerox was not worried: Low cost meant low quality. All of American industry in the 1970s was reacting similarly to world competition—so assured were they of their superior quality and technology. They imagined they were untouchable.

American products were considered luxury, state of the art, and superior in quality to any foreign competitor's. The Japanese in particular posed no threat, because their products were seen as cheap, unreliable, and even laughable in quality.

After World War II, as Japan struggled to rise from the ashes, the label "Made in Japan" was a joke in the United States. But, with the help of Dr. William Edwards Deming (an American, ironically), Japan's production philosophies and quality turned around. By the 1970s, Japan was catching up. Costs were still low, but the product no longer was inconsequential in quality.

In 1970, Xerox all but monopolized the almost $2 billion copier industry. By 1977, although the industry market had quadrupled, Japanese market share had dramatically increased, IBM made a significant impact, and Xerox's share was drastically reduced. In 1974, the Japanese introduced the cheap and efficient plain paper copiers, while Xerox continued using coated paper. From 1975 to 1978, Japanese firms such as Ricoh, Canon, and Konishiroku (not including Fuji Xerox) gained 25 percent of the world market for slow copiers.

Not only were competitors producing faster but the toner (liquid ink) that the Japanese were using was less expensive than Xerox's dry powder, and the parts used were less complex, mass produced, more reliable, and easier to fix. In addition, aggressive advertising and pricing by the Japanese allowed them to sell, rather than lease, their copiers, which released tied-up capital. Xerox was being outproduced and underpriced.

It was in 1979 that Xerox finally rallied and began to make the changes necessary for survival. Although Xerox stood at 36 in the Fortune 500 listings early in 1979, such managers as then-chairman and CEO C. Peter McColough had the foresight to see that they had to do better than simply relax to stay ahead of competitors.[1]

David Kearns, elected president and CEO in 1982, took the risk, bent the rules, and used creativity to make the necessary changes at Xerox. Kearns's total quality strategy gave Xerox employees the tools they needed to compete in the global market.

Xerox Looks to Quality Improvement

When CEO David Kearns decided that Xerox was ready for significant changes, the corporate attitude concerning quality was the first thing to be scrutinized. As he had learned, "the better the quality, the lower the overall costs." This massive cultural change would be accomplished through extensive training. In 1983, Xerox implemented a "Quality through Leadership" program that had three objectives:

To improve profits as reflected in higher return on assets.

To improve customer satisfaction.

To improve market share.

Kearns at first believed all three of these goals to be equally important, and he did not want one to overshadow the others. Soon, however, conflicts became unavoidable. To increase the return on assets, employees would try to cut costs. These actions sometimes would be at the expense of customer satisfaction and, hence, market share would decline. At this time it was necessary to prioritize these goals: Customer satisfaction became No. 1.

The "QTL" program cost an estimated $125 million and 4 million man-hours of work. It produced a 40 percent increase in customer satisfaction and a 60 percent decrease in complaints. It involved every level of the company from top to bottom. The orientation phase of the program took six months to complete. It took four years of training to reach the entire organization with the QTL message. Each supervisor learned from his supervisor, then trained and inspected his direct reports. Managers became coaches and a team approach was adopted.

After having promoted the "Leadership through Quality" campaign, employees came to the conclusion, however, that promotions were not always based on criteria related to quality. The "Role Model Manager" concept was then created.[2] New criteria were developed to guide promotion decisions, based on leadership characteristics fundamental to the total quality concept.

By 1989, 75 percent of Xerox workers had participated in the drive for perfect quality, on more than 7,000 quality improvement teams. Spending for training was increased to 2.5 to 3.0 percent of annual revenues.[3]

TQC became the buzzword at Xerox—total quality control. This "has nothing to do with checking quality as your products roll off the assembly line," said Kearns. "It is empowering employees to take responsibility for quality."[4] Allowing the responsibility to be shifted to lower levels was of prime importance in reducing costs, especially for the largest supplier of cut-sheet paper in the world. In 1989, Xerox produced 600,000 tons of paper.

To attain quality in every area, role models were chosen: L.L. Bean for distribution, American Express for collection, and American Hospital Supply Corporation on automated inventory control. These companies were selected as the most outstanding in these respective areas. Xerox investigated how these companies achieved their success and established goals for its employees as well as methods for achieving them. This process is known as competitive benchmarking, which is "the continuous process of measuring products, services, and practices against the company's toughest competitors or those companies renowned as industry leaders."[5] Benchmarking is the means by which practices required to achieve new goals are discovered. It forces continual focus on the environment. Xerox was one of the earliest U.S. proponents of benchmarking and institutionalized the practice in its organization.

Finally, Kearns realized that quality begins with suppliers. It is important to include suppliers in the quality program, and it is difficult to monitor 5,000 suppliers, so Xerox cut its base of vendors to 300 to gain more control over the quality of inputs and to reduce costs.

Quality Costs

Three different types of costs are involved in product production, and there are trade-offs within these types as methods vary. The goal of management is to reduce total costs, and it is most effective to do this by improving quality from the start.

1. *Prevention costs.* When defect-free products are demanded, prevention costs escalate. Each worker must be certain that each task is done perfectly the first time. The cost of this quality and perfection is prevention cost.

2. *Appraisal costs.* As the number of defects approaches zero, there becomes no necessity to inspect. The cost of inspectors and other ways of detecting defects drops to nothing.

3. *Internal and external failure costs.* Internal failure costs are experienced when defects are noted before shipping. External costs occur when flaws are not detected until after shipping. Both are reduced to zero when perfect quality is attained.

As the quality improves, prevention costs escalate, but the decline in appraisal costs and internal and external failure costs more than offset this increased expense. It is much cheaper to do it right the first time. As Dr. Deming had told the Japanese in 1946, and later told David Kearns, the closer a company comes to producing with zero defects, the less money is necessary for quality control.

Production techniques were examined to determine ways to eliminate defects from the beginning, with the focus on producing products with no defects, as opposed to the earlier focus of simply catching all of the products below certain standards as they came off the assembly line. Suppliers were included in this drive. Xerox cut its supplier base to have more control over supply quality, and it became more demanding in terms of specifications.

The focus on producing no defects at each step in the production process reduces costs considerably. The cost to repair a mistake, or a defect, increases geometrically as the defective product moves away from the point of defect in the assembly or production process. For example, it may take only a few seconds of time and a few cents to correct a mistake while a product is in the production process. Once the defective product leaves the plant and gets into the hands of the final consumer, it may cost weeks of time and thousands of dollars to correct the same mistake.

If production operations are of perfect quality, there is no need for quality control, recalls, rejections, or repairs on machines necessitated by production faults. It is, therefore, very cost effective to use TQM as a philosophy for how to do business.

Through this focus on costs, manufacturing costs were reduced by more than 20 percent (despite inflation), the time needed to bring a new product to market was reduced by 60 percent, and quality improved. These improvements were possible without any factories being closed or any of the manufacturing being moved offshore.[6]

Hard Work Is Rewarded

The changes at Xerox implemented by Kearns were far-reaching. They included reorganizing the research and development staff and the marketing force, with the objective of viewing new products as systems. McCologh was the first to describe Xerox as an information company, as opposed to a copier company. Xerox was one of the first companies to conclude that the "Industrial Age" is over and the "Information Age" has begun.

With this definition, "myopic marketing" was avoided, and Xerox began to develop its electronic "Office of the Future," with an office communications network and a new word processing system. The Ethernet network was similar to IBM's System Network architecture in that it connected many offices that were in one building, or in a group of buildings, but unlike IBM, Xerox's system did not need a mainframe. Working with Digital Equipment Corporation, a leader in the field, Xerox soon installed this high technology in the White House and Congress.

Although Xerox was still big in the upper end of the industry, management began to concentrate more on the lower end. Steps were taken to begin marketing in China and India, two of the biggest untapped plain-paper-copier markets. By working closely with Fuji Xerox, Xerox Corporation was able to learn more efficient and less costly ways of producing a more reliable product.[7]

By 1988, Xerox's management decided to undertake an extensive strategic review. The results of this endeavor led to savings of $60 million in the first year,[8] and winning the Malcolm Baldrige National Quality Award in 1989.

A decade after the implementation of these changes, the results were astounding. Customer satisfaction, the return on assets ratio, and market share rose steadily. It took a while for the turnaround to take place—results were not immediate. Most of the key decisions were made in 1979, yet the upward swing did not become apparent until five years later. This was due partially to the sharp recession in the early 80s—the economy was at its worst in 1984.

The rise in customer satisfaction was due primarily to the increased involvement of employees, who now are directly responsible for keeping customers happy. As one executive says, "Employees are closest to the customer," so they would know best how to please the customer. Employees also are promised more job security. After the heavy layoffs in 1981 and 1982, Xerox agreed to abide by a no-layoff policy in 1983. Management stuck by this, even through the difficult years of 1983 and 1984.

Employees were included in more management decisions. Line workers and others, closer to the action, were invited to add their input concerning ways to improve production and service through quality improvement teams. By working with the unions instead of fighting them, union leadership was committed to the company's excellence. More money was spent on training employees.

With a smaller number of more closely monitored suppliers, the number of defect-free products rose to 99.95 percent; but, although they received the highest honor for a quality company, David Kearns was not happy—they had not yet reached 100 percent defect-free.

To qualify for the Malcolm Baldrige award, a company must be outstanding in these areas:

Leadership.

Information and analysis.

Planning.

Human resource utilization.

Quality assurance.

Quality results.

Customer satisfaction.

Leadership. In a company seeking a quality award, leadership must be exhibited not as an authoritarian style management but as a two-way system. Upper management must delegate much authority and decision making to line supervisors. Input from workers must be solicited. Leaders should be open to opinions and changes, keeping goals in sight but being flexible enough to adapt to environmental changes within or outside of the company. Public responsibility as exhibited by senior executives also plays a crucial role in determining the quality of leadership. (100 pts. in the Baldrige competition. See exhibit, "Examination Categories and Items.")

Information and analysis. This area examines the breadth and depth of the data collected and utilized by the corporation. Impressive benchmarks should have been set in terms of quality planning, evaluation, and improvement. Analysis techniques are scrutinized. (70 pts.)

Planning. To successfully compete in this area, a company must have mapped out, in some depth, both short-term and long-term management strategies. These plans must realize company goals, but they also must be flexible enough to change with unforeseen occurrences. (60 pts.)

Human resource utilization. Management must utilize the workforce to maximize its potential. Employees should feel involved in the company, and feel that they have contributed to making the company successful. All should be trained in quality production. Recognition and praise should be given often, on an equal basis. Morale should be maintained at a high level. (150 pts.)

Quality assurance. Tracing a product from its development through manufacturing, a company must be able to show how quality was assured in each stage. Each product should have been developed to meet key quality requirements, and it should have been constructed with the highest-quality materials from suppliers. Continual assessment and improvements must be made. (140 pts.)

Quality results. This category relies heavily on the activity of a firm's key competitors. Industry trends in quality improvement and levels must be assessed, along with the achievements of the industry's world leaders. After summarizing these trends and levels for business processes, operations, and support services, supplier quality must be discussed. For a product to be of superior quality, it must begin with superior materials. (180 pts.)

Customer satisfaction. Customer expectations are examined, as are corporate relationships with the customers. Information gained from these relationships, as well as complaints submitted, should be analyzed and utilized by management to improve quality. Customer satisfaction is compared with that of others in the industry. (300 pts.)

As shown in the exhibit, a perfect quality score would add up to 1,000 points.

In the words of Robert Mosbacher:

> The winners of this award have made quality improvement a way of life. Quality is their bottom line, and that kind of can-do attitude makes for world-class products and services.

Examination categories and items–Malcolm Baldrige National Quality Award

Examination categories/items	Maximum points	
1.0 Leadership:		
1.1 Senior executive leadership	40	
1.2 Quality values	15	
1.3 Management for quality	25	
1.4 Public responsibility	20	**100**
2.0 Information and analysis:		
2.1 Scope and management of quality data and information	20	
2.2 Competitive comparisons and benchmarks	30	
2.3 Analysis of quality data and information	20	**70**
3.0 Strategic quality planning:		
3.1 Strategic quality planning process	35	
3.2 Quality goals and plans	25	**60**
4.0 Human resource utilization:		
4.1 Human resource management	20	
4.2 Employee involvement	40	
4.3 Quality education and training	40	
4.4 Employee recognition and performance measurement	25	
4.5 Employee well-being and morale	25	**150**
5.0 Quality assurance of products and services:		
5.1 Design and introduction of quality products and services	35	
5.2 Process quality control	20	
5.3 Continuous improvement of processes	20	
5.4 Quality assessment	15	
5.5 Documentation	10	
5.6 Business process and support service quality	20	
5.7 Supplier quality	20	**140**
6.0 Quality results		
6.1 Product and service quality results	90	
6.2 Business process and support service quality	50	
6.3 Supplier quality results	40	**180**
7.0 Customer satisfaction		
7.1 Determining customer requirements and expectations	30	
7.2 Customer relationship management	50	
7.3 Customer service standards	20	
7.4 Commitment to customers	15	
7.5 Complaint resolution for quality improvement	25	
7.6 Determining customer satisfaction	20	
7.7 Customer satisfaction results	70	
7.8 Customer satisfaction comparison	70	**300**
Total points		**1,000**

Source: This case was prepared by Neil H. Snyder, the Ralph A. Beeton Professor of Free Enterprise, University of Virginia; Katherine Lilley, McIntire School, University of Virginia; and Deborah Francis, University of South Carolina.

Case Incidents

Robot repercussion

Victor Principal, vice president of industrial relations for General Manufacturing, Inc., sat in his office reviewing the list of benefits the company expected to realize from increasing its use of industrial robots. In a few minutes, he would walk down to the labor-management conference room for a meeting with Ralph McIntosh, president of the labor union local representing most of the company's industrial employees. The purpose of this meeting would be to informally exchange views and positions preliminary to the opening for formal contract negotiations later in the month, which would focus on the use of computer-integrated robotics systems and the resulting impact on employment, workers, and jobs.

Both Principal and McIntosh had access to similar information flows relevant to industrial robots, including the following. Unlike single-task machines, installed in earlier stages of automation, robots can be programmed to do one job and then reprogrammed to do another one. The pioneering generation of robots is mainly programmed to load machines, weld, forge, spray paint, handle materials, and inspect auto bodies. The latest generation of robots includes vision-controlled robots, which enable the machines to approximate the human ability to recognize and size up objects by using laser-beam patterns recorded by television cameras and transmitted to "smart" computers. The computer software interprets and manipulates the images relayed by the camera in a "smart" or artificially intelligent way.

Experts concluded that the impact of robot installation on employment would be profound, although the extent of the worker replacement was not clear. The inescapable conclusion was that robot usage had the capacity to increase manufacturing performance and to decrease manufacturing employment.

Principal walked down to the conference room. Finding McIntosh already there, Principal stated the company's position regarding installation of industrial robots: "The company needs the cooperation of the union and our workers. We don't wish to be perceived as callously exchanging human workers for robots." Then Principal listed the major advantages associated with robots: (1) improved quality of product as a result of the accuracy of robots; (2) reduced operating costs, as the per-hour operational cost of robots was about one-third of the per-hour cost of wages and benefits paid to an average employee; (3) reliability improvements, as robots work tirelessly and don't require behavioral support; and (4) greater manufacturing flexibility, because robots are readily reprogrammable for different jobs. Principal concluded that these advantages would make the company more competitive, which would allow it to grow and increase its workforce.

McIntosh's response was direct and strong: "We aren't Luddites racing around ruining machines. We know it's necessary to increase productivity and that robotic technology is here. But we can't give the company a blank check. We need safeguards and protection." McIntosh continued, "We intend to bargain for the following contract provisions:

1. Establishment of labor–management committees to negotiate *in advance* about the labor impact of robotics technology and, of equal importance, to have a voice in deciding how and whether it should be used.
2. Rights to advance notice about installation of new technology.
3. Retraining rights for workers displaced, to include retraining for new positions in the plant, the community, or other company plants.
4. Spreading the work among workers by use of a four-day workweek or other acceptable plan as an alternative to reducing the workforce.

McIntosh's final sentence summed up the union's position: "We in the union believe the company is giving our jobs to robots to reduce the labor force."

Their meeting ended amiably, but Principal and McIntosh each knew that much hard bargaining lay ahead. As Principal returned to his office, the two opposing positions were obvious. On his yellow tablet, Principal listed the requirements as he saw them: (1) A clearly stated overall policy was needed to guide negotiation decisions and actions; (2) it was critical to decide on a company position regarding each of the union's announced demands and concerns; and (3) a plan must be developed.

As Principal considered these challenges, he idly contemplated a robot possessing artificial intelligence and vision capability that could help him in his work. Immediately a danger alarm sounded in his mind. A robot so constructed might be more than helpful and might take over this and other important aspects of his job. Slightly chagrined, Principal returned to his task. He needed help—but not from any "smart" robot.

Source: J. Champion and J. James, *Critical Incidents in Management: Decision and Policy Issues,* 6th ed. (Burr Ridge, Ill.: Richard D. Irwin, 1989).

Implementing strategic change

James Fulmer, chief executive officer of Allied Industries, reviewed three notes he had exchanged with Frank Curtis, director of fiscal affairs, now president of a company owned by Allied. The two executives were going to meet in a few minutes to discuss problems that had recently surfaced. During the past decade, Allied had aggressively pursued a growth objective based on a conglomerate strategy of acquiring companies in distress. CEO Fulmer's policy was to appoint a new chief operating officer for each acquisition with instructions to facilitate a turnaround. Fulmer reviewed two of the notes he had written to Curtis.

Date: January 15:
Memorandum

To: Frank Curtis, Director of Fiscal Affairs, Allied Industries

From: James Fulmer, Chairman, Allied Industries

Subject: Your Appointment as President, Lee Medical Supplies

You are aware that Allied Industries recently acquired Lee Medical Supplies. Mr. John Lee, founder and president of the company, has agreed to retire, and I am appointing you to replace him. Our acquisitions group will brief you on the company, but I want to warn you that Lee Medical Supplies has a history of mismanagement. As a distributor of medical items, the company's sales last year totaled approximately $300 million, with net earnings of only $12 million. Your job is to make company sales and profits compatible with Allied standards. You are reminded that it is my policy to call for an independent evaluation of company progress and your performance as president after 18 months.

Date: September 10:
Memorandum

To: Frank Curtis, President, Lee Medical Supplies

From: James Fulmer, Chairman, Allied Industries

Subject: Serious Problems at Lee Medical Supplies

In accord with corporate policy, consultants recently conducted an evaluation of Lee Medical Supplies. In a relatively short period of time, you have increased sales and profits to meet Allied's standards, but I am alarmed at other aspects of your performance. I am told that during the past 18 months, three of your nine vice presidents have resigned and that you have terminated four others. An opinion survey conducted by the consultants indicates that a low state of morale exists and that your managerial appointees are regarded by their subordinates as hard-nosed perfectionists obsessed with quotas and profits. Employees report that ruthless competition now exists between divisions, regions, and districts. They also note that the collegial, family-oriented atmosphere fostered by Mr. Lee has been replaced by a dog-eat-dog situation characterized by negative management attitudes toward employee feelings and needs. After you have studied the enclosed report from the consultants, we will meet to discuss their findings. I am particularly concerned with their final conclusion that "a form of corporate cancer seems to be spreading throughout Lee Medical Supplies."

As Fulmer prepared to read the third note, written by Frank Curtis, he reflected on his exit interview with the consultants. While Fulmer considered Curtis a financial expert and a turnaround specialist, his subordinates characterized Curtis as an autocrat and better suited to be a Marine boot camp commander.

Date: September 28:
Memorandum

To: James Fulmer

From: Frank Curtis

Subject: The So-Called Serious Problems at Lee Medical Supplies

I have received your memorandum dated September 10, and reviewed the consultants' report. When you appointed me to my present position I was instructed to take over an unprofitable company and make it profitable. I have done so in 18 months, although I inherited a family-owned business that by your own admission had been mismanaged for years. I found a group of managers and salespeople with an average company tenure of 22 years. Mr. Lee had centralized all personnel decisions so that only he could terminate an employee. He tolerated mediocre performance. All employees were paid on a straight salary basis, with seniority the sole criterion for advancement. Some emphasis was given to increasing sales each year, but none was given to reducing costs and increasing profits. Employees did indeed find the company a fun place to work, and the feeling of being a part of a family did permeate the company. Such attitudes were, however, accompanied by mediocrity, incompetence, and poor performance.

I found it necessary to implement immediate strategic changes in five areas: the organization's structure, employee rewards and incentives, management information systems, allocation of resources, and managerial leadership style. As a result, sales areas were reorganized into divisions, regions, and districts. Managers who I felt were incompetent and/or lacking in commitment to my objectives and methods were replaced. Unproductive and mediocre employees were encouraged to find jobs elsewhere. Authority for staffing and compensation decisions was decentralized to units at the division, region, and district levels. Managers of those units were informed that along with their authority went responsibility for reducing costs and for increasing sales and profits. Each unit was established as a profit center. A new department was established and charged with reviewing performance of those units. Improved accounting and control systems were implemented. A management-by-objectives program was developed to establish standards and monitor performance. Performance appraisals are now required for all employees. To encourage more aggressive action, bonuses and incentives are offered to managers of units showing increased profits. A commission plan based on measurable sales and profit performances has replaced straight salaries. Resources are allocated to units based on their performance.

My own leadership style has probably represented the most traumatic change for employees. Internal competition is a formally mandated policy throughout the company. It has been responsible for much of the progress achieved to date. Progress, however, is never made without costs, and I recognize that employees are not having as much fun as in the past. I was employed to achieve results and not to ensure that employees remain secure and happy in their work. Don't let a few crybabies unable to adjust to changes lead you to believe that problems take precedence over profits. Does it mean that I am not people oriented if I believe it is unlikely that a spirit of aggressiveness and competitiveness can coexist with an atmosphere of cooperativeness and family orientation? Do you feel that we are obligated to employees because of past practices? Frankly, I thought I had your support to do whatever was necessary to get this company turned around. In our meeting, tell me if you think my approaches have been wrong and, if so, tell me what I should have done differently.

Just as Fulmer finished reviewing the third memorandum, his secretary informed him that Curtis had arrived for their scheduled meeting. He realized he was undecided about how to communicate to Curtis his ideas and beliefs regarding how changes in an organization can best be implemented. One thing he did know: He didn't appreciate how Curtis had expressed his views in his memorandum, but he recognized that he probably should set aside emotions and respond to the questions Curtis posed.

Source: J. Champion and J. James, *Critical Incidents in Management: Decision and Policy Issues,* 6th ed. (Burr Ridge, Ill.: Richard D. Irwin, 1989).

Company Directory

A

ABB Flakt
(Subsidiary of Asea Brown Boveri, Inc.)
650 Ackerman Road
Columbus, OH 43202
(614) 261-2000
Sales: $200,000,000
Employees: 2,000

Advanced Micro Devices, Inc.
915 De Guigne Street
Box 3453
Sunnyvale, CA 94088
(408) 732-2400
Sales: $1,650,000,000
Employees: 11,250
http://www.amd.com

Aetna Life & Casualty Co.
151 Farmington Avenue
Hartford, CT 06156
(860) 273-0123
Sales: $17,120,200,000
Employees: 42,631
http://www.aetna.com

Allied Signal, Inc.
101 Columbia Road
Morristown, NJ 07962-2497
(973) 455-2000
Sales: $11,830,000,000
Employees: 86,400
http://www.alliedsignal.com

Amdahl Corporation
1250 East Arques Avenue
Sunnyvale, CA 94088-3470
(408) 746-6000
Sales: $862,000,000
Employees: 7,000
http://www.amdahl.com

American Airlines, Inc.
(Subsidiary of American Corporation)
P.O. Box 619616 DFW Arpt Street
Dallas, TX 65261-9616
(817) 355-1234
Sales: $14,400,000,000
Employees: 102,400
http://www.americanair.com

American Broadcasting Companies, Inc.
(Subsidiary of Capital Cities/ABC Inc.)
77 W. 66th Street
New York, NY 10023
(212) 456-7777
Sales: NA
Employees: NA
http://www.abctelevision.com

American Express Company
200 Vesey Street
American Express Tower
New York, NY 10285-4805
(212) 640-2000
Sales: $14,170,000,000
Employees: 100,188
http://www.americanexpress.com

American Motors Co.
(Subsidiary of Chrysler Corporation)
27777 Franklin Road
Southfield, MI 48034
(313) 827-1000
Sales: $4,030,000,000
Employees: 22,500
http://www.americanmotors.com

Ameritech
30 S. Wacker Drive
Chicago, IL 60606
(312) 750-5000
Sales: $11,710,000,000
Employees: 71,300
http://www.ameritech.com

Amoco Corp.
200 East Randolph Drive
Chicago, IL 60601
(312) 856-6111
Sales: $28,900,000,000
Employees: 46,700
http://www.amoco.com

Ampex
500 Broadway
Redwood City , CA 94063-3199
(650) 367-2011
Sales: $526,450,000
Employees: 3,000
http://www.ampex.com

Anheuser Busch Companies, Inc.
One Busch Place
St. Louis, MO 63118
(314) 577-2000
Sales: $11,500,000,000
Employees: 43,345
http://www.anheuser-busch.com

A&P Company, Inc.
2 Paragon Drive
Montvale, NJ 07645
(201) 930-4000
Sales: $557,157,000
Employees: 4,600
http://www.aptea.com/index.htm

Apple Computers, Inc.
One Infinite Loop
Cupertino, CA 95014
(408) 996-1010
Sales: $8,000,000,000
Employees: 11,800
http://www.apple.com

ARCO Pipe Line Co.
(Subsidiary of Atlantic Richfield Company)
5900 Cherry Avenue
Long Beach, CA 90805
(310) 428-9000
Sales: $48,000,000
Employees: 280
http://www.arco.com

Argus Corporation Ltd.
(Subsidiary of Ravelston Corporation Limited)
10 Toronto Street
Toronto, Canada M5C 2B7
(416) 363-8721
Sales: $20,560,000,000
Employees: 22,000
http://www.argusresearch.com

ASEA Brown Boveri
(Subsidiary of ABB ASEA Brown Boveri, Ltd.)
900 Long Ridge Road
Stamford, CT 06902
(203) 329-8771
Sales: NA
Employees: NA
http://www.abb.com

Ashland Oil
1000 Ashland Dr.
Russell, KY 41169
(606) 329-3333
Sales: $9,500,000,000
Employees: 33,000
http://www.ashland.com

Atlantic Richfield Co.
515 South Flower Street
Los Angeles, CA 90071-2256
(213) 486-3511
Sales: $15,000,000,000
Employees: 31,300
http://www.arco.com

AT&T Co.
550 Madison Avenue
New York, NY 10022
(212) 605-5500
Sales: $34,900,000,000
Employees: 365,000
http://www.att.com

Automatic Data Processing
One ADP Boulevard
Roseland, NJ 07068
(201) 994-5000
Sales: $2,220,000,000
Employees: 21,000
http://www.adp.com

Avon Products, Inc.
1345 Avenue of the Americas
New York, NY 10105-0196
(212) 282-5000
Sales: $3,450,000,000
Employees: 34,500
http://www.avon.com

B

Bally Engineered Structures
20 N. Front Street
Bally, PA 19503
(610) 845-2311
Sales: $25,000,000
Employees: 400

Banc One Corp.
100 E. Broad Street
Columbus, OH 43271-0261
(614) 248-5800
Sales: $80,000,000,000
Employees: 42,800
http://www.bankone.com

Bankers Trust Company
(Subsidiary of Bankers Trust New York Corp.)
One Bankers Trust Plaza
130 Liberty St.
New York, NY 10006
(212) 250-2500
Sales: NA
Employees: 12,500
http://www.bankerstrust.com

Bank of America National Trust and Savings Association
(Subsidiary of BankAmerica Corp.)
555 California Street
San Francisco, CA 94104
(415) 622-3456
Sales: NA
Employees: 78,500
http://www.bankamerica.com

Bausch & Lomb
One Bausch & Lomb Place
Rochester, NY 14604-2701
(716) 338-8444
Sales: $1,870,000,000
Employees: 14,500
http://www.bausch.com

Baxter Healthcare Corp.
(Subsidiary of Baxter International, Inc.)
One Baxter Parkway
Deerfield, IL 60015
1-800-422-9837
Sales: $6,700,000,000
Employees: 40,900
http://www.baxter.com

Bayer AG
Werk Leverkusen
Leverkusen, Germany 51368
+49-214-308-992
Sales: NA

Employees: 164,400
http://www.bayer-ag.de/bayer/indexe.htm

L. L. Bean, Inc.
Casco Street
Freeport, ME 04033
(207) 865-4761
Sales: $368,000,000
Employees: 1,920
http://www.llbean.com

The Bear Stearns Companies, Inc.
245 Park Avenue
New York, NY 10167
(212) 272-2000
Sales: $2,420,000,000
Employees: 7,454
http://www.bearstearns.com

Bechtel Group
50 Beale Street
San Francisco, CA 94105-1895
(415) 768-1234
Sales: $7,000,000,000
Employees: 21,200
http://www.bechtel.com

Bell Atlantic Corp.
1095 Avenue of the Americas
New York, NY 10036
(212) 349-2121
Sales: $13,000,000,000
Employees: 71,400
http://www.bellatlantic.com

Bell & Howell
5215 Old Orchard Road
Skokie, IL 60077-1076
(847) 470-7660
Sales: $675,000,000
Employees: 5,718
http://www.bellhowell.com

BellSouth Corp.
1155 Peachtree Street N.E.
Atlanta, GA 30309-3610
(404) 249-2000
Sales: $15,880,000,000
Employees: 95,100
http://www.bellsouthcorp.com

Bertelsmann
(Subsidiary of Bertlesmann Aktiengesellschaft)
1540 Broadway
New York, NY 10036
(212) 782-1000
Sales: $2,300,000,000
Employees: 5,100
http://www.bertelsmann.de/

Best Products Company, Inc.
P.O. Box 26303
Richmond, VA 23260
(804) 261-2000
Sales: $1,400,000,000
Employees: 18,500

Bethlehem Steel Corp.
1170 Eighth Avenue
Bethlehem, PA 18016-7699
(610) 694-2424
Sales: $4,320,000,000
Employees: 20,500
http://www.bethsteel.com

BMW
Petuelring 130
D-80788 Munich, Germany
+49-89-38-20
Sales: DM27,180,000,000
Employees: 70,950
http://www.bmw.com

The Boeing Co.
7755 East Marginal Way South
Seattle, WA 98108
(206) 655-2121
Sales: $25,400,000,000
Employees: 123,000
http://www.boeing.com

Bombay Company, Inc.
550 Bailey Avenue
Fort Worth, TX 76107
(817) 347-8200
Sales: $231,740,000
Employees: 2,900
http://www.bombayco.com

Borg-Warner Corp.
200 South Michigan Avenue
Chicago, IL 60604
(312) 322-8500
Sales: $3,330,000,000
Employees: 78,000

Brio Industries, Inc.
160-7400 River Rd.
Richmond, British Columbia
Canada, V6X 1X6
(604) 214-9733
Sales: $1,850,000
Employees: 60
http://www.brio-ind.com

Bristol-Myers Squibb Co.
345 Park Avenue
New York, NY 10154-0037
(212) 546-4000
Sales: $11,440,000,000
Employees: 49,500
http://www.bms.com

British Petroleum Co.
One Finsbury Circle
Britannic House
Moor Lane
London, England EC242BU
44-71-496-4000
Sales: £40,280,000,000
Employees: 130,100
http://www.bp.com

British Telecommunications
81 Newgate Street
London, England EC1A7 AJ, UK
+44-171-356-5000
Sales: $17,100,000,000
Employees: 156,000
http://www.bt.com

Brooks Brothers
346 Madison Avenue
New York, NY 10017
(212) 682-8800
Sales: NA
Employees: 3,075

Browning Ferris
757 N. Eldridge
Houston, TX 77079
(281) 870-8100
Sales: $3,500,000,000
Employees: 29,400
http://www.bfi.com

Burger King Corp.
(Subsidiary of Grand Metropolitan plc)
17777 Old Cutler Road
Miami, FL 33157
(305) 378-7011
Sales: $6,100,000,000
Employees: 42,000
http://www.burgerking.com

C

Canon Business Machines, Inc.
(Subsidiary of Canon, Inc.)
3191 Red Hill Avenue
Costa Mesa, CA 92626
(714) 556-4700
Sales: $50,000,000
Employees: 150

Carnival Corp.
3655 N.W. 87th Avenue
Miami, FL 33178-2428
(305) 599-2600
Sales: $1,560,000,000
Employees: 1,400
http://www.carnival.com

Caterpillar, Inc.
100 Northeast Adams Street
Peoria, IL 61629
(309) 675-1000
Sales: $11,620,000,000
Employees: 51,200
http://www.caterpillar.com

CBS, Inc.
51 W. 52nd Street
New York, NY 10019-6188
(212) 975-4321
Sales: $3,500,000,000
Employees: 6,000
http://www.cbs.com

Chase Manhattan Corp.
270 Park Ave.
New York, NY 10017-2036
(212) 270-6000
Sales: $11,420,000,000
Employees: 31,100
http://www.chase.com

Chevron Corp.
575 Market St.
San Francisco, CA 94105
(415) 894-7700
Sales: $33,000,000,000
Employees: 55,123
http://www.chevron.com

Chiat/Day/Mojo Inc. Advertising
320 Hampton Drive
Venice, CA 90291
(310) 314-5000
Sales: NA
Employees: 300

Chiquita Brands International
(Subsidiary of American Fin Corp.)
250 E. 5th Street
Cincinnati, OH 45202
(513) 784-8000
Sales: $2,530,000,000
Employees: 45,000
http://www.chiquita.com

Chrysler Corp.
1000 Chrysler Drive
Auburn Hills, MI 48326
(248) 576-5741
Sales: $43,600,000,000
Employees: 123,000
http://www.chrylercorp.com

Citibank
(Subsidiary of Citicorp)
399 Park Avenue
New York, NY 10043
(301) 714-5326
Sales: NA
Employees: 81,000
http://www.citibank.com

Citicorp
399 Park Avenue
New York, NY 10043
(301) 714-5326
Sales: $32,200,000,000
Employees: 88,500
http://www.citibank.com

Coast Gas Industries, Inc.
885 Salinas Road
Watsonville, CA 95076
(408) 724-3200
Sales: $180,000,000
Employees: 275

The Coca-Cola Co.
One Coca-Cola Plaza N.W.
Atlanta, GA 30313
(404) 676-2121
Sales: $13,900,000,000
Employees: 31,312
http://www.cocacola.com

Colgate-Palmolive
300 Park Avenue
New York, NY 10022
(212) 310-2000
Sales: $7,140,000,000

Employees: 29,000
http://www.colgate.com

COMPAQ Computer Corp.
20555 SH 249
Houston, TX 77070
(281) 370-0670
Sales: $7,190,000,000
Employees: 9,500
http://www.compaq.com

Consolidated Natural Gas
CNG Tower
625 Liberty Avenue,
22nd Fl. CNG Tower
Pittsburgh, PA 15222-3199
(412) 227-1000
Sales: $3,180,000,000
Employees: 8,000
http://www.cng.com

Control Data Corp.
8100 34th Avenue
Minneapolis, MN 55420
(612) 853-8100
Sales: $3,670,000,000
Employees: 38,800

Cooper Tire and Rubber Co.
Lima and Western Avenues
Findlay, OH 45840
(419) 423-1321
Sales: $1,190,000,000
Employees: 7,600
http://www.coopertires.com

Adolph Coors Co.
17735 W. 32nd Ave.
Golden, CO 80401
(303) 279-6565
Sales: $1,580,000,000
Employees: 6,200

Corning Glass Works
Houghton Park
Corning, NY 14830
(607) 974-9000
Sales: $4,040,000,000
Employees: 39,000

Cowles Media Corp.
4 High Ridge Park
Stamford, CT 06905
(203) 321-1788
Sales: $256,000,000
Employees: 3,260
http://www.cowles.com

CSX
One James Center
901 E. Cary St.
Richmond, VA 23219-4031
(804) 782-1400
Sales: $8,940,000,000
Employees: 47,000
http://www.csx.com

Cyrix Corp.
2703 N. Central Expressway
Richardson, TX 75080
(214) 894-8387
Sales: $125,100,000
Employees: 185
http://www.cyrix.com

D

Dana Corp.
4500 Dorr Street
Toledo, OH 43615
(419) 535-4500
Sales: $5,400,000,000
Employees: 40,000
http://www.dana.com

Data General Corp.
4400 Computer Drive
Westboro, MA 01580
(508) 898-5000
Sales: $1,230,000,000
Employees: 6,500
http://www.dg.com

Days Inns of America, Inc.
(Subsidiary of Tollman-Hundley
Lodging Corp.)
339 Jefferson Road
Parsippany, NJ 07054
(973) 428-9700
Sales: $117,800,000
Employees: 3,193
http://www.daysinn.com

Dell Computer Co.
One Dell Way
Round Rock, TX 78682
(800) 915-3355
Sales: $2,870,000,000
Employees: 5,000
http://www.dell.com/

Delta Air Lines, Inc.
Hartsfield International Airport
Atlanta, GA 30326
(404) 765-2600
Sales: $12,000,000,000
Employees: 73,533
http://www.delta-air.com/

Digital Equipment Corp.
111 Powder Mill Rd.
Maynard, MA 01754
(978) 493-5111
Sales: $14,370,000,000
Employees: 92,000
http://www.digital.com

Domino's Pizza, Inc.
30 Frank Lloyd Wright Dr.
Ann Arbor, MI 48106-0997
(313) 930-3030
Sales: $296,000,000
Employees: 51,300
http://www.dominos.com

Domino Sugar Corp.
1114 Avenue of the Americas
Baltimore, MD 10036
(212) 789-9700
Sales: $1,300,000,000
Employees: 7,729

The Dow Chemical Co.
2030 Willard H. Dow Center
Midland, MI 48674
(517) 636-1000
Sales: $18,660,000,000
Employees: 62,000
http://www.dom.com/homepage/
index.html

Dow Corning Corp.
2200 W. Salzburg Rd.
Midland, MI 48686
(517) 496-4000
Sales: $1,760,000,000
Employees: 8,691
http://www.dow.com

Dow Jones & Co., Inc.
200 Liberty Street
New York, NY 10281
(212) 416-2000
Sales: $1,930,000,000
Employees: 10,000
http://www.dowjones.com

**William Dudek
Manufacturing Co.**
4901 W. Armitage Avenue
Chicago, IL 60639
(312) 622-2727
Sales: $3,000,000
Employees: 50

Du Pont
1007 Market Street
Wilmington, DE 19898
(302) 774-1000
Sales: $37,100,000,000
Employees: 114,000
http://www.dupont.com

E

Eastern Airlines
(Sudsidiary of Continental
Air Holdings, Inc.)
Miami International Airport
Miami, FL 33148
(305) 873-2211
Sales: $1,500,000,000
Employees: 19,000

Eastman Kodak Co.
343 State Street
Rochester, NY 14650
(716) 724-4000
Sales: $16,360,000,000
Employees: 137,750
http://www.kodak.com

Eaton Corp.
1111 Superior Avenue N.E.
Cleveland, OH 44114-2584
(216) 523-5000
Sales: $4,400,000,000
Employees: 50,000
http://www.eaton.com

Electro-Biology, Inc.
6 Upper Pond Road
Parsippany, NJ 07054
(201) 299-9022
Sales: $28,000,000
Employees: 350

Elizabeth Arden
1345 Avenue of the Americas
New York, NY 10105
(212) 261-1000
Sales: NA
Employees: 3,428
http://www.utee.com/arden/

Emerson Electric Co.
8000 West Floussant Avenue
St. Louis, MO 63136
(314) 553-2000
Sales: $8,170,000,000
Employees: 71,600
http://www.emersonelectric.com

Equitable Life Assurance Society
787 Seventh Avenue
New York, NY 10019
(212) 554-1234
Sales: $60,000,000,000
Employees: 20,000
http://www.equitable.com/
equitablelifepage.htm

Exxon Corp.
1251 Avenue of the Americas
New York, NY 10020-1198
(212) 333-1000
Sales: $74,400,000,000
Employees: 145,000
http://www.exxon.com

F

Federal Express Corp.
2007 Corporate Avenue
Memphis, TN 38132
(901) 369-3600
Sales: $7,800,000,000
Employees: 93,000
http://www.fedex.com/

**Federal National
Mortgage Association**
3900 Wisconsin Avenue N.W.
Washington, D.C. 20016
(202) 752-7000
Revenues: $16,050,000,000
Employees: 2,400
http://www.fanniemae.com

Firestone Tire & Rubber Co.
(Division of
Bridgestone/Firestone, Inc.)
One Bridgestone Park
P. O. Box 140991
Nashville, TN 37214-0991
(615) 231-3442
Sales: NA
Employees: NA
http://www.bridgestone-usa.com

First Boston Corp.
(Subsidiary of First Boston, Inc.)
Park Avenue Plaza
New York, NY 10055
(212) 909-2000
Sales: $1,300,000,000
Employees: 4,040

Fleet Financial Group, Inc.
One Federal St.
Boston, MA 02110-2010
(617) 346-4000
Sales: $4,680,000,000
Employees: 25,200
http://www.fleet.com

Food Lion, Inc.
2110 Executive Dr.
Salisbury, NC 28145
(704) 633-8250
Sales: $7,600,000,000
Employees: 60,000
http://www.foodlion.com

Ford Motor Co.
American Road
Dearborn, MI 48121-1899
(313) 322-3000
Sales: $108,520,000,000
Employees: 332,700
http://www.ford.com

The Foxboro Co.
(Subsidiary of Siebe plc)
600 N. Bedfort St.
East Bridgewater, MA 02333
(508) 543-8750
Sales: $597,780,000
Employees: 4,700
http://www.foxboro.com

Fox Television Stations, Inc.
5746 Sunset Boulevard
Los Angeles, CA 90028
(213) 856-1001
Sales: NA
Employees: 1,250

Funco, Inc.
10120 W. 76th Street
Minneapolis, MN 55344
(612) 946-8883
Sales: $50,500,000
Employees: 380
http://www.funcoland.com

G

Gateway Foods, Inc.
(Subsidiary of Scrivner, Inc.)
P.O. Box 1957
LaCrosse, WI 54602
(608) 785-1330
Sales: NA
Employees: 500

General Dynamics Corp.
3190 Fairview Park Drive
Falls Church, VA 22042-4523
(703) 876-3000
Sales: $7,830,000,000
Employees: 107,000
http://www.gdeb.com/pr/corpinfo

General Electric Canada
2300 Meadowvale Boulevard
Mississauga, Ontario
Canada L5N 5P9
(416) 858-5100
Sales: $1,420,000
Employees: 4,248

General Electric Co.
3135 Easton Turnpike
Fairfield, CT 06432
(203) 373-2211
Sales: $60,600,000,000
Employees: 222,000
http:/www.ge.com

General Foods Corp.
(Subsidiary of Philip Morris Companies, Inc.)
250 North Street
White Plains, NY 10605
(914) 335-2500
Sales: NA
Employees: 55,000

General Mills, Inc.
One General Mills Boulevard
Minneapolis, MN 55426
(612) 540-2311
Sales: $8,130,000,000
Employees: 121,300
http://www.generalmills.com

General Motors Corp.
100 Renaissance Ctr.
Detroit, MI 48243-7301
(313) 556-5000
Sales: $130,220,000,000
Employees: 711,000
http://www.gm.com

Glaxo Holdings
Clarges House
Berkeley Avenue
Greenford, Middlesex, England
W1Y 8DH
44-71-493-4060
Sales: $1,500,000
Employees: 40,000

The Goodyear Tire & Rubber Co.
1144 East Market Street
Akron, OH 44316
(216) 796-2121
Sales: $11,640,000,000
Employees: 121,586
http://www.goodyear.com/

The Greyhound Corp.
Greyhound Tower
Phoenix, AZ 85077
(602) 248-4000
Sales: NA
Employees: 38,100

Grumman
1111 Stewart Avenue
Bethpage, NY 11714
(516) 575-0574
Revenues: $4,040,000,000
Employees: 28,900

Guinness
39 Portman Square
London, England W1H 9HB
44-71-486-0288
Sales: £4,660,000
Employees: 23,264

H

Hallmark Cards, Inc.
2501 McGee Trafficway
Kansas City, MO 64141
(816) 274-5111
Sales: $3,400,000,000
Employees: 22,000

John Hancock
John Hancock Plaza
Boston, MA 02117
(617) 572-6000
Assets: $36,220,000,000
Employees: 19,000

Hanna-Barbera, Inc.
(Subsidiary of Turner Broadcasting System, Inc.)
3400 Cahuenga Boulevard
Hollywood, CA 90068
(213) 851-5000
Sales: $59,700,000
Employees: 500

Harley-Davidson, Inc.
3700 W. Juneau Avenue
Box 653
Milwaukee, WI 53201
(414) 342-4680
Sales: $1,220,000,000
Employees: 5,600
http://www.harley-davidson.com

Hasbro, Inc.
1027 Newport Avenue
Pawtucket, RI 02861
(401) 431-8697
Sales: $2,730,000,000
Employees: 10,000
http://www.hasbro.com

Heineken
Tweede Weteringplant Soen
101720 Amsterdam, Netherlands 21
Sales: $9,500,000
Employees: 42
http://www.heinken.com

H. J. Heinz Co.
600 Grant Street
Pittsburgh, PA 15219
(412) 456-5700
Sales: $7,100,000,000
Employees: 37,700

Hewlett-Packard Co.
3000 Hanover Street
Palo Alto, CA 94304
(650) 857-1501
Sales: $20,320,000,000
Employees: 97,000
http://www.hp.com

Hilton Hotels Corp.
9336 Civic Center Drive
Beverly Hills, CA 90210
(213) 278-4321
Sales: $1,390,000,000
Employees: 34,000
http://hilton.com

Honda
1-1, 2-chome,
Minami-Aoyama, Minato
Tokyo, Japan 107 Ku
81-3-3423-1111
Sales: $37,450,000,000
Employees: 31,036
http://www.honda.co.jp

Honeywell, Inc.
Honeywell Plaza
Minneapolis, MN 55408
(612) 951-1000
Sales: $5,960,000,000
Employees: 52,300
http://www.honeywell.com/

I

Intel Corp.
2200 Mission College Blvd
Santa Clara, CA 95052-8119
(408) 765-8080
Sales: $8,780,000,000
Employees: 24,600
http://www.intel.com/

International Business Machines (IBM)
Old Orchard Road
Armouk, NY 10504
(914) 765-1900
Sales: $62,720,000,000
Employees: 235,000
http://www.ibm.com

International Harvester Co.
(Stringers International Co.)
1000 Desoto Street
Clarksdale, MS 38614
(601) 624-4305
Sales: NA
Employees: 25

J

Johnson & Johnson
1 Johnson & Johnson Plaza
New Brunswick, NJ 08933
(732) 524-0400
Sales: $14,130,000,000

Employees: 81,600
http://www.jnj.com

Jostens, Inc.
5501 Norman Center Drive
Minneapolis, MN 55437
(612) 830-3300
Sales: $827,000,000
Employees: 8,000
http://www.jostens.com

K

Kellogg Co.
1 Kellogg Square
Battle Creek, MI 49016-3599
(616) 961-2000
Sales: $6,300,000,000
Employees: 16,500
http://www.kelloggs.com

Kentucky Fried Chicken
(Subsidiary of PepsiCo)
P.O. Box 32070
Louisville, KY 40232
(502) 456-8300
Sales: $3,000,000,000
Employees: 30,000

Kidder Peabody Group, Inc.
10 Hanover Square
New York, NY 10005
(212) 510-3000
Sales: $582,000,000
Employees: 5,700

Kindercare Learning Centers, Inc.
600 NE Holladay, Ste. 1400
Portland, OR 97232
(503) 872-1300
Sales: $437,200,000,000
Employees: 19,000

Kmart Corp.
3100 West Big Beaver Road
Troy, MI 48084
(248) 643-1000
Sales: $34,160,000,000
Employees: 320,000
http://www.kmart.com

Kollmorgen Corp.
347 King St.
Northhampton, MA 01060
(413) 586-2330
Sales: $185,540,000
Employees: 1,660

Kroger Co.
1014 Vine Street
Cincinnati, OH 45202
(513) 762-4000
Sales: $22,320,000,000
Employees: 170,000
http://www.kroger.com

L

Laidlaw Industries
(Subsidiary of Laidlaw, Inc.)
669 Airport Freeway
Suite 400
Hurst, TX 76053
(817) 282-7580
Sales: $942,000,000
Employees: 9,420

Lever Brothers Co.
(Subsidiary of Unilever
United States, Inc.)
390 Park Avenue
New York, NY 10022
(212) 688-6000
Sales: $2,100,000,000
Employees: 4,900

Levi Strauss & Co.
(Subsidiary of Levi Strauss
Assoc., Inc.)
1155 Battery Street
Levi's Plaza
San Francisco, CA 94111-1230
(415) 501-3939
Sales: $5,900,000,000
Employees: 36,400
http://www.levistrauss.com

Lincoln Electric Co.
22801 St. Clair Avenue
Cleveland, OH 44117-1199
(216) 481-8100
Sales: $846,000,000
Employees: 6,600
http://www.lincolnelectric.com

Arthur D. Little, Inc.
25 Acorn Park
Cambridge, MA 02140-2390
(617) 498-5000
Sales: $341,000,000
Employees: 2,400
http://www.adlittle.com

Lockheed Corp.
4500 Park Granada Boulevard
Calabasas, CA 90405
(818) 876-2000
Sales: $13,070,000,000
Employees: 71,000

Louisiana-Pacific Corp.
111 S.W. Fifth Avenue
Portland, OR 97204
(503) 221-0800
Sales: $2,500,000,000
Employees: 13,000
http://www.lpcorp.com

Louisville Gas & Electric
(Subsidiary of Louisville Gas &
Electric Energy Corp.)
220 W. Main Street
Louisville, KY 40202
(502) 627-2000
Sales: $775,130,000
Employees: 2,800
http://www.louisville.ky.us/lge.htm

LTV Corp.
200 Public Sq.
Cleveland, OH 44114-2308
(216) 622-5000
Sales: $7,040,000,000
Employees: 54,800
http://www.ltvsteel.com

M

R. H. Macy and Co., Inc.
151 West 34th Street
New York, NY 10001
(212) 695-4400
Sales: $6,970,000,000
Employees: 54,000

Marriott Corp.
Marriott Drive
Washington, D.C. 20058
(301) 897-9000
Sales: $4,240,000,000
Employees: 214,000
http://www.marriott.com

Martin Marietta Corp.
6801 Rockledge Drive
Bethesda, MD 20817
(301) 897-6000
Sales: $9,440,000,000
Employees: 92,786

Mary Kay Cosmetics
16251 Dallas Pkwy
Dallas, TX 75248
(972) 687-6300
Sales: $486,000,000
Employees: 100,000
http://www.marykay.com

Matsushita Electronic Co. of America
(Subsidiary of Matsushita
Electric Industrial Co., Ltd.)
1 Panasonic Way
Secaucus, NJ 07094
(201) 348-7000
Sales: NA
Employees: 7,000

Mattel, Inc.
333 Continental Boulevard
El Segundo, CA 90245-5012
(310) 252-2000
Sales: $2,700,000,000
Employees: 17,500
http://www.barbie.com

Mazda Motor Manufacturing (USA) Corp.
(Subsidiary of Mazda
Motor Corp.)
1 Mazda Drive
Flat Rock, MI 48134
(313) 782-7800
Sales: NA
Employees: 600

McCaw Cellular Communications, Inc.
(Subsidiary of AT&T Corp.)
5400 Carillon Point
Kirkland, WA 98033
(206) 827-4500
Sales: $2,190,000,000
Employees: 3,500

McDonald's Corp.
1 McDonald's Plaza
Oakbrook, IL 60523
(630) 623-3000
Sales: $14,400,000,000
Employees: 174,000
http://www.mcdonalds.com

McDonnell Douglas Corp.
Lambert St. Louis Airport
St. Louis, MO 63166
(314) 232-0232
Sales: $14,490,000,000
Employees: 127,926

MCI Communications Corp.
1801 Pennsylvania Avenue
Washington, D.C. 20006
(202) 872-1600
Sales: $11,920,000,000
Employees: 34,000
http://www.mci.com

The Mead Corp.
Courthouse Plaza, N.E.
Dayton, OH 45463
(937) 495-6323
Sales: $4,790,000,000
Employees: 21,600
http://www.mead.com

Merck & Co., Inc.
One Merck Drive
Box 100
Whitehouse Station, NJ 08889
(908) 423-1000
Sales: $10,500,000,000
Employees: 47,100
http://www.merck.com

Mervyn's
(Subsidiary of
Dayton-Hudson Corp.)
25001 Industrial Boulevard
Hayward, CA 94545
(415) 785-8800
Sales: $2,862,300,000
Employees: 44,600

Metro-Goldwyn-Mayer, Inc.
2500 Broadway St.
Santa Monica, CA 90404
(310) 449-3000
Sales: $690,100,000,000
Employees: 830
http://www.mgmua.com

Microsoft
One Microsoft Way
Redmond, WA 98052
(425) 882-8080
Sales: $4,650,000,000
Employees: 15,000
http://www.microsoft.com

Miller Brewing Co.
(Subsidiary of Philip Morris Companies, Inc.)
3939 West Highland Boulevard
Milwaukee, WI 53201
(414) 931-2000
Sales: $2,914,000,000
Employees: 1,618

Herman Miller, Inc.
855 E. Main Avenue
Zeeland, MI 49464-0302
(616) 772-3300
Sales: $885,670,000
Employees: 5,400
http://www.hermanmiller.com/

Mirage Resorts, Inc.
3400 Las Vegas Boulevard South
Las Vegas, NV 89109
(702) 791-7111
Sales: $953,300,000
Employees: 12,000
http://www.mirageresorts.com

Mitsubishi Motors
5-33-8 Shiba
Minato-ku
Tokyo, Japan 108
3-3456-1111
Sales: $19,850,000,000
Employees: 27,603
http://www.mitsubishi-motors.co.jp

Mobil Corp.
3225 Gallows Road
Fairfax, VA 22037-0001
(703) 846-3000
Sales: $63,470,000,000
Employees: 63,700
http://www.mobil.com

Monsanto Co.
800 North Lindbergh Boulevard
St. Louis, MO 63167
(314) 694-1000
Sales: $7,900,000,000
Employees: 33,797
http://www.monsanto.com

J. P. Morgan & Co., Inc.
60 Wall Street
New York, NY 10260-0060
(212) 483-2323
Sales: $1,590,000,000
Employees: 15,193
http://www.jpmorgan.com

Morgan Stanley Group, Inc.
1251 Avenue of the Americas
New York, NY 10020
(212) 703-4000
Revenues: $11,160,000,000
Employees: 8,249

Motorola, Inc.
1303 East Algonquin Road
Schaumburg, IL 60196
(847) 576-5000
Sales: $16,960,000,000
Employees: 102,000
http://www.mot.com

MTV Networks, Inc.
(Subsidiary of Viacom International)
1515 Broadway
New York, NY 10036
(212) 258-8000
Sales: $675,000,000
Employees: 1,700

N

NationsBank Corp.
101 N. Tryon Street
NationsBank Plaza
Charlotte, NC 28246
(704) 386-5000
Sales: $10,400,000,000
Employees: 760
http://www.nationsbank.com

NCR Corp.
1700 South Patterson Boulevard
Dayton, OH 45479
(937) 445-5000
Sales: $4,310,000,000
Employees: 62,000
http://www.ncr.com

Nestlé
800 N. Brand Blvd
Glendale, CA 91203
(818) 549-6000
Sales: NA
Employees: 22,000
http://www.nestle.com

New Jersey Bell Telephone Co.
540 Broad Street
Newark, NJ 07102
(201) 649-9900
Sales: $2,500,000,000
Employees: 19,700

The News Corp., Ltd.
Two Holt Street
Sydney, NSW
Australia 2010
61-2-9288-3000
Sales: $7,400,000,000
Employees: 24,700
http://www.newscorp.com

Nexagen, Inc.
2860 Wilderness Place
Boulder, CO 80301
(303) 444-5893
Sales: $1,890,000
Employees: 526

Nike, Inc.
One Bowerman Drive
Beaverton, OR 97005-6453
(503) 671-6453
Sales: $3,790,000,000
Employees: 9,000
http://info.nike.com

Nissan Motor Corp.
(Subsidiary of Nissan Motor Co., Ltd., Tokyo, Japan)
18501 South Figueroa Street
Carson, CA 90247
(213) 532-3111
Sales: $14,415,180,000
Employees: 3,000

Nordstrom, Inc.
1501 Fifth Avenue
Seattle, WA 98101-1603
(206) 628-2111
Sales: $3,590,000,000
Employees: 31,000
http://www.nordstrom-pta.com

Northern Telecom, Inc.
(Subsidiary of Northern Telecom Ltd.)
200 Athens Way
Nashville, TN 37228-7388
(615) 734-4000
Sales: NA
Employees: 20,000
http://www.nortel.com

Nucor Corp.
2100 Rexford Road
Charlotte, NC 28211
(704) 366-7000
Sales: $2,250,000,000
Employees: 5,900
http://www2.nue.com/nbs

O

Office Depot, Inc.
2200 Old Germantown Road
Delray Beach, FL 33445
(561) 278-4800
Sales: $2,580,000,000
Employees: 25,000

Olin Corp.
501 Merritt Seven
Norwalk, CT 06856-4500
(203) 750-3000
Sales: $2,420,000,000
Employees: 12,400

Olsten Corp.
175 Broad Hollow Rd.
Melville, NY 11747-8905
(516) 844-7800
Sales: $1,960,000,000
Employees: 1,200
http://www.olsten.com

Oryx
47341 Bayside Pkwy.
Fremont, CA 94538
(510) 249-1144
Sales: $3,000,000
Employees: NA
http://www.oryxtech.com

Owens-Corning Fiberglas Corp.
Fiberglas Tower
Toledo, OH 43659
(419) 248-8000
Sales: $2,940,000,000
Employees: 17,000

P

Pacific Gas & Electric
77 Beale Street
San Francisco, CA 94105-1814
(415) 973-7000
Sales: $10,600,000,000
Employees: 23,000
http://www.pge.com

J. C. Penney Co., Inc.
6501 Legacy Drive
Plano, TX 75024-3698
(972) 431-1000
Sales: $19,580,000,000
Employees: 193,000
http://www.jcpenney.com

People's Bank
(Subsidiary of People's Mutual Holdings)
850 Main Street
Bridgeport, CT 06604-4913
(203) 338-7171
Sales: $337,600,000
Employees: 2,500
http://www.peoples.com

PepsiCo, Inc.
700 Anderson Hill Road
Purchase, NY 10577-1444
(914) 253-2000
Sales: $25,020,000,000
Employees: 423,000
http://www.pepsico.com

Perkin-Elmer Corp.
761 Main Avenue
Norwalk, CT 06859-0001
(203) 762-1000
Sales: $1,010,000,000
Employees: 6,000
http://www.perkin-elmer.com

Philips
(Subsidiary of Philips Industries, Inc.)
4801 Springfield Street
Dayton, OH 45431
(513) 253-7171
Sales: $945,000,000
Employees: 279

Pillsbury Co.
(Subsidiary of Gramet Holdings Corp.)
Pillsbury Center
200 South 6th Street
Minneapolis, MN 55402
(612) 330-4966
Sales: $6,120,000,000
Employees: 68,000

Pitney Bowles, Inc.
1 Elmcroft Road
Stamford, CT 06926-0790
(203) 356-5000
Sales: $3,540,000,000
Employees: 32,539

Pizza Hut, Inc.
(Subsidiary of PepsiCo)
9111 E. Douglas
Wichita, KS 67207
(316) 681-9000
Sales: $6,400,000,000
Employees: 151,000

Polaroid Corp.
549 Technology Square
Cambridge, MA 02139
(617) 386-2000
Sales: $2,250,000,000
Employees: 12,359
http://www.polariod.com

Polycast
(Subsidiary of the Jessup Group, Inc.)
402 S. Byrkit
Mishawaka, IN 46544
(219) 259-1259
Sales: $120,000,000
Employees: 733

Pratt & Whitney
(Subsidiary of United Technologies Corp.)
400 Main Street
Cumberland, RI 02864
(401) 333-6000
Sales: $3,500,000
Employees: 30

Price/Costco, Inc.
10809 120th Avenue N.E.
Kirkland, WA 98033
(206) 828-8100
Sales: $15,500,000,000
Employees: 18,100

The Procter & Gamble Co.
One Procter & Gamble Plaza
Cincinnati, OH 45202
(513) 983-1100
Sales: $30,430,000,000
Employees: 80,350
http://www.pg.com

Prudential-Bache Properties, Inc.
One Seaport Plaza
New York, NY 10292
(212) 214-2178
Sales: NA
Employees: 11,000

Publix Stores, Inc.
1395 6th Street N.W.
Winter Haven, FL 33881
(813) 688-1188
Sales: $27,000,000
Employees: 279

R

Raychem Corp.
300 Constitution Drive
Menlo Park, CA 94025
(415) 361-3333
Sales: $1,500,000,000
Employees: 11,000

RCA Corp.
(Subsidiary of General Electric Co.)
30 Rockefeller Plaza
New York, NY 10020
(212) 621-6000
Sales: NA
Employees: 80,000

Reebok International, Ltd.
100 Technology Center Drive
Stoughton, MA 02072
(781) 341-5000
Sales: $2,890,000,000
Employees: 4,220
http://www.reebok.com

Reflexite Corp.
120 Darling Drive
Avon, CT 06001
(203) 676-7100
Sales: $40,000,000
Employees: 350

Reuters
410 11th Avenue South
Hopkins, MN 55343
(612) 935-6921
Sales: $26,300,000
Employees: 230

RJ Reynolds Tobacco Co.
(Subsidiary of RJR Nabisco, Inc.)
401 N. Main Street
Winston-Salem, NC 27101
(336) 741-5000
Sales: $8,100,000,000
Employees: 14,000
http://www.rjrt.com

RJR Nabisco, Inc.
1100 Reynolds Boulevard
Winston-Salem, NC 27102
(919) 773-2000
Sales: $16,595,000,000
Employees: 130,000

Rockwell International Corp.
600 Anton Blvd., Ste 700
Costa Mesa, CA 92626-7147
(714) 424-4200
Sales: $10,840,000,000
Employees: 77,028
http://www.rockwell.com

Rohn and Haas Co.
100 Independence Mall West
Philadelphia, PA 19106
(215) 592-3000
Sales: $3,260,000,000
Employees: 13,000
http://www.rohmhass.com

Rubbermaid, Inc.
1147 Akron Road
Wooster, OH 44691-6000
(330) 264-6464
Sales: $2,110,000,000
Employees: 12,371
http://www.rubbermaid.com

Ryder System, Inc.
3600 N.W. 82nd Avenue
Miami, FL 33168
(305) 593-3726
Sales: $4,220,000,000
Employees: 40,000
http://www.ryder.com

S

Safeway, Inc.
5918 Stoneridge Mall Rd.
Pleasonton, CA 94588-3229
(510) 467-3000
Sales: $15,210,000,000
Employees: 124,000
http://www.safeway.com

J. Sainsbury
Stamford House
Stamford Street
London, England SE1 9LL
+44-171-695-6000
Sales: $11,220,000,000
Employees: 79,974
http://www.sainsburys.co.uk

Saks Fifth Avenue
(Subsidiary of Investcorp.)
12 E. 49th Street
New York, NY 10017
(212) 940-4048
Sales: $1,400,000,000
Employees: 8,000

Savin Corporation
(Subsidiary of CDC Data Systems, Ltd.)
9 West Broad Street
Stamford, CT 06904-2270
(203) 967-5000
Sales: $198,000,000
Employees: 1,900

Scandinavian Airlines
138-02 Queens Boulevard
Jamaica, NY 11453
(718) 657-2575
Sales: $166,000,000
Employees: 610

Scott Paper
Scott Plaza
Philadelphia, PA 19113
(610) 522-5000
Sales: $4,750,000,000
Employees: 25,900

Seagram International
(Subsidiary of Seagold Vineyards Holding Corp.)
375 Park Avenue
New York, NY 10152
(212) 572-7000
Sales: $3,150,000,000
Employees: 10,200

Sears Roebuck & Co.
3333 Beverly Rd.
Hoffman Estates, IL 60179
(847) 286-2500
Sales: $50,840,000,000
Employees: 363,000
http://www.sears.com

Shaklee
(Subsidiary of Y-S Holding Corp.)
444 Market Street
San Francisco, CA 94111
(415) 954-3000
Sales: $480,000,000
Employees: 3,300

Shell Oil Co.
(Subsidiary of Shell Petroleum, Inc.)
One Shell Plaza
900 Louisiana
Houston, TX 77002
(713) 241-6161
Sales: $21,090,000,000
Employees: 22,212
http://www.shellus.com

Shenandoah Life Insurance Co.
2301 Brambleton Avenue S.W.
Roanoke, VA 24015
(703) 985-4400
Sales: $131,800,000
Employees: 212

Siemens Corp.
(Subsidiary of Siemens AG)
1301 Avenue of the Americas
New York, NY 10019
(212) 258-4000
Sales: $3,980,000,000
Employees: 376

Smith Barney
(Subsidiary of Travelers, Inc.)
388 Greenwich St.
New York, NY 10103
(212) 816-6000
Sales: $950,000,000
Employees: 7,500
http://www.smithbarney.com

Solectron Corp.
777 Gilbraltar Drive
Milpitas, CA 95035
(408) 957-8500
Sales: $1,460,000,000
Employees: 6,000
http://www.solectron.com

Sony Corp. of America
(Subsidiary of Sony Corp.)
9 West 57th Street
New York, NY 10019
(212) 371-5800

Sales: $2,000,000,000
Employees: 6,900

Southwest Airlines Co.
2702 Love Field Dr.
Dallas, TX 75235
(214) 792-4000
Sales: $2,300,000,000
Employees: 11,400
http://www.iflyswa.com

The Sperry Co., Inc.
9146 U.S. Highway 52
Brookville, IN 47012
(317) 647-4141
Sales: NA
Employees: 300

Spiegel, Inc.
3500 Lacey Road
Downers Grove, IL 60515-5432
(630) 986-8800
Sales: $2,600,000,000
Employees: 12,000
http://www.spiegel.com

Sprint Corp.
2330 Shawnee Mission Parkway
Westwood, KS 66205
(913) 624-3000
Sales: NA
Employees: NA
http://www.sprint.com

Square D
1415 S. Roselle Road
Palatine, IL 60067
(708) 397-2600
Sales: $1,720,000,000
Employees: 19,300

The Standard Oil Co.
(Subsidiary of British Petroleum Co. plc)
200 Public Square
Cleveland, OH 44114
(216) 586-4141
Sales: $14,780,000,000
Employees: 41,600

State Farm Mutual Auto Insurance Co.
One State Farm Plaza
Bloomington, IL 61701
(309) 766-2311
Sales: $22,000,000,000
Employees: 49,752

Sun Microsystems
901 San Antonio Rd.
Palo Alto, CA 94303
(650) 960-1300
Sales: $4,310,000,000
Employees: 12,500
http://www.sun.com

Sunoco
(Subsidiary of Sun Co., Inc.)
36 York Mills Road
Northyork, Ontario
Canada M2P 2C5
(416) 733-7300
Sales: $1,500,000,000
Employees: 4,115

T

Taco Bell
(Subsidiary of PepsiCo)
17901 Von Karmen Avenue
Irvine, CA 92714
(714) 863-4500
Sales: $1,470,000,000
Employees: 47,000

TCI International, Inc.
222 Caspian Drive
Sunnyvalle, CA 94089
(408) 747-6100
Sales: $28,260,000
Employees: 140
http://www.tcibr.com

Teleflex Inc.
155 South Limerick Road
Royersford, PA 19468
(215) 948-5700
Sales: $175,000,000
Employees: 3,500

Tenneco, Inc.
1275 King St.
Greenwich, CT 06831
(203) 863-1000
Sales: $14,400,000,000
Employees: 90,000
http://www.tenneco.com

Texaco, Inc.
2000 Westchester Avenue
White Plains, NY 10650
(914) 253-4000
Sales: $46,200,000,000
Employees: 54,400
http://www.texaco.com

Texas Instruments Inc.
13500 North Central Expressway
Dallas, TX 75265
(972) 995-2011
Sales: $4,920,000,000
Employees: 77,800
http://www.ti.com

The Thermos Co.
300 N. Martingale Road
Schaumburg, IL 60173
(708) 240-3150
Sales: NA
Employees: 2,000

3M
3M Center
St. Paul, MN 55144-1000
(612) 733-1110
Sales: $8,600,000,000
Employees: 84,300
http://www.mmm.com

Time Warner, Inc.
1275 Rockefeller Plaza
New York, NY 10019
(212) 484-8000
Sales: $14,500,000,000
Employees: 41,700
http://pathfinder.com/corp

Toshiba International Corp.
(Subsidiary of Toshiba Corp.)
350 California Street
Suite 700
San Francisco, CA 94104
(415) 434-2340
Sales: $201,000,000
Employees: 506

Toyota Motor Sales USA, Inc.
(Subsidiary of Toyota Motor Corp.)
19001 South Western Avenue
Torrance, CA 90509
(310) 787-1310
Sales: $5,000,000,000
Employees: 2,200

Toys "Я" Us, Inc.
395 West Passaic Street
Rochelle Park, NJ 07662
(201) 845-5033
Sales: $2,444,903,000
Employees: 28,600

The Travelers Corp.
One Tower Square
Hartford, CT 06183-1050
(203) 277-0111
Sales: NA
Employees: 30,000

Triangle Industries, Inc.
900 Third Avenue
16th Floor
New York, NY 10022
(212) 230-3000
Sales: $1,640,000,000
Employees: 14,000

TRW, Inc.
1900 Richmond Road
Cleveland, OH 44124-3760
(216) 291-7000
Sales: $5,490,000,000
Employees: 82,400
http://www.trw.com

U

Ultra Pac, Inc.
21925 Industrial Boulevard
Rogers, MN 55374
(612) 428-8340
Sales: $11,590,000
Employees: 75

Unilever
(Subsidiary of Nederlandse Unilever Bedrijuen)
390 Park Avenue
New York, NY 10022-4698
(212) 888-1260
Sales: $8,110,000,000
Employees: 30,600

Union Carbide Corp.
Old Ridgebury Road
Section C-2
Danbury, CT 06817-0001
(203) 794-2000
Sales: $9,000,000,000
Employees: 46,900
http://www.unioncarbide.com

Union Pacific Corp.
1717 Main St., Ste 5900
Dallas, TX 75201-4605
(214) 743-5600
Sales: $7,560,000,000
Employees: 233
http://www.up.com

Unisys Corp.
Township Line & Union Meeting Roads
Blue Bell, PA 19424
(215) 986-4011
Sales: $5,030,000,000
Employees: 100,000
http://www.unisys.com

United Airlines, Inc.
(Subsidiary of Allegis Corp.)
1200 Algonquin Road
Elk Grove Township, IL 60007
(847) 700-4000
Sales: $52,900,000,000
Employees: 54,300
http://www.ual.com

United Parcel Service of America, Inc.
55 Glenlake Pkwy. NE
Atlanta, GA 30328
(770) 828-6000
Sales: $8,610,000,000
Employees: 160,000
http://www.ups.com

United Technologies Corp.
Main and Pearl Streets
Hartford, CT 06101
(860) 728-7000
Sales: $15,600,000,000
Employees: 193,000
http://www.utc.com

US Air
2345 Crystal Drive
Arlington, VA 22227
(703) 872-7000
Sales: $6,260,000,000
Employees: 53,700
http://www.usairways.com

US Steel
(Subsidiary of USX Corp.)

600 Grant Street
Pittsburgh, PA 15219-4776
(412) 433-1121
Sales: NA
Employees: NA
http://www.ussteel.com

USX Corp.
600 Grant Street
Pittsburgh, PA 15219
(412) 433-1121
Sales: $18,060,000,000
Employees: 45,592

Viacom, Inc.
(Subsidiary of National Amusements, Inc.)
1515 Broadway
New York, NY 10036
(212) 258-6000
Sales: $2,000,000,000
Employees: 4,900
http://www.viacom.com

Volkswagen
Wolfsburg, Germany
05-36190
Phone: 49-53-61-90
Sales: $68,070,000,000
Employees: 267,038
http://www.vw.com

Wal-Mart Stores
702 8th Street
Bentonville, AR 72716-8611
(501) 273-4000
Sales: $11,900,000,000
Employees: 150,000
http://www.wal-mart.com

The Walt Disney Co.
500 South Buena Vista Street
Burbank, CA 91521
(818) 560-1000
Sales: $1,370,000,000
Employees: 30,000
http://www.disney.com

Warner Communications
75 Rockefeller Plaza
New York, NY 10019
(212) 484-8000
Sales: $2,230,000,000
Employees: 8,000

Waste Management
3003 Butterfield Road
Hinsdale, IL 60521
(630) 572-8800
Sales: $4,480,000,000
Employees: 42,600
http://www.wastemanagement.com

Westinghouse Electrical Corp.
Six Gateway Center
Pittsburgh, PA 15222
(412) 244-2000
Sales: $10,700,000,000
Employees: 133,000

Weyerhaeuser Co.
33663 32nd Drive S.E.
Federal Way, WA 98003
(206) 924-2345
Sales: $5,200,000,000
Employees: 41,700

Whirlpool
2000 M63 N.
Benton Harbor, MI 49022-2692
(616) 923-5000
Sales: $6,290,000,000
Employees: 39,400
http://www.whirlpool.com

WHYCO Chromium Co.
Thomaston, CT 06787
(203) 283-5826
Sales: $14,000,000
Employees: 200

Woolworth Corp.
233 Broadway
Woolworth Building
New York, NY 10279-0003
(212) 553-2000
Sales: $9,800,000,000
Employees: 73,000

X

Xerox Corp.
800 Long Ridge Road
Stamford, CT 06904
(203) 968-3000
Sales: $8,730,000,000
Employees: 98,500
http://www.xerox.com

Z

Zale Corp.
901 West Walnut Hill Lane
Irving, TX 75038-1003
(214) 580-4000
Sales: NA
Employees: 9,900

Zenith
1000 Milwaukee Avenue
Glenview, IL 60025-2493
(847) 391-7000
Sales: $2,610,000,000
Employees: 32,000
http://www.zenith.com

Glossary

A

360-degree appraisal Process of using multiple sources of appraisal to gain a comprehensive perspective of one's performance.

accommodation A style of dealing with conflict involving cooperation on behalf of the other party but not being assertive about one's own interests.

accountability The expectation that employees perform a job, take corrective action when necessary, and report upward on the status and quality of their performance.

accounting audits Procedures used to verify accounting reports and statements.

activity-based costing (ABC) A method of cost accounting designed to identify streams of activity, and then to allocate costs across particular business processes according to the amount of time employees devote to particular activities.

adapters Companies that take the current industry structure, and its future evolution, as givens.

administrative management A classical management approach that attempted to identify principles and functions that managers could use to achieve superior organizational performance.

affective conflict Emotional disagreement directed toward other people.

arbitration The use of a neutral third party to resolve a labor dispute.

assessment center A managerial performance test in which candidates participate in a variety of exercises and situations.

assets The values of the various items the corporation owns.

authority The legitimate right to make decisions and to tell other people what to do.

autocratic leadership A form of leadership in which the leader makes decisions on his or her own and then announces those decisions to the group.

autonomous work groups Groups that control decisions about and execution of a complete range of tasks—acquiring raw materials, performing operations, quality control, maintenance, and shipping.

avoidance A reaction to conflict that involves either ignoring the problem by doing nothing at all, or by de-emphasizing the disagreement.

B

balance sheet A report that shows the financial picture of a company at a given time and itemizes assets, liabilities, and stockholders' equity.

barriers to entry Conditions that prevent new companies from entering an industry.

behavioral approach A leadership perspective that attempts to identify what good leaders do—that is, what behaviors they exhibit.

benchmarking The process of comparing the organization's practices and technologies with those of other companies.

bootlegging Informal efforts by managers and employees to create new products and new processes.

boundaryless organization Organization in which there are no barriers to information flow.

bounded rationality A less-than-perfect form of rationality in which decision makers cannot conduct a complete, rational analysis because decisions are complex and complete information is unavailable.

brainstorming A process in which group members generate as many ideas about a problem as they can; criticism is withheld until all ideas have been proposed.

broker Persons who assemble and coordinate participants in a network.

budgeting The process of investigating what is being done and comparing the results with the corresponding budget data to verify accomplishments or remedy differences. Also called budgetary controlling.

buffering Creating supplies of excess resources in case of unpredictable needs.

bureaucracy A classical management approach emphasizing a structured, formal network of relationships among specialized positions in the organization.

bureaucratic control The use of rules, regulations, and authority to guide performance.

business ethics The moral principles and standards that guide behavior in the world of business.

business incubators Protected environments for new, small businesses.

business judgment rule allows management wide latitude in policy if the policy can be justified.

business plan A formal planning step in starting a new business that focuses on the entire venture and describes all the elements involved in starting it.

business strategy The major actions by which a business competes in a particular industry or market.

C

cafeteria benefit program Employee benefit programs in which employees choose from a menu of options to create a benefit package tailored to their needs.

carrying capacity The ability of a finite resource to sustain a population.

centralized organization An organization in which high-level executives make most decisions and pass them down to lower levels for implementation.

certainty The state that exists when decision makers have accurate and comprehensive information.

charismatic leader A person who is dominant, self-confident, convinced of the moral righteousness of his or her beliefs, and able to arouse a sense of excitement and adventure in subordinates.

chief technology officer (CTO) Executive in charge of technology strategy and development.

clan control Control based on the norms, values, shared goals, and trust among group members.

coaching Dialogue with a goal of helping another be more effective and achieve his or her full potential on the job.

coalition building Finding other organizations or groups of voters that share political interests on a particular legislative issue.

coalitional model Model of organizational decision making in which groups with differing preferences use power and negotiations to influence decisions.

cognitive conflict Issue-based differences in perspectives or judgments.

cohesiveness The degree to which a group is attractive to its members, members are motivated to remain in the group, and members influence one another.

collaboration A style of dealing with conflict involving emphasizing both cooperation and assertiveness in order to maximize both parties' satisfaction.

communication The transmission of information and meaning from one party to another through the use of shared symbols.

comparable worth Principle of equal pay for different jobs of equal worth.

competitive environment The immediate environment surrounding a firm; includes suppliers, customers, competitors, and the like.

competitive intelligence Information that helps managers determine how to compete better.

compliance-based ethics programs Company mechanisms typically designed by corporate counsel to prevent, detect, and punish legal violations.

compromise A style of dealing with conflict involving moderate attention to both parties' concerns.

computer-integrated manufacturing The use of computer-aided design and computer-aided manufacturing to sequence and optimize a number of production processes.

concentration A strategy employed for an organization that operates a single business and competes in a single industry.

concentric diversification A strategy used to add new businesses that produce related products or are involved in related markets and activities.

conceptual and decision skills Skills pertaining to a manager's ability to recognize complex and dynamic issues, examine the numerous and conflicting factors such issues involve, and resolve the problems for the benefit of the organization and its members.

concurrent control The control process used while plans are being carried out, including directing, monitoring, and fine-tuning activities as they are performed.

conflict Opposing pressures from different sources. Two levels of conflict are psychological conflict and conflict that arises among individuals or groups.

conglomerate diversification A strategy used to add new businesses that produce unrelated products or are involved in unrelated markets and activities.

conservation An environmental philosophy that seeks to avoid waste, promote the rational and efficient use of natural resources, and maximize long-term yields, especially of renewable resources.

contingencies Factors that determine the appropriateness of managerial actions.

contingency perspective An approach to the study of management proposing that the managerial strategies, structures, and processes that result in high performance depend on the characteristics, or important contingencies, of the situation in which they are applied.

contingency plans Alternative courses of action that can be implemented based on how the future unfolds.

continuous process A process that is highly automated and has a continuous production flow.

control The process of measuring progress toward planned performance and applying corrective measures to ensure that performance is in line with managers' objectives.

controlling The management function of monitoring progress and making needed changes.

cooperative strategies Strategies used by two or more organizations working together to manage the external environment.

coordination The procedures that link the various parts of the organization for the purpose of achieving the organization's overall mission.

coordination by mutual adjustment Units interact with one another to make accommodations so as to achieve flexible coordination.

coordination by plan Interdependent units are required to meet deadlines and objectives that contribute to a common goal.

core competencies The unique skills or knowledge an organization possesses that give it an edge over competitors.

corporate constituency programs Organizational efforts to identify, educate, and motivate individuals to take political action that could benefit the organization.

corporate legitimacy A motive for organizational involvement in the public policy process. The assumption is that organizations are legitimate to the extent that their goals, purposes, and methods are consistent with those of society.

corporate social responsibility Obligation toward society assumed by business.

corporate social responsiveness The process companies follow and the actions they take in the domain of corporate social responsibility.

corporate strategy The set of businesses, markets, or industries in which an organization competes and the distribution of resources among those entities.

cost competitiveness Keeping costs low in order to achieve profits and price so that they are attractive to consumers.

culture shock The disorientation and stress associated with being in a foreign environment.

current ratio A liquidity ratio which indicates the extent to which short-term assets can decline and still be adequate to pay short-term liabilities.

custom-made solutions The combination of ideas into new, creative solutions.

customer service The speed and dependability with which an organization can deliver what customers want.

D

debt-equity ratio A leverage ratio which indicates the company's ability to meet its long-term financial obligations.

decentralized organization An organization in which lower-level managers make important decisions.

defenders Companies that stay within a stable product domain as a strategic maneuver.

delegation The assignment of new or additional responsibilities to a subordinate.

democratic leadership A form of leadership in which the leader solicits input from subordinates.

demographics Measures of various characteristics of the people who comprise groups or other social units.

deontology Focuses on rights of individuals.

departmentalization Subdividing an organization into smaller subunits.

design for environment (DFE) A tool for creating products that are easy to recover, reuse, or recycle.

development Teaching managers and professional employees broad skills needed for their present and future jobs.

development project A focused organizational effort to create a new product or process via technological advances.

devil's advocate A person who has the job of criticizing ideas to ensure that different viewpoints are fully explored.

dialectic A structured debate comparing two conflicting courses of action.

dialogue A discourse in which members explore complex issues from many viewpoints in order to come to a common deeper understanding.

differentiation An aspect of the organization's internal environment created by job specialization and the division of labor.

differentiation strategy A strategy an organization uses to build competitive advantage by being unique in its industry or market segment along one or more dimensions.

discount the future Weight short-term costs and benefits more heavily than longer-term costs and benefits.

discussion A type of discourse in which each person attempts to win a debate by having his or her view accepted by the group.

diversity training Programs that focus on identifying and reducing hidden biases against people with differences and developing the skills needed to effectively manage a diversified workforce.

division of labor The assignment of different tasks to different people or groups.

divisional organization Departmentalization that groups units around products, customers, or geographic regions.

domain defense Activities intended to counter challenges to the organization's legitimacy.

downsizing The planned elimination of positions or jobs.

downward communication Information that flows from higher to lower levels in the organization's hierarchy.

dynamic network Temporary arrangements among partners that can be assembled and reassembled to adapt to the environment.

E

ecocentric management has as its goal the creation of sustainable economic development and improvement of quality of life worldwide for all organizational stakeholders.

economic responsibilities are to produce goods and services that society wants at a price that perpetuates the business and satisfies its obligations to investors.

economies of scale Reductions in the average cost of a unit of production as the total volume produced increases.

economies of scope Economies in which materials and processes employed in one product can be used to make other, related products.

effectiveness The degree to which the outputs of the organization correspond to the outputs desired by organizations and individuals in the external environment.

efficiency The ratio of outputs to inputs.

egoism An ethical system defining acceptable behavior as that which maximizes consequences for the individual.

emergent strategy The strategy that evolves from all the activities engaged in by people throughout the organization.

empowerment The process of sharing power with employees, thereby enhancing their confidence in their ability to perform their jobs and their belief that they are influential contributors to the organization.

entrepreneurial orientation The tendency of an organization to engage in activities designed to identify and capitalize successfully on opportunities to launch new ventures by entering new or established markets with new or existing goods or services.

entrepreneurial venture A new business having growth and high profitability as primary objectives.

entrepreneurship The act of forming a new organization of value.

environmental movement An environmental philosophy postulating that the unintended negative effects of human economic activities on the environment are often greater than the benefits, and that nature should be preserved.

environmental scanning Searching for and sorting through information about the environment.

environmental uncertainty Lack of information needed to understand or predict the future.

equifinality Principle that states there are many avenues to the same outcome, and not just one best way.

equity theory A theory stating that people assess how fairly they have been treated according to two key factors: outcomes and inputs.

ERG theory A human needs theory developed by Alderfer postulating that people have three basic sets of needs which can operate simultaneously.

ethical climate of an organization refers to the processes by which decisions are evaluated and made on the basis of right and wrong.

ethical issue Situation, problem, or opportunity in which an individual must choose among several actions that must be evaluated as right or wrong.

ethical responsibilities Meeting other social expectations, not written as law.

ethics The system of rules governing the ordering of values.

executive champion An executive who supports a new technology and protects the product champion of the innovation.

expatriates Parent-company nationals who are sent to work at a foreign subsidiary.

expectancy Employees' perception of the likelihood that their efforts will enable them to attain their performance goals.

expectancy theory A theory proposing that people will behave based on their perceived likelihood that their effort will lead to a certain outcome and on how highly they value that outcome.

external audit An evaluation conducted by one organization, such as a CPA firm, on another.

external environment All relevant forces outside a firm's boundaries, such as competitors, customers, the government, and the economy.

extinction Withdrawing or failing to provide a reinforcing consequence.

extrinsic reinforcers Reinforces given to a person by the boss, the company, or some other person.

F

failure rate The number of expatriate managers of an overseas operation that come home early.

feedback control Control that focuses on the use of information about previous results to correct deviations from the acceptable standard.

feedforward control The control process used before operations begin, including policies, procedures, and rules designed to ensure that planned activities are carried out properly.

Fiedler's contingency model of leadership effectiveness A situational approach to leadership postulating that effectiveness depends on the personal style of the leader and the degree to which the situation gives the leader power, control, and influence over the situation.

filtering The process of withholding, ignoring, or distorting information.

final consumer Those who purchase products in their finished form.

flexible benefit programs Benefit programs in which employees are given credits to spend on benefits that fit their unique needs.

flexible factories Manufacturing plants that have short production runs, are organized around products, and use decentralized scheduling.

flexible processes Methods for adapting the technical core to changes in the environment.

forcing A style of dealing with conflict involving competitiveness, strong focus on one's own goals and little or no concern for the other person's goals.

forecasting Method for predicting how variables will change the future.

framing effects A psychological bias influenced by the way in which a problem or decision alternative is phrased or presented.

frontline managers Lower-level managers who supervise the operational activities of the organization.

functional organization Departmentalization around specialized activities, such as production, marketing, human resources, etc.

functional strategies Strategies implemented by each functional area of the organization to support the organization's business strategy.

functions of management The four basic management processes consisting of planning, organizing, leading, and controlling.

G

garbage can model Model of organizational decision making depicting a chaotic process and seemly random decisions.

genius of the "and" The ability to pursue multiple goals at once.

glass ceiling An invisible barrier that makes it difficult for certain groups, such as minorities and women, to move beyond a certain level in the organizational hierarchy

global organization model An organization model consisting of a company's overseas subsidiaries and characterized by centralized decision making and tight control by the parent company over most aspects of worldwide operations. Typically adopted by organizations that base their global competitive strategy on low cost.

global start-up A new venture that is international from the very beginning.

goal A target or end that management desires to reach.

goal displacement A condition that occurs when a decision-making group loses sight of its original goal and a new, possibly less important goal emerges.

goal-setting theory A motivation theory that states people have conscious goals that energize them and direct their thoughts and behaviors toward one end.

grapevine Informal communication network.

group maintenance behaviors Actions taken to ensure the satisfaction of group members, develop and maintain harmonious work relationships, and preserve the social stability of the group.

groupthink A phenomenon that occurs in decision making when group members avoid disagreement as they strive for consensus.

growth need strength The degree to which individuals want personal and psychological development.

H

Hawthorne Effect People's reactions to being observed or studied resulting in superficial rather than meaningful changes in behavior.

Hersey and Blanchard's situational theory A life cycle of leadership developed by Hersey and Blanchard postulating that a manager should consider an employee's psychological and job maturity before deciding whether task performance or maintenance behaviors are more important.

hierarchy The authority levels of the organizational pyramid.

high-involvement organization A type of organization in which top management ensures that there is consensus about the direction in which the business is heading.

horizontal communication Information shared among people on the same hierarchical level.

host-country nationals Natives of the country where an overseas subsidiary is located.

human capital The knowledge, skills, and abilities of employees that have economic value.

human relations A classical management approach that attempted to understand and explain how human psychological and social processes interact with the formal aspects of the work situation to influence performance.

human resources management (HRM) Formal systems for the management of people within the organization. Divided into three major areas: staffing, rewarding, and designing work.

hygiene factors Characteristics of the workplace, such as company policies, working conditions, pay, and supervision, that make a job more satisfying.

I

illusion of control People's belief that they can influence events, even when they have no control over what will happen.

incremental model Model of organizational decision making in which major solutions arise through a series of smaller decisions.

independent entrepreneur An individual who establishes a new organization without the benefit of corporate sponsorship.

independent strategies Strategies that an organization acting on its own uses to change some aspect of its current environment.

informing A team strategy that entails concentrating first on the internal team process to achieve a state of performance readiness, then informing outsiders of its intentions.

innovation A change in technology; a departure from previous ways of doing things.

innovation Introduction of new products.

instrumentality The perceived likelihood that performance will be followed by a particular outcome.

integration The degree to which differentiated work units work together and coordinate their efforts.

integrity-based ethics programs Company mechanisms designed to instill in people a personal responsibility for ethical behavior.

intermediate consumer Customers who purchase raw materials or wholesale products before selling them to final customers.

internal audit A periodic assessment of a company's own planning, organizing, leading, and controlling processes.

international organization model An organization model that is composed of a company's overseas subsidiaries and characterized by greater control by the parent company over the research function and local product and marketing strategies than is the case in the multinational model.

interpersonal and communication skills People skills; the ability to lead, motivate, and communicate effectively with others.

intrapreneurs New venture creators working in big corporations.

intrinsic reward Reward a worker derives directly from performing the job itself.

ISO 9000 A series of quality standards developed by a committee working under the International Organization for Standardization to improve total quality in all businesses for the benefit of both producers and consumers.

J

job analysis A tool for determining what is done on a given job and what should be done on that job.

job enlargement Giving people additional tasks at the same time to alleviate boredom.

job enrichment Changing a task to make it inherently more rewarding, motivating, and satisfying.

job maturity The level of the employee's skills and technical knowledge relative to the task being performed.

job rotation Changing from one routine task to another to alleviate boredom.

just-in-time (JIT) A system that calls for subassemblies and components to be manufactured in very small lots and delivered to the next stage of the production process just as they are needed.

K

Kohlberg's model of cognitive moral development Classifies people into one of three categories based on their level of moral judgment.

L

labor relations The system of relations between workers and management.

laissez-faire A leadership philosophy characterized by an absence of managerial decision making.

large batch Technologies that produce goods and services in high volume.

law of effect A theory formulated by Edward Thorndike in 1911 stating that behavior that is followed by positive consequences will likely be repeated.

Leader-Member Exchange (LMX) theory Highlights the importance of leader behaviors not just toward the group as a whole but toward individuals on a personal basis.

leading The management function that involves the manager's efforts to stimulate high performance by employees.

lean manufacturing An operation that strives to achieve the highest possible productivity and total quality, cost effectively, by eliminating unnecessary steps in the production process and continually strives for improvement.

learning organization An organization skilled at creating, acquiring, and transferring knowledge, and at modifying its behavior to reflect new knowledge and insights.

legal responsibilities To obey local, state, federal, and relevant international laws.

liabilities The amounts a corporation owes to various creditors.

life-cycle analysis (LCA) A process of evaluating all inputs and outputs to determine the total environmental impact of the production and use of a product.

line departments Units that deal directly with the organization's primary goods and services.

logistics The movement of the right goods in the right amount to the right place at the right time.

low-cost strategy A strategy an organization uses to build competitive advantage by being efficient and offering a standard, no-frills product.

M

macroenvironment The most general environment; includes governments, economic conditions, and other fundamental factors that generally affect all organizations.

make-or-buy decision The question an organization asks itself about whether to acquire new technology from an outside source or develop it itself.

management The process of working with people and resources to accomplish organizational goals.

management audits An evaluation of the effectiveness and efficiency of various systems within an organization.

management by objectives (MBO) A process in which objectives set by a subordinate and supervisor must be reached within a given time period.

management myopia Focusing on short-term earnings and profits at the expense of longer-term strategic obligations.

management teams Teams that coordinate and provide direction to the subunits under their jurisdiction and integrate work among subunits.

managing diversity Managing a culturally diverse workforce by recognizing the characteristics common to specific groups of employees while dealing with such employees as individuals and supporting, nurturing, and utilizing their differences to the organization's advantage.

market control Control based on the use of financial and economic information.

mass customization The production of varied, individually customized products at the low cost of standardized, mass-produced products.

matrix organization An organization composed of dual reporting relationships in which some managers report to two superiors, a functional manager, and a product manager.

maximize A decision realizing the best possible outcome.

mechanistic organization A form of organization that seeks to maximize internal efficiency.

media richness The degree to which a communication channel conveys information.

mentors Higher level managers who help ensure that high-potential people are introduced to top management and socialized into the norms and values of the organization.

middle-level managers Managers located in the middle layers of the organizational hierarchy, reporting to top-level executives.

mission An organization's basic purpose and scope of operations.

monolithic organization An organization that has a low degree of structural integration—employing few women, minorities, or other groups that differ from the majority—and thus has a highly homogeneous employee population.

moral philosophy Principles, rules, and values people use in deciding what is right or wrong.

motivation Forces that energize, direct, and sustain a person's efforts.

motivators Factors that make a job more motivating, such as additional job responsibilities, opportunities for personal growth and recognition, and feelings of achievement.

moving Instituting the change.

multicultural organization An organization that values cultural diversity and seeks to utilize and encourage it.

multinational organization model An organization model that consists of the subsidiaries in each country in which a company does business, with ultimate control exercised by the parent company.

N

need hierarchy A conception of human needs organizing needs into five major types, and postulating that people satisfy them one at a time from bottom to top.

needs assessment An analysis identifying the jobs, people, and departments for which training is necessary.

negative reinforcement Removing or withholding an undesirable consequence.

network organization A collection of independent, mostly single-function firms.

nonprogrammed decisions New, novel, complex decisions having no proven answers.

norms Shared beliefs about how people should think and behave.

North American Free Trade Agreement (NAFTA) An economic pact that combined the economies of the United States, Canada, and Mexico into the world's largest trading block.

O

one-way communication A process in which information flows in only one direction—from the sender to the receiver, with no feedback loop.

open-book management Practice of sharing with employees at all levels of the organization vital information previously meant for management's eyes only.

operational planning The process of identifying the specific procedures and processes required at lower levels of the organization.

opportunity analysis A description of the product or service, an assessment of the opportunity, an assessment of the entrepreneur, specification of activities and resources needed to translate your idea into a viable business, and your source(s) of capital.

optimizing Achieving the best possible balance among several goals.

organic structure An organizational form that emphasizes flexibility.

organization A managed system designed and operated to achieve a specific set of objectives.

organization chart The reporting structure and division of labor in an organization.

organization culture The set of important assumptions about the organization and its goals and practices that members of the company share.

organizational behavior modification (OB Mod) The application of reinforcement theory in organizational settings.

organizing The management function of assembling and coordinating human, financial, physical, information and other resources needed to achieve goals.

orientation training Training designed to introduce new employees to the company and familiarize them with policies, procedures, culture, and the like.

outcome A consequence a person receives for his or her performance.

outplacement The process of helping people who have been dismissed from the company to regain employment elsewhere.

P

parading A team strategy that entails simultaneously emphasizing internal team building and achieving external visibility.

parallel teams Teams that operate separately from the regular work structure, and exist temporarily.

participation-in-decision-making Dimension of the range of leadership behaviors—autocratic to democratic—that managers perform in involving their employees in making decisions.

path-goal theory A theory that concerns how leaders influence subordinates' perceptions of their work goals and the paths they follow toward attainment of those goals.

perception The process of receiving and interpreting information.

performance appraisal Assessment of an employee's job performance.

performance gap The difference between actual performance and the desired performance.

planning The management function of systematically making decisions about the goals and activities that an individual, a group, a work unit, or the overall organization will pursue in the future.

plans The actions or means that managers intend to use to achieve organizational goals.

plural organization An organization that has a relatively diverse employee population and makes an effort to involve employees from different gender, racial, or cultural backgrounds.

political action committees (PACs) Political action groups that represent an organization and make donations to candidates for political office.

positive reinforcement Applying valued consequences that increase the likelihood that a person will repeat the behavior that led to it.

power The ability to influence others.

principle of exception A managerial principle stating that control is enhanced by concentrating on the exceptions or significant deviations from the expected result or standard.

proactive change A response that is initiated before a performance gap has occurred.

probing A team strategy that requires team members to interact frequently with outsiders, diagnose their needs, and experiment with solutions.

procedural justice Using fair process in decision making and making sure others know that the process was as fair as possible.

product champion A person who promotes a new technology throughout the organization in an effort to obtain acceptance and support for it.

profit and loss statement An itemized financial statement of the income and expenses of a company's operations.

programmed decisions Decisions encountered and made before, having objectively correct answers, and solvable by using simple rules, policies, or numerical computations.

project and development teams Teams that work on long-term projects but disband once the work is completed.

prospectors Companies that continuously change the boundaries of their task environments by seeking new products and markets, diversifying and merging, or acquiring new enterprises.

psychological contract A set of perceptions of what employees owe their employers, and what their employers owe them.

public affairs department A department that monitors key events and trends in the organization's political and social environments, analyzes their effects on the organization, recommends organizational responses, and implements political strategies.

punishment Administering an aversive consequence.

Q

quality The excellence of a product, including such things as attractiveness, lack of defects, reliability, and long-term dependability.

quality circles Voluntary groups of people drawn from various production teams who make suggestions about quality.

quality of work life (QWL) programs Programs designed to create a workplace that enhances employee well-being.

R

reactive change A response that occurs when events in the environment have already affected the firm's performance; problem-driven change.

ready-made solutions Ideas that have been seen or tried before, or follow the advice of others who have faced similar problems.

recruitment The development of a pool of applicants for jobs in the organization.

reflection Process by which a person attempts to repeat and clarify what he or she believes the other person is saying.

refreezing Strengthening the new behaviors that support the change.

reinforcers Positive consequences that motivate behavior

relationship-motivated leadership Leadership that places primary emphasis on maintaining good interpersonal relationships.

relativism bases ethical behavior on the opinions and behaviors of relevant other people.

reliability The consistency of test scores over time and across alternative measurements.

resources Inputs to a system that can enhance performance.

responsibility The assignment of a task that an employee is supposed to carry out.

return on investment (ROI) A ratio of profit to capital used, or a rate of return from capital.

right to work Legislation that allows employees to work without having to join a union.

rightsizing A successful effort to achieve an appropriate size at which the company performs most effectively.

risk The state that exists when the probability of success is less than 100 percent.

roles Different sets of expectations for how different individuals should behave.

S

satisfice To choose an option that is acceptable although not necessarily the best or perfect.

scenario A narrative that describes a particular set of future conditions.

selection Choosing from among qualified applicants to hire into an organization.

self-designing teams Teams with control over the design of the team, as well as the responsibilities of autonomous work groups.

self-managed teams Autonomous work groups in which workers are trained to do all or most of the jobs in a unit, have no immediate supervisor, and make decisions previously made by first-line supervisors.

semiautonomous work groups Groups that make decisions about managing and carrying out major production activities, but still get outside support for quality control and maintenance.

sexual harassment Conduct of a sexual nature that has negative consequences for employment.

shapers Companies that try to change the structure of their industries, creating a future competitive landscape of their own design.

side street effect As you head down a road, unexpected opportunities begin to appear.

simultaneous engineering A design approach in which all relevant functions cooperate jointly and continually in a maximum effort aimed at producing high-quality products that meet customers' needs.

situational analysis A process planners use, within time and resource constraints, to gather, interpret, and summarize all information relevant to the planning issue under consideration.

situational approach Leadership perspective proposing that universally important traits and behaviors do not exist, and that effective leadership behavior varies from situation to situation.

skunkworks A project team designated to produce a new, innovative product.

small batches Technologies that produce goods and services in low volume.

small business A business having fewer than 100 employees, independently owned and operated, not dominant in its field, and not characterized by many innovative practices.

smoothing Leveling normal fluctuations at the boundaries of the environment.

social facilitation effect Working harder when in a group than when working alone.

social loafing Working less hard and being less productive when in a group.

sociotechnical systems An approach to job design that attempts to redesign tasks to optimize operation of a new technology while preserving employees' interpersonal relationships and other human aspects of the work.

span of control The number of subordinates who report directly to an executive or supervisor.

specialization A process in which different individuals and units perform different tasks.

speed Fast and timely execution, response, and delivery of results.

spin-off A new company started by managers who create independent businesses that split from the parent corporation.

staff departments Units that support line departments.

stakeholders Groups and individuals who affect and are affected by the achievement of the organization's mission, goals, and strategies.

standard Expected performance for a given goal; a target that establishes a desired performance level, motivates performance, and serves as a benchmark against which actual performance is assessed.

standardization Establishing common rules and procedures that apply uniformly to everyone.

stockholders' equity The amount accruing to the corporation's owners.

stonewalling The use of public relations, legal action, and administrative processes to prevent or delay the introduction of legislation and regulation that may have an adverse impact on the organization.

strategic alliance A formal relationship created among independent organizations with the purpose of joint pursuit of mutual goals.

strategic control system A system designed to support managers in evaluating the organization's progress regarding its strategy and, when discrepancies exist, taking corrective action.

strategic goals Major targets or end results relating to the organization's long-term survival, value, and growth.

strategic leadership Behavior that gives purpose and meaning to organizations.

strategic management A process that involves managers from all parts of the organization in the formulation and implementation of strategic goals and strategies.

strategic maneuvering The organization's conscious efforts to change the boundaries of its task environment.

strategic planning A set of procedures for making decisions about the organization's long-term goals and strategies.

strategic retreat Efforts to adapt products and processes to changes in the political and social environments while minimizing the negative effects of those changes.

strategic vision The long-term direction and strategic intent of a company.

strategy A pattern of actions and resource allocations designed to achieve the organization's goals.

structured interview Selection technique that involves asking each applicant the same questions and comparing their responses to a standardized set of answers.

substitutes for leadership Factors in the workplace that can exert the same influence on employees that leaders would provide.

subsystems Interdependent components of a system.

subunits Subdivisions of an organization.

superordinate goals Higher-level goals taking priority over specific individual or group goals.

supervisory leadership Behavior that provides guidance, support, and corrective feedback for the day-to-day activities of work unit members.

survivor's syndrome Loss of productivity and morale in employees who remain after a downsizing.

sustainable growth Economic growth and development that meet the organization's present needs without harming the ability of future generations to meet their needs.

switching costs Fixed costs buyers face when they change suppliers.

SWOT analysis A comparison of strengths, weaknesses, opportunities, and threats that help executives formulate strategy.

synergy The sharing of benefits across system parts, resulting in a whole that is greater than the sum of its parts.

system A set of interdependent parts that processes inputs into outputs.

systems theory A theory stating that an organization is a set of interdependent elements, which in turn are interdependent with the external environment.

T

tactical planning A set of procedures for translating broad strategic goals and plans into specific goals and plans that are relevant to a distinct portion of the organization, such as a functional area like marketing.

task performance behaviors Actions taken to ensure that the work group or organization reaches its goals.

task specialist An individual who has more advanced job-related skills and abilities than other group members possess.

task-motivated leadership Leadership that places primary emphasis on completing a task.

team A small number of people with complementary skills who are committed to a common purpose, set of performance goals, and approach for which they hold themselves mutually accountable.

team training Training that provides employees with the skills and perspectives they need to work in collaboration with others.

technical innovator A person who develops a new technology or has the key skills to install and operate the technology.

technical skill The ability to perform a specialized task involving a particular method or process.

technology The systematic application of scientific knowledge to a new product, process, or service.

technology audit Process of clarifying the key technologies upon which an organization depends.

technology life cycle A predictable pattern followed by a technological innovation starting from its inception and development to market saturation and replacement.

teleology Considers an act to be morally right or acceptable if it produces a desired result.

termination interview A discussion between a manager and an employee about the employee's dismissal.

third-country nationals Natives of a country other than the home country or the host country of an overseas subsidiary.

time-based competition (TBC) Strategies aimed at reducing the total time it takes to deliver a product or service.

top-level managers Senior executives responsible for the overall management and effectiveness of the organization.

total organization change Introducting and sustaining multiple policies, practices, and procedures across multiple units and levels.

total quality management An integrative approach to management that supports the attainment of customer satisfaction through a wide variety of tools and techniques that result in high-quality goods and services.

tragedy of the commons A term describing the environmental destruction that results as individuals and businesses consume finite resources (i.e., the "commons") to serve their short-term interests without regard for the long-term consequences.

traditional work groups Groups that have no managerial responsibilities.

training Teaching lower-level employees how to perform their present jobs.

trait approach A leadership perspective that focuses on individual leaders and attempts to determine the personal characteristics that great leaders share.

transactional leaders Management through business transactions in which leaders use their legitimate, reward, and coercive powers to give commands and exchange rewards for services rendered.

transfer price Price charged by one unit for a product or service provided to another unit within the organization.

transformational leader A leader who transforms a vision into reality and motivates people to transcend their personal interests for the good of the group.

transnational organization model An organization model characterized by centralization of certain functions in locations that best achieve cost economies; basing of other functions in the company's national subsidiaries to facilitate greater local responsiveness; and fostering of communication among subsidiaries to permit transfer of technological expertise and skills.

transnational teams Work groups composed of multinational members whose activities span multiple countries.

two-factor theory Herzberg's theory describing two factors affecting people's work motivation and satisfaction.

two-way communication A process in which information flows in two directions—the receiver provides feedback and the sender is receptive to the feedback.

tyranny of the "or" The belief that things must be either A or B, and cannot be both; that only one goal and not another can be attained.

U

uncertainty The state that exists when decision makers have insufficient information.

unfreezing Realizing that current practices are inappropriate and that new behavior must be enacted.

union shop An organization with a union and union security clause specifying that workers must join the union after a set period of time.

unity-of-command principle A structure in which each worker reports to one boss, who in turn reports to one boss.

universalism The ethical system upholding certain values regardless of immediate result.

upward communication Information that flows from lower to higher levels in the organization's hierarchy.

utilitarianism An ethical system which states that the greatest good for the greatest number should be the overriding concern of decision makers.

V

valence The value an outcome holds for the person contemplating it.

validity The degree to which a selection test predicts or correlates with job performance.

value chain Sequence of activities that flow from raw materials to the delivery of a product or service.

vertical integration The acquisition or development of new businesses that produce parts or components of the organization's product.

vigilance A process in which a decision maker carefully executes all stages of decision making.

virtual office A mobile office in which people can work anywhere, as long as they have the tools to communicate with customers and colleagues.

virtue ethics A perspective that what is moral comes from what a mature person with "good" moral character would deem right.

vision A mental image of a possible and desirable future state of the organization.

voluntary responsibilities Additional behaviors and activities that society finds desirable and that the values of the business dictate.

Vroom-Yetton-Jago model A situational model of leadership that focuses on how leaders go about making decisions.

work teams Teams that make or do things like manufacture, assemble, sell, or provide.

Notes

Chapter One

1. G. Hamel, "Managing out of Bounds," *Financial Times Mastering Management,* 1997
2. R. Henkoff, "Smartest and Dumbest Managerial Moves of 1994," *Fortune,* January 16, 1995, pp. 48–97.
3. Ibid.
4. T. Ehrenfeld, "The New and Improved American Small Business," *Inc.,* January 1995, pp. 34–45.
5. "Manufacturing Innovation," *Black Enterprise,* August 1991, p. 86.
6. M. Loeg, "How's Business?" *Fortune,* January 16, 1995, pp. 135–36.
7. R. Webber, "General Management Past and Future," *Financial Times Mastering Management,* 1997.
8. C. Bartlett and S. Ghoshal, 1997, "The Myth of the Generic Manager," *California Management Review,* Fall, *40,* 92–116
9. L. R. Sayles "Doing Things Right: A New Imperative for Middle Managers," *Organizational Dynamics,* Spring 1993, pp. 5–14.
10. A. Hadley, *The Straw Giant* (New York: Random House, 1986)
11. C. Quintanilla, "New Airline Fad: Faster Airport Turnarounds," *The Wall Street Journal,* August 4, 1994, pp. B1, B2.
12. A. Farnham, "America's Most Admired Company," *Fortune,* February 7, 1994, pp. 50–54.
13. E. E. Lawler III, *The Ultimate Advantage* (San Francisco: Josey-Bass, 1992).
14. Henoff, "Smartest and Dumbest Managerial Moves of 1994."
15. Lawler, *The Ultimate Advantage.*
16. Henoff, "Smartest and Dumbest Managerial Moves of 1994."
17. Ibid.
18 Lawler, *The Ultimate Advantage.*
19. Ehrenfeld, "The New and Improved American Small Business."
20. T. Ehrenfeld, "The Demise of Mom and Pop?" *Inc.,* January 1995, pp. 46–48.
21. Ibid.
22. D. A. Garvin, "Manufacturing Strategic Planning," *California Management Review,* Summer 1993, pp. 85–106.
23. T. Agins, "Fashion Knockoffs Hit Stores before Originals as Designers Seethe," *The Wall Street Journal,* August 8, 1994, pp. A1, A4.
24. Loeb, "How's Business?
25. N. Hutheesing, "10 to Watch," *Forbes,* November 3, 1997, pp. 150–54.
26. D. Kirkpatrick, "Now Everyone in PCs Wants to Be Like Mike," *Fortune,* September 8, 1997, pp. 47–48.
27. Ibid.
28. Ibid.
29. R. Katz, "Skills of an Effective Administrator," *Harvard Business Review* 52 (September–October), pp. 90–102.
30. H. Mintzberg, "The Manager's Job: Folklore and Fact," *Harvard Business Review* 53 (July–August 1975), pp. 49–61.
31. A. Deutschman, "The Trouble with MBAs," *Fortune,* July 29, 1991, pp. 67–79.
32. S. Lehrman, "Putting Management Potential to the Test," *Bryan–College Station Eagle,* December 8, 1985, p. 3F.
33. N. Nohria and J. Berkley, "Whatever Happened to the Take-Charge Manager?" *Harvard Business Review,* January–February 1994, pp. 129–37.
34. J. Guyon, "Why Is the World's Most Profitable Company Turning Itself Inside Out?" *Fortune,* August 4, 1997, pp. 52–57.
35. T. Peters, "Prometheus Barely Unbound," *The Executive,* November 1990, pp. 70–84.
36. W. J. Holstein, "The Stateless Corporation," *Business Week,* May 14, 1990, pp. 98–105.
37. M. Murray, "Era Is Nearing an End as Heinz' Johnson Assumes More Control," *The Wall Street Journal,* March 11, 1997, pp. 1, 12.
38. A. C. Copetas, "European Workers Brace for Change as EMC Nears," *The Wall Street Journal,* April 17, 1997, p. 2.
39. R. Cole, P. Bacdayan, and B. J. White, "Quality, Participation, and Competitiveness," *California Management Review,* 1993, pp. 68–81.
40. T. Peters, *Liberation Management* (New York: Alfred A. Knopf, 1992).
41. P. Senge, *The Fifth Discipline* (New York: Doubleday, 1990); R. Hodgetts, F. Luthans, and S. Lee, "New Paradigm Organizations: From Total Quality to Learning to World-Class," *Organizational Dynamics,* Winter 1994, pp. 5–19.
42. D. K. Smith, *Taking Charge of Change* (Reading, MA: Addison-Wesley, 1996).
43. E. E. Lawler III, *From the Ground Up: Six Principles for Building the New Logic Corporation* (San Francisco: Jossey-Bass, 1996).
44. Nohria and Berkley, "Whatever Happened to the Take-Charge Manager?"
45. W. Kiechel III, "A Manager's Career in the New Economy," *Fortune,* April 4, 1994, pp. 68–72.
46. Ibid.
47. B. O'Brian, and G. Stern, "Nonstop Networking Propels an Accountant into U.S. Big Leagues," *The Wall Street Journal,* March 20, 1997, pp. 1, 2.
48. Peters, *Liberation Management.*
49. J. Kotter, *The New Rules: How to Succeed in Today's Post-Corporate World* (New York: The Free Press, 1995).
50. Ibid.

Chapter One Appendix

1. C. George, *The History of Management Thought* (Englewood Cliffs, NJ: Prentice Hall, 1972).
2. Ibid.
3. A. D. Chandler, *Scale and Scope: The Dynamic of Industrial Capitalism* (Cambridge, MA: Belknap Press of Harvard University Press, 1990).
4. Ibid.
5. J. Baughman, *The History of American Management* (Englewood Cliffs, NJ: Prentice Hall, 1969), chap. 1.
6. George, *The History of Management Thought,* chaps. 5–7; F. Taylor, *The Principles of Scientific Management* (New York: Harper & Row, 1911).
7. J. Case, "A Company of Businesspeople," *Inc.,* April 1993, pp. 79–93.
8. H. Kroos and C. Gilbert, *The Principles of Scientific Management* (New York: Harper & Row, 1911).
9. H. Fayol, *General and Industrial Management,* trans. C. Storrs (Marshfield, MA: Pitman Publishing, 1949).
10. George, *The History of Management Thought,* chap. 9; J. Massie, "Management Theory," in *Handbook of Organizations,* ed. J. March (Chicago: Rand McNally, 1965), pp. 387–422.
11. C. Barnard, *The Functions of the Executive* (Cambridge, MA: Harvard University Press, 1938).
12. George, *The History of Management Thought;* Massie, "Management Theory."
13. E. Mayo, *The Human Problems of Industrial Civilization* (New York: Macmillan, 1933); F. Roethlisberger and W. Dickson, *Management and the Worker* (Cambridge, MA: Harvard University Press, 1939).
14. A. Maslow, "A Theory of Human Motivation," *Psychological Review* 50 (July 1943), pp. 370–96.
15. A. Carey, "The Hawthorne Studies: A Radical Criticism," *American Sociological Review* 32, no. 3 (1967), pp. 403–16.

16. M. Weber, *The Theory of Social and Economic Organizations,* trans. T. Parsons and A. Henderson (New York: Free Press, 1947).
17. George, *The History of Management Thought,* chap. 11.
18. D. McGregor, *The Human Side of Enterprise* (New York: McGraw-Hill, 1960).
19. C. Argyris, *Personality and Organization* (New York: Harper & Row, 1957).
20. R. Likert, *The Human Organization* (New York: McGraw-Hill, 1967).
21. L. von Bertalanffy, "The History and Status of General Systems Theory," *Academy of Management Journal* 15 (1972), pp. 407–26; D. Katz and R. Kahn, *The Social Psychology of Organizations,* 2nd ed. (New York: John Wiley & Sons, 1978).
22. J. Thompson, *Organizations in Action* (New York: McGraw-Hill, 1967); J. Galbraith, *Organization Design* (Reading, MA: Addison-Wesley, 1977); D. Miller and P. Friesen, *Organizations: A Quantum View* (Englewood Cliffs, NJ: Prentice Hall, 1984).

Chapter Two

1 Lee Smith, "Air Power," *Fortune,* July 7, 1997, pp. 134–36; "Industry Awaits Impact of Boeing Merger," *Industrial Distribution,* February 1997, pp. 15–16; "And Then There Were Two," *Financial World,* April 15, 1997, p. 70.
2. William Pesek, Jr., "Trading Points: Has Wall Street Noticed that Budget Gap Is Lowest in 15 Years?" *Barron's* 77, no. 6 (February 10, 1997), p. MW12; "Balanced Budget, Yes. Amendment, No." *Business Week,* February 10, 1997, p. 136.
3. Judith J. Friedman and Nancy DiTomaso, "Myths about Diversity: What Managers Need to Know About Changes in the U.S. Labor Force," *California Management Review* 38, no. 4 (Summer 1996), pp. 54–77.
4. Matthew Klein, "Holes in the Smoke Screen," *American Demographics* 19, no. 7 (July 1997), p. 31; Christine Jordan Sexton, "Florida Supreme Court Upholds Tobacco Liability Law," *National Underwriter* 199, no. 29 (July 15, 1996), p. 46; "Tobacco Firms Offer $360 Billion," *Business Insurance* 31, no. 25 (June 23, 1997), pp. 1, 45.
5. Jonathan R. Laing, "Just Spiffy," *Barron's* 77, no. 12 (March 24, 1997), pp. 37–42; Matthew J. Kiernan, "Get Innovative or Get Dead," *Business Quarterly* 61, no. 1 (Autumn 1996), pp. 51–58.
6. David J. Collis and Cynthia A. Montgomery, *Corporate Strategy: Resources and Scope of the Firm* (Burr Ridge, IL: McGraw-Hill/Irwin, 1997).
7. Roger Hallowell, "Southwest Airlines: A Case Study Linking Employee Needs Satisfaction and Organizational Capabilities to Competitive Advantage," *Human Resource Management* 35, no. 4 (Winter 1996), pp. 513–34; Wendy Zeller, "Greyhound Is Limping Badly," *Business Week,* August 22, 1994, p. 32.
8. Interested persons can check out their webpage at http://www.amazon.com/.
9. Arthur Sherman, George Bohlander, and Scott Snell, *Managing Human Resources,* 11th ed. (Cincinnati, OH: Southwestern Publishing, 1998).
10. Brent Schlender, "The Adventures of Scott McNealy: Javaman," *Fortune,* 136, no. 7 (October 13, 1997), pp. 70–78.
11. P. Kotler, *Marketing Management: Analysis, Planning, Implementation and Control,* 9th ed. (Englewood Cliffs, NJ: Prentice Hall, 1990).
12. Aaron A. Buchko, "Conceptualization and Measurement of Environmental Uncertainty: An Assessment of the Miles and Snow Perceived Environmental Uncertainty Scale" *Academy of Management Journal* 37, no. 2 (April 1994), pp. 410–25.
13. Abdalla F. Hagen, "Corporate Executives and Environmental Scanning Activities: An Empirical Investigation." *SAM Advanced Management Journal* 60, no. 2 (Spring 1995), pp. 41–47; Richard L. Daft, "Chief Executive Scanning, Environmental Characteristics, and Company Performance: An Empirical Study," *Strategic Management Journal* 9, no. 2 (March/April 1988), pp. 123–39; Masoud Yasai-Ardekani, "Designs for Environmental Scanning Systems: Tests of a Contingency Theory," *Management Science* 42, no. 2 (February 1996), pp. 187–204.
14. Sumantra Ghoshal, "Building Effective Intelligence Systems for Competitive Advantage," *Sloan Management Review* 28, no. 1 (Fall 1986), pp. 49–58; Kenneth D. Cory, "Can Competitive Intelligence Lead to a Sustainable Competitive Advantage?" *Competitive Intelligence Review* 7, no. 3 (Fall 1996), pp. 45–55.
15. Paul J. H. Schoemaker, "Multiple Scenario Development: Its Conceptual and Behavioral Foundation," *Strategic Management Journal* 14, no. 3 (March 1993), pp. 193–213.
16. Robin T. Peterson, "An Analysis of Contemporary Forecasting in Small Business," *Journal of Business Forecasting Methods & Systems* 15, no. 2 (Summer 1996), pp. 10–12; Spyros Makridakis, "Business Forecasting for Management: Strategic Business Forecasting," *International Journal of Forecasting* 12, no. 3 (September 1996), pp. 435–37.
17. Irving DeToro, "The 10 Pitfalls of Benchmarking," *Quality Progress* 28, no. 1 (January 1995), pp. 61–63.
18. Martin B. Meznar, "Buffer or Bridge? Environmental and Organizational Determinants of Public Affairs Activities in American Firms," *Academy of Management Journal* 38, no. 4 (August 1995), pp. 975–96.
19. David Lei, "Advanced Manufacturing Technology: Organizational Design and Strategic Flexibility," *Organization Studies* 17, no. 3 (1996), pp. 501–23; James W. Dean Jr. and Scott A. Snell, "The Strategic Use of Integrated Manufacturing: An Empirical Examination," *Strategic Management Journal* 17, no. 6 (June 1996), pp. 459–80.
20. C. Zeithaml and V. Zeithaml, "Environmental Management: Revising the Marketing Perspective," *Journal of Marketing* 48 (Spring 1984), pp. 46–53.
21. Willem P. Burgers, "Cooperative Strategy in High Technology Industries," *International Journal of Management* 13, no. 2 (June 1996), pp. 127–34; Jeffrey E. McGee, "Cooperative Strategy and New Venture Performance: The Role of Business Strategy and Management Experience," *Strategic Management Journal* 16, no. 7 (October 1995), pp. 565–80.
22. Richard A. D'Aveni, *Hypercompetition—Managing the Dynamics of Strategic Maneuvering* (New York, The Free Press 1994); Michael A. Cusumano, "Strategic Maneuvering and Mass-Market Dynamics: The Triumph of VHS over Beta," *Business History Review* 66, no. 1 (Spring 1992), pp. 51–94.
23. R. Miles and C. Snow, *Organizational Strategy, Structure, and Process* (New York: McGraw-Hill, 1978).

Chapter Three

1. T. Peters, *Liberation Management* (New York: Alfred A. Knopf, 1992).
2. M. McCall and R. Kaplan, *Whatever It Takes: Decision Makers at Work* (Englewood Cliffs, NJ: Prentice Hall, 1985).
3. B. Bass, *Organizational Decision Making* (Homewood, IL: Richard D. Irwin, 1983).
4. J. March, "Bounded Rationality, Ambiguity, and the Engineering of Choice," *Bell Journal of Economics* 9 (1978), pp. 587–608.
5. D. Messick and M. Bazerman, "Ethical Leadership and the Psychology of Decision Making," *Sloan Management Review,* Winter 1996, pp. 9–22.

6. G. A. Garvin, "Building a Learning Organization," *Harvard Business Review,* July–August 1993, pp. 78–91.
7. McCall and Kaplan, *Whatever It Takes.*
8. K. MacCrimmon and R. Taylor, "Decision Making and Problem Solving," in *Handbook of Industrial and Organizational Psychology,* ed. M. D. Dunnette (Chicago: Rand McNally, 1976).
9. Q. Spitzer and R. Evans, *Heads, You Win! How the Best Companies Think* (New York: Simon & Schuster, 1997).
10. C. Gettys and S. Fisher, "Hypothesis Plausibility and Hypotheses Generation," *Organizational Behavior and Human Performance* 24 (1979), pp. 93–110.
11. E. R. Alexander, "The Design of Alternatives in Organizational Contexts: A Pilot Study," *Administrative Science Quarterly* 24 (1979), pp. 382–404.
12. P. Nayak and J. Ketteringham, *Breakthroughs* (New York: Rawson Associates, 1986).
13. R. Abelson and A. Levi, "Decision Making and Decision Theory," in *The Handbook of Social Psychology,* vol. 1, 3rd ed., ed. G. Lindzey and E. Aronson (New York: Random House, 1985).
14. Spitzer and Evans, *Heads, You Win!*
15. J. O'Toole, *Vanguard Management: Redesigning the Corporate Future* (Garden City, NY: Doubleday, 1985).
16. McCall and Kaplan, *Whatever It Takes.*
17. Spitzer and Evans, *Heads, You Win!*
18. K. Labich, "Four Possible Futures," *Fortune,* January 25, 1993, pp. 40–48.
19. McCall and Kaplan, *Whatever It Takes.*
20. M. B. Stein, "Teaching Steelcase to Dance," *New York Times Magazine,* April 1, 1990, pp. 22ff.
21. D. Siebold, "Making Meetings More Successful," *Journal of Business Communication* 16 (Summer 1979), pp. 3–20.
22. I. Janis and L. Mann, *Decision Making* (New York: Free Press, 1977); Bass, *Organizational Decision Making.*
23. J. W. Dean Jr. and M. Sharfman, "Does Decision Process Matter? A Study of Strategic Decision-Making Effectiveness," *Academy of Management Journal* 39 (1996), pp. 368–96.
24. R. Nisbett and L. Ross, *Human Inference: Strategies and Shortcomings* (Englewood Cliffs, NJ: Prentice Hall, 1980).
25. Messick and Bazerman, "Ethical Leadership."
26. T. Bateman and C. Zeithaml, "The Psychological Context of Strategic Decisions: A Model and Convergent Experimental Findings," *Strategic Management Journal* 10 (1989), pp. 59–74.
27. Messick and Bazerman, "Ethical Leadership."
28. N. Adler, *International Dimensions of Organizational Behavior* (Boston: Kent, 1990).
29. K. M. Eisenhardt, "Speed and Strategic Choice: How Managers Accelerate Decision Making," *California Management Review* 32 (Spring 1990), pp. 39–54
30. Q. Spitzer and R. Evans, "New Problems in Problem Solving," *Across the Board,* April 1997, pp. 36–40.
31. G. W. Hill, "Group versus Individual Performance: Are n + 1 Heads Better than 1?" *Psychological Bulletin* 91 (1982), pp. 517–39.
32. N. R. F. Maier, "Assets and Liabilities in Group Problem Solving: The Need for an Integrative Function," *Psychological Review* 74 (1967), pp. 239–49.
33. Ibid.
34. R. Cosier and C. Schwenk, "Agreement and Thinking Alike: Ingredients for Poor Decisions," *The Executive,* February 1990, pp. 69–74.
35. A. Amason, "Distinguishing the Effects of Functional and Dysfunctional Conflict on Strategic Decision Making: Resolving a Paradox for Top Management Teams," *Academy of Management Journal* 39 (1996), pp. 123–48.
36. K. Eisenhardt, J. Kahwajy, and L. J. Bourgeois III, "Conflict and Strategic Choice: How Top Management Teams Disagree," *California Management Review,* Winter 1997, pp. 42–62.
37. Cosier and Schwenk, "Agreement and Thinking Alike."
38. Ibid.
39. C. Knowlton, "How Disney Keeps the Magic Going," *Fortune,* December 4, 1989, pp. 115–32.
40. P. LaBerre, "The Creative Revolution," *Industry Week,* May 16, 1994, pp. 12–19.
41. J. V. Anderson, "Weirder than Fiction: The Reality and Myths of Creativity," *Academy of Management Executive,* November 1992, pp. 40–47; J. Krohe Jr., "Managing Creativity," *Across the Board,* September 1996, pp. 17–21.
42. A. Farnham, "How to Nurture Creative Sparks," *Fortune,* January 10, 1994, pp. 94–100; T. M. Amabile, "A Model of Creativity and Innovation in Organizations," in *Research and Organizational Behavior,* ed. B. Straw and L. Cummings, vol. 10 (1988), pp. 123–68.
43. R. Sutton and A. Hargadon "Brainstorming Groups in Context: Effectiveness in a Product Design Firm," *Administrative Design Quarterly* 41 (1996), pp. 685–718.
44. Dean and Sharfman, "Does Decision Process Matter?"
45. K. Eisenhardt, J. Kahwajy, and L. J. Bourgeois III, "How Management Teams Can Have a Good Fight," *Harvard Management Review,* July–August 1997, pp. 77–85.
46. J. E. Jackson and W. T. Schantz, "Crisis Management Lessons: When Push Shoved Nike," *Business Horizons,* January–February 1993, pp. 27–35.
47. C. M. Pearson and I. I. Mitroff, "From Crisis Prone to Crisis Prepared: A Framework for Crisis Management," *The Academy of Management Executive,* February 1993, pp. 48–59.
48. J. Hickman, and W. Crandall, "Before Disaster Hits: A Multifaceted Approach to Crisis Management," *Business Horizons,* March–April 1997, pp. 75–79.
49. I. Mitroff, L. K. Harrington, and E. Gai, "Thinking about the Unthinkable," *Across the Board,* September 1996, pp. 44–48.
50. G. Meyers with J. Holusha, *When It Hits the Fan: Managing the Nine Crises of Business* (Boston: Houghton Mifflin, 1986).
51. McCall and Kaplan, *Whatever It Takes.*

Chapter Four

1. J. Bracker and J. Pearson, "Planning and Financial Performance of Small Mature Firms," *Strategic Management Journal* 7 (1986), pp. 503–22; Philip Waalewijn and Peter Segaar, "Strategic Management: The Key to Profitability in Small Companies," *Long Range Planning* 26, no. 2 (April 1993), pp. 24–30.
2. Aramark annual report, 1997.
3. "American, British Airways Form Cargo Alliance." *Transportation & Distribution* 37, no. 8 (August 1996), p. 20; "American Airlines, British Airways Alliance Stirs up Controversy," *Logistics Management* 35, no. 8 (August 1996), pp. 21–22.
4. Patricia Sellers, "Can Wal-Mart Get Back the Magic?" *Fortune,* April 29 1996, pp. 130–36.
5. David J. Collis and Cynthia A. Montgomery, *Corporate Strategy: Resources and the Scope of the Firm* (Burr Ridge, IL: Richard D. Irwin, 1997).
6. R. Ashkenas, D. Ulrich, T. Jick, and S. Kerr, *The Boundaryless Organization* (San Francisco: Jossey-Bass, 1995).
7. Shell Oil company documents, 1997.
8. Arthur A. Thompson and A. J. Strickland III, *Strategic Management: Concepts and Cases,* 8th ed. (Burr Ridge, IL: Richard D. Irwin, 1995), p. 23.
9. Roger Hallowell, "Southwest Airlines: A Case Study Linking Employee Needs Satisfaction and Organizational Capabilities to Competitive

Advantage," *Human Resource Management* 35, no. 4 (Winter 1996), pp. 513–34.

10. Collis and Montgomery, *Corporate Strategy.*
11. Ibid.
12. Thomas D. Sugalski, "Resource Link: Re-establishing the Employment Relationship in an Era of Downsizing," *Human Resource Management* 34, no. 3 (Fall 1995) pp. 389–403.
13. Robert C. Camp, "A Bible for Benchmarking, by Xerox," *Financial Executive* 9, no. 4. (July/August 1993) pp. 23–27. See, also, Dawn Anfuso, "At L. L. Bean, Quality Starts with People," *Personnel Journal* 73, no. 1 (January 1994), p. 60.
14. Robert E. Hoskisson, "Corporate Divestiture Intensity in Restructuring Firms: Effects of Governance, Strategy, and Performance," *Academy of Management Journal* 37, no. 5 (October 1994) pp. 1207–51; S. Gannes, "Merck Has Made Biotech Work," *Fortune,* January 19, 1987, pp. 58–64; Mark Maremont, "Why Kodak's Dazzling Spin-Off Didn't Bedazzle," *Business Week,* June 28, 1993, p. 34; Emily S. Plishner, "Eastman Chemical Spins Out of the Kodak Family Portrait," *Chemical Week,* 152, no. 24 (June 23, 1993), p. 7.
15. Stratford Sherman, "Why Disney Had to Buy ABC," *Fortune* 132, no. 5 (September 4, 1995), p. 80.
16. M. Porter, *Competitive Advantage* (New York: Free Press, 1985), pp. 11–14.
17. "Toys 'Я' Us Faces International Challenge," *Discount Store News* 33, no. 10 (May 16, 1994), pp. 86–88.
18. Anne Faircloth, "One-on-One Shopping," *Fortune,* July 7, 1997, pp. 235–236.
19. Robert Simons, "How New Top Managers Use Control Systems as Levers of Strategic Renewal," *Strategic Management Journal* 15, no. 3 (March 1994), pp. 169–89; Stephen Bungay, "Creating a Strategic Control System," *Long Range Planning* 24, no. 3 (June 1991), pp. 32–39; P. Lorange, M. Morton, and S. Ghoshal, *Strategic Control* (St. Paul, MN: West Publishing, 1986), p. 10; Colin Eden, "Evaluating Strategy—Its Role within the Context of Strategic Control," *Journal of the Operational Research Society* 44, no. 9 (September 1993), pp. 853–65.

Chapter Five

1. M. E. Guy, *Ethical Decision Making in Everyday Work Situations* (New York: Quorum Books, 1990).
2. O. C. Ferrell and J. Fraedrich, *Business Ethics: Ethical Decision Making and Cases,* 3rd ed. (Boston: Houghton Mifflin, 1997).
3. Ibid.
4. Guy, *Ethical Decision Making.*
5. Ferrell and Fraedrich, *Business Ethics.*
6. L. Kohlberg and D. Candee, "The Relationship of Moral Judgment to Moral Action" in *Morality, Moral Behavior, and Moral Development,* ed. W. M. Kurtines and J. L. Gerwitz (New York: John Wiley & Sons, 1984).
7. L. K. Trevino, "Ethical Decision Making in Organizations: A Person-Situation Interactionist Model," *Academy of Management Review,* pp. 601–17.
8. Ferrell and Fraedrich, *Business Ethics.*
9. J. Krohe Jr., "Ethics Are Nice, but Business Is Business," *Across the Board,* April 1997, pp. 16–22.
10. Ibid.
11. J. Badarocco Jr. and A. Webb, "Business Ethics: A View from the Trenches," *California Management Review,* Winter 1995, pp. 8–28.
12. G. Laczniak, M. Berkowitz, R. Brookes, and J. Hale, "The Business of Ethics: Improving or Deteriorating?" *Business Horizons,* January–February 1995, pp. 39–47.
13. S. Brenner and E. Molander, "Is the Ethics of Business Changing?" in *Ethics in Practice: Managing the Moral Corporation,* ed. K. Andrews (Cambridge, MA: Harvard Business School Press, 1989).
14. R. T. De George, *Business Ethics,* 3rd ed. (New York: Macmillan, 1990).
15. T. P. Paré, "Jack Welch's Nightmare on Wall Street," *Fortune,* September 5, 1994, pp. 40–48.
16. J. B. Ciulla, "Why Is Business Talking about Ethics? Reflections on Foreign Conversations," *California Management Review,* Fall 1991, pp. 67–80.
17. R. E. Allinson, "A Call for Ethically Centered Management," *Academy of Management Executive,* February 1995, pp. 73–76.
18. Krohe, "Ethics Are Nice."
19. D. Messick and M. Bazerman, "Ethical Leadership and the Psychology of Decision Making," *Sloan Management Review,* Winter 1996, pp. 9–22.
20. Krohe, "Ethics Are Nice."
21. C. Handy, *Beyond Uncertainty: The Changing Worlds of Organizations* (Boston: Harvard Business School Press, 1996).
22. R. A. Cooke, "Danger Signs of Unethical Behavior: How to Determine if Your Firm Is at Ethical Risk," *Journal of Business Ethics,* April 1991, pp. 249–53.
23. Ciulla, "Why Is Business Talking about Ethics?"
24. A. Farnham, "State Your Values, Hold the Hot Air," *Fortune,* April 19, 1993, pp. 117–24.
25. L. S. Paine, "Managing for Organizational Integrity," *Harvard Business Review,* March–April 1994, pp. 106–17.
26. F. Hall and E. Hall, "The ADA: Going beyond the Law," *The Academy of Management Executive,* February 1994, pp. 7–13; A. Farnham, "Brushing Up Your Vision Thing," *Fortune,* May 1, 1995, p. 129.
27. Paine, "Managing for Organizational Integrity."
28. Krohe, "Ethics Are Nice."
29. Guy, *Ethical Decision Making;* D. Kirrane, "Managing Values: A Systematic Approach to Business Ethics," *Training and Development Journal,* November 1990, pp. 53–60.
30. R. P. Nielson, "What Can Managers Do about Unethical Management?" *Journal of Business Ethics,* May 1987, pp. 309–20.
31. L. Preston and J. Post, eds., *Private Management and Public Policy* (Englewood Cliffs, NJ: Prentice Hall, 1975).
32. Ferrell and Fraedrich, *Business Ethics.*
33. Ibid.
34. D. Quinn and T. Jones, "An Agent Morality View of Business Policy," *Academy of Management Review* 20 (1995), pp. 22–42.
35. Ibid.
36. Ibid.
37. K. E. Goodpaster, "Business Ethics and Stakeholder Analysis," *Business Ethics Quarterly* 1 (1991), pp. 53–73.
38. Quinn and Jones, "An Agent Morality View of Business Policy."
39. D. C. Korten, *When Corporations Ruled the World* (San Francisco: Berrett-Koehler, 1995).
40. Handy, *Beyond Certainty.*
41. Quinn and Jones, "An Agent Morality View of Business Policy."
42. Handy, *Beyond Certainty.*
43. D. Turban and D. Greening, "Corporate Social Performance and Organizational Attractiveness to Prospective Employees," *Academy of Management Journal* 40 (1997), pp. 658–72.
44. M. Baucus and D. Baucus, "Paying the Piper: An Empirical Examination of Longer-Term Financial Consequences of Illegal Corporate Behavior," *Academy of Management Journal* 40 (1997), pp. 129–51.
45. Handy, *Beyond Certainty.*
46. J. O'Toole, "Doing Well by Doing Good: The Business Enterprise Trust Awards," *California Management Review,* Spring 1991, pp. 9–24.

47. J. Collins and J. Porras, *Built to Last: Successful Habits of Visionary Companies* (London: Century Business, 1996).
48. Ibid.
49. R. Ackerman and R. Bauer, *Corporate Social Responsiveness* (Reston, VA: Reston, 1976).
50. M. B. E. Clarkson, "A Stakeholder Framework for Analyzing and Evaluating Corporate Social Performance," *Academy of Management Review* 20 (1995), pp. 92–117.
51. Ibid.
52. Kanter, *World Class* (New York: Touchstone, 1995), p. 192.
53. Ibid., pp. 192–94.
54. Ibid.
55. J. Gale and R. A. Buchholz, "The Political Pursuit of Competitive Advantage: What Business Can Gain from Government," in *Business Strategy and Public Policy: Perspectives from Industry and Academia,* ed. A. A. Marcus, A. M. Kaufman, and D. R. Beam (Westport, CT: Greenwood Press, 1987), pp. 31–41.
56. T. Parsons and C. Perrow, *Complex Organizations,* 2nd ed. (Glenview, IL: Scott, Foresman, 1979).
57. B. Baysinger, "Domain Maintenance as an Objective of Business Political Activity," *Academy of Management Review* 9 (1984), pp. 248–58.
58. P. Andrews, "The Sticky Wicket of Evaluating Public Affairs: Thoughts about a Framework," *Public Affairs Review* 6 (1986), pp. 94–105.
59. S. Lusterman, *The Organization and Staffing of Corporate Public Affairs* (New York: Conference Board, 1987).
60. C. Zeithaml, G. Keim, and B. Baysinger, "Toward an Integrated Strategic Management Process: An Empirical Review of Corporate Political Strategy," in *Strategic Management Frontiers,* ed. John H. Grant (Greenwich, CT: JAI Press, 1988), pp. 377–93.
61. G. Keim and C. Zeithaml, "Corporate Political Strategy and Legislative Decision Making," *Academy of Management Review,* 1986, pp. 828–43.
62. J. Post, "Managing as if the Earth Mattered," *Business Horizons,* July–August 1991, pp. 32–38.
63. C. J. Corbett and L. N. Van Wassenhove, "The Green Fee: Internationalizing and Operationalizing Environmental Issues," *California Management Review,* Fall 1993, pp. 116–33.
64. N. Walley and B. Whitehead, "It's Not Easy Being Green," *Harvard Business Review,* May–June 1994, pp. 46–51.
65. "The Challenge of Going Green," letters, *Harvard Business Review,* July–August 1994, pp. 37–50.
66. F. Rice, "Who Scores Best on the Environment," *Fortune,* July 26, 1993, pp. 114–22.
67. P. Shrivastava, "Ecocentric Management for a Risk Society," *Academy of Management Review* 20 (1995), pp. 118–37.
68. Ibid.
69. Ibid.
70. Ibid.
71. Ibid.
72. M. Russo and P. Fouts, "A Resource-Based Perspective on Corporate Environmental Performance and Profitability," *Academy of Management Journal* 40 (1997), pp. 534–59.
73. L. Grant, "Monsanto's Bet: There's Gold in Going Green," *Fortune,* April 14, 1997, pp. 36-38.
74. A. Fisher, "The World's Most Admired Companies," *Fortune,* October 27, 1997, pp. 40–58.
75. G. Pinchot & E. Pinchot, *The Intelligent Organization,* 1996, San Francisco: Berrett Koehler.
76. S. L. Hart "Beyond Greening: Strategies for a Sustainable World," *Harvard Business Review,* January–February 1997, pp. 66-76.

Chapter Five Appendix B

1. F. Rice, "Who Scores Best on the Environment," *Fortune,* July 26, 1993, p. 114–22.
2. A. Brown, "Business Leaders Respond to Rio with Self-Regulation," *International Herald Tribune,* June 23, 1997, p. 17.
3. Ibid.
4. K. Dechant and B. Altman, "Environmental Leadership: From Compliance to Competitive Advantage," *The Academy of Management Executive,* August 1994, pp. 7–20.
5. R. Stavins, letter in "The Challenge of Going Green," *Harvard Business Review,* July–August 1994, pp. 37–50.
6. N. Walley and B. Whitehead, "It's Not Easy Being Green," *Harvard Business Review,* May–June 1994, pp. 46–51; C. J. Corbett and L. N. Van Wassenhove, "The Green Fee: Internationalizing and Operationalizing Environmental Issues, *California Management Review,* Fall 1993, pp. 116–33.
7. Walley and Whitehead, "It's Not Easy Being Green."
8. "The Challenge of Going Green."
9. Ibid.
10. F. B. Cross, "The Weaning of the Green: Environmentalism Comes of Age in the 1990s," *Business Horizons,* September–October 1990, pp. 40–46.
11. "The Challenge of Going Green."
12. H. Ellison, "Saving Nature while Earning Money," *International Herald Tribune,* June 23, 1997, p. 18.
13. E. Smith and V. Cahan, "The Greening of Corporate America," *Business Week,* April 23, 1990, pp. 96–103.
14. M. E. Porter, "America's Green Strategy," *Science,* April 1991, p. 168.
15. A. Kleiner, "What Does It Mean to Be Green?" *Harvard Business Review,* July–August 1991, pp. 38–47.
16. D. C. Kinlaw, *Competitive and Green: Sustainable Performance in the Environmental Age* (Amsterdam: Pfeiffer & Co., 1993).
17. Rice, "Who Scores Best on the Environment."
18. J. O'Toole, "Do Good, Do Well: The Business Enterprise Trust Awards," *California Management Review,* Spring 1991, pp. 9–24.
19. Rice, "Who Scores Best on the Environment?"
20. O'Toole, "Do Good, Do Well."
21. G. Hardin, "The Tragedy of the Commons," *Science* 162 (1968), pp. 1243–48.
22. D. Kirkpatrick, "Environmentalism: The New Crusade," *Fortune,* February 12, 1990, pp. 44–55.
23. Ibid.
24. R. Carson, *The Silent Spring* (Boston: Houghton Mifflin, 1962); R. Paehlke, *Environmentalism and the Future of Progressive Politics* (New Haven: Yale University Press, 1989), pp. 13–41, 76–143; R. Nash, ed., *The American Environment* (Reading, MA: Addison-Wesley, 1968); R. Revelle and H. Landsberg, eds., *America's Changing Environment* (Boston: Beacon Press, 1970); L. Caldwell, *Environment: A Challenge to Modern Society* (Garden City, NY: Anchor Books, 1971); J. M. Petulla, *Environmental Protection in the United States* (San Francisco: San Francisco Study Center, 1987).
25. B. Commoner, *Science and Survival* (New York: Viking Press, 1963); B. Commoner, *The Closing Circle: Nature, Man and Technology* (New York: Bantam Books, 1971).
26. R. Paehlke, *Environmentalism and the Future of Progressive Politics* (New Haven: Yale University Press, 1989)
27. P. Shrivastava, "Ecocentric Management for a Risk Society," *Academy of Manage ment Review* 20 (1995), pp. 118–37.
28. B. Commoner, *The Closing Circle: Nature, Man and Technology* (New York: Bantam Books, 1971).
29. Paehlke, *Environmentalism.*
30. Ibid.
31. Ibid.

32. P. Hawken, J. Ogilvy, and P. Schwartz, *Seven Tomorrows: Toward a Voluntary History* (New York: Bantam Books, 1982); Paehlke, *Environmentalism.*
33. Porter, "America's Green Strategy."
34. C. Morrison, *Managing Environmental Affairs: Corporate Practices in the U.S., Canada, and Europe* (New York: Conference Board, 1991).
35. Ibid.
36. Kleiner, "What Does It Mean to Be Green?"
37. K. Fischer and J. Schot, *Environmental Strategies for Industry* (Washington, DC: Island Press, 1993).
38. Rice, "Who Scores Best on the Environment?"
39. Dechant and Altman, "Environmental Leadership."
40. Ibid.
41. Ibid.
42. Ibid.
43. H. Ellison, "Saving Nature while Earning Money."
44. Dechant and Altman, "Environment Leadership."
45. Smith and Cahan, "The Greening of Corporate America."
46. J. Elkington and T. Burke, *The Green Capitalists* (London: Victor Gullanez, 1989); M. Zetlin, "The Greening of Corporate America," *Management Review,* June 1990, pp. 10–17.
47. Smith and Cahan, "The Greening of Corporate America."
48. J. Stevens, "Assessing the Health Risks of Incinerating Garbage," *EURA Reporter,* October 1989, pp. 6–10.
49. L. Blumberg and R. Gottlieb, "The Resurrection of Incineration" and "The Economic Factors," in *War on Waste,* ed. L. Blumberg and R. Gottlieb (Washington, DC: Island Press, 1989).
50. L. Blumberg and R. Gottlieb, "Recycling's Unrealized Promise," in Blumberg and Gottlieb, *War on Waste,* pp. 191–226.
51. J. Elkington, "Towards the Sustainable Corporation: Win-Win-Win Business Strategies for Sustainable Development," *California Management Review,* Winter 1994, pp. 90–100.
52. Dechant and Altman, "Environmental Leadership."
53. Brown, "Business Leaders Respond to Rio with Self-Regulation."
54. H. Ellison. ,"Joint Implementation Promotes Cooperation on World Climate," *International Herald Tribune,* June 23, 1997, p. 21.
55. Corbett and Van Wassenhove, "The Green Fee."
56. Ibid.
57. Ibid.
58. Ibid.
59. Elkington, "Towards the Sustainable Corporation."
60. F. S. Rowland, "Chlorofluorocarbons and the Depletion of Stratospheric Ozone," *American Scientist,* January–February 1989, pp. 36–45.
61. Elkington, "Towards the Sustainable Corporation."
62. Corbet and Van Wassenhove, "The Green Fee."
63. H. Ellison,"Joint Implementation Promotes Cooperation on World Climate."
64. Elkington, "Towards the Sustainable Corporation."
65. H. Ellison, "The Balance Sheet," *International Herald Tribune,* June 23, 1997, p. 21.
66. Ibid.

Chapter Six

1. "European Foreign Policy: Unity by Machinery?" *The Economist,* March 2, 1996, pp. 46–47; "European Union: Wishful Thinking," *The Economist,* September 24, 1994, pp. 84–85.
2. "EU: MNCs Face New Challenges as Frontiers Merge," *Crossborder Monitor* 2, no. 10 (March 16, 1994), p. 1; Jane Sasseen, "EU Dateline," *International Management* 49, no 2. (March 1994), p. 5.
3. J. Perez-Lopez, G. Schoepfle, and J. Yochelson, eds., *EC 1992: Implications for U.S. Workers* (Washington, DC: U.S. Department of Labor, 1990).
4. T. Peters, "Prometheus Barely Unbound," *The Executive,* November 1990, pp. 70–84.
5. Jean Chretien. "APEC: Directions for 1997," *Presidents & Prime Ministers,* no 6 (November/December 1996, p. 28–29; "APEC Action Plan," *Presidents & Prime Ministers* 5, no. 1 (January/February 1996), pp. 27–28; "The Opening of Asia," *The Economist,* November 12, 1994, pp. 23–26; "It's Time to Open All of Asia's Markets," *Business Week,* November 14, 1994.
6. Nora Lustig, "The 1982 Debt Crisis, Chiappis, NAFTA, and Mexico's Poor," *Challenge* 38, no. 2. (March/April 1995), pp. 45–50; Nadine M. Post. "Accent Is on Cities, NAFTA," *ENR* 234, no. 6 (February 13, 1995), p. 18; Rachel Kaplar, "Mexico, Here We Come," *International Management* 49, no. 5 (1994), pp. 44–46; Bran Christine, "NAFTA's Effect on the Mexican Economy," *Risk Management* 41, no. 6 (1994), p. 32; Richard L. Thomas, "NAFTA Changes the Game: A U.S. Perspective," *Bank Management* 70, no. 3 (May/June 1994), pp. 55–58; Alan L. Rosas, Lawrence W. Whitehead, and Maria T. Morandi, "The Nitty-Gritty of the Ratification Debate: NAFTA's Environmental Issues and Opportunities," *Business Mexico* 3, no. 9 (September 1993), pp. 42–45.
7. P. Belli, "Globalizing the Rest of the World," *Harvard Business Review,* July/August 1991, pp. 50–55.
8. "World Bank Recommendations to Promote Economic Growth in the Middle East and North Africa," *Middle East Executive Reports* 18, no. 11 (November 1995), p. 27; Andreas Savvides, "Economic Growth in Africa." *World Development* 23, no. 3 (March 1995), pp. 449–58.
9. Roger Ahrens, "Going Global," *International Business* 9, no. 7 (July/August, 1996), pp. 26–30; Bill Javetski, "Old World, New Investment," *Business Week,* October 7, 1996, pp. 50–51.
10. "Foreign Direct Investment in the Triad: A Framework for Understanding Regionalization in the 1990s," *International Executive* 39, no. 1 (January/February 1997), pp. 67–81; "U.S. Direct Investment Abroad: Detail for Historical-Costs Position and Related Capital and Income Flows," *Survey of Current Business* 76, no. 9 (September 1996), pp. 98–128; "Recent Trends in Foreign Direct Investment," *Financial Market Trends* 67 (June 1997), pp. 15–29.
11. "Current International Trade Position of the U.S.: Imports Outpace Exports; Balance with Japan Improves," *Business America* 117, no. 6 (June 1996), pp. 35–37.
12. Hillary Rosner. "FTD, 800-Flowers Face New Reality with Web." *Brandweek* 37, no. 2 (January 8, 1996), p. 9; Matt Roush. "Antitrust Concerns at FTD," *Advertising Age* 66, no. 5 (January 30, 1995), p. 12.
13. C. A. Bartlett and S. Ghoshal, *The Transnational Solution: Managing Across Borders* (Boston: Harvard Business School Press, 1989).
14. Steven E. Prokesch, "Making Global Connections at Caterpillar," *Harvard Business Review* 74, no. 2 (March/April 1996), pp. 88–89.
15. Chang H. Moon, "The Choice of Entry Modes and Theories of Foreign Direct Investment," *Journal of Global Marketing* 11, no. 2 (1997), pp. 43–64; Isabelle Maignan, and Bryan A Lukas, "Entry Mode Decisions: The Role of Managers' Mental Models," *Journal of Global Marketing* 10, no. 4 (1997), pp. 7–22.
16. Maureen Nevin Duffy, "3M Lauds China Government Help," *Chemical Marketer Reporter* 251, no. 1 (January 6, 1997), p. 19.

17. Charlene Marmer Solomon, "Staff Selection Impacts Global Success," *Personnel Journal,* January 1994, pp. 88–101.
18. Nancy J. Adler and Susan Bartholomew, "Managing Globally Competent People," *Academy of Management Executive* 6, no. 3 (1992), pp. 52–65; Cecil G. Howard, "Profile of the 21st-Century Expatriate Manager," *HRMagazine,* June 1992, pp. 93–100.
19. Scott A. Snell, Charles C. Snow, Sue Canney Davison, and Donald C. Hambrick, "Designing and Supporting Transnational Teams: The Human Resource Agenda," *Human Resource Management,* 1998; Charles C. Snow, Scott A. Snell, Sue Canney Davison, and Donald C. Hambrick, "Use Transnational Teams to Globalize Your Company," *Organizational Dynamics,* Spring 1996, pp. 50–67.
20. Donald C. Hambrick, James W. Fredrickson, Lester B. Korn, and Richard M. Ferry, "Reinventing the CEO," *21st Century Report* (Korn/Ferry and Columbia Graduate School of Business, 1989).
21. Charlene Marmer Solomon, "Danger Below! Spot Failing Global Assignments," *Personnel Journal,* November 1996, pp. 78–85.
22. Reyer A. Swaak, "Expatriate Failures: Too Many, Too Much Cost, Too Little Planning," *Compensation & Benefits Review,* November/December 1995, pp. 50–52.
23. Howard, "Profile of the 21st-Century Expatriate Manager."
24. Nancy J. Adler, "Global Leadership: Women Leaders," *Management International Review* 37, no. 1 (Special issue, 1997), pp. 171–96; Nancy J. Adler and Fadna N. Israeli "Competitive Frontiers. Women Managers in a Global Economy," *Organization Studies* 16, no. 4 (1995), pp. 724-25. See also Nancy J. Adler, "Pacific Basin Managers: A Gaijin, Not a Women," *Human Resource Management* 26, no. 2 (1987), pp. 169–91; Hilary Harris, "Women in International Management: Opportunity or Threat?" *Women in Management Review* 8, no. 5 (1993), pp. 9–11.
25. Gretchen M. Sprietzer, Morgan W. McCall, and Joan D. Mahoney, "Early Identification of International Executive Potential," *Journal of Applied Psychology* 82, no. 1 (1997), pp. 6–29; Ronald Mortensen, "Beyond the Fence Line," *HRMagazine,* November 1997, pp. 100–109; "Expatriate Games," *Journal of Business Strategy,* July/August, 1997, pp. 4–5; "Building a Global Workforce Starts with Recruitment," *Personnel Journal* (Special Supplement), March 1996, pp. 9–11.
26. Gunnar Beeth, "Multicultural Managers Wanted," *Management Review,* May 1997, p. 21.
27. David Stamps, "Welcome to America," *Training,* November 1996, pp. 23–30.
28. Linda K. Trevino and Katherine A. Nelson, *Managing Business Ethics: Straight Talk about How to Do It Right* (New York: John Wiley & Sons, 1995).
29 Patricia Digh, "Shades of Gray in the Global Marketplace," *HRMagazine,* April 1997. pp. 91–98.
30. Charlene Marmer Solomon, "Put Your Global Ethics to the Test," *Personnel Journal,* January 1996, pp. 66–74.
31. Digh, "Shades of Gray;" Ashay B. Desai and Terri Rittenburg, "Global Ethics: An Integrative Framework for MNEs," *Journal of Business Ethics* 16 (1997), pp. 791–800; Paul Buller, John Kohls, and Kenneth Anderson, "A Model for Addressing Cross-Cultural Ethical Conflicts," *Business & Society* 36, no. 2 (June 1997), pp. 169–93.

Chapter Seven

1. R. Hisrich and M. Peters, *Entrepreneurship: Starting, Developing, and Managing a New Enterprise* (Burr Ridge, IL: Richard D. Irwin, 1994).
2. J. A. Timmons, *New Venture Creation* (Burr Ridge, IL: Richard D. Irwin, 1994).
3. G. T. Lumpkin and G. G. Dess, "Clarifying the Entrepreneurial Orientation Construct and Linking It To Performance, " *Academy of Management Review,* 1996, Volume 21, pp. 135–72.
4. R. W. Smilor, "Entrepreneurship: Reflections on a Subversive Activity," *Journal of Business Venturing 12* (1997), pp. 341–46.
5. W. Megginson, M. J. Byrd, S. R. Scott Jr., and L. Megginson, *Small Business Management: An Entrepreneur's Guide to Success,* 2nd ed. (Boston: Irwin McGraw-Hill, 1997).
6. Timmons, *New Venture Creation.*
7. T. Peters, "Thrashed by the Real World," *Forbes,* April 7, 1997, p. 100.
8. G. Pinchot, "How Intrapreneurs Innovate," *Management Today,* December 1985, pp. 54–61.
9. A. Marsh, "Promiscuous Breeding" *Forbes,* April 7, 1997, pp. 74–77.
10. B. O'Reilly, "The New Face of Small Business," *Fortune,* May 2, 1994, pp. 82–88.
11. Smilor, "Entrepreneurship," p. 341.
12. H. Aldrich, *Ethnic Entrepreneurs: Immigrant Business in Industrial Societies* (Newbury Park, CA: Sage, 1990).
13. A. E. Serwer, "Lessons from America's Fastest-Growing Companies," *Fortune,* August 8, 1994, pp. 42–60.
14. E. I. Altman, "Why Businesses Fail," *Journal of Business Strategy,* Winter 1983, pp. 15–35.
15. "How It Really Works: Introduction," *Business Week,* August 25, 1997, pp. 48–49.
16. P. Elstron, "It Must Be Something in the Water," *Business Week,* August 25, 1997, pp. 84–87.
17. T. Fuller, "Malaysia's Wired 'Super-corridor,' " *International Herald Tribune,* November 15–16, 1997, pp. 1, 6.
18. A. Ebeling, "The Three Icons of the Old West," *Forbes,* November 17, 1997, pp. 152–54.
19. J. Collins and J. Porras, *Built to Last* (London: Century, 1996).
20. Ibid.
21. K. H. Vesper, *New Venture Mechanics* (Englewood Cliffs, NJ: Prentice Hall, 1993).
22. B. Schlender et al., "Cool Companies, Part 1," *Fortune,* July 7, 1997, pp. 50–60.
23. Ibid.
24. Vesper, *New Venture Mechanics.*
25. E. Schonfeld, "The Space Business Heats Up," *Fortune,* November 24, 1997, pp. 52–60.
26. Ibid.
27. Ibid.
28. Vesper, *New Venture Mechanics.*
29. Timmons, *New Venture Creation.*
30. "Do Universities Stifle Entrepreneurship?" *Across the Board,* July/August 1997, pp. 32–38.
31. M. Sonfield and R. Lussier, "The Entrepreneurial Strategy Matrix: A Model for New and Ongoing Ventures," *Business Horizons,* May–June, 1997, pp. 73–77.
32. Hisrich and Peters, *Entrepreneurship.*
33. Ibid.
34. W. A. Sahlman, "How to Write a Great Business Plan," *Harvard Business Review,* July–August 1997, pp. 98–108.
35. Ibid.
36. Ibid.
37. Schlender et al., "Cool Companies."
38. Sahlman, "How to Write a Great Business Plan."
39. Ibid.
40. Ibid.
41. Ibid.
42. H. H. Stevenson, "A Perspective on Entrepreneurship," Harvard Business School Case No. 9-384-131.
43. S. McCartney, "Michael Dell—and His Company—Grow Up," *The Wall Street Journal,* January 31, 1995, pp. B1, B4.
44. A. F. Brattina, "The Diary of a Small-Company Owner," *Inc.,* May 1993, pp. 79–89, and June 1993, pp. 117–22.
45. L. Kroll, "My Partner, My Father," *Forbes,* June 2, 1997, pp. 66–70.
46. W. P. Barrett, "The Perils of Success," *Forbes,* November 3, 1997, pp. 129–37.

47. Ibid.
48. Ibid., p. 132.
49. O'Reilly, "The New Face of Small Business."
50. C. Burck, "The Real World of the Entrepreneur," *Fortune,* April 5, 1993, pp. 62–81.
51. Serwer, "Lessons from America's Fastest-Growing Companies," pp. 42–60.
52. R. Blunden, "A Framework for the Empirical Study of Venture Discontinuance," in *The Spirit of Entrepreneurship,* ed. R. G. Wycham et al. (Vancouver, BC: International Council of Small Business, 1987), p. 159.
53. P. F. Drucker, "How to Save the Family Business," *The Wall Street Journal,* August 19, 1994, p. A10.
54. Barrett, "The Perils of Success," p. 137.
55. L. Kroll, "The Graduates," *Forbes,* November 3, 1997, pp. 138–42.
56. B. Oviatt and P. P. McDougall, "Global Start-ups: Entrepreneurs on a Worldwide Stage," *Academy of Management Executive* 9, (1995), pp. 30–43.
57. Ibid.
58. Ibid.
59. M. Hordes, J. A. Clancy, and J. Baddaley, "A Primer for Global Start-ups," *Academy of Management Executive* 9, (1995), pp. 7–11.
60. Ibid.
61. R. M. Kanter et al., "Driving Corporate Entrepreneurship," *Management Review,* April 1987, pp. 14–16.
62. I. Chithelen, "Work in Progress," *Forbes,* November 12, 1990, pp. 226–27.
63. R. M. Kanter, *The Change Masters* (New York: Simon & Schuster, 1983).
64. D. Clark, "How a Woman's Passion and Persistence Made 'Bob'," *The Wall Street Journal,* January 10, 1995, pp. B1, B8.
65. Collins and Porras, *Built to Last.*
66. Kanter et al., "Driving Corporate Entrepreneurship."
67. Ibid.
68. J. Argenti, *Corporate Collapse: The Causes and Symptoms* (New York: John Wiley & Sons, 1979).
69. Kanter et al., "Driving Corporate Entrepreneurship."
70. G. T. Lumpkin and G. G. Dess, "Clarifying the Entrepreneurial Orientation Construct and Linking It to Performance," *Academy of Management Review* 21 (1996), pp. 135–72.
71. T. Bateman and J. M. Crant, "The Proactive Dimension of Organizational Behavior," *Journal of Organizational Behavior,* 1993, pp. 103–18.
72. A. E. Serwer, "Michael Dell Turns the PC World Inside Out," *Fortune,* September 8, 1997, pp. 38–44.
73. Lumpkin and Dess, "Clarifying the Entrepreneurial Orientation Construct."
74. Collins and Porras, *Built to Last.*
75. G. Pinchot and E. Pinchot, *The Intelligent Organization* (San Francisco: Berrett-Koehler, 1996).

Chapter Eight

1. L. LaPlante, "Org Chart Revisited," *Computerworld,* April 29, 1996, pp. 32–33; R. Cooke, "Structuring Your 'Org' Chart," *Credit Union Management* 19, no. 9 (September 1996), pp. 28–29; H. Stieglitz, "What's Not on the Organization Chart," *The Conference Board Record,* November 1964, pp. 44–59.
2. B. L. Thompson, *The New Manager's Handbook* (Burr Ridge, IL: Richard D. Irwin, 1995).
3. P. Lawrence and J. Lorsch, *Organization and Environment* (Homewood, IL: Richard D. Irwin, 1969).
4. Ibid.; Thompson, *The New Manager's Handbook.* Also see S. Sharifi and K. S. Pawar, "Product Design as a Means of Integrating Differentiation," *Technovation* 16, no. 5 (May 1996), pp. 255–64; W. B. Stevenson and J. M. Bartunek, "Power, Interaction, Position, and the Generation of Cultural Agreement in Organizations," *Human Relations* 49, no. 1 (January 1996), pp. 75–104.
5. J. D. Edwards, "Measuring Influence Distribution in a Public Organization: A Test of the Control Graph Technique," *Public Administration Quarterly* 20, no. 4 (Winter 1997), pp. 477–504.
6. J. Bacon, *Corporate Boards and Corporate Governance* (New York: The Conference Board, 1993); N. R. Augustine, "The 20th Century Company Meets the 21st Century Board," *Directors and Boards* 21, no. 1 (Autumn 1996), pp. 14–24.
7. John A. Byrne, Ronald Grover, and Richard A. Melcher. "The Best and the Worst Boards," *Business Week,* December 8, 1997, pp. 90–98.
8. A. J. Michels, "Chief Executives as Idi Ahmin?" *Fortune,* July 1, 1991, p. 13; C. M. Daily and D. R. Dalton, "CEO and Board Chair Roles Held Jointly or Separately: Much Ado About Nothing?" *Academy of Management Executive* 11, no. 3 (August 1997), pp. 11–20.
9. D. C. Hambrick and M. Geletkanycz, "The External Ties of Top Executives: Implications for Strategic Choice and Performance," *Administrative Science Quarterly* 42, no. 4 (December 1997), pp. 654–81; D. Greening, "Managing Industrial and Environmental Crises," *Business and Society* 36, no. 4 (December 1997) 334–61.
10. P. Carillo and R. Kopelman, "Organization Structure and Productivity: Effects of Subunit Size, Vertical Complexity, and Administrative Intensity on Operating Efficiency," *Group and Organization Studies* 16 (1991), pp. 44–59. See also "When Slimming May Cut More Than the Fat," *Management Today,* April 1996, p. 8.
11. D. Van Fleet and A. Bedeian, "A History of the Span of Management," *Academy of Management Review* 2 (1977), pp. 356–72.
12. G. Spreitzer, "Social Structural Characteristics of Psychological Empowerment," *Academy of Management Journal* 39, no. 2 (April 1996), pp. 483–95.
13. C. Ogden, "How I Coped with Chaos at the White House," *Fortune* 135, no. 5 (March 17, 1997), pp. 146–48; O. Pollar, "Management: Giving up Control," *Successful Meetings* 45, no. 1 (1996), p. 75; S. Bushardt, D. Duhon, and A. R. Fowler, Jr., "Management Delegation Myths and the Paradox of Task Assignment," *Business Horizons* 34 (March–April 1991).
14. E. Beaubien, "Legendary Leadership," *Executive Excellence* 14, no. 9 (September 1997), p. 20; "How Well Do You Delegate," *Supervision* 58, no. 8 (August 1997), p. 26; J. Mahoney, "Delegating Effectively," *Nursing Management* 28, no. 6 (June 1997), p. 62; J. Lagges, "The Role of Delegation in Improving Productivity," *Personnel Journal,* November 1979, pp. 776–79.
15. G. Matthews, "Run Your Business or Build an Organization?" *Harvard Management Review,* March–April 1984, pp. 34–44.
16. T. Peters, "Letting Go of Controls," *Across the Board* 28 (June 1991), pp. 14–18.
17. R. Boehm and C. Phipps, "Flatness Forays," *McKinsey Quarterly* 3 (1996), pp. 128–43; W. Zellner, "Go-Go Goliaths," *Business Week,* February 13, 1995, pp. 64–70.
18. E. E. Lawler III, "New Roles for the Staff Function: Strategic Support and Services," in *Organizing for the Future,* J. Galbraith, E. E. Lawler III, & Associates (San Francisco: Jossey-Bass, 1993).
19. Michael Porter, *Competitive Advantage: Creating and Sustaining Superior Performance,* (New York: Free Press, 1985).
20. R. Duncan, "What Is the Right Organization Structure?" *Organizational Dynamics* 7 (Winter 1979), pp. 59–80.
21. J. Galbraith, "The Business Unit of the Future," in Galbraith, Lawler & Associates, *Organizing for the Future.*

22. Ibid.; Boehm and Phipps, "Flatness Forays." See also R. K. Chung, "The Horizontal Organization: Breaking Down Functional Silos," *Business Credit* 96, no. 5 (May 1994), pp. 21–24.

23. R. Duncan, "What Is the Right Organization Structure?"

24. J. K. McCollum, "The Matrix Structure: Bane or Benefit to High Tech Organizations?" *Project Management Journal* 24, no. 2 (June 1993), pp. 23–26; R. C. Ford, "Cross-Functional Structures: A Review and Integration of Matrix," *Journal of Management* 18, no. 2 (June 1992), pp. 267–94; H. Kolodny, "Managing in a Matrix," *Business Horizons,* March–April 1981, pp. 17–24.

25. J. Barker, "Conflict Approaches of Effective and Ineffective Project Managers: A Field Study in a Matrix Organization," *Journal of Management Studies* 25, no. 2 (March 1988), pp. 167–78; G. J. Chambers, "The Individual in a Matrix Organization," *Project Management Journal* 20, no. 4 (December 1989), pp. 37–42, 50; S. Davis and P. Lawrence, "Problems of Matrix Organizations," *Harvard Business Review,* May–June 1978, pp. 131–42.

26. C. Bartlett and S. Ghoshal, "Matrix Management: Not a Structure, a Frame of Mind," *Harvard Business Review* 68 (July–August 1990), pp. 138–45.

27. Davis and Lawrence, "Problems of Matrix Organizations."

28. J. G. March & H. A. Simon, *Organizations* (New York: John Wiley & Sons, 1958); J. D. Thompson, *Organizations in Action* (New York: McGraw-Hill, 1967).

29. C. Alter. "An Exploratory Study of Conflict and Coordination in Interorganizational Service Delivery Systems," *Academy of Management Journal* 33, no. 3 (September 1990), pp. 478–502.

30. M. Tushman and D. Nadler, "Implications of Political Models of Organization," in *Resource Book in Macro Organizational Behavior,* ed. R. H. Miles (Santa Monica, CA: Goodyear, 1980).

Chapter 9

1. N. Nohria and J. Berkley, "An Action Perspective: The Crux of the New Management," *California Management Review*, Summer 1994, pp. 70–92.

2. Ibid.

3. T. Burns and G. Stalker, *The Management of Innovation* (London: Tavistock, 1961). See also B. Dumaine, "The Bureaucracy Busters," *Fortune,* June 13, 1991, pp. 36–50; D. A. Morand, "The Role of Behavioral Formality and Informality in the Enactment of Bureaucratic versus Organic Organizations," *Academy of Management Review* 20, no 4, (October 1995), pp. 831–72.

4. Burns and Stalker, *The Management of Innovation.*

5. D. Nadler, J. Hackman, and E. E. Lawler III, *Managing Organizational Behavior* (Boston: Little, Brown, 1979).

6. Dumaine, "The Bureaucracy Busters."

7. B. Buell and R. Hof, "Hewlett-Packard Rethinks Itself," *Business Week,* April 1, 1991, pp. 76–79.

8. D. Robey, *Designing Organizations,* 3rd ed. (Homewood, IL: Richard D. Irwin, 1991).

9. "Why Big Might Remain Beautiful," *The Economist,* March 24, 1990, p. 79.

10. W. Zellner, "Go-Go Goliaths," *Business Week,* February 13, 1995, pp. 64–70.

11. R. Henkoff, "Keeping Motorola on a Roll," *Fortune,* April 18, 1994, pp. 67–78.

12. M. Selz, "Small Manufacturers Display the Nimbleness the Times Require," *The Wall Street Journal,* December 29, 1993, pp. A1, A2.

13. L. Berton, "Big Accounting Firms, Striving to Cut Costs, Irritate Small Clients," *The Wall Street Journal,* April 24, 1994, pp. A1, A8.

14. B. Morris, "He's Smart, He's Not Nice, He's Saving Big Blue," *Fortune,* April 14, 1997, pp. 68–74; D. Kirkpatrick, "Gerstner's New Vision for IBM," *Fortune,* November 15, 1993, pp. 119–26; D. Depke, "IBM and Apple: Can Two Loners Learn to Say 'Teamwork'?" *Business Week,* July 22, 1981, p. 25.

15. R. Henkoff, "Keeping Motorola on a Roll."

16. W. Cascio, "Downsizing: What Do We Know? What Have We Learned?" *Academy of Management Executive,* February 1993, pp. 95–104.

17. Ibid.; M. Hitt, B. Keats, H. Harback, and R. Nixon, "Rightsizing: Building and Maintaining Strategic Leadership and Long-Term Competitiveness," *Organizational Dynamics,* Fall 1994, pp. 18–31; R. E. Stross, "Microsoft's Big Advantage—Hiring Only the Supersmart," *Fortune,* November 25, 1996, pp. 159–62; R. Lieber, "Wired for Hiring: Microsoft's Slick Recruiting Machine," *Fortune,* February 5, 1996, pp. 123–24.

18. Hitt, Keats, Harback, and Nixon, "Rightsizing."

19. Ibid.

20. Cascio, "Downsizing."

21. J. Galbraith, "Organization Design: An Information Processing View," *Interfaces* 4 (Fall 1974), pp. 28–36. See also S. A. Mohrman, "Integrating Roles and Structure in the Lateral Organization," in *Organizing for the Future,* J. Galbraith, E. E. Lawler III, & Associates, (San Francisco: Jossey-Bass, 1993).

22. Walden Paddlers, personal communication.

23. Galbraith, "Organization Design;" Mohrman, "Integrating Roles and Structure."

24. K. Ohmae, *The Mind of the Strategist: Business Planning for Competitive Advantage* (New York: Penguin Books, 1982), Chap. 8.

25. K. Ishikawa, *What Is Total Quality Control? The Japanese Way,* trans. David J. Lu (Englewood Cliffs, NJ: Prentice Hall, 1985).

26. Bureau of Business Practice, *ISO 9000: Handbook of Quality Standards and Compliance* (Needham Heights, MA: Allyn and Bacon, 1992).

27. R. Blackburn and B. Rosen, "Total Quality and Human Resources Management: Lessons Learned," *The Academy of Management Executive* 7, no. 3 (1993), pp. 49–66.

28. M. Price and E. E. Chen, "Total Quality Management in a Small, High-Technology Company," *California Management Review,* Spring 1993, pp. 96–117. See also, G. Easton, "The 1993 State of U.S. Total Quality Management: A Baldrige Examiner's Perspective," *California Management Review,* Spring 1993, pp. 32–54.

29. Bureau of Business Practice, *ISO 9000.*

30. Price and Chen, "Total Quality Management."

31. T. Stewart, "Reengineering: The Hot New Management Tool," *Fortune,* August 23, 1993, pp. 41–48.

32. J. Champy, *Reengineering Management* (New York: HarperBusiness, 1995). See also M. Hammer and J. Champy, *Reengineering the Corporation* (New York: HarperCollins, 1992).

33. Joan Woodward, *Industrial Organization: Theory and Practice* (London: Oxford University Press, 1965).

34. O. Port, "Custom-Made, Direct from the Plant," *Business Week,* 1994 Special Issue, pp. 158–59.

35. J. Martin, "Give 'em Exactly What They Want," *Fortune,* November 10, 1997, pp. 283–85; B. J. Pine II, B. Victor, and A. Boynton, "Making Mass Customization Work," *Harvard Business Review,* September–October 1993, pp. 108–19; Port, "Custom-Made."

36. J. Johansen, U. S. Karmarker, D. Nanda, and A. Seidmann "Computer Integrated Manufacturing: Empirical Implications for Industrial Information Systems," *Journal of Management Information Systems* 12, no. 2 (Fall 1995), pp. 59–83. See also M. A. Youndt, S. A. Snell, J. W. Dean, Jr., and D. P. Lepak, "Human Resource Management, Manufacturing Strategy, and Firm

Performance," *Academy of Management Journal* 39, no. 4 (1996), pp. 836–67; R. Schroeder and M. Pesch, "Focusing the Factory: Eight Lessons," *Business Horizons,* September–October 1994, pp. 76–81.

37. D. Upton, "The Management of Manufacturing Flexibility," *California Management Review,* Winter 1994, pp. 72–89.
38. J. Womack and D. Jones, "From Lean Production to the Lean Enterprise," *Harvard Business Review,* March–April 1994, pp. 93–103.
39. A. Taylor III, "How Toyota Defies Gravity," *Fortune,* December 8, 1997, pp. 100–108; "Lean Manufacturing Systems Have Big Payoff," *Purchasing* 123, no. 1 (1997), pp. 221–27.
40. Womack and Jones, "From Lean Production to the Lean Enterprise."
41. J. D. Blackburn, *Time-Based Competition* (Homewood, IL: Richard D. Irwin, 1991); B. Wagner and L. Digman, "The Relationships between Generic and Time-Based Strategies and Performance," *Journal of Managerial Issues* 9, no. 3, (Fall 1997), pp. 334–54; E. H. Kessler, A. K. Chakrabarti, "Innovation Speed: A Conceptual Model of Context, Antecedents, and Outcomes," *Academy of Management Review* 21, no. 4, (1996), pp. 1143–92.
42. R. Henkoff, "Delivering the Goods," *Fortune,* November 28, 1994, pp. 64–78.
43. Ibid.
44. Ibid.
45. M. Tucker and D. Davis, "Key Ingredients for Successful Implementation of Just-in-Time: A System for All Business Sizes," *Business Horizons,* May–June 1993, pp. 59–65.
46. M. Tucker and D. Davis, "Key Ingredients for Successful Implementation of Just-in-Time: A System for All Business Sizes," *Business Horizons,* May–June 1993, pp. 59–65. See also J. Funk, "Just-in-Time Manufacturing and Logistical Complexity: A Contingency Model," *International Journal of Operations & Production Management* 15, no. 5 (1995), pp. 15–19; Z. Zhu and P. H. Zhiwei, "Defining Critical Elements in JIT Implementation: A Survey," *Industrial Management + Data Systems* 95, no. 8 (1995), pp. 21–29; G. Bassett, *Operations Management for Service Industries* (Westport, CT: Quorum Books, 1992).
47. J. D. Kasarda and D. A. Rondinelli, "Innovative Infrastructure for Agile Manufacturers," *Sloan Management Review* 39, no. 2 (Winter 1998), pp. 73–81.
48. D. Gerwin, "Integrating Manufacturing into the Strategic Phases of New Product Development," *California Management Review,* Summer 1993, pp. 123–36.
49. G. Hamel and C. K. Prahalad, "Competing for the Future," *Harvard Business Review,* July–August 1994, pp. 122–28.
50. G. Hamel and C. K. Prahalad, *Competing for the Future* (Boston: Harvard Business School Press, 1994).
51. R. E. Miles and C. C. Snow, *Fit, Failure, and the Hall of Fame* (New York: Free Press, 1994). See also D. Cravens, S. Shipp, and K. Cravens, "Reforming the Traditional Organization: The Mandate for Developing Networks," *Business Horizons,* July–August 1994, pp. 19–28; R. Miles and C. Snow, "Organizations: New Concepts for New Forms," *California Management Review* 28 (Spring 1986), pp. 62–73.
52. S. Tully, "The Modular Corporation," *Fortune,* February 8, 1993, pp. 106–15.
53. D. Cravens, S. Shipp, and K. Cravens, "Reforming the Traditional Organization: The Mandate for Developing Networks," *Business Horizons,* July–August 1994, pp. 19–28.
54. Tully, "The Modular Corporation.
55. Ibid.
56. Miles and Snow, *Fit, Failure, and the Hall of Fame.*
57. R. M. Kanter, "Becoming PALs: Pooling, Allying, and Linking across Companies," *Academy of Management Executives* 3 (August 1989), pp. 183–93.
58. B. A. Stertz, "In a U-Turn from Past Policy, Big Three of Detroit Speed into Era of Cooperation," *The Wall Street Journal,* June 28, 1991, pp. B1, B4
59. R. Osborn and C. Baughn, "Forms of Interorganizational Governance for Multinational Alliances," *Academy of Management Journal* 33 (1990), pp. 503–19.
60. R. M. Kanter, "Collaborative Advantage: The Art of Alliances," *Harvard Business Review,* July–August 1994, pp. 96–108.
61. Ibid.
62. Ibid.
63. P. Senge, *The Fifth Discipline* (New York: Doubleday Currency, 1990). See also M. E. McGill and J. W. Slocum, Jr., *The Smarter Organization: How to Build a Business That Learns and Adapts to Marketplace Needs* (New York: John Wiley & Sons, 1994).
64. D. A. Garvin, "Building a Learning Organization," *Harvard Business Review,* July–August 1993, pp. 78–91.
65. Ibid.
66. E. E. Lawler III, *The Ultimate Advantage: Creating the High-Involvement Organization* (San Francisco: Jossey-Bass, 1992); E. E. Lawler III, "Total Quality Management and Employee Involvement: Are They Compatible?" *The Academy of Management Executive,* February 1994, pp. 68–76; E. E. Lawler III, "Executives' Behavior in High-Involvement Organizations," in *Making Organizations Competitive,* ed. R. Kilmann (San Francisco: Jossey-Bass, 1991).
67. Lawler, "Executives' Behavior in High-Involvement Organizations."
68. Lawler, "Total Quality Management and Employee Involvement."
69. R. Ashkenas, D. Ulrich, T. Jick, and S. Kerr, *The Boundaryless Organization: Breaking the Chains of Organizational Structure* (San Francisco: Jossey-Bass, 1995); R. W. Keidel, "Rethinking Organizational Design," *Academy of Management Executive,* November 1994, pp. 12–27.

Chapter Ten

1. "The Importance of HR," *HRFocus,* March 1996, p. 14. See also William J. Rothwell, "Trends in HRM," Commerce Clearing House and Society for Human Resource Management, 1996.
2. Thomas A. Stewart, *Intellectual Capital* (New York: Doubleday, 1997); Carolyn Walkup, "Companies Vie for Workers as Labor Pool Evaporates," *Nation's Restaurant News* 29, no. 8 (February 20, 1995), pp. 1, 4; W. B. Johnston, "Global Work Force 2000: The New World Labor Market," *Harvard Business Review,* March–April 1991, pp. 115–27.
3. James P. Clifford, "Job Analysis: Why Do It and How It Should Be Done," *Public Personnel Management* 23 (Summer 1994), pp. 321–40; Ronald A. Ash, "Job Analysis in the World of Work," in *The Job Analysis Handbook for Business, Industry, and Government,* ed. Sidney Gall (New York: John Wiley & Sons, 1988); E. L. Levine, *Everything You Always Wanted to Know about Job Analysis: A Job Analysis Primer* (Tampa, FL: Mariner Publishing, 1983).
4. Michael T. Brannick, Joan P. Brannick, and Edward L. Levine, "Job Analysis, Personnel Selection, and the ADA," *Human Resource Management Review* 2, no. 3 (1992), pp. 171–83; S. R. Burchett and K. P. DeMeuse, "Performance Appraisal and the Law," *Personnel,* July 1985, pp. 29–37.
5. David E. Terpstra, "The Search for Effective Methods," *HRFocus,* May 1996, pp. 16–17; L. Amante, "Help Wanted: Creative Recruitment Tactics," *Personnel* 66, no. 10 (1989), pp. 32–36. See also Jean Powell Kirnan, John A. Farley, and Kurt F. Geisinger, "The Relationship between

Recruiting Source, Applicant Quality, and Hire Performance: An Analysis by Sex, Ethnicity, and Age," *Personnel Psychology* 42, no. 2 (Summer 1989), pp. 293–308; David F. Caldwell and A. Austin Spivey, "The Relationship between Recruiting Source and Employee Success: An Analysis by Race," *Personnel Psychology* 36, no. 1 (Spring 1983), pp. 67–72; Thomas J. Hutton, "Increase the Odds for Successful Searches," *Personnel Journal,* November 1995, pp. 1–5; R. D. Gatewood and H. S. Fields, *Human Resource Selection* (Hinsdale, IL: Dryden Press, 1987); B. Schneider and N. Schmitt, *Staffing Organizations* (Glenview, IL: Scott, Foreman, 1986); R. D. Arvey and R. H. Faley, *Fairness in Selecting Employees,* 2nd ed. (Reading, MA: Addison-Wesley Publishing, 1998).

6. Allan Halcrow, "Employees Are Your Best Recruiters," *Personnel Journal* 67, no. 11 (November 1988), pp. 42–49; P. G. Swaroff, L. A. Barclay, and A. R. Bass, "Recruiting Sources: Another Look," *Journal of Applied Psychology* 70 (1985), pp. 720–28.
7. Patrick Scheetz, "Best, Worst Majors for Job-Hunting Grads," *USA Today,* May 29 1996, p. 11B; "Pop Quiz: How Do You Recruit the Best College Grads?" *Personnel Journal,* August 1995, pp. 12–18; Shannon Peters Talbott, "Boost Your Campus Image to Attract Top Grads," *Personnel Journal,* March 1996, pp. 6–8; Holly Rawlinson, "Scholarships Recruit Future Employees Now," *Recruitment,* a supplement of *Personnel Journal,* August 1988, p. 14; V. R. Lindquist and F. S. Endicott, *Trends in the Employment of College and University Graduates in Business and Industry,* 40th annual report (Evanston IL: Northwestern University Press, 1986).
8. James M. Conway, Robert A. Jako, and Deborah F. Goodman, "A Meta-Analysis of Interrater and Internal Consistency Reliability of Selection Interviews," *Journal of Applied Psychology* 80, no. 5 (October 1995), pp. 565–79; Malcolm Wheatley, "The Talent Spotters," *Management Today,* June 1996, pp. 62–64; Michael McDaniel, Deborah L. Whetzel, Frank L. Schmidt, and Steven D. Maurer, "The Validity of Employment Interviews: A Comprehensive Review and Meta-Analysis," *Journal of Applied Psychology* 79, no. 4 (August 1994), pp. 599–616; Elaine D. Pulakos, Neal Schmitt, David Whitney, and Matthew Smith, "Individual Differences in Interview Ratings: The Impact of Standardization, Consensus Discussion, and Sampling Error on the Validity of a Structured Interview," *Personnel Psychology* 49, no. 1 (Spring 1996), pp. 85–102; Michael A. Campion, James E. Campion, and Peter J. Hudson Jr., "Structured Interviewing: A Note on Incremental Validity and Alternative Question Types," *Journal of Applied Psychology* 79, no. 6 (December 1994), pp. 998–1002; R. A. Fear, *The Evaluation Interview* (New York: McGraw-Hill, 1984).
9. Christopher E. Stenberg, "The Role of Pre-employment Background Investigations in Hiring," *Human Resource Professional* 9, no. 1 (January/February 1996), pp. 19–21; L. Barani, "Background Investigations: How HR Stays on the Cutting Edge," *HRFocus* 70 (June 1993), p. 12; "The Final Rung: References," *Across the Board,* March 1996, p. 40; M. G. Aamondt, D. A. Bryan, and A. J. Whitcomb, "Predicting Performance with Letters of Recommendation," *Public Personnel Management* 22 (Spring 1993), pp. 81–90; Robert L. Brady, "Employee Loses Defamation Suit over Bad Reference," *HRFocus* 73, no. 7 (July 1996), p. 20; Glenn Withiam, "Complexities of Employee References," *Cornell Hotel and Restaurant Administration Quarterly* 37, no. 3 (June 1996), p. 10; Bureau of National Affairs, *Employee Selection Procedures: ASPA-BNA Survey No. 45* (Washington, DC: U.S. Government Printing Office, 1983).
10. Seymore Adler, "Personality Tests for Salesforce Selection: Worth a Fresh Look," *Review of Business* 16, no. 1 (Summer/Fall 1994), pp. 27–31. See also M. R. Barrick and M. K. Mount, "The Big Five Personality Dimensions and Job Performance: A Meta-Analysis," *Personnel Psychology* 44 (1991), pp. 1–26; Daniel P. O'Meara, "Personality Tests Raise Questions of Legality and Effectiveness," *HRMagazine,* January 1994, pp. 97–100; Jeffrey A. Mello, "Personality Tests and Privacy Rights," *HRFocus* 73, no. 3 (March 1996), pp. 22–23; Bureau of National Affairs, *Employee Selection Procedures.*
11. Samuel Greengard, "Genetic Testing: Should You Be Afraid?" *Workforce* 76, no. 7 (July 1997), pp. 38–44; Robert Ellis Smith, "Corporations Fail the Fair Hiring Test," *Business and Society Review* 88 (Winter 1994), pp. 29–33; Judy D. Olian, "AIDS Testing for Employment Purposes? Facts and Controversies," *Journal of Business and Psychology* 3, no. 2 (Winter 1988), pp. 135–53; Eric Rolfe Greenberg, "Workplace Testing: Who's Testing Whom?" *Personnel* 66, no. 5 (May 1989), pp. 39–45; David Warner, "Rules on Medical Tests for New Hires," *Nation's Business* 79 (August 1991), pp. 29–31. See also Jonathan A. Segal, "Pre-employment Physicals under the ADA," *HRMagazine* 37 (October 1992), pp. 103–7; John F. Kirch, "Worry Free Drug Testing?" *Security Management* 40, no. 8 (August 1996), p. 10; "Drug Testing Grows, AMA Study Finds," *Managing Office Technology* 41, no. 7 (July 1996), p. 23; Paul Farrell, "Pass or Fail: Managing a Drug and Alcohol Testing Program," *Risk Management* 43, no. 5 (May 1996), pp. 34–37.
12. Patrick M. Wright, Michele K. Kacmar, Gary C. McMahan, and Kevin Deleeuw, "P=f(M × A): Cognitive Ability as a Moderator of the Relationship between Personality and Job Performance," *Journal of Management* 21, no. 6 (1995), pp. 1129–2063; Therese Hoff Macan, Marcia J. Avedon, Matthew Paese, and David E. Smith, "The Effects of Applicants' Reactions to Cognitive Ability Tests and an Assessment Center," *Personnel Psychology* 47, no. 4 (Winter 1994), pp. 715–38; Paul R. Sackett and Daniel J. Ostgaard, "Job-Specific Applicant Pools and National Norms for Cognitive Ability Tests: Implications for Range Restriction Corrections in Validation Research," *Journal of Applied Psychology* 79, no. 5 (October 1994), pp. 680–84; F. L. Schmidt and J. E. Hunter, "Tacit Knowledge, Practical Intelligence, General Mental Ability, and Job Knowledge," *Current Directions in Psychological Science* 2, no. 1 (1993), pp. 3–13; Bruce J. Avolio and David A. Waldman, "An Examination of Age and Cognitive Test Performance across Job Complexity and Occupational Types," *Journal of Applied Psychology* 75 (February 1990), pp. 43–50; Bureau of National Affairs, *Employee Selection Procedures.*
13. Florence Berger and Ajay Ghei, "Employment Tests: A Facet of Hospitality Hiring," *Cornell Hotel and Restaurant Administration Quarterly* 36, no. 6 (December 1995), pp. 28–31; Malcolm James Ree, Thomas R. Carretta, and Mark S. Teachout, "Role of Ability and Prior Job Knowledge in Complex Training Performance," *Journal of Applied Psychology* 80, no. 6 (December 1995), pp. 721–30. Bureau of National Affairs, *Employee Selection Procedures.*
14. "If the Shoe Fits," *Security Management* 40, no. 2 (February 1996), p. 11; Samuel Greengard, "Are You Well Armed to Screen Applicants?" *Personnel Journal* (December 1995), pp. 84–95; Peter Bullard, "Pre-employment Screening to Weed Out Bad Apples," *Nursing Home* 43, no. 5 (June 1994), pp. 29–31; Malcolm C. McCulloch, "Can Integrity Testing Improve Market Conduct?" *LIMRA's MarketFacts* 15, no. 2 (March/April 1996), pp. 15–16; Bureau of National Affairs, *Employee Selection Procedures.*
15. D. S. Ones, C. Viswesvaran, and F. L. Schmidt, "Comprehensive Meta-Analysis of Integrity Test Validities: Findings and

Implications for Personnel Selection and Theories of Job Performance," *Journal of Applied Psychology* 78 (August 1993), pp. 679–703. See also Gilbert Fuchsberg, "Attorney General in New York Urges Integrity Test Ban," *The Wall Street Journal,* March 6, 1991.

16. Lewis Newman, "Outplacement the Right Way," *Personnel Administrator* 34, no. 2 (February 1989), pp. 83–86; Rocki-Lee DeWitt, "The Structural Consequences of Downsizing," *Organization Science* 4, no. 1 (February 1993), pp. 30–40; L. Reibstein, "Survivors of Layoffs Help to Lift Morale and Instill Trust," *The Wall Street Journal,* March 13, 1986, p. 13.
17. See *Adair v. United States,* 2078 U.S. 161 (1908). See also Leonard B. Mandelbaum, "Employment-at-Will: Is the Model Termination Act the Answer?" *Labor Law Journal* 44, no. 5 (May 1993), pp. 175–285; S. A. Youngblood and L. Bierman, "Due Process and Employment-at-Will: A Legal and Behavior Analysis," in *Research in Personnel and Human Resource Management,* Vol. 3, ed. K. Rowland and G. Ferris (Greenwich, CT: JAI Press, 1985), pp. 185–230; C. Schwoerer and B. Rosen, "Effects of Employment-at-Will Policies and Compensation Policies on Corporate Image and Job Pursuit Intentions," *Journal of Applied Psychology* 74 (1989), pp. 653–56.
18. Dick Grove, *Discipline without Punishment* (New York: American Management Association, 1996); Jeffrey A. Mello, "The Fine Art of the Reprimand: Using Criticism to Enhance Commitment, Motivation, and Performance," *Employment Relations Today* 22, no. 4 (Winter 1995), pp. 19–27; J. R. Redecker, "Discipline, Part 1: Progressive Systems Work Only by Accident," *Personnel* 62 (October 1985), pp. 8–12; A. W. Bryant, "Replacing Punitive Discipline Policy Capturing Approach," *Personnel Psychology* 43 (Spring 1990), pp. 117–34.
19. J. Jannotta, "Stroh's Outplacement Success," *Management Review,* January 1987, pp. 52–53. See also John E. Lyncheski, "Mishandling Terminations Causes Legal Nightmares," *HRMagazine* 40, no. 5 (May 1995), pp. 25–30.
20. *Employer EEO Responsibilities* (Washington, DC: Equal Employment Opportunity Commission, U.S. Government Printing Office, 1996); Nancy J. Edman and Michael D. Levin-Epstein, *Primer of Equal Employment Opportunity,* 6th ed. (Washington, DC: Bureau of National Affairs, 1994).
21. Robert Gatewood and Hubert Field, *Human Resource Selection,* 3rd ed. (Chicago, IL: Dryden Press, 1994), pp. 36–49; R. A. Baysinger, "Disparate Treatment and Disparate Impact Theories of Discrimination: The Continuing Evolution of Title VII of the 1964 Civil Rights Act," in *Readings in Personnel and Human Resource Management,* ed. R. S. Schuler, S. A. Youngblood, and V. L. Huber (St. Paul, MN: West Publishing, 1987).
22. "Uniform Guidelines on Employee Selection Procedures," *Federal Register* 43, no. 166 (August 25, 1978), pp. 38290–309. See also *A Professional and Legal Analysis of the Uniform Guidelines on Employee Selection Procedures* (Berea, OH: American Society for Personnel Administration, 1981).
23. "1995 Industry Report," *Training* 32, no. 10 (May 1996), pp. 37–82. See also B. Filipczak, "Training Cheap," *Training* 32, no. 10 (May 1996), pp. 28–34; "Training Industry Report Highlights 1995's Big Trends," *Personnel Journal* 75, no. 1 (January 1996), p. 25; "Education," *The Wall Street Journal,* February 9, 1991, p. R5.
24. A. P. Carnevale, *America and the New Economy: How New Competitive Standards Are Radically Changing American Workplaces* (San Francisco: Jossey-Bass, 1991); Marc Hequet, "Doing More with Less," *Training* 31 (October 1995), pp. 77–82; Filipczak, "Training Cheap."
25. Sandra N. Phillips, "Team Training Puts Fizz in Coke Plant's Future," *Personnel Journal* 75, no. 1 (January 1996), pp. 39–42. See also George Bohlander and Kathy McCarthy, "How to Get the Most from Team Training," *National Productivity Review,* Autumn 1996, pp. 25–35.
26. For more information, see Kenneth Wexley and Gary Latham, *Increasing Productivity through Performance Appraisal* (Reading, MA: Addison-Wesley, 1994). See also H. J. Bernardin and R. W. Beatty, *Performance Appraisal: Assessing Human Behavior at Work* (Boston: Kent Publishing, 1984).
27. Mark Edwards and Ann J. Ewen, "How to Manage Performance and Pay with 360-Degree Feedback," *Compensation and Benefits Review* 28, no. 3 (May/June 1996), pp. 41–46. Also see Mary N. Vinson, "The Pros and Cons of 360-Degree Feedback: Making It Work," *Training and Development* 50, no. 4 (April 1996), pp. 11–12; John F. Milliman, Robert F. Zawacki, Carol Norman, Lynda Powell, and Jay Kirksey, "Companies Evaluate Employees from All Perspectives," *Personnel Journal* 73, no. 11 (November 1994), pp. 99–103; R. S. Schuler, *Personnel and Human Resource Management* (St. Paul, MN: West Publishing 1984).
28. Arthur Sherman, George Bohlander, and Scott Snell, *Managing Human Resources,* 11th ed. (Cincinnati, OH: Southwestern Publishing, 1998). See also W. A. Schiemann, "The Impact of Corporate Compensation and Benefit Policy on Employee Attitudes and Behavior and Corporate Profitability," *Journal of Business and Psychology* 2 (1987), pp. 8–26.
29. Garry M. Ritzky, "Incentive Pay Programs That Help the Bottom Line," *HRMagazine* 40, no. 4 (April 1995), pp. 68–74; Steven Gross and Jeffrey Bacher, "The New Variable Pay Programs: How Some Succeed, Why Some Don't," *Compensation and Benefits Review* 25, no. 1 (January–February 1993), p. 51; G. T. Milkovich and J. M. Newman, *Compensation* (Plano, TX: Business Publications, 1987).
30. Theresa Welbourne and Luis Gomez-Mejia, "Gainsharing: A Critical Review and a Future Research Agenda," *Journal of Management* 21, no. 3 (1995), pp. 559–609; Denis Collins, "15 Lessons Learned from the Death of a Gainsharing Plan," *Compensation and Benefits Review* 28, no. 2 (March–April 1996), pp. 31–40.
31. Thomas H. Patten and Mark G. Damico, "Survey Details Profit-Sharing Plans: Is Revealing Allocation Formulas a Performance Incentive?" *National Productivity Review* 12, no. 3 (Summer 1993), pp. 383–94; J. Savage, "Incentive Programs at Nucor Corporation Boost Productivity," *Personnel Administrator,* August 1981, pp. 33–36.
32. Kenneth W. Chilton, "Lincoln Electric's Incentive System: A Reservoir of Trust," *Compensation and Benefits Review* 25, no. 6 (November 1994), pp. 29–34. See also D. W. Meyers, *Human Management: Principles and Practice* (Chicago: Commerce Clearing House, 1986).
33. *Wage and Hour Manual, BNA Policy and Practice Series* (Washington, DC: Bureau of National Affairs, 1986).
34. Richard Scholl and Elizabeth Cooper, "The Use of Job Evaluation to Eliminate Gender-Based Pay Differentials," *Public Personnel Management* 20, no. 1 (Spring 1991), pp. 1–17; E. A. Cooper and G. V. Barret, "Equal Pay and Gender: Implications of Court Cases for Personnel Practices," *Academy of Management Review,* 1984, pp. 84–94.
35. Sherman, Bohlander, and Snell, *Managing Human Resources,* p. 374; Milkovich and Newman, *Compensation.*
36. C. Trost, "In Minnesota, 'Pay Equity' Passes Test, but Foes See Trouble Ahead," *The Wall Street Journal,* May 10, 1984, p. 27.
37. T. Gup, "The Curse of Coal," *Time,* November 4, 1991, pp. 54–64.

38. Linda Kahn, *Primer of Labor Relations,* 25th ed. (Washington, DC: Bureau of National Affairs Books, 1994); A. Sloane and F. Witney, *Labor Relations* (Englewood Cliffs, NJ: Prentice Hall, 1985).
39. S. Premack and J. E. Hunter, "Individual Unionization Decisions," *Psychological Bulletin* 103 (1988), pp. 223–34.
40. Robert Sinclair and Lois Tetrick, "Social Exchange and Union Commitment: A Comparison of Union Instrumentality and Union Support Perceptions," *Journal of Organizational Behavior* 16, no. 6 (November 1995), pp. 669–79. See also Premack and Hunter, "Individual Unionization Decisions."
41. David Meyer, "The Political Effects of Grievance Handling by Stewards in a Local Union," *Journal of Labor Research* 15, no. 1 (Winter 1994), p. 33; A. O. Hirchman, *Exit, Voice, and Loyalty: Responses to Decline in Firms, Organizations, and States* (Cambridge, MA: Harvard University Press, 1970).
42. George Bohlander and Donna Blancero, "A Study of Reversal Determinants in Discipline and Discharge Arbitration Awards: The Impact of Just Cause Standards," *Labor Studies Journal* 21, no. 3 (Fall 1996), pp. 3–18; A. A. Malinowski, "An Empirical Analysis of Discharge Cases and the Work History of Employee Reinstated by Labor Arbitrators," *Arbitration Journal* 36 (1981), pp. 31–46.
43. Courtney Gifford, *Directory of U.S. Labor Organizations, 1996 Edition* (Washington DC: Bureau of National Affairs, 1996); E. E. Lawler III and S. Mohrman, "Unions and the New Management," *Academy of Management Executive,* 1987, pp. 293–300.
44. J. H. Foegen, "Labor Unions—Don't Count Them Out Yet!" *Academy of Management Executives,* February 1989, pp. 67–69; H. Love, A. L. Barrett Jr., and L. Ozley, "The Transformation of National Steel Corporation," in *Corporate Transformation,* ed. R. Kilmann and T. J. Covin (San Francisco: Jossey-Bass, 1988).

Chapter Eleven

1. "Charting the Projections: 1994–2005," *Occupational Outlook Quarterly,* Fall 1995, pp. 1–27. See also Ronald E. Kutscher, "Outlook 1990–2005: Major Trends and Issues," *Occupational Outlook Quarterly,* Spring 1992, pp. 2–5.
2. Ibid.; "Four by Four," *Training and Development Journal,* February 1989, pp. 13–21.
3. "Tomorrow's Jobs," *Occupational Outlook Handbook,* 1992–1993 ed. (Washington, DC: Bureau of Labor Statistics, May 1992), pp. 8–14; Kutscher, "Outlook 1990–2005."
4. *Employment and Earnings,* (Washington, DC: Bureau of Labor Statistics, U.S. Department of Labor, July 1996), p. 152. See also Nancy Perry, "More Women Are Executive VPs," *Fortune,* July 12, 1993, p. 16.
5. Tom Dunkel, "The Front Runners," *Working Woman,* April 1996, pp. 30–35, 72, 75; Rosemary Cafasso, "The Diversity Gap," *Computerworld,* June 1996, pp. 35–37; Gillian Flynn, "Do You Have The Right Approach to Diversity?" *Personnel Journal,* October 1995, pp. 68–75; Amanda Troy Segal and Wendy Zellner, "Corporate Women," *Business Week,* June 8, 1992, pp. 74–78.
6. Arthur Sherman, George Bohlander, and Scott Snell, *Managing Human Resources,* 11th ed. (Cincinnati, OH: Southwestern Publishing, 1998); Mark Maremont, "Abuse of Power," *Business Week,* May 13, 1996, pp. 86–98; Jennifer Laabs, "Sexual Harassment," *Personnel Journal,* February 1995, pp. 36–45.
7. "Tomorrow's Jobs;" K. Kovach and J. Pearce, "HR Strategic Mandates for the 1990s," *Personnel,* April 1990, pp. 50–55; Margaret L. Usdansky, "Minority Majorities in One in Six Cities," *USA Today,* June 9, 1993, p. 10A; "Charting the Projections: 1994–2005;" "The Immigrants," *Business Week,* July 13, 1992, pp. 114–22; Jaclyn Fierman, "Is Immigration Hurting the U.S.?" *Fortune,* August 9, 1993, pp. 76–79; B. Dicken and R. Blomberg, "Immigrants—Can They Provide the Future Labor Force?" *Public Personnel Management,* Spring 1991, pp. 91–100.
8. Sherman, Bohlander, and Snell, *Managing Human Resources;* Asra Q. Nomani, "Labor Letter," *The Wall Street Journal,* November 7, 1996, p. A1.
9. "An ADA Checklist for Implementation and Review," *HRFocus,* July 1994, p. 19. See also *ADA Compliance: The Complete Planning and Practice Guide,* (Business & Legal Reports, Inc., 1993); Stephen Overall, "Firms Hire Fewer Disabled People in Unskilled Jobs," *People Management,* November 16, 1995, p. 10.
10. S. Meisinger, "The Americans with Disabilities Act: Begin Preparing Now," Society for Human Resource Management, legal report, Winter 1991.
11. J. Peters, "How to Bridge the Hiring Gap," *Personnel Administrator,* October 1989, pp. 76–85.
12. "Charting the Projections: 1994–2005." See also Kutscher, "Outlook 1990–2005;" "Tomorrow's Jobs."
13. Ibid.
14. "An ADA Checklist for Implementation and Review." See also *ADA Compliance;* "Overall, Firms Hire Fewer Disabled People in Unskilled Jobs;" Rudy M. Yandrick, "A Strategy for Managing Behavioral Problems at Work," *HRMagazine* 41, no. 6 (June 1996), pp. 150–60; "320-Pound Woman Wins $100,000 Legal Appeal over Lost Job," *Arizona Republic,* November 24, 1993, p. A3; "Low Literacy," *Training and Development,* January 1994, p. 12; Donald J. Ford, "Toward a More Literate Workforce," *Training and Development,* November 1992, pp. 52–55.
15. Michael A. Verespej, "The Education Difference," *Industry Week* 245, no. 9 (May 6, 1996), pp. 11–14; Richard D. Zalman, "The Basics of In-house Skills Training," *HRMagazine* 34, no. 2 (February 1990), pp. 74–78; Ron Zemke, "Workplace Illiteracy—Shall We Overcome?" *Training* 26, no. 6 (June 1989), pp. 33–39; Teresa L. Smith, "The Basics of Basic-Skills Training," *Training and Development* 49, no. 4 (April 1995), pp. 44–46; Teresa L. Smith, "Job Related Materials Reinforce Basic Skills," *HRMagazine,* July 1995, pp. 84–90; J. Oberle, "Teaching English as a Second Language," *Training,* April 1990, pp. 61–67.
16. Shari Caudron, "Don't Make Texaco's $175 Million Mistake," *Workforce,* March 1997, pp. 58–66. See also Peter Wright, Stephen Ferris, Janine Hiller, and Mark Kroll, "Competitiveness through Management of Diversity: Effects on Stock Price Valuation," *Academy of Management Journal* 38, no. 1 (February 1995), pp. 272–87.
17. N. Adler, *International Dimensions of Organizational Behavior,* 3rd ed. (Boston: PWS–Kent, 1997); T. Cox and S. Blake, "Managing Cultural Diversity: Implications for Organizational Competitiveness," *Academy of Management Executives* 5 (August 1991), pp. 45–56.
18. "Successful Companies Realize that Diversity Is a Long-Term Process, Not a Program," *Personnel Journal,* April 1993, p. 54.
19. Adler, *International Dimensions of Organizational Behavior;* Cox and Blake, "Managing Cultural Diversity."
20. Adler, *International Dimensions of Organizational Behavior.*
21. Flynn, "Do You Have The Right Approach to Diversity?"; Caudron, "Don't Make Texaco's $175 Million Mistake."
22. A. Livingston, "What Your Department Can Do," *Working Woman,* January 1991, pp. 59–60.
23. Leslie E. Overmyer Day, "The Pitfalls of Diversity Training," *Training and Development* 49, no. 12 (December 1995),

pp. 24–29; Sara Rynes and Benson Rosen, "A Field Survey of Factors Affecting the Adoption and Perceived Success of Diversity Training," *Personnel Psychology* 48, no. 2 (Summer 1995), pp. 247–70; "Quick-Fix Diversity Efforts Are Doomed," *Training,* January 1995, pp. 18–19; Dawn Anfuso, "All Colgate Asks for Is a Little Respect," *Personnel Journal* 74, no. 10 (October 1995), p. 49; L. Foxman and W. Polsky, "Cross-Cultural Understanding," *Personnel Journal,* November 1989, pp. 12–14.

24. Cox and Blake, "Managing Cultural Diversity."
25. Nancy L. Mueller, "Wisconsin Power and Light's Model Diversity Program," *Training and Developmen*t, March 1996, pp. 57–60; T. Cox, "The Multicultural Organization," *Academy of Management Executives* 5 (May 1991), pp. 34–47; Shari Caudron, "Training Can Damage Diversity Efforts," *Personnel Journal* 72, no. 4 (April 1993), pp. 51–62; B. Geber, "Managing Diversity," *Training,* July 1990, pp. 23–30.
26. N. Perry, "The Workers of the Future," *Fortune,* Spring–Summer 1991, pp. 68–72.
27. *Opportunity 2000* (Indianapolis: Hudson Institute, 1988).
28. Cox and Blake, "Managing Cultural Diversity."

Part Three Intergrating Case

1. Gloria M. Curry, "Package Delivery Service: The Options Are Plentiful," *Office,* August 1989, pp. 60–62.
2. Charles Arthur, "The War in the Air," *Business* [U.K.], November 1989, pp. 60–66.
3. Erik Guyot, "Air Courier Fight for Pacific Business," *Asian Finance* [Hong Kong], July 15, 1990, pp. 22–23.
4. James T. McKenna, "Airline Boosts International Cargo Services to Protect Market Shares," *Aviation Week & Space Technology,* November 20, 1989, pp. 124–25.
5. Dean Foust, "Mr. Smith Goes Global," *Business Week,* February 13, 1989, pp. 66–72.
6. Frederick W. Smith, "Empowering Employee," *Small Business Reports,* January 1991, pp. 15–20.
7. Perry A. Trunick, "Leadership and People Distinguish Federal Express," *Transportation & Distribution,* December 1989, pp. 18–22.
8. "Federal Express Spreads Its Wings," *Journal of Business Strategy,* July–August 1988, pp. 15–20.
9. Foust, "Mr. Smith Goes Global."
10. "Federal Express Spreads Its Wings." pp. 3–10.
11. Erik Calonius, "Federal Express Battle Overseas," *Fortune,* 1990, December 3, 1990, pp. 137–40.
12. Foust, "Mr. Smith Goes Global."
13. James Ott, "Board Decision Muddle Rules on Union Role after Merger," *Aviation Week & Space Technology,* August 28, 1989, p. 68.
14. Foust, "Mr. Smith Goes Global."

Chapter Twelve

1. W. Bennis and B. Nanus, *Leaders* (New York: Harper & Row, 1985), p. 27.
2. Ibid.
3. Ibid., p. 144.
4. J. Kouzes and B. Posner, *The Leadership Challenge,* 1st ed. (San Francisco: Jossey-Bass, 1987).
5. Ibid.
6. Ibid.
7. E. C. Shapiro, *Fad Surfing in the Boardroom* (Reading, MA: Addison-Wesley, 1995).
8. J. Kouzes, and B. Posner, *The Leadership Challenge,* 2nd ed. (San Francisco: Jossey-Bass, 1995).
9. Ibid.
10. W. Bennis, and Townsend, *Reinventing Leadership* (New York: William Morrow, 1995).
11. Ibid.
12. Kouzes, and Posner, *The Leadership Challenge* (1987).
13. J. A. Conger, "The Dark Side of Leadership," *Organizational Dynamics* 19 (Autumn 1990), pp. 44–55.
14. J. P. Kotter, "What Leaders Really Do," *Harvard Business Review* 68 (May–June 1990), pp. 103–11.
15. A. Zaleznik, "The Leadership Gap," *The Executive* 4 (February 1990), pp. 7–22.
16. G. Yukl, *Leadership in Organizations,* 3rd ed. (Englewood Cliffs, NJ: Prentice Hall, 1994).
17. R. House and R. Aditya, "The Social Scientific Study of Leadership. Quo Vadis?" *Journal of Management* 23, (1997), pp. 409–73.
18. R. E. Kelly, "In Praise of Followers," *Harvard Business Review* 66 (November–December 1988), pp. 142–48.
19. Bennis & Townsend, *Reinventing Leadership.*
20. R. Heifetz and D. Laurie, "The Work of Leadership," *Harvard Business Review,* January–February 1997, pp. 124–34.
21. Kelly, "In Praise of Followers."
22. J. R. P. French and B. Raven, "The Bases of Social Power," in *Studies in Social Power,* ed. D. Cartwright (Ann Arbor, MI: Institute for Social Research, 1959).
23. G. Yukl and C. Falbe, "Importance of Different Power Sources in Downward and Lateral Relations," *Journal of Applied Psychology* 76 (1991), pp. 416–23.
24. Ibid.
25. Ibid.
26. R. M. Stogdill, "Personal Factors Associated with Leadership: A Survey of the Literature," *Journal of Psychology* 25 (1948), pp. 35–71.
27. S. Kirkpatrick and E. Locke, "Leadership: Do Traits Matter?" *The Executive* 5 (May 1991), pp. 48–60.
28. G. A. Yukl, *Leadership in Organizations,* 2nd ed. (Englewood Cliffs, NJ: Prentice Hall, 1989).
29. Heifetz and Laurie, "The Work of Leadership."
30. J. P. Kotter, *The General Managers* (New York: Free Press, 1982).
31. S. Zaccaro, R. Foti, and D. Kenny, "Self-Monitoring and Trait-Based Variance in Leadership: An Investigation of Leader Flexibility across Multiple Group Situations," *Journal of Applied Psychology* 76 (1991), pp. 308–15.
32. R. Hooijberg, J. G. Hunt, and G. Dodge, "Leadership Complexity and Development of the Leaderplex Model, *Journal of Management* 23 (1997), pp. 375–408.
33. J. Misumi and M. Peterson, "The Performance-Maintenance (PM) Theory of Leadership: Review of a Japanese Research Program," *Administrative Science Quarterly* 30 (June 1985), pp. 198–223.
34. Ibid.
35. G. Graen and M. Uhl-Bien, "Relationship-Based Approach to Leadership: Development of Leader-Member Exchange (LMX) Theory of Leadership over 25 Years: Applying a Multi-level Multi-domain Perspective," *Leadership Quarterly* 6, no. 2 (1995), pp. 219–47.
36. House & Aditya, "The Social Scientific Study of Leadership."
37. Ibid.
38. J. Wagner III, "Participation's Effect on Performance and Satisfaction: A Reconsideration of Research," *Academy of Management Review,* April 1994, pp. 312–30.
39. R. White and R. Lippitt, *Autocracy and Democracy: An Experimental Inquiry* (New York: Harper & Brothers, 1960).
40. A. Tannenbaum and W. Schmidt, "How to Choose a Leadership Pattern," *Harvard Business Review* 36 (March–April 1958), pp. 95–101.
41. E. Fleishman and E. Harris, "Patterns of Leadership Behavior Related to Employee Grievances and Turnover," *Personnel Psychology* 15 (1962), pp. 43–56.

42. R. Likert, *The Human Organization: Its Management and Value* (New York: McGraw-Hill, 1967).
43. R. Blake and J. Mouton, *The Managerial Grid* (Houston: Gulf, 1964).
44. Misumi and Peterson, "The Performance-Maintenance (PM) Theory."
45. Tannenbaum and Schmidt, "How to Choose a Leadership Pattern."
46. V. Vroom and P. Yetton, *Leadership and Decision-Making* (Pittsburgh: University of Pittsburgh Press, 1973).
47. V. Vroom and A. Jago, *The New Leadership: Managing Participation in Organizations* (Englewood Cliffs, NJ: Prentice Hall, 1988).
48. R. J. House and R. Aditya, "The Social Scientific Study of Leadership. Quo Vadis?" *Journal of Management* 23 (1997), pp. 409–23.
49. Vroom and Jago, *The New Leadership*; R. Field and R. House, "A Test of the Vroom-Yetton Model Using Manager and Subordinate Reports," *Journal of Applied Psychology* 75 (1990), pp. 362–66.
50. R. J. House, "A Path Goal Theory of Leader Effectiveness," *Administrative Science Quarterly* 16 (1971), pp. 321–39.
51. J. Howell, D. Bowen, P. Dorfman, S. Kerr, and P. Podsakoff, "Substitutes for Leadership: Effective Alternatives to Ineffective Leadership," *Organizational Dynamics* 19 (Summer 1990), pp. 21–38.
52. B. M. Bass, *Leadership and Performance Beyond Expectations* (New York: Free Press, 1985).
53. R. J. House, "A 1976 Theory of Charismatic Leadership," in *Leadership: The Cutting Edge,* ed. J. G. Hunt and L. L. Larson (Carbondale, IL: Southern Illinois University Press, 1977).
54. M. Potts and P. Behr, *The Leading Edge* (New York: McGraw-Hill, 1987).
55 Ibid.
56. House & Aditya, "The Social Scientific Study of Leadership."
57. B. M. Bass, "Leadership: Good, Better, Best," *Organizational Dynamics,* Winter 1985, pp. 26–40.
58. Ibid.
59. Bennis and Nanus, *Leaders.*
60. B. Bass, B. Avolio, and L. Goodheim, "Biography and the Assessment of Transformational Leadership at the World-Class Level," *Journal of Management* 13 (1987), pp. 7–20.
61. K. Albrecht and R. Zemke, *Service America* (Homewood, IL: Dow Jones–Irwin, 1985).
62. B. Bass, "Does the Transactional-Transformational Paradigm Transcend Organizational and National Boundaries?" *American Psychologist* 22 (1997), pp. 130–42.
63. G. Spreitzer, and R. Quinn, "Empowering Middle Managers to Be Transformational Leaders," *Journal of Applied Behavioral Science* 32 (1996), pp. 237–61.
64. Ibid.
65. J. Huey, "The New Post-Heroic Leadership," *Fortune,* February 21, 1994, pp. 42–50.
66. Ibid.
67. P. Block, *The Empowered Manager* (San Francisco: Jossey-Bass, 1991).
68. Ibid.
69. Kouzes & Posner, *The Leadership Challenge* (1995).
70. M. McCall, *High Flyers.* (Boston: Harvard Business School Press, 1998).
71. F. E. Fiedler, *A Theory of Leadership Effectiveness* (New York: McGraw-Hill, 1967).
72. P. Hersey and K. Blanchard, *The Management of Organizational Behavior* (Englewood Cliffs, NJ: Prentice Hall, 1984).
73. Yukl, *Leadership in Organizations.*

Chapter Thirteen

1. R. Kreitner and F. Luthans, "A Social Learning Approach to Behavioral Management: Radical Behaviorists 'Mellowing Out,'" *Organizational Dynamics,* Autumn 1984, pp. 47–65.
2. D. Katz and R. L. Kahn, *The Social Psychology of Organizations* (New York: John Wiley & Sons, 1966).
3. E. Locke, "Toward a Theory of Task Motivation and Incentives," *Organizational Behavior and Human Performance* 3 (1968), pp. 157–89.
4. R. H. Schaffer, "Demand Better Results—and Get Them," *Harvard Business Review* 69 (March–April 1991), pp. 142–49.
5. T. Mitchell and W. Silver, "Individual and Group Goals When Workers Are Interdependent: Effects on Task Strategies and Performance," *Journal of Applied Psychology* 75 (1990), pp. 185–93.
6. P. C. Early, T. Connolly, and G. Ekegren, "Goals, Strategy Development, and Task Performance: Some Limits on the Efficacy of Goal Setting," *Journal of Applied Psychology* 74 (1989), pp. 24–33; C. E. Shalley, "Effects of Productivity Goals, Creativity Goals, and Personal Discretion on Individual Creativity," *Journal of Applied Psychology* 76 (1991), pp. 179–85.
7. J. Main, "Is the Baldridge Overblown?" *Fortune,* July 1, 1991, pp. 62–65.
8. E. Thorndike, *Animal Intelligence* (New York: Macmillan, 1911).
9. S. C. Faludi, "At Nordstrom Stores, Service Comes First—but at a Big Price," *The Wall Street Journal,* February 20, 1990, pp. A1, A16.
10. K. Butterfield, L. K. Trevino, and G. Ball, "Punishment from the Manager's Perspective: A Grounded Investigation and Inductive Model," *Academy of Management Review* 39 (1996), pp. 1479-1512.
11. S. Kerr, "On the Folly of Rewarding A, While Hoping for B," *Academy of Management Journal* 18 (1975), pp. 769–83.
12. J. Weber, "Farewell, Fast Track," *Business Week,* December 10, 1990, pp. 192–200.
13. A. Bennett, "When Money Is Tight, Bosses Scramble for Other Ways to Motivate the Troops," *The Wall Street Journal,* October 31, 1990, pp. B1, B5.
14. V. H. Vroom, *Work and Motivation* (New York: John Wiley & Sons, 1964).
15. A. H. Maslow, "A Theory of Human Motivation," *Psychological Review,* July 1943, pp. 370–96.
16. M. Wahba and L. Birdwell, "Maslow Reconsidered: A Review of Research on the Need Hierarchy Theory," *Organizational Behavior and Human Performance* 15 (1976), pp. 212–40.
17. F. Rose, "A New Age for Business?" *Fortune,* October 8, 1990, pp. 156–64.
18. C. Bartlett and S. Ghoshal, "Changing the Role of Top Management: Beyond Strategy to Purpose," *Harvard Business Review,* November–December 1994, pp. 79–88.
19. Weber, "Farewell, Fast Track."
20. C. Alderfer, *Existence, Relatedness, and Growth: Human Needs in Organizational Settings* (Glencoe, IL: Free Press, 1972).
21. C. Pinder, *Work Motivation* (Glenview, IL: Scott, Foresman, 1984).
22. D. McClelland, *The Achieving Society* (New York: Van Nostrand Reinhold, 1961).
23. D. McClelland and R. Boyatzis, "Leadership Motive Pattern and Long-Term Success in Management," *Journal of Applied Psychology* 67 (1982), pp. 737–43.
24. N. Adler, *International Dimensions of Organizational Behavior,* 2nd ed. (Boston: Kent, 1991); G. Hofstede, *Cultures and Organizations* (London: McGraw-Hill, 1991).
25. T. M. Amabile, "A Model of Creativity and Innovation in Organizations," in *Research in Organizational Behavior,* ed. B. M. Staw and L. L. Cummings (Greenwich, CT: JAI Press, 1988), pp. 10, 123–67.
26. C. M. Ford, "A Theory of Individual Creative Action in Multiple Social Domains," *Academy of Management Review* 21 (1996), pp. 1112–42.

27. G. Oldham, and A. Cummings, "Employee Creativity: Personal and Contextual Factors at Work," *Academy of Management Journal* 39 (1996), pp. 607–34.
28. T. Amabile, R. Conti, H. Coon, J. Lazenby, and M. Herron, "Assessing the Work Environment for Creativity," *Academy of Management Journal* 39 (1996), pp. 1154–84.
29. M. Campion and G. Sanborn, "Job Design," in *Handbook of Industrial Engineering,* ed. G. Salvendy (New York: John Wiley & Sons, 1991).
30. B. G. Posner, "Role Changes," *Inc.,* February 1990, pp. 95–98.
31. M. Campion and D. McClelland, "Interdisciplinary Examination of the Costs and Benefits of Enlarged Jobs: A Job Design Quasi-Experiment," *Journal of Applied Psychology* 76 (1991), pp. 186–98.
32. F. Herzberg, *Work and the Nature of Men* (Cleveland: World, 1966).
33. J. R. Hackman, G. Oldham, R. Janson, and K. Purdy, "A New Strategy for Job Enrichment," *California Management Review* 16 (Fall 1975), pp. 57–71.
34 T. Ehrenfeld, "Cashing In," *Inc.,* July 1993, pp. 69–70.
35. D. Fenn, "Bottoms Up," *Inc.,* July 1993, pp. 58–60.
36. R. Rechheld, "Loyalty-Based Management," *Harvard Business Review,* March–April, 1993, pp. 64–73.
37. A. Bianchi, "True Believers," *Inc.,* July 1993, pp. 72–73.
38. Ibid.
39. J. Finegan, "People Power," *Inc.,* July 1993, pp. 62–63.
40. Ibid.
41. T. Peters and N. Austin, *A Passion for Excellence* (New York: Random House, 1985).
42. Ehrenfeld, "Cashing In."
43. Finegan, "People Power."
44 Campion and Sanborn, "Job Design."
45. A. Haasen, "Opel Eisenach GMBH—Creating a High-Productivity Workplace," *Organizational Dynamics,* Spring 1996, pp. 80–85.
46. Ibid.
47. Peters and Austin, *A Passion for Excellence.*
48. K. Thomas and B. Velthouse, "Cognitive Elements of Empowerment: An 'Interpretive' Model of Intrinsic Task Motivation," *Academy of Management Review* 15 (1990), pp. 666–81.
49. Price Waterhouse Change Integration Team, *Better Change* (Burr Ridge, IL: Richard D. Irwin, 1995).
50. E. E. Lawler III, *The Ultimate Advantage: Creating the High Involvement Organization* (San Francisco: Jossey-Bass, 1992).
51. G. M. Spreitzer, "Social Structural Characteristics of Psychological Empowerment," *Academy of Management Journal* 39 (1996), pp. 483–504.
52. J. Kouzes and B. Posner, *The Leadership Challenge* (San Francisco: Jossey-Bass, 1995).
53. Price Waterhouse Change Integration Team, *Better Change.*
54. J. Jasinowski and R. Hamrin, *Making It in America* (New York: Simon & Schuster, 1995).
55. J. Adams, "Inequality in Social Exchange," in *Advances in Experimental Social Psychology,* ed. L. Berkowitz (New York: Academic Press, 1965).
56. W. C. Kim and R. Mauborgne, "Fair Process: Managing in the Knowledge Economy," *Harvard Business Review,* July–August 1997, pp. 65–75.
57. Ibid.
58. D. Henne and E. Locke, "Job Dissatisfaction: What Are the Consequences?" *International Journal of Psychology* 20 (1985), pp. 221–40.
59. R. E. Walton, "Improving the Quality of Work Life," *Harvard Business Review,* May–June 1974, pp. 12, 16, 155.
60. E. E. Lawler III, "Strategies for Improving the Quality of Work Life," *American Psychologist* 37 (1982), pp. 486–93; J. L. Suttle, "Improving Life at Work: Problems and Prospects," in *Improving Life at Work,* ed. J. R. Hackman and J. L. Suttle (Santa Monica, CA: Goodyear, 1977).
61. S. L. Robinson, "Trust and Breach of the Psychological Contract," *Administrative Science Quarterly* 41 (1996), pp. 574–99.
62. E. W. Morrison and S. L. Robinson, "When Employees Feel Betrayed: A Model of How Psychological Contract Violation Develops," *Academy of Management Review* 22 (1997), pp. 226–56.
63. D. Rousseau, "Changing the Deal while Keeping the People," *Academy of Management Executive* 10 (1996), pp. 50–58.
64. E. Ridolfi, "Executive Commentary," *Academy of Management Executive* 10 (1996), pp. 59–60.
65. E. E. Lawler III, *From the Ground Up* (San Francisco: Jossey-Bass 1996).
66. Ibid.
67. Kim and Mauborgne, "Fair Process."
68. Rousseau, "Changing the Deal while Keeping the People;" Kim & Mauborgne, "Fair Process."

Chapter Fourteen

1. S. Cohen and D. Bailey "What Makes Teams Work: Group Effectiveness Research from the Shop Floor to the Executive Suite," *Journal of Management* 23 (1997), pp. 239–90.
2. B. Dumaine, "Who Needs a Boss?" *Fortune,* May 7, 1990, pp. 52–60.
3. Ibid.
4. K. Wexley and S. Silverman, *Working Scared* (San Francisco: Jossey-Bass, 1993).
5. B. Dumaine, "The Trouble with Teams," *Fortune,* September 5, 1994, pp. 86–92.
6. E. E. Lawler III, *From the Ground Up* (San Francisco: Jossey-Bass, 1996).
7. Wexley and Silverman, *Working Scared.*
8. Lawler, *From the Ground Up.*
9. Dumaine, "The Trouble with Teams."
10. Lawler, *From the Ground Up.*
11. R. M. Kanter, "Championing Change: An Interview with Bell Atlantic's CEO Raymond Smith," *Harvard Business Review,* January–February 1991, pp. 118–130.
12. R. Heifetz and D. Laurie, "The Work of Leadership," *Harvard Business Review,* January–February 1996, pp. 124–34.
13. Lawler, *From the Ground Up.*
14. Dumaine, "Who Needs a Boss?"
15. D. Nadler, J. R. Hackman, and E. E. Lawler III, *Managing Organizational Behavior* (Boston: Little, Brown, 1979).
16. M. Cianni and D. Wnuck, "Individual Growth and Team Enhancement: Moving toward a New Model of Career Development," *Academy of Management Executive* 11 (1997), pp. 105–15.
17. Cohen and Bailey, "What Makes Teams Work."
18. J. Katzenback and D. Smith, "The Discipline of Teams," *Harvard Business Review,* March–April 1993, pp. 111–20.
19. J. Zenger and Associates, *Leading Teams* (Burr Ridge, IL: Business One Irwin, 1994).
20. S. Cohen, "New Approaches to Teams and Teamwork," in J. Galbraith, E. E. Lawler III, and Associates, *Organizing for the Future* (San Francisco: Jossey-Bass, 1993).
21. Cohen and Bailey, "What Makes Teams Work."
22. Ibid.
23. R. Banker, J. Field, R. Schroeder, and K. Sinha, "Impact of Work Teams on Manufacturing Performance: A Longitudinal Field Study," *Academy of Management Journal* 39 (1996), pp. 867–90.
24. D. Yeatts, M. Hipskind, and D. Barnes, "Lessons Learned from Self-Managed Work Teams," *Business Horizons,* July–August 1994, pp. 11–18.
25. B. Kirkman and D. Shapiro, "The Impact of Cultural Values on Employee Resistance to Teams: Toward a Model of Globalized

Self-managing Work Team Effectiveness," *Academy of Management Review* 22 (1997), pp. 730–57.

26. B. Macy and H. Isumi, "Organizational Change, Design, and Work Innovation: A Meta-analysis of 131 North American Field Studies—1961–1991," *Research in Organizational Change and Development* 7 (1993), pp. 235–313.
27. Ibid.
28. B. W. Tuckman, "Developmental Sequence in Small Groups," *Psychological Bulletin* 63 (1965), pp. 384–99.
29. C. Snow, S. Snell, S. Davison, and D. Hambrick, "Use Transnational Teams to Globalize Your Company," *Organizational Dynamics,* Spring 1996, pp. 50–67.
30. C. J. G. Gersick, "Time and Transition in Work Teams: Toward a New Model of Group Development," *Academy of Management Journal* 31 (1988), pp. 9–41.
31. J. R. Hackman, *Groups That Work (and Those That Don't)* (San Francisco: Jossey-Bass, 1990).
32. Zenger and Associates, *Leading Teams.*
33. Dumaine, "The Trouble with Teams."
34. J. Case, "What the Experts Forgot to Mention," *Inc.,* September 1993, pp. 66–78.
35. A. Nahavandi and E. Aranda, "Restructuring Teams for the Reengineered Organization," *Academy of Management Executive,* November 1994, pp. 58–68.
36. J. Katzenback and D. Smith, *The Wisdom of Teams* (Boston: Harvard Business School Press, 1993).
37. Nadler, Hackman, and Lawler, *Managing Organizational Behavior.*
38. P. Petty, "Behind the Brands at P&G: An Interview with John Smale," *Harvard Business Review,* November–December 1985, pp. 78–80.
39. T. Peters and N. Austin, *A Passion for Excellence* (New York: Random House, 1985).
40. T. Kidder, *The Soul of a New Machine* (Boston: Little, Brown, 1981).
41. Nadler, Hackman, and Lawler, *Managing Organizational Behavior.*
42. Katzenback and Smith, "The Discipline of Teams."
43. Ibid.
44. C. Meyer, "How the Right Measures Help Teams Excel," *Harvard Business Review,* May–June 1994, pp. 95–103.
45. Meyer, "How the Right Measures Help Teams Excel."
46. Lawler, *From the Ground Up.*
47. M. Erez, "Is Group Productivity Loss the Rule or the Exception? Effects of Culture and Group-Based Motivation," *Academy of Management Journal* 39 (1996), pp. 1513–37.
48. Katzenbach and Smith, "The Discipline of Teams."
49. P. Pascarelloa, "Compensating Teams," *Across the Board,* February 1997, pp. 16–22.
50. R. Wageman, "Interdependence and Group Effectiveness," *Administrative Science Quarterly* 40 (1995), pp. 145–80.
51. Cianni and Wnuck, "Individual Growth and Team Enhancement."
52. Lawler, *From the Ground Up.*
53. Wellins, Byham, and Dixon, *Inside Teams.*
54. Ibid.
55. J. O'Toole, *Vanguard Management: Redesigning the Corporate Future* (New York: Doubleday, 1985).
56. R. F. Bales, *Interaction Process Analysis: A Method for the Study of Small Groups* (Reading, MA: Addison-Wesley, 1950).
57. Katzenback and Smith, *The Wisdom of Teams.*
58. R. Wellins, R. Byham, and G. Dixon, *Inside Teams* (San Francisco: Jossey-Bass, 1994).
59. C. Stoner and R. Hartman, "Team Building: Answering the Tough Questions," *Business Horizons,* September–October 1993, pp. 70–78.
60. S. E. Seashore, *Group Cohesiveness in the Industrial Work Group* (Ann Arbor, MI: University of Michigan Press, 1954).
61. Banker et al., "Impact of Work Teams on Manufacturing Performance."
62. B. Mullen and C. Cooper, "The Relation Between Group Cohesiveness and Performance: An Integration," *Psychological Bulletin* 115 (1994), pp. 210–27.
63. Seashore, *Group Cohesiveness in the Industrial Work Group.*
64. B. Lott and A. Lott, "Group Cohesiveness as Interpersonal Attraction: A Review of Relationships with Antecedent and Consequent Variables," *Psychological Bulletin,* October 1965, pp. 259–309.
65. Hackman, *Groups That Work.*
66. W. Bennis, *Organizing Genius* (Reading, MA: Addison-Wesley, 1997).
67. Cianni and Wnuck, "Individual Growth and Team Enhancement."
68. K. Jehn, "A Multimethod Examination of the Benefits and Detriments of Intragroup Conflict," *Administrative Science Quarterly* 40 (1995), pp. 245–82.
69. Wellins, Byham, and Dixon, *Inside Teams.*
70. D. G. Ancona, "Outward Bound: Strategies for Team Survival in an Organization," *Academy of Management Journal* 33 (1990), pp. 334–65.
71. Ibid.
72. L. Sayles, *Leadership: What Effective Managers Really Do, and How They Do It* (New York: McGraw-Hill, 1979).
73. Ibid.
74. Stoner and Hartman, "Team Building."
75. D. Tjosvold, *Working Together to Get Things Done* (Lexington, MA: Lexington Books, 1986).
76. M. Blum and J. A. Wall Jr., "HRM: Managing Conflicts in the Firm," *Business Horizons,* May–June 1997, pp. 84–87.
77. Ibid.
78. J. A. Wall Jr. and R. R. Callister, "Conflict and Its Management," *Journal of Management* 21 (1995), pp. 515–58.
79. K. W. Thomas, "Conflict and Conflict Management," in *Handbook of Industrial and Organizational Psychology,* ed. M. D. Dunnette (Chicago: Rand McNally, 1976).
80. K. W. Thomas, "Toward Multi-Dimensional Values in Teaching: The Example of Conflict Behaviors," *Academy of Management Review* (1977), pp. 484–89.

Chapter Fifteen

1. P. Senge, *The Fifth Discipline* (New York: Doubleday, 1990).
2. Ibid.
3. L. Penley, E. Alexander, I.E. Jernigan, and C. Henwood, "Communication Abilities of Managers: The Relationship to Performance," *Journal of Management* 17 (1991), pp. 57–76.
4. W. V. Haney, "A Comparative Study of Unilateral and Bilateral Communication," *Academy of Management Journal* 7 (1964), pp. 128–36.
5. W. V. Haney, *Communication and Interpersonal Relations: Text and Cases* (Homewood, IL: Richard D. Irwin, 1986).
6. D. Tannen, "The Power of Talk: Who Gets Heard and Why," *Harvard Business Review,* September–October 1995, pp. 138–48.
7. Ibid.
8. Ibid.
9. Ibid.
10. Ibid.
11. L. K. Larkey, "Toward a Theory of Communicative Interactions in Culturally Diverse Workgroups," *Academy of Management Review,* April 1996, pp. 463–91.
12. C. Argyris, "Good Communication That Blocks Learning," *Harvard Business Review,* July–August 1994, pp. 77–85.
13. Ibid.
14. Ibid.
15. C. Deutsch, "The Multimedia Benefits Kit," *The New York Times,* October 14, 1990, sec. 3, p. 25.

16. T. W. Comstock, *Communicating in Business and Industry* (Albany, NY: Delmar, 1985).
17. J. Taylor and W. Wacker, *The 500 Year Delta: What Happens after What Comes Next* (New York: HarperCollins, 1997).
18. W. Ruch and M. Crawford, *Business Communication* (New York: Merrill, 1991).
19. M. J. Cronin, "Knowing How Employees Use the Intranet Is Good Business," *Fortune,* July 21, 1997, p. 65.
20. R. Rice and D. Case, "Electronic Message Systems in the University: A Description of Use and Utility," *Journal of Communication* 33 (1983), pp. 131–52; C. Steinfield, "Dimensions of Electronic Mail Use in an Organizational Setting," *Proceedings of the Academy of Management,* San Diego, 1985.
21. J. Solomon, "As Electronic Mail Loosens Inhibitions, Impetuous Senders Feel Anything Goes," *The Wall Street Journal,* October 12, 1990, pp. B1, B8.
22. B. Glassberg, W. Kettinger, and J. Logan, "Electronic Communication: An Ounce of Policy Is Worth a Pound of Cure," *Business Horizons,* July–August 1996, pp. 74–80.
23. Ibid.
24. Ibid.
25. K. Edelman "Open Office? Try Virtual Office," *Across the Board,* March 1997, p. 34.
26. S. Shellenbarger, "Overwork, Low Morale Vex Office Staff," *The Wall Street Journal,* August 17, 1994, pp. B1, B4.
27. Ibid.
28. "Home Alone: The Job," *Collections & Credit Risk,* May 1997, p. 23.
29. J. Stuller, "Overload," *Across the Board,* April 1996, pp. 16–22.
30. Taylor and Wacker, *The 500 Year Delta.*
31. Ibid.
32. R. Tetzeli, "Surviving Information Overload," *Fortune,* July 11, 1994, pp. 32–35.
33. Ibid.
34. T. W. Malone, "Is Empowerment Just a Fad? Control, Decision Making and IT," *Sloan Management Review,* Winter 1997, pp. 23–35.
35. J. W. Medcof, "Challenges in Managing Technology in Transnational Multipartner Networks," *Business Horizons,* January–February 1996, pp. 47–54.
36. R. Lengel and R. Daft, "The Selection of Communication Media as an Executive Skill," *Academy of Management Executive* 2 (1988), pp. 225–32; L. Trevino, R. Daft, and R. Lengel, "Understanding Managers' Media Choices: A Symbolic Interactionist Perspective," in *Organizations and Communication Technology,* ed. J. Fulk and C. Steinfield (London: Sage, 1990).
37. J. Fulk and B. Boyd, "Emerging Theories of Communication in Organizations," *Journal of Management* 17 (1991), pp. 407–46.
38. P. G. Clampitt, *Communicating for Managerial Effectiveness* (London: Sage, 1991).
39. Ibid.
40. T. J. Larkin and S. Larkin, "Reaching and Changing Frontline Employees," *Harvard Business Review,* May–June 1996, pp. 95–104.
41. Ibid.
42. M. McCall, M. Lombardo, and A. Morrison, *The Lessons of Experience: How Successful Executives Develop on the Job* (Lexington, MA: Lexington, 1988).
43. C. M. Kelly, "Effective Communications—Beyond the Glitter and Flash," *Sloan Management Review,* Spring 1985, pp. 69–74.
44. K. Reardon, *Persuasion in Practice* (London: Sage, 1991).
45. N. Nohria and B. Harrington, *Six Principles of Successful Persuasion* (Boston: Harvard Business School Publishing Division, 1993).
46. R. Ashkenas, D. Ulrich, T. Jick, and S. Kerr, *The Boundaryless Organization* (San Francisco: Jossey-Bass, 1995).
47. H. K. Mintz, "Business Writing Styles for the 70's," *Business Horizons,* August 1972. Cited in *Readings in Interpersonal and Organizational Communication,* ed. R. C. Huseman, C. M. Logue, and D. L. Freshley (Boston: Allyn & Bacon, 1977).
48. C. D. Decker, "Writing to Teach Thinking," *Across the Board,* March 1996, pp. 19–20.
49. M. Forbes, "Exorcising Demons from Important Business Letters," *Marketing Times,* March–April 1981, pp. 36–38.
50. C. Krauthammer, "Make It Snappy: In Praise of Short Papers, Short Speeches, and, Yes, the Sound Bite," *Time* July 21, 1997, p. 84.
51. W. Strunk Jr. and E. B. White, *The Elements of Style,* 3rd ed. (New York: Macmillan, 1979); H.R. Fowler, *The Little Brown Handbook* (Boston: Little, Brown, 1986).
52. G. Ferraro, "The Need for Linguistic Proficiency in Global Business," *Business Horizons,* May–June 1996, pp. 39–46.
53. Ibid.
54. C. Chu, *The Asian Mind Game* (New York: Rawson Associates, 1991).
55. Ferraro, "The Need for Linguistic Proficiency in Global Business."
56. Comstock, *Communicating in Business and Industry.*
57. M. Korda, *Power: How to Get It, How to Use It* (New York: Random House, 1975).
58. A. Mehrabian, "Communication without Words," *Psychology Today,* September 1968, p. 52. Cited in M. B. McCaskey, "The Hidden Message Managers Send," *Harvard Business Review,* November–December 1979, pp. 135–48.
59. Ferraro, "The Need for Linguistic Proficiency in Global Business."
60. *Business Horizons,* May–June 1993. Copyright 1993 by the Foundation for the School of Business at Indiana University. Used with permission.
61. "Too Many in the New Workforce Are Lacking Basic Skills," *Research Alert,* November 15, 1996, p. 5.
62. A. Athos and J. Gabarro, *Interpersonal Behavior* (Englewood Cliffs, NJ: Prentice Hall, 1978).
63. "Have You Heard about Sperry?" *Management Review* 69 (April 1980), p. 40.
64. J. Kouzes and B. Posner, *The Leadership Challenge* (San Francisco: Jossey-Bass, 1995).
65. G. Graham, J. Unruh, and P. Jennings, "The Impact of Nonverbal Communication in Organizations: A Survey of Perceptions," *Journal of Business Communications* 28 (1991), pp. 45–62.
66. D. Upton and S. Macadam, "Why (and How) to Take a Plant Tour," *Harvard Business Review,* May–June 1997, pp. 97–106.
67. Ibid.
68. N. Adler, *International Dimensions of Organizational Behavior,* 2nd ed. (Boston: Kent, 1991).
69. Chu, *The Asian Mind Game.*
70. W. C. Redding, *Communication within the Organization: An Interpretive Review of Theory and Research* (New York: Industrial Communication Council, 1972). Cited in F. M. Jablin, "Superior-Subordinate Communication: The State of the Art," *Psychological Bulletin* 86 (1979), pp. 1201–22.
71. Penley et al, "Communication Abilities of Managers."
72. J. W. Koehler, K. W. E. Anatol, and R. L. Applebaum, *Organizational Communication: Behavioral Perspectives* (Orlando, FL: Holt, Rinehart & Winston, 1981).
73. J. Waldroop and T. Butler, "The Executive as Coach," *Harvard Business Review,* November–December 1996, pp. 111–17.
74. T. Judge and J. Cowell, "The Brave New World of Coaching," *Business Horizons,* July–August 1997, pp. 71–77.
75. Ibid.
76. J. Gutknecht and J. B. Keys, "Mergers, Acquisitions, and Takeovers: Maintaining Morale of Survivors and Protecting

Employees," *Academy of Management Executive,* August 1993, pp. 26–36.

77. D. Schweiger and A. DeNisi, "Communication with Employees Following a Merger: A Longitudinal Field Experiment," *Academy of Management Journal* 34 (1991), pp. 110–35.
78. J. Case, "The Open-Book Managers," *Inc.,* September 1990, pp. 104–13.
79. J. Case, "Opening the Books," *Harvard Business Review,* March–April 1997, pp. 118–27.
80. T. R. V. Davis, "Open-Book Management: Its Promise and Pitfalls," *Organization Dynamics,* Winter 1997, pp. 7–20.
81. Ibid.
82. W. V. Ruch, *Corporate Communications* (Westport, CT: Quorum, 1984).
83. Ashkenas et al., *The Boundaryless Organization.*
84. Ruch, *Corporate Communications.*
85. Ashkenas et al., *The Boundaryless Organization.*
86. Koehler, Anatol, and Applebaum, *Organizational Communication.*
87. Ashkenas et al., *The Boundaryless Organization.*
88. D. K. Denton, "Open Communication," *Business Horizons,* September–October 1993, pp. 64–69.
89. R. L. Rosnow, "Rumor as Communication: A Contextual Approach," *Journal of Communication* 38 (1988), pp. 12–28.
90. K. Davis, "The Care and Cultivation of the Corporate Grapevine," *Dun's Review,* July 1973, pp. 44–47.
91. N. Difonzo, P. Bordia, and R. Rosnow, "Reining in Rumors," *Organizational Dynamics,* Summer 1994, pp. 47–62.
92. Ibid.
93. Ashkenas et al., *The Boundaryless Organization.*
94. Ibid.
95. R. M. Hodgetts, "A Conversation with Steve Kerr," *Organizational Dynamics,* Spring 1996, pp. 68–79.
96. Ibid.
97. R. M. Fulmer, "The Evolving Paradigm of Leadership Development," *Organizational Dynamics,* Spring 1997, pp. 59–72.
98. Ibid.
99. Ashkenas et al., *The Boundaryless Organization.*

Chapter Sixteen

1. James C. Collins, and Jerry I. Porras, *Built to Last: Successful Habits of Visionary Companies* (New York: HarperBusiness, 1994).
2. Management Control Systems and Strategy: A Critical Review, " *Accounting, Organizations and Society* 22, no. 2 (February 1997), pp. 207–32; "Time Stealing," *Forbes,* December 20, 1982, p. 9.
3. W. G. Ouchi, "Markets, Bureaucracies, and Clans," *Administrative Science Quarterly* 25 (1980), pp. 129–41.
4. D. Robey and C. A. Sales, *Designing Organizations* (Burr Ridge, IL: Richard D. Irwin, 1994); M. W. Morgan, "Measuring Performance with Customer-Defined Metrics," *Quality Progress* 29, no. 12 (December 1996), pp. 31–33.
5. R. Basu and N. Wright, "Measuring Performance against World Class Standards," *IIE Solutions* 28, no. 12 (December 1996), pp. 32–35; P. Drucker, "Permanent Cost Cutting," *The Wall Street Journal,* January 11, 1991, p. A10.
6. D. M. Strong, "IT Process Designs for Improving Informational Quality and Reducing Exception Handling: A Simulation Experiment," *Information Management* 31, no. 5 (January 1997), pp. 251–63; J. T. Burr, "Keys to a Successful Internal Audit," *Quality Progress* 30, no. 4 (April 1997), pp. 75–77.
7. "Behind the UPS Mystique: Puritanism and Productivity," *Business Week,* June 6, 1990, pp. 66–73.
8. T. Wall, J. M. Corbett, R. Martin, C. Clegg, and P. Jackson, "Advanced Manufacturing Technology, Work Design, and Performance: A Change Study," *Journal of Applied Psychology* 75 (1990), pp. 691–97.
9. R. Henkoff, "Make Your Office More Productive," *Fortune,* February 25, 1990, pp. 40–49.
10. R. C. Davis, *The Fundamentals of Top Management* (New York: Harper & Row, 1951); J. Donnelly Jr., J. Gibson, and J. Ivancevich, *Fundamentals of Management* (Plano, TX: Business Publications, 1981).
11. W. J. Bruns Jr. and F. W. McFarlan, "Information Technology Puts Power in Control Systems," *Harvard Business Review,* September–October 1987, pp. 89–94; Strong, "IT Process Designs for Improving Informational Quality."
12. C. Griffin and W. Stewart, "Take Stock, Then Take Charge," *PEM: Plant Engineering & Maintenance* 21, no. 4 (September 1997), p. 26; F. Pomeranz, "Preemptive Auditing: Future Shock or Present Opportunity?" *Journal of Accounting, Auditing, and Finance,* Summer 1979, pp. 352–56.
13. A. M. Rabinowitz, "Rebuilding Public Confidence and Organizational Controls," *CPA Journal* 66, no. 1 (January 1996), pp. 30–34; R. Buchele, "How to Evaluate a Firm," *California Management Review,* Fall 1962, pp. 5–17.
14. G. A. Ewert, "How to Sell Internal Auditing," *Internal Auditor* 54, no. 5 (October 1997), pp. 54–57; J. T. Burr, "Keys to a Successful Internal Audit," *Quality Progress* 30, no. 4 (April 1997), pp. 75–77.
15. R. Henkoff, "Cost Cutting: How to Do It Right," *Fortune,* April 9, 1990, pp. 40–49.
16. P. C. Brewer and L. A. Vulinec, "Harris Corporation's Experiences with Using Activity-Based Costing," *Information Strategy: The Executive's Journal* 13, no. 2 (Winter 1997), pp. 6–16; Terence P. Pare, "A New Tool for Managing Costs," *Fortune,* June 14, 1993, pp. 124–29; Robert Ochs and John Bicheno, "Activity-Based Cost Management Linked to Manufacturing Strategy," *IM,* January–February 1991, pp. 11–16; W. M. Baker, "Take Another Look at Activity-Based Costing," *Industrial Management* 38, no. 1 (January/February 1996), pp. 19–23.
17. K. Merchant, *Control in Business Organizations* (Boston: Pitman, 1985); C. W. Chow, Y. Kato, and K. A. Merchant, "The Use of Organizational Controls and Their Effects on Data Manipulation and Management Myopia," *Accounting, Organizations, and Society* 21, nos. 2/3 (February/April 1996), pp. 175–92.
18. E. E. Lawler III and J. Rhode, *Information and Control in Organizations* (Pacific Palisades, CA: Goodyear, 1976).
19. J. Veiga and J. Yanouzas, *The Dynamics of Organization Theory,* 2nd ed. (St. Paul, MN: West, 1984).
20. Lawler and Rhode, *Information and Control in Organizations.*
21. L. Schiff, "Downsizing Workplace Stress," *Business & Health* 15, no. 1 (November 1997), pp. 45–46; S. Albrecht, "Are Your Employees the Enemy?" *HRFocus* 74, no. 4 (April 1997), p. 21.
22. Lawler and Rhode, *Information and Control in Organizations;* D. Robey, *Designing Organizations* (Homewood, IL: Richard D. Irwin, 1991).
23. Lawler and Rhode, *Information and Control in Organizations.*
24. W. H. Newman, *Constructive Control.* (Englewood Cliffs, NJ: Prentice Hall, 1975).
25. T. A. Stewart, "Why Budgets Are Bad for Business," *Fortune,* June 4 1990, pp. 179–90.
26. Henkoff, "Make Your Office More Productive."
27. Bruns and McFarlan, "Information Technology."

28. Lawler and Rhode, *Information and Control in Organizations;* J. A. Gowan, Jr. and R. G. Mathieu, "Critical Factors in Information System Development for a Flexible Manufacturing System," *Computers in Industry* 28, no. 3 (June 1996), pp. 173–83.
29. T. A. Stewart, "Do You Push Your People Too Hard?" *Fortune,* October 22, 1990, pp. 121–28.
30. S. Tully, "The CEO Who Sees Beyond Budgets," *Fortune,* October 22, 1990, pp. 121–28.
31. Merchant, *Control in Business Organizations.*
32. S. K. Sia, and B. S. Neo, "The Impacts of Business Process Re-engineering on Organizational Controls," *International Journal of Project Management* 14, no. 6 (December 1996), pp. 341–48; Kevin P Coyne and Renee Dye, "The Competitive Dynamics of Network-Based Businesses," *Harvard Business Review* 76, no. 1 (January–February 1998), pp. 99–109.
33. T. A. Stewart, "CEO Pay: Mom Would be Proud," *Fortune* 135, no. 6 (March 31, 1997), pp. 119–20; Brian Dumaine, "A Knockout Year for CEO Pay," *Fortune,* July 25, 1994, pp. 94–103; "Worthy of His Hire?" *The Economist,* February 1, 1992, pp. 19–22.
34. S. A. Snell and J. W. Dean Jr., "Strategic Compensation for Integrated Manufacturing: The Moderating Effects of Jobs and Organizational Inertia," *Academy of Management Journal* 37, no. 5 (1994), pp. 1109–40; M. A. Youndt, S. A. Snell, J. W. Dean Jr., and D. P. P. Lepak, "Human Resource Management, Manufacturing Strategy, and Firm Performance," *Academy of Management Journal* 39, no. 4, Special Issue (1996), pp. 836–66.
35. Michael Macoby, "Managers Must Unlearn the Psychology of Control," *Research Technology Management,* January–February 1993, pp. 49–51.
36. William C. Taylor, "Control in an Age of Chaos," *Harvard Business Review,* November–December 1994, pp. 64–76. See also Kevin Kelly, *Out of Control: The Rise of New-Biological Civilization* (Reading, MA: Addison-Wesley, 1994); Collins and Porras, *Built to Last;* G. Pascal Zachary, *Showstopper! The Breakneck Race to Create Windows NT and the Next Generation at Microsoft* (New York: Free Press, 1994)
37. V. Sathe, *Culture and Related Corporate Realities* (Homewood, IL: Richard D. Irwin, 1985); A. Reichers and B. Schneider, "Climate and Culture: An Evolution of Constructs," in *Organization Climate and Culture,* ed. B. Schneider (San Francisco: Jossey-Bass, 1990).
38. Collins and Porras, *Built to Last;* T. Deal and A. Kennedy, *Corporate Culture: The Rites and Rituals of Corporate Life* (Reading, MA: Addison-Wesley, 1982); T. Peters and R. Waterman, *In Search of Excellence* (New York: Harper & Row, 1982).
39. R. Leifer and P. K. Mills, "An Information Processing Approach for Deciding upon Control Strategies and Reducing Control Loss in Emerging Organizations," *Journal of Management* 22, no. 1 (1996), pp. 113–37; V. Hope and J. Hendry, "Corporate Culture Change—Is It Relevant for the Organisations of the 1990s?" *Human Resource Management Journal* 5, no. 4 (Summer 1995), pp. 61–73.

Chapter Seventeen

1. C. Snow and E. Ottensmeyer, "Managing Strategies and Technologies," in *Strategic Management in High Technology Firms,* ed. M. Lawless and L. Gomez-Mejia (Greenwich, CT: JAI Press, 1990); H. Bahrami and S. Evans, "Stratocracy in High Technology Firms," *California Management Review* 30 (Fall 1987), pp. 51–66.
2. Donna C. L. Prestwood and Paul A. Schumann Jr., "Revitalize Your Organization," *Executive Excellence* 15, no. 2 (February 1998), p. 16; Carliss Y. Baldwin and Kim B. Clark, "Managing in an Age of Modularity," *Harvard Business Review* 75, no. 5 (September–October 1997), pp. 84–93; U. E. Gattiker, *Technology Management in Organizations* (Newbury Park, CA: Sage, 1990).
3. James M. Utterback, *Mastering the Dynamics of Innovation* (Boston: Harvard Business School Press, 1994).
4. Gary P. Pisano, *The Development Factory: Unlocking the Potential of Process Innovation* (Boston: Harvard Business School Press, 1996); Utterback, *Mastering the Dynamics of Innovation.*
5. E. M. Rogers, *Diffusion of Innovation,* 3rd ed. (New York: Free Press, 1983). Also see Hugh M. O'Neill, Richard W. Pounder, and Ann K. Buchholtz, "Patterns in the Diffusion of Strategies across Organizations: Insights from the Innovation Diffusion Literature," *Academy of Management Review* 23, no. 1 (January 1998), pp. 98–114.
6. Ibid.
7. M. E. Porter, *Competitive Strategy* (New York: Free Press, 1980); Joseph G. Monroe, "Technology and Competitive Advantage—The Role of General Management," *Research Technology Management,* March–April 1993, pp. 16–25.
8. J. A. Schumpeter, *The Theory of Economic Development* (Boston: Harvard University Press, 1934). See also E. M. Neiva, "Chain Building: The Consolidation of the American Newspaper Industry, 1955–1980," *Business and Economics* 24, no. 1 (Fall 1995), pp. 22–27.
9. G. Day and J. Freeman, "Burnout or Fadeout: The Risks of Early Entry into High Technology Markets," in Lawless and Gomez-Mejia, *Strategic Management in High Technology Firms;* Shaker A. Zahra, Sarah Nash, and Deborah J. Bickford, "Transforming Technological Pioneering in Competitive Advantage," *Academy of Management Executive* 9, no. 1 (1995), pp. 17–31.
10. "Kodak Settles with Polaroid," *New York Times,* July 16, 1991, p. D8; N. Byrnes and A. Hardman, "Cold Shower," *Financial* 162, no. 19 (September 28, 1993), pp. 38–39.
11. M. Imai, *Kaizen: The Key to Japan's Competitive Success* (New York: Random House, 1986). For a recent interview with Imai, see "An Interview with Masaaki Imai: Ongoing Improvement," *Executive Excellence* 14, no. 19 (October 1997), pp. 11–12.
12. B. O'Reilly, "Drugmakers under Attack," *Fortune,* July 29, 1991, pp. 48–63; D. Bandow, "The FDA Can Be Dangerous to Your Health," *Fortune* 134, no. 9 (November 11, 1996), p. 56.
13. D. M. Schroeder, "A Dynamic Perspective of the Impact of Process Innovation upon Competitive Strategies," *Strategic Management Journal* 11 (January 1990), pp. 25–42.
14. "Fool's Paradise," *The Economist,* February 3, 1990, p. 81.
15. Ibid.
16. Martyn Pitt and Ken Clarke, "Frames of Significance: Technological Agenda-Forming for Strategic Advantage," *Technology Analysis & Strategic Management* 9, no. 3 (September 1997), pp. 251–69.
17. F. Barbetta, "Motorola's Iridium; The Clock is Ticking," *Business Communications Review* 27, no. 2 (February 1997), p. 16; Theodore B. Kinni, "A Ma Bell for the Space Age," *Industry Week,* March 21, 1994, pp. 71–72; Theodore B. Kinni, "Boundary-Busting Teamwork," *Industry Week,* March 21, 1994, pp. 72–74; Charles F. Mason, "Scientific-Atlanta Wins IRIDIUM Deal," *Telephony* 226, no. 6 (February 1994), p. 10; "IRIDIUM: A Closer Look," *Telecommunications* 27, no. 12 (December 1993), p. 27.
18. Pitt and Clarke, "Frames of Significance."
19. Keith Naughton "Detroit's Impossible Dream?" *Business Week,* March 2, 1998, pp. 66–67.
20. Jimmy Carter, "Corporate Giving Is Part of the Solutions Equation; Philanthropy: When Business Works with Individuals, Government and Nonprofits to Do Good, Success

Is Boundless," *Los Angeles Times,* February 19, 1998, p. B9; Nancy Walsh D'Epiro, "Targeting River Blindness," *Patient Care* 31, no. 16 (October 15, 1997), p. 18.

21. Pitt and Clarke, "Frames of Significance."
22. Rogers, *Diffusion of Innovation;* C. Hildebrand, "Tech-crastination," *CIO* 11, no. 9 (February 15, 1998), p. 22.
23. E. von Hipple, *The Sources of Innovation* (New York: Oxford University Press, 1988).
24. Ibid.
25. K. M. Eisenhardt and C. B. Schoonhoven, "Resource-Based View of Strategic Alliance Formation: Strategic and Social Effects in Entrepreneurial Firms," *Organization Science* 7, no. 2 (March/April 1996), pp. 136–50; T. Peters, "Get Innovative or Get Dead (Part 1)," *California Management Review,* Fall 1990, pp. 9–26.
26. P. Adler and K. Ferdows, "The Chief Technology Officer," *California Management Review,* Spring 1990, pp. 55–62; Joseph Maglitta, "Meet the New Boss," *Computerworld,* March 14, 1994, pp. 80–82.
27. Melanie Warner, "The New Way to Start Up in Silicon Valley," *Fortune* 137, no. 4 (March 2, 1998), pp. 168–74; Leon Richardson, "The Successful Entrepreneur," *Asian Business,* July 1994, p. 71; Charles Burck, "The Real World of the Entrepreneur," *Fortune,* April 5, 1993, pp. 42–55.
28. D. L. Day, "Raising Radicals: Different Processes for Championing Innovative Corporate Ventures," *Organization Science* 5, no. 2 (May 1994), pp. 148–72; Clifford Siporin, "Want Speedy FDA Approval? Hire a 'Product Champion,'" *Medical Marketing & Media,* October 1993, pp. 22–28; Clifford Siporin, "How You Can Capitalize on Phase 3B," *Medical Marketing & Media,* October 1994, pp. 72–72.
29. "Face Value: The Mass Production of Ideas, and Other Impossibilities," *The Economist* 334, no. 7906 (March 18, 1995), p. 72; Benjamin Schneider, Sarah K. Gunnarson, and Kathryn Niles-Jolly, "Creating the Climate and Culture of Success," *Organizational Dynamics* 23, no. 1 (Summer 1994), pp. 17–29; Thomas J. Martin, "Ten Commandments for Managing Creative People," *Fortune,* January 16, 1995, pp. 135–36.
30. Lisa K. Gundry, Jill R. Kickul, and Charles W. Prather, "Building the Creative Organization," *Organizational Dynamics* 22, no. 2 (Spring 1994), pp. 22–36; Thomas Kuczmarski, "Inspiring and Implementing the Innovation Mind-Set," *Planning Review,* September–October 1994, pp. 37–48.
31. R. Neff, "Toray May Have Found the Formula for Luck," *Business Week,* June 15, 1990, p. 110.
32. "Stimulating Creativity and Innovation," *Research Technology Management* 40, no. 2 (March/April 1997), pp. 57–58; Z. J. Czajkiewicz and T. R. Wielicki, "CIM—A Journey to Manufacturing Excellence," *Computers and Industrial Engineering* 27, no. 1 (September 1994), pp. 91–94; T. Peters, "Get Innovative (Part 2)," *California Management Review* 33, no. 2 (Winter 1991), pp. 9–23.
33. H. Kent Bowen, Kim B. Clark, Charles A. Holloway, and Steven C. Wheelwright, "Development Projects: The Engine of Renewal," *Harvard Business Review,* September–October 1994, pp. 110–20; C. Eden, T. Williams, and F. Ackermann, "Dismantling the Learning Curve: The Role of Disruptions on the Planning of Development Projects," *International Journal of Project Management* 16, no. 3 (June 1998), pp. 131–38.
34. Steven C. Wheelwright and Kim B. Clark, *Revolutionizing Product Development* (New York: Free Press, 1992), pp. 49–50.
35. E. Trist, "The Evolution of Sociotechnical Systems as a Conceptual Framework and as an Action Research Program," in *Perspectives on Organizational Design and Behavior,* ed. A. Van de Ven and W. F. Joyce (New York: John Wiley & Sons, 1981), pp. 19–75; Alfonso Molina, "Insights into the Nature of Technology Diffusion and Implementation: The Perspective of Sociotechnical Alignment," *Technovation* 17, nos. 11/12 (November/December 1997), pp. 601–26; J. C. Spender, "Making Knowledge the Basis of a Dynamic Theory of the Firm," *Strategic Management Journal* 17 (Winter 1996), pp. 45–62.
36. S. Zuboff, *In the Age of the Smart Machine* (New York: Basic Books, 1988); Scott A. Snell and James W. Dean Jr., "Strategic Compensation for Integrated Manufacturing: The Moderating Effects of Jobs and Organizational Inertia," *Academy of Management Journal* 37, no. 5 (1994), pp. 1109–40; M. A. Youndt, S. A. Snell, J. W. Dean Jr., and D. P. Lepak, "Human Resource Management, Manufacturing Strategy, and Firm Performance," *Academy of Management Journal* 39, no. 4, Special Issue (1996), pp. 836–66.

Chapter Eighteen

1. C. Giffi, A. Roth, and G. Seal, *Competing in World-Class Manufacturing: America's 21st Century Challenge* (Homewood, IL: Business One Irwin, 1990)
2. R. M. Kanter, *World Class: Thriving Locally in the Global Economy* (New York: Touchstone, 1995).
3. T. G. Gunn, *21st Century Manufacturing* (New York: HarperBusiness, 1992).
4. Giffi, Roth, and Seal, *Competing in World-Class Manufacturing.*
5. J. Collins and J. Porras, *Built to Last* (London: Century, 1996).
6. Ibid.
7. Ibid.
8. D. A. Nadler, "Managing Organizational Change: An Integrative Approach," *Journal of Applied Behavioral Science* 17 (1981), pp. 191–211.
9. J. Stanislao and B. C. Stanislao, "Dealing with Resistance to Change," *Business Horizons,* July–August 1983, pp. 74–78.
10. J. P. Kotter and L. A. Schlesinger, "Choosing Strategies for Change," *Harvard Business Review,* March–April 1979, pp. 106–14.
11. G. Johnson, *Strategic Change and the Management Process* (New York: Basil Blackwell, 1987); K. Lewin, "Frontiers in Group Dynamics," *Human Relations* 1 (1947), pp. 5–41.
12. E. H. Schein, "Organizational Culture: What It Is and How to Change It," in *Human Resource Management in International Firms,* ed. P. Evans, Y. Doz, and A. Laurent (New York: St. Martin's Press, 1990).
13. M. Beer, R. Eisenstat, and B. Spector, *The Critical Path to Corporate Renewal* (Cambridge, MA: Harvard Business School Press, 1990).
14. E. E. Lawler III, "Transformation from Control to Involvement," in *Corporate Transformation,* ed. R. Kilmann and T. Covin (San Francisco: Jossey-Bass, 1988).
15. D. Hellriegel and J. W. Slocum, Jr., *Management,* 4th ed. (Reading, MA: Addison-Wesley, 1986).
16. J. O'Shea and C. Madigan, *Dangerous Company: The Consulting Powerhouses and the Businesses They Save and Ruin* (New York: Times Books, 1997).
17. Ibid.
18. P. Harris, *New World, New Ways, New Management* (New York: American Management Association, 1983).
19. Schein, "Organizational Culture."
20. E. E. Lawler III, *From the Ground Up* (San Francisco: Jossey-Bass, 1995).
21. Kotter and Schlesinger, "Choosing Strategies for Change."
22. Lawler, *From the Ground Up,* p. 134.
23. Ibid.
24. Ibid.
25. Nadler, "Managing Organizational Change."
26. B. Schneider, A. Brief, and R. Guzzo, "Creating a Climate and Culture for

Sustainable Organizational Change," *Organizational Dynamics,* Spring 1996, pp. 7–19.

27. The Price Waterhouse Change Integration Team, *Better Change: Best Practices for Transforming Your Organization* (Burr Ridge, IL: Irwin, 1995).
28. N. Nohria and J. Berkley, "Whatever Happened to the Take-Charge Manager?" *Harvard Business Review,* January–February 1994, pp. 128–37.
29. Lawler, *From the Ground Up.*
30. The Price Waterhouse Change Integration Team, *Better Change.*
31. Ibid.
32. J. Kotter, *Leading Change* (Boston: Harvard Business School Press, 1996).
33. Lawler, *From the Ground Up.*
34. Kotter, *Leading Change.*
35. Schneider, Brief, and Guzzo, "Creating a Climate and Culture."
36. R. Beckhard and R. Harris, *Organizational Transitions* (Reading, MA: Addison-Wesley, 1977).
37. Kotter, *Leading Change.*
38. O'Shea and Madigan, *Dangerous Company.*
39. Kotter, *Leading Change.*
40. D. Smith, *Taking Charge of Change* (Reading, MA: Addison-Wesley, 1996).
41. G. Hamel, "Killer Strategies That Make Shareholders Rich," *Fortune,* June 23, 1997, pp. 22–34.
42. G. Hamel and C. K. Prahalad, *Competing for the Future* (Boston: Harvard Business School Press, 1994).
43. B. J. Pine, B. Victor, and A. Boynton, "Making Mass Customization Work," *Harvard Business Review,* September–October 1993, pp. 108–19
44. J. W. Slocum, Jr., M. McGill, and D. Lei, "The New Learning Strategy: Anytime, Anything, Anywhere," *Organizational Dynamics,* Autumn 1994, pp. 33–47.
45. Pine, Victor, and Boynton, "Making Mass Customization Work."
46. W. Zellner and D. Griesing, "Go-Go Goliaths," *Business Week,* February 13, 1995, pp. 64–70.
47. M. J. Kiernan, "The New Strategic Architecture: Learning to Compete in the Twenty-First Century," *The Academy of Management Executive,* February 1993, pp. 7–21.
48. M. Magnet, "Let's Go for Growth," *Fortune,* March 7, 1994, pp. 60–72.
49. Ibid.
50. Ibid.
51. O'Shea and Madigan, *Dangerous Company.*
52. Magnet, "Let's Go for Growth."
53. O'Shea and Madigan, *Dangerous Company.*
54. Ibid.
55. Hamel and Prahalad, *Competing for the Future.*
56. Ibid.
57. H. Courtney, J. Kirkland, and P. Viguerie, "Strategy under Uncertainty," *Harvard Business Review,* November–December 1997, pp. 66–79.
58. Ibid.
59. Hamel and Prahalad, *Competing for the Future.*
60. J. Kotter, *The New Rules: How to Succeed in Today's Post-Corporate World* (New York: The Free Press, 1995).
61. Ibid.
62. Ibid.
63. Lawler, *From the Ground Up;* Kotter, *The New Rules.*
64. Lawler, *From the Ground Up.*
65. M. Peiperl and Y. Baruck, "Back to Square Zero: The Post-Corporate Career," *Organizational Dynamics,* Spring 1997, pp. 7–22.
66. Ibid.
67. Kotter, *The New Rules.*
68. G. Binney, and C. Williams, *Leaning into the Future* (London: Nicholas Brealey, 1997).

Part Five Integrating Case

1. Joseph F. McKenna, "The Great Expectations of David Kearns," *Industry Week,* June 17, 1991, p. 34.
2. G. M. Herrington, "The Catch-22 of Total Quality Management," *Across the Board,* September 1991.
3. M. Katherine Glover, "The Quest for Excellence," *Business America,* November 20, 1989, pp. 2–11.
4. David Kearns, "Quality in Copiers, Computers, and Floor Cleaning," *Management Review,* February 1989, pp. 61–63.
5. R. C. Camp, "Learning from the Best Leads to Superior Performance," *Journal of Business Strategy* 13, no. 3 (1992), pp. 3–6.
6. Paul Allaire and Norman Rickard, "Quality and Participation at Xerox," *Journal for Quality and Participation,* March 1989, pp. 24–26.
7. Subrata N. Chakravarty, "Xerox—Back on the Road to Success," *Forbes,* July 7, 1980, pp. 40–42.
8. *1990 Moody's Industrial Manual,* pp. 4381–89.

Name Index

A

B

C

D

E

F

N

O

P

Subject Index

D

E

F

G

P

Q

R